"No other guide has as much to offer . . . these books are a pleasure to read."

Gene Shalit on the *Today Show*

★ ★ ★ ★ ★ (5 star rating) "Crisply written and remarkably personable. Cleverly organized so you can pluck out the minutest fact in a moment. Satisfyingly thorough."

Réalités

"The information they offer is up-to-date, crisply presented but far from exhaustive, the judgments knowledgeable but not opinionated."

New York Times

"The individual volumes are compact, the prose succinct, and the coverage up-to-date and knowledgeable . . . The format is portable and the index admirably detailed."

John Barkham Syndicate

"They contain an amount of information that is truly staggering, besides being surprisingly current."

Detroit News

"These guides address themselves to the needs of the modern traveler demanding precise, qualitative information . . . Up-beat, slick, and well-put-together."

Dallas Morning News

". . . Attractive to look at, refreshingly easy to read, and generously packed with information."

Miami Herald

"These guides are as good as any published, and much better than most."

GW00703252

Stephen Birnbaum Travel Guides

Canada
Caribbean, Bermuda, and the Bahamas
Disneyland
Europe
Europe for Business Travelers
Florida for Free
France
Great Britain and Ireland
Hawaii
Italy
Mexico
South America
United States
USA for Business Travelers
Walt Disney World

CONTRIBUTING EDITORS

Jeremy Addis
Tom Barrington
Isabel Bass
Cathy Beason
Susan Braybrooke
Karen Cure
Jeff Davidson
James Davie
Michael Dervan
Robin Dewhurst
Bonnie Dudley Edwards
R. D. Eno
Ronald Faux
Michael Finlan
Trevor Fishlock
Bryn Frank
Emily Greenspan
Ida Grehan
Susan Grossman
David Hanly
Ben Harte
Constance Hill
David Hoyle
Paul Hughes

Peter Johnston
John B. Keane
Michael Leech
Nancy Lyon
Carole Martin
Alexandra Mayes
Robin Mead
Ann Millman
Daphne Pochin Mould
Ann Nugent
Tony O'Riordan
David Owen
John Preston
Patricia Tunison Preston
Alan Reeve-Jones
Allan Rokach
Anne-Maree Sheehan
George Stacpoole
Colin Toibin
Marcia Wallace
Sean White
David Wickers
Diane Wood
Carol Wright

COVER
Robert Anthony

SYMBOLS
Gloria McKeown

MAP
Etta Jacobs

A Stephen Birnbaum Travel Guide

Birnbaum's
GREAT BRITAIN
and IRELAND
1988

Stephen Birnbaum
EDITOR

Brenda Goldberg
EXECUTIVE EDITOR

Kristin Moehlmann
Barbara Benton
Associate Editors

Kathleen McHugh
Eleanor O'Neill
Assistant Editors

Stephen Coleman
Editorial Assistant

HOUGHTON MIFFLIN COMPANY / BOSTON 1987

For Alex, as always

This book is published by special arrangement
with Eric Lasher and Maureen Lasher.

Copyright © 1987 by Houghton Mifflin Company

ISBN: 0-395-44533-7
ISSN: 0749-2561 (Stephen Birnbaum Travel Guides)
ISSN: 0884-1195 (Great Britain and Ireland)

Printed in the United States of America

Q 10 9 8 7 6 5 4 3 2 1

Contents

ix   **A Word from the Editor**

1   **How to Use This Guide**

GETTING READY TO GO

All the practical travel data you need to plan your vacation down to the final detail.

When and How to Go

9   What's Where
11   When to Go
18   Traveling by Plane
29   Traveling by Ship
33   Touring by Car
36   Touring by Rail
41   Touring by Bus
44   Package Tours
50   Camping and Caravanning, Biking, and Hiking

Preparing

56   Calculating Costs
59   Entry Requirements and Documents
60   Planning a Trip
61   How to Pack
63   How to Use a Travel Agent
64   Insurance
67   Hints for Handicapped Travelers
70   Hints for Traveling with Children
73   Hints for Single Travelers
76   Hints for Older Travelers
78   Medical and Legal Aid and Consular Services

On the Road

82   Credit and Currency
86   Accommodations and Reservations
92   Tipping

93 Shopping
96 Sports
98 Time Zones and Business Hours
99 Mail, Telephone, and Electricity
100 Drinking and Drugs
102 Customs and Returning to the US

Sources and Resources

104 Tourist Information Offices
107 Theater and Special Event Tickets
107 Camera and Equipment
110 Genealogy Hunts
114 Books and Magazines
115 Words to the Wise

PERSPECTIVES

A cultural and historical survey of Britain and Ireland's past and present, their people, politics, and heritage.

Britain

119 History
135 Literature
144 Architecture
148 Traditional Music and Dance
153 Food and Drink

Ireland

160 History
168 Literature
176 Architecture
178 Traditional Music and Dance
181 Food and Drink

THE CITIES

Thorough, qualitative guides to each of the 21 cities most often visited by vacationers and businesspeople. Each section, a comprehensive report of the city's most appealing attractions and amenities, is designed to be used on the spot. Directions and recommendations are immediately accessible because each city guide is presented in consistent form.

187	Bath	315	Galway
199	Belfast	324	Glasgow
207	Brighton	337	Kilkenny
219	Bristol	346	Limerick City
231	Cambridge	354	London
245	Canterbury	386	Oxford
254	Cardiff	399	Stratford-upon-Avon
264	Chester	411	Waterford
274	Cork	420	Wexford
285	Dublin	429	York
302	Edinburgh		

DIVERSIONS

A selective guide to more than 15 active and cerebral vacations, including the places to pursue them where the quality of experience is likely to be highest.

For the Body

443	Great Golf
448	Tennis
450	Horsing Around
461	Wonderful Waterways and Coastal Cruises
467	Gone Fishing
481	Freewheeling by Two-Wheeler
488	Stalking and Shooting
491	Great Walks and Mountain Rambles

For the Mind

504	Marvelous Museums
515	The Performing Arts
528	Feis and Fleadh: The Best Festivals
538	Antiques and Auctions
550	Ancient Monuments and Ruins

For the Experience

563 Pub Crawling
573 Rural Retreats
588 Stately Homes and Great Gardens
594 Tea Shops and Tea Gardens
599 Mead and Meat Pies: Historical Banquets
602 Shopping Spree

DIRECTIONS

The most spectacular routes and roads; most arresting natural wonders; and most magnificent castles, manor houses, and gardens — all organized into 19 specific driving tours.

Great Britain

621 Southeast England
635 Channel Islands
641 Southwest England
660 The Cotswolds
670 The Lake District
680 Scottish Lowlands
694 Scottish Highlands
707 Scottish Islands
721 Wales

Northern Ireland

739 Antrim Coast

Irish Republic

750 Southeast Ireland: Dublin to New Ross
758 South-Central Ireland
768 West Cork
773 The Ring of Kerry and the Beara Peninsula
786 The Dingle Peninsula
795 Clare
802 Connemara
812 Southern Mayo
817 Donegal

827 **Index**

A Word from the Editor

This guide to Great Britain and Ireland was the initial volume of an entirely new phase in our travel guide series. Whereas our first half-dozen guides covered rather broad geographic areas, this in-depth examination of Great Britain and Ireland was our first guide to treat the world's most popular travel destinations in considerably greater detail than is possible in an "area" book. Our guidebooks to France and Italy have continued this direction.

Such treatment in depth only reflects an increasingly apparent trend among travelers — the frequent return to treasured foreign travel spots. Once upon a time, even the most dedicated travelers would visit distant parts of the world no more than once in a lifetime — usually as part of that fabled old Grand Tour. But greater numbers of would-be sojourners are now availing themselves of the increasingly easy opportunity to visit favored parts of the world over and over again.

So where once it was routine to say that you'd "seen" a particular country after a very superficial, once-over-lightly encounter, the more perceptive travelers of today recognize that it's entirely possible to have only skimmed the surface of a specific travel destination even after having visited that place more than a dozen times. Similarly, repeated visits to a single site permit true exploration of special interests, whether they be sporting, artistic, or intellectual in nature. Multiple visits also allow an ongoing relationship with foreign citizens sharing similar interests, and an opportunity to discover and appreciate different perspectives on a single field of endeavor.

For those of us who spent the last several years working out the special system under which we present information in this series, the luxury of being able to devote nearly as much space as we like to just a quartet of countries is as close to guidebook heaven as any of us expects to come. But clearly, this is not the first guide to what were once called the British Isles — one suspects that guides of one sort or another have existed at least since Caesar's legions crossed the English Channel. Guides to Great Britain and Ireland have existed literally for centuries, so a traveler might logically ask why a new one is necessary at this particular moment.

Our answer is that the nature of travel to Great Britain and Ireland, and even the travelers who now routinely make the trip, have changed dramatically of late. For the past 2,000 years or so, travel to and through Britain and Ireland was an extremely elaborate undertaking, one that required extensive advance planning. Even as recently as the 1950s, a person who had actually been to England, Scotland, Ireland, or Wales could dine out on his or her experiences for years, since such adventures were quite extraordinary and usually the province of the privileged alone.

With the advent of jet air travel in the late 1950s, however, and of increased-capacity, wide-body aircraft during the 1960s, travel to and around once distant lands became extremely common. In fact, in more than two decades of nearly unending inflation, air fares may be the only commodity in the world that has actually gone down in price. And as a result, international travel is now well within the budgets of mere mortals.

Attitudes, as well as costs, have changed significantly in the last couple of decades. Beginning with the so-called flower children and hippies of the 1960s, international travel lost much of its aura of mystery. Whereas their parents might have chosen a superficial sampling of London or Dublin, these young people, motivated as much by wildly inexpensive "youth fares" as by the inclination to see the world, simply picked up and settled in various parts of Europe for an indefinite stay. While living as inexpensively as possible, they usually adopted with great gusto the local lifestyle and generally immersed themselves in things European.

Thus began an explosion of travel to and in Great Britain and Ireland. And over the years, the development of inexpensive charter flights and packages fueled and sharpened the new American interest in and appetite for more extensive exploration.

Now, as we reach the last few years of the 1980s, those same flower children who were in the forefront of the modern travel revolution have undeniably aged. While it may be impolite to point out that they are probably well into their untrustworthy 30s (and mostly firmly enmeshed in establishment activities), their original zeal for travel remains undiminished. For them it's hardly news that the way to get to Dover is to head toward Canterbury, make a right, and then wait for white cliffs to appear. Such experienced and knowledgeable travelers have decided precisely where they want to go and are more often searching for ideas and insights to expand their already sophisticated travel consciousness. And — reverting to their youthful instincts and habits — they are after a deeper understanding and fuller assimilation of the British and Irish milieus. Typically, they visit single countries (or even cities) several times and may actually do so more than once in a single year.

Obviously, any new guidebook to Great Britain and Ireland must keep pace with and answer the real needs of today's travelers. That's why we've tried to create a guide that's specifically organized, written, and edited for this more demanding modern audience, one for whom qualitative information is infinitely more desirable than mere quantities of unappraised data. We think that this book and the other guides in our series represent a new generation of travel guides, one that is especially responsive to modern needs and interests.

For years, dating back as far as Herr Baedeker, travel guides have tended to be encyclopedic, seemingly much more concerned with demonstrating expertise in geography and history than in any analysis of the sorts of things that more frequently concern a typical tourist. But today, when it is hardly necessary to tell a traveler where London is located, it's hard to justify devoting endless pages to historical perspectives. As suggested earlier, it's not impossible that the guidebook reader may have been to Great Britain and Ireland nearly as often as the guidebook editor, so it becomes the responsibility of that editor to provide new perceptions and to suggest new directions to make the guide genuinely valuable.

That's exactly what we've tried to do in our series. I think you'll notice a different, more contemporary tone to the text, as well as an organization and focus that are distinctive and more functional. And even a random examination of what follows will demonstrate a substantial departure from the standard guidebook orientation, for we've not only attempted to provide information of a different sort but we've also tried to present it in a context that makes it particularly accessible.

Needless to say, it's difficult to decide precisely what to include in a guidebook of this size — and what to omit. Early on, we realized that giving up the encyclopedic approach precluded the inclusion of every single route and restaurant, which actually helped define our overall editorial focus. Similarly, when we discussed the possibility of presenting certain information in other than strict geographical order, we found that the new format enabled us to arrange data in a way that we feel best answers the questions travelers typically ask.

Large numbers of specific questions have provided the real editorial skeleton for this book. The volume of mail I regularly receive seems to emphasize that modern travelers want very precise information, so we've tried to address these needs and have organized our material in the most responsive way possible. Readers who want to know the best restaurants in Cardiff or the best golf courses in Scotland will have no trouble whatever finding that data in this guide.

Travel guides are, understandably, reflections of personal taste, and putting one's name on a title page obviously puts one's preferences on the line. But I think I ought to amplify just what "personal" means. I do not believe in the sort of personal guidebook that's a palpable misrepresentation on its face. It is, for example, hardly possible for any single travel writer to visit thousands of restaurants (and nearly as many hotels) in any given year and provide accurate appraisals of each one. And even if it were possible for one human being to survive such an itinerary, it would of necessity have to be done at a dead sprint and the perceptions derived therefrom would probably be less valid than those of any other intelligent individual visiting the same establishments. It is, therefore, impossible (especially in an annually revised and updated guidebook *series* such as we offer) to have only one person provide all the data on the entire world.

I also happen to think that such individual orientation is of substantially less value to readers. Visiting a single hotel for just one night or eating one hasty meal in a given restaurant hardly equips anyone to provide appraisals that are of more than passing interest. No amount of doggedly alliterative or oppressively onomatopoeic text can camouflage a technique that is specious on its face. We have, therefore, chosen what I like to describe as the "thee and me" approach to restaurant and hotel evaluation and, to a somewhat more limited degree, to the sites and sights we have included in the other sections of our text. What this really reflects is personal sampling tempered by intelligent counsel from informed local sources, and these additional friends-of-the-editor are almost always residents of the city and/or area about which they have been consulted.

Despite the presence of several editors, a considerable number of writers and researchers, and numerous insightful local correspondents, very precise editing and tailoring keep our text fiercely subjective. So what follows is purposely designed to be the gospel according to Birnbaum, and it represents as much of my own taste and insight as is humanly possible. It is probable, therefore, that if you like your cities genteel and your mountainsides uncrowded, prefer small hotels with personality to huge high-rise anonymities, and can't tolerate fresh fish that's been relentlessly overcooked, we're likely to have a long and meaningful relationship. Readers with dissimilar tastes may be less enraptured.

I also should point out something about the person to whom this guidebook is directed. Above all, he or she is a "visitor." This means that such elements as restaurants have been specifically picked to provide the visitor with a representative, enlightening, stimulating, and above all, pleasant experience. Since so many extraneous considerations can affect the reception and service accorded a regular restaurant patron, our choices can in no way be construed as a definitive guide to resident dining. We think we've listed all the best places, in various price ranges, but they were chosen with a visitor's viewpoint in mind.

Other evidence of how we've tried to tailor our text to reflect changing travel habits is most apparent in the section we call DIVERSIONS. Where once it was common for travelers to spend a foreign visit nailed to a single spot, the emphasis today is more likely to be directed toward pursuing some active enterprise or special interest while seeing the surrounding countryside. So we've selected every activity we could reasonably evaluate and organized the material in a way that is especially accessible to activists of either an athletic or cerebral bent. It is no longer necessary, therefore, to wade through a pound or two of extraneous prose just to find the very best crafts shop or the quaintest country inn within a reasonable radius of your destination.

If there is a single thing that best characterizes the revolution in and evolution of current holiday habits, it is that most travelers now consider travel a right rather than a privilege. Travel today translates as the enthusiastic desire to sample all of the world's opportunities, to find that elusive quality of experience that is not only enriching but comfortable. For that reason, we've tried to make what follows not only helpful and enlightening but the sort of welcome companion of which every traveler dreams.

Finally, I should point out that every good travel guide is a living enterprise; that is, no part of this text is cast in bronze. In our annual revisions, we refine, expand, and further hone all our material to serve your travel needs even better. To this end, no contribution is of greater value to us than your personal reaction to what we have written, as well as information reflecting your own experiences while using the book. We earnestly and enthusiastically solicit your comments on this book and your opinions and perceptions about places you have recently visited. In this way, we will be able to provide the most current information — including the actual experiences of the travel public — and to make those experiences more readily available to others. So please write to us at 60 E 42nd St., New York, NY 10165.

We sincerely hope to hear from you.

STEPHEN BIRNBAUM

How to Use This Guide

A great deal of care has gone into the organization of this guidebook, and we believe it represents a real breakthrough in the presentation of travel material. Our aim has been to create a new, more modern generation of travel books and to make this guide the most useful and practical travel tool available today.

Our text is divided into five basic sections, in order to best present information on every possible aspect of a vacation in Britain or Ireland. This organization itself should alert you to the vast and varied opportunities available as well as indicating all the specific, detailed data necessary to plan a trip. You won't find much of the conventional "quaint villages and beautiful scenery" text in this guide; we've chosen instead to use the available space for more useful and practical information. Prospective itineraries tend to speak for themselves, and with so many diverse travel opportunities, we feel our main job is to explain them and to provide the basic information — how, when, where, how much, and what's best — to allow you to make the most intelligent choices possible.

What follows is a brief summary of the five sections of this book and what you can expect to find in each. We believe that you will find both your travel planning and en route enjoyment enhanced by having this book at your side.

GETTING READY TO GO

This compendium of practical travel facts is a sort of know-it-all companion that provides all the precise information necessary to go about creating a trip. There are entries on more than 30 separate topics, including how to travel, what preparations to make before leaving, what to expect in the different countries, what the trip is likely to cost, and how to avoid problems. The individual entries are specific, realistic, and cost-oriented.

We expect that you will use this section most in the course of planning your trip, for its ideas and suggestions are intended to facilitate the often confusing planning period. Entries are intentionally concise in an effort to get directly to the meat of the matter. This information is further augmented by extensive lists of sources for more specialized information and some suggestions for obtaining travel information on your own.

PERSPECTIVES

Any visit to an unfamiliar destination is enhanced and enriched by understanding the cultural and historical heritage of that area. We have, therefore, provided just such an introduction to Great Britain and Ireland, their past and present, people, architecture, literature, music and dance, and food and drink.

THE CITIES

Individual reports on the 21 cities most visited by tourists and businesspeople have been researched primarily by professional journalists on their own turf. Useful at the planning stage, THE CITIES is really designed to be taken along and used on the spot. Each report offers a short-stay guide to its city within a consistent format: an essay, introducing the city as a historic entity and a contemporary place to live; *At-a-Glance,* a site-by-site survey of the most important (and sometimes most eclectic) sights to see and things to do; *Sources and Resources,* a concise listing of pertinent tourist information, meant to answer a myriad of potentially pressing questions as they arise — from the address of the tourist office to where to find the best night spot, to see a show, to play golf, or to get a taxi; and *Best in Town,* our cost-and-quality choices of the best places to eat and sleep on a variety of budgets.

DIVERSIONS

This very selective guide is designed to help travelers find the very best places in which to pursue a wide range of physical and cerebral activities without having to wade through endless pages of unrelated text. With a list of more than 15 theme vacations — for the body, the mind, and the experience — DIVERSIONS provides a guide to the special places where the quality of experience is likely to be highest. Whether you seek golf courses or fishing boats, luxurious hotels or atmospheric pubs, each entry is the equivalent of a comprehensive checklist of the absolute best in Britain and Ireland.

DIRECTIONS

Here are 19 itineraries that range all across the countryside, along the most beautiful routes and roads, past the most spectacular natural wonders, through the most historic cities and countryside. DIRECTIONS is the only section of this book to be organized geographically, and its itineraries cover the touring highlights of England, Scotland, Wales, Northern Ireland, and the Irish Republic in short, independent journeys of 3 to 5 days' duration. Itineraries within each country can be connected for longer trips or used individually for short, intensive explorations.

Each entry includes a guide to sightseeing highlights; a cost-and-quality guide to accommodations and food along the road (small inns, castle hotels, hospitable farms, country and off-the-main-road discoveries); and suggestions for activities.

Although each of the sections of the book has a distinct format and a special function, they have all been designed to be used together to provide a complete package of travel information. To use this book to full advantage, take a few minutes to read the table of contents and random entries in each section to get an idea of how it all fits together.

Pick and choose information from the different sections. Assume, for example, that you have always wanted to take that typically English vacation, a walking tour through rural England, but you never really knew how to organize it or where to go. Turn first to the hiking section of GETTING READY TO GO, as well as the chapters on planning a trip, accommodations, and climate and clothes. These short, informative entries provide plenty of practical information. But where to go? Turn next to DIRECTIONS. Perhaps you choose to walk the 100-odd-mile Cotswold Way. Your trip will certainly begin and end in London, and for a complete rundown on that fabulous city, you should read the London chapter of THE CITIES. Finally, turn to DIVERSIONS to peruse the chapters on sports, hotels, antiques, and other activities in which you are interested to make sure you don't miss anything in the neighborhood.

In other words, the sections of this book are building blocks to help you put together the best possible trip. Use them selectively as a tool, a source of ideas, a reference work for accurate facts, and a guide to the best buys, the most exciting sights, the most pleasant accommodations, the tastiest food — *the best travel experiences* that you can have.

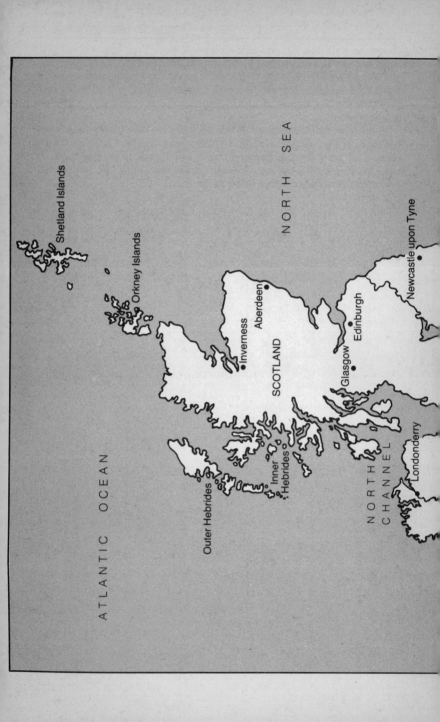

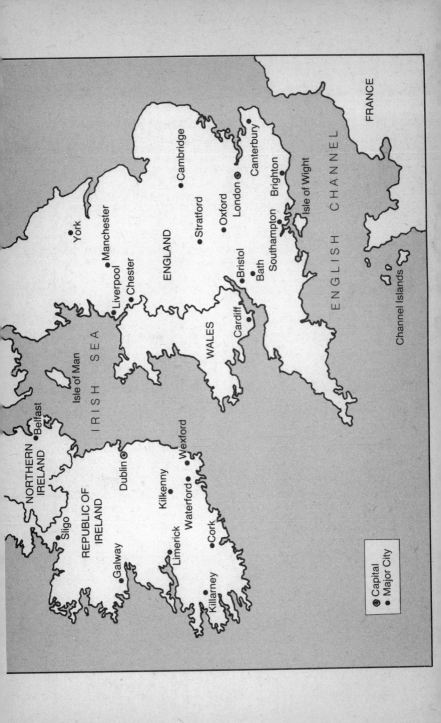

GETTING READY TO GO

When and How to Go

What's Where

 The islands that make up Great Britain and Ireland — which together used to be known as the British Isles — lie in the North Atlantic immediately off the northwest coast of France, separated from the Continent by the English Channel, the Strait of Dover, and the North Sea. Dover, on the southeast tip of England, and Calais, in the northwestern corner of France, are only 25 miles from each other. Included in the scattering of tiny islands nearby that are part of Great Britain are the Channel Islands; the Isle of Man; the Orkneys, Hebrides, and Shetlands off the coast of Scotland; and others.

England, Scotland, and Wales (Great Britain) together with Northern Ireland are the major entities that compose the United Kingdom. Northern Ireland, a province of the UK, consists of six counties — Antrim, Armagh, Down, Fermanagh, Londonderry, and Tyrone — and covers an area of some 5,000 square miles in the northeastern part of the island of Ireland. There are 26 counties in the Irish Republic. In total, the United Kingdom covers some 94,000 square miles and has a population of 56 million, 1.5 million of whom live in Northern Ireland. Physically, England dominates its island, covering well over half the area that extends from the southern coast along the English Channel to Newcastle, at the edge of the Scottish Lowlands. Wales abuts England on the west, projecting into St. George's Channel, which separates it from Ireland. Scotland forms the northern third of the island. The Irish Republic covers some 26,600 square miles, the lion's share of the island it shares with Northern Ireland; it has a population of about 3.5 million.

ENGLAND

Broadly speaking, England is rather flat in the south and east and mountainous in the north and west. Like all generalizations, however, this one has a striking exception — the southwestern peninsula, which is dominated by two large wild moorlands, Dartmoor and Exmoor. The more southerly, Dartmoor, is a granite-based, desolately beautiful region of rugged hills and bogs; the gentler Exmoor is a heather-clad plateau creased by deep valleys cradling tiny, whitewashed villages.

The south and east of England are low-lying lands crossed by ranges of rolling hills and gently sculpted by slow-moving rivers. The highlands here are paradoxically called "the Downs." Much of the area is now "Londonized," but it's still possible to find delightfully rural and provincial towns.

To the north, the lowlands merge imperceptibly with the Midlands, a mining and manufacturing region centered on Birmingham. The landscape, although often marred by industry, is subtly attractive, especially around the Derbyshire hills and the Peak National Park. The Midlands slope away to East Anglia, a large tract of flat and beautifully still countryside, whose citizens retain a strong regional identity. At the coast the land slips quietly into the North Sea; here, there are many deserted beaches; peaceful wildlife reserves; and the famous Broads, haunt of sailors and fishermen.

The great backbone of England is the Pennine chain, a mountain range which runs north from South Yorkshire to Scotland. Although surrounded on three sides by heavily populated cities, the Pennines remain remarkably wild. To the west is the Lake District, where volcanic rocks and glaciation have combined to produce a stunning landscape of mountains, woods, and lakes. England's highest mountain, Scafell Pike (3,210 feet), dominates this region, loved by hikers and campers. In the east, the North York Moors, cut by fast-flowing rivers into a patchwork of dales, reach northward to a very secluded corner of England, Northumberland. No industry has ever penetrated here, or large town ever grown up. Even the roads hesitate; only river valleys like Coquetdale penetrate the heart of this wild region.

SCOTLAND

Emerging without fuss from northern England, the Lowlands of Scotland are a region of broad valleys and rounded green hills, quite unlike the stereotypical image of wild Scotland, but no less beautiful. Farther north, however, above the Highland Boundary Fault, that wilder Scotland begins; here are the towering mountains, cascading waterfalls, and deep forests. The Fault runs right through Loch Lomond, Britain's largest stretch of inland water, which is dotted with tiny islands. In the east are the Trossachs ("the Bristly Country"), an uncivilized thicket of birch, oak, and heather crowding Lochs Katrine, Archay, and Venachar. This is the heart of the romantic Sir Walter Scott region, immortalized in his long poem, *The Lady of the Lake*.

North again are the Highlands proper, running from Fort William in the southwest, up the coast to Cape Wrath at the northern tip of the country to the Highland capital, Inverness. The mountains here are often snow-capped in summer, and the rivers have sliced through the harsh slopes to feed dense pine forests. In the far west the Atlantic has taken charge and carved long rugged fingers from the land, leaving sea-filled valleys between them. Off that remote coast are the Hebrides — a group of rocky islands flung into the ocean. Largest and perhaps best of all is Skye, "the Faery Isle," a volcanic wonderland softened by rivers and mists that is still serenely remote from the present century and breathtakingly beautiful.

WALES

Wales is ringed with huge castles, reminders of those days when its people were kept under strict control by their nervous English neighbors. The need for caution has gone, but the sense of difference between the two countries still persists and is reflected by the striking change of scenery as you cross from the green and gentle hills and valleys of English "Border Country" to the rugged mountains of Wales.

The Brecon Beacons of the south and center are the heart of wild Wales. Their highest point, Pen-y-Fan, is 2,906 feet above sea level and the roads give up long before reaching its heights. But pony trails abound, and it's very easy to forget civilization as you trot along past slate outcroppings and thundering waterfalls. The Pembrokeshire coast in southwestern Wales is considered the most spectacular in all Britain. Here, the mountains rush headlong into the sea, only sometimes softened by sandy bays and quiet creeks. The industrial towns of Port Talbot, Swansea, and Cardiff are located along the southern coast. The people there make their livings refining and shipping the coal and iron ore carved from mines in the steep and isolated valleys of South Wales.

Wales is at its most dramatic, however, in the far northwest. Here, its highest mountains, the Snowdon Massif (3,560 feet at the highest peak) look down over range upon range of slate-brown mountains and valleys, rushing rivers, and huge lakes. The drive from Barmouth on the coast inland to Dolgellau follows the Maddach Estuary, with the Cadair Idris mountains towering above you. This experience will banish forever any misconceptions you may have of Britain's countryside being flat and tame. But to experience the full beauty of Snowdonia, you must leave the car and walk or climb in the mountains themselves.

NORTHERN IRELAND

Most people who have never visited Northern Ireland — or "Ulster," as it is often called — think of it as a drab, gray, and beleaguered country. Although it's true that "the troubles" persist, the scenery is far from drab and the welcome as warm as any you will receive. In the southeast, the majestic Mountains of Mourne really do sweep down to the sea around Kilkeel — you'll see at once why they are sung about. Along the Antrim coast, fierce and perpendicular headlands leap into the ocean on all sides, but inland are green and lush pastures watered by serene loughs (a lake in Ireland is a *lough,* the same as a *loch* in Scotland) and hugged by gently heaving hills. Lough Neagh, the largest lake in the United Kingdom, covers 153 square miles in the middle of the country and is bordered by five of the six counties. A major feature of the landscape in the southwest corner of Ulster is the watery, forested county of Fermanagh, which has more than 150 islands in its largest lake, Lough Erne.

IRISH REPUBLIC

Prim whitewashed cottages surrounded by verdant pastures and flowering hedgerows — this is the conventional image of Eire. But, in fact, Irish terrain is remarkably more varied for so small a country and can change abruptly in a matter of miles. In the northwest — counties Donegal, Mayo, and Galway — the landscape is stark and the vegetation brushy. Innumerable stone walls march without hesitation up steep mountainsides, where shaggy cattle graze stubbornly on the rocky land. To the south, the forbidding hills of northern County Clare, which appear to be almost paved with stone, give way to rolling, velvety meadows and powdery strands. The highest mountains in Ireland are in the southwest — on the Dingle, Kerry, and Beara peninsulas. Here sandstone ridges such as the Macgillycuddy's Reeks and the Caha and Slieve Mish mountains were shaped by Ice Age glaciers, which also left behind scores of lakes and valleys. More gentle is the southern coast of Ireland — a seascape of quiet coves, saltwater marshes, and little fishing villages — and the southeastern coast, a resort area popular for its sunny weather and sandy beaches. Just south of Dublin is the scenic Glendalough Valley, ringed by mountains, watered by two lakes, and scattered with ancient Christian ruins. The midlands, an area stretching roughly from Dublin west to Limerick, is a low-lying plain with many lakes and bogs. The green fields here are rived with black trenches from which turf has been cut, and the air is sweet with the smell of turf fires.

When to Go

 For North Americans as well as Europeans, the period from mid-May to mid-September has long been — and remains — the peak period for travel, the traditional vacation time. As far as the weather is concerned, Great Britain and Ireland are at their best then: cooler and more comfortable than many other, less temperate, destinations on the Continent, where a summer heat wave is almost a foregone conclusion. It should be superfluous to point out, however, that neither country is a single-season vacation area, and more and more vacationers who have a choice are considering the advantages of off-season travel. Though many of the lesser tourist attractions may close for the winter — especially from December through Easter in rural areas — the major ones are open and they are less crowded, as are the cities. During the off-season, British and Irish life is seen at its most natural, a lively social and cultural season is underway, and, what's more, it's generally less expensive.

For some, the most convincing argument in favor of off-season travel is the economic one. In fall and especially in winter, air fares drop and hotel rates go down. Relatively inexpensive package tours become available and the independent traveler can get farther on less, too. Europe is not like the Caribbean where high season and low season are precisely defined and rates drop off automatically on a particular date. But many British hotels lower rates or offer cut-rate "mini-break" packages (for stays of more than one day, especially over weekends) from October through April, and hotel rates in Ireland tend to be at their lowest from January through March. Savings can be as much as 20%, unless high-season rates continue to prevail because of an important local event — such as the Spring Show in Dublin. Many smaller guesthouses and bed-and-breakfast houses (B&Bs) close off-season in response to reduced demand, but there are still plenty of places to stay.

CLIMATE: Most people want to travel when the weather is best. To the extent that it is mild, with no beastly hot summers or bone-chilling winters eliminating chunks of the calendar from the options, the weather in both Great Britain and Ireland cooperates to make them multiseasonal destinations. Warm currents from the Gulf Stream soften extremes of temperature and even provide the surprising touch of palm trees in downtown Dublin and in western Scottish gardens.

The climate is hardly perfect, however. For one thing, you probably won't come home with a suntan, even in summer. There is a reason for those renowned peaches-and-cream complexions and the reason is moisture, meaning frequently overcast skies, or even rain. To avoid disappointment, expect the worst, and you might be pleasantly surprised at how infrequently it actually happens. Remember, also, that though winters are not the marrow-freezing scourges of the northern US and Canada, they are damp, and central heating is usually inadequate by North American standards. Mid-October through mid-March is admittedly not an ideal time for touring the Scottish or Irish countryside, though it may be suitable for those with special outdoor interests such as fishing and hunting.

London is very much a city of the temperate zone. With occasional exceptions, summers tend to be moderately warm, with few days above 75°F (24°C), and winters moderately cold, with few days dropping below 30°F (−1°C). Spring and autumn tend to be comfortable, with little more than a sweater or light overcoat required. Umbrellas or raincoats are necessary, but legends about London's incessant rain are exaggerations. The truth is that the weather in London is often unreliable and unpredictable, with beautiful mornings turning into dreary afternoons and vice versa. Yet London has less rainfall than Rome, which is known as a sunny city. It simply thins its rain out and spreads it over more days: not hard, driving rains, but showers.

Though changeability is typical of British weather, it is safe to say that the farther north and west you go from the heart of England, the wetter it gets. This is because winds moving from west to east drop their rain over Britain's mountainous backbone and proceed over the rest of the country a good deal drier. In Edinburgh, a day with no rain is a rarity, even in summer. Mists are not unknown either, and when the wind blows, put millstones in your shoes. On the other hand, temperatures usually don't go below freezing in winter or over 70°F (21°C) in summer. A mackintosh with a zip-in lining that fits over everything you own is a recommended survival kit. In the Scottish Highlands and islands, chances for good weather are best May through September. Cloudy days are a matter of course, but this doesn't mean the sun never shines. Days get very long in the summer and there is daylight well into the June night in northernmost areas.

Ireland's climate tends to be even more consistently showery than Britain's. Because of westerly winds coming from the Atlantic, it, too, has heavier rainfall in the west than in the east, but because of the country's small size, it has relatively uniform temperatures throughout. Summers are cool and winters are mild. In Dublin, average winter temperatures range from 39° to 45°F (4° to 7°C), with January and February the coldest months; average summer temperatures range from 61° to 70°F (16° to 21°C), with July and August the warmest months. Lightweight wools are worn even in summer. April is the driest month in Ireland and May and June are the sunniest months.

The chart below lists seasonal temperature ranges for specific British and Irish cities and should give a better idea of what weather conditions to expect and, therefore, what to pack.

AVERAGE TEMPERATURES (in °F)

	January	*April*	*July*	*October*
Aberdeen, Scot.	36°–43°	40°–49°	52°–63°	43°–54°
Bath, Eng.	38°–49°	40°–54°	54°–67°	41°–52°
Belfast, N. Ire.	36°–43°	40°–54°	52°–65°	45°–56°
Brighton, Eng.	43°–49°	43°–56°	58°–65°	47°–52°
Bristol, Eng.	40°–47°	38°–56°	54°–67°	45°–58°
Cambridge, Eng.	34°–43°	40°–58°	54°–72°	43°–59°
Cardiff, Wales	36°–45°	41°–56°	54°–68°	47°–58°
Chester, Eng.	38°–45°	40°–54°	54°–68°	45°–58°
Cork, Ire.	36°–49°	41°–56°	54°–68°	45°–58°
Dover, Eng.	36°–45°	43°–54°	58°–68°	49°–59°
Dublin, Ire.	34°–47°	40°–56°	52°–68°	43°–58°
Edinburgh, Scot.	34°–43°	40°–52°	52°–65°	45°–54°
Galway, Ire.	40°–49°	43°–54°	56°–68°	49°–58°
Glasgow, Scot.	34°–41°	40°–54°	52°–67°	43°–56°
Inverness, Scot.	34°–43°	38°–50°	52°–63°	43°–54°
Killarney, Ire.	41°–50°	45°–56°	54°–70°	49°–59°
Limerick, Ire.	36°–47°	41°–56°	54°–67°	45°–58°
Liverpool, Eng.	36°–45°	41°–52°	56°–67°	47°–56°
London, Eng.	36°–45°	40°–56°	56°–72°	45°–58°
Manchester, Eng.	36°–43°	41°–56°	56°–70°	45°–58°
Oxford, Eng.	34°–45°	41°–58°	54°–72°	45°–58°
Stratford-upon-Avon, Eng.	36°–47°	41°–56°	52°–76°	43°–59°
York, Eng.	36°–47°	41°–54°	58°–72°	43°–56°

SPECIAL EVENTS: Many travelers may want to time a trip to coincide with a special event. The highlight of a sports lover's trip may be attendance at the British or Irish championships of his or her game. For a music lover, a concert in a great cathedral may be a thrilling experience and much more memorable than seeing the same church on a sightseeing itinerary. A folklore festival can bring nearly forgotten traditions alive or underscore their continuing significance in modern life.

In both Great Britain and Ireland, the calendar of such events is a busy one from spring through fall, but there is still much that is happening in winter. In London, the cultural season proceeds at a pace that few other cities can match. Museums and galleries mount special exhibitions; ballet and opera take place at Covent Garden and the Coliseum; concerts are held at the Royal Festival Hall, Royal Albert Hall, and Queen Elizabeth Hall; and the theater is everywhere. Other cities and towns, whatever their size, promote their own smaller cultural programs. Winter is also the height of the soccer and rugby season throughout the island, and curling and other winter sports are under way in Scotland. The grouse-hunting season in the Highlands opens in mid-August and runs to mid-December. In Ireland, a land of horse lovers, there's racing practically all year round; fishing for one species or another is also possible all year; and winter is the hunting season. Somewhere a bloodstock sale, a rugby match, or a festival of drama, music, or dancing is taking place.

The events below are the major ones, listed according to the months in which they usually occur. Since there can be variations from year to year, check with the British Tourist Authority, the Northern Ireland Tourist Board, or the Irish Tourist Board for the exact dates of anything you wouldn't want to miss and for current schedules of fairs, festivals, and other events. It is also possible to book tickets in advance for many of the major festivals through a US firm, Edwards & Edwards, 1 Times Square Plaza, New York, NY 10036 (phone: in New York State, 212-944-0290; elsewhere, 800-223-6108).

GREAT BRITAIN

February

Crufts Dog Show: Over 8,000 canine entries, representing over a hundred breeds, compete for the "best of show" title. London.

March

Oxford vs. Cambridge Boat Race: Since 1829 and Cambridge is ahead. The big event in intercollegiate rowing takes place on the Thames between Putney and Mortlake and can be viewed from the towpath. London.

April

Shakespeare Theatre Season: Shakespeare's plays performed in the town of his birth by the outstanding cast of the Royal Shakespeare Company. Season runs until January. Stratford-upon-Avon.

Grand National Steeplechase: Britain's most famous jumping race, with all Britain betting on the outcome. Aintree Racecourse, Liverpool.

Badminton Horse Trials: Major event on the equestrian calendar: dressage, cross-country, and show jumping. Badminton.

London Marathon: A marathon run through the streets of London, including historic areas.

May

Chichester Festival Theatre Season: Drama festival with four plays running for 5 months in modern Festival Theatre. After London, a good place to catch top-flight British productions. Chichester.

Pitlochry Festival Theatre Season: Five months of summer theater in a Scottish Highlands resort. Pitlochry.

Brighton Festival: Music and theater plus fringe events and fireworks in this seaside resort. Some performances in the Royal Pavilion. Brighton.

Chelsea Flower Show: Acres of flowers, shrubs, trees, and flower arrangements set up on the grounds of the Royal Hospital. London.

Bath International Festival: Two weeks of choral and chamber music, art and film shows, lectures, garden and walking tours throughout the lovely Georgian town. Bath.

Glyndebourne Festival Opera: Over 2 months of first-rate opera. At intermission festival-goers in formal dress dine in the restaurant or picnic on the lawn. Near Lewes, East Sussex.

June

The Derby: The world's most famous horse race, run since 1780 when Lord Derby didn't make the winner's circle but did win the toss of a coin that gave his name to the event. Epsom Racecourse, Epsom, Surrey.

Aldeburgh Festival: A 2-week music festival founded by composer Benjamin Britten. Concerts — emphasis is on new works — take place in churches, houses, and in the Snape Maltings Concert Hall. Aldeburgh.

Mid-Wales Festival of the Countryside: A series of more than 40 events celebrating the rural attractions of Wales. Held from June through September at various locations throughout Wales.

York Mystery Plays and Festival of the Arts: Recreation of 14th-century mystery plays by 200 citizens of York. Held every 4 years (the next one is in 1988), it takes over 3 weeks and includes an arts festival with symphony and chamber concerts, choral music, and ballet. York.

Trooping the Colour: The Queen's official birthday parade and the pageantry of royal Britain at its best; from Buckingham Palace to Horse Guards Parade and back. London.

Royal Ascot: Part of the London season, the June meeting at Ascot Racecourse is attended by the Queen, members of the royal family, and high society in hats. Ascot.

Wimbledon Lawn Tennis Championships: The world's most prestigious tennis tournament and another part of the London season — there's a royal box at center court — lasting two full weeks. All-England Lawn Tennis and Croquet Club, London.

July

Henley Royal Regatta: The international rowing regatta is watched from grandstands or from boats moored to the riverbank; another fashionable gathering on the London social calendar. Henley-on-Thames.

City of London Festival: Orchestral, choral, and chamber concerts, as well as arts events, in St. Paul's Cathedral, the Mansion House, the Guildhall, the Tower of London, and other spots within the square-mile City of London. London.

Llangollen International Musical Eisteddfod: An extremely popular festival of choral music, folk music, and dancing that draws more than 10,000 competitors from over 30 countries yearly to a small town in Wales. *Eisteddfod* is the Welsh word for "session," and this one is 5 days of song in foreign tongues and colorful national costumes. Llangollen.

British Grand Prix: Top British motor race. Held in even-numbered years at Brands Hatch, near Dartford, and in odd-numbered years at Silverstone, near Towcester.

British Open Golf Championship: One of golfing's great moments. First played in 1860, it now moves annually from course to prestigious course in England and the sport's ancestral home in Scotland.

August

Royal National Eisteddfod of Wales: A celebration of the Welsh language and culture and the chance to hear some of those famous Welsh choirs; arts and crafts contests and the "chairing of the bard" ceremony. Site alternates yearly between North and South Wales.

Cowes Week: International sailing festival at the headquarters of British yachting. Cowes, Isle of Wight.

Three Choirs Festival: Founded in the early 18th century and considered Europe's oldest continuing music festival — in this case, choral music. Held annually in rotation in the three cathedral cities of Gloucester, Worcester, and Hereford.

Edinburgh International Festival: Several festivals crammed into one 3-week extravaganza: the main music and drama festival with performing artists of world renown; the Festival Fringe, shoestring to big-time productions by amateurs and professionals who come at their own expense; the Military Tattoo, a nightly concert spectacle of pipe bands and kilted regiments on the esplanade of Edinburgh Castle; the Film Festival; the Jazz Festival; the Book Festival. Edinburgh.

September

Farnborough Air Show: Biannual aerospace exhibition and display of flying. Farnborough.

Braemar Royal Highland Gathering: Best known of the Scottish Highland gatherings takes place near Balmoral Castle under the patronage of the Queen; piping, dancing, and Highland games such as "putting the stone" and "tossing the caber." Braemar.

October

Horse of the Year Show: A major show-jumping event. Wembley, London.

National Gaelic Mod: The Mod is to Scotland what the Eisteddfod is to Wales — a week of song, dance, and storytelling, this time in Gaelic. Site varies from year to year.

State Opening of Parliament: The Queen rides in the Irish State Coach from Buckingham Palace to the Houses of Parliament; ceremony inside is closed to the public but the procession can be seen en route. London. (It is sometimes held at the beginning of November.)

November

London to Brighton Veteran Car Run: Antique cars leave Hyde Park Corner, London, and drive to Brighton in celebration of the turn-of-the-century day on which a law requiring cars to be preceded by a man waving a red flag was dropped from the books.

Lord Mayor's Procession: Colorful parade of the newly elected Lord Mayor who rides from the Guildhall to the Royal Courts of Justice in an antique, horse-drawn carriage attended by costumed bodyguards. London.

IRISH REPUBLIC AND NORTHERN IRELAND

March

St. Patrick's Week: Celebrations throughout the Republic give the patron saint his due. Parades and other festivities in Cork, Dublin, Dundalk, Kilkenny, Killarney, Limerick, Sligo, Waterford, and Wexford. In Northern Ireland, there's an important pilgrimage to Slemish Mountain, County Antrim, where the saint tended sheep as a boy, as well as musical and other events in and around Downpatrick, where he is said to have established Ireland's first monastery.

April

Cork International Choral and Folk Dance Festival: An international choir competition with folk dancing exhibitions. Cork.

World Championships in Irish Dancing: Dancers from around the world compete with Ireland's best, chosen in national championships in February. Site changes from year to year; last year the event was held in Galway.

May

Spring Show and Industries Fair: A week-long trade and livestock show with daily horse jumping competitions — like a huge country fair in the heart of Dublin and one of the city's two biggest annual events. Dublin.

Pan Celtic Week: Representatives of Scotland, Wales, Cornwall, the Isle of Man, Brittany, and Ireland compete in song, dance, and sports. Killarney.

Fleadh Nua: Pronounced "flah," this is a festival of traditional music, the second most important one in Ireland. Ennis.

Festival of the Galway Tribes and Families: A giant reunion, with banquets, entertainment, and a week's worth of talk about ancestors.

Dundalk International Maytime and Amateur Drama Festival: Music, sports, social events, and an international drama festival. Dundalk, County Clare.

Writers' Week: Lectures, workshops, competitions, and camaraderie for writers. Listowel, County Louth.

June

Festival of Music in Great Irish Houses: A week or so of classical concerts in beautiful 18th-century mansions. Dublin.

July

Orangemen's Day and the Sham Fight: Colorful parades in Belfast and other cities and a sham fight at Scarva in County Down commemorate the Battle of the Boyne.

International Folk Dance Festival: Dancers from Ireland and other countries converge in Cobh, County Cork, for this event.

August

Dublin Horse Show: An outstanding sporting and social event attracting horse fans and the smart set from around the Emerald Isle, across the Irish Sea, and from Europe and America. International jumping competitions daily, auctions, band concerts, arts and crafts exhibits, folk dances, dinner dances — it's the gathering of the year. Dublin.

Puck Fair: Actually a 3-day livestock sale, and an excuse to keep the Guinness flowing. Men of the village capture a wild billy goat who, beribboned, watches over the festivities from a pedestal above the square. Killorglin, County Kerry.

Ancient Order of Hibernians' Processions: Parades, religious services, and sports events commemorate Lady Day. Various cities in Northern Ireland.

Connemara Pony Show: The famous ponies strut their stuff on the third Thursday of the month. Clifden, County Galway.

Yeats International Summer School: Two weeks of lectures, seminars, and discussions of his work and its background, an entire course with a certificate on completion. Tourists can participate with single admission tickets. Sligo.

Fleadh Cheoil na hÉireann: An All-Ireland Fleadh and the year's most important gathering of traditional Irish musicians. Some compete and some just play, and for 3 days there is music everywhere. Site changes from year to year.

Ould Lammas Fair: A very popular and traditional Irish fair held annually since the 16th century. Ballycastle, Northern Ireland.

Rose of Tralee International Festival: One of the country's biggest bashes. A folk festival, dancing and singing, and endless opportunities for merriment occur around the central event: the selection of the Rose of Tralee from a bouquet of fair, young lasses of Irish descent who congregate at County Kerry from around the globe. Tralee.

September

All-Ireland Hurling Final and All-Ireland Football Final: Two rousing finales to a season of Gaelic sports. The hurling final is traditionally held in Croke Park on the first Sunday in September and the Gaelic football final follows two Sundays later. Dublin.

Waterford International Festival of Light Opera: Amateur groups from Britain and Ireland vie to give the best performance of a musical or operetta, and for 2 weeks the pubs stay open late. Waterford.

Galway Oyster Festival: The Lord Mayor opens the first oyster of the season, inaugurating two days of feasting on oysters, brown bread, and Guinness stout. Clarenbridge, Galway.

October

Cork Film Festival: Still an important week on the calendar of international film festivals, though on a smaller scale than before. Cork.

The Guinness Jazz Festival: A popular event featuring top-notch jazz musicians and vocalists from all over the world. Cork.

Dublin Theatre Festival: A fortnight of new plays by Irish playwrights plus imported productions and plenty of opportunity to discuss them. Dublin.

Castlebar International Song Contest: Devoted to popular music, it's one of the most important song contests in Europe. Castlebar.

Wexford Opera Festival: Rarely performed 18th- and 19th-century operas are staged in the small, restored Georgian Theatre Royal, and recitals, concerts, exhibitions, and balls go on elsewhere. The 12-day gala has an international reputation. Wexford.

November

Belfast Festival at Queen's: Three weeks of classical music, folk music, jazz, opera, ballet, drama, and film at Queen's University. Belfast.

Traveling by Plane

The air space between North America and Europe is the most heavily trafficked in the world. It is served by dozens of airlines, almost all of which sell seats at a variety of prices under widely different terms. It is not uncommon for passengers sitting side by side on the same wide-body jet to have paid fares varying by hundreds of dollars for their respective seats, and all too often the traveler paying more would have been equally content with the terms of a less expensive ticket. Because you probably will spend more for your air fare than for any other single item in your travel budget, it's a good idea to know something about the kinds of flights available, bargain arrangements, and the latest wrinkles in the scheduled and charter airline scene.

SCHEDULED FLIGHTS: Airlines offering regularly scheduled flights from the United States to Great Britain, many on a daily basis, are: Air America, Air India, Air New Zealand International, American Airlines, British Airways, British Caledonian, Continental, Delta, Eastern, El Al, Kuwait Airways, Northwest Orient, Pan Am, Piedmont, TWA, and Virgin Atlantic.

Gateways – At present, direct flights to Great Britain depart from Anchorage, Atlanta, Baltimore, Boston, Chicago, Dallas/Fort Worth, Denver, Detroit, Honolulu, Houston, Los Angeles, Miami, Minneapolis/St. Paul, Newark, New York, Orlando, Philadelphia, Pittsburgh, St. Louis, San Francisco, Seattle, Tampa, and Washington, DC. As defined here, a direct flight is one requiring no change of plane between the starting and terminating cities, though the flight may not necessarily be nonstop. Airlines also consider flights involving a change of plane as direct flights as long as the flight number remains the same. With direct flights thus defined, many more US cities serve as gateways to Britain. Scheduled flights from the US land at London's Heathrow and Gatwick airports, at Manchester International Airport, and at Glasgow's Prestwick Airport.

Aer Lingus operates daily scheduled flights to Ireland from New York in summer (six times a week in winter), and direct, nonstop, flights from Boston three times weekly in summer. All Aer Lingus flights land first at Shannon International Airport in the west of Ireland, then terminate at Dublin Airport in the east. Northwest Orient also currently has direct scheduled flights from New York to Shannon (one to three times weekly, depending on season) and from Boston to Shannon (with a frequency ranging from no service in winter to daily flights at the height of the season). In spring and summer, some of these flights go on to Dublin. Pan Am flies nonstop from New York to Shannon one to three times weekly, depending on season, and Delta flies nonstop from Atlanta to Shannon up to five times weekly in spring and summer (off-season flights from Atlanta to Shannon take off twice weekly but are routed via London).

Fares – Perhaps the most common misconception about fares on scheduled airlines is that the cost of the ticket determines the quantity and quality of the service you'll receive on the flight. This is true to a certain extent, but a far more realistic rule of thumb is that the less you pay for your ticket, the more restrictions and qualifications you'll encounter before you get on the plane (as well as after you get off).

These qualifying aspects usually relate to the months in which you travel, how far in advance you purchase your ticket, the minimum and maximum time you remain abroad, your willingness to make up your mind concerning a return date at the time of booking, and your ability to stick to your decision. Your ticket will fall into one of several fare categories being offered by scheduled carriers flying between the US and Great Britain and Ireland. These are first class, business, economy, and advance purchase excursion (APEX).

In a class by itself is the Concorde, the supersonic jet developed by France and Britain that cruises at speeds of 1,350 miles per hour and makes transatlantic crossings in half the time of subsonic jets. British Airways offers Concorde service to London from New York, Washington, DC, and Miami. Service is one class (lavish care, with champagne and caviar all the way). The fare is considerably more expensive than that for first class on a subsonic carrier, but for some the gift of time is worth the price.

1. *First Class:* In general, a first-class, round-trip ticket costs five or six times the APEX fare — quite a lot to pay for free earphones and a glass of champagne in your own special section of the plane. But the atmosphere is certainly classier — especially on the wide-body jets — and there are the added comforts of more leg room, more spacious seats, and, increasingly, "sleeper" seats. No advance booking is necessary, no minimum or maximum stay required, no cancellation penalty, and tickets can be purchased for one-way or round-trip travel. On most first-class fares, unlimited free stopovers are allowed — an incredible bonus on a long trip. If you're planning to visit countries besides Great Britain or Ireland, you could stop over in any number of cities en route to your most distant destination, provided that certain set, but generous, maximum permitted mileage limits are respected. Note that it is not easy to inform yourself of stopover possibilities. It takes a good travel agent, working with the airline's rate desk (to which the public doesn't normally have access) to apprise you fully of stopover privileges.

2. *Business Class:* Not too long ago, there were only two classes of air travel: first class and all the rest (usually called economy). But because passengers paying full economy fares — business travelers for the most part — traveled in the same compartment as passengers flying for considerably less on various discount fares, the airlines introduced special frills to compensate those paying the full price. Thus, business class came into being, though many airlines have their own names for it, such as Clipper Class on Pan Am, Ambassador Class on TWA, Super Club on British Airways, and Executive Class on Aer Lingus. A separate cabin or cabins, usually toward the front of the plane, is the norm. Liquor and headsets are free, and there may be a greater number of selections on the menu as well as a separate counter for speedier check-in. Seats are generally roomier, and there may be more leg and shoulder space between passengers than in the rear of the cabin.

Like first class, you travel on any scheduled flight you wish, you may buy a one-way or a round-trip ticket, and the ticket is valid for a year. There are no minimum- or maximum-stay requirements, no advance booking is necessary, and you are not subject to any cancellation penalties. In addition, the fare allows the same unlimited free stopover privileges as first class. On some transatlantic routes, airlines have introduced business fares at two price levels. When this is the case, the higher fare usually allows unlimited free stopovers in the classic sense, using other carriers if need be, while the lower fare allows none or only those that can be completed on the same carrier.

3. *Economy:* The terms of this fare may vary slightly from route to route and from airline to airline, and some airlines sell more than one type of economy fare. Those that offer business class also tend to offer economy tickets for substantially less than business class, the saving effected by limiting the frills (you pay for the liquor and headsets, you check in with the masses) and by reducing the stopover privileges. Other airlines may have one fare (which may be called "regular economy") allowing unlimited stopovers and a second, less expensive fare (it may be called "special economy") limiting them in some way. Thus, many prospective full-fare economy passengers prefer to upgrade themselves to business class if they need an unrestricted ticket or if comfort is a priority; if not, they buy an APEX. Common to all economy fares, however, is their relative convenience. As is the case with the higher-priced tickets, they can be bought for a flight up to the minute of take-off if seats are available, and if the ticket is round-trip, the return reservation can be made any time you wish — months before you leave or the day before you return. They are valid for a year, after which they can be renewed if not used (but you must pay any price increase that may have occurred in the meantime), and if you ultimately decide not to fly at all, your money will be refunded. While both first-class and business-class fares remain the same year-round, economy fares have traditionally varied in price from a basic (low-season) price, in effect most of the year, to a peak (high-season) price in summer, but this is changing. Some economy fares now remain the same year-round, and some have three price seasons: basic (or low), shoulder, and peak.

4. *Advance Purchase Excursion (APEX):* Excursion fares have been the traditional bargain fares. They apply to round trips only, and they have minimum- and maximum-stay requirements. In the past, excursions had neither advance booking requirements nor cancellation penalties, they often permitted one stopover (which had to be paid for) in each direction, and they had "open jaws," which meant that you could fly to one city and depart from another, arranging and paying for your own transportation between the two. But the traditional excursion fares have been replaced on almost all the airlines by the APEX, or advance purchase excursion, which is essentially an excursion ticket with strings attached. Passengers sit with and receive the same services as economy passengers even though they have paid significantly less for their seats, but, in return, they are subject to certain restrictions. The ticket is usually good for a minimum of 7 days abroad and a maximum, currently, of 6 months abroad in the case of tickets to Great Britain and Ireland. As its name implies, it must be paid for in full a certain number of days (usually 21) before departure. The drawback to the APEX is that it penalizes travelers who change their minds. Both the departing and return flights must be reserved at the time you buy the ticket, and there is a penalty of $50 to $100 or more for changing or canceling a reservation before travel begins or while you are abroad. No stopovers are allowed on the APEX, but it is sometimes possible to create an open-jaw effect by buying an APEX on a split ticket basis; i.e., flying to Shannon and returning from London. The total fare would be half the price of an APEX to Shannon plus half the price of an APEX to London. In general, Advance Purchase

Excursions across the Atlantic are sold at basic, shoulder, and peak rates, and may include surcharges for weekend flights.

Standby fares are elusive on flights to many European cities but are fairly common between the US and London, less common between the US and Ireland. However, they are available from time to time. Although the definition of standby varies somewhat from airline to airline, it generally means that one buys a ticket for the desired flight usually no sooner than the day of anticipated departure, and then one literally "stands by" at the airport on the chance that a seat will be available. Once aboard, however, a passenger enjoys the same meal service and frills (or lack thereof) as the economy-fare passengers. Something else to look into are GIT (group inclusive tour) and ITX (independent tour excursion) fares. These "tour-basing" fares are for group or independent travelers prepurchasing a minimum of ground arrangements at their destination. In the past, they were among the least expensive fares, but with the advent of discount fares such as the APEX, they have all but disappeared from some air routes, or their price tags are the equivalent of other discount fares.

Travelers looking for the least expensive air fares should, finally, scan the travel pages of their newspapers for announcements of special promotions. These are the airline industry's equivalent of a sale and may be offered not only to encourage travel during slow seasons but also to inaugurate and publicize new routes.

Another way to fly for less is with one of the smaller airlines that consistently manage to offer bargain rates. You will probably note early on in your research that there is little, if any, difference in the prices charged by the main carriers for a ticket in the same fare category between the same two cities. In addition to other factors, the economics of the marketplace tends to rule, with airlines rushing to match any new package of fares and conditions proposed by a competitor or risk being priced out of business. But some airlines — frequently those that were once strictly supplemental, or charter, airlines — can provide a lot for less because of lower overhead, uncomplicated route networks, and other limitations in their service. Note that even though the difference in price between a ticket on a low-fare airline and an APEX carrier may sometimes be negligible, the former may still be the better buy because the ticket may be governed by fewer restictions.

At present, two of these low-fare airlines fly to Great Britain. Virgin Atlantic flies from Newark to London's Gatwick Airport daily year-round and from Miami to Gatwick two or more times a week, depending on season. For information and reservations, call 201-623-0500 or 800-862-8621. For Miami-Gatwick reservations, call 305-871-3554. The airline sells tickets in several fare categories, including business class, economy, APEX (which can be purchased one-way), and a variation of standby, called "Same Day Saverfare."

A new entrant in the smaller airline field is Air America, which flies from Los Angeles via Baltimore/Washington, DC, to Gatwick twice weekly. All tickets are in the same category, a 21-day advance purchase fare, which also includes one-way trips.

Also among the smaller airlines to be considered for budget air travel is Icelandair, which has long been known as a source of low-cost flights to Europe. It flies from New York, Baltimore/Washington, DC, Chicago, Detroit, and Orlando to Reykjavik and Luxembourg, and although connections can be made from those points to London, the airline is a better choice for travelers visiting continental Europe than for those wishing to visit Great Britain. For reservations and tickets, contact a travel agent or Icelandair (phone: 212-967-8888 or 800-223-5500).

Discount fares can appear and disappear quickly. Special promotional fares, for instance, may be offered to inaugurate a new route, to drive a new competitor off an old route, or to encourage travel in slow seasons. Check with all the airlines serving your intended destination and call each one several times — you will most likely receive quotes that vary from day to day and from reservations clerk to reservations clerk. When you think you've obtained a good deal, make your booking, but be sure to read the fine print for specifications about duration of stay, cancellations, and so on.

Finally, if you don't have the time and patience to investigate personally all possible air departures and connections for a proposed trip, remember that a travel agent can be of inestimable help. A good agent has at hand the information on what flights go where, when, and what categories of tickets are available on each. Most also have automated reservation tie-ins with a major carrier, in which case information on seat availability on all flights for the day you want to leave can result in reservation and confirmation in a matter of minutes.

Reservations – When making plane reservations through a travel agency, ask the agent to give the airline your home phone number as well as a daytime business number. All too often the airline has only an agency number as the official contact for changes in flight plans. Especially during the winter, weather conditions sometimes hundreds or even thousands of miles away can wreak havoc with flight schedules. The airlines are fairly reliable about getting this sort of information to passengers if they can reach them, but often they can't if the agency is closed for the night or the weekend. Specify to your travel agent that you want a home phone contact provided to the airline, and if you have any doubts, call the airline and do it yourself.

Most return reservations from international destinations are automatically canceled after the required reconfirmation period (usually 72 hours before the flight) has passed. If you look at the back of your airline ticket, you'll see the need to reconfirm specifically spelled out. Don't let yourself be lulled into a false sense of security by the "OK" on your ticket next to the number and time of a returning flight. That only means that a reservation has been entered: *A reconfirmation is still necessary.*

Seating – Where you sit can make a real difference in your comfort on the flight. Airline seats are usually assigned on a first-come, first-served basis when you check in, although some airlines permit you to reserve a seat when you purchase your ticket and some go a step further by allowing you to visit a ticket office prior to departure to secure an actual boarding pass for the flight. There are a few basics to consider in choosing a spot. You must decide first of all whether you want to sit in a smoking or nonsmoking section and whether you prefer a window, aisle, or middle seat. A window seat protects you from aisle traffic and gives you a view (provided it is not over a wing), while an aisle seat enables you to get up and stretch your legs without disturbing anyone. Middle seats are least desirable for most people, and seats in the last row are the most undesirable of all, since they seldom recline all the way.

The amount of leg room you'll have (as well as chest room when the seat in front of you is in a reclining position) is determined by pitch, a measurement of the front to rear spacing between seats. Since airplanes have tracks along which this spacing can be adjusted, the amount of pitch is a matter of airline policy and unrelated to the type of plane you fly in. First-class and business-class seats have the greatest pitch, a fact that figures prominently in airline advertising. In economy class, the standard pitch on transatlantic flights is 34 inches, not quite comfortable for most people, and on some low-fare airlines and charter flights, it can be as little as 31 or 32 inches — downright cramped. Passengers with long legs are advised to choose a seat directly behind a door or emergency exit, since these seats often have greater-than-average pitch, or a bulkhead seat, which is a seat in the first row of a cabin. (But steer clear of the first row if you want to watch the movie.) The number of seats abreast, another factor determining comfort, depends on a combination of airline policy and airplane dimensions. First class and business class, again, have the fewest seats per row. Economy class generally has 9 seats per row on a DC-10 or an L-1011, making either one slightly more comfortable than a 747, on which there are 10 seats per row. However, charter flights on DC-10s and L-1011s can have 10 seats per row and be noticeably more cramped than 747 charters, where the seating remains at 10 per row.

Smoking – US regulations regarding smoking on airplanes require that nonsmoking sections must be enlarged to accommodate all passengers who want to sit in them, provided they have confirmed reservations and do not arrive late for the flight. Cigar- and pipe-smoking are banned even from the smoking sections. These regulations apply to domestic flights and to flights by US carriers departing from or returning to the US, not to flights by foreign carriers into or out of the US.

Flying with Children – As a general rule, a child under 2 years of age (and not occupying a seat) flies overseas at 10% of whatever fare the accompanying adult is paying. A second child without a second adult pays the fare applicable to children ages 2 through 11. In most cases, this amounts to 50% of an adult first-class, business, or economy fare and two-thirds of an adult APEX fare. (On flights for which economy tickets are sold at two price levels, children may be charged either half or two-thirds of the adult economy fare.)

Most airlines have portable bassinets available. On some planes they hook into a bulkhead wall; on others they are placed on the floor in front of you. Ask about obtaining one when you make your reservation, and when checking in, request a bulkhead or other seat that has room enough in front to use it. (On longer flights, the bulkhead seats generally are reserved for families traveling with small children.) Even if you do use a bassinet, babies must be held during takeoff and landing. Do not plan on using your own bassinet aloft until you've checked with the airline you'll be flying. Some airlines prohibit their use during flight; others may require that they be strapped into a seat and that a child's fare rather than an infant's fare be paid. Airline policy regarding infant safety seats also varies widely, even though the Federal Aviation Administration has approved the use on planes of those manufactured after January 1, 1981 (so don't remove the label).

Meals – It is possible to order many kinds of special meals for your flight if you give the airline 24 hours' notice. The range of available cuisines and diets includes high protein, vegetarian, kosher, Muslim, low calorie, low sodium, and infants' and children's meals.

Getting Bumped – A special air travel problem is the possibility that an airline will accept more reservations (and sell more tickets) than there are seats on a given flight. This is entirely legal and is done to make up for the inevitable passengers who don't show up for a flight for which they have reservations. If the airline has oversold the flight and everyone does show up, the airline is subject to stringent rules laid down to protect travelers.

The airline first seeks ticketholders willing to give up their seats voluntarily in return for a negotiable sum of money or some other inducement, such as an offer of upgraded seating on the next flight or a voucher for a free trip at some other time. If there are too few volunteers, the airline may bump passengers against their wishes. Anyone inconvenienced in this way, however, is entitled to an explanation of the criteria used to determine who does or does not get on the flight, as well as to compensation if the resulting delay exceeds certain limits. If the airline can put the bumped passengers on an alternate flight that will get them to their planned destination within 1 hour of their originally scheduled arrival time, no compensation is owed. If the delay is more than an hour, but less than 2 hours on a domestic flight and less than 4 hours on an international flight, the bumped passengers must be paid denied-boarding compensation equivalent to the one-way fare to their destination (subject to a maximum of $200). If the delay is more than 2 hours beyond the original arrival time on a domestic flight or more than 4 hours on an international flight, the compensation must be doubled, up to but not exceeding the sum of $400. (These rules do *not* apply to inbound flights from abroad, even on US carriers.) The airline may also offer bumped travelers a voucher for a free flight instead of the denied-boarding compensation. The passenger can choose either the money or the voucher (the dollar value of which may be no less than the monetary compensation to which the passenger is entitled). The voucher is not a substitute for the bumped passenger's original ticket — the airline continues to honor that as well.

The rules also do not apply if the flight is canceled or delayed, or if a smaller aircraft is substituted, due to mechanical problems. In such cases, some airlines provide amenities to stranded passengers, but these are strictly at the individual airline's discretion. Deregulation of the airlines has meant the traveler must find out for himself what he is entitled to receive. A useful booklet, *Air Travelers' Fly Rights,* is available for $2.75 from the Superintendent of Documents, US Government Printing Office, Washington, DC 20402; stock number 003-006-00106-5.

Baggage – Travelers flying from the US to Europe may face two different kinds of regulations. On a US flag airline or on a major international carrier, each passenger is allowed one or more pieces of carry-on luggage, which must fit easily under a seat on the plane. The total combined dimensions (length, width, and depth) of the piece or pieces must be less than 45 inches. In addition, each first-class passenger is allowed to check two bags, neither of which may exceed a total of 62 inches (combined length, width, and depth) or, usually, 70 pounds. Economy- and promotional-fare passengers are also allowed two bags in the cargo hold, the total combined dimensions of *both* together not to exceed 107 inches and, usually, neither one to exceed 70 pounds. On some airlines, business-class passengers are given the first-class allowance; on others, the economy-class allowance. Children paying 50% or more of an adult fare have the same baggage allowance as a full-fare passenger; infants paying 10% of an adult fare are entitled to only one piece of baggage whose combined dimensions may not exceed 45 inches. Additional, oversize, or overweight bags are assessed at a flat rate.

On European local or trunk carriers, however, you may find your luggage subject to the old weight determination under which economy-fare and discount passengers are allowed only 44 pounds total of luggage without additional charge. First-class and, sometimes, business passengers are allowed 66 pounds total.

To reduce the chances of your luggage going astray, remove all airline tags from previous trips and label each bag *inside and out,* preferably with your business address rather than your home address, to prevent potential thieves from knowing whose house might be unguarded. Lock everything and double-check the tag that the airline attaches to make sure it is coded for your destination. Experienced travelers add an adhesive label to the outside of the bag showing the airline, the flight number, and a temporary address at their destination. If your bags are not in the baggage claim area after your flight, or if they're damaged, report the problem to airline personnel *immediately.* Fill out a report form on your lost or damaged luggage and hold on to a copy of it and your claim check. If you must surrender the check to claim a damaged bag, get a receipt for it to prove that you did, indeed, check baggage on the flight. Most airlines have emergency funds to dispense to passengers stranded away from home without luggage, but if it turns out your bags are truly lost and not simply delayed, do not there and then sign any paper indicating you'll accept a settlement offer. Since the airline is responsible for the value of your bags within certain statutory limits, you should take time to assess the extent of your loss (see *Insurance,* GETTING READY TO GO). It's a good idea to keep records indicating the price you paid for the bags and their contents because these help to eliminate arguments.

CHARTER FLIGHTS: By actually renting a plane or at least booking a block of seats on a specially arranged flight, charter operators can offer travelers air transportation — often coupled with a hotel room, meals, and other arrangements — at costs lower than most economy or excursion fares on scheduled flights. Charters were once the only air fare bargains available, but this is no longer the case. In recent years, the numerous promotional fares on scheduled airlines have often been nearly as low, especially on the most competitive routes, and their terms have usually been more flexible. Nevertheless, after a few lean years, the charter business is staging a strong comeback. The savings possible on the flights varies considerably depending on the countries to which they are headed (some governments do not allow charters to land at all; others allow them to undercut scheduled fares by a wide margin). Among the current offerings, charter flights to Great Britain and Ireland are common, a sign that they still represent good value.

Charter travel once required that an individual be a member, of fairly long standing, of an organization, club, or other "affinity" group whose main purpose was not travel. Newer "public charters" are more flexible. Public charters are open to anyone, whether part of a group or not; they have no advance booking requirements; and they have no minimum-stay requirements. They allow the passenger to book a one-way flight, and those with routes to several different cities usually allow passengers to "mix and match" flights, that is, to fly to one city and return from another. (*Note:* These are American regulations, and they do not control the charter laws in other countries. For example, if you want to book a one-way foreign charter back to the US, you may find advance booking rules are in force.) The operator may offer air-only charters, selling the flight alone, or charter packages, which include the flight plus a combination of land arrangement such as accommodations, meals, tours, or car rental.

Bookings – Charter operators rent planes from scheduled airlines or from specialized charter airlines, then offer the flights to the public either directly through advertisements or through travel agents. Passengers buy tickets from the operator or the agent, not from the airline owning the plane. Keep in mind while reading the ads and the brochures that most charters have little of the flexibility of regularly scheduled flights regarding changes of flight dates, cancellations, and refunds; the price you pay for saving money is the risk of losing some or a lot of it if you cannot stick to your plans. Keep in mind, too, that by virtue of the economics of charters, the plane will almost always be full, so it will be crowded, though not necessarily uncomfortable. If you do decide to take a charter, read the contract carefully and note:

1. Stipulations regarding cancellation by the consumer. It cannot be repeated often enough that if you are forced to cancel your trip, you can lose much and possibly all of your money unless you have cancellation insurance, which is a *must* (see *Insurance,* GETTING READY TO GO). Frequently, if you cancel well in advance (often 6 weeks or more), you may forfeit only a $25 or $50 fee. If you cancel only 2 or 3 weeks before the flight, there may be no refund at all unless you or the operator can supply a substitute passenger.

2. Stipulations regarding cancellations and major changes made by the charterer. Charter flights may be canceled by the operator up to 10 days before departure for any reason, usually underbooking. Your money will be returned in 2 weeks in this event, but that may leave you too little time to make new arrangements. (The charter may *not* be canceled within 10 days of departure except for circumstances — such as natural disasters or political upheavals — that make it physically impossible to perform the flight.) Charterers may also make "major changes," such as in the date or place of departure or return, but if you don't accept these changes, you are entitled to cancel and receive a full refund. In addition, they are permitted to assess a surcharge (for fuel or other rising costs) of up to 10% of the air fare up to 10 days before departure. If the price increase is more than 10%, that, too, is considered a major change giving you the right to a full refund — though, again, if you cancel, you may have too little time to make alternate plans. Prices may not be increased at all within 10 days of departure.

3. Instructions concerning the payment of the deposit and the balance, and to whom

the check is to be made payable. Ordinarily, checks are made out to an escrow account, which means that the charter company can't spend your money until your flight has been completed and, in the event that completion never occurs, there is a reserve of cash for refunds. But if you or your travel agent makes your check out to the charter company directly, this protection is automatically lost. The charter company should be bonded (usually by an insurance company), and you should know the name of the bonding agent. If you want to file a claim against the charter company, the claim should be sent to the bonding agent within 60 days of the date of your scheduled return flight.

DISCOUNT TRAVEL SOURCES: An excellent source of information on economical travel opportunities is the *Consumer Reports Travel Letter,* published monthly by Consumers Union. It keeps abreast of the travel scene on a variety of fronts, including package tours, rental cars, insurance, and more, but it is especially helpful for its coverage of air fares and hotel discounts, offering guidance on all the options from scheduled flights on major or low-fare airlines to charters and discount sources. For a year's subscription, send $37 to Consumer Reports Travel Letter, Subscription Dept., Box 5248, Boulder CO 80322.

Still another way to take advantage of bargain air fares is open to those who have a flexible schedule. A number of organizations, usually set up as last-minute travel clubs and functioning on a membership basis, routinely keep in touch with travel suppliers to help them dispose of unsold inventory at discounts of between 15% and 60%. A great deal of the inventory consists of complete tour packages and cruises, but some clubs offer air-only charter seats and, occasionally, seats on scheduled flights. Members pay an annual fee and receive the toll-free number of a telephone hot line to call for information on imminent trips. In some cases, they also receive periodic mailings with information on upcoming trips for which there is more advance notice. Despite the suggestive names of the clubs providing these services, last-minute travel does not necessarily mean that you cannot make plans until literally the last minute. Trips can be announced with as little as a few days' or as much as two months' notice, but the average is from one to four weeks before departure. It does mean that your choice at any given time is limited to what is offered, and if your heart is set on a particular destination, you might not find what you want, no matter how attractive the bargains. Among these organizations are:

Discount Travel International, Iven Bldg., 114 Forest Ave., Suite 205, Narberth, PA 19072 (phone: 215-668-2182; or 800-228-6500). Annual fee: $45.

Encore Short Notice, 4501 Forbes Blvd., Lanham, MD 20706 (phone: 301-459-8020). Annual fee: $36 per person, $46 per family.

Last-Minute Travel Club, 132 Brookline Ave., Boston MA 02215 (phone: 617-267-9800). Annual fee: $30 per person, $35 per couple or family.

Moment's Notice, 40 E 49th St., New York, NY 10017 (phone: in New York State, 212-486-0503; elsewhere, 800-221-4737). Annual fee: $45.

On Call to Travel, PO Box 11622, Portland, OR 97211 (phone: 503-643-7212 collect). Annual fee: $45.

Stand Buys Ltd., 311 W Superior, Suite 404, Chicago, IL 60610 (phone: in Illinois, 312-943-5737 or 800-972-5858; elsewhere, 800-367-4443). Annual fee: $45.

Worldwide Discount Travel Club, 1674 Meridian Ave., Miami Beach, FL 33139 (phone: 305-534-2082). Annual fee, $50.

NET FARE SOURCES: The newest notion for supplying inexpensive travel services comes from travel agents who offer individual travelers "net" fares. Defined simply, a net fare is the bare minimum amount at which an airline or tour operator will carry a prospective traveler. It doesn't include the amount that would normally be paid to the travel agent as commission. Traditionally, such travel agent commissions amount to about 8% on international tickets and 10% on domestic fares — not counting significant additions to these commission levels that are payable retroactively when agents sell more than a specific volume of tickets or trips for a single supplier. Instead of making their income from conventional commissions, these agencies assess a fixed fee that may or may not provide a bargain for travelers; it requires a little arithmetic to determine whether you're better off with a net travel agent or one who accepts conventional commissions.

One of the first to offer this type of pricing is *McTravel* (92335 Sanders Rd., Northbrook, IL 60062; phone: in Illinois, 312-876-1116; elsewhere, 800-331-2941), who will write a domestic ticket for $10 and an international ticket for $20 (providing that travelers make their own reservations directly through the airlines). Based on these fees, operative at press time, any international trip for which the ticket costs more than $400 looks like a good net buy, while the breakeven on domestic tickets is somewhat lower. There's also the opportunity to economize further by making your own airline reservations, then asking *McTravel* only to write/issue your ticket. For travelers who reside outside the Chicago area, business may be transacted by phone, and purchases may be paid by using a credit card.

CONSUMER PROTECTION: Consumers who feel they have not been dealt with fairly by an airline should make their complaints known. Begin with the customer service representative at the airport where the problem occurs. If he or she cannot resolve the complaint to your satisfaction, write to the airline's consumer office, explaining what reservations you held, what happened, the names of the employees involved, and what you expect the airline to do to remedy the situation. Send copies (never the originals) of the tickets, receipts, and other documents to back up your claims.

If you still receive no satisfaction and if the problem concerns lost baggage, compensation for getting bumped, smoking rules, charter regulations, or unfair or deceptive practices by an airline, write to the Consumer Affairs Division, Room 10405, Office of Intergovernmental and Consumer Affairs, US Department of Transportation, 400 Seventh St., SW, Washington, DC 20590, or call Consumer Affairs at 202-366-2220. Even so, consumer complaints should still be addressed initially to the airline that provoked them.

The Department of Transportation's consumer booklet *Fly Rights* is a good introduction to regulations governing the airlines. To obtain a copy, send $1, check or money order, to Consumer Information Center, Dept. 165-P, Pueblo, CO 81009.

A charter flight or package should always be chosen with care. When you consider a charter, ask your travel agent who runs it and check out the company. The Better Business Bureau in the company's home city can tell you the number of complaints, if any, lodged against it in the past.

ON ARRIVAL: Heathrow, Britain's main international airport, is 15 miles from central London, and the trip into town can be easily made on the London underground (subway) from Heathrow Central Station at the airport itself. Piccadilly Line tube trains leave every 4 to 10 minutes, depending on the time of day, and operate between 5 AM (5:50 AM on Sundays) and 11:45 PM daily. Stops are convenient to most of London's main hotel areas, and the line feeds into the rest of the London underground network. The fare varies according to destination: Heathrow to Central London, about a 45-minute trip, costs between £1.50 and £2 (it's about £18 plus tip by taxi). London Regional Transport's two express Airbus services connect Heathrow with Victoria Station (A1) and with Euston Station (A3), as well as major hotel areas, for £3. A cab ride from Heathrow to Central London will cost approximately £20.

Gatwick, 29 miles from central London, is not linked to the underground, but it does have its own rail station. Gatwick express trains, for which tickets can be purchased from US Britrail Travel International offices, leave for London's Victoria Station every

15 minutes from 5:30 AM to 10 PM. The trip takes 30 minutes and costs £4.60. The new "Airliner" 11-seat luxury minibus service provides direct transportation to London from Heathrow's Coach Travel Centre and Gatwick's coach waiting room. Prices are £4 and £6, respectively, and the trip takes 1 hour. Flights from the US also serve Manchester and Glasgow. Manchester International Airport is 10 miles from central Manchester; express buses leave the International Arrivals Terminal every half-hour for the Chorlton Street Bus Station, Piccadilly, and Victoria Rail Station. Fare for the approximately 30-minute trip is £1. Glasgow's Prestwick Airport is 35 miles from the center of the city, reached by bus to the Anderston Cross Bus Station in about 1¼ hours; fare £2.70.

If you arrive at Ireland's Shannon International Airport in the west, CIE (Córas Iompair Éireann, the National Transportation Company) buses will take you to the Limerick Railway Station in downtown Limerick, the nearest city, 15 miles away. Departures are every half-hour during morning and evening hours of peak traffic, otherwise once an hour (to midnight). The bus ride is about 45 minutes long and the fare is IR£3.25. If you prefer to take a taxi, you'll pay about IR£10. From Limerick there are an average of six trains a day to Dublin, a 2½ hour trip to the east coast. CIE buses connect Dublin Airport, 6 miles north of the city, with Busaras (Dublin's Central Bus Station) on Store Street every 40 minutes up to midnight; the fare is IR£2.50. The taxi fare to a similar city-center location will be about IR£8.

Daily air service between London and Dublin is provided by British Airways, Aer Lingus, Ireland's Ryanair, and Britain's Dan-Air Services, and internal services are abundant in both countries. In Great Britain, several airlines, including British Caledonian, have scheduled flights to other British and Irish cities and islands. British Airways runs many shuttle flights daily between London and Manchester, Glasgow, and Edinburgh, and British Airways and British Midland both have daily flights between London and Belfast. (An express bus service connects with most flights arriving at Belfast Airport. The journey time to Great Victoria Street Station in the center of the city is 40 minutes and the fare is £1.80.) In Ireland, Aer Lingus provides domestic service between Shannon and Dublin, Dublin and Cork, and Cork and Shannon. Aer Arann schedules flights between Galway and the Aran Islands in Galway Bay.

Intra-European Fares – Those who intend to travel by plane to countries in Europe beyond Great Britain and Ireland will find that, although bargain fares between some cities (London and Amsterdam, for instance) have been introduced and less-impressive discount promotional fares exist for other routes, flights between European cities tend to be quite expensive, especially one-way trips. The European Common Market has been focusing on airfares recently, and various diplomatic and legal actions may soon lead to increased competition — and far lower fares. In the meantime, however, the high cost of European fares can be avoided by careful use of stopover rights on the higher-priced transatlantic tickets — first class, business class, and full-fare economy. If your ticket doesn't allow stopovers, ask about excursion fares such as PEX (a type of excursion that must be paid for at the time the reservation is made and that has minimum and maximum stay requirements and cancellation penalties), Super PEX, and APEX for round-trips, and Eurobudget for one-way trips. If the restrictions that govern them allow you to use them (frequently the minimum stay requirement means staying over a Saturday night), you save as much as 35% to 50% off full-fare economy. Note that these fares, which once could be purchased only after arriving in Europe, are now sold in the US and can be purchased before departing.

BUCKET SHOPS: Still another recourse is the London bucket shop, a flourishing industry given the British government's pro-consumer stance regarding airline competition. The majority of London bucket shops (discount travel agencies selling air tickets for less than what the airlines themselves would sell them) specialize in long-haul routes to the Middle East, Far East, Australasia, Africa, and Latin America, rather than in flights to other European countries. But many of the long-haul flights make interim stops in Europe, and discounted tickets for the intra-European segments are often available. Bucket shops can be located most easily in London's Sunday newspapers: The *Times, Express, Observer,* and *Telegraph* are best. *Time Out,* a weekly magazine with information on what's going on in London, also features discount air travel information. Although there is no longer anything shady about bucket shops, it is always wise to be wary. Visit the premises in person, if possible. If you are quoted a price that is dramatically lower than that of other bucket shop offerings to the same city, consider the possibility that the ticket may be stolen. A reputable bucket shop should allow you to pay a deposit; don't pay in full until you have checked with the carrier that a confirmed reservation exists in your name — and the ticket is in hand.

Traveling by Ship

 Alas, the days when steamships reigned as the primary means of transatlantic transportation are gone, days when Italy, France, Sweden, Germany, Norway, the Netherlands, and England — and the US — had fleets of liners that offered luxurious week-plus trips across the North Atlantic.

But one ship remains for this type of service: Cunard's *Queen Elizabeth 2.* For seagoing enthusiasts, the *QE2* is the most impressive vessel afloat — as well as one of the largest — and is as comfortable as ever after several months in drydock for refurbishment during the winter of 1986–87. The QE2 is scheduled for approximately a dozen round-trip transatlantic crossings from April through December. Although the ship normally sets its course from New York to Southampton, England (a 5-day trip), and returns directly to the US, on a few of the crossings, it proceeds from Southampton to Cherbourg, France, before beginning the return trip. Similarly, on some crossings, the ship calls at Boston, Baltimore, Philadelphia, and Port Everglades, Florida, in addition to New York, thus giving non–New Yorkers a choice of points to embark or disembark. Transatlantic crossings are not inexpensive. Last year the one-way, per-person cost of the 5-day trip was from $1,250 (for the least expensive, two-in-a-cabin, transatlantic-class accommodations) to $7,555 (for one of the most luxurious travel experiences imaginable). Cunard has brought an ocean voyage aboard a luxury liner within reach of the ordinary traveler, however, by introducing an air/sea package in conjunction with British Airways. The one-way ticket to Europe by sea includes an economy return air fare from London to any of 57 North American cities — a free flight home, in essence, provided certain length-of-stay restrictions are respected (first-class *QE2* passengers must complete all travel within 40 days and transatlantic-class passengers, within 20 days, or the air allowance is cut in half). The allowance can be applied to an upgraded air ticket if desired, and if you want to splurge, you can even fly home on the supersonic Concorde, provided you make up the considerable difference between your air allowance and the Concorde fare (which at press time is $799). Cunard also packages various land tours of Britain, Ireland, and the Continent that can be added to the basic air/sea offer. For information, contact Cunard, 555 Fifth Ave., New York, NY 10017 (phone: in New York State, 212-661-7777; elsewhere in the US, 800-221-4770).

One other ship, the Polish Ocean Lines' *Stefan Batory,* crosses the Atlantic with some frequency, though it is on a much more modest scale than the *QE2.* The passenger vessel makes up to six crossings a year between Montréal and Gdynia, Poland, calling at London and Rotterdam en route. The cost of one-way passage to London in 1987 ranged from $775 to $1,365 per person, double occupancy. For information, contact McLean Kennedy Passenger Services, 410 St. Nicolas St., Montréal, Québec H2Y 2P5, Canada (phone: 514-849-6111).

An interesting transatlantic crossing possibility for those who have the time is what is referred to in the industry as a "positioning" cruise. This is the sailing of a US- or Caribbean-based vessel from its winter season berth to the city in Europe from which it will be offering summer cruise programs. Eastbound positioning cruises take place at particular times in the spring; westbound return in the fall. Since ships do not make the return trip until ready to position themselves for the next cruise season, most lines offering positioning cruises have some sea/air arrangement that allows passengers to fly home economically — though the cruises themselves are not an inexpensive way to travel.

Among the ships that regularly offer positioning cruises are Cunard/NAC's *Vista-fjord,* formerly of Norwegian American cruises, Royal Viking Line's *Royal Viking Sea* and *Royal Viking Sky,* and Royal Cruise Line's *Royal Odyssey.* Itineraries and ports of call vary from year to year, however, and in any given year, there may be no positioning cruise allowing passengers to disembark at or near a British port. Typically, the ships set sail from Florida or San Juan, Puerto Rico, and cross the Atlantic to any of a number of European ports — Málaga, Barcelona, Genoa, Naples, Venice, Piraeus, Cherbourg, Le Havre, Southampton — where the trip may be broken before proceeding to cruise European waters (i.e., the Mediterranean, the Baltic or Black sea, through the Norwegian fjords). Passengers may stay aboard for the basic transatlantic segment alone or for both the crossing and the subsequent European cruise. In 1987, the *Royal Viking Sea* made an eastbound positioning cruise from Fort Lauderdale, allowing passengers to disembark at a British port (Southampton). Prices range from $5,064 to $14,304 per couple for the 11-day trip. (There was also a 24-day crossing from Fort Lauderdale via Southampton to Copenhagen.) At the end of the summer, the ship returned from Southampton to New York on a leisurely 27-day cruise that included calls at Glengarriff and Dublin, in Ireland. The *Vistafjord*'s itinerary from Fort Lauderdale via New York and Southampton to Hamburg was also available as a 16-day segment from Fort Lauderdale to Southampton for $4,939 to $13,759 per couple, or as a 13-day cruise from New York to Southampton. The Royal Odyssey followed a more southerly course on its eastbound crossing, but its westbound crossing at the end of the season was an 8-day cruise from Southampton to New York, priced from $1,248 to $2,648 per person, double occupancy, including a two-night London hotel package preceding departure. For information, contact Cunard/NAC, 555 Fifth Ave., New York, NY 10017 (phone: 212-661-7777 in New York State; elsewhere, 800-221-4770); Royal Viking Line, 750 Battery St., San Francisco, CA 94111 (phone: 415-398-8000 in California; elsewhere, 800-422-8000); or Royal Cruise Line, One Maritime Plaza, Suite 660, San Francisco, CA 94111 (phone: 415-956-7200).

FREIGHTERS: An alternative to cruise ships is travel by freighter. These are cargo-carrying ships that also take a limited number of passengers (usually about 12) in reasonably comfortable accommodations. The idea has romantic appeal, but there are a number of drawbacks to keep in mind. Though freighters are usually less expensive than cruise ships, they are not the least expensive means of crossing the Atlantic (excursion or even economy air fare is less expensive). Accommodations and recreational facilities vary, but freighters are not cruise ships and aren't designed to amuse passengers, so it is important to enjoy the idea of the freighter itself. Schedules are erratic, and the traveler must fit his or her schedule to that of the ship. While there are freighters that cross the Atlantic to European ports — such as Rotterdam — where ferries offer convenient and inexpensive transport to Britain, at press time, only one freighter line was carrying passengers from the US to a British port. In 1987, Lykes Line carried a maximum of six passengers in three double cabins on a 14-day crossing from Galveston and New Orleans to Felixstowe (northeast of London), calling at Rotterdam and Bremerhaven en route. The one-way per-person fare was $1,400 for a double stateroom and $1,500 for a double suite. For information, contact Lykes Line,

Lykes Center, 300 Poydras St., New Orleans, LA 70130 (phone: in Louisiana, 504-523-6611; elsewhere, 800-535-18610). Another line, Polish Ocean Lines, took six passengers once weekly on a 9- to 11-day trip from Port Newark, NJ, to Le Havre (less than 6 hours by ferry from Portsmouth), Rotterdam, and Bremerhaven. For information, contact Gydnia America Line, 39 Broadway, New York, NY 10006 (phone: 212-952-1280).

For sailing dates and other information, contact: Freighter World Cruises, 180 S Lake Ave., Suite 335, Pasadena, CA 91101 (phone: 818-449-3106); Pearl's Freighter Tips, 175 Great Neck Rd., Great Neck, NY 11021 (phone: 212-895-7646 or 516-487-8531); TravLtips Cruise and Freighter Travel Association, PO Box 188, Flushing, NY 11358 (phone: 718-939-2400).

INLAND WATERWAYS: Cruising the canals and rivers of Europe is becoming more and more popular, probably in reaction to the speed of jet travel and the rush to do as much as possible in a minimum period of time. A river cruiser, barge, or traditional canal narrowboat averages only about 5 miles an hour, covering in a week of slow floating the same distance a car would travel in a few hours of determined driving. Passengers see only a small section of foreign countryside, but they see it with a detail and intimacy simply impossible through any other means of conveyance.

Both Great Britain and Ireland have waterways ideal for cruising. The River Thames is a favorite itinerary, navigable for 125 miles; another follows the quiet flow of the River Avon from Stratford-upon-Avon to Tewkesbury, where it joins England's longest river, the Severn. Also popular are the rivers, lakes, and interconnecting waterways of the Norfolk Broads in East Anglia; the quiet, less trafficked Fens, just west of the Broads; and several hundred miles of old narrow canals in the Midlands that were crucial to the development of the Industrial Revolution. Here, only traditional narrowboats — from 30 to 70 feet long but never more than 6 feet 10 inches in the beam — can navigate, because the canals, some as narrow as 20 feet, have locks a uniform 7 feet across. In Ireland, the River Shannon and its lakes, Lough Ree and Lough Derg, cut north to south through a good part of the country, and the Grand Canal traverses its heart from Shannon Harbour to Dublin. A branch of the canal runs south to meet the River Barrow, navigable on to Waterford. Above the Shannon's source, the scenic lakeland of 50-mile-long Lough Erne is also popular with cruisers.

There are two ways to cruise the inland waterways: by self-skippered boat or by booking aboard a hotel boat. If you choose to be your own skipper, you will be shown how to handle the craft, and told whom to call if you break down, but once you cast off, you and your party — the boats hold from 2 to 12 people — will be on your own. You do your own cooking or eat at pubs along the way, help lock keepers operate the gates, and even operate untended locks yourself.

The alternative is to cruise on a hotel boat — a converted barge or narrowboat. These carry up to 12 guests in Great Britain, in addition to the crew. (Hotel narrowboats often travel in pairs, with crew aboard the first and guests following behind.) You can charter the boat and have it all to yourself or join other guests aboard. Cruises are usually from four to seven nights, and accommodations can be simple or quite luxurious. When reading the brochure, note the boat's facilities (most have private cabins but shared bathrooms) as well as the itinerary and any special attractions. Some cruises feature gourmet food; some make a point of visiting historic spots; and some seek out good locations for antique shopping.

The BTA publishes *UK Waterway Holidays*, a free booklet listing some three dozen British boatyards offering narrowboat rentals or hotel boat cruises through UK Waterway Holidays Ltd., a consortium of the British Waterways Board and the Association of Pleasure Craft Operators. This group, and two other large British companies, Blake's Holidays and Hoseason's Holidays, representing approximately 120 and 90 individual boatyards, respectively, all have agents in the US. The Irish Tourist Board publishes an information sheet, "Cruising on Inland Waterways," with particulars on Irish companies — the majority of which rent self-skippered boats. The firms listed below will provide information or arrange your whole holiday afloat.

Bargain Boating, Morgantown Travel Service: Books self-skippered boats in Great Britain and Ireland. 127 High St., Morgantown, WV 26505 (phone: 304-292-8471).

Dial Travel, Dial Britain: Books self-skippered boats and hotel boat cruises; agents for UK Waterway Holidays. PO Box 1034, Hunt Valley, MD 21030 (phone: in Maryland, 301-683-4310; elsewhere, 800-424-9822).

Floating Through Europe: Operates a hotel barge on the Thames and a pair of hotel wideboats on the Avon. 271 Madison Ave., 10th floor, New York, NY 10016 (phone: in New York State, 212-685-5600; elsewhere, 800-221-3140).

Skipper Travel Services: Books self-skippered boats and hotel boat cruises in Great Britain and Ireland; agents for UK Waterway Holidays and Hoseason's Holidays. 210 California Ave., PO Box 60309, Palo Alto, CA 94306 (phone: 415-321-5658).

FERRIES: Numerous ferries link Great Britain and Ireland with each other and with the rest of Europe. Nearly all of them carry both passengers and cars — you simply drive on and drive off in most cases — and nearly all of the routes are in service year-round. Space for cars should be booked as early as possible, especially for July and August crossings, even though most lines schedule more frequent departures during the summer months.

Among the ferries to Great Britain is the fleet of Sealink ships, jointly operated by British, Dutch, Belgian, and French partners. Sealink connects Hoek van Holland (Netherlands) with Harwich; the French ports of Calais and Dunkerque with Dover; Boulogne with Folkestone; Dieppe with Newhaven; and Cherbourg with Weymouth (no winter service).

Other ferry services between Europe and Great Britain operate from Bergen and Stavanger (Norway) to Newcastle, from Bergen to Lerwick, and from Kristiansand and Oslo to Harwich; from Göteborg (Sweden) and Esbjerg (Denmark) to Newcastle and Harwich; and from Hamburg to Harwich. There are ferries from Scheveningen (Netherlands) to Great Yarmouth, from Rotterdam to Hull, and from Vlissingen to Sheerness; from Zeebrugge (Belgium) to Hull, Felixstowe, and Dover; and from Oostende to Dover. Ferries from French ports operate from Dunkerque to Ramsgate; from Calais and Boulogne to Dover; from Le Havre, Ouistreham, and Cherbourg to Portsmouth; from St. Malo to Portsmouth and the Channel Islands; and from Roscoff to Plymouth. There is even a ferry from Plymouth to Santander, Spain, via Brittany Ferries of Portsmouth.

Hoverspeed hovercraft carry both cars and passengers on a cushion of air across the Channel between Calais or Boulogne and Dover. Service is daily year-round, but since hovercraft travel a few feet above the surface of the water, they can be obstructed by waves and are grounded when the Channel is rough. When weather is good, however, they make the crossing in about 35 minutes (compared to the 1¼ to 1¾ hours it takes by ferry). Passengers-only Jetfoil service, also daily, connects Dover with Oostende in approximately 1¾ hours (3¾ to 4¾ hours by ferry).

Irish Continental Line ferries to Ireland from the Continent leave Le Havre several times weekly year-round for Rosslare Harbour and once weekly in summer for Cork; Cherbourg twice weekly April through September for Rosslare Harbour; and Roscoff once weekly year-round for Cork. Between Great Britain and Ireland there are daily, year-round Sealink services from Fishguard, Wales, to Rosslare Harbour and from Holyhead, Wales, to Dun Laoghaire. Both trips take about 3½ hours. Other ferry lines make daily trips from Holyhead to Dublin directly (3½ hours), from Liverpool to

Dublin (7 to 9 hours), and Rosslare Harbour (4 hours). Ferry services to Northern Ireland connect Liverpool to Belfast in 9 hours, and the Scottish port of Cairnryan to Larne in 2 hours' time. The Sealink ferry travels between Stranraer, Scotland, and Larne in 2¼ hours.

Regularly scheduled car and passenger ferries travel from various mainland ports to the Orkney and Shetland islands, the Inner and Outer Hebrides, the Isle of Man, and the Isles of Scilly. Sealink ferries connect the mainland to the Channel Islands and the Isle of Wight, and for holders of the BritRail Pass, travel to the latter is free.

Most ferry arrivals and departures are well served by connecting passenger trains or buses, and in the case of Sealink ships, Hoverspeed hovercraft, or the Jetfoil, passengers can buy through train tickets from London to cities such as Dublin, Amsterdam, Brussels, or Paris that include the ferry portion of the trip. The London to Paris route on through services by trainhovercraft/train takes about 5½ hours; London to Brussels by train/ship/train, about 7½ hours (a train/jetfoil trip will get you to Brussels even faster — in 5½ hours); London to Dublin by train/ship/train, about 9½ hours. For Sealink schedules and prices, contact BritRail Travel International offices in North America (see *Touring by Rail* for addresses); for information on other ferry services, contact the British or Irish tourist offices or the P. & O. European Ferries Center, PO Box A, Saltillo, PA 17253 (phone: 814-448-3945 or 800-458-3606), the US representative of several ferry lines. Many operators offer reduced rates for round-trip excursions, midweek travel, or off-season travel.

Touring by Car

 Once you've mastered the trick of keeping to the left side of the road, you'll find both Great Britain and Ireland ideally suited for driving tours. Distances between major cities are reasonable and the historical and cultural density is such that a visitor can use the flexibility of a car to maximum advantage, covering large amounts of territory visiting major sites or spending the same amount of time equally absorbed motoring from village to village. (See DIRECTIONS for our choices of the most interesting driving itineraries.)

But driving isn't an inexpensive way to travel. Gas prices are higher in Europe than in North America, and car rentals are not necessarily less costly. Most people will make arrangements for their rental from the US, and it is important to explore every alternative before making your choice.

RENTING A CAR: There are several options for getting wheels abroad, including leasing, but most people simply rent a car through a travel agent or international rental firm before they go or, once they are in Europe, from a local company. Another possibility, also arranged before departure, is to rent the car as part of a broader package. Arrangements of this sort are known variously as fly-drive, self-drive, or go-as-you-please packages or car tours.

Renting from the US – Travel agents can arrange foreign rentals for clients, but you can also do it yourself. The British Tourist Authority and the Irish Tourist Board can supply brochures of numerous British and Irish car rental companies, many of which have US representatives through whom you can make arrangements directly. Indeed, Godfrey Davis, Britain's largest company, is the British link in the worldwide chain of National Car Rental, and the large Irish firm Murray's Rent a Car is the Irish link. To rent from either of these, call National (known in Europe as Europcar; phone: 800-328-4567). You can also do it yourself by calling the international divisions of the other familiar car rental names such as Hertz (phone: 800-654-3131), Avis (phone: 800-331-1212), Budget (phone: 800-527-0700), and Dollar Rent a Car (known in

Europe as InterRent; phone: 800-421-6868). All publish directories listing the foreign locations in which they operate and all quote weekly flat rates based on unlimited mileage with the renter paying for gas. (Time and mileage rates, i.e., a basic per-day or per-week charge, plus a charge for each mile driven, are generally only to the advantage of those who plan to do very little driving.) It is also possible to rent a car before you go by contacting any of a number of smaller, less well known US companies that do not operate worldwide but specialize in European auto travel, including leasing and car purchase in addition to car rental. These firms — some are listed below — act as agents for a variety of European suppliers, offer unlimited mileage almost exclusively, and frequently manage to undersell their larger competitors by a significant margin. Comparison shopping is always necessary, however, because the company that has the least expensive rentals in one country may not necessarily have the least expensive in another, and even the international giants offer discount plans whose conditions are easy to fulfill. Hertz's Affordable Europe, Avis's Supervalue Europe, and similar plans offered by Budget and National allow discounts of 15% to 30% off their usual rates provided the car is reserved a certain number of days in advance of departure (usually 2 to 7), is rented for a minimum period (usually a week), and, in some cases, is returned to the location that supplied it.

No matter which firm you choose, the first factor influencing the cost of a rental is the type and size of car. Rentals are based on a tiered price system, with different sizes of cars often listed as A (the smallest and least expensive) through F, G, or H (the largest and most expensive). The larger the car, the more it costs to rent in the first place and the more gas it consumes, but for some people the greater comfort and extra luggage space of a larger car may make it worth the additional expense. Be warned, too, that few European cars have automatic transmission; those that have it cost more and must be requested specifically at the time of booking. Collision damage waiver protection (see *Insurance*) is optional, but it is another daily expense if you choose to take it. Other costs are drop-off charges (if the car is left in a city other than the one in which it was picked up) and local taxes. The value-added tax rate on car rentals is 15% in Great Britain and Northern Ireland, and only 10% in the Irish Republic. This tax is *not* included in the rental price quoted. Finally, currency fluctuation is another factor to consider. Most brochures quote prices in dollars, but these dollar amounts are frequently only guides; an amount in European currency is the actual charge. In the end, you may pay more or less than expected if there has been a significant change in the rate of exchange. Some companies guarantee rates in dollars, but this is not always an advantage. If the dollar is growing consistently stronger overseas, for instance, you would be better off with rates guaranteed in local currency.

There are legitimate bargains in car rentals provided you shop for them. Call the familiar car rental names whose toll-free numbers are given at the beginning of this section and ask about their special discount plans. Also call the smaller companies listed below. The latter may well offer lower rates, but you must begin early because the best deals may be booked to capacity quickly and may require payment 14 to 21 days before delivery.

Auto-Europe, PO Box 1097, Camden, ME 04843 (phone: in Maine, 207-236-8235; elsewhere, 800-223-5555).

The Cortell Group, 3 E 54th St., New York, NY 10022 (phone: in New York State, 800-442-4481; elsewhere, 800-223-6626).

Europe by Car, 1 Rockefeller Plaza, New York, NY 10020 or 9000 Sunset Blvd., Los Angeles, CA 90069 (phone: in New York State, 212-581-3040 or 800-223-1516; in California, 213-272-0424 or 800-252-9401; in Washington, DC, 202-338-1755).

The Kemwel Group, 106 Calvert St., Harrison, NY 10528 (phone: 800-468-0468).

Fly/Drive – Airlines, charter companies, tour operators, and even independent travel agents offer fly/drive packages. Typically, they used to include round-trip airfare and a car waiting at the airport, plus one night's free lodging in the gateway city. Increasingly, in place of the night's lodging, a block of prepaid accommodations vouchers, one for each night of the stay, is included, along with a list of hotels that accept them. Tour prices vary according to the category of hotels used and there are budget plans using accommodations such as bed-and-breakfast houses or farmhouses. The greater the number of establishments participating in the scheme, the more freedom you have to range at will during the day's driving and still be near a place to stay for the night. For instance, vouchers of the Hertz Affordable Europe hotel plan (available to customers of the Affordable Europe discount rental plan) are good at 1,500 participating properties in Great Britain. Except for the first night's stay, which is reserved before you leave the US, most packages require you to make day-to-day advance reservations en route, but there are less flexible car tours that provide a car, a hotel plan, and a prearranged itinerary that permits no deviation because the hotels are all reserved in advance. Deluxe tours of this type are packaged by Auto Venture, Abercrombie & Kent International, and others.

Local Rentals – It is a commonplace that the least expensive way to rent a car is to wait until you are in Europe. However, before setting off blithely on a trip expecting that bargain rates will be the rule once you are abroad, consider a few points. Rates lower than those uncovered in your pre-trip research can certainly be found by searching out small, strictly local, car rental companies overseas, whether in less than prime locations in major cities or in more remote cities and towns. But sometimes the individual entrepreneur in a given town turns out to be the local link in a larger chain that is the supplier of the stateside agency whose prices you were hoping to beat. Obviously, deals do exist abroad, but to find them you must be willing to invest a sufficient amount of vacation time comparison shopping on the scene. You must also be prepared to return the car to the location that rented it — drop-off possibilities are likely to be limited. Brochures of some of the smaller car rental companies without US representation can be picked up at the BTA or the Irish Tourist Board, and they can serve as a useful basis of comparison. The BTA booklet *Vehicle Hire,* which lists the addresses and prices of small firms in Britain and Northern Ireland, is especially useful. Overseas, the car hire section of the local Yellow Pages is a good place to begin.

If you intend to rent a car only occasionally, relying mainly on other means of transportation, bear in mind that Godfrey Davis–Europcar operates Rail-Drive booths in 75 British railroad stations and 27 airports. A car can be reserved before you board the train and it will be waiting for you at your destination. There is a 10% discount on rentals to BritRail Pass holders. (A special BritRail Pass/Godfrey Davis package that includes a BritRail Pass for unlimited train travel for 8, 15, or 22 days plus a Europcar with unlimited mileage for 4, 8, or 12 days is sold by BritRail Travel International offices in North America. See *Touring by Rail,* GETTING READY TO GO.)

DRIVING: A US citizen driving in Great Britain or Ireland must have a valid driver's license from his or her state of residence; proof of liability insurance is also required and is a standard part of any car rental contract, but if you are traveling in your own car, you must carry an International Insurance Certificate, known familiarly as a Green Card, available through your automobile insurance broker. The British and the Irish both drive on the left-hand side of the road and for this reason the steering wheel is on the right-hand side of the car. The switch is confusing at first but it is possible to adjust in enough time to enjoy the trip. Seat belts are compulsory for the driver and front seat passenger, and both Britain and Ireland are zealous in prosecuting drunken drivers, routinely administering Breathalyzer tests and imposing heavy fines or even jail sentences. If you've been drinking, do as the natives do and walk home, take a cab, or make sure that a licensed member of your party sticks strictly to seltzer water.

Unlike the rest of Europe, distances are measured in miles and they are registered as such on the speedometer — although on main roads and around city centers in Ireland, mileage signs are being changed to kilometers (occasionally giving the distinct impression you're getting farther from a place as you approach it). British speed limits are 70 mph on motorways (expressways) and dual carriageways (4-lane highways), 60 mph on single carriageways (single-lane highways), and 30 mph in towns or built-up areas — unless other limits are posted. In the Irish Republic, the speed limit is 50 mph on the open road and 30 to 40 mph in towns and built-up areas. Pictorial direction signs are standardized according to the International Roadsign System and their meanings are indicated by their shapes — triangular signs mean danger; circular signs give instructions; and rectangular signs are informative.

Excellent road maps are published by Britain's two main automobile clubs, the Automobile Association, or AA (Fanum House, Basingstoke, Hampshire RG21 2EA), and the Royal Automobile Club, or RAC (49 Pall Mall, London SW1Y 5JG). Both have more than one series available — national, regional, local, and town maps in varying scales — and both publish maps of Ireland as well.

The British Travel Bookshop (40 W 57th St., New York, NY 10019) carries a selection of AA maps covering England, Scotland, and Wales. John Bartholomew & Son, Ltd., a Scottish map company, puts out a series of motoring maps (including maps of Ireland) that are stocked in many book stores and map shops around the US. A catalogue of the full line can be obtained by writing to the company at 12 Duncan St., Edinburgh EH9 1TA. Michelin publications — red and green guides as well as road maps — are distributed extensively throughout the country; for information, write Michelin's US headquarters (Michelin Guides and Maps, PO Box 3305, Spartanburg, SC 29304-3305; phone: 803-599-0850). The American Automobile Association publishes a map of Great Britain and Ireland and also a European tour planning map, which are available from the travel agencies in most AAA offices. The AAA is a source of other travel information, and if you are a member, you can take advantage of the services of the AA, with whom the AAA has a reciprocal agreement. An automatic temporary membership in one or the other of the British clubs — giving visitors access to their emergency rescue services — is also usually a part of the standard car rental contract. Both the AA and the RAC (the AA is the larger and operates in Ireland, too) patrol major routes and maintain roadside telephone boxes for use in case of a breakdown.

Gasoline – Called petrol in Britain and Ireland, it is sold by the imperial gallon in both countries, a measure that is a bit larger than the US gallon. One imperial gallon equals 1.2 US gallons; or one imperial gallon equals 4.5 liters and one US gallon equals 3.8 liters. Gas prices everywhere rise and fall depending on the world supply of oil, and the American traveling overseas is further affected by the prevailing rate of exchange, so it is difficult to say precisely what fuel will cost when you travel. It is not difficult to predict, however, that in both Britain and Ireland fuel costs will run substantially higher than you are accustomed to paying in the United States.

Touring by Rail

Perhaps the most economical, and often the most satisfying, way to see a lot of a foreign country in a relatively short time is by rail. It is the quickest means of transportation between two city centers up to 300 miles apart (beyond that distance a flight would be quicker, even counting commuting time from airport to city center). But time isn't really the point. Travel by train is a way to keep moving and to keep seeing at the same time, and not the least of its pleasures is the opportunity it offers to meet the people along the way. With the many special fares and discounts available to visitors, train travel is an almost irresistible bargain.

GREAT BRITAIN: While North Americans have been raised to depend on their cars, Europeans have long been able to depend on public transportation. In fact, the novel idea of carrying passengers by rail occurred to the British first and, in 1825, train travel was born. Today, British Rail, the national railroad company, operates no fewer than 15,000 trains a day, a number exceeded only by the West Germans. As an example of present-day service, consider the *Flying Scotsman,* one of the most famous of British trains since the middle of the 19th century. Originally, it did not truly fly, but today it is one of British Rail's new high-speed Inter City 125 trains on the London to Edinburgh route, making the 393-mile journey in a mere 4 hours and 35 minutes of travel. Other Inter City 125 trains, so called because they operate at speeds up to 125 mph for long stretches of track, lead from London to Bath and Bristol, to Cardiff and Swansea, to Exeter, Plymouth, and Penzance, and to Birmingham, Manchester, and Sheffield, among other routes. The rest of British Rail's Inter City express services are fast and frequent, connecting cities and major towns with few intermediate stops. Counting local and suburban lines as well, there are few places in England, Scotland, and Wales that can't be reached by rail.

Fares on British trains are based not only on the distance traveled but also on the quality of accommodations the passenger chooses. Both the Inter City and the Inter City 125 expresses have first-class and second-class (or economy) cars; although on many local routes, especially rural ones, trains may have one class only, corresponding to second class. On most trains, seats are arranged in open cars, though there still remain a few older cars with seating in compartments. In general, seats in first class are two abreast facing two more abreast across a table. On the other side of the aisle, two single seats face each other across a smaller table. The seats are wider than those in second class and are adjustable. Second-class seats are also arranged around tables, but there are two abreast on both sides of the aisle and they are nonadjustable. For the extra comfort that it provides, first-class travel costs roughly 50% more than second-class travel, and because of this, is generally less crowded. But anyone electing to travel second class — as most of the British do — can count on service that compares favorably with that found anywhere in North America.

Round-trip tickets (called "return" tickets in Great Britain) generally cost double the price of one-way (or single) tickets. There are ways to economize, however, if you travel when most Britons are hard at work and not riding the rails. One such discount is the Saver Ticket, which affords a substantial savings on a day's outing if you depart after the morning rush hour and return after the evening rush has subsided. Weekend returns also provide substantial savings if you leave on a Friday, Saturday, or Sunday, and return on the Saturday, Sunday, or Monday of the same weekend. Other discounts are available, so inquire. The Triple Ticket saves money on day trips from London to any three cities chosen from a list of about two dozen. A version for first-class travel is sold in the US; one for second-class travel, in London. To save even more, consider buying one of the variety of rail passes allowing unlimited travel within a set time period. Some are meant for foreign tourists only and must be bought before you go (see below).

Most of the Inter City trains have either a restaurant car, where a full lunch or dinner costs about £7 to £12 excluding wine and tip, or a buffet car offering simpler, less expensive snacks and drinks, including alcoholic ones. If you're sure you will want to eat en route, however, it's a good idea to inquire beforehand exactly what meal service is offered on the train you'll be traveling. Seats in the dining car should be reserved either before boarding or through the steward very early in the trip.

Sleeping cars are found on night trains to Scotland, the north and west of England,

and Wales. The sleeper supplement is a standard £15 addition to the price of a first- or second-class ticket, even if you're traveling on a discounted ticket. You will have a single compartment to yourself in first class (couples share connecting single compartments); in second class you'll share double accommodations, one in the top bunk, the other below. Lone travelers are paired with a stranger of the same sex, though they may occasionally have a compartment all to themselves. In either first or second class, there is a wash basin in the compartment, and a morning wake-up is provided by the attendant who leaves hot coffee or tea and biscuits at the door, free of charge. As a matter of course, you'll be awakened one-half hour before your stop, but if that is not enough time for you, tell the attendant the night before at what time you want to get up. Passengers traveling to the end of the line may stay in their bunks until 7 AM or 7:30 AM, even if the train is scheduled to arrive earlier than that.

Naturally, it is best to travel light enough to keep your suitcase with you on the overhead rack, but if you have quite a bit of luggage, it can be loaded on to the baggage car found on nearly every train. No claim ticket is issued, so label your things inside and out. If you are getting off at an intermediate station, make your way to the baggage car as you approach your stop and supervise the unloading yourself. It is not the attendant's responsibility to do it for you even if you have printed your destination conspicuously on the bag. Most stations have porters or self-service carts, though you may find either or both in short supply when you need one. Baggage can be checked overnight at the Left Luggage facilities in most stations or in 24-hour lockers in some.

Both first- and second-class seats on most Inter City trains can be reserved in advance, either before you leave home or after your arrival in Great Britain. Reservations may reduce flexibility, but they are advisable during the summer on certain popular routes such as London-Edinburgh, London-Glasgow, London-Manchester, and London to points southwest. Sleeper reservations are necessary and should be made as far in advance as possible. Reservations can be made through travel agents or BritRail Travel International offices in North America (addresses below) or, in Great Britain, at British Rail Travel Centers set up to help passengers with bookings and information on all services offered by British Rail. The British Travel Center at 4/12 Regent St. in London (open 9–5, Monday through Friday) offers the broadest services; others are at most of London's main railway stations, at Heathrow and Gatwick airports, and at railway stations in many other cities.

The multiplicity of London's train stations requires an explanation. There are 11 principal ones, each the starting point for trains to a particular region, with occasional overlapping of routes. The ones the tourist is most likely to encounter include King's Cross, departure point for Northeast England and Eastern Scotland including Edinburgh; St. Pancras, for trains going due north from London as far as Sheffield; Euston, serving the Midlands, North Wales including Holyhead and ferries for Dun Laoghaire, Ireland, Northwest England, and Western Scotland including Glasgow; Paddington, for the West Country and South Wales including Fishguard and ferries to Rosslare, Ireland; Victoria, for Gatwick Airport and, along with Charing Cross Station, for departures to Southeast England; and Liverpool St. Station, for departures to East Anglia and to Harwich for ferries to the Continent and to Scandinavia. Though stations are interconnected via London's underground (subway) system, allowing passengers to avoid busy surface streets while transferring from one to the other, you should still leave plenty of time to make the change. Note also, for your travels in other parts of Britain, that London is not the only city with more than one station.

Drivers should be aware of British Rail's car-carrying trains, called Motorail, operating principally between London and Scotland and between London and the West Country. Motorail allows car owners to take to the rails for long distances while their car travels with them on a flatcar. Book well in advance for this, especially in the summer. Another service for motorists is the Rail-Drive booth, found in 75 rail stations throughout Great Britain, operated by Godfrey Davis–Europcar. Passengers can reserve a car before boarding the train and find it waiting for them at the station of their destination. Special rates apply for holders of the BritRail Pass and Rail-Drive packages can be arranged through BritRail Travel International offices in North America before you leave home.

Britainshrinkers are another British Rail enterprise. These are all-inclusive escorted tours out of London, either day trips or overnighters, combining fast rail travel with more leisurely sightseeing by bus. The Britainshrinker to Brighton, for example, departs London's Victoria Station at 9AM on Thursdays, includes a morning visit to the Royal Pavilion — with time for browsing and lunch by the sea — and an afternoon visit to Arundel Castle, and arrives back at Victoria Station by 6 PM the same day. There are thirteen other 1-day itineraries and six overnight tours of 2 or 4 days' duration. Britainshrinkers, available April through November only, can be booked through BritRail Travel International offices in North America or at the British Rail Travel Centers in London stations.

Sealink ships cross the Channel and the North Sea to Belgium, the Netherlands, and France, and the Irish Sea to Ireland. They also link the Isle of Wight and the Channel Islands to the mainland. While many other shipping companies provide the same car and passenger ferry services, Sealink connections allow a traveler to buy a through train ticket from London to Paris, Brussels, Amsterdam, Rotterdam, The Hague, or Dublin, with no need to make separate arrangements for the sea portion of the journey. Travel is by rail to the water, where the ship waits, equipped or not with sleeping cabins depending on the length of the trip. Passengers walk to the ship and, on the other shore, they board a waiting train to complete the journey — referred to as the "boat train." Through train tickets from London to Paris can also be bought using Hoverspeed hovercraft rather than Sealink ship. These skim across the surface of the water with their cargo of passengers and autos, crossing the Channel from Dover to Boulogne or Calais in about 35 minutes (versus 1¼ to 1¾ hours by ship). Similarly, passengers-only Jetfoil service can be used on the trip from London to Belgium, Luxembourg, and the Netherlands. (Note: Reservations are essential for Jetfoil.)

Sealink connections to Dublin leave London's Euston Station for Holyhead, Wales, proceed from there by ferry to Dun Laoghaire, Ireland, and then by train to Dublin's Connolly and Heuston stations. Sealink connections to southern Ireland leave Paddington Station in London and cross the Irish Sea from Fishguard, Wales, to Rosslare Harbour. Another Sealink service leaves Stranraer, Scotland, for Larne, Northern Ireland.

IRELAND: In the Irish Republic, the government-owned Córas Iompair Éireann (CIE, or the National Transportation Company) operates the railroads as well as the country's intercity buses. Main rail routes radiate from Dublin to Belfast, Northern Ireland, and to Sligo, Westport, Galway, Cork, Limerick, Killarney and Tralee, Waterford, and Wexford. There are also services between Dublin and the ferry ports of Dun Laoghaire and Rosslare, and between Rosslare and Limerick. Shannon Airport is connected by bus with Limerick from where there are several trains daily to Dublin and Cork.

Dublin has three principal train stations — Connolly, Heuston, and Pearse — and, as in London, it is important to be sure from which station your train will leave. Distances are not great: From Dublin to Belfast, Northern Ireland, on the nonstop city-to-city express is a 2½-hour trip, and trips from Dublin clear across the heart of the country to Galway or south to Cork take just under 3 hours. Because of these distances, there is no need for sleeping cars on Irish trains, but you will find either a restaurant or a buffet car or, at the least, light refreshments available on most main routes.

The only class of travel in Ireland is called standard. Where seat reservations are possible, as on certain main routes, they can be made as far as 3 months in advance, though not from North America.

Baggage can be checked through to your destination between any two stations in the Republic, but not between the Republic and Northern Ireland nor between Ireland and Great Britain — because of customs inspections. Since you keep it with you, keep it light, because porters are not easy to find as you get on and off the Irish Sea ferries. Most stations have Left Luggage areas where baggage can be checked overnight.

Trains between Dublin and Belfast are operated in cooperation with Northern Ireland Railways whose own routes in the northern "six counties" (Ulster) are few: Belfast to Londonderry via Ballymena and Coleraine, Belfast to Bangor, and Belfast to Larne. Travel on these is either standard class or first class.

PASSES: The Eurailpass, the first and best known of all rail passes, is not valid for travel in Great Britain or Northern Ireland, though the Republic of Ireland is a member of the Eurail network. There is no dearth of alternative rail passes in Great Britain or Northern Ireland, however, and they not only save you a considerable amount of money, they can also save you time. Since they are validated by an information clerk on the day of your first trip, they spare you the trouble of standing in ticket lines — which can be very long in the peak travel season.

The BritRail Pass is the most extensive, offering unlimited travel throughout England, Wales, and Scotland, and is issued for either first-class or economy travel for periods of 8, 15, or 22 days, or for 1 month, with children from 5 through 15 years traveling at half fare in each of the eight categories. The BritRail Youth Pass, for those 16 through 25, allows unlimited travel in economy accommodations, and the BritRail Senior Citizen Pass allows anyone 65 or over to travel in first class at less than first-class rates. A Eurail Youth Pass, available to travelers under 26 years of age, features unlimited second-class travel throughout 16 European countries.

There is no doubt that the BritRail Pass is a bargain. At press time, the cost of an 8-day adult economy pass was $149, roughly the same as that of one round-trip fare between London and Edinburgh, which was $136. Unfortunately, the usefulness of the pass stops at the Irish shore, and there isn't another pass that is valid for travel in both countries. The Eurailpass, entitling holders to 7, 15, or 21 days, or 1, 2, or 3 months of unlimited first-class travel throughout 16 European countries, is accepted on Irish trains, but unless you are combining a visit to Ireland with sightseeing on the Continent, it is not as economical as Ireland's Rambler Ticket. Rambler Tickets are good for unlimited travel in standard class (you pay a supplement for super-standard if and when you want it), and come in four versions: 8 or 15 days by rail or bus alone or 8 or 15 days by both. The latter combination should be considered, since trains in Ireland do not take you everywhere, and rail and bus routes are well integrated. The tickets can be bought either before you leave, from any travel agency or from CIE Tours International (address follows), or after you arrive, at any CIE railway booking office in Ireland (Dublin, Limerick, Cork, Waterford, and Galway railway stations) or from CIE, 35 Lower Abbey St., Dublin. (The Youth Rambler Ticket, for those between the ages of 14 and 26, must be purchased in the US; it is good for 8, 15, or 30 days.) The Rambler Ticket can be used only in the Irish Republic, not in Northern Ireland, and although it allows unlimited bus travel, use of city bus lines is excluded. Another pass, the Irish Overlander, costs $139 and is valid for both the Irish Republic and Northern Ireland. It allows unlimited train and bus travel for 15 days and can be bought from CIE Tours International in the US, from the CIE Booking Office in Dublin, or from the Northern Ireland Railways office at Belfast Station or Ulsterbus offices in Belfast. CIE will accept credit cards.

Some other passes are worth investigating if you plan to thoroughly explore a limited region. The Scottish Highlands and Islands Travelpass, for instance, provides unlimited train and bus travel in the Scottish Highlands plus ferry service to the larger Scottish islands, and includes round-trip transportation between either Glasgow or Edinburgh and the Highlands area. A 7- or 14-day Travelpass can be obtained through BritRail Travel International offices in North America; 8- or 12-day versions can be obtained in Great Britain. All are valid from March through October only. Other rail passes — among them the Freedom of Scotland ticket, the Rail Runabout Ticket (for Northern Ireland), and regional Railrovers — are designed primarily for use by British citizens who cannot take advantage of the BritRail Pass. They are sold locally and limited to the selected region, usually on a seasonal basis. For rail buffs, there is even the Great Little Trains of Wales–Wanderer Ticket, good for as many scenic trips as desired on the eight quaint, narrow-gauge steam railways of Wales. Tickets are issued for 8 consecutive days (good from March 28 to September 20) and can be bought at any of the railways at the time of your first trip, though you can write ahead for details, timetables, or the ticket to Brecon Mountain Railway, Pan Station, Merthyr Tydfil, Mid Glamorgan CF48 2UP, Wales.

FURTHER INFORMATION: The *Eurail Guide,* by Kathryn Saltzman Turpin and Marvin Saltzman ($10.95), discusses routes, rates, and all the ins and outs of Eurail-passes and other special rail deals around the world in complete detail. It contains information on Great Britain, too, though the Eurailpass is not valid there, and is an excellent buy for the serious rail traveler. The most revered and most accurate world-wide railway book is the hefty *Thomas Cook Continental Timetable,* issued monthly and available in a few travel bookstores or from the Forsyth Travel Library, PO Box 2975, Shawnee Mission, KS 66201, for $15.95 plus $2.50 postage ($2.50 for UPS or Priority Mail). You can order it by phone and pay by credit card by calling 913-384-0496. Thomas Cook also publishes an excellent *Rail Map of Europe,* available from the same source for $6.95. If purchased together, the cost is $21.95, plus the same $2.50 postage charge.

BritRail Travel International offices in North America provide information on all British Rail services, make reservations, sell tickets and rail passes, and distribute a free catalogue, *Go Brit Rail.* Addresses are: 630 Third Ave., New York, NY 10017 (phone: 212-599-5400); 800 South Hope St., Suite 603, Los Angeles, CA 90017 (phone: 213-624-8787); Cedar Maple Plaza, 2305 Cedar Springs, Dallas, TX 75201 (phone: 214-748-0860); 94 Cumberland St., Toronto, Ontario M5R 1A3 (phone: 416-929-3333); and 409 Granville St., Vancouver, British Columbia V6C 1T2 (phone: 604-683-6896). BritRail's *Travel Times,* a booklet-sized summary of the main Inter City train services between major tourist centers in England, Wales, and Scotland, is available free from these offices. To buy a Rambler Ticket, or for information on train travel in Ireland, contact CIE Tours International, 122 E 42nd St., New York, NY 10168 (phone: in New York City, 212-972-5600; elsewhere in the US, 800-CIE-TOUR). This office also makes available a free timetable of train services in the Irish Republic.

Touring by Bus

Going from place to place by bus may not be the fastest way to get there, but that may possibly be the only drawback to bus travel. A persuasive argument in its favor is its cost: Short of hitchhiking, traveling by bus is the least expensive way to cover a long distance. On the average, a bus ticket between two cities in the United Kingdom costs about half the price of the corresponding train ticket; in the Irish Republic, about two thirds of the train fare. For this amount, you will travel comfortably, if not always speedily, to your destination, enjoying an equally scenic view. The bus trip from London to Edinburgh takes 9 or 10 hours, for instance, and you could cover the same territory in 4½ to 4¾ hours aboard a high-speed train, but since high-speed trains are not in operation everywhere, the time differential on most routes is not as extreme. Buses can also take you to outposts remote from the railroad tracks, if you're so inclined, especially in Ireland where train service is more limited than it is in Great Britain. A map of the bus routes of either country is not much different from a road map: If the way is paved, you can be sure a bus — some bus — is assigned to travel it. The network of express buses — those traveling long distances with few stops en route — is only slightly less extensive. Because of this, both Great Britain and Ireland are particularly well-suited to bus travel.

It should be noted that to the British, only the bus that takes you from stop to stop in town is known as a bus; the vehicle that takes you from city to city or on a tour is called a coach. Express coach service throughout Great Britain is operated jointly by National Express, serving England and Wales, and by Scottish Citylink Coaches, part of the Scottish Bus Group. In Northern Ireland, Ulsterbus operates the buses.

National Express and the Scottish Bus Group offer a number of discounts on their already quite economical bus fares. A round-trip ticket (called a return ticket) usually costs twice the one-way fare, but if you're traveling on off-peak days or coming back the same day, you can buy a round-trip ticket that may cost no more than the one-way (called single) ticket. Ask also about midweek and weekend returns for savings that are less extraordinary, though still worthwhile. And if you're planning to use the bus regularly, consider buying one of the bus passes or cards discussed below. Remember that children between the ages of 5 and 16 receive a reduction of one third off normal fares, as do travelers over 60 years of age. For each paying adult, one child under five travels free.

London's main bus depot is the Victoria Coach Station on Buckingham Palace Road. The National Express information office in the station and the new Coach Travel Centre at 13 Regent St. (phone: 730-0202) supply information and timetables and handle bookings. If you are leaving from London during peak travel periods it is advisable to book well in advance.

In the Irish Republic, the state-owned Córas Iompair Éireann (CIE, or the National Transportation Company) operates the trains, the long-distance or provincial buses, and the city buses of Dublin, Cork, Limerick, Waterford, and Galway. There are reduced rates for midweek and weekend return trips and a number of bus passes are available. CIE's main booking office in Dublin, at 59 Upper O'Connell St. (phone: 787-777), and the Central Bus Station (phone: 742-941), provide timetables, maps, and information on how to get anywhere in Ireland by bus or train, as well as tickets. All long-distance buses leave from the Central Bus Station (Busaras) on Store St.

CIE also operates a series of half- or full-day tours by sightseeing bus from major cities. From Dublin, for instance, there are about two dozen itineraries, including city sightseeing itineraries. Tours leave also from Shannon, Limerick, Tralee, Killarney, Cork, Waterford, Wexford, Galway, Sligo, and other cities.. They begin as early as March in some areas and are run through September or October, though many are run at the height of the summer only. Departures are daily or several times weekly and prices range from IR£4.50 to IR£20. Information is available from CIE Tours International, 122 E 42nd St., New York, NY 10168 (phone: in New York City, 212-972-5600; elsewhere in the US, 800-CIE-TOUR).

BUS PASSES AND CARDS: Several bus passes and discount cards make the bus even more of a bargain in Britain and Ireland. None of these have to be bought before you go, though most of them can be bought here and it's a good idea to investigate them as you plan your trip.

For Great Britain, there's the Britexpress Card, offered by National Travel (NBC) Ltd. It costs $10 and allows the bearer a one-third discount off one-way and round-trip fares for any number of trips taken during a 30-day period over the entire National Express and Scottish Citylink networks, and on selected services of other companies.

Meant for overseas visitors only, the card can be bought through a travel agent before departure or directly from National Express's US agents, The Kemwel Group, 106 Calvert St., Harrison, NY 10528 (phone: 800-468-0468) or Worldwide Marketing Associates, 7136 W Grand Ave., Chicago, IL 60635 (phone: in Illinois, 312-889-6015; elsewhere, 800-621-3405). In Britain you can buy it, with a passport as ID, at Green Line information centers at Heathrow and Gatwick airports, at the National Express office in Victoria Coach Station, at the Coach Travel Centre in Regent Street, and at the Glasgow and Edinburgh bus stations.

Not strictly for buses, the Scottish Highlands and Islands Travelpass allows unlimited travel for a specified period of time by bus and rail in the Highlands area of Scotland, on ferry services to the Scottish islands, and on transporation to the Highlands and islands area from Glasgow or Edinburgh. It is good, too, for travel on the post buses that in some rural areas of Scotland carry mail and the occasional passenger. The Travelpass, valid from March through October and issued for a period of either 7 or 14 days, can be obtained in Great Britain (from British Rail offices, Scottish Bus Group offices, Caledonian MacBrayne Ltd. offices, or by writing to Hi-Line, Holiday Lodge, Bridgend Rd., Dingwall IV15 9SL, Scotland) or through BritRail Travel International offices in North America.

Since the same company (CIE) runs both buses and trains in the Irish Republic, it is only natural that Irish passes are valid for both bus and train travel. The Rambler Ticket is sold for 8 or 15 days of unlimited travel, and either version is available for rail or bus travel alone or in a bus and rail combination. (Use of city bus service is excluded.) The tickets, valid only in the Irish Republic, can be bought from a travel agent or from CIE Tours International in the US (address above), at the CIE Booking Office in Dublin, and at the Dublin, Limerick, Cork, Waterford, and Galway railway stations. Another combination bus and rail pass, the Irish Overlander, is valid for 15 days of unlimited travel in both the Irish Republic and Northern Ireland. It, too, is sold by CIE Tours International in the US and by the CIE Booking Office in Dublin, as well as by Northern Ireland Railways and Ulsterbus offices in Belfast.

The Freedom of Northern Ireland ticket is a bus-only pass, valid for 1 or 7 days' travel on all Ulsterbus services in Northern Ireland. Buy it at bus stations in Northern Ireland.

Though bus timetables can be picked up overseas, it may be useful to have them on hand to help you plan before you go. National Express coach guides come out twice yearly (summer and winter schedules, including Scottish Citylink services) and cost £7 each by sea mail and £10 each air mail. Write to National Express Ltd., Projects Office, 4 Vicarage Rd., Edgbaston, Birmingham B15 3ES.. The *Provincial and Expressway Bus Timetable* of CIE routes in the Irish Republic is available (in very limited quantities) free from CIE Tours International. For services in Northern Ireland, write to Ulsterbus Ltd., 10 Glengall St., Belfast, BT12 5AB. Specify the region you are interested in or ask for the complete package of timetables (no charge).

Many city bus lines have their own tourist discount schemes that are a help to anyone who expects to do a lot of moving around in town. Not only do they save money, they also spare the bearer the bother of digging in pockets and handbags for small change. London Regional Transport, the authority that runs the city's buses and underground (subway) trains, offers a multitude of such passes, but the main one is the London Explorer Pass for 3, 4, or 7 days of unlimited travel on the bus and the underground within the whole of greater London. Trips by underground and Airbus between Heathrow Airport and central London are included. The pass can be obtained from BritRail Travel International before departure or purchased in London at numerous underground ticket offices and London Regional Transport travel information centers. There is also a 1-day off-peak Travelcard, good for unlimited bus and underground travel within a specified zone; the 1-day Bus Pass, good for unlimited travel outside central

London only; and the Golden Rover Ticket, valid on Green Line Coaches and London Country buses for a day or a weekend of travel. These are available from almost any tube (subway) or bus station, as well as from the bus driver. Other cities have other bus bargains, so if you're interested, always ask before you buy — there's bound to be something available. If you don't use one of the unlimited travel tickets, remember that in London and Dublin there is no flat bus fare. The rate varies with the distance traveled and there is usually a conductor or driver to tell you how much you owe. Remember, also, always to "queue up" at the bus stop not only in Great Britain, but in Ireland, too.

Package Tours

 If the thought of buying a package for travel to and through Europe conjures up visions of a race through ten countries in as many days with a busload of frazzled fellow passengers as companions, you should be aware that packages need not be that way at all. For one thing, not all packages are package tours, and the one you buy does not necessarily have to include any organized touring at all, nor will it necessarily provide you with traveling companions either. If it does, however, you'll find that people of all sorts — many just like yourself — are taking advantage of packages today because they are economical and convenient, save the purchaser an immense amount of planning time, and exist in such variety that it's virtually impossible for the Europe-bound traveler not to find one that fits at least the majority of his or her preferences. With continuing inflation, packages have emerged as one of the best of travel buys.

In essence, a package is a combination of travel services that can be purchased as a single booking. It may include any or all of the following: transatlantic transportation, local transportation (and/or car rentals), accommodations, some or all meals, sightseeing, entertainment, transfers to and from the hotel at each destination, taxes, tips, escort service, and a variety of incidental features that might be offered as options at additional cost.

In other words, a package may be any combination from a fully escorted tour offered at an all-inclusive price to a simple fly/drive booking allowing purchasers to do exactly as they please. Its principal advantage is that it saves money; invariably the cost of the combined arrangements is well below the price that would be paid if all the elements included were bought individually. An important additional feature is that because these elements are purchased at the same time, travelers are left free to devote their full attention to the trip — the burdensome details settled.

The lower prices that are possible through package travel come about as a result of high-volume participation. The tour packager negotiates for services in wholesale quantities — blocks of hotel rooms to be used during a given period of time, group meals, busloads of ground transportation, and so on — and thus purchases them at a lower per-person price. Even after markups and commissions are added, the retail tour price is still reasonably below what independent travelers would pay if planning such a trip on their own. Most packages, however, are subject to restrictions governing the duration of the trip and require total payment by a given time before departure.

Packages are put together by tour operators or wholesalers, some retail travel agencies, airlines, charter companies, hotels, and even special interest organizations, and what goes into them depends on who is organizing them. The most common type, assembled by tour wholesalers and sold through travel agents, can run the gamut from deluxe everything to simple tourist-class amenities or even bare necessities. Fly/drive and fly/cruise packages are usually the joint planning efforts of airlines and, respectively, car rental organizations and cruise line operators. Charter flight programs may range from little more than air fare and a minimum of ground arrangements to full-scale tours or vacations. There are also hotel packages organized by hotel chains or associations of independent hotels and applicable to stays at any combination of member establishments; resort packages covering arrangements at a specific hotel; and special interest tours, which can be once-only programs organized by particular groups through a retail agency or regular offerings packaged by a tour operator. They can feature food, music or theater festivals, a particular sporting activity or event, a commemorative occasion, even scientific exploration. Since most packages are bought through travel agents, a good one is the best guide to help sort through this abundance. The agent will be able to provide information not only on packages of general interest but also on the specialized ones, even though the latter can sometimes be booked either through an agent or the packager, particularly if the program caters to a small number of people and is limited to one or a few departures annually. (In our discussion of sample packages below, addresses of tour operators are given if they accept bookings directly from the public.)

To determine whether or not a package — or more specifically, which package — fits your travel plans, start by evaluating your interests and your needs, deciding how much and what you want to see and do. Gather whatever package tour information is available for dates that fit your time schedule and read the brochures carefully to determine exactly what is included. Tour brochures almost always highlight — in eye-catching type — the lowest price at which a tour is offered. This price, however, may be available off-season only, at the lowest-priced hotel among several in the program (which, nonetheless, may be quite satisfactory), or in such limited numbers that there is a waiting list. Note, too, that prices quoted in brochures are almost always based on double occupancy: The rate listed is for each of two people sharing a double room. If traveling alone, the supplement for single accommodations can raise the price considerably (see *Hints for Single Travelers*).

Increasingly, in this age of ever-changing air fares, brochures seldom include the price of the airline ticket in the price of the package. Applicable air fares from various gateway cities are usually listed separately, as extras, and have to be added to the total price of the ground arrangements. Before doing this, get the latest quote from the airline, because the air fares in the brochure may well be out of date by the time you read them. If the brochure gives more than one category of sample fares per gateway, your travel agent or airline tour desk clerk will be able to tell you which one applies to the package you choose, depending on when you travel, how far in advance you book, and other factors. When the brochure does include round-trip transportation in the package price, don't forget to add the round-trip transportation cost from your home to the departure city to come up with the total cost of the package. Check the brochures for the following: what exactly is included in the tour price — and what isn't; what meals are included in the price; class of hotels; amount of refund in case of cancellation before departure; can the operator cancel the tour if too few people sign up; can the operator unilaterally increase the price.

Read the responsibility clause (usually at the end of the descriptive literature) very carefully. Here the tour operator frequently expresses the right to change services or schedules as long as you are offered equivalent arrangements; this clause also absolves the operator of responsibility if circumstances beyond human control affect the operation of the tour.

One of the consumer's biggest problems is finding enough information to judge the reliability of a tour packager, since individuals seldom have direct contact with the firm putting the package together. Usually, a retail travel agent intervenes between customer and tour operator, and much depends on the candor and cooperation of the agent. You should ask a number of questions about the tour you are considering. For example: Has the agent ever used the package provided by this tour operator before? How long has the tour operator been in business? Which and how many companies are involved in the package? If air travel is by charter flight, is there an escrow account in which deposits will be held, and, if so, what is the name of the bank?

This last question is very important. The law requires that tour operators deposit every charter passenger's deposit and subsequent payment in a proper escrow account. Money paid into such an account cannot legally be used except to pay for the costs of a particular package or as a refund if the trip is canceled. To ensure the safe handling of your money, make out your check to the escrow account — by law the account number must appear in the operator-participant contract, and it's usually found in that mass of minuscule type on the back. Write the details of the charter, including the destination and dates, on the face of the check; on the back, print the words "For Deposit Only." Your travel agent may prefer that you make your check out to him, saying that he will then pay the tour operator the fee minus his commission. But it is perfectly legal to write your check this way and the agent should have sufficient faith in the tour operator to trust him to send the proper commission. If your agent objects too vociferously to this procedure, consider taking your business elsewhere, because if you don't make your check out to the escrow account you lose your escrow protection should the trip be canceled or the tour operator or travel agent fail. Furthermore, recent bankruptcies in the travel industry have served to point out that even the protection of escrow may not be enough to safeguard your payments. Increasingly, insurance is becoming a necessity (see *Insurance*).

The United States Tour Operators Association (USTOA) publishes "How to Select a Package Tour," a brochure designed to answer consumer questions. For a free copy, write to: USTOA, 211 E 51st St., Suite 12B, New York, NY 10022.

SAMPLE PACKAGES TO GREAT BRITAIN AND IRELAND: There are dozens and dozens of packages available to Great Britain and Ireland today, visiting one or both of the countries, exploring a selected region, or stopping in London or Dublin only. Especially broad is the choice of escorted sightseeing tours by motorcoach — anywhere from 7 days to 3 weeks or more in length — with an array of itinerary possibilities available. Typically, breakfast is almost always included, whereas the number of lunches and dinners may vary considerably. The hotel accommodations used are first class or better, with private baths or showers in all rooms, though some tour wholesalers offer less expensive alternatives to their standard tours by downgrading the quality of the lodgings.

An equally common type of package available to Great Britain and Ireland is an arrangement often described in brochures as a self-drive or go-as-you-please tour. What's usually included is the use of a rented car and a block of as many prepaid hotel vouchers as needed for the length of your stay, along with a list of participating hotels at which the vouchers are accepted. Most often, only your first night's accommodation will be reserved; from then on you book a room one stop ahead as you drive from place to place. In other cases, all the hotels are booked before you leave (or you can opt to book them, for a fee), requiring that you stick closely to a suggested route. Most operators offering these packages offer budget versions as well. There are plans using only simple bed-and-breakfast houses or farmhouses, plans mixing standard hotels with farmhouses, plans allowing an extended stay at one hotel or farmhouse. CIE Tours International, for example, offers a variety of alternatives. Vouchers can be bought for first-class hotels, farmhouses, or town and country homes (B&Bs) in either Great Britain or Ireland or both. One plan combines Ireland, Scotland, and Britain on a 15-day package. Abercrombie & Kent International (1420 Kensington Rd., Oak Brook, IL 60521; phone: 312-954-2944 or 800-323-7308), on the other hand, offers tailor-made "Country Houses of Britain and Ireland" packages, all deluxe. On each itinerary, a specific hotel — all are converted manor houses, castles, and other stately homes

— is to be reached each night, and each itinerary can be bought in either a self-drive or chauffeured version.

As one of the world's greatest cities, London is by itself of interest to visitors and many tour operators have packaged it that way. Basically, the package includes transfers between airport and hotel, a choice of hotel accommodations (with breakfast) in several price ranges, plus any number of other features that you may not need or want but would lose valuable time arranging if you did. Among these are one or two half-day conducted sightseeing tours of the city; passes for unlimited travel by subway or bus; discount cards for shops, museums, and restaurants; membership in and admission to clubs, casinos, and discotheques; and car rental for some or all of your stay — usually a week, though 3-, 5-, and even 14-day packages are available.

With the addition of theater tickets, the basic London package turns into a show tour, one of the most popular city programs. British Airways has a 6-night tour, for instance, that includes hotel accommodations, 7 days of unlimited subway and bus travel, tickets to three plays or musicals, dinner at a theme restaurant, and other features.

A staple among special-interest packages to Great Britain and Ireland is the golf tour. The main ingredient is a chance to play at some of the oldest and best courses in the world: St. Andrews, Turnberry, Gleneagles, Troon, and Carnoustie in Scotland; the Killarney, Ballybunion, Portmarnock, and Royal Dublin courses in the Irish Republic; the Royal Portrush and the Royal County Down courses in Northern Ireland. A fly/drive arrangement is usually involved, with rental car, hotel accommodations for a week or two, often one dinner per day, and some greens fees included. There are packages allowing you to spend an entire week at one course, to play only Irish or only Scottish courses or to combine them, and special packages permitting you to both play golf and attend the British Open when it's held. BTH Holidays (185 Madison Ave., New York, NY 10016 (phone: in New York State, 212-684-1820; elsewhere, 800-221-1074) and International Golf (PO Box 819, Champlain, NY 12919; phone: 514-933-2771) both have self-drive golf packages and tours by escorted motorcoach, and the latter include escorted sightseeing itineraries for nongolfers in the group. Golf Intercontinental (205 E 42nd St., Room 1514, New York, NY 10017; phone: in New York State, 212-661-6565; elsewhere, 800-223-6114) offers tours for serious golfers only. Many more golf packages are available, so ask your travel agent.

Among other sports-oriented packages are the seven Wimbledon tennis packages run by Keith Prowse & Co. Ltd., 234 W 44th St., New York, NY 10036 (phone: in New York State, 212-398-1430; elsewhere, 800-223-4446). The most popular packages include seats for 4 days of play on the center and #1 courts and tickets to either the men's final and ladies' semifinals or to the ladies' final and men's semifinals. Two firms that offer packages focused around — and guaranteeing entrance in — marathons are *Grimes Travel* (250 W 57th St., New York, NY 10019; phone: in New York State, 212-307-7797; elsewhere, 800-832-7778) and *Marathon Tours* (108 Main St., Boston, MA 02129; phone: 617-242-7845). *Grimes Travel* offers a 6-night stay in Dublin for the October marathon; *Marathon Tours* offers a week in London for the spring marathon — the world's largest — as well as a one-week package to Dublin for the October marathon.

Inland waterway trips on canal boats or river barges are another type of special interest package that can be enjoyed in either Great Britain or Ireland. They're becoming increasingly popular and are discussed at length in *Traveling by Ship*, GETTING READY TO GO. For enthusiasts of other outdoor activities, there are one-week (and longer) horseback riding holidays that combine rural village itineraries in England, Ireland, and the Scottish border with overnight accommodations at local inns (FITS Equestrian, 2011 Alamo Pintado Rd., Solvang, CA 93463; phone: 805-688-9494). The choices — but not for beginners — include 6 days of riding the Connemara Trails (nights are spent in hotels), 8 days polishing skills at the Greystones Equestrian Center at Castle Leslie in County Monaghan, as well as an 8-day package in the vicinity of Lough Derg that stresses both riding and cuisine. A variety of biking packages and hiking trips through the moors and bogs of Ireland, rural England, or the Scottish Highlands are other possiblities. For more information, see *Camping and Caravanning, Biking, and Hiking. Mountain Travel* has developed 2- to 3-week itineraries that range in difficulty from easy day hikes to strenuous hiking and climbing. Contact Mountain Travel, 1398 Solano Ave., Albany, CA 94706 (phone: 415-527-8100; for reservations only, 800-227-2384).

The American fascination with British upper-class life has prompted a number of nonsporting special-interest packages. The gardens that typically surround England's stately homes are the focus of the 10-day English Country Gardens package offered by *Esplanade Tours,* 581 Boylston St., Boston, MA 02116 (phone: 617-266-7465). *In the English Manner* (PO Box 936, Alamo, CA 94507; phone: 415-935-7065) is another company that specializes in individualized tours to English gardens, among other places. *Lynott Tours* offers The Crafts of Ireland, a 10-day escorted motorcoach tour whose participants see Waterford crystal, Belleek pottery, and Donegal tweeds being made; attend Aran knitting demonstations; talk to quilters and lace makers; visit a design center; and spend a day at a school where they get to learn something about a craft.

Other special-interest packages include music and opera tours, the specialty of Dailey-Thorp, Inc., 315 W 57th St., New York, NY 10019 (phone: 212-307-1555). Its offerings include events in England, Scotland, and Ireland, and regularly combines a visit to the Wexford Opera Festival in October with opera and sightseeing in London. Mystery tours are becoming increasingly popular. The Rendezvous with Murder package run by ICTS/InterContinental Travel Systems (4133 Taylor St., San Diego, CA 92110; phone: in San Diego, 619-299-4217; elsewhere in California, 800-457-9515; elsewhere in the US, 800-428-7462) spends 11 days meeting authors and visiting sites associated with famous British mystery novels; a "murder weekend," with a crime to be solved by participants, is included. Christmas packages are a good way to avoid the disappointment of discovering a country virtually shut down for the holidays, and ICTS (address above) offers one of the best: The 12 Days of Christmas, which includes a variety of English Christmas festivities as well as deluxe hotel and manor accommodations. Faith Tours (270 Sunrise Hwy., Rockville Centre, NY 11570), which specializes in tours geared to Roman Catholic travelers, offers trips to the shrine at Knock and other Irish sights on two of its tours, one combining Ireland and Lourdes and the other Ireland and Great Britain.

EUROPEAN PACKAGES BOOKED IN BRITAIN: For years, experienced travelers have known that some of the least expensive tours of Europe could be booked abroad and that British tour operators offered the best of all possible deals. Often, for less than half the price of a scheduled air ticket from London to Athens and back, the smart shopper could pick up the flight plus a week's worth of adequate, if spartan, accommodations and even some meals. Then the expenses of British packagers began to rise with inflation and the bargains became less enticing. But many British operators continue to cater to the budget end of the market and they still manage to put together a good deal (which becomes even more attractive to Americans when the exchange rate is favorable). With their local clientele in mind they tend to specialize in tours from London to the Continent, and thus the assortment of budget tours of their own country and Ireland is less broad. Their basic tours, though competitively priced, frequently do not fall into the budget category, but more and more companies are adding a selection of 3- or 4-day mini-tours that save money because they cover only a limited area. Some of these are so economically priced that two or more of them together can still cost less than a single, longer, standard tour covering approximately the same territory.

The following are some of Britain's major high-volume or economy-minded tour operators. Some have become familiar names in this country recently because they have opened US offices and begun to market some or all of the tour offerings in their British catalogues directly to the American public — i.e., booking one of their packages is no different from booking the package of an American tour operator. Almost all of the rest have at least a representative in the US to handle American bookings. Note that most of these offices or representatives prefer to deal with travel agents rather than individuals. Note also that because of the extra costs involved in making arrangements from this end, packages booked here can run 5% to 15% more than if booked in Britain; and if you attempt to book through the British office by mail, your request will most likely be referred to the US representative. Clearly, you will save money by waiting until you are in England to book, but you will be taking a chance that the package you want will still be open at the last minute.

Cosmos of London: In 1987, this firm specializing in low-cost motorcoach tours of Europe offered 42 tour series, of which six were tours of Britain or Ireland. Breakfast daily and slightly more than half the dinners were included, and almost all rooms had private facilities. Cosmos matches singles wishing to share a room to avoid the single supplement. For information, contact Cosmos Tours, 95-25 Queens Blvd., Rego Park, NY 11374 (phone: in New York State, 718-268-7000; elsewhere, 800-221-0090). Bookings must be made through a travel agent. The London office, Cosmostourama, is at 180 Vauxhall Bridge Rd., London SW1V 1ED (phone: 834-7412).

Frames National: Reasonably priced coach tours of both Europe and Great Britain and Ireland are available through Frames, and though the company is not primarily budget oriented, it offers a series of low-cost minitours of England, Scotland, and Wales. Frames National's US agent, Tourpak International, The Kemwel Group, 106 Calvert St., Harrison, NY 10528 (phone: 800-468-0468), prefers bookings through travel agents. The London office is at 97 Southampton Row, London WC1 B4B2 (phone: 637-4171).

Glenton Tours: This long-established company is a specialist in first-class but relatively inexpensive motorcoach tours of Great Britain (over 30 itineraries), and it also has two tours visiting Ireland. Most prices are based on accommodations with private bath. The US representative is Worldwide Marketing Associates, 7136 W Grand, Chicago, IL 60635 (phone: in Illinois, 312-889-6015; elsewhere in the US 800-621-3405). Head offices in London are at 114 Peckham Rye, London SE15 4JE (phone: 639-9777).

Globus-Gateway: Probably the tour operator used most by Americans, Globus-Gateway offers 10 motorcoach tours of Great Britain or Ireland, with hundreds of departure dates to choose from, in addition to 40 tours elsewhere in Europe. Breakfast and dinner daily are included in the price of most tours, and all accommodations have private baths. Bookings through travel agents only. Globus-Gateway's US and London addresses and phone numbers are the same as those of Cosmos (see above).

Thomson Holidays: Great Britain's largest tour operator owns its own airline, Britannia Airways, and its coach tours venture as far afield as the foothills of the Himalayas. Thomson is also known for a broad selection of Mediterranean holiday packages that include round-trip air fare (from Britain) and a week or two or more of villa or apartment rental. Write to Thomson Holidays, Rochester House, 2 Belvedere Rd., London SE19 2HQ (phone: 653-8899).

Thomson Vacations: Thomson's US affiliate offers US-originating (from Chicago, Detroit, Los Angeles, and San Francisco) coach tours to Europe (including Great Britain and Ireland). For information, contact Thomson Vacations, 100

NW Point Blvd., Elk Grove Village, Chicago, IL 60007 (phone: 312-640-1150 or 800-222-6400), but book through a travel agent.

Townsend Thoresen: Best known as the major ferry service for crossings from Great Britain to Northern Ireland and the Continent, this firm also represents 23 ferry companies. Bookings in the US are handled by the company's European Ferries Center, PO Box A, Main St., Saltillo, PA 17253 (phone: in Pennsylvania, Alaska, or Hawaii, 814-448-3945; elsewhere in the US, 800-458-3606; in Canada, 800-433-4230), which will deal with the public. The London office is at 127 Regent St., London W1R 8LB (phone: 437-7800; 734-4431).

Trafalgar Tours: Not strictly a budget company, it offered an extensive selection of tours on the Continent in 1986 as well as thirteen tours of Great Britain and Ireland, including four budget-conscious CostSaver tours on which savings were realized by mixing tourist- and first-class hotels. Bookings are made only through travel agents or Trafalgar Tours, 21 E 26th St., New York, NY 10010 (phone: in New York City, 212-689-8977; elsewhere, 800-854-0103). The office of the London affiliate, Trafalgar Travel Ltd., is at 15 Grosvenor Place, London SW1X 7HH (phone: 235-7090).

Another British tour operator to investigate is Thomas Cook, the best known of all tour operators headquartered in London. Its name is practically synonymous with the Grand Tour of Europe, but Cook's tours span the world, with itineraries ranging from deluxe to moderate, including some of the budget variety as well. You can book a tour directly through any one of its offices in major cities of North America or through any travel agency. Thomas Cook's headquarters are in London at 45 Berkeley St., Piccadilly, London W1A 1EB (phone: 499-4000).

Camping and Caravanning, Biking, and Hiking

CAMPING AND CARAVANNING: In Great Britain and Ireland, sites for camping and caravans (as recreational vehicles are called) are plentiful. Most are open from Easter through October and they fill quickly at the height of the summer season, so it's a good idea to arrive early in the day if you haven't been able to reserve a pitch in advance. Caravanning is extremely popular with European vacationers and many parks cater more to the caravanner than to the tent dweller, but in neither country are campers or caravanners restricted to the official sites. Using private property, however, requires the permission of the landowner or tenant first — as well as the responsibility to leave the land exactly as you found it in return for the hospitality. When in difficulty, remember that tourist information offices throughout Britain and Ireland can direct you to sites in the areas they serve.

Many comprehensive guides to sites are available. The British Tourist Authority publishes *Britain: Camping & Caravan Parks,* a free guide to sites in England, Scotland, Wales, and Northern Ireland, with the directions to, charges for, and facilities of each. The AA guide, *Camping and Caravanning in Britain,* published by the Automobile Association of Great Britain, Fanum House, Basingstoke, Hampshire RG21 2EA, England, is available from the British Travel Bookshop ($11.95, plus $3 handling charge), as well as from many other bookstores that specialize in travel. It lists about 1,000 campsites inspected and rated by the AA and provides other information of interest to campers. A leaflet, "Come Camping in the Forest," describing camping and caravan sites in Britain's forests, is available free from the Forestry Commission, 231

Corstorphine Rd., Edinburgh EH2 7AT, Scotland. The Northern Ireland Tourist Board publishes the free booklet *Northern Ireland: Camping and Caravan Parks* listing over 100 sites; it is available from Tourist Information Centres in Northern Ireland and from all BTA offices. The Irish Tourist Board also publishes the yearly guide *Caravan & Camping Parks,* listing all sites meeting the board's minimum standards. Listings include a grading of the facilities, descriptions of the sites, and fees. The booklet is distributed free at Irish Tourist Board offices in North America.

The International Camping Carnet, issued by the international camping organization Fédération Internationale de Camping et Caravanning, is a pass that is useful in Europe, entitling the bearer to discounts at some sites and often accepted in place of a passport when the campground owner wants to hold a document as security until you've paid your bill. It is not necessary for camping in Great Britain and Ireland, but it does open the gates to the sites operated exclusively for their members by two major groups, the Camping and Caravanning Club of Great Britain and Ireland and the Caravan Club. The Camping and Caravanning Club (11 Grosvenor Pl., London SW1 WOEY) publishes a free annual guide to its own and other British and Irish sites, and provides information and assistance to members, foreign visitors with the carnet, and foreign visitors without the carnet who become temporary members. The Caravan Club (East Grinstead House, London Rd., East Grinstead, West Sussex RH19 1UA) publishes a guide to its sites plus over 3,500 farm sites. The International Camping Carnet is available in the US from the National Campers and Hikers Association (4804 Transit Rd., Bldg. 2, Depew, NY 14043; phone: 716-668-6242) for a family membership fee of $23, which includes camping information and membership in the association.

Camping equipment is available for sale or rent throughout Great Britain and Ireland, and rentals can be booked in advance through any number of outfitters. The above mentioned guides to camping and caravanning contain lists of outfitters and the national tourist offices in the US can supply information on reliable dealers. Rentals of recreational vehicles can also be arranged from the US through several companies, including:

Auto-Europe, PO Box 500, Yorktown Heights, NY 10598 (phone: in New York State, 800-942-1309; elsewhere, 800-223-5555).

The Cortell Group, 3 E 54th St., New York, NY 10022 (phone: in New York State, 800-442-4481; elsewhere, 800-223-6626).

Europe by Car, 1 Rockefeller Plaza, New York, NY 10020 or 9000 Sunset Blvd., Los Angeles, CA 90069 (phone: in New York State, 212-581-3040; in California, 800-252-9401; elsewhere, 800-223-1516).

The Kemwel Group, 106 Calvert St., Harrison, NY 10528 (phone: 800-468-0468).

Reservations should be made well in advance as the supply is limited and the demand great. Generally, two types of vehicles are offered: minibuses customized in various ways for camping, often including elevated roofs; and larger coach-type vans. Towed vehicles can be hired overseas, but are not usually offered by companies in the US.

If you plan to rent a caravan in Britain or Ireland and use it on the Continent as well, make sure that whatever you drive is equipped to deal with the electrical and gas standards of all countries on your itinerary. There are differences, for instance, between the bottled gas supplied in Britain and on the Continent. You should either have a sufficient supply of the type your camper requires or equipment that can use either type. If you're towing a camper, note that nothing towed is automatically covered by the liability insurance of the primary vehicle; the primary vehicle's Green Card must carry a specific endorsement for the towed vehicle. Whether driving a camper or towing, it is essential to have some idea of the terrain you'll be encountering en route, since grades can sometimes be too steep for certain vehicles to negotiate and some roads are off limits to towed caravans.

A packaged camping tour abroad is a good way to have your cake and eat it too. The problems of advance planning and day-to-day organizing are left to someone else, yet you still reap the savings benefits that shoestring travel affords. Be aware, however, that these packages are usually geared to the young, with ages 18 to 35 as common limits. Transfer from place to place is by bus as on other sightseeing tours, but overnights are in tents and meal arrangements vary. Often there is a general food fund that covers meals in restaurants or in the camp; sometimes there is a chef and sometimes the cooking is done by the participants themselves. An organization called Camping Tours of Europe, Ltd., 40 Underhill Blvd., Syosset, NY 11791 (516-496-7400), markets the camping tours of two British tour operators.

Horse-drawn Caravans – A caravan vacation in an entirely different spirit is possible in Ireland, one country where it is common to tour in a horse-drawn wagon. The vehicle is barrel-shaped in Gypsy style and has bunks for up to four people and a gas stove for cooking. No experience in handling the horse is required: The company that rents the caravan teaches harnessing and unharnessing plus the basics of horse care before you set out. Not much ground can be covered this way (rentals are usually by the week) but the caravan bases are generally located in very scenic areas that are pleasant to explore in depth. Most companies provide a route to follow, pointing out where to find bathroom facilities and the best spots to stop for the night. Cost of renting the caravan starts at approximately $205 per week, including oats for the horse, but not supplementary charges for any grazing the animal might do as you park for the night. The Irish Tourist Board has a list of operators to contact to reserve a horse-drawn caravan, something you should do well in advance if you want to have one at the height of the summer.

BIKING: For young or energetic travelers, the bicycle offers a marvelous way to see a country, especially where the terrain is conducive to easy cycling as it is in Great Britain, one of the most popular of European destinations for foreign tourists on two wheels. Much of the country is rolling hills and, except for the environs of industrialized cities, nearly traffic-free secondary roads can be found almost everywhere, threaded neatly through picturesque stretches of countryside. There is even less traffic in Ireland, a country that tends to be flat to rolling in its middle, hilly on the coast, and scenic throughout. Biking has its drawbacks, of course: You can carry little baggage, travel is slow, and you are exposed to the elements, which in both Great Britain and Ireland means a mild climate with cool evenings — and the ever-present possibility of showers.

Whether you travel independently or join an organized cycling tour, a valuable book to help you prepare for all contingencies is *Bicycle Touring in Europe* by Karen and Gary Hawkins (Pantheon Books; $6.95). The BTA's booklet *Cycling* provides information on various aspects of biking in Britain and also describes several suggested routes. Bicycles can be rented economically in most cities and towns. (*Note:* Because of insurance regulations, few companies in Great Britain rent powered cycles to North Americans. Those that do are listed in the brochure entitled *Britain: Motorcycle Holidays.*) In Ireland, there are over 100 Raleigh Rent-a-Bike dealers; the Irish Tourist Board distributes a leaflet listing them, or you can write for it directly to TI-Irish Raleigh Ltd., Broomhill Rd., Tallaght, County Dublin, Ireland (phone: 521-888). Mopeds, motorcycles, and scooters cannot be rented in Ireland.

Detailed maps allow you to find scenic byways as well as the route that goes around the mountain, not up it. Maps are available from a number of sources, but those of the Bartholomew National series (on a scale of 1:100,000 — 1 centimeter of map equals 100,000 centimeters or 1 kilometer of road) or GT series (1:253,440 — 1 centimeter of map equals approximately 2.5 kilometers of road) are particularly useful for Great Britain and Ireland. If unavailable in your local map store, these can be ordered from John Bartholomew & Son Ltd., 12 Duncan St., Edinburgh EH9 1TA, Scotland, or, if you are a member, through the Cyclists Touring Club. This group, Britain's largest cycling association, not only runs organized tours for cyclists, but also has a number of planned routes available in pamphlet form for bikers traveling on their own. It also helps members plan custom-made tours and publishes a yearly handbook as well as magazines. For information on joining, write to the CTC at Cotterell House, 69 Meadrow, Godalming, Surrey GU7 3HS, England. When the going gets rough, remember that arduous parts of the journey can be avoided by loading your bicycle on the luggage van of a train. Bicycles are generally transported free on British trains, except on Inter City 125 routes, which have special arrangements for bicycles in the guard's van (there's a £3 charge on weekdays), Motorail car-carrying services, or boat trains to the Continent. It's a good idea to check with the station the day before your departure. On Irish trains, they travel at approximately one-quarter the standard (second-class) fare. There's a $24 bicycle supplement fee for Rambler ticketholders.

More than one organization offers bike tours of Great Britain and Ireland. An advantage of such a tour is that shipment of equipment — your bike — is handled by organizers, and the shipping fee is included in the total tour package. Travelers simply deliver the bike to the airport, already disassembled and boxed; shipping boxes can be obtained from most bicycle shops with little difficulty. Bikers not with a tour must make their own arrangements with the airline, and there are no standard procedures for this. Some international carriers provide shipping cartons for bikes and charge only a nominal fee. Other airlines don't provide cartons and may charge as much as $50 or more. Another attraction of *some* organized tours is the existence of a "sag wagon" to carry extra luggage or you and your bike, too, when you can't pedal another mile. Accommodations on tours can vary from campgrounds and hostels to hotels, and as a result, tour prices also vary.

Among the groups sponsoring yearly bike tours to Europe are the American Youth Hostels (which also sponsors hiking tours) and its local chapters or councils. The 1987 summer program of the national organization (PO Box 37613, Washington, DC 20013; phone: 202-783-6161) included a 16-day tour of England with accommodations in hostels; versions of the tour were geared to adults 18 and up, to teenagers 14 to 18 only, and to mixed ages. Another itinerary featured 21 days of cycling through England, Ireland, and Wales. The Metropolitan New York Council of American Youth Hostels (75 Spring St., New York, NY 10012; phone: 212-431-7100), a local AYH affiliate with a particularly broad tour program, offered six bicycle trips to Great Britain in 1987, four of which were for teenagers and two, including a 15-day tour of England, limited to adults. Overnights on all six were spent in hostels and camping. Cyclists not traveling on tours should nevertheless familiarize themselves with the activities of the AYH organization since membership in it is a prerequisite for staying at most youth hostels abroad. There is no age limit to membership in AYH, and hostels in Great Britain and Ireland do not impose an upper age limit for use of their facilities. (For more information on hostels, see *Hints for Single Travelers.*) In addition, the Metropolitan New York Council's free catalogue, *Information & Equipment,* is a useful planning aid for cyclists, hikers, and campers.

The International Bicycle Touring Society is another nonprofit membership organization that regularly sponsors low-cost bicycle tours around the US and Canada and overseas. Tours to England, Scotland, and Ireland were among the foreign itineraries on the 1987 program. Participants must be over 21 and are usually between 30 and 60 years old. A sag wagon goes along and accommodations are in inns and hotels. For information, send a $2 plus a 39¢ SASE to IBTS at 2115 Paseo Dorado, La Jolla, CA 92037 (phone: 619-459-8775). You may also want to investigate the tours of Britain and the Continent offered to members of Britain's Cyclists Touring Club (address above). Join early if you decide to participate.

Hundreds of organizations sponsoring biking tours have sprung up around the country in response to the explosion of interest in this form of travel. The League of American Wheelmen (Bicycle USA, Suite 209, 6707 Whitestone Rd., Baltimore, MD 21207; phone: 301-944-3399) publishes an annual list of tour operators in the US and abroad and can put you in touch with biking groups in your area. For $3 they will send you a copy of their tour list.

HIKING: The British Tourist Authority, the Irish Tourist Board, and the Northern Ireland Tourist Board distribute information sheets on walking and mountaineering and there are several other sources of information for those intent on getting about on their own steam. The Ramblers Association, 1/5 Wandsworth Rd., London SW8 2LJ, publishes *Guides to Local Walking,* listing guidebooks and maps for walkers, and *Long Distance Footpaths,* with details of a number of long-distance routes. The British Mountaineering Council, Crawford House, Precinct Centre, Booth St. E, Manchester M13 9RZ, furnishes advice on mountaineering and rock climbing and a list of qualified guides. The Federation of Mountaineering Clubs of Ireland, 20 Leopardstown Gardens, Blackrock, County Dublin (phone: 01-881266), can be contacted for information and advice, and will provide a list of general and regional walking and climbing guidebooks that can be ordered through its office or bought at bookstores in Ireland. *Irish Walk Guides,* a series of six regional guidebooks published by Gill and Macmillan, are sold in bookstores throughout Ireland, north and south. Each contains full details of the best hill walks in the area, maps, and notes on climate, flora and fauna, and mountain safety. *The Open Forest,* a guide to state parks and forests, is available free from the Irish Tourist Board in Ireland, as is *Hill Walking and Rock Climbing.*

If you are hiking on your own, without benefit of a guide or group, a map of the trail you plan to use is a must. Ordnance Survey maps of the Landranger series, on the scale of 1¼ inches to 1 mile (1:50,000), cover the whole of Britain, and the Outdoor Leisure series, ideal at 2½ inches to 1 mile (1:25,000), includes all of the more popular areas. The British Travel Bookshop carries a very limited selection of the maps; more are available by mail order from Stansfords (12-14 Long Acre, London WC2P 9LP) and from Hatchard's (187 Piccadilly, London W1). For a price list of similar maps of Ireland, write to the Ordnance Survey Office, Phoenix Park, Dublin (Wicklow Way is an especially popular hiking/walking map for those touring on foot); and for Northern Ireland, contact the Government Bookstore, Chichester St., Belfast 1 (phone: 232-2-34488). Having studied the map, choose a route in keeping with your physical condition, and stick to the defined path unless you are an experienced hiker and know the area well. Let someone know where you are going and when you expect to be back — if the hike is impromptu, leave a note on your car. Always know your own limits.

All you need to set out on a simple hike are a pair of sturdy shoes and heavy socks; jeans or long pants to keep branches, nettles, and bugs off your legs; a canteen of water; a hat to protect you from the sun; and, if you like, a picnic lunch. It is a good idea to dress in layers, so that you can peel off a sweater or two to keep pace with the rising sun and put them back on as the sun goes down. Make sure, too, to wear clothes with pockets or bring a pack to keep your hands free. Some useful and important pocket or pack stuffers include a jackknife, waterproof matches, and a compass.

If you prefer to travel as part of an organized group, see the January/February issue of *Sierra* magazine for the Sierra Club's annual list of foreign outings, or contact the Sierra Club Outing Department, 730 Polk St., San Francisco, CA 94109 (phone: 415-776-2211). Distances are usually traveled in minibuses and overnights are in inns, bed and breakfast farmhouses, or, occasionally, campgrounds, but variations in 1987 included a combined hiking and biking trip to Ireland. *Mountain Travel,* a company specializing in adventure trips around the world, offered four 15- to 17-day walking tours of Great Britain and Ireland in 1986. Itineraries were graded according to difficulty; travel between areas of interest was by minibus; and accommodations were in small hotels and guesthouses. Contact Mountain Travel, 1398 Solano Ave., Albany, CA 94706 (phone: 415-527-8100; for reservations outside California, 800-227-2384). The experienced hiker may want to contact AYH's national headquarters (address above) or any local council for information about AYH hikes, which have included England and Ireland in recent years.

Preparing

Calculating Costs

$ After the 1985 explosion of US travelers headed to the Continent, travel to Europe from North America declined in 1986, due in part to fears of terrorist activity but at least equally to a steady weakening of the US dollar abroad. But although prices in Europe, including Great Britain and Ireland, increased at a rate of roughly 20% to 30% in 1987, the continued availability of discount fares and charter flights made it possible for last year's travelers to reduce the cost of transatlantic transportation easily. Package programs can still lessen the price of a vacation in Britain or Ireland, because the group rates obtained by the tour packager are usually much less expensive than the tariffs paid by someone traveling on a freelance basis, that is, paying for each element — airfare, hotel, meals, car rental — separately.

Although generally more expensive than the Mediterranean countries, Britain is not one of the most costly countries in Europe. The British Tourist Authority (40 W 57th St., New York, NY 10019) has been very successfully campaigning to call the attention of potential visitors to the low-cost options available for almost every entry in the traveler's budget. Some BTA publications stress this theme, among them a *Bed & Breakfast in Britain* brochure, an introduction to a most reasonable and pleasant way to bring down the high cost of housing for the tourist. In the same spirit, the Irish Tourist Board — the dollar is going even further in Ireland these days — distributes a leaflet, "Free Attractions in Ireland," which describes 80 of the country's free attractions.

There are many variables that affect the cost of a vacation, but the major expenses are transportation, accommodations, and food, the latter two of which are especially affected by fluctuations in the exchange rate — that is, how much of a given foreign currency the dollar will buy. A number of other expenses must be allowed for: local transportation, sightseeing, shopping, and miscellaneous items such as admission tickets, drinks, local taxes, and tips.

The easiest way to put a ceiling on the price of all these things is to consider buying a package tour. If it is a totally planned and escorted one, with almost all transportation, rooms, meals, sightseeing, local travel, tips, and the like, included and prepaid, you will know beforehand almost exactly what the trip will cost and the only surprise will be the one you spring on yourself by succumbing to some irresistible but expensive souvenir rather than the trifles you intended. The various types of packages available are discussed in *Package Tours*, GETTING READY TO GO, but a few points bear repeating here. Not all packages are package *tours*. There are loosely organized arrangements in which some features (transatlantic transportation, rooms, transfers) are included but others such as sightseeing and dining are left to your own discretion. More and more, even experienced travelers are being won over to the idea of packaged travel, not only for the convenience and the planning time saved, but above all for the money saved. Whatever elements you choose to have in your package the organizer has gotten for you wholesale — and they are prepaid.

The possibility of prepaying for elements of your trip is an important point to consider even if you intend to be strictly independent, with arrangements entirely of your own making and all bought separately. You may not be able to match the price of the wholesale tour package, but at least you will have introduced an element of predictability into your accounting, thus reducing the risk that some budget-busting expense along the way might put a damper on the rest of your travel plans. With the independent traveler in mind, we suggest below some of the ways to pin down the cost of a trip beforehand, but there are two further variables that will influence the cost of your holiday whether you buy a package or do it all yourself. One is timing. If you are willing to visit during the less-trafficked off-season months when transatlantic air fares are lower, you'll find the rates at many hotels lower also. Keep in mind those periods that are generally referred to as the shoulder months, between the traditional low and high seasons (approximately late March to mid-May and late September through November). Costs are only a little less than in high season but the weather should be agreeable and you won't be bucking the crowds that can force a traveler without a hotel reservation into the most expensive hostelry in town in peak months. Another factor that will influence the cost of your trip is whether you will be traveling alone or as one of a pair. The prices quoted for package tours are almost always based on double occupancy of hotel rooms and the surcharge — or single supplement — for a room by yourself can be quite hefty. If you are shopping for a hotel room on your own you'll find that there are many more double rooms than single rooms and that the price of a single is roughly two-thirds that of a double.

TRANSPORTATION: Airfare is really the easiest cost to pin down, though the range and variety of flights available may be confusing initially. A detailed explanation of the various categories is given in *Traveling by Plane,* GETTING READY TO GO. Essentially the traveler can choose from one of several categories of scheduled flights — ranging in expense from first class, which presumably no vacation traveler needs, to APEX and standby — or charters.

In earlier sections of GETTING READY TO GO we discussed the various means of travel within Europe: rented car, bus, or train. The most important factor in determining which of these to use is the amount of traveling you plan to do and the length of time you will be abroad. If you intend to move about a great deal between cities, a pass allowing unlimited travel by rail or bus or both is likely to be the most economical form of transport. The passes are quite reasonably priced and those that can be bought before you go are especially attractive provided they are valid in all the areas you plan to visit. If road touring is your object, you should look into fly/drive arrangements versus straight rentals and compare the rates offered by some of the smaller US firms specializing in car travel in Europe with the rates and the discount plans offered by some of the large, familiar names in car rental (see *Touring by Car*). Always look for the flat rate based on unlimited mileage.

ACCOMMODATIONS: Room costs run a very wide gamut. Most expensive — and that can be $150 and up for a double room in London — will be international hotels with a full complement of business services. (There is no sacred edict stating that travelers must put up at deluxe hotels, however, and by skipping over the great small hotels, inns, and guesthouses, you might be missing a very special experience.) At the opposite end of the scale are the bed-and-breakfast houses, where you can spend the night in surroundings that may be homey or spartan, but are almost always clean and adequate. B&B's average about $18 per person per night in Britain, $14 in Ireland, but they are not easy to find in London where, as in any metropolis, space is at a premium and few private homes have the spare room to rent to passing strangers. Nevertheless, budget accommodations in central London do exist, and the BTA publishes the recently expanded *London Value Hotels,* which lists double room accommodations ranging from £27 to £45 per person per night. The Irish Tourist Board also provides a list of B&B establishments. Two additional options for those staying for an extended period are the "holiday let" or "self-catering holiday" and the home exchange. In the first case, you actually rent an apartment; in the second, you and a foreign family exchange homes for an agreed-upon period of time.

If you want to travel but also want to eliminate the element of surprise from your accommodations budget, you can take advantage of the hotel voucher schemes that frequently come as part of a fly/drive package. You receive a block of prepaid vouchers and a list of hotels that accept them as total payment for a night's stay, but if you want to upgrade your lodgings from time to time, there is often another set of hotels that accept the same vouchers upon payment of a supplement.

In Britain, slightly lower hotel rates can be expected off-season — from October through April. Many hotels offer "mini-break" packages, that is, a discount for a stay of 2 or more nights, usually over a weekend, and though these discounts may be in effect any time of the year, they are most common when demand is low. In Ireland, rates are lowest from January through March. (For a discussion of the range and variety of places to stay in Great Britain and Ireland, see *Accommodations,* GETTING READY TO GO.)

FOOD: Restaurant dining — particularly in the better eating establishments of major tourist cities — is, comparatively speaking, going to hit your purse, wallet, or credit card hardest. If you're an independent traveler and taking all of your meals out, allow roughly $35 to $50 a day for food. That includes breakfast, because increasingly in large urban hotels, the breakfast that comes with the price of the accommodations is Continental (coffee and rolls), or there is an extra charge for the full English or Irish breakfast. That amount should also cover taxes and a service charge and perhaps a carafe of table wine at dinner — but you won't be splurging. The estimate is based on fixed menu meals, which can at least provide a tasty and occasionally imaginative food selection, but no predinner cocktails. If you want to order a dinner of your choice in one of the major cities, be prepared for the tab to rise much higher. Notice, however, that we said that *dining* is going to hit your wallet hard. If you're up to a steady diet of fish and chips, you can get by on less. And there is some relief out in the countryside where the breakfast that comes with the bed in the typical B&B can still be a filling one, apt to hold you straight through midday, though even travelers on a severe budget are advised not to skip lunch. Pub lunches in general are becoming more and more imaginative everywhere and they're probably the best food buy you'll encounter.

Our restaurant choices are listed in the *Best in Town* sections of CITIES and in the *Checking In* and *Eating Out* sections of each tour route in DIRECTIONS. The basis for selection has been to give the best value for the money. The restaurants are rated as expensive, moderate, or inexpensive, and approximate price ranges for those labels in the given area are supplied.

LOCAL TAXES: A sales tax or VAT (Value Added Tax) is affixed to both goods and services. In Great Britain, the standard rate is 15%, whether on overnight room accommodations or on goods purchased in local stores. In Ireland, the tax on accommodations is 10%; on goods, 10% to 25%. In both Britain and Ireland, all advertised prices must by law include VAT. The VAT on purchases can be avoided by having the goods sent directly to your home address — if the store is willing to do so. In addition, some stores operate a "retail export" scheme, whereby you pay the tax, have a VAT relief form validated by a customs clerk as you leave the country, mail the form to the store, and receive a check in pounds in return.

SERVICE CHARGES: Increasingly, hotels and restaurants include a 10% to 15% charge on the cost of rooms and food to cover gratuities. Again, this may not be specified at the time of making reservations, so ask in advance. At restaurants, visitors should ask if a service charge is included in the bill submitted at the end of a meal. Even when such charges are included, an additional tip is appropriate if the service has been exceptional or if the service charge is minimal.

Other expenses, such as the cost of local sightseeing tours, will vary from city to city.

Official tourist information offices are plentiful in both countries and most of the better hotels will have a concierge or someone else at the front desk able to provide a rundown on the cost of local tours and full-day excursions in and out of the city. Special discount passes for tourists providing unlimited travel by the day or the week on regular city transportation are available in most large cities. An Open to View ticket ($29 from BritRail offices in the US) provides a month of free admissions to more than 600 British historic sites — such as Stonehenge, Longleat House, Hampton Court, and Windsor Castle — that are privately owned or the properties of the National Trust or the Ancient Monuments division of the Department of the Environment, both of which are charged with the preservation of national treasures. The ticket comes with a booklet listing the properties and the hours they are open. Entrance to major museums is usually free.

Entry Requirements and Documents

A valid US passport is the one document required for travel to either the United Kingdom or the Irish Republic, and you must have one for re-entry into the US. No visas are necessary. As a *general* rule, possession of a US passport entitles the bearer to remain in these countries for up to 3 months as a tourist; study, residency, or work necessitate acquiring completely different documents and considerably more laborious procedures are involved.

Vaccination certificates are required by authorities only if the traveler is entering from an area of contagion as defined by the World Health Organization. Because smallpox is considered eradicated from the world, there are only a few countries that continue to require visitors to have a smallpox vaccination certificate. You will certainly not need one to travel to the UK or the Irish Republic, or to return to the US.

New passports are now valid for 10 years from the date of issue (5 years for those under age 18). The expired passport itself is not renewable but must be turned in along with your application for a new and valid one (you will get it back, voided, when you receive the new one). Delivery can take as little as 2 weeks or as long as a month, and anyone applying for a passport for the first time should allow at least 4 weeks for delivery — even 6 weeks during the high season, from approximately mid-March to mid-September. In an emergency, a passport can be issued in as little time as one business day, but you will have to present an airline ticket with a confirmed reservation for a specific and imminent date to qualify for such special handling — obviously, you should resort to this only in a genuine emergency. Go directly to the nearest passport office to plead your case. For emergencies occurring outside business hours, there is a 24-hour telephone number in Washington, DC (202-634-3600), which can put you in touch with a State Department duty officer who may be able to expedite your application. Or call the Washington Passport Agency between the hours of 8 AM and 5 PM at 202-523-1673.

Normal passports contain 24 pages, but frequent travelers can request a 48-page passport at no extra cost. Every individual, regardless of age, must have his or her own passport. Family passports are no longer issued.

Passport renewal can be done by mail, but anyone applying for the first time or anyone under 18 renewing a passport must do so in person at one of the following places:

1. The State Department passport offices in Boston, Chicago, Honolulu, Houston, Los Angeles, Miami, New Orleans, New York City, Philadelphia, San Francisco, Seattle, Stamford, CT, and Washington, DC.
2. Any of 1,000 US post offices with designated acceptance facilities.

Application blanks are available at all these offices and must be presented with:

1. Proof of US citizenship. This can be a previous passport or one in which you were included. If you are applying for your first passport and you were born in the United States, your birth certificate is the required proof. If you were born abroad, a Certificate of Naturalization, a Certificate of Citizenship, a Report of Birth Abroad of a Citizen of the United States, or a Certification of Birth is necessary.
2. Two 2 × 2-inch front-view photographs in color or black and white taken within the previous 6 months. These must be taken by a photographer rather than by a machine.
3. Cash, check, or money order for the $7 execution fee (not required if you are renewing a passport), and the $35 passport fee ($20 for those under 18).
4. Proof of identity. Again, this can be a previous passport, or a driver's license, a Certificate of Naturalization or of Citizenship, or a government ID card with a physical description or a photograph. Failing any of these, you should be accompanied by a friend of at least 2 years' standing who will testify to your identity. Credit cards or social security cards do not suffice as proof of identity.

Passports can be renewed by mail on forms obtained at designated locations only if the expired passport was issued no more than 12 years before the date of the application for renewal and if it was not issued before the applicant's 16th birthday. Send the completed form with the expired passport, two photos (signed in the center of the back), and $35 (no execution fee required) to the nearest passport agency office.

■**SHOULD YOU LOSE YOUR PASSPORT ABROAD:** Immediately report the loss to the nearest US consulate. You can get a 3-month temporary passport directly from the consulate, but you must fill out a "loss of passport" form and follow the same application procedure — and pay the same fees — as you did for the original. It's likely to speed things up if you have a record of your passport number and the place and date of its issue.

Planning a Trip

123 For most travelers, a week-plus trip to Great Britain and/or Ireland can be too expensive for an "I'll take my chances" type of vacation. Hence a little planning is crucial. This is not to say that you have to work out your itinerary in minute detail before you go, but to suggest that by considering where you want to go, what you want to do, and how much you want to spend, you'll find it much easier to avoid delays, unexpected expenses, and the need to alter your plans because of unforeseen developments. In thinking out your trip, start with the following basics:

1. How much time will you have to spend?
2. Do you want to visit one, a few, or many different places?
3. When do you plan to travel? (It can make a considerable difference in what's open at your destination as well as in the cost of transportation and accommodations.)
4. How much money do you have to spend on your trip?
5. Do you want an unstructured trip (in which you'll be on your own when you get to your destination), or would you prefer the company and schedule of an escorted tour?

With firm answers to these major questions, start reviewing literature on the areas in which you're most interested. The British and Irish tourist boards in the US are ready sources for brochures or other information on their respective cities and countrysides (their addresses are listed in *Tourist Information Offices*). Other good sources of information are airlines, hotel representatives, and travel agents, who should be well supplied with literature from wholesalers and tour operators who organize packages and other travel arrangements to Europe. In other words, up-to-date travel information is plentiful and you should be able to accumulate not only everything you want to know about the places you plan to visit, but also about the tours and packages that are available to each. See *Package Tours*.

You can now make almost all of your own travel arrangements if you have the time to follow through with hotels, airlines, tour operators, and so on. But you'll probably save considerable time and energy if you have a travel agent make reservations and arrangements for you. The agent also should be able to advise you of alternative arrangements of which you may not be aware. Only very rarely will these services cost you any money and they may even save you some (see *How to Use a Travel Agent*). Well before departure (depending on how much in advance you make your reservations), the agent will supply you with a packet that includes all your tickets and hotel confirmations, and often a day-by-day outline of where you'll be when, along with a detailed list of whatever flights or trains you're taking.

Before your departure, find out what the weather will be like at your destination. Consult *When to Go* for a chart of average temperatures in various cities as well as a list of special events that may occur during your stay. See *How to Pack* for further details on the weather and what clothes to take. And if you're planning an extended stay in a particular city or region, you'll find it useful to read a bit about the area's history, its food specialties, people, and places of interest, especially if you are visiting for the first time.

Put your house in order: Pay all the bills, cancel newspapers, and arrange for mail to be held at the post office; have a good friend check the pipes and water the plants, and generally don't advertise your departure.

Make a list of any valuable items you are carrying with you, including credit card numbers and the serial numbers of your traveler's checks. Put copies in your luggage to facilitate identification in case of loss. Put your name and business address — *but never your home address* — on a label on the exterior of your luggage.

Review your travel documents. If you are traveling by air, check to see that your ticket has been filled in correctly. The left side of the ticket should have a list of each stop you will make (even if you are only stopping to change planes), beginning with your departure point. Be sure that the list is correct, and count the number of carbons to see that you have one for each plane you will take. If you have confirmed reservations, be sure that the column marked "status" says "OK" beside each flight. Have in hand vouchers or proof of payment (preferably from the hotels themselves) for any reservations for which you've paid in advance; this includes hotels, transfers to and from the airport, sightseeing tours, car rentals, special events, and so on.

How to Pack

 The goal is to remain perfectly comfortable, neat, clean, and adequately fashionable wherever you go, but to actually pack as little as possible. The main obstacle to achieving this end is habit: Most of us wake each morning with an entire wardrobe hanging in our closets, and we assume that our suitcase should offer the same variety. Not so; only our anxiety about being caught short makes us treat a suitcase like a mobile closet, and you can eliminate even the anxiety (and learn to travel lightly) by following two firm packing principles:

1. Organize your travel wardrobe around a single color — blue or brown, for example — that allows you to mix, match, and layer clothes. Holding firm to one color scheme will make it easy to eliminate items that don't harmonize; and by picking clothes for their adaptability and compatibility with your basic color, you will put together the most extensive wardrobe with the fewest pieces of clothing.
2. Use laundries to renew your wardrobe. Never overpack to ensure a supply of fresh clothing — shirts, blouses, underwear — for each day of a long trip. Businesspeople routinely use hotel laundries to wash and clean clothes and, if these prove too expensive, there are laundromats in most towns of any size.

CLIMATE AND CLOTHES: Although Britain and Ireland are farther north than most of the US — London, sitting astride latitude 51°30′, is a bit north of Québec's Gaspé Peninsula — the climate is generally much milder. The Gulf Stream, which warms the coasts of both countries, brings moderate temperatures year-round, with few subzero winters or blistering hot summers. Daily temperatures in Britain's coldest months (December, January, February) hover around 35° or 40°F (2° or 5°C) and summers generally average about 70°F (21°C). Similarly, Ireland's winter temperatures rarely dip below 40°F (5°C) and summer temperatures usually rise no higher than 70°F (21°C). The stereotype about English and Irish weather being wet is true: It rains often throughout the year, and even on fairly clear days the outside atmosphere still feels damp.

The temperate climate makes packing rather simple, if not altogether lightweight. A versatile item of clothing you'll find indispensable in both Great Britain and Ireland is a raincoat, preferably with a zip-out lining and a hood. The removable lining lets you adapt to temperature changes and the hood is better suited (and less cumbersome) than an umbrella for the fine, misty rain. Other appropriate apparel would be a warm wool sweater or jacket, even in summer (tweeds are worn year-round). And finally — since the best touring of castles, cathedrals, and countryside is on foot — pack a comfortable pair of walking shoes. Generally speaking, your fall wardrobe will probably have everything that's needed for the trip. For more detailed weather information, see *When to Go.*

FASHION: In London, you'll see a lot of chic, trendy dressing, and in Dublin, more relaxed, conservative attire. For a special dinner at one of the finest restaurants in either city, men should take along a suit or sports jacket and women a suit or cocktail dress. Otherwise, be guided by your own tastes and wear whatever makes you feel comfortable.

PACKING: A recommended packing procedure is the so-called layering method, designed to get everything in and out of a bag with as few wrinkles as possible. Heavy items go on the bottom and sides, and corners are stuffed with such articles as socks, underwear, shoes, handbags, and bathing suits. Then layer on the more easily wrinkled items, such as shirts and slacks, dresses and skirts, even jackets. Pack them with as few folds as possible. On the top layer put immediate needs, such as pajamas, sweater, raincoat, and the like. Make the layers even and the total contents of your bag as full and firm as possible to keep things from shifting around during transit.

TRAVELING WRINKLE-FREE: While packing, interleave each layer of clothes with plastic cleaning bags, which will help preserve pressed clothes while they are in the suitcase. Unpack your bags as soon as you get to a hotel. Nothing so destroys freshly cleaned and pressed clothes as sitting for days in a suitcase. Finally, if something is badly wrinkled and can't be professionally pressed before you must wear it, hang it overnight in a bathroom where the bathtub has been filled with very hot water; keep the bathroom door closed so the room becomes something of a steam room. It really works miracles.

SOME FINAL PACKING HINTS: Try to select toiletries and cosmetics that come in plastic containers. Glass-bottled liquids should be placed in plastic bags. If traveling overnight, put a few necessary toiletry items in a purse, a shoulder bag, or some other small, easily carried case. Add an emptied airline bag to your suitcase; you'll find it handy for overnight trips, beach outings, or for carrying purchases home. Don't ever put necessities such as medicine, travel documents, cash, or credit cards in your checked luggage; keep them in a piece of hand luggage that you carry.

How to Use a Travel Agent

 A reliable travel agent remains your best source of service and information for planning a trip abroad whether you already have a specific itinerary that only requires reservations or need extensive help in sorting through the maze of air fares, tour offerings, hotel packages, and the scores of other arrangements that may be required for a trip overseas.

You should know what you want from a travel agent to be able to evaluate what you are getting. It is perfectly reasonable to expect your travel agent to be a thorough travel specialist, with information about your destination, and, even more crucial, a command of current air fares, package tours, charters, ground arrangements, and other wrinkles in the travel scene.

To make the most intelligent use of a travel agent's time and expertise, you should know something of the economics of the industry. As a client, you traditionally pay nothing for the services performed by the agent; it's all free, from advice on package tours to reserving a river cruise. Any money that the travel agent makes on the time spent arranging your itinerary — booking hotels, resorts, or flights, or suggesting activities — comes from commissions paid by the suppliers who provide these services — the airlines, hotels, and so on. These commissions generally run anywhere from 7% to 15% of the total cost of the service. In some cases an agent may ask you to pay a fee for very personalized attention such as planning a custom-made itinerary or making reservations at places that do not pay commissions, such as a small country inn or guesthouse. In most instances, however, you'll find that agents provide their traditional services at no charge to you.

This system implies two things you should be alert to concerning your relationship with any travel agent.

1. You will get better service if you arrive at the agent's desk with your basic itinerary already planned. Know roughly where you want to go, what you want to do, and how much you want to spend. Use the agent to make bookings (which pay commissions) and to advise you on facilities, activities, and alternatives within the parameters of the basic itinerary you have chosen. You get the best service when you are requesting commissionable items. As there are few commissions on camping or driving-camping tours, an agent is unlikely to be very enthusiastic about helping to plan one. The more vague your plans, the less direction you can expect from most agents. If you walk into an agency and say "I have two weeks in June, what shall I do?" you will most likely walk out with nothing more than a handful of brochures. So do your homework.
2. Be watchful. There is always the danger that an incompetent or unethical agent will send you to a place that offers the best commissions rather than the best facilities for your purposes.

You should choose a travel agent with the same care with which you would choose a doctor or lawyer. You will be spending a good deal of money on the basis of the agent's judgment, and you have a right to expect that judgment to be mature, informed, and interested. At the moment, unfortunately, there are no real standards within the industry to help you gauge an agent's competence, and the quality of individual agents varies enormously. While several states are in the process of drawing up legislation for licensing agents — which would at least ensure that anyone acting as a travel agent has met some minimum standards — only a very few at present have any form of registration on their books. Perhaps the best-prepared agents are those who carry the initials CTC (Certified Travel Counselor) after their names. This means that they have worked in the travel industry for at least 5 years and have completed the 18-month course of study conducted by the Institute of Certified Travel Agents of Wellesley, Massachusetts, indicating a relatively high level of expertise.

An agent's membership in a trade association can be another useful guideline. The American Society of Travel Agents (ASTA) and the smaller but highly respected Association of Retail Travel Agents (ARTA) require member agents and agencies to abide by a code of ethics. If you feel you have been improperly dealt with, complaints about an ASTA member can be made to ASTA's Consumer Affairs Department, 4400 MacArthur Blvd., NW, Washington, DC 20007 (phone: 202-965-7520). Complaints about an ARTA member's service can be made to ARTA, 25 S Riverside Ave., Croton-on-Hudson, NY 10520 (phone: 914-271-9000). But keep in mind that these are industry organizations and they do not guarantee the ethics, competence, or financial soundness of their members.

Perhaps the best way to find a travel agent is by word of mouth. If the agent (or agency) has done a good job for your friends over a period of time, it probably indicates a certain level of commitment and concern. But always ask for the name of the specific agent with whom they dealt, for it is that individual who will serve you, and quality can vary widely within a single agency.

Once you've chosen an agent, be entirely candid. Budget considerations rank at the top of the candor list, and there's no sense in wasting the agent's (or your) time poring over itineraries that you know you can't afford. Similarly, if you like a fair degree of comfort, that fact should not be kept secret from your travel agent, who may assume that you wish to travel on a tight budget even when that's not the case.

Insurance

 It is unfortunate that most decisions to buy travel insurance are impulsive and are usually made without any real consideration of the traveler's existing insurance policies. Too often the result is the purchase of needlessly expensive short-term policies that duplicate existing coverage and reinforce the tendency to buy coverage on a trip-by-trip basis rather than to work out a total and continuing travel insurance package that might well be more effective and economical.

Therefore, the first person with whom you should discuss travel insurance is your own insurance broker — not a travel agent or the clerk behind the airport insurance counter. You may well discover that the insurance you already carry — homeowner's policies and/or accident, health, and life insurance policies — protect you adequately while you travel, and that your real needs are in the more mundane areas of excess value insurance for baggage or trip cancellation insurance.

To make insurance decisions intelligently, however, you should first understand the basic categories of travel insurance and what they are designed to cover. Then you will be able to determine what is missing in the broader context of your personal insurance needs and be in a position to choose the most economical way of filling the gap — through riders on existing policies; with one-shot short-term policies; through a special program put together for the frequent traveler; or with a combination policy sold by insurance companies through brokers, tour operators, and travel agents.

There are six basic categories of travel insurance: baggage and personal effects; personal accident and sickness; trip cancellation and interruption; default and/or bankruptcy; flight (to cover death or injury); automobile (for driving your own or a rented car).

BAGGAGE AND PERSONAL EFFECTS INSURANCE: If baggage and personal effects are included in your current homeowner's policy, check with your broker about the necessity for a special floater to cover you for the duration of a trip. The object is to protect your bags and their contents in case of damage or theft anytime during your travels. Only limited protection is provided by the airline. For most international flights, including domestic portions of international flights, the airline's liability limit is approximately $20 per kilo ($9.07 per pound) for checked baggage and $400 per passenger for unchecked baggage. (On domestic flights, the limit of liability on most airlines is $1,250 per passenger.) But these limits, which should be specified in the finer print of your ticket, represent maximums, and to be awarded even this amount you'll have to provide an itemized list of lost property. If you're including new and/or expensive items, be prepared to back up your claim with sales receipts or other proofs of purchase.

If you are carrying goods worth more than the maximum protection offered by the airline, you should consider excess value insurance, available from the airlines at an average, currently, of 50¢ per $100 worth of coverage. This insurance can be purchased at the airline counter when you check in, though you should arrive early to fill out the necessary forms and to avoid holding up other passengers checking in. Excess value insurance is also included in certain of the combination travel insurance policies discussed below.

■**ONE NOTE OF WARNING:** Be sure to read the fine print of any excess value insurance policy; there are often specific exclusions, such as money, tickets, furs, gold and silver objects, art, and antiques. And remember that insurance companies ordinarily will pay only the depreciated value of the goods rather than their replacement value. To best protect the items you're carrying in your luggage, have photos made of valuables, and keep a record of the serial numbers of such items as cameras, typewriters, radios, and so on. This will establish that you do, indeed, own the objects. If your luggage disappears en route or is damaged, deal with the situation immediately, at the airport, train station, or bus station. If an airline loses your luggage, you will be asked to fill out a Property Irregularity Report before you leave the airport. If your property disappears elsewhere, make a report to the police at once.

PERSONAL ACCIDENT AND SICKNESS INSURANCE: This covers you in case of illness on the road (hospital and doctor's expenses, lost income, and so on). In most cases it is a standard part of existing health insurance policies, though you should check with your broker to be sure that your policy will pay for medical expenses incurred abroad.

TRIP CANCELLATION AND INTERRUPTION INSURANCE: Most package tours, cruises, and charter flights require full payment a substantial period of time before departure. Although cancellation penalties vary (they are listed in the fine print in every tour brochure, and before you purchase a package tour you should know exactly what they are), rarely will you get more than 50% of your money back if forced to cancel within a few weeks of leaving. Any refund of money paid for a charter flight canceled even well in advance may depend on your being able to supply a substitute passenger. Therefore, if you book a package tour or charter flight, you should have trip cancellation* insurance to guarantee a full refund should you, a traveling companion, or a member of your immediate family get sick, forcing you to cancel your trip or *return home early*. The key here is not to buy just enough insurance to guarantee full reimbursement in case of cancellation. The proper amount of coverage should be sufficient to reimburse you for the cost of having to catch up with a tour after its departure or having to travel home at the full economy air fare if you have to forgo the return trip of a discounted flight (such as an excursion with advance purchase requirements), and especially if you have to forgo the return portion of a charter.

Cancellation insurance designed to cover a specific package is frequently offered by tour operators. Otherwise, it can be bought through travel agents or from insurance companies or their agents as part of a combination travel insurance policy. Read any policy carefully before you buy it, and be sure the one you choose provides enough money to get you home from the farthest point on your itinerary should you have to fly on a scheduled flight. Also, be sure to check the specific definition of "family members" and "preexisting medical conditions." Some policies will not pay if you become ill from a condition for which you have received treatment in the past.

DEFAULT AND/OR BANKRUPTCY INSURANCE: Trip cancellation insurance usually protects you in the event that you, the traveler, are unable to take — or complete — your trip. A recent innovation is coverage in the event of default and/or bankruptcy on the part of the tour operator, airline, or other travel supplier. In some travel insurance packages this contingency is included in the trip cancellation portion of the coverage; in others, it is a separate feature. Either way, it is becoming increasingly pertinent. Whereas most travelers have long known to beware of the possibility of default or bankruptcy when buying a charter flight or charter tour, in recent years more than a few respected scheduled airlines have unexpectedly revealed their shaky financial condition, sometimes leaving stranded ticketholders in their wake. Moreover, the value of escrow protection of a charter passenger's funds has lately come into question. While default/bankruptcy insurance will not ordinarily result in reimbursement in time for you to pay for new arrangements, it can ensure that you will eventually get your money back, and even independent travelers buying no more than an airplane ticket may want to consider it.

Note, however, that because of differing state insurance regulations, default and/or bankruptcy insurance is not universally available. In addition, it can be expensive. In its absence, consider using credit cards to pay for travel arrangements whenever possible. The federal Fair Credit Billing Act permits purchasers to refuse payment for credit card charges where services have not been delivered, so the potential onus of dealing with a receiver for a bankrupt airline falls on the credit card company. Do not assume that another airline will automatically honor the ticket you're holding on a bankrupt airline, since the days when virtually all major carriers subscribed to a default protection program are long gone. Some airlines may voluntarily step forward to accommodate stranded passengers, but this is now an entirely altruistic act.

FLIGHT INSURANCE: Airlines have carefully established limits of liability for the death or injury of passengers. For international flights these are printed right on the ticket: a maximum of $75,000 in case of death or injury. But remember, these limits of liability are not the same thing as insurance policies; they merely state the *maximum* an airline will pay in the case of death or injury, and every penny of that is usually subject to a legal battle.

This may make you feel that you are not adequately protected. But before you buy last-minute flight insurance from an airport vending machine, as many passengers do, consider the purchase in light of your total existing insurance coverage. A careful review of your current policies may reveal that you are already amply covered for accidental death, sometimes up to three times the amount provided for by the flight insurance you're buying in the airport.

Be aware that airport insurance, the kind you typically buy at a counter or from a vending machine, is among the most expensive forms of life insurance coverage available anywhere, and that even within a single airport, rates for approximately the same coverage can vary. Often the vending machines are more expensive than coverage sold over the counter, even when policies are with the same national company.

If you buy your ticket with an American Express, Diners Club, or Carte Blanche credit card, you are issued automatic accident and accidental death insurance at no extra cost. American Express automatically provides $100,000 coverage; Carte Blanche, $150,000; Diners Club, $650,000. American Express offers additional coverage at extremely reasonable prices, but a cardholder must sign up for it in advance: $3 per ticket buys $250,000 worth of flight insurance, and $5.50 buys $500,000 worth; $11 provides $1 million worth of coverage.

AUTOMOBILE INSURANCE: Public liability and property damage (third-party) insurance are compulsory in the United Kingdom and the Irish Republic whether you drive your own car or a rental. Every car rental contract includes this coverage, but has a deductible ranging from $400 to $1,000. Optional collision damage waiver protection, usually costing from $4 to $8 per day, relieves the renter from paying the deductible amount in the event of an accident. Your car rental contract (with the appropriate insurance box ticked off) will suffice as proof of insurance. If you drive your own car, you must carry an International Insurance Certificate (called a Green Card), available through insurance brokers in the US.

COMBINATION POLICIES: A number of insurance companies offer all-purpose travel insurance packages that include baggage, personal accident and sickness, and trip cancellation insurance, and, sometimes, default and bankruptcy protection. They cover you for a single trip and are sold by travel agents, insurance agents, and others. One such policy is Travel Guard, endorsed by the American Society of Travel Agents (ASTA) and available through travel agents.

Hints for Handicapped Travelers

Roughly 35 million people in the US alone suffer from some sort of disability. At least half this number are physically handicapped. Like everyone else today, they — and the uncounted disabled millions around the world — are on the move. More than ever before the disabled are demanding facilities they can use comfortably, and they are being heard. Accessibility, both here and abroad, is being brought up to more acceptable standards every day.

PLANNING: It is essential to make travel arrangements well in advance and to specify to all services involved the degree of your disability or restricted mobility. Fortunately, there are some excellent organizations to help you begin. Rehabilitation International/USA (RIUSA) is a national organization that provides information and services to the disabled and is affiliated with similar organizations in over 77 foreign countries. RIUSA publishes the *International Directory of Access Guides,* a free listing of over 450 access guides both domestic and international with information on where to write for them. For a copy of the guide, send $1 to RIUSA, Access Guide, 1123 Broadway, Suite 704, New York, NY 10010 (phone: 212-972-2707).

Mobility International/USA (MIUSA), the US branch of Mobility International, a nonprofit British-based organization with affiliates in some 35 countries, offers advice and assistance to disabled travelers who are members — including information on accommodations, access guides, and study tours. Write to Mobility International USA (MIUSA), PO Box 3551, Eugene, OR 97403 (phone: 503-343-1284, voice and TTY). MIUSA publishes *A World of Options: A Guide to International Educational Exchange,*

Community Service, and Travel for Persons with Disabilities. The book is $11 for members, or $13 for nonmembers (price includes postage). MIUSA also publishes a newsletter that is available by subscription for $10.

The Travel Information Center at Moss Rehabilitation Hospital is a free service designed to help handicapped people plan trips. It cannot make travel arrangements but will supply information about particular cities or countries or any special interests you have. Write to the Travel Information Center, Moss Rehabilitation Hospital, 12th St. and Tabor Rd., Philadelphia, PA 19141 (phone: 215-329-5715, ext. 2468).

To keep abreast of developments in travel for the handicapped as they occur, you may want to join the Society for the Advancement of Travel for the Handicapped (SATH). Membership in SATH, a nonprofit organization whose members include travel agents, tour operators, and other travel suppliers, as well as consumers, costs $40 ($20 for students) and the fee is tax deductible. SATH publishes a quarterly newsletter and can provide information on travel agents or tour operators in the US and overseas who have experience or an interest in travel for the handicapped. Send a stamped, self-addressed envelope to SATH, 26 Court St., Brooklyn, NY 11242 (phone: 718-858-5483).

An excellent book to consult is Louise Weiss's *Access to the World: A Travel Guide for the Handicapped* (Facts on File; $14.95). Ms. Weiss provides extensive information on transportation and hotels and offers sound tips for the disabled traveler abroad. Check the library for Mary Meister Walzer's *A Travel Guide for the Disabled: Western Europe* (Van Nostrand Reinhold), which gives a country-by-country listing of hotels and restaurants along with their access ratings and other useful information. Frommer's *A Guide for the Disabled: The United States, Canada, & Europe* (Simon & Schuster; $10.95), by Frances Barish, contains a chapter on London. There is also a travel magazine — *The Itinerary* — for people with disabilities. It comes out every other month with information on accessibility, listings of tours, news of devices, travel aids, and special services as well as numerous general travel hints and costs $9 a year ($16 for two years). To subscribe, write *The Itinerary,* PO Box 1084, Bayonne, NJ 07002 (phone: 201-858-3400).

The British Tourist Authority's *Britain for the Disabled* (free) contains helpful information on a variety of topics concerning the handicapped; and the section on Great Britain and Northern Ireland in RIUSA's *International Directory of Access Guides* mentioned above is especially comprehensive. Many of the publications listed were prepared by and are available directly from the Royal Association for Disability and Rehabilitation (RADAR), 25 Mortimer St., London W1N 8AB, to whom you may want to write for an up-to-date price list. A central source of information on facilities in the Republic of Ireland is the National Rehabilitation Board, 25 Clyde Rd., Dublin 4, Ireland.

Regularly revised hotel guides using the "symbol of access" to point out accommodations suitable for wheelchair-bound guests include the AA/BTA *Hotels and Restaurants in Britain* ($18.95 plus $3.25 handling charge), sold at the British Travel Bookshop, and the *Michelin Red Guide to Great Britain and Ireland,* sold in general bookstores ($14.95). The Irish Tourist Board also uses the symbol in its annual *Guide to Hotels and Guesthouses,* but its *Accommodation and Restaurant Guide for Disabled Persons,* available free from US offices, is an actual access guide and much more useful.

It should be noted that almost all of the material published with disabled travelers in mind deals with the wheelchair-bound traveler for whom architectural barriers are of prime concern. A problem that will restrict the movement of another category of handicapped, blind people, is the very strict enforcement of anti-rabies laws in both the United Kingdom and the Irish Republic. Any dogs brought into either country must spend 6 months in quarantine — and seeing-eye dogs are not exempt.

AIR TRAVEL: Disabled passengers should always make reservations well in advance and should provide the airline with all relevant details of their condition when doing so. These details include information on mobility, toileting, whether or not you use oxygen, and whether airline-supplied equipment such as a wheelchair or portable oxygen will be necessary. Be sure that the person you speak with understands fully the degree of your disability — the more details provided, the more effective the help that can be given. Then, the day before the flight, call back to make sure that all arrangements have been taken care of, and on the day of the flight, arrive early so that you can be boarded before the rest of the passengers. Carry a medical certificate with you, stating your specific disability or the need to carry particular medicine. (Some airlines require the certificate and you should find out the regulations of the airline you'll be flying well beforehand.) In most cases, you can be wheeled as far as the plane, and sometimes right onto it, in your own wheelchair; if not, a boarding chair may be used. Your own wheelchair will be folded and put in the baggage compartment and should be tagged as escort luggage to assure that it's available at planeside immediately upon landing rather than in the baggage claim area.

The Airport Operators Council International puts out a guide to over 470 airports here and abroad called *Access Travel: A Guide to Accessibility of Airport Terminals.* It includes detailed information on Heathrow, Gatwick, and Stansted airports in England; Aberdeen, Edinburgh, Glasgow, and Prestwick in Scotland; and Cork, Dublin, and Shannon airports in Ireland. For a free copy, write to ACCESS AMERICA, Consumer Information, Pueblo, CO 81009. The British airports are discussed in a series of airport access guides prepared by the British Airports Authority and called *Who Looks After You at Heathrow Airport?* (or Gatwick Airport, Stansted Airport, and so on). To receive a copy, write to the British Airports Authority, Masefield House, Gatwick Airport, Gatwick, West Sussex RH6 0HZ, filling in the name of the airport that interests you.

TRAVEL BY SHIP: Cunard's *Queen Elizabeth 2* is considered to be the best-equipped ship for the handicapped — all but the top deck is accessible. The *QE2* crosses the Atlantic regularly from April through November, between New York and its home port of Southampton, England, sometimes calling at Cherbourg, France. Be sure to provide the ship'd management with details of your condition and a physician's letter.

TRAVEL BY CAR, BUS, OR TRAIN: The best solution to getting around is to travel with an able-bodied companion who can drive. Another option is to hire a chauffeur-driven auto. As for doing the driving yourself, it is extremely difficult in Europe to find rental cars adapted with hand controls for the disabled. One company that does supply them is Kenning Car Hire Ltd., at 477–479 Green Lanes, Palmers Green, London N13.

Bus travel is not recommended for travelers who are totally wheelchair bound unless they have someone along who can lift them on and off or they are members of a group tour designed for the handicapped and using a specially outfitted bus. Local personnel may be willing, but there are often regulations prohibiting them from actually picking up a passenger. If you have some mobility, however, you'll find employees usually quite happy to help you board and exit.

Travel by train is becoming more feasible especially in Britain where many newer trains have removable seats in first class that can accommodate a wheelchair up to 24½ inches wide. The number of destinations (London to Liverpool, Manchester, Glasgow, Edinburgh, Bristol, the west of England, and South Wales among them) is still limited and lavatories on even these trains are still not accessible, though most trips are not long; major stations, however, have restroom facilities for the handicapped. On other trains, passengers can arrange to travel in the guard's van, that is, the baggage car. Wheelchair passengers travel at one-third off the applicable standard fare (unless they occupy a normal seat) and arrangements, either to ride in the guard's van or to have seats removed, or for an escort at stations, must be made through the area manager in advance. *British Rail: A Guide for Disabled People,* an access guide to railway stations, is available through RADAR (address above). For more information on British trains, contact BritRail Travel International offices in New York, Chicago, Dallas, or Los Angeles; for information on Irish trains, contact CIE Tours International, 122 E 42nd St., New York, NY 10168 (phone: in New York City, 212-972-5600; elsewhere in New York State, 800-522-5258; elsewhere in the US, 800-CIE-TOUR).

TOURS: The following travel agencies or tour operators specialize in making group or individual arrangements for the handicapped traveler and all have experience in travel to Great Britain or Ireland. Programs for the physically impaired are run by specialists who have traveled in advance or have thoroughly researched hotels, restaurants, and places of interest to be sure they present no insurmountable obstacles.

Evergreen Travel Service/Wings on Wheels Tours, 19505 L, 44th Ave. W, Lynnwood, WA 98036 (phone: 206-776-1184; in Washington State, 800-562-9298; elsewhere, 800-435-2288). Handles cruises, group tours, and individual arrangements for the physically disabled and the blind.

Flying Wheels Travel, Box 382, Owatonna, MN 55060 (phone: 507-451-5005 or 800-533-0363). Handles tours and individual arrangements for the physically disabled and the elderly.

The Guided Tour, 555 Ashbourne Rd., Elkins Park, PA 19117 (phone: 215-782-1370). Offers some tours for the physically handicapped but is more geared to the developmentally disabled.

Interpretours, Encino Travel Service, 16660 Ventura Blvd., Encino CA 91436 (phone: 818-788-4118 or 818-788-4515, voice and TTY). Arranges independent travel, cruises, and tours for the deaf, with an interpreter as tour guide.

Travel Horizons Unlimited, 11 E 44th St., New York, NY 10017 (phone: 212-687-5121). Arranges tours, and independent travel for those who require hemodialysis.

Hints for Traveling with Children

What better way to be receptive to the experiences you will encounter than to take along the young, wide-eyed members of your family? And what better place to take them than Great Britain and Ireland, where you'll find tales of King Arthur's Court and Robin Hood, not to mention the leprechauns, fairies, and little people lurking around every bend. Your children's company does not have to be a burden or their presence an excessive expense. The current generation of discount air fares makes flights to these countries a good deal less expensive than a decent summer camp. Or why not send them to summer camp in the Irish countryside while you do some touring? Gaeltacht vacations are offered for children during the summer months in Irish-speaking regions; here they can learn a bit about the language, folklore, and traditions of the Irish people. Riding holidays and pony trekking, as well as traditional camps, are popular in England, Scotland, Wales, and Northern Ireland.

If, however, you'd like to keep the family together, you can rent a cottage or visit a family farm in the countryside. The British and Irish tourist offices have information on how to make arrangements for any of these vacations.

A family trip will be an investment in your children's futures, making geography and history come alive to them, and a sure memory that will be among the fondest you will share with them someday. Their insights will be refreshing to you; their impulses may take you to unexpected places with unexpected dividends. At whatever age, the experience will be invaluable to them. It is necessary, however, to take some extra time to prepare for the trip.

Here are several hints for making a trip with children easy and fun.

1. Children should be part of planning the trip, and preparations should begin about a month before you leave, using maps, atlases, travel magazines, and travel books to make clear exactly where you are going and how far away it is. Part of the excitement of the journey will be associating the tiny dots on the map with the very real places the children visit a few weeks later. You can show them pictures of streets and scenes in which they will stand within a month. Don't shirk history lessons, but don't burden them with dates. Make history light, anecdotal, pertinent, but most of all, fun. Read them Irish folklore, teach them a Highland fling, set them to tracing their ancestral roots.

2. Children should be in on the planning of the itinerary, and where you go and what you do should reflect some of their ideas. If they know enough about architecture and geography before they go, they will have the excitement of recognition when they arrive, and the illumination of seeing how something is or is not the way they expected it to be.

3. Give children specific responsibilities. The job of carrying their own flight bags and looking after their personal things, along with some other light travel responsibility, will give them a stake in the journey.

PACKING: Choose your own and your children's clothes wisely. Take only drip-dry, wrinkle-resistant articles, comfortable shoes — sneakers or sandals — and a few things to keep warm and dry. But limit packing to a minimum. No one likes to carry added luggage, and you'll be surprised that, when abroad, clothes are about the last thing on your mind.

It is a good idea to take along as many handy snacks as you can squeeze into the corners of your suitcases. These should include things like raisins, nuts, sucking candy, and crackers (especially for the tots). Don't worry if your supply is quickly depleted — airports and train stations are well stocked with such items.

Along with these few edibles, pack a special medical kit (see *Medical and Legal Aid Abroad*) and some packaged towelettes for dirty fingers. Have your children choose a few favorite toys to bring along. Pens, crayons, and paper take up the least amount of room and can be put to use during long car trips or train rides. You might also encourage your children to draw what they see around them. Any way you can think of to help them assimilate their new experiences will increase their enjoyment.

PLANNING: Give children who can read books on Britain and Ireland. The British Travel Bookshop (40 W 57th St, New York, NY 10019) has a "Discovering" series, and some of the titles will especially appeal to children — *Discovering Kings and Queens, Discovering Ghosts,* and *Discovering Preserved Railways* ($3.25 each, plus $2 handling per order). It also offers the nicely illustrated *Stonehenge* ($3.25), a history book for children 11 and older, and the new *Children's Guide to London* ($8.95), designed for family trips and featuring information on everything from the Tower of London to the city's unique Museum of Childhood. *Irish Book Loft* (232 Madison Ave., New York, NY 10019) specializes in Irish books and records and has paperbacks and cassettes on Irish fairies, genealogy, history, and folklore. Miroslav Sasek's travel series for children, published by Macmillan and available in general bookstores, includes *This Is Ireland.* David Macaulay's *Castle* (Houghton Mifflin), which uses text and drawings to show how castles were built in Wales in the 13th century, is particularly suited to helping children understand the many castles they may see in Great Britain; *Cathedral,* by the same author, is also appropriate.

GETTING THERE AND GETTING AROUND: Begin early to investigate all available discount and charter flights as well as any package deals and special rates offered by the major airlines. Booking is sometimes required up to 2 months in advance. You may well find that charters offer no reductions for children, but the major scheduled airlines invariably do. As a general rule, a child under 2 years of age flies to Europe at 10%

of the fare paid by the accompanying adult as long as the child is kept on the adult's lap. (Don't despair, though. If there are empty seats around you, no one will object to your putting the child down, and armrests are generally removable.) A second child under 2 without a second adult flies to Europe at the same fare applicable to children from 2 through 11, which is usually half an adult economy fare and two thirds an adult APEX fare. Given advance notice, airlines provide special infant seats and children's meals. For landings and takeoffs, have a bottle or pacifier on hand for the infants and some gum or sucking candy for older children. This will keep everyone swallowing properly and ensure against earaches caused by rapid changes in air pressure. Newborn babies, whose lungs may not be able to adjust to the altitude, should not be taken aboard an airplane. (Note: Some airlines refuse to carry pregnant women in their eighth or ninth month, for fear of the hazards of an in-flight birth. Check with the airline ahead of time.)

By ship, children (ages 1 through 12) usually travel at a considerably reduced fare. On British trains, children travel free under age 5 and at half fare from ages 5 through 15. On Irish trains (and buses), they travel free under 3 years of age and at half fare from ages 3 through 15. Britain's BritRail Pass and the Irish Republic's Rambler Ticket, which offer unlimited travel within a set period of time, are similarly discounted. The Eurailpass, also valid in Ireland, is half price for children ages 4 through 12. Buy these passes before you leave the US. Northern Ireland Railways' unlimited travel pass, the Rail Runabout, is half price to children under 16; the Freedom of Northern Ireland bus pass is also discounted for children under 16. Both can be bought only in Northern Ireland. The Britexpress Pass, bought either in Britain or through travel agents in the US, lets children 5 through 16 years ride the bus in England, Scotland, and Wales at about 30% the price of an adult pass.

ACCOMMODATIONS: Often a cot will be placed in a hotel room at little or no extra charge. If you wish to sleep in separate rooms, special rates are sometimes available for families in adjoining rooms. You might want to look into accommodations along the way that will add to the color of your trip; there are, for instance, many country inns, farmhouses, and cottages throughout the British and Irish countrysides that could prove a delightful experience for the whole family. And don't forget castles, many of which double as hotels. Your children will love them. Camping facilities are often situated in beautiful, out-of-the-way spots and are generally good, well equipped, and less expensive than any hotel you will come across.

WHAT TO SEE AND DO: For specific suggestions on what to see and do in the various cities, see the individual city reports in THE CITIES. There are several excellent publications that focus on the interests of the young visitor and provide helpful hints for parents. Agencies to contact if you want to send your child to summer camp or a riding school are listed in *Young Visitors to Britain,* put out by the BTA; it will even tell your child how to find a British pen pal. Also ask the BTA about an organization called Universal Aunts, Ltd. This group has a wide range of services including picking a child up at an airport or train station, babysitting, and conducting children's tours. The Irish Tourist Board publishes dozens of fact sheets on every topic of interest, i.e., folklore, summer schools, camps, and regions where Irish is still spoken.

There are some general things to remember when traveling with children. First and foremost, don't forget that their attention span is far shorter than an adult's. They don't have to see every museum to learn something from their trip; watching, playing with, and talking to other children can be equally enlightening experiences. Try to break up the day into short, palatable segments: no more than a morning or afternoon dedicated to any one activity, be it travel or sightseeing. Also, remember the places that children the world over love to visit: zoos, country fairs, amusement parks, beaches, and nature trails, many of which are listed in the publications previously mentioned.

Hints for Single Travelers

Just about the last trip in human history in which the participants were neatly paired was the voyage of Noah's Ark. Ever since, passenger lists and tour groups have reflected the same kind of asymmetry that occurs in real life, as countless individuals set forth to see the world unaccompanied (or unencumbered, depending on your outlook) by spouse, lover, friend, or relative.

There are some things to be said for traveling alone. For one thing, it forces you to see more; it requires that you be self-reliant, independent, and responsible. It also requires you to be more outgoing, with the result that you tend to meet more people than you would traveling in a pair. Unfortunately, it also turns you into a second-class citizen.

For the truth is that the travel industry is not yet prepared to deal economically with people who vacation by themselves. Most travel bargains, including package tours, hotel accommodations, resort packages, and cruises, are based on *double-occupancy* rates. This means that the per-person price is offered on the basis of two people traveling together and sharing a double room. For exactly the same package, the single traveler will have to pay a surcharge, called the "single supplement," which can add as much as 30% to 55% to the basic per-person rate.

Don't despair, however. There are scores of inexpensive guesthouses, small hotels, and B&Bs throughout Great Britain and Ireland. These smaller accommodations offer a cozy atmosphere and prices that are still quite reasonable for the single traveler. Given your unencumbered state, you may want to consider an organization catering to people interested not only in seeing the sights abroad but also in meeting the people en route. The United States Servas Committee keeps a worldwide list of hosts willing to take visitors into their homes as guests for a 2-night stay. (See the section on Home Stays, *Accommodations and Reservations,* GETTING READY TO GO.)

If you prefer to have your arrangements taken care of for you, a number of options have emerged. Cosmos, the British tour operator specializing in budget motorcoach tours of Europe, offers "Guaranteed Share," a plan whereby singles who wish to share rooms are matched by the tour escort with like-minded individuals and charged the basic tour price. If a suitable partner can't be found, Cosmos will pay the single supplement, though those who elect to stay on their own must pay the supplement. Cosmos tours can be booked through travel agents. Singleworld (444 Madison Ave., New York, NY 10022; phone: in New York City, 212-758-2433; elsewhere, 800-223-6490), which organizes its own packages and also books singles on the cruises and tours of others, similarly arranges shared accommodations if requested, charging a one-time surcharge that is much less than the single supplement would be.

Singleworld — actually a club joined either through travel agents or direct for a yearly fee of $18, paid at the time of booking — is one of the many organizations catering solely to single vacationers of all ages. Some charge minimal membership fees; others offer their services free. But the basic service offered by all is the same — to match the unattached person with a compatible travel mate. Perhaps the most recent innovation along these lines is the creation of organizations that "introduce" the single traveler to other single travelers, somewhat like a dating service. Travel Companion Exchange (PO Box 833, Amityville, NY 11701; phone: 516-454-0880) is one such. Functioning on a membership basis (fees range from $3 to $11 per month, depending on age), members fill out a lengthy questionnaire to establish a personal profile and write a listing much like an ad in a personal column. The listing is free to other members, who can request a copy of the complete questionnaire and then go on to make contact to plan a joint vacation. Travel Share International, based in Santa Barbara, is another referral service that pairs single travelers — primarily professionals between 35 and 65 — with travel companions. Its bimonthly directory, "Key to Adventure," profiles members and their areas of interest. More detailed descriptions and even photographs of members can be requested, but contacting the potential companion is up to the member. A six-month membership is $59; a year-long membership is $99. Contact Travel Share International, PO Box 30365, Santa Barbara, CA 93130 (phone: 805-682-9955).

Two specific groups of single travelers deserve special mention: women and students. Among the organizations catering directly to women travelers is Estilita Grimaldo's Womantours (5314 N Figueroa St., Los Angeles, CA 90042; phone: 213-255-1115), which arranges group and individual travel programs for women. Countless women do travel by themselves in Britain and Ireland. Such a venture need not be feared. In fact, most British and Irish cities are considerably safer than American cities and, in some cases, friendlier. One lingering inhibition many female travelers still harbor is that of eating alone in public. The trick here is to relax, because solo diners are no longer an uncommon sight nor scorned.

A large number of single travelers are students. There are many benefits for students abroad, and the place to begin is by applying for an International Student Identity Card (ISIC) before leaving home. Reductions on train and air fares, and free entry to most museums and other exhibits are only some of the advantages of this card; it also includes medical and accident insurance for overseas travel. Applications require a $10 fee, a passport-sized photograph, and proof that you are a full-time student (this means a letter or bill from your school registrar with the school's official seal; high school and junior high school students can use their report cards). To apply, write to the Council on International Educational Exchange (CIEE), 205 E 42nd St., New York, NY 10017 (phone: 212-661-1414), or visit one of the CIEE's 21 regional offices (call the number above for locations). This organization, which administers a variety of work, study, and travel programs for students, also sponsors charter flights to Europe which are open to the public.

Special transportation discounts are available to students and youth in both Britain and Ireland. CIE, the Irish Republic's National Transportation Company, has a Youth Rambler Ticket for those between the ages of 14 and 26. It allows the holder 8, 15, or 30 days of unlimited travel by rail or bus or by a combination of the two. The ticket must be purchased before going overseas (from travel agents or CIE Tours International, in New York). Eurail's Youthpass, for those under 26, is accepted in the Irish Republic, but is not really economical unless you are traveling through several other countries on the Eurail network (which does not include Great Britain).

In Great Britain, British Rail offers the BritRail Youth Pass for anyone age 16 through 25. The Youth Pass permits unlimited train travel in economy class throughout England, Scotland, and Wales for 8-, 15-, or 22-day or 1-month time periods.

(The addresses and phone numbers of BritRail Travel International and CIE Tours International are listed in *Touring by Rail,* GETTING READY TO GO.)

For accommodations, keep in mind that youth hostels are plentiful throughout Great Britain and Ireland. These are a sure place to meet people your own age and are generally clean, well located, and always inexpensive. Hostels are run by the hosteling associations of some 60-plus countries that make up the International Youth Hostel Federation (IYHF); membership in one of the national associations affords access to the hostels of the rest. To join the American affiliate, American Youth Hostels (AYH), write to the national office at PO Box 37613, Washington, DC 20013-7613 (phone: 202-783-6161), or contact the local AYH council nearest you. Membership costs $20 for people between age 18 and 59; $10 for anyone outside those limits. (If joining by mail, add $1 for postage.) The *AYH Handbook,* which lists hostels in the US, comes with your AYH card; the *International Handbooks,* listing hostels worldwide (volume one covers Europe and the Mediterranean), may be purchased for $7.95 (plus $2 postage) each. Should you go abroad without an AYH card, you can get an International Youth Hostel Federation guest card (for the equivalent of about $18) by contacting one of the four national YHA associations in Great Britain and Ireland. For hostels in England and Wales, contact the YHA at Trevelyan House, 8 St. Stephen's Hill, St. Albans, Hertfordshire AL1 2DY, or at 14 Southampton St., London WC2E 7HY; in Scotland, Scottish Youth Hostels Association, 7 Glebe Crescent, Stirling FK8 2JA; in Northern Ireland, Youth Hostel Association of Northern Ireland, 56 Bradbury Pl., Belfast BT7 1RU; in the Irish Republic, Irish Youth Hostel Association (An Oige), 39 Mountjoy Square, Dublin 1. These associations also publish handbooks to hostels in their areas. In addition, the Irish Tourist Board publishes an information sheet, *Youth Hostels,* listing them, and the British Tourist Authority publishes *Britain: Youth Accommodation,* listing hostels and other budget accommodations including university facilities (where stays of 1 or 2 weeks are permitted). For more information, contact either the BTA or the British Universities Accommodation Consortium, PO Box U32, University Park, Nottingham, Nottinghamshire NG7 2RD, England.

The YMCA and the YWCA also run economical accommodations and have separate offices to contact for information. You can get a list of Ys in Great Britain by writing to the National Council of YMCAs, 640 Forest Rd., Walthamstow, London E17 3DZ, or the National Council of YWCAs, 2 Weymouth St., London W1 4AX. For a listing of YMCAs and YWCAs in London, write YMCA, 35 Craven Terr., Lancaster Gate, London W2 3EL; or YWCA, Accommodation and Advisory Service, 16 Great Russell St., London WC1B 3LR. These agencies will not make bookings for travelers, however; reservations must be made directly with the specific Y of choice.

There are many private houses and farms throughout the countryside that make a pleasant home base and a chance to meet local people. The BTA publishes a booklet titled *Britain: Stay on a Farm,* which lists working farms in both Great Britain and Northern Ireland, while the Northern Ireland Tourist Board publishes its own useful booklet titled *Farm and Country Holidays,* listing country homes and working farms. The Irish Tourist Board also has information on these accommodations in its *Irish Homes* guide. On many farms, the traveler will get a room and a hearty breakfast for as little as $10 a day.

And there's always camping. Virtually any area of the countryside in Great Britain or Ireland has a place for you to pitch your tent and enjoy the scenery. There are numerous national parks, and, with permission, you can camp on private acres of farmland. Many of the campsites have showers, laundry rooms, public phones, eating facilities, and shops. Both the Irish and British tourist authorities have booklets listing sites and their facilities, as well as places to rent camping equipment.

If you're at least 18 years old and a full-time student in a US college or university, you can work in Ireland for up to 4 months and in Britain for up to 6 months at any time of the year. For information on the types of jobs available and where they're located, contact the Council on International Educational Exchange (address above). The pay is low, but it will help cover the cost of your trip.

Summer study programs are popular and courses diverse: literature, language, history, politics, folklore, music, painting, and crafts. For information on specific courses, colleges, their costs, and requirements, send for *Discover Young Ireland* from the Irish Tourist Board, *Young Travellers to Britain* from the BTA, and *Study in Britain* from British Information Services, 845 Third Ave., New York, NY 10022 (212-752-5747 in New York City; elsewhere, 800-223-5339).

Hints for Older Travelers

Reduced air fares, special package deals, the dollar's high exchange rate, and more free time are just some of the factors that have helped bring the world closer to the approximately 30 million Americans over age 65. Senior citizens are an ever-growing segment of the travel population, and the trend among them is to travel more frequently and for longer periods of time. Retired travelers can also take advantage of off-season travel, avoiding crowds and escaping higher prices. In addition, overseas, as in the US, discounts are frequently available.

PACKING: Bear in mind that you will not always find central heating in guesthouses, restaurants, and other public places. Take along a warm sweater (even summer evenings can be cool) and a raincoat (see *How to Pack* and *When to Go,* GETTING READY TO GO) — but remember that one secret to happy traveling is to *pack lightly.* Most common toilet articles, in familiar brands, are available just about anywhere you go. Be sure to take with you any medication you need, enough to carry you through without a prescription for the duration of your trip; pack it separately in a carryall in case your luggage is lost or detoured, along with a note from your doctor for the benefit of airport authorities. It is also wise to take along a few common medications — aspirin and something for stomach upset may come in handy. If you are diabetic or have cardiac problems, carry your medical records. Remember that Medicare will not cover you abroad — but Britain's free medical care is extended to foreign guests in (but only in) emergencies. A number of organizations exist to help you avoid or deal with a medical emergency overseas. For further information on these services, see *Medical and Legal Aid Abroad,* GETTING READY TO GO. A word of caution — don't overdo it. Allow time for some relaxing each day to refresh yourself for the next scheduled sightseeing event. Traveling across time zones can be exhausting. Plan on spending at least one full day resting before you start touring. If you're part of a group tour, be sure to check the planned itinerary thoroughly. Some package deals sound wonderful because they include all the places you've ever dreamed of visiting. In fact, they can become so hectic and tiring that you'll be reaching for a pillow instead of your camera.

PLANNING: In the US, many hotel and motel chains, airlines, car rental companies, bus lines, and other travel suppliers offer discounts to older travelers. Some of these discounts, however, are extended only to bona fide members of certain senior citizens organizations. Because the same organizations frequently offer package tours to both domestic and international destinations, the benefits of membership are twofold. Those who join can take advantage of discounts as individual travelers and also reap the savings that group travel affords. In addition, because the age requirements for some of these organizations are quite low (or nonexistent), the benefits can begin to accrue early. Among the organizations dedicated to helping you see the world are:

American Association of Retired Persons (AARP): Travel programs designed exclusively for AARP members cover the globe and include a broad range of escorted motorcoach tours, hosted holidays in European cities and resorts, regional tours of rural areas of Europe, and cruises. Offers Medicaid Supplement Plan. Membership is open to anyone age 50 and above, whether retired or not; dues are $5 a year or $12.50 for 3 years. 1909 K St., NW, Washington, DC 20049 (phone: 202-872-4700).

The Mature Outlook: Membership is available at $7.50 per year for either an individual or a couple and is open to anyone age 50 and older. A changing schedule of tours is offered every year. PO Box 1205, Glenview, IL 60025 (phone: in Illinois, 312-291-7900; elsewhere, 800-336-6330).

National Council of Senior Citizens: The roster of tours offered by this organization is different each year, but the emphasis is always on keeping costs low, and Great Britain and Ireland are frequent destinations. The annual membership fee is $10 per individual or $14 per couple. There is no age requirement; most members are over 50, however. 925 15th St., NW, Washington, DC 20005 (phone: 202-347-8800).

Many tour operators specialize in group travel for older persons. Grand Circle Travel, Inc., which caters exclusively to the over-50 traveler, packages a huge variety (no continent is left untrod) of escorted tours, cruises, and extended vacations in one spot. It has numerous itineraries to Great Britain and Ireland. Contact Grand Circle at 347 Congress St., Boston, MA 02210 (phone: 800-221-2610). Gadabout Tours offers escorted tours to many North American destinations but also has tours to Europe including Great Britain and Ireland. For information, write Gadabout Tours, 700 E Tahquitz-McCallum Way, Palm Springs, CA 92262 (phone: in California, 619-325-5556 or 800-521-7309; elsewhere, 800-952-5068)), or see a travel agent.

Educational travel is another choice open to older people. Interhostel, a program sponsored by the Division of Continuing Education of the University of New Hampshire, sends travelers back to school at cooperating institutions in various European countries, including Great Britain and Ireland. Participants attend lectures on the history, economy, politics, and cultural life of the country they are visiting, go on field trips to pertinent points of interest, take part in activities meant to introduce them to their foreign contemporaries, and also do some conventional sightseeing. Trips are for 2 weeks, accommodations are on campus in university residence halls or off campus in modest hotels (double occupancy). Groups are limited to 35 to 40 participants who are at least 50 years old (or younger if a participating spouse is at least 50), physically active, and not in need of special diets. For further information, contact Interhostel, UNH Division of Continuing Education, Verrette House, 6 Garrison Ave., Durham, NH 03824 (phone: 603-862-1147).

Similar to Interhostel is Elderhostel, a nonprofit organization offering educational programs at a huge number of schools in the US and Canada as well as at cooperating institutions overseas, a great many of which are in Great Britain. Programs run from 1 week nationally to 3 weeks internationally, and arrangements to remain abroad at the end are possible. Accommodations are in residence halls and meals are taken in student cafeterias. Elderhostelers must be at least 60 years old (or younger if a spouse or companion qualifies), in good health, and not in need of special diets. For information, write to Elderhostel, 80 Boylston St., Suite 400, Boston, MA 02116 (phone: 617-426-7788).

A word of caution: Don't overdo it. Allow time for some relaxing each day to refresh yourself for the next scheduled activity. Traveling across time zones can be exhausting. Plan on spending at least one full day resting before you start touring. If you're part of a group tour, be sure to check the planned itinerary thoroughly. Some package deals sound wonderful because they include all the places you've ever dreamed of visiting. But, in fact, they can become so hectic and tiring that you'll be reaching for a pillow instead of your camera.

An excellent book to read before embarking on any trip, domestic or foreign, is Rosalind Massow's *Travel Easy: The Practical Guide for People Over 50,* available for $8.95 from AARP Books, 1909 K St., NW, Washington DC 20049 (phone: 202-872-4700). It discusses a host of travel-related subjects, from choosing a destination to getting set for departure, with chapters on transportation options, tours, cruises (including a rundown on who's who aboard a cruise ship and whom to tip), avoiding health problems, and handling dental emergencies en route.

DISCOUNTS: BritRail offers a Senior Citizen Pass for those 65 and older. It permits unlimited first-class train travel through England, Scotland, and Wales at the economy fare and is valid on Sealink ships to the Isle of Wight and on the Lake Windermere steamers. The Senior Citizen Seapass gives you all the benefits of the rail pass in addition to one-way or round-trip passage to Ireland or the Continent. Both are available for 7, 14, or 21 days or 1 month and must be purchased before entering Great Britain. Northern Ireland Railways' Rail Runabout Ticket, bought in Northern Ireland and good for 7 consecutive days of unlimited train travel, is half price to senior citizens. Many other discounts on transportation in Great Britain and Ireland are not limited to senior citizens. Excellent books for budget-conscious older travelers are: *The Discount Guide for Travelers Over 55* by Caroline and Walter Weintz (E. P. Dutton; $7.95) and *The Senior Citizen's Guide to Budget Travel* in Europe (Pilot Books; $3.95).

Refer to the *Touring by Bus* sections of GETTING READY TO GO.

Medical and Legal Aid and Consular Services

MEDICAL AID: The surest way to return home in good health is to be prepared for common medical problems en route. So before we describe the health facilities available in Great Britain and Ireland, here are some tips to consider while still in the US.

Prepare a compact and personal medical kit including Band-Aids, first-aid cream, nose drops, insect repellent, aspirin, an extra pair of prescription glasses or sunglasses if you wear them, Lomotil or an equivalent for diarrhea, Dramamine or an equivalent for motion sickness, a thermometer, and a supply of those medicines you take regularly. In the corner of your kit, keep a list of all the drugs you have brought and their purpose as well as a copy of your doctor's prescriptions (or a note from your doctor). This could come in handy if you are ever questioned by police or airport authorities about why you are carrying drugs. It is also a good idea to ask your doctor to prepare a medical identification card that includes such information as your blood type, your social security number, any allergies or chronic health problems you have, and your medical insurance number. Check with your insurance company on the applicability of your policy while abroad; many do not apply or are not accepted in Europe. Older travelers should know that Medicare does not make payments out of the country, and — contrary to lingering popular belief — Britain's National Health Service (see below) does not provide free medical care to visitors, except in a few instances.

If your policy does not protect you while you're traveling, there are programs specifically designed to fill such a gap. International Underwriters/Brokers has two comprehensive packages, one of which is HealthCare Abroad and the other, Health-Care Global. For as little as $1 per day, HealthCare Global provides $25,000 in accident, illness, medical evacuation, and other coverage for travelers. There is an age limit of 65, but no medical examination is required. For $3 per day (minimum 10 days, maximum 90 days), HealthCare Abroad offers significantly better coverage in terms of dollar limits, and the age limit is 75. Features such as trip cancellation and baggage insurance are optional. For further information, write to HealthCare Abroad, 243 Church St. Rest., Vienna, VA 22180 (phone: in Virginia, 703-255-9800; elsewhere, 800-237-6613).

Other organizations provide a variety of medical services for travelers. *Medic Alert*

Foundation International sells identification tags that specify that the wearer has a health problem that may not be readily apparent to a casual observer. A heart condition, diabetes, epilepsy, or severe allergies are the sorts of things that these badges were developed to communicate, conditions that, if unrecognized at a time when emergency treatment is necessary (a time when you may be unable to speak for yourself), can result in tragic treatment errors. In addition to the identification emblems, the foundation maintains a central file (telephone number clearly inscribed on the ID badge) from which your complete medical history is available 24 hours a day via a telephone call. The one-time membership fee of from $20 to $38 depends upon the type of emblem you select — from stainless steel to 10K gold-filled. For information contact: Medic Alert, PO Box 1009, Turlock, CA 95381-1009 (phone: in California, 209-668-3333 or 800-344-3226; elsewhere, 800-228-6222).

Assist-Card International provides a number to call — 24 hours a day, 365 days a year — where complete emergency medical assistance can be arranged, including ambulance or air transportation to the proper treatment facilities, local lawyers for a case that is the by-product of an accident, and up to $5,000 in bail bonds for a judicial proceeding that is similarly the result of an accident. The organization will also arrange for a flight home if a traveler is unable to complete a trip because of illness or an accident, and will pay any necessary fare differential. This organization also pays the first $3,500 in medical expenses and provides 80% coverage up to $10,000, including 100% of prescriptions. In 1987 fees for the Assist-Card varied according to the length of the trip abroad and ranged from $40 for a 5-day card to $220 for a 90-day itinerary to $320 for up to 120 days. For information, contact: Assist-Card Corporation of America, 444 Brickell Ave., Suite M130, Miami, FL 33131 (phone: in Florida, 305-381-9959; elsewhere in the US, 800-874-2223; in Canada, 800-641-2223).

International Association for Medical Assistance to Travelers (*IAMAT*) provides members with a directory of affiliated medical centers in over 100 countries to be called for a list of participating English-speaking doctors who have also agreed to a set payment schedule. A nonprofit organization, IAMAT appreciates donations, with a suggested minimum of $5; for $20, a set of worldwide climate charts detailing weather and sanitary conditions will be included. To join, write well in advance of your trip to IAMAT, 417 Center St., Lewiston, NY 14092 (phone: 716-754-4883).

International SOS Assistance also offers a program to cover medical emergencies while traveling. Members are provided with telephone access — 24 hours a day, 365 days a year — to a worldwide, monitored, multilingual network of medical centers. A phone call brings assistance ranging from telephone consultation to transportation home by ambulance or aircraft, and in some cases transportation of a family member to the place where you are hospitalized. The first $1,000 of sickness or accident bills are insured ($25 deductible). The service can be purchased for a week ($15; additional coverage is $2 per day), a month ($45), or a year ($195). For information contact: International SOS Assistance, Inc., PO Box 11568, Philadelphia, PA 19116 (phone: in Pennsylvania, 215-244-1500; elsewhere, 800-523-8930).

Intermedic provides a directory of physicians in 170 cities in over 90 countries including Great Britain and Ireland. The annual fee is $6 for an individual and $10 for a family. Each physician listed has provided Intermedic with data on his or her medical education, professional experience, and hospital affiliation; and each has indicated a willingness to respond promptly to calls from traveling Intermedic members. They have also agreed in writing to a ceiling on fees for any initial visit. For information contact: Intermedic, Inc., 777 Third Ave., New York, NY 10017 (phone: 212-486-8900).

In Great Britain and Northern Ireland, the National Health Service provides free medical aid to tourists *only* for treatment in hospital accident and emergency wards and for the diagnosis and treatment of certain communicable diseases. Most visitors (excepting nationals of Common Market countries or of those with which the United

Kingdom has reciprocal agreements) are liable for all other medical charges, including hospitalization resulting from an accident or emergency. In the Irish Republic, where the General Medicine Service provides either free hospital coverage or free total health care for nearly all citizens, tourists (except from Common Market countries) must pay for all treatment, even in emergencies.

If a bona fide emergency occurs in Great Britain, the fastest way to receive attention may be to take a taxi to the emergency room ("casualty department" in England) of the nearest hospital. An alternative is to dial 999, the free nationwide emergency number used to summon the police and fire trucks and ambulances. Since British ambulance dispatchers are accustomed to taking calls from doctors only, state immediately that you are a foreign tourist and then the nature of your problem and your location.

In Ireland, night emergency service rotates among hospitals and you should call 999, the nationwide emergency number here, too, to find out which one in a given area is on duty. The same number can be dialed for an ambulance, but as in Britain, a taxi may be a faster way to reach help. Ambulances in both countries are meant primarily for transportation, and beyond the attendant's expertise in cardiopulmonary resuscitation, few are equipped to give treatment en route.

If you need a doctor for something less than an emergency in Great Britain, there are several ways to find one. Ask at your hotel or check the local post office where neighborhood NHS physicians are supposed to be listed (though they often aren't). You can also dial 999 for help in locating a doctor. What you will get is the name of a general practitioner, since in Britain, specialists almost always see patients upon referral only. If you're in London, an additional way to find a doctor is to call the consular division of the US embassy, which keeps a list of local doctors in private practice. (Most British doctors work within the National Health Service system, though they are allowed to see private patients. Some practice privately only, and there are more of these in London than elsewhere in England, and many more in England than in Scotland or Wales.) For many travelers, this is the best solution. For one thing, a private doctor may be willing to see you more quickly than the local NHS general practitioner. For another, if you know it's a specialist you need, one in private practice will usually see you without a general practitioner's referral. When you do get the appointment, you'll be going to the doctor's "surgery" (office), where he or she keeps surgery hours.

In the Irish Republic GMS doctors may also treat visitors as private patients. To find one in a nonemergency situation, consult the regional health board (there are eight of them) for a list of GMS general practitioners approved for the area served. The office of the Eastern Health Board, which serves Dublin, is at 1 James's St., Dublin (phone: 757951). Private practice is quite common in Ireland, but even doctors working within the General Medicine Service — not on a prepaid salary as British physicians are — tend to schedule tourists quickly. In addition, though general practitioners deliver primary care here, too, there is no violation of protocol in approaching a specialist directly. Call the appropriate department of a teaching hospital or, in Dublin, the US embassy, which also maintains a list of doctors. Remember that if you are hospitalized in the Republic, you will have to pay even in an emergency. You can choose to be put in a private wing, but a bed on the ward is much less expensive.

Pharmacies in both countries are called "chemists." It is difficult, if not impossible, to find one willing to fill a foreign prescription. Exceptions are made in emergencies — a diabetic needing insulin, for instance — but even in an emergency you will more than likely be supplied only enough of a drug to last until a local doctor can write a prescription. Take what you need with you.

LEGAL AID ABROAD: It is often far more alarming to be arrested abroad for an infringement of the law than at home. Not only are you alone among strangers, but the punishment can be worse. Granted, the American consulate can advise you of your rights and provide a list of lawyers, but it cannot interfere with local due process.

The best advice is to be honest and law abiding. If you are issued a traffic ticket, pay it. If you are approached by drug hawkers, ignore them. Penalties for possession of marijuana and other narcotics are generally more severe than in the US.

CONSULAR SERVICES: There is one crucial place to keep in mind when outside the US — namely, the United States consulate. If you are injured or become seriously ill, the consulate will direct you to medical assistance and notify your relatives. If, while abroad, you become involved in a dispute that could lead to legal action, the consulate, once again, is the place to turn. And in case of natural disasters or local civil unrest, consulates around the world handle the evacuation of US citizens if such a procedure is necessary. Keep in mind, though, that nowhere does the consulate act as an arbitrator or ombudsman on an American citizen's behalf. The consul has no power, authorized or otherwise, to subvert, alter, or contravene the legal processes, however unfair, of the country in which he or she serves. Nor can a consul oil the machinery of a foreign bureaucracy or provide legal advice. The consul's responsibilities do include providing a list of lawyers, information on local sources of legal aid, assignment of an interpreter if the police have none, informing relatives in the US, and the organization and administration of any defense monies sent from home. If a case is tried unfairly or the punishment seems unusually severe, the consul can make a formal complaint to the authorities. In a case of what is called "legitimate and proven poverty" — of an American stranded abroad without funds — the consul will contact sources of money such as family or friends in the US, make application for aid to agencies in foreign countries, and, as a last resort, arrange for repatriation at government expense. Consuls will not lend money.

Do not expect the consulate to help you with trivial difficulties such as canceled reservations or lost baggage. The consulate is primarily concerned with the day-to-day administration of services such as issuing passports and visas; providing notarial services; the distribution of VA, social security, and civil service benefits to resident Americans; depositions; extradition cases; and reports to Washington of births, deaths, and marriages of US citizens. There is no US consulate in the Irish Republic, but US Embassy's Consular Service serves the same function; the US embassy is at 42 Elgin Rd., Ballsbridge, Dublin 4 (phone: 688777). In Great Britain, the US consulate is at 24/31 Grosvenor Sq., London W1A 1AE (phone: 499-9000); and in Northern Ireland, at Queen's House, 14 Queen St., Belfast BT1 6EQ (phone: 228239).

On the Road

Credit and Currency

 It may seem hard to believe, but one of the greatest (and least understood) costs of travel is money itself. If that sounds simplistic, consider the fact that you can lose as much as 30% of the value of your dollars simply by changing money at the wrong place or in the wrong form. So your single objective in relation to the care and retention of your travel funds is to make them stretch as far as possible. And when you do spend money, it should be on things that expand and enhance your travel experience, not on unnecessaries. This requires more than merely ferreting out the best air fare or the most charming budget hotel. It means being canny about the management of money itself.

TRAVELER'S CHECKS: Most people understand the necessity of protecting travel funds from loss or theft by carrying them in the form of replaceable and/or refundable traveler's checks rather than cash. An equally good reason to carry them is that they invariably get a better rate of exchange than cash does — usually by at least 1%. The reasons for this are rather technical, but it is a fact of travel life not to be ignored.

That 1% won't do you much good, however, if you have already spent it buying your traveler's checks. Several of the major traveler's check companies charge 1% for the privilege of using their checks; others don't — but the issuing institution (i.e., the particular bank at which you purchase them) may itself charge a fee. Thomas Cook checks issued in US currency are free if you have made your travel arrangements through its travel agency, for example; Barclay Bank Visa checks are also free if purchased at a Barclay branch office. American Express checks are free to AAA members, and Bank of America checks are free at the bank's branches in California. What's more, if you purchase traveler's checks at a bank in which you maintain significant accounts (especially commercial accounts of some size), you may find that the bank will absorb the 1% fee as a courtesy.

The traveler's checks listed below are readily recognized and convertible in all areas of Great Britain and Ireland. However, there are some important facts to be aware of when using traveler's checks: Don't assume that restaurants, smaller shops, or other establishments in hamlets and villages are going to have change for checks in large denominations; don't expect change in US currency except at banks and international airports; and, most important, while it's possible to get refunds for lost or stolen checks during regular business hours, weekend refunds can be quite difficult.

We cannot overemphasize the importance of knowing how to replace lost or stolen checks. All of the traveler's checks companies have selling agents around the world, both in their own name and at other associated agencies (usually, but not necessarily, banks) where refunds can be obtained during business hours. Be sure to make a photocopy of the refund instructions that the issuing institution gives you at the time of purchase. Keep one list in your wallet, but keep the copy with other "emergency information," stashed away in the bottom of your luggage. This emergency packet should include an accurate listing of the serial numbers of your traveler's checks, the purchase receipt, your passport number and date of issue, the numbers of any credit cards you have with you, and any other bits of information you can't bear to be without. The serial numbers and purchase receipt will certainly facilitate refund arrangements if the checks are lost or stolen. Here is a list of the major companies issuing traveler's checks and the number to call for refunds:

American Express: To report lost or stolen checks in the continental US, call 800-221-7282; in Alaska and Hawaii, call 800-221-4590; from Ireland and the United Kingdom, call the nearest American Express office, London 930-4411, or Brighton, England, 369-3555; from elsewhere outside the US, call the nearest American Express office or 801-968-8300, collect.

Bank of America: To report lost or stolen checks in the US except Hawaii and Alaska, call 800-227-3460. From those states or outside the US, call 415-622-3800, collect.

Barclay's Bank: To report lost or stolen checks in the US except California, call 800-227-6811; in California, 415-574-3200; in Alaska and Hawaii, 800-227-6830. From Europe, Ireland, and anywhere in Great Britain, call 01-937-8091, collect.

Citicorp: To report lost or stolen checks in the US, including Alaska and Hawaii, call 800-645-6556. Outside the US, call 813-623-1709, collect.

MasterCard: To report lost or stolen checks in the US except New York State, Alaska, and Hawaii, call 800-223-9920; from those states and from outside the US, call 212-974-5696, collect; in Great Britain and Ireland, call 1-438-1414 (London Refund Centre).

Thomas Cook MasterCard: To report lost or stolen checks in the US including Alaska and Hawaii, call 212-974-5696, collect. From Europe and Ireland, call 733-63200, collect; from within the United Kingdom, dial 733-502995, which is toll-free. In Europe, you can also call the nearest branch of Thomas Cook. (Note: If you have no success reaching any of these, try calling 212-974-5696, collect, from anywhere in the world — it just won't be as efficient.)

Visa: To report lost or stolen checks, call 800-227-6811; in California, 800-632-0520; in Alaska and Hawaii, 800-227-6830; outside the US, 415-574-7111, collect. From Europe, you can also call London 937-8091.

TIP PACKS: It's not a bad idea to buy a *small* amount of pence and pounds in advance of your departure. But note the emphasis on small, because exchange rates for these "tip packs" are uniformly vile. Their advantages are threefold: You become familiar with the currencies (really the only way to guard against being cheated during your first few hours in a new country); you are guaranteed some money should you arrive when a bank or exchange counter isn't open or available; and you don't have to depend on hotel desks, porters, or taxi drivers for change. But a tip pack is the only foreign currency you should buy before you leave. Although foreign currency traveler's checks are available from American Express and Thomas Cook, for example, the exchange rates are usually worse than you will get in banks abroad, and the wisest advice is to carry the bulk of your travel funds abroad with you in US dollar traveler's checks.

CREDIT CARDS: There are two essentially different kinds of credit cards available to consumers in the United States, and travelers must decide which kind best serves their interests. "Convenience" cards — American Express, Diners Club, Carte Blanche are the most widely accepted — cost the cardholder a basic membership fee but put no limit on the amount the cardholder may charge on the card in any month. However, the entire balance must be paid in full at the end of each billing period (usually a month), so the cardholder is not actually extended any credit — although deferred payment plans can usually be arranged for some types of purchases.

"Bank" cards, on the other hand, are often issued free, although some banks now charge a fee. They are real credit cards in the sense that the cardholder has the privilege of paying a minimum amount ($\frac{1}{36}$ is not untypical) of the total balance in each billing period. For this privilege, the cardholder is charged an interest rate — about 1½% a month or 18% a year for the cards listed below — on the balance owed. In addition, there is a maximum set on the amount the cardholder can charge to the card, which represents the limit of credit the card company is willing to extend. Major bank cards are Visa (formerly BankAmericard) and MasterCard (formerly Master Charge). In Great Britain and Ireland, MasterCard is sometimes called Access.

One of the thorniest problems of using credit cards abroad has to do with the rate of exchange at which any purchase is charged. The fact is that the exchange rate in effect on the date that you make a foreign purchase has nothing at all to do with the rate of exchange at which your purchase is billed to you on the invoice you receive months later in the US. The amount American Express charges is ultimately a function of the exchange rate in effect on the day your charge is received at an American Express service center. (There is, incidentally, a 1-year limit on the time that a shop can take to forward its charge slips to American Express's clearinghouse.) At Diners Club, three banks are called on the day foreign exchange transactions arrive and customers are given the best rate, that is, the one most favorable to the dollar. The rate Visa uses to process an item is the wholesale rate in effect on the day that Visa receives the transaction from its merchant's bank. Thus, though up to 30 days may pass between the date of your purchase and the date Visa converts it, the conversion rate is usually close to the one prevailing about 11 days after your purchase, assuming that the foreign merchant deposits the sales draft in his bank within a week and that the bank processes it through its interchange in three to five days.

The principle at work in this credit-card–exchange-rate roulette is simple, but very hard to predict. You make a purchase at a particular dollar-versus-local-currency exchange rate. If the dollar gets stronger in the time between purchase and billing, your purchase actually costs you less than you anticipated. If the dollar drops in value during the interim, you pay more than you thought you would. There isn't much you can do about these vagaries except follow one very broad, very clumsy rule of thumb: If the dollar is doing well at the time of purchase, its value increasing against the local currency, use your credit card on the assumption it will still be doing well when billing takes place. If the dollar is doing badly, assume it will continue to do badly and pay with traveler's checks. If you get badly stuck, your only recourse is to complain.

In any case, all types of credit cards are handy additional means to avoid carrying a lot of cash. However, establishments you may encounter abroad may not honor *all* major cards, and you'll find it helpful to have several cards with you on your trip. Following is a list of credit cards that have wide international use, with some of their key features of greatest significance to travelers and a telephone number for further information:

American Express: Emergency personal check cashing at American Express or representatives' offices (up to $200 cash in local currency, $1,000 in traveler's checks); emergency personal check cashing for guests at participating hotels (up to $250 in US and Canada, $100 elsewhere) and, for holders of airline tickets, at participating airlines in the US (up to $50). Extended payment plan for cruises, tours, and airline tickets. $100,000 free travel accident insurance on plane, train, bus, and ship if ticket was charged to card; up to $1,000,000 additional low-cost flight insurance available. Contact: American Express Card, PO Box 39, Church St. Station, New York, NY 10008 (phone: 800-528-4800).

Carte Blanche: Emergency personal check cashing at participating Hilton hotels in the US (up to $1,000) and for guests at other participating hotels and motels (up to $250 per stay). Extended payment plan for airline tickets. $650,000 free travel accident insurance on plane, train, and ship if ticket was charged to card. Contact: Carte Blanche, PO Box 5824, Denver, CO 80217 (phone: 800-525-9135).

Diners Club: Emergency personal check cashing at participating Citibank branches worldwide (up to $1,000, with a minimum per check of $50 in the US and $250 overseas); emergency personal check cashing for guests at participating hotels and motels (up to $250 per stay). Extended payment plan for all charges can be arranged if you've been a cardmember for at least 5 months and your account is not 30 days past due at the time of extension application. $650,000 free travel accident insurance on plane, train, and ship if ticket was charged to card. Contact: Diners Club, PO Box 5824, Denver, CO 80217 (phone: 800-525-9135).

MasterCard: Cash advance at participating banks worldwide. Interest charge on unpaid balance and other details are set by issuing bank. Check with your bank for information.

Visa: Cash advance at participating banks worldwide. Interest charge on unpaid balance and other details are set by issuing bank. Check with your bank for information.

FOREIGN EXCHANGE: Rule number one is as simple as it is inflexible. Only change your money at banks, where your dollars always buy the greatest amount of foreign currency. Unless someone holds a gun to your head, never, repeat never, exchange dollars for foreign currency at hotels, restaurants, or retail shops, where you are sure to lose a significant amount of your dollar's buying power.

Rule number two: Estimate your money needs carefully; if you overbuy you lose twice — buying and selling back. Every time you exchange money, someone is making a profit, and rest assured, it isn't you. Use up your foreign currency before leaving.

Rule number three: Don't buy money on the black market. The exchange rate may appear to be better, but it is a common practice to pass off counterfeit bills to unsuspecting foreigners who aren't familiar with the local currency.

Rule number four: Learn the local currency quickly and keep aware of daily fluctuations in the exchange rate. These are listed in major newspapers, including the *International Herald Tribune,* for the preceding day. Rates change to some degree daily. For rough calculations it is quick and safe to use round figures, but for purchases and actual currency exchanges, carry a small pocket calculator.

The basic currency unit in both Britain and Ireland is the pound — either the pound sterling or the Irish pound (or punt). Though the Irish pound once maintained parity with the pound sterling, it is now linked to EEC currencies; British money and Irish money are no longer interchangeable and they have different exchange rates vis-à-vis the American dollar. In both countries, however, the pound is divided into 100 units called pence. In Britain, these are distributed in a 100p (£1) coin as well as 50p, 20p, 10p, 5p, 2p, and 1p coin denominations; in Ireland, in 50p, 10p, 5p, 2p, 1p and ½p coins. The British halfpenny ceased to be legal tender at the end of 1984. Paper money is issued in Ireland in IR£100, IR£50, IR£20, IR£10, IR£5, and IR£1 notes; in Britain, in £50, £20, £10, and £5 notes. The Bank of England stopped printing £1 notes on December 31, 1984, and any £1 notes remaining in circulation ceased to be legal tender on December 31, 1985. However, banks in Scotland and Northern Ireland also print versions of the £1 note and these are likely to continue circulating. Be aware that you may still find shillings, equal to 5p, in circulation, leftovers of the pre-decimal currency system. Also note that Republic of Ireland currency is no longer accepted in Northern Ireland.

Accommodations and Reservations

From elegant, centuries-old resorts to modest and inexpensive guesthouses, you can be comfortable and well cared for on almost any budget in either Great Britain or Ireland. Our selection of accommodations, which embraces this wide range of possibilities, is included in the *Best in Town* sections of the CITIES and in the *Checking In* and *Eating Out* sections of each tour route in DIRECTIONS. Also consult the brochures and booklets we cite in the discussions below. Some of these are available free from the British and Irish tourist offices; where appropriate, we've given prices of those which must be purchased from the British Travel Bookshop (40 W 57th St., New York, NY 10019). The handling charge is $2 and up, depending on the value of the order (sent via first-class mail).

ACCOMMODATIONS: Hotels, Guesthouses, and Inns – Although there is no official rating system for British hotels, they tend to fall into rough categories. Hotels can be large or small, chain-operated or independent, new and of the "international standard" type or well-established and traditional. There are resort hotels with recreation facilities and motels with almost no facilities. Breakfast is usually included in the quoted price of any room, and it is usually a full one of juice, coffee or tea, rolls, cereal, and eggs and bacon, though there is a growing tendency in the larger urban hotels to substitute a Continental breakfast (coffee and rolls) or to charge separately for the full one. Most rooms in better hotels come with private baths; the closer to the budget end of the scale and beyond the city centers, the more likely it is that the room will have a wash basin with hot and cold water and access to a public bathroom in the hall. A service charge of 10% to 15% may be added to bills at some properties in addition to a compulsory 15% Value Added Tax. Hotels, motels, guesthouses, and inns with four rooms or more are required to display minimum and maximum room prices in a manner that clearly shows what is included. If not clear, be sure to ask in advance what the final tab will be since the extras can add considerably to the bill. (To reduce it, consider traveling off-season, and investigate the hotel "mini-breaks" offered by many British chains. These packages allow a discount for stays of 2 nights or more, usually weekends, and can be in effect at any time of the year.) The AA publication *Hotels and Restaurants in Britain* ($18.95 at the British Travel Bookshop), which lists room prices inclusive of extras, is currently the most comprehensive guide to British hotels. It does not include establishments in Northern Ireland, however. These are listed in the Northern Ireland Tourist Board's official annual *Northern Ireland: All the Places to Stay* ($2.95). Note that unlike hotels in Great Britain, those in Northern Ireland are graded according to an official rating system similar to the one (described below) followed by the Irish Tourist Board in the Irish Republic. For those interested in information on London alone, the London Tourist Board's *Where to Stay in London* ($4.50) is a good book to consult and is available at the British Travel Bookshop.

Guesthouses are to Britain what pensions are to the Continent. Also called private hotels or board residences, they are generally small, family-run, and most often in the budget category. A special group of commended guesthouses provides outstanding service and costs more; see *Commended Country Hotels, Guest Houses and Restaurants,* a free BTA publication. Also see *Scotland: Hotels and Guesthouses* and *Wales: Hotels and Guesthouses;* available through the British Travel Bookshop for $7.95 and $8.25, respectively. Unlike hotels, guesthouses do not provide meals for nonguests and unlike inns, they usually are not licensed to serve alcohol. The standard practice is for breakfast to be included in the room price and some, though not all, offer an evening meal if desired. Prices are typically from $15 to $30 per person, and for this, there is usually no private bath nor is there always running water in the bedroom. Guesthouses are found everywhere and especially at seaside resorts where the vacationing British keep them heavily booked all summer long.

Inns are also of particular interest to travelers attracted by the prospect of sampling the lodging of another age. There are inns dating back to medieval times and many more not quite so old that have nevertheless been in business for centuries. An inn was, first of all, a wayside watering place for travelers passing on foot, horseback, or by coach, but laws requiring the innkeeper to provide food for the drinkers and accommodations for the diners turned innkeepers into hoteliers. The focal point of an inn is still its public bar, and the number of rooms is usually, therefore, limited; some in city centers do not provide accommodations at all. What remains of bygone days is the charm of thatched roofs, timbered façades, cobblestone courtyards, beamed ceilings, and the occasional four-poster bed. Heating and hot and cold water in the rooms have been added, though private bathrooms are usually lacking. Inns are found in any price range, from $15 per person and up. The BTA's free *Stay at an Inn* lists a selection of them found in historic towns all over Britain.

Most of the rooms for rent in the Irish Republic are listed in one of two publications issued yearly by Bord Fáilte, the Irish Tourist Board. *Discover Ireland: Hotels and Guesthouses* details regularly inspected accommodations registered with the Tourist Board and maximum prices are quoted. Hotels are graded in five categories (A*, A, B*, B, and C), but behind those letter grades may be found anything from a luxurious, turreted castle redolent of Irish history to a large, modern, and functional high-rise or a simple, family-run hostelry. Guesthouses are similarly rated (A, B*, B, and C), and though it is sometimes difficult to distinguish between some of the smaller, family-run hotels and the guesthouses, the latter are almost always family enterprises and tend to be more informal and personal in their hospitality. The official dividing line is the meal service: The hotel dining room is open to nonresidents. Guesthouses cater exclusively to their guests, and in some cases will serve breakfast only (generally a full one and included in the room price), though usually a partial or full board plan by the day or the week will be available. Guesthouses, too, can vary in atmosphere from old, reconverted Georgian residences to brand-new, built-for-the-purpose premises. Bathroom facilities vary considerably: in an A* hotel, most rooms have private bathrooms; in an A guesthouse, some rooms with private bath may be available; in either hotel or guesthouse, where a private bath is lacking, the room will have hot and cold running water. In all Irish accommodations, the price quoted must include the Value Added Tax (18% on rooms, 23% on food and drink). A service charge of from 10% to 15% is usually added to hotel and guesthouse bills.

Castle Hotels – Among the most interesting of Britain's and Ireland's accommodations are the castle and country house hotels, specializing in the traditional atmosphere and hospitality typical of a great country estate. Formerly country homes, ancestral mansions, and family castles before their conversion to hotels, they are noteworthy for their architectural features and surrounding gardens or parklands, their river- or lakeside settings, or locations in dell, dale, and mountain. The real attraction, however, is the history associated with so many of them and their antique decor, undisturbed by the modern amenities (TV, private baths) that have been added. Prices are not economy class — from $35 and up per person, including breakfast. Some of these properties are members of the prestigious French hotel association Relais et Châteaux (catalogue available for $10 from travel bookshops or from David Mitchell & Company, 200 Madison Ave., New York, NY 10016; phone: 212-696-1323). Others are listed in the BTA's free *Commended Country Hotels, Guest Houses and Restaurants*. For further suggestions, contact the British and Irish tourist offices.

B&Bs – Britain's "bed-and-breakfast" houses provide precisely what the name implies. Though any hotel, inn, or guesthouse does the same, it is unusual for a B&B to offer the extra services found in other establishments, and consequently, the B&B route is often the least expensive way to go. With the exception of London, where they are scarce, they are found anywhere there are extra rooms to let in a private house and a landlady or landlord willing to attend to the details of this homespun form of hospitality. Private baths are rare; in recompense, the breakfasts are hearty, home-cooked, and as often as not, served along with some helpful tips on what to see and do and a bit of family history to add to the local lore. Prices average about $10 per person per night, breakfast included. Few BTA publications list B&Bs but those of the regional tourist boards often do; the Scottish Tourist Board publishes *Scotland: Bed and Breakfast* ($5.50); the Wales Tourist Board prints *Wales: Bed and Breakfast* ($5.25); and the English Tourist Board publishes *Where to Stay: Farmhouses, Bed and Breakfast and Inns in England* ($5.25). In addition, the Tourist Information Centre in any British town will have a list of local B&Bs.

The Irish Tourist Board's *Irish Homes* guide lists accommodations in town and country homes. Though not cited as such, these are the Irish equivalent of British B&Bs, the extra rooms of private homes to which adjustments have been made to meet the Tourist Board's inspection standards. Rarely will you find a private bathroom, but there is hot and cold running water in nearly all rooms in homes approved by the Tourist Board and listed in the guide. Costing about $10 per night here, too, breakfast included, B&Bs are perfect places to spend 1 or 2 nights as you tour the countryside, though you can stay longer since many offer weekly rates for partial board and some for full board.

Farmhouses – In both Great Britain and Ireland, farm families put up guests on a similar basis: for a night or two or by the week, with weekly half-board plans available. Listings with the Irish Tourist Board, in the BTA's *Stay on a Farm* and the Northern Ireland Tourist Board's *Farm and Country Holidays* carry a brief description of each farm, allowing travelers to pick a traditional one or a modern one, a dairy farm over a sheep farm, one with ponies to ride, or one near a river for fishing. If the peace and quiet and the coziness of the welcome are appealing, a farmhouse can be an ideal base from which to explore a region by car or by foot, and an especially good idea for those traveling with children.

Home Exchanges – An alternative for families content to stay in one place while on vacation is a home exchange. It is an exceptionally inexpensive way to ensure comfortable, reasonable living quarters with amenities that no hotel could possibly offer. Often the trade includes a car; almost always it means living in a new community in a manner the average hotel guest never experiences. Several companies publish directories of individuals and families willing to trade homes with others for a specified period of time. In some cases, you must be willing to list your home in the directory; in others, you can subscribe without appearing in it. Arrangements for the actual exchange take place directly between you and the homeowner. There is no guarantee that you will find a listing in the area in which you are interested, but there are directories with hundreds or thousands of listings in North America and in Europe, including Great Britain and Ireland. One organization that provides such information is the *Vacation Exchange Club* (12006 111th Ave., Youngtown, AZ 85363; phone: 602-972-2186), which handles some 6,000 listings, about one-quarter of which are in Great Britain and Ireland. Subscriptions cost $24.70 a year, for which the subscriber receives two directories (a late winter edition and a follow-up edition in early spring) plus a listing in one of them. The directories without the subscriber's listing cost $16.

Flats, Homes, and Cottages – Another alternative to hotels for the visitor content to stay in one spot for a week or more is to actually rent a house or apartment (called a "flat" in Britain and Ireland). Known as a "holiday let" or a "self-catering holiday," a furnished rental has both the advantages and disadvantages of living "at home" abroad. It is certainly less expensive than a first-class hotel for the same period of time (though luxury rentals are available, too); it has the comforts of home, including a kitchen, which means savings on food; it gives a sense of the country that a large hotel often cannot. On the other hand, a certain amount of housework is involved because if you don't eat out, you have to cook, and though some holiday lets come with a cleaning person, most don't.

The BTA publishes *Holiday Homes* and *Apartments in London,* two free booklets that give information on rental agencies and properties in Great Britain. Further guides to self-catering accommodations are published by the English, Scottish, and Welsh Tourist Boards and are available from the British Travel Bookshop. The Irish Tourist Board distributes booklets prepared by regional tourism organizations in Ireland listing houses and apartments for rent along with the names of the owners to contact to make arrangements. Finally, there are companies in the US that arrange rentals in Europe; they handle booking and confirmation paperwork, generally for a fee included in the rental price. Those listed below have many properties in Great Britain, fewer in Ireland:

> *At Home Abroad:* British cottages and country houses; in Ireland, one castle, a fishing lodge, and some elegant country houses. Photographs of properties can be requested by mail for a $50 registration fee. 405 E 56th St., Apt. 6H, New York, NY 10022 (phone: 212-421-9165).
>
> *Villas International Ltd.:* Specializes in London flats, also has country houses, from cottages to castles, throughout Great Britain and Ireland; no registration fee. 71 W 23rd St., New York, NY 10010 (phone: in New York State, 212-929-7585; elsewhere, 800-221-2260).

In Ireland, it is possible to rent traditional thatch-roofed cottages specially built with all modern conveniences. Located mostly in small towns on the southwest seaboard, these picturesque dwellings have a romantic appeal all their own. On the practical side, however, they are fairly inexpensive, can be rented by the week, month, or summer season, and have modern kitchens and baths that make them a sensible choice for families with small children. For a brochure, write Shannon Development, 757 Third Ave., New York, NY 10017 (phone: 212-371-5550), or contact Rent-an-Irish-Cottage Limited, Shannon Airport House, Shannon International Airport, County Clare, Ireland. Another group of cottages, without thatched roofs, is found on Galway Bay. Contact the Irish Tourist Board or Galway Bay Cottages, Barna, County Galway, Ireland. Cottage vacations are also offered by several tour operators specializing in Ireland.

Home Stays – Travelers are often impressed by the hospitality extended to them in small family-run guesthouses and B&Bs in Britain and Ireland. Often, catering to guests is not the proprietor's sole or even main means of support, and more than once you'll come away feeling you've been one of the family. This being the case, it is sometimes difficult to draw a line between a stay as a paying guest in a commercial establishment, and a "home stay" — where you also pay for your accommodations and any food or extras you consume. There is a distinction, however, basically one of intent on the part of both the hosts and the guests: You must want to get to know each other and be willing to exert the extra effort to do so.

Beyond that, there are other differences. Almost always, you, alone or with your family, will be the only party staying with your hosts. And though the cost of meals (except breakfast) is not included in the cost of the stay — because most travelers want to sample at least a few of the local restaurants — when you do eat at home, you sit down at the table with the rest of the family. It is quite common especially to have the first night's dinner at home and it is not unusual for hosts to arrange a dinner party later in the stay so you can meet some of their friends. There can be further participation in family activities, too, depending on how much of your time you want "organized" and always remembering that your hosts are most likely not on vacation as you are.

The better services that arrange home stays visit prospective hosts and choose only those genuinely interested in meeting foreigners and making their stay a memorable experience. The host, in fact, is probably better screened than you, the guest. The usual procedure is for you to fill out a questionnaire giving personal information such as the names and ages of family members, occupations, special interests, plus character and/ or credit references. The service then selects a few possibilities and lets you make the final decision. Often there is a minimum stay (usually 3 to 5 nights) and sometimes a maximum (2 weeks, for instance, though most travelers don't want to stay that long in one place while touring overseas). The entire cost of the stay is usually paid in advance, whereas any charges for meals or other extras are paid in cash to the host on departure. To avoid embarrassment, the service advises you beforehand what the host will be charging for any meals you do decide to take.

The following organizations arrange home stays with British families, and two of them have a few Irish families who open their homes to guests, too. Last year costs of these programs ranged from about $25 to about $120 per night per couple, with an average of from $65 to $75 per night. Single rates are also available and there are reductions for children.

> *At Home in England,* 66 Edgewood Ave., Larchmont, NY 10538 (phone: 914-834-
> 3944). Over 100 homes in England, including central London, Scotland, and
> Wales; one castle and a few other homes in Ireland. Note: This program is also
> available from British Airways.
> *In the English Manner,* PO Box 936, Alamo, CA 94507 (phone: 415-935-7065).
> About 70 homes, ranging from cottages and castles in England, Scotland, Wales,
> and Ireland, to central and suburban London flats; London rentals also availa-
> ble.

If the thought of paying anything for your keep means to you that you are not truly a guest, there is another organization, the United States Servas Committee, Inc., which maintains a list of hosts throughout the world willing to throw open their doors to foreigners entirely free of charge. The aim of this nonprofit peace program is to promote international understanding, and every effort is made to discourage freeloaders. Servas will send you an application form and the name of the nearest of some 150 volunteer interviewers around the US for you to contact. After the interview, if you're approved, you'll receive documentation certifying you as a Servas traveler (allow 6 to 8 weeks from the initial contact with Servas). There is a membership fee of $45 for an individual and a deposit of $15 to receive the host list, refunded on its return. The list gives the name, address, age, occupation, and other particulars of the hosts, including languages spoken. From then on it is up to you to write them directly, and Servas makes no guarantee that you will be accommodated. If you are, you'll normally stay 2 nights. Servas stresses that you should choose only people you really want to meet and that for this brief period you should be interested mainly in your hosts, not in sightseeing. It also suggests that one way to show your appreciation once you've returned home is to become a host yourself. The minimum age of a Servas traveler is 18 (however, children under 18 may accompany their parents), and though quite a few are young people who've just finished college, there are travelers (and hosts) in all age ranges and occupations. At present there are over 450 listings in Great Britain and Ireland. Contact Servas at 11 John St., Room 706, New York, NY 10038 (phone: 212-267-0252).

RESERVATIONS: Advance hotel reservations are recommended year-round in the major cities. In high season — June through September — the advice to book ahead extends to resorts and popular tourist sites from coast to coast and across the Irish Sea.

To the extent that you are able to settle on a precise itinerary beforehand, it is best to reserve accommodations before you go. The simplest way is to leave it all to a travel agent who will provide this service for free if the hotel, inn, or guesthouse in question pays agents a percentage. The British and Irish accommodations guides use a symbol to show which of the establishments listed do pay such a commission. If the one you pick doesn't, the travel agent may charge a fee to cover costs or you may have to make the reservation yourself.

The do-it-yourself method is fairly simple if you intend to stay mainly in hotels that are members of chains or groups, whether British or Irish ones with US representatives or American ones with hotels overseas. Naturally, the more links in the chain, the more likely that an entire stay can be booked with a minimum number of letters or phone calls to one central reservations system. Either a travel agent or the British and Irish tourist offices will be able to tell you who in the US represents a particular hotel.

To reserve a room in a hotel that's not represented in the US, it may be necessary to telephone or write directly. Be sure to give full details of your requirements and several alternate dates, if possible. You will probably be asked to send a deposit in the amount of one night's lodging, payable by foreign draft; in return, be sure to get written confirmation of your reservation. One shortcut, if the request is made a minimum of 4 weeks in advance, is to write to the Central Reservation Service of the Irish Tourist Board — Bord Fáilte, 14 Upper O'Connell St., Dublin 1 (phone: 735209), which will reserve, free of charge, any of the accommodations listed in its official accommodations guides. A similar service for reserving London hotels only (and stays of at least 2 nights) is provided by the London Visitors and Convention Bureau, 26 Grosvenor Gardens, London SW1W ODU, and requires a minimum of 6 weeks' notice. A small fee is charged, which is later deducted from the hotel bill.

If the hotel you want has no rooms available for your chosen dates, take heart. Making reservations early is usually the best advice, but sometimes making them later gives equally good results. What was unavailable 6 months in advance may suddenly become available 6 days — or even 6 hours — before your arrival. Should that not occur, there will almost always be some cancellation in one hotel or another on the date you arrive and there are services geared to help you find them. Tourist Information Centres (TIC's) in most British ports of entry (seaports, airports, railroad terminals) will reserve a room in the locality for a small fee (usually no more than 7p, except in London) or a refundable deposit or both. The London Tourist Board's Tourist Information Centres in the Heathrow Airport Underground Station and Victoria Railway Station will book hotels and budget accommodations such as guesthouses, but not hostels. The desks of numerous hotel booking agencies, charging similar fees or deposits, are also found in rail stations and airports. These can make same-day or advance reservations for London or other parts of Britain, as can the central reservations offices of the various hotel chains and groups. In the Irish Republic, Tourist Information Offices located throughout the country and at Shannon and Dublin airports and the ferry ports of Dun Laoghaire and Rosslare Harbour will make a reservation for a small fee to cover costs. In Dublin proper, offices are on Upper O'Connell St., at the address and phone number given above.

Britain's Tourist Information Centres and Ireland's Tourist Information Offices can also be put to use by those who prefer to give full rein to their wanderlust unhampered by hotel reservations made too far in advance. In Great Britain, any TIC displaying a Tourist Accommodation Service sign (a bed appears on it) can supply information and book a room in its locality once you've arrived there. Some provide a further Book-a-Bed-Ahead (BABA) service. Go early in the day before starting out for your destination and, for a fee, usually £1.75 or a refundable deposit or both, a staff member will phone ahead to make a reservation — provided you're going to an area that also has a BABA service. The network is thicker in Wales (where it's called a Bed Booking

Service) and Scotland than in England; Northern Ireland is without BABA service. You must claim your room relatively early: Bookings are provisional and are usually released at 6 PM each evening. Book-a-Bed-Ahead can also handle B&B accommodations, though these can be found almost as easily by just keeping an eye out for the signs on windows and gateposts or, in small villages, by asking any policeman or shopkeeper who in the area rents rooms. In Ireland, all Tourist Information Offices are equipped, for a small fee, to help with advance reservations in other parts of the country.

A word about overbooking: The international travel boom has brought with it some abuses that are pretty much standard operating procedure in any industry facing demand that outstrips supply, and this problem is certainly not unique to Britain or Ireland. Hotels overbook rooms on the assumption that a certain percentage of no-shows is inevitable. When cancellations don't occur and everybody with a reservation arrives as promised, you may find yourself holding a valid reservation for which no room exists. Though there's no sure way to avoid overbooking, there are ways to minimize the risk.

First, always carry evidence of your confirmed reservation with you. This should be a direct communication from the hotel to you or your travel agent and should specify the exact dates and duration of your accommodations and the price. Absolutely the weakest form of confirmation is the voucher slip a travel agent routinely issues, since it carries no official indication that the hotel has verified your reservations.

Even better is the increasing opportunity to guarantee hotel reservations by giving the hotel (or its reservation system) the number of your credit card and agreeing that the hotel is authorized to charge you for that room no matter what. It's still possible to cancel if you do so before 6 PM of the day of your reservation (sometimes 4 PM in resort areas), but when you do cancel under this arrangement, make sure you get a cancellation number to protect you from being billed erroneously.

Tipping

Throughout Britain and Ireland, the practice of including a service charge — generally 10–15% — as part of basic hotel and restaurant bills is relatively common. It has the advantage of eliminating any question about how much and whom to tip, but it confounds North Americans who are not always used to the custom. The threat is that a traveler unaware of the "service included" policy may leave additional gratuities that are redundant and unnecessary.

A restaurant menu will usually state whether a service charge is added automatically to the bill, but if you don't find this notice indicated, don't hesitate to ask the waiter at the time your bill is presented. If the tip has been added, no further gratuity is expected — though it's a common practice in Britain and Ireland for diners to leave a few extra pence on the table. The emphasis is on "few," and 50p is usually quite adequate. If no service charge has been included on your bill, tip 10% to 15% of the basic amount. By all means, leave less if you want to penalize poor service or more to reward excellent and especially efficient attention. In the finest restaurants, where a multiplicity of servers are present, plan to tip 5% to the captain in addition to the standard 15% for your waiter. The sommelier who has opened and served your wine is entitled to a gratuity of approximately £1 per bottle.

It's not necessary to tip the maitre d' of any restaurant unless he has been especially helpful in providing a table or has helped to arrange a special party. In instances where tipping the maitre d' is appropriate, the range of tips normally varies between £2 and £5. In allocating gratuities at a restaurant, pay particular attention to what has become the standard credit-card charge form, which now includes separate places for indicating gratuities for waiters and/or captains. If these separate boxes do not appear on the charge slip presented to you, simply ask the waiter or captain how these separate tips should be indicated.

There is virtually no tipping in pubs — unless you become something of a regular and care to offer the barman an occasional drink. It is not uncommon, however, to leave a few pence for a barmaid; and if you are served at a table in a bar or cocktail lounge, a small gratuity — 50p — is usual.

As in restaurants, you will normally find a service charge of from 10 to 15% included in your final hotel bill at most British and Irish hotels. No additional gratuities are required — or expected — beyond this billed service charge. It is unlikely, however, that you will find a service charge added to bills in small guesthouses or modest bed-and-breakfast establishments. In these cases, let your instincts be your guide; no tipping is expected by members of the family who own the house, but it is a nice gesture to leave something for others — such as a dining room waiter or a maid — who may have helped you. A gratuity of 50p per night is adequate in these cases.

If a hotel does not automatically add a service charge, it is perfectly proper to ask to have an extra 10–15% added to your bill, to be distributed among those who served you. This may be an especially convenient solution in a large hotel, where it's difficult to determine just who out of a horde of attendants actually performed particular services. If you prefer to distribute tips yourself, a chambermaid generally is tipped at the rate of 50p per day, or £2 to £3 per week. Tip the concierge or hall porter for specific services only, and the amount of such gratuities should depend on the level of service provided. Doormen and/or porters are generally tipped at the rate of 50p per bag for carrying luggage, and you may want to add a small additional amount if a doorman helps with cab or car. Other miscellaneous tips to hotel staff depend entirely on the service rendered.

Once upon a time, taxi drivers in Britain and Ireland would give one a rather odd look if presented with a tip for a taxi fare, but times have changed and 10–15% of the amount on the meter is now a standard gratuity. Porters in airports expect to be compensated at the rate of about 50p per bag in both Britain and Ireland. Ditto porters who carry your bags in railway or bus stations.

Theater ushers are not tipped in either country, though it is common to purchase a program from the person who shows you to your seat. Sightseeing tour guides are usually tipped, and members of a tour may discuss a total amount among themselves and contribute equally to this gratuity.

Shopping

Browsing through the department stores, street markets, auction houses, fabulous small shops, and crafts centers of Great Britain and Ireland will undoubtedly be one of the highlights of your trip. You may not be quite as ebullient about prices as you might have been a few years ago, but there is still plenty of value left for the money and enough quality and craftsmanship to make many an item irresistible. To help steer you toward the best, several sections of this book are devoted to shopping. In CITIES, individual city reports include a listing of specific stores, boutiques, and markets, as well as descriptions of special shopping streets where they exist. And in DIVERSIONS, there are sections that tell not only where to find antiques and other collectibles, but also — for those who have yet to experience this stimulating form of acquisition — how to buy them at auctions.

WHAT TO BUY: Cashmere sweaters and Shetland wool knits are enduring British classics, as are Harris tweeds, ancestral tartans, and cotton and silk Liberty prints, whether sold by the yard or made up into fashionable clothes. Burberrys and Jaeger are good labels, and there are lesser-priced sports clothes at Marks and Spencer stores around the country. Harrods in London is Europe's largest department store and it should be on your sightseeing list even if it's not on your shopping list. Its motto, *Omnia, Omnibus, Ubique* (Everyone, Everything, Everywhere), gives a pretty good idea of the range of its activities. Shopping can also be mixed with sightseeing in the famous food department at Fortnum and Mason, purveyor of groceries to the Royal Family — which may explain the formality of swallow-tailed coats on its salesclerks (pronounced "clarks"). There are still some antiques left in Britain, in spite of the shiploads consigned to US dealers. In London, try the Bermondsey–New Caledonia Market — a dealers' market — very early Friday mornings for a chance at what might turn up in an expensive shop later in the day, unless you spot it first. The showrooms of Sotheby's and Christie's, probably the most famous art and antique auctioneers in the world, are open for viewing. If you attend the daily sales, however, don't move a muscle or blink an eye unless you've brought money — lots of it. New and used china comes from quality suppliers such as Minton, Royal Doulton, Staffordshire, Aynsley, and Wedgwood, and new and used books from any number of shops on London's Charing Cross Road, including one (Foyles) with a stock of over four million volumes.

In Ireland, crafts are thriving. Products in traditional and modern styles and combinations of the two are found in craft centers, workshops, and stores throughout the country. Details are in the *Irish Crafts* information sheet available from Irish Tourist Board offices in the US. Typical of the work currently being done are the highly prized white wool sweaters and berets knit on the western seacoast and on the Aran Islands, earthenware pottery in modern but natural shapes, and exceedingly well executed silver and gold jewelry in contemporary styles. Donegal tweed has been handloomed for centuries on the Donegal coast of northwest Ireland, and a jacket made of it could be one of the most durable you've ever owned. Pearly Belleek china, luminous Waterford crystal, and Irish lace or linens endow any table with elegance, and Irish smoked salmon goes well with such a setting.

HOW TO SHOP ABROAD: The goods are enticing, but even so, quality goods are not necessarily less expensive in a fashionable boutique in the capital city of the country from which they came than they are in an equally fashionable US store. To be sure, do some homework before you go and arrive prepared with a list of the goods you want — as specific as possible, with brands or labels — and the cost of each in the US. In some cases, you will find it less expensive to buy abroad, but frequently you will find it is not, and knowing the difference is crucial to a successful shopping trip. Once you've arrived, it is still necessary to comparison shop as much as time permits, bearing in mind that articles can be less costly the closer you get to their point of manufacture, and least expensive of all in the factory that makes them — if it sells to the public. You'll get a better price on Donegal tweeds, for instance, at small factories and shops in County Donegal than in Dublin, and Scottish woolens and knitwear are less costly at mill outlet stores in Scotland than in shops in either Edinburgh or London. On the other hand, Waterford glass cannot be bought at the factory (though you can tour it), and since its wholesale price is standard within Ireland, its retail price will vary from shop to shop depending on markup only. In England, the Royal Doulton, Spode, Minton, and Wedgwood factories at Stoke-on-Trent do have retail shops on the premises, but, in order not to undercut their own retailers, they do not sell at discounted prices. (Two of them — Wedgwood and Spode — have "seconds" shops where you can pick up china with slight imperfections at up to half off the ordinary retail price.)

If your itinerary won't allow combing the countryside in search of sources, and if you can time your visit accordingly, perhaps the best bargains in almost anything British may be had at sale time: two weeks in January and one week in July when the majority of London's department stores and specialty shops offer their wares at substantial reductions. Londoners wait for the sales, not to mention the rest of the British and hordes of shoppers from the Continent, so expect some of the usual local reserve to disappear as all engage in a frantic fight for some of the world's most coveted merchandise.

DUTY-FREE SHOPS: If common sense tells you that it is always less expensive to buy goods in an airport duty-free shop than to buy them at home or in the streets of a foreign city, you'd best be aware of some basic facts. Duty-free, first of all, does not mean that the goods you buy will be free of duty when you return to the US. Rather, it means that the shop has paid no import tax acquiring goods of foreign make because the goods are not to be used in the country, which is why duty-free goods are available only in the restricted passengers-only area of international airports or are delivered to departing passengers on the plane. In a duty-free store, you save money only on goods of foreign make because they are the only items on which import tax would be charged in any other store. There is usually no saving on locally made items, although in countries that impose VAT taxes (see below) that are refundable to foreigners, the prices in airport duty-free shops are also minus this tax, sparing travelers the often cumbersome procedures they would otherwise have to follow to obtain the refund. Beyond this, there is little reason to delay buying local souvenirs until you reach the airport. In fact, because airport duty-free shops usually pay high rents, the locally made goods sold in them may well be more expensive than they would be in a downtown store. The real bargains are foreign goods, but — let the buyer beware — not all foreign goods are automatically less expensive in an airport duty-free shop. Spirits, smoking materials, and perfumes are fairly standard bargains, but when buying cameras, watches, clothing, chocolates and other foods, and luxury items, be sure to know what they cost elsewhere. Terrific savings do exist (they are the reason for such shops, after all), but so do overpriced items that an unwary shopper might find equally tempting.

There are several airport duty-free shops in Great Britain and Ireland, but Shannon International Airport's Duty-Free Shop was the world's first and remains one of the most renowned. Here, there are savings to be had on foreign goods — Lalique crystal, Swiss watches, French perfumes — though not necessarily on Irish-made goods. If you haven't been able to scout out your souvenirs at the source, however, they should cost no more at Shannon than at Irish shops in downtown areas and certainly less than they would back home. And it may be convenient to buy them here rather than carry them with you throughout your trip, provided you're willing to take a chance on finding the desired item in the right size and color and provided you arrive at the airport in enough time to do your shopping. Shannon also operates a mail-order service that can be used long after you've left Ireland. You'll have to pay the import duty on items you order, but since your purchases are free of a retail store's markup, you will still pay less than you would in a stateside specialty shop. You can get the mail-order catalog as you pass through Shannon or request it from Shannon Development, 757 Third Ave., New York, NY 10017 (phone: 212-371-5550). By studying a copy before you go, you'll be better equipped to compare the quality and prices of the merchandise you'll encounter as you shop overseas.

VALUE ADDED TAX: Commonly abbreviated as VAT, this is a tax levied by various European countries and added to the purchase price of most merchandise. The standard VAT rate in Great Britain and Northern Ireland is 15% (children's clothes, books, food, and transportation exempt), while in the Irish Republic it ranges from 10% to 25% — the higher rate applies to luxury goods such as watches, jewelry, furs, glass, and cameras (food and transportation exempt). The tax is intended for residents (and is already included in the price tag), but visitors are required to pay it, too, unless they have purchases shipped directly by the store to an address abroad. If they pay the tax and take purchases with them, however, visitors are entitled to a refund under the retail export schemes in operation in both countries. To obtain the refund, show the salesperson your passport and ask for a VAT relief form, which will be filled out on the premises. As you leave the country, have the form validated at the customs desk that's usually next to passport control and mail it back to the store at the adjacent post box (stores generally supply stamped, self-addressed envelopes for this purpose). Not all stores participate in this export scheme and some that do require a minimum purchase below which they refuse to process the forms. They may also deduct a small charge from your refund for providing the service.

If your shopping was done by credit card, the VAT refund will probably appear as a credit (in dollars) to your account. If your purchases were paid for in cash, your refund will be made by check in the currency of the country in which the purchase was made. Your own US bank may assess a fee, anywhere from $5 to as high as $15 or more, for converting a check into US dollars. Far less costly is sending your foreign currency check (after endorsing it) to Ruesch International, 1140 Nineteenth St., NW, Suite 320, Washington, DC 20036 (phone: 800-424-2923). The flat fee for conversion of foreign currency checks to US dollars is only $2.

Sports

 Castles and churches, museums and monuments are all part of the European experience, testimony to what fired the mind and stoked the soul of a country in days gone by. Another part of the experience is meeting the people. Day by day, you will see them going calmly about their daily lives. To see them at their most energetic, however, it helps to see them involved in the pastimes they are most passionate about: in other words, sports. In Great Britain and Ireland these include games that are hardly known in the US as well as games that are the ancestors of our own national pastimes. Among them, along with where and when to see both the players and the spectators at their enthusiastic best, are the following:

SOCCER: If attendance records are a guide, this is the most popular sport in Britain, where it's called football and was called football long before the Americans began to play anything remotely resembling it. After rugby came on the scene, the London Football Association was formed in 1863 to protect the purity of the original football, which then became known as "association football," and eventually as "soccer," through constant repetition of the abbreviation for the word "association." Whatever it's called, this is the game that fills the papers with predictions and details of players' salaries, and draws huge crowds — lately very unruly ones — to the stadiums. The season runs from August to May, with games played on Saturday afternoons or evenings. To see what it's all about, follow the crowds to the grounds of some of the most popular professional clubs in the London area: Arsenal, Highbury Stadium, Avenell Rd., N5 (phone: 359-0131); Chelsea, Stamford Bridge Grounds, Fulham Rd., SW6 (phone: 385-5545); Tottenham Hotspur, 748 High Rd., N17 (phone: 808-1020); West Ham United, Boleyn Park, Green St., E13 (phone: 470-1325). Top teams outside London are Manchester United, Liverpool, and Ipswich. The Football Association Cup Final, an event the equivalent of the World Series, takes place at Wembley Stadium, London (phone: 902-1234), before a crowd of 100,000. Football tickets are usually bought at the stadium about an hour before the match, but for the Cup Final they're usually sold out in advance to club members. Rest assured it will be on the telly. For a schedule, contact the Football Association, Ltd., 16 Lancaster Gate, London W2 3LW (phone: 262-4542), or any BTA office in the US.

RUGBY: A schoolboy at the great English public school at Rugby invented something new in 1823 by picking up the soccer ball (football) and running forward with it, contrary to the rules. Soccer was basically a kicking game, but carrying the ball and tackling became part of the new sport, formalized in 1871 when the Rugby Football Union came into being. Exported to the US, rugby developed into American football, which it resembles — somewhat. In Britain, rugby is an amateur sport, played from September to April on Saturday afternoons by school and university teams, county teams, hospital teams, and by anyone else who can bring together the requisite 15 players per side. Anyone who's seen the game will remember the "set scrum," one means by which play begins, when forwards of opposing teams, like two compact and only apparently disorderly phalanxes, push and shove against each other for possession of the ball. Rugby has been described as a "ruffian's sport, played by gentlemen," and play proceeds in a rugged fashion without protective equipment. The most important matches — including international ones such as England vs. Wales, Scotland, or Ireland — are played in southwest London at Twickenham, stadium and headquarters of Rugby Union's controlling body (Whitton Rd., Twickenham; phone: 892-8161). Cardiff, Wales, is another stronghold and the place to see a match there is in Cardiff Arms Park. In Edinburgh, go to the Murrayfield Rugby Ground.

Rugby League, an offshoot of Rugby Union, is both an amateur and a professional sport played according to a different set of rules by teams of 13 players. Its stronghold is in the north of England — Lancashire and Yorkshire, principally — but the Rugby League Challenge Cup Final takes place at London's Wembley Stadium in May.

CRICKET: Soccer and rugby move at a fast pace, but anyone on a tight schedule may not have time to take in a cricket match, which takes a leisurely 3 to 5 days to finish, though some 1-day competitions have been introduced. British — in fact English — to the core (it's been dated as far back as the 12th or 13th century and rules existed by 1744), the very name of the game has come to signify fair play, and what is "not cricket" is conduct not befitting a gentleman and a sportsman. (Cricket never made it in the American colonies though an early form of baseball was similar to it.) The season runs from mid-April to early September and matches are played by university teams and by professional county teams. International, or test, matches take place annually. The most famous ever was that won by Australia over Britain in 1882, the morning after which London's shocked *Sporting Times* ran an obituary for British cricket, announcing that its remains would be cremated. Since then, any Great Britain–Australia test match is played for the "Ashes," which repose in an urn that never leaves the Cricket Memorial Gallery at Lord's Cricket Ground, London — not even if Australia wins. Lord's Cricket Ground, home of the Marylebone Cricket Club, the sport's governing body, is *the* place to see a game (St. John's Wood Rd., London NW8; phone: 289-1615). Next best place is The Oval (Kennington, London SE11; phone: 735-4911), home of the Surrey County Cricket Club and site of the 1882 humiliation.

POLO: No one is sure where it came from — somewhere in central Asia probably — but it got to Britain via India where enthusiastic British army officers discovered it and brought it home. The first match seems to have been played on the outskirts of London in 1871. From the beginning it has been a rich man's sport, since it takes a lot of money to maintain a string of polo ponies and a string of them is necessary: The game is a fast and punishing one for the horses and the player will change mounts more than once during a game. There are some 500 players in Britain, and the fact that Prince Charles is among them helps to keep the game very much alive. The Hurlingham Polo Association (Ambersham Farm, Ambersham, Midhurst, West Sussex GU29 0BX; phone: 07985-277) is polo's governing body. To see a match, go to Smith's Lawn, Windsor Great Park, Windsor, or to Cowdray Park, Midhurst, West Sussex, on summer weekends.

CURLING: Scotland participates in the football and Rugby Union frenzy, but it has its own pastimes, too. Besides golf, which began here, there is curling, a major winter sport that probably began here, and if not, at least developed here. Curling has been almost as successful an export as golf, and there are now many more curlers in Canada than in Scotland, but the Scots have been curling since the 16th century and the Royal Caledonian Curling Club, founded in 1838, is the governing body of the sport. In this game, the player slides a curling stone — up to 44 pounds of round, polished, and flattened granite, with a handle at the top for the grip — across the ice toward a goal or tee, using a broom to sweep the way clear in front of the stone as it swishes home. The sweeping melts the ice a bit, drawing the stone on. There are four players per team and the team that wins is the one with the most stones closest to the tee. Curling rinks are found all over Scotland, in cities such as Glasgow, Edinburgh, Aberdeen, Dundee, and Inverness, as well as in smaller cities and at the winter sports complex at Aviemore, where championship games take place.

HIGHLAND GAMES: You'll see plenty of kilts and plenty of sheer brute strength at these traditional annual athletic meets. The history of the games goes back as far as the 11th century. They take place along with clan gatherings and bagpipe and dance competitions all over the Scottish Highlands during the summer and the calendar is especially busy in August and early September. Even the Queen attends the Braemar Royal Highland Gathering, the best known of the Highland games, held not far from Balmoral Castle on the first Saturday in September. Most of the games are running and throwing events and they're usually entered by professionals. The main event at many a gathering is a sport called "tossing the caber," actually a tree trunk of considerable weight that must be "tossed" from a vertical position — if the athlete can manage it. The caber at the Braemar games, all 19 feet and 120 pounds of it, has been tossed, but rarely. Rules of the Scottish Games Association require that the caber start out bigger and heavier than any of the athletes can handle but that it can be cut down if it can't be tossed. Once someone has been successful, however, the caber stays as it is. Besides Braemar, other important games are the Portree Highland Games on the Isle of Skye, the Cowal Highland Gathering at Dunoon, and the Aboyne Highland Games.

GAELIC FOOTBALL: The Irish have two national sports, both thrillers. They developed their own form of football and it's the fastest and roughest one of all, though not nearly as rough as it used to be when a game was more an outburst of territorial rivalry than a sport. A particularly vicious encounter prompted the formation of the Gaelic Athletic Association in 1884 and with it a set of rules. Thus purged of its brutality but not of its passion, the game emerged resembling both soccer and rugby, but more the latter than the former. Teams represent Ireland's 32 counties and as the season progresses through the summer, hardly an Irish soul remains unmoved by the spectacle. The All-Ireland Football Final packs them into Dublin's Croke Park (phone: 74-31-11) for the day of reckoning, traditionally the last Sunday in September.

HURLING: The other Irish national game is fast and dangerous and unique to the Emerald Isle. Played on a field by two teams of 15 players each, the instrument of aggression is the hurley, or *camán* — a 3-foot-long wooden blade of a stick with a curved tip to catch, run with, then use to hurl a leather-covered ball, or *sliotar,* toward the goalpost. The ball moves faster than the speed of light, the hurley sticks whirl, and opportunities for insult or injury are rife. Also a summer game, the hurling season unfolds with the Gaelic football season and reaches its own conclusion at Croke Park in the All-Ireland Hurling Final — usually the first Sunday in September. The football final follows at the end of the month and closes out the sports calendar.

Time Zones and Business Hours

TIME ZONES: Both Britain and Ireland fall into the Greenwich Mean Time zone. Measured from Greenwich, England, at longitude 0°0′, it is the base from which all other time zones are measured. Areas in zones west of Greenwich have earlier times and are called Greenwich Minus; those to the east have later times and are called Greenwich Plus. For example, New York City is 5 hours earlier than Greenwich, England (Greenwich Minus 5); when it is noon in Greenwich, it is 7 AM in New York.

Because both nations move their clocks an hour ahead in the spring and an hour back in the fall, corresponding to daylight-saving time in the US, the same differential between time zones is maintained nearly all year.

British and Irish timetables use a 24-hour clock to denote arrival and departure times, which means that hours are expressed sequentially from 1 AM. For example, the departure of a train at 6 AM will be announced as "0600"; whereas one leaving at 6 PM will be noted as "1800." A departure at midnight would be "2400."

BUSINESS HOURS: In Great Britain, Northern Ireland, and the Irish Republic, most businesses are open Mondays through Fridays from 9 AM to 5 or 5:30 PM. Shops follow roughly the same schedule, from 9 AM to 5:30 or 6 PM, except that they are also open on Saturdays. In small towns and villages they may close for an hour at lunchtime, and there is at least one weekday when they close at 1 PM. Some stores in Dublin skip the early closing and simply don't open on Mondays; a few in London close early on Saturdays. Larger stores in British and Irish shopping centers stay open till 8 or 9 PM at least one day a week (Thursdays in most cases, but Wednesdays for some London stores, and Thursdays *and* Fridays for many Irish stores).

Banking hours in Great Britain and Northern Ireland are 9:30 AM to 3:30 PM, with a break for lunch (12:30 to 1:30 PM) in Scotland and Northern Ireland. A few banks in Northern Ireland are also open Saturday mornings. In the Irish Republic, banking hours are 10 AM to 3 PM, also with a lunch break (12:30 to 1:30 PM) but also with late hours at least one day a week (Thursdays till 5 PM in Dublin). Most British and Irish banks are closed on Saturdays, Sundays, and public holidays (called bank holidays), although major airport banks are open 7 days a week. Most Barclay's Bank branches are open Saturday mornings as is the Commercial Bank at Grafton and Dame streets in Dublin.

Post offices in Great Britain are open Mondays through Fridays from 9 AM to 5:30 PM and on Saturdays from 9 AM until 12:30 or 1 PM. In Ireland, they are usually open Mondays through Saturdays, from 9 AM to 5:30 PM. Main post offices in London and Dublin keep longer hours and Sunday hours.

Mail, Telephone, and Electricity

 MAIL: "Poste Restante" is the equivalent of our general delivery and is probably the best way to have your mail sent if you do not have a definite address. The central or main post office in each city or town handles Poste Restante, so make sure you call at the correct office when inquiring after your mail.

American Express holds mail free of charge for clients only. You must be able to show an American Express card, traveler's checks, or a voucher proving you are on one of the company's tours to avoid paying for mail privileges. Those who aren't clients must pay a nominal fee each time they ask if they have received mail whether they actually have a letter or not. There is also a forwarding charge for clients and nonclients alike. A list of American Express addresses in Britain and Ireland is contained in the pamphlet *Services and Offices* available from the nearest US branch of American Express.

US embassies and consulates abroad do not accept mail for tourists. They will, however, help out in emergencies, if you need to receive important business documents or personal papers, for example. It is best to inform them either by separate letter or cable, or by phone if you are in the country already, that you will be using their address for this purpose.

TELEPHONE: Direct dialing within the country, between nations, and overseas is possible in both London and Dublin. There are a lot of digits involved once you start dialing outside the national borders, but by avoiding operator-assisted calls, costs are cut considerably and rates are reasonable. Except for calls made through hotel switchboards. One of the most unpleasant surprises foreign travelers encounter is the amount they find tacked on to their hotel bill for telephone calls, because foreign hotels routinely add surcharges that can be the equivalent of a daily room rate. It's not at all uncommon to find 300% or 400% added on to telephone charges.

Until recently, the only recourse against this unconscionable overcharging was to call collect when phoning from abroad, or to use a telephone credit card (available through a simple procedure from any local US phone company). American Telephone & Telegraph has put together Teleplan, to set limits on surcharges for calls made by hotel guests from their rooms. Teleplan is currently in effect in virtually all the hotels in Ireland, in the Comfort Hotels International in Great Britain, and in all Hilton International hotels. Teleplan agreements stipulate a flat amount for credit card or collect calls (currently between $1 and $10) and a flat percentage (between 20% and 100%) on calls paid for at the hotel. For further information, contact the International Information Service, AT&T Communications, 635 Grand St., Pittsburgh, PA 15219 (phone: 800-874-4000), and ask for the *Teleplan* brochure.

Until Teleplan becomes universal, it's wise to ask the surcharge rate *before* calling from your hotel. Similarly, it's still a good idea to use your telephone credit card, if you have one, and if not, to place your call collect or place the call and ask your party to call you right back. If none of these choices is possible, make your international calls from the local post office or special telephone center to avoid the surcharges.

While the British telephone system is fairly reliable, making connections in Ireland can sometimes be hit or miss — all exchanges are not always in operation on the same day. If you dial a number and can't get through, you'll just have to try later or the next day. So be warned: If you have to make an important call — to make a reservation in another city, for instance — do it a few days ahead of time.

ELECTRICITY: A useful brochure is *Foreign Electricity Is No Deep Dark Secret,* published by the Franzus Company (free; send a stamped, self-addressed envelope to them at 352 Park Ave. S, New York, NY 10010; phone: 889-5850). It provides information about converters and adapter plugs for electrical appliances to be used abroad but manufactured for use in the US. The United States runs on 110-volt, 60-cycle alternating current; Great Britain, Northern Ireland, and the Irish Republic all run on 220- or 240-volt, 50-cycle alternating current. The large difference between US and European voltage means that without a converter, the motor of a US appliance used overseas would run at twice the speed it's meant to and would quickly burn out. You can solve the problem by buying a lightweight converter to transform foreign voltage into the domestic kind (there are two types of converters, depending on the wattage of the appliance), or by buying dual-voltage appliances that convert from one to the other at the flick of a switch (hair dryers of this sort are common). The difference between the 50-cycle and 60-cycle currents will cause no problem — the appliance will simply run more slowly — but you will still have to deal with differing socket configurations before plugging in. Sets of plugs for use worldwide can be bought at hardware stores.

Drinking and Drugs

DRINKING: It is more than likely that some of the warmest memories of your trip will be moments of conviviality shared over a drink in a neighborhood pub. You'll find that hard liquors, wines, and brandies are distilled to the same proof and often are the same labels as those you'll find at home;

however British and Irish beers and ales tend to be about 5% higher in alcoholic content and have quite a different flavor from those brewed in the US.

You'll want to try each country's specialties. Scotch whisky and English ale are the favorites in British pubs. Whisky may be tempered with a little water or ice, and ale comes cellar-chilled or sometimes refrigerated. In the pubs of Ireland, Guinness stout, a dark, syrupy beer with a thick creamy head and a pronounced bitterness, is the favorite. (For a more thorough discussion of British and Irish beverages, see *Food and Drink*, PERSPECTIVES, and *Pub Crawling*, DIVERSIONS.)

Pub hours in Britain and Ireland vary slightly and confuse everyone. To make matters even worse, the regulations relating to "opening hours" have recently been changed. In England — and not in any other country in Great Britain — the old regulations allowed a pub to open at 11 AM, serve drinks until 3 PM, then close until 5:30 PM, and remain open until 11 PM. A recent amendment to these regulations eliminated the 3 to 5 PM closing, but *only* for those establishments in which a "real" meal is available and on the table with your beer mug during that period. It's too early to appraise how the broad range of pub owners will adopt this change since the meal specified under the new rules must be one that is eaten with a knife and fork. Normal "pub grub" munchies — sandwiches, or finger foods such as Scotch eggs, for example — don't qualify. Sunday hours are shorter: noon to 2 PM and 7 to 10 PM. And to confuse you completely, opening and closing hours in Scotland, Wales, and Northern Ireland are entirely different from those in England. In addition, there are local quirks as well, such as places in Scotland that stay open all afternoon and those in parts of Scotland and Wales that close all day Sunday. In some parts of Northern Ireland, the pubs are open from 11:30 AM to 11 PM Mondays through Saturdays and are closed all day Sunday, though hotels and restaurants retain the right to serve alcoholic beverages.

Pub hours are yet again different in the Republic of Ireland. Here all pubs are open from 11:30 AM to 11:30 PM (only till 11 PM in the winter) on Mondays through Saturdays. In Dublin and in major cities, they officially close from 2:30 to 3:30 PM every afternoon for a hiatus known to all as the "holy hour." On Sundays throughout the Republic, pubs are open from noon to 10 PM at night, with some closing from 2 to 4 PM.

As in the US, national taxes on alcohol affect the prices of liquor in Britain and Ireland. Prices for mixed drinks are about the same as at home. Local beers and ales are reasonably priced, so take this opportunity to savor them at the source.

Two caveats: The legal age for drinking is 18 in both Great Britain and Ireland. Those under 18 are allowed into pubs but, of course, cannot be served alcoholic beverages. When setting off to do some serious pub crawling, leave your car behind and make alternate plans for transportation back to the hotel. There are strict laws against drunk driving in both Britain and Ireland and they are adamantly enforced.

DRUGS: There is a ready supply of hashish and other drugs in London and certain other cities just as there is in the US, but don't be deluded into believing that this easy access denotes a casual attitude on the part of authorities. The moderate legal and social acceptance that marijuana has won in the US has no counterpart in either country. The best advice is, simply, don't mess with drugs; and for heaven's sake never cross a border carrying any illegal or controlled substance. Customs officials make routine, random searches and will throw the book at any offender, which can mean imprisonment for possessing the smallest amount of a drug. (If you carry medicines that contain a controlled drug, make sure you have a current doctor's prescription.) There isn't much that the American consulate can do for drug offenders beyond providing a list of lawyers. Having broken a local law, your fate is in the hands of the local authorities.

Ironically, you can get in almost as much trouble coming through US customs with over-the-counter drugs picked up abroad that contain substances that are controlled in the US. Cold medicines, pain relievers, and the like often have codeine or codeine derivatives that are illegal except by prescription in the US. Throw them out before you leave for home.

Customs and Returning to the US

Customs allowances for US citizens returning from abroad were most recently revised in January 1983, although allowances for incoming currency and its equivalent were raised in November 1984. The most meaningful change for the tourist is the increase in the individual duty-free exemption: You may now bring in articles totaling $400 without paying duty on them, provided they accompany you and are for personal use. A flat 10% duty based on the "fair retail value in country of acquisition" is assessed on the next $1000 worth of merchandise brought in for personal use or gifts. Any amounts over $1,400 are dutiable at a variety of rates.

Families traveling together may make a joint declaration to customs, a procedure that permits one member to exceed his or her duty-free exemption to the extent that another falls short. Families may now also pool purchases dutiable under the flat rate amount. A family of three, for example, would be eligible for up to a total of $3,000 at the 10% flat duty rate (after each member had used up his or her $400 duty-free exemption) rather than three separate $1,000 allowances. This grouping of purchases is extremely useful when considering the duty on a high-tariff item, jewelry or a fur coat, for example. Individuals are allowed 1 carton of cigarettes (200) and 1 liter of alcohol if over 21. Alcohol above this allowance is liable for both duty and the Internal Revenue tax. Antiques that are 100 or more years old and accompanied by proof from the seller of that fact, are duty-free, as are paintings and drawings if done entirely by hand (frames, however, are dutiable).

Personal exemptions can be used once every 30 days and in order to be eligible an individual must have been out of the country for more than 48 hours. If any portion of the exemption has already been used once within any 30-day period, or if your trip is less than 48 hours long, the duty-free allowance is cut to $25. The allotment for individual "unsolicited" gifts mailed from abroad (only one per day per recipient) has been raised to $50 retail value per gift. These gifts do not have to be declared and are not included in your duty-free exemption.

Clearing customs is a simple procedure. Forms are distributed by airline or ship personnel before arrival. If your purchases total no more than the duty-free $400 limit, you need only fill out the identification part of the form and can make your declaration orally to the customs inspector. If entering with more than $400 worth of goods, a written declaration must be submitted. It is illegal not to declare dutiable items; you are smuggling, and the penalty can be anything from stiff fines and seizure of the goods to prison sentences. It simply isn't worth doing. Nor should you go along with the suggestions of foreign merchants who offer to help you secure a bargain by deceiving customs officials in any way. Such transactions are frequently a setup using the foreign merchant as an agent of US Customs. Another agent of US Customs is TECS, the Treasury Enforcement Communications System, a computer that is being used to store all kinds of pertinent information on returning citizens. There is a basic rule to buying goods abroad, and you should never contravene it: If you can't afford the duty on something, don't buy it. Your list or verbal declaration should include all items purchased abroad as well as gifts received abroad, purchases made at the behest of others, repairs, and anything brought in for sale. Do not include in the list items that do not accompany you, i.e., purchases that you have mailed or had shipped home. These are dutiable in any case, even if for your own use and even if the items that accompany your return from the same trip do not exhaust your $400 duty-free exemption. In fact, it is a good idea, if you have accumulated too much while abroad, to mail home any personal effects (made and bought in the US) that you no longer need rather than your foreign purchases. These personal effects pass through customs as "American Goods Returned" and are not subject to duty.

Gold, gold medals, bullion, and up to $10,000 in currency or negotiable instruments may be brought into the US without being declared in writing, but you must declare them verbally to the customs officer as you enter. Sums over $10,000 must be declared in writing. Drugs are totally illegal with the exception of physician-prescribed medication. It's a good idea to travel with no more than you actually need of any medication and to have the prescription on hand and a letter from your doctor (especially if you are carrying a syringe — even if it's for your insulin shots) in case any question arises either abroad or reentering the US.

Customs implements the rigorous Department of Agriculture regulations concerning the importation of vegetable matters, seeds, bulbs, and the like. Living vegetable matter may not be imported without an import permit and everything must be inspected, permit or not. Processed foods and baked goods are usually okay. Meats are generally restricted, and regulations depend on the country of origin and manner of processing.

Customs agents are businesslike, efficient, and not unkind. During the peak season, clearance can take time, but this is generally because of the strain put on capacity by a number of jumbo jets disgorging their passengers at the same time, not unwarranted zealousness on the part of the customs people.

A final word: The US Customs Service publishes a free kit of pamphlets with customs information, including *Know Before You Go,* a basic discussion of customs requirements pertaining to all travelers; *International Mail Imports; Pets, Wildlife, US Customs; Travelers' Tips on Bringing Food, Plant, and Animal Products into the United States; GSP and the Traveler; Pocket Hints; Currency Reporting; Importing a Car;* and *Trademark Information for Travelers.* For the entire kit or individual pamphlets, write or call the US Customs Service, PO Box 7407, Washington, DC 20044 (phone: 202-566-8195), or contact any of the seven regional offices (listed in telephone directories under "Treasury Department") in Boston, Chicago, Houston, Los Angeles, Miami, New Orleans, and New York.

Sources and Resources

Tourist Information Offices

Below is a list of national tourist offices in the United States and in Great Britain and Ireland. These organizations can provide travel and entry information, and literature is usually free. British Tourist Authority and Irish Tourist Board offices in North America are best equipped to handle written or telephone inquiries from potential visitors on this side of the Atlantic. When requesting travel brochures and maps, state your particular areas of interest regarding hotels, restaurants, special events, tourist attractions, guided tours, and sports facilities.

There are numerous regional tourism organizations as well as more than 700 Tourist Information Centres located in towns throughout England, Scotland, Wales, and Northern Ireland, and more than 70 Tourist Information Offices in the Irish Republic. These furnish information and handle inquiries by mail and, where numbers are given, also by telephone. Offices are generally open Mondays through Fridays. Some are open in summer only and others year-round. For a complete listing of all local information centers, seasonal and otherwise, contact the national tourist offices.

IN THE US

British Tourist Authority, 40 W 57th St., New York, NY 10019 (phone: 212-581-4700); 350 S Figueroa St., Suite 450, Los Angeles, CA 90071 (phone: 213-628-3525); John Hancock Center, Suite 3320, 875 N Michigan Ave., Chicago, IL 60611 (phone: 312-787-0490); Cedar Maple Plaza, Suite 210, 2305 Cedar Springs, Dallas, TX 75201 (phone: 214-720-4040).

Irish Tourist Board, 757 Third Ave., New York, NY 10017 (phone: 212-418-0800); 29 E Madison, Suite 200, Chicago, IL 60602 (phone: 312-444-1987); 1199 Broadway, Suite 349, Burlingame, CA 94010 (phone: 415-583-1605).

Northern Ireland Tourist Board, 40 W 57th St., New York, NY 10019 (phone: 212-765-5144).

ENGLAND

London Visitors and Convention Bureau, 26 Grosvenor Gardens, London SW1 0DU (phone: 01-730-3488).

Cumbria Tourist Board, Ashleigh, Holly Rd., Windermere, Cumbria LA23 2AQ (phone: 09662-4444).

East Anglia Tourist Board (includes Cambridgeshire, Essex, Norfolk, and Suffolk), Toppesfield Hall, Hadleigh, Suffolk 1P7 5DN (phone: 0473-822922).

East Midlands Tourist Board (includes Derbyshire, Leicestershire, Lincolnshire, Northamptonshire, and Nottinghamshire), Exchequergate, Lincoln LN2 1PZ (phone: 0522-31521).

English Tourist Board, Thames Tower, Black's Rd., Hammersmith, London W6 9EL (phone: 01-846-9000).

Heart of England Tourist Board (includes Gloucester, Hereford and Worcester, Shropshire, Staffordshire, Warwickshire, and West Midlands), 2-4 Trinity St., Worcester, Worcestershire WR1 2PW (phone: 0905-613132).

Northumbria Tourist Board (includes Cleveland, Durham, Northumberland, and Tyne and Wear), Aykley Heads, Durham City, Co. Durham DH1 5UX (phone: 0385-46905).

North West Tourist Board (includes Cheshire, High Peak District of Derbyshire, Greater Manchester, Lancashire, and Merseyside), The Last Drop Village, Bromley Cross, Bolton, Lancashire BL7 9PZ (phone: 0204-591511).

South East England Tourist Board (includes East Sussex, Kent, Surrey, and West Sussex), 1 Warwick Park, Tunbridge Wells, TN2 5TA (phone: 0892-40766).

Southern Tourist Board (includes Eastern and Northern Dorset, Hampshire, and the Isle of Wight), Town Hall Centre, Leigh Rd., Eastleigh, Hampshire SO5 4DE (phone: 0703-616027).

Thames and Chilterns Tourist Board (includes Bedfordshire, Berkshire, Buckinghamshire, Hertfordshire, and Oxfordshire), 8 Market Place, Abingdon, Oxfordshire OX14 3UD (phone: 0235-22711).

West Country Tourist Board (includes Avon, Cornwall, Devon, West Dorset, Somerset, and Wiltshire, and the Isles of Scilly), Trinity Ct., 37 Southernhay E, Exeter, Devon EX1 1QS (phone: 0932-76351).

Yorkshire and Humberside Tourist Board (includes Humberside and North, South, and West Yorkshire), 312 Tadcaster Rd., York YO2 2HF (phone: 0904-707961).

CHANNEL ISLANDS

Alderney Recreation and Tourism Committee, States Office, St. Anne's, Alderney (phone: 0481-822994).

States of Guernsey Tourist Committee, PO Box 23, St. Peter Port, Guernsey (phone: 0481-23552).

Herm Island Administrative Office, Herm Island, Via Guernsey (phone: Herm 4, or 0481-22377).

States of Jersey Tourism Committee, Weighbridge, St. Helier, Jersey (phone: 0534-78000).

Sark Tourist Information Officer, Sark (phone: 0481-83-2345).

ISLE OF MAN

Isle of Man Tourist Board, 13 Victoria St., Douglas, Isle of Man (phone: 0624-74323).

ISLE OF WIGHT

Isle of Wight Tourist Board, 21 High St., Newport, Isle of Wight PO30 1JS (phone: 0983-524343).

SCOTLAND

Scottish Tourist Board, 23 Ravelston Terr., Edinburgh EH4 3EU (phone: 031-332-2433).

Aviemore and Spey Valley Tourist Organisation, Main Rd., Aviemore, Inverness-shire PH22 1PP (phone: 0479-810363).

City of Edinburgh District Council, 3 Princes St., Edinburgh EH2 2QP (phone: 031-557-2727).

Dumfries and Galloway Tourist Board, Douglas House, Newton Stewart, Wigtownshire DG8 6DQ (phone: 0671-2549).

Fort William and Lochaber Tourist Board, Travel Centre, Fort William, Inverness-shire PH33 6AN (phone: 0397-3781).

Greater Glasgow Tourist Board, 35-39 St. Vincent Pl., Glasgow G1 2ER (phone: 041-227-4894).

Inverness, Loch Ness and Nairn Tourist Board, 23 Church St., Inverness IV1 1EZ (phone: 0463-234353).

Loch Lomond, Stirling and Trossachs Tourist Board, Beechwood House, St. Ninians Rd., Stirling FK8 2HU (phone: 0786-70945).

Oban, Mull and District Tourist Board, Boswell House, Argyll Sq., Oban, Argyll PA34 4AN (phone: 0631-63122).

Orkney Tourist Board, Information Centre, Broad St., Kirkwall, Orkney KW15 1DH (phone: 0856-2856).

Outer Hebrides Tourist Board, 4 S Beach St., Stornoway, Isle of Lewis PA87 2XY (phone: 0851-3088).

Perthshire Tourist Board, PO Box 33, George Inn La., Perth PH1 5LH (phone: 0738-27958).

St. Andrews and North East Fife Tourist Board, 2 Queens Gardens, St. Andrews, Fife KY16 9TE (phone: 0334-74609).

Scottish Borders Tourist Board, Municipal Buildings, High St., Selkirk TD7 4JX (phone: 0750-20555).

Shetland Tourist Organisation, Information Centre, Market Cross, Lerwick, Shetland ZE1 0LU (phone: 0595-3434).

South West Ross and Isle of Skye Tourist Board, Tourist Information Centre, Portree, Isle of Skye IV51 9BZ (phone: 0479-2137).

Note: Scotland has more than 30 regional tourism bodies. Those listed above handle areas most frequently of interest to visitors.

WALES

Wales Tourist Board, Brunel House, 2 Fitzalan, Cardiff CF2 1UY (phone: 0222-499909).

Mid Wales Tourism Council (includes parts of Dyfed, Gwynedd, and Powys), Canolfan Owain Glyndwr, Machynlleth, Powys SY20 8EE (phone: 0654-2653).

North Wales Tourism Council (includes Clwyd and most of Gwynedd), 77 Conwy Rd., Colwyn Bay, Clwyd LL29 7LN (phone: 0492-31731).

South Wales Tourism Council (includes parts of Dyfed and Powys, Gwent, Mid, South, and West Glamorgan), Ty Croeso, Gloucester Pl., Swansea SA1 1TY (phone: 0792-465204).

IRISH REPUBLIC

City of Dublin Region, 14 Upper O'Connell St., Dublin 1 (01-747733).

Cork/Kerry Region, Tourist House, Grand Parade, Cork (phone: 021-273251).

Donegal/Leitrim/Sligo Region, Aras Reddon, Temple St., Sligo (phone: 071-61201).

Eastern Region (includes Dublin, Kildare, Louth, Meath, and Wicklow counties), St. Michael's Wharf, Dun Laoghaire, County Dublin (phone: 01-806984).

Midland Region (includes Cavan, Laois, Longford, Monaghan, Roscommon, and Westmeath counties), Dublin Rd., Mullingar, County Westmeath (phone: 044-48650).

Mid-Western Region (includes Clare, Limerick, and northern Tipperary counties), The Granary, Michael St., Limerick (phone: 061-317522).

South-Eastern Region (includes Carlow, Kilkenny, southern Tipperary, Waterford, and Wexford counties), 41 The Quay, Waterford (phone: 051-75788).

Western Region (includes Galway and Mayo counties), Aras Fáilte, Eyre Square, Galway (phone: 091-63081).

NORTHERN IRELAND

Northern Ireland Tourist Board, River House, 48 High St., Belfast, BT1 2DS (phone: 0232-231221).

Theater and Special Event Tickets

Both the British Tourist Authority and the Irish Tourist Board can supply information on the many special events and festivals that take place in Britain and Ireland, though they cannot in all cases provide the actual program or detailed information on ticket prices. In more than one section of this book you will come across mention of events to spark your interest — everything from music festivals and special theater seasons to sporting championships — along with addresses to write for descriptive brochures, reservations, or tickets. Since many of these occasions are sometimes booked well in advance, if there is something you would surely not want to miss, you should think about having your booking in hand before you go. If you do write, remember that any request from the US should be accompanied by an international reply coupon to ensure a response (send two of them for an airmail response — you can obtain the coupons from any post office). Actual tickets can usually be paid for by an international postal money order or by foreign draft.

Tickets for London shows, sports events, and opera, ballet, and concert performances that are part of the regular cultural seasons in London and elsewhere can be bought before you go from the following agencies. (They may also be able to supply tickets to some of the more popular special events.)

    Edwards & Edwards, One Times Sq. Plaza, New York, NY 10036 (phone: in New York State, 212-944-0290; elsewhere, 800-223-6108). Provides tickets for Edinburgh's International Festival and the Stratford-Upon-Avon Shakespeare season as well as theater and cultural events in London. Booking fee: $7 to $9 per ticket.

    Keith Prowse & Co. Ltd., 234 W. 44th St., New York, NY 10036 (phone: in New York State, 212-398-1430; elsewhere in the US, 800-223-4446). Theater, concerts, sporting events in London, plus Stratford-upon-Avon and the Edinburgh Military Tattoo. Booking fee: $9 per ticket.

    London Stages, 18455 Burbank Blvd., Suite 5-N, Tarzana, CA 91356 (phone: 818-881-8433). Handles events in London and Stratford-upon-Avon only. Service charge of $5 per ticket.

Camera and Equipment

Vacations are everybody's favorite time for taking pictures. After all, most of us want to remember the places we visit — and show them off to others — through spectacular photographs. Here are a few suggestions to help you get the best results from your travel picture-taking.

BEFORE THE TRIP: If you're taking your camera out after a long period in mothballs, or have just bought a new one, check it thoroughly before you leave to prevent unexpected breakdowns and disappointing pictures.

1. Shoot at least one test roll, using the kind of film you plan to take along with you. Use all the shutter speeds and f-stops on your camera, and vary the focus to make sure everything is in order. Do this well in advance of your departure so there will be time to have film developed and to make repairs, if they are necessary. If you're

in a rush, most large cities have custom labs that can process film in as little as an hour. Repairs, unfortunately, take longer.

2. Clean your camera thoroughly, inside and out. Dust and dirt can jam camera mechanisms, scratch film, and mar photographs. Remove surface dust from lenses and camera body with a soft camel's-hair brush. Next, use at least two layers of crumpled lens tissue and your breath to clean lenses and filters. Don't rub hard and don't use water, saliva, or compressed air on lenses or filters because they are so easily damaged. Persistent stains can be removed by using a Q-tip moistened with liquid lens cleaner. Anything that doesn't come off easily needs professional attention. Once your lenses are clean, protect them from dirt and damage with inexpensive skylight or ultraviolet filters.

3. Check the batteries for both the camera and the light meter and take along extras just in case yours wear out during the trip. They can be a nuisance to find, especially abroad.

EQUIPMENT TO TAKE ALONG: Keep your gear light and compact. Items that are too heavy or bulky to be carried comfortably on a full-day excursion will likely stay in your hotel room.

1. Most single lens reflex (SLR) cameras come with a 50mm, or "normal," lens, a general purpose lens that frames subjects within an approximately average angle of view. This is good for street scenes taken at a distance of 25 feet or more and for full-length portraits shot at 8 to 12 feet. You can expand your photographic options with a wide-angle lens such as a 35mm, 28mm, or 24mm. These give a broader than normal angle of view and greater than normal "depth of field," that is, sharp focus from foreground to background. They are especially handy for panoramas, cityscapes, and for large buildings or statuary from which you can't step back. For extreme close-ups, a macro-lens is best, but a screw-on magnifying lens is an inexpensive alternative. Telephoto lenses, 65mm to 1000mm, are good for shooting details from a distance (as in animal photography), but since they tend to be heavy and bulky, unless you anticipate a frequent need for them, omit them from vacation photography equipment. A zoom, which is a big lens but relatively light, has a variable angle of view so it gives a range of options. Try a 35mm to 80mm; beware of inexpensive models that give poor quality photographs. Protect all lenses with skylight or ultraviolet filters, which should be removed for cleaning only. A polarizing filter helps to eliminate glare and reflection and to achieve fully saturated colors in very bright sunlight. Take along a couple of extra lens caps (they're the first things to get lost) or buy an inexpensive lens cap "leash."

2. Travel photographs work best in color. Good slide films are Kodachrome 64 and Fujichrome 50, both moderate- to slow-speed films that provide saturated colors and work well in most outdoor lighting situations. For very bright conditions, try slower film like Kodachrome 25. If the weather is cloudy, or you're indoors with only natural light, use a faster film, such as Kodachrome or Ektachrome 200 or 400. These can be "pushed" to higher speeds. Recently there are even faster films on the market for low-light situations. The result may be pictures with whiter, colder tones and a grainier image, but high-speed films open up picture possibilities that slower films can not.

Films tend to render color in slightly different ways. Kodachrome brings out reds and oranges. Fujichrome is noted for its yellows, greens, and whites. Agfachrome mutes bright tones, producing fine browns, yellows, and whites. Anticipate what you are likely to see, and take along whichever types of film will enhance your results. You might test films as you test your camera (see above).

If you prefer film that develops into prints rather than slides, try Kodacolor 100 or 400 for most lighting situations. Vericolor is a professional film that gives excellent results, especially in skin tones, but suffers shifts in color when subjected to temperature extremes; take it along for people photography *if* you're sure you can protect it from heat and cold. All lens and filter information applies equally to print and slide films.

How much film should you take? If you are serious about your photography, pack one roll of film (36 exposures) for each day of your trip. Film is especially expensive abroad, and any leftovers can be bartered away or brought home and safely stored in your refrigerator. Processing is also more expensive abroad and not as safe as at home. If you are concerned about airport security X-rays damaging your undeveloped film (X-rays do not affect processed film), store it in lead-lined bags sold in camera shops. This possibility is not as much of a threat as it used to be, however. In the US, incidents of X-ray damage to unprocessed film (exposed or unexposed) are minimal because low-dosage X-ray equipment is used virtually everywhere. As a rule of thumb, photo industry sources say that film with speeds up to ASA 400 can go through security machinery in the US five times without any noticeable effect. Overseas, the situation varies from country to country, but at least in Western Europe the trend is also toward equipment that delivers less and less radiation. While it is doubtful that one exposure would ruin your pictures, if you're traveling without a protective bag you may want to ask to have your photo equipment inspected by hand, especially on a prolonged trip with repeated security checks. (Naturally, this is possible only if you're carrying your film and camera on board with you; it's a good idea anyway, because it helps to preclude loss or theft or the possibility at some airports that checked baggage will be X-rayed more heavily than hand baggage.) In the US, Federal Aviation Administration regulations require that if you request a hand inspection, you get it, but overseas the response may depend on the humor of the inspector. One type of film that should never be subjected to X-rays, even in the US, is the new, very high speed film with an ASA rating of 1,000. If you are taking some of this overseas, note that there are lead-lined bags made especially for it. Finally, the walk-through metal detector devices at airports do not affect film, though the film cartridges will set them off.

3. A small battery-powered electronic flash unit, or "strobe," is handy for very dim light or at night, but only if the subject is at a distance of 15 feet or less. Flash units cannot illuminate an entire scene, and many museums do not permit flash photography, so take such a unit only if you know you will need it. If your camera does not have a hot-shoe, you will need a PC cord to synchronize the flash with your shutter. Be sure to take along extra batteries.

4. Invest in a broad camera strap if you now have a thin one. It will make carrying the camera much more comfortable.

5. A sturdy canvas or leather camera bag, preferably with padded pockets — not an airline bag — will keep equipment organized and easy to find.

6. For cleaning, bring along a camel's-hair brush that retracts into a rubber squeeze bulb. Also, take plenty of lens tissue and plastic bags to protect equipment from dust.

SOME TIPS: For better pictures, remember the following pointers:

1. *Get close.* Move in to get your subject to fill the frame.
2. *Vary your angle.* Shoot from above or below — look for unusual perspectives.
3. *Pay attention to backgrounds.* Keep it simple or blur it out.
4. *Look for details.* Not just a whole building, but a decorative element; not just an entire street scene, but a single remarkable face.
5. *Don't be lazy.* Always carry your camera gear with you, loaded and ready for those unexpected moments.

Genealogy Hunts

It's possible to trace your ancestors by mail, or to do your research stateside using the thousands of reels of microfilmed records on file at the Church of Latter Day Saints' genealogical library in Salt Lake City. Or you can hire a professional genealogist. But nothing is quite as satisfying as flipping through the records on your own and actually visiting the area where your ancestors lived. Thanks to an abundance of records kept throughout the ages in Britain, the descendants of yeoman and middle-class families can trace their heritage back to the 1400s; but even if your pedigree is not quite so grandiose, there's a good chance that you'll be able to worship in a church where some great-great-great-great-grandfather was married, or walk up to the house where his children were born, or read a will written in his own hand, or photograph his moss-covered gravestone in some peaceful country churchyard. When you're doing the research in person, the process is more efficient than by mail, since you can follow up clues on the spot.

It goes without saying, however, that you can't even begin to search abroad until you've laid the groundwork at home. You need to know not only the name of your emigrant ancestor, but also the dates of his birth and emigration. You must also have a general idea of where he came from. The names of his relatives can also be useful. From there, you'll be able to consult parish registers and the archives of various public record offices and genealogical libraries. Note: Don't forget about the realignment of British counties that took place in 1974; many records were relocated at that time.

Before you begin, you may want a copy of the Irish Tourist Board's free information sheet called "Tracing Your Ancestors," which offers an excellent summary of genealogical sources and procedures. Another useful guidebook is the British Tourist Authority's *Step-by-Step Guide to Tracing Your Ancestors* ($8.50), available at the British Travel Bookshop (see *Books and Magazines*).

ENGLAND AND WALES

In the mid-16th century, England united with Wales, so, although the Welsh have their own language, the two countries' records are essentially one and the same.

The search is easiest if your ancestor emigrated after 1837, when civil registration of births, marriages, and deaths was introduced in both countries. The General Register Office, St. Catherine's House, 10 Kingsway, London WC2B, 6JP, houses the records, and like most in Britain, they're indexed, but to get particulars you have to request a certificate, the preparation of which takes a day or two.

Birth certificates give date and place where the event occurred; the child's forenames; his father's name and occupation; his mother's name and maiden surname; her usual residence if the birth took place elsewhere; and the name and address of the person providing the information.

Marriage certificates give the names of the contracting parties; their ages (most of the time, that is; and you must remember that some people stretched the truth a bit); their fathers' names and occupations; the date and place of the marriage; and the names of the witnesses.

A death certificate records the date, place, and cause of death, plus the deceased's name, age, occupation, and usual residence (if different from the place of death), and the name and address of the person furnishing the data.

The details on a birth certificate usually tell you enough so that you can look for the parents' marriage certificate, and the marriage certificate will usually give you the information you need to find the records of the births of the two parties.

Once you know the addresses, you may get further information from returns of the censuses taken decennially from 1841 on and now housed at the Census Room of the Public Record Office, Land Registry Building, Portugal St., London WC2, as far as the year 1881. Later returns are held by the General Register Office, St. Catherine's House (address above). Complete data from later returns become available only after a century has passed from the census date, but partial information from the 1891 and 1901 censuses is available in some circumstances.

These and other British records should lead you, if your American research did not already, to the period before 1837. In this era, it's the registers of the 14,000 parish churches in England and Wales that are your most valuable source. Gaps in their listings of baptisms, marriages, and burials do exist, but some volumes date from as early as 1538, when the law requiring the clergy to keep such records went into effect. Copies of many of them are at the Society of Genealogists, a private genealogical library open to the public for a fee at 14 Charterhouse Buildings, London EC1M 7BA; the library has catalogues of the copies that can be found here and elsewhere. Where no copies exist, you can find out the originals' whereabouts from the appropriate County Record Office. (A list of County Record Offices' addresses has been published by Her Majesty's Stationery Office, London.) When you do locate the parish, use *Crockford's Clerical Directory* to find the name and address of the clergyman who currently has custody of the records. Make an appointment as far in advance as possible so that you can be sure that the clergyman will have time to show you his records.

The above-mentioned County Record Offices provide other valuable information. Many well-to-do folk were married by license in the good old days, and records of the proceedings can often be found in the County Record Offices. (Others are housed in the Lambeth Palace Library, London SE1 7JU, and the Guildhall Library, Aldermanbury, London EC2P 2EJ, which has an extensive collection of the material on London.)

Various centralized indexes of vital records, available in genealogical libraries, can also be useful. *Boyd's Marriage Index,* which covers the period from 1538 to 1837, is only one.

Among the genealogist's best tools are wills, especially in Wales, where, until the mid-19th century, surnames changed with each generation as in Scandinavian countries. The information you find in a will can often clarify relationships of people whose names you've found mentioned elsewhere, and the particulars are almost always reliable. Sometimes you can make up charts for several generations of a family from just one will. If the document (or a copy) was proved since 1858, you'll find it at The Principal Probate Registry, Somerset House, The Strand, London WC2R 41LB. Before 1858, wills were proved in a variety of courts, depending on the deceased's holdings. If they were varied and widespread, the will was generally proved in the Prerogative Court of Canterbury (PCC), if the deceased lived in the southern half of England; or, if he lived in the north, in the Prerogative Court of York. The PCC records, which begin in 1383 and are indexed, are at the Public Record Office, Chancery La., London WC2A 1LR; the York probate records, which date from 1389, are at the Borthwick Institute, St. Anthony's Hall, Peasholme, York YO1 2PW, and are indexed to 1858. (By appointment only, so write well in advance of your visit.)

When, sooner or later, you hit a snag in your research, you can get help at the Society of Genealogists. In addition to the parish register transcripts, it houses a vast general index of names, a 7-million-entry marriage index, and a collection of documents relating to some 13,000 families, plus material for Scottish, Welsh, and Irish families and for English families abroad. When you need professional help, consult the College of Arms, Queen Victoria St., London EC4V 4BT. The British Travel Bookshop carries *Discovering Your Family Tree* ($3.25) and *Discovering Surnames* ($3.25), which are not restricted to English and Welsh families only (postage depends on amount ordered; call 212-765-0898 or write 40 W 57th St., New York, NY 10019, and ask for their booklist).

SCOTLAND

Many Scots, including boatloads of prisoners boarded against their will, crossed the Atlantic in the 17th and 18th centuries during the political turmoil that followed the deposition of the Catholic king James II and the struggle of his grandson Charles Edward Stuart, or "Bonnie Prince Charlie" (1720–88), to regain the throne. Flora Macdonald, who helped in the escape of this romantic fellow after his defeat, in 1746, at Culloden Moor, was just one of the Scottish immigrants of this period.

Tracing these families, and others, can be relatively simple here, for in addition to the fact that the records are remarkably thorough to begin with, they're all centrally located. The General Register Office for Scotland, New Register House, Princes St., Edinburgh EH1 3YT, contains not only the records of births, marriages, and deaths since the beginning of compulsory registration in 1855, but also information from about 4,000 old parish registers dealing with Scotland's 900 parishes before compulsory registration. The earliest of these dates back to 1553, although more commonly they begin in the 17th or 18th century. The fact that married women are also often listed under their maiden names makes your work just that much easier. To make matters better yet, New Register House is also the repository for the returns of the decennial census from 1841 onward, and those up to and including that of 1891 may be consulted.

Wills, justiciary records, deeds, services of heirs, and other legal documents are also in Edinburgh, at the Scottish Record Office in H. M. General Register House, Princes St., Edinburgh EH1 3YY. Registers of sasines, a Scottish document dealing with the descent of land, are also available here.

Although these records may be all you need, there are also many books, articles, and unpublished materials that may help you work out any knotty problems you encounter. The Scots Ancestry Research Society, 3 Albany St., Edinburgh EH1 3PY and the Scottish Genealogy Society, 21 Howard Pl., Edinburgh EH3 5JY, can help you directly or provide you with the names of professional searchers. Margaret Stuart's *Scottish Family History: A Guide to Works of Reference on the History and Genealogy of Scottish Families* (1930), Joan Ferguson's *Scottish Family Histories Held in Scottish Libraries* (1960), and G. F. Black's *Surnames of Scotland* (1962) may also prove helpful. You may also be interested in contacting the Scottish Tartans Society and Museum, Davidson House, Drummond St., Comrie, Perthshire PH6 2DW, a noncommercial cultural organization that maintains an enormous fund of information about tartans.

THE REPUBLIC AND NORTHERN IRELAND

It was the great potato famine of 1846–48 that drove 4 million Irish across the Atlantic, but several thousand came before that, and hundreds of thousands have come in the years since then. In general, just where you look for the records of your forebears will depend on whether they came from the north or the south.

Some Protestant marriages on the island were recorded beginning in 1845, and civil registration of births, deaths, and marriages in general began in 1864.

When you're researching ancestors who lived in the south, you'll find Catholic marriage records from 1864 to the present and Protestant marriage records from 1845 at the General Register Office, 8-11 Lombard St. E, Dublin 2. Births, marriages, and deaths that occurred before civil registration began may be recorded in parish registers. Roman Catholic registers are normally still held by the parish priest. Most are on microfilm in the National Library (address below), but in some cases permission from the parish priest is necessary. Most of the *surviving* Church of Ireland registers are held by the local clergy. Unfortunately, more than half of them burned in the great fire of 1922, along with most probate records and the census records from 1813 to 1851.

This may make your research difficult, but various other records do exist. The Tithe Applotment Books, containing the names of people whose holdings were subject to tithe in the 1820s and 1830s, are especially useful. You'll find them in the Public Records Office of Ireland, Four Courts, Dublin 7. This office also holds the census records for 1901 and 1911; original wills proved since 1904 and copies of many earlier wills; copies of some Church of Ireland parish registers; and a wide variety of other records. Deeds, leases, mortgages, settlements, and other records of transactions relating to property, dating from as early as 1708, are recorded at the Registry of Deeds, Henrietta St., Dublin 1.

When all else fails, visit the National Library, Kildare St., Dublin 2. Here you'll find the library's Genealogical Office as well as all manner of books, manuscripts, directories, family histories, and genealogical and historical journals, and also various deeds, letters, and other papers relating to a number of Irish families. If your ancestors were Presbyterian, you can get help from the Presbyterian Historical Society, Church House, Fisherwick Place, Belfast BT1 6DU.

If your ancestors lived in the north of Ireland, you may find the records you need in either Dublin or Belfast. Records of births, marriages, and deaths from the beginning of civil registration until 1922 are in the General Register Office in Dublin, while post-1922 records are in Belfast at the General Register Office, Oxford House, 49-55 Chichester St., Belfast BT1 4HL. Although the 1922 fire destroyed many old wills, some thousands of copies, notes, and extracts, as well as the Tithe Applotment Books and many other documents relating to the people of the northern part of Ireland are preserved at the Public Record Office of Northern Ireland, 66 Balmoral Ave., Belfast BT9 6NY. On the other hand, the records of the Registry of Deeds in Dublin and of the Genealogical Office in Dublin can be useful. When your trail turns cold, you can get help from the Irish Genealogical Association, 164 Kingsway, Dunmurry, Belfast BT17 9AD, whose US agent is Ruth B. Green, Shamrock Travel, 6623 Meadowbrook Dr., Fort Worth, TX 76112 (phone: 817-457-1993). Also of assistance is the Ulster Historical Foundation, 66 Balmoral Ave., Belfast BT9 6NY, (phone: 661621), whose US agent is Donna Hotaling, All Ireland Heritage, 2255 Cedar La., Vienna, VA 22180 (phone: 703-560-4496). Both of these agents lead heritage tours, and the latter also publishes a quarterly magazine, *All Ireland Heritage* ($24 per year subscription).

Especially useful, no matter where in Ireland your ancestors hailed from, is *The Handbook on Irish Genealogy* (1973), published by Heraldic Artists, Ltd., 3 Nassau St., Dublin 2. It contains lists of parish registers for the Roman Catholic, Church of Ireland, and Presbyterian churches, plus useful maps, and more. Other Irish genealogical materials are available from the same source and from Historic Families, 8 Fleet St., Dublin 2; *The Irish Ancestor, An Illustrated Journal* may also help. Write Ms. Rosemary ffolliott, The Glebe House, Fethard, County Tipperary.

SPECIAL PROBLEMS

If your ancestor did not belong to the established church of the land, you may have difficulties at first, but there are special genealogical societies and/or guides for just about any sect you can name. The records of the Society of Friends, for instance, are a dream — superbly indexed and organized. Information about the Huguenots, the French Protestants who came in great waves from the late 16th century and especially around 1685 following the revocation of the Edict of Nantes, can be pursued by writing to the Huguenot Society of London, 54 Knatchbull Rd., London SE5. Research into Jewish ancestry can be slow going because of frequent name changes. The Jewish Historical Society of England, 33 Seymour Pl., London W1H 5AP, is a great resource.

For help locating societies concerned with other groups, contact the big genealogical libraries in the country of your ancestors' origin.

Books and Magazines

Throughout GETTING READY TO GO, numerous books and brochures have been recommended as good sources of further information on a variety of topics. In many cases these have been publications of the British Tourist Authority or the Irish Tourist Board, and are available free through their offices. Others can be found in the travel section of any good general bookstore. In addition, there are several bookstores and mail-order houses — such as the British Travel Bookshop mentioned frequently in the foregoing text — that specialize in books about Great Britain or Ireland, especially those not published in the US. Their addresses are given here:

British Travel Bookshop, 40 W 57th St., 3rd Floor, New York, NY 10019 (phone: 212-765-0898). Carries a complete line of books and maps on all areas of Britain, including AA- and BTA-produced material and other books by major and little-known publishers. Open 9 AM to 5 PM, Mondays through Fridays.

British Gifts, PO Box 26558, Los Angeles, CA 90026. Mail order only. Stocks a large selection of maps and books on Britain, including AA and BTA publications.

Irish Book Loft, 232 Madison Ave., New York, NY 10019 (phone: 212-481-3056). Carries just about any kind of book pertaining to Ireland — literature, history books, guide books — along with records, cassettes, and maps. Open 10 AM to 6:30 PM, Mondays through Fridays; 11 AM to 5 PM, Saturdays.

Irish Books & Media, 2115 Summit Ave., St. Paul, MN 55105 (phone: 612-647-5678). It's not a bookstore, but a mail-order house specializing in all kinds of books from Ireland — history, fiction, biographies, as well as travel.

Keshcarrigan Bookshop, 90 West Broadway, New York, NY 10007 (phone: 212-962-4237). Sells a variety of Irish books and records and is a good place to look for out-of-print volumes. Keshcarrigan is the largest supplier of books in Gaelic outside of Dublin. Open 11 AM to 5 PM weekdays; noon to 5 PM Saturdays.

The Rivendell Book Shop, 109 St. Mark's Place, New York, NY 10009 (phone: 212-533-2501). Specializes in books on Cornish, Welsh, Irish, and Scottish history, religion, mythology, and folklore. Records and tapes are also available. Open noon to 8 PM, Mondays through Saturdays.

The following stores specialize in travel also, but not in travel to any particular country or continent. You'll find books on Great Britain and Ireland on the shelves along with guides to the rest of the world, and you may even come across some old Baedekers.

Book Passage, 51 Tamal Vista, Corte Madera, CA 94925 (phone: in California, 415-927-0960; elsewhere, 800-321-9785). Travel guides, maps to all areas of the world. Free catalogue available.

Forsyth Travel Library, PO Box 2975, Shawnee Mission, KS 66201 (phone: 913-384-0496). Travel guides and maps, over the counter and by mail order. Free catalogues.

Gourmet Guides, 1767 Stockton St., San Francisco, CA 94133 (phone: 415-391-5903). Travel guides and maps, along with cookbooks. Free catalogues.

The Travel Suppliers, 727 N Placentia Ave. Fullerton, CA 92631 (phone: 714-528-

2502). Books and maps, plus travel paraphernalia from luggage to voltage converters. Catalogues.

Traveller's Bookstore, 22 W 52nd St., New York, NY 10019 (phone: 212-664-0995). Comprehensive collection of travel guides and maps. Catalogue ($1.50 including postage).

Before or after your trip you may want to subscribe to magazines that specialize in information about Britain or Ireland. *In Britain,* a monthly, and *Ireland of the Welcomes,* a bi-monthly, are both published by the respective tourist boards; the magazines usually spotlight various parts of the countryside and contain sketches about contemporary and historical personalities. Subscriptions: *In Britain,* Box 1238, Allwood, Clifton, NJ 07012 ($22.90 for 1 year, or $2.50 for one issue at the British Travel Bookshop); *Ireland of the Welcomes,* PO Box 84, Limerick, Irish Republic ($12 for 1 year, $20 for 2). *Inside Ireland,* published independently by two women, Brenda Weir and Gill Bowler, is a quarterly newsletter that reports on a wide variety of topics — shopping, real estate, the arts, restaurants and pubs, retirement in Ireland, and the like. A subscription ($30 for 1 year) also entitles you to use their information service and to receive special supplements dealing with genealogy, accommodations, and other subjects. There are subscriber discounts on car rentals, cottage rentals, and shopping. For a sample copy of the newletter ($1), write: *Inside Ireland,* Rookwood, Stocking Ln., Ballyboden, Dublin 16, Irish Republic.

Words to the Wise

 "Two people divided by the same language" is how Oscar Wilde described the transatlantic relationship between Britain and the US. He had a point. Below are some common British and Irish terms followed by their standard American translations.

aubergine: eggplant
bespoke: custom-made
biscuit: cookie or cracker
black spot: blind curve in the road
bonnet (car): hood
boot (car): trunk
candy floss: cotton candy
car park: parking lot
chemist's shop: drugstore
chips: french fries
coach: long-distance bus
cotton: thread
cotton wool: absorbent cotton
crisps: potato chips
cul-de-sac: dead end
dual carriageway: divided highway
dynamo (car): generator
face flannel: washcloth
flat: apartment
flyover: overpass
gear lever: gearshift
hire purchase: installment plan
jar: a glass of whiskey, stout, or other alcoholic beverage

jumper: sweater
left luggage office: baggage room
lift: elevator
loch: lake
loo, lavatory, WC: bathroom
lorry: truck
mackintosh, mac: raincoat
nappy: diaper
off licence/wine merchant: liquor store
overtake: pass
petrol: gasoline
pram: baby carriage
public school: private school
queue: stand in line
quid: pound
rasher: slice of bacon
reception: front desk
return ticket: round-trip ticket
roundabout: traffic circle
silencer (car): muffler
single ticket: one-way ticket
stalls (theater): orchestra seats
stone: measure of weight equal to 14 pounds
surgery: doctor's or dentist's office
trainers: sneakers
trunk call: long-distance call
underground, tube: subway
wellingtons: rubber boots

PERSPECTIVES

Britain

History

Who built Stonehenge? Alas, we don't really know. Britain is an island and its earliest history is a succession of invasions and immigrations. In one of these waves the original inhabitants of Britain disappeared, leaving behind great stone circles like those at Stonehenge and Avebury, built about 2000 BC, and primitive flint tools, but no trace of their language or heritage.

The Bronze Age reached Britain sometime after 1600 BC, brought by a race of people known as the "Beaker Folk," identified by their tools fashioned from Cornish tin and Irish copper, and pottery of a distinctively idiosyncratic shape.

THE CELTS

In the seventh century BC there arrived on the island the first tribes of whom there is a definite historical record. These were the Celts, a race of warriors, artists, and bards who decorated their shields with intricate abstract designs and forged their weapons from iron. They brought with them a priestly caste called the Druids, who led them in worshiping a pantheon of nature spirits in groves of trees and administered the tribes' systems of law and education. Remains of an Iron Age village can be seen at Maiden Castle in Dorset.

About 75 BC the Belgae (present day Belgium is named for them) settled in England. A chief of the Belgae, Cymbeline (ca. AD 5–40), who gave his name and very little else to a play by Shakespeare, is the first identifiable figure in British history. He minted coins that bore his own image and established a tribal capital at Colchester. Cymbeline died just before the second Roman invasion in AD 43.

THE ROMANS

Julius Caesar landed in Britain at Dover with an expeditionary force in 55 BC primarily to cut off communication between tribal chiefs on the island and those in Gaul. But it was not until Claudius's personal expedition nearly a century later that a permanent garrison was established and that conquest began in earnest.

At first the Celtic tribes resisted the Romans fiercely, chiefly under Caractus, son of Cymbeline, who was captured and taken to Rome, and Boadicea, the first of a series of remarkable women in British history, who was the chief of a Norfolk tribe, the Iceni. It was only after Boadicea's defeat and suicide by poison in AD 61 that the Pax Romana finally prevailed in the southern part of England.

In the north, skirmishes continued for decades, prompting Emperor Hadrian, who had visited Britain in 121, to have built (ca. 122–127) the 73½-mile-long wall that stretches from the Tyne River in northeast England to Solway Firth in southwest Scotland and is named for him.

Until 450, Britain south of the wall was the Roman province of Britannia, a source for the empire's Cornish tin, grain, and slaves.

The impact of Roman civilization was indelible, not least in the establishment of a capital where the Thames River becomes narrow enough to ford. They named it Londinium — London. Other towns flourished too, among them Eboracum (York), Lindum (Lincoln), Devana Castrum (Chester), and Aquae Sulis (Bath), where sections of the ancient baths can still be seen. In addition, the conquerors built for military purposes the famous Roman Roads, among them the Fosseway, part of which is today a quiet country road in southern Warwickshire.

The street plans of many English towns betray Roman origins, although the schools where Greek and Roman law were taught and the villas with their remarkably sophisticated central heating systems lie buried beneath rubble and grass.

ANGLES, SAXONS, AND JUTES

In the middle of the fourth century, piratic raids of the Province of Britannia by the Scoti, an Irish race, and the Picts, inhabitants of present-day Scotland, increased, while a series of Saxon tribes of the Teutonic race penetrated the southeast of the country. Cut off from supply routes by the Teutonic conquest of Gaul and faced with the disintegration of the empire in Rome, the Roman legions withdrew from Britain. Lacking a trained army of their own, the native Celts fled to the western fringes of their land, where their descendants flourish today. The territory they left was occupied not only by the Saxons, but also by their kinfolk from northern Germany, the Jutes, and by the tribe that gave its name to the southern half of Britain, the Angles. These loosely knit tribes gradually coalesced into what became known as the Heptarchy — the seven kingdoms of Wessex (the West Country), Essex (Southeastern England north of London), Sussex, Kent, East Anglia, Mercia (the Midlands) and Northumbria (Northern England). Occasionally one king among the seven would achieve primacy and it was during the supremacy of Ethelbert of Kent that Augustine the Monk (St. Augustine of Canterbury) arrived in southeast England in 597.

CHRISTIANITY

There had been Roman Christians in the service of the Empire, among them the father of Patrick, the Apostle of Ireland, and Irish missionaries had established isolated Christian settlements on the Celtic fringe in the northwest of England and the west of Scotland. But the descendants of the Teutonic invaders in most parts of England had not been converted.

Much of English history can be told in a series of anecdotes and the first is probably that concerning the conversion of England. The story goes that Pope Gregory I (St. Gregory the Great) was walking in Rome one day when he spotted some handsome flaxen-haired youths in chains.

"Who are they?" he asked.

"Angles," he was told, "pagans."

"Not Angles," the Pope replied, "angels!" And he decided that their country belonged to Christ.

Thus, Augustine the Benedictine, charged with the task, presented himself to King Ethelbert, who gave the monk and his companions some land at Canterbury, and founded the see that is still first in authority in England.

Contact with the Celtic church led to conflict. The customs of the Roman monks were less austere than those of the Irish and they calculated the date of Easter by different means. When they met at the Synod of Whitby in 664 the differences were settled and the Celtic church submitted to Rome, which was to dominate England spiritually for the next 870 years.

There followed a golden age of monastic learning and religious art, especially manuscript illumination. Missionaries from the British church were known all over Europe. Theodore of Tarsus, Archbishop of Canterbury from 690 to 699, introduced the Roman system of bishoprics and parishes and initiated national synods that brought the rival kingdoms together for the first time. How well he succeeded is proven by the title of St. Bede's *Ecclesiastical History of the English People,* published ca. 731, which suggests that by this date the inhabitants of the country were accustomed to thinking of "England" as a unit.

Certainly the Mercian king Offa (reigned 757–796) thought so. He was the first king to sign himself on charters as *Rex Anglorum* (King of the English), the existence of other kings notwithstanding. Offa is perhaps best remembered for Offa's Dyke, the entrenchment he built as a barrier against the Welsh on the border of England and Wales. Parts of the dyke are well preserved. Offa's burial place, Offchurch in Warwickshire, is an exquisite village not far from Stratford-upon-Avon.

It was in Offa's reign that the first of the Danish raids on the English coast took place. These were followed by a series of Viking onslaughts, until only the Kingdom of Wessex, under the first English national hero, Alfred the Great (849–899), was offering resistance. Alfred is remembered by all English schoolchildren for a particular legend. The story goes that after a particularly unsuccessful skirmish with the Danes he was forced to flee to the Somerset fens where he took refuge with an old peasant woman who did not recognize him. The woman gave him shelter and food and asked him to watch some oaten cakes that she had placed on the fire. Alfred began to think of his next campaign and the cakes started to burn. When the old woman returned she scolded the shabby king roundly. Whether or not the story is true it is certain that his mind was frequently occupied with defeating — or compromising with — the Danish invaders. At the Peace of Wedmore in 878 defeat and compromise came hand in hand. Having temporarily bested the Danes, Alfred extracted a promise from their chief, Guthrun, that he would become a Christian and leave England in peace, and they divided the country between them. The line of demarcation ran roughly from southeast to northwest, with

Alfred taking the southern part, including London. The northern part was ceded to Danish immigrants and became known thereafter as the Danelaw, the territory where the rules and customs of Denmark flourished.

Alfred was not only a warrior, he was also a scholar; as the first translator from Latin to English of St. Bede's *History,* he is acknowledged to be one of the fathers of English literature. He invited European scholars to his court, instituted schools, and directed the foundation of the *Anglo-Saxon Chronicle,* ca. 891, the sole source of much of our knowledge of early Christian England.

Alfred's son, Edward (reigned 899–924), began the reconquest of the Danelaw, which was completed under Edward's son, Athelstan (reigned 924–939). The Vikings were christianized and absorbed into Anglo-Saxon society. One Dane, Oda, became Archbishop of Canterbury in 924.

In 991 the Viking raids began again, led by Sven Forkbeard, king of Denmark. By 1013 Sven was acknowledged ruler of England and the English king Ethelred the Unready fled to Normandy. Sven's son Canute (reigned 1017–35), although the son of a conqueror, was revered by subsequent generations of Englishmen, largely because of his treatment of some sycophantic courtiers. Legend has it that among Canute's entourage were some who considered him to be — or said that they considered him to be — semi-divine. They claimed that if he wished he could turn back the tide. When the rumor came to Canute's ears he took his court to the shore where he sat in his throne commanding the tide to recede. When it didn't, he reminded the offenders of the difference between the honor that belonged to God and that which belonged to the king.

Canute, through his sons, also ruled Norway and Denmark. When he died, ruling such a large northern empire proved too difficult for his heirs. In 1042 Danish rule ended in England and Ethelred's son, Edward (reigned 1042–66), came from Normandy to claim his crown.

The saintly Edward, known as the Confessor, had little taste or flair for kingship. His main preoccupation was with religion (in 1065 he founded the Church of St. Peter which later became famous as Westminster Abbey), and he was politically and physically dominated by the powerful Earl Godwin of Wessex, whose son Harold succeeded the childless Edward to the throne in 1066.

THE NORMAN CONQUEST

When Harold Godwinsson (1022?–66) arrived at Hastings to meet the Norman invaders, he was already the triumphant victor over his brother Tostig and Harold III of Norway in a decisive battle at Stamford Bridge on September 25, 1066. He was killed at the Battle of Hastings on October 14, by a Norman arrow that penetrated one of his eyes. A 23-foot-long embroidery attributed to William the Conqueror's wife, Matilda, illustrates the incident. Called the Bayeux tapestry, it is housed in the Bayeux Museum in Normandy.

By Christmas Day, the Conqueror, William I (1027?–87), the illegitimate son of Robert I of Normandy and a tanner's daughter, had been crowned king of England. There were to be other invasions of England, but this was the last to succeed. It is from this point on that England stops being constantly on the defensive, and becomes a country determined to expand. The culmination of this desire was reached in the vast empire ruled from London in the reign of Victoria.

Resistance to William was never very effective. The Saxon rebels, ill-equipped and generally disorganized, were no match for the Norman cavalry clad in chain mail and garrisoned in fortified keeps. The most famous outlaw was Hereward the Wake, a Saxon chieftain from Lincolnshire, who made one valiant last stand in the fens of the Isle of Ely. Hereward's exploits made him a folk hero. He is known as the Last of the English.

Perhaps the greatest legacy William left was the *Domesday* (or *Doomsday*) *Book,* a record of a survey made in 1085–86 of every parcel of land in England, who owned it, and who had owned it.

William was succeeded in England by his son, William II (reigned 1087–1100), called William Rufus because of his ruddy complexion. William II made enemies of the church by the sale of church lands, and of the people by ruthless taxation. He was killed while hunting in the New Forest by what history has politely termed a stray arrow, and was followed by his brother, Henry I (reigned 1100–1135), known as Henry Beauclerk (the fine clerk), for his ability to read and write. During Henry's reign an accounting system for administering the income and expenditure of the realm was introduced. This system was the nucleus of the modern exchequer. Henry also appointed justices to travel into the provinces to see that the laws of the realm were administered fairly, causing him to be known as the Lion of Justice. Henry's only son, William, died in 1120 in what has become known as the Wreck of the White Ship in the English Channel. Legend has it that after the death of his heir, the king was never again known to smile. His only remaining child was a daughter, Matilda (1102–67), who at the age of 23 became the widowed empress of Germany and at 26 the countess of Anjou. In 1126, 1131, and again in 1133, Henry had required a group of powerful English barons — and, most notably, his nephew Stephen of Blois (1097–1154) — to acknowledge Matilda as Henry's successor to the throne. On Henry's death in 1135, Stephen repudiated his oath and had himself declared king. The result was an era of civil war and anarchy during which, men said, "the heavens slept." Following the death of Stephen's son, Eustace (1153), Matilda's son Henry was accepted as heir apparent.

Henry II (1135–89), by his marriage to the remarkable Eleanor of Aquitaine and through his succession to possessions in Normandy and Anjou, was the lord of a large part of France, a fact that was to dominate English history for nearly 250 years. Henry is best remembered for his quarrel with Thomas à Becket, his former crony, which brought to a head the conflict between church and state.

THE CHURCH IN THE MIDDLE AGES

The church in Henry's time was an almost autonomous organization existing side by side with the secular authority represented by the king. The right to invest archbishops and bishops with symbols of their office had been won for the church by Thomas's predecessor, St. Anselm, in 1107, making the pope, and not the king, supreme authority in ecclesiastical matters. The visible power of the church in Henry II's day was everywhere. Many of the cathedrals that are one of England's glories today were in their infancy in Henry's reign: Durham Cathedral, the most perfect example of Norman architecture in Britain, was consecrated in 1093, Ely in 1083, Winchester in 1093, and Norwich in 1096. In addition the great Cistercian abbeys of Rievaulx, Jervaulx, and Fountains, and the Benedictine houses at Selby and Whitby and other places served to remind the king of the power of the church. The crisis with Becket reached its climax over who should prosecute those men in Holy Orders who had broken the law — "criminous clerks," as they were called. The crown and its justices, said Henry. The church, said Thomas. It was more than a matter of church and state, however. Thomas à Becket had been Henry's closest friend and as Chancellor of England had lived as à sybarite. On his appointment to the archbishopric of Canterbury his personal habits had become austere and the authority he acknowledged was not Henry's but that of the church. Henry, so the story goes, was heard to mutter, "Will no one rid me of this troublesome priest?" and shortly afterward Thomas was murdered by four knights of Henry's entourage. The murder shocked the whole Christian world. Within 3 years Thomas had been canonized and Henry was forced to do penance at his shrine. Canterbury became a place of pilgrimage surpassed in Europe only by Santiago de Compostela in Spain. Its importance was immortalized in Chaucer's *Canterbury Tales,* while the crisis between the two former friends has inspired numerous biographies and dramas, the most famous of which are Anouilh's *Becket* and T. S. Eliot's *Murder in the Cathedral.*

Henry's son Richard I, called Richard the Lion-Hearted (1157–99), has appealed to movie-makers rather than dramatists — especially as the king who reigned during the exploits of the legendary Robin Hood. Although he was king for 10 years, Richard spent only 2 of them in England. In the popular imagination Richard is a benign and just monarch, the very antithesis of his sinister brother, John Lackland. The truth about Richard is more complicated. He was chivalrous, brave, war loving, and homosexual. His devotion to the Third Crusade seems to have arisen from a taste for military combat as much as a desire to bear witness to the glory of God. The most romantic story concerning Richard tells of his release from captivity in Germany. On his way home from the Crusade in 1190 he was taken prisoner by Leopold II, margrave of Austria. Richard's favorite troubador, Blondel de Nesle, wandered through Europe singing a song known only to the two of them. As he sang outside Dürstein Castle, Blondel heard a voice responding to his song and was able to tell Richard's friends where he was incarcerated.

There are no romantic stories about King John (1166–1216). He is best known as the king who was forced to accept the Magna Carta by his barons at Runnymede in June 1215. The charter set forth the principle that the king was not absolute and that he was required to observe the rights of subjects and communities. There is no written constitution in Britain and to this day the Magna Carta is one of the most important documents in British constitutional history.

John's son, Henry III (1207–72), succeeded to the throne as a 9-year-old boy. The quarrels with powerful barons that had marred his father's reign were even more serious during that of Henry. In 1258, a group of noblemen under the leadership of Henry's brother-in-law, Simon de Montfort, forced Henry to acknowledge the Provisions of Oxford, which effectively handed over power to a council of 15 members. Henry repudiated the provisions in 1261 and thereby started a 6-year struggle with his barons, during which de Montfort was killed at the battle of Evesham in 1265.

In spite of the constant atmosphere of crisis between the king and the barons, cultural life in England flourished during Henry's reign. Three great colleges of Oxford University were founded during this period: University College (1249); Balliol (1263); and Merton (1264). At the same time the Franciscan philosopher and scientist Roger Bacon (ca. 1214–94) made Oxford the greatest center of learning in Europe.

Henry's son, Edward I (1239–1307), found himself more often in conflict with his Welsh and Scottish neighbors than with his barons. He completed the conquest of Wales in 1282, and in 1301 had his son (later Edward II, 1284–1327), who had conveniently been born in the castle at Carnarvon in North Wales, declared prince of that country. The title Prince of Wales has usually been given to the eldest son of the sovereign ever since. Edward's struggle to become overlord of Scotland was ultimately less successful, although history remembers him as the Hammer of the Scots and he removed the ancient coronation stone of the Scottish kings from Scone, the Scottish royal seat. It now sits under St. Edward's chair in Westminster when the sovereign is crowned.

Edward II is best remembered from the play by Elizabethan dramatist Christopher Marlowe that depicts the monarch's infatuation with his favorite, Piers Gaveston, earl of Cornwall, and his murder in particularly brutal circumstances at Berkeley Castle in Gloucestershire. His son, Edward III (1312–77), came to the throne in 1327 when he was 15 years old, though he was effectively controlled by his mother, Isabella, and her lover, Roger de Mortimer, earl of March, until the latter's execution in 1333.

THE HUNDRED YEARS WAR

Much of Edward's reign was focused on the series of wars that became known as the Hundred Years War, caused by disputes over English holdings in France; trouble between the great weaving cities of Flanders, which were allies of the English, and their French overlords; and French aid to the Scots. To exacerbate matters Edward assumed the title king of France, claiming that the salic law, which debars succession to or through females, applied in France. (It did and even if it didn't, there were at least five senior claimants). The title king of France remained incorporated in the English crown until the reign of George III in the nineteenth century. The two most famous battles of the Hundred Years War — Crécy in 1346 and Poitiers in 1356 — did much to establish the reputation of the king's heir, Edward, the Black Prince, as a legendary figure of heroism and chivalry in English history.

The other single dominating feature of Edward III's reign was the Black

Death, the epidemic disease that according to some estimates reduced the population of England by one-half. The resulting labor shortage accelerated the change from a society of laborers bound to a single master to one where freelance services could be offered, and the country never again returned to the system of servile tenure. When during the reign of the Black Prince's son, Richard II (1377–99), landlords tried to resurrect that system, they were repulsed by the Peasants' Revolt of 1381. (It was led by two men of Kent, Wat Tyler and Jack Straw; a pub called *Jack Straw's Castle* now stands on the high point of Hampstead Heath, London, where he is said to have assembled his followers.)

Richard's reign ended in abdication; he was replaced by his first cousin, Henry Bolingbroke (IV), son of John of Gaunt (who was duke of Lancaster and fourth son of Edward III). Taking advantage of Richard's unpopularity, Henry had himself "elected" king by Parliament, thereby bringing the house of Lancaster to the throne.

Between 1400 and 1406 Henry had to contend with four rebellions against his authority. His son Henry V (1387–1422) (Shakespeare's Prince Hal) avoided such occurrences by concentrating his subjects' minds once again on the long drawn-out struggle with France. Following his victory at Agincourt on October 25, 1415, over vastly superior French forces, Henry was assured of the support of his countrymen for the house of Lancaster. He had himself declared regent of France and heir to Charles VI, whose daughter, Isabella, he married.

The son they produced, the ill-fated Henry VI (1421–71), succeeded his father in 1472 when he was barely 9 months old. "Henry VI, in infant bonds crowned king/Of whose state so many had the managing/That they lost France and made his England bleed," wrote Shakespeare accurately in his epilogue to *Henry V*.

Henry VI's appetite for war was minimal. He was more concerned with religion and literature, and in spite of the virtually endless turmoil of his reign, managed to found Eton College near Windsor in 1440 and King's College at Cambridge in 1441. The military successes of his father in France were gradually whittled away, as France rallied under Joan of Arc (burned 1429) and other leaders. By the end of the Hundred Years War in 1453, Gascony, Maine, Normandy, Bordeaux, and Bayonne were controlled by the French, leaving Calais as the only English possession in France.

In England, the great nobles made rich by the wars and by the recently introduced farming of sheep kept increasingly large retinues that amounted to small private armies. These semi-independent chieftains fought with one another and terrorized their neighbors uncontrolled by the king or the council that ruled in his name. In 1450, tired of the virtual anarchy around them, about 30,000 men from Kent and Sussex marched on London under one Jack Cade and demanded that Henry's kinsman and heir, Richard, duke of York, be admitted to the ruling council. During two brief periods during which Henry was judged insane, Richard acted as Lord Protector of the realm. In 1454 when the king recovered, Richard was unwilling to yield his power and there followed what is probably the most famous family feud in history, the Wars of the Roses (1455–85).

THE WARS OF THE ROSES

To understand the rationale behind this struggle it is necessary to resort to some genealogy. Both Henry VI and Richard were descended in the direct male line from Edward III, Henry via Edward's fourth son, John of Gaunt (duke of Lancaster), Richard from the fifth son, Edmund (duke of York). In addition, however, Richard was descended through his mother from Edward's third son, Lionel, duke of Clarence, giving him the superior claim according to the English laws of succession. The white rose on the crest of the house of York and the red rose adopted as the badge of the house of Lancaster gave this dreary 30-year quarrel its name.

Henry's antipathy to war notwithstanding, his wife, Margaret of Anjou, was determined to secure the inheritance for their son, Edward, born in 1453, even after Henry was taken prisoner following the battle of Northampton in 1460 and had acknowledged Richard as his heir. A year later Richard was dead and his son was proclaimed king as Edward IV (lived 1442–83) and the kings of the house of Lancaster were declared by Parliament to have been usurpers. Except for a brief period in 1470–71 when Henry was restored, Edward managed to hold on to his throne for 20 years, although until the death of Henry (probably by murder) in the Tower of London in 1471, the picture was one of battles, victories, reversals, and more victories.

A dozen years later in 1483 another king of the Yorkist dynasty, Edward V, who had succeeded his father when he was 12 years old, was to die in the tower. Whether he and his younger brother (known to history as the "little princes in the tower") were murdered by command of their uncle, Richard III (1452–85), has never been satisfactorily established. We do know that Richard was prepared to go to the extraordinary lengths of marrying his niece, Elizabeth of York, Edward V's sister, to secure his position. (He was refused.) Although Richard's dealings with his people were remarkable for his sense of justice and his accessibility (Shakespeare's monster is largely a brilliant invention), the old dynastic rivalry ruined him. In 1485, at Bosworth Field in Leicestershire, he was killed in battle by the forces of Henry Tudor, earl of Richmond, the surviving heir to the claims of the house of Lancaster. The crown of England was found in a bush, and the Wars of the Roses ended.

THE TUDORS

Henry Tudor (1452–1509) was crowned Henry VII and married Elizabeth of York, thus uniting the two houses. His reign was remarkable for an expansion in learning and knowledge of the outside world. William Caxton's printing press had been established at Westminster in 1477 and Thomas Malory's *Le Morte d'Arthur* published in 1485. Under a patent from Henry VII dated March 15, 1496, John Cabot sailed from the West Country port of Bristol and reached North America in the vicinity of Cape Breton in Canada. English claims on the American continent were later based on this discovery.

Henry Tudor's son Henry VIII (1491–1547) is probably the best-known king in English history, not least for his six wives. Henry's struggle with the papacy over his divorce from Katherine of Aragon and his marriage to Anne Boleyn has tended to obscure his early religious fervor. In 1521 he wrote the *Assertion of the Seven Sacraments,* a rebuttal of Martin Luther. For his pains he received the title Defender of the Faith from Pope Leo XI, a title which the English sovereign bears to this day.

Thirteen years later in 1534 the Defender of the Faith became the founder of the Church of England when Henry caused the Act of Supremacy to be passed. The act declared that the king and his successors were the supreme head of the church and clergy in England. Among those executed for refusal to take the oath confirming the act were the Bishop of Rochester, St. John Fisher, and Henry's erstwhile friend and chancellor, St. Thomas More. Religious orders were dissolved and many great abbeys and monasteries sold to the highest bidder. The hauntingly beautiful ruins of Fountains Abbey in Yorkshire and Tintern Abbey in Wales date from this period. Henry's marital exertions notwithstanding, all his descendants were dead by the end of 1603.

In the meantime there were three more Tudor monarchs. The first was Edward VI (1537–53), Henry's sickly son by Jane Seymour, who gave his name to the King Edward VI Grammar Schools, i.e., free college preparatory schools around England, the most famous of which is the school that William Shakespeare attended in Stratford. Edward was succeeded by Henry's daughter by Katherine of Aragon, Mary I, whose attempt to restore Catholicism and consequent decimation of the Protestant bishops caused her to be known as Bloody Mary. And finally there was Elizabeth I, the Virgin Queen (1533–1603). During Elizabeth's reign the European renaissance came into full bloom in England, most notably in the person of William Shakespeare (1564–1616). The school where he learned his little Latin and less Greek still stands in Stratford and is one of the most perfect spots in the country for soaking up the atmosphere of Elizabethan England.

This period also saw the ascendancy of England's sea power as demonstrated by Sir Francis Drake, who became the first Englishman to circumnavigate the globe (1577–80), and Sir Walter Raleigh, who in 1596 sailed 300 miles up the Orinoco River in Central America. The English superiority at sea culminated in the defeat in 1588 of the Great Armada from Spain — a fleet of 362 ships and 3,165 cannon — which had been sent to conquer England in the name of Catholicism.

Both Elizabeth and her people were victims of inflation. An influx of precious metals from the New World and the expansion of the wool trade had brought enormous changes to the economic structure of England. The value of the revenues that by tradition and hereditary right accrued to the Crown dwindled. To save money Elizabeth was frequently obliged to take to the road, traveling with her court from great house to great house to be entertained at the cost of the leading noblemen of England. One such "progress," or journey, to Lord Leicester's at Kenilworth Castle, has been immortalized in the novel *Kenilworth* by Sir Walter Scott.

The poor took to the road, too, in Elizabeth's reign, though in rather less luxury than the queen. Land that had traditionally been put under the plough was enclosed for sheep pasturage, which required a smaller labor force. The displaced laborers — "sturdy beggars," as they were known — wandered from place to place seeking employment and, quite incidentally, inspired the children's nursery rhyme, "Hark, hark, the dogs do bark, the beggars are coming to town . . ."

In 1601 Parliament passed the Poor Law charging individual parishes with the welfare of the needy.

Elizabeth's reign was marred only by the execution of her cousin, Mary Queen of Scots (1542–87), at Fotheringhay Castle in Northamptonshire. Mary had been a rallying point for Catholics after Elizabeth had been declared a bastard by Pope Paul IV. Mary's apparent implication in a plot to assassinate Elizabeth forced the Tudor queen to sign her death warrant, a decision which biographers tell us was to haunt her for the rest of her life.

It was to James VI of Scotland, who as Mary's son was the real heir in any case, Elizabeth left the throne in her will, and he hurried to London to be also crowned King James I of England in 1603. His accession united the two kingdoms in his person though they were to have separate parliaments for another 104 years.

THE STUARTS

There had been a Stuart on the throne of Scotland ever since Robert II succeeded in 1371. Robert was the grandson through his mother of the famous Robert the Bruce who, according to legend, regained hope and courage after defeat in battle by observing the patience with which a spider wove its web. He was the descendant also of King Duncan who had been slain by Macbeth in 1040, who in turn was the descendant of the ancient Irish High Kings. For several hundred years the single outstanding feature of Scottish history was one of wars with England, often in alliance with France. Mary Queen of Scots was herself half French, had spent her childhood in France, and was the widow of a French king before marrying James VI's father. In Scotland to this day there are French words in use — *gigot* for a leg of lamb comes to mind — that are not heard in England outside French restaurants.

James I was pedantic — the Wisest Fool in Christendom men called him — superstitious, and susceptible to the flattery of many male favorites. The warm reception the English offered him initially cooled when it became clear that he did not understand the English parliamentary system or the religious changes taking place. He managed to offend both Puritans and Catholics by his intransigence, and the latter prepared to assassinate him when he opened Parliament on November 5, 1605. The gunpowder to be used in the plot was discovered in the cellars of the Houses of Parliament and one of the conspirators, Guy Fawkes, was arrested. On any November 5, Guy Fawkes Day, visitors can see bonfires dotting the countryside and effigies of Fawkes being burned.

James authorized the publication of the Bible that bears his name and is one of the masterpieces of written English.

Charles I (1600–1649), who succeeded James in 1623, had even less success in dealing with Parliament than his father. In 1628 it adopted the Petition of Right, a statement of civil liberties that prohibited the billeting of soldiers with civilians; arrest on unspecified charges; martial law in peacetime; and all forms of taxation not approved by Parliament itself. Charles assented to the petition in return for financial subsidies for which he was desperate, then promptly violated it by exacting by force the ancient taxes known as "tonnage and poundage."

From 1629 to 1640 he ruled without Parliament; in 1641 Parliament in turn issued the Grand Remonstrance, which set out in full its grievances against the king. On January 3, 1642, Charles went to the House of Commons in an attempt to arrest five of its members. He failed, and the Commons withdrew to the Guildhall (in the heart of the city of London), where they were protected by citizens of the metropolis. Charles made his way to York where he was joined by 65 members of the Commons and 32 peers. When he raised the standard at Nottingham in August 1642, the Civil War had begun.

THE CIVIL WAR, 1642–46

English schoolboys used to reenact the Civil War between the Cavaliers (the Royalists) and the Roundheads (Puritan Parliamentarians under Oliver Cromwell) the way American schoolboys play cowboys and Indians. The romantic hero in this otherwise bleak period was Prince Rupert of the Rhine, Charles's nephew, who distinguished himself first of all at the bloody battle of Edgehill in northern Oxfordshire. Charles's strength was further diminished by defeats at Marston Moor in 1644 and Naseby in 1645. In 1647 he fell into the hands of parliamentary forces, and was tried and convicted of treason "for laying war against Parliament." On January 30, 1649, he was beheaded in Whitehall, London, an act regarded by Royalists then and now as regicide.

THE COMMONWEALTH, 1649–60

The Commonwealth was dominated from the start by Oliver Cromwell, who in 1653 assumed the title of Lord Protector. The title and office of king, as well as the House of Lords, were abolished. Parliament met regularly but acted merely as the instrument for Cromwell, who was virtually a dictator, rigidly enforcing the puritanical laws that had been enacted and using the army to collect taxes. When he died in 1659 his son, Richard, became Protector. Richard managed to hold the office for only a few months since he was unable to control the army. He became known to history as Tumbledown Dick.

THE RESTORATION

Puritan supremacy and military control engendered a strong reaction and by the spring of 1660 public opinion was clearly in favor of inviting Charles II to return to England from the Continent, to which he had fled. His resumption of the crown, however, was subject to certain conditions; these were accepted by Charles in the Declaration of Breda (April 14, 1660), in which he proclaimed among other things an amnesty to all not especially excluded by Parliament. When Charles entered London on May 29, 1660, there were several days of rejoicing. His reign is remembered in the popular imagination as a kind of English bacchanalia. Public dancing was permitted once more and the theaters were reopened.

The licentious mood of the times was superbly chronicled by Samuel Pepys (1633–1703), the Prince of Gossips, in his diaries.

The era was not entirely frivolous, however. In 1662 the Royal Society, generally agreed to be the world's most celebrated organization for stimulating scientific research, was founded. In 1665–66, Sir Isaac Newton formulated the theory of gravity, thus changing our understanding of physical laws.

More somber was the Great Plague of April 1665 and the Great Fire of London, which burned 450 acres of the city between September 2 and 9, 1666. It is because so many structures were destroyed by the fire that there exists today the present St. Paul's Cathedral as well as 40 or so other beautiful churches designed by the brilliant architect, Sir Christopher Wren, in an effort to rebuild London.

Charles left no legitimate heirs, although by one of his many mistresses he is the ancestor of the Princess of Wales, the former Lady Diana Spencer.

Charles's brother, James II (1633–1701), assumed the throne in 1685. He was a convert to the Roman Catholic faith in a country where Parliament had passed in 1673 the Test Act, which excluded from public office all those who refused, among other things, to take communion according to the rite of the Church of England. He was moreover formed in the same autocratic Stuart mold as his father and grandfather. By his first wife, he fathered two daughters, both brought up as Protestants. A subsequent marriage (after his conversion) to a devout Catholic, and the birth of his son, James, on June 10, 1688 (known in history as the Old Pretender), proved intolerable to both the Tory and Whig parties in England. On June 29 seven Whig and Tory leaders invited William of Orange (who was James's son-in-law and also his nephew) to come to London and take the throne. He arrived there on December 19 and on December 22 James fled to France.

William and his wife, Mary, were crowned in February 1689 and reigned jointly until Mary's death in 1694, after which William reigned alone until 1702. In 1701, when it seemed clear that both William and his successor, Princess Anne (James II's younger daughter, later Queen Anne; reigned 1702–14), would die childless, Parliament passed the Act of Settlement declaring that the sovereigns of Great Britain were to be Protestant. The crown was settled on Sophia of Hanover, a granddaughter of James I, and her Protestant heirs.

Some Scottish Jacobites — supporters of the house of Stuart; *Jacobus* is Latin for James — objected to the act and planned to offer the Scottish throne to James Stuart, the Old Pretender. To avoid this, in Queen Anne's reign an Act of Union was passed (1707), establishing one parliament for the United Kingdom and adopting one flag, the crosses of St. George and St. Andrew known as the Union Jack.

THE HANOVERIANS

In spite of the union, Jacobite risings were launched in 1715 just a few months after the son of Sophia of Hanover came to the throne as George I (reigned

1714–27) and again in 1719. Both failed miserably and Jacobite aspirations lay dormant until 1745 when the Young Pretender, James's son, Charles, popularly called Bonnie Prince Charlie (1720–88), landed in Scotland and penetrated as far south as Derby in England before he and his army were dispersed.

Neither George I nor his son George II (reigned 1727–60) cared much for living in Britain, and public affairs fell increasingly into the hands of ministers. Chief among these was Sir Robert Walpole (1676–1745), First Lord of the Treasury to George I and George II, and generally recognized as the first British "Prime Minister and First Lord of the Treasury." It is from Walpole's day that the British cabinet has usually been drawn from the party forming the majority in the House of Commons.

Ministers controlled not only affairs in the United Kingdom but an increasingly vast overseas empire based largely on the European demand for sugar and tobacco, and on the slave trade. By the Treaty of Paris (1763), which ended the Seven Years War between Britain and France, the United Kingdom gained Canada and all the French territories east of the Mississippi, Grenada in the West Indies, Florida, Senegal, and confirmation of her possessions in India.

Twenty years later, by another Treaty of Paris (September 23, 1783), Britain was forced to acknowledge the independence of the United States. This act represented the final repudiation of the North American policy of George III (1738–1820). Throughout the struggle with the colonists the king had displayed a stubbornness and shortsightedness that were not always characteristic of the way he tried to rule at home. By 1782, however, much of the popularity he had once enjoyed in England had waned. His acquiescent minister, Lord North, who had mismanaged the war with the colonies, resigned, and in 1783 George, whose mental instability was becoming more obvious, was forced to accept the younger William Pitt (1759–1806) as prime minister. Pitt's rise to power marked the end of any significant influence that the British sovereign could exercise over Parliament.

The loss of the United States was assuaged by the addition to the colonial map of Australia and New Zealand, discovered by Captain James Cook in 1771, and by the territories won as a result of the Napoleonic Wars, 1803–15. These wars had added two names to the long litany of English heroes: Lord Nelson, victor of the sea battle of Trafalgar on October 21, 1805, and the Duke of Wellington, who defeated Napoleon at Waterloo, June 18, 1815. The territories awarded to Britain in the subsequent carve-up of the world included Ceylon, Trinidad, Tobago, Malta, Mauritius, and the Cape Colony of South Africa.

THE INDUSTRIAL REVOLUTION

The final defeat of Napoleon naturally inspired a period of national rejoicing. It also added 400,000 men to the ranks of the unemployed — and the dissatisfied.

Since George III's accession in 1760, England had changed radically. Technology based on the use of wood for fuel and wind and water for power had given way to one in which power was based on steam, particularly for raising coal from mines. The appearance of James Watt's steam engine in 1769 marked the summit of this development.

The all-important cotton textile industry was revolutionized by a series of inventions that resulted in a tremendous increase in output. The landscape in the mining areas of the North and the Midlands changed completely. The Midland coal fields became known as the Black Country.

In Lancashire large cotton mills sprang up across the county. Birmingham, equidistant from England's main ports, became a large manufacturing center.

People poured from the countryside to find jobs in the new urban industrial areas. Legislation controlling conditions of employment was nonexistent. Women and children, as well as men, could be required to work for as long as they were able to stand up. With a pool of cheap female and child labor available, male breadwinners and their families often starved. By 1843, during Queen Victoria's reign (1837–1901), there were 200,000 inmates in workhouses.

The sort of life led by the poor in the early nineteenth century has been brilliantly described in the novels of Charles Dickens (1812–70).

REFORM

The population shifts caused by the Industrial Revolution had done nothing to change the way that Britain was represented geographically in Parliament. "Rotten boroughs" — districts where the population had declined considerably — still returned two members, whereas big industrial cities such as Birmingham elected none.

Ninety-nine percent of the 400,000 soldiers demobilized in 1815 had no vote. They were, moreover, to suffer like their fellow countrymen from two pieces of legislation designed to favor the rich, especially landowners. One was the 1815 Corn Law, which virtually excluded all foreign corn from Britain, thereby raising the price of bread. The other was the abolition in 1816 of the 10% income tax. The popular agitation, food riots, and calls for reform that followed culminated in the Peterloo Massacre of 1819, when armed horsemen cut down listeners at a large open air parliamentary reform meeting at Manchester.

The reign of George IV (1820–30) saw two pieces of legislation that signaled that Parliament and the small segment of the population that it represented (about 420,000 out of 23 million people) were resigned to change. One was a more favorable Corn Law (1828) permitting grain to be imported at any time and fixing the duties so that prices remained reasonably low. The other was the Catholic Emancipation Act (1829), which restored to Catholics many of the privileges that had been removed by the Test Act, including the right to sit in Parliament.

It was the Great Reform Bill of 1832 in the reign of William IV (1830–37) that marked the beginning of democracy in Britain. Although it added only 800,000 people to the rolls, it redistributed 143 seats. Among the large cities finally enfranchised were Manchester and Birmingham.

Parliament's social conscience prevailed. The following year, in 1833, slavery was abolished in the colonies and a Factory Act was passed forbidding the employment of children under 9 and regulating work hours.

Under two of Queen Victoria's prime ministers, Benjamin Disraeli (1804–81), a Conservative, and William Gladstone (1809–98), a Liberal, Reform Bills in 1867 and 1884 added close to 3 million male voters to the electoral rolls, most of them from the working classes.

Women over 30 were given the vote in 1918, but it was not until 1928 that they shared the franchise equally with men and were permitted to vote at 21.

The Victorian era produced a number of remarkable men and women besides those responsible for electoral reform, among them Florence Nightingale (1820–1910), the founder of modern nursing; the poet Lord Tennyson (1809–1902), who is buried in Westminster Abbey; and the social reformer Lord Shaftesbury (1801–85). It was also the era when Karl Marx (1818–83) sat for years in the Reading Room of the British Museum writing *Das Kapital* while the peaceful revolution he declared impossible got under way all around him.

The enfranchisement of urban workers under Disraeli and Gladstone resulted in the formation of the Labour Party in 1900, which has always tended to prefer a mild, pragmatic form of socialism to the more revolutionary kind proposed by Marx. Since 1924 the Labour and Conservative parties have alternated in office with almost predictable regularity except for periods of National Government — government with ministers drawn from all major parties — during times of national emergency. The last of these was from 1940 to 1945, during World War II, under the leadership of Winston Churchill (1874–1965) whose panache as a wartime leader made him a hero along the lines of Nelson and Wellington.

The House of Lords — the upper house of Parliament — lost the last vestiges of its power in 1911 during the administration of Prime Minister David Lloyd George (1863–1942). In that year the Parliament Act was passed denying the lords any power over a bill involving finance and circumscribing the delay they could exercise over other legislation.

The creation of hereditary peers (i.e., lords who can pass on to their heirs their titles and the privileges of sitting in the House of Lords) was discontinued during the 1960s when a system of life peerages was introduced to provide the chamber with able men and women who could contribute to national debates. The House still provides the government with senior ministers however. Lord Carrington, Foreign Secretary in the administration of Britain's first woman Prime Minister Margaret Thatcher (appointed 1979), is a hereditary peer who sits in the House of Lords.

The other hereditary institution, the Crown, appears likely to flourish. Victoria's heirs, Edward VII (1901–10), George V (1910–36), Edward VIII (1936; abdicated and became the duke of Windsor), George VI (1936–52), and Elizabeth II (1952–present) have all succeeded to the throne quite smoothly. Even the sting of the abdication crisis was quickly overwhelmed by the impending threat of World War II.

The monarchy today has little more than the power "to be consulted, to encourage, and to warn," as political theorist Walter Bagehot wrote in 1867. But although the monarch no longer has the right to dissolve Parliament, she has the right to refuse to dissolve it. That is to say that if a prime minister should resign because of lack of support in the House of Commons the monarch has the right to ask someone else to form a government if she believes that that person can command a majority in the House.

Perhaps the most useful function of the monarchy in the twentieth century is its role as the head of the Commonwealth, that loosely knit group of countries that were formerly a part of the British Empire.

As the ranking member of the Commonwealth and a comparatively recent member of the European Economic Community (the Common Market), Britain forms a political bridge between its former possessions and Western Europe. In addition, it still frequently serves as arbiter and mediator in disputes among and between its former possessions. British influence, though clearly diminished, remains a substantive force in world affairs.

Literature

 Until the late eighteenth century, it was fashionable for cultivated British travelers to be appalled by much of the local scenery. They dismissed mountain landscapes as "horrid" — a word that, to Latin scholars of the day, meant "uncouth" or "shaggy." They preferred to pull down the carriage blinds, or better still, to remain in London.

Then along came Wordsworth and Scott. William Wordsworth (1770–1850) set forth the Lake District as nourishment for the eye, and found in mountaintops an inspiration for the spirit. Meanwhile, Walter Scott (1771–1832) quite consciously turned the Scottish Highlands and borders to literary ends in his novels and poems. Thus, in the nineteenth century, cliffs suddenly became glamorous, mountains fashionable, and ravines a romantic enthusiasm. Nineteenth-century excursionists filled the Scottish Trossachs, armed with Scott's popular narrative poem, *The Lady of the Lake.*

Even today, our perceptions of British landscapes are shaped by the experience of literature. What would the world think of the Lake District if Wordsworth, Coleridge, and Southey had not lived and worked there? Similarly, the novels of Thomas Hardy (1840–1928) have bestowed a cosmic significance on the heaths and tumuli of Dorset: "To persons standing alone on a hill during a clear midnight such as this, the roll of the world eastward is almost a palpable movement" (*Far from the Madding Crowd*).

Authors such as Hardy impose an image of their own creation on a countryside. The reader traveling through the region cannot escape it. Is he seeing Dorset or is he experiencing Hardy's Wessex? A more fantasy-minded tourist might even pursue the haunts of the fictional characters. For example, Dorchester, where Hardy was educated and where he lived for the first 40 years of his life, is the Casterbridge of his novels; Woolbridge Manor, near Wool, has been identified as the Wellbridge Manor of *Tess of the D'Urbervilles;* and in Bindon Abbey you can see the empty stone coffin in which Angel Clare laid Tess.

The traveler in a more cheerful mood might follow Mr. Pickwick and the

Pickwick Club on their Dickensian travels. Eatanswill, of the Eatanswill Election, where Mrs. Leo Hunter gave her fancy-dress breakfast, is actually Sudbury, in Essex. And so on . . .

A BRIEF CHRONOLOGY: MEDIEVAL TIMES

"Anon." was the first English author, and among the first literary figures were monastic chroniclers who — working chiefly at Canterbury, Peterborough, and Winchester — laboriously compiled *The Anglo Saxon Chronicle,* that mixture of history, rumor, and poetry drawn from earliest times to the twelfth century. England then was a country of marsh and forest.

Chaucer (ca. 1345–1400), the author of *The Canterbury Tales,* is the first great name among English poets. He is known to have gone to France with Edward III's army, to have served in the medieval equivalent of the diplomatic service, and to have been appointed, in 1374, controller of customs in the City of London. There he lived above Aldgate, one of the eastern gateways to that then walled city. Aldgate is now just another commercial street, and the closest one can come to Chaucer is a plaque on an undistinguished building in Whitechapel that marks his former residence.

During the fifteenth century, in Westminster, William Caxton set up his famous printing press, the first in England. English literature in the vernacular was given a tremendous boost, and the reading public greatly increased. *The Canterbury Tales* was one of the works that were set on Caxton's press. Another was Sir Thomas Malory's *Le Morte d'Arthur,* a prose translation of a French story that has permeated English literature. The legend of King Arthur is memorably retold in Tennyson's *Idylls of the King* and in *Camelot,* the modern musical version. Sir Thomas wrote his Arthurian work in Newgate Prison, where the wayward knight was jailed for a variety of crimes that included assault, extortion, jail breaking, poaching, a cattle raid, armed robbery, and attempted murder. Newgate Prison is no more; the Old Bailey, London's Central Criminal Court, now stands in its place.

SHAKESPEARE AND STRATFORD-UPON-AVON

In the sixteenth century, during the reign of Queen Elizabeth, Shakespeare burst upon the stage, and the English language reeled. There are those who would argue that Shakespeare, an actor with no education beyond that provided by Stratford's grammar school, could not have written Shakespeare's plays. They must be the works of Francis Bacon — too well born to admit their authorship. Or else, they must be the works of Christopher Marlowe — too widely believed murdered in a tavern brawl to risk the publicity. But let us accept, along with the vast majority, that the Shakespeare who wrote the plays, and who seems to have coined half the English language, was that same young man who came to London from Warwickshire in the 1580s and found employment as an actor.

The Elizabethan age already was one of popular enthusiasm for the theater — an English enthusiasm that has continued to the present day. But the theaters were regarded with suspicion by city government, and so they were built in what were then the rural suburbs of London. The first, The Theatre, was erected in 1577 at Shoreditch, to the east of the city. The Globe was in Southwark, on the far bank of the Thames. Just north of the City — for sixteenth-century London has now become merely the banking quarter of a much greater whole — a blue plaque is set into a blank wall in an undistinguished street. It reads: GOOD MASTER EDWARD ALLEYN'S FORTUNE THEATRE STOOD ON A SITE NEAR HERE IN 1600.

The stage was then patronized by men of culture and by the populace, the "groundlings" — by the circle and the pit. Thus the Shakespearean plays alternated elevated themes with scenes of low comedy. With a flourish of trumpets the captains and the kings depart, stage left; enter stage right the drunken porters, the punning clowns.

Although his theatrical career was centered in or near London, Shakespeare has put Stratford-upon-Avon on the map. If Shakespeare had not been born there, Stratford would be no more than a Warwickshire market town, much like a hundred other small English towns.

In 1769 the actor David Garrick — mindful, no doubt, of how much he owed his own career to parts like Richard III — superintended the first annual celebration of Shakespeare's birthday. Stupendous rainfalls dimmed the event slightly; several persons were drowned and several events had to be abandoned. Nevertheless, the town caught on as a focus of literary pilgrimage. No building associated with Shakespeare is not a museum. The site of his own demolished house has become a memorial garden, and even Anne Hathaway's cottage has been visited by millions paying tribute to literature.

April 23, the feast day of England's patron saint, George, is also celebrated, by happy chance, as the birthday of its patron poet. On the nearest Saturday to that date, the whole town still turns to ceremony: The diplomatic corps journeys up from London; flags of all the nations are flown; processions are formed; and wreaths are laid. Even before Garrick, Stratford was becoming a place of literary enthusiasm. A subsequent owner of New Place — an imposing residence in the center of Stratford that Shakespeare bought in 1597, retired to in 1610, and died in in 1616 — was much harassed by curious tourists. Strangers would knock at his door and want to see the mulberry tree under which the great man wrote. So, in 1756, the new owner cut the mulberry tree down. (A local opportunist bought the timber and turned it into souvenirs, for which there was already a demand.) In 1759, mainly to spite his fellow townsmen, he demolished the house itself. Its site is now a garden, stocked with the trees, herbs, and flowers mentioned in the plays.

Meanwhile, the curious — having paid their orthodox respects at the tomb in Stratford Church — were already visiting Shakespeare's birthplace in Henley Street. There were no birth certificates in those days; but Stratford must be reckoned Shakespeare's birthplace, since his parents, John and Mary Shakespeare, are known to have been living there in 1564. The house was passed from his granddaughter (and last direct descendant) to his great-nephew's family, to whom it belonged until 1806. In the late eighteenth and early nineteenth century, the tenants of the house were not above exhibiting spurious relics, and at least one made a good income from favoring visitors with fragments cut from "Shakespeare's very own chair."

On Thursday, September 16, 1847, the house was put up for auction as "the truly heart-stirring relic of a most glorious period, AND OF ENGLAND'S IMMORTAL BARD." The sale was not unforeseen. Committees had been set up, and theatrical benefits and charity concerts had been held to raise money. The house was bought for £3,000.

It was a solid sixteenth-century house, half-timbered and mullioned, built of local materials. A surprising amount of the original fabric remains: the flagstones knew Shakespeare's feet; the timbers were familiar to his hand.

The original intention was to entrust the house to the government. Instead, the committees found themselves perpetuated as the Shakespeare Birthplace Committee (recognized by Act of Parliament in 1891 as the Shakespeare Birthplace Trust). Between 1857 and 1864 much was done to restore the house to its original condition. An eighteenth-century brick facing on part of the building was removed. Dormer windows were restored in accord with the evidence of the earliest engraving (published in 1769). The adjoining properties were removed to reduce the risk of fire, for when Shakespeare was born the house was part of a row.

In the ensuing years the same Trust acquired the home of Shakespeare's wife, Anne Hathaway; Hall's Croft, a medieval house in which the poet's daughter Susanna lived after her marriage; and Mary Arden's house, birthplace of the poet's mother at Wilmcote, a few miles northwest of the town. The trust has also established the Shakespeare Centre and a reference collection.

In 1879 the *Shakespeare Memorial Theatre* was built beside the river. Burned down in 1926 (the surviving library wing is a monument to the florid architectural piety of the nineteenth century), it was replaced by the present theater in 1932. This is the home of the *Royal Shakespeare Company,* which presents the plays of Shakespeare and others in both London and Stratford.

In the villages that surround Stratford, idyllic cottages are inhabited by nationally known actors and actresses. With Shakespeare himself as the principal local industry, the town has an abundance of hotels, many with Shakespearean names, and a superabundance of gift shops and craft centers.

THE SEVENTEENTH CENTURY

Meanwhile, a whole school of metaphysical poetry was flourishing — with religious subject matter; neatly turned verse; and sharp, direct, and often elaborate metaphor. John Donne (1573–1631) was the central figure among these poets. In youth he was a dissolute man about town; in age, a saintly City preacher and dean of St. Paul's Cathedral. You will find his effigy in St. Paul's — it is one of the few monuments to have survived the 1666 Fire of London. Characteristically, he sat for it in life, wearing his shroud.

Donne was the first chaplain of Lincoln's Inn, one of the Inns of Court to which English barristers belong. Each of the Inns of Court has many literary associations, for many English authors have studied law. An appetite for the picturesque will take the visitor to London to Lincoln's Inn. There, when a senior member dies, it is the custom for the chapel bell to be tolled, and the visitor might call to mind Donne's most celebrated lines: "Never send to know for whom the bell tolls; it tolls for thee."

The seventeenth century was also the time of John Milton (1608–74), a giant in English literature, a university man (Christ's College, Cambridge), and a poet in Latin and Hebrew as well as English. Born in London, Milton lived there when he wrote *Paradise Lost* and its sequel, *Paradise Regained.* He was buried in St. Giles, Cripplegate, a medieval church that survives in the middle of the extravagantly modern architecture of London's Barbican. He was a first-rate scholar, and one of the last men ever to master just about all that was known. (Today, of course, that is impossible.) When he was a very young man, he decided to become the greatest English poet of all time — and he did.

THE EIGHTEENTH CENTURY

A dominant figure of the second half of the eighteenth century was Dr. Samuel Johnson (a doctor of laws) — essay writer, pamphleteer, novelist, and author of the very influential *Dictionary of the English Language* (1755). Dr. Johnson is, perhaps, most renowned as one of the greatest conversationalists who ever lived. Fortunately, much of his talk was faithfully recorded for us by his biographer, James Boswell. To cite just one example, Dr. Johnson once declared, with typical authority, "When a man is tired of London, he is tired of life, for there is in London all that life can afford."

This man, who rejoiced so vigorously in the sociability of literary London, lived for a time (1749–59) in a house in Gough Square, an alley to the north of Fleet Street. That house still stands and here the visitor may intrude into the past, for it is open to the public. The house contains not only a collection of portraits and letters but also something much less tangible, the flavor of the man's life.

THE NINETEENTH CENTURY

The last century was a time of many literary greats — so many, that we cannot even attempt to mention all of them. They ranged from the Romantic poets — Wordsworth, Coleridge, Byron, Shelley, and Keats — to such novelists as Charles Dickens, the Brontë sisters, and Jane Austen. It can hardly have occurred to Jane Austen that Chawton Cottage, where she lived from 1809 to 1817, would become a place of public show, for her work was secret and her novels were published anonymously. Jane Austen died in obscurity in 1817, at the age of 42.

The cottage still stands in the Hampshire village of Chawton, where Austen lived with her widowed mother and her sister Cassandra. Today it is owned by the Jane Austen Trust. While living there she revised *Sense and Sensibility* and *Pride and Prejudice* and wrote *Emma* and *Persuasion.* She worked in the common sitting room, where she was always ready to slip her paper under a blotter when she heard that famous creak of the door. (The door is there; the creak has gone.) This sitting room, though a small and unassuming room in a small and seemly house, has seen the creation of those perfect portraits of provincial life and universal character.

Long before the Austens moved in and fitted it up, Chawton Cottage may have been a posting inn; the road that idles past was then the main road to Winchester. It is known that the house declined into laborers' dwellings before it was restored by the Trust. Today, however, it is as nearly as possible the house that Jane Austen knew. Some of the original furniture has found its way back. On the table stands part of a dinner service whose purchase is recorded in a surviving letter. Her bedroom upstairs still overlooks the yard, the bakehouse/laundry, and the outhouse containing her mother's donkey cart.

There may be souvenirs on sale in the parlor, letters in frames on the walls, yet one feels that at any moment Jane Austen may return from walking up to the big house. No matter that the village pond opposite has long been filled in. No matter that the motorway whines past a few hundred yards away.

A scant mile from Chawton is the town of Alton, with its main street bedizened with shopfronts. Here it is still possible to imagine the younger Miss Bennets (*Pride and Prejudice*) walking in search of officers, to imagine good Miss Bates (*Emma*) about her marketing.

Finally, there is Bath — the place where nearly all her marvelous characters "take the waters." Before she moved to Chawton and after her father retired from his rectorship, Jane Austen's family actually lived in Bath. One of their homes, 4 Sydney Place, is marked with a plaque. The beauty of Bath today is that so little has changed. Fashionable society abandoned Bath in about 1840 and began to take other waters abroad. So where the honeyed stone terraces of the eighteenth century end, the suburbs of the 1920s begin. Apart from a vast new hotel in the center of town, few thought it worthwhile to tear down, redevelop, or embellish nineteenth-century Bath.

If Jane Austen were to do anything so uncharacteristic as to haunt a place, her sprightly specter in sprigged muslin would find everything in Bath just as she remembered it. And one could do worse than follow her as one's guide — to walk, "with great elasticity," down Milsom Street with Catherine Morland, to wait opposite Union Passage for John Thorpe to pull up in his gig, to loiter outside the Pump Room until Isabella and Catherine appear in hotly indifferent pursuit of young men (all from *Northanger Abbey*) . . . or to enter the Assembly Rooms and see exactly where Anne Elliot encountered Captain Wentworth (*Persuasion*).

Bath remains to this day a trim, precise city, peopled by characters, whether fictional or historic, who lived at precise addresses. Dickens's Mr. Pickwick and his party settled in lodgings in Royal Crescent; Mr. Pickwick, like Isabella and Catherine, frequented the Pump Room. It was out of a house in Royal Crescent that his friend Mr. Winkle was locked while only half awake and half dressed. It was from No. 11 Royal Crescent that the playwright Sheridan went off with the singer Elizabeth Linley. Does it matter which is fiction and which is fact?

Fiction has inspired many a reader to dream about the Yorkshire moors. The most renowned of these dreamers, the nineteenth-century American poet Emily Dickinson, wrote "I never saw a moor/I never saw the sea" —

and indeed, she never did. Airplane and railroad, however, have brought many a twentieth-century visitor to the heather-studded moors.

And with good reason. Even if the domineering Reverend Patrick Brontë had never been incumbent of the Yorkshire village of Haworth in the 1840s, the moors around it would now be accounted scenic. But the Reverend Mr. Brontë had three daughters (not to mention a dissolute son who was Emily's model for the fictional Heathcliff). By writing *Wuthering Heights, Jane Eyre,* and *The Tenant of Wildfell Hall,* Emily, Charlotte, and Ann Brontë imbued mere topography with literary associations and implications; and the Brontë Society, restoring the parsonage and opening it to the public, has turned a minor entry in the gazetteer into an international shrine.

You can draw your own map of nineteenth-century literary Britain — almost infinitely. For example, Salisbury in Wiltshire is a much visited town. It has a cathedral; it has history; it has Stonehenge nearby. But as good a reason as any for visiting Salisbury is the small fact that "wandering one midsummer evening round the purlieus of Salisbury Cathedral," Anthony Trollope (1815–82) "conceived the story of *The Warden.*" And from *The Warden* grew all of Trollope's Barchester novels.

Thomas Hardy's birthplace is a small thatched cottage on the outskirts of Dorchester. It is approached by a 10-minute walk through woods; the interior is open by appointment only, and then only the parlor.

No doubt the greatest English novelist of all, however, was Charles Dickens, whose work greatly influenced a legion of writers — including one as remote from him in time and place as Dostoyevsky. Dickens began life as a journalist and wrote his novels at a hectic rate in weekly parts. Like Shakespeare, Dickens was enormously popular. Many thousands of readers on both sides of the Atlantic eagerly awaited those weekly installments.

Dickens (1812–70) lived much of his life in London. The tourist who goes down to the Thames at Blackfriars where the cars now speed along the riverbank, cannot be sure whether he is seeking out the young David Copperfield, sent to wash and label bottles at Murdstone and Grinby's warehouse, or the young Charles Dickens, miserably employed in a blacking factory a little farther upstream. But success came to the young Dickens, and he established his reputation — with the completion of *The Pickwick Papers* and the writing of *Oliver Twist* and *Nicholas Nickleby* — at about the time he, his wife, and his young son came to live at No. 48 Doughty Street, near the Gray's Inn Road (1837). The house, now owned by the Dickens Fellowship, is open to the public.

Walter Scott (1771–1832), as any traveler in Scotland discovers, made much of this country in his own image, or at least in the image of ancient romance, which he marshaled in his novels. His novels take the characters of history — some of it quite recent in his day — and turn them into a more compelling reality. It would be difficult for many people to say whether the character of, for example, Jeannie Deans, heroine of *The Heart of Midlothian,* was an invention or not. For it is a novel, like so many of Scott's, full of real events (in this case Edinburgh's Porteous Riots of 1736) and historical characters, among them Queen Caroline.

One finds the same imprecision about location. In *The Bride of Lammer-*

moor the castle, Wolf's Crag, is taken by many to be Fast Castle on the east coast. The author himself wrote evasively that the position of Fast Castle "seems certainly to resemble that of Wolf's Crag as much as any other, while its vicinity to the mountain ridge of Lammermoor renders the assimilation a probable one." (Mountain ridge is a bit steep for the Lammermuir Hills, but that is the effect that Scott has on scenery.) Certainly Ellen's Isle in Loch Katrine owes much of its fame to its part in *The Lady of the Lake.*

There is no imprecision about Scott's own residences. For most of his active life he lived in Edinburgh, at 39 Castle Street, a house identified by a small statuette above the door. Otherwise, it is inaccessible, for it is now a legal office. From there, having made a fortune and lost it, he finally retired to the baronial pile he had designed at Abbotsford, near Galashiels. This is now a monument to Scott the novelist and antiquarian, opened to the public by his descendants.

Relics of Scott, Robert Louis Stevenson, and Robert Burns are in Edinburgh in a museum called Lady Stair's House, romantically situated in an alley off the High Street. Much of Burns's literary output was produced in Edinburgh, although Ayrshire, from whence he came, and to which he returned, is scattered with memorials to him, and places associated with him.

Robert Louis Stevenson (1850–94) was perhaps the writer who described the city of Edinburgh with the greatest sympathy. He was born at 8 Howard Place, then on the northern fringes of the town, but grew up at 17 Heriot Row, just across Queen Street Gardens from 39 Castle Street. From the Heriot Row windows he looked down on Leerie the lamplighter (*A Child's Garden of Verses*). In consumptive adulthood he lived in Bournemouth (Hardy's Sandbourne), in America, and in Samoa. But he always looked back to Edinburgh.

Even *Treasure Island* is said to have its Edinburgh associations: The map of the island, it is claimed, was based on an island in a small ornamental pond in Queen Street Gardens. *Kidnapped,* that most Scottish of books, follows the Lowlander David Balfour in his flight with Alan Breck, during the aftermath of the Jacobite uprising of 1745. *Kidnapped* is an exhilarating adventure yarn, but its account of the journey from the western coast of Mull, through Appin, over Rannoch Moor and down through Balquhidder to Stirling also constitutes an excellent guidebook for any visitor to the Highlands.

THE TWENTIETH CENTURY

The London of today has grown into an amorphous region. But even its remotest suburb has some literary interest, some chance association with authorship. Among its greatest literary interpreters have been Charles Dickens and Virginia Woolf. The novels of Dickens were written at a journalistic gallop; Virginia Woolf composed hers with agonizing care. Her novels are often accounted "difficult," but in them, and in her shorter writings, she creates a scene, composed of random moments in time, which lives more strongly than the actual streets she is describing. One cannot board a No. 11 bus down the Strand without remembering Elizabeth Dalloway's taking an impetuous, allusive omnibus ride from Westminster to Chancery Lane (*Mrs. Dalloway*).

Virginia Woolf was a Londoner. She was born, in 1882, at 22 Hyde Park Gate, a tall confident house that still overlooks the south side of the park. After her father's death she moved to Bloomsbury, living first with her brother and sister, later with her husband, Leonard Woolf, in a number of houses: 46 Gordon Square, 29 Fitzroy Square, 52 Tavistock Square (Dickens, too, had once lived in this square; both their houses have been demolished), and finally in Mecklenburgh Square.

Her eye was acute, and her imagination imposed its own enhancing order on the streets and squares of the London of 60 years ago. In *Mrs. Dalloway* she has pinned down Mayfair — every brick, every leaf — on an early summer morning. In *Night and Day* and *Jacob's Room* she has done the same for the Strand, Bloomsbury, and Holborn.

There may be little of the picturesque in the town of Eastwood and the Nottinghamshire coalfields, but D. H. Lawrence was not only born there but set many of his novels in the area and peopled the novels with characters drawn from life. You can walk the streets of Eastwood and pass from *The White Peacock* to *Women in Love* to *Sons and Lovers.* Here, in Devonshire Drive, is the very house in which the Brangwen sisters lived. Here at Gresley, just a few hundred yards off the M1 motorway, is the church where they came to watch the wedding (*Women in Love*) . . .

The nineteenth century was the great age of English theater. Ornate palaces were built in every suburb and provincial town and theatrical companies toured the country by way of the recently developed railways. However, the nineteenth century produced no great playwrights until the last couple of decades, when Oscar Wilde and George Bernard Shaw began to write for the stage.

Yet Shaw, who lived until 1950, rightly belongs to the twentieth century. And it was Shaw himself, with that unflappable sense of his own importance, who left his house at Ayot St. Lawrence, just north of London, to the National Trust. This was his home from 1906 until 1950, and it came to the Trust exactly as he had lived in it, with his books, his papers, and his furniture.

Harold Nicolson's *Diaries and Letters* records the rather macabre story of how he, as Chairman of the Trust, went down to inspect Shaw's bequest in 1950. There he found "all his hats, and coats and nailbrushes etc." and, on the garden paths, spread a few days before, the ashes of Shaw himself, "like the stuff put down for slugs."

BLUE PLAQUES
AND THE NATIONAL TRUST

Unleashed on his or her literary trail, a visitor to London will find a number of buildings marked with blue commemorative plaques. Some, on modern structures, merely hint that someone — Coleridge or Dryden — "lived in a house on this site." Others designate a surviving house: These very steps up to this very door represented security to some great writer; this doorknob was familiar to his or her hand; these, perhaps, were the very panes of glass through which he or she viewed the passing world. A few literary figures are remembered by more than a plaque affixed to a wall. The National Trust is the custodian of many a literary shrine; it preserves and opens to the public such important homes as No. 24 Cheyne Row, London, where Thomas Carlyle lived from 1834 until his death in 1881; Wordsworth's birthplace in Cockermouth, Cumbria; and Lamb's House, Rye, East Sussex, where Henry James spent the summers from 1898 until his death in 1916, and where he wrote *The Ambassadors* and *The Golden Bowl.*

Architecture

Britain has castles and cathedrals that can hold their own with those of Europe, but its domestic architecture — stately homes, farms, cottages, and parish churches — best expresses the character of the people and the progress of British life through the ages. Many stately homes are open to the public and can be visited and viewed in detail. Take a half-day's trip out of London — no matter the direction — and you can enjoy the rich heritage of old homes and cottages that everywhere remain part of Britain's daily life. Many a village pub — where you can stop for a beer, lunch at the bar, or partake of a more formal dining room repast — will date from Elizabethan times or earlier. (Some say the Old Chesil Rectory pub at Winchester is the oldest in the country.)

Many of these indigenous buildings have grown or have been altered over the years, so that their style is not pure, nor their history unalloyed. Tales of their derivation may be as varied as the people you talk to about them — but their authenticity and their central role in the life of their localities are beyond dispute.

Walk through the village streets, go into the pubs, spend some moments in the parish churches, and you will begin to experience the flavor of English life, as articulated in its buildings. Get off the main road, take almost any byroad in Kent, Surrey, or Sussex, and you will be surprised at the number of old village centers that survive on the very fringes of the major metropolitan areas in this very crowded land.

Remains of Roman villas can be seen here and there in England; a particularly fine one is found at Bignor in Sussex.

In addition, quite a number of Saxon churches or parts of churches survive in England, predating the Norman Conquest of 1066. The earliest Saxon churches were built of timber with neither aisles nor towers. Later versions, such as Bradford on Avon in Wiltshire or Earl's Barton in Northamptonshire, have blunt, crudely decorated towers and reproduce in stone the earlier types of wooden ornamentation. An interesting part-Saxon church, in the attractive sailing village of Bosham on Chichester Harbour, Sussex, is said to commemorate the spot where the Saxon king Canute "told the sea to go back." And many churches in East Anglia have the round towers that hark back to Saxon times.

Brought in by William the Conqueror in 1066, Norman architecture is equivalent to the style known on the Continent as Romanesque. In Britain, the Norman period extended from the Conquest to the latter part of the twelfth century, when the Gothic style was born. Norman abbey churches and cathedrals are numerous in England, for the period of the conquest was a period of building and rebuilding.

Romanesque structures of this period are typically heavy and solid, with round arches. Architectural historian Nikolaus Pevsner described their Englishness as "an articulation . . . that conveys to us at once a feeling of certainty and stability . . . There is no wavering here — as there was none in the ruthless policy of William the Conquerer in subduing and normalizing England. Blunt, massive, and overwhelmingly strong are the individual forms which architects used in these early buildings, sacred as well as secular."

Winchester Cathedral (1080–90) is an example of early Norman architecture; Durham Cathedral (1093–1130) is High Romanesque. The latter anticipates the Gothic style in its vaulting over the choir. This is probably the earliest example of rib vaulting in Europe. Pevsner cites the White Tower at the Tower of London and the keep of Colchester Castle in Essex as examples of the massive, almost brutal English secular architecture of the Norman period.

During the latter part of the twelfth century Gothic architecture flowered in England as it did in Europe. With its pointed arches, flying buttresses, fully developed rib vaulting, and its elaborate stained glass windows, this style introduced a new concept of religious space. The Gothic combined structural clarity with a coherent expression of interior space and an honest use of materials. So much engineering skill was martialed in its soaring surge toward heaven, that even today "Gothic" and "cathedral" are almost synonymous in most people's minds.

The earliest English example of developed Gothic is the east end of Canterbury Cathedral, which was started by William Sens in 1175. Lincoln (begun 1192) and Salisbury (about 1220) are fine, mature examples of the early English Gothic period. Wells (dedicated in 1239), with its carved west front, was one of the few to escape the ravages of Oliver Cromwell. In the fourteenth century its famous inverted arches were added to support the tower, which was then in danger of collapse.

Wells marks the transition to the decorated style of the middle Gothic period. This was the period when the famous octagon at Ely Cathedral was built to replace an earlier tower that had collapsed into the church. (Some of the most dramatic feats of ecclesiastical architecture were corrections of earlier structural deficiencies!) Many of the boldest and most celebrated castles in Wales were also erected at the end of the thirteenth century, among them Harlech, Conway, and Caernarvon.

The Gothic period went out with the perpendicular style, which was almost the antithesis of its immediate predecessor. Here the emphasis was on strong, simple vertical and horizontal elements, large windows with fine, repetitive tracery, and fan vaulting. St. George's Chapel, Windsor (1474), and King's College Chapel, Cambridge (1446–1515), are supreme examples of this architectural period. Do not miss King's College Chapel. The whole of Cambridge, easily accessible by train from London, is well worth a visit — but King's College Chapel, with its powerfully simple exterior and delicately ornate interior, speaks directly to the heart. If you get there in the afternoon, try to catch evensong at about 3 or 3:30, sung in candlelight by one of the finest men-and-boy's choirs in the world.

The return to classical (especially Italian) principles and influences, known as the Renaissance, swept Europe in the fifteenth century, began to appear in England during the reign of Henry VII, and took hold in the reign of Henry VIII.

Throughout the Tudor and Jacobean periods, several influences combined to shape English architecture: the devotion to large, mullioned windows, typical of the perpendicular Gothic style; the French and Italian Renaissance preoccupation with symmetry; and decorative motifs — especially an ornamentation known as strap-work, that originated in the Netherlands. Longleat House in Wiltshire (1568), Hardwick Hall in Derbyshire (1591–97), Hatfield House in Hertfordshire (1608–12), and Audley End in Essex (1603) each in its own way demonstrates a balance between these architectural forces.

Inigo Jones (1573–1652) — painter, stage designer, and architect — introduced the purity of Palladian forms to English architecture, marking this important transition with his Queen's House, Greenwich (1616). But it was Sir Christopher Wren (1632–1723), England's most renowned architect, who created England's own unique expression of classical and baroque architecture. Wren's masterpieces are fortunately very much in evidence today, notably St. Paul's Cathedral and numerous fine city churches. Many of Wren's structures suffered severe damage in the blitz of World War II, and have since been faithfully restored and rebuilt.

The classical purity of Palladianism reappeared in Bath, with John Wood the Elder's (1704–54) planning of Queen Square and with his son John Wood the Younger's (1728–81) design of Royal Crescent. Also in the classical tradition was John Nash (1752–1835), whose Regent Street and Regent's Park frontages in London are world famous. There are Georgian or Regency Squares in many cities, but perhaps the most beautiful are in Dublin. These too are designed in the spirit of classical symmetry.

Architecturally, the late eighteenth century and most of the nineteenth century must be characterized as a period of historical revival and a looking back to the past for inspiration. At first, neoclassicism appeared with a return to "first principles," meaning the nobility and simplicity of Greek art. As the nineteenth century advanced, neoclassicism was abandoned in favor of the revival of specific — and sometimes superficially applied — styles of the past.

Pattern books were produced to enable architects to provide their patrons with buildings designed in the style of their choice, whether this was Gothic, Norman Provincial, Greek Revival, or French Renaissance. Among the eighteenth- and nineteenth-century stylistic revivals, however, there were vigorous and original architects and approaches to architecture, that, to some extent, anticipated the future. Robert Adam (1728–92), generally considered a master of the purest neoclassical expression, in fact interpreted Greek and Roman themes in a highly personal way. His Syon House, Middlesex, is an example of the delicacy of his detail and the transparent quality of his space. Sir John Soane (1753–1837), who clothed his buildings in overtly neoclassical forms, could not quite conceal his romantic and picturesque leanings. His No. 13 Lincoln's Inn Fields, London (now the Sir John Soane Museum), is not to be missed.

At the same time, in the mid-nineteenth century, another influence was sweeping away much of the fabric of the past. Industrialization brought new construction techniques, using iron and glass with apparently limitless possibilities, and causing as much anxiety as optimism. Joseph Paxton exploited this technology in his daring design of the famed and ill-fated Crystal Palace (1851). Structural tours de force were also displayed in a number of new iron bridges.

Initially, these developments caused architects to retreat in fear into increasingly effete imitations of the past, leaving the real breakthroughs in design to the engineers. But ultimately, modern architecture was born in response to both the perils and the challenges of the machine.

At first this response took the form of an attempt to master or to arrest the power of the machine by a deliberate return to hand craftsmanship in every aspect of life. Author, art critic, and social reformer John Ruskin thought that handicrafts would reawaken the medieval pride in collective work and ameliorate the impersonal effects of industrialization. And in 1861, British designer, socialist, and poet William Morris formed the Arts and Crafts Movement, which aimed to bring the beauty of individual craftsmanship into every home in the land. Morris's home, The Red House at Bexley Heath in Kent, was designed by Philip Webb in 1859, and set a standard for the picturesque style of residential architecture that was to follow.

Richard Norman Shaw (1831–1912) and Charles Annesley Voysey (1857–1941) were the chief exponents of the picturesque architectural style. Sometimes, a certain austerity appeared in their work that can be regarded as foreshadowing the modern movement in England. In Glasgow, Charles Rennie Mackintosh (1868–1928) was also influenced by Morris, and created his own highly original, historically premodern designs. His most notable works include the tea shops he did for Miss Cranston and the now-famous Glasgow School of Art (1897–99).

Two parallel developments, the work of the Chicago School in America, and that of the Bauhaus in Germany, finally brought modern architecture to the attention of the whole world. In Chicago in the 1880s and 1890s, the skyscraper evolved — a tall building with steel skeletons that removed any load-bearing function from the walls. A parallel development was the elevator. These two inventions changed the face of corporate architecture.

At about the same time, at the Bauhaus in Germany, architect Walter Gropius (1883–1969) was introducing a new architectural aesthetic based on industrial technology and modern materials. He preached the doctrine that a building's form must be lean and clean, derived from and expressive of its essential function.

Britain was comparatively slow to embrace the international style of the modern movement. However, in the 1950s, such men as Sir Leslie Martin, Eric Lyons, and Lord Llewelyn-Davies were pioneers in prefabricated schools and housing. The postwar housing at Roehampton has achieved world renown. Britain has also been in the vanguard of modern town planning, taking a leadership role in the evolution of the concept of the garden city or the new town. These self-contained communities do not depend, as the typical suburbs do, on London or on other metropolitan centers. Sir Ebenezer Howard (1850–

1928) was the father of this movement, and Letchworth, started in 1903, was the earliest garden city and is worth a visit. Welwyn Garden City, Hampstead Garden Suburb, and, more recently, Cumbernauld New Town in Scotland, are interesting examples of the evolution of the idea of the new town.

The bombing of London, especially in the area around St. Paul's, created opportunities for postwar urban development. A number of high-rise towers have been built, against the strenuous opposition of those who viewed them as destructive to London's lovely skyline, and to the scale and environmental quality of the city. The towers have gone up, nonetheless, though few have any architectural distinction. The Barbican Development, the new Stock Exchange, and Chartered Accountants Hall are some of the most interesting high-rises in the City of London area. New Zealand House, Thamesmead, Brunswick Center, The Economist Building, and the Institutes of Education and Law are also new London buildings worth a second look.

Having attempted in a few short pages to trace the history and development of English architecture — with its chief exponents and some pivotal buildings of each period — we must return to the starting point — to England's domestic architecture. The grand and not-so-grand country houses, the town squares, the villages, country towns, inns, and farmhouses — these are the soul of English architecture. One sees them wherever one travels. Many grand and more modest houses are open to the public. Although there are a number of books about them, the best source of basic information is the British National Trust, which owns and operates so many.

As you travel through England, you will be struck by regional differences in building styles and materials. If you study some of these buildings, you will learn something about their local character and about the periods of their origin. Especially striking are the black-and-white timbered houses of Cheshire and Shropshire. Gawsworth Hall near Macclesfield, Little Moreton Hall near Congleton, and the Feathers Inn, Ludlow, are three of the finest. In Kent, the oasthouses for drying the hops to make beer are indigenous architectural forms worth a detour to see.

The Cotswolds (chiefly Gloucestershire) are noted for the yellowish-gray stone used on almost all buildings, old and new. Some Cotswold villages, such as Bibury, Broadway, Castle Combe, and Stow-on-the-Wold represent English vernacular architecture at its most enchanting. Here brick, flint, tile, slate, timber, and thatch make their appearance throughout the country. Their color palettes and patterns weave themselves into their background with an environmental integrity that we strive for in modern forms and materials and cannot find.

Traditional Music and Dance

 There's more to dance in Britain than Scotland's Highland Fling: England and Wales both have traditions of their own which mirror distinctive cultures. It all adds up to a rich inheritance — surprising, perhaps, in so small an island.

The origins of British ceremonial dance are said to lie in pagan and primitive rituals — in magic and myths, in seasonal celebrations, and in fertility and luck-bringing rites. Historians argue about dates and derivations, but certainly some of the oldest surviving ceremonial dances are rooted in the Stone, Neolithic, and Iron ages. Later the dances were variously influenced by the invading Celts, Jutes, Angles, Saxons, and Scandinavians.

Probably the earliest music for dance was provided by the chanting of the dancers, and rhythmic sounds produced on any domestic or hunting implements at hand. Primitive instruments included drums, bagpipes, other pipes such as flute and recorder, and reed instruments.

In pagan times ritual dancing was essential to existence, and later both ritual and social folk dances were enjoyed as a form of merrymaking and as a relief from the daily battle for survival. The early Christian church abhorred pagan revelry, as did the Puritans in later times, but neither group succeeded in putting an end to dancing. It was the Industrial Revolution in the nineteenth century that did the most damage, shifting communities toward a more impersonal lifestyle. All was not lost, however.

Imagine a tranquil village amidst England's verdant Oxfordshire countryside on a warm spring day, the village green lined with spectators intently watching six dancing men who are dressed in white trousers and shirts, with bells tied below their knees, wearing black bowler hats decorated with flowers and ribbons, and carrying white handkerchiefs. In this scene you have one of the most famous of all surviving English ritual ceremonial dances, the Cotswold morris.

The costume described is the one worn by the Bampton morris dancers, who perform annually in Bampton each Spring Bank Holiday Monday. The dancers are accompanied by a single musician, playing either a fiddle or a melodeon (a Viennese accordion), and by two "characters," one of whom bears a cake impaled on a sword and the other, a Fool, who carries a pig's bladder and teases people. The whole performance is wrapped in an atmosphere of jollity, with everyone reacting good-humoredly to the Fool's mocking taunts and acting as if they believe that tasting the cake will bring good luck.

There are other traditional Cotswold morris teams near Bampton, which also perform locally in spring and summer, in Abingdon, Chipping Camden, and Headington. The dancers usually wear white costumes, black shoes, and bells; they carry either handkerchiefs or, for use in rhythmic "combat," wooden sticks — but there are many differences in the colorful accessories peculiar to the individual teams. There are variations too in each team's dances, and although the steps themselves are simple, the skill lies in coping with the changing rhythms and patterns; any irregular ringing of the bells soon draws attention to the offender. Though the dancers are amateurs they take enormous pride in their performances.

No one is certain whence came the word *morris*. There was a widely held belief that it derived from the dark-skinned Moors of Spain, and though this is now dismissed, it did seem to make sense in connection with another tradition, the Processional Morris of the Britannia Coconut Dancers, for which the dancers blacken their faces.

The Britannia Coconut Dancers or, as they are often called, the Britannia Nutters, perform throughout the Saturday before Easter in the Lancashire town of Bacup. The eight men of the team carry mill bobbins and garlands of colorful rags. They dress in a ritual disguise of white hats, red and white decorated shirts, black breeches, long white socks, and clogs, and dance through the streets to the accompaniment of a brass band.

Since the sixteenth century traditional instruments that accompanied morris dancing have been the pipe and tabor (a small drum), which are played simultaneously by a single musician; but fiddles, melodeons, and concertinas are also popular nowadays.

Sword dances are a tradition of the northeast, having developed in all probability from the weapon dances of the ancient Romans, which in turn were once part of a pagan rite possibly even older than the forerunners of the morris dance. Sword dances used to be associated with sword plays, and though the plays as such have now disappeared the dances still contain an element of drama that is exemplified by the retention of characters such as Tommy (a king) and Betsy (a half-man, half-woman creature).

There are two distinct types of sword dance, the long sword (stiff), which is danced in Flamborough (Humberside), Grenoside and Handsworth (South Yorkshire), and Loftus, Skelton, and Guisborough (Cleveland); and the short or rapper sword (flexible), which is the specialty of the Royal Earsdon Sword Dancers at Earsdon near Newcastle-on-Tyne.

The steps consist of complex mixtures of walks, runs, and (in the rapper) fast "jigging with shuffles." Swords are linked to symbolize the unbroken ring of life, and periodically they are plaited together into a many-sided lock, which is then held up by the captain of the team for the approval of the crowd. The rapper sword dance has no counterpart elsewhere. It is a more athletic dance than the long sword dance, which might be said to resemble the style of "soldiers at the double."

Sword dances are performed between Boxing Day (the first weekday after Christmas) and Plough Monday (the first or second Monday in January), to the accompaniment of a single musician with pipe, accordion, or fiddle, by teams of five to eight men. Dancers wear either military-type uniforms or white shirts and stylish versions of miners' "long shorts" with colorful sashes and rosettes for decoration.

The 'Obby 'Oss Procession may be seen in two towns in the West Country: Padstow (Cornwall) and Minehead (Somerset). Both ceremonies are held in early May and involve men dressed as horses parading through the town with their attendants. Of the two, the Padstow 'Obby 'Oss ceremony on May 1 is the more celebrated. It starts at midnight the night before when selected "mayers" go round the town singing, and then early next morning they decorate the streets with festive greenery. The 'Oss emerges midmorning and dances through the streets for the rest of the day accompanied by the mayers, a teaser, and a memorable May Day tune, played on melodeons, accordions, and drums. Superstition plays an integral part in these dances, and the locals enter into the ceremonies with enthusiasm, convinced that the 'osses are lucky.

Each year, on the first Monday after the first Sunday after September 4, you can see the ancient Abbots Bromley (Staffordshire) horn dance. It is believed to have originally been a fertility ritual, but this is played down nowadays — the villagers prefer to associate it more with the traditions of the deer hunt. Six male dancers, dressed in Tudor costume, carry reindeer horns, and since three are clothed in white and three in black it is supposed that they symbolize good and evil. Four characters escort the dancers, the Fool, the Hobby Horse, the Maid Marian (a man-woman figure), and Robin Hood with his bow and arrow, and they all parade through the village streets entertaining the crowds with plenty of dancing and tomfoolery. The Horse ensures that the two musicians with melodeon and triangle are kept up to snuff by persistently and rhythmically clacking his jaws!

There is another form of dance tradition in England quite separate from these ritual ceremonial dances, the social or country dances. These are done purely for enjoyment, by men and women together, and even by children. They developed in the rural communities and, quite separately, in the ballrooms and drawing rooms of the aristocracy.

Among the most popular country dances were those which celebrated May Day. To this day people still enjoy the traditions that have developed from the old customs, such as dancing round the Maypole and choosing the May Queen. Oldest of all the surviving dances is the world-famous Helston furry dance, which is performed each year on or about May 8 in Helston (Cornwall) to celebrate the passing from darkness (winter) into light (spring). The dance, which is accompanied by the Helston Town Band, is processional and during the day there are three separate processions: for children, for formally dressed adults, and for anyone in the mood to make merry.

In the sixteenth century court dances were formal and dignified, but during the reign of Elizabeth I the courtiers were introduced to rustic dances, first as entertainment and then for participation; and almost inevitably the traditions began to mingle and lived on under the collective title of country dances.

These dances enjoyed their greatest popularity in the eighteenth century, after which they gradually went out of favor. In the early twentieth century they were revived by Cecil Sharp. With tireless enthusiasm he collected and chronicled hundreds of dances, tunes, and songs. He founded the English Folk Dance Society, which later became the English Folk Dance and Song Society and which rekindled interest everywhere. From this countless affiliated clubs have sprung, and nowadays you may be sure that every night somewhere in town or country there are informal dances or *ceilidhs* (evenings of traditional music, song, and dance).

If you come to England looking for folk dance and music you would do well to begin your search at Cecil Sharp House, home of the English Folk Dance and Song Society (2 Regents Park Rd., London NW1 7AY, phone: 485-2206). They welcome visitors and will let you browse in the library among the specialized books (predominantly British and American). There are also magazines, photographs, tapes, pamphlets advertising events and festivals, and a bookshop — and if you peep into the main hall you may even see some dancing! Overseas members currently pay an annual subscription of £5.85.

In Scotland there are no longer either ritual ceremonial dances or dance-dramas: The only traditional dances that survive come from the Highlands and undoubtedly most famous of all is the Highland fling.

The name comes from the flinging action made by the working foot as it moves sharply inward to the lower calf of the supporting leg. Though its origins probably lie in battle traditions it is an elegant dance. But there must be a "fire in the feet," and the dancer, his weight balanced on his toes, must make intricate cutting, beating, kicking, and flinging movements with enough verve and agility to astonish his audience.

Seann triubhs ("shabby trousers") is another favorite Highland dance. It is said that during the '45 Rebellion (the Jacobite uprising of 1745) men had to wear tartan trews (trousers) instead of kilts, and this dance is symbolic of that period and the attempts that were made to "shake off" the trousers. However much truth there is in that story, *seann triubhs* is an extremely graceful traveling dance that mixes cutting, beating, and kicking movements with pirouettes, balances, and attractive circlings of the arms.

There is only one hilt-and-point sword dance in Scotland that resembles the English tradition: the Papa Stour sword dance, still performed in the Shetland Island of Papa Stour. The Highland sword dance is performed between the angles made by two swords placed on the ground in the form of a cross, and though the dancer must show plenty of vigor he also has to be extremely delicate so as to avoid touching the swords with his feet as they beat, step, and jump.

Elaborate costumes are worn for these dances, consisting of kilt, velvet jacket (or shirt and tie), plaids (lengths of tartan placed over the shoulders), a sporran (animal-skin pouch) attached to a chain round the waist, and ghillies (soft flat black shoes). Women wear similar costumes, but without the sporran. Traditionally the most popular accompanying instrument is the bagpipe, though jew's-harp, fiddle, and melodeon are also common. The best place to see Highland dancing is at one of the many Highland Games that take place between mid-July and mid-September. The Games of Braemar and Dunoon are especially popular for dancing.

Just when country dances began to go out of vogue in England in the early nineteenth century they became immensely popular in Scotland, and have remained so to this day, although had it not been for the formation in 1923 of the Scottish Country Dance Society, less authenticity might have prevailed.

These dances are vivacious or graceful, and in the main they fall into three groups, strathspeys, reels, and jigs, with hundreds of variations of each. The men wear kilts and the women white dresses and tartan sashes. Originally the bagpipe was the most popular accompanying instrument, but it has now been superseded by the fiddle.

Scottish country dancing has a worldwide following these days, and many foreign visitors join the (now) Royal Scottish Country Dance Society's annual summer school at St. Andrews. There are performances and casual gatherings all over Scotland throughout the year as well as competitions, festivals, and displays at Highland Games. During the summer months, there is even dancing in the streets of Edinburgh. For more information contact Miss M. M. Gibson, the Royal Scottish Country Dance Society, 12 Coates Crescent,

Edinburgh EH3 7AF (phone: 225-3854), and the Scottish Tourist Board, 23 Ravelston Terr., Edinburgh EH4 3EU (phone: 332-2433).

Surprisingly, since the Welsh are renowned for their musical traditions, there is less apparent love of dance, and little is known about the early folk dances. In the Middle Ages there were many popular dances including chains, rounds, reels, and morris dances, but with the establishment of the Chapel in Wales in the late eighteenth century these merrymakings were forced to a halt. The people were obliged to concentrate on religion, and consequently their musical talents became vested in their great choral tradition.

The instrument that dominates is the harp. Wales boasts the triple harp which, with its three rows of strings, is considered by some to be the finest harp in existence. Undoubtedly it lends itself to dancing, though the fiddle and flute are also popular. The only dance that has survived in an unbroken tradition is the clog and broom dance. It is vigorous, and quite tricky to perform: The dancer makes fast tapping steps around the broom as it lies on the ground, or he may pick it up and jump over it. Nowadays some of the best dancers delight in introducing inventive tricks into it.

It was not until 1949, with the formation of the Welsh Folk Dance Society, that attempts were made to salvage what was left of the dances. It also has made great efforts to ensure that authentic costumes survive, and these are usually quaint and charming: breeches, waistcoats, and shirts for men; and pretty blouses, long skirts with lace aprons, and caps, or the well-known, tall, flat-topped black hats for women.

You'll find plenty of dance displays at the International Musical Eisteddfod in July at Llangollen or the Royal National Eisteddfod of Wales (which alternates each August between North and South Wales), and the many smaller ones which crop up all over Wales during the summer. Information can be obtained from Mrs. Jean Huw Jones, Dolawenydd, Betws, Ammanford, Dyfed SA18 2HE (phone: 2837), and the Wales Tourist Board, 3 Castle St., Cardiff CF1 2RE (phone: 27281).

Food and Drink

 The image most Americans have of British food is that of a massive roast beef, surrounded by plainly cooked vegetables, baked potatoes, and a little gravy. No elaborate sauces or violent flavors. Unfortunately, cost has driven the roast beef of old England into decline, but you can still sample its splendor in "carvery" rooms in major London hotels, where huge joints of beef, pork, and lamb are featured. Many "medieval banquet" restaurants also serve meals styled to resemble feasts of the past — from the sixteenth century to Victorian times. These, however, aim more for drama than for authenticity, and the visitor must go elsewhere for genuine "Old English" dishes. In an effort to promote traditional foods and recipes, the British Tourist Board created the "Taste of England, Scotland, and Wales" distinction. You'll see this noted on many menus, and tourist board booklets list the establishments that serve traditional fare.

BREAKFAST: A SUBSTANTIAL MEAL

"Breakfast first, business later," declared British writer William Makepeace Thackeray. Standard breakfast fare includes grapefruit or juice, eggs and bacon, with tomatoes, mushrooms, or sausages, followed by toast, marmalade, and tea or coffee.

Some country house hotels have preserved the Edwardian tradition of serving kidneys and kedgeree. (The latter, a fish and rice mixture flavored with curry, is particularly good for soaking up and salving any excesses of the night before.) A mixed grill of lamb chops, sausages, liver, kidney, mushrooms, and tomatoes also may be served as a late breakfast dish, and potted and cold meats, brawn (a cold, pressed pig meat), and finnan haddock are also popular.

Regional sausages, such as Cumberland ring sausages, can still be found. And in Lancashire and Scotland, Suffolk, or black, pudding is famous. It's made with pig's blood and served sliced with grilled bacon and eggs. Potato cakes, crisply fried, are served in some places, and in Wales and north Cornwall, a seaweed called "laverbread" is fried with the bacon. Kipper, a bony smoked fish that's quite salty, is another breakfast staple.

Is it any wonder that novelist Somerset Maugham once commented that to eat well in Britain, one should eat breakfast three times a day?

TEA: A BRITISH TRADITION

"Everything stops for tea" is an English saying, and rare is the worker who can get through his day without tea breaks. The afternoon tea meal was started in about 1780 by the duchess of Bedford as a gossipy way of filling in the time between early lunch and late dinner. A whole industry of teacups, special china, cake stands, embroidered cloths, linen, and tea forks for the cakes grew up, and a precise ritual soon evolved around a silver teapot and sugar bowl with little tongs.

This graciousness has disappeared in today's hurried times. Visitors, however, can still test out Rupert Brooke's lines "Stands the church clock at ten to three?/And is there honey still for tea?" Honey or country preserves, particularly strawberry jam, go with scones, which are rather like an American biscuit. Other cakes include Victoria sponge rock and fairy (iced) cakes, Battenburg, and Madeira. In Scotland, teas are substantial, and they include fruitcakes like Dundee and tea breads, which are halfway between cakes and breads in consistency. In Wales, bacon, fish, pancakes, and *bara brith* ("speckled bread") are eaten.

In Devon and Cornwall, tea is served with thick, clotted cream, and regional cakes follow sandwiches and scones. "Tea" also refers to the early evening meal in the north, and in country districts (especially in Shropshire) one may still find signs for "farm teas." These are often quite substantial — including salads, ham, or fish. The "strawberry tea" is a happy summer event during the Wimbledon tennis fortnight and the Henley regatta: A bowl of fresh strawberries and cream is served with tea.

In the smaller villages and towns, there used to be many shops where local ladies served tea and homemade cakes; this was considered a respectable occupation for "spinsters" ever since a Miss Cranston set up the country's first tea room in Glasgow's Sauchiehall Street in 1904. These days, tea shops come and go, and some consider high tea to be an endangered meal.

Nevertheless, the afternoon high tea ritual is still maintained in all its glory by such hotels as the *Lygon Arms* in Broadway in the Cotswolds, which serves crumpets and tea cakes in winter. And teas at the *Ritz, Dorchester,* or *Brown's* hotels in London are tops: At any one of these hostelries, monogrammed Irish linen covers the high little round tables (the stiffly corseted Edwardian ladies sat higher than today's women) and thin cucumber, cress, cheese, tomato, egg, or smoked salmon sandwiches are followed by scones, clotted cream, and strawberry. Finally, delicate petit fours and pastries are served. A choice of Indian and China teas is traditional. (For a more extensive selection of tea shops and tea gardens see DIVERSIONS.)

THE MAIN COURSE

As we have said, Britain is famous for its good roast meats, such as chicken, turkey, and duckling, as well as game in season — pheasant, grouse, quail, partridge, venison, and hare. However, there are many outstanding meat dishes besides the traditional roast, including meat pies, puddings, and stews.

In the little Cotswold village of Broadway, the butcher shop called *Collins* still practices the old art of making raised pies. Typically, the pies have carefully molded, high sides and are filled with game from local shoots. So special are *Collins*'s pies that *Harrods* and *Fortnum and Mason* keep specially monogrammed pie molds there.

Perhaps more familiar to most Americans is the steak and kidney pie, which when served in London sometimes also contains mushrooms or oysters. More economical recipes use less expensive cuts of meat. For example, Lancashire hot pot utilizes the neck end of lamb, and tripe and onions is a northern favorite. On the banks of the Mersey River the word *scouse* may be heard more than seen on a menu. It is a diminutive for *lobscouse,* a lamb, beef, and vegetable stew and is such a favorite with Liverpudlians that they are nicknamed Scouses. And Robert Burns called the Scottish favorite, haggis, the "chieftain o' the puddin race." It is a dish made of the innards of a sheep, minced with suet and oatmeal, and it's traditionally served with "tatties and neeps," or potatoes and turnips. Haggis is now often offered on hotel menus as an appetizer.

In the Midlands, where ham and bacon are especially loved, little pieces of bacon turn up in boiled, hot, gray peas. Pork crackling is rendered down to make "scratchings" and is often sold in pubs in packets and eaten like potato chips. The great hams of the country are in York, where they are cured by dry salting. York hams are said to have derived their original flavor from smoking in the oak sawdust of timbers used in the building of York's cathedral. Bradenham ham, made since 1781, is dry-cured, pickled in molasses for a month, and matured for 3 months thereafter. Suffolk Seager ham is rounded with a dark brown finish. It is cured in brine, black treacle, and molasses and then it is smoked.

The Dunmow flitch is a side of bacon traditionally presented every 3 years to the most harmoniously married couple in this Essex town. You may also come across the bacon "clanger," a pastry roll of bacon, onion, and herbs that originated in Oxfordshire. Sometimes it has a sweet filling at one end and is savory at the other, so that a worker in the fields could take his whole meal in one neat pack.

Practicality mixed with poverty was the origin of the Cornish pasty that was made for the tin miner (many of whom immigrated to Colorado, where pasties are still served at the miners' festival). Triangular in shape, so it can slip into a pocket, the pasty contained potato, vegetables, and whatever scraps of meat were available. It was said that the pasty was hard enough to withstand a fall down the mine shaft.

And now a word about the trimmings: *Tracklement* is the lovely old English word for a condiment to go with meat. Cumberland sauce with ham or pâté is one old delight, red currant jelly goes with lamb, and there are many chutneys. Mustard is the major meat accompaniment, declared by George I to be his favorite. *Colman's* mustard shop in Bridewell Lane, Norwich, is a replica of a nineteenth-century grocer's shop and sells many blends. Other English mustards include *Taylors,* English vineyard mustards, and whole grain mustards by *Crabtree and Evelyn.* Horseradish cream — they say the best horseradish root comes from country graveyards — is a pungent root that is grated, mixed with cream, and served with roast beef.

Because it's an island, Britain has a plentiful supply of fish and seafood. Cod is king and it is usually served up as the ubiquitous fish fingers. Turbot is served with hollandaise sauce, and Dover sole and mackerel traditionally served with gooseberry sauce. Herrings, pilchards (which are popular tinned in oil for teas), bloaters from Yarmouth, and sprats are traditional fish. Salmon is the luxury fish, caught in Scotland and in bigger English rivers like the Wye. In summer it is served poached hot with hollandaise sauce or cold with mayonnaise and cucumber. Smoked salmon is a glory that is principally found in Scotland, and smoked mackerel and trout are served as appetizers with horseradish sauce.

Oysters from East Anglia and Cornwall, shrimp from Lancashire's Morecambe Bay, lobsters, mussels, and Dublin Bay prawns are all popular, if expensive. Londoners like small shellfish such as whelks or cockles; these are skewered on a pin and sold from stalls in the East End. They also enjoy eels, jellied or made into pies with a green parsley sauce. Whitebait may open a meal, and on the Severn River in spring, elvers (baby eels) are eaten in competitions to see who can consume the most.

Fish and chips, the age-old British favorite, can be enjoyed in impressive, chandelier-hung surroundings at *Harry Ramsden's* in Guisley, Yorkshire. Other recommended places for a fish-and-chip pilgrimage are the *Gainsboro* at Hull, *Bryan's* fish restaurant at Headingly, and *Mother Hubbard's* at Girlington near Bradford.

Eleanor Roosevelt once remarked, "The English have ten green vegetables and eight of them are brussels sprouts." Although vegetables are often a weak spot on the British menu, there are some exceptions. Spring is heralded by the arrival of little new potatoes cooked with a sprig of mint and served with melted butter. Cold mashed potatoes and leftover cabbage are often mixed together and fried for breakfast or for light family meals. In England this is known as "bubble and squeak" and in Scotland as "rumbledethumps" — because of the elbow grease that goes into beating it. And "pan haggerty" — thinly sliced potatoes, onions, and grated cheese — is pan fried in Northumbria. Early in the summer there is samphire, a marsh plant that is eaten like asparagus in East Anglia. Asparagus itself is ready in June and is expensive, but like strawberries and salmon, it's a sign of the British summer.

DESSERTS

A "good pud" is seen as a threat to most dieters, but traditional puddings live on in Britain, aided by memories of the nostalgic treats of childhood. Before North Sea oil and central heating, Britons kept warm with a whole repertoire of suet puddings: Kentwell pudding, in which a lemon and butter and sugar were encased in suet pastry; spotted dicks, suet with dried fruit; or castle, treacle, mattress, and cabinet puddings. Bread and butter pudding cooked with dried fruit and milk was another favorite, and Christmas pudding served after the turkey is probably the richest of all: It's dark with fruit and alcohol and it is served with custard, rum, or brandy butters.

Not all puddings are heavy. Syllabub was made originally by pouring fresh cow's milk from a height onto lemon and wine mixtures. Junkets are a light, creamy affair made in the West Country: indeed, visits to the dairy to eat this became so popular that the word *junket* is now synonymous with a party outing. Another confection was a puree of rhubarb and gooseberries mixed with thick cream. And trifle is a year-round favorite — it's sponge cake, soaked in sherry, layered with raspberry jam or fruit, and topped with custard and cream.

A most famous pudding — which can also be eaten cold with jam for dessert — is the Yorkshire pudding usually served with roast beef. Yorkshire women claim only they can make it properly, though a local competition to find the champion pudding maker was won lately by a Chinese chef.

But puddings are by no means the only dessert specialties to be found in Britain. Many baked products can be sampled and bought from the weekly Women's Institute markets (a list is available from the National Federation of Women's Institutes, 39 Eccleston St., London SW1W 9NT). These small, friendly regional markets are a good way to meet local people.

Gingerbread, a specialty of the Lake District, is made daily in *Sarah Nelson's* shop in Grasmere. In this area, gingerbread alphabets were once used to teach children to read. Shortbread is Scotland's favorite, while in Richmond, Surrey, "maids of honour tarts," named for Anne Boleyn's ladies, are still sold. The *Old Bakewell Pudding* shop in Bakewell, Derbyshire, sells tarts with almonds and raspberry jam. Yorkshire's parkin, based on oatmeal, treacle, and ginger, is made traditionally on November 5, Bonfire Night. Also in Yorkshire, apple pie is a favorite dish customarily eaten with a slice of cheese. The locals are fond of the rhyme: "Apple pie without a slice of cheese is like a kiss without a squeeze."

As for fruit, Scottish raspberries from Speyside are excellent in flavor. Outstanding among the late summer fruits in Britain are apples, pears, and plums, particularly damsons and greengages. Britons often mix soft fruits with black and red currants to make a "summer pudding;" the fruit is puréed and put in a crust made of dried bread.

BREADS AND CHEESES

Among British breads are bloomers, baps (soft Scottish breakfast rolls), coburgs, cobs, pistols (round-shaped loaves), and cottage loaves (two rounds on top of each other). Biscuits (cookies and crackers) include Dorset knobs — dried, rusklike tidbits that go with cheese — and Bath Olivers — thin water biscuits invented in the eighteenth century for dieters by Dr. Oliver, Bath's first spa physician.

England has nine national cheeses, of which Stilton is king. A veined blue cheese from Leicestershire, it is traditionally served with port. Cheshire cheese, which comes in patriotic red, white, and blue versions, was much loved by Samuel Johnson; his favorite Fleet Street pub in London is named *The Cheshire.* Lancashire cheese spreads and toasts well. Derby is the rarest, and sage Derby, veined with the herb, was originally made for Christmas. Caerphilly was once made in Wales, and now it's made in Somerset. Easily digestible, Caerphilly was the chosen snack of coal miners cramped at the pit face. Cheddar from the Mendip Hills goes well in a fruit pie pastry.

"New" cheeses are brought out regularly. These include red Windsor, veined with red wine; Cotswolds, a double Gloucester with onions and chives; Walton, a blend of Cheddar and Stilton; Ilchester, a cheddar mixed with beer, spices, and chives; and Labra, the first ewe's milk cheese to be made since the Middle Ages.

In certain areas, you can visit farms to see cheeses being made. In Scotland many national cheeses are made in Orkney, including Dunlop, Caboc (rolled in oats), and Castle Stuart blue cheeses.

A NOTE ON BEVERAGES

The pub or "local" is a Briton's home away from home; it's an informal place to talk and drink. Most British beer is warm and heavy, so often the lagers served chilled are more to the visitors' taste. Local breweries persist and such brews as Adnams of Southwold with their Fishermen's ale, Doddington, Theakstons, Ruddles, Toby Cobbold of Ipswich, and Greene King of Bury St. Edmunds are served mainly in their own regions. "Real ale" bars are springing up around the country these days — even at some railway stations. A few unusual pub drinks are black beer from Leeds, which is made from malt and cane sugar mixed with rum, whisky, or lemonade; shrub, which was used as a West Country mix to sweeten sea-tainted rum in the old smuggling days; and lovage, an herbal pick-me-up that is also from the West Country.

Cider is a traditional drink from the West Country and Hereford. It's based on fermented apples and is sold fresh. (The sweetness varies.) Some leading cider producers own pubs that specialize in cider. In the West Country, some pubs sell "scrumpy," the raw farm-brewed cider that has a deceptive ox-felling power; so much so, that the police are not eager that it be sold to tourists. Mead is a honeysweet drink dating from before Christian times. It is still made in Cornwall and on the island of Lindisfarne, where the factory is open to the public.

Although Britain has always been thought of as a beer-drinking country, wine is rapidly becoming popular as well. Today you can find wine lists that offer selections from California to Australia, and from Chile to Charente. In addition, Britain is reviving its native vineyards, which declined during the Middle Ages, when most of France — and French wine — was under the control of the English crown. The English Vineyards Association numbers over 400 growers, who produce 180,000 bottles per year. Among the best-known names are Hambledon and Pilton Manor in Somerset, both of which have days when they are open for visitors. Adgestone from the Isle of Wight is one of the most prized wines, and Beaulieu comes from Lord Montagu's estate in Hampshire. Merrydown in Sussex also produces English country wines made from elderberries, red currants, and apples.

And though pubs advertise Harvey Wallbangers and other cocktails, the more conservative Briton will have a sherry before a formal meal and a glass of port (known as the "Englishman's drink") afterward. On hot summer days, many find a gin and tonic cooling, and a whisky and soda is good any time. But even though gin, vodka, and other spirits are made in Britain, Scotch is the most popular — more than 200 brands are produced and consumed. So much Scotch is sold that they say the duty on its sale pays for the nation's defense budget! (For a more complete discussion of beers, ales, and liquors, as well as the selection of the best watering holes in Britain, see *Pub Crawling,* DIVERSIONS.)

Ireland

History

Imagine that you are standing on a windswept headland, a country of lush green glens behind you, the tumultuous sea at your feet. A beautiful girl approaches you, an orphan, she says, but of noble lineage, who tells you a tale so full of romance and heroism and piety and cruelty and *sturm und drang* that you cannot decide whether to laugh or cry, but still find yourself listening enraptured to her compelling voice.

This is Ireland, and the Irish themselves are inclined to surrender to her charms. For centuries, they have been compounding a political and social mythology out of songs, legends, and history, and the heroes of that mythology — Finn MacCool, Brian Ború, Patrick Sarsfield, Wolfe Tone, Daniel O'Connell, and Charles Parnell — remain the controlling models for modern Ireland's political and social behavior. When Patrick Pearse, a leader of the 1916 Easter Rebellion, invoked the Ulster hero Cu Chulainn while British troops besieged his little band in the Dublin General Post Office, he rallied his men with an image from the nation's antiquity. The revival of the Irish language, a cornerstone of government policy, affirms the continuity of the Irish Republic with its remotest antecedents. No other nation in Europe requires an understanding of its most distant past to complete an understanding of its present.

THE CELTS

The Celts were a family of Indo-European warrior aristocracies related by language, religion, mastery of horsemanship, and a flammable temperament that kept them always at each other's throats. From their arrival in Ireland between 500 and 50 BC, the Celtic clans warred ceaselessly among themselves for territory, tribute, and cattle. Sensitive and superstitious, they were terrorized by their priests (druids) and master-poets (*filidhe;* pronounced *fee-lee*), whose curses carried weight with the gods and in whose memories reposed the only record of tribal histories, genealogies, and myth. These learned, almost Brahmanic castes maintained their own training academies and provided the only source of social unity among the various tribes.

The family was the fundamental Celtic social unit from which all rights and authority flowed. Tribal alliances were matters of military convenience rather than treaty, and not until the fifth century AD did the Irish establish the semblance of a central power. Even then, the High King, ruling from the Hill of Tara, drew his authority not from law but from the tacit consensus of the legislative assemblies of tribal chieftains and nobles. The O'Neill High Kings, whose dynasty endured until the eleventh century, invoked a national spirit by convening the first such assembly — though each tribe had previously conducted its own and continued to do so. The O'Neills also raised a standing army (the Fianna), but even after the Ulaid of Ulster — last of the Celtic tribes to resist Gaelic dominance — were subdued in 851, their control of Ireland remained tenuous.

Gaelic civilization flourished unconsumed by the Roman Empire in what W. B. Yeats would call "the Celtic Twilight." Its decentralized social structure evolved without interference, and when, in the fifth century, Christianity was introduced by St. Patrick, the new church adapted itself at once to this design. Abbeys and monasteries patronized by local chieftains and entirely independent of diocesan authority became the seats of church power; out of touch with Rome, the Irish clung to old doctrines long after they had been abandoned or revised elsewhere in Christendom. Yet, the monasteries nourished a lively intellectual life; graduates of the poetic academies, attracted by the ascetic ethos, flocked to the monasteries and abbeys, learned to write, and created the stunningly illuminated manuscripts in which the oral literature of the nation was first written down. By decree of Columcille (St. Columba), a Gaelic prince, poet, and founder of the first native order, lay poets were officially employed in every royal court after 575. The literary arts thus enjoyed the patronage of both church and state.

When the barbarians inundated Europe in the fifth century, Christian learning crawled to high ground in Ireland. As the deluge subsided, Irish missionaries ventured over the European continent, founding monasteries, restoring literacy, and resuscitating the faith amid the ruins of Hellenic civilization. John Scotus Erigena (which means "Irish-born") and his contemporary, Sedulius Scotus, taught in the palace schools founded by Charlemagne and the monasteries of Ireland received students from abroad; but while this lively traffic earned Ireland the epithet "Isle of Saints and Scholars," it turned Rome's efforts to reforming the doctrinally wayward church and bringing it under central control.

In 795, Ostmen, the predatory Vikings, commenced their raids along the Irish coast, leveling monasteries and torching whole libraries. These Norse pirates built a string of garrisons along the eastern coast, proclaiming themselves kings and establishing Ireland's first cities and ports. The fractious Gaels were helpless to dislodge these ferocious and well-organized intruders. Late in the tenth century, an obscure chieftain from Clare, Brian Ború, overthrew the Danish king of Limerick and, by three usurpations, dispossessed the O'Neills and declared himself High King of Ireland. For a few short years, Brian united the tribes of Ireland behind his leadership; he routed the Danes from their chief stronghold, Dublin, at the Battle of Clontarf in 1014. Brian, alas, lost his life in the battle, and the Irish relapsed into squabbling over succession to the Tara monarchy.

THE NORMAN INVASION

Though their dominance had been broken, the Norsemen remained in Ireland as sailors and merchants, intermarrying with the Gaels and assimilating the native culture. In 1166 they joined with the chiefs of Leinster to overthrow their king, Dermot MacMurrough, who fled to England where he formed an alliance with some Norman adventurers whom he hoped would restore him to his realm. In 1169, these mail-clad buccaneers landed on the Baginburn headland in Waterford, and in 2 years had seized Leinster for their leader, Richard Fitz-Gilbert de Clare, known as "Strongbow." MacMurrough died soon after. Before these brilliant, methodical soldiers the Irish had no defense. In 1171 Strongbow and the rest of the Normans resentfully acknowledged themselves subjects of Henry II, and the High King Rory O'Connor recognized Henry as his sovereign in return for control over all unconquered areas. Ireland had become the property of the English crown.

The Normans marked their holdings with a line called the "Pale," a thin strip of land on the eastern coast. But as Norman and Gael intermarried, the former became, as the saying goes, more "Irish than the Irish themselves." (The Irish referred to the Normans as "Old Foreigners," while the English called those who had gone native "degenerate English.") By 1261, the Gaels had adopted Norman military techniques, putting an end to their conquests, while the Normans had taken up the Gaelic language and culture, maintaining poets and commissioning manuscripts like any native chieftain.

The rapprochement displeased the English. In 1297, to consolidate the colony and muster troops from it for his Scottish wars, Edward I convened an Irish Parliament at Kilkenny, which was hostile to the Gaels and assimilated Normans. By 1366, the Parliament had promulgated statutes to separate the "races," but these were largely ignored by a very mixed population. The Normans had built cities, introduced English common law, and mingled names like Bourke, Butler, and Carey with O'Brien, O'Neill, and O'Donnell. Culturally distinct from England and uncomfortable as colonials, the Normans declared parliamentary independence in 1460.

THE PLANTATION

The Reformation and the Tudor monarchy put an end to their adventure. In 1541, Henry VIII compelled the Irish Parliament to recall his sovereignty. He then asserted his authority to govern the Irish church, as he had already done in England, and imposed the "plantation" policy, under which native Irish and some "degenerate English" landholdings were seized and regranted to loyal English fortune seekers. Resistance to the policy centered in Ulster, where the chieftains Red Hugh O'Donnell and Hugh O'Neill, setting aside old rivalries, formed the Tyrone Confederation and, in the first of Ireland's revolutions, rose against Henry's "new earls" (as those who literally bought titles and rights to the land were called). Promises of Spanish assistance were obtained, and from 1594 to 1603 the Tyrone Confederation rebelled with some success against the English. In 1601, a Spanish fleet sailed into Kinsale on the southern coast, and the English Lord Mountjoy turned to attack them, whereupon O'Donnell and O'Neill swept down from the north to besiege the besiegers. The Spanish pressed for a decisive engagement; O'Neill argued for attrition, but O'Donnell forced the issue. The Battle of Kinsale was fought on Christmas Eve, 1601, and the Hispano-Gaelic alliance, insufficiently prepared, went down in defeat. The defeated earls, O'Donnell and O'Neill, were permitted to return to Ulster; but after a few years of suffering English rule, they sailed in self-imposed exile to the Continent in 1607, an event often called the "Flight of the Earls."

The plantation policy went forward apace. In Ulster, barely one tenth of the land was retained by its native inhabitants; the rest was planted with Presbyterian colonists from Scotland, dissenters in their own country. In 1641, Norman soldiers, unemployed and wandering the countryside, enlisted with the Irish chiefs of Ulster in another uprising. The Irish Parliament, now sitting at Dublin, expelled its Catholic members, who gathered at Kilkenny to proclaim a provisional government.

Presiding over this revolution was Owen Roe O'Neill; nephew of Hugh and a statesman of some sophistication, he envisioned for Ireland a centralized and autonomous native government. After Owen Roe's victory over parliamentary forces at Benburb in 1646, Charles I, facing Cromwell's insurgence at home, offered a treaty that would have reversed the plantation policy; but the Catholic clergy, holding out for emancipation from the Protestant crown, persuaded Owen Roe to reject it. After deposing the king in 1649, Cromwell turned to the reconquest of Ireland, and in September stormed the town of Drogheda, slaughtering 3,500 inhabitants in reprisal for earlier revolutionary terrorism. Owen Roe's death in November signaled the collapse of the resistance. Limerick and Galway capitulated in 1652, and 30,000 Irish soldiers followed their chiefs into exile in what the Irish remember as "the Flight of the Wild Geese."

The Cromwellian Act of Settlement in 1652 extended the plantation policy; Irish lands were seized and distributed among demobilized English soldiers and the financiers of the reconquest. The Catholic Church was outlawed and its properties confiscated. Towns were seeded with English burgesses and native merchants were relocated to the perimeters. The common people were reduced to virtual slavery as tenants on lands immemorially theirs. By 1655, what remained of the Gaelic nation languished among the stony acres west of the Shannon. By 1688, Protestants, though they comprised a tiny minority of its population, owned 78% of all the land in Ireland.

STUART vs. ORANGE

With the ascension of James II, a Catholic, in 1685, England's policies in Ireland were somewhat liberalized. But James was deposed in 1688 and fled to France. In 1689 he moved to Ireland, where he hoped to establish, in this Catholic nation, a base from which to recover his throne. Catholic France rallied to the Jacobites (as his followers were called) and sent a fleet to Kinsale in 1689. But Protestant Europe as determinedly supported William of Orange, James's Protestant successor. Things came to a head on July 1, 1690, when a mixed army of Danes, Germans, French Huguenots, and English overwhelmed the Jacobites at the Battle of the Boyne. The Irish army, under Patrick Sarsfield, fell back and retrenched beyond the Shannon. They then sallied forth to meet the Protestants at the Battle of Aughrim, and, when defeated again, Sarsfield gathered the remains of his army behind the walls of Limerick and indomitably withstood two lengthy English sieges before finally obtaining favorable terms of surrender, which London was largely to ignore. Sarsfield and his men, like the earls some 40 years before them, fled in exile to France. (Sarsfield joined the French army and died in battle in 1693, crying: "Oh, that this were for Ireland.")

ROBERT EMMET, WOLFE TONE — IRISH PROTESTANT PATRIOTISM

The hope of Irish freedom dashed, England imposed the Penal Codes in 1695, the apartheid statutes by which Catholics were denied nearly all rights at law and reduced to serfdom. (In the words of one Lord Chancellor: "The law does not take into account the existence of such a person as an Irish Roman Catholic.") Yet while the Penal Codes ensured the privileges of the Ascendancy, they also effectively tied most of the Protestant gentry — but not the Protestant magnates — to the land, while tariffs restricted the economy. Furthermore, although the Dublin Parliament was supposedly autonomous in most areas, in fact it merely rubber-stamped the acts of Westminster. All Catholics and many Protestants chafed under the English yoke. In 1791 the Protestant patriot Wolfe Tone founded the United Irishmen, which — inspired by the French revolution — attempted to bring together Catholics and Protestants in common cause against the English government. The movement gained strength quickly in Ireland, but was suppressed in 1794. Wolfe Tone fled to Paris to raise an army of liberation, and, in 1798, Ireland's third revolution broke out in Wexford. Tone and a French fleet hurried to its aid, but the ragtag rebels, led by two priests, John Murphy and Michael Murphy, were crushed at Vinegar Hill (Waterford) before the fleet could arrive. The French, surrounded at Castlebar (County Mayo), surrendered, and Tone, denied an honorable execution before a firing squad and condemned instead to the gallows, slit his throat. In 1801, the Act of Union abolished the Irish Parliament and absorbed Ireland into a United Kingdom. Revolution erupted for the fourth time in 1803, led this time by Robert Emmet, but it collapsed in confusion on the brink of success, and Emmet, whose stirring speech from the scaffold embedded itself in the Irish memory, was hanged.

CATHOLIC EMANCIPATION

In 1793, a Catholic Relief Bill had ostensibly restored all Catholic rights except that of holding elective office, an omission that rendered the rest meaningless. In 1823, Daniel O'Connell, the brilliant Kerry lawyer and orator, organized the Catholic Association which, by tithing its members a penny a month, became an organ of legal defense and agitation and the underground government of the Gaelic nation. O'Connell was a peerless organizer, and when defiant voters in Clare elected him to Westminster in 1828, the orchestrated mass movement behind him so intimidated England that he was seated, accomplishing full Catholic emancipation in a stroke.

In 1830, leading a substantial Irish voting bloc in Parliament, O'Connell embarked on a campaign to repeal the Union. Committed to reform within the constitution, activism within the law, and loyalty to the crown, O'Connell threw his party's support behind the Whigs, counting on their backing the repeal movement if they displaced the Tories. But Prime Minister Melbourne's Whig government, once elected, reneged, supported by a Protestant Ascendancy determined to protect its property and power under the Union by force if necessary. The Irish masses stood ready to take up arms at the first word from O'Connell; the Young Ireland party, led by journalist Charles Gavin Duffy and poet Thomas Davis, urged O'Connell to abandon his pacifist principles and lead them in revolution. O'Connell had no such intention. Instead, in 1842–43, he organized and addressed a series of "monster meetings" — rallies in support of repeal; at the one held at Tara, nearly a million people assembled peacefully to hear him speak in the open air. The meetings were perfectly legal, but the English government — mindful of O'Connell's tremendous influence — sent troops to surround the meeting held at Clontarf and threatened violence if the crowd did not disperse. Though he was within his rights, and though the assembly could probably have overwhelmed the soldiers, O'Connell canceled the meeting. The next year, he and Duffy were arrested and convicted of sedition. Though the House of Lords later reversed the verdict, O'Connell emerged from 2 months in prison largely stripped of his influence. He split with Young Ireland in 1846; momentum passed to its leaders, and he died in 1847.

THE IRISH FAMINE

In that year, the potato, staple of the common people, succumbed to blight for the second time and the Great Famine descended over Ireland. It was a catastrophe beyond description; starvation, dysentery, and cholera decimated the population, and tens of thousands fled to America. Ireland lost about 2 million people between 1845 and 1855, yet Britain stuck to its free trade philosophy and intervened as little as possible on the theory that private enterprise would eventually sort things out. Relief aid actually decreased as the famine worsened. Yet, throughout this Irish holocaust, food was exported from Ireland to pay rents to absentee landlords in England. Great estates went bankrupt and passed into the hands of profiteers who thought nothing of evicting their destitute and starving tenants.

In 1848, under the leadership of William Smith O'Brien and spurred by the writings of John Mitchel (who had been deported to Australia for publishing the seditious journal *United Irishman*), what remained of Young Ireland staged and bungled an armed insurrection. Its participants followed Mitchel to Australia. For almost a decade, the nationalist movement lay dormant and the Irish language and economy languished through neglect. Industrialization was financed by London only in Ulster, which attached itself commercially to the industrial northwest of England, alienating itself still further from the rest of Ireland, where there were virtually no manufacturers. Circumstances were preparing Ulster for separation.

HOME RULE

After the collapse of the repeal movement, the nationalists regrouped behind the Home Rule proposal, which would have restored at least a measure of autonomy to the Irish nation. After 1875, the leader of the Home Rule party at Westminster was Charles Stewart Parnell, an Irish Protestant and charismatic leader who implemented the policy of "obstruction," or withholding his considerable political support to gain concessions for Ireland. Parnell's tactical brilliance secured the admiration and cooperation of William Gladstone, the Liberal Prime Minister; despite their efforts, however, the Home Rule Bill was twice defeated in Parliament. Shortly thereafter, Parnell suffered a serious blow to his reputation: Two British civil servants were murdered in Dublin's Phoenix Park, and *The Times* published a forged letter allegedly from Parnell condoning the killings. Then, in 1888, a divorce proceeding revealed Parnell's liaison with a colleague's wife; he was condemned by Protestant England and Catholic Ireland, his followers dropped away, and he died in disgrace 3 years later at 45.

Nationalist leadership passed to the Sinn Féin (Ourselves Alone), a party founded in 1902 by Arthur Griffith, who favored an independent Irish Parliament. Despite the resistance of Ulster's Orangemen, a society formed to protect the privileges and liberties of Protestants, and the organization of the paramilitary Ulster Volunteers, a Home Rule Bill was finally enacted in 1914. But the Orange militants had succeeded in amending the bill to give Ulster's six counties, with their Protestant majority, the option of seceding from Ireland and remaining in the Union. The outbreak of World War I fatally delayed implementation of the bill, and Ireland, on the eve of its independence, stood divided against itself.

EASTER RISING

The Easter Rebels of 1916 looked to England's enemy, the Germans, for aid as Hugh O'Neill had looked to the Spanish and Tone to the French. Organized as the Irish Volunteers, their emissary to Berlin, Roger Casement, was captured by the British while returning to warn that German support would not be forthcoming. (Casement was convicted before a military court and hanged.) This was on Good Friday, 1916. The Volunteers canceled what was to have been a national insurgence, but the Dublin contingent, hopeless of success, rose to martyrdom on Easter Monday. The 1,200 Volunteers seized strategic buildings around the city; on the steps of the General Post Office, leader Patrick Pearse read the proclamation of an Irish Republic. British troops, ordered to dislodge the rebels, left central Dublin in ruins. Seventeen rebel leaders — including Pearse, Thomas McDonough, John McBride, Joseph Plunkett, and James Connolly — died before a firing squad. Public outrage at the executions persuaded the British to commute the sentences of

William Cosgrave, later president of the Free State, and Eamon de Valera, later president of the provisional government of the republic.

The martyrs, none of them important figures before death, became national heroes afterward. In the elections of 1919, Sinn Féin scored a landslide victory in parliamentary elections, but the deputies refused to take their seats, convening instead the Dáil Éireann (Assembly of Ireland) under de Valera's presidency and proclaiming the Republic once again. England implemented Home Rule, exempting from it the six counties of Ulster, but the Dáil would accept nothing short of total independence. Ireland burst into violence: The IRA under Sinn Féin leader Michael Collins waged a bloody guerrilla war with the Black and Tans, England's paramilitary police force to whom countless atrocities were attributed; British police fired on the crowds at a sporting event in Dublin's Croke Park; army barracks came under regular attack. The ordinary functions of government dissolved in subversion. In 1921, Griffith and Collins negotiated a treaty with Britain by which a new state, Saorstát Éireann (Irish Free State) was created as a Dominion in the Commonwealth and under the crown. The Dáil accepted the treaty, but de Valera rejected it and was repudiated by the Dáil. Griffith became the Free State's first president, and Collins, fearing a civil war, made overtures to de Valera, assuring him privately there would be no oath of allegiance to the crown in a new Irish constitution. But de Valera remained adamant and organized an "underground Republic" with himself as president, Sinn Féin as its party, and the IRA as its militia; it would acknowledge neither the crown nor the partition of Ireland.

IRISH FREE STATE

In 1922, incensed by a Free State constitution that embodied the terms of the treaty, IRA troops occupied the Four Courts, the building in Dublin that houses the superior courts of Ireland. Under enormous pressure from Britain, the Free State moved in troops and gunboats, and a few days later commenced a series of raids on Republican headquarters in Dublin hotels. Republicans and Free Staters were at war. Political unity once again escaped the Irish, and the country quaked with assassinations and skirmishes. Griffith died in August and Collins a few days later in an ambush near Cork. In 1923, de Valera declared a cease-fire. He agreed to enter the Dáil in 1927, whereupon Sinn Féin drew away from him to the leftist frontier of Republican intransigence. De Valera founded a new party, Fianna Fáil, whose members he urged to take the oath of allegiance to the crown as he had done — with "mental reservations." Fianna Fáil acquired a majority in 1932 and a new government, headed by De Valera, was formed. A new constitution was promulgated in 1937, declaring the nation the Republic of Eire and abolishing the oath. In 1949, Eire withdrew from the Commonwealth; at the same time, Britain, to establish a legal basis for partition, referred the question to the heavily Protestant Ulster Parliament at Stormont, which put the issue of Union before a popular referendum whose outcome was never in doubt.

PARTITION

Since then, the industrialized cities of Northern Ireland — Belfast and Derry — and many of the larger towns have divided into sectarian camps. In the 1960s, a Catholic civil rights movement agitated for Catholic representation at Stormont in proportion to the Catholic population, which brought a violent response from the Protestants, to whom the cause seemed synonymous with reunification with the Republic. The IRA, now an extra-legal militia outlawed even in the Republic, came to the defense of the Catholic constituency. Confronted by virtual civil war, which Stormont was powerless to stop since it represented only one side, Britain suspended the Northern Ireland legislature in 1972. Stepping between the warring factions, the British army became a target of IRA hostility, along with the paramilitary Ulster Defense Force. But now, bound by the legal precedent of the 1949 referendum, Britain has no way of withdrawing from Ulster without a majority mandate, and Ulster has no way of forming a government to which both sides can consent and thereby impose law and order without British intervention.

Ulster-Protestants are proud of their heritage and fearful of losing not only property but some of their rights and liberties as British subjects under the Irish Republican constitution, which embodies the moral doctrines of the Catholic Church. Efforts within the Republic to conciliate Ulster by expunging from the constitution clauses — such as that against divorce — offensive to Protestants have proven futile. Further, Ireland's economy is weak and agricultural, plagued by unemployment and inadequate social services; while Northern Ireland is industrial and shares the benefits of the British welfare system. The Republicans, however, have never acknowledged Britain's authority over any portion of Ireland, and regard partition as an act of gerrymandering by an illegitimate power. The intransigence of both sides makes reconciliation seem unlikely, despite recent agreements and attempts at rapprochement between the British and Irish prime ministers.

Literature

 In Ireland, the magic of language has from the earliest times conferred a special and exalted status on those who command it. The poets of ancient Ireland had a reputation for supernatural powers and may have belonged to a caste that practiced sorcery. Even in the modern era, men of letters have been accorded high political honors unheard of in other countries. Douglas Hyde (1860–1949), one of those responsible for the revival of the Irish language and literature through the founding of the Gaelic League in 1893, became president of the Republic in 1938, and the poet and Nobel laureate W. B. Yeats (1865–1939) served as a senator from 1922 to 1928. In addition, the Irish language has imparted to the English speech of the country a haunting music and a distinctive, cantering rhythm.

The *filidhe* (master-poets of the Celts) earned their prestige by subjecting themselves to a rigorous course of training at bardic academies where the curriculum demanded memorization of lengthy sagas and learning composition in complex meters. Many graduates of the academies were attracted by monastic life, and their manuscripts and magnificent calligraphy and illumination made them Europe's preeminent students of literature. Between the eighth and sixteenth centuries these monks transcribed the oral traditions of which they were the living archives and, by keeping them in circulation, preserved them for posterity.

From various manuscript sources scholars can reconstruct the two great saga cycles, that of the Red Branch warriors of Ulster province and that of Finn MacCool and his Fenian band (the Fianna). The Ulster cycle constitutes a portion of the tribal history of the Uliad, who gave their name to the northernmost of Ireland's five provinces, and seems to have become current during the first century BC, though a quantity of older lore had been incorporated in the cycle. The king of the Ulidians in the cycle is Conchobar (pronounced Con-a-choor), whose castle stood at Emain Macha near modern Keady, County Armagh. But the protagonist is Cu Chulainn, the Hound of Ulster, offspring of the sun god and hero of the tribe.

The cycle centers around the Tain Bo Cualinge (The Cattle-Raid of Cooley), an epic narrative in which the semilegendary Queen Maeve of Connaught leads an expeditionary force toward Cooley (near Dundalk) to steal Conchobar's prized Brown Bull. Cu Chulainn single-handedly holds the invading army at bay while the Ulstermen recover from a 9-days' illness.

Cu Chulainn adds to the conventional virtues of courage and honor an impulsive disdain for any check to his appetites. He is the arch-individualist, a larger-than-life figure who postpones his first encounter with the Connaughtmen to keep a date with a woman, and who slays in single combat his best friend and his only son despite the promptings of human tenderness. His daring and determination together with a roguish impetuosity established a comic tradition in Irish literature.

Cu Chulainn was specifically a hero of the men of Ulster. But, between the commencement of the O'Neill dynasty and the height of the Norse incursions, Irish society was challenged to transcend the old clan loyalties for the sake of military unity. This was achieved politically in the person of Brian Ború and in literature through the Fenian cycle, which was the first truly national, rather than tribal, epic.

Finn MacCool, his son Oscar, his grandson Ossian, and his comrades Diarmiat and Cailte commanded the Fianna, the standing army of professional warriors said to have been mustered to the service of Cormac Mac Art, son of the founder of the Tara monarchy, in the third century AD. The Fenians were, from the outset, national rather than tribal heroes. Unlike the Ulster cycle, composed mostly in prose and incorporating myths in a highly learned manner, the Fenian cycle springs directly from popular folklore and employs a ballad meter to which the music of the common people easily adapted itself. It is more immediate and dramatic. Its characteristic form is the monologue or dialogue and its setting is the Christian era into which some Fenian hero has survived to speak, often to St. Patrick, of bygone days of glory. Not originally a product of the bardic academies, the Fenian cycle did not enter the courtly repertoire until the twelfth century, by which time it had already displaced the Ulster sagas in popular favor.

In contrast to Cu Chulainn, champion of a civilized nobility, the Fenians choose to live outside the pale of settlements and courts, preferring the woods and wilds. They are hunters rather than soldiers, akin to the gods of nature and place worshiped in the vernacular religion. It is from the Fenian tradition that Irish poetry receives its extraordinary sensitivity to nature:

> Arran of the many stags,
> The sea strikes against its shoulder . . .
> Skittish deer are on her peaks,
> Delicious berries on her manes . . .
> — *The Colloquy of the Old Men,*
> a Fenian romance from a
> 15th-century manuscript,
> translated by Myles Dillon

From the stories themselves flow the lyrical richness of Irish poetry, the sweetness and nostalgia of popular folk song, and the whole romantic spirit, dash, and panache of Irish history. The Fenian cycle inaugurates a dramatic and intensely personal literary style, which became the expressive mode of the Irish nation and provided the archetype of the outlaw brotherhood in which the nineteenth-century revolutionaries cast themselves.

The *filidhe* and its elite tradition were destroyed by the social upheavals caused by the plantation policy which replaced Irish landowners with English and later Scottish colonists prepared to offer allegiance to the crown. It was not until the eighteenth century, however, that it was finally extinguished. As late as 1781, a young schoolteacher from Clondagach, County Clare, who had educated himself in the metrical complexities of bardic composition, published an epic satire in the Irish language called *The Midnight Court,* in which the women of Ireland indict the men for contempt of matrimony and obtain a conviction in the court of the Fairy Queen. The poem is elegant, racy, and dreamlike, but its ribaldry proved too strong for a public taste narrowed by oppressive works that were pious and patriotic. The poem was suppressed, though portions of it can be heard recited from memory in some modern Irish-speaking households. Merriman, last of the *filidhe,* wrote nothing more and died in 1805.

Literature in English has been written in Ireland since the fourteenth century, but many of the Anglo-Irish literati owe little to the national traditions. Irish was the native tongue, and the native populace, denied and excluded from educational institutions by the Penal Codes, produced a glorious but impermanent body of unwritten poetry.

The chief educational institution in Ireland was Trinity College, Dublin, founded in 1591 as a university for the Protestant gentry. Trinity was the intellectual nursery of an extraordinary series of writers whose work places them more properly in a history of English rather than Irish literature. Yet their remarkable singularity of expression was one that could only have been nurtured in an environment where talk, conversation, language, provided the main indoor entertainment.

Chronologically, the first of these writers was Jonathan Swift (1667–1745), author of *Gulliver's Travels,* who is buried in St. Patrick's Cathedral, Dublin, of which he was dean. Next was William Congreve (1670–1729), author of one of the greatest comedies in the English language, *The Way of the World.* Then comes Oliver Goldsmith (1730?–74), the son of a Church of Ireland clergyman who is most famous for his play *She Stoops to Conquer* and his friendship with Dr. Samuel Johnson. Finally there is Oscar Wilde (1854–1900), the flamboyant author of the play *The Importance of Being Earnest* and the novel *The Picture of Dorian Gray.*

Two Dubliners who did not attend Trinity need to be mentioned in this category. One is Richard Brinsley Sheridan (1751–1816), the descendant of a famous Anglo-Irish family, whose masterpieces include *The Rivals* and *The School for Scandal.* The other is George Bernard Shaw (1856–1950), widely considered to be the greatest dramatist in the English language after Shakespeare. Shaw spent his first 20 years living in seedy gentility in Dublin. Even after he left to take up residence (and literary sovereignty) in London he never failed to involve himself in Irish affairs whether it concerned Parnell's divorce or Casement's homosexuality. Indeed he is one of the few writers in history who is as famous for his political curmudgeonry as he is for his great works (*St. Joan; Pygmalion; Heartbreak House*). A statue of him by Prince Paul Troubetskoy stands outside the National Gallery of Ireland, to which he left a substantial part of his fortune.

Occasionally the Protestant Ascendancy did produce a writer who was truly Irish in sympathy. One of these was Thomas Moore (1779–1852). Moore was a friend and the eulogizer of Robert Emmet (executed 1803), the prototype of the sort of Irishman who is both Protestant and nationalist. Emmet himself deserves a place in Irish literature for his speech from the scaffold which contains the immortal words, "Let no man write my epitaph . . ." Moore was a literary, though not a militant, patriot who wrote in the plaintive style of Irish folk song, often to popular airs. Songs like "The Minstrel Boy" and "The Harp That Once Through Tara's Halls" were ambassadors from romantic Ireland to the English gentry and helped revise their image of the Irish as crude and barbarous.

In 1842, *The Nation* magazine began publishing the poems and translations of James Clarence Mangan and Samuel Fergusson. Their work, infused with the energy and misty grandeur of the Irish language, excited interest in ancient literature, particularly the Fenian cycle. Its vibrant tapestry of hunts and fatal love, journeys to the underworld, battles between mortals and ghosts, sojourns in fairyland, and tone of wistful longing for the lost ardor of youth appealed to the romantic temperament of the times.

But the burgeoning political and literary movement did not achieve the status of a renaissance until the appearance of the work of W. B. Yeats (1865–1939), whose early imitations of folk poetry grafted French symbolism onto Irish folklore. Introduced to the Ulster cycle by his friend and patroness of the Irish Literary Renaissance, Lady (Augusta) Gregory, Yeats became fascinated by the figure of Cu Chulainn and meditated upon this image of the kind of reckless and heroic action he admired but shrank from in many poems.

William Butler Yeats was an unlikely Irishman. Son of an atheist father, the portraitist J. B. Yeats; grandson of the dandyish Church of Ireland rector at Drumcliff, County Sligo; brother of the expressionist painter Jack Yeats — William Butler Yeats was a member of various occult societies, an admirer of the English and a defender of the Ascendancy, a member of London literary society, and in his youth, one of those bohemian aesthetes whose tastes and style were schooled by the lyrical poetry of A. C. Swinburne, the humanist doctrines of Walter Pater, and the heroic fantasies of William Morris. Yet, he was also an ardent supporter of Charles Parnell, briefly a member of the Fenian Brotherhood, and a student of Irish folklore. Debarred from religious belief by the skepticism inherited from his father, Yeats invented a personal cosmology in which the clash and union of opposites, represented by the phases of the moon, become the dynamic force in history. ("By opposition, square and trine . . ." he says in the poem "In Memory of Major Robert Gregory.") The great poems of his middle years take their intellectual structure from this esoteric and enchantingly bizarre mythology, which perfectly expressed the contradictions of his own nature. Passionately attached to the peasantry, in whom he saw the wellspring of Ireland's creative energy, Yeats was equally passionately the champion of the Ascendancy, whom he regarded as Ireland's intellectual elite capable of giving coherent shape to the emotions of the masses. In his last years he abandoned his highly personalized mysticism to return with new freedom to the subject matter of his earliest days. Pathologically shy, Yeats was nevertheless proud and a trifle vain of his striking good looks. He became one of Ireland's leading public men and it was, ironically, this status rather than his years of obsession with mysticism and folklore that inspired his greatest poem, "Among School Children," with its famous last line "How can we know the dancer from the dance?"

Yeats often found himself embroiled in controversy because of the parochialism of the Dublin public, whose tastes were circumscribed by oppression and a conservative church. Yeats's own verse was not the source of his troubles; rather it was his defense of his friends and colleagues — Synge, Joyce, O'Casey. That he was a patriot, albeit an eccentric one, a celebrant of the Easter Rising, and, in his youth, a slightly uncomfortable agitator, did not go unrewarded; in 1922 he was appointed a senator of the Irish Free State. In debate, he spoke magnificently and pugnaciously against censorship, and also against the constitutional prohibition of divorce, which he characterized as an insult to the Protestant minority. He helped to found the Abbey Theatre, now a national institution, but when angry mobs stormed the stage, infuriated at a reference to women's undergarments in Synge's *Playboy of the Western World,* Yeats stepped before the curtains and sternly reproached them. When they did it 20 years later over the appearance of a prostitute in O'Casey's *The Plough and the Stars,* Yeats confronted them a second time, booming at them: "You have disgraced yourselves again!" Ireland loves drama, and Yeats provided drama in abundance. In return, Ireland grudgingly offered him its adoration for the splendor and valor of his quixotic idealism.

Yeats believed that great poetry must be rooted in place and "The Lake Isle of Innisfree," "The Fiddler of Dooney," "The Man Who Dreamed of Faeryland," and others of his early poems are set close to Sligo town. But the most important landmarks in his verse are Knocknarea, atop of which stands the pile of stones known as Queen Maeve's Cairn, and Ben Bulben, the limestone mesa on the other side of Sligo Bay. Between these two mountains, spectral horsemen called Dananns were said to ride each night:

> The host is riding from Knocknarea
> And over the grave of Clooth-na-Bare;
> Caoilte tossing his burning hair,
> And Niamh calling *Away, come away* . . .
> ("The Hosting of the Sidhe," ca. 1899*)

To these horsemen, Yeats, buried in Drumcliffe churchyard at the foot of Ben Bulben, addressed himself in his epitaph:

> *Cast a cold eye*
> *On life, on death.*
> *Horseman, pass by!*
> ("Under Ben Bulben," 1938)

Yeats's work is among the glories of modern literature (he won the Nobel Prize in 1923), yet he was unstintingly generous and supportive of other writers. He encouraged the younger Anglo-Irish writer, John Millington Synge, to rediscover his roots by visiting the Aran Islands in Galway Bay. Synge's sojourn on Inishmaan, as well as in other Irish-speaking regions, inspired him to combine the realism of Ibsen with the wild, fantastical speech of the Irish countryside in plays that treated the life of Ireland's impoverished rural proletariat with Chekovian irony and unsentimental honesty. Synge never romanticized, and his plays have no heroes. Christy Mahon, protagonist of *The Playboy of the Western World,* finds himself suddenly a celebrity in a strange village after confessing to the murder of his own father, and the object, thanks to his prestige, of the affections of Pegeen Mike, the daughter of a publican. When Christy proves innocent of the crime, Pegeen turns on him in a paroxysm of disappointment because, having shown himself to be more tender than wicked, he lacks the notoriety to elevate her life beyond its drudgery; in the last line of the play, having "lost her only playboy of the western world," she realizes, too late, that she loves him. In *Riders to the Sea,* set in the Aran Islands, an old woman accepts the drowning of her last surviving son with a chilly stoicism that is at once tragic and appalling. Synge's is a vision without comfort, as bleak as Dreiser's, and as perversely comic as Chekhov's.

Synge died in 1909 at the age of 38, but not before he had given the Abbey Theatre and the playwrights of Ireland a dramatic style, often vulgarized, alas, into "peasant-quality" plays in which quaintness and condescending coyness displace Synge's unsparing realism. Synge invented a dialect in which the idioms and constructions of Irish are rendered directly into English. So exquisite a tool did this dialect become that Synge used it to splendid effect in his translations of Petrarch and Villon. But no other playwright could manage the trick.

*"The Hosting of the Sidhe," from *The Collected Poems of W. B. Yeats* (New York: Macmillan, 1956). © The Macmillan Company 1956. Reprinted by permission of Macmillan Inc., Macmillan London Ltd., M. B. Yeats, and Anne Yeats.

Synge's example, and Yeats's solicitous encouragement, bore fruit in the work of the next great Abbey playwright, Sean O'Casey (1884–1964). Born in the Dublin slums, O'Casey, a Protestant, was the first figure of the Literary Renaissance to spring directly from the proletariat and to make the urban working class the subject of his attention. O'Casey needed no synthetic dialect; the speech of Dublin came naturally to him. His politics, however, came as a mild shock to his colleagues — most especially Yeats, whom O'Casey remembered with wry affection in his memoirs — for he professed to be Communist. Equally shocking to the public was his insistence on showing Dublin's raw backside. The presence of a prostitute in *The Plough and the Stars* together with the meeting of revolutionary patriots in the unholy precincts of a pub, provoked riots at the play's premiere. Two years later, embittered at *The Plough's* reception and furious because Yeats refused to produce his next play, *The Silver Tassie,* O'Casey moved to England, never to return. Nothing he wrote thereafter quite equaled his early works, which also included *Juno and the Paycock* and *Shadow of a Gunman.*

O'Casey's social passion, his sense of grievance, and his identification with his working-class characters left him more vulnerable than Yeats and Synge to sentimentality; yet, his affection for the outlaw and the outcast recalls the Fenian tradition and rescues his early plays from bathos. O'Casey's spiritual successor among Irish playwrights was Brendan Behan (1923–1964). Housepainter, drunkard, and self-made intellectual, Behan, between 1956 and 1958, disposed of his mammoth talent in three works — *Borstal Boy,* his memoir of life in a British reformatory where he was imprisoned for revolutionary terrorism on English soil; *The Quare Fellow,* a drama of prison life under the pall of an inmate's imminent execution; and his magnum opus, *The Hostage,* after which he subsided into notoriety and drink.

Behan's last words, spoken to the nun at his hospital bedside, were: "God bless you, sister, and may all your sons be bishops." He lived and wrote with Rabelaisian gusto. In 1937, he joined the outlawed Irish Republican Army and gave his youth to the cause, although he grew to distrust the fanaticism he saw in it. *The Hostage* is a kind of tragic farce in which an IRA contingent, commanded by a bizarre Ascendancy enthusiast, seizes a young British soldier and holds him hostage in a Dublin brothel on Nelson Street where the residents include, among the working girls, two outrageous homosexuals, a devout and lascivious spinster, and an innocent housemaid who falls in love with the hostage. The Republicans threaten to kill the prisoner in order to force the reprieve of two of their own facing execution in a Belfast jail. The play is punctuated by songs that lampoon Irish piety, by dances and jokes, and, finally, by the gunfire of a police raid in which the hostage is tragically killed. Characters frequently address the audience, the accompanist remains onstage throughout, and no pretense is made that this is anything but theater; yet it captures the emotions anyway having dispensed with every theatrical convention except the heart's truth.

James Joyce (1882–1941), the titan of Irish prose, exempted himself from the Literary Renaissance — he referred to Yeats's Celtic Twilight as the "Cultic Toilette" — and at age 22 expatriated himself to the Continent. He took with him a handsome but intellectually unprepossessing shopgirl, Nora Barnacle, who became for him the personification of Dublin, in the environs of which Joyce set everything he ever wrote.

Joyce's insistence on fixing his most obscure works to the real, even trivial, details of the city he remembered, amounted to the most creative obsession in modern letters. As a young man, growing up in a middle-class home, educated in Catholic prep schools and at Trinity College, Joyce had been attracted to the realism of Ibsen and learned Norwegian to read his plays in the original.

Ulysses, the huge novel that established Joyce's preeminent reputation, follows Leopold Bloom, a Dublin Jew, his wife, Molly, and young Stephen Daedalus, Joyce's surrogate, in their minute-by-minute progress through a single day — June 16, 1904 — in Dublin. Joyce employed a stream-of-consciousness technique to record the random associations of his characters' thoughts. Readers were shocked by the eroticism of these interior monologues, and the book was until quite recently banned in Ireland. Yet Dubliners who managed to obtain copies were fascinated by the many living personalities parading across the pages and by the accuracy with which Joyce had observed and remembered the city, its features, and its speech. What few realized was how brilliantly Joyce had transformed the details of Dublin life — newspaper articles from June 16, 1904, brand-name household goods, idioms of local patois — into symbols of Europe's mythological and psychic heritage represented by *The Odyssey,* the novel's controlling metaphor. Nor do many readers appreciate Joyce's love for his characters until Molly Bloom's long interior soliloquy on the edge of sleep.

On "Bloomsday," June 16, of every year, dedicated Joyceans gather in Dublin to retrace the routes followed by *Ulysses*'s characters: from the Martello Tower (a Napoleonic era fortress) where Joyce, like Stephen Daedalus, lived in his student days, through the city, past nearly every point of interest or importance, to Eccles Street, where the Blooms resided. Fans of Joyce's next and last book, *Finnegans Wake,* are rather few. It is probably the most frustrating and impenetrable book ever written, for here language itself is the subject. Nearly every one of the book's 237,600 words has several meanings at once. Joyce, master of nearly every European language, enlisted them all to create this huge stream-of-consciousness work — the sleeping, dreaming thought-flow of the Earwicker family of Dublin, whose matriarch, Ann (known also as Anna Livia Plurabelle), is at once the spirit of the Liffey River and the form of the book.

Joyce's works belong to the Red Branch line — comic, cosmic, larger-than-life — but Samuel Beckett, briefly his secretary in the 1930s and another Dublin expatriate to the Continent, belongs to no tradition, though he shows the influence of Joyce and Synge. A founding member of the avant-garde, and Ireland's third Nobel Prize winner (after Yeats and Shaw), Beckett's enigmatic plays and novels seem less overtly Irish than the works of his compatriot although here and there in *Waiting for Godot* one hears echoes of the Irish music hall, and the astute reader or listener will realize that *Play* is set in Foxrock, a Dublin suburb. Beckett, the quintessential absurdist, displays in works as dauntingly obtuse in starkness as *Finnegans Wake* the characteristic daring and individualism of the Irish.

Ireland has dispensed fine writing to the world — this is no provincial tradition — with astonishing abundance in this century. Among the lesser-known luminaries, some of whom have fallen into the shadows of the gods, are Frank O'Connor, memoirist, essayist, translator, and chronicler nonpareil of literary Ireland; Patrick Kavanagh, Ireland's only beat poet; Louis Mac-Neice, the Belfast poet; Flann O'Brien (*At Swim-Two-Birds*), surrealist virtuoso; Denis O'Donoghue, the literary critic; playwrights Brian Friel and Hugh Leonard, who have enjoyed notable successes on Broadway; poets Thomas Kinsella and Seamus Heaney; and, to run on and on, Padraic Colum, Denis Johnstone, Iris Murdoch, Brian Moore, Edna O'Brien, Liam O'Flaherty, Sean O'Faoilain . . . as though all the vital energies of the nation, pent up through 700 years of oppression, were erupting. The spectacle of the Irish literary explosion is without parallel in history.

Architecture

Ireland is full of picturesque ruins and ancient structures, which is part of its charm for Americans unaccustomed to architecture older than a few centuries. Along every Irish road and river lie Stone Age tombs, ruined abbeys, decayed or restored castles, Palladian-style manor houses, and stately Georgian mansions. And the thatched and whitewashed or fieldstone cottages in the remoter regions are most appealing with their timeless, homespun simplicity.

The oldest structures, some of which have been dated to 3000 BC, are the megalithic monuments — the tumuli and stone circles at Carrowmore in County Donegal and Carrowkeel in County Sligo; the passage grave complex at Brugh na Boinne in County Meath; and the decorated standing stones and dolmens scattered about the countryside. Whether these monuments were built by an indigenous people or by immigrants is not known, but they are similar to those found in Europe and England; Stonehenge is perhaps the best-known example. It is thought that these structures were prehistoric shrines, and that the Celts, who began arriving in Ireland around 500 BC, also endowed the sites with religious or magical significance.

The earliest Celtic structures are the *dúns,* fortresses enclosed by dry-stone walls and often built atop megalithic shrines or ring-forts. The walls served both to keep cattle in and protect the settlement from attack. The most famous and impressive of the fortresses is Dún Aengus on the Aran isle of Inishmore in Galway Bay. Dún Aengus is a semicircle; its open side is a cliff that drops precipitously 266 feet to the roiling Atlantic, giving the impression that the missing half of the circle had collapsed into the ocean in some terrible cataclysm. Other notable ringed fortresses include Tara in County Meath and Grianán of Aileach in County Donegal.

Early Celtic dwellings were built of timber and wattle and have not survived. In treeless areas people lived in stone dwellings; their *clocháns* (beehive huts) were constructed in corbelled fashion, with the stones overlapping each other. The early Christian churches were also built in the beehive style, although some variations were introduced — such as a rectangular shape and a pitched roof. Two examples are Skellig Michael off the Kerry coast, and the Gallerus Oratory in County Kerry; both are thought to date to the eighth century.

The round tower is another relic of early Christian architecture. Ranging in height from 70 to 120 feet, slightly tapered, and topped by a conical roof, these were bell towers as well as places of refuge where monks hid from Viking invaders. (The doorway was located high above the ground and when under attack the inhabitants withdrew the adjoining ladder for safety.) A fine example of an early Christian round tower is the freestanding, eleventh-century structure at Glendalough in County Wicklow.

Irish monastic and ecclesiastic architecture further developed with the introduction to Ireland of the Romanesque style during the twelfth century. It was embraced with some enthusiasm by native artisans, and ornate stone carvings — human and animal heads, chevrons, interlace, and foliage — decorate the arches, doorways, capitals, and sometimes windows of the churches of this period. The Chapel of Cormac, situated on the Rock of Cashel in County Tipperary, is the earliest Irish Romanesque structure in the country and Clonfert Cathedral in County Galway is perhaps the most ornate; both have heavily embellished portals.

The invasion of the Normans in 1170 changed the face of Irish architecture forever, for they brought with them from England and Wales the designs and styles, proportions, shapes, and decorative devices prevalent there. Eager to colonize, they began a flurry of cathedral- and castle-building that lasted from the twelfth to the seventeenth century. The numerous churches constructed during this period tended to be large and Gothic in style, with tall lancet windows and pointed arches; St. Patrick's Cathedral in Dublin is a fine example. The typical Norman fortress had a square stone keep enclosed by curtain walls linking four circular corner towers. King John's Castle in Limerick City, built in 1210, combines all of these features. The towerhouse, a structure favored by both Norman and native Irish, dates to between the fifteenth and seventeenth century. Most of them were built, however, just after the Statute of 1429 which offered a £10 subsidy to any person building such a tower within the Pale. The so-called £10 houses were fortified dwellings built of stone, four or five stories high, with narrow slitted windows and a steeply pitched roof. A very simple Norman-built towerhouse is Donore Castle in County Meath.

During the late seventeenth century, domestic dwellings began to look less like fortresses and more like the classical mansions popular in England. This meant that houses were often built of brick, with hipped roofs and dormer windows, as exemplified by Beaulieu in County Louth. Very soon, however, the Irish and English imagination was captured by Palladianism, a reinterpretation of the design principles evolved by Italian architect Andrea Palladio in the mid-sixteenth century. The arrangement of columns and arches in the façade of Bellamont Forest in County Cavan is a typical Palladian motif.

The eighteenth century saw the architectural expansion and enhancement of Ireland's urban centers — Belfast, Cork, Dublin, Limerick, and Waterford. During this period Dublin received a heady endowment of new buildings designed in the classical style — incorporating elements from ancient Greek and Roman architecture — such as Trinity College, the Four Courts, the Custom House, and the Parliament buildings (now the Bank of Ireland). Georgian architecture was also popular, and elegant Georgian squares — gracious greens presided over by tall brick townhouses with pillared doorways and distinctive fanlights — appeared not only in Dublin (Fitzwilliam and Merrion squares), but also in Limerick City (Newtown Pery) and in Belfast (Donegall Square). Neoclassicism remained in vogue during the nineteenth century, although Irish architects also flirted briefly with various revivals of the Gothic style (St. Finbarr's Cathedral in Cork), Italianate (the Custom House in Belfast), and Edwardian (Belfast City Hall).

The common dwellings of Ireland remained virtually unchanged from earliest Celtic times: They were usually only one room heated by a central fireplace that vented its smoke through a hole in the roof. Stables and byres were built adjacent, although animals sometimes shared the living quarters in the interest of warmth. The central hearth style with hipped roof was most common in the eastern counties, while homes in the northwest had a bed alcove and room extensions. In the southwest, gables appeared, rising above the thatching, which replaced stone as the common roofing material. Two-story dwellings did not appear until the late nineteenth century, when, after the depopulation caused by the famine, efforts were made to eliminate the thatched cottages altogether and replace them with more modern accommodations.

Today, the art of thatching has been practically lost, though many old vernacular houses are still in use. Departing visitors whose route back to Shannon Airport takes them through Adare, County Limerick, can see an especially pretty row of thatched houses on their way through town, and chances are they'll also see a thatcher at work, because the roofs are meticulously kept. The traditional style has also been revived somewhat in villages of thatched cottages — with open fireplaces and flagstone floors, as well as electricity, modern heating, and plumbing — built for the use of vacationers. But more than likely, what the visitor will remember most is the haunting picture of the same simple dwellings scattered forlorn and deserted throughout the Irish countryside, left to decay when their owners left for a better life elsewhere. The history of Ireland is indeed told in its architecture.

Traditional Music and Dance

The harp is the instrument most associated with Ireland from ancient times; it was used for centuries by learned bards who entertained the royal Gaelic courts with recitations of poetry and sagas. After the dissolution of the Gaelic courts ordered by the Cromwellian Act of Settlement in 1652, the bards scattered to the countryside, where they mingled with folk poets, and a general intermarriage of their styles ensued. The classical airs that evolved from such collaboration — "The Coolun," "Roisin Dubh," and "Eileen Aroon" — present a refinement and gravity uncommon in folk music.

The harpers traveled among the houses of the rural gentry, playing traditional songs and creating new ones on commission. The greatest of these harpers was Turlough O'Carolan (1670–1738), whose compositions wed a certain European sophistication (perhaps acquired in Dublin) with a native Irish sensibility: Though his melodies are quite lengthy and complex, they also flirt now and again with the popular gapped scales, never losing touch with the folk spirit. Some have become staples of modern Irish ensembles.

Another instrument always associated with Ireland is the bagpipe. The *uilleann* (pronounced ill-en) pipes differ from those played in Scotland in that the bellows is pumped with the elbow, a softer reed is used, the drones are slung across the leg of the seated player, and there are keys that change the drone notes when depressed with the heel of the right hand, enabling the player to produce chords. The *uilleann* has been called the "Irish organ," for it is capable of extremely rich, resonant sound, though, with its straps and harnesses, it resembles an instrument of torture. The west of Ireland, particularly County Clare, was until recently the home of fine Irish piping; but the recent rise in popularity of Irish music throughout the world has persuaded numbers of young Irish (who might otherwise have belabored guitars) to take up the arduous study of this noble and exacting instrument.

While traditional dance music is played on pipes as well as fiddles, the "big airs" — the slow and majestic classical tunes — are especially moving when played on the expansive pipes. Of the older generation of pipers, only Seamus Ennis is still alive, though many recordings of great pipers like Willy Clancy and Leo Rowesome are available. Three of the best younger pipers are Paddy Maloney, of The Chieftains, Finbar Furey, of the Furey Brothers, and the virtuosic Joe McKenna. The McPeakes of Belfast were three generations of harpers, pipers, and singers led by Frank McPeake, reputed to have been the first piper skilled enough to sing to his own accompaniment.

The piper produces the melody — trills, grace notes, and other flourishes — by moving his fingers to open or close the holes of the chanter, or pipe. Flutes and pennywhistles are played in the same way, without tonguing. The great Sligo fiddler Michael Coleman, who emigrated to America and recorded here in the 1920s, evolved a similar ornamental style for his instrument, one which has since become the standard. The musical embellishments used by fiddlers, pipers, flutists, and pennywhistlers perfectly suits the structure of Irish dance music — the jigs, reels, and hornpipes — in which a sinuous and fluid melody rushes along with scarcely a pause for breath, diving and soaring with dizzying exuberance. The stuttering throb of the *bodhrán* (a hand-held drum beaten with a double-headed stick) gives the music an irresistible rhythmic momentum more like jazz or flamenco than anything in the other Celtic musical traditions.

The music of County Kerry tends to be less hectic and more regularly cadenced than that of the rest of the country. Some scholars believe it represents an older style. Polkas and schottisches, not found elsewhere in Ireland, are performed in Kerry, as are longer, more elegant dances. A fine example of the latter, which will seem more classical and less Irish to the average listener, and more like the harp music of Carolan, is the work of Eugene O'Donnell, the fiddler.

The Connemara region on Ireland's far western coast, a rocky and forbidding region north of Galway City, is famous for its singers and for its stately, mysterious ballads. The vocal technique resembles that of piping and Sligo fiddling; some of the notes are changed or the tempo slowed and the melody is delivered with a multitude of embellishments. The effect can be quite fascinating, as if you were listening to dance music in slow motion. The recordings of Joe Heany of Carna provide excellent examples of the ballad style.

Ensembles of singers or musicians are not traditional in Ireland. Solo playing was the rule until the 1920s when record companies began to demand lively and audible renditions of dance tunes to supply the dance market in America; this prompted musicians to seek accompanists. During the 1950s, Sean O'Riada, a "serious" composer and harpsichordist, hearing the *ceildhe* (dance) bands that had begun to form and sounded, as someone wrote, "like a tree full of blackbirds," conceived the idea of arranging Irish music for an orchestra of traditional instruments. He gathered a group of fiddlers, pipers, accordionists, whistlers, flutists, and drummers in Dublin and taught them their parts by ear (few could read music). The delightful result was Ceolteori Cualain, the first sophisticated folk music ensemble, for whom O'Riada provided many orchestrations, which — though they were enriched with harmonies, counterpoint, even rudimentary fugues — never lost their simplicity and drive.

During the 1960s, the Clancy Brothers and Tommy Makem found an audience among folk music fans in America, and introduced them to a species of Irish music worlds away from "Mother Macree" and the other products of the Hibernian division of Tin Pan Alley. Their repertoire included revolutionary and patriotic songs (as well as that pungent Irish subgenre, the antiwar song), sea chanties, and children's songs, all of them delivered with robust good humor and taste. Since the disappearance of the harpers in the nineteenth century, music had rarely been a professional undertaking among the Irish, but the Clancys stimulated a new interest, and before long Ireland was in the midst of a ballad boom. Among the more successful groups were The Dubliners, a group of four — later five — men including Ronny Drew, a flamenco guitarist and master of the Dublin street-ballad, and Barney McKenna, a wizard who pioneered the application of the Sligo style to the tenor banjo. The Dubliners have proven a durable institution, though, like most Irish musicians who want to earn a living by their art, they have had to seek audiences in England and on the Continent.

After the death of Sean O'Riada, a party of his alumni formed The Chieftains to carry on his style and bring it to a wider audience. They tightened the O'Riada sound and began running tunes together in patchwork medleys, sometimes juxtaposing contrasting sounds for dramatic effect. The Chieftains fathered a generation of such ensembles in Ireland and Scotland as well as America, where "Celtic" bands have begun to proliferate. Among the best Irish bands are Planxty, Sweeny's Men, The Bothy Band, and De Danann;

they preserve the charm and melodic richness of traditional music but deliver it with the instrumental daring and emotional impact of rock.

Music clubs have lately begun to spring up in various Irish cities so that now musicians — who previously gathered only in a few pubs or at government-sponsored summer music festivals — may perform regularly. Concerts are rare, though, and you must search pretty far in the country to find local pubs where musicians play (see *Where to Hear Traditional Irish Music,* DIVERSIONS). For years, music was like conversation to the Irish: They would no sooner pay for a song than for a chat.

Food and Drink

 Ireland's location and climate have combined to produce an agricultural abundance: Its lush grasslands support a thriving livestock industry, resulting in good beef, lamb, and pork; its extensive waters yield a fine harvest of fish and seafood: sole, plaice, mackerel, sea trout, salmon, lobster and crab, prawns and scallops, oysters and mussels; its soil and mild climate nurture barley, wheat, sugar beets, and potatoes — as well as other vegetables, when Irish farmers can be persuaded to grow them.

At its best, Irish food is fresh, nourishing, and prepared simply. There are some regional variations and a few local specialties, but the real geographical division is between the coast and the interior. On the coast, which is heavily visited by travelers, food is on the whole good and presentation attractive. The flat heart of the country has barely emerged from the dark English provincial ages that dominated food in Ireland for a century and a half. The "commercial hotel" — the haven of the turn-of-the-century English business traveler — established a horrendous food pattern that is only now breaking up. A typical meal here consisted of Windsor soup (a nondescript liquid full of floury lumps) and overdone roast beef, crowded on the plate by watery, overcooked vegetables and bathed in a thicker version of the soup called "gravy." This repast concluded with a heavy pudding doused in a nasty, viscous, yellow liquid miscalled "custard." You will rarely find this meal now in its pristine horror, but elements of "commercial" cooking still survive in the midlands and the wary traveler must forage around a little for better food.

That dire warning noted, we will now discuss *real* Irish food. The timing of meals in Ireland is important. The Irish food day is divided into three main meals and almost as many side events. The weight-conscious visitor will simply have to pick and choose and try to be selective.

A typical Irish breakfast starts with porridge (a flavorsome boiled oatmeal topped with cream) and continues through a main course of bacon and eggs accompanied by fried tomatoes, toast, and orange marmalade. The eggs you can have any style and the bacon is good though not cooked crisply. You may also be served a black or white pudding (both are kinds of blood pudding) or even kidney or liver. Tea is recommended over coffee; with rare exceptions the Irish do not make coffee well. They make their tea strong and with milk; inform them if you want it weak and with lemon.

A breakfast alternative offered on the coast is plaice, a delicate-tasting flounder-style fish, or fresh mackerel if they are running. Try both for a new and delightful breakfast experience.

Instead of toast you may be served a coarse, wholemeal "brown bread" — homebaked, nutty, and delicious — or "soda bread" — plain white, usually made *without* raisins (unlike the unauthentic version often served in American restaurants).

The midmorning snack — a cup of tea or coffee with a biscuit (cookie) or sweet bun — is very popular in urban Ireland: Some temples to the practice are *Bewley's Oriental Cafés* in Dublin (sinfully sweet sticky buns and coffee topped with Jersey cream), *Lydon House* in Galway, and *Thompson's* in Cork. Over such matins, much business is conducted, gossip exchanged, and romances started or continued.

To dine or not to dine is a big question for the traveler. For most Irish people, particularly those in the countryside, luncheon is the main meal, taken about one o'clock, and usually consists of soup, meat (beef or chicken), vegetables (peas, cabbage, carrots, and usually potatoes), and dessert (the Irish call them sweets). The latter are generally puddings or pastries. Here or there, you may encounter carrageen sweets; these are molded jelly with extract of Irish moss, a species of seaweed, flavored with lemon rind and served with heavy cream or fruit. They are mild and subtle and entirely pleasant. Cheese is often offered as an alternative to dessert. Irish cheese is good and some hotels have a tempting cheeseboard that includes French and other European varieties. If you are staying with an Irish family, follow custom — otherwise do as you like. Most hotels and restaurants feature a formal midday meal, and a saving grace is that although fundamentally the same meal as that served in the evening it costs up to 50% less.

The alternatives to a full hot lunch are luckily multiplying in Ireland. Hotel coffee shops or lounges will serve cold plates of smoked salmon, chicken, salads, or sandwiches. The Irish pub — which hitherto concentrated on one thing, drink — is gradually extending its menu from sandwiches (which are thin and bready by American standards), to include soup, cold plates, salads, and hot meat pies. Watch for signs that say "Pub Grub." Another option in some towns are fish-and-chip shops; the fish (usually whiting) is good, the chips delicious, and the price low.

Or you may prefer to skip lunch and sustain yourself until the main evening meal by having afternoon tea. This fine English institution is, like many other colonial relics, slowly fading from Ireland. Afternoon tea is undeniably a spiritual refreshment; it can rise to ritual, however, when it includes delicate finger sandwiches of ham, chicken, or cucumber; strips of toast with honey; chocolate eclairs; heavy fruitcakes; or wedges of apple tart with cream. You can indulge in such an experience at *Hunters* hotel in Ashford, County Wicklow; or *Rathmullan House,* in Rathmullan, County Donegal.

The domestic Irish evening dinner meal is usually called tea or supper — "high tea" if you want to distinguish it verbally from the afternoon version. In winter it might be quite a substantial meal — a mixed grill (sausage, bacon, kidney, a small piece of steak, and a lamb chop), steak and French fries, or fish in the coastal areas; in summer, it may be something lighter, such as boiled eggs with toast or bread and jam, or a plate of sliced cold chicken or ham. Tea is rounded off with cake, a fruit tart, pudding, or scones.

Among the traditional Irish dishes for which you should lunge when they are offered are oxtail soup, Irish stew (simmered layers of onion, potato, and mutton), and fresh salmon — in season — for which the country is justifiably famous. Seafood, surprisingly, has only recently become popular in Ireland, though the coastal waters abound with prawns, lobster, mussels, and oysters. Each October, at the beginning of the oyster harvest, a festival is held in Galway City, during which bushels of bivalves meet their doom in a deluge of porter (a dark beer). Briefly thereafter, oysters become available in the shops. Another delicacy sometimes served in restaurants is the periwinkle, a tiny sea snail that is boiled, picked from the shell with sewing needles or wooden pikes, and eaten. Dipped in melted butter laced with garlic, the winkle need not blush before the escargot.

At fairs or horse races, you may notice little bags of dried seaweed being sold as though it were candy; this is dulse, and it makes a tasty, salty "chaw" — a fine accompaniment to a glass of stout.

This brings us to the subject of drink. The favored beverage is stout, or porter, a dark, pungent brew served by the "jar," with a head like thick cream and a reputation for being able to support life single-handedly. Guinness is the largest brewer, though other brands are locally obtainable outside Dublin. (Guided tours are no longer conducted at the Guinness brewery on St. James's Gate, but an audiovisual show is offered and visitors are still invited to sample the famous stout.) Good lager and ale, like stout, are drawn at room temperature; the Irish regard the American custom of taking such beverages icy cold with the wry detachment of the anthropologist. They privately think it is a custom suitable only for savages. A dash of sweetened lime juice in a glass of beer makes a refreshing drink called, unsurprisingly, lager and lime.

Most Irish bartenders do not mix drinks, and wines, except for brandy, are not widely available. The spirits of choice are gin, Scotch, and Irish whiskey. The whiskey distributed for home consumption is far smoother than the youthful export stuff, though of slightly lower proof. It is, like the great malt whiskeys of Scotland, a straight liquor, unblended, and it has a distinctive fruity bouquet and trace of sweetness. Don't miss a chance to sample that famous after-dinner treat — Irish coffee, a tantalizing concoction of hot coffee and whiskey topped with a thick layer of gently whipped cream. (For a more complete discussion of beers, ales, and liquors, as well as a selection of the best watering holes in Ireland, see *Pub Crawling,* DIVERSIONS.)

THE CITIES

THE CITIES

BATH

Bath was meant to be a beautiful city, and it is. Anchored in the valley of the River Avon and reverberating up seven surrounding hills in the southwest corner of the Cotswolds, its location alone would have been promising. But for close to 2,000 years, the ancient city — known as Aquae Sulis to its Roman founders — remained undistinguished except as the site of Britain's only hot springs, a place to come and "take the waters." It was a remarkable eighteenth-century urban planning effort that made Bath the splendid Georgian city that it is today. Then the haphazard parts, including the striking abbey, were unified along classical lines in tier upon tier of crescents, terraces, and squares climbing from the banks of the river. As a result, Bath still calls itself the first planned city in England, and visitors who see its warm, honey-colored stones set against the rich green of lawn, tree, and wooded hillside will probably agree.

The city's past emerges from legend with the Romans who, in approximately AD 54, established an elaborate system of baths here along with a temple to Sulis Minerva, a combination of the Celtic deity Sul and the Roman goddess of wisdom, Minerva. The town grew to become a famous health resort and remained one until the Romans left Britain in the early fifth century. After that, Aquae Sulis declined rapidly and the Roman baths sank back into the warm mud.

The Saxons built an abbey in 781, such a fine one that it was chosen as the site of the coronation in 973 of King Edgar as the first king of England in a ceremony that has remained a model for the coronation of all subsequent English kings and queens. The city's fame was short-lived, however, though the sick continued to be drawn to medieval baths raised over the salubrious mineral springs by builders unaware of the ancient prototypes buried underground. As the visitors soaked in the Cross Bath (dating from the seventh century), the King's Bath (built smack on top of the Romans' reservoir in the twelfth century), and others, Bathonians made a better living in the wool trade — Chaucer's Wife of Bath was one of the successful makers of cloth.

With the patronage of royalty in the late seventeenth century, Bath began to regain its reputation as a first-class spa. The wife of King James II, Mary of Modena, bore a healthy son after a stop at the Cross Bath. His daughter, Queen Anne, later made several trips. Once kings and queens and their entourages, members of court, country gentry, and notables from all walks of life began to take the cure or just luxuriate, Bath was suddenly fashionable among both the healthy and the sick.

Today's city of elegant squares and crescent streets is the labor of love of three eighteenth-century gentlemen. Richard "Beau" Nash arrived in 1705. He was an honest gambler from Wales, a social catalyst who found his calling when he took on the job of master of ceremonies, in charge of public entertainments. Nash was the equivalent of a modern fund raiser and public relations person for Bath. He found the money to pave roads, light streets, and endow the Royal Mineral Water Hospital, which survives as the Royal National Hospital for Rheumatic Diseases. He became an arbiter of taste and comportment, laying down rules of etiquette that were not to be broken. Duels were suppressed, smoking in public prohibited, improper dress ridiculed, corruption in the sedan chair business wiped out. Within a generation, the sheer force of his personality had made Bath the second capital of English society.

A Cornish postal clerk named Ralph Allen arrived next. He eventually became postmaster, made a fortune from the mail business, and bought the limestone quarries on the southern hill of the city, Combe Down. Bath's pale stone was as yet untested for building purposes, so Allen engaged a Yorkshire architect, John Wood, as technical adviser. It was a master stroke. Thus supplied with financial backing and building material, the talented Yorkshireman proceeded to impose architectural order on the gay whirl of the city, designing not simply single buildings but entire rows, crescents, and squares in accordance with the Neoclassical principles of the Palladian style. Queen's Square, North and South Parade, and the Circus are all his.

Wood's grand conceptions were not realized in full, not even by his son, another John Wood, who carried on the father's work and added his own to the Bath landscape. The younger Wood's Assembly Rooms enclosed the Georgians' amusements and dalliance in aesthetically suitable wrappings. While the frivolity endured, they were the essence of Bath. But his ultimate expression was the Royal Crescent, a beautiful scimitar of a street whose grandeur seems almost out of keeping with a city this size, one that was never in itself of great consequence in the affairs of state, though almost anyone of consequence — in government, the arts, or society — spent time here.

Visitors to Bath today see much of it as the Georgians left it, despite bombing damage during World War II, population growth (now at 85,000), and the development of light industry. Bathonians have a history of carefully safeguarding their heritage and preserving their architecture, even to the point where residents whose tree-lined gardens are visible to tourists receive a maintenance grant from the city's "tree fund." Blending the past with the present to create a congenial whole is one of the marvels of Bath. It still provides the feeling of a city truly built in a gentler age, a time immortalized in the novels of Jane Austen and Tobias Smollett. It's a pervasive feeling that's hard to shake in Bath — as if one would want to. Instead, reinforce it by walking up to the Royal Crescent at dusk. As the honey-colored stones darken to gray, the lights of the city twinkle across the dark shadows of Royal Victoria Park as softly as gas lamps. It's easy to imagine you're in an England more than two and a half centuries old.

BATH AT-A-GLANCE

SEEING THE CITY: The up-and-down setting of this city on seven hills provides more than one spot for an overall view. If you have a car, drive north up Lansdown Road and see Bath unfold beneath you or, even better, go to the opposite side of town: From Widcombe Hill or North Road you face directly onto Bath Abbey, the Royal Crescent, and the Pump Room.

SPECIAL PLACES: Bath's tourism "musts" are conveniently situated right in the heart of town. The hot baths of Aquae Sulis may have given the city its start in the 1st century, but the most commanding building is undoubtedly the later abbey, the massive square-towered edifice that dwarfs its surroundings from almost every angle. Still later came the Assembly Rooms, the Pump Room, and glorious streets, squares, and crescents that have helped to make Bath the architectural gem that it is.

Roman Baths – The baths are Britain's most complete Roman remains, fed by the country's only hot water springs. The establishment, with its magnificent Great Bath, flourished between the 1st and 5th centuries AD as one of the most famous health resorts of the Roman Empire, then fell into ruin. The springs themselves — gushing to the surface at a temperature of 110°F and a rate of more than 300,000 gallons a day — remained in use for various later baths, however, including the King's Bath, built by 12th-century Normans over the Roman reservoir and spring, next to the by-then-buried Roman baths. Rediscovery of the latter began in the 18th century, and they are still being excavated today. The treasures preserved in the accompanying museum include coins, gemstones, pewter tableware, mosaics, and a gilt-bronze head of the goddess Sulis Minerva, to whom a temple on the site was dedicated. Many of the objects were found in the most recent excavations beneath the floor of the King's Bath, where the ancients had thrown them as offerings to the sacred spring. (Among the more unusual finds are the curses inscribed on lead invoking the aid of the goddess in bringing grief to an enemy.) Excavations in the area of the original temple precinct, underneath the Pump Room, are now complete. Open daily except Christmas Day and Boxing Day. Admission charge includes entrance to the Roman Baths and the Pump Room. Abbey Church Yard (phone: 61111 or 65043 evenings and weekends).

Pump Room – Upstairs from the baths, this grand hall was built at the end of the 18th century. It was one of the town's social centers and continues as a meeting place for both natives and tourists. The mineral water pumped to the fountain in the bay window is the same therapeutic drink that Sam Weller of *Pickwick Papers* thought tasted like "warm flat-irons." Glasses of the tepid, cloudy water are available for sampling in the Pump Room for 25p. Or enjoy some Bath buns and coffee and listen to the Pump Room Trio play its daily morning concert (afternoons on Sundays) on the platform under the balcony, a tradition dating to the days of Beau Nash. Open daily during the summer; in winter, there's a grand piano recital in the afternoon. The admission charge to the Roman Baths includes the Pump Room; a combined ticket admits you to the Assembly Rooms and the Museum of Costume on Bennett St. as well. Abbey Church Yard (phone: 61111 or 65043 evenings and weekends).

Bath Abbey – A Saxon abbey and a Norman cathedral occupied this site before the present church was begun in 1499. The cathedral had fallen into ruin when Bishop Oliver King, Bishop of Bath and Wells, was inspired to rebuild the church by a dream, which is represented by the angels ascending ladders into heaven carved on the west front. Though its predecessor was much larger, Bath Abbey is no disappointment. Inside, daylight pours through sparkling panes of glass in the tall clerestory windows (the abbey is sometimes called the Lantern of the West for this reason), illuminating the famous fan vaulting, a pale and delicate example of English perpendicular architecture. The 19th-century east window over the altar, unusual for its square top, was damaged in World War II and restored by the great-grandson of its original designer. Note also the medieval carving of the Prior Birde Chantry next to the sanctuary and, at the northeast corner of the church, the modern Edgar Window showing the coronation of the man thought to have been the first king of all England, in 973. (Visitors cannot wander around during services.) Abbey Church Yard.

Assembly Rooms – Designed by John Wood the Younger, these opened in 1771 as a fashionable gathering place where concerts, dancing, card games, and light refreshments could be enjoyed in surroundings of appropriate elegance. Such light-mindedness was scorned in the Victorian age, and from the mid-19th century on the Bath Assembly Rooms fell into disrepair, then were restored to their former splendor in 1938 only to be gutted, except for the shell, by a World War II bombing raid. What the visitor sees today is a faithful reconstruction of the rooms carried out with the aid of detailed 18th-century engravings. The ballroom, lit by five crystal chandeliers that were safely packed away at the outbreak of the war, looks like a giant blue and white Wedgwood confection, and the tearoom is no less delectable a creation in a pinkish tone. Downstairs is the Museum of Costume, with an array of 18th-century finery along with exhibitions dating from 1560 to the present, making up one of the largest costume collections in the world. Open daily. Admission charge for museum only. Bennett St. (phone: 61111 or 65025 evenings and weekends).

Royal Crescent – The sheer stateliness of Bath's showpiece of residential architecture rarely fails to impress. The Royal Crescent is the supreme achievement of John Wood the Younger and is considered to be the finest crescent in Europe. Begun in 1767, it consists of 30 pale amber Georgian stone houses whose 114 Ionic columns support a continuous cornice the length of the curving whole. Ironwork fences, the sidewalk, and the cobblestone street repeat the curve, wrapping it around a sweeping segment of Royal Victoria Park. The Bath Preservation Trust has restored No. 1 Royal Crescent as a Georgian residence and museum of 18th-century cooking. Open daily except Mondays, March through October. Admission charge. At the end of Brock St. (phone: 28126).

Circus – Another example of Georgian town planning, this is possibly the greatest achievement of John Wood the Elder, who began it in 1754. It is a stately ring of regally proportioned and identically faced stone townhouses surrounding a circular green of lawn and huge spreading plane trees. Each of its three sections is composed of 11 houses fronted by columns in Doric, Ionic, and Corinthian tiers. Wood designed one of the houses — No. 7 — for William Pitt, MP for Bath and later prime minister of England, and many other celebrities have lived here over the years, including the painter Thomas Gainsborough (No. 17) and the explorer David Livingstone (No. 13). At the north end of Gay St.

Pulteney Bridge – Bath's version, on a smaller scale, of the Ponte Vecchio in Florence. Built in 1770 by Robert Adam, this shop-lined structure on three arches connects Grand Parade and Bridge Street to Argyle Street, and even if you don't window-shop, you'll be across it before you know it. Below the bridge is the boomerang-shaped Pulteney Weir, recently redesigned for the purposes of flood control.

Holburne of Menstrie Museum – The former Sydney Hotel (built in 1796–97) houses a superb collection of silver, glass, porcelain, bronzes, furniture, and paintings by English masters such as Sir Joshua Reynolds and Thomas Gainsborough. A wide range of 20th-century craftwork, including textiles, pottery, furniture, and calligraphy, is on display in a crafts study center. Closed January; afternoon teas are served in the garden in summer. Admission charge. Great Pulteney St. (phone: 66669).

Prior Park – A handsome Georgian mansion overlooking the city, Prior Park was designed for Ralph Allen by John Wood the Elder. Allen had bought the local Combe Down stone quarries and Wood was a proponent of the Palladian style in architecture. When stone and style came together in early buildings such as Prior Park, begun in 1735, it was a forecast of things to come for Bath. Alexander Pope and Henry Fielding visited here (Allen is Squire Allworthy in Fielding's *Tom Jones*), but today Prior Park is a boys' school. The grounds and chapel are open daily. Admission charge to the grounds. About 1 mile southeast of Bath (phone: Combe Down 832752).

American Museum in Britain – Its 18 period rooms range from a 17th-century New England saltbox to a mid-19th-century New Orleans mansion, plus such other curiosities as a Colonial Massachusetts tavern, a replica of George Washington's garden at Mount Vernon, the captain's cabin of a Yankee whaling boat, and an old-fashioned country store. The museum is in Claverton Manor, a Neoclassical home of 1820. Open afternoons April through October daily except Mondays; otherwise by appointment. 2.5 miles east of town (phone: 60503).

Huntingdon Heritage Centre – Exhibitions of Bath's city model, as well as its architectural heritage. Open Tuesdays through Fridays. The Vineyards (phone: 333895).

■**EXTRA SPECIAL:** Just outside Bath, the Kennet and Avon Canal winds lazily along leafy banks. Opened in 1810, the long-neglected canal has now been re-dredged and brought back to life for pleasure craft. On Saturday and Sunday afternoons in spring and summer, a waterbus plies between Bath and Folly Swing Bridge, the prettiest section of the canal. In the spring you stand an excellent chance of passing broods of newborn ducklings and cygnets splashing about under their mothers' watchful gaze. You can also enjoy a cruise on the River Avon aboard the *Scenic I,* which runs daily on the hour from 11 AM to 7 PM upstream from Pulteney Weir opposite the Parade Gardens. For details on other boat trips, check with the Tourist Information Centre. It's also lovely to walk alongside the canal on the old towpath where horses drew barges long ago.

SOURCES AND RESOURCES

TOURIST INFORMATION: On-the-spot details about Bath can be obtained from the Tourist Information Centre (phone: 62831) opposite the Roman Baths and Pump Room in the Abbey Church Yard. An excellent *Bath Official Guide Book* is available from the information center and most bookstores. Christopher Ansley's *New Bath Guide,* a satirical look at 18th-century Bath society, was an immediate hit when it was first published in 1766, and it is still carried in some local bookstores.

City of Bath honorary guides — known as the mayor's guides — will take you on a free, approximately 1¾-hour walking tour if you wish; they're carefully trained, unpaid volunteers, and they frown on tips. Tours leave the Abbey Churchyard (outside the Pump Room); for exact times, consult the notice board outside the Pump Room entrance or ask at the information office.

Marion Carter provides a private guide service using qualified, registered professional guides for walks in Bath and car tours in the surrounding area (phone: 312901).

Local Coverage – The daily (except Sundays) *Bath & West Evening Chronicle* has details of events taking place in the city. The Tourist Information Centre also publishes the monthly *What's On.*

GETTING AROUND: Bus and Train – Trains depart from the Bath Spa station on Dorchester St. at Manvers St. For information, call British Rail (phone: 63075). *Badgerline* and *National Express* operate the city buses and long-distance coaches, which leave from the bus station, also on Manvers Street. Open-top bus tours are offered in warm weather. For tour and bus information call the station at 64446.

MUSEUMS: In addition to those mentioned in *Special Places,* others are:

Artsite Gallery – Reopened in 1985 after extensive refurbishment, it features a number of exhibitions accompanied by recorded interviews with the artists. Closed Mondays. Linley House, 1 Pierrepont Pl. (phone: 60394).

Beaux Arts Gallery – Works by contemporary artists and ceramicists. Closed Sundays. 13 York St. (phone: 64850).

Burrows Toy Museum – Children's games, dolls, and other toys of the last two centuries. Open daily. York St. (phone: 61819).

Camden Works – The 190-million-year history of Bath stone, the preserved contents of a Victorian brass foundry, an aerated mineral water factory, and engineering works. Closed Fridays, October to Easter. Julian Rd. (phone: 318348).

Herschel House and Museum – Former home of Sir William Herschel, the astronomer who discovered the planet Uranus. Astronomical and musical exhibits. Open Wednesdays, Saturdays, and Sundays from April through October; open Sundays from November through February; closed March. 19 New King St. (phone: 336228).

Geology Museum – Fossils from the rocks of North Somerset. Closed Sundays. 18 Queen Sq. (phone: 28144).

Museum of Bookbinding – A reconstruction of a 19th-century bindery. Open weekdays. Manvers St. (phone: 66000).

National Center of Photography – The Royal Photographic Society's display of original Victorian photographs, early cameras, and changing contemporary exhibitions. Closed Sundays. Milsom St. (phone: 62841).

Victoria Art Gallery – Paintings, etchings, prints, porcelain, and Bohemian glass. Closed Sundays. Bridge St. (phone: 61111 or 65024 evenings and weekends).

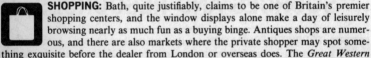

SHOPPING: Bath, quite justifiably, claims to be one of Britain's premier shopping centers, and the window displays alone make a day of leisurely browsing nearly as much fun as a buying binge. Antiques shops are numerous, and there are also markets where the private shopper may spot something exquisite before the dealer from London or overseas does. The *Great Western Antique Centre,* Bartlett St., is one of these; closed Sundays. Its many stalls sell everything from Victrolas and antique tiled stoves to old buttons still on the card. The *Bartlett Street Antique Market,* just across the street, is another, full of stalls doing business daily except Sunday. The *Bath Antique Market,* Guinea La., occurs only on Wednesdays, as does the nearby *Paragon* antiques market, both of which attract dealers from all over the west of England.

A taste of old Bath can be found at the *Bath Market,* in the Guildhall on Bridge Street. Butchers, fishmongers, secondhand books, and fruit-and-vegetable stalls spill over one another in an atmosphere that reeks of tradition and is authentic right down to the sawdust scrunching beneath your feet. A cheery, bustling place, especially on dark winter evenings. Open daily, except Sundays, from 9 AM.

A short selection of Bath's many fine shops follows. The majority of the city's stores stay open six days a week, closing on Sundays, but a few also close on Mondays.

Bath Stamp & Coin Shop – For collectors or beginners. 12–13 Pulteney Bridge (phone: 63073).

Catherine – Quite simple the best place for delicious Belgian Leonidas chocolates — so precious that they are sold by the gram. 18 Northumberland Pl. (no phone).

Chapter and Verse Bookshop – The proprietors claim to be able to procure any book from any place faster than anyone else, but with more than 25,000 titles in stock, there can't be many left. The shop has a huge section devoted to Bath and local history. 9–10 High St. (phone: 64654.

Corridor Stamp Shop – Similar to the *Bath Stamp and Coin Shop,* but stamps only. Look for it, if only to make sure you pass through the narrow, glass-covered arcade where it is located. 7a The Corridor (phone: 63368).

Jim Garrahy's Fudge Kitchen – It's difficult to wait until you're back out on the street before sampling the results of this shop's 1830s recipes for chocolate, mint, walnut, and other mouth-watering fudges. Union Passage (phone: 62277).

Highland Clothing Co. – The place for cashmere, lambswool, Braemar knitwear, and tartans. Rooftop restaurant. 2a Bath St. (phone: 66144).

Gift Horse – Glass paperweights, board games, and other British products. Classic hand-marbled stationery and desk accessories. 14 Union Passage (phone: 66093).

Global Village – Bright handicrafts, kitchenware, folk art, and costumes from near and far. 4–5 Green St. (phone: 64017).

Jolly's – A department store with everything from fashion to food. Milsom St. (phone: 66201).

E. P. Mallory & Son – Again, two shops. Old jewelry and silver at 5 Old Bond St. (phone: 65443); modern jewelry, silver, and china at 1/4 Bridge St. (phone: 65885).

Mementos of Bath – Souvenirs of the Roman Baths and the rest of Bath — even a record of the Pump Room Trio. Roman Baths (phone: 61111).

National Trust Shop – Linens, preserves, toiletries, crafts, and handknit woolens, many produced exclusively for the National Trust. 14 Abbey Church Yard (phone: 60249).

Papyrus Fine Paper – For stationery, scrolls, handmade books and albums, pens, and inks. 25 Broad St. (phone: 63418).

Poppy at the Glove Shop – One of the few specialty glove shops in England, the shop also stocks leather handbags, scarves, belts, and costume jewelry. 19 Green St. (phone: 65320).

Rossiter's – A row of several shops that sell lovely housewares and decorative items for the home — kitchenware, china tea services, chintz fabrics, and more. 40 Broad St.

Scoops – A new shop, featuring ultramodern kitchenware, can accommodate bulk purchases. *Bureau de Change* on the premises. 26 Milsom St. (phone: 66066).

Timothy Solloway – Fine linens, British and imported, for kitchen, bed, and bath. 3 Church St. (phone: 66463).

Wellow Crafts – Traditional crafts from about 180 artisans. Among the many items are knitwear and patchwork quilts. Kingsmead Sq. (phone: 64358).

 SPECIAL EVENTS: The highlight of the year is the *Bath International Festival of Music,* 2 weeks of musical events of exceptional quality in late May and early June, which includes the *Bath Contemporary Art Fair.* For concerts and operas, the festival uses the town's handsome old halls, including the Assembly Rooms, the Guildhall Banqueting Room, and the Theatre Royal, while choral and organ performances take place in Bath Abbey or in nearby Wells Cathedral. Reservations are required, and bookings can be made by mail from the first week in April. For details, write to the Bath Festival Office, Linley House, 1 Pierrepont Pl., Bath BA1 1JY. The schedule of the Bath *Georgian Festival Society* is available in the Pump Room. The *Royal Bath and West Show,* the biggest agricultural show in the West Country, is held each year at the end of May at Shepton Mallet, 20 miles south of the city. Several antiques fairs are held in Bath each year. Most notable is the West of England Antiques Fair, which takes place in May at the Assembly Rooms.

 SPORTS: The *Sports and Leisure Centre* on the Recreation Ground has some indoor sports and swimming as well as a sauna, a solarium, and an electric golf trainer. Across the river via North Parade Bridge (phone: 62563).

Boating – *Bath Boating Company,* Forester Rd. (phone: 66407), has skiffs and punts for hire. Information about boat trips on the Avon as well as on the Kennet and Avon Canal is available at the Tourist Information Centre (phone: 62831).

Cricket – The *Bath Cricket Club* (phone: 25935) plays at the North Parade Cricket Ground across the river and just to the south of the Sports and Leisure Centre. The *County Cricket Festival* is held in June when you'll see some even better teams compete on the Recreation Ground. Consult the newspaper or the monthly events list put out by the information center for specifics.

Fishing – For a license to fish in the River Avon and the Kennet and Avon Canal, apply at the Wessex Water Authority, Broad Quay, or at a local fishing tackle dealer.

Golf – *Entry Hill,* just a mile from downtown, is Bath's newest golf club. The 9-hole course is open daily and membership is not necessary (phone: 834248). Bath's other leading golf clubs are on the outskirts of town. The *Lansdown Golf Club,* an 18-hole course about 2 miles north of town on Lansdown, accepts visitors (phone: 22138); the *Kingsdown* course (18 holes) is a century old and overlooks Box Valley (phone: 742530); another 18-holer, the *Bath Golf Club* is the oldest of them all, next door to Sham Castle (phone: 63834).

Horse Racing – The *Bath Races* take place a few times each month from April through September at the racecourse on Lansdown, 2 miles north of town (phone: 66375).

Rugby – The *Bath Rugby Football Club* (phone: 25192) plays its home games on the Recreation Ground. The monthly events list keeps track of the dates and times.

Soccer – *Twerton Park,* about a mile west of Bath via the Lower Bristol Rd., is the scene of the *Bath City Football Club* (phone: 23087) games. Consult the events list.

Swimming – The pool at the *Sports and Leisure Centre* on the Recreation Ground (North Parade Rd.; phone: 62563) is open year-round.

 THEATER: *Bath's Theatre Royal,* in The Sawclose at the end of Barton St. (phone: 65065), dates from 1805 and has reopened after major renovations. Once again it provides an intimate setting for comedy, drama, musicals, opera, ballet, concerts, and a traditional Christmas pantomime. The theater also stages pre-London openings and is a regional base for the National Theatre. The *Bath Puppet Theatre* (phone: 312173) overlooks the picturesque Pulteney Weir (beside the famous bridge), and performs on weekends and school holidays.

 MUSIC: Concerts of classical music presented in unusual surroundings by leading artists are part of the 2-week Bath International Festival of Music beginning in late May (see *Special Events*). The rest of the year, music by local and visiting groups can be heard at the *Theatre Royal* and elsewhere. The Pump Room Trio holds forth with concerts of light orchestral music in the Pump Room mornings throughout the year; during the summer there are band concerts in the Parade Gardens on Sunday afternoons. Pubs with live jazz nightly or several nights weekly include *The Entertainer,* North Parade, next door to the *Fernley* hotel (phone: 61603), and *The Bell,* 103 Walcot St. (phone: 25998).

 NIGHTCLUBS AND NIGHTLIFE: The quiet dignity of the place means that Bath is unlikely to win an award as Britain's most swinging city. What happens, happens in the pubs, and in night spots such as *Rumours,* opposite the Theatre Royal (phone: 63993); and *Moles,* 14 George St. (phone: 333423), which features a live band.

 SINS: When you've partaken of Bath buns in the Pump Room, indulge yourself further with a Sally Lunn (a pastry not quite as sweet as a Bath bun, to be eaten toasted, with butter or clotted cream) at *Sally Lunn's House* on North Parade Passage (phone: 61634). Sally's house is supposed to be the oldest in Bath (built in 1482, and recent excavations of the basement have unearthed kitchenware dating back to Roman times). The buns have been served here since she herself, a pastry cook, first dreamed them up in the 17th century.

For less tasteful sins, consult the barman or hotel porter.

BEST IN TOWN

 CHECKING IN: Bath has a number of memorable hotels and a few truly outstanding ones. Summer visitors, particularly in July or August, must book well in advance. The Tourist Information Centre, Abbey Church Yard (phone: 60521), can help make arrangements. Expect to pay $80 or more for a double room with breakfast at hotels listed in the expensive category; between $50 and $75 at those listed as moderate; and under $50 at any listed as inexpensive.

Priory – Without a doubt, one of Britain's best country hotels. A Gothic house built in 1835, its 15 rooms are furnished with antiques. In the quiet gardens is a heated swimming pool in use from spring through fall. The restaurant is divided in two: *Brown Dining Room* and the *Terrace* (see *Eating Out*). It's about a mile from the center of Bath. Closed the first two weeks in January. Wopton Rd. (phone: 331922). Expensive.

Royal Crescent – The centerpiece of the Royal Crescent, this elegant and historic Georgian hostelry is part of Bath's architectural heritage. There are 36 super-deluxe rooms, but to really splurge, spend a night in one of the extra-special apartments. The Sir Percy Blakeney Suite, for example, has a 17th-century canopied bed, pale blue sofas, an Oriental carpet, and a white and gold ceiling of intricate gesso swirls. On summer days, cocktails and tea are served in the garden. 15 & 16 Royal Crescent (phone: 319090). Expensive.

Ston Easton Park – Peter and Christine Smedley's Palladian country manor, 12 miles outside of Bath, won the Egon Ronay Hotel of the Year award within months of opening in 1982. A grandfather clock ticks in the library, a log fire crackles throughout the winter, and the 20 guestrooms (several with four-poster beds) overlook 300 acres of landscaped parkland. Ston Easton (phone: 076121-631). Expensive.

Francis – In an entirely different spirit, this 90-room property forms the southern side of Queen Square, built by John Wood the Elder between 1729 and 1736. Damaged by World War II, the hotel has been rebuilt in its original style, and furnishings reflect the period. Queen Sq. (phone: 24257). Expensive to moderate.

Ladbroke Beaufort – Bath's most modern hotel has 124 rooms (with an additional 60 planned for 1988) and is built over a municipal parking lot on the banks of the Avon overlooking the river and Pulteney Bridge. There is no period charm here; it rates for efficiency, convenience, and comfort. Walcot St. (phone: 63411). Expensive to moderate.

Fernley – This 18th-century building opposite the Parade Gardens is just a 2-minute walk to the Pump Room, Roman Baths, and Abbey. Most of the 47 rooms have private baths. There's also a salad bar, *Magnums,* a French brasserie, and *No. 3 North Parade,* an adjoining restaurant with a tearoom. 1 North Parade (phone: 61603). Expensive to moderate.

Number Nine – Tucked away on one of Bath's most charming, secluded walkways in the heart of the city, this building is a bona fide historical property with scores of antiques to prove it. The 8 rooms are individually decorated, one with a four-poster bed; another has a Jacuzzi. Closed in January. Miles Buildings (phone: 25462). Expensive to moderate.

Bath – Only minutes from the city center, Bath's newest hotel has 96 luxurious rooms and is superbly sited alongside Widcombe Basin and the river. Widcombe Basin (phone: 338855). Moderate.

Gainsborough – A mile from the center, here is a small country house providing bed and breakfast set in an acre of garden. All 16 rooms have private baths and two have four-poster beds. Weston La. (phone: 311380). Moderate.

Jane's – Its bistro-style restaurant, tearoom, health spa, and disco give this little hotel a fresh, bubbly atmosphere. It has 26 modern rooms and is close to city center. 7 Manvers St. (phone: 65966). Moderate.

Lansdown Grove – A modernized Georgian mansion, this is on Lansdown hill, facing south over the city. The 40 rooms are pleasantly decorated; all have private baths, and some have balconies with lovely views. Lansdown Rd. (phone: 315891). Moderate.

Pratt's – As historic as any hotel in Bath, *Pratt's* is in South Parade, a John Wood design of the 1740s. It has 47 modern, comfortable rooms, all with private baths. Saturday night dinner dances are held in winter months. South Parade (phone: 60441). Moderate.

Royal York – Queen Victoria slept here in 1830, when she was still a princess and the hotel was still an old coaching inn. More than half of the 52 large rooms have private baths. George St. (phone: 61541). Moderate.

Redcar – Not far from the center of town, near Henrietta Park, the hotel is part of a mellowed stone Georgian terrace and has 31 well-equipped rooms. 27 Henrietta St. (phone: 69151). Moderate.

Somerset House – This small Georgian no-smoking house has just 1 single and 8 double rooms, which accounts for owners Jean and Malcolm Seymour's personal service and very good home-cooked meals (which include ingredients from their garden). 35 Bathwick Hill (phone: 66451). Inexpensive.

County – Friendly and unpretentious, this 25-room hotel has a restaurant, grill room, and three bars. Only half the rooms have private baths. 18–19 Pulteney Rd. (phone: 66493). Inexpensive.

Parkside Guest House – Nicely placed on the fringe of Royal Victoria Park, close to the Royal Crescent and the Botanical Gardens, this pleasant inn offers vegetarian meals on request. 11 Marlborough La. (phone: 29444). Inexpensive.

 EATING OUT: The range of restaurants in Bath is broad: English, French, Italian, Greek, Indian, Chinese, and many more. Expect to pay $55 to $60 and up for a meal for two with wine at restaurants listed below as expensive; from $35 to $55 at the moderate ones; and less than $35 at the inexpensive ones. At the numerous wine bars and fast-food establishments, two people can eat simply for less than $10.

Hole in the Wall – It doesn't sound like much, but this beamed restaurant with flagstones in the basement of a Georgian building has been one of Bath's most prestigious eating spots for a number of years. The cuisine is mostly French and usually superb, and there is great variety. Reservations are advised, especially for Saturday night. (There are also 8 rooms available.) Closed Sundays and three weeks over the Christmas holidays. 16 George St. (phone: 25242). Expensive.

Old Mill – This is a hotel-restaurant on the River Avon about 2.5 miles from town. Good English cooking is the specialty; traditional Sunday lunches are served, too. Tollbridge Rd., Batheaston (phone: 858476). Expensive.

Priory – Dinner is a grand occasion here, and you can choose to have it either in the Georgian *Brown Dining Room* with period furniture and paintings or in the *Terrace* overlooking the courtyard. The cuisine is primarily French and there is an extensive wine list. Weston Rd. (phone: 331922). Expensive.

Flowers – On the ground floor of three beautifully converted 18th-century courtesans' houses, this restaurant is brightly decorated in pastel colors and its walls are crammed with artwork. Traditional English food is the specialty. Closed Sundays and Mondays, and a week at Easter, two weeks at Christmas, and most of August. 27 Monmouth St. (phone: 313774). Expensive to moderate.

Clos du Roy – French food, neither classic nor nouvelle but imaginative creations by owners Philippe and Emma Roy. Open daily. 7 Edgar Buildings, George St. (phone: 64356). Moderate.

Le Jardin – This lively, plant-filled restaurant prepares both English and French dishes. The fish and poultry specialties are among the best choices, particularly the turbot in Cornish crab sauce. Closed for lunch on Mondays. 2 George St. (phone: 63341). Moderate.

Medley – An upscale café that serves three meals a day and features some interesting items like mussel pâté. 33 Brock St. (phone: 311955). Moderate.

La Pentola – Down the stairs at the river end of North Parade, the stone-vaulted room that is the restaurant's dining area was once a cellar for the patrician home above. The fare is strictly Italian and rated among the town's better values. Closed Sundays and Mondays. 14 North Parade (phone: 24649). Moderate.

Popjoy's – Beau Nash lived with his mistress Juliana Popjoy in this Georgian house, which is now one of the best restaurants in Bath. High-quality English dishes are made from seasonal produce (the menu changes every two months). Closed Mondays in winter. Sawclose (phone: 60494). Moderate.

Il Romano – One of Bath's few upmarket Italian restaurants, this is a friendly, efficient establishment where plates are piled high with steak, fish, and pasta. 1 Barton St. (phone: 26572). Moderate.

Theatre Vaults – This restaurant, in the vaults of the restored Theatre Royal, has quickly gained a good reputation for reasonably priced and tasty lunches and suppers. Open daily. Barton St. (phone: 65074). Moderate.

Woods – The two dining rooms, basically Georgian including the fireplaces, have been attractively updated with modern cane seating and finished off in tones of beige, burnt orange, and dark red. English and French cooking are featured and it's advisable to book. Closed Sundays and Mondays. 9–13 Alfred St. (phone: 314812). Moderate.

KT's – Places like this are now a familiar High Street sight, featuring a light and airy decor combined with such hearty, healthy fare as hamburgers, stuffed potatoes, lentil lasagna, and vegetarian moussaka. Open for lunch and dinner daily. 4–5 Grand Parade (phone: 61946). Moderate to inexpensive.

Pasta Galore – A new eatery serving pasta in all shapes and forms. Open lunch and evenings daily except Sundays. 31 Barton St. (phone: 63861). Moderate to inexpensive.

Sweeney Todd's – This friendly, boisterous restaurant on Bath's main shopping street serves good pizza and hamburgers. 15 Milsom St. (phone: 62368). Moderate to inexpensive.

Bink's – Although it calls itself a coffee shop, this place serves remarkably good hot and cold meals in a pleasant atmosphere. Afternoon tea is served here in true English style — scones, jam, and clotted cream. *Bink's* will also pack you a lunch to go. Open daily. Abbey Church Yard (phone: 66563). Inexpensive.

Canary – Peer through the multipaned windows facing the narrow street to see a profusion of small tables set in a bower of flowery wallpaper. This busy, licensed tea shop serves one-dish meals such as quiche, omelettes, and salads as well as a wonderfully confusing selection of cakes for tea. Closed evenings. 3 Queen St. (phone: 24846). Inexpensive.

Clarets – A downstairs wine cellar and restaurant with contemporary styling and a youngish, sophisticated clientele. Open daily except Monday evenings and Sunday lunchtimes for drinks, meals, or snacks. In summer, tables are set up outside. 7 Kingsmead Sq. (phone: 66688). Inexpensive.

David's Coffee Shop – A handkerchief-sized café serving homemade Continental cakes and pastries and delicious sandwiches. Open daily. 17 Pulteney Bridge (phone: 64636). Inexpensive.

Francis – Even if you're not staying here, stop by for the weekday buffet lunch in the elegant surroundings of the *Roman Bar.* Pile your plate with cold cuts and salad, add a pint of ale, and consume it smugly — it's not at all a bad deal. Queen Sq. (phone: 24257). Inexpensive.

Moon and Sixpence – This is an attractive wine bar–restaurant in a restored courtyard (self-service during the day; waiters in the evenings) serving enticing fish, meat, and salads. During the summer, outdoor tables surround a lovely fountain. Open daily. Just off Broad St. (phone: 60962). Inexpensive.

Monk's Coffee House – Strategically set opposite the Pump Room and Roman Baths, a good place for light meals, coffee, and snacks. 7 Abbey Church Yard (phone: 60759). Inexpensive.

Rajpoot Tandoori – A quiet, elegant restaurant featuring Raj curries and tandoori barbecues. 4 Argyle St. (phone: 66833). Inexpensive.

Walrus and Carpenter – Beefburgers, chili con carne, and steaks are the choices in this attractive restaurant on a corner near the Theatre Royal. Open evenings only. 28 Barton St. (phone: 314864). Inexpensive.

SHARING A PINT: At first glance, the *Saracen's Head,* 42 Broad St., looks like an ersatz antique. In fact, it is said to be the oldest pub in town. The building was completed in its present form in 1713 and Charles Dickens stayed here in 1835 while it was still an inn (the display case in the wall has a few items from his time). While bending your elbow, be sure to appreciate the original plasterwork in the beamed ceiling. Around the corner on Green St., there's the *Old Green Tree,* and if business is brisk, you'll have to squeeze in. Its tiny bar, smoking lounge, and snug are paneled in dark wood and all is very friendly, intimate, and cozy. The *Rummer,* in a renovated Regency building on Newmarket Row along Grand Parade opposite the Pulteney Weir, looks like a restaurant in someone's living room. Actually, it, too, is a pub, and although bar snacks are served all day, you can sit graciously at those tables with just a drink. The *Grapes,* Westgate St., occupies a lovely old building — white walls, dark beams, etched glass in the doorway — and the mood is lively. The *Huntsman,* North Parade, manages to be almost all things to all people. The main lounge bar of this establishment is filled at lunch with office workers and with tourists who come for the great variety of fast, honest food. Downstairs, the noisy Cellar Bar is frequented by students and other youth. Upstairs, there's a quiet restaurant. The *Huntsman* is sprawling and comfortable, and the entrance toward the river is claimed to be the oldest shopfront in Bath.

BELFAST

As the capital of Northen Ireland, Belfast has made international headlines for many years. Most Americans are aware that since 1969 the city has been plagued by political, religious, and terrorist activity. However, because most of the violence is directed toward specific targets, tourists have not been drawn into it and the citizenry seems to take the security measures in stride and carries on with life almost normally. Visitors are unlikely to see many outward signs of "the troubles." A security check on vehicles approaching Belfast's Aldergrove International Airport is possible, though rare. And although some of the barriers still stand as mute testimony to the strife, pedestrians no longer face parcel inspections upon entering or leaving the city center, which remains off-limits to private cars. Because of the restrictions on traffic, large areas of Belfast's reinvigorated downtown have been reborn as pedestrian shopping districts — with such a profusion of flowers, baskets, benches, and trees that the city was recognized in the 1986 Beautiful Britain in Bloom competition.

For travelers trying to appreciate the origins of "the troubles," a look at Belfast's history proves invaluable. Belfast, or *Béal Feirste* in Irish, means "mouth" of the Farset, a stream that flows into the River Lagan. It was the natural harbor and strategic defense position formed by the Lagan and Belfast Lough that prompted various marauders over the centuries — Anglo Norman, Scottish, and Irish — to establish a castle here. By the sixteenth century, the area was controlled by the O'Neills, earls of nearby Tyrone. After the defeat at Kinsale in 1601 of the great Irish chieftain Hugh O'Neill, the lands were confiscated by the English Crown; in 1603, they were granted by Elizabeth I to Sir Arthur Chichester, governor of Carrickfergus, who built a new castle and supplanted the native Irish with English and Scottish colonists. (This was the era of "the plantation of Ireland.") In 1613 Belfast was granted a charter of incorporation and allowed two (Protestant) representatives to the British Parliament. In the years that followed, the Catholic Irish rose up in revolt several times, with no success; they suffered under harsh Penal Codes, which usurped their property, outlawed their religion, and denied their civil rights.

Soon after the revocation of the Edict of Nantes in 1685, Belfast was washed by a new wave of settlers — this time French Huguenots fleeing religious persecution. They brought with them improved weaving methods, which spurred the town's fledgling linen industry into rapid expansion throughout the eighteenth century. In addition to linen, the development of rope-making, engineering, tobacco, and sea trade, infused Belfast's economy, causing the town to double in size every ten years. During this period Roger Mulholland, a local architect, drew up a plan dividing the town into a grid of streets for construction and development. The grid included Donegall

Square and was bordered roughly by Wellington Place and Chichester, Great Victoria, May, and Howard streets. Along these avenues many elegant Georgian buildings were erected by Belfast's prosperous linen merchants.

In 1791, Wolfe Tone, the son of a Protestant Dublin tradesman who was inspired by the American and French revolutions and influenced by radical Belfast Presbyterians, formed the Society of United Irishmen in Belfast. Espousing social as well as political reforms, the society's goal was "to substitute the common name of Irishmen in place of the denominations of Protestant, Catholic, and Dissenter." As Belfast became a center of dissent against the British, the United Irishmen supported an effort by both Presbyterians and Catholics to rid Ireland of English rule. Uprisings in 1798 proved unsuccessful, including a June 7 attack on Antrim, during which the Irish sang the *Marseillaise.* The United Irishmen's leader, Henry Joy McCracken, later was hanged in Belfast. Wolfe Tone's Belfast-born ideas of an Irish republic attractive to all the Irish, together with the uprisings, constituted a watershed for the ideal of a united Ireland. Unfortunately, the concept collapsed into sectarianism soon after.

Economically, Belfast continued to burgeon during the nineteenth century, aided by the Act of Union (which made Ireland part of Great Britain) and by the growth of its shipbuilding industry. Belfast was fancifully called "the Athens of the North" for its patronage of the arts, and most of its gracious architecture (designed by the famous Charles Lanyon) dates from this era. Unfortunately, the city's prosperity was not shared by all its citizens; the Irish Catholics were still excluded from representation in London, better housing, and sometimes even employment.

In 1920, after much bloody struggle by the Irish for self-government, Britain enacted the Home Rule Bill, which established two new Parliaments — one each in Dublin and Belfast. In 1921, a treaty was signed, formally creating an Irish Free State consisting of 26 mostly southern counties and leaving the 6 northern counties to choose between union with the new republic or with Britain. The Protestant-dominated Belfast Parliament chose the latter course, and the new entity called Northern Ireland was born.

Because the Republic of Ireland remained neutral in World War II, Ulster (a historical name now synonymous with Northern Ireland), became strategically vital to the Allied cause. The first American contingent of GIs arrived in Belfast in January 1942, and, by the end of that year, there were 100,000 American troops in the province preparing for the Normandy invasion. Generals Eisenhower and Patton oversaw the troop training in Northern Ireland for the massive D-Day venture.

Today, Belfast, second in size only to Dublin, is a sturdy, red brick, industrial city ringed by beautiful bluish-purple hills that shelter ancient castles and echo with Irish folklore. Although bothered by continued high unemployment (as in the republic), a glance around downtown Belfast reveals few visual remnants of prior urban renewal projects or overt terrorist activity. Its basically prosperous appearance reflects the city's role as commercial and cultural capital of the country, but until the smoldering internecine conflicts are finally resolved, a shadow will continue to darken Belfast's future.

BELFAST AT-A-GLANCE

SEEING THE CITY: The best views of Belfast are seen from the top of Cave Hill, 2 miles north of the city. To the south is the Old City, dominated by the copper-domed City Hall in Donegall Square; to the west is Lough Neagh, the largest lake in Ireland. Carrickfergus, Holywood, and Bangor also can be seen from the hill, and on a clear day the Isle of Man may be visible.

SPECIAL PLACES: Many of the streets in the 18th-century Old City have been made pedestrian walkways and shopping arcades, where automobiles are prohibited. This poses no problem, as Belfast is a small city best seen by foot. A 1½-mile walking tour is described in the "Belfast Civic Festival Trail" brochure available at the Tourist Board office at 48 High Street.

CITY CENTER

City Hall – A statue of Queen Victoria stands in front of this imposing pillared and corniced gray stone structure capped by a 173-foot-high copper dome. Completed in 1906, its interior is richly decorated in the elaborate Edwardian style with stained glass and marble. It is one of Ireland's most outstanding buildings. Tours are conducted Wednesday mornings. Make reservations by calling the Department of Leisure Services (phone: 220202). Donegall Sq. S.

St. Malachy's Church – This is a fine example of the lavish Gothic Roman Catholic churches built in Ireland during the 19th century. Note especially its remarkable fan-vaulted ceiling, virtually dripping with intricate and lovely plasterwork, similar to that found in Henry VII's Chapel at Westminster Abbey in London. Alfred St.

Royal Courts of Justice – An imposing building, finished in 1933, the "four courts" is constructed of Portland stone and was a gift from Britain. Chichester St.

Albert Memorial – Looking a little incongruous among parking lots and office buildings, this 35-meter memorial honoring Prince Albert (Queen Victoria's consort) is often called Belfast's Big Ben, since it bears such a striking resemblance to London's famous tower. This one, however, has settled slightly to one side, which earned it another nickname, "Belfast's leaning tower." At the river end of High St.

Custom House – This squarish and solid-looking building was designed by the architect Sir Charles Lanyon in the richly corniced, somewhat grand Italianate style, which was popular in Ireland in the mid-19th century. Sculptures of Britannia, Neptune, and Mercury decorate the pediment on the seaward side. Custom House Square.

St. Anne's Cathedral – This church, which has been under construction since 1899 and therefore combines many architectural styles, is distinguished by some fine Irish-Romanesque carving and sculpture. Church of Ireland. Donegall St.

St. Peter's Cathedral – Completed in 1866, the building is noted for its soaring twin spires, and a circular carving by the doorway depicting angels freeing St. Peter from prison. Roman Catholic. St. Peter's Square.

First Presbyterian Church – Completed in 1783 and where John Wesley preached in 1789. The church has a lovely interior. Rosemary St.

ENVIRONS

Port of Belfast – Poised cranes and cables are stock elements looming above this busy port, the largest in Ireland. Shipbuilding remains a primary occupation, and numerous ocean liners have been constructed or repaired here. The noted Harland & Wolff (H&W) shipyard grew from two acres in 1858 to 300 in the mid-20th century.

Once the world's largest shipyard and long renowned for innovative ship design and sophisticated engine and hull construction, H&W today boasts the world's largest dry dock. On April 2, 1912, the *Titanic* set out from its H&W birthplace to Southampton, England, for her maiden voyage. Just 12 days later, *Titanic* struck an iceberg and, in 3 hours, the glamorous, "virtually unsinkable," ocean liner sank.

Stormont – A mile-long road leads uphill through the estate, with its extensive gardens, to the moribund Parliament House, once the seat of Northern Ireland's legislature. Two statues on the grounds remind visitors of Ulster's political reality: One, at the juncture of the approach avenues, is of Lord Carson, the Dublin lawyer who kept Belfast British during and after World War I; the other, in the main entrance hall of the Parliament building, is of Lord Craigavon, Northern Ireland's first prime minister, best known for his anti-Republican slogans, "Not an inch" and "No surrender." Upper Newtownards Rd., just east of the city.

Belfast Castle – Of very recent vintage (1870), this mansion — with its turrets, tower, gables, and ornate carving — is a fine example of the romantic Scottish baronial style imported to this area during the plantation of Ulster. Given to the city in 1934 by a former mayor of Belfast, the earl of Shaftsbury, the estate is now open to the public. Antrim Rd., north of the city.

Cave Hill – About 2 miles north of the city, Cave Hill is a lovely afternoon's diversion. You can take a stroll through the Hazelwood Gardens and Belfast Zoo, or climb to the craggy hill's summit (1,188 feet) and MacArt's Fort, an ancient earthwork.

Queen's University – When founded in 1845, the school was associated with colleges in Galway and Cork; in 1909, it broke away to become independent. Its original red brick, Tudor buildings designed by Charles Lanyon are now only a small fraction of the many buildings that make up the university complex. In November the Belfast Festival at Queen's is held at the university, with a multitude of events offered — film, music, and drama. The *Queen's Film Theatre* is also open to the public. University Rd.

■**EXTRA SPECIAL:** Between Queen's University and the Ulster Museum lies Belfast's 28-acre Botanic Garden, the showpiece of which is the charming Palm House glass conservatory. A famous Victorian-era Belfast landmark, the Palm House was begun in 1839 and it predates London's Kew Gardens' conservatory. It features one of the earliest examples of a curvilinear cast-iron glasshouse. The colorful floral displays in the cool left wing, tropical right wing, and 37-foot high center dome are open to the public year-round. University Rd.

SOURCES AND RESOURCES

TOURIST INFORMATION: The Northern Ireland Tourist Board, River House, 48 High St., Belfast BT1 2DS (phone: 246609), offers information, maps, and leaflets on the area. At the back entrance to city hall you can pick up the *Belfast City Council Reference Guide,* and at bookshops ask for *The Visitor's Guide to Northern Ireland* (Hunter Publishing; $10.95) by Rosemary Evans. For help in tracing your ancestral roots, contact the Ulster Historical Foundation, 66 Balmoral Ave., Belfast BT9 6NY (phone: 661621).

Local Coverage – The *Belfast Telegraph,* the *Newsletter,* and the *Irish News* are all published daily. Check the *Belfast Telegraph* for entertainment listings.

GETTING AROUND: As we have said, Belfast's inner core is off-limits to private cars, so you will need to take a bus or walk. You may wish to travel outside the city, however, and so listed below are facilities for doing just that.

Bus – For the airport and points south, go to the Ulsterbus Station on

Great Victoria St.; for points north, to the one on Oxford St. For information about schedules and departures, call 320011.

Car Rental – Several car rental agencies are represented at Aldergrove International Airport, including *Avis,* 173 Airport Rd. (phone: Crumlin 52333); *Godfrey Davis,* 181 Airport Rd. (phone: Crumlin 53444); and *Hertz* (phone: Crumlin 52533). In the city try *McCauslands,* 21–31 Grosvener Rd (327211).

Sightseeing Tours – *Citybus* conducts 3½-hour tours of greater Belfast weekdays at 2 PM, from Easter through September. The colorful commentary provided by the drivers is a bit of Belfast "crack" (chat) that should not be missed. Highlights include city center landmarks, the Queen's University district, the shipyards, Stormont, and the Belfast Zoo. Departure is from Castle Place, opposite the British Home Store; tours includes afternoon tea. £2.50. *Citybus* also has tours to the Ulster Folk and Transport Museum (phone: 246485).

Taxi – There are taxi ranks at the main bus and rail terminals and at city hall. Or, call *Fast Taxi* (phone: 58011); *Dial-A-Cab* (phone: 797777); *Able Taxi* (phone: 241999); or *Fon A Cab* (phone: 233333).

Train – The Belfast Central Station provides service to all destinations in the Republic as well as Northern Ireland; trains for the car ferry crossing to Stranraer, Scotland, leave from York Road Station. For all information, call 230310.

 SHOPPING: The highlights of Belfast's shopping scene are china, crystal, linens, woolens, and antiques. Especially recommended are: *John and Charlotte Lambe,* known for 18th- and 19th-century furniture, paintings, and silver (19 Shore Rd.); *Sinclair's Antique Gallery,* specializing in fine jewelry and silver (26 Arthur St.); and *The Bell Gallery,* which handles Irish paintings (13 Adelaide Pk.). Irish linen is still woven in Belfast and Northern Ireland, but a great deal is exported. It is available at *Samuel Lamont & Sons, Ltd.,* (Stranmillis Embankment) in large supply, including sheets. Smyths/Simpson Irish Linen (8 Callender St.) stocks quality linens along with needlework and textile crafts. *Hall's Linen* (23 Queen's Arcade) and *Irish Linen Store* (Fountain Centre, College St.) also have fine linen goods. For those particularly interested in handcrafts, the free booklet *A Guide to Northern Ireland Crafts and Craftsmen* provides the names, addresses, and specialties of Irish artisans in the six counties as well as Belfast. Pick up a copy of the booklet at Local Enterprise Development Unit, 17 Linenhall St., one block from City Hall. Crafts are usually on display and some may be for sale.

 SPECIAL EVENTS: The *Ulster Harp National,* Northern Ireland's most important steeplechase, is held at Downpatrick Race Course in February. The boisterous *Battle of the Boyne Parade* (also called Orangemen's Day), the largest in Ireland, marches through Belfast every July 12. In late summer the city holds its *International Rose Trials* at Sir Thomas and Lady Dixon Park, an event that draws rose aficionados from around the world. The *Belfast Festival* at Queen's University in November is an international arts symposium, with presentations of music, drama, and films.

 SPORTS: Fishing – Despite all the commercial shipping coming in and out of Belfast, fishing can be very good in Belfast Lough. It is best known for its coalfish, pollack, and whiting, but small skate are sometimes taken at Ballymaconnell Point, near Bangor, and it's worth trying for cod from the rocks around Blackhead Lighthouse. The area is best fished, however, from a small boat with an outboard motor.

Golf – There are ten 18-hole courses: *Balmoral,* 518 Lisburn Rd. (phone: 668514); *Malone,* Drumbeg, Dunmurry (phone: 612758); *Helen's Bay* (phone: Helen's Bay 852815); *Fortwilliam,* Downview Ave. (phone: 771770); *Clandeboye,* Conlig, Newtownards (phone: Bangor 270767); *Knock,* Dundonald (phone: Dundonald 3251);

Carnalea, Station Rd., Bangor (phone: Bangor 461368); *Belvoir Park,* 73/75 Church Rd. (phone: 641159); *Royal Belfast,* Craigavad, Holywood (phone: Holywood 2165); and *Bangor,* Bangor (phone: Bangor 3922).

Sailing – The nearest place to hire a sailboat is the *Strangford Sailing School,* Skettrick Island, Killinchy, County Down (phone: Killinchy 541592).

Swimming – The centrally located *Maysfield Leisure Centre* (phone: 241633) and *Avoneil Leisure Centre* (phone: 51564) have indoor pools.

Tennis – Tennis and squash courts are also at the *Maysfield Leisure Centre* and the *Avoneil Leisure Centre.*

 MUSEUMS: Belfast's museums of note include the following:

Arts Council Gallery – Contemporary Irish and international art. Bedford House, Bedford St.

Octagon Gallery – This gallery also exhibits the best work done by local artists. Orpheus Building, York St.

Ulster Folk and Transport Museum – Begun in 1958, this 136-acre indoor and outdoor complex depicts Northern Ireland's social history. It consists of a gallery of artifacts that offer an evolutionary explanation of rural Ulster life, complemented by 19 building — among them a linen mill, spade mill, church, schools, forge, thatched cottiers' cottage, and different styles of terrace and farmhouses — removed stone by stone from the Ulster countryside. Each building is furnished circa 1900 and has a guide in attendance. Small admission fee. Off Bangor Rd. in Cultra, seven miles northeast of Belfast.

Ulster Museum – On the grounds of the Botanic Gardens, the collections here include Bronze Age horns and pottery, Celtic personal ornaments, early Christian and medieval antiquities (including facsimiles of the 8th- and 9th-century *Book of Kells* and *Book of Armagh*), Irish art, glass and silver, and a display of life in Ireland covering 9,000 years. The most popular exhibit is the *Girona* treasure, an amazing hoard of gold and silver coins, jewelry (one gold chain weighs 4 pounds and is more than 8 feet long), and other artifacts recovered from a Spanish galleon wrecked off the Giant's Causeway 400 years ago. Noted Belgian underwater archaeologist Robert Stenuit salvaged the treasure in 1968, during some 6,000 hours of diving time. University Road.

 THEATER: The *Grand Opera House,* adjacent to the Europa hotel on Great Victoria St., is Belfast's finest theater. Drama, ballet, concerts, and other entertainments are scheduled throughout the year. For recorded information, call 249129; for advance booking, call 241919. The *Lyric Players Theatre,* Ridgeway St. (phone: 660081 or 669660), features Irish drama and the classics. The *Arts Theatre,* Botanic Ave. (phone: 224936 or 242819), offers popular plays and musicals. The *Group Theatre,* Bedford St. (phone: 229685), presents mostly amateur theatricals, some of which are quite good.

 MUSIC: The *Ulster Orchestra* gives concerts at Ulster Hall, 30 Bedford St.; inquire about tickets at the box office (phone: 229685). You can hear traditional Irish music at the *Errigle Inn,* Ormeau Rd., Mondays; *Sunflower Bar,* Corporation St., Fridays; *Blackthorn Bar,* Church St., Tuesdays and Saturdays; *Madden's,* Smithfield, most nights; *Rotterdam,* Pilot St., most nights; *Duke of York,* off Lower Donegall St., Fridays and Saturdays.

NIGHTCLUBS AND NIGHTLIFE: Belfast's nightlife has improved dramatically of late, although many non-hotel bars still shutter at 11:30 PM. The *Europa* offers live music nightly except Sundays and Mondays; and *Pip's International,* on Dublin Rd., is a where the young at heart and limber of limb go to dance. Most hotels sponsor dinner dances Saturday nights.

BEST IN TOWN

CHECKING IN: Belfast, like other Irish cities, offers a range of accommodations, from sleek, modern hotels to charming, old hostelries. Expect to pay $90 and up for a double in a hotel listed as expensive; and between $40 and $60 in moderate. Staying at a guesthouse or farmhouse can be considerably less expensive — rates begin at $20 to $25 for 2, and include full Irish breakfast. A listing of such lodgings is included in the brochure *All the Places to Stay,* available from the Northern Ireland Tourist Board.

Conway – Some 5 miles from the city center, it offers attractive grounds, an outdoor pool, and 76 rooms. Dunmurry (phone: Dunmurry 612101). Expensive.

Culloden – On 12 acres of secluded gardens and woodland overlooking Belfast Lough, this former bishop's palace may be Northern Ireland's most luxurious hotel. Its 76 beautifully appointed rooms are done in silks and velvets, and the elegant dining room and public areas are filled with antiques. The bar is part of what was once the bishop's chapel. Craigavad (phone: Holywood 5223). Expensive.

Dunadry Inn – Located not far from the airport, this atmospheric inn has had past lives as a linen, then a paper mill. The huge lawn was where the linen was once laid to whiten in the sun. Beetling machines can be seen in the bar, and old mill cottages provide the lodging space. The full-service inn has 64 rooms. 2 Island-reagh Drive (phone: Templepatrick 32474). Expensive.

Europa – This 200-room modern high-rise hotel is right in the city center, near the Opera House and other sites of interest. Its restaurants and bars are popular meeting places for Belfasters, and there's live music nightly, except Sundays and Mondays. Great Victoria St. (phone: 245161). Expensive.

Wellington Park – In the prettier part of Belfast, this refurbished Georgian building has 54 modern rooms and a restaurant. It's a good choice during the International Arts Festival. 21 Malone Rd. (phone: 661232). Expensive.

Old Inn – The thatched portion of the inn was built about 1614 and smugglers were said to have used the inn until the close of the 18th century. There are many handsome, old pieces of furniture throughout the inn, and what the rooms lack in size they make up in charm. The Old English suite has twin brass four-poster beds, and the Azalea Suite has cupboard beds with drapes. Some of the 26 rooms lack private baths, but each has a washbasin. In the back of the inn is a tea garden overlooking Crawfordsburn Glen. Just off the Bangor Rd., 15 Main St., Crawfordsburn (phone: Helen's Bay 853255). Moderate.

EATING OUT: Most Belfast hotels have their own dining rooms. For dinner out, try *Restaurant 44,* 44 Bedford St. (phone: 244844; reservations essential); *La Belle Epoque,* 103 Great Victoria St. (phone: 223244); or the *Strand,* 12 Stranmillis Rd. (phone: 682266). Several other restaurants can be found in Belfast's suburbs and surrounding small towns. These include: the *Cartwheel,* 44 High St., Bangor (phone: Bangor 456362); the *Schooner,* 30 High St., Holywood (phone: Belfast 428880); the *Hansom Cab,* 35 Railway St., Lisburn (phone: Lisburn 74652).

In addition, the Northern Ireland Tourist Board publishes an annual booklet called *Let's Eat Out in Northern Ireland* (£1) that includes an extensive list of eating places in Belfast and throughout the province.

SHARING A PINT: Just across Great Victoria Street from the *Europa* hotel are two atmospheric old pubs, the *Crown,* with stained-glass windows and polished wood snugs, and *Robinson's,* with a big stone fireplace and mahogany bar. Also try *Drury Lane,* 2 Amelia St. (for an after-theater dinner); the *Beaten Docket,* 48 Great Victoria St.; *Morning Star,* 17 Pottinger's Entry (old pub atmosphere, lunch only). Most pubs offer light lunches, some have pub-grub dinners; all are closed Sundays.

BRIGHTON

Brighton straddles 7 miles of breezy English Channel coast and although it is England's oldest and most famous seaside resort, it is also a colorful, cosmopolitan town in its own right, with great character, style, and vitality. No winter ghost town this; it bustles all year round.

Brighton has never been prim. In less permissive days, when an illicit weekend was still naughty, Brighton was the place for it. Only an hour (on the train from London) left the maximum time available for a romantic interlude in one of the numerous private and discreet (though distinctly unromantic) local hotels. Famous men kept their mistresses here in elegant bayfronted houses bordering quiet seaview squares. The city people brought their manners, fashions, and entertainments with them and nicknamed their coastal capital "London-on-Sea." This liberal attitude lingers. Brighton has more than its fair share of amusements, hotels, restaurants, theaters, pubs, shops, and sports facilities. It also has a great number of eccentrics and oddballs who wander around unremarked, basking in the town's liberalism and adding to its appeal.

None of this happened by chance, for Brighton was established by one of the greatest eccentrics of all time — the Prince Regent who eventually became King George IV of England. This spoiled, wayward, and extravagant libertine first visited Brighton in 1783, lured by the new fashion for sea bathing hailed as a cure-all by another eccentric, Dr. Richard Russell of nearby Lewes. The prince loved the place and promptly set about building the most exotic palace in Europe, just across the fields from the narrow, cobbled streets that once made up the original medieval fishing town of Brighthelmstone.

Famous worldwide for its bizarre beauty, the Royal Pavilion he conjured up sits like a beige Oriental fantasy in the middle of a formal English garden. Outside, it resembles a Mogul palace; inside, the decor carries a fancy for lavish chinoiserie to the limit. It became the hub of the Prince Regent's glittering and cultured social circle, but not everyone thought it beautiful. Wags at the time commented not only on its onion domes, but also referred to turnips and a "considerable number of bulbs of the crown-imperial, the narcissus, the hyacinth, the tulip, the crocus, and others . . ." To one critic it seemed the dome of St. Paul's had gone to Brighton and pupped. When the Prince Regent became king in 1820, he lost interest in the completed palace, but his successor, King William IV, enjoyed summers here and Queen Victoria stayed here, too, but reportedly was not amused.

The Royal Pavilion set the tone for the future: Regency Brighton was extravagant and gay. The narrow streets of the fishing village became the home of hostelries, restaurants, and boutiques. Theaters, music halls, parks, and gardens sprouted around the Pavilion, and Brighton became the country's most fashionable resort, graced by a splendid pier at each end of the seafront.

Its popularity has continued from those Regency days. Although most of its 3 million visitors a year now come only for the day or weekend instead of the formerly traditional fortnight, a new university and arts college, an impressive new yachting marina, and a growing convention trade have all combined to add a new dimension to the town and make it far more vital and cultured than most resorts. Brighton also has a distinct cosmopolitan flavor, thanks to its proximity to the Continent. French, German, Italian, Spanish, and Scandinavian students were quick to take advantage of it, using the town as a first base for their English-language schooling.

Most visitors still head directly for the beaches, but these are for the hardy rather than the knowledgeable sun worshiper. The shorefront consists of shingle stones rather than soft sand, and the tides can be strong, fueled by bracing breezes. To the west, the beaches are cleaner, quieter, and fringed by the lawns of Brighton's stately and (dare one say it) staid neighbor, Hove.

The central beaches are boisterous, friendly, and the first to become crowded with families. Here are the amusement arcades, bumper cars, fish and chip cafés, cockles and whelks stalls, paddling pools, putting greens . . . in short, all the slightly sleazy glories of the traditional English seaside resort that are not to be missed. The crowning glory of this candy-floss (cotton candy) mile is the Palace Pier, complete with café, fishing platforms, and boat rides as well as endless slot machines and fun fair thrills. Sadly, the West Pier — far prettier but less well placed for attracting day-trippers — has been closed for some time, although plans to restore it to its former glory are under way.

Heading east past the center of town, England's famous white cliffs begin their gradual climb toward Dover. The beaches become rockier and narrower and virtually disappear at high tide. But at low tide they are a delight for shrimp catchers and seapool ponderers. The quaint and largely unspoiled village of Rottingdean, 4 miles east of the center of Brighton in the gentle, rolling hills of the Sussex Downs, is the perfect focal point for these uncommercialized, untamed beaches that still belong to the true sea lover.

Lining Brighton's main seafront and stretching into spacious garden squares behind it are hundreds of hotels and guesthouses, large and small, good and bad. Most are in Regency style with bay fronts, balconies, and wrought-iron trimmings, but there are some good modern hotels as well, a result of the thriving conference trade. Beyond the seafront, the heart of the town lies focused on the narrow streets of the original village and the shopping streets that grew up around it and the Royal Pavilion. Cosmopolitan Brighton lives in these "Lanes," with art shops, bookstores, boutiques, antiques stalls, and the best restaurants, cafés, pubs, and wine bars. There's something for every taste and pocketbook here and the whole area of the Lanes is perfect for people-watching or browsing. Residents use this part of town as much as visitors, even in high summer, and if prices are a little inflated, perhaps the atmosphere is worth it!

Real local color is still farther afield, however, and is very easy to miss. It centers on Gloucester Road and Kensington Gardens, in the area between

Brighton's railway station and the Dome. This whole section was once nearly a slum until a timely preservation order made it trendy again. Now the little flat-fronted laborer's houses are snapped up by aspiring executives who commute to London. It is also the main student quarter and the starting point for many of the newest fashions, and it is certainly the best place for spotting the real eccentrics or one of the many famous actors who live or retire here. It is still possible to find bargains in the junk shops, and the local pubs and cafés may be scruffy but they're full of interesting people.

Between this highly metropolitan scene and the seaside razzmatazz, Brighton offers a full range of entertainments, holiday sports, and sights. Few visitors have sufficient time to see it all, let alone the beautiful surrounding Sussex countryside. But the beauty of this lovely, liberal place is that you can spend as little as a day or as much as a year here and still come away satisfied.

BRIGHTON AT-A-GLANCE

SEEING THE CITY: The best view is from the end of the Palace Pier, which is at the junction of Marine Parade and the Old Steine. On the clearest days you can see the whole sweep of the coast from Worthing to Beachy Head. To the west, the Peace Statue marks the boundary of Brighton and the start of Hove Lawns. To the east is the impressive seawall of the Marina with the white cliffs above. In between is the entire Brighton seafront. Don't neglect the pier itself, a splendid Victorian structure of iron and steel, wood and glass, lined with amusement halls, slot machines, sun decks, fishing platforms, and endless candy-floss (cotton candy) and hot doughnut stalls. The Palace Pier is open every day of the year, hours depending on the season.

For a spectacular, if expensive, night view, hotels such as the *Metropole* or the *Norfolk Resort* hotel, both on King's Rd., have rooftop rooms for dinner or dancing. After attending a concert at the Brighton Centre, stop in at its less expensive *Skyline* restaurant, which also has a very good view.

SPECIAL PLACES: You'll be doing a lot of walking — browsing through the old quarter, ambling along the seafront promenade, visiting the dazzling Brighton Pavilion — within a fairly centralized area of an otherwise sprawling town. For the sights outside the center, take the local bus, unless something more characteristic, such as the electric railway or the open-topped excursion buses mentioned below, is indicated.

CENTRAL BRIGHTON

Royal Pavilion – A Mogul palace bedecked with minarets, onion domes, terraces, and trellises, this was the creation of Brighton's prime mover and shaker, the Prince Regent who became King George IV of England. It was begun modestly in 1786 and was rebuilt in its present extravagant form by the English architect John Nash (who also laid out Regent's Park and Regent Street in London and redesigned Buckingham Palace) from 1815 to 1821. The state and private apartments are arranged with superb Regency and Chinese furniture and works of art, including many original pieces on loan from Queen Elizabeth II and probably the best show of gold plate in all of England. Open daily (phone: 603005).

The Regency Exhibition, now at the Pavilion year-round, is spectacular, with the huge Banqueting Room set with silver, gold, porcelain, and glass from the period. Other marvelous rooms include the Saloon, the North and South Drawing Rooms, the King's Apartments, and the Great Kitchen, which has the original mechanical spits, over 500 pieces of copperware, and tables showing the preparation of a banquet. The magnificent Music Room, tragically destroyed by fire in 1975, has been restored. The Royal Pavilion Lawns have deck chairs and regular summer performances by the Pavilion Trio band. The Royal Pavilion is also the scene of some of the musical events of the Brighton Festival, held in May. Open daily, from late September to June, 10 AM to 5 PM; from early June until late September, open 10 AM to 6:30 PM; closed Christmas and Boxing Day. Admission charge. Town center, above the Old Steine (phone: 603005).

The Lanes – The roughly square mile of narrow, paved alleys that made up the original village can only be visited on foot. This area is Brighton's Old Town and it's full of atmosphere and character, with countless shops for buying or browsing, including particularly good ones for books or antiques. Shop around to find the best price, however, especially if you're looking at antique jewelry. Entrances to the Lanes are all clearly marked and the easiest to spot are on East Street, North Street, Ship Street, and Middle Street. Look for Duke's Lane, just off Ship Street, cunningly created out of backyards and filled with boutiques. Brighton Square, another of the more modern additions, is the center of the Lanes, with benches and a café-bar ideal for watching the world go by, Continental style.

King's Road – This is the main seafront road. Steps and slopes lead down from it to the central beaches and the lower promenade with cafés, amusement halls, and all the traditional seaside entertainment. Fish and chips wrapped in newspaper, jellied eels, peanuts, ice cream, cotton candy, and Brighton rock candy are the things to eat, washed down with a pot of tea that will be served on a tin tray if you want to take it to the beach for a picnic. It's inexpensive and very cheerful, but rent a deck chair because you might find bits of tar on the pebbles. The Palace Pier end of the King's Road is most rowdy. Opposite the beach at East Street, the Old Fish Market is used for mending nets and fishermen sell their wares from the beach, about 100 yards away. The Beach Deck near the *Grand* hotel is another entertainment area with outdoor concerts and games for children. Toward Hove, the scene becomes more sedate, with singsong pubs replaced by boating ponds and putting greens. If you prefer grass to stony beaches, try the Lawns at Hove.

Volk's Railway and Peter Pan's Playground – Britain's first public electric railway opened in 1883 and still runs along the edge of Brighton's easterly beaches. The track starts 200 yards east of Palace Pier and extends 1 mile to the western perimeter of the Marina. The ride is inexpensive, and passengers travel in little wooden carriages with open sides and yellow roofs. Take it out to the Marina, then stroll back at sea level along Madeira Drive, passing Peter Pan's Playground and Fun Fair. The alternative is to return via the high-level Marine Parade with its ornate Victorian ironwork — the walk is quieter and gives better views. There is a temperamental lift opposite Peter Pan's but don't rely on it working. Volk's Railway runs from Easter until October; Peter Pan's Playground is open from Easter through October.

Brighton Art Gallery and Museum – Close to the gardens of the Royal Pavilion and housed in buildings originally intended as stables for the palace, the gallery contains Brighton's fine collection of Old Masters and English watercolors and a good collection of pottery and porcelain. It also has the most important collection of 20th-century Continental and English decorative art in the country. Worth seeing as well — the history of Brighton's seaside and the inspired Costume Museum. Closed Mondays. Free. Church St. (phone: 603005).

Brighton Centre – One of Europe's largest conference and exhibition complexes, the Centre also hosts major concerts and entertainment. There's the *Skyline* restaurant, a cocktail bar that overlooks the English Channel, and facilities for banquets and dances. Kings's Rd. (phone: 203131; box office: 202881).

Brighton Marina – This ambitious construction, the largest yachting marina in Europe, was built against the odds of gale force winds and tumultuous seas and opened in May 1979, by the Queen. Immense breakwaters protect the inner harbor and have an enviable record for fishing catches. The marina has berths for nearly 2,000 yachts, a selection of historic boats, a chandlery, and a boatyard. An added attraction is the HMS *Cavalier*, a 2,000-ton destroyer that was one of the last Royal Navy warships in service during World War II. Special events are arranged throughout the year, but recent private acquisition of the marina involves plans for a multimillion-pound residential and commercial complex, so fewer events are taking place until construction is complete. Open daily from 9 AM until dusk. Reach it by Volk's Railway, any of the city's open-topped buses, or by car — there is good parking. Small admission charge. Marine Dr., Black Rock, 1½ miles east of the Palace Pier (phone: 693636).

St. Nicholas's Churchyard – Brighton is full of quiet green corners tucked away out of sight of the main roads and easy to miss. St. Nicholas's Churchyard is one of the prettiest and is perfectly placed for a rest after shopping in nearby Western Road. It's a short walk up the steep hill of Dyke Road (which starts just above the Clock Tower) to the shallow brick steps that lead into the peaceful grounds surrounded by the gray flint walls characteristic of the area. The church itself is not always open but has a 12th-century Norman font and some excellent stained-glass windows. The top end of the churchyard leads into a small park.

ENVIRONS

Preston Manor – Two miles out from the Old Steine along the main London Road is this charming 18th-century country house set in beautiful parkland. It has original furnishings of the 18th to 20th centuries, including some fine silver and paintings, all arranged as they would have been during the life of the family that owned it. Open Tuesdays through Sundays 10 AM to 5 PM; closed Mondays except bank holidays. Small admission charge. Buses No. 5a or No. 5b from the Old Steine take about 10 minutes (phone: 552101).

Booth Museum of Natural History – Not too far away from Preston Manor, this is an entirely different kind of museum. It houses a large collection of British birds, stuffed and displayed in their natural habitats, an exhibit of both British and exotic butterflies, an exhibit of skeletons illustrating evolution, and a new Geology of Sussex gallery. Admission fee. Open weekdays except Thursdays 10 AM to 5 PM, Sundays 2 PM to 5 PM. 194 Dyke Rd., close to the Seven Dials (phone: 552586).

British Engineerium – Various Victorian steam engines — and the impressive Easton and Anderson steam engine of 1876 — puff efficiently away every Sunday in the engine houses of this museum. A huge number of Victorian mechanical inventions and other engineering exhibits are displayed in the restored 19th-century water pumping station. Open daily except Christmas, 10 AM to 5 PM. Admission fee. Nevill Rd., Hove, 3 miles from Brighton center (phone: 559583).

Stanmer Park – A natural park in the downland of Sussex is the setting for a village preserved as it was at the turn of the century. There are farmyards, a duck pond, a woodland park, and a rural museum that's open Sundays and Thursdays in summer; most other parts are open daily. Lewes Rd., 4 miles northeast of Brighton center, just before the University of Sussex campus.

Devil's Dyke – This famous beauty spot is 700 feet above sea level. The devil is supposed to have dug a chalk pit here to let in the sea and drown the pious folk of Sussex. The attempt failed but the view is spectacular. Near Poynings, 8 miles from Brighton center.

Charleston Farmhouse – This 18th-century building was the favorite country retreat of the Bloomsbury clan of artists, writers, and intellectuals during the 1920s and 1930s. Regular visitors to the house in its heyday included Virginia Woolf, economist John Maynard Keynes, Benjamin Britten, T. S. Eliot, and Bertrand Russell. The house has been fully restored by Vanessa Bell (Virginia Woolf's sister) and Duncan Grant. Firle, 6 miles east of Lewes (phone: 0321-83265).

■ **EXTRA SPECIAL:** When the weather allows, open-topped excursion buses run along the seafront to Rottingdean, a picturesque Sussex village set on the cliff tops in downland countryside. Steps and slopes lead to the undercliff walk edging narrow rocky beaches and to the open-air saltwater swimming pool — a sun trap that catches reflections off the white cliffs above it. A very pretty High Street has some good pubs and curio shops as well as the general stores typical of a small village. The *Plough Inn* is on the village green. Rudyard Kipling lived in Rottingdean and adjoining his house on the green is *The Grange,* a small art gallery and museum that has displays of his letters and books as well as frequent temporary exhibitions. The Grange is open Mondays, Tuesdays, Thursdays, and Saturdays 10 AM to 5 PM; and Sundays 2 PM to 5 PM (phone: 31004). Rottingdean village is 4 miles east of Brighton, easily reached by several buses, including the open-topped ones.

SOURCES AND RESOURCES

TOURIST INFORMATION: The main Tourist Information Centre is at Marlborough House, 54 Old Steine, near North St. (phone: 23755). There is an information kiosk open in the summer only on King's Rd. opposite West St. Hove's Tourist Information Centre is at the Town Hall, Norton Rd. (phone: 775400). All three carry books, maps, guides, and leaflets. The British Tourist Authority's *Guide to Brighton* (10p) gives a brief outline of attractions and lists accommodations. It has an adequate map but a better one will cost 55p, or there are various street-by-street guides for about £1, all available at bookstores and newsstands. *In and Around Sussex* (50p) is good for attractions up to 30 miles from Brighton. There is also a guide for disabled visitors. The information center has all of these. The BTA publishes a good general leaflet available free of charge at its US offices.

Local Coverage – The *Brighton Evening Argus* is on sale everywhere from noon onward, usually with a good entertainment section. The weekly *Brighton and Hove Express* and *What's On* are both sold at newsstands.

GETTING AROUND: Central Brighton is ideal for walking — the best parts are all fairly close. Outside the main center, the town gets hilly.

Bus – The best way to get around both the town and the county. Three private companies (*Brighton and Hove Buses, Southdown Services,* and *Brighton and Hove Bus and Coach Company*) operate from either the Pool Valley bus station (schedules and ticket offices are here) or the Old Steine. Some buses require the exact fare so take loose change with you or buy a Travelcard for unlimited weekly travel in the Brighton area (£6.50 from any post office or at the bus station). A MasterRider card allows unlimited travel on all buses within a 35-mile radius of the city (£12 per week). Regular local fares start at 15p. For information on local buses, call 606141; for regional services, 606600.

Car Rental – All main firms are represented but traffic is congested, and car parking is scarce and by meter in the center. Unless you're planning an excursion, you're better off without a car.

Tourbus – From mid-June to mid-September, guided tours aboard double-decker buses provide a good introduction to the city. Tickets and timetables are available at the Tourist Information Centre.

Taxi – There are reliable taxi stands at the railroad station and at the intersection of East and North streets. You may be able to hail a cab in the street and they are good at responding to telephone calls. To order one, phone *Streamline Cars* at 27282.

MUSEUMS: In addition to those mentioned in *Special Places,* museums of interest are:

Aquarium and Dolphinarium – Performing dolphins in the 1,000-seat dolphinarium and a varied display of freshwater, marine, and tropical fish, sea lions, and turtles in the mock Gothic underground galleries of Britain's largest aquarium. Other attractions include a flight simulator and an indoor children's adventure playground. Marine Parade (phone: 604234).

Hove Museum of Art – Coins, medals, watches, dolls, miniatures, plus a good modern exhibition. 19 New Church Rd., Hove (phone: 779410).

SHOPPING: Churchill Square is Brighton's pride — a new, modern precinct with all the major chain stores including *Habitat* (called *Conran's* in the states), the furniture and housewares store. It's next to the original shopping street off Western Road, near its eastern end. In the vicinity of Churchill Square, Western Road runs into North Street, giving almost 2 miles of prime shopping; the inexpensive and cheerful shops and stalls of Gardner Street, Bond Street, and the Lanes lead off North Street. Best buys are antiques, bric-a-brac, secondhand books, and local paintings and crafts, plus traditional English glass, china, and woolens. Most shops stay open until 8 PM on Thursdays. Shops to look into include the following:

Avison's Belgian Chocolates – Morello cherries, hazelnut pralines, and speciality chocolates tempt the eye and the mouth in an enticing window display. 19 Preston St. (phone: 28015).

Friends – A fascinating leather shop, either for buying things ready-made or the materials to make them yourself. The store also does first-class repairs to all leather goods. 29 Bond St. (phone: 27607).

Graffiti – An assortment of brightly colored novelty gifts — including cards, bags, notepaper, and balloons. 17 Cranbourne St. (phone: 27777).

Hanningtons – The smartest store in town, selling furniture, china, and glass as well as men's and women's clothing. North St. (phone: 29877).

Kokoro – A rare antiquarian bookshop with some precious volumes, historic documents, and manuscripts. 36 Duke St. (phone: 25954).

Lawleys – Good for china and glass. 25 North St. (phone: 26068).

Pecksniff's Bespoke Perfumery – Bath salts, perfumes, soaps, skin care products, and a wide range of self-serve potpourri. 45–46 Meeting House La.(phone: 28904).

Jo Webb – An unusual collection of old and new music boxes in every shape and size. Prince Albert St. (no phone).

SPECIAL EVENTS: The *Brighton Festival* in May provides a full program of music, theater, dance, and other entertainment, all detailed in the festival program available from February on. For information, write to the Brighton Festival Office, Marlborough House, Old Steine, Brighton, East Sussex BN1 1EQ, England.

The *London to Brighton Veteran Car Run* takes place the first Sunday in November. Antique cars — the "Old Crocks" — make their annual pilgrimage from Hyde Park Corner in London to Madeira Drive in Brighton in celebration of the day in 1896 when a law requiring all motor cars to be preceded by a man waving a red flag was finally dropped. A *Historic Commercial Vehicle Rally,* every year in May, is a runner-up to the Old Crocks. Trucks, fire engines, ambulances, and the like take part.

SPORTS: You can wear yourself out at the *King Alfred Leisure Centre* playing badminton or table tennis, bowling, swimming in the palm-fringed pool, scooting down the waterslides called "flumes," or taking a sauna, then finishing off in the café or bar. Open all year. Kingsway, Hove (phone: 734422).

Cricket – For a modest entry fee you can watch a match — called a fixture — at the *Sussex County Cricket Ground,* Eaton Rd., Hove. The local tourist office has a calendar of fixtures.

Fishing – Good catches are sea whiting, mackerel, occasionally plaice, and very occasionally cod. The best place to fish is at the *Brighton Marina* (phone: 693636). Free. During the summer, only angling club members can fish from the Palace Pier: Try your luck at the groynes (breakwaters) instead. Those toward Hove, where there are fewer boats and swimmers, are preferable. No charges or permits for this.

Golf – The *East Brighton Golf Club,* Roedean Rd., has one of the best courses in the area, with magnificent views over sea, downs, and Marina. Visitors are welcome. Several buses from the Old Steine pass it (phone: 603989). The municipal *Hollingbury Park Golf Club,* Ditchling Rd., has 18 reasonable holes open to all. The No. 26 bus from the Old Steine takes you right there (phone: 552010). If you prefer to take the game very casually, try the two pitch-and-putt courses on either side of the Roedean school on the way to Rottingdean. You can rent clubs, balls, and tees, and hit away happily without embarrassment.

Greyhound Racing – *Coral Stadium,* Nevill Rd., Hove, has races three times a week (twice in winter) from 7:45 PM. Telephone 731028 or 720757 for a table in the excellent restaurant that overlooks the course.

Horse Racing – The *Brighton Races* meet 17 times a year between April and October at the *Brighton Racecourse,* Race Hill (phone: 29801, ext. 426).

Soccer – There's a good support for the *Brighton and Hove Albion* — known locally as the *Seagulls.* Games are played from late August to mid-April at the Brighton and Hove Albion Ground on Goldstone Rd., Hove (phone: 739535).

Tennis – Twelve parks have public courts. The main ones are in *Preston Park,* 10 hard courts in all, easily seen from the London Road. Another 10 courts are on the other (west) side of the road away from the main park in a section called the Rockery. There's no racquet hire, nor can you book any of the public courts. Just take a chance and turn up, but be prepared to wait during July and August.

THEATER: The *Theatre Royal,* New Rd. (phone: 28488), has pre-London runs and variety with weekly changes in the bill. Some good, some bad. Other productions are at the *Gardner Centre Theatre,* a modern theater-in-the-round at the University of Sussex, Falmer (phone: 685861).

MUSIC: You can hear all kinds. Big pop and rock concerts are at the 5,000-seat *Brighton Centre,* Russell Rd. (phone: 202881). The *Dome,* 29 New Rd., slightly smaller with 2,000 seats, stages classical, light, pop, rock, and variety events, including some with international celebrities (phone: 682127). *St. Peter's Church,* London Rd., has occasional organ concerts, and several pubs have folk, jazz, and rock groups and informal singsongs.

NIGHTCLUBS AND NIGHTLIFE: This tends to be bright, breezy, and informal, with the emphasis on the young and noisy. Apart from the pubs, which are crowded in summer, activity centers on *Kingswest,* an entertainment complex on King's Road close to the West Street intersection. It contains three night spots. *Busbys* (phone: 25899) is for the smartly dressed (no jeans) over-21 crowd. *Coasters Fun* (phone: 25897) caters to a younger and more trendy clientele, but still no jeans. The music is live, usually pop and rock. The *Top Rank Suite* (phone: 25895) varies from night to night, sometimes live music, sometimes disco. Farther along the King's Rd., the *Metropole* hotel's lively new club, the *Metro*, is open until 2 AM (phone: 775432). Check the *Argus* for details. There are four casinos: in the *Metropole* hotel (phone: 775432), *Sergeant York's*, 88 Queen's Rd., near the station (phone: 26514), the *International Casino Club*, 6 Preston St. (phone: 725101), and *Hove Sporting Club*, 28 Fourth Ave., Hove (phone: 72026). Several hotels and restaurants have dinner dances or cabarets.

 SINS: The first public nudist beach in the country opened officially in Brighton in April 1980. If you care to defy the winds, the pebbles, and the rubberneckers, the beach is just west of the Marina.

BEST IN TOWN

 CHECKING IN: The best hotels are those with a sea view and even inexpensive ones can be found overlooking the eastern or western ends of the beaches. At an expensive hotel a twin room with private bathroom and TV will cost about $55 to $60 per person, including breakfast, tax, and service. A moderate hotel will cost about $35, and the simplest private hotel (guesthouse) will run from $15 to $25, but this will not include a private bathroom. The better hotels offer reduced weekly rates in June, July, and August, when there is no convention business in town, and many also offer year-round holiday (including weekend) bargains (the "Brighton for All Seasons and all Reasons" brochure, available at the Tourist Information Centre, lists them all). Do not turn up without a reservation from August through June, which is traditionally the prime convention season. There are also holiday flat-lets available with prices from $90 to $350 per flat per week, depending on the size.

Bedford – Tall, modern, spacious, comfortable, and a little impersonal, but one of the best in town, with 126 rooms. King's Rd. (phone: 29744). Expensive.

Grand – Right in the center of the seafront, this is the old and very attractive queen of Brighton hotels. Its Victorian architecture is at its best in the lobby and on the landings. Reopened in the fall of 1986, the hotel has undergone extensive restoration since the IRA bombing of 1984 and now features an indoor pool, sauna/solarium, fitness center, and nightclub. King's Rd. (phone: 21188). Expensive.

Granville – Several of owner Audry Simpson's 26 rooms feature Jacuzzis, Greek baths, and four-poster beds. A solarium is also on the premises. *Trog's* restaurant, a separate entity below the hotel, serves imaginative French food and fine wines. 125 King's Rd. (phone: 26722). Expensive.

Metropole – A large, modernized period hotel, it has good facilities, including its own health club and casino, plus a garage. It also has an attached exhibition hall, and since it's the main conference hotel in Brighton, it's one of the first to fill. King's Rd. (phone: 775432). Expensive.

Norfolk Resort – Toward the Hove end of the seafront and recently reconstructed, it still sports its attractive and bright Regency exterior. An expansion has increased the room total to 115, and facilities now include a swimming pool, health club, and American-style cocktail bar, plus a rooftop nightclub and restaurant. King's Rd. (phone: 738201). Expensive.

Old Ship – On the seafront close to the Lanes, much of its original style and charm is intact, especially in the 200-year-old banquet room once used by the Prince

Regent. The 155 rooms vary from simple singles to lavish delights with antique four-poster beds. King's Rd. (phone: 29001). Expensive.

Queens – Now under new ownership, this luxury hotel has 78 rooms, 12 suites, and 4 restaurants. Extensive leisure facilities include a Turkish bath and a gym. 1–5 King's Rd. (phone: 727316). Expensive.

Wheeler's Sheridan – This is a landmark of red Edwardian brick at a noisy corner of the seafront, but its location is outweighed by its plushness — velvet, brass, and crystal — and atmosphere. Its 56 rooms are very popular with regular customers, so book ahead. 64 King's Rd. (phone: 23221). Expensive.

Royal Albion – Built in 1826, this hotel became one of the town's most fashionable properties during the 1920s. All 115 rooms overlook either the sea or Steine Gardens. Old Steine (phone: 29202). Expensive to moderate.

Lanes – This hotel has 20 rooms, all with bath; most have an excellent sea view. 70 Marine Parade (phone: 674231). Moderate.

Olde Place – If you can't stay here or prefer to be in the center of town, this traditional, oak-beamed village inn is still worth a visit for a meal. High St., Rottingdean (phone: 31051). Moderate.

Prince Regent – There are many small hotels in this elegant, airy square facing the West Pier. This one with 18 rooms was recently restored in full Regency style, and the accent is on friendly service. 29 Regency Sq. (phone: 29962). Moderate.

Royal Crescent – One mile from the center, this 51-room hotel has a strong Regency flavor, a friendly atmosphere, and excellent views. It's close to the Kemptown area, with some interesting little shops nearby. 100 Marine Parade (phone: 606311). Moderate.

Le Flemings – Small but enterprising, with a bar, comfortable furnishings, and a pretty courtyard. 12 rooms. 12a Regency Sq. (phone: 27539). Inexpensive.

Marina House – Just a few yards from the seafront, this nicely furnished little hotel is run by a cheery husband and wife team. 8 Charlotte St. (phone: 605349). Inexpensive.

Preston Resort – Two miles from the town center, close to Preston Manor and Park, this is a good stop for the motorist. It's a modern, attractive 20-room hotel with parking and it's close to the main London-Brighton Road. 216 Preston Rd. (phone: 507853). Inexpensive.

Twenty One – A tiny (6 room) Victorian house with a terrace, it has built up a solid reputation as a fine hotel in a style reminiscent of a sophisticated private house. Lots of stairs, so don't arrive with heavy suitcases. Closed Decmeber 22 to January 25. 21 Charlotte St. (phone: 686450). Inexpensive.

 EATING OUT: Brighton is fortunate to have a greater variety of restaurants than most cities its size. Just about every style of cooking is available, including the usual range of Indian, Chinese, and Italian, and better than average Greek. Local fish is delicious, whether it costs 50p and is served in a newspaper or sets you back £10 in an exclusive restaurant. There are some good spots with inexpensive fast food, and there's a healthy sprinkling of better restaurants with excellent and imaginative fare. At the less expensive restaurants you can still get a simple English three-course set meal for under $10 per person. In the moderate ones, a meal with a fair amount of skill in its preparation and presentation will cost about $20, including house wine. The most expensive ones in town cost about $28 to $35 each, including wine, with service added.

English's Oyster Bar – If you can treat yourself well only once, do it here. The restaurant is 150 years old, converted from 400-year-old fisherman's cottages in the Lanes. Reservations necessary. Closed Christmas and Boxing Day. 29–31 East St. (phone: 27980). Expensive.

French Connection – Once a Georgian fisherman's cottage, this is now an intimate and romantic restaurant known for its unusual French, English, and fish dishes. Service is especially friendly. Closed Sundays and Christmas day. 11 Little East St. (phone: 24454). Expensive.

Wheeler's Oyster Rooms and Restaurant – The seafood is unsurpassed and it's served in Edwardian elegance. Reservations are necessary, since this is one of the oldest and best-known restaurants in the region. Closed Christmas, New Year's Day, and Boxing Day. 17 Market St. (phone: 25135). Expensive. The management here also runs *Wheeler's Sheridan Tavern,* a hotel restaurant serving similar fare. 64 King's Rd. (phone: 28372). Expensive.

Fudges – On the seafront, in the basement of a grand Victorian building that was rescued from dereliction in 1984, and hugely popular for its good, traditional English fare. Open for lunch and dinner. 127 King's Rd. (phone: 205852). Expensive to moderate.

Lawrence – A tiny, tasty place serving unusual and imaginative dishes with an emphasis on English produce. Open for lunch and dinner (reservations only, on Sundays). Closed Christmas. 40 Waterloo St. (phone: 772922). Moderate.

Le Grandgousier – This is tiny, too, and informal. Everyone shares one huge table and tucks into the simply cooked food. The choice is limited, but it's great fun and good value. Closed Saturday lunch, all day Sunday, and Christmas week, but usually open until midnight for dinner. 15 Western St. (phone: 772005). Moderate.

Al Forno – Owned by two brothers (who also run *Al Duomo,* at 7 Pavilion Building; phone: 26741), this simple and crowded Italian place is great for pizzas and pastas. Outdoor dining in summer. Closed Mondays, Sunday lunch, and Christmas. 36 East St. (phone: 24905). Moderate to inexpensive.

Caprice Carvery – You'll have to leave the center of Brighton, but it's well worth the trip — you may carve as much as you want from the roasts. Open daily. Third Ave., Hove (phone: 778737). Moderate to inexpensive.

Browns – The atmosphere is light, bright, and busy, with sanded floors, white walls, and palms. This is the best of the hamburger-spaghetti palaces, open every day with continuous service. 3–4 Duke St. (phone: 23501 and 23502). Inexpensive.

Crusts – The kind of bistro now familiar on the British restaurant scene — decorated with plants, elegant coatstands, and bentwood chairs — serving hot, substantial, value-for-your-money food: burgers, baked potatoes, and salads. Bring your own wine (corkage charge) or visit *Crusts Wine Bar,* opposite. 24 Market St. (phone: 26813). Inexpensive.

Food for Friends – Tulips on the tables, still-lifes on the walls, plants hanging from the ceiling, classical music on the turntable, and delicious casseroles and wholesome salads served by a young, cheerful staff to a fast-moving (but never-ending) queue of Brightonites. 17a–18 Prince Albert St. (phone: 736236). Inexpensive.

 SHARING A PINT: It's difficult to choose from the wide selection of pubs in Brighton. The *Belvedere,* 159 King's Rd. Arches, close to the Palace Pier, is a boisterous, beachside bar — don't dress up. The *Colonnade Long Bar,* New Rd., is next to the Theatre Royal and used during intermissions; it has Victorian decor and a good selection of playbills. Don't miss *Cricketers* on Black Lion St., the town's oldest pub. The original parts, dating back to 1549, include the stables and coachyard, and there are old mirrors and marble and brass tables. The *Bedford Tavern,* 30 Western St., is simple and unassuming but if you're passing by, pop in to see its collection of heraldry. *Dr. Brighton's,* on King's Rd. by Market St. is a traditional-looking pub with good, hot food. The *Druid's Head,* Market Pl., The Lanes, is an Old World pub with beams and decorative horse brasses. Once a smugglers' haunt, it now belongs to the fashionable young set. The *King and Queen,* Marlborough Pl., an amusing imitation of a Tudor beer garden, overlooks the Victoria Gardens. It's good for families — there's an aviary for diversion. The *Royal Pavilion Tavern,* Castle Sq., is a popular central pub with old oak panels and beams and extensive hot and cold snacks. In Rottingdean, the *Black Horse,* High St., is a genuine village pub, with a comfortable and friendly large bar and the original snug — the tiny bar for women.

BRISTOL

A century ago, as described in the pages of Robert Louis Stevenson's *Treasure Island,* a wide-eyed visitor could wander the docks of Bristol, sniffing in the smell of tar in the salt air, marveling at the figureheads of ships that had been far over the world and the "many old sailors, with rings in their ears, and whiskers curled in ringlets, and tarry pigtails, and their swaggering, clumsy sea-walk . . ." It was a scene that any movie mogul would have been proud to conjure up on a Hollywood back lot.

Naturally, Bristol looks like that no more. Now it's a large, modern, lively city with isolated patches of medieval antiquity reaching through the centuries. Walk along the quayside of the harbor today and see the characteristic old warehouses that, until recently, were empty and decaying. Now they have been restored as museums and arts and exhibition centers. The former freight yards and great cranes are now idle — poignant reminders of Bristol's former prowess as a great trading port — but these, too, are being restored to preserve an important part of the city's railway and dockside heritage. Now pleasure craft, visiting naval warships, and even a few restored traditional sailing boats grace the quaysides. For the visitor, this striking view around the harbor is further enhanced by the backdrop of Bristol's city center, dominated by the towers of the cathedral and, behind them, the university buildings.

Bristol had been an important port since the eleventh century. During the Middle Ages, its merchants and seafarers traded in wine, stacking the wharves and cellars with Bordeaux from France, sherry from Spain, and port from Portugal. By the fifteenth century it was known for an enterprising maritime boldness that attracted sailors from Europe bent on discovery. John Cabot came from Italy, found backing by a local merchant, and set sail in 1497 to become the first explorer to reach the American mainland. The customs officer who awarded Cabot a pension was Richard a Meryk, and to this day some Bristolians believe that it was he, and not Amerigo Vespucci, who gave his name to the New World.

Cabot was followed by other explorers, then by thousands of early American settlers who stepped off European soil here and sailed to a new life. Having played its part in the discovery of America, Bristol did its share in developing it, financing colonization efforts, trading in Virginia tobacco and West Indian sugar. A less glorious chapter in its history was its involvement in the black slave trade, on the proceeds of which Bristol merchants grew fat, while the Quakers and John Wesley and his Methodists, who were all influential here, railed against it.

"All shipshape and Bristol fashion" is an English phrase meaning everything methodical and orderly, recalling the days when this West of England city was dominated by the masts of tall ships from all corners of the world.

In Bristol, unlike most other seafaring cities, the docks are in the heart of the town rather than at its edge. That the ships are no longer there is the result of an error of judgment on the part of the earliest Bristolians. The city grew at the confluence of the Avon and Frome rivers, 7 miles inland from where the Avon — which rises and falls with close to the highest tide in the world — flows out into the Severn estuary. Fear of piracy caused the medieval inhabitants to plant themselves far upstream, a less than ideal location that made docking a tricky business of picking the right moment to set out upriver or risk getting stuck in the mud at low tide. Even berthed ships were in danger of breaking up in the tidal sweep.

To remedy this, the city channeled the Avon into a new cut in the early eighteenth century, creating a "floating harbor" with a constant level of water for ships to tie up in. But by then, much transatlantic trade had already been lost to Liverpool. Ironically, the situation was not helped by the presence of Isambard Kingdom Brunel, the pioneering British engineer who built the largest vessels of his day, thereby inspiring even larger ones — which couldn't make it up the Avon to Bristol. By the end of the nineteenth century, new docks had been built downstream at Avonmouth and Portishead, but, alas, they came too late to prevent the decline in Bristol's maritime fortunes.

The cityscape underwent further change as a result of World War II. The blitz of 1940–41 damaged some 9,000 buildings, including the medieval core (the original castle that used the Avon and the Frome as its moat had been razed centuries before on the orders of Cromwell). Throughout history the tallest structures in Bristol had been the spires and towers of churches, but with postwar reconstruction came the first tall office blocks. Now it is necessary to walk between walls of concrete and glass for a glimpse of the churches, as fine as those in any medieval city, and the other reminders of Bristol's heritage — remains of early monasteries and Georgian squares and terraces — that survive.

For many devotees, Bristol's most charming part is suburban Clifton, perched on the Clifton and Durdham Downs above the city and the Avon Gorge. Begun as a dormitory in the healthful high air for visitors to the Hot Well spa at the foot of the gorge, Clifton then became a fashionable place to live. The spa had only a brief moment of glory in the early eighteenth century (Bath was more popular), but Clifton was left with Georgian crescents to compete with those of Bath, and large, graceful Victorian villas. When the wealthy moved out early in this century, Clifton lost its cachet, but many of its houses have since been restored and it is now a quiet residential quarter with shops and bistros and a villagelike atmosphere appealing to young sophisticates.

Still, Clifton is far from the reality of a commercial, manufacturing city of nearly half a million people. The more distant suburb of Filton, one of the largest aerospace capitals in the world and the hub of Bristol's aircraft industry (the supersonic Concorde came off the production line here), is closer to the old spirit of adventure, perhaps, but the heart of the city is really in the waterways, its most characteristic visual feature. Although life in the harbor is only the ghost of what it once was, the docks remain a museum of Britain's mercantile past.

BRISTOL AT-A-GLANCE

 SEEING THE CITY: From the top of the Cabot Tower on Brandon Hill there is a spectacular bird's-eye view of the center of Bristol and much of the surrounding area. It's quite a climb, however, and the view is almost as good from the base of the tower. The panorama is dominated by church spires, venerable stone buildings, and waterways, and it provides a surprise. Bristol has a generous amount of open space for a city whose past has been linked so strongly with commercial and maritime matters, and you'll see a lot of greenery among the old buildings and new office blocks.

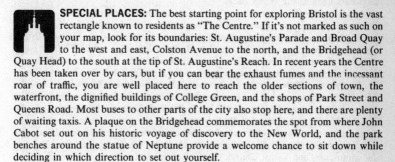 **SPECIAL PLACES:** The best starting point for exploring Bristol is the vast rectangle known to residents as "The Centre." If it's not marked as such on your map, look for its boundaries: St. Augustine's Parade and Broad Quay to the west and east, Colston Avenue to the north, and the Bridgehead (or Quay Head) to the south at the tip of St. Augustine's Reach. In recent years the Centre has been taken over by cars, but if you can bear the exhaust fumes and the incessant roar of traffic, you are well placed here to reach the older sections of town, the waterfront, the dignified buildings of College Green, and the shops of Park Street and Queens Road. Most buses to other parts of the city also stop here, and there are plenty of waiting taxis. A plaque on the Bridgehead commemorates the spot from where John Cabot set out on his historic voyage of discovery to the New World, and the park benches around the statue of Neptune provide a welcome chance to sit down while deciding in which direction to set out yourself.

CENTRAL BRISTOL

Bristol Cathedral – The Cathedral Church of the Holy and Undivided Trinity was founded in the 12th century as an Augustinian monastery. The Norman chapter house, which dates from this earliest period, should not be missed. Other older parts are the 13th-century Elder Lady chapel and the 14th-century choir and Eastern Lady chapel (with the Jesse window), while the nave is the work of a Victorian architect faithful to the original style. Particularly interesting, if you have the time to study them, are the 16th-century misericords in the choir on which monks — who were not allowed to sit during services — leaned. They're beautifully carved and all different, some with serious and some with humorous scenes. College Green (phone: 24879).

Council House – This graceful, curved, 20th-century red brick building across the street from the cathedral is the headquarters of Bristol's municipal administration. The golden unicorns on either end of the roof are symbolic of the city, also to be found on its coat of arms. Since this is a working building, tours of the interior are by special arrangement and for groups only. College Green (phone: 266081).

Georgian House – Once the home of a merchant wealthy from West Indian trade, this is now a museum maintained as though the merchant and his family still lived in it. It was built in 1790 and the furnishings, all of local manufacture, are Georgian in period. Open daily except Sundays from 10 AM to 5 PM. 7 Great George St. (phone: 299771, ext. 237).

City Museum and Art Gallery – The museum has extensive collections in the fine and applied arts, archaeology and history, geology and natural history, but visitors pressed for time will find exhibits of Bristol blue — and green, amethyst, and white — glass not too far beyond the lobby. The building next door to the museum, looking much older than it is, is the 20th-century neo-Gothic Wills Memorial Building of the

University of Bristol. It houses the 10-ton Great George bell, which sounds hourly in E flat. Open daily except Sundays from 10 AM to 5 PM. Queens Rd. (phone: 299771).

King Street – This cobbled street was laid out in the 1660s and remains one of the most picturesque in Bristol. The pink buildings at its western end are the Merchant Venturers' Almshouses, built in the 17th century for retired seamen. Next is the 18th-century Old Library, now a restaurant. Farther along, the Palladian Coopers' Hall, a guildhall built in 1743, has become the entrance to the Theatre Royal, since 1766 one of the leading stages in the country and the present home of the Bristol Old Vic Company. Several other 17th-century edifices line the street, which ends with a group of buildings as appealingly half-timbered and gabled as you'll see anywhere. Built in 1664, these houses eventually became *Ye Llandoger Trow,* an inn where Daniel Defoe is supposed to have met the man he transformed into Robinson Crusoe, and which still operates as a pub and restaurant. King Street stops at an original stretch of Bristol quayside known as the Welsh Back.

Corn Street – The four bronze "nails," or trading tables, on which 16th- and 17th-century merchants counted out their money ("paid on the nail") characterize this section of Bristol. The heart of the medieval city was at the crossing of Corn, Broad, High, and Wine streets and the area later became Bristol's center of banking and commerce. Corn Street, especially, is an amalgam of worthy and workaday 18th- and 19th-century buildings as well as the home of the new Tourist Information Centre at No. 35. Two to compare are the Exchange (1743), behind the nails, designed by John Wood the Elder as a market and meeting place for merchants, and the ornately carved palazzo (1854) across from it, now Lloyd's Bank. Behind the Exchange is the St. Nicholas Market, a warren of stalls covered over in the 18th century and still going strong daily except Sunday. Several interesting churches include All Saints (Corn St.), with Norman foundations; St. Nicholas's (St. Nicholas St.), dating from the 1760s and now a museum; and Christ Church (Broad St.), an 18th-century replacement of an earlier church. (The mechanical men who strike the quarter hours on its clock were on the older building, too.) Walk to the end of Broad Street and you'll come to St. John's Gate, the only survivor of Bristol's nine medieval gateways.

John Wesley's New Room – In contrast to the other, imposing churches to be visited in Bristol, the world's first Methodist chapel is a spare and simple house of worship. John Wesley built it in 1739 and he and his brother preached here for 40 years. Their living quarters are upstairs. Open 10 AM to 4 PM (closed from 1 to 2 PM); closed Wednesdays and Sundays. 36 The Horsefair.

THE HARBOR

Bristol's historic harbor extends from Temple Meads in the east to Clifton Suspension Bridge in the west and comprises some 6 miles of waterfront in the historic core of the city. Major development of the harbor's tourism potential is already under way, including the construction of conference and exhibition centers, a shopping and entertainment complex, Redcliffe Caves, and a science-technology center.

Bristol Maritime Heritage Centre – This striking, modern building was opened in 1985 and houses artifacts and displays which tell the city's maritime history. Free admission. Open daily. Great Western Dock, Gas Ferry Rd., off Cumberland Rd.

St. Mary Redcliffe – The church Queen Elizabeth I described as "the fairest, goodliest, and most famous parish church in England" was built mostly in the 14th and 15th centuries near enough to the city docks to be a merchant seaman's last and first call at the beginning and end of a voyage. It is an outstanding example of Perpendicular architecture, and it positively presides over what has since become a rather dull stretch of the Bristol cityscape. Inside, the nave and choir soar to a ceiling ornamented with more than 1,200 carved and gilded bosses. As you enter, note the unusual hexagonal shape and the very pretty stained-glass windows of the outer north porch, which dates to 1290, and the black marble pillars of the late-12th-century inner north porch, the oldest part of the church. Redcliffe Way.

SS *Great Britain* – Following the SS *Great Western,* the SS *Great Britain* was the second nautical accomplishment of Isambard Kingdom Brunel. When it floated out from Bristol in 1843, it was not only the first iron-hulled screw steamship in the world, it was also the largest liner on the seas. The *Great Western,* which had been the first transatlantic steam vessel, is no more; the *Great Britain,* fortunately, is. Shipwrecked and abandoned in the Falkland Islands in 1886, its return to the city in 1970 was a nostalgic and emotional occasion. It is now being restored at the British Maritime Heritage Centre dock, where it was built. Open daily from 10 AM to 6 PM in summer and to 5 PM in winter. Admission charge. Great Western Dock, Gas Ferry Rd., off Cumberland Rd. (phone: 20680).

CLIFTON

Clifton Suspension Bridge – Bristol's most famous landmark is another of Isambard Kingdom Brunel's achievements. The bridge has a 702-foot span, 245 feet above the high water level of the Avon Gorge, and though it adds an attractive focal point to the Clifton scene, it is entirely functional. Before it opened in 1864, people crossed the river in a basket on a cable. Since then, pilots have flown underneath it and suicides have been attempted (some successfully) from it. The city's favorite story is that of the young woman who jumped after a lover's quarrel in 1885 — she parachuted gently in her petticoats to a soft landing in the mud and lived to a ripe old age.

Clifton Cathedral – The Cathedral Church of Saints Peter and Paul is the headquarters of the Roman Catholic diocese of Clifton. Completed in 1973, it is considered an important work of contemporary church architecture, designed to reflect the most recent changes in the form of liturgical worship. Visitors are welcome inside to see its modern works of art. Pembroke Rd. (phone: 738411).

Clifton and Durdham Downs – Bristol's largest and most popular open space covers more than 400 acres on the north side of the city. Bristolians play football on the Downs in winter, cricket in summer, and walk on the green expanse year-round.

Zoological Gardens – The Bristol zoo is one of the best in Britain. It has more than 1,000 animals, birds, reptiles, and fish, but it is most famous for its white tigers. There are also extensive gardens. Closed Christmas Day. Admission charge. Clifton Down (phone: 738951).

ENVIRONS

Bristol's location is in itself a drawing card for tourists: the rolling Cotswold hills, the magnificent Cheddar Gorge, and the scenic walking country in and around the Wye Valley are all accessible by car or Tourist Centre sightseeing buses. Other outlying sights include:

Blaise Castle House Museum – Blaise Castle itself is nothing but a Gothic folly, a sham structure built in 1766 to decorate the grounds of this estate. Blaise Castle House Museum, set up in the estate's real 18th-century mansion, is a folk museum of costumes, toys, crafts, and other reminders of West Country life in days gone by. The landscaped grounds contain woodlands, walkways, the remains of an Iron Age hill fort, and a number of attractions for children. Open Wednesdays to Saturdays from 2 to 5 PM. Henbury, 4 miles northwest of Bristol (phone: 506789).

■**EXTRA SPECIAL:** You can sample dockside Bristol easily enough on foot by walking from the Bridgehead along Narrow Quay, over the Prince Street Bridge and onto Prince's Wharf, beyond which is Wapping Wharf with the SS *Great Britain* at its far end. (A helpful *Maritime Walks* guidebook is available at the City Information Centre.) Another choice is the ferrybus. During the season it plies the

Floating Harbour from Narrow Quay, making various stops including the *Great Britain.*

SOURCES AND RESOURCES

 TOURIST INFORMATION: The City Information Centre (phone: 293891) at Colston House on Colston St. can supply brochures, maps, and general information. It's open weekdays from 9 AM to 5 PM and on Saturdays from 9 AM to 12:30 PM. For 40p, you can pick up the *Bristol Official Visitors Guide,* which is a comprehensive introduction to all aspects of the city and includes several walking tours to cover its sights. Other walking tour guides are available, including a "Walkabout" series on individual routes. *The Bristol Heritage Walk* brochure describes a route that is marked on the streets it follows. If you're in town from May through September, try one of the regular walking tours led by Bristol's Corps of Guides. They leave once a day from late April through September at 11 AM, departing from the Neptune Statue at the Bridgehead, and include an *Old City* walk, a *Christmas Steps* walk, and a *Harbour* walk. In addition, walking tours of Clifton are arranged every Sunday from the end of March through September. All walks cost 60p and last approximately 1½ hours. The exact time of departure is posted outside the information center, at the Exchange, or near Neptune's statue at the Bridgehead.

Local Coverage – The morning *Western Daily Press* and the *Bristol Evening Post* are the two dailies, while the fortnightly *Venue* magazine covers what's on and where to go in and around the city.

GETTING AROUND: You may want to take a bus or taxi to Clifton, but the rest of Bristol is walkable, with one word of warning. Traffic speeds around and out from the Centre in all directions, and little provision seems to have been made for pedestrians to interrupt it. There are a few traffic lights (all pedestrian operated) and a few striped zebra crossings (where the pedestrian has the right of way once he or she steps from the curb), but you'll see many a Bristolian paused on the verge of a dash at the sight of any break in the two-way onslaught.

Bus and Train – The *Bristol City Line* operates bus services within the city and throughout the surrounding area, including the inexpensive and friendly yellow minibuses that run approximately every 10 minutes, and also conducts sightseeing tours during the summer months. Most city bus routes include a stop in the Centre; long-distance coaches operate out of the bus station on Marlborough Street, north of the Broadmead shopping center. For information on bus schedules, call 553231 from 8 AM to 9 PM, or 558211 for details on tours. For train information, call Temple Meads Railway Station, Temple Gate, (phone: 294255), from 8 AM to 10 PM.

Car Rental – The major national and international companies are represented.

Taxi – You'll have no trouble getting a taxi in the Centre for the trip out, but for the return, you'll probably have to call one. Numerous cab companies are listed in the Yellow Pages.

MUSEUMS: In addition to those discussed in *Special Places,* Bristol has a number of other interesting museums.

Bristol Industrial Museum – Machinery, especially that connected with transport — including horse-drawn carriages and a model of the Concorde cockpit — in a transit shed in the city docks. Open Saturdays through Wednesdays from 10 AM to 5 PM, but closed from 1 to 2 PM. Prince's Wharf (phone: 299771, ext. 290).

Harvey Wine Museum – An illustration of how wine is made, plus collections of old wine bottles, wineglasses and decanters, and silver decanter labels. The well-known wine company has set up the museum, which can be visited by appointment Mondays through Thursdays and on Fridays from 10:30 AM to 12:30 PM and 2:30 to 4:30 PM. 12 Denmark St. (phone: 277661).

National Lifeboat Museum – Britain's only museum dedicated to housing and restoring rescue vessels. On the quayside of the historic harbor, next to the Industrial Museum. (phone: 213-389).

St. Nicholas's Church Museum – A church converted to an ecclesiastical museum of silver, vestments, and church art including an altarpiece by William Hogarth. Admission is free, but there is a charge to do a rubbing in the Brass Rubbing Centre downstairs. Open daily except Sundays from 10 AM to 5 PM. St. Nicholas (phone: 299771, ext. 243).

Red Lodge – A 16th-century house preserved with its 18th-century alterations and furnishings of both periods. Open daily except Sundays from 2 to 5 PM. Park Row (phone: 299771, ext. 236).

Temple Meads Terminus – Designed by Isambard Kingdom Brunel and opened in 1840, this was once the grandest railway station in Europe. It's now undergoing extensive restoration. (phone: 292688).

SHOPPING: Bristol's stores are many, drawing shoppers from all over the west of England and from South Wales. You'll find almost anything, though the emphasis is on the needs of the town shopper rather than tourist preferences. Broadmead is a very large, modern shopping center around a pedestrian mall — department stores, supermarkets, and other stores are legion here. Smaller, more expensive shops are found along Park Street, Queens Road, Whiteladies Road, and all along Canon's Road below the Watershed Media Centre. For local color, browse through the vegetables, crockery, parakeets, and other things in the St. Nicholas Market any day except Sunday. Daily except Sundays, from 9 AM to 3:30 PM, an antiques and crafts market takes place in the nearby Exchange. For more antiques and small boutiques, visit The Mall and its environs in Clifton, also. The Clifton Antiques Market, 26/28 The Mall, is open from 10 AM to 6 PM Tuesdays through Saturdays.

Alexander Gallery – Fine art dealers and publishers. 122 Whiteladies Rd. (phone: 739582).

Banks of Bristol – Antique reproduction specialists selling chairs, tables, and household goods. 71 Park St. (phone: 28306).

Bristol Craft Centre – Jewelers, potters, weavers, leatherworkers, an embroiderer, and others market what they make on the same premises at 6 Leonard La., an exceedingly narrow passage from Corn to Small St., entered from the opening beside 31 Corn St. (phone: 23182).

Bristol Guild – All manner of arts and crafts shops sell their wares here, from kitchenware and decorative furnishings to basketware and pottery. The traditional (but hard to find) Bristol chocolates called "Guilberts" can also be purchased here. 66–70 Park St. (phone: 25548).

Les Chatteries – Health food galore as well as nuts, coffee, preserves, mustards, handmade chocolates, and their own brand of multiflavored ice cream. Canon's Rd. (phone: 20969).

City Museum and Art Gallery Shop – Handmade reproductions of Bristol blue glass are on sale here, as well as posters, prints, and other souvenirs. Queens Rd. (phone: 299771).

Debenham's – An excellent department store with goods from furs to furnishings. The Horsefair (phone: 291021).

Dingles – Also a department store, more exclusive than *Debenham's,* and with a noteworthy food hall. Queens Rd. (phone: 215301).

George's – Three very good bookshops, all on Park Street: No. 89 for general books, No. 81 for academic books, and No. 52 for fine arts books (phone: 276602).

 SPECIAL EVENTS: The water and wine that played such a part in Bristol's past come together fittingly one week in July in the *World Wine Fair and Festival,* the city's biggest annual event. Exhibitors come to the Bristol Exhibition Complex, two refurbished warehouses on the Floating Harbour just below the Bridgehead, from all over the world, stands are set up for visitors to sample wines not usually available for general consumption, and fireworks displays light up the city docks. The docks are also the focus of other events, including the *Bristol Boat Show* in April or May, the *Bristol Grand Prix* power boat race in June, and the *Bristol Harbour Regatta and Rally of Boats* in July. In August, the sky over Ashton Court Estate, 825 acres of park on the other side of the Clifton Suspension Bridge, is full of multicolored hot-air balloons taking part in the *Bristol International Balloon Fiesta.*

 SPORTS: Four sports centers provide facilities for squash, badminton, bowls, and various team games. The largest of these is the *Whitchurch Sports Centre,* Bamfield, Whitchurch (phone: 833911), south of the city. Whitchurch is open daily, has a sauna and bar, and is also the scene of spectator events such as basketball and hockey games and karate matches.

Cricket – The *Gloucestershire County Cricket Club* (phone: 46743) plays at the *County Ground,* Nevil Rd., from the end of April through early September.

Greyhound Racing – Call the Bristol Stadium, Stapleton Rd. (phone: 511919), for the latest racing schedule.

Rugby – The *Bristol Rugby Club* (phone: 514448) is based at the *Memorial Ground,* Filton Ave.; the *Clifton Rugby Club* (phone: 500445), at Cribb's Causeway.

Soccer – The *Bristol City Football Club* plays at Ashton Gate (phone: 632812); the *Bristol Rovers Football Club* plays at the *Eastville Stadium* (phone: 511050). Most games are on Saturdays at 3 PM.

Swimming – Bristol has 11 indoor pools open daily (closing at noon on Sundays). The outdoor pool at Oakfield Place, Clifton, is open daily from mid-May to early September.

 THEATER: Bristol has made a name for itself in British theatrical history. The famous *Theatre Royal,* King St. (phone: 24388), opened in 1766, is the oldest continuously active theater in Britain. Since World War II it has been the home of the Bristol Old Vic Company, one of the most respected repertory groups in the land. The Bristol Old Vic does both classic and new plays, but if you have a choice, see a Shakespearean or other old comedy, because they're especially suited to the splendor of the Georgian setting. The company also plays at the *New Vic,* a second, modern auditorium next door (but sharing entrance and box office with the *Theatre Royal*). While almost as large, the *New Vic* is meant for informal and experimental theater and can be used for theater-in-the-round. Finally, you'll see smaller productions at the *Little Theatre* (phone: 291182), inside Colston Hall on Colston St., where the Little Theatre Company presents its productions as well. The Bristol Old Vic Theatre School (phone: 733535) gives several performances yearly at all the aforementioned theaters or at the *Vandyck Theatre* on Park Row, home of the University of Bristol Drama Department. As the first such department in a British university, this is another part of Bristol's theatrical tradition. The *Bristol Hippodrome,* St. Augustine's Parade (phone: 299444), seats 2,000 and hosts touring companies such as the Royal

Shakespeare Company and the National Theatre Company. It is also the stage for visiting opera and ballet. The *Watershed,* Britain's first media and communications center, at 1 Canon's Rd. (phone: 276444), and the *Arnolfini Arts Centre,* 16 Narrow Quay (phone: 299194), are dockside warehouses that have been converted to contemporary arts centers, with cinemas, galleries, and stage facilities, restaurants, and bars.

MUSIC: *Colston Hall,* Colston St. (phone: 22957), is Bristol's main venue for all types of musical performances, from classical to pop. The Bournemouth Symphony Orchestra and the Bournemouth Sinfonia play a regular season of concerts — the Harveys Bristol Series — from October to April. *St. George's,* a refurbished Neoclassical church on Brandon Hill (phone: 428431) serves as an important classical music site with a full program of lunchtime concerts. Touring opera and ballet companies stage their productions at the *Bristol Hippodrome,* St. Augustine's Parade (phone: 299444), and concerts of 20th-century music are the specialty of the *Arnolfini Arts Centre* (address above), which showcases the contemporary in all the arts. Recitals are held in many of Bristol's churches, including Bristol Cathedral, Clifton Cathedral, St. Mary Redcliffe, the Lord Mayor's Chapel on College Green, and St. George's Church on Charlotte St. University of Bristol students put on concerts, often at lunchtime, in the *Wills Memorial Building,* Queens Rd.

NIGHTCLUBS AND NIGHTLIFE: Bristol's nightlife compares well with that of any city outside London. There are more than 20 nightclubs, including *Yesterdays,* 15 King St. (phone: 297670), which has five bars, two discotheques, a restaurant, and a fast-food counter; the *Reeves Club and Cabaret Room* at *Arno's Court* hotel, 470 Bath Rd. (phone: 711461); *Misty's* at 48 Park St. (phone: 24422); and *Platform One,* Clifton Down Station (phone: 739171).

BEST IN TOWN

CHECKING IN: Bristol is not the prime tourist destination that prestigious Bath is, but as an important commercial center and the object of many an expense account traveler, it's no less expensive than its neighbor. A wide range of accommodations is available, however, and if you book in advance, you should be able to find a room at the right price almost any time of the year. Look in Clifton for the broadest choice of reasonably priced small hotels and guesthouses. Few of Bristol's hotels are right in the center of town, and those that are tend to be in the expensive category. As a rough guide, expect to pay more than $75 a night for a double room at an expensive hotel, between $50 and $75 at a moderate one, and $30 to $50 at an inexpensive one. A hearty English breakfast should be included in the rate, but a growing number of the top hotels now offer room only.

Grand – This large, lovely Victorian has had a facelift and now sports a scrubbed stone exterior above the row of brown and gold striped awnings that line the street. Gracious and extensively modernized inside; right in the historic center. Broad St. (phone: 291645). Expensive.

Holiday Inn – Just like any other *Holiday Inn* you know. This modern, multi-story hotel has 284 spacious rooms, a sauna, indoor swimming pool, gym, restaurants, and bars. It's convenient to the Broadmead shopping center, with a courtesy car operating to and from the railroad station on weekdays. Lower Castle St. (phone: 294281). Expensive.

Ladbroke Dragonara – Swish and modern, with 200 luxurious rooms, it's close to the city center and to the railroad station. Traffic races by out front and the setting is unglamorous, but the beautiful church of St. Mary Redcliffe does dress up the neighborhood. There are 204 rooms. Redcliffe Way (phone: 20044). Expensive.

Thornbury Castle – A 16th-century country house that once played host to King Henry VIII and Anne Boleyn. It became known as a restaurant that served bacon from its own pig farm and wine from its own vineyard. While the pigs have gone, the highly regarded wine remains, and the castle now offers 12 cozy rooms above the restaurant. Thornbury (phone: 0454-418511). Expensive.

Avon Gorge – This solid white block of Victoriana perches on the edge of Clifton overlooking the Avon Gorge and the Clifton Suspension Bridge. A recent expansion has brought the total number of rooms to 83, all with private bath or shower. If you don't get one gorge-side, enjoy the view at tea on the terrace. Sion Hill, Clifton (phone: 738955). Moderate.

Hawthorns – In Clifton, only about half a mile from the Park Street shops. It has 170 rooms (though not all with bath) and a wide range of entertainment. Woodland Rd., Clifton (phone: 731260). Moderate.

St. Vincent Rocks – This Regency hotel is a smaller (46 rooms, all with private bath) alternative to the *Avon Gorge* hotel down the road. It, too, overlooks the gorge and has an enviable view of the Clifton Suspension Bridge. Sion Hill, Clifton (phone: 739251). Moderate.

Unicorn – It's smarter than its unappealingly modern front on Prince Street would lead you to believe. Go around back and you're right among the cobblestones, chains, and bollards of Narrow Quay and the harbor. Contemporary styling inside (192 rooms) and a popular waterfront bar. Prince St. (phone: 294811). Moderate.

Glenroy – Comfortable and small (49 rooms), and part of one of Clifton's attractive 19th-century squares. About half of the rooms have private bath. 30 Victoria Sq., Clifton (phone: 739058). Inexpensive.

Seeley's – A serviceable place, this, too, is in Clifton, not far from the Park Street shops. About half of the 60 rooms have private baths (some have Jacuzzis) and all have TV, radio, and tea-making facilities. Finishing touches include a sauna, solarium, and invigorating spa baths. 19–27 St. Paul's Rd., Clifton (phone: 738544). Inexpensive.

 EATING OUT: As one of the largest cities outside London, you'd expect Bristol to be well endowed with good restaurants, and it is. There are some excellent eating places in the hotels and some equally good ones outside, in central Bristol and Clifton, offering traditional English, Chinese, French, Indian, Italian, or other cuisine. In addition, the city has two floating pub-restaurants. To sample local fare, try Severn salmon, Cheddar-cooked ham, jugged hare, and pigeon pie. A meal for two with wine will cost more than $45 at a restaurant listed as expensive, $35 to $45 at one listed as moderate, and less than $35 at an inexpensive one.

Gornys – Friendly service and imaginatively cooked food are what draw people to this Swiss-French restaurant run, in fact, by a German. Open for dinner only; closed Sundays, Mondays, the month of August, and two weeks at Christmas. Reservations are essential. 13 Cotham Rd. (phone: 426444). Expensive.

Harveys – The wine cellar of the famous firm of wine merchants is no ordinary place: frogs' legs among the appetizers, specialties such as beef Wellington or venison cutlets with juniper berries and gin, and four sauces for the duck. The bill of French and English fare is bountiful and the wine list will never cramp your style. Closed Saturday lunch, Sundays, and public holidays. 12 Denmark St. (phone: 277665). Expensive.

Kiln – Part of the *Ladbroke Dragonara* hotel, this unusual round restaurant with a fixed-price carvery as well as an à la carte menu, is actually a 200-year-old kiln for the making of Bristol glassware. Dancing on Saturdays. Redcliffe Way (phone: 20044). Expensive.

Restaurant du Gourmet – Three floors of a terraced house make up this French restaurant. The atmosphere is intimate but the menu is extensive. Closed Sundays and Mondays; dinner only on Saturdays, when you should be sure to reserve a table. 43 Whiteladies Rd. (phone: 736230). Expensive.

The Bridge – In the *St. Vincent Rocks* hotel, this restaurant has a wall of windows from which to admire the Clifton Suspension Bridge and, though enclosed, is decorated with numerous photos of old Bristol. English and French dishes are featured and roast meats are served from a carving trolley. Sion Hill (phone: 739251). Moderate.

Colley's Supper Rooms – Arrive punctually at 7:45 PM for a wonderful six-course supper. There is no menu in the conventional sense, but plenty of variety. Judging by the fact that the place is often booked solid weeks ahead, people are happy with the arrangement. Closed Sundays for lunch and all day Mondays. 153 Whiteladies Rd. (phone: 730646). Moderate.

51 Park Street – Owner Bruce Isaacs is a firm believer in the motto "Come in and eat as much or as little as you like, when you like." His young staff rush between the potted plants, elegant chairs, tables, and coatstands to serve Continental breakfast and brunches (including eggs Benedict) to a never-ending stream of students, Bristolians, and tourists. The paddle fans and discreet music add to the atmosphere. 51 Park St. (phone: 28016). Moderate.

Michael's – Here you can feast on such delicacies as cream of Stilton soup, fresh salmon trout in a mushroom sauce, and passion fruit sorbet. The ornate Victorian dining room, converted from an old garage, is filled with flowers, curios, and tables of assorted shapes and sizes; the bar with chaise longues, stuffed birds, and a fireplace. Reservations are advisable. Open for dinner daily except Sundays and for lunch on Sundays from mid-September until Easter. 129 Hotwell Rd. (phone: 276190). Moderate.

Rajdoot – Authentic Punjabi cuisine — including the charcoal, clay oven barbecues of tandoori cooking — is served in an elegant setting. Test your palate on a quail or lobster curry. Open for lunch and dinner daily, though not for Sunday lunch. Reservations are essential for the evening meal. Closed bank holidays. 83 Park St. (phone: 28033). Moderate.

Vintners – Despite the rather cavernous atmosphere, good wines and delicious hot food are served here. Open for breakfast, with live music at lunchtime and seating available in the back garden during summer. St. Stephen's St. (phone: 291222). Moderate.

Bloomers – The 18th-century Old Library premises are now fresh and folksy inside, with lights hanging low over antique pine tables, chairs copied from those in an old farmhouse kitchen, and lots of potted plants. Stick to the fish and meat pies or have one of the more imaginative entrées, such as pan-fried veal coated in Stilton and breadcrumbs. Three-course "gourmet specials" are served especially for the customer in a hurry. Closed Saturdays for lunch and all day Sundays. Old Library, King St. (phone: 291111). Inexpensive.

Trattoria da Renato – Actors and actresses from the Old Vic across the street congregate here. The walls are covered with their photos and the tables are attractively covered with pink napery topped by white lace. Food is Italian. Closed Saturday lunch and Sundays. 19 King St. (phone: 298291). Inexpensive.

SHARING A PINT: The *Full Moon,* 1 North St., is supposed to be the oldest pub in Bristol — something by that name was already marked as "a very ancient hostellerie" on a map of the city in the 13th century. If you go in the summer, sit outside at the tables in the old stableyard. Jazz pubs are a special feature of Bristol nightlife and one of the best is the *Old Duke,* at the Welsh Back end of King St. It is jamming and jammed 6 nights a week from 8:30 PM (Sundays noon to 2 PM). If you can't get in, go across the street to *Ye Llandoger Trow,* where there are three small bars (and two 2nd-floor restaurants) in the 17th-century building, one with a beautifully carved fireplace and the coziest of table nooks under the stairs. Another popular pub left over from the 17th century is *Ye Shakespeare,* 78 Victoria St., a note of charm in an otherwise plain neighborhood. In Clifton, *The Royal Oak,* 50 The Mall, is the place to go for traditional brews and atmosphere — stone walls, oak beams, and seating at high-backed oak settees. While you're at it, you might just as well drink a toast of Bristol milk (sherry), so called according to a 17th-century clergyman, author, and wit, because it was the "first moisture" tasted by infants in this wine-importing city.

CAMBRIDGE

Cambridge's bold claim to being the most beautiful city in Britain is based on the majestic architecture of its several colleges. The distinction is not often disputed (except by its rival, Oxford, the country's other bastion of knowledge and medieval design). Each year, millions of visitors flock to this small city to marvel at its masterpieces of cut stone, stained glass, and carved wood, and to breathe its rarefied and scholarly atmosphere. They also come to Cambridge for an experience Oxford cannot match: a quiet punt ride up the "Backs" on the River Cam, which slides lazily past the colleges' back lawns (hence the name), and is edged by lush green banks and drooping willows. One nineteenth-century tourist, Henry James, described the Backs as "the loveliest confusion of gothic windows and ancient trees, of grassy banks and mossy balustrades, of sun-checquered avenues and groves, of lawns and gardens and terraces, [and] of single arched bridges spanning the little stream . . ." Lesser tourists have come to much the same conclusion on postcards written to the folks back home.

This city of great tranquillity and beauty has long historical roots. Cambridge was established in AD 43 as a Roman camp on a hill overlooking a natural ford in the River Cam at its upper navigable limit. The camp blossomed into a trading town, as the Romans built roads connecting Colchester, the garrison town to the southeast, with Lincoln, a settlement in the north. In the fifth century, the area was overrun and conquered by the Saxons. St. Bene't's (a contraction for St. Benedict's) Church dates from this period; its Saxon tower stands today. In the eleventh century, the Normans, too, invaded Cambridge, and under instructions from William the Conqueror built a castle to defend the town against rebels led by Hereward the Wake.

Details about early scholarly stirrings in Cambridge are vague. There was a monastery in the nearby town of Ely, and, in 1209, when students retreating from a hostile townsfolk streamed here from Oxford, these monks may have set up a center of learning. Whatever the case, by the mid-thirteenth century the university was firmly established and by 1284 the first college founded, then called St. Peter's, later Peterhouse. During the fourteenth and fifteenth centuries, eleven more colleges were founded and several hostels were built to house the students.

Today, education is Cambridge's main industry (there are 35 colleges and about 12,000 students), but the university, like Oxford, retains its original medieval organization. Each of the colleges is a self-governing entity within a decentralized university system. Each drafts its own rules and holds title to its own property. While the university provides lectures, conducts examinations, and awards degrees, it is the individual colleges that control admissions and determine the subjects an undergraduate should "read."

Strictly speaking, the term "university" refers not to its imposing granite structures but rather to the community of people involved — the chancellor, masters, and fellows and scholars, to be exact. The chancellor governs the university as a whole, aided by the vice-chancellor, who supervises the various administrative personnel and is chairman of the principal university bodies. Each college is presided over by a master, who heads a staff of fellows (commonly referred to as "dons"). The dons conduct weekly tutorials (discussions of an assignment with a student), give lectures, and do their own academic research. The position of don is as much an identity as a job; one tried to explain the mystique in this way: "Being a don at Cambridge is more than a job. It is a way of life. If he will never be rich, he is at least his own master . . . He lives in surroundings compared to which any other city whose university tempts him to move appears so often shabby and ugly. That is why so few move."

Many scholars feel the same attachment to Cambridge — with good reason. Ever since the Middle Ages the colleges have traditionally provided for their members' every need. Each self-sufficient enclave includes a dining room, with an imposing high table where the master and fellows dine apart from (and a bit above) the undergraduates; a chapel; a library; and common rooms as well as private rooms where students live. More important, many colleges have remained unchanged over the centuries. Cambridge has spawned some of the most influential figures in politics, the arts, and science — people like Cromwell, Pepys, Newton, Darwin, Wordsworth, and Byron. What undergraduate would not delight in writing at Samuel Pepys's desk or wielding the same silverware as Oliver Cromwell?

Cambridge, like any institution that reaches so far into the past, is plagued as well as enriched by traditions out of step with the modern world. Perhaps because of its monastic beginnings, the university has always disciplined students rather rigorously. For example, until fairly recently, the college gates were locked at 11 PM. As each college is surrounded in a rather prisonlike way by high walls often crowned with a row of spikes, there was no easy way to get in if you tarried too long. This hardly deterred spirited carousers, however, and the famous night climbs of Cambridge have spawned many a British mountaineer.

As a result of this and other episodes, the emphasis at Cambridge upon dignity and discipline has become somewhat legendary. Consider the oft-told tale of the student who tried to turn the ancient rules to his own advantage. In studying the university statutes he discovered that he had the right, while sitting for an examination, to demand a tankard of ale from the proctor. His request was grudgingly granted and the ale brought in . . . but not without a price. For it seems that the statute, set down in the fourteenth century, also made it compulsory to wear a sword after dark. The next evening the student was found and fittingly — if somewhat uncomfortably — attired.

CAMBRIDGE AT-A-GLANCE

 SEEING THE CITY: Head straight for Great St. Mary's, the University Church in King's Parade, and climb to the top for a fine view of the city. For an alternative perspective stroll up Castle Mound, once the site of Cambridge's castle, whose stonework was gradually removed over the years and used in the construction of the colleges.

SPECIAL PLACES: Every tour of Cambridge should begin at its heart — the colleges, all of which are open in part to the public. A word of warning, however: The colleges are not museums, but private places where people live and work, and Cambridge's 3 million yearly visitors create an enormous problem, especially in spring and summer when students are preparing for exams. To some extent, the situation would be like finding your own backyard on the itinerary of every tour of England. What's more, the colleges receive no income from tourists, so visiting their courts (the counterparts of Oxford's quads) should be considered a great privilege and quiet behavior only common courtesy.

In general, visitors are allowed to walk around the courts (but not on the grass, which remains the privilege only of fellows); visit the chapels and some gardens; and occasionally go into other designated areas, such as libraries or dining halls. Members of the college live off a "staircase," as the names at the bottom will indicate, but unless you are visiting a friend or relative in residence you won't be allowed to wander into these private quarters. The colleges are also sometimes closed to visitors — for example, from May to the end of June, when examinations are being taken. Notices to this effect are posted at the gate; if in doubt, check with the porter in the college lodge.

The selection of colleges below is by no means exhaustive, but it does include those most interesting architecturally and most centrally located. If you have time to visit only a few of them, King's and Trinity should be at the top of the list. Nearby Queens' and St. John's (and perhaps the entire area between them) would be both worthwhile and easy to reach, and you'd still have time to explore the Backs. Some of the colleges not mentioned below are Peterhouse (founded in 1284); Gonville and Caius, pronounced "Keys" (1348); St. Catherine's (1473); Sidney Sussex (1596); and Downing (1800). Then there are the three colleges founded for women, namely Girton (1869; out of town and far removed from the lusty male population); Newnham (1871; novelist Margaret Drabble studied here); and New Hall (1954; probably Cambridge's most controversial building — judge for yourself). Last, the three newest colleges are Churchill (1960; way out of town, inspired by Sir Winston's wish to encourage scientific and technological studies); Fitzwilliam (1966; affectionately called Fitzbilly); and Robinson, opened by the queen in 1981.

THE COLLEGES

Corpus Christi College (1352) – Because the Old Court has changed little since it was built in the 14th century, it provides a glimpse at medieval college organization. Then four students shared a room but each had his own study cubicle — hence the difference in the size of the windows. In the 16th century, one of the cubicles would have been used by the great English dramatist Christopher Marlowe, when he was a student here. The library, containing a priceless collection of Anglo-Saxon manuscripts (nearly 40 of them, saved from the libraries of monasteries dissolved by Henry VIII and including an important copy of the *Anglo-Saxon Chronicle*) is open Tuesdays and

Thursdays during the term. The chapel is open daily. Be warned: the college is said to have a resident ghost. Trumpington St.

Pembroke College (1347) – The college was founded by Marie de Valence, countess of Pembroke, and some of the buildings of her time survive. The chapel (built in 1663–66) was Sir Christopher Wren's first building, designed while he was a professor at Oxford. Wren's uncle, who had been imprisoned in the Tower of London and intended the chapel as thanksgiving for his release, told his nephew that since he was a mathematician, he ought to be capable of building a chapel. Wren was and did, in a classical style new to Cambridge. The college is also known for its gardens. Trumpington St.

Queens' College (1448) – Founded by Margaret of Anjou and Elizabeth Woodville, the respective queens of Henry VI and Edward IV, Queens' has a lovely red brick First Court built in the 15th century and decorated with a sundial in the 17th century. But its pièce de résistance is the New Court. The cloister around it, also 15th century, supports a wonderful example of 16th-century domestic architecture called the President's Lodge (Queens' does not have a master), an evocative building of timber and plaster that is put to good use in May Week as a backdrop for the college's productions of Shakespeare. Also of interest is the Mathematical Bridge, a copy of an original (1749) that was held together on geometrical principles without nails, nuts, or bolts but that, once taken apart by some curious Victorians, couldn't be put back together without the fastenings. Sir Basil Spence's Erasmus Building (1959) was one of the first modern contributions to college architecture (Erasmus, the Renaissance theologian, lived at Queens' in 1511–14). Queens' La.

King's College (1441) – Of the grand design that Henry VI had for the college he founded, only the chapel was ever realized. It was not until 1724, when the Fellows' Building was added, that an actual court began to take shape where Henry intended one; until then, students lived in an older court that is no longer part of the college. But the magnificent Gothic chapel, begun in 1446 and completed 90 years later, largely as the founder planned it, is not only Cambridge's best-known building, it is also often acclaimed the finest building in England — and all this majesty had been meant initially for the private worship of only seventy scholars. The initial stage of construction ended in 1461 when Henry was deposed (the level that had been reached at that point is visible in a change in color of the stone). Edward IV and Richard III financed further work, but it was Henry VII who began the final stage and left money for its completion, which explains the rose of his Tudor father and the portcullis of his Beaufort mother, symbols carved everywhere as decoration. The chapel has the largest fan-vaulted ceiling in existence; original 16th-century stained glass, the gift of Henry VIII, in all but one (and part of another) of its windows; and an intricately carved wood organ screen bearing the initials of Henry VIII and Anne Boleyn, another gift. Behind the altar is Rubens's *Adoration of the Magi,* donated in the 1960s after having set a record for the highest price ever brought by a painting at auction. The chapel is open daily, but be prepared for unpredicted closings due to choir practice or recording sessions. The King's College Chapel Choir is very well known, so if you get a chance, go and listen. Notices of concerts are usually posted on the doorway. Evensong is held at 5:30 PM on weekdays (excluding Mondays) and 3:30 PM on Sundays during university terms only. King's Parade.

Clare College (1338) – Though one of the oldest colleges, its original buildings were destroyed by fire and the present ones date only from the 17th century. They rank among the university's most handsome, however, and Clare's bridge is the oldest (1640) and one of the prettiest on the Cam. The college is also known for the elegance of its 18th-century wrought-iron gates and for the delightful Fellows' Garden on the other side of the river. The garden is normally open from 2:45 to 4:30 PM on weekdays. Trinity La.

Trinity Hall (1350) – Originally, all the colleges were called halls and the people who lived in them were the college. Gradually, the latter word became more inclusive in meaning and, by the 19th century, most of the halls had changed their names. Because a Trinity College already existed, Trinity Hall is the only Cambridge college known by its old name. Traditionally the college for lawyers, its Front Court dates from the 14th century, but it was refaced in the 18th century. You'll get a better idea of Trinity's early days by seeing the 16th-century Tudor brick library, especially pretty in summer when the flowers bordering it are in bloom. Trinity La.

Trinity College (1546) – Founded by Henry VIII, Trinity is the largest college in Cambridge and home to more than 800 students. The school has a distinguished roster of alumni: Francis Bacon, John Dryden, Isaac Newton, Thomas Macaulay, Alfred Lord Tennyson, Bertrand Russell, six British prime ministers, over 20 Nobel Prize winners, and Prince Charles, not to mention Lord Byron, who was eventually "sent down," expelled, for rooming with a pet bear and bathing naked in the fountain at the center of the Great Court, the source of the college's water supply. The Great Court, the largest court or quad in either Cambridge or Oxford, is the creation of Thomas Nevile, master of the college in the late 16th and early 17th centuries. He also began Nevile's Court; the long cloister on the north side is where Newton worked out his theory of sound (stand at its west end and stamp your foot to hear the echo he timed to measure the speed of sound). Nevile's Court became complete only at the end of the 17th century with the addition of Christopher Wren's library — and the sight of the sun resplendent on the glass of the Wren Library's many windows is still one of the most memorable in Cambridge. The library is open to the public from noon to 2 PM on weekdays, and from 10:30 AM to 12:30 PM on Saturdays during term (it's lavish with carved wood inside and some of its treasured manuscripts are usually on display). Nevile's dining hall (again, Cambridge's largest) is between the two courts and is normally open from 2 to 3 PM during the summer vacation, except on Sundays. Trinity St.

St. John's College (1511) – An enormous, rather austere place, this is the second largest of the Cambridge colleges, with buildings spanning the centuries. The beautiful gatehouse, ornate with the arms of the founder, Lady Margaret Beaufort (mother of Henry VII), is in its original state, the Second and Third courts date from the late 16th and early 17th centuries respectively, but across the River Cam are the 19th-century neo-Gothic New Court and the ultramodern Cripps Building. The two parts of the college are connected by the covered Bridge of Sighs (1831), picturesque despite the bars on the windows to keep undergraduates inside. William Wordsworth was a St. John's student; he later wrote of its "three gloomy courts," in the first of which (much altered since the founding) he had an "obscure nook." St. John's St.

Magdalene College (1542) – Built in the 15th century to house Benedictine monks studying at Cambridge, Magdalene (pronounced Mawdlen) was founded as an actual college in the 16th century, and its First Court has buildings of both centuries. It is a favorite of the British aristocracy, but its most famous student was Samuel Pepys, who left his library to his old school, including the manuscript of his famous diary. The library — arranged in presses Pepys himself provided — is open daily except Sundays from 11:30 AM to 12:30 PM, and from 2:30 to 3:30 PM. Across the street from the college are old buildings that Pepys himself would have seen. Magdalene St.

Jesus College (1496) – This is another college with a religious background. Founded on the site of a convent that dated from the 12th century, Jesus, too, has parts that are older than it is, including the chapel — though the pre-Raphaelite stained glass (by Edward Burne-Jones and Ford Madox Brown) and ceilings (by William Morris) came about during a 19th-century restoration. The college is approached via a long, brick-walled avenue known as the "chimney," but once past the 15th-century gate tower, the grounds are spacious, with gardens and a delightful Tudor Cloister Court.

Alistair Cooke, a journalist and commentator on the American scene, was a Jesus undergraduate, as were Laurence Sterne and Samuel Taylor Coleridge. Jesus La.

Christ's College (1505) – This was the first of the two colleges Lady Margaret Beaufort founded at Cambridge, and, as at St. John's, her coat of arms above the gate makes a highly ornamental entranceway. John Milton was a student at Christ's (he wrote many early poems here and a later one, "Lycidas," was written in memory of a college fellow) as was Charles Darwin. The beautiful Fellows' Garden (open 10:30 AM to noon and 2 to 4 PM on weekdays) contains a mulberry tree traditionally associated with Milton. St. Andrew's St.

Emmanuel College (1584) – Sir Walter Mildmay, Queen Elizabeth's chancellor of the exchequer, founded this college on the site of a 13th-century Dominican friary that had been dissolved by Henry VIII. The monastic buildings were converted to college use (the friary church became the dining hall), then other buildings followed, including the chapel and its colonnade (1668–73) designed by Sir Christopher Wren. Emmanuel was meant to educate clergymen and it became a center of Protestant theology, but because of their Puritan sympathies, many of its graduates went to America in the early 17th century. Among them was John Harvard, who died at the age of 31, leaving $1,600 and 320 books for the foundation of Harvard University. St. Andrew's St.

OTHER CAMBRIDGE SIGHTS

Fitzwilliam Museum – The private treasure trove that Viscount Fitzwilliam donated to the university, along with the funds for a building to house it, is one of the oldest public museums in the country. Opened in 1848, it contains Middle Eastern, Egyptian, Greek, and Roman antiquities and European ceramics, manuscripts, paintings, drawings, and miniatures of all periods. The paintings and drawings — from Flemish and Italian Old Masters through French Impressionism to modern English art — are in the gallery upstairs, open between 2 and 5 PM daily. The rest is in the downstairs gallery, open from 10 AM until 2 PM. Both galleries are open Sundays from 2:15 to 5 PM, and closed Mondays. The museum also sponsors temporary exhibitions. Trumpington St. (phone: 69501).

Senate House – This classical Georgian building of the 1720s was designed by the English architect James Gibbs (who also designed the Fellows' Building next to the King's College Chapel), and it, too, belongs to the university. When illuminated at night, its Corinthian details make it look almost like an edible confection, and each June it becomes the suitably stylish setting for the ceremony of General Admission to Degrees — graduation, that is. King's Parade.

Round Church – Built in the same distinctive shape as the Holy Sepulcher Church in Jerusalem, the Norman Round Church dates from about 1130. It is one of only five Round Churches still surviving in England. Bridge St.

Folk Museum – Crafts, tools, kitchen and farm equipment, toys, and furniture are among the many objects on display in a series of rooms meant to illustrate life in Cambridge and the surrounding countryside in the last few hundred years. The building itself was formerly a pub (*The White Horse Inn*) and in the courtyard is an 18th-century shopfront, one of several large relics salvaged from Cambridge's past. Open Mondays through Saturdays and Sunday afternoons. Admission charge. Corner of Castle and Northampton sts. (phone: 355159).

Brass Rubbing Centre – Don't let the thought of working in a cold, damp, and dimly lit church put you off the idea of brass rubbing; in Cambridge, there's a cozy do-it-yourself workshop with 70 brasses to choose from. The brasses are replicas of monuments to real people (mostly minor gentry — the very wealthy invested in more elaborate stoneworks) dating back to the time of the Crusaders. The price for making your own rubbing ranges from £2 to £6 depending on the size of the brass you choose and includes the use of all materials plus basic instruction for novices. If you can't summon the necessary effort — and brass rubbing is hard work — the center also sells finished rubbings. Open 10 AM to 5 PM, Tuesdays through Saturdays (Mondays also, in July and August). Wesley Church Library, King St. (phone: 61318).

Scott Polar Research Institute – The small museum here is dedicated to the famous explorer and to polar exploration. Letters, diaries, and photographs of Robert Falcon Scott's expedition to the South Pole are on display along with souvenirs of other expeditions and displays describing the geography and geology of the Antarctic and current polar research. Open daily except Sundays from 2:30 to 4 PM. Lensfield Rd. (phone: 337733).

Botanic Gardens – These are the university's research gardens, open to the public Mondays through Saturdays and summer Sundays. You'll find the hothouses very inviting on cold days (in winter, the Cambridge east winds seem to blow uninterrupted all the way from Siberia). Entrances on Bateman St., Trumpington Rd., Brooklands Ave., and Hills Rd. (phone: 337733).

American Military Cemetery – More than 3,800 American servicemen who fought in World War II from British bases are buried in these beautifully landscaped grounds. The names of another 5,125 who lie in unknown graves are inscribed on the Memorial Wall. On the Madingley Rd., 4 miles outside the city (phone: Madingley 210350).

■**EXTRA SPECIAL:** One of the most stylish ways to enjoy Cambridge is to hire a punt — a long, flat-bottomed, square-nosed boat that is both steered and propelled by means of a long pole that you push into the mud of the river bottom. It sounds difficult, looks easy, and, in practice, is somewhere between the two. Be prepared for ridicule from the onlookers along the grassy banks, especially if you go around in circles or, heaven help you, get the pole stuck in the mud and forget to let go. Either explore the Backs, a beautiful stretch of river behind the college and past splendid lawns, gardens, and drooping willows, or go on a lengthier excursion up the river to Grantchester for tea. The two routes are separated by a weir. Scuda-more's Boat Yards, a famous Cambridge name in punting, offers punts for self-drive hire at two locations, one at Quayside, off Bridge Street, and another at Mill Lane, near Silver Street (but go to the latter if you're aiming for Grantchester). The cost is £3.20 an hour, plus a £25 deposit. Don't forget to stand at the back of the boat, especially if you have recently been to Oxford where they stand at the front. The deposit is deductible *if* you return. There is also chauffeured punt service with champagne, strawberries, and cream.

SOURCES AND RESOURCES

TOURIST INFORMATION: The Tourist Information Center, on Wheeler Street (phone: 322640), is open weekdays from 9 AM to 6 PM (9 AM to 5:30 PM November through February) and on Saturdays from 9 AM to 5 PM. From May through September, it is also open on Sundays (10:30 AM to 3:30 PM). The center offers guided tours of the colleges and through the intricate maze of small streets and alleyways around them. The tours last approximately 2 hours, cost £1.75, and depart daily most of the year and on Saturdays only from mid-November through March. You can check the schedule by calling the number above. Historic Cambridge walking tours are conducted Monday through Saturday evenings from mid-June to mid-August; tours leave from the center and cost £1.85. For information on all university departments, including museums, use the general university phone number: 337733.

For an aerial view, half-hour flights on four-seater light aircraft are available at nearby Bourne airport for approximately £15 per person. For booking details, contact the Tourist Information Center (address above).

The center sells a comprehensive selection of guides to Cambridge. These include the *Cambridge Official Guide, A Brief Guide to Cambridge* and *Where to Eat In and Around Cambridge.* Available free are a city map and pamphlets on the area's events, accommodations, campsites, bike rentals, car rentals, bookshops, and antiques shops.

Most of Cambridge's bookstores (see *Shopping*) carry a broad range of guidebooks including many, "picturebooks" filled with lush photographs. Try to find *Look at Cambridge* and *Historic Cambridge* by John Brooks, *Cambridge* by Kenneth Holmes, and *Royal Cambridge* by Marion Colthorpe, which describes the many royal visits to the city since Queen Elizabeth I.

Local Coverage – Check the *Cambridge Evening News,* the city's daily paper.

GETTING AROUND: Cambridge and London are linked by frequent trains from Liverpool Street Station, travel time about 1½ hours. The Cambridge railway station is a long walk away from the center of town, so take the bus that waits in the front of the station or a taxi (which will cost roughly £2.50).

Bicycles – Most students and some academics travel around by bike. You can rent one from *University Cycle and Electrical,* 9 Victoria Ave. (phone: 355517), or from *Cambridge Cycle Hire,* 118 Mill Rd. (phone: 314333). A day's hire will run about £2.50, and a week's £5, with a deposit of around £20.

Boat – A sightseeing alternative for enjoying Cambridge and the surrounding countryside is a three-day or a one-week cruise on board the *Westover Boat Company's* converted narrow boats. Summer only. (phone: 0860-516343).

Bus – For inexpensive links to other towns in East Anglia and London, try the bus; the station is on Drummer St.

Car Rental – Try *Godfrey Davis* at 315 Mill Rd. (phone: 248198) or *Marshall's Car Hire,* Jesus La. (phone: 62211).

Taxi – Two of the biggest taxi companies are *Camtax,* 26 Victoria Rd. (phone: 313131), and *United,* 123a Hills Rd. (phone: 352222). Apart from the trip into town from the station or visits to places outside the city such as the American Military Cemetery, you're unlikely to need a cab, since most of the places of interest in town are within walking distance of each other.

MUSEUMS: In addition to those described in *Special Places,* Cambridge has a number of other interesting museums. The best of these are:

Kettles Yard Art Gallery – Permanent collection of modern art including works by Henri Gaudier-Brzeska, Ben Nicolson, and Christopher Wood, and changing exhibits of contemporary art and crafts. Permanent collection open daily 2 to 4 PM; exhibition gallery open daily except Sundays, 12:30 to 5:30 PM, Sundays, 2 to 5:30 PM. Northampton St. (phone: 352124).

Museum of Classical Archaeology – Casts of Greek and Roman sculpture. Open weekdays, 9 AM to 1 PM and 2:15 to 5 PM, and Saturdays from 10 AM to 1PM. Sidgwick Ave.

Sedgwick Museum of Geology – Geological specimens by the hundreds. Open weekdays, 9 AM to 1 PM and 2 to 5 PM, and Saturdays during the university's full term from 9 AM to 1 PM. Downing St. (phone: 333456).

University Museum of Zoology – Displays on marine life, birds, insects, and mammals, as well as fossil specimens. Open weekdays, 2:15 to 4:45 PM. Downing St. (phone: 336600).

Whipple Science Museum – Early microscopes, telescopes, astronomical and navigational equipment, surveying instruments, slide rules, and electrical apparatus. Open weekdays, 2 to 4 PM, during university term only, as well as the first Sunday in every month. Free School La. (phone: 334500).

SHOPPING: The marketplace in Market Square, on ever-so-flat Market Hill, has been a shopping area since medieval times. The stalls, sheltered by brightly colored canopies, are open for business year-round daily except Sundays. Most sell fruits and vegetables and inexpensive clothing, but one or two sell items of interest to visitors, including gifts, records, and secondhand books.

Cambridge abounds in bookstores that stock much more than just academic tomes. *Heffers of Cambridge,* an establishment with many branches, has its main bookstore at 20 Trinity St. (phone: 358351); other branches include a children's bookshop at 30 Trinity St. (phone: 356200); and paperback shops at 13 Trinity St. (phone: 61815) and 31 St. Andrew's St. (phone: 354778). *Sherratt & Hughes* (formerly *Bowes & Bowes*), the oldest bookshop in England, has presided over its corner location on Trinity and Market streets for the last 400 years; *Deighton, Bell & Co.* at 13 Trinity St. (phone: 353939) offers rare and fine books; and *G. David,* a Cambridge institution for second-hand books, has shops at 3 and 16 St. Edward's Passage (phone: 354619).

The city has three main shopping areas. The first starts at St. John's Street and continues down Trinity Street, along King's Parade (with colleges on one side and old shop buildings on the other, some dating from the 16th century), and into Trumpington Street. The second begins at Magdalene Bridge and runs down Bridge Street, Sidney Street, St. Andrew's Street, and Regent Street. The third is recently developed Grafton Centre, 10 minutes from downtown, with both department stores and small, exclusive boutiques.

Antiques Etcetera – A magpie's nest of Victoriana, including watches and clocks, silver, and jewelry. 18 King St. (phone: 62825).

Barratts – A 200-year-old china and glass emporium with a vast selection of crystal (Waterford, Stuart, Webb, Edinburgh) and china (Wedgwood, Royal Doulton, Minton, Spode, Royal Crown Derby, Royal Worcester). 2 St. Mary's Passage (phone: 66711).

The Friar's House – Crammed with fine crystal and porcelain and the best selection of collector's paperweights in East Anglia. Open daily. Bene't St., behind King's Parade (phone: 60275).

Primavera – Pottery, glass, cards, tiles, clothes, toys, corn dollies, clay Suffolk cottages, and many other pretty items. 10 King's Parade (phone: 357708).

Ryder and Amies – Caters to the university's demand for badges, plaques, cufflinks, crested ties, and college rugby shirts (various colors); also carries Shetland tweed ties and tartan berets. 22 King's Parade (phone: 350371).

Scots Corner – Shelves and tables piled high with kilts, tartans, tweeds, and fine Scottish knitwear. 11 Bridge St. (phone: 61534).

W & G Taylor – Tweeds and tartan items as well as a range of deerstalker hats and 6-foot-long striped scarves (available in different colors, depending upon college allegiance). It also has the largest selection of hats in Cambridge. 5 Trinity St. (phone: 350510).

Textile Studio – An exclusive collection of stunning ball gowns and wedding dresses (all designed to order) in addition to an assortment of textiles, knitwear, and other gift items. 3 Free School La. (phone: 313583).

SPECIAL EVENTS: Most university events take place during the university terms — there are three a year — and more toward the end of the term than the beginning. The most celebrated is *May Week,* which actually takes place in June and is closer to a fortnight than a week. It is the busiest time on the social calendar, enhanced by a general feeling of relief at the end of the working year, particularly in the wake of final examinations. Many college and university societies put on displays of their activities, the most delightful of which are the plays and concerts held on the college lawns (to which the public may go). Each year several colleges hold elaborate balls — the May Balls — at which members and their guests (though outsiders can sometimes buy tickets — ask at the porters' lodge) dance from dusk till dawn, enjoy champagne buffets, and, if still going strong, punt up to Grantchester for breakfast.

Late in June, the *Midsummer Fair* takes place on Midsummer Common — as it has since the Middle Ages. During the last two weeks in July, the city sponsors the *Cambridge Festival,* the most important part of which is a series of concerts and recitals in such historic settings as the King's College and St. John's College chapels and the Senate House. There are also art exhibitions, dramatic presentations, a fireworks display, and an Elizabethan feast. The weekend *Folk Festival* at Cherry Hinton Hall closes the month.

 SPORTS: Both the university and town hold regular sporting events throughout the year. During the winter months, soccer and rugby are the most popular, and in the summer, cricket. The college playing fields are dotted around the town; you'll find many of these indicated on the tourist office map. Schedules of events are posted on the notice boards in the porters' lodges of the individual colleges.

Fishing – In the Cam, naturally. A rod license can be obtained for about £3 wherever you rent tackle.

Golf – There are public courses at Gog Magog, Babraham Rd., Bar Hill, and Girton.

Riding – There are several stables in the area, including *Miss E. Pickard's School* at New Farm Stables, Bourn (phone: 934-501), 8 miles west of Cambridge. The charge is around £7.75 per hour.

Rowing – A major university sport, competition reaches a crescendo in March when eights from Oxford and Cambridge clash on the Thames in London. The rest of the year, college boat clubs, as well as local school and town clubs, row downriver from Midsummer Common. You'll often see eights, fours, pairs, and single sculls practicing on the river, but watch out for the almost equally frequent coach bicycling along the towpath. With one hand gripping the handlebars and the other clutching a megaphone, he won't be looking where he's going, so be sure to keep out of his way. Traditional racing can't be done on the Cam, because it isn't wide enough for two boats to row side by side. Instead they race in a line. Sometimes as many as 15 boats participate in a single competition, each starting off at one-and-a-half-length intervals behind the other. The object is to catch up with the one in front and overlap the stern — hence the name of the race, "Bumps." University *Bumps* take place in February and during May Week (in June), city *Bumps* in July, on a course between Baitsbite Lock and Stourbridge Common. The best place to watch is from the towpath at Fen Ditton.

Walking – Choose from among the area's several enjoyable walking trails — along the Cam towpaths; across the meadows to Grantchester, so beloved by the poet Rupert Brooke; down the Coe Fen Nature Trail (which starts at the bridge near the rough car park off Barton Road). Other trails are recommended in the Tourist Information Centre's booklet, *More Country Walks Around Cambridge.*

 THEATER: The *Arts Theatre* at Peas Hill (phone: 352000) puts on modern and classic plays, ballet, opera, light opera, and other musical productions by local and touring companies. It also stages the annual Footlights Review in June, a satirical presentation that gave birth to such eminent wits as David Frost, Dudley Moore, Jonathan Miller, and John Cleese. The university's *Amateur Dramatic Club (ADC) Theatre* on Park St. (phone: 359547) has an excellent reputation and puts on a broad selection of plays during the university term.

MUSIC: There are many concerts and recitals in Cambridge throughout the year, including large choral works by the Cambridge University Music Society and the King's College Chapel choir; organ recitals in Great St. Mary's and the King's College Chapel; and many other solo appearances. Details and times are posted on notice boards in the college porters' lodges as well as in several restaurants, cafés, bookstores, and the various faculty buildings.

 NIGHTCLUBS AND NIGHTLIFE: Despite the city's youthful population, there isn't much taking place in the small hours, mainly because the undergraduates have to be back in their dorms then. The few discos in town include *Ronelles* in Heidelberg Gardens, Lion Yard (Thursday night is for the "oldies" — those over 25; Wednesdays are free for women); and *Route 66* on Wheeler St. (opposite the tourist office). Both places serve reasonably priced meals and cocktails. Note that no jeans, T-shirts, or sneakers are allowed and men must wear jackets and ties.

 SINS: Cambridge doesn't have a red-light district. The greatest sin in such an academic environment, surpassing even lust, is sloth, whether it's lounging around in the sunshine on the lawns; loafing in a punt (while someone else struggles with the pole); or else lying propped on one elbow watching a game of cricket at Fenner's, the university's cricket grounds. If you prefer to indulge in gluttony, try a sticky and scrumptious Chelsea bun from the famed *Fitzbillies Cake Shop.* Two locations: 52 Trumpington St., just across the road from the Fitzwilliam Museum; and 50 Regent St.

BEST IN TOWN

 CHECKING IN: Cambridge offers few moderate or expensive hotels, but numerous inexpensive bed-and-breakfasts. During the summer and particularly toward the close of the school year (the end of May, beginning of June), when the influx of tourists is further bolstered by parents and other relatives visiting students, it is difficult to get a room. For May Week you'll need to reserve at least 2 months in advance. Although the tourist office provides a booking service for visitors who arrive without a room reservation, don't expect it to perform miracles on short notice. In Cambridge and environs you'll pay $75 and up for a double room at an expensive hotel; between $45 and $75 at a moderate one; under $45 at an inexpensive one.

Cambridgeshire Moat House – It more than compensates for its out-of-town location with a plethora of sports facilities — an 18-hole championship golf course, tennis courts, squash courts, sauna, and a large, heated, indoor swimming pool. All 100 rooms have private bath and shower. Bar Hill, 4.5 miles northwest of Cambridge on the A604 (phone: 0954-80555). Expensive.

Garden House – The town's most luxurious hotel, it's close to the city center yet set amid three acres of gardens that reach down to the river, where punting and fishing are possible. At dusk, sip cocktails on the lawn before tackling the extensive restaurant menu, including typical English dishes. All the 117 bedrooms (there are 10 suites, each named after a Cambridge college) have private bathroom and shower, and most have small balconies overlooking the gardens and river. Granta Pl. (phone: 63421). Expensive.

Post House – Overlooking a lake, just 1½ miles from the center of town, this recently opened establishment has an appealing countrified atmosphere, 120 rooms, a restaurant, and a heated indoor pool. Lakeview, Bridge Rd., Impington (phone: 022-023-7000). Expensive.

Gonville – Next to the green called Parker's Piece, this modern hotel is lacking in atmosphere but has a good restaurant. Light refreshments are served on the sheltered patio during summer. Gonville Pl. (phone: 66611). Expensive to moderate.

University Arms – An imposing structure on the edge of Parker's Piece, the *Arms* has belonged to the same family since 1891. The oak-paneled dining room, which overlooks the park and has a grand fireplace, also boasts an impressive wine list that includes several house wines bottled by the proprietor. There are three bars, one with 100 different types of whiskey. 116 rooms, all with bath. Regent St. (phone: 351241). Expensive to moderate.

Arundel House – This converted Victorian terrace building overlooks the river and Jesus Green and offers a cozy atmosphere, friendly service, and all modern conveniences. 53 Chesterton Rd. (phone: 67701). Moderate.

Helen – There is a charming, Italian-style garden in front of this 25-room hotel, a mile from town and a 10-minute walk from the railway station. 167/69 Hills Rd. (phone: 246465). Moderate.

Rosswill Guest House – There's a warm, friendly welcome from Bill and Muriel Halliday in their comfortable townhouse overlooking the River Cam and Jesus Green. With 13 spacious rooms and ample parking, it's a 10-minute walk from the city center. 17–19 Chesterton Rd. (phone: 67871). Moderate.

Royal Cambridge – Spanning several Regency houses, this completely modernized hotel is on the main London-Cambridge road (A10), close to the city center. 74 rooms, most with private bathrooms. Trumpington St. (phone: 351631). Moderate.

Five Gables Farm – This Tudor farmhouse has oak beams, working fireplaces, and a relaxing rural setting. Open May through September only. Buck's La., Little Eversden, about 7 miles southwest of Cambridge (phone: Comberton 2236). Inexpensive.

EATING OUT: Although Cambridge is generally rated poorly as an eating town, it is well served by several eating houses in the inexpensive (less than $20 for dinner for two) and moderate (between $20 and $35) categories. Most of these offer extremely good value and large helpings — the latter is an especially important consideration in a town where most of the potential customers are students.

Don Pasquale – One of the city's top restaurants, with a somewhat Italian menu. The pheasant roasted with capers, onions, parsley, and white wine sauce is especially recommended. 12 Market Hill (phone: 67063). Expensive to moderate.

Jean Louis – This classic French restaurant has lots of eye appeal since it's housed in one of Cambridge's cottages at the foot of Castle Hill. The menu has delicious meat and fish dishes. 15 Magdalene St. (phone: 315232). Expensive to moderate.

Shades – A highly versatile menu, mainly English dishes, served in an upstairs restaurant (snacks are available downstairs in the wine bar). The desserts, which are occasionally dreamed about in lectures, can be consumed while admiring the view of King's College from the window. Closed Sundays and Mondays; wine bar open daily. 1 King's Parade (phone: 359506). Expensive to moderate.

Fagin's – A French restaurant, richly decorated on the inside with retired cinema seats and marble-topped tables. 33 Bridge St. (phone: 62054). Moderate.

Footlights – Mexican and English cuisine, as well as occasional live jazz and folk music, are the highlights of this cocktail bar–restaurant — as young and lively as the Grafton Centre in which it's located. Fitzroy St. (phone: 323434). Moderate.

Taj Mahal – The best of Cambridge's dozen-plus Indian restaurants. Try the spicy lamb Pasanda. 37 Regent St. (phone: 353835). Moderate.

Eraina – A cosmopolitan taverna with a menu composed of multiple choices, including Italian, Chinese, Austrian, and Greek dishes as well as charcoal-broiled steaks, roasts, and a selection of 21 omelets. A favorite among office workers. Open daily. 2 Free School La. (phone: 68786). Moderate to inexpensive.

Old Orleans – Get your tortilla chips and Dixie desserts at this new Southern-style barbecue smokehouse, serving everything from seafood gumbo soup to char-grilled barbecue ribs and a wide selection of cocktails. Open daily, 11 AM to midnight. Miller's Yard, 10/11 Mill Lane (phone: 322777). Moderate to inexpensive.

Varsity – Another Greco-Cambridge restaurant, with Franco-Anglo influences, and chips served more or less with everything. The clientele is composed mainly of students enjoying a break from college dinners. There are three dining rooms; the main floor is the best for people-watching. 35 St. Andrew's St. (phone: 356060). Moderate to inexpensive.

Belinda's Coffee/Wine Bar and Beer Cellar – This self-service restaurant is actually a renovated underground maze of spacious passages. Selections are from a freshly prepared hot and cold buffet, and seating is at counters and tables. Good wine list. 14 Trinity St. (phone: 354213). Inexpensive.

Fitzwilliam Museum Coffee Room – Pâté with tasty breads, homemade quiche, cheesecake, French pastries, and good coffee are among the fare. Closed Sundays and Mondays; otherwise open 10:30 AM to 4 PM. Trumpington St. Inexpensive.

Martin's – Its rock cakes and homemade doughnuts are in constant demand; hot meals and thick sandwiches are also available. The place is filled with students during the school term, but looks a little empty and sad at other times. Closed evenings. 4 Trumpington St. (phone: 61757). Inexpensive.

Pentagon – An impressive array of hot and cold dishes is displayed. Halfway up the stairs to the *Arts Theatre*, it features photos of actors past and present. St. Edward's Passage (phone: 359302). Inexpensive.

Nettles – A minuscule vegetarian–health food café with a delicious range of foods, including nut loaf and *muesli* with fruit. Open only for lunch (9 AM to 3 PM); closed Sundays. 6 St. Edward's Passage (phone: 350983). Inexpensive.

Sweeney Todd's – A pizza and hamburger joint in an old water mill — you can watch the water gushing over the wheel as you eat. Newnham Rd. (phone: 67507). Inexpensive.

For cream teas try *Auntie's Tea Shop* in St. Mary's Passage (open daily); *The Orchard* at Grantchester (open summers only; closed Wednesdays); *The Barn* at Fen Ditton (open Tuesdays, Wednesdays, Thursdays, Saturdays, and Sundays only during the summer); and *Hobb's Pavillion,* a converted cricket pavilion overlooking Parker's Piece, where healthy lunches are very reasonably priced (closed Sundays and Mondays). An even creamier affair can be enjoyed at the *Copper Kettle,* 4 King's Parade, where the treats include American-style cheesecake and baba au rhum with pineapple and fresh cream.

SHARING A PINT: Cambridge has many more pubs than colleges, and most of them serve real ale. The *Eagle* on Bene't St. is one of the oldest in the country. A 17th-century coaching inn, it has a gallery overlooking a courtyard where outside drinking (and eating) is popular during the summer. Also on Bene't St. is the *Bath,* with traditional bitter and draught cider as well as mature cheeses and hearty breads. The *Baron of Beef* on Bridge St. is a woody, beamy, Old World student haunt. Tucked away at the end of Thompsons La., the *Spade and Beckett* has a peaceful garden looking onto the river. The *Fort St. George in England,* Midsummer Common, is a gathering spot for rowing enthusiasts; you can sip ale and watch the boats at the same time. The *Ancient Druids* in Grafton Centre brews its own beer on the premises.

CANTERBURY

Despite the vast damage inflicted by World War II bombing raids (and subsequent rebuilding and development), there remains enough sheer history in Canterbury to give the impression of time's having stopped somewhere along the line and only recently started again to admit the automobile, electricity, and indoor plumbing. The cathedral, begun in the eleventh century and finally completed in the 16th, towers moodily over the pubs and shops crouching nearby; half-timbered, whitewashed little houses line the narrow streets; and the River Stour, long ago plied by seagoing ships, now drifts slowly past brilliant flowerbeds and under arching stone bridges. Countless ghosts walk the passageways unseen, and after dark you can almost hear the chanting of monks on their journey from cloister to dining hall.

But Canterbury's history stretches a good deal farther back than the Middle Ages. The first settlement of any size known to have flourished in the area dates to about 300 BC. In about 75 BC, these poorly organized natives were conquered by the Belgae, a tribe from across the Channel; still later, in 54 BC, Roman troops led by Julius Caesar stormed and took one of the Belgic fortified camps. A full-scale invasion was launched by Emperor Claudius during the next century, and it was after this victory that the Romans settled in permanently. They called the place Durovernum Cantiacorum and built roads connecting the city with other settlements to the north and south. You can still see traces of the Roman period around Canterbury. For example, the medieval city walls were built upon the original Roman foundations and an intricately tiled Roman pavement is found in Butchery Lane.

During the fifth century Britain was invaded and conquered by the Saxons; by 560 the city had forsaken its Roman identity to become Canterbury (actually Cantwarabyrig), the capital of the Saxon kingdom of Kent, ruled by Ethelbert. It was with the arrival in 597 of St. Augustine — sent by the pope to convert Ethelbert and his subjects to Christianity — that Canterbury assumed its new and final role of cathedral city. For in the years that followed, Augustine became archbishop (and primate of all England), founded the Abbey of Sts. Peter and Paul (now called St. Augustine's Abbey), and established the first cathedral.

The city was racked by several invasions during the ensuing years — the Vikings, Danes, and Normans all destroyed much that they found and built anew (including the cathedral). The incident that really put the city on the map, however, was the murder of Thomas à Becket in 1170.

Becket, for years a trusted advisor to King Henry II, was named archbishop of Canterbury in 1162. Thus began a long power struggle between the two over who was the final authority on church matters. Regarded by some as a traitor, Becket was slain in his own cathedral by four of the king's knights. He was soon canonized a saint and the place where he fell declared a shrine. (The shrine was destroyed in 1538, and now only a plaque marks the spot.) People from all over the world began to flock here by the thousands to honor the martyr. So popular was the pilgrimage to Canterbury that Geoffrey Chaucer chose it as the narrative vehicle for his bawdy classic, *Canterbury Tales,* in which each pilgrim tells his story as the group journeys together to the shrine.

Canterbury can claim many literary connections in addition to this most famous one to Chaucer: The dramatist Christopher Marlowe was born here in 1564 and educated at the King's School; you may be able to catch a performance of one of his plays at the new Marlowe Theatre in The Friars. Some three centuries later, the playwright and novelist W. Somerset Maugham, also a King's alumnus, sent the protagonist in *Of Human Bondage* to school here. R. H. Barham, the nineteenth-century humorist, was born in St. George's Parish and set parts of his series *The Ingoldsby Legends* in Canterbury. Joseph Conrad, although born in Poland, became one of England's great adventure writers and is buried near Westgate. St. Dunstan's is the setting for several episodes of Charles Dickens's novel *David Copperfield;* in fact, the hotel called the House of Agnes on St. Dunstan's Street is supposedly the building Dickens had in mind when he described the home of Agnes Wickfield.

A day's stroll will take you past most of these landmarks, retracing the real or fictitious footsteps of the city's illustrious native sons. If you just let your imagination run a bit as you wander through Canterbury's prim gates and gardens, you'll soon begin to sense its less decorous past — when the pious thronged the city's crowded streets, the taverns roared a welcome, and the scaffold threatened the woebegone wrongdoer.

CANTERBURY AT-A-GLANCE

SEEING THE CITY: As you approach Canterbury — by car on Route A2 from London, from Dover in the southeast, or from Whitstable a few miles to the north — you are immediately aware of the towering hulk of the cathedral, floodlit by night and somberly gray in the daytime, and no less impressive than it was at the true dawn of England's history. There are three viewpoints you shouldn't miss. The first, for a panorama, is the high plateau called Eliot Causeway on the campus of the University of Kent-at-Canterbury, about 2 miles along the road to Whitstable. Admission is free, but visitors are not particularly encouraged. The second is the summit of the Westgate Tower, a massive piece of fortification abutting the City Wall. Admission charge. The third is the roof of the multistory parking lot on Gravel Walk. From here you can see the town's remaining ancient buildings (most were wiped out by wartime bombing). Admission by courtesy of the management.

SPECIAL PLACES: Although you've seen the splendor of the cathedral from a distance, you haven't experienced the vastness of its frontage. Walk along the busy shop-lined stretch of Mercery Lane, leading from the middle of High Street, and into the broad patio called Buttermarket. Immediately opposite is the Christ Church Gate; through here you enter another world. From west to east ranges the South West Tower, built in 1460, and behind it the added North West

Tower of 1840. Then comes the Nave, dating from 1400, and east of that the noble Bell Harry Tower, raised in 1500. Next are the South East Transept, originating in 1126, and the Choir, put up during the restoration of 1184. The dates given relate only to the superstructure; the main work was started more than 400 years earlier. It is here, in the open, away from the clamor of traffic and trade, that you first experience the sensation of stepping into medieval history.

CANTERBURY CATHEDRAL

The traceable story goes back to the time of Ethelbert, king of Kent, who in 597 granted the site now occupied by the cathedral to St. Augustine, the Christian missionary from Rome. Building began in 602. Little is known of subsequent events until the disastrous fire of 1067, the year following the Conquest, after which the cathedral was completely rebuilt from its foundations. The history of the present fabric therefore starts with the work of reconstruction carried out by the first Norman archbishop, Lanfranc, in 1070. A hundred years later the infamous murder of Archbishop Thomas à Becket led to continuing pilgrimages and the common acceptance of Canterbury Cathedral as the "Mother Church of the realm."

The Nave – Take a good look at this cavernous, majestic, peaceful enclosure. Designed in about 1400 by Henry Yevele, the architect of Westminster Hall and the nave of Westminster Abbey, it is an example of Perpendicular Gothic and has long been regarded as one of the greatest architectural masterpieces in the world. An interesting and unexplained oddity is that if you stand near the center, at the western end, and view the whole length of the building through the choir screen, the presbytery, and Trinity Chapel, you will notice that the cathedral is not set in a straight line. The eastern part inclines toward the south, or, from your point of view, the right. Exactly behind you is the West Window, with its figure of Adam in the act of digging (this window has been removed for restoration but will be returned). This dates from 1178, and is probably the earliest action picture in existence, by which is meant that until then all church windows showed only immobile and flat outlines not in sequence. Similar illustrated windows appear in all parts of the vast church, forming a rich gallery of medieval artwork. The brilliant jewel-tone windows high in the clerestory look merely decorative from floor level, but with good binoculars you can see more detail, and the fascinating and often lighthearted tales unfold like a current newspaper cartoon. The so-called Poor Man's Bible illustrates scenes from the Old and New Testaments for the illiterate populace, miracles supposedly performed at Becket's shrine, and homely little accounts of 13th-century life.

The Tomb of the Black Prince – Edward of Woodstock, son of King Edward III, became Prince of Wales, but was survived by his father and never succeeded to the throne. He is remembered as a hero of the battles of Crécy and Poitiers and a tireless patron of the cathedral. It was under his sponsorship that Henry Yevele was able to carry out major rebuilding in the crypt and also design the Westgate and a considerable portion of the city walls. In 1363 the Black Prince married Joan, the Fair Maid of Kent; this match and the subsequent marriage of their daughters to almost all claimants to the throne resulted in the start of the York and Tudor dynasties. His shrine and tomb, with a replica of all the royal knightly regalia displayed nearby, may be seen in the south aisle of Trinity Chapel. It is considered among the most splendid memorials in England.

The Crypt – This is the oldest part of the cathedral, with a low roof and rounded arches in pure Norman style, its rather frightening severity relieved by grotesque and deliberately humorous carvings on the capitals (top part) of the pillars. Also on view is the original regalia of the Black Prince.

The Martyrdom – The site where Thomas à Becket was slain by four French knights — Fitzurse, de Moreville, de Tracy, and le Breton — on December 29, 1170, is in the northwest transept at the western end of the crypt. The four, with their retainers, were sent on this evil mission because Archbishop Becket refused to place the demands of his king, Henry II, above those of the church. A shrine venerating the saint was erected after his death, although only the original steps remain, worn down by countless thousands of feet over the centuries.

The Choir (or Quire) – This might be called the jewel of the cathedral, because of the sparkling beauty of its glasswork, the oldest examples of which are the Twelve Miracle Windows.

The Cloisters, the Chapter House, the Green Court, the King's School – To see the cathedral's entire interior takes the better part of a day, but be sure to make time for the peripheral buildings that date from when the whole was a Benedictine monastery. The Cloisters, leading from the Chapter House, are virtually "corridors in the vale of time." If as you stroll through the passageway called the Dark Entry you encounter the ghost of a certain Nell Cook, don't be alarmed — you're not the first. The story of her origin is obscure and her occasional appearances are rarely sinister — so far anyway. Beyond the Green Court, and traditionally associated with the cathedral itself, is the King's School, the oldest public school in the land. (The term "public" is really a misnomer for "private"; this is a very expensive and exclusive private boys' school.) The King's School is architecturally notable for its handsome Norman staircase.

WITHIN THE OLD CITY WALLS

About half of the initial wall structure still stands; the walkway atop it makes a fascinating hike in good weather. In the Poor Priest's Hospital you can see the 150-year-old *Invicta,* a steam-powered locomotive designed by George Stephenson, and a working remnant of one of the earliest passenger railways in the world.

The Westgate – The next most imposing of Canterbury's historic buildings is at the extreme end of St. Peter's Street, following on from High Street, 5 minutes' walk in a westerly direction from the cathedral. As a relic it is magnificent, but it has a grisly history: Construction of the Westgate Towers was started at the order of Simon of Sudbury in 1380, during the reign of Richard II. In the following year, it became the city gaol (jail), which it remained until 1829. Today it is a museum exhibiting a collection of arms and armor, shackles, manacles, fetters, and instruments of torture; and the old prison cells still retain their original doors and fittings. Even the timbers of the dreaded gallows are here, a macabre reminder that prisoners were hanged for sometimes quite trivial offenses. Open daily except Sundays from April to September, 10 AM to 1 PM and 2 to 5 PM; October to March, 2 to 4 PM.

Dane John – Nothing to do with Danes, but a prominent feature of central Canterbury, with its prehistoric mound giving fine views of the red tile Tudor houses in the neighborhood. The name comes from the Norman-French word *donjon,* meaning a castle or keep, or — more chillingly — a dungeon. Dane John lies southwest of the cathedral, about 5 minutes' walk from Christ Church Gate.

The Norman Castle – A vast ruin now, but it still possesses one of the largest Norman keeps in the country. It was built between 1070 and 1094 and has been several times surrounded and captured and was once the royal prison for the County of Kent. Like the Westgate, it has a grim history of cruelty and mayhem. When the fanatical Mary I was on the throne, many Protestants were imprisoned here before being burned at the stake for their religious opinions. The Norman Castle is at the junction of Castle St. and Rheims Way.

OUTSIDE THE PERIMETER

St. Dunstan's – The section of Old Canterbury beyond the Westgate and leading toward the railway crossing on Whitstable Road. A good place of call is the *House of Agnes,* now a hotel on St. Dunstan's Street (see *Best in Town*), reputedly the one

Dickens had in mind as the house of Agnes Wickfield in *David Copperfield*. The interesting old *Falstaff Inn* is nearly opposite, and a door or so away is a small, cozy pub called the *Bishop's Finger*. (The name refers to the ring worn by medieval bishops.)

St. Augustine's Abbey – Founded by St. Augustine, with the support of King Ethelbert, in AD 602. Largely a ruin, but an important and still beautiful relic of Canterbury's past, particularly the finely restored Fyndon Gate. Reached from the Quenin Gate of the cathedral.

ENVIRONS

Chilham Castle Keep – A 15-minute drive due south of Canterbury is Chilham Castle, the home of Viscount Massereene and Ferrard and one of the finest houses in Kent. The Jacobean house is not open to the public, but the splendidly preserved Norman keep remains an attraction for visitors throughout the year. Its quite glorious setting in 300 acres of forest is also a good reason to visit.

Howlett's Zoo Park – The largest breeding colony of gorillas outside the US, run by John Aspinall and his family. There's also a fine collection of great cats and free-roaming herds of deer and antelope. Bekesbourne (phone: 721286).

Fordwich – Drive to Sturry, 4 miles north of Canterbury on Rte. A28. Turn right at the signpost. The tiny former Cinque Port on the River Stour is less than a minute away. It is an exquisite little town of some 300 inhabitants and is remarkable for having the smallest town hall in England, delightful to look at and scarcely bigger than a farmworker's cottage. Nobody knows how old the structure is, but the records show that extensive repairs were carried out as recently as 1474. Here again, you'll see instruments of torture. The stocks are outside in the courtyard, their oaken clamps worn slim from centuries of use; the small prison is in one corner; and overlooking the river stands the crane that once lowered condemned miscreants into the water for drowning. Beside it is the ducking chair for the correction of shrewish wives, and in the town hall itself you can inspect the room set aside for drying them off. An excellent place for lunch is the *George and Dragon*, round the corner from the town hall (see *Best in Town*).

■**EXTRA SPECIAL:** In late September or early October is the annual Canterbury Festival, with a costumed procession through the streets followed by events such as plays and concerts. During the third week of July, a series of choir and orchestra concerts are given at the King's School and in the environs of the cathedral. The musical performances are very well done and performed in glorious surroundings, but wear something warm — it can get very chilly in the evenings. Buy tickets at Forwood Bookings, 37 Palace St. (phone: 55600).

SOURCES AND RESOURCES

TOURIST INFORMATION: The Tourist Information Center is at 13 The Longmarket (phone: 66567), close to the cathedral. It stocks the usual helpful guidebooks, brochures, and maps and is open daily except Sundays from 9:30 AM to 4:30 PM year-round. Guided tours of the city leave Longmarket daily at 2:15 PM from May until September; the fee is 75p. To arrange additional or out-of-season tours, consult the Guild of Guides, Arnett House, Hawks La. (phone: 459779).

Local Coverage – The *Kentish Gazette* weekly includes a useful Town Crier supplement, which lists all local events. You can find it at Kent County Newspapers Ltd., 9 St. George's Pl. (phone: 68181).

The Tourist Information Center also carries *What's on '87*, a quarterly booklet with a comprehensive list of events in the Canterbury area.

 GETTING AROUND: As Canterbury is very small, the best form of transportation is your own two feet. However, you may decide to visit some of the outlying areas, in which case you'll need to know about alternate modes, discussed below.

Bus – Forty-minute bus tours leave every hour from 10 AM to 4 PM daily except Sundays. From the bus station on St. George's Lane (near *Riceman's Department Store*), you can catch buses to Dover, Folkestone, Deal, and Margate (all about an hour's ride). Call for information: 66151.

Taxi – Quick and courteous cab service is available at all times. Try *Austen's Taxis* (phone: 454105); *Bishop's Taxis* (phone: 65566); *Canterbury Radio Taxis* (phone: 60333); or *Taylor's Taxis* (phone: 456363). (Remember you need a 10p coin for the telephone.)

Car Rental – There are many car rental firms in Canterbury; among them are: *U-Drive Rentals* (phone: 69366); *Canterbury Motor Co. Ltd.* (phone: 451791, ext. 51); *Hertz* (phone: 65654); *Invicta* (phone: 60354); *Dane Valley* (phone: 710590). There is adequate, low-cost car parking in the city.

 MUSEUMS AND GALLERIES: Religious articles are displayed in Canterbury's churches and cathedral. The city's most interesting museums are *The Royal Museum and Art Gallery*, 18 High St. (the Beaney Institute), which incorporates *Buff's Regimental Museum* and chronicles the area's history and archaeology; the *Westgate*, St. Dunstan's St., which has a collection of weapons and armor; the new *Heritage Museum*, housed in the 13th-century Poor Priests' Hospital on Stour St., which offers a walk through the city's history; and the *Roman Pavement*, Butchery La., which shelters the remains of a Roman mosaic floor and other artifacts. For information on any of these four, call 452747. *The Drew Gallery*, 16 Best La. (phone: 458759), holds exhibitions of contemporary paintings, sculpture, prints, and ceramics by local, national, and international artists. *Denne Hill* in Womenswold, about 8 miles southeast of Canterbury (phone: 831452), is a fascinating Victorian house filled with more than 200 modern artworks. The house is also an occasional venue for contemporary music and theater.

 SHOPPING: Canterbury's compact size makes it a shopper's dream. For a wide selection of the basic necessities, try *Riceman's Department Store*, opposite the bus station; *Debenham's*, on Guildhall St.; or *Marks and Spencer*, 4 St. George's St. If your hobby is antiques, spend a morning in Palace St. — turn right out of Christ Church Gate of the cathedral, and first right again. There are many antiques shops along here; a few to look for are: *Five Centuries Antiques*, No. 18; *The Aristocrat*, No. 19; *Parker-Williams Antiques*, No. 22. Pottery collectors should be sure to stop in at *The Canterbury Pottery* on the far side of Buttermarket, just before Mercery La. *The Indoor Market* on St. Peter's St. (closed Sundays) is usually a collector's and bargain hunter's paradise. *The Tube* is one of Cantebury's trendiest clothes stores; it's in the Marlowe shopping arcade. For a special experience walk down to *The Old Weavers' House*, at 1–3 King's Bridge, across from the County Hotel in High St. This is one of the most spectacular 17th-century houses in the city; and features a weaving room, a tea garden, coffee shop, and ducking stool poised over the Stour. Stone jewelry, crafts, and brass rubbings are sold here, and river tours can be arranged.

SPORTS: Cricket – Canterbury is cricket territory; to watch this very British game at its best, go to the *Kent Country Cricket Club* at St. Lawrence Ground, off Old Dover Rd. (phone: 63421). Tickets are available at the gate.

Golf – The well-kept, 18-hole *Canterbury Golf Club,* Littlebourne Rd. (phone: 63586), is open to the public. Players with established handicaps are preferred, but novices are not discouraged. Clubs may be rented.

Swimming – The Kingsmead indoor swimming pool on Kingsmead (phone: 69817) is open to the public. Admission fee.

Horseback Riding – Horses can be hired at two stables about 5 miles due north of Canterbury: *High Rews Equestrian Centre,* Canterbury Rd., Herne Common (phone: Herne Bay 62678); *Homecroft Riding Stables,* Canterbury Rd., Herne Common (phone: Herne Bay 2065).

THEATER: Canterbury has only one commercial playhouse, the *Marlowe,* at The Friars, which opened in the spring of 1984 (phone: 67246). The *Gulbenkian Theatre* of the University of Kent on St. Giles La. (phone: 69075) is generally open to the public during the university terms only; its offerings include plays, recitals, concerts, and lectures. Check the newspapers for schedules.

NIGHTCLUBS AND NIGHTLIFE: There's not much after-dark entertainment in Canterbury. However, one possibility is *Alberry's Wine and Food Bar,* 38A St. Margaret St. (phone: 452378), for an enjoyable evening of eating and drinking and, on Monday, Tuesday, and Thursday nights, listening to live music downstairs in its Roman cellar. *Crotchets Wine Bar,* 59 Northgate, (phone: 458857), has more than 60 wines on its list, a garden, and, most nights, live jazz.

SINS: Another dismal failure. Any sins actually committed should either be kept to yourself or reported to the Dean and Chapter.

BEST IN TOWN

CHECKING IN: In Canterbury, you must book well in advance, because the city welcomes about 2 million visitors during the summer. Most of the hotels listed below are smallish, but make up for this shortcoming with their cheerful and attentive service. None, however, is in the true luxury class except for nearby *Eastwell Manor,* in Ashford. For a double room in the hotels we list below, expect to pay $50 to $85 per night in those noted as expensive; $30 to $50, moderate; and $20 to $30, inexpensive.

County – First licensed in 1629, it is considered the best in Canterbury and is richly decorated and furnished in antiques. The hotel's restaurant specializes in Continental cuisine. 74 rooms; parking available. High St. (phone: 66266). Expensive.

Eastwell Manor – This turreted, rambling country house hotel offers 24 luxurious, spacious rooms furnished with antiques, and an accomplished kitchen, all set amid extensive gardens. This is a first-class choice for visitors who long to experience life in an elegant rural setting. Eastwell Park, Ashford (phone: 0233-35751). Expensive.

Slatters – Part Tudor, part Queen Anne, and part Roman, but mostly modern, this 32-room hotel is just 200 yards from the Cathedral and continuously busy. Parking. St. Margaret's St. (phone: 463271). Expensive.

Abbots Barton – At this large country house surrounded by its own attractive grounds, you'll find logfires and a quiet, old-fashioned ambience; good food; and solid, comfortable furniture. In short, it's the perfect home base for families. Facilities include 50 modern rooms (43 with private baths) and parking. 37 New Dover Rd. (phone: 60341). Moderate.

George and Dragon – This charming 16th-century inn near the River Stour has 13 rooms. Its restaurant, which serves steak dinners, also offers a very fine hot and cold buffet lunch. Fordwich, near Sturry (phone: 710661). Moderate.

Georgian Guest House – If you're a little eccentric, you'll find yourself one of the family at this 15th-century B&B, full of antiques. 69 Castle St. (phone: 461111). Inexpensive.

Ann's Guest House – A family-run, Victorian house, featuring four-poster beds in most of its 19 rooms, and good parking facilities. 63 London Rd. (phone: 68767). Inexpensive.

EATING OUT: Although it's a country town, Canterbury boasts a few very fine restaurants, where you can have an expertly prepared meal for a reasonable price. There are also some cozy little eateries in the surrounding area, which you may decide to include on a day tour out of town. In general, a meal for two, excluding wine, tips, and drinks, will run about $35 to $50 in a place listed as expensive, $20 to $35 in a moderate one, and under $20 in an inexpensive one.

Beehive – In the Middle Ages, the *Beehive* was a pub conveniently located across the way from the cattle market; in the 18th century, it was a smugglers' lair. Today it's one of Canterbury's best restaurants — a small and intimate place specializing in Continental food. Reservations necessary. 52 Dover St. (phone: 61126). Expensive.

Duck Inn – This snug little restaurant, in a 16th-century cottage and warmed by a roaring fire, is noted for its very good French cooking. It's about 5 miles outside Canterbury, near the village of Bridge on the road to Dover. The best transportation is a taxi. Reservations necessary. Closed Mondays and Tuesdays. Pett Bottom (phone: 830354). Expensive.

Ristorante Tuo e Mio – Just the place for a rich, satisfying Italian lunch or dinner with plenty of fresh produce and pasta available. Top it off with a sinful zabaglione. Parking is not too good, so walk instead. Closed Mondays and Tuesdays for lunch. Reservations necessary. 16 The Borough (phone: 61471). Expensive.

House of Agnes – Referred to in Dickens's *David Copperfield,* it's now a hotel as well as a restaurant. The kitchen prepares good hearty English home cooking. Reservations necessary. 71 St. Dunstan's St. (phone: 65077). Moderate.

Marlowe's – Fresh flowers decorate the tables at this friendly eatery, which features health foods and a salad bar. Open daily. St. Peter's St. (phone: 464569). Moderate.

Queen Elizabeth – This authentic Tudor building, once the cathedral's guesthouse where Elizabeth I reputedly stayed, is now a pleasant restaurant known for its good lunches and teas. High St. (phone: 464080). Moderate to inexpensive.

Tascolls Wine Bar – A lively spot filled with potted plants, wooden tables, and twenties jazz, its blackboard menu lists a variety of homemade items and a wide selection of wines. Live music on Fridays. Closed Sundays. 49/50 Castle St. (phone: 60381). Inexpensive.

Caesars – A student haunt, with huge hamburgers and generous portions of ribs and other transatlantic dishes. 46 St. Peter's St. (phone: 456833). Inexpensive.

Manhattan Transfer – Choose from ten original New York pizzas, all freshly made on the premises, followed by American desserts. Dinner only; closed Mondays. 41 Broad St. (phone: 459174). Inexpensive.

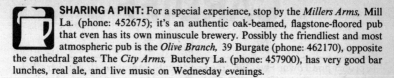

SHARING A PINT: For a special experience, stop by the *Millers Arms,* Mill La. (phone: 452675); it's an authentic oak-beamed, flagstone-floored pub that even has its own minuscule brewery. Possibly the friendliest and most atmospheric pub is the *Olive Branch,* 39 Burgate (phone: 462170), opposite the cathedral gates. The *City Arms,* Butchery La. (phone: 457900), has very good bar lunches, real ale, and live music on Wednesday evenings.

CARDIFF

"A proper fine Towne" was how the seventeenth-century cartographer Christopher Saxton described Cardiff. And today it's a proper fine city: handsome, spacious, and genial, with a definite sense of its own importance. It is, after all, the capital city of the principality of Wales. And it has a capital feel about it. You sense right away that it is at the center of things. It is a busy headquarters for commerce, industry, government, the arts, and communications. And it has perhaps the most attractive city center in all of Britain — the "Welsh Washington," as it's called.

From London, Cardiff is 2½ hours away on the M4 (Swansea) motorway, or less than 2 hours by the 125-mph super-train, nicknamed the "Welsh Bullet." And the Central Station sign says *Caerdydd*/Cardiff in salute to the two languages of Wales, hinting at the history, pride, and fascination of this singular land. Welsh, spoken by one fifth of the principality's 2.8 million people, is Wales's distinction among nations; and its story is a central part of the history of the Welsh people.

In Cardiff you'll see the language (it's older than English, dating from the sixth century) written on all manner of signs. You're sure to see the word *Croeso* — "welcome" — and the Welsh mean it. And you'll hear the language spoken in the streets and shops and on radio and television.

But you won't hear it a lot. For one thing Cardiff is in southeast Wales, and the strongly Welsh-speaking areas are in the north and west. Cardiffians, however have their own distinctive twang, one of the many strands from which the city's character is woven. It is a multilayered and cosmopolitan place (twinned with Nantes in France, Stuttgart in Germany, and Xiamen in China), an outward-looking, modern European city of warm people, as well as a storehouse of the history of a fascinating area — three of the thirteen Welsh signatories of the Declaration of Independence were sons of Cardiff, and Dr. Richard Price, who drafted the basis, came from nearby Bridgend.

Cardiff is Europe's youngest capital city, awarded the status by Queen Elizabeth in 1956, at a time when nationalist feeling in Wales was demanding some recognition of the principality's special identity within the United Kingdom. Other towns applied for the honor, but Cardiff was the home of the Welsh Office, headquarters of all Welsh administration, and the Temple of Peace, which administers all liaison between Wales and the United Nations. With such administrative prowess and a population of 277,000, the city had the scale, background, and facilities to make it a realistic contender.

Diligent Romans built a no-nonsense little Cardiff beside the River Taff as part of their network of conquest. It served as a fort and trading post. The Roman stones, still visible around the first 2 feet of the castle walls, were already old when the Normans arrived in the eleventh century and built their own castle.

On a mound they raised a keep, a noble medieval fist, and it remains intact: one of the finest examples of its kind in Britain. Castle, moat, and green are right in the city center and Cardiffians like to saunter or doze on the green on summer days.

King Edward I of England conquered stubborn Wales in the thirteenth century. But 100 years or so later, in 1404, the Welsh political comet Owain Glyndwr fanned the embers of resistance, started a war of independence, and sacked Cardiff. Eventually he lost his struggle, but five centuries later Cardiff was generous enough to erect a marble statue of the hero in its opulent city hall.

Roundheads took the town from Royalists in Britain's seventeenth-century civil war. But for nearly 200 years after that life was peaceful enough. Cardiff bloomed quietly, a market town, seaport, and occasional bolt-hole for pirates prowling the Bristol Channel.

Then the Industrial Revolution came. Up in the winding green valleys, spoking from Cardiff's hub, men tore out coal to fuel factories, furnaces, mills, ships. The coal was sent to Cardiff, first by mule, then barge, then rail, for onward shipment to British cities and the world.

The new Cardiff soared on the dizzy spiral of the great coal rush, the central event in post-1800 Welsh history. The riches of the valleys poured in. The Taff ran black. Tycoons multiplied. With Welsh coal at the heart of British economic expansion Cardiff became the world's greatest coal port. The Cardiff Coal Exchange is still there in dockland, monument to an age, a stately Victorian edifice in Coalowner Gothic. Look at it, and in your mind's eye you can see the frockcoated financiers making their fortunes.

In its heyday, Cardiff's dockland was called Tiger Bay. It was a teeming, noisy, rumbustious Dodge City of pubs, little houses, and bordellos. Today, old Tiger Bay has gone; for it was a time as well as a place. The slums have been cleared and the area is often cited as an example of an integrated multiracial community of long standing. And its people prefer you to use its proper name: Butetown.

During Cardiff's Victorian and Edwardian expansion, its top citizens consolidated its position as chief city of Wales. Among lawns, shrubs, and boulevards they built their halls of government and culture: city hall, county hall, museum, law courts, university, and others, all laid out in a grand magisterial sweep. Meanwhile, the burgeoning middle classes built lovely villas in places like Cathedral Road.

One of the most pleasant things about Cardiff is that its heart remains village-sized. And the castle, the business center, shops, restaurants, pubs, hotels, station, rugby stadium, museum, theaters, galleries, and parks can all be reached comfortably on foot.

You can traverse the city by way of parks, greens, and footpaths; and the stroll across Llandaff Fields to Llandaff, the secluded village within the city, with its cathedral, pubs, and cottages, is a great favorite (see *Special Places*).

One of the famous parks, though, is not a park at all: Cardiff Arms Park is a temple of rugby football, a game to which Welshmen devote blood, sweat, and tears. On big-match Saturdays the city seems to vibrate with emotion, song, and excitement. The Red Dragon flag of Wales is hoisted aloft and almost everyone seems to have a leek or a daffodil, the national emblems, pinned to hat or coat. To be in Cardiff on one of these days is to experience a certain kind of Welshness, humorous and exuberant, in the raw.

CARDIFF AT-A-GLANCE

SEEING THE CITY: Right in the middle of town is the best place to get a feel for Cardiff: the castle. It is open almost every day of the year. Cross the moat bridge, go through the gate house, turn left, and make for the clock tower. From here you get a sentry's-eye view of the castle itself, the River Taff, the Arms Park, Sophia Gardens Cricket Ground, and busy shopping streets. You can also see the famous "animal wall" — a row of sculptures of beasts and birds perched on battlements. You can see Bute Park, stretching off in the direction of Llandaff cathedral; and the pristine towers, domes, and greenery of Cathays Park (pronounced Catt-hays). Much the same view can be had from a slightly different vantage point, the roof garden of the castle. This is a piece of delicious Victorian extravagance, with its delightful shrubs, murals, mosaics, and fountains. On the northwest edge of Cardiff is The Wenallt, an area of rolling woodland from which you get a superb view of Cardiff, laid out on its coastal plain, and of the Bristol Channel.

SPECIAL PLACES: Although Cardiff owes much of its importance and growth to coal, there has been over the years a conscious effort to keep its center free of grime. The city fathers of the last century dreamt they dwelt in marble halls — and set about making that dream come true. The Cardiff they made is, at its center, a place of gracefulness and greenery. And its compactness means that, for the most part, you can park the car and walk to the principal sights; and are never far from a little restaurant or a jolly pub; or stretch of grass where you might like to do as the locals do and chat, read, gaze, or snooze.

CITY CENTER

Civic Center – At the end of the 19th century, the city bought 60 acres from the Marquess of Bute for what is today's Civic Center. A short walk from the main shopping area, it includes all of Cardiff's most impressive buildings: the Castle, City Hall, National Museum, and Welsh Office, plus the University College and the Institute of Science and Technology. Built with white Portland stone, they are all ganged around a war memorial on the fringe of Bute Park. Wide avenues make the Center an attractive walking area, particularly during evening civic functions, when the fountains and buildings are floodlit.

Cardiff Castle – Nineteen hundred years of history are stored here. The Roman walls are 10 feet thick and, as you can see, the stone keep on its *motte,* or mound, was built to last when it was erected in the 13th century to show the local people who was boss. The castle has always been lived in, and the third marquess of Bute, one of Wales's great coal moguls, ordered the renovations and extensions that give the place its unique appearance. He commissioned the architect William Burges to design a nobleman's indulgence. The result is the Baroque and charming place you enjoy today, full of color, exquisite murals, carvings, and painted ceilings and windows. There is a table with a hole in it, through which a vine emerged, enabling the marquess and guests to pluck fresh grapes. Part of the castle is now used for civic receptions and banquets (medieval banquets are held every evening except Sundays yearround; phone 372737 for booking and information). Other rooms and towers house the museum of the Welsh Regiment. A visit to the castle includes an excellent conducted tour, although you can wander on your own amongst the peacocks if you prefer. Admission charge (phone: 31279).

National Museum of Wales – A short walk from the castle is one of Britain's finest museums. Huge and airy, it offers a broad-ranging and detailed introduction to Wales in all aspects. It has a remarkable collection of carved Celtic standing stones and crosses; a host of national treasures; and a gallery housing, among much else, the work of artists like Augustus John and his sister Gwen, and an outstanding collection of Impressionist paintings. Apart from its large permanent collection, the National hosts touring art exhibits. Museum Ave., Cathays Park. Open daily except Mondays from 10 AM until 5 PM, Sundays from 2:30 to 5 PM. Free (phone: 397951).

City Hall – Next to the museum, it is distinguished by its clock tower and ornate stonework. Inside is the Marble Hall with its statues of the great men of Welsh history. Closed weekends.

Cathays Park – Pink-surfaced avenues, blossom, shrubs, walks, statuary, and buildings of an almost Athenian aspect. The Welsh are rightly proud of it.

ENVIRONS

St. John's Church – A landmark in Cardiff since the 15th century, with its tall pinnacled tower in the Perpendicular style. It is the heart of the city's commercial and shopping district and is a 2-minute walk from the castle.

Llandaff Fields – On these tree-lined meadows in summer, boys are playing baseball (surprisingly popular in these parts) or cricket, maybe dreaming of playing first-class cricket one day at Sophia Gardens, the handsome ground in the city center. This is a lovely setting for the game that is a British passion and a mystery to foreigners. Why not go for a few hours and enjoy trying to understand the ritual? In winter the boys will be playing rugby and dreaming of playing in the red shirt for Wales at Cardiff Arms Park.

Llandaff – Two miles from the city center. You can reach it by walking across Llandaff Fields, or by bus. Llandaff is a charming enclave: Somehow it has retained a sleepy village air with its neat and solid Victorian houses, inns, whitewashed deanery, and a village green from which a path leads to the cathedral, beautiful and discreet in its hollow. St. Teilo founded a settlement here in the 6th century, which is how Llandaff got its name: *Llan* (church) and *taff*, from the River Taff. The cathedral dates from the 12th century. It fell into disrepair and was at one time a beer house and cattle shelter. It was restored in the 19th century, wrecked in an air raid in 1941, and restored once more. One of its most striking features, and still controversial, is Epstein's aluminum figure of Christ, which dominates the nave.

Old Bishops Palace – In keeping with the rest of Llandaff: peaceful gardens among ancient walls, a place for reflection.

Butetown – Cardiff's famous and notorious Tiger Bay of days gone by. Time was when seafaring men from many parts of the world settled in this dockland area and created a vibrant, tough, and often seamy and squalid community. Things have changed a lot, and though Bute Town is still a lively, mixed community, it prides itself on its respectability. The coal trade isn't what it was, but the docks are still very important. And it's interesting to see the imposing shipping and banking offices and the Coal Exchange, built in the great days of the coal rush. There's a museum here, the Welsh Industrial and Maritime Museum (phone: 481919), which displays the machinery that powered early industrial growth and other pioneering equipment. Admission free. From High Street in the city center you can get a bus to the museum, in the heart of Butetown.

Castell Coch – With its turretted, fairy-tale-like towers, the Red Castle dominates the northern pass into Cardiff from the South Wales valleys. Built by William Burges, who was also partially responsible for Cardiff Castle, it was designed as a hunting lodge for the Third Marquess of Bute. Its remarkable fantastic (in the literal sense of the word) interior includes a carved wooden ceiling as well as wooden parrots along the gallery. Open daily 9:30 AM to 6:30 PM mid-March to mid-October; off-season hours are 9:30 AM to 4 PM, except Sundays from 2 to 4 PM. Admission charge. Taffs Well (phone: 810101).

Roath Park – Some 100 acres, with an attractive lake. You can rent a rowboat very cheaply (just keep away from the serious young lads fishing from the banks); admire the geese camped on the island; and pause at the miniature lighthouse, a memorial to the Antarctic hero, Captain Scott, who sailed from Cardiff to make his ill-fated expedition to the South Pole.

Dyffryn Gardens – These are a few miles west of the city center, on Rt. A48 at St. Nicholas. On the way down the winding country road (where you can get a good feel for the lovely Vale of Glamorgan) you can stop at the Tinkinswood long barrow, one of the finest examples of a Neolithic burial chamber to be found in Wales: It has a 40 ton capstone. Dyffryn House (phone: 593328) is a spacious mansion with 70 acres of spacious grounds to match. It has masses of flowers, shrubs, and trees. And it has a teahouse. So it's a perfect place in which to wind down and draw breath. It is open from April to September, and weekends in October, and admission is £1. You can reach Dyffryn by bus from the station, No. X1 or No. 231.

■**EXTRA SPECIAL:** Out on the edge of the Vale of Glamorgan, 4½ miles from the city center, at St. Fagan's, is one of Cardiff's most pleasant treats, the *Welsh Folk Museum* (phone: 569441). You can spend an absorbing day here and be astonished that time seems to fly by so quickly. In the 100-acre estate around the newly renovated Tudor mansion are an original cottage, farmhouses, barns, a smithy, a tollhouse, a chapel, tannery, cockpit, woolen factory, and other buildings. Each one once stood in some part of rural Wales, was carefully taken apart, its stones and slates and beams numbered, then reconstructed in the sheep-grazed meadows of St. Fagan's. The furnishings and equipment are authentic too, and you can wander through the houses, upstairs and downstairs, to see how Welsh people lived through the centuries. You'll note the cozy fireside beds and the lovespoons that young men carved for their sweethearts: The more intricate the carving the deeper the passion! St. Fagan's tells the story of the people of Wales. The attendants are jolly, helpful, and all speak Welsh. In addition to the authentic buildings, St. Fagan's has a large museum, a buttery, and a restaurant. Open daily from 10 AM to 5 PM, Sundays from 2:30 PM; admission charge. Take the No. 32 bus, which leaves from the station every hour on the hour.

SOURCES AND RESOURCES

TOURIST INFORMATION: In the Welsh language the name of the Wales Tourist Board is Bwrdd Croeso Cymru — literally translated as Wales Welcome Board. It gives you an idea of how the Welsh feel about showing visitors their land. The Board's office in Cardiff is in the center, at 3–6 Bridge Street, near the new Holiday Inn (phone: 27281). Here visitors can get maps, guidebooks, leaflets, and personal advice and directions (open Mondays through Saturdays 9:30 AM to 6 PM). The paperwork is high quality, and the advice is bright and friendly. There is also a 24-hour computerized "Infopoint" information display in the window. Visitors can also get information about Cardiff from the Public Relations Officer, City Hall, Cardiff (phone: 822000).

The Wales Tourist Board publishes an excellent, clear, and colorful map of Wales.

And there are good cheap maps and guides to Cardiff available at newsagents and bookshops like *W. H. Smith* and *Menzies.* You'll find a wide selection of books about Wales in *Lears* on St. Mary St. and *Oriel* in Charles St.

Local Coverage – The city's Public Relations Office publishes brochures, books, and a useful guide called *Events in Cardiff* each month. And you can get information about restaurants and entertainments from the Wales Tourist Board. Daily movie, theater, and concert listings are in the *Western Mail,* published every morning except Sunday, and the *South Wales Echo,* Cardiff's afternoon paper.

GETTING AROUND: Buses – At its heart Cardiff is a walker's city. But there's a bus network that operates until late at night. Cardiff Buses (phone: 396521) runs a good variety of tours in summer months using open-topped double-decker buses, starting from Greyfriars Road. There's an information kiosk at the bus station.

Car Rental – Most major national and international firms have offices in Cardiff: *Hertz* (phone: 24548); *Avis* (phone: 42111); *Godfrey Davis* (phone: 498978, 497110).

Taxi – Cabs (*thacsis*) don't cruise as a rule. The Wales Tourist Board has a good taxi list, and there are plenty of firms in the Yellow Pages. *Castle Cabs* (phone: 394929), *City Centre Cars* (phone: 488888), *Amber Cars* (phone: 378111, 378378), and *Metro Cabs* (phone: 464646) are among those offering 24-hour service. There are cab ranks at Central station and the Friary in the city center.

Trains – Good rail services to the suburbs, outlying towns, valleys, and villages and fast intercity services. Valley Line local trains run from both Central and Queen Street stations. Information from British Rail, Central Station (phone: 28000).

MUSEUMS: In addition to those described in *Special Places,* the following museums are of interest.

Chapter Centre for the Arts – One of the largest in Europe, with cinemas, theater, workshops, and touring exhibitions of contemporary works. Market Rd. (phone: 396061).

Ffotogallery – Wales' leading photography gallery changes exhibits monthly. 31 Charles St. (phone: 41667).

Oriel Art Gallery – Exhibitions change about every three weeks. 53 Charles St. (phone: 395548).

St. David's Hall – Take the escalators up to all six floors for the free exhibitions of modern art, mostly by local artists. Closed Sundays. Working St. (phone: 42611).

Turner House Art Gallery – Plymouth Rd., Penarth (phone: Penarth 708870).

SHOPPING: The shopping in Cardiff is excellent. There's a wide range of goods, expensive and bargain, in big stores, little stores, and friendly boutiques. The main shopping streets are Queen Street, Working Street, The Hayes, and St. Mary Street, nearly all pedestrianized and, like all the city's attractions, well signposted. St. David's Centre is a huge, modern enclosed arcade with branches of the major chain stores, boutiques, and supermarkets (including Marks and Spencer, and Debenhams). It is particularly lively at lunchtime. By contrast, the city's famous shopping arcades (Dominion, Queen Street, Castle, Morgan, Royal, and Oxford) contain smaller, specialty shops, many selling Welsh craftwork — woolen products, beautiful bedspreads, flannel, pottery, and woodwork. There's a smaller, fast-developing shopping area out near Roath, on Wellfield Road, with a number of specialty shops and whole-foods restaurants.

Cardiff Indoor Market – All the bustle, noise, and color of Wales, with a wide range of goods and accents. Welsh lamb is a specialty in the butchers' stalls; *bara brith,* a kind of fruit bread, is offered at the bakers' stalls. And try some *laverbread,* a Welsh delicacy. It's a thick black seaweed, something of an acquired taste, delicious with ham or bacon. Another Welsh favorite you'll find here is cockles. Closed Wednesdays and Sundays. Entrance in St. Mary St. or the Hayes.

Castle Welsh Crafts and Woollens – Designer fashions, plus traditional quality woolens. 1 Castle St. (phone: 43038).

Charisma Chocolates – There's Thayer's real dairy ice cream on sale, or sink your teeth into a freezing liter of champagne sorbet for less than $4. 46-48 Royal Arcade (phone: 371081).

Howells of Cardiff – One of the major department stores, with almost everything, especially a good range of glassware, china, and gifts. Also a smart delicatessen and restaurant. St. Mary St. (phone: 31055).

Jacob's Warehouse – A crafts and antiques market. Open Thursdays and Saturdays. W Canal Wharf.

H. J. Lear Ltd. – The largest in Cardiff, with two floors of paper and hardbacks, including maps and guidebooks of the area. 13 Royal Arcade (phone: 395036).

David Morgan – Another big department store in the city center. The Hayes (phone: 21011).

Jan Stedman – A modern, friendly shop selling trendy women's lingerie, swimwear, and trinkets. 24 Morgan Arcade (phone: 372537).

Things Welsh – Pottery, crafts, woolens, metalwork, all of good quality. Duke St. Arcade (phone: 33445).

TSP Inter – They will design and print "I'm not a tourist" or any other motif on your baseball cap, T-shirt, or jeans. 14–16 Morgan Arcade (phone: 387013).

Wally's Delicatessen – A well-stocked deli counter at the back (the specialty was Belgian pâté when we called), plus shelves loaded with Oriental delicacies, herbs, dried pulses, whole grains, and wines. 46 Royal Arcade (phone: 29265).

 SPECIAL EVENTS: The *Cardiff Searchlight Tattoo* is a military pageant held every 2 years in the arena of Cardiff Castle. The *Llandaff Festival of Music* is growing in stature and is held every June. A big rugby match is always a special event: You're unlikely to get tickets for an international, but less important matches are just as passionate and exciting. The *Cardiff Festival of Music* (classical) convenes for three weeks in late November to December.

 SPORTS: Visitors are welcome to use the wide range of sporting facilities at the *Western Leisure Centre* (phone: 593592) and the *Heath Sports Centre* (phone: 755607).

Ice Skating – Available at *Cardiff Ice Rink,* Hayes Bridge Rd. (phone: 383451).

Riding – You can rent horses at *Cardiff City Riding School,* Pontcanna Fields, a few miles west of Cardiff (phone: 383908).

Rugby – This is a national passion and the immensely popular *Cardiff Rugby Club* plays at the *Cardiff Arms Park National Rugby Stadium.*

Sailing – There's boat rental and anchorage at *Penarth,* 5 miles south of Cardiff.

Swimming – Go to the *Wales Empire Pool* on Wood St. (phone: 382296), where you can also have a Turkish bath and sauna.

 THEATER: *The New,* in Park Pl. (phone: 3948), stages productions by the internationally renowned Welsh National Opera, ballet, pre-London plays, and pantomime in the winter. *The Sherman,* in Senghennydd Rd. (phone: 30451), is a modern theater that puts on plays by major professional groups and sometimes by local amateur groups. The small "workshop" theater is known for its fringe productions. The *Chapter Arts Centre,* on Market Rd. (phone: 396061), features regular theater productions and daily movies. There's also a small restaurant on the premises which is well-patronized by local students. Moving Being, Wales' leading experimental theater group, appears regularly at *St. Stephen's Theatre Space*, West Bute St. (phone: 498885). Show schedules can be found in the local papers.

MUSIC: "Praise the Lord — we are a musical nation," one of Dylan Thomas's characters said. And Cardiff does its best to live up to that with a regular program of concerts. *St. David's Hall*, a new 2,000-seat national concert and conference center on Working St., presents a wide variety of musical entertainment — classical, jazz, rock, and folk — as well as sports, films, lectures, and other large-scale events (phone: 42611 for information; 371236 for box office). Lunchtime concerts can be heard here, in *City Hall*, and at the *BBC Wales* concert hall in Llandaff.

NIGHTCLUBS AND NIGHTLIFE: Cardiffians take their evening pleasure with some enthusiasm. They like to go out to dinner and take quite a long time over the meal: They're not fast-food folk. And they like propping up a bar, talking and listening to music. You'll find it easy to join them in any of these activities. Cardiff also has a number of nightclubs; these include *Mont Merence*, 45 Charles St. (phone: 29142) and *Bumpers*, Castle Arcade (phone: 32654).

SINS: For the wheelers and dealers, there's gambling at *Les Croupiers*, 32 St. Mary St. (phone: 382810) and at *Sloane's*, Westgate St. (phone: 43899). You might find striptease or topless bars here or there in the city, but Cardiff is not renowned for these art forms.

BEST IN TOWN

CHECKING IN: Wales has always been popular with travelers, and some of its hotels are justly famous. Moreover, standards have been improved considerably during the past few years. If you want the tops in comfort and class in Cardiff you'll have to pay top dollar, but in the more modest places you will find considerable comfort, excellent home-cooked food, a warm welcome, and a bill that doesn't make you pale. Consult the Tourist Board, which has lists of recommended and inspected hotels. A double with breakfast in a hotel in the expensive category will cost $70 to $90; in the moderate, $50 to $70; and in the inexpensive, as low as $20.

Celtic Manor – This 19th-century manor house is a few miles outside Cardiff, off the M4, but is definitely worth consideration. Special features include huge bedrooms that overlook the flower-filled wooded gardens of Chepstow and the *Patio* conservatory/restaurant. Coldra Woods, Newport (phone: 0633-413000). Expensive.

Holiday Inn – Cardiff's newest hotel boasts 190 rooms and all the modern conveniences, including a pool, gym, sauna, spa bath, and piano bar. Hayes Bridge Rd. (phone: 399944). Expensive.

Inn on the Avenue – Just off the M4, this first-class hotel has 152 rooms, all with private bath. Restaurant, pool, gym, beauty salon, and helipad; parking available. Circleway E (phone: 732520). Expensive.

Park – Considered the best, with a gracious, spacious air and an attentive staff. There are 108 rooms and two very good restaurants — the *Caernarfon Room* and the *Theatre Garden*. Parking. Park Pl. (phone: 383471). Expensive.

Post House – Up to date and very comfortable, it's a bit out of town at Pentwyn, so you really need a car. Good eating and plenty of sports facilities to work it off. 150 rooms. Pentwyn (phone: 731212). Expensive.

Beverley – Comfortable and friendly with a good restaurant. 18 rooms. 75 Cathedral Rd. (phone: 43443). Moderate.

Crest – This hotel has 160 smart, modern, and comfortable rooms with all the facilities. Bilingual signs and notices are a pleasant nod of respect to the old language. Westgate St. (phone: 388681). Moderate.

Lincoln – Welshman Keith Baines spent 24 years in the US before returning with his American wife to join two large Victorian houses to form this comfortable 18-room hotel. Guests craving an "authentic" American breakfast will be happy to find that the menu includes such items as honest-to-goodness pancakes with maple syrup and eggs Benedict. 118 Cathedral Rd. (phone: 395558). Moderate.

Royal – One of Cardiff's long-established and most dependable hotels, with 67 rooms. In the center of town on St. Mary St. (phone: 383321). Moderate.

Cedars – In a pleasant and quiet suburb, it's comfortable and has a restaurant. 25 rooms. Fidlas Rd., Llanishen (phone: 752163). Inexpensive.

Hayes Court – This is representative of a number of good, clean, comfortable, and rather homely hotels, not far from the city center. It has a restaurant and a liquor license; there's also a sauna. 160 Cathedral Rd. (phone: 30420). Inexpensive.

 EATING OUT: Cardiff is a cosmopolitan city and this is reflected in its restaurants, tastes, and menus. While you're here, though, be sure to try the local specialties, such as Welsh lamb. Likewise don't miss fresh Welsh salmon or *sewin*, a kind of trout. Pluck up courage and taste *laverbread* — remember it's not bread but seaweed. For starters, you'll find *cawl* (broth) in its various forms delicious. And to round off a meal, homemade pies and fruit tarts are usually good. Some restaurants, mainly the less expensive ones, serve food throughout the day and evening. Others stick to the usual lunch and dinner hours, and these places accept major credit cards. Eating out in Cardiff is less expensive than in London. Expect to pay $35 and up for dinner for two, including wine and tips in places listed as expensive; $20 to $35 in a moderate restaurant; and under $20 for an inexpensive meal.

Spanghero's – Named after a rugby hero, this establishment is known for its accomplished French nouvelle cuisine carefully prepared and beautifully presented by celebrated chef David Evans. For those who need to watch their budgets rather than their waistlines, there are less expensive meals in the informal wine bar. Westgate House, Westgate St. (phone: 382423). Expensive.

Gibson's – One of the capital's most enjoyable restaurants, at which the proprietress almost always scores a bull's eye with her French cooking. There's a good atmosphere, a friendly staff, and wines to match. Reservations required. A little off the beaten track at 8 Romilly Crescent (phone: 41264). Expensive to moderate.

Harvesters – Be sure to bring a robust appetite — the food here is British with a Welsh flavor, that is, hearty but rather plain. Try the homemade soup and the delicious game casserole. Open daily except Sundays for dinner; closed for 3 weeks in August. Reservations recommended. 5 Pontcanna St. (phone: 32616). Expensive to moderate.

Savastano's – The reason Jimmy Savastano's place is usually busy, and the customers keep on coming back, is because it provides a happy, delicious, and informal eating experience. Italian specialties; veal dishes are especially good. Reservations recommended. 302 North Rd., Gabalfa (phone: 621018). Expensive to moderate.

Landaf Celebrity – There are two entrances to this establishment: one in St. David's Hall and the other on Working Street. The wholesome, if unimaginative, dishes include traditional Welsh roast, shoulder of Welsh lamb with mint, and farmhouse chicken with bacon roll. Closed Sundays. Working St. (phone: 27211). Moderate.

Truffles – A conservative menu of steaks, fish, and the like, with a downstairs tearoom. Church St. (phone: 44958). Closed Sundays. Moderate.

Armless Dragon – A bright, cheery place with a number of surprising specialties, including shark curry, Welsh laverbread balls, wild rabbit, and rack of Welsh lamb. Closed Saturday lunch and Sundays. 97 Wyvern Rd. (phone: 382357). Moderate.

Yr Ystafell Gymraeg – The name means "the Welsh Room" and, not surprisingly, the restaurant is furnished with Welsh antiques. You'll find many enjoyable native dishes here: Choose from cockles, laverbread, and lamb. The steak and kidney pie is lovely and so is the cawl. Reservations recommended. Closed Saturday lunch and Sundays. 72-74 Whitchurch Rd., Gabalfa (phone: 42317, 397660). Moderate.

Riverside – A successful Cantonese restaurant, this place is a cut above average and offers a great variety of dishes, all cooked by talented hands. It also serves an interesting Chinese beer. Open daily from noon to midnight. Reservations recommended. 44 Tudor St., Riverside (phone: 372163). Moderate.

Blas ar Gymru – A recent winner of the Road and Car Taste of Britain award (RAC) for Wales, this cozy eatery serves up generous helpings of good, wholesome, traditional Welsh dishes like cawl (a thick vegetable, leek, and lamb soup) and gower cockle and bacon pie, all washed down with local wine or mead. 48 Crwys Rd. (phone: 382132). Moderate.

Arnolds – Americans say that this hamburger joint is as good as the best back home. Bright and breezy atmosphere, with All-American desserts like apple pie, colossal ice cream dishes, and cheesecake, too. Albany Rd (phone: 499893). Inexpensive.

The Louis – It's open all day and serves traditional meals from a large menu. Just the place for traditional high tea, with friendly waitresses and plenty of room. St. Mary St. (phone: 25722). Inexpensive.

Tandoori Mahal – Typical of the many Indian restaurants in Cardiff, this restaurant offers authentic tandoori (clay oven) cooking served by a friendly staff. 98 Albany Rd., Roath Park (phone: 491500). Inexpensive.

Zio Pin – A lively Italian restaurant serving pizza, homemade pasta, and calzones. Albany Rd. (phone: 485673). Inexpensive.

Crumb's Salad – As the name suggests, the house specialty here is salad — of many varieties — including vegetable, rice, and fruit. Open daily except Sundays for lunch only. 33 Morgan Arcade (phone: 395007). Inexpensive.

Peppermint Lounge – Just the place if you have the munchies, featuring homemade burgers and a full range of cocktails. 34 Woodville Rd. (phone: 374403). Inexpensive.

Le Rombouts Coffee House – The comforting aroma of freshly brewed coffee hits you long before you reach the front door. Sit downstairs for a bowl of soup, a roll, and a coffee or, if you have something more formal in mind, upstairs for goulash, ravioli, or salad. 19 Morgan Arcade (phone: 388391). Inexpensive.

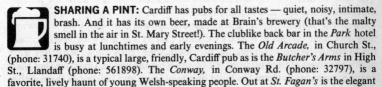 **SHARING A PINT:** Cardiff has pubs for all tastes — quiet, noisy, intimate, brash. And it has its own beer, made at Brain's brewery (that's the malty smell in the air in St. Mary Street!). The clublike back bar in the *Park* hotel is busy at lunchtimes and early evenings. The *Old Arcade,* in Church St., (phone: 31740), is a typical large, friendly, Cardiff pub as is the *Butcher's Arms* in High St., Llandaff (phone: 561898). The *Conway,* in Conway Rd. (phone: 32797), is a favorite, lively haunt of young Welsh-speaking people. Out at *St. Fagan's* is the elegant *Plymouth Arms* (phone: 569130), where you can eat well, too.

CHESTER

The red sandstone walls surrounding the old city of Chester are the only city walls in Britain to have come down to the twentieth century very nearly intact. For the last three centuries they have been a pleasant place to walk to get a better view of one of the most medieval-looking of British cities. Before that, however, these walls did their share of preserving it. Though it's now been more than 300 years since Chester's streets have seen any fighting, the walls are a reminder that it has been a military city for all its nineteen centuries of existence.

The original town — called Deva or Castra Legionis, fortress of the legions — was laid out by the battle-tested veterans of the Roman Twentieth Legion (conquerors of the Celtic warrior-queen Boadicea) when Britain became the newest province of the Empire only decades after the Crucifixion. Centuries after the Romans had abandoned Britain, Hugh Lupus suppressed the local tribes, thus gaining the Earldom of Chester (a title held ever since by the monarch's eldest son). He built the castle at Chester from which Edward I set out from here to crush the rebellious Welsh, binding them into submission in the thirteenth century with a chain of coastal fortresses from Flint to Caernarvon. Later still, Chester's position astride the route to Ireland was of strategic importance to Charles I, who expected reinforcements from his armies there, during the mid-seventeenth-century Civil War between the King and his Parliament. Charles watched the defeat of his army at the battle of Rowton Moor (1645) and fled the city, only to go on to eventual execution.

Since Roman times, there have always been soldiers in Chester. Even now it is the home of an active unit, the First Battalion, The King's Regiment, and the permanent depot of its own county regiment, the Cheshire Regiment, first formed three centuries ago. This military presence has stamped itself firmly on the city. The four main streets follow the line of the main roadways laid out inside the Roman fort almost 2,000 years ago, and where they meet at Chester Cross, the Church of St. Peter is built on the foundations of the Roman headquarters building and the residence of the military commander. The lines of many of the smaller back streets echo the layout of the Roman barracks, granaries, and storehouses.

Even the Rows, Chester's aboveground network of shopping walkways, may owe their origins to the city's distant past as a military fortress. According to one of the more convincing theories (no one really *knows* why they were built), the ruins of the buildings left by the Romans were so massive that their Saxon successors preferred to build on top of them and in front of them rather than labor to remove the weighty stonework. The surviving rows follow the four main streets — Bridge Street, Watergate Street, Northgate Street, and Eastgate Street — that existed within the Roman fortress, and even the one exception, a now-vanished set of rows down Lower Bridge Street, lies along the Roman road from the fort to the Dee crossing — a road that would also have been lined with Roman buildings. (Complaints that shops in the rows were dark — Daniel Defoe was among the complainers — led to a theory that they were deliberately built to keep the wares of Chester's merchants from scrutiny in broad daylight, but this theory is not taken seriously.)

Chester's military history has left a practical legacy. Before mechanization, armies marched — whatever Napoleon might have said — on their own two feet, and this is a city designed as much for today's pedestrian, shopper, or tourist, as it was for yesterday's infantryman. The almost-complete circuit of the city walls, built on the north and east over the original Roman ramparts but extended to the south and west probably by Saxon engineers to take the city's defenses closer to the river, links with the Rows to form a network of walkways completely free from the traffic below. In addition, the four main city streets are now being turned into a pedestrian area, and though it will be some years before cars are finally banished, traffic levels within the walls are already low enough to give a feeling of the city before the coming of the automobile.

One reason Chester still possesses so many links with the past is that it has been in decline, in a sense, ever since the Middle Ages. Originally a major port, the silting-up of the Dee eventually killed the seaborne trade with Ireland and America. Remedies were tried, but in the end, shipping moved to Liverpool on the nearby River Mersey (at the time, an obscure fishing village), and with it went the industrialization and urbanization that would have obliterated the old Chester forever.

Instead, the city found a new role as a prosperous market town, a trading center between northwest England and North Wales, and a destination for 1.5 million tourists a year who are treated to the sight of as picturesque a town as any in old England. Boswell told Johnson it pleased his fancy more than any town he ever saw, and Nathaniel Hawthorne wrote of its "houses of very aged aspect, with steep, peaked gables."

Yet in spite of the abundance of black and white half-timbering, Chester's buildings are today largely the work of Victorian restorers and rebuilders. Fortunately, they were enthralled by the traditional Cheshire "magpie" decoration, and their revival designs give the city a unity of style that bridges the centuries. Among the Georgian brick and Victorian plaster are genuine ancient houses such as the Leche House and Bishop Lloyd's House dating from the sixteenth and early seventeenth centuries. Near them is God's Providence House — so called because its inhabitants survived the plague in centuries gone by — built in the same era but rebuilt, more richly decorated, 200 years later. It's entirely typical of Chester that the real and the reproduction are so intermingled and, sometimes, virtually indistinguishable.

CHESTER AT-A-GLANCE

 SEEING THE CITY: In a city as tightly packed as Chester, there's no single spot for a panoramic vista. The Grosvenor Bridge across the Dee, the longest single masonry arch in the world when it was completed in 1832, gives a good view down onto the racecourse and the river and across to the city skyline behind the western ramparts of the city walls. But for a closer view of the city's bustle, pick a spot on the Rows overlooking Chester Cross, where you can lean on the old balustrades and watch the world go by. Tuesdays through Saturdays from April to September, at noon and 3 o'clock, the town crier Michael Chittenden stands by the Cross in top hat, blue frockcoat, and yellow waistcoat and breeches — the 19th-century uniform of the city bellman — to bring the citizens up to date on the day's events. Another means of seeing the city is aboard a horse-drawn narrowboat that plies a section of the Shropshire Union Canal. Boats are docked at the Tower Wharf on Whipcord La. (phone: 390059) and run from Easter to September.

SPECIAL PLACES: Chester's compact layout, not to mention its tougher-than-average parking problems, make it an ideal city to explore on foot. Pubs, restaurants, museums, and shops are all within a few minutes' walk of one another. For the more energetic, the 2-mile circuit of the city walls (see *Extra Special*) is a useful connecting link to the cathedral and the river, where tree-lined walks and rows of benches make an ideal spot to end a walking tour.

Rows – Chester's above-pavement-level pedestrian shopping "streets" or galleries were built in the Middle Ages over the main roads of the original Roman fortress. Bridge Street and Eastgate Street Rows have the most cosmopolitan shops, Northgate Street Rows have survived, with gaps and changes of level, but Watergate Street Row has the strongest flavor of the past, with its antique and curio shops and magnificent old houses such as the Leche House. This was built in the mid-16th century as the town residence of the Leche family, so called because they were originally "Leeches," or surgeons, to King Edward III in the 1300s. Another magnificent house is Bishop Lloyd's House, built in the early 17th century for Dr. George Lloyd who was Bishop of Sodor and Man from 1600 to 1604 and Bishop of Chester from 1604 to 1615. The house, reconstructed in the 19th century, contains elaborate carvings (including the three-legged crest of the Isle of Man) and broad windows on the front, which were a local fashion and which turn up again in the Falcon Inn and the Bear and Billet Inn on Lower Bridge Street, where the original Rows have all but vanished. Leche House is now an antique shop; you must arrange a visit to Bishop Lloyd's House in advance.

Cathedral – Not originally a cathedral at all, this was founded in 1093 by Hugh Lupus, the Norman earl of Chester and alleged nephew of William the Conquerer, as the Benedictine Abbey of St. Werburgh. The abbey was broken up in 1540 when Henry VIII dissolved England's monasteries, and the following year the church became the cathedral of the new diocese of Chester. You can still see the monks' dining room, the choir stalls, the cloisters where they studied, and part of the shrine to St. Werburgh (an Anglo-Saxon abbess who died ca. AD 700), which attracted pilgrims from all over the north of England during the Middle Ages. Outside, the new bell tower (1975) is the first separate one to be added to an English cathedral in 500 years. St. Werburgh St.

Castle – At the city end of the Grosvenor Bridge, these colonnaded buildings don't look much like a castle today. The original Norman fortress on its superb defensive position overlooking the river and the Old Dee Bridge was completely transformed between 1788 and 1822 to house the Assize Courts. Behind the Georgian court building (now housing Chester's Crown Courts), the 750-year-old Agricola Tower is the only part of the medieval castle that survives. It can be viewed on request — ask at the Cheshire Military Museum — and the court buildings can be seen from the Public Gallery when the courts are in session. Castle St.

Abbey Square – The low arch of the 14th-century Abbey Gateway, where the Chester Miracle Plays were performed in the Middle Ages, is on the eastern side of Town Hall Square. Through the gateway is Abbey Square, a peaceful oasis of cobble-stones and Georgian houses, scarcely changed in 200 years. From the opposite corner of the square, Abbey Street leads to the Kaleyard Gateway, a gap in the city walls that once gave access to the abbot's private garden.

Old Dee Bridge – Until the opening of the Grosvenor Bridge 150 years ago, all traffic across the river had to use this narrow medieval bridge, built on the site of the Roman crossing more than seven centuries ago. It leads from the city to the old suburb of Handbridge, called Treboeth or "Burned Town" by the Welsh who burned it more than once during cross-border raids before they were subdued in the 13th century.

River Dee and the Groves – The name comes from that given by the Romans to both town and river — Deva. Below the city walls is the Groves, Chester's tree-lined riverside promenade, with seats used by fishermen, by audiences for the Sunday brass-band concerts, and by picnickers watching the boats. Here you can rent motorboats and rowing skiffs (but watch out for the weir just above the Old Dee Bridge) or you can leave the navigation to others and book a trip on one of the large passenger launches going upriver to Heronbridge and the tranquil charm of Eccleston village. You can come back by boat, by city bus from Eccleston, or by foot along the riverbank path through the Meadows on the Handbridge side.

■**EXTRA SPECIAL:** Chester's walls are nearly complete, which makes them unique in Britain, and a first-class way to explore the city. Start by climbing to the top of the Eastgate arch, crowned by the much-photographed clock commemorating Queen Victoria's Diamond Jubilee in 1897 and symbolizing Chester to exiles all over the world. Follow the wall southward and near the modern Newgate arch. You'll see the foundations of one of the corner towers of the original Roman fort. Across Vicar's Lane is the excavated half of the amphitheater the Romans used for gladiatorial contests as well as for drills and weapons training, while next to the Newgate, the old Wolfe or Wolfeld Gate gives an idea of just how narrow the Roman and medieval city gates must have been. Beyond the Newgate arch you come eventually to six short flights of steps — the Wishing Steps. According to local tradition, if you make a wish, run from the bottom to the top, then down and back again without drawing breath, your wish will come true!

As the walls swing west, there's a good view of the river and the old bridge. After crossing the Bridgegate arch, rebuilt and widened like the other city gates in the 18th century, you come to the only gap in the walls, beside County Hall. Look for the signposts on the other side of the hall and rejoin the ramparts as they turn north beside the Castle. You pass the racecourse on the Roodee — a recreation area first used for racing in 1540, making Chester Races the oldest in the country. Tours of the Roodee building are available by arrangement (phone: 0244-313126). You also pass the Watergate arch before reaching the old Bonewaldesthorne's Tower in the northwestern corner of the defenses and the Water Tower at the end of a spur wall. When the Water Tower was built in the 14th century, the river was so close it flowed through the archway.

The northern face of the walls is the most impressive of all, since the original ditch that ran full circuit was widened and deepened here in the 18th century as part of Chester's canal. You'll pass the Goblin Tower, nicknamed Pemberton's Parlour after a local rope-maker who sat in comfort to watch his workers toiling below, then, close to the Northgate, a bastion called Morgan's Mount, after the commander of a royalist battery placed here in the Civil War siege of 1645. If you look out over the parapet, you'll see the precarious Bridge of Sighs spanning the giddy drop to the canal. It was used to take prisoners from the notorious Northgate Jail across to the Chapel of St. John for a last service before their execution.

Finally, the northeastern corner of the walls is crowned by King Charles's Tower, built on the site of the original Roman tower. Here Charles I is supposed to have stood while his army was crushed on the field of Rowton Moor in

September 1645. He fled afterward, begging the city to hold out for 10 more days. When Chester finally surrendered to Parliament 5 months later, its citizens were starving and weak from disease, but its walls still held the enemy at bay.

SOURCES AND RESOURCES

 TOURIST INFORMATION: You'll find local guides, handouts, lists of events, maps, and a monthly *What's On* bulletin at the Tourist Information Centres at the Town Hall, Northgate St. (closed Sundays; phone: 40144, 49026 evenings and weekends); Chester Visitor Center, Vicar's La. (open daily; phone: 313126); and Grosvenor Precinct, 24 St. Michael's Square (closed Sundays; phone: 48612). Guided tours of the city leave from the Town Hall and the Visitor Centre regularly throughout the day; official guides wear a Blue Badge. If you want to spend an evening in an English home, you can arrange it by calling Mr. and Mrs. Richardson (phone: 678868), Mr. and Mrs. Brockley (phone: 380749), or Mr. and Mrs. Read (phone: 051-3396615), who organize this free, friendly service, any day from 5 to 7 PM. You can even hire a town crier, Roman Legionary, or Tudor lady to make a special greeting!

For advice on where to eat, the *Chester Restaurant Guide,* distributed at the Tourist Information Centre at Town Hall and Chester Visitor Centre, Vicars Lane, covers the city and surrounding area (for dinners as well as lunches) in great detail.

Local Coverage – Five newspapers report on town events: the *Chester Chronicle,* whose files include issues that give day-to-day coverage of the American Revolution, appears Fridays, the *Chester Observer* on Wednesdays, the *Chester Express* and the *Chester Mail* on Tuesdays, and the *Evening Leader* on weekdays. There is also some coverage in the *Liverpool Daily Post* (mornings) and the *Liverpool Echo* (evenings).

 GETTING AROUND: Bus – The Chester Corporation operates services inside the city area. Contact one of the city's information centers for details. Crosville Motor Services, with an enquiry office (phone: 381515) at the Delamere Street bus station, operates services outside the city.

Car Rental – For travel outside the city, it makes sense to rent a car. There are local offices of *Avis,* 128 Brook St. (phone: 311463), *Budget,* Lower Bridge St. (phone: 313431), and *Hertz,* Sealand Rd. (phone: 374705).

Taxi – Chester's complex parking arrangements make cabs a good idea in the city area. Cab stands are in front of the Town Hall and outside the Railway station on City Road. You can flag down the licensed black taxicabs anywhere you see them, or you can book cabs in advance from *Chester Radio Taxis* (phone: 372372).

 MUSEUMS: Chester has several museums devoted to preserving and presenting its long history. Among them are:

Boat Museum – Climb aboard the narrowboats on the Shropshire Union Canal to see demonstrations of 19th-century living and working conditions on the canal. Dockyard Rd., Ellesmere Port (phone: 051-355-5017).

Cheshire Military Museum – Three centuries of the Cheshire Regiment, including service in America and India, and the campaign under General Sir Charles James Napier who annexed the Indian province of Sind for the British in 1843 and announced his success with the terse Latin *Peccavi,* meaning "I have sinned." Chester Castle.

Chester Heritage Centre – A slide show on the history of Chester, before and after photographs of the restoration of its buildings, and a changing exhibition on the city's heritage. St. Michael's Church, Bridge St. Row (phone: 317948).

Chester Visitor Centre – Video presentations of the city's 2,000-year history and a lifesize reconstruction of an 1850s street scene, replete with sounds and smells, old shop and pub fronts transported from the Rows, a Brass Rubbing center, and a coffee and lunch bar in an old oak-beamed school. Vicars La. (phone: 318916).

Grosvenor Museum – The main museum is named after Hugh Lupus Grosvenor, first duke of Westminster, who donated part of the site on which the museum was built in the 1880s. It contains many relics of Chester's Roman past, natural history exhibits, paintings, and silver. Grosvenor St. (phone: 21616).

King Charles's Tower – Models and relics of Civil War Chester. City Walls.

Toy Museum – A collection of fascinating antique playthings. Bridge St. Row (phone: 316251).

 SHOPPING: Most of the best shops are along the elevated walkways of the Rows and the arcades leading off them, above the traffic and covered from the weather. One of the best is Godstall Lane (off Eastgate Row), a narrow alley with women's clothing shops, a *Pennine Woolskin* shop, and *Roberts' Specialty Tea and Coffee Shop,* which serves samples at outside tables. Antiques shops and silversmiths (see *Sins*) are especially good, as are the clothes shops, from expensive fashion stores to an ever-changing but constantly replaced selection of ultracheap boutiques.

Adams Antiques – Unusual cabinets, chandeliers, and board games for discerning collectors. 65 Watergate Row (phone: 319421).

Laura Ashley – Victorian-style dresses, children's clothes, wallpaper, and fabrics. Watergate Row (phone: 316403).

Blakes – Old family bakehouse, virtually unchanged since Victorian days. Shop early in the day, as the delicious homemade bread and misshapen but tasty cakes and pies tend to sell out by midafternoon. Watergate St. Row (phone: 25933).

Boodles and Dunham – One of the oldest jewelers in town. 52 Eastgate St., next door to the *Grosvenor* hotel (phone: 26666).

Brown's of Chester – The city's premier department store, founded in the reign of the same George III who presided over the loss of the American colonies. It's now owned by Debenham's store chain, but much of the old style still survives. Particularly good for women's clothes and perfumes. Eastgate St. (phone: 20001).

Duttons – A health food shop and, a bit farther down the road, a wine store. Godstall La., off Eastgate St. opposite Brown's (phone: 21488).

Flying Machine – General gift shop. Basement "Cookshop" is bolstered by Roman pillars, which formed part of the Principia (headquarters) of the Fortress of Deva. The scale of the original building is illustrated by a lifesize mural. 21-23 Northgate (phone: 316955).

Golfers World – Equipment and British woolens for golfers. 15 Watergate Row (phone: 318497).

Indesign – Designers of rustic, knobby wooden chairs and chests that look as though they're still growing. Some textiles and ceramics, too. 38 Watergate St. (phone: 29459).

William Jones – Specialty foods — coffee, Chinese and Indian teas, chocolates, sausages and pies, cheeses, bacon. In Owen Owen's Bridge St. store (phone: 21555).

Three Kings Studios – Pottery plus other work from more than 70 local artists and craftsmen. Lower Bridge St. (phone: 317717).

Tudor Antiques – A tiny shop packed with dollhouses, dolls, their clothes, and (increasingly hard to find) teddy bears. Lower Bridge St. (no phone).

SPECIAL EVENTS: There's top-class flat racing at the *Chester Races* three times a year: the 3-day Chester Cup meeting the first week of May, 2 days in mid-July, and in late August or early September. *Beating Retreat,* a military ceremonial with a display of massed bands, takes place on the Castle grounds in late May. The nearby village of Kelsall stages a *Folk Festival* featuring concerts and Morris dancing on the late May bank holiday. The *Chester Summer Music Festival,* in mid-July, is a week's worth of orchestral concerts, recitals, and choral works.

 SPORTS: Chester's multisport leisure center, *Northgate Arena,* opened in 1977. It has squash courts, badminton courts, and a swimming pool with palm trees, rocks, children's paddling area, and training pool. Corner of Victoria Rd. and St. Oswalds Way (phone: 380444).

Cricket – For those who want to experience the mysteries of the British national game for themselves, *Chester Boughton Hall Cricket Club* has home matches every Saturday afternoon and some Sundays from May to late September at the Filkins Lane ground.

Golf – There are clubs for hire at the 9-hole municipal golf course at Westminster Park (phone: 673071). Visitors with a temporary membership also have access to the 18-hole courses at the *Chester Golf Club,* Curzon Park (phone: 677760); the suburban *Upton-by-Chester Golf Club* (phone: 381183) and *Vicars Cross Golf Club* (phone: 35174); and the *Eaton Golf Club* at Eccleston (phone: 680474).

Horseback Riding – Both experienced riders and novices can try *Waverton Riding and Livery Centre* (phone: 335202).

 THEATER: Local repertory productions and some touring productions take place in the *Gateway Theatre,* Hamilton Pl. (phone: 40393), and in the *Clwyd Theatre* at Mold, 12 miles away (phone: 95-55114). Liverpool's wider choice of theaters is only 45 minutes away by car.

 MUSIC: Occasional concerts are to be heard in the Town Hall, the cathedral, the *Gateway Theatre* (see above), or at the *Clwyd Theatre* in Mold (phone: 95-55114). The local *Chester Symphony Orchestra* or visiting artists and ensembles do the honors. Much more happens in summer when the week-long Chester Summer Music Festival (July) is devoted to it.

 NIGHTCLUBS AND NIGHTLIFE: *High Society,* Love St. (phone: 43448), is predominantly a disco with occasional live music, as are *Caverns,* 39-41 Watergate St. (phone: 20619); *Blimpers,* City Rd. (phone: 314794); *Rendezvous,* Northgate St. (phone: 27141); and *Cinderella Rockerfella,* 144 Foregate St. (phone: 314981). For a more refined atmosphere, the *Plantation Inn* hotel, Liverpool Rd. (phone: 374100), has dinner and dancing every evening from 7:30 PM, and the *Rowton Hall* hotel, Whitchurch Rd. (phone: 335262), has a dinner dance every Saturday from 8 PM. In the city, there are dinner dances on Saturday nights at the *Chester Grosvenor* hotel, Eastgate St. (phone: 24024), and the *Plantation* hotel, Liverpool Rd., (phone: 274100). For folk music buffs, there's a folk evening every Monday at 8:30 PM in the *Bear and Billet,* Lower Bridge St. (phone: 21272) and at 8 PM every Friday in the *Bull and Stirrup,* Upper Northgate St. (phone: 371167). There is live cabaret at the *Regency* hotel, 6 miles from the city center at South Wirral (phone: 051-339-8101), and the *Merseyview Country Club* (phone: 0928-33108).

 SINS: If avarice means coveting beautiful things from the past or present, then this is the place to indulge that foible. For centuries, Chester's silversmiths were so famous that the city had its own Assay Office off Watergate Street where the Chester hallmark was stamped on their handiwork. Today you can buy fine gold, silver, and jewelry from specialists like *Boodle and Dunthorne,* by the Grosvenor Hotel on Eastgate St. (phone: 26666); from *Lowe's,* 11 Bridge St. Row (phone: 25850); or from *Brown's,* 2 Eastgate Row (phone: 24357). For antiques in the wider sense, try the shops down Watergate Row. Among them, *Erica and Hugo Harper* at #27 (phone: 23004), *Wellesley Wilson* at #29 (phone: 23836), and *Chester Antiques* at #49 (phone: 311768) sell anything from a silver spoon to a full dinner service, from a delicate miniature to something as substantial as a Georgian table or a Welsh dresser.

BEST IN TOWN

CHECKING IN: Hotels in Chester fall into three categories: the old and expensive, the new and moderately expensive, and the small and inexpensive. For the top-of-the-range hotels in the city center, expect to pay up to $150 for a double room with bath. This includes breakfast, which rates as a meal in its own right. Out-of-town hotels and motels charge about $150 for a double, but with breakfast extra. Best values are found at the smaller hotels which charge about $40 to $70 per night for a double.

Chester Grosvenor – Built between 1863 and 1866, this has a reputation as Chester's best hotel, an old and luxurious establishment with superb service, an excellent restaurant, and a pianist in the tea lounge. All 108 rooms have private bath. Access to nearby health club. Eastgate St. (phone: 24024). Expensive.

Blossoms – Built in the 16th century, with later face lifting outside, modernized inside, this remains a hotel in the traditional manner — sweeping staircases, thick carpeting, and 72 comfortable rooms, all with private bath. St. John St. (phone: 23186). Expensive to moderate.

Queen – Built to serve the adjacent railway station, this is a classic Victorian hotel, though it has been brought well into the 20th century. All its 90 rooms have private baths. City Rd. (phone: 28341). Expensive to moderate.

Abbots Well – This converted country house is an elegant hotel-motel on the southern edge of the city. It has a good restaurant and 127 rooms, all with private bath. Whitchurch Rd. (phone: 332121). Moderate.

City Walls and **Cromwell Court** – An elegant Georgian house next to the walls on the western side of the city. In addition to 17 rooms (all with bath), 10 apartments have been added next door, along with a restaurant, sauna, and gym. City Walls Rd. (phone: 313416). Moderate to inexpensive.

Ye Olde King's Head – One of the city's oldest inns (it dates from the 16th century) with a lovely timbered dining room. There are only 10 rooms, none with private bath. 48 Lower Bridge St. (phone: 24855). Moderate to inexpensive.

Cavendish – This is actually a beautifully restored and elegantly furnished Edwardian house with 20 rooms, set in its own landscaped gardens on the edge of town. There is tennis, croquet, boating, fishing, and golf near at hand. 42-44 Hough Green (phone: 675100). Inexpensive.

Pied Bull – Passengers used to board the stage for London at this old coaching inn. It's a cheerful pub with 8 rooms. Northgate St. (phone: 25829). Inexpensive.

EATING OUT: Chester's choice of restaurants is surprisingly good. You could eat in a different place every night for a month and still not cover the whole list. Generally, prices are lower than in larger cities: $60 for two, including wine, is the absolute top. Most restaurants will set you back less than $40, and by choosing carefully you can get away with a meal for two for $25 or less. Some of the foreign restaurants — Swiss, French, Italian, Greek, Mexican — offer a lot for the money, and the best value of all must be the hot and substantial Indian curries and the more exotic Chinese specialties.

Craxton Wood – A delicious meal in the French restaurant of this country house hotel might consist of *bûchette de saumon, truite en papillote,* fresh vegetables, and a Black Forest tart. (There are also 13 guest rooms and a suite with lots of antique furnishings.) Closed Sundays, all bank holidays, the last 2 weeks in August, and for 1 week at Christmas. Puddington, 5 miles north of the city on the main Parkgate Rd. (A540) (phone: 051-3394717). Expensive.

Rossett Hall – This is a luxury restaurant in a Georgian country house, with first-class cooking and top-quality local cheeses. Closed Sunday evenings. Follow the A483 road south 5 miles to the village of Rossett, then look for Rossett Hall behind the long wall on the right-hand side of the road in the center of the village. Wrexham Rd., Rossett (phone: 570867). Expensive.

Chester Grosvenor – The main hotel dining room serves classic French cooking (trout, veal, lamb) and does it impeccably. Closed December 24–26. Down in *Harvey's,* there are other hot and cold dishes (closed Sundays). Eastgate St. (phone: 24024). Expensive in the main restaurant, moderate in the restaurant.

Boat Inn – Every inch of the 15-mile drive to this country pub and restaurant is worth it. The setting above the beautiful upstream reaches of the Dee is incomparable. Pheasant and fresh Dee salmon are on the menu in season, along with vintage clarets and Burgundies. Follow A483 to Wrexham (12 miles south), then take A539 and look for the sign for Erbistock. Erbistock, Clwyd (phone: 0978-780143). Expensive to moderate.

Pippa's – The menu is French bistro, the setting stylish, and the resident jazz pianist provides excellent entertainment. Closed Sundays. 58 Watergate St. (phone: 313721). Expensive to moderate.

Blue Bell – In the city's oldest medieval inn, this restaurant offers a traditional menu of English fare such as halibut with grapes or orange and lemon pork, with not a chip to be seen. Afternoon tea available. Closed Sundays. 65 Northgate St. (phone: 317758). Moderate.

Abbey Green – Organically grown vegetables and quiches made the eggs of free-range chickens are on the inventive vegetarian menu at this Victorian house. Aperitifs and coffee are served in the "withdrawing" room. 2 Abbey Green, Northgate St. (phone: 313251). Moderate to inexpensive.

Jade Cantonese – Most Chinese restaurants in Britain are Cantonese (via Hong Kong), but this is the only one in Chester to offer a full Cantonese menu. Behind its rather garish façade are delicious, subtle flavors, crisp vegetables, and a genuine mixture of Chinese diners among the clientele. Closed Sundays. 43 Watergate St. Row (phone: 21455). Moderate to inexpensive.

Paris Brioche – A French patisserie serving fresh goods at breakfast. Or take out their delicious cakes, sandwiches, or French filled rolls. Closed Sundays. 39 Bridge St. (phone: 312594). Moderate to inexpensive.

Watergate Wine Bar – Below street level in an oak-filled, 12th-century crypt, this eatery is popular for its atmosphere and its extraordinary menu, featuring curried parsnip soup, pears with stilton mousse and tarragon, and pheasant with wine and grapes. Champagne brunch on Sundays. Watergate St. (phone: 20515). Moderate to inexpensive.

Aphrodite's – Here you can dine in the same room as Charles I, though not from the same menu. This Greek restaurant is in the restored Gamul House, which was the home of Sir Francis Gamul, mayor of Chester and host to the king during the mid-17th-century Civil War siege. Greek specialties such as dolmades and moussaka and Greek and Cypriot wines are served in the main restaurant. Lower prices prevail in the street-level taverna. Closed Sundays. Gamul House, Lower Bridge St. (phone: 319811). Inexpensive.

Great American Disaster – As close as you're likely to get to a genuine hamburger and definitely the only place in Chester for anything approaching American cooking. Other specialties are steak and chicken, french fries (chips), baked potatoes, salads, apple pie, American beer, coffee, Coke. 14 Lower Bridge St. (phone: 318973). Inexpensive.

Sidoli's – Spread over two floors, this restaurant serves homemade pasta and other Italian dishes, including pizza. The ice cream is also homemade. Closed Sundays. 25 Northgate St. (phone 44068). Inexpensive.

60's – Southern style chicken and Mexican burritos are served in a dark, cocktail-bar ambience. Music Hall Passage (phone: 318515). Inexpensive.

SHARING A PINT: Pubs are the center of Chester life. In the old days they were simply places to drink and chat, but now most of them serve food, too, and the best of them give even good restaurants a run for their money. The *Boat House,* at the upstream end of the Groves next to the school and club boathouses, used to be a real rowing man's pub, with faded photographs of long-gone oarsmen and autographed oarblades on the wall. Now a noisy, cheerful, busy River Bar has been added, full of young people and music, but with an unmatchable view of the Dee. The *Bear and Billet* on Lower Bridge St. is a beautiful 17th-century half-timbered house turned into a popular and friendly pub offering food as well as drinks. It once belonged to the earls of Shrewsbury who enjoyed the profits from the tolls of the adjacent Bridgegate. (Before going in, look up: Payment was often in kind, hence the doors high in the gable where a hoist was used to lift goods to and from the roof storehouse.) *Duke's,* set in modern surroundings in Mercia Sq., is one of the new generation of wine bars. It serves wine by the glass, draught and bottled beers, plus a hot dish-of-the-day. The *Albion Inn,* close to the walls on Park St., is just the opposite, a real, old-fashioned, cozy, back-street Chester pub with draught beer from the wood and the traditional steak and kidney pie, black pudding and mushy peas, bread and cheese, and treacle tart. The *Town Crier,* opposite the railway station on City Rd., is a newly renovated establishment that serves traditional ales as well as meals. Other drinking haunts favored by locals include the *Pied Bull* on Northgate St., *Custom House Inn* on Watergate St., and *Boot Inn* on Eastgate St.

CORK

The Irish Republic's second city is a bustling, zesty, highly individual place, quite different from Dublin in appearance and atmosphere. Though it lacks the capital's Georgian uniformity, it makes up for the defect in visual variety, mixing the romance of mock-Gothic outlines with the moderation and proportion of the classical style. Dublin is flat and Cork is up and down on hills; Dublin is a somber tone, Cork variegated, light and dark, as its local stones. And while Dublin, as capital, was burdened with an alien tradition of subservience, Cork cultivated a spirit of defiance that earned it the nickname Rebel Cork. It is a busy, assertive, self-made place where Jack is as good as his master and frequently tells him so.

The making of Cork was the River Lee, which flows not only through, but in and around, the city as it approaches its great estuary. In its valley it formed a great marsh with islands that became, as in Venice, the foundation of the town and the source of its Gaelic name, Corcaigh, meaning "a marshy place." The first actual settlement was, as might be expected, a little Gaelic monastery founded in the sixth century by an obscure but still beloved abbot-bishop named Barra of the Fair Hair, or Finbar. The monastery, on a hill south of the river where the present St. Finbarre's Cathedral stands, grew in power and it was probably its reputation for wealth that enticed the Vikings in their longboats up the estuary and through the sinuous marsh. They first founded a trading post here in the eighth century and within 50 years they had fortified one of the islands to become the right and tight little city of Cork.

In time, the Vikings became subjects of the Gaelic prince of the area, MacCarthy Mor, but they nevertheless maintained a degree of independence in their island city under their own *jarl,* or ruler, until the Norman invasion forced them to switch allegiance. In the turbulent centuries that followed, the inhabitants of Cork city acquired a reputation for independent-mindedness even to rebellion. King John (as prince) gave them a charter in 1185, they were back under the MacCarthys by 1195, they were given a more prestigious charter by the king in 1199, and another new one in 1241, but in 1495 they nearly seized the crown itself when they received the pretender to the throne, Perkin Warbeck, and escorted him to England to proclaim him king of England and lord of Ireland.

While Dublin's monuments are castle and parliament house and the homes of the great nobles, Cork within its island walls had shops and warehouses and banks. It was essentially a trading town and still is. In the eighteenth century, it became the great supply port for the American colonies, sending out beef, bacon, and butter, and during the Napoleonic Wars it was the larder of the British army and navy. Gradually, rows of houses began to rise along the winding creeks between the islands and at last Cork expanded beyond its walls and up the sides of the river valley.

As the merchants made money, they developed an appreciation of civilized amenities. Cork silver and glass became tasteful and elegant. A Cork school of painters developed; the neoclassical subjects of James Barry and Robert Fagan, the townscapes of Nathaniel Grogan, and the historical panoramas of Samuel Forde and Daniel Maclise can be admired in the Crawford Municipal Art Gallery. Talk has always been a strong art form in Cork; the accent is singsong and musical, but it conceals a sharp verbal wit used to deadly effect on native and visitor. The wordsmiths met in drinking clubs and debating societies and produced a circle of essayists and poets including William Maginn, a Johnsonian schoolmaster and satirist, and Francis Sylvester O'Mahony ("Father Prout"), a mocking ex-priest, both of whom scored in the literary reviews when they emigrated to London, and a gentle lyric poet, J. J. Callanan, who died young in Lisbon.

The nineteenth century also produced some distinguished architecture in Cork. First the brothers Pain, pupils of John Nash, came from London and built bridges, jails, a courthouse, some lovely town houses with gentle Regency bowfronts, and the delightful Gothic fantasy, Blackrock Castle, at the end of the Marina walk. They were succeeded by the Deane family, builders of churches, banks, and Cork's University College. From their firm, in turn, emerged Benjamin Woodward, a genius of the neo-Gothic whose best work is in Dublin and Oxford.

Cork in the twentieth century is chronicled in the short stories of Seán O'Faoláin and Frank O'Connor, both natives. It is still a workaday city; shops, warehouses, and factories are part of its fabric. But it is also a good talking town, a great eating-out town, a sports-mad town. During the War of Independence (1919–21) it was a wellspring of nationalistic fervor, losing two mayors and many public buildings to the cause. Since then, it has withstood the worst assaults of modernization, though its cramped island site has given it some real traffic problems, which the city's 136,000 inhabitants manage to live with in their own spirited way. They are a most competent people whose response to good fortune and bad is a mocking laugh and a musical burst of anecdote.

CORK AT-A-GLANCE

 SEEING THE CITY: The north slope of the river valley is dominated by the tower of St. Anne's Church, better known simply as Shandon steeple. Cross the river and climb the tower to an outside balcony. The city will be at your feet, the flat marsh area with its busy streets surrounded by what Edmund Spenser called "The spreading Lee, that like an island fayre / Encloseth Corke with his divided floode." The Lee here forms a north channel and a south channel, and between them is the compact central island known as the "flat of the city." Patrick Street, or St. Patrick Street, which is the main artery crossing the island, was itself once an open river channel, as were the Grand Parade and the South Mall. In the 18th century you would still have seen ships afloat in these channels, but by 1800 the waterways had been turned into thoroughfares for the traffic on foot, hoof, and wheel that crowded into the city's business district. Quieter, more reflective parts of Cork are the slopes that rise to the south and north of the central island. The Gothic towers of St. Finbarre's Cathedral and the graceful Gothic quadrangles of the university are on the far slope, and churches, convents, and hospitals are to the right and left beneath you on the near slope.

SPECIAL PLACES: The "flat of the city" is the hub of activity in Cork, and a walk along Patrick Street (affectionately called "Pana" by residents, with a dying fall on the *a*) and its subsidiary arteries is as traditional an activity as the European evening promenade. Going east to west, it is properly done on the left path, in order to have a view of the better-preserved right side of the street with its delicately bowfronted 18th-century houses (the left side had to be replaced when British troops burned the street in 1920). Patrick Street leads to the Grand Parade, which runs straight to the south channel of the river and has some traditional weather-slated bowfronts remaining from the 18th century. At the south channel, the Grand Parade meets the South Mall, now the financial district. Here, a few characteristic merchants' houses remain from the days when the South Mall was still an open waterway. Doors at street or water level open onto basement storerooms so that boats could be unloaded easily, and high outside steps lead up to the merchants' living quarters above their merchandise. Walking is the best way to see the flat of the city, and when you are ready to cross to the north or south banks, you'll find numerous bridges spanning the still-flowing channels.

FLAT OF THE CITY

Father Matthew Statue – This memorial to Father Theobald Matthew, the "apostle of temperance," is the work of the celebrated 19th-century Irish sculptor John Henry Foley, who also created the monument to Daniel O'Connell in Dublin and was one of several artists responsible for the Albert Memorial in London. Father Matthew, a superior of the Capuchin Order in Cork, was known not only for his crusade in the cause of temperance but also for his work among the poor, especially during the mid-19th-century famines. The statue is a central point of reference in Cork City. Patrick St. at Patrick Bridge.

Crawford Municipal Art Gallery – The gallery is housed in a red brick building put up in the early 18th century as the city's Custom House. It contains a select collection of works by painters of the 20th-century Irish School: Orpen, Lavery, and Yeats; a good representation by artists of the earlier Cork School: Barry, Grogan, Forde, and Maclise; and some fine examples of Cork silver and glass. Open weekdays from 9:30 AM to 5:30 PM, Sundays from 9 AM to 1 PM. Emmet Pl.

Church of Saints Peter and Paul – Opened in 1868, this excellent Gothic Revival church by E. W. Pugin is typical of Cork in its casing of red sandstone and its dressing of white limestone. Off Paul St.

Coal Quay Market – This outdoor flea market is open for business daily (except Sundays), not on the quays, but on a street running from the Grand Parade to Coal Quay. No longer colorful and not exactly sweet-smelling, it takes place in front of a market building with good classical frontage, now privately owned. Corn Market St.

English Market – Fruit, vegetables, fish, and meat — including local specialties such as drisheen (blood pudding or blood sausage) and tripe — are displayed and sold in a stylish late-18th-century market arcade under a cast-iron and glass roof. When the market is in full swing, daily except Sundays, the scene is animated and the stallholders are full of Cork esprit and chat. Entrances off Patrick St., Princes St., and Grand Parade.

Court House – The Pain brothers, James and George Richard, designed this stately building with Corinthian porticoes in 1835. Sir Walter Scott, among others, admired it. Washington St.

South and North Main Streets – When Cork was still enclosed by walls, its main gates were at the South Gate Bridge and the North Gate Bridge. Between the two ran the spine of the medieval city, worth walking today for its atmosphere redolent of food and housewares shops. The much-altered 18th-century Protestant Christ Church, South Main St., is on the site of a medieval parish church that dated from the Normans and was probably the church in which Edmund Spenser married Elizabeth Boyle, his Irish bride, in the 16th century. Another of Cork's medieval parish churches (there were two of them) was off North Main Street, in the vicinity of which there are also many lanes — such as Portney's Lane — that once housed merchants and craftsmen.

Mercy Hospital – When it was built in the 18th century, this was the Mansion House of the mayor of Cork. The handsome building with its Italianate front is the work of the Sardinian architect Davis Ducart; the good stucco ceiling inside is by Patrick Osborne of Waterford. The building is now a hospital, but it's open to visitors during normal business hours. Henry St.

Holy Trinity Church – The church of the Capuchin friars, also known as the Father Matthew Memorial Church, is from the 1830s. Internally, it is a charming Regency Gothic creation by George R. Pain. The lantern spire by Coakley, which complements it externally, is a graceful later addition enhanced by the riverside setting. Father Matthew Quay.

NORTH BANK

St. Patrick's Bridge – This mid-19th-century bridge is a very satisfactory classical construction in white limestone. The view from it — upriver over the city's churches, convents, and other institutions, and downriver to the ships — is quintessential Cork. Patrick's Hill, a precipitous street housing fashionable doctors, leads up the north bank from the bridge and it's almost worth the climb for another view over the city. End of Patrick St.

St. Anne's Church, Shandon – The quaint pepper-box tower of this Protestant church, built from 1722 to 1726, is the symbol of Cork. Shandon steeple rises in square tiers to its cupola and weather vane crowned by a golden fish and, as in the old jingle — "Red and white is Shandon steeple / Party coloured like the people" — it has two red sides and two white sides, a combination that is a signature of many Cork buildings. From the top of the steeple, look out over the river valley and note the source of the color scheme: one slope of red sandstone and an opposite one of silvery white limestone. The Shandon churchyard is the last resting place of Francis S. O'Mahony, a fitting spot because it was he, under the pen name Father Prout, who wrote "The Bells of Shandon," a song that made both bells and church famous. Open from 9:30 AM to 6 PM in summer, from 10:30 AM to 4:30 PM the rest of the year. Church St.

St. Mary's Dominican Church – Kearns Deane, a member of the very prominent family of Cork architects responsible for several of the city's classical buildings, designed this church with the solid portico in 1832. Inside, there is a tiny carved ivory madonna of 14th-century Flemish origin. Pope's Quay.

St. Patrick's Church – A flurry of construction in the classical style took place in early-19th-century Cork. Another good example is this church by George R. Pain (1836) at the foot of the handsome hillside suburbs of Tivoli and Montenotte. The elegant lantern is modeled on the Temple of the Winds in Athens. Lower Glanmire Rd.

SOUTH BANK

Red Abbey – Nothing is left of the abbey of the Canons of St. Augustine except the tower of its church. It is the solitary relic of the early Cork monasteries and, indeed, of medieval Cork. When the duke of Marlborough besieged the city in 1690, he put a cannon on the tower and directed his fire at the city walls across the south channel of the Lee. Before leaving the spot, walk around the corner to Dunbar Street for a look at St. Finbar's South, known also as the South Chapel, an unusually early (1766) Catholic church (there are very few 18th-century Catholic churches in Ireland) with an altarpiece by John Hogan, one of the most important Irish sculptors of the last century. Off Mary St.

Elizabeth Fort – The massive curtain walls are what is left of a 17th-century fort that once housed the Cork garrison. Today, a modern police station stands incongruously within the walls. Off Barrack St.

St. Finbarre's Cathedral – Though somewhat foreshortened on its confined site — where the city's patron saint chose to put his monastery in the 6th century — this Protestant cathedral is considered to be a brilliant essay in French Gothic by William Burges, an English architect who also designed Cardiff Castle and the quadrangle of Yale University. It was built between 1867 and 1879 to replace an earlier church, which itself replaced a medieval church damaged in the siege of 1690. (Only a cannonball remains of that one, found 40 feet above the ground in the tower.) Burges's three spires are most successful and his interior detail is rich and inventive. Bishop St.

University College – The main quadrangle is a gem of 19th-century collegiate architecture (reminiscent of the colleges at Oxford) by Thomas Deane and his partner, Benjamin Woodward. Later additions do not quite maintain the initial high standard, but the Honan Chapel on the grounds, architect James J. McMullen's 1915 revival of 12th-century Irish-Romanesque style, has interesting exterior details and is stuffed with treasure inside: stained-glass windows, embroideries, tabernacle enamels, and a joyous mosaic floor. The chapel usually closes during school holidays. Western Rd.

■ **EXTRA SPECIAL:** *Fota Island* is the home of the ornamental estate that belonged to the Smith-Berry family, once earls of Barrymore, and is now owned by University College Cork. Its centerpiece, Fota House, was built in the 1820s by Sir Richard Morrison, who created some of Ireland's finest Neoclassical interiors, and it stands today as a splendid example of Regency architecture. The rooms are all fully furnished with Irish pieces from the 18th and 19th centuries and fitted with rich period wallpapers and curtains. Most notable, however, are the Irish landscape paintings, dating from the 1750s to the 1870s and constituting the most comprehensive private collection of its kind. On the grounds of the estate are an arboretum, a bee garden, and a wildlife park covering 70 acres of parkland, woods, and lagoons. Fota House is open April through September, Mondays to Saturdays from 11 AM to 6 PM, Sundays from 2 to 6 PM; the rest of the year, Sundays and holidays only from 2 to 6 PM. Fota Island is on the main road to Cobh, about 16 miles southeast of Cork in Carrigtwohill (phone: 021-812555).

SOURCES AND RESOURCES

TOURIST INFORMATION: The Cork-Kerry tourism office, Grand Parade (phone: 273251), offers information, guidebooks, maps, and leaflets. You can purchase two helpful booklets here, *The Cork Guide* (60p) and the excellent *Tourist Trail* (50p), a walking guide to Cork. For books and pamphlets on the city's history and background, visit Liam Ruiseal's bookshop around the corner at 49–50 Oliver Plunkett St.

Local Coverage – The *Cork Examiner* is the one they call "de payper." It's the morning daily, full of local color. The *Evening Echo,* essential for entertainment information, comes out every evening, and the *Cork Weekly Examiner,* a potpourri of current happenings, appears every Tuesday.

GETTING AROUND: In the "flat of the city," walking is easier and faster than going by bus or car because of congested traffic, restricted parking, and one-way circuits. Car drivers should observe the local disc parking system — it works. Books of 10 disc tickets cost IR£2 in tobacco and newspaper shops and garages. In addition, Cork has two new multi-story parking garages, both situated along the banks of the River Lee downtown — one at Lavitts Quay and the other at Merchants Quay. Both are open Monday through Saturday (20p per hour).

Bus and Train – A good city bus service radiates from the Father Matthew Statue. County buses, long-distance buses, and day tours leave from the Bus Station in Parnell Pl., a block east of the statue. CIE operates summer bus tours of the city as well as excurions to Killarney, Bantry Bay, Limerick, and Tipperary (phone: 503399, ext. 318). Trains leave from Kent Station, Lower Glanmire Rd., on the northern bank of the Lee. For bus and train information by phone, call 504422.

Car Rental – All major international and national firms are represented. Consult the local Yellow Pages.

River Cruises – From mid-May to mid-August, there are afternoon and evening cruises around Cork Harbor and excursions to Fota Island. Schedules and rates are available from the tourist office or Marine Transport, Cobh (phone: 811485).

Taxi – Cab ranks are at the stations and in the middle of Patrick St., opposite the Savoy Centre and at most hotels. Otherwise, you can call one from your hotel (phone: 231568, 502211, 961311, or 502680).

Walking Tours – During July and August, free guided walking tours depart Tuesday and Thursday evenings from the tourist office on Grand Parade (phone: 966833). Daytime tours are conducted from mid-June to mid-September, Mondays and Fridays at 3 PM and Saturdays at 11 AM (phone: 885405 or 273251). More extensive tours are organized by Discover Cork Guided Tours, "Belmont," Douglas Rd. (phone: 293873).

MUSEUMS: Paintings and sculpture by Irish artists and others are in the *Crawford Municipal Art Gallery* (see *Special Places*). The *Cork Public Museum,* Fitzgerald Park, contains interesting displays of Cork history from the earliest times to the present, and the surrounding park has a pleasant riverside walk and sculptures by Seamus Murphy, a well-known Cork stone carver who became a sculptor. The museum is closed Saturday afternoons and Sundays; the park is open daily (contact the tourist office for the exact hours, which vary with the season). Off Mardyke Rd., a promenade parallel to Western Rd.

SHOPPING: As to be expected of the Republic's second largest metropolitan area, Cork is an excellent shopping center, offering a variety of goods. Major department stores are on Patrick Street; small shops and boutiques abound on Princes and Oliver Plunkett streets. And if you're in town on a Thursday, Friday, or Saturday, be sure to stop at the *Cork Antique Market,* 4 Tuckey St. Some of the more rewarding places to stop off during the course of a spree are the following:

Barry's Tea – A provision shop par excellence, stocking not only exquisite teas and area cheeses but also the delightful Hadji Bey Turkish Delight, a candy manufactured in Cork, and a wide selection of vintage wines. 7 Princes St. (phone: 270995).

Blarney Woolen Mills – One of the country's busiest craft emporia, known for fine knits produced on the premises. Also stocks crystal, china, and other gift items. Open daily. Blarney. (phone: 85280).

Cash's Department Store – Cork's equivalent of Dublin's *Switzer's* sells a general range of linens, woolens, tweeds, glassware, and other goods. 18 Patrick St. (phone: 964411).

Cork Arts Society Gallery – Frequent exhibitions by local artists. Closed Sundays and Mondays. 16 Lavitt's Quay (phone: 505749).

Crafts of Ireland – Housed in a former wine cellar, this "all Irish" collection includes batik, candles, glass, graphics, leatherwork, pottery, toys, weaving, wood-turning, and wrought-iron work. 65 Patrick St. (phone: 275864).

Fitzgerald – Established in 1860, this shop features Burberry coats and Bally shoes at half US prices as well as Irish tweeds and cashmere knitwear. 24 Patrick St. (phone: 270095).

House of Donegal – The best source for classic trench coats and custom rainwear, all fashioned on the premises with linings of Donegal tweed or silk. Tweed suits, coats, jackets, tartans, and capes are also made to order. 6–8 Paul St. (phone: 272447 or 502387).

Irish Home Crafts – A tiny place chock full of Irish crochet, tweeds, handknits, pottery, art, jewelry, and patchwork. 7 Marlborough St. (phone: 273379).

Ireland Today Irish Glass Shop – A variety of local glassware, plus the chance to see an authentic craftsman at work. 78 Oliver Plunkett St. (phone: 273294).

Stephen Pearce – Housed in a former tea warehouse and candy factory (original cogs and wheels are in evidence), this modern bi-level shop sells the pottery-work of its namesake, as well as a range of crafts of more than 50 other Irish artisans. Paul St. (phone: 272324).

Presents – One of the city's better antiques shops as well as a fine source of sheepskin rugs and handmade craftwork. 75 Oliver Plunkett St. (phone: 275549).

Queen's Old Castle – A traditional department store elegantly converted to a varied shopping mall that includes cafés for the weary. Grand Parade.

Savoy Centre – Also a shopping mall, this one splendidly set in the Art Deco surroundings of a former cinema. Patrick St.

 SPECIAL EVENTS: Cork is a festive town. In April it hosts the *Country Music Festival;* then in early May comes the *International Choral and Folk Dance Festival,* with colorful and tuneful choirs and lively dancers competing from all over the world. Its well-established *Film Festival* of short and feature-length films takes place in September or October, and in late October the town is hopping and bopping with the *Jazz Festival.* For information, contact the tourist office on Grand Parade.

 SPORTS: Golf – Several hospitable golf courses surround the city and welcome visitors daily or every weekday. The 18-hole *Cork Golf Club* is at Little Island (phone: 353263), about 6.5 miles from the center. Others to try are the *Douglas Golf Club* (phone: 291086), about 3 miles away; the *Muskerry Golf Club* (phone: 85297), about 8 miles away; and *Monkstown Golf Club* (phone: 841225), at Monkstown, a village on the western shore of Cork Harbour, about 5 miles from Cork city. Greens fees average $5 to $10.

Greyhound Racing – Betting is brisk Mondays, Wednesdays, and Saturday nights at the *Cork Greyhound Stadium* on Western Rd. Details available in the *Cork Examiner.*

Hurling and Gaelic Football – Cork's *Páirc Uí Chaoimh* stadium on the Marina Walk east of town is the headquarters of Gaelic hurling and football in the south. Matches — of one or the other game — take place most Sunday afternoons through the summer season, and Rebel Cork is a power to be reckoned with in hurling especially.

Riding – Four stables are convenient to the city: *Ballywilliam Riding Centre,* Cobh (phone: 811908); *Hitchmough Riding School,* Monkstown (phone: 371267); *Pine Grove Riding Centre,* White's Cross (phone: 503857); and *Hennessy's Riding School,* White's Cross (phone: 506238). Rates are from $6 to $12 per hour.

Rugby and Soccer – Both are played at the *University Grounds,* Mardyke Walk. See the sports pages of the *Cork Examiner* for match times.

Sailing – Cork Harbour is a sailor's paradise and the *Royal Cork Yacht Club* (phone: 831440), now with headquarters downriver in Crosshaven, welcomes visitors from other clubs.

Tennis – Visitors are welcome at the *Church of Ireland Sports Club,* Garryduff, Rochestown (phone: 294029).

 THEATER: The *Cork Opera House,* Emmet Pl. (phone: 270022), is a modern replacement of a romantically decayed theater that burned down in the 1950s. Drama and musical comedies, opera, and ballet are all staged here. The *Everyman Playhouse,* Father Matthew St. (phone: 276287), offers seasons of new plays, foreign and Irish. The *Ivernia Theatre* on the Grand Parade (phone: 272703) is a showcase for Irish drama as well as classical, popular, and folk music. The *Irish National Ballet,* born and based in Cork (but often on tour), performs regularly at the Everyman Theatre and will soon have a home at the new international ballet center next to the Shandon Church. Check with the Tourist Office or the *Evening Echo* for details.

 MUSIC: For a relatively small city, Cork is fairly rich in music. There are regular lunch-hour concerts of classical music in summer, evening ones the rest of the year. Check at the tourist office, or call the Cork School of Music (phone: 965583). Traditional Irish music is provided several nights a week during the summer at the new Cork-Kerry Tourism *Entertainment Centre* behind the tourist office on Grand Parade. See the tourist office for both schedules and tickets. Irish ballads can be heard nightly at *DeLacy House,* 74 Oliver Plunkett St.

 NIGHTCLUBS AND NIGHTLIFE: The disco scene is lively. Recommended are *Sables,* on Pembroke St.; *Bogarts* at the Savoy Centre; *Zoe's* on Oliver Plunkett St.; *Spider's,* Washington St.; *Coco's,* in the Victoria Hotel; the *Oscar Club,* in the Ashley Hotel; and *Club Oasis,* on Grand Parade. Check the hotels for cabaret and dancing and see the *Evening Echo,* the best paper for entertainment listings, for other events.

 SINS: Ask any sailor.

BEST IN TOWN

 CHECKING IN: Cork can be jam-packed in high season, so reservations are recommended. Hotels vary from the sleek modern one on the outskirts to the downtown dowagers that have been upgraded with bathrooms and coffee shops. Expect to pay $80 and more for a double in the expensive category (with Irish breakfast more common than not); rooms in the moderate category run from $50 to $75; in inexpensive, $50 or less. If you arrive without a reservation, you will not be left out in the cold. The tourist office in Grand Parade will always help and Cork has a range of good, inexpensive guesthouses at $30 and less for a double.

Arbutus Lodge – If you want to get as close as possible to what some consider the best restaurant in Cork, and perhaps in Ireland, head for this elegant mansion amid gardens overlooking the city and the river. The Georgian decor is enhanced by a collection of modern Irish art. There are 20 small but good rooms, all with bath. Montenotte (phone: 501237). Expensive.

Ballymaloe House – Dating from the 17th century with extensions and a chunky stone keep from the 14th-century Fitzgerald castle, this ivy-walled "old family home" consists of a 400-acre farm replete with grazing sheep and ponies, 25 rooms, and even a cooking school. There is extra lodging space in the upgraded courtyard area, the gatehouse, and the gate lodge. Guests and outsiders alike enjoy first-class meals (see *Eating Out*). Ballymaloe also has a swimming pool, tennis courts, and 9-hole golf course. Shanagarry (phone: 021-652531). Expensive.

Imperial – The dowager of them all, stately in the middle of the South Mall and close to everything, took shape on the drawing board of Thomas Deane. The grande dame is not as starchy as she looks; in fact, all 93 rooms have been renovated with an Art Deco flair, and now include private bath. Meals in the very competent French restaurant, *La Duchesse,* are served to the accompaniment of piano music. South Mall (phone: 965333). Expensive.

Jurys – On the banks of the River Lee, with views of St. Finbarre's Cathedral, this modern, 200-room hotel is only a 5-minute walk from the main shopping district. It features the seafood cuisine of *The Fastnet,* a sing-along bar, and the domed, atrium-style pavilion, with an indoor-outdoor heated pool, saunas, squash courts, and a gym. Western Rd. (phone: 966377). Expensive.

Longueville House – One of Ireland's leading country houses, this 18th-century Georgian mansion is set on a 500-acre wooded estate, 20 miles north of Cork. All 18 rooms have private baths, and the inn is celebrated for the award-winning *Presidents' Restaurant* and its vineyard, which produces a unique Irish white wine. Mallow (phone: 022-27156). Expensive.

Metropole – This dowager, too, manages to keep up appearances. Behind the Victorian (1892)façade of brick and limestone are 125 rooms, all with color TV and phones, most with bath. On the north bank close to the railway station and ferryport. MacCurtain St. (phone: 508122). Expensive.

Silver Springs – Another modern hotel on the fringes. Rooms are no-nonsense, all 72 with baths. If you are lucky, yours will have a delightful view of the river and passing ships. There is a handy coffee shop as well as a restaurant. Glanmire Rd. (phone: 507533). Expensive.

Blarney – Convenient for anyone anxious to kiss the legendary Blarney Stone, this modern 76-room establishment has a peaceful country setting. All rooms have private bath and the restaurant, which features nightly entertainment, faces Blarney Castle. Blarney (phone: 85281). Moderate.

Innishannon – Just 15 miles outside Cork is this riverside hotel on 9 acres of gardens and woodlands. Built as a private mansion in 1720, it now has 13 guestrooms (all with private bath), a bowfronted dining room, a lounge-library, and a conservatory. Innishannon (phone: 775121). Moderate.

Lotamore House – A sprawling Georgian residence situated on four acres along the River Lee, this house is just a five-minute drive from downtown Cork. Recently refurbished, all 20 rooms have private baths, orthopedic beds, TVs and telephones, while the public rooms retain an 18th century aura — from a sweeping staircase, ornate plasterwork, and crystal chandeliers to the 1791 drawing room fireplace. Dublin Rd., Tivoli (phone: 822344). Inexpensive.

 EATING OUT: Cork, to say it again, is a good eating-out town, largely because the residents eat out quite a bit. Do not ignore the hotel dining rooms; some of them offer very good value and one in particular may be the best in Ireland. In addition to the restaurants below, the natives frequent good restaurants half an hour or so from Cork (see *Kinsale* in the West Cork tour route in DIRECTIONS). Dinner for two without wine or tips will cost $50 and up in places listed as expensive; $30 to $45 in the moderate ones; under $30 in the inexpensive ones.

Arbutus Lodge – Having won all the awards, it still keeps up its standard for excellent and innovative cooking. The seafood is superb (most things are). Try the "tasting" menu if it is on — you'll get to sample up to a dozen different dishes. A distinguished wine list delights even the most discriminating customers. Reservations are a must. Major credit cards. Montenotte (phone: 501237). Expensive.

Ballymaloe House – The food is simple and fresh; nearly everything is grown on the property. Begin with the watercress soup, smoked mackerel, or homemade Danish pâté; follow with summer turkey braised in butter and fresh herbs, roast beef with three sauces, or French casserole of roast pork with Normandy mustard; and top it all with a board of area cheeese, fruit tarts, cake, and coffee with Ballymaloe chocolates. Marvelous. Open for lunch and dinner. Shanagarry (021-652531). Expensive.

Lovetts – French cuisine is served in this period house in the suburbs. Seafood is especially recommended; don't miss the brown bread ice-cream. Reservations necessary. Major credit cards. Churchyard La., off Well Rd., Douglas (phone: 294909). Expensive.

Jacques – A self-service eatery by day is transformed into a romantic bistro and wine bar each evening. The imaginative dinner menu ranges from cassoulet of shellfish to noisettes of lamb with apricot stuffing, roast quail, or chicken Dijon. Homemade desserts include a heavenly almond meringue filled with chocolate cream and rum. 9 Phoenix St. (phone: 502387). Moderate.

Oyster Tavern – This traditional chophouse is an inner-city favorite. The whitebait and sole are memorable. Busy, so you may have to wait in the bar, which is pleasant. Market La., off Patrick St. (phone: 272635 or 272716). Moderate.

Glassialleys – In Cork parlance, glassialleys are marbles, and this small café near the Cork Opera House is well known for its marble-topped tables and glass marble decor. The menu is an eclectic blend of seafood, steaks, and burgers, with hints of Mexican, Greek and Chinese flavoring. 17 Drawbridge St. (phone: 272305). Moderate to inexpensive.

Mary Rose – Shoppers find the two branches of this all-day restaurant handy for coffee and pastries, light lunches, snacks, salads, and dinner. In the Queens Old Castle and Savoy shopping centers. (phone: 507762). Inexpensive.

SHARING A PINT: Cork's pub system is unusual for Ireland in that it is made up, as in Britain, of independent houses and "tied" ones linked to a particular brewery. Some bars serve only Beamish stout, some only Murphy's (the local brews); the independent ones serve both, and Guinness as well. Up to the mid-1950s it was possible to tell who sold what from the outside. Beamish pubs had a classic black and gold nameplate and were called the *Malt Shovel,* the *Black Swan,* the *Winning Post,* and the *Office* — ("I was delayed at the Office, dear"). The Murphy pubs had a cream and brown trim and usually sailed under their owners' names. Then some irreverent design genius came along and put them both in nondescript contemporary lettering. Inside, however, they keep their individuality. The *Long Valley,* Winthrop St., is a traditional pub where you can sample both Beamish and Murphy's stouts. *Le Château,* right in the middle of Patrick St., is crowded but pleasant. On Drawbridge St., just beside the Opera House, audience and actors meet for good talk and the occasional song at the *Grand Circle. Beechers Inn,* Faulkners La., is convenient to the office of the *Cork Examiner,* so the usual liquids come with the customary quota of newspaper rumors. Across the river on the hill beside the old Elizabeth Fort, the *Gateway,* Barrack St., is supposed to be the oldest pub in Cork. It dates from the 17th century and it is credible that the duke of Marlborough drank here;

certainly legions of his military followers through the centuries did. Good lunchtime eating and drinking pubs include the *Mutton Lane Inn* on Mutton Lane off Patrick St., *Maguire's Pennyfarthing Inn* on Grand Parade, the *Shandon Tavern* on Lavitt's Quay, and *Dan Lowrey's Seafood Tavern* on MacCurtain St. And *Henchy's,* 40 St. Luke's, in the Corkhills, is a fine place to sip a pint and listen to the distinctive Cork accent.

DUBLIN

This friendly city is steeped in a history often troubled, sometimes splendid; a city of wide Georgian streets, elegant squares, magnificent doorways; of memorable sunsets that bathe the eighteenth-century red brick façades until the houses seem to glow with their own fire and the very windows seem made of gold; a city of ancient churches and cathedrals thrusting their hallowed spires and towers against the skyline; a city where the English language acquires a unique dimension, and where the dark, creamy-headed Guinness stout flows abundantly in companionable pubs. This is a city like no other European capital; set like a jewel in the sweep of Dublin Bay; behind, to the south, rise the Dublin hills and the Wicklow Mountains. Through the city the River Liffey — James Joyce's Anna Livia Plurabelle — wends its leisurely way to the sea, spanned, as it passes through Dublin, by eleven bridges.

Once, there was only one bridge. Indeed, it was not so much a bridge as a mere ford in the river, and it stood approximately where the Father Matthew Bridge stands today. It was built by the first Celtic inhabitants of what is now Dublin. When they came here, we cannot be sure; what is certain is that, by AD 140, they were well established on this site. The Celts themselves probably referred to the spot by a name that endures to this day in the official Gaelic Baile Atha Cliath, the Town of the Ford of the Hurdles.

It was not, however, until the coming of the Vikings, or Norsemen, that Dublin as we now know it began to take shape. The old Celtic settlement had at no time been a place of national importance; its significance was as a ford of the Liffey en route to the ancient royal capital of Tara. In the year AD 837, 65 Viking longboats sailed into Dublin harbor and up the mouth of the River Liffey. These early Viking settlers established themselves a little downstream from the old Celtic settlement, on a spot where the Poddle, which now flows underground, entered the Liffey, causing it to form a dark pool, or *dubh linn*. The Vikings referred to their settlement by these two Gaelic words, and the anglicized version became the city's modern English name. Dublin rapidly became the focal point of the Viking invasion of Ireland. Then, as the Vikings began to see that trading was ultimately more profitable than plunder and as they began to settle and intermarry in their new homeland, Dublin became a major center for their extensive European trade. Not long after their arrival they were converted to Christianity and in 1034 erected a cathedral, which became the nucleus of modern Christ Church. The cathedral stood in the center of Viking Dublin and allows us to place the ancient city accurately.

Just over three centuries after the coming of the Vikings, new invaders swept Ireland. In 1169 the first contingent of Normans landed on the beach of Bannow, in County Wexford. Two years later, the powerful baron Richard Gilbert de Clare, otherwise known as Strongbow, arrived at the gates of Dublin with a thousand men. The city was taken by storm; its Viking king and inhabitants were forced to flee. Thereafter Dublin became the center of the English conquest, as it had become the center of the Viking conquest.

Not long afterward, it became necessary to fortify the city. For this purpose Dublin Castle was built not far from the old Viking cathedral. The cathedral itself had been taken over by Strongbow not long before, and a new and larger edifice erected in its place. The city walls were built along with the castle. (Their remains can be seen at St. Audeon's Arch, below Christ Church.) Thus medieval Dublin began to take shape, small in size and surrounded by walls.

In shape and in size Dublin did not alter greatly until the arrival of a new viceroy, or king's representative, in 1662 heralded Dublin's rise to a definitive national importance. Dublin, under James Butler, duke of Ormonde, became and remained the central arena for Ireland's social, political, and cultural life.

Butler, believing that the stability of a government should be reflected in public works, began municipal improvements almost immediately. The solitary, medieval Dublin Bridge was joined by four new bridges across the river; the Phoenix Park (to this day the largest enclosed urban park in the world) was walled and several new streets were built.

Dublin's importance as a city and as a seaport increased enormously in that time. It was, however, in the eighteenth century that Dublin was truly to flourish. During this century it became one of the most brilliant and sparkling capitals in all Europe. The strong movement toward parliamentary independence that took place at this time was reflected in the splendid Parliament House (now the Bank of Ireland in College Green), commenced in 1729, the first in a series of great public buildings. Extensive rebuilding was carried out on Dublin Castle and Trinity College. The Wide Streets Commission was set up. It was as if the city were proudly preparing for the unprecedented position of importance it would occupy when, in 1782, parliamentary independence was conceded to Ireland by the British Parliament.

Great buildings followed one another in dizzying succession — Leinster House, the Royal Exchange, the Mansion House, the Four Courts, the Custom House. Irish classical architecture, in all its gravity, beauty, and balance, reached full maturity. It flowered in public buildings and private houses, spacious squares and elegant streets. This was Georgian Dublin (various king Georges sat on the British throne in the period): the Dublin of Henry Grattan, Oliver Goldsmith, Jonathan Swift, Bishop Berkeley and Edmund Burke, David Garrick and Peg Woffington. Handel himself conducted the world première of his *Messiah* in this glittering city, whose center was concentrated in the area between Dublin Castle and the Parliament House.

Architecturally, Dublin reached its zenith in the eighteenth century. Henceforward, its brilliance was to be sculpted in the written word rather than in stone. The next century saw an end to the halcyon days of Home Rule; with the dismantling of the Parliament, Dublin's political and social life suffered a blow from which it was not to recover easily. By contrast, its literary life began to flower, for in the nineteenth century two great literary movements were born in Dublin — the Gaelic League and the Irish Literary Renaissance. Between them, the two movements revived and romanticized the early legends and history of Ireland. The literary renaissance — spearheaded by William Butler Yeats, Lady Augusta Gregory, Douglas Hyde, and

John Millington Synge, to name but a few — placed a splendid and indelible mark on twentieth-century English literature. (Equally renowned are Irish or Ireland-born writers not directly associated with the Gaelic League renaissance, men like Samuel Beckett, who won the Nobel Prize for Literature in 1969 and who was born in Dublin in 1906; George Bernard Shaw, who wrote in England but was born in Dublin; and Brendan Behan.) The movement found its greatest expression in the creation of the Abbey Theatre, associated forever with the brilliant plays of Sean O'Casey; for many years the Abbey was the most famous theater in the world. The Gaelic League, on the other hand, had more popular appeal; with its dream of the restoration of the Gaelic language and the reestablishment of a separate Irish cultural nation, it provided a great deal of the inspiration for the Easter Rebellion of 1916.

This uprising was concentrated in Dublin. It sparked the 5-year War of Independence, which culminated in the Anglo-Irish Treaty of 1921 (whereby Ireland gained the status of Free State). The signing of the treaty was followed by Civil War in 1922–23, during which many buildings that had escaped damage in 1916 suffered badly. Today, happily, all the heirlooms of the eighteenth century have been restored to their original grandeur.

Dublin today, with a population of 1 million, is far larger than it has been at any other stage of its history. Nevertheless, it is still an eminently walkable city. The crossroads of medieval and eighteenth-century Dublin remain the center of interest. Within a half-mile radius of the Bank of Ireland on College Green lie the cathedrals, the museums, Dublin Castle, the great Georgian public buildings, the parks, and the shops. All are neatly enclosed by the Royal Canal to the north and the Grand Canal to the south.

Besides sightseeing, a visitor should sample Dublin's abundant cultural offerings, especially its theaters. But the true focal point of Dubliners' social life is the pub, and it is there you must go to find them. Dublin can be a comfortable, "down home" place to visit, so slow down and enjoy it. If you do, you will find that there is an endearing earthiness about Dublin, a quality which inspired James Joyce to refer to his native city in off-color, though affectionate, terms as "strumpet city in the sunset" and "dear, dirty Dublin."

DUBLIN AT-A-GLANCE

SEEING THE CITY: Views of this essentially flat city are best from a number of restaurants in the surrounding hills; particularly nice is *Killakee House* in Rathfarnham (phone: 932645 or 932917). Or see Dublin from afar in the neighboring Wicklow Mountains.

SPECIAL PLACES: Central Dublin is very compact. Since traffic can move slowly, by far the best way to see the city is on foot. A good idea is to take one of the CIE (Córas Iompair Éireann, National Transport Company) sightseeing tours. These last for about 3 hours and are an excellent and enjoyable way of getting one's bearings. They leave from the Central Bus Station, Store St. (phone: 746301). Gray Line also operates tours, 3 Wilton Pl. (phone: 744466). Then, armed with Dublin Tourism's splendid, signposted *Tourist Trail,* the determined sightseer should set off on foot to see and experience as much of Dublin as time allows.

SOUTH DOWNTOWN

Merrion Square – This is the loveliest of all Dublin's Georgian squares, a study in balance and elegance, evoking the graciousness of a vanished age. Note particularly the variety of fan-lighted doorways. Have a look at #1, where the young Oscar Wilde lived with his celebrated parents, the surgeon Sir William Wills Wilde and poetess "Speranza"; #42, home of Sir Jonah Barrington, 18th-century barrister and raconteur; #58, where Daniel O'Connell lived, "the Liberator" who won Catholic Emancipation in 1829; #70, home of tragic Sheridan Le Fanu, author of sinister tales such as *Uncle Silas* and *Through a Glass Darkly* — after his wife's death in 1858 he shut himself up there, appearing only after nightfall to walk in the shadows of Merrion Square; #82, where William Butler Yeats, poet and Nobel Prize winner, lived. Today, the only house in the square used as a private dwelling is #71, where well-known couturière Sybil Connolly has her home and studio.

Leinster House – When young Lord Kildare, earl of Leinster, chose to build a mansion here in 1745, all of fashionable Dublin protested, for at that time the north side of the city was the fashionable side. Undaunted, he went ahead with his plan, asserting that "Where I go, fashion will follow." His prophecy came true. The house Lord Kildare built is said to resemble the White House, whose architect, James Hoban of Carlow, studied in Dublin after the completion of Leinster House. The building was purchased in the 19th century by the Royal Dublin Society, and in 1921 the Parliament of the new Irish Free State chose the building as its meeting place. Leinster House continues to be the meeting place of the Dail (House of Representatives) and Seanad (Senate). When the Dail is in session, you may watch from the visitors' gallery. Apply for tickets at the main gate. Kildare St., Merrion Sq. (phone: 789911).

National Museum – When Leinster House belonged to the Royal Dublin Society, it became the nucleus of a complex of cultural buildings — the National Gallery, the National Library, the Museum of Natural History, and the National Museum. These are all worth visiting, but the National Museum especially should not be missed. There is a collection of gold objects dating from the Bronze Age to early Christian times almost without parallel in Western Europe. Admission is free. Kildare St. (phone: 765521).

Genealogical Office – Formerly in Dublin Castle, this is the office of Ireland's Chief Herald, the ideal starting point for an ancestry hunt. 2 Kildare St. (phone: 608670).

St. Stephen's Green – Not far from Merrion Square lies St. Stephen's Green, one of the loveliest of Dublin's many public parks. It is on 22 acres with gardens, a waterfall, and an ornamental lake. It's an excellent place to come in summer, to sit and watch working Dublin take its lunch; bands play on the bandstand in July and August.

Mansion House – Dublin preceded London in building a Mansion House for its lord mayor in 1715. In the Round Room the Declaration of Irish Independence was adopted in 1919, and the Anglo-Irish Treaty of 1921 was signed there. The Round Room is usually open to visitors. Dawson St. (phone: 762852).

Trinity College – Dawson Street descends to meet Trinity College, the oldest university in Ireland, founded by Elizabeth I of England on the site of the 12th-century Monastery of All Hallows. Alumni of the college include Oliver Goldsmith, Edmund Burke, Jonathan Swift, Bishop Berkeley (pronounced "bark-lee," who also lent his name to incorrectly pronounced Berkeley in California), William Congreve, Thomas Moore, Sheridan Le Fanu, and Oscar Wilde, to name but a few. No trace of the original Elizabethan structure remains; the oldest surviving part of the college dates from 1700. The Long Room, Trinity's famous library, is the longest single chamber library in existence. It contains a priceless collection of 800,000 volumes and 3,000 ancient manuscripts and papyri. The library's chief treasure is the *Book of Kells,* an 8th-century manuscript transcription of the four gospels described as the "most beautiful book in the world." Closed Saturday afternoons and Sundays. Admission charge from April to October. College Green (phone: 772941).

Parliament House – Facing Trinity College is the monumental Parliament House, now the Bank of Ireland. Built in 1729 and regarded as one of the finest examples of the architecture of its period, this was the first of the great series of 18th-century public buildings in Dublin. As its name implies, it was erected to house the Irish Parliament in the century that saw the birth of Home Rule. College Green (phone: 776801).

Dublin Castle – As you move away from College Green, Dame Street leads westward toward the older part of the city, where the early Viking and Norman settlers chose to establish themselves.

Castles have gone up and down on the site of the present castle. A Celtic *rath* was almost certainly followed by a wooden Viking fortress and this in turn was supplanted by the great stone castle erected by John of England in the 13th century. The castle was for 400 years the center of English rule in Ireland; for much of this time it had as grim a reputation as the Tower of London. Although the present building is essentially 18th century, one of the four towers that flanked the original moated castle survives as the Record Tower. The 15th-century Bedford Tower was the state prison; the Georgian State Apartments, formerly the residence of the English viceroys, were beautifully restored between 1950 and 1963 and are now used for state functions. St. Patrick's Hall in the State Apartments was the scene of the inauguration of Ireland's first president, Douglas Hyde; here, too, President John F. Kennedy was made a freeman of Dublin.

The Bedford Tower, the Chapel Royal, and the State Apartments can be visited for a small admission charge. Dublin Castle (phone: 777129).

Christ Church Cathedral – Not far from Dublin Castle, the massive shape of Christ Church Cathedral crowns the hill on which the ancient city stood. Founded in 1038 by Viking King Sitric Silkenbeard of Dublin, Christ Church was demolished in the 12th century and rebuilt by the Norman Richard Gilbert de Clare (Strongbow), who is buried within its walls. The cruciform building has been much restored through the centuries, but the beautiful pointed nave and the wonderful stonework remain virtually unchanged. These walls have witnessed many dramatic scenes in the course of Irish history. Christ Church today is the Church of Ireland (Protestant) Cathedral for the Diocese of Dublin. The vaulted crypt remains one of the largest in Ireland. In front of this cathedral Dubliners traditionally gather to ring in the New Year. You can visit the cathedral and crypt. Christ Church Pl. (phone: 778099).

St. Audoen's Arch and the City Walls – The 13th-century church of St. Audoen is Dublin's oldest parish church. It was founded by early Norman settlers, who gave to the church the name St. Ouen, or Audoen, after the patron saint of their native Rouen. Close to the church is a flight of steps leading down to St. Audoen's Arch, the sole surviving gateway of the medieval city walls. Open daily; free (phone: 791855).

St. Patrick's Cathedral – Christ Church stood within the old walled city. One of its 12th-century archbishops, John Comyn, felt that while he remained under municipal jurisdiction he could not achieve the temporal power for which he thirsted. Accordingly, he left the city walls and built a fine palace within a stone's throw of Christ Church. Today St. Patrick's is the national cathedral of the Church of Ireland. By the 19th century both cathedrals were in a state of considerable disrepair. Henry Roe, a distiller, came to the aid of Christ Church, restoring it at his own expense; Sir Benjamin Lee Guinness of the famous brewing family came to the assistance of St. Patrick's — hence the saying in Dublin that "Christ Church was restored with glasses, St. Patrick's with pints!"

The early English interior of St. Patrick's is very beautiful; the nave is the longest in Ireland. The cathedral's particular fascination, however, lies in its wealth of monuments, especially the Geraldine Door, the Cork Memorial, and the monument to Dame St. Leger. The greatest interest of all, though, is in the long association with St. Patrick's of Jonathan Swift, author of *Gulliver's Travels* and dean of the cathedral for 32 years. Within these walls he is buried, beside his loving Stella. On a slab near the entrance is carved the epitaph he composed for himself, which Yeats described as the greatest epitaph in literature. Open to visitors. St. Patrick's Cathedral (phone: 754817).

Guinness Brewery – Founded in 1759 by Arthur Guinness with a mere £100, Guinness's today is the largest exporting stout brewery in the world. The former Guinness Hop Store, on Crane Street adjacent to the main brewery, was once the storage building for the ingredients for the world-famous dark stout, and the aroma remains. Now it is a public hall showcasing traveling displays, art shows, technological works, and contemporary arts. The Visitors Centre shows an audio-visual presentation about the making of the famous brew, complete with free samples. Also of note are the Guinness Museum and the Cooper's Museum. Small admission charge for the rotating exhibitions (phone: 756701).

Royal Hospital – One of Ireland's oldest public buildings, this 17th-century treasure was restored to the tune of IR£20 million and reopened in 1985 on its 300th anniversary. Originally built as a home for aged veterans, it is now a magnificent museum. Displays range from National Museum pieces to traveling art exhibitions from as far away as China. The restoration of the Grand Hall/dining room has been rated as one of Europe's finest achievements of the century. Also used for public concerts (check the Dublin newspapers). Surrounding the building are 50 acres of grounds, including an 18th-century formal garden, a courtyard, sculpture park, and "Bully's Acre," the resting place of many 11th-century Irish chieftains. Admission charge. Kilmainham (phone: 718666 or 719147).

NORTH DOWNTOWN

Four Courts – Almost across the river from Guinness's lies the stately Four Courts of Justice, dating from the apogee of the 18th century. The building was begun by Thomas Cooley and completed by James Gandon, the greatest of all the Georgian architects. Court sittings (Supreme and High) are open to the public. Free. Inns Quay (phone: 725555).

St. Michan's Church – Not far from the Four Courts is St. Michan's, a 17th-century church built on the site of a 10th-century Viking church. The 18th-century organ is said to have been played by Handel when he was in Dublin for the first public performance of *Messiah*.

Of more immediate interest, perhaps, is the extraordinary crypt, with its remarkable preservative atmosphere: Bodies have lain here for centuries without decomposing and you can, if you feel so inclined, shake the hand of an 8-foot-tall Crusader! Open on weekdays and Saturday mornings. Small admission charge. Church St. (phone: 724154).

Moore Street – A left turn past the historic General Post Office leads down Henry Street; the second turn to the right off Henry Street is Moore Street. In this street, among the fruit and flower sellers, you can hear the true voice of Dublin — lively, warm, voluble, speaking an English that is straight Sean O'Casey.

Municipal Gallery of Modern Art – Beyond the Garden of Remembrance (a memorial to those who died for Irish freedom), on the north side of Parnell Square, is Charlemont House, designed by Sir William Chambers in 1764. Lord Charlemont, for whom the house was designed, was a great patron of the arts; it is fitting that his house became, in recent times, the Municipal Gallery of Modern Art. The gallery should not be missed; it has an outstanding collection of Impressionist paintings, and more recent artists such as Picasso, Utrillo, and Bonnard are well represented, to say nothing of such prominent Irish painters as Sir William Orpen, John B. Yeats (the poet's father), and Jack Yeats. Closed Mondays. Admission is free. Parnell Sq. (phone: 741903).

Abbey Theatre – Alas, the original Abbey Theatre, founded by Yeats and Lady Gregory on the site of the old city morgue, is no more. In 1951, at the close of a performance of O'Casey's *Plough and the Stars* — a play that ends with Dublin blazing in the aftermath of rebellion — the theater itself caught on fire and was burned to the ground. The New Abbey, designed by Michael Scott, one of the country's foremost architects, opened in 1966 on the site of the original building. The lobby, which can be seen daily (except Sundays), contains interesting portraits of those connected with the theater's early successes. Performances nightly (except Sundays). Abbey St. (phone: 744505).

Custom House – This masterpiece of Georgian architecture adorns the north bank of the Liffey, to the east of O'Connell Street. It was the chef d'oeuvre of James Gandon and is one of the finest buildings of its kind in Europe. It is now occupied by government offices and is closed to the public; it should, nonetheless, be seen at close range: the carved riverheads that form the keystones of the arches and entrances are splendid. Custom House Quay (phone: 742961).

SUBURBS

Phoenix Park – Northwest of the city center, the Phoenix Park is the largest enclosed urban park in the world. Within its walls are the residences of the president of the republic and the US ambassador. The park covers 1,760 acres, beautifully planted with a great variety of trees. Among the attractions are the lovely People's Gardens, the herd of fallow deer, the horse-race course, and the Zoological Gardens. Dublin Zoo is said to be the most beautiful zoo in Europe; it also has a most impressive collection of animals and holds several records for lion breeding. The park and zoo are open daily (the park is free; small charge for the zoo; phone: 213021 or 771425).

Chester Beatty Library – Founded by an American, naturalized British resident in Ireland, this library is considered to be the most valuable and representative private collection of Oriental manuscripts and miniatures in the world. The "copper millionaire with a heart of gold," Chester Beatty willed his marvelous library to the people of Dublin. Open Tuesdays through Fridays. No admission charge. 20 Shrewsbury Rd., Ballsbridge (phone: 692386).

Malahide Castle – In a north city suburb of Dublin, Malahide Castle has only recently been opened to the public. For eight centuries this was the home of the Talbots of Malahide. Magnificently furnished in period style (mostly 18th century) with part of the very valuable National Portrait Collection on view, it is well worth a visit. Admission charge. Malahide, Co. Dublin (phone: 452337).

Newbridge House and Park – Built in 1740, this country mansion is full of memorabilia of the Cobbe family, including original hand-carved furniture collected through the years, portraits, memoirs, day books, a museum of world travels, and an extensive doll collection. Downstairs, visitors can view a kitchen and laundry room from 1760, complete with ancient implements. The wooded grounds (365 acres) have picnic areas and walking trails. Five miles north of Dublin Airport and 12 miles from the city center, Newbridge can be comfortably combined with an excursion to nearby Malahide Castle. Admission charge; open from June through October, weekdays, 10 AM to 5 PM; Sundays, 2 to 6 PM. From November through March, it is open only on Wednesday and Sunday afternoons, 2 to 5 PM. Off the Dublin/Belfast Rd. (N1) at Donabate, Co. Dublin (phone: 436534 or 436535).

■ **EXTRA SPECIAL:** The beautiful Boyne Valley is one of Ireland's most storied and evocative sites, and it makes an easy and interesting day trip. Leave Dublin by the Navan road, passing through Dunshaughlin (which takes its name from a church founded by St. Seachnall, a companion of St. Patrick). Six miles south of Navan, signposted to the left, is the Hill of Tara. Although only some grassy mounds and earthworks recall a splendid past, it is impossible to remain unmoved by the site's history: This is "Royal Tara," where High Kings of Ireland were crowned on the Lia Fail (the Stone of Destiny) before time began. And it was here, at the tribes' great triennial Feis of Tara, that laws were enacted and revised. Now, as Moore writes in his immortal song, "No more to chiefs and ladies bright / The harp of Tara swells / The chord alone that breaks at night / Its tale of ruin tells."

Returning to the Navan road, you will pass the striking ruins of 16th-century Athlumney Castle on the east bank of the Boyne, about 1.5 miles from Navan. Continue on through Donaghmore, with its remains of a 12th-century church and a round tower. Nearby, below the Boyne Bridge, lies Log na Ri — the Hollow of the King — where people once used to swim their herds of cattle ceremoniously across the river, to protect them from the "little people" and from natural disasters.

The village of Slane lies on one of the loveliest stretches of the Boyne. There are some delightful Georgian houses, but the history of this small town goes back far beyond the 18th century. It was on the hill that overlooks Slane that St. Patrick lit the Paschal Fire on Holy Saturday, AD 433, and drew upon himself the wrath of the High King's druids. Patrick emerged victorious from the ensuing confrontation, and Christianity began its reign in Ireland. On the slopes of the hill are the remains of an ancient earthen fort and the ruins of a 16th-century church. Quite apart from archaeological interest, the climb up Slane Hill is well worth the effort — rewarding the energetic with fine views across the tranquil Boyne Valley to Trim and Drogheda. Just outside the town lies the estate of Slane Castle, a 19th-century castellated mansion in which the present occupant, Lord Mountcharles, has opened a fine restaurant (phone: 041-24207).

Downstream from Slane is Brugh na Boinne — the Palace of the Boyne — a vast necropolis over 4,000 years old. Here, beneath a chain of tumuli, kings of Ireland were laid to rest in passage graves of remarkable complexity. The tumuli of Dowth, Knowth, and Newgrange in particular are of major interest, both for their extent and the amazing diversity of their sculptured ornamentation. Newgrange is one of the finest passage graves in all of Western Europe, and it has been opened to the public. There is a permanent archaeological exhibition and guided tours are available. Closed Mondays.

Continuing down the Boyne Valley, you reach Drogheda, an ancient town that has witnessed many a dramatic scene in the course of Irish history, the most famous of which was the defeat of James II by William of Orange on July 12, 1690. Other reminders of its past include: the 13th-century St. Laurence's Gate, the only surviving of the original ten gates in this once walled city; the ruins of 13th-century St. Mary's Abbey; the Norman motte and bailey of Millmount; and the fine Millmount Museum; St. Peter's Church, where the head of St. Oliver Plunkett, martyred archbishop of Armagh, is enshrined.

Five miles north of Drogheda, you reach Monasterboice, an ancient monastic settlement noteworthy for one of the most perfect high crosses in Ireland — the intricately carved 10th-century Cross of Muireadach. Southwest of Monasterboice are the impressive ruins of Mellifont Abbey. Dating from 1142, this was the first Cistercian foundation in Ireland and heralded a whole new style of ecclesiastical architecture. Note especially the remains of the gate house, and the octagonal lavabo.

Return to Dublin via the N1.

SOURCES AND RESOURCES

TOURIST INFORMATION: For general information, brochures, and maps before your visit, contact the Irish Tourist Board, 757 Third Ave., New York, NY 10017 (phone: 212-418-0800). For on-the-spot information and assistance, call the Dublin Tourism Tourist Information Offices at Dublin Airport (phone: 376387) and 14 O'Connell St. (phone: 747733). The Tourist Information Offices will advise you on all aspects of your stay in Ireland and will make theater bookings and hotel reservations anywhere in the country. They also sell *Dining in Ireland* and *The Dublin Guide* (also at most bookstores).

The *Tourist Trail,* published by Dublin Tourism and available at its offices, is an excellent walking guide to the city. Another invaluable Dublin Tourism publication is *Dublin — Useful Information.* The best city map is the Ordnance Survey Dublin Map; less detailed but generally adequate maps are also available.

Local Coverage – *In Dublin,* published fortnightly, covers every conceivable activity in Dublin, including theater, cinema, music, exhibitions, sports, and cabarets. *What's On in Dublin* and *Tourism News* are published monthly by Dublin Tourism and are available at its offices. Main daily newspapers are: the *Irish Times,* the *Irish Independent,* and the *Irish Press;* main evening papers are the *Evening Herald* and the *Evening Press.*

GETTING AROUND: Airport – Dublin Airport is north of the city at Collinstown. In normal traffic, a trip from the airport to downtown takes 35 to 40 minutes, with an average taxi fare of IR£12. And *CIE (Córas Iompair Éireann, National Transport Company)* operates bus service (see below) timed to meet all flights, between the airport and the central bus station.

Bus – *CIE* operates rail and bus transport not only in Dublin but nationwide. Cross-city bus routes are extensive. The fare is collected after the passenger is seated (exact fare is not required). Although Dublin has no subway, a new commuter rail system, *Dublin Area Rapid Transport* (*DART*), runs from central Dublin along the bay as far north as Howth and as far south as Bray. It is swift, dependable, and safe at all hours.

Day tours from Dublin are operated by *CIE* from the Central Bus Station, Store St. A wide range of tours is available (phone: 746301). Guided walking tours of various parts of the city are also available; check with the tourist office for times and meeting points.

All information regarding bus and rail travel throughout the republic can be obtained by calling 787777. An official bus and rail timetable is available at newsstands.

Taxi – There are stands throughout the city, especially near main hotels, and cabs can also be hailed in the streets. Your first conversation with a Dublin cab driver will assure you that you are in fact in Ireland. Among the companies that operate a 24-hour radio service are *Blue Cabs* (phone: 761111), *Irish Taxi Co-op* (phone: 766666), and *National Radio Cabs* (phone: 772222).

Car Rental – Many Dublin firms offer excellent self-drive facilities. Advice and brochures are available from tourist offices.

MUSEUMS: The National Museum, the Heraldic Museum, and the Royal Hospital are described in *Special Places.* Dublin is also the home of the *Dublin Civic Museum,* South William St., the *National Wax Museum,* off Parnell Square, the *Irish Jewish Museum,* 3/4 Walworth Rd., off Victoria

St., and the *Museum of Childhood,* The Palms, 20 Palmerstown Park, Rathmines, a private collection of antique dolls and toys (small admission charge; phone: 973223).

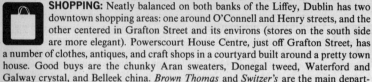 **SHOPPING:** Neatly balanced on both banks of the Liffey, Dublin has two downtown shopping areas: one around O'Connell and Henry streets, and the other centered in Grafton Street and its environs (stores on the south side are more elegant). Powerscourt House Centre, just off Grafton Street, has a number of clothes, antiques, and craft shops in a courtyard built around a pretty town house. Good buys are the chunky Aran sweaters, Donegal tweed, Waterford and Galway crystal, and Belleek china. *Brown Thomas* and *Switzer's* are the main department stores on Grafton Street; *Arnott's, Roche's,* and *Clery's* are fine stores in the O'Connell and Henry streets area. The famous *Kilkenny Design Centre* has a marvelous store on Nassau Street, with a wide range of Irish goods. Some other recommended shops are:

Laura Ashley – Fashion and fabrics for the home, adults, and children, by the English designer. 7 Dawson St. (phone: 791260).

Best of Irish – A wide range of Irish goods — crystal, china, handknits, jewelry, linens, and tweeds can be found here. Open daily. Next to the Westbury Hotel, on Harry St., off Grafton St. (phone: 791233).

Bewley's Cafés Ltd. – A Dublin landmark, it's an emporium of coffees and teas of all nations, with tempting candy selection as well. Sampling of both coffees and teas is encouraged. Only the Grafton Street shop has waitress service. 78/79 Grafton St. (phone: 776761).

Chez Nous – Handmade sweets and other confections. 15 Lad La. (phone: 762503).

Cleo Ltd. – For over 50 years, one of Dublin's most fashionable sources for hand-knitted and handwoven cloaks, caps, suits, coats, and shawls. 18 Kildare St. (phone: 761421).

Sybil Connolly – Ireland's reigning couturière; her romantic ballgowns of finely pleated Irish linen are indeed special. 71 Merrion Sq. (phone: 767281).

Paul Costelloe – Designer of ready-to-wear for women. 42 Drury St. (phone: 711598).

Pat Crowley – Silky and seductive blouses and dresses. 14 Duke St. (phone: 710219).

Eason & Son Ltd. – Jam-packed with tomes and paperbacks, maps, records, and stationery. 40-42 Lower O'Connell St. (phone: 733811).

Patrick Flood – Silver and gold jewelry in traditional Irish designs. Unit 14, 1st floor, Powerscourt House Centre (phone: 770615).

Fred Hanna – Booksellers to Trinity College. New and used books; excellent books and maps on Ireland. 28/29 Nassau St. (phone: 771255).

Heraldic Artists – A good source for family crests, flags, scrolls, and genealogy tomes. 3 Nassau St. (phone: 762391).

House of Ireland – Quality Irish and European goods — from Aynsley, Lladro, Spode, Wedgwood, Waterford, and Hummels to hand-knits, kilts, linens, shillelaghs, and Irish Sweeps tickets. 37/38 Nassau St. and 64/65 Dawson St. (phone: 714543).

Irish Cottage Industries – Sweaters, tweeds, and anything else hand-knit, hand-crocheted, handwoven, or hand-braided. 44 Dawson St. (phone: 713039).

H. Johnston Ltd. – Traditional blackthorn walking sticks. 11 Wicklow St. (phone: 771249).

Kapp and Peterson – Tobaccos and hand-carved pipes for men and women. 55 Grafton St. (phone: 714652).

Kevin & Howlin Ltd. – Men's ready-to-wear and made-to-measure clothing. The store now carries some women's tweeds. 31 Nassau St.

Mullins of Dublin – For coats of arms emblazoned on parchments, plaques, even door knockers. 36 Upper O'Connell St. (phone: 741133).

Fergus O'Farrell – For more than 25 years, this has been a showcase for quality Irish crafts — from woodcarvings and brass door knockers to beaten copper art; also handmade candles, stationery, and prints from 19th-century woodcuts. 62 Dawson St. (phone: 770862).

Sheepskin Shop – Just the spot to stock up on high quality sheep and lambskin suits and coats, as well as a variet selection of leather trousers, suits, and jackets. 20 Wicklow St. (phone: 719585).

Tara Woollen Mills – A little off the beaten track, in a converted factory along the docks on the eastern edge of the Liffey, this new enterprise offers quality woollens at bargain prices. There is also a self-service restaurant and a wide selection of Irish and Scottish products. Custom House Quay (phone: 787279).

Tower Design Craft Centre – Once a sugar refinery, this newly renovated 1862 tower houses the workshops of more than 30 innovative craftspeople — with work ranging from heraldic jewelry, Irish oak woodcarvings, and hand-cut crystal to stained glass, toys, and fishing tackle. Self-service restaurant also on premises. Ideal for a rainy day. Pearse St. (phone: 775655).

Waltons Musical Instrument Galleries – Bagpipes and Irish harps as well as records. 2-5 N Frederick St. (phone: 747805).

 SPECIAL EVENTS: Outstanding annual events include *St. Patrick's Day* on March 17, with a parade and many other events; an *Irish Music Festival (Feis Cheoil)* in May; the *Festival in Great Irish Houses* in June, for concerts by international celebrities in Georgian mansions near Dublin; *Bloomsday,* June 16, when fans of James Joyce gather from around the world to follow the circuitous path through Dublin that takes Leopold Bloom from morning until late at night in *Ulysses;* the *Horse Show,* the principal sporting and social event of the year, in August; the *Dublin Theatre Festival* in September and October, featuring new plays by Irish authors, and the *Dublin Marathon,* on the last Monday of October. For details about these and other events, inquire at the Tourist Office (see above).

 SPORTS: Bicycling – Irish Raleigh Industries operates *Rent-a-Bike* at a number of city firms (phone: 521888). Two downtown shops offering bicycling rentals are *King of the Road,* 65 Mespil Rd. (phone: 687923), and *N. Ryan,* 115 Upper Dorset St. (phone: 305090). Charges average IR£4 per day or IR£20 per week.

Gaelic Games – Football and hurling are two fast and enthralling field sports; important matches are played at *Croke Park.* For details, see the calendar of events in *In Dublin* or call Croke Park (phone: 743111).

Golf – There are over 30 courses within easy reach of Dublin; visitors are welcome at all clubs on weekdays, but gaining admission can be more difficult on weekends. Two of the finest courses in the world, *Portmarnock* (phone: 323082) and *Royal Dublin* (phone: 337153), are just north of the city and should not be missed.

Greyhound Racing – An exciting spectator sport, this can be seen regularly at two tracks, each an 8-minute ride from the city center: *Shelbourne Park Stadium* and *Harold's Cross Stadium.* Details in *In Dublin* or at the Tourist Office.

Horse Racing – *Phoenix Park* is the site of races in the city, but the course is straight, not circular, which makes for frustrating viewing. You may see the start, the middle, or the end, but you won't see the whole race. Better is the very famous racecourse, *Curragh,* about a mile outside the town of Kildare in County Kildare. It's less than an hour's drive from Dublin. Six miles south of the city, Leopardstown has a very modern racecourse.

Horseback Riding – A list of riding establishments close to Dublin and registered with the Irish Horse Board is available at Tourist Offices.

Tennis – Ireland has a new international facility — the Irish Lawn Tennis Association Tennis Centre — about a 15-minute taxi ride from the city center. With 4 indoor and 4 outdoor courts, this first-rate tennis spot is open daily from 7 AM to midnight, year-round. Equipment rental at Pro Shop. *Dublin Sport* hotel, Kilternan (phone: 953729). There are a few public courts, generally outdoor, in and around Dublin where visitors can play for a small fee. The most central is Herbert Park, Ballsbridge (phone: 684364).

 THEATER: For complete program listings see the publications listed above. There are eight main theaters in the city center; smaller groups perform in the universities, in suburban theaters, and occasionally in pubs and hotels. The main theaters are the *Abbey* and the *Peacock,* both at Lower Abbey St. (phone: 744505); the *Gate* (the theater of Michael MacLiammoir and Hilton Edwards), Cavendish Row (phone: 744045); the *Gaiety,* South King St. (phone: 771717), mostly for revues, musicals, and opera; the *Olympia,* Dame St. (phone: 778962), for everything from revues to straight plays; the *Eblana,* Store St. (phone: 746707), a small theater offering mostly modern comedy; the *Focus,* Pembroke Pl. (phone: 763071) for Russian and Scandinavian works; the *Project Arts Centre,* 39 E Essex St. (phone: 713327), very avant-garde.

For children, the *Lambert Puppet Theatre* in the suburb of Monkstown will prove irresistible. Clifton La., Monkstown (phone: 800974).

It is always advisable to reserve in advance for theater in Dublin. You can make bookings at theaters, tourist offices, the information desks of *Switzer's* and *Brown Thomas* stores, Grafton St., and the central ticket bureau (phone: 794455). Most of the theaters accept telephone reservations.

 MUSIC: The National Concert Hall, Earlsfort Terrace, off St. Stephen's Green (phone: 711888), is the center of Dublin's active musical life and the home of the *RTE* (*Radio Telefis Éireann*) *Symphony Orchestra. RTE* performances are held regularly as are a variety of other concerts. For a schedule, phone the concert hall or check local publications. In April and September the *Dublin Grand Opera Society* holds its spring and winter seasons at the Gaiety Theatre. Traditional Irish music is a must. Sessions are held at many places around town by an organization called *Comhaltas Ceoltóirí Éireann* (phone: 800295); ballad sessions are held nightly except Sundays in the *Abbey Tavern,* Howth, 10 miles north of the city on the coast (phone: 322006). Many pubs have music on an informal basis — *O'Donoghue's* in Merrion Row is one of the most famous (and least comfortable). Try also *Toner's* and the *Baggot Inn,* both in Lower Baggot St., *Kitty O'Shea's* on Upr. Grand Canal St., or *Foley's* on Merrion Row. There are many other listings in *In Dublin.*

 NIGHTCLUBS AND NIGHTLIFE: There is little in the way of large-scale cabaret-cum-dancing in Dublin; swinging Dublin tends to congregate on the discothèque scene. Premises range from the large, lively places where an escort is not necessarily required to small, intimate clubs. Most discothèques only have wine licenses.

Among the more established discothèques on a rapidly changing scene are the large and lively *Annabel's* in the *Burlington* hotel; *Raffles* in the *Sachs; Barbarella's* and *Jules,* both off Merrion Row; *Flamingo's* in the *Parkes,* on Stillorgan Rd.; *Blinkers* at Leopardstown racecourse, and *Rumours* on O'Connell St. Smaller, more intimate clubs are mainly to be found in the Leeson Street area: try *Maxwell Plums, Bojangles, Samantha's, Styx,* and *Aphrodite's.* The most famous traditional cabaret in Dublin is the established *Jurys Cabaret;* nightly except Mondays (phone: 605000). Also good are the *Braemor Rooms,* Churchtown (phone: 988664), *Doyle's Irish Cabaret* at the *Burlington* (phone: 605222); and *Clontarf Castle* dinner show (phone: 332271).

 SINS: Drinking is the pet vice of the Irish; local sources say the Liffey runs dark with Guinness and "even the damned island is shaped like a diseased liver!"

Dublin's "sin strip," Leeson Street, is not outstandingly — but perhaps sufficiently — sinful.

BEST IN TOWN

 CHECKING IN: Since the late 1970s, with the opening of the 5-star deluxe *Berkeley Court* and the *Westbury* and the refurbishment of the *Shelbourne* and *Jurys,* Dublin's hotels have risen a bit, but they are still hardly at the top of world-class standards. Expect to pay more than $100 for a double room in hotels classified as expensive; $60 to $80 is moderate; $50 and less is inexpensive. A room with Irish breakfast for two in a private home in a residential neighborhood will cost $30 or less.

Note: The Tourist Board offers a list of hotels they have inspected and graded; they also have a computerized reservation service all over Ireland (see *Sources and Resources*).

Berkeley Court – The flagship of the P. V. Doyle Group and the first Irish member of the Leading Hotels of the World group. Close to the city in the leafy suburb of Ballsbridge, the *Berkeley* combines graciousness with modern efficiency. Contemporary and antique furnishings harmonize, and the service is exceptionally warm. There are 220 rooms, 6 suites with Jacuzzis, an excellent dining room, a conservatory-style coffee shop, a health center with indoor pool and saunas, and a shopping arcade. Lansdowne Rd. (phone: 601711). Expensive.

Bloom's – Centrally located, this intimate hotel has a high commitment to service. Its 86 rooms have color TV, air conditioning, trouser pressing, free mixers and ice, and direct-dial telephones. Every corridor has an ice cabinet and a shoeshine. Fine dining is offered in the *Trinity Room* restaurant, and there are two lively bars, *Bogie's* and *Yesterday's.* Anglesea St. (phone: 715622). Expensive.

Burlington – Ireland's largest hotel, with 500 rooms, was completely refurbished in 1985. Restaurants include an international dining room, the *Sussex,* and the cozy *Rib and Tackle Room* for beef and seafood. Trendy *Mespil Bar,* with its cheery hanging plants, globe lights and brass, has a popular lunch buffet. A musical revue is performed at *Doyle's Irish Cabaret* on summer evenings, and there's year-round entertainment in *Annabels* lounge. Leeson St. (phone: 605222). Expensive.

Gresham – Once considered one of the grandest of Dublin hotels, the *Gresham* has changed ownership a number of times and has come to rest in the Ryan Holdings Group. Though you could hardly call it grand these days, the hotel has, in the past, attracted such luminaries as Princess Grace and Prince Rainier, Elizabeth Taylor and Richard Burton, Louis Armstrong, and Bing Crosby. Upper O'Connell St. (phone: 746881). Expensive.

Jurys – Another modern hotel, the former *Inter-Continental,* is in Ballsbridge opposite the American embassy. Taking center stage are a new multistory skylit lobby and the dome-shaped Pavilion atrium, with a indoor-outdoor pool, health center, cocktail bar, lounge and *The Kish,* a seafood restaurant. Its 314 bedrooms are large and well appointed, and there are hair dryers and terrycloth robes in the tile bathrooms. Despite the hotel's size, there are nice personal touches (amenity baskets and fruit bowls). The *Embassy Room* offers Irish and international cuisine. There is also the 23-hour *Coffee Dock*. For entertainment, *Jurys* offers Ireland's longest running and most famous cabaret. The newly enlarged *Dubliner Bar* is particularly pleasant. Northumberland Rd. (phone: 605000). Expensive.

Shelbourne – This venerable hotel, a nice mixture of the dignified and the lively, is now more polished than ever after a $5 million facelift. Some rooms are truly splendid — particularly the front rooms on the second floor. Many are supremely comfortable, if compact. But the sense of history in the creaky-floored hallways and the glittering function rooms and the varied clientele — from socialites to literati — make this establishment especially appealing. The *Horseshoe Bar* is one of the livelier fixtures of Dublin pub life, while the new *Aisling* restaurant, with its 1826 plasterwork and trio of Waterford crystal chandeliers, is a showcase for modern Irish cuisine. St. Stephen's Green (phone: 766471). Expensive.

Westbury – The newest luxury addition to the Doyle Hotel Group, it has a fashionable location as the centerpiece of a chic new mall of shops and restaurants. The management emphasizes elegance, and the 150 rooms have canopied beds and an abundance of mahogany and brass furnishings. Private suites with Jacuzzis are also available. Among the restaurants here, the most noteworthy is the grand *Russell Room.* Grafton St. (phone: 791122). Expensive.

Ariel House – A homey guesthouse with 15 rooms and a restaurant with a wine license. One block from the DART station for easy commuting to the city center. Room rates include full breakfast. 52 Lansdown Rd. (phone: 685512). Moderate.

Montrose – Similar to (but larger than) the *Tara Tower,* near the National Radio and Television Studios and across the road from the new Belfield campus of University College, Dublin. About 10 minutes' drive from the city center, on a well-serviced bus route. Its 190 bedrooms are comfortable, and there is a good restaurant. Amenities include a grill, bars, health center, hairdressing salon, and souvenir shop. Stillorgan Rd. (phone: 693311). Moderate.

Skylon – Midway between downtown and the Dublin Airport, this modern north side hostelry has 100 rooms all done in a colorful Irish motif. The hotel also features a restaurant/grill that stays open until midnight. Upr. Drumcondra Rd. (phone: 379121). Moderate.

Tara Tower – Ten minutes' drive from the city center, on a well-serviced bus route, this modern hotel is comfortable and very reasonably priced. The 100 bedrooms come with radio, television, and telephone and many overlook Dublin Bay. The lobby is small, but there is a good restaurant-grill that's open until midnight. Merrion Rd. (phone: 694666). Moderate.

Anglesea Townhouse – Near the American Embassy, this Edwardian residence is the home of Helen Kirrane, who spoils her guests with hearty breakfasts of fresh fish, homemade breads and scones, fresh juices, baked fruits, and warm cereals. Heirlooms and family antiques add to the ambience of this jewel of a B&B (all 8 rooms have private bath-shower, TV, and direct dial phones). 63 Anglesea Rd., Ballsbridge (phone: 683877). Inexpensive.

Egan's House – With 19 rooms, all with private baths, this is another comfortable guesthouse. 7 Iona Park (phone: 303611). Inexpensive.

Iona House – Another guesthouse, with 12 rooms and an restaurant/coffee shop serving breakfast through late snacks. 5 Iona Park (phone: 306217). Inexpensive.

Mount Herbert – Close to the city center, this well-run family-owned property has 96 rooms, a new health facility, and a fairly good restaurant. No bar (wine license only) but a very pleasant atmosphere. 7 Herbert Rd. (phone: 684321). Inexpensive.

EATING OUT: Where food is concerned, Ireland, first and foremost an agricultural country, has outstanding raw materials. But truly distinctive and innovative Irish cuisine really does not exist. There are traditional dishes such as Irish stew, Dublin coddle, bacon and cabbage, but this kind of dish is a rara avis on the menu of most of the better restaurants, being looked down upon as too common to prepare for discriminating diners.

Where the serving of its enviable agricultural produce is concerned, Ireland's top restaurants can compare with the best anywhere. Dublin offers a wide range of first-class restaurants, a somewhat more restricted range of moderately priced establishments, and a number of fast-service, inexpensive eating places.

Dinner for two without wine will cost $50 and up in expensive restaurants; $30 to $45 is moderate; below $30 is inexpensive. Reservations are always recommended, especially at expensive and moderate establishments. Unless noted otherwise, most are closed Sundays and holidays.

Berkeley Court – One of the best of the hotel restaurants, this is an elegant, lavishly appointed room; its prize-winning chef produces highly satisfactory cuisine. Open daily. Lansdowne Rd. (phone: 601711). Expensive.

Celtic Mews – In an old Georgian mews with a warm, welcoming atmosphere, this is one of Dublin's original fine dining spots. Entrécs range from pheasant and lobster to classic Irish stew. Dinner only. 109a Lr. Baggot St. (phone: 760796). Expensive.

Le Coq Hardi – Run by owner/chef John Howard, twice Gold Medal winner in the prestigious Hotelympia/Salon Culinaire contest, this is a gracious Georgian establishment. Its extensive à la carte menu offers many house specialties such as Mr. Howard's renowned *caneton à l'orange.* Reservations essential. Major credit cards. 35 Pembroke Rd., Ballsbridge (phone: 689070). Expensive.

Ernie's – Master seafood chef Ernie Evans earned a far-reaching reputation at the *Towers* hotel on the Ring of Kerry. Still specializing in fruits de mer, he now works magic on dishes like Valencia scallops, garlic prawns, and fresh salmon. Dinner only; closed Sundays and Mondays. Mulberry Gardens, Donnybrook (phone: 693300). Expensive.

Grey Door – Open since 1978, this restaurant has achieved an enviable reputation for fine Russian and Finnish cuisine. The wine list is good and the more adventurous imbiber can sample such rarities as Russian champagne. The setting behind this elegant doorway in the heart of Georgian Dublin is intimate, rather like dining in a private home. 23 Upper Pembroke St. (phone: 763286). Expensive.

King Sitric – A superb small restaurant, right on the bay, serves perfectly cooked fish and excellent wines in a tastefully restored old house. The service is also very good. It also specializes in game birds such as grouse and snipe. East Pier, Howth (phone: 325235). Expensive.

Locks – This French provincial restaurant is on the banks of the Grand Canal near Portobello Bridge. Only the freshest produce is used for such dishes as wild salmon and breast of pigeon. 1 Windsor Terr., Portobello (phone: 752025). Expensive.

Lord Edward – Strictly for seafood lovers (no meat on the menu), this restaurant is in a tall, Victorian building opposite historic Christ Church Cathedral, in the older part of the city. The seafood is prepared and served in the classic French style. Reservations essential. Major credit cards. 23 Christ Church Pl. (phone: 752557). Expensive.

Patrick Guilbaud – This trendy place for French nouvelle cuisine draws an equally stylish crowd. Specialties include breast of duck in cider sauce, veal kidneys and sweetbreads, lamb's tongue and brill, and bacon in curry sauce. 46 James Pl., off Baggot St. (phone: 764192). Expensive.

White's on the Green – The gathering place for media stars, celebrities, and expense account diners. Elegantly appointed, with the air of a Georgian garden. Dublin's newest "in" spot features French nouvelle cuisine and the finest service traditions. Menu ranges from veal sweetbreads with fennel and celery to roasted wild salmon or panaché of lamb with fresh tarragon. 119 St. Stephen's Green (phone: 751975). Expensive.

Coffers – Around the corner from *Bloom's* hotel, this small, comfortable restaurant specializes in steaks — varying from a plain fillet to a pork steak cooked in fresh apples and Pernod. It features a special pre-theater dinner daily except Sundays. 6 Cope St. (phone: 715900, 715740). Moderate.

Gallery 22 – A pleasant, garden-like atmosphere pervades this restaurant near the *Shelbourne* on St. Stephen's Green. The innovative menu includes seafood pancakes, rack of lamb, sea trout, and fillet steak with vermouth sauce. A pre-theater dinner is also offered. 22 St. Stephen's Green (phone: 686169). Moderate.

La Grenouille – A French-style bistro next to the Powerscourt Townhouse Center. Each dish on the limited menu is cooked to order. Choices range from rack of lamb or poulet in blue cheese sauce to steak and duck, all served with an array of fresh vegetables. Open daily for dinner, a rarity in Dublin. 64 S William St. (phone: 779157). Moderate.

Rudyards – It occupies three floors of a tall, narrow house in Crown Alley and offers a combination of mildly exotic Continental dishes, from spinach-stuffed pancakes to navarin of lamb, pasta, and tomato pie and beef in orange sauce. No reservations. 15 Crown Alley, off Dame St. (phone: 710846). Moderate to inexpensive.

Unicorn – Established in 1939, this small Italian restaurant is a favorite with Irish politicians and literati. All pastas and sauces are made by owners Renato and Nina Sidoli. Open for lunch and dinner daily except Sundays. Merrion Ct., off Merrion Row (phone: 762182 or 688552). Moderate to inexpensive.

Bad Ass Cafe – One of the newest, brightest, and liveliest restaurants to hit town in some time. Famed as much for its (loud!) rock music and videos as for its great pizza. Steaks are another specialty. Crown Alley, behind the Central Bank on Dame St. (phone: 712596). Inexpensive.

Captain America's – Specializes in "genuine American hamburgers," Tex-Mex, and barbecue dishes, served with American beer and rock music. Open daily. Grafton Court, 1st floor, Grafton St. (phone: 715266). Inexpensive.

Casper & Giumbini's Drink and Food Emporium – A really lively restaurant with some traditional Irish dishes, such as Irish stew (not always easy to come by in Irish restaurants!). There's also an exotic range of cocktails and a selection of international beers. Saturday and Sunday brunch is served. 6 Wicklow St. (phone: 794347). Inexpensive.

Kilkenny Kitchen – This bright, self-service restaurant in the Kilkenny Design Centre makes a perfect stop for morning coffee, lunch, or afternoon tea (no dinner) during a day of shopping. There's a limited but tasty choice of dishes and very good salads. Kilkenny Shop, Nassau St. (phone: 777066). Inexpensive.

Pancake HQ – The emphasis here is on salads, seafood, hamburgers, and steaks, and lavish dessert pancakes are a specialty of the house. The atmosphere is cheerful, and the clientele tends to be fairly young and lively. 5 Beresford Pl. (phone: 744657). Inexpensive.

SHARING A PINT: Until you have been in a pub, you have not experienced Dublin. Here Dubliners come to pursue two serious occupations: drinking and conversation. Many pubs are ugly and modern, complete with Muzak and plastic, but plenty of traditional pubs remain — noisy, companionable places where you can pursue friendly ghosts of bygone Dublin in an unhurried atmosphere. Some favorites are the *Horseshoe Bar* in the *Shelbourne Hotel*, St. Stephen's Green (phone: 766471), favored by the uppity, horsey set; the *Bailey*, at 2 Duke St. (phone: 773055), a literary pub that actually displays the door of nearby 7 Eccles St., where Joyce's Molly and Leopold Bloom lived; *O'Donoghue's*, off St. Stephen's Green, for Irish ballads; the *Palace Bar* on Fleet St., a traditional haunt of journalists and literati; *Mulligans* of Poolbeg St., renowned for the quality of its pint, appreciated equally by the dock workers and students (from nearby Trinity College), who form its main clientele; the *Stag's Head*, Dame Ct. (a great haunt of the legal profession), which serves hearty hot lunches at reasonable prices; *Neary's*, Chatham St., which offers delicacies like smoked salmon and oysters in season; the *Brazen Head*, Bridge St., and *Davy Byrne's*, 21 Duke St., for plain drinking and gab; *Doheny and Nesbitts* on Merrion Row, which is always known simply as "Nesbitts" — try the bar, not the modernized upstairs lounge; and last, but very far from least, the utterly delightful *Ryans*, Parkgate St., with its shining mirrors, its courteous barmen, and its snugs where guests can drink quietly.

WINE BARS: A popular addition to the Dublin scene are wine bars, which generally offer light meals and good wines at moderate prices. Some exceptionally pleasant examples of the genre are:

Kilmartin's – Originally owned by a turf accountant (or bookie), its new owners retained both the name and the racing decor. Run by two young women, both Cordon Bleu cooks, Kilmartin's offers a limited but excellent menu. The house wine is particularly good. 19 Upper Baggot St. (phone: 686674).

Shrimp's – Tiny, but charmingly decorated, it is not the place to air your most intimate thoughts. The food, however, is tempting and you can choose from a good range of wines. 1 Anne's La. (phone: 713143).

Mitchell's – In the cellar (where else!) of Mitchell's Wine Merchants, this is where swinging Dubliners lunch. The menu is somewhat limited, but the helpings are large, the cooking quite good, and the desserts mouth-watering. Alas, it's not open in the evenings. Get there before 12:30, or you'll find yourself in for a long wait at lunchtime (which you can while away by sampling some of Mitchell's splendid wines). 21 Kildare St. (phone: 680367).

The Táin – The emphasis here is on modern Irish design, although the background music is often a melodious ancient harp. Steaks are the specialty but there are also such delights as curried prawn soup, smoked Wicklow trout, and crudité salads. Powerscourt Townhouse Centre, 59 S William St. (phone: 791517).

Timmerman's – Arched ceilings, old church pews, and empty wine barrels dominate the decor of this unique spot. The menu is simple — quiches, lasagne, steaks, corned beef, and a variety of fruits and vegetable salads. A popular choice to accompany wine is a platter of 15 different Irish cheeses. Music in the evenings. Powerscourt Townhouse Centre, 59 S William St. (phone: 717425 or 794186).

EDINBURGH

Other beautiful and famous urban centers such as Rome or San Francisco may share the distinction of being built on hills, but Edinburgh, a stark and in some ways still medieval city whose streets have often flowed with blood, alone can claim to be built on extinct volcanoes.

Astride one of these, high above the houses where Edinburgh's 440,000 inhabitants dwell, looms Edinburgh Castle, a portentous fairy tale structure that often makes visitors gasp the first time they see it. It seems almost supernatural, with ancient stonemasonry rising out of volcanic rock as if there were no dividing line between the two.

From the seventh century on, there was a fortress where Edinburgh Castle now stands, and as life in the Middle Ages became more civilized, life within the fortress spilled onto the long sloping ridge — carved by glaciers ages after the volcanic era — that runs down from Edinburgh Castle to the foot of Arthur's Seat, another extinct volcano, crowning Edinburgh's central park. The ridge, with its clusters of high stone and wood tenements, its one thin, snakelike public street, its cathedral, and its tollbooth, was (and still is) the securing knot at the center of Scotland's legal, commercial, and artistic fiber.

Walking around central Edinburgh today is sheer joy. There's very little need for a map; it's hard to get lost. Every time you reach a hilltop, there's a glorious vista of the sweeping fusion of earth, sky, and sea, and every glance up an alley reveals fantastic steeples, jagged, smoking, chimney-potted skylines, or beauteous rotund domes. The city lights its most imposing public buildings at night, and they are legion, spread out over a series of precipices and valleys. Nature provides incredible sunsets, the product of Scotland's unique slowly fading evening light (the "gloaming") and rapid change in the evening temperature. Legend and romance are at every hand. Somebody famous lived in almost every residence.

At the head of the legend and romance brigade are the arch Presbyterian John Knox and Mary, Queen of Scots, both of whom dominated life in the Edinburgh of the late sixteenth century. (Not that they dominated it together. When Mary arrived in Edinburgh in the autumn of 1561 as Scotland's very young and very Catholic new queen, Knox described the event in his diary as God having fouled the air with black fog and seeping rain.) The political and religious strife attendant upon Mary's reign is notorious, as are her two marriages and the three deaths associated with them, the last of these her own (she was beheaded by her cousin Queen Elizabeth I of England, to whom she had fled for asylum). Mary lived in Holyrood Palace, by the abbey at the base of Arthur's Seat. John Knox lived up the ridge from her near St. Giles's Cathedral, within the city gates. Both residences are extant and open to the public today.

Their Edinburgh reached its full flower around the end of the seventeenth century, when the tenements along the ridge had grown 15 (or more) tottering stories high and housed uncounted numbers of people, all of whom threw their garbage into the central street, warning those below with nothing more than the terse cry *"Gardez-loo!"* Buildings frequently collapsed. Water could be had only from one of the city's six wells, called *pennywells* (their sites are still marked today), and inhabitants would line up with buckets from 3 AM on to be sure of some water.

These cramped and malodorous conditions, plus a plethora of alehouses and a police force made up of decrepit Highlanders back from European wars, no doubt had something to do with the locals' favorite sport, rioting on fete days, parade days, and the king's birthday. Riots occasioned by more serious events were frequent also and occurred regularly in every age up to the Victorian and even beyond. Famous instances are the assassination of a wealthy councillor, John MacMorran, by dissatisfied youths at the Royal High School (sixteenth century); "Cleanse the Causeway," a battle in the streets between two noble families, the Douglases and Hamiltons (seventeenth century); the Jenny Geddes affair, in which a Presbyterian fishwife caused pandemonium by throwing a stool at a dean who was reading the new Episcopal service book in St. Giles's Cathedral — the first event in the British Civil War (seventeenth century); the Porteous Riots, immortalized by Sir Walter Scott in *The Heart of Midlothian* (eighteenth century); and the trial of William Burke, whose sale of his victims' corpses to the University of Edinburgh's medical luminaries did so much to further the international reputation of that great institution (nineteenth century). Religious riots have scarred the city's history repeatedly, although the last one was back in the 1930s.

Obviously this wizened medieval town had to spread out somehow, and luckily, in the second half of the eighteenth century, its by now thoroughly Protestant God sent it an increase in trade and prosperity. City fathers erected a wealth of new buildings on another ridge to the north — known as the New Town, connected to the Old Town by bridges. The classically proportioned beauty of New Town buildings, many of which were designed by the world-renowned British architect Robert Adam, is a testament to what is generally regarded as Edinburgh's golden age, part of the so-called Scottish Enlightenment. It was a great age not only for architects but for writers, publishers, philosophers, and politicians. Throughout the city, taverns became the sites of ongoing seminars. Among many other well-known people of the time, David Hume, Adam Smith, and James Boswell were Edinburgh men.

Today's Edinburgh has lost some of its traditional vibrancy and color, though it is certainly safer and cleaner. The near stranglehold the Presbyterian Church of Scotland attained on the social institutions during Queen Victoria's reign meant that industriousness, temperance, and respectability — all the middle-class virtues — took supreme command of the city. About 60% of the present inhabitants are white-collar workers, an unusually high proportion, which helps keep the local flavor staid.

Nonetheless, signs are that things are livening up. Since 1979, an avalanche of flashy pubs, nightspots, and restaurants has shattered the city's sober air. Edinburgh has always been favored by geography, situated as it is on the Firth of Forth, an inlet in the North Sea, and surrounded by woods, rolling hills, and lochs (lakes). It is not only a national capital but a port whose chief exports include whisky, coal, and machinery; a large brewing center; and a center for nuclear and electronics research.

And though the idea of a Scottish Assembly at Edinburgh — favored by a majority of Scottish voters — was set aside on a technicality a few years ago, a groundswell of agitation for Scotland's greater control of its own affairs remains. Who can say whether Edinburgh's second golden age is at hand? Perhaps not all its volcanoes are extinct.

Certainly the smell of sulfur has been ominously in the air, as the ancient capital has been suffering the repercussions of Thatcherism's bitter conflicts. Increased government pressure on the BBC has resulted in the shelving of plans for a National Broadcasting Centre for Scotland and for the transfer of news and current affairs to Glasgow. Labour party victories in local government elections have been offset by government privatization of Edinburgh city transport, which has led to at least temporary transport chaos, if not an actual Streetcar War. The Edinburgh Festival (see *Extra Special*) has been caught in the crossfire, weakened by government slashing of arts budgets and local Labour Council charges of elitism. In fact, the Festival has continued to maintain high standards, and, despite continuing pressure, the theater pageant is reviving, rejuvenated.

If anything, occasional disasters heighten the innumerable triumphs of what is undoubtedly the world's greatest arts festival. The low-budget Film Festival can't be Cannes, but its stature increases steadily. Unfortunately, mismanagement, anti-apartheid boycotts, and underfunding made the Commonwealth Games of 1986 a financial disaster, and Edinburgh's complacency has been additionally jolted by a growing preference for Glasgow as the site of future sporting events. The old Glasgow taunt that Edinburgh is "fur coat and nae knickers" has all too much relevance in a cold financial climate. The capital has had to look to its laurels, which means, among other things, that tourists are currently taken far less for granted.

EDINBURGH AT-A-GLANCE

 SEEING THE CITY: Edinburgh has many wonderful views; on a clear day, there are striking panoramas from the top of any of its extinct volcanoes. To the north lies the sparkling Firth of Forth and, beyond it, the ancient kingdom of Fife. To the south are the lovely Pentland Hills and surrounding plowed farmlands. Look eastward, where the giant Bass Rock, off the coast of Berwickshire, meets your eye. Look westward to see across the whole nation to Ben Lomond, nearly on the west coast of Scotland! If you have a car, drive up Arthur's Seat (the road begins just by Holyrood Palace), park at Dunsapie Loch, and walk to the uppermost height (a steep and furzy climb — wear flat shoes and watch out for falling sheep). If you have no car, see the city from Edinburgh Castle.

SPECIAL PLACES: The "Royal Mile" is the name given to the oldest part of the city, the road that runs downhill from Edinburgh Castle to Holyrood Palace. It comprises four contiguous streets: Castle Hill, the Lawnmarket, High Street, and the Canongate. Since the entire citizenry of Edinburgh lived and worked for centuries either on or just off these four streets, the Royal Mile is practically groaning with objects and sites of historic fascination: 16th- and 17th-century houses, well preserved, with their adjacent courtyards and closes; residences of famous writers and distinguished thinkers; St. Giles's Cathedral, the High Kirk of Edinburgh, with its 17th-century spire in the shape of the Scottish crown; excellent museums; the classical City Chambers; and the building where Scotland's Parliament met from 1639 until union with England's in 1707. For additional details, see *The Royal Mile: Brief Guide,* an excellent walking companion, available for 30p from the tourist office.

THE ROYAL MILE

Edinburgh Castle – The oldest building in Edinburgh is part of the castle structure, a tiny ethereal chapel built by Queen Margaret, the wife of the Malcolm who features in *Macbeth.* King James VI of Scotland (later James I of England) was born here. The Scottish Regalia, including Sceptre and Crown, are on display. These disappeared after the union of Scotland with England and were found, over a hundred years later, by Sir Walter Scott (who was leading a government commission appointed to look for them) in an old locked box. Emotion ran so high that his daughter, who was present on the occasion, fainted when he lifted the lid. Also in the castle is the Scottish National War Memorial, honoring Scots who died in the two world wars.

Outlook Tower Visitor Centre – A short distance east of the castle, climb up 98 steps, walk outside, and find yourself face to face with church spires. The camera obscura, actually a periscope, throws a revolving image of nearby streets and buildings onto a circular table, while one of the tower's denizens gives an excellent historical talk. Downstairs is a very good book shop carrying everything from Lady Antonia Fraser's best-selling biography of Mary, Queen of Scots, to gleaming coffee table volumes about one of the national obsessions, Scotch whisky. Open daily, 9:30 AM to early evening. Admission charge. Castle Hill (phone: 226-3709).

Parliament House – Built from 1632 to 1640, after Charles I suggested that it replace the Collegiate buildings of St. Giles's Cathedral, this historic sanctum once housed Scotland's Parliament and is today the country's supreme court. Until 1982, tourists could enter only by written request. Its showpiece is the Great Hall, with a fine hammer-beam roof and walls laden with portraits by Raeburn and other famous Scottish artists. Closed Saturdays through Mondays. Upper High St. (phone: 225-2595).

St. Giles's Cathedral – A church of some sort has stood here for over 1,000 years. The medieval building here was named for the Athenian saint Egidius (Giles). St. Giles's has often been showered by flying religious fur, especially at the time of the Reformation. In 1559–60 soldiers were put on guard at the church and many of its treasures hidden in private Catholic homes; Protestant nobles nonetheless ravaged the altars. Later, English troops came to their aid and stripped St. Giles's from top to bottom. It was at this stage that John Knox, a prime mover in this sequence of events, was made minister of St. Giles's. His unmarked grave is believed to be under Parliament Square, just outside St. Giles's. Open daily. Upper High St. (phone: 225-4363).

Mercat Cross, or Market Cross – Near the east door of St. Giles's stands a monument erected by W. E. Gladstone, prime minister of Britain off and on from 1868 to 1894. Here was the crossroads at which proclamations were read out and public hangings took place, until well into the 19th century. It was also the commercial focal point of old Edinburgh, the place being so thick with butchers, bakers, merchants, burgesses, lawyers, tinkers, tailors, farmers, drovers, and fishmongers that the town council issued ordinances requiring each trade to occupy its own separate neighboring street or close (hence the names you see on the entrances to the closes as you go down the Royal Mile: Fleshmarket Close, Advocates' Close, and so on). City tradesmen never obeyed these ordinances, however, and the Mercat Cross remained as colorful as ever until the city began to spread out in the second half of the 18th century. High St., by St. Giles's.

Advocates' Close and Anchor Close – These are typical of the many narrow alleys that gave access to the inns and taverns that were so much a part of Edinburgh's 18th-century cultural life. Doors to these places (taverns no longer) were topped by stone architraves dating from the 16th century and bearing inscriptions like "Blissit Be God of Al His Gifts" or "Spes Altera Vitae" (these two examples are still in Advocates' Close today). In Anchor Close was Douglas's, where the poet Robert Burns habitually drank. Entrances of both closes are from High St.

John Knox's House – Legend says that Scotland's fieriest preacher of all time lived here, but historians say no. However, legend has won, and this attractive 15th-century dwelling was preserved when most of its neighbors were razed during the widening of High Street in 1849. Open October through March, 10 AM to 4 PM; 10 AM to 5 PM the rest of the year. Closed Sundays. Admission charge. 45 High St. (phone: 556-6961).

Acheson House – When King Charles I was crowned at Edinburgh in 1633, Sir Archibald Acheson, baronet, was his secretary of state. Acheson built this house, a small courtyard mansion, the only one of its kind in Edinburgh, in the same year. It was the height of elegance in its day, yet 100 years later it had become a popular brothel and 200 years after that was inhabited by 14 families, though it had been built to house one. It was bought and restored by the marquess of Bute in 1935, whereupon, despite its history, it was leased to the Canongate Kirk for a manse! Today it houses the Scottish Craft Centre, where you can buy all sorts of attractive, handmade items. Closed Sundays. Free. 140 the Canongate (phone: 556-8136).

Canongate Kirkyard – Opposite Acheson House. Pause long enough to read the long list — mounted on a plaque — of notables buried there. The Canongate.

Scottish Stone and Brass Rubbing Centre – Visitors may rub any of the brasses or stones on show. Materials are provided for a fee that probably won't come to over £4. The brass commemorating Robert Bruce, king of Scotland from 1306 to 1329, is very impressive. In addition to being nice souvenirs, your own finished products make beautiful gifts. Closed Sundays. Canongate Tollbooth Annex, 163 Canongate (phone: 225-1131).

Holyrood Palace – A royal retreat since the beginning of the 16th century, the palace is where Queen Elizabeth II stays when she is in residence in Edinburgh today. It is made of stone, a huge, imposing round-towered edifice befitting kings and queens. Most of what you see of it now was built by Charles II from 1671, but it is chiefly associated with Mary, Queen of Scots, who lived in it well before that for six contentious, sensational years. The old part, still extant, contains her bedroom and the supper room in which David Riccio, her secretary, was brutally murdered before her very eyes by a gang of armed men that included her jealous husband, her cousin Lord Darnley. By the side of the palace, within its spacious grounds, are the picturesque ruins of Holyrood Abbey and the lodge known as Queen Mary's Bath House, where she reputedly bathed in red wine. A guide will take you through it all, sparing no gory details. Closed Sundays from November through March and when the queen is in town. Admission charge. At the bottom of the Canongate (phone: 556-7371).

BEYOND THE ROYAL MILE

Princes Street Gardens – Princes Street is modern Edinburgh's Main Street, its Broadway, and its Fifth Avenue. The gardens stretch nearly the street's whole length on the south side, where the old Nor' Loch, which was used in medieval times as the castle moat, once stood. The city spends thousands of pounds every year to keep the gardens opulent with flowers. In summer months (June–September) there are concerts, children's shows, variety acts, and do-it-yourself Scottish country dancing (to professional bands) here. Gates close at dusk. Princes St.

National Gallery of Scotland – Smack in the middle of Princes Street Gardens, on a man-made embankment called the Mound, is this exquisite museum, opened in 1859. It contains paintings by British and European masters from the 14th century to Cézanne. Open daily. Free. The Mound (phone: 556-8921).

Scott Monument – Sir Walter Scott is certainly one of Edinburgh's favorite sons — his face even decorates all Bank of Scotland notes, even though he was the most famous bankrupt in Scottish history. The elaborate 200-foot Gothic monument on the east end of Princes Street Gardens helps make Edinburgh's skyline the ornamental marvel it is. Its 287 steps take you to the summit. (Don't attempt it if you suffer vertigo.) Closed weekends. Admission charge. Princes St. (phone: 225-2424, ext. 6596).

New Town – To the north of Princes Street lies the largest Neoclassical townscape in Europe, built between the 1760s and 1830s. Assiduous conservation means that little has changed externally in these streets, squares, and crescents. Three of the more interesting ones are Charlotte Square (designed by Robert Adam), Moray Place, and Ann Street. The New Town Conservation Centre, 13A Dundas St. (phone: 556-7054), arranges guided tours of the area; closed weekends.

Georgian House – On the most gracious square in the elegant New Town, the National Trust for Scotland has furnished a house in period style and opened it to the public. The kitchen is a wonderland of utilitarian objects that would have belonged to a typical high-class late-18th-century ménage. Fascinating audio-visual sessions on the history and topography of the New Town come with the admission price. Open daily April through October; weekends only November to mid-December; closed mid-December through March. 7 Charlotte Sq. (phone: 225-2160).

Edinburgh Zoo – Opposite the Pentland Hills, away from the city center, en route to the western suburb of Corstorphine, is a zoo with a view and the world's most famous penguins, the largest colony in captivity. Every afternoon at 2:30, from April to October, they perform their delightful Penguin Parade through the park grounds. Open daily. Admission fee. Corstorphine Rd., Murrayfield (phone: 334-9171).

Grassmarket – This ancient street is flanked by many cozy eateries, elegant shops, and seedy-looking flophouses. The West Bow, off the street's east end, has some intriguing boutiques. Leading from the Grassmarket is Cowgate, with the 16th-century Magdalen Chapel (phone the Scottish Reformation Society to see it: 225-1836).

Dean Village – This 800-year-old grain milling town on the Water of Leith is over 100 feet below the level of much of the rest of the city and a good place to soak up local color. In summer the woodland walk along the river is popping with bohemians who live in the next village, Stockbridge. End of Bell's Brae (turn left off Queensferry St. onto Bell's Brae as you approach Dean Bridge from the west end of Princes St.).

■**EXTRA SPECIAL:** The Edinburgh International Festival is held every year during the last three weeks of August. It features the best-known, most highly regarded performers in opera, music, theater, and dance. Each year brings different orchestras, soloists, theater and opera companies — all are usually topnotch.

Accompanying the festival proper is the phenomenal Edinburgh Festival Fringe, an orgy of over 1,000 productions by amateur and lesser-known professional companies from Europe, Britain, and the US who come to Edinburgh at their own expense to strike a blow for art and for themselves. Perhaps the most celebrated Fringe success story was Tom Stoppard's *Rosencrantz and Guildenstern Are Dead.*

Coinciding with the first two weeks of the International Festival is the Edinburgh International Film Festival. Entries are screened at 88 Lothian Road, where the rest of the year Filmhouse (phone: 228-6382) offers a varied diet of classics and art movies in bijou surroundings with outstanding restaurant and bar facilities.

And the Edinburgh Military Tattoo, a spectacular concert in full Highland dress by the massed pipe bands of Her Majesty's Scottish regiments, blasts forth most nights during the festival on the Castle Esplanade.

The Edinburgh Jazz Festival convenes during the second week of the International Festival. Pick up the succession of lively concerts at the Edinburgh Festival Club, in the Edinburgh University Staff Club, 9/15 Chambers St. (phone: 226-5639).

Those interested are advised to reserve tickets — and hotel space — as far in advance as possible, especially for the most popular attractions such as the Tattoo. A detailed festival brochure is available at the British Tourist Authority in New York (see *Sources and Resources*) by April. You can book reservations through a travel agent or write directly to the individual events. For the International Festival, it's the Festival Box Office, 21 Market St., Edinburgh EH1 1BW (phone: 226-4001); for the Tattoo, the Tattoo Office, 22 Market St., Edinburgh EH1 1QB (phone: 225-1188); and the Edinburgh Festival Fringe Society, 170 High St. (phone: 226-5257 and 226-5259; reservations, 226-5138).

SOURCES AND RESOURCES

TOURIST INFORMATION: For information in the US, contact the British Tourist Authority, 40 W 57th St., New York, NY 10036 (phone: 212-581-4700); in Edinburgh, the City of Edinburgh Tourist Centre, Waverley Market, 3 Princes St., Edinburgh EH2 2QP (phone: 557-2727), offers information, maps, and leaflets. The Edinburgh office stocks all City of Edinburgh publications. On sale there is the *Edinburgh Official Guide,* updated annually. In it is a reasonable working map of downtown areas, with places of interest marked. A good, more detailed map is the Edinburgh number of the *Geographia Street Atlas and Index* series, on sale at most local bookshops. The pamphlets on Edinburgh history and legend at the *Camera Obscura* bookshop (see *Special Places*) will add greatly to your appreciation of what you see of the city. Each costs about $3. Also check the Ticket Centre, Tattoo Office, Waverley Bridge (phone: 225-3732), open weekdays, 10 AM to 5 PM, as well as on weekends in July and August. The US Consulate is at 3 Regent Terr. (phone: 556-8315).

Local Coverage – The *Scotsman,* morning daily; the *Edinburgh Evening News,* evening daily; *What's On,* published monthly by the city, listing forthcoming happenings; another *What's On,* a free, privately owned monthly, is available in most hotel lobbies; *Leisureline Service,* a recorded daily telephone prospectus from May through September (phone: 246-8041); and *The List,* a comprehensive Glasgow and Edinburgh events guide (phone: 558-1192). Also, see the *Festival Times* during the Edinburgh Festival.

GETTING AROUND: Airport – Edinburgh Airport is about a half-hour from the center of town; the average taxi fare is £7. An "Airlink" bus, #100, travels from the airport to Waverley Bridge, making stops en route at the *Caledonian* hotel and at Haymarket and Murrayfield (phone: 226-5087). The tourist desk at the Edinburgh Airport (phone: 333-2167) will provide information.

Bus – *City Transport* headquarters is at 14 Queen St. (phone: 554-4494), parallel to Princes St., two blocks away. Route maps are no longer available, because routes are subject to change every three months. The Tattoo Office at Market St. and Waverley Bridge also houses a City Transport Information Bureau, where details on each current bus route (except for St. Andrew Square Bus Station) can be obtained. Passengers can reach most places from Princes St.; exact fare required. The Tourist Board office can provide information on bus tours of the city and countryside. Longer-distance buses go from St. Andrew Square Bus Station, St. Andrew Sq. (phone: 556-2126).

Car Rental – All major national firms are represented.

Taxi – There are cabstands at St. Andrew Square Bus Station and in Waverley Station, off Princes St. Or phone *City Cabs* (phone: 228-1211), *Central Radio Taxis* (phone: 229-5221), or *Radiocabs* (phone: 225-6736 or 225-9000).

Train – The main railway station is Waverley Station at Princes St. and Waverley Bridge (phone: 556-2451).

 MUSEUMS: The city runs three museums of local history: *Huntly House,* the Canongate (phone: 225-2424, ext. 6689); *Canongate Tollbooth,* the Canongate (phone: 225-2424, ext. 6638); and *Lady Stair's House* (a Burns, Scott, and Stevenson museum), Lawnmarket (phone: 225-2424, ext. 6593). The *Scottish National Gallery* is described in *Special Places.* Other museums are:

Central Library – An outstanding collection of maps, prints, photographs, books, and newspapers. The Reference, Scotland, and Edinburgh rooms are invaluable. George IV Bridge (phone: 225-5584).

DeMarco Gallery – Headquarters for avant-garde art. St. Mary's Church, Blackfriars St. (phone: 557-0707).

Edinburgh Wax Museum – With every notorious Scot from Macbeth to Billy Connolly, and a particularly effective gruesome Chamber of Horrors that makes Mme. Tussaud's look like a high school prom. Admission charge. 142 High St.(phone: 226-4444).

Lauriston Castle – A 16th-century home decorated entirely with Edwardian antiques. Off Cramond Rd. S (phone: 336-2060).

Museum of Childhood – Antique toys, games, dolls, and costumes, all beautifully explained and arranged. 38 High St. (phone: 225-2424, ext. 6638).

National Library of Scotland – Exhibits on Scotland's literati through the ages. George IV Bridge (phone: 226-4531).

Royal Scottish Museum – A museum of natural history, science, and technology, great for kids. Chambers St. (phone: 225-7534).

Scottish National Gallery of Modern Art – Matisse to Picasso. Belford Rd. (phone: 556-8921).

Scottish National Portrait Gallery/The National Museum of Antiquities – These museums are on two sides of one building. 1 Queen St. (phone: 556-8921).

 SHOPPING: Princes Street is Edinburgh's main shopping street, chock-a-block with a variety of stores. In addition, at the east end of Princes Street is Waverley Market, a large, modern shopping mall with Waverley Station at its base and the Tourist Office on the roof. Open daily until 6 PM, except Thursdays until 7 PM. The best buy is in Scottish tartans and woolens. Also worth a look are antiques — particularly Victoriana — in the area around St. Stephen's Street in Stockbridge. Bone china and Scottish crystal are attractive, and don't miss the shortbread, which is on sale everywhere. We especially recommend the following shops:

Debenham's – A branch of the London firm, with clothes, accessories, cosmetics, and more. 109-112 Princes St. (phone: 225-1320).

Edinburgh Woollen Mill – A good, inexpensive alternative to the *Scotch House* at 62 Princes St. (phone: 225-4966); 453 Lawnmarket (phone: 225-1525); and 51 High St. (phone: 556-9786).

Jenner's Department Store – Sells everything, especially bone china and Scottish crystal. A particularly good selection of fine food items, ideal for packing fancy picnics. Princes and St. David's sts. (phone: 225-2442).

Janet Lumsden – Antique silver, jewelry, glass, and porcelain. 51A George St. (phone: 225-2911).

Pitlochry Knitwear – Bargains in Scottish products, especially sweaters, kilts, and ladies' suits. 28 North Bridge (phone: 225-3893).

Scotch House – Classy, expensive woolens such as kilts, sweaters, tweeds, scarves, shawls, and mohairs. 60 Princes St. (phone: 556-1252).

 SPECIAL EVENTS: The *Edinburgh International Festival* and the concurrent *Edinburgh Festival Fringe* and *Edinburgh International Film Festival* are held every year during the last three weeks in August. (For details, see *Extra Special.*) The *Edinburgh Folk Festival* occurs in early spring (for details, contact the Folk Festival office, Skilling Hill, Temple, near Edinburgh; phone: 830-0298).

 SPORTS: Golf – Scotland's national mania. A letter from your home club president or pro should get you into any of the city's 22 courses (you'll usually need it only for the posh, private ones like *Royal Burgess, Bruntsfield,* both in suburban Barnton, and *Muirfield* — home of the world's oldest group of plays, the Honourable Company of Edinburgh Golfers — in nearby Gullane). Clubs can be rented. Full details on public courses are listed in the *Edinburgh Official Guide* and in the free leaflet *Golf in Scotland,* both available at the tourist office.

Skiing – *Hillend Ski Center* on the Pentland Hills is the largest artificial slope in Britain. Equipment for hire. Open daily 9:30 AM to 9 PM, weekends May through August 9:30 AM to 5 PM (phone: 445-4433).

Swimming – Have a dip in the luxurious *Royal Commonwealth Pool,* built for the 1970 Commonwealth Games. Open weekdays, 9 AM to 9 PM, weekends, 10 AM to 4 PM. Dalkeith Rd. (phone: 667-7211). For other sports, consult your *Edinburgh Official Guide.*

 THEATER: The *King's,* 2 Leven St. (phone: 229-1201), and the *Royal Lyceum,* Grindlay St. (phone: 229-9697), are Edinburgh's two main venues. Although productions at the *King's* are considered mediocre, the *Royal Lyceum* has been gaining a reputation for its interesting work. The *Playhouse,* 20 Greenside Pl. (phone: 557-2590), is a converted cinema where musical productions are staged. The *Traverse,* 112 West Bow (phone: 226-2633), a theater club with an avant-garde image and a much higher standard. The *Netherbow,* 43 High St. (phone: 556-9579), and *Theatre Workshop,* 34 Hamilton Pl. (phone: 225-7942), mount small-scale, artistic productions. Schedules are in the dailies and in *The List.*

 MUSIC: Classical music is the city's overriding passion. Highbrow musical events are held at *Usher Hall,* Lothian Rd. (phone: 228-1155), where the *Scottish National Orchestra* holds performances on Friday nights at 7:30. The *Scottish Opera Co.,* which has excellent standards, has seasons at the *King's,* and also at the *Playhouse* (see *Theater* for addresses), where other famous names in both classical and nonclassical music give concerts. For chamber music and occasional jazz, try *Queen's Hall,* Clerk St. (phone: 668-3456). The Scottish Chamber Orchestra often performs International Lunchtime Concerts (except during the Festival) on Mondays at 1 PM in Assembly Rooms, George St. Tickets at Tattoo Office, Waverley Bridge, and at Usher Hall. At *St. Mary's Cathedral,* Palmerston Pl. (phone: 225-6293), evensong is sung on weekday afternoons at 5:15 by a trained choir with boy sopranos. Also, countless amateur groups swell the city's halls and churches. Details are available in the dailies and in *The List.*

NIGHTCLUBS AND NIGHTLIFE: Edinburgh isn't exactly Las Vegas; it isn't even Philadelphia. Discos here are usually filled with a very young crowd, but you could risk the following if you're under thirty: *Zenatec,* 56 Fountainbridge (phone: 229-8522 or 229-7733); *Cinderellas Rockerfellas,* 99 St. Stephen St. (phone: 556-0266); and *Outer Limits* (teenagers leave at 11 PM so others can roll up to an after-hours bar), W Tollcross (phone: 228-3252). Jazz and folk music can be heard at bars and hotels around the city; check the *Evening News'* Nightlife page or *What's On* magazine. *Fire Island,* 127 Princes St. (226-4660), is the city's gay (male) disco.

SINS: You have to know somebody.

BEST IN TOWN

CHECKING IN: In Scotland, it is practically impossible to get a room without an accompanying kippers-to-nuts Big Scottish Breakfast (you pay for it whether you eat it or not). Expect to shell out $110 and up for a double with breakfast in the hotels listed below as expensive; $85 to $110 for those in the moderate category; between $50 and $85 for the cheapies-but-goodies in the inexpensive range. Unless otherwise noted, hotels accept all major credit cards. Should you find it impossible to get into any of our selected hotels, City of Edinburgh District Council at the airport, and in town at Waverley Market, 3 Princes St. (phone: 557-2727), has an accommodations service covering all of Edinburgh and the surrounding district.

Caledonian – A large, Edwardian, former railroad hotel with 254 rooms, 2 dining rooms, and 3 bars. Recently completely refurbished, it boasts great views of Edinburgh Castle. The new decoration is very engaging, and the rooms have been made infinitely more appetizing. Celebrities love it. Phones in rooms. West end of Princes St. (phone: 225-2433). Expensive.

Carlton Highland – This building has been remarkably transformed from an old department store into a grand and sophisticated Victorian hotel. Recently opened with 207 rooms, 2 dining rooms, and a bar. North Bridge, off Princes St. (phone: 556-7277). Expensive.

Dalhousie Castle – Originally built during the 12th century and enlarged ever since (Queen Victoria once stayed here). Now it's a luxury country house hotel with 24 rooms. About 8 miles south of Edinburgh (phone: Gorebridge 2-0153). Expensive.

Edinburgh Sheraton – This new, honey-colored hotel, just off Princes Street, seems architecturally incongruous in the neighborhood, but it can't be beat for its range of modern amenities: 263 very well equipped rooms, a health club and gym, sauna and whirlpool, swimming pool, parking, bar, and restaurant. 1 Festival Sq. (phone: 229-9131). Expensive.

George – The best in town. It is in the New Town, between Charlotte and St. Andrew squares, and is known for its gracious comfort. It has 195 bedrooms, 2 dining rooms, and a long bar. Phones in rooms. 19-21 George St. (phone: 225-1251). Expensive.

Howard – Its flower-filled window boxes are the last word in winsomeness. It has 25 rooms, with phones (and, surprisingly for a hotel this size, private baths). 32-36 Great King St. (phone: 557-3500). Expensive.

North British – A former British Rail hotel, it's large (200 rooms), recently refurbished, and overlooks the Castle and Princes Street Gardens. Its restaurant, the *Cleikum,* serves authentic Scottish cuisine. Princes St. (phone: 556-2414). Expensive.

Post House – An ultramodern, all-conveniences affair, this is a good place to be if you have a car (it's beside the zoo, outside the city center). Its low-priced coffeehouse is less stuffily British than almost anywhere else. Breakfast optional. Its 208 rooms all have phones. Corstorphine Rd. (phone: 334-8221). Expensive.

Ladbroke Dragonara – A flashy, contemporary property away from the center of things but with a beautiful view of the Water of Leith and close to Dean Village and the Museum of Modern Art. There are 146 rooms and two restaurants. 69 Belford Rd. (phone: 332-2545). Expensive to moderate.

Braid Hills – Muriel Spark fans will remember that this is where Miss Jean Brodie, by then past her prime, took tea. An old, established family-run, 70-room hotel in the southern suburbs toward the Pentland Hills. 134 Braid Rd. (phone: 447-8888). Moderate.

Donmaree – This sweet little family hotel, in a respectable suburb, has 17 rooms. 21 Mayfield Gardens (phone: 667-3641). Moderate to inexpensive.

Galloway Guest House – Not as well equipped as the *Donmaree,* but more centrally located, just off the panoramic Dean Bridge. Dinner served off-season only. Guests have limited access to the kitchen; none of the 10 rooms has a phone. No credit cards. 22 Dean Park Crescent (phone: 332-3672). Inexpensive.

Melville Castle – This was the family seat of "King Harry the Ninth" or Henry Dundas, the first Viscount Melville, the Tory Lord Advocate who ruled Scotland from Westminster by a system of patronage during the late 18th and early 19th centuries. It's superbly romantic and highly historic. It has 21 rooms, most with phones. On the A7, approaching Dalkeith, about 6 miles (10 km) south of Edinburgh — ask for directions (phone: 663-6633). Inexpensive.

 EATING OUT: Reports on Scottish food vary from calling it a joke to claiming it is at least superior to English cooking. Still, visitors might want to try some of the following specialties: cock-a-leekie soup (chicken and leek), salmon, haddock, trout, and Aberdeen Angus beef. Skip any offering of haggis, except on a purely experimental basis. Scones originated in Scotland, and shortbread shouldn't be missed. Restaurants usually keep the city's formal hours (lunch until 2:30, dinner anywhere from 6). Expect to pay $85 and up for dinner for two, excluding wine and tips, in establishments listed as expensive; $50 to $85 in moderate establishments; and $50 and under in inexpensive places.

Beehive Inn – Among the fittings in this Old Town restaurant is a cell door from the very old town jail. Steaks and fish are served from an open charcoal grill and are followed by luscious desserts. Closed Sundays. Major credit cards. 18 Grassmarket (phone: 225-7171). Expensive.

Cosmo's – Edinburgh's link to Rome. Everybody who works here is fiercely Italian, as is the menu. Fabulous seafoods and veal, and a cocktail bar made of imported Italian marble. Closed Sundays and Mondays. Reservations necessary. Major credit cards. 58A Castle St. (phone: 226-6743). Expensive.

Howtowdie – White tablecloths and glass cases full of taxidermists' birds set the tone at this Highland-style establishment long famed for its ritzy image and traditional Scottish cooking. Reservations necessary. Closed Sundays. 27a Stafford St. (phone: 225-6291). Expensive.

Prestonfield House – A 300-year-old country estate within its own peacock-laden park grounds. Candlelit dinners in rooms with tapestries, paintings, and blazing open fires. French cooking. Reservations necessary. Major credit cards. Off Priestfield Rd. (phone: 667-8000). Expensive.

Pompadour – The facinating lunch menu here is a steadily unfurling history of Scots cooking, while dinners feature French cuisine. In the *Caledonian* hotel, Princes St. (phone: 225-2433). Expensive.

L'Auberge – A discreet, indeed positively diplomatic, restaurant that serves French fare, most notably fish and game. Open daily. 56 St. Mary's St. between Cowgate and Canongate (phone: 556-5888). Moderate.

Blake's – An upmarket establishment (formerly *Nimmo's*) serving à la carte seafood, steak, and rack of lamb. There's also a charming wine bar. Reservations suggested. 101 Shandwick Pl. (phone: 556-1177). Moderate.

Shamiana – Tandoori (Indian) food at its finest. Everything is cooked from scratch with delicate spices. Pale pink tablecloths, bone china, waitresses in saris, give the place a rarefied air. Evenings only; closed Sundays. Reservations necessary. Major credit cards. 14A Brougham St. (phone: 228-2265). Moderate.

Skipper's – A jolly waterfront workers' café, serving seafood caught fresh daily. Reservations necessary. 1a Dock Pl., Leith (phone: 554-1018). Moderate.

Stockbridge Steak House – Under new management, still offering steak but also stressing other examples of Scottish and Irish cuisine. 42 St. Stephen St. (phone: 226-5877). Moderate.

Arches – The dining room adjoining this bustling university-area bar has very good lunches and elegant dinners. Closed Sundays. 66-67 South Bridge (phone: 556-0200). Moderate to inexpensive.

Merchant's – Trendy French bistro, white tablecloths, silver, crystal, and waitresses wearing trousers. Also a green parrot that sleeps at lunchtime and can be pacified at dinner with monkey-nut. 17 Merchant St. (phone: 225-4009). Moderate to inexpensive.

Henderson's Salad Table – This cafeteria-style vegetarian's heaven-on-earth may keep diners standing in line for as long as 15 minutes, but it's worth it. Piles of salads, hot pots, opulent desserts available continuously day and evening. Closed Sundays, except during Festival. 94 Hanover St. (phone: 225-2131). Inexpensive.

Madogs – American fare (and some Mexican dishes) are served in a setting of wicker chairs, potted palms, pop music, and big glossy photos of Hollywood heroes. Closed Sundays, October to May. Reservations necessary at lunchtime and Friday and Saturday nights. Major credit cards. 38a George St. (phone: 225-3408). Inexpensive.

Scots – The successful successor to *Mermans*. The decor is batik, but the crowd is a mixed bag — artists, tourists, and businesspeople. Closed Mondays and Saturday lunch; closed Sundays, September to April. Reservations recommended. 8-10 Eyre Pl. (phone: 556-1177). Inexpensive.

SHARING A PINT: Until recently, boozing was restricted to puritanical hours. But now it's possible to imbibe from 11 AM to 11 PM, and a few places have opened up where the taps keep flowing until the wee hours. Among the best pubs: the *Abbotsford,* 3 Rose St. (phone: 225-5276), is a haunt of Scotland's "Makars" (playwrights and poets) and journalists; *Bennett's,* Leven St. (phone: 229-5143), is a noisy but atmospheric theater-district pub with a Victorian hangover; the *Beau Brummel,* 99 Hanover St. (phone: 225-4680), is a neo-Regency plush artifact in mid-city; and the *Tilted Wig,* 3 Cumberland St. (phone: 556-1824), facetiously known as the "Wilted Twig," is notable for its uncompromising trendiness and has a clientele of bar-hogging English smoothies, whom you can scatter at a stroke by standing in the doorway shouting, "Nigel, your MG's on fire!" And for enjoyable courtyard drinking facilities, join the crowd of university students at the *Pear Tree,* 38 W Nicolson St., off Buccleuch St. (phone: 667-7796). If you enjoy folk music, try the *Fiddler's Arms,* 9-11 Grassmarket (phone: 229-2665).

Rutherford's, Drummond St., off South Bridge opposite Old College, was much frequented by Robert Louis Stevenson and Arthur Conan Doyle when they were Edinburgh University students in the 1870s, although while within its portals they never knowingly met. *Stewart's,* across the road, is a fine working-class pub, and if the private back room is free, you and your friends can occupy it for an old-fashioned disputatious Scottish enquiry into philosophy — see Scott's *Guy Mannering. Preservation Hall,* 9 Victoria St. (phone: 226-3816), opposite *Bookfare* bookshop, is large, commodious, ornamented with fine epigraphs against drink, and offers rock music evenings. *Mather's,* 25 Broughton St. (phone: 556-6754) is the ecumenical watering-hole for left-wing labour, nationalist, and sexual politicos. Opulent barges sometimes carry licences in tourist season on the Leith waterfront. Find out at the *Waterfront Wine Bar,* 1c Dock Pl., Leith (phone: 554-7427). Also try *The Seagull's Nest,* 57 The Shore, Leith (phone: 554-8784). Both offer bar lunches.

GALWAY

The ancient port city of Galway hangs on to a romantic past that has been seasoned as much by myth as by reality. It isn't the glory of the early Gaelic kingdoms that haunts the local folk memory so much as the swashbuckling days of the Spanish Main. It was then that the prevailing sou'westerlies speeded tall ships toward Galway from the ports of Spain. In the fifteenth and sixteenth centuries, the two places were engaged in a rich, bustling commerce and the image of noble Spanish *hidalgos* swaggering through the cobbled streets of Galway still burns bright in the imagination.

Galway is proud of its medieval Spanish connection, almost to the point of forgetting that the really potent influence in shaping the city was Anglo-Norman. The citizenry sees the hand of Spain everywhere, and indeed some of the old back-street town houses and courtyards are faintly reminiscent of things *español*. Down near the docks, the celebrated Spanish Arch is an extension of the fortress walls that protected the old city and likely got its name from the Spanish sailors who once frequented the nearby alehouses.

Galway nurtures the fables of a colorful past in other ways. Its most famous legend is that of the mayor who hanged his own son. This archetype of the stern father was one James Lynch Fitzstephen who, in 1493, condemned his son Walter as a murderer. Apparently, Walter had killed a visiting Spaniard for stealing his girlfriend. So popular was Walter throughout Galway that no one could be found to hang him, so the father had to do it himself. A stone memorial window marks the execution spot today. Even though gray-bearded historians have debunked this story in modern times, the stone window still stands and most Galwegians are loyal to the legend.

There's a stronger ring of truth to another much-told story, that of Christopher Columbus discovering Galway before he ever clapped a weather eye on America. It is held that he called here and prayed in St. Nicholas's Church, en route to the uncharted western seas. It might be considered an auspicious stopping-off place for any would-be discoverer, because this particular St. Nicholas was the patron saint of sea voyagers.

Whatever the truth of the Columbus story, it is hard to shake the faith of Galway people in their own notable explorer and saint, Brendan. They and many other Irish people believe St. Brendan discovered the New World centuries before the Italian upstart. Naturally, Brendan sailed from Galway port.

Galway's origins go back long before the sixth-century St. Brendan and Christian times. There were settlements on its river in pagan days. The Irish for Galway is Gaillimh (pronounced *Goll*-iv) and there's a legend that the name comes from a princess, Gaillimh, who was drowned in the river. Nowadays, the river is called the Corrib and its surging waters rushing into Galway Bay are the pulsing soul and spirit of the city. In summertime, legions of silver salmon swarm in from the Atlantic feeding grounds in response to the immemorial mating call and fight their way upriver to the headwaters where they were spawned. That used to be one of the more uplifting sights in Galway, and it still is in a way, though the salmon have been thinned out by pollution and the genocidal nets of the factory ships.

It was the Normans, and not the Spaniards or anyone else, who developed Galway into a thriving mercantile city. In the thirteenth century they hopscotched from Britain to Ireland with the help of a pope and a traitorous Irish prince, and when their armies reached Galway they quickly subdued the native tribes, taking over the city. They built stout walls around it to keep out the wild Irish, and then, in a matter of decades, became more Irish than the Irish themselves. Much later, in the mid-seventeenth century, Cromwell smashed his iron fist on the city and reinforced the chains of conquest.

Galway became known as the City of the Tribes because of the 14 dynastic merchant families that controlled its wealth and fortune for several centuries. Outside the walls, across the river, the relics of the ancient Irish civilization survived in the fishing village called the Claddagh, which spreads out from Nimmo's Pier at the estuary of Galway Bay. Its thatched cottages have been torn down and replaced by drab, utilitarian homes, but it still manages to hold on to its own identity and remain aloof from Galway City.

From the middle of the nineteenth century until quite recently, Galway was a port for passenger liners plying the Atlantic between the United States and Europe. The passage was not always comfortable. During the potato famine of the 1840s, thousands of starving Irish peasants sailed from Galway to the New World aboard vessels whose abysmal conditions won them the chilling name "coffin ships."

Only in recent years has Galway become industrialized. It has grown in size in the past two decades and has ventured warily into the era of affluence. Progress has altered the leisurely rhythm of life in the city and introduced a more frantic tempo, but it's still a small town, really. The old charm lingers on, particularly in its back streets and alleyways. It is there that in fanciful moments you can almost hear the thrum of Spanish guitars and the clack of Castilian castinets.

Well, why not?

GALWAY AT-A-GLANCE

SEEING THE CITY: There are no really great vantage points from which to get an overall view of Galway City. The best bet for a bird's-eye reconnoiter is from atop the *Great Southern* hotel, which is right in the middle of things in front of the railway station on Eyre Square. From the *Claddagh Bar and Grill* in the penthouse you can look across the rooftops of the city and get a general feel of what it might be like out there. An inquiry at reception will get you up to the rooftop almost anytime (phone: 64041).

SPECIAL PLACES: Galway is a small town (population 30,000), so you can see just about everything worth seeing in a single day. What's more, you can do it on foot. A walk through the city streets — making sure not to miss out on those history-haunted back lanes — is highly recommended. Galway weather is infuriatingly temperamental and rain clouds are never far off, but even in the gentle drizzle of the famous Irish "soft day," you can set off with a mac and cover the whole town without risk of drowning. You might even walk out to Salthill, the seaside resort that's about 1 ½ miles from downtown and where, if the clouds have decamped, you can catch one of the best views of the sun going down on Galway Bay.

Eyre Square – This is the heart of the city and the place you'll probably see first. It once was the Fair Green (where livestock and produce were sold), and is now named after one of the ruling merchant tribes, the Eyres. (Charlotte Brontë got the title of her famous novel when she saw the name Jane Eyre on a gravestone during a visit to Galway.) The original pastoral appearance of the green was destroyed by local authorities in an outrageous act of philistinism during the 1960s when they poured concrete sidewalks along its edges. The park within the square is named after John F. Kennedy in memory of his Galway visit. There's a fascinating statue of a quirky gnome of an Irish writer called Padraic O Conaire at the northern end. A splendid cut stone doorway of a type seen in the better homes of long ago also stands in the park, this one from the home of another of the tribes, the Brownes.

St. Nicholas's Church – This is the place where Columbus is said to have prayed before sailing off to discover America. Originally built by the Anglo-Normans in 1320, it was greatly added to down the centuries. After the Reformation, the church became the prize in a tug-of-war between Protestants and Catholics and changed hands a number of times before Cromwell's forces finally secured it for the Protestants. Outside the church, you can also wander through the country market that is set up on Saturday mornings. Market St.

Lynch Memorial Window – Just up the street from the church, this stone window marks the spot where the mayor of the city, James Lynch Fitzstephen, is supposed to have hanged his son Walter for murder in 1493. It isn't the actual window through which the luckless lad exited into the next world — it was carved some 200 years later. The hanging story is a good one but almost certainly untrue. Market St.

Lynch's Castle – The ubiquitous Lynch tribe that gave so many mayors to the city originally lived in this 16th-century building, regarded as the finest town castle in all Ireland. It's now a bank but has been lovingly restored and preserved. Shop St. at the intersection called the Four Corners.

Salmon Weir – The centuries-old salmon fishery is below the Salmon Weir Bridge opposite the new Catholic cathedral. This is a pleasant place to pass an hour in summer watching the salmon on their way up to the spawning grounds.

Catholic Cathedral – On the site of a former jailhouse opposite the Salmon Weir Bridge, this is new, though inspired by Renaissance and other church architecture of the past. It is a large building but not remarkably lovely. Earl's Island.

Spanish Arch – The best-known landmark in Galway. The arch was built in 1594 as an addition to the old town wall and as protection for Spanish ships docking nearby to unload their wines. There's a museum now attached to the Arch (see *Sources and Resources*) through which you can climb to the top and look across the Corrib to the Claddagh. Beside Wolfe Tone Bridge where the river enters the sea.

Claddagh – This district was originally a fishing village where the native Irish clung to their old culture in defiance of the usurping Anglo-Normans within the walls. Claddagh people no longer fish nor speak Irish, but they still proudly maintain a sense of separateness from the city. The famous Claddagh ring — two hands clasping a heart surmounted by a crown — was fashioned by local goldsmiths and was the traditional wedding band. Cross the Corrib at Wolfe Tone Bridge and you're in the Claddagh.

Salthill – Galway's seaside resort is really part of the city, a mere 1 ½ miles from downtown. Salthill has three sandy beaches on Galway Bay but invariably the weather is hostile to sunbathing and surfing. When the weather is good, swimming is safe and there's no crowding on the beaches. The Leisureland complex that dominates the seafront has a huge heated indoor swimming pool and Coney Island–style amusements for children and adults. Southwest of Galway, reachable by frequent buses from Eyre Sq.

Franciscan Abbey – Built in 1836, the abbey is on the site of a 13th-century friary that was founded by the De Burgos (Burkes), the first Norman lords of Galway. St. Francis St.

University College – The original building, completed in 1849, was modeled in neo-Gothic style on some of the colleges at Oxford. Built as a nondenominational institution, it was once condemned by the Catholic bishops as godless and Catholics were forbidden to attend, but they ignored the ban. A small university, it has a friendly, unstuffy atmosphere; someone will always be glad to show you around. Main entrance to the campus is off University Rd. (phone: 24411).

■ **EXTRA SPECIAL:** Generally, Galway is a quiet place but it does have its moments. In the fall it lets down its hair and stages the closest approximation of *la dolce vita* you'll find in Ireland. This is the *Galway Oyster Festival,* held every year over a very long and vertiginous weekend in September. A most sybaritic occasion, it has many more temptations than the oysters everyone ostensibly comes to eat.

The organized events of the festival are rather expensive and must be booked in advance. It's also advisable to reserve a hotel room, especially if you plan to stay at the *Great Southern* — the center of the festival — or at any of the other better hotels in Galway. To attend all the events of the festival, from Friday night to Sunday morning, including a reception and dinner, festival banquet, lunch, oyster tasting, and recuperative Irish coffee "morning after," costs about $200 per sore head. This does not include hotel, nor does it include the heavy run on your pocket during a weekend of intensive socializing that involves much buying of booze. Count on an outlay of at least $350 for the weekend. For details, call the tourist office (phone: 63081) or write to Áras Fáilte, Eyre Sq., Galway.

Another festive occasion is *Galway Race Week,* beginning on the last Monday of July. This is a synonym for 6 days of heavy gambling on the ponies running at Ballybrit racetrack within walking distance of the city center. It also entails heroic drinking round the clock and heavy poker sessions in hotel bedrooms, all earthy and great fun even if you don't like horses.

Finally, don't leave Galway without visiting the Aran Islands (see *Connemara* tour, DIRECTIONS), and, oh, go ahead and take part in one of those medieval banquets in Dunguaire Castle (see *County Clare* tour, DIRECTIONS). Information on both of these is available from the tourist office.

SOURCES AND RESOURCES

TOURIST INFORMATION: For comprehensive information and advice, first go to the tourist office, Áras Fáilte, just south of the western side of Eyre Sq. During the summer, another office is open on the Promenade in Salthill (phone for either office: 63081). Pick up all of the free literature and maps including, when available, the Galway Junior Chamber of Commerce's listing of summer events in Galway and Salthill. A small booklet, *Tourist Trail of Old Galway,* describes a walking tour and costs 45p at the tourist office.

Hardiman's *History of Galway* is the definitive work on the city's past and can be bought at the Connacht Tribune newspaper office on Market St. or at *Kenny's Bookshop,* High St. For more detailed sources, try the County Library in the Hynes Building, St. Augustine St.

Local Coverage – Two weeklies, the *Connacht Tribune* and the *Connacht Sentinel,* and two giveaways, *The Galway Advertiser* and the *New Galway Observer,* provide strictly local news.

GETTING AROUND: If the weather allows, you can walk all over the city without great stress.

Bus – The central departure point for all city buses is the west side of Eyre Sq. City bus service stops at 11:30 PM. Buses for points outside the city leave from the railway station behind the *Great Southern* hotel. (The only trains leaving the station are for Dublin and intervening stops.) All buses and trains are run by CIE, which also operates touring coaches (phone: 62131).

Car Rental – It's best to pick up your car at the port of arrival in Ireland, usually Shannon or Dublin, where the major rental companies operate. *Avis* has a Galway office at the Áras Fáilte tourism office (phone: 68901). *Hertz* is at Headford Rd, Galway (phone: 61837).

Taxi – Plenty of cabs are available and they're not too costly. Go to the central cabstand on the north side of Eyre Sq. or phone 7888, 55919, or 63333.

MUSEUMS: Galway's only museum is the *Galway City Museum.* Though it's tiny, it houses a range of exhibitions that highlight the city's past. A spiral staircase from the museum takes you onto the top of the Spanish Arch, from which you can look across the Corrib to the Claddagh.

SHOPPING: Good values are to be found in native knitwear and homespun tweeds as well as Irish glass, bone china, Connemara marble, and other ornamental ware.

Blue Cloak Boutique – Fashions of the times at moderate cost. 31 Upper Abbeygate St. (phone: 7785).

Browne Doorway – This tiny gift boutique is crammed with Irish-made pottery, silverware, tapestries, linen, woolens, and the work of local painters. Eyre Sq., beside the *Great Southern* hotel (phone: 65757).

Lydon Boutique – High-class, with-it fashions for smart young ladies. It's expensive, but you get value. Shop St. (phone: 66205).

Moon's – A large, American-style department store stocked with quality items. William St. (phone: 65254).

O'Maille's – Everything is wholesomely Irish — Aran sweaters, Donegal tweeds, and shapeless Connemara hats. Pricey but worth it. Dominick St. (phone: 62696).

Anthony Ryan – A fine store for men's and women's fashions. 18 Shop St. (phone: 62733 or 67061).

Treasure Chest – This name belongs to two separate shops run by the same firm, both of them stylish and with a dazzling display of quality wares, including Irish crystal, pottery, woolens and tweeds, Irish traditional craftwork, and, most notably, classic Irish crocheted garments. William St. (the bigger shop) and Eglinton St. (phone: 63862).

SPECIAL EVENTS: The *Galway Oyster Festival* and *Galway Race Week* are held in September and July respectively. (See *Extra Special* for details.) The *Galway Arts Festival* usually takes place in July or August, with classical music, poetry readings, art exhibitions, and theatrical happenings.

SPORTS: Boating and Sailing – Rowboats and outboards can be hired for trips up the Corrib River and into Lough Corrib, the big lake upstream. Contact *Frank Dolan,* 13 Riverside, Galway City (phone: 65841). For all types of sailing on Galway Bay, contact the *Galway Bay Sailing Centre,* Rinville, Oranmore (phone: 94527).

Fishing – A license must be bought and a fee paid to fish for salmon at the Weir, which has an international reputation among anglers. For details and booking, call the Galway Fishery (phone: 62388). There's free fishing for brown trout on Lough Corrib, but, again, you'll need a license if you're after salmon. Boats can be hired. Phone *Des Moran,* Knockferry Lodge, Knockferry, Rosscahill (phone: 80122), or the tourist office (phone: 63081). To go sea angling for shark, contact *Elmer Kavanagh,* 2 Victoria Pl., Galway City (phone: 64789).

Golf – There's a challenging 18-hole course in Salthill where visitors are welcome (phone: 22169 or 21827).

Swimming – The beaches at Salthill are superb if the weather is good. If not, there's the indoor pool at *Leisureland* on the seafront in Salthill, open every day (phone: 21455).

 THEATER: The *Druid Theatre,* Chapel La. (phone: 68617), has evolved into one of the most exciting theatrical centers in Ireland. It stages traditional and avant-garde productions at irregular intervals, with both lunchtime and evening performances. There's an Irish-language theater — *An Taibhdhearc* (pronounced An *Thigh*-vark) — which has been producing plays in Irish for over 50 years. The emphasis during the tourist season is on traditional Irish music and dance interspersed with a short play in Irish, so heavily mimed that no knowledge of the language is needed. The theater is on Middle St. (phone: 62024).

 MUSIC: Traditional Irish music is heard in many pubs in Galway and Salthill; consult the local papers to keep track of these sessions.

 NIGHTCLUBS AND NIGHTLIFE: The fact that there are no true nightclubs does not mean life ceases at midnight. Most hotels have drinking sessions until near dawn. Some bars, too, continue serving illegally after closing time (11:30 PM in summer, 11 PM in winter, except Sundays when it's an hour earlier) and discreet inquiry will gain you access to these. There are a number of late-night discos, mostly for young people (the generation gap has a higher threshold in Ireland and below 40 can be "young"), and again you'll have to check the local newspapers for what's happening where. One of the best discos is *Krystals,* Thursdays, Fridays, and Saturdays in the basement of the *Great Southern* hotel, Eyre Sq. (phone: 64041). In summer, most Salthill hotels have cabarets and discos. One of the livelier Salthill discos is *CJ's Night Club* in the *Monterey* hotel (phone: 24017).

 SINS: Sin is acceptable in Galway as long as you don't take pleasure in it. A cautious step-by-step approach of considerable subtlety is advised in overtures to the opposite sex. Once you have won confidence, all is possible. Useful hint: A lot of drinking can be presumed in almost any social encounter in Galway, so if you can keep your alcohol level down, you will have a decided advantage over more drunken rivals. Galway has no red-light district.

BEST IN TOWN

 CHECKING IN: The better hotels in Galway have become expensive, though it's still possible to find some moderately priced ones that are good. A few have adopted the American plan and no longer include breakfast in the room rate. Where breakfast is included, it's the gargantuan Irish meal of bacon, eggs, and sausages — usually very good and you pay for it whether you eat it or not. In the following listing, assume that a private bath is included unless otherwise specified. Expensive means $40 to $55 a night for a double room; the moderate category is $25 to $40; and inexpensive rates range from $20 to $25.

Ardilaun House – Once the stately home of an aristocratic scion, the building and grounds still retain a patrician aura. It's hidden away among trees and shrubs on Taylor's Hill, the best address in town (phone: 21433). Expensive.

Corrib Great Southern – This younger sister of the big Victorian hotel on Eyre Square aspires to similar standards. It's modern and comfortable. Dublin Rd. (phone: 55281). Expensive.

Great Southern – A superior hotel, with 120 of the most comfortable rooms in Galway. Its elegant foyer is the center of social life in the city and an easy place to strike up new friendships. The food in the *Claddagh Grill* is great; a heated swimming pool and sauna are welcome bonuses. Eyre Sq. (phone: 64041). Expensive.

Anno Santo – For those who prefer the quiet life, here is a classy, intimate place with a relaxed atmosphere. Specify private bath. Threadneedle Rd., Salthill (phone: 22110). Moderate.

Galway Ryan – All 96 rooms in this modern hotel have bath and shower, television, and direct-dial phones. There is also a playroom for both adults and children. Food is conventional and wholesome. During the summer, musical entertainment and discos are a nightly feature. Dublin Rd. (phone: 53181). Moderate.

Skeffington Arms – This is a small and homey place where you get friendly attention. Specify bath here, too. Eyre Sq. (phone: 63173). Moderate.

Adare House – An outstanding guesthouse if bed and breakfast is all that's required (they don't serve other meals). Fine comfortable rooms, tastefully decorated. Extremely good value. Father Griffin Pl. (phone: 62638). Inexpensive.

 EATING OUT: Strangers to Galway should not venture into any restaurant without having it *reliably* recommended; there are a few shoddy places best avoided. However, the city does have some exceptionally good eating places and some of the better ones are in hotels. Don't expect anything too adventurous because the cuisine generally is quite unsophisticated, with simple, unadorned dishes. Native beef and lamb are among the world's best, so it's hard to go wrong with straight steaks or chops. Surprisingly, perhaps, good seafood is hard to come by, though the places we list are all versatile with fish. In season, Galway salmon from the Corrib River is superlative, and during the "r" months the oysters from the bay are possibly the best on the entire globe. To eat well, stick to the expensive restaurants, though there are a number of commendable ones in the moderate range. Except for those we recommend, stay away from inexpensive joints. Expect to pay $45 and up for dinner for two with wine in the expensive category and $35 to $45 in the moderate bracket. Credit cards are accepted. A service charge is included in all bills, but a tip is expected all the same! Note that most of the restaurants listed open briefly for lunch, then close and reopen for a 2- or 3-hour dinner period, usually from 7 PM on. Since several are out of town, it's a good idea to check on their hours before you get in the car.

Ardilaun House – With its decorous wood paneling and glass chandeliers, this restaurant retains a 19th-century ambience. The food is conventional but of very high order, and it's a popular dining place for families. Fresh meats and fish are the specialties. Taylor's Hill (phone: 21433). Expensive.

Paddy Burke's – Strictly a pub until the bar food began winning awards, *Paddy Burke's* still has a bar at which Galwegians gather at dusk to imbibe either Guinness or draft lager and munch bar fare like smoked salmon, Galway oysters in season, and rich fish pâté. The large room on the left is now a proper restaurant, offering mussel soup, baked salmon, foil-baked fresh fish, and luscious fried scallops. Clarenbridge (phone: 091-96107). Expensive.

Casey's Westwood – It has a neo-Georgian decor and a menu emphasizing French and Irish cooking, with the freshest ingredients. Dangan Upper, Newcastle, right by the University College (phone: 21442). Expensive.

Claddagh Grill – On the top floor of the *Great Southern* hotel and the finest all-around restaurant in the city. Try the wonderful lamb from Connemara or the Corrib salmon. The Continental dishes are good, too. *Great Southern* hotel, Eyre Sq. (phone: 64041). Expensive.

Drimcong House – A lovely old country house now serves as the backdrop for one of Ireland's best restaurants. Like the decor, the cuisine is elegant yet unpretentious, and the service super-efficient yet unobtrusive. Specialties include excellent wild game, spiced beef, salmon, and oysters. It is a dining experience not to be missed. One mile past Moycullen village on N59 (phone: 85115). Expensive.

Eyre House – Undistinctively modern but crisply fresh in appearance, this restaurant serves a fine five-course dinner from 6 PM onward. Fresh fish and rib roast are specialties. Reservations recommended. Open daily. Eyre Sq. (phone: 62396). Expensive.

La Taverna – Mama mia! The only Italian restaurant in western Ireland and a good one, too, with a full range of pasta dishes. Try the particularly fine Bolognese tagliatelle and lasagna. There's also a worthy Italian wine cellar to complement the food. 169 Upper Salthill (phone: 23174). Expensive.

Moran's of the Weir – This lovely thatched pub on the edge of the water is the most famous place in Ireland for oysters, but at other times of the year there are smoked salmon, mussel soup, and other seafoods. Pub hours. On the road to Limerick, 10 miles out of the city; turn right just before the village of Kilcolgan (phone: 96113). Expensive.

Salthill – The food at this hotel is always good but especially so on Irish nights, when the menu is planned around such native foodstuffs as lamb, salmon, oysters, and prawns. The Promenade, Salthill (phone: 22711). Expensive.

Silver Teal – An Irish restaurant that has a way with French sauces. The seafood dishes are opulent; there are lobster and pheasant in season. Moycullen village, 7 miles north on the road to Oughterard (phone: 85274). Expensive.

Ty-ar-mor – You'll have to travel a few miles out of the city to get to this one, too. It's a Breton restaurant atmospheric with nets and lobster pots, in the seaside village of Barna. Seafood and crêpes are the specialties and the cuisine is *très bon*. Reservations recommended. Sea Point, Barna (phone: 69186). Expensive.

Rabbitt's – Oysters and other succulent sea dishes are the specialty of the house in this 100-year-old bar/restaurant, brought back to life recently through a major refurbishment. 23-25 Forster St. (phone: 66490 or 62215). Moderate.

Skeffington Arms – The hotel's dining room serves the best steak in town, but the scallops and duck are also memorable. It's delightfully informal and friendly. Eyre Sq. (phone: 63173). Moderate.

Lydon House – Downstairs is a good, stand-up, fast-food eatery; upstairs is a more formal, sit-down restaurant with an orthodox but tasty menu. 5 Shop St. (phone: 61131). Moderate to inexpensive.

McSwiggan's – Meticulous restoration work has turned this place into a Victorian shrine, with gilded mirrors and beautiful mahogany woodwork. Marvelous pub grub and booze are dispensed downstairs in the saloon, and upstairs there's a quietly elegant atmosphere for formal sit-down meals of exceptionally high quality. Eyre St. (phone: 61970 and 68917). Moderate to inexpensive.

Brasserie – Tacos, pizzas, and such in a nice setting with open fireplace. 19 Middle St. (phone: 61610). Inexpensive.

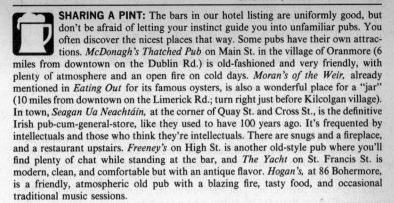

SHARING A PINT: The bars in our hotel listing are uniformly good, but don't be afraid of letting your instinct guide you into unfamiliar pubs. You often discover the nicest places that way. Some pubs have their own attractions. *McDonagh's Thatched Pub* on Main St. in the village of Oranmore (6 miles from downtown on the Dublin Rd.) is old-fashioned and very friendly, with plenty of atmosphere and an open fire on cold days. *Moran's of the Weir,* already mentioned in *Eating Out* for its famous oysters, is also a wonderful place for a "jar" (10 miles from downtown on the Limerick Rd.; turn right just before Kilcolgan village). In town, *Seagan Ua Neachtáin,* at the corner of Quay St. and Cross St., is the definitive Irish pub-cum-general-store, like they used to have 100 years ago. It's frequented by intellectuals and those who think they're intellectuals. There are snugs and a fireplace, and a restaurant upstairs. *Freeney's* on High St. is another old-style pub where you'll find plenty of chat while standing at the bar, and *The Yacht* on St. Francis St. is modern, clean, and comfortable but with an antique flavor. *Hogan's,* at 86 Bohermore, is a friendly, atmospheric old pub with a blazing fire, tasty food, and occasional traditional music sessions.

GLASGOW

"The Second City of the Empire" — this grand sobriquet belonged to Glasgow through the long and glorious reign of Queen Victoria, when only London surpassed the famous northern megalopolis in size, wealth, and might. From a tiny seventh-century cathedral town on a tributary of the River Clyde, Glasgow grew to be an international industrial capital, the world's foremost shipbuilding center, and a pioneer in mining, railroading, canal cutting, ironworking, steam engineering, and scientific invention and development. From the time of James Watt (1736–1819), who was a Glasgow man, the city never looked back.

Today Glasgow is Britain's third most visited city (after London and Edinburgh), renowned for its magnificent and extensive Victorian architecture. Greek, Gothic, Venetian, Beaux-Arts, Renaissance, Art Nouveau — you name it, Glasgow's effervescent coterie of nineteenth-century architects copied it and went it one better. All over central Glasgow, public buildings the size of a chain of Alps capture the pomp and circumstance of the Victorian age, while in the west end, private residences from the same period show an unrivaled variety and graceful delicacy of line. Unbelievably, many of the elaborate string-corniced wonders in the city center were built as warehouses!

Although Scottish nationalists today bitterly lament the union of the English and Scottish parliaments in 1707, it was in fact this move which put Glasgow on the capitalist map. Freed at last from stringent laws prohibiting Scottish trade with the American colonies, city merchants now exploited Glasgow's relative proximity to the open sea. While cargoes from London were attacked by pirates in the English Channel, and London's ships waited days for each other to load so they could sail in fleets for protection, Clyde clippers zoomed carefreely to Virginia. In exchange for Scottish muslins and linens, Glasgow merchants acquired tobacco, and acquired it much faster than their English competitors, whom they undersold. Soon Glaswegian tobacco merchants were supplying half of Europe. They became known as "tobacco lords," married into each others' families, and produced dynasties that endured to corner many a new kind of market when the American Revolution severely curtailed tobacco profits.

As the Industrial Revolution gathered momentum, pressure to increase the efficiency of the Clyde, which was too shallow to allow heavy ships to service Glasgow's ports, became fierce. Parliament approved a plan to strip away miles of adjacent factories and build in their stead high quaysides acting as dikes. Steam dredgers and the development of underwater blasting did the rest. By 1886, 58 million cubic yards of waste and sludge had been dispatched and the whole riverbed had been lowered by about 29 feet. No mere "muddling through" was good enough for Glasgow in those iron-willed days; when

Man fought Nature, Nature lost. As Glaswegians put it, "The Clyde Made Glasgow and Glasgow Made the Clyde."

Daniel Defoe glowingly described Glasgow's spacious streets and beautifully proportioned houses (a striking contrast to the Edinburgh of the same period), and visiting writers in later generations noted how eager the natives were to point these out. Signs of civic pride, past and present, are everywhere. Glaswegians have long had a penchant for showing off, witness, since Victorian times, the large number of official and unofficial parades, elaborate world's fair–type exhibitions and crowded sailings down the Clyde in open boats. The city crest, bearing symbols associated with Glasgow's founder and patron saint, St. Mungo, appears on everything, even the sides of city buses. Museums are municipal, free, and very special, especially the Transport Museum (see *Special Places*), where you can sense how wheels have become an absolute cult for Glaswegians in the climate of nostalgia and waning power that is the aftermath of their enormous share of the Industrial Revolution.

Perhaps logically, perhaps paradoxically, the gargantuan civic pride of Glaswegians is nowhere more evident than within the city's widely famous slum subculture, associated primarily with a southside district called the Gorbals. Its raw, swaggering, laugh-loving idiom is epitomized today in the art of comedian Billy Connolly. The virile mix of football, folklore, hard drink, and Red politics was fanned and molded in the nineteenth century by whole new populations that poured into the Clyde Valley from Catholic Ireland and the Scottish Highlands. The small, staid old Presbyterian Glasgow of tobacco lord days, in which stick-brandishing officials known as "bum baillies" beat the behinds off offenders caught strolling in the streets during church, hardly knew how to absorb the shock. This was the origin of much of Glasgow's present orange-green antipathy, exemplified by the rivalry between the Rangers and Celtic soccer teams.

Glasgow's slums have been of momentous importance to British political history. In 1922, Glasgow constituencies elected ten Socialist MPs, all local orators who had become noted for their high-minded, left-wing ideals. They and their followers were known as the Red Clydesiders. Two years later, Ramsay MacDonald, also a Scot, became Britain's first Labour prime minister. Today the Labour party, often eclipsed in England in parliamentary elections, would sink without Glasgow's support.

But the road to political significance was a hard one for Glasgow. During World War I the city was *urbs non grata* at Westminster because of strikes in its ship and munitions yards. Public rallies, furthermore, exhorted Glaswegians to enlist for no form of combat short of a full-scale workers' revolution. With years of exploitation behind them, Glasgow's slum dwellers were on a galloping high. Housewives organized a rent strike by shouting propaganda from the tops of middens (shacks containing communal garbage) in tenement backcourts. By Bloody Friday, January 31, 1919, strikes of all kinds were widespread in Glasgow and multitudes gathered in George Square to hear Prime Minister Lloyd George, up from London for the purpose, speak from the steps of the City Chambers. Rioting ensued, 50 people were injured, two important Red Clydesiders went to jail, and the next day armed troops and tanks blazed into the city. Yet somehow this token taste of blood had cleared the air, and within a few days most strikers returned to work and the tanks disappeared.

Glasgow today is a mass of contradictions. It has a greater variety of quality cultural events than Edinburgh (except during the Edinburgh Festival), yet it also has one of the highest crime rates in Europe. Right in its middle, near its most elegant buildings, are streets in a state of shameful dereliction. The Gorbals and other tenement areas have been bulldozed and refitted with faceless skyscraper apartments, yet the rambunctiousness and camaraderie of the days when 30 people shared one toilet, and every drink was a half of whisky knocked back with a pint of beer to chase it, linger on.

The Second City, however, is gone. Elevated motorways on concrete slabs thread their way over parts of Glasgow's once-majestic urban scene, and the Clyde, which sent the ringing din of riveting from its busy docks all over the city, is still. Population has declined from over a million to around 750,000 and Birmingham has outstripped Glasgow as London's runner-up in size. Yet at least half of all Scots still live within 20 miles of Glasgow, and engineering and printing, to say nothing of textile, food, drink, tobacco, and chemical industries, soldier on, despite rising unemployment. Whither now? There are Scottish nationalists who believe that, given the failure of efforts to bring the country a degree of autonomy via less drastic means, Glasgow's best bet might be for Scotland to go for complete independence.

GLASGOW AT-A-GLANCE

SEEING THE CITY: Getting an overhead gander at Glasgow is almost like finding the Holy Grail. The city is devoid of rooftop restaurants and publicly accessible steeples. Make your way to Glasgow University (buses No. 44 and No. 59 leave frequently from the city center for University Avenue), and storm the Gothic vaults of the main university building, architect Sir George Gilbert Scott's elephantine monstrosity built on Gilmorehill in 1870. Ask for the lodge of the "Bedellus," who with his magic key will unlock a door that leads to the steps to the top of Glasgow University Tower. If you can stand the climb, the reward is spectacular: Just below you is lovely Kelvingrove Park, with the River Kelvin winding through. Across the river is Kelvingrove Art Gallery, on a hill above a wooded glade. South of you is the River Clyde, and southeast is downtown Glasgow. Be sure to phone the Bedellus to make arrangements beforehand, otherwise you'll be in for a long wait. The best time to visit is Fridays at 2 PM. University of Glasgow (phone: 339-8855).

SPECIAL PLACES: One way to see Glasgow is to take it period by period. But start in the middle of things, with Victorian Glasgow, because it is this era that is the essence of the city. Except for the Transport Museum, (which is relocating to Kelvin Hall in April 1988), the surviving Victoriana listed below is quite conveniently placed. The rest of the sights — Medieval Glasgow, the Old Merchants' City, Modern Glasgow, and Clydeside attractions — are not far afield either, but don't expect to cover everything the same day. If you visit from June through September, hop aboard *Discovering Glasgow '88,* the zany, 2-hour, 14-mile bus tour of the city that costs £3 for adults and departs at 2 PM daily from the Trans-Clyde Travel Centre in St. Enoch Square (phone: 226-4826 and 636-3190).

VICTORIAN GLASGOW

George Square – Also called Glasgow's Valhalla, this intriguing mix of equal parts statues, flower plots, picnickers, and pigeons was originally laid out in 1781 and named after King George III. It came into its own in Victorian times, when most of the grandiose buildings now surrounding it were constructed. Since Bloody Friday it has been the undisputed central focal point of the city.

City Chambers – William Young, a local boy who made good in London, designed Glasgow's Italian Renaissance city hall, and Queen Victoria officially opened it in 1888 to the roars of 600,000 spectators. Inside, the loggia, staircases, and grand banqueting hall, with their sumptuous interplay of granite, mosaics, marble, and stone, make a millionaire's mansion look like a log cabin. Guided tours begin at 10:30 AM and 2:30 PM weekdays (except Thursdays and when a banquet is in progress). George Sq. (phone: 221-9600).

Merchants' House – Opposite George Square's west side is the Glasgow Chamber of Commerce building, built in 1877 by native architect John Burnet (the ungainly upper three stories spoiling the effect of the domed turret were added later). Glasgow invented chambers of commerce in 1659 when its Merchant Guild erected a house, unique at that time, from which to minister to the widowed and orphaned of the collective merchant poor. That building — and that institution — was this one's ancestor. (Glasgow's Trades Guild, not to be outdone by its archrival, followed suit with a similar institution and eventually built the elegant Trades House of 1794, designed by the renowned Scottish architect, Robert Adam. This is on nearby Glassford St. and is well worth a look.) Open 9 AM to 5 PM, unless a special meeting is taking place. 7 W George St. (phone: 204-2121).

Buchanan Street, Gordon Street – For row after nonstop row of massive, public architectural Victoriana, nowhere in the world beats this!

Tenement House – Recently opened by the National Trust for Scotland, this is an example of a Scottish middle-class turn-of-the-century household and provides an interesting look at life in Victorian Britain. Open daily, 2 to 5 PM, but arrange for admission beforehand (phone: 552-8391).

Museum of Transport – In 1962, a huge turnout of Glaswegians wept openly as they watched a parade of trams from all eras make a farewell memorial run through the streets. The trams were then lovingly roundhoused and became the nucleus of this museum. Also present are vintage cars, trains, and fire engines of Scottish design, plus a bevy of brightly painted Victorian items: traction engines, craftsmen's carts, carriages, even a one-horse open sleigh. The oldest bicycle in the world is here, looking like a couple of mill wheels. There is also an extensive nautical exhibition — pictures and models only — at which you can brush up your Clydeside history. The Museum of Transport should reopen in its new location, Kelvin Hall, in April 1988.

Necropolis – Every tombstone is a virtual Parthenon in this graveyard of Glasgow's wealthy Victorian industrialists. Save a few gasps for the *pièce de résistance,* the huge, round, double-decked Menteith Mausoleum (date: 1842; recipe: gingerbread) on the east side beside a bird's-eye view of a local brewery. The towering statue of John Knox was erected in 1833 (before the brewery). Keep clear of the place after 4:30 PM, when it fills up with imbibers, petty thieves, glue sniffers, and (possibly) resurrectionists. Open all day. Across the Bridge of Sighs off Cathedral Sq.

MEDIEVAL GLASGOW

Glasgow Cathedral – A perfect specimen of pre-Reformation Gothic architecture, this was the only church on the Scottish mainland to have its inner structure spared during pillaging by 16th-century Protestant zealots bent on destroying "monuments of idolatry." Its 15th-century carved stone choir screen, separating the aristocracy at the front of the building from the plebians at the back, was saved through petitioning by Glaswegian stonemasons: Such was the prestige of the Glasgow trade guilds. Have a look also at the remarkable fan vaulting in the crypt over the tomb of Glasgow's patron saint, St. Mungo, and at the chair Oliver Cromwell sat in when he visited Glasgow in 1650 (Glasgow was lucky because at most places he visited he was too busy burning and wrecking to sit down.) The chairs Queen Elizabeth and Prince Philip sit in when they worship in Glasgow Cathedral can be seen (the queen turns Presbyterian automatically when she hits the Scottish border). Open 9:30 AM to 7 PM on weekdays, 2 to 5 PM Sundays, from April through September; closing at 4 PM daily from October through March. Cathedral Sq. (phone: 552-0220).

Provand's Lordship – Just opposite the cathedral is the oldest house in Glasgow, built about 1471. It was the town house of the prebend, or provand, of a nearby country see. Imagine a colony of such buildings extending up and down the adjacent streets and you will have an idea of the Glasgow of Mary Queen of Scots's time. The house was closed in 1980 for restoration and repair and reopened in 1983 as a period museum. Open weekdays 10 AM to 5 PM, 2 to 5 PM Sundays.

THE OLD MERCHANTS' CITY

Glasgow Cross – This was the heart of the city in the 18th century, before George Square took over. The large reproduction of an etching you saw on a wall of Merchants' House shows what it used to be like looking west down the Trongate. Today, the Tolbooth steeple (1626) and the Tron Church steeple (1636) are all that's left from earlier times. The Edinburgh stagecoach stopped in Glasgow Cross, carrying newspapers from the capital, and Glasgow's merchants conducted their morning business and sipped their "meridians," or noonday rums, in the Tontine Hotel, opposite the Tron Church. If you see the "scaffies," or city street sweepers, leaning on their brooms chatting garrulously together at 4:30 each afternoon, eating ice cream bought from a van beside the Tolbooth steeple, they are perhaps acting under the influence of a folk memory two centuries old. You can't see anything better than this for local color! Intersection of Gallowgate, Trongate, Saltmarket, and High St.

Sterling's Library – The main part of this structure, now a library, was the mansion of William Cunningham, the most famous tobacco lord of all. Ask at the front desk for the historical pamphlet. Closed Wednesdays and Sundays. Royal Exchange Sq., off Queen St. (phone: 221-1876).

MODERN GLASGOW

Glasgow School of Art – This is the most famous building in Glasgow and one of the most famous buildings of its period in the world — Charles Rennie Mackintosh's finest example of the style poet laureate John Betjeman called "Beardsley-esque baronial." Its east wing was completed in 1899, the rest, with additions to the east wing, in 1909. Ironically, Mackintosh, an architect, interior designer, and artist of the avant-avant-garde, won the competition for the design of the school because his plan was the cheapest to build! Today, few dispute his unqualified genius. The library especially, with its almost infinite attention to the tiniest decorative details, is exquisite. Open on weekdays, 10:30 to 11:30 AM and 2:30 to 3:30 PM. The porters conduct informal guided tours and relevant literature is for sale in the office. 167 Renfrew St. (phone: 332-9797).

John Logie Baird Plaque – You'll find it by the door of the room where Baird invented television (if he invented it — he is said to have been anticipated by an obscure Irish curate), in the main hall of the University of Strathclyde. The Scottish inventor demonstrated a true television system in 1926. Open on weekdays 9 AM to noon and 2 to 4 PM. George St., just east of George Sq. (phone: 552-4400).

BY CLYDESIDE

Custom House Quay – The Glasgow Corporation has fitted out its disused dock-sides with flower-decked walkways. Bands play here in summer, and discos blare at night, while the anchored *Carrick* casts a silent eye upon all. The *Carrick,* a contemporary of the famous clipper *Cutty Sark,* holds the world sailing ship record of 65 days from Australia to London. Custom House Quay adjoins Clyde St.

Clyde Street – Continuing east, you'll see on your left the 17th-century, Dutch tower of Glasgow's *original* Merchants' House, preserved for its magnificence when the house itself was razed. At No. 64 to No. 76 the world's most pretentious fish market, dated 1873, is dripping with sculpted rosettes and topped with winged horses. The building, once derelict, has been transformed into a classy new market similar to London's Covent Garden called Briggait (phone: 332-7244). At the end of Clyde Street, around the corner to the left along the Saltmarket, are the Justiciary Courthouses, with Doric porches, where the last public hanging in Glasgow, that of the dashingly notorious conman and poisoner Dr. Edward William Pritchard, occurred in 1865.

Glasgow Green – This is the oldest public park in Europe, and it has certainly seen a lot of action! The heart-rending statue at the west entrance was erected in 1881 by temperance reformers, after which massive turnouts of public temperance pledgers were a common sight on the green for decades. During World War I, you couldn't see the grass for the sea of tweed caps at Red Clydesiders' rallies. The green was also for centuries the site of Glasgow's chief washhouse and bleaching lawn: Foreign visitors commented on the brazenness of the local washerwomen, who lifted their skirts about their thighs to dance barefoot on the dirty clothes stewing in their tubs. It was on Glasgow Green one fine Sunday afternoon in 1765 that James Watt, playing hookey from church, had a vision of the steam condenser that changed the history of the world. Open all day. The west entrance is opposite the Justiciary Courthouses in the Saltmarket.

People's Palace – You never know what you'll find at this museum of local history, since the city owns more objects than it can possibly display at once and keeps changing the show. The place is impressionistic and fun, with everything from theatrical bills and political pamphlets to elaborate wrought-iron streetlights and fountains and the ridiculous pouting stone faces that once adorned the façade of the Tontine Hotel. There are exhibits from every century. Open daily 10 AM to 5 PM; Sundays 2 to 5 PM. East side of Glasgow Green (phone: 554-0223).

Scottish Exhibition and Conference Centre – The queen opened this structure in 1985 as a site for major auto and trade shows as well as top-name entertainment. Five interlinked halls are grouped around a glass-covered concourse housing restaurants, cafeterias, and gift shops. Off Finnieston St. at the site of the old *Queen's Dock,* on the banks of the River Clyde (phone: 248-3000).

■**EXTRA SPECIAL:** How about a trip on the last seagoing paddle steamer in the world, the *Waverley?* From spring until early fall, the Paddle Steamer Preservation Society operates this charming craft on one-day round trips from Anderston Quay, Glasgow, to scenic spots, beyond the Firth of Clyde. As you cruise the Clyde you'll see the cranes and derricks in the dockyards that once supplied over half the world's tonnage of oceangoing ships. Have lunch in the restaurant (with bar) on board, or bring sandwiches. For full details, contact Waverley Excursions Ltd., Waverley Terminal, Anderston Quay (phone: 221-8152).

SOURCES AND RESOURCES

TOURIST INFORMATION: The Greater Glasgow Tourist Board Office, 35 St. Vincent Pl. (phone: 227-4880), has stacks of free leaflets recommending things to see and do not only in Glasgow but throughout Scotland. Open 9 AM to 9 PM Mondays through Saturdays, 10 AM to 6 PM Sundays. Ask at the desk for the official city guidebook, *1988 Greater Glasgow,* and for *Arrival,* a monthly booklet with a comprehensive diary of local entertainment (no charge for these items). Bartholomew publishes a complete map of Glasgow, available at the Tourist Board Office for the reduced price of 85p (more in bookshops). John Smith and Son, booksellers, 57–61 St. Vincent St. (phone: 221-7472), carries *Glasgow at a Glance* (about £5). This is your bible, chronologically wrapping up every important building in town with an erudite blurb and a stunning picture, so don't leave it behind in your hotel. Short historical paperbacks about Glasgow are on sale, too, plus a selection of touring and restaurant guides and maps.

Local Coverage – The *Glasgow Herald* is the one respectable morning daily; the evening daily is the *Evening Times.* A valuable monthly guide to Glasgow and Edinburgh events is *The List,* available at newsstands for 50p. It also contains excellent features and reviews.

GETTING AROUND: Rule No. 1 is to use your feet in the George Square district — you can't view Victorian architecture properly unless you wallow in it. Buchanan, Gordon, and Sauchiehall streets are pedestrian zones. For information (including timetables) about available public transport (bus, rail, and subway) operated by Transclyde, contact the Travel Centre, St. Enoch Sq. (phone: 226-4826). Also check at the Trans Centre (St. Vincent St.), where you can obtain weekly or monthly travel passes called Transcards. Major changes in the public transport system have occurred, so be sure to check with the Travel Centre or the Tourist Board Office.

Bus and Subway – Glasgow's bus system was once a model of urban transport, but since deregulation in October 1986, it leaves something to be desired. Schedules change every three months and some routes have too many buses, causing traffic congestion, while other areas are left without adequate service. For information, phone 332-9644, 226-4826, or 248-7432.

Subway trains run every 5 minutes (none on Sundays or after 7 PM). The system's stops are listed in *Greater Glasgow* or on a city center map. Hillhead Station is a good alighting point for west end shops and restaurants.

Car Rental – Renting a car is recommended because there is plenty to lure you out of downtown Glasgow. All the major firms are in the yellow pages.

Taxi – Taxis are still reasonably priced at 80p for the first mile and 20p for each addition 1/6-mile. There is increasing demand for taxis following the chaos caused by deregulation of the buses, and at night they are harder to find than ever. To visit places such as the Burrell Collection, phone for a taxi in advance: *Albany Radio Cars* (phone: 556-6161 or 357-1717); *Croft Radio Cars* (phone: 644-2344, 331-2769, 641-8786, and 644-3514); *Radio Cars* (phone: 880-5050, 881-5050, 882-5050, 883-5050, 638-5050, and 445-5050); or *Radio Cars Glasgow* (phone: 649-3333).

Train – Central Station on Gordon St. (phone: 204-2844) and Queen Street Station (phone: 204-2844) are the city's major terminals. Both stations provide regular local service, and a bus connects the two.

MUSEUMS: The *Transport Museum* and the *People's Palace,* described in *Special Places,* are high on the list of things to see. But the most important of Glasgow's museums is the fabulous Burrell Collection, listed below with others worth a visit. Admission free; openings hours, unless otherwise stated, are 10 AM to 5 PM, Mondays through Saturdays, 2 to 5 PM Sundays.

Art Gallery and Museum – British and European paintings including Rembrandt's *Man in Armor* and Dali's *Christ of St. John of the Cross* in addition to natural history, ethnography, and the decorative arts. Organ recitals take place in the promenade at 3 PM every Saturday. Closed Sunday mornings. Kelvingrove Park (opposite Kelvin Hall) on Dumbarton Rd. (phone: 334-1134).

Burrell Collection – Bequeathed to Glasgow by Sir William Burrell, a millionaire ship owner (and opened to the public in 1983), this dazzling, 8,000-piece collection contains Cézannes, Rembrandts, Ming vases, Halses, sculptures, and tapestries. It can be difficult to find Pollok House, so ask for directions at the information bureau or call the gallery itself. On the Pollok House grounds (phone: 649-7151).

Haggs Castle – An ornate castelated late-16th-century structure containing the original kitchen with cauldrons, spits, and barrels, and a Victorian nursery. A children's activity workshop — butter making, spinning, weaving and more — takes place on Saturday afternoons (reservations necessary on local holidays) in a nearby cottage, and the landscape includes a knot garden. 100 St. Andrews Dr. (phone: 427-2725).

Hunterian Museum – Geological, anthropological, and historical collections, and Roman relics. Open 9:30 AM to 5 PM weekdays, 9:30 AM to 1 PM Saturdays. In the main building of Glasgow University, Gilmorehill, off University Ave. (phone: 339-8855, ext. 221).

Hunterian Art Gallery – Paintings, drawings, prints, and furniture by (among others) Whistler and Charles Rennie Mackintosh. Open 9:30 AM to 5 PM weekdays, 9:30 AM to 1 PM Saturdays. Hillhead St. (phone: 339-8855, ext. 7434).

Pollok House – Works by El Greco, Goya, Murillo, and William Blake, plus antique furniture, silver, porcelain, and glass, all displayed in a house designed by William Adam, the father of the famous family of Scottish architects, and completed in 1752 (later additions by Sir Rowand Anderson were begun in 1890). It is surrounded by extensive park grounds. 2060 Pollokshaws Rd. (phone: 632-0274).

Royal Highland Fusiliers Museum – Three centuries of the Glasgow and Ayrshire Regiment: uniforms, weapons, medals, and pictures. Open 9 AM to 4:30 PM Mondays through Thursdays, 9 AM to 4 PM Fridays. 518 Sauchiehall St. (phone: 332-0961).

SHOPPING: Tuesday or Saturday is early closing day (1 PM) for some shops, though most city-center establishments remain open daily, often including Sundays in recent years. Local wares include woolens, pottery, crystal, Victorian bric-a-brac, jewelry, shortbread, and whisky. Here's what's where:

Argyll Arcade – Gift items, jewelry, and clothing shops are found here, but the arcade itself is something to see. Built in 1828 by John Reid, there's a magnificent mosaic roof best viewed from the Buchanan Street entrance. Also of interest is the historic Sloan's Arcade Café.

Candleriggs Market – Converted from an old fruit market in 1982, this is a good place to hobnob with residents and inspect local wares. Open Fridays, Saturdays, and Sundays only. 71–73 Albion St. (phone: 552-5908).

Fraser's – This four-tiered, balconied, Victorian-vintage department store with central court, glass-paneled ceiling, and a couple of hundred feet of suspended chandelier offers English bone china, clothes, linens, Edinburgh crystal, food delicacies, or just a beautiful breath of rarified air. 21 Buchanan St. (phone: 221-3880).

Iona Shop – Specialists in Celtic jewelry, including hand-crafted pieces of silver and polished Scottish stone. In the Argyll Arcade, the L-shaped passage between Argyll and Buchanan streets that is Glasgow's famous diamond and jewelry center (phone: 221-9038).

Lawrie's – The sort of place where the landowning milord buys his deerstalking "breeks" (breeches). Kilts, skirts, jackets, pure wool plaids, tweeds, mohairs, accessories, and souvenirs. Highland dress made to order and clan tartans traced for visitors unsure of their Scottish connections. 110 Buchanan St. (phone: 221-0217) and 38 Renfield St. (phone: 221-9047).

Lawrie Renfrew's – Fishing equipment, free in-the-know advice to fishermen, and the-one-that-got-away sessions with the rest of Mr. Renfrew's clientele. Gone fishin' Thursdays. 514 Great Western Rd. (phone: 334-3635).

Saltoun Pottery – Hand-thrown mugs and jugs designed by talented Glaswegian Nancy Smillie. 24 Ruthven St. (phone: 334-4240).

Savoy Centre – This new, self-contained shopping complex, clean and well maintained, has 160 shops selling almost anything. Off Sauchiehall St.

Upstairs Downstairs – Eastern objects and imported Indian clothes for women, in joyous native designs. 625 Great Western Rd. (phone: 334-9623). Visit also *Eurasia Crafts,* 528 Great Western Rd. (phone: 339-3933), and *Koh-i-noor Crafts,* 173 Byres Rd. (phone: 339-2884).

Victorian Village – Antiques, roomfuls of ornaments and old lace. Beethoven's Pastoral wafts through the adjoining corridors while you browse or dawdle in the charming tearoom. 57 W Regent St. (phone: 332-0703).

For an authentic taste of old-fashioned Glasgow street-vending, try *Paddy's Market,* by the railway arches in Shipbank Lane, or the *Barras* ("barrows"), east of Glasgow Cross, where they sell everything from "wee fleas" to white elephants.

SPECIAL EVENTS: Parades, band concerts, sports competitions, beauty contests, and disco dancing are what goes on in summertime at community festivals, and every Glasgow district has one, usually in late May or June. Get the complete list from the Greater Glasgow Tourist Board Office. The *Scottish National Orchestra (SNO) Proms* — 14 concerts with famous guest soloists and conductors — alternate among Edinburgh, Glasgow, Aberdeen, and Dundee in summer. The Proms have nothing to do with dancing, but the final night in Edinburgh is traditionally an orgy of well known musical tours de force. Contact the SNO, 3 La Belle Pl., Glasgow G3 7LH (phone: 332-7244). *The Glasgow International Folk Festival* takes place in early July; for details, contact the Arts Centre, 12 Washington St. (phone: 221-4526).

Every May there is the *Mayfest,* a major international arts festival (phone: 221-0232). The Prince and Princess of Wales will open the *Garden Festival* in April 1988 at the Scottish Exhibition and Conference Centre. From April 28 to September 26, visitors can enjoy exotic flowers and plants and a variety of food and entertainment. For information, phone 429-8855.

SPORTS: Boating – Try *Hogganfield Park* and *Queen's Park* (details in *Greater Glasgow '88*).

Fishing – The Firth of Clyde, the ocean, and the upland waterways near Glasgow are all popular. The Glasgow Information Bureau has a free leaflet, *Scotland for Deep Fishing.* Or ask Lawrie Renfrew (see *Shopping*).

Golf – Get *Golf in Scotland,* a free leaflet, from the Greater Glasgow Tourist Board Office. It supplies details of the championship courses along the Ayrshire coast as well as the Glasgow courses. Rent equipment from a pro shop and have ready an introductory letter from your home club secretary.

Hiking – Glasgow has 7,000 acres of municipal green space, much of it woodland, in over 70 parks. *Greater Glasgow '88* describes attractions in the larger parks. The Glasgow Information Bureau has guides to the trails for 15p.

Horseback Riding – The *Kilmardinny Farm and Riding Establishment Ltd.,* Milngavie Rd., Bearsden (phone: 942-4404), is your best bet.

Soccer – It's called football here, and in Glasgow football is just about synonymous with the two home teams, the *Celtic* and *Rangers.* Kickoff is 7:30 PM on Wednesdays and 3 PM on Saturdays from August through May. Celtic Park, at 95 Kerrydale St., is the *Celtic* home stadium, and Ibrox Park, on Edmiston Dr., is the home of the *Rangers.* Get tickets from the turnstiles prior to the games and take no intoxicating beverages; police may search you. League playoffs and cup finals are at Hampden Park on Somerville Dr. It's fair to say that football violence is now much less evident in Scotland than in England, but *Rangers* crowds still make anti-Catholic noises.

 THEATER: Since 1942, the *Glasgow Citizens Theatre,* in deepest Gorbals on Gorbals St. (phone: 429-0022), has been famous throughout Scotland for its vigorous experimentalism, high standard of performance, and lusty approach to what are usually considered highbrow classics. Closed June through August. The *Pavilion,* Renfield St. (phone: 332-0478), is the inheritor of the rich "Scotch comic" music hall tradition that Glasgow has given the world — *vide* Harry Lauder. Pre-London runs and large amateur (dramatic society) productions are at the *King's,* Bath St. (phone: 248-5153). *The Mitchell Theater,* Granville St. (phone: 221-3198), has variety acts and light musicals. There is also a handful of locales where the flower of upcoming young artistic Glasgow unfolds its petals: the *Glasgow Print Studio and Drama Centre,* 128 Ingram St. (phone: 552-0704); the *Athenaeum Theatre,* in the Royal Scottish Academy of Music and Drama building on Buchanan St. (phone: 332-5294); and the amazing *Third Eye Centre,* 350 Sauchiehall St. (phone: 332-7521), which publishes its own glossy monthly brochure describing events on its premises including plays, mime, dance, cabaret acts, jazz, films, talks, poetry readings, appearances by folk and rock groups, and workshops in dramatic arts for all ages. Open Tuesdays through Saturdays, 10 AM to 5:30 PM, Sundays 2 to 5:30 PM, and evenings when events are scheduled; while you're there, stop in at the bar, café, or trendy bookshop. The *Glasgow Film Theatre* (for art films) is at 12 Rose St. (phone: 332-6535). The *Tron Theatre Club,* 38 Parnie St. (phone: 552-4267), stages trendy new productions by small professional companies.

MUSIC: The restored *Theatre Royal* on Hope St. (phone: 331-1234), originally built in 1882, is the elegant headquarters of the prestigious Scottish Opera Company. Other national opera companies perform there, too (as do professional theater groups). *City Hall,* Candleriggs (phone: 552-1850), and *Henry Wood Hall,* Claremont St. (phone: 221-4952), are the places for important orchestral and classical concerts, supplemented by *Glasgow Cathedral,* which often hosts choral and sacred works. Also in Candleriggs is the Ticket Centre (phone: 552-5961), where you can reserve tickets for the *King's* and *Mitchell* theaters and *City* and *Kelvin* halls. Rock rolls in the *Apollo Theatre* on Renfield St. (phone: 332-9221). Bagpiping and Highland and Scottish country dancing must be traced to city parks and to small parish halls — have a look at your copy of *Time Glasgow.* As for jazz, Glasgow's jazz king is Frank Pantrini. His incomparable sextet plays the pub and restaurant circuit. Check the dailies for where. The City of Glasgow Municipal Club runs a Grand Ole Opry house nightly, plus Saturday afternoons, at Paisley Road Toll (phone: 429-5396).

NIGHTCLUBS AND NIGHTLIFE: The safest course is to chart a theater evening with a restaurant meal afterward. This will steer you clear of the restless natives whose idea of a Big Night Out is a long crawl from one mobbed, fuming pub to another, the progression marked by rantings, singing, and battles of wit. Gambling halls and dance hangouts can have an unadorned and, to a tourist, tawdry air. Oasis in the wilderness: *Charlie Parker's,* Royal Exchange Sq. (phone: 248-3040), specializes in drinks and dinner; upstairs is the *Pzazz* disco (phone: 221-5323); open Thursdays through Sundays. Other night spots of note are *Cardinal Folly,* Pitt St. (phone: 332-1111), and *Ultratec,* Wellington St. (phone: 333-0493). Keep an eye out also for establishments with occasional cabaret acts, such as *Halibee's Design Studios,* 55 Ruthven La. (phone: 334-8560), which has jazz and folk nights, a vegetarian menu, and no bar (customers bring their own bottles). Glasgow's gay pub is currently *Vintner's,* 312 Clyde St. (phone: 221-2089), and its gay disco is *Bennet's,* 88 Glassford St. (phone: 552-5761). (*Gay Scotland,* a monthly magazine available at most bookshops, will provide more information.)

Pubs clank shut at 11 PM. Consult your copy of *Wining and Dining in Glasgow* for restaurants that have extended-hours licenses to serve drinks with food after the pubs close. You can drink until 2 AM in the overnight-guests-only bar of your hotel without having to eat.

SINS: It's impossible to sin with much panache in Glasgow, unless you invent your own method. How about streaking naked across the top of the City Chambers' Jubilee Pediment while rolling a barrel of whisky to pour on the city police when they invite your descent? (The real sin here would be in the waste of the whisky.)

BEST IN TOWN

CHECKING IN: A well-known Scottish television executive recently defined a typical Glasgow hotel as a "reasonable, functional, bathroom's-got-a-bath, bedroom's-got-a-bed kind of place." Comfort you'll certainly get, but don't expect to be overwhelmed by the picturesque. The price of a room includes breakfast, whether you eat it or not, and top-class establishments will want you to show your mettle by guzzling prunes, porridge, herrings, eggs, bacon, sausages, tomatoes, coffee, and toast, all in one sitting. Private baths are available. Our hotels in the expensive range charge anywhere from $80 and more a night per double; moderate hotels charge $60 to $80 per double; and inexpensive hotels $45 to $60 per double. Guesthouses and bed-and-breakfasts are a lot less expensive. Lists of these for Glasgow, Renfrew, Strathkelvin, and Monklands are available in *Greater Glasgow '88.*

Albany – Where the visiting pop stars stay — this is a slick 248-room flat-topped box with a big-city image. Inside, it's soft lights, carpets, and chrome. One of the two dining rooms is a popular carvery serving Scottish fare. Bothwell St. (phone: 248-2656). Expensive.

Holiday Inn – Yes, it's one of *the* Holiday Inns and has everything from individual mini-bars in the 296 rooms to a heated indoor Jacuzzi whirlpool. Argyll St. (phone: 226-5577). Expensive.

Hospitality Inn – Glasgow's newest hotel has 316 rooms that contain all the ultra-modern conveniences. It also has two restaurants, *Prince of Wales,* which serves French food, and *Garden Café,* which has an American-style menu of steaks, burgers, chili, and fried chicken. 36 Cambridge St. (phone: 332-3311). Expensive.

One Devonshire Gardens – Stately, distinguished townhouse where one can feel like a 19th-century aristocrat. Eight unusually designed rooms; restaurant. West Glasgow (phone: 339-2001). Expensive.

Stakis Pond – There are 134 rooms in this somewhat lethargic modern hotel in the west end. The name comes from the usable boating pond, which it overlooks, and it's a good place for kids. Great Western Rd. (phone: 334-8161). Expensive.

Beacon's – Consider it a bit of historic Glasgow in the form of a charming Victorian terraced house with 36 rooms and period decor. Edward VII once stayed here. The view across Kelvingrove Park to the town of Paisley and the hills beyond is glorious. 7 Park Terr. (phone: 332-9438). Moderate.

Central – An architecturally distinguished railway hotel of the 1880s, the *Central* is next to Central Station. It's spacious and gracious in the Victorian mode, but it was built right over a streetful of slum houses, so it may be haunted by the home-loving ghosts of the dispossessed. Sumptuous bedrooms (219). Gordon St. (phone: 221-9680). Moderate.

Sherbrooke Castle – The bar here is the neighborhood pub, ideal for helping you forget you're a tourist. This elegant old 9-room mansion-house is on a knolltop on the city's south side. 11 Sherbrooke Ave. (phone: 427-4227). Moderate.

Stakis Grosvenor – This pure white 93-room Victorian showpiece in the West End, opposite the Botanic Gardens, is elegance incarnate. Grosvenor Terr. (phone: 339-8811). Moderate.

Marie Stuart – Bill Tennent, a local television personality, runs this grand old house with 8 rooms well south of the Clyde. Glaswegians like it for wakes and weddings. 46–48 Queen Mary Ave. (phone: 424-3939). Inexpensive.

EATING OUT: Native food, dismissed with a laugh by the ignorant because of the names of some of its dishes ("haggis," "powsowdie," "cullen skink"), can actually be delicious. Top of the Scottish gastronomic pops are Aberdeen Angus steak, lamb with rowanberry jelly, venison, moor grouse, salmon, and trout. For a meal for two expect to pay over $50 at restaurants listed as expensive; $30 to $50 at restaurants listed as moderate; and under $30 at restaurants listed as inexpensive. This selection does not include any of Glasgow's numerous pubs with catering facilities, fish and chips shops, and plastic-age fried chicken or burger joints. Time your hunger pangs carefully. Most restaurants are traditionally open for lunch from noon until 2:30 PM and for dinner from 5 PM or 7 PM until 11 PM or so. Few are open continuously throughout the day and few are open on Sundays.

Poacher's – The trendiest restaurant in town is in an old farmhouse off a narrow lane in the west end. Decor is dark green with matching shrubbery. The menu (Scottish fare — something different cooked fresh every day) is recited. Book ahead. Closed Sundays. Ruthven Lane off Byres Rd. (phone: 339-0932). Expensive.

L'Ariosto – High-backed pine chairs, tiled floor, dim lighting, soft music, and lots of lovers' nooks make this romantically and classily Italian. The bill of fare doesn't stop at spaghetti. Dancing Tuesday through Saturday nights. Closed Sundays. 92/94 Mitchell St. (phone: 221-8543 and 221-0971). Expensive to moderate.

Fountain – Small and unpretentious, this restaurant is in the London image, known for its expense-account lunches. Menu is international, with emphasis on French cuisine. Closed Saturday lunch and Sundays. 2 Woodside Crescent, Charing Cross (phone: 332-6396). Expensive to moderate.

Colonial – This establishment prides itself on being Glasgow's top restaurant, but now serves modern Scottish food. Eat here and you'll see the unseen face of business Glasgow. Closed Sundays. 25 High St. (phone: 552-1923). Moderate.

La Parmigiana – Italian cuisine served here, by jolly Italian waiters. Striped awning outside, bijou-type intimacy within. Dining is accompanied on Fridays and Saturdays by the strains of "O Sole Mio" and other gems sung to the tune of a small guitar. Closed Sundays. 445 Great Western Rd. (phone: 334-0686). Moderate.

Trattoria Caruso – Food is Italian plus basic British. Across the street from the Theatre Royal, this is popular with actors and theatergoers. An extension to the dining area is a chic new pizza parlor. Closed Sundays. 311/313 Hope St. (phone: 331-2607). Moderate to inexpensive.

Ad Lib Mid Atlantic – Steaks and real beef hamburgers, piped disco music, and posters of glamorous American celebrities are all part of the effort to make Yankees feel at home and Glaswegians feel they're not. Cocktails are a specialty. Open Mondays through Saturdays noon to 2 AM, Sundays 6 PM to 1 AM. 111 Hope St. (phone: 248-7102). Inexpensive.

Café Gandolfi – Genuine 1930s bits and pieces (like the overhead propeller fan), a larger-than-life delicatessen, comestibles, taped 1930s jazz, and animated intellectual chat. Closed Sundays. 64 Albion St. (phone: 552-6813). Inexpensive.

Café Pumpernickel – A pleasant, friendly place specializing in light lunches and afternoon teas. Good for quietly relaxing after a hard day's shopping or sightseeing. 25 Parnie St., near Glasgow Cross (no phone). Inexpensive.

Rogano – Seafoods are a specialty, and there's an oyster bar in this pub-restaurant, which media people and talkative about-towners have claimed as their own. Its antique fixtures include mirrors and glass paneling adorned with sea themes. Closed Sundays. 11 Exchange Pl. (phone: 248-4055). Inexpensive.

Shenaz – You'll be met by a venerable ancient in a turban and led to a candlelit table. Order lager, not wine, with your exotic Indian fare. Open for lunch and dinner weekdays; dinner only on Sundays. 53 Berkeley St. (phone: 248-4804). Inexpensive.

Ubiquitous Chip – No, this is not a fish and french fries outlet. The menu caters to the discriminating palate, featuring local delicacies when they are in season. And the glassed-in courtyard with a fountain and an Art Deco water lily mural pleases the eye, too. Closed Sundays. 12 Ashton La. (phone: 334-5007). Inexpensive.

Willow Tea Room – Another great hideaway to recuperate in during a hectic day, it serves light meals and beverages. Particularly noteworthy, it was designed by Charles Rennie Mackintosh, the noted Art Nouveau architect from Glasgow. 217 Sauchiehall St. (phone: 332-0521). Inexpensive.

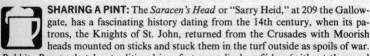 **SHARING A PINT:** The *Saracen's Head* or "Sarry Heid," at 209 the Gallowgate, has a fascinating history dating from the 14th century, when its patrons, the Knights of St. John, returned from the Crusades with Moorish heads mounted on sticks and stuck them in the turf outside as spoils of war. *Babbity Bowster* hotel, a traditional inn, features a lively café bar (without the usual din-creating machinery) with live music, mainly traditional and classical, in an 18th-century building. 16/18 Blackfriars St. For a touch of the Franco-Scottish "auld alliance", try *Fouquet's Wine Bar and Brasserie,* 7 Renfield St. *Scott's Corner* at 923 Sauchiehall St. offers local color, including "live weekend entertainment," somewhat obviously with the tourist in mind. The younger set may find the smart decor of *Austin's,* 183 Hope St., sufficiently swinging. Intellectuals make tthemselves at home in the bar at the *Tron Theatre Club* (closed Mondays), 63 Trongate. The *Waterloo Bar,* recently refurbished, has a live DJ Thursdays and Sundays and is open to midnight except Sundays. *Foxy's,* 311 Argyle St., has background music at lunchtime. But Glasgow is crawling with pubs, and if you stay any length of time you will soon find your own favorites.

KILKENNY

Ireland's best-preserved medieval town is the minute inland city of Kilkenny, 75 miles southwest of Dublin. Beginning as a tiny Gaelic settlement around the monastery of St. Canice (whence its Irish name, *Cill Chainnigh,* "the cell of Canice"), it came to prominence under the Normans when their leader, Strongbow, seized it in 1170 and built a fortification on the hill over the River Nore. The walled town was peopled with a purposeful community of Norman families, of whom ten — "Archdeakin, Archer, Cowley, Langton, Ley, Knaresborough, Lawless, Raggett, Rothe and Shee . . ." as an old list rhymes them off — distinguished themselves particularly and rose to power. Between the Gothic cathedral at one end and the strong castle at the other, the houses, inns, shops, new friaries, and the merchants' parish church crowded inside the city walls on the high bank of the river.

Its reputation as a stable and industrious market town thus established, Kilkenny then went on to achieve some notoriety. In the early fourteenth century, a formidable Norman woman named Dame Alice Kyteler, daughter of a banker, prosperous survivor of four husbands, and wealthy herself through moneylending (a practice, not incidentally, frowned upon by the church), was accused of witchcraft by Richard le Drede, bishop of Ossory, the local see. Dame Alice was supported by Arnold le Poer, the seneschal, and many powerful friends; the bishop, by the law and the commission he had from the Pope to extirpate heresy. A Kilkenny friar records the confrontation: "On Monday . . . the lady Alice Kyteler was tried, found guilty, condemned as a heretic for divers sorceries, manifold heresies, offering sacrifices to demons . . ." Though her powerful friends resisted and even imprisoned the bishop, he and the authority of the Church won that round. Dame Alice fled to Scotland, her maid Petronilla was burned at the stake in her stead, and Le Poer died in prison. The bishop did not get off scot-free either. He was accused of heresy and had to flee to the papal court in Avignon.

Several decades later, the name Kilkenny became associated with infamy. As elsewhere in Ireland, the Normans had been intermarrying with the Irish and "going native" in other ways, too. Such fraternization was perceived as a threat by the English king who by now feared being left with too few trustworthy settlers to rule the island on his behalf. Consequently, a parliament held in Kilkenny in 1366 (the city was important enough to be a regular meeting place, along with Dublin, of the Irish Parliament the Normans had instituted) passed the Statutes of Kilkenny. These forbade the Normans to marry the Irish, prohibited them from adopting the Irish language, customs, or dress, and segregated native Irish everywhere beyond the walls of towns.

From the end of the fourteenth century and for centuries thereafter, the castle of Kilkenny was occupied by the Butlers, earls of Ormonde, the most powerful family in medieval Ireland and long in the forefront of Irish history.

They lived peaceably with the Gaelic chieftains, but at the same time were rich from royal favor. They married into the royal family, hosted royal visits, and acted frequently as the king's deputy in Ireland. Under their protection Kilkenny was spared the worst horrors of Henry VIII's Reformation and the devastating cycle of rebellion and repression that ensued during the reign of Elizabeth. The Butlers conformed to Protestantism and the city monasteries were silently suppressed, becoming civic property. John Bale, an English friar appointed the first conforming bishop of Ossory, smashed statues in the cathedral and wrote fiery sectarian pamphlets, but he is better remembered in Kilkenny for the morality plays he wrote and had performed at the Market Cross, which once stood near the center of High Street.

The city could not totally escape the racial and religious conflict of the times, however. When another revolt — the Ulster Rebellion, which would be brutally crushed by Oliver Cromwell — broke out in 1641, Kilkenny became the seat of the independent Irish Parliament set up by Anglo-Irish and Old Irish Catholics united in their common defense. It met from 1642 to 1648, presided over by Lord Mountgarrett, a member of a minor Catholic branch of the Butlers, while the earl, the king's man, sat on the fence. Though the confederation went so far as to establish a mint, manufacture weapons, raise an army, and receive ambassadors, it fell apart from within when its Norman and Irish factions began to disagree, and it disbanded in confusion. In 1660, Cromwell arrived to take Kilkenny for the English Parliament.

After the ritual window-breaking and statue-smashing in St. Canice's Cathedral, Cromwell's rule in Kilkenny was less bloody than elsewhere. Families involved in the parliament were banished west of the Shannon, "to Hell or Connaught," along with the rest of the propertied Catholics who had opposed the Protector. Those from Kilkenny never went, however; they secretly hung around the city until the Restoration brought back the king and a Butler again, now duke of Ormonde, as his viceroy. The duke managed to bring about a return of some of the lands confiscated from Kilkenny's leading citizens, but they and the city never quite recovered from the events of the century and never regained their former influence.

It is perhaps due to the long dark years of decline that followed that so much of Kilkenny's early architecture remains intact — the city was simply not prosperous enough to tear things down and rebuild them on a grand scale, nor was there any need to do so. The gloom began to lift with a cultural revival in the nineteenth century and dispersed completely in recent years, leaving only a lingering air of quaintness to temper the changes of a city now in expansion. The Butlers have been gone from the castle since the 1930s but they characteristically and munificently presented it to the people. Its beautiful gardens and park are there, the art gallery has a notable collection of portraits, and the dukes' fine stables have become the Kilkenny Design Workshops, a nursery of modern design talent. The Rothes' house has been restored as a museum and library; the Shee almshouse has now been refurbished. Once a year, Kilkenny Arts Week has music resounding through castle and cathedral. The little medieval city that witnessed so much Irish history is still the integral core of a busy and modern, yet still traditional community.

KILKENNY AT-A-GLANCE

SEEING THE CITY: Kilkenny lies in two neat crescents on either side of a river valley basin and does not afford heights for the sweeping panoramic view. If you stand in the terraced rose garden in front of Kilkenny Castle, you can survey the city's limits from the castle behind you to the compact gray St. Canice's Cathedral in the distance, while the river below gives drama and movement. From here, though, you'll be looking *through* the town, catching its recurrences of church spire and Tholsel clock tower. The reverse view is from the top of the round tower at the cathedral (small entrance fee), but it is so high up that the city becomes a gray mass; the climb is not recommended for those with vertigo.

SPECIAL PLACES: The street that straggles from the castle to the cathedral is Kilkenny's Royal Mile. It starts at the castle gates as the Parade, an oblong plaza with the castle's classical stables and a decorous row of Georgian houses on one side and a tree-lined promenade, the Mayor's Walk, along the garden wall on the other. High Street, Kilkenny's main commercial street, comes next, with the medieval just under the surface of its respectable Georgian face. The Tholsel, "the house of taxes," is the mid-point of High Street. Beyond it on the right a unique Kilkenny feature occurs at intervals — the slips, or arched, stepped alleyways giving access to the street at river level. Dashing down slips and side alleys is very much part of sightseeing and shopping in Kilkenny. After High Street, the thoroughfare widens again as Parliament Street, and you see the restored Rothe House and the classical courthouse. Then it narrows to medieval size for Irishtown and leads you to St. Canice's Steps at the foot of the cathedral.

Kilkenny Castle – Kilkenny's most imposing monument looms grandly through trees over the river at the southeastern end of town. The Norman conqueror Strongbow had put up earthen fortifications here and his successor in the early 13th century, William the Earl Marshall, replaced them with an irregular quadrangle of curtain walls reinforced by a fat round tower at each of the four corners. The Butler family, Norman earls of Ormonde, bought it in 1391 and from then on it, and they, dominated the city. Though the family in residence remained the same for over five centuries, the castle itself underwent many changes. When the earls became dukes in the 17th century, it was rebuilt as a French château; it was made Gothic in another major reconstruction in the 19th century. The gardens and park are open to the public in daylight hours and the interior may be visited (guided tours are available). Particularly notable is the 19th-century Gothic-revival picture gallery. Designed by Benjamin Woodward, it has a painted hammer-beam roof by J. Hungerford Pollen and a fine collection of Butler family portraits. The old castle kitchen serves home-cooked snacks, tea, and coffee. Open daily June through September; closed Mondays in winter. Admission fee. The Parade (phone: 21450).

Kilkenny Design Workshops – This cupola-crowned classical group of buildings with a semicircular courtyard once formed the castle's stables. The horses' stalls originally had decorated plaster ceilings, whereas the grooms occupied plainer and more cramped quarters upstairs. Since 1965 the buildings have housed the government-sponsored Kilkenny Design Workshops , where everything from traditional craft products to electronic hardware is designed for Irish manufacturers, and young Irish designers get some work experience. Visitors are not allowed in the workshops, but the splendid showroom and shop on the premises sells products designed or made here as well as goods made all over the country that come up to the Workshops' high standards (see *Shopping*). Open daily. The Parade (phone: 22118).

Shee Alms House – One of the few surviving Tudor almshouses in Ireland was founded in 1582 by Sir Richard Shee "for the accommodation of 12 poor persons." The charity, thus begun by one of Kilkenny's leading families, endured for three centuries. After the adjoining St. Mary's Church became Protestant during the Reformation, a chapel in the almshouse was used for Catholic services. In the present century, the house has served as a storehouse, but it has been refurbished and now holds the city's tourist information office. Upstairs is a model of Kilkenny as it was in 1642, when the Confederation Parliament made it the capital of Ireland — a status that lasted just a few years. Rose Inn St.

St. Mary's Church – Parts of this church are believed to date from the 13th century. A fine display of Tudor and Stuart grave monuments is housed in the north transept. St. Mary's La.

High Street – Kilkenny's main street has undergone considerable change through the centuries, but a pause here and there still helps to recall its earlier days. Nos. 17, 18, and 19 hide a Tudor house (built in 1582) that belonged to the Archers, another of the town's ten leading families, and you can see their crest above the door. Behind it are the remains of the "Hole in the Wall," a supper house famous enough in the late 18th and early 19th centuries to have merited a verse: "If you ever go to Kilkenny/Ask for the Hole in the Wall/You may there get blind drunk for a penny/And tipsy for nothing at all." On the north side of High St. about 100 yards from the main cross-street, look above the shop fronts, and you'll see a Tudor gable with the impaled arms of Henry Shee and his wife, Frances. He was a mayor of Kilkenny in the early 17th century and this was their town house.

Tholsel – The Saxon word for "the house of taxes" is another name for Kilkenny's town hall. Built in the mid-18th century, it has open arcades that provide a market below and support a fine Georgian council chamber above. High St.

Rothe House – John Rothe built this solid Tudor merchant's house — actually three houses around two courtyards, with room for shop, storage, and living quarters — in 1594. Rothe was a member of another of Kilkenny's important families, and his wife Rose was an Archer. After the Rothes lost the house in the 17th century because of their association with the Confederation of Kilkenny, it eventually became a school. Finally, the Kilkenny Archaeological Society bought it, restored it, and opened it in 1966 as a library and historical museum. Open Sunday afternoons year-round and weekdays from April through October; open Tuesday, Friday, and Saturday afternoons the rest of the year. Tours are held weekdays at 3 PM in the summer. Admission charge. Parliament St. (phone: 22893).

St. Francis Abbey – This one-time Franciscan friary is on the premises of the 18th-century Smithwicks Brewery, desolate among beer casks and empty crates but still worth seeing. It was founded in the 13th century by Richard the Marshall and suppressed, along with the rest of the Irish monasteries, in the 16th century. The seven-light east window and the bell tower with its unusual supporting figures are from the 14th century. Off Parliament St.

Black Abbey – The church of the Dominicans, or Black Friars, is on high-walled Abbey Street just beyond Black Freren Gate, the last remaining gate in the city walls. Its history is similar to that of the Franciscan abbey; both were founded and suppressed at approximately the same time, though the Black Abbey survives today as an active Dominican priory. Immediately after suppression, however, townspeople built thatched huts within its walls and it was for a time used as a courthouse before being reclaimed, restored, and opened again for worship. Abbey St.

St. Canice's Cathedral – This building, raised in the 13th century by the first

Norman bishop, Hugh de Rous, occupies the site of the early Irish monastery of St. Canice and a later Romanesque-style church. A plain cruciform structure, it is nevertheless impressive for its size — the second largest medieval cathedral in Ireland — and its simplicity. The Master of Gowran (a mason who also worked on a neighboring church at Gowran) contributed some vigorous stone carving, in the west doorway particularly, but the renowned stained glass of the east window survived the Reformation only to be smashed to bits by Cromwell's troops, who also left the cathedral roofless and did considerable damage to its many monuments. The church's collection of 16th- and 17th-century tomb sculptures, many by the O'Tunneys, a local family of sculptors, is still remarkably rich, however, and its hammer-beam roof (a product of a later restoration) is notable. Outside, the round tower predates the cathedral, though its roof is not the original one. St. Canice's Library, established 300 years ago, has 3,000 old volumes. Reached via St. Canice's Steps, which are linked to St. Canice's Pl. by Velvet La. Open 9 AM to 1 PM and 2 to 5 PM daily.

■ **EXTRA SPECIAL:** *Kilkenny Arts Week* takes place at the end of August or the beginning of September. It is basically a music festival, with lunchtime recitals and grand evening concerts in the castle and cathedral, the classical music interspersed with programs of traditional music and folk song. Poetry readings — some well-known writers have read their work here — are another fundamental ingredient, as are art exhibitions and street theater. It is a friendly, all-join-in event that actually lasts for 9 days, each one ending at the Arts Week Club, where the social side of the festival goes on until the wee hours. For information, write the tourist office at the Shee Alms House, Rose Inn St., Kilkenny.

SOURCES AND RESOURCES

TOURIST INFORMATION: In Kilkenny, the Tourist Information Office, Shee Alms House, Rose Inn St. (phone: 21755), has information, maps, and leaflets. The city map is free; the *Kilkenny Guide* costs 50p. A Kilkenny craft guide is free.

Local Coverage – *The Kilkenny People* is published on Wednesdays. The three Dublin morning dailies are also available. Local events are posted weekly in the Tholsel arcade on High St.; details on daily happenings are available at the tourist office.

GETTING AROUND: Kilkenny is a walkable city, and there is no city bus service. From castle to cathedral is just over a mile. You might need a taxi to get to the railway station, which is a little farther away.

Bus and Train – CIE buses and trains serve McDonagh Station, John St. Upper (phone: 22024).

Car Rental – The nearest rental points are *Tully* in Carlow (phone: 0503-31257) and *Bolands* in New Ross (phone: 051-21213) but either will pick up and set down at the Kilkenny tourist office (address above) where bookings can be made.

Taxi – Cabs are available from *Delaney's* (phone: 22457), *Drennan* (phone: 62138), *Farrell* (phone: 65949), *Larkin* (phone: 62622), *Martin* (phone: 22979), and *O'Brien* (phone: 61333).

Walking Tours – Guided historical walking tours leave at 10:30 AM, and 12:15, 3, and 4 PM from the tourist office (address above) daily except Sunday mornings in summer, and cost IR£2.

MUSEUMS: In addition to the Butler family's distinguished portrait collection, the *Kilkenny Castle* art gallery features occasional traveling exhibitions. The restored *Rothe House* contains the Kilkenny Archaeological Society's museum of local history. See *Special Places.*

SHOPPING: The presence of the Kilkenny Design Workshops has led to a proliferation of choice craft shops in Kilkenny. The town also has literary associations (Jonathan Swift, among others, attended Kilkenny College) and a good bookshop. (Most shops are closed Thursday afternoons.)

Allen & Sons – Good selection of Waterford glass, which they will pack safely and dispatch to overseas addresses duty free. 94 High St. (phone: 22258).

Liam Costigan – Modern jewelry by a Kilkenny Design Workshop graduate. Colliers La. (phone: 62408).

Rudolf Heltzel – Exquisite modern jewelry, this time by a pioneer Kilkenny Design Workshop teacher. 10 Patrick St. (phone: 21497).

Kilkenny Bookshop – It includes a good section on Ireland. St. Kieran's St. (phone: 65054).

Kilkenny Design Shop – An Aladdin's cave of modern Irish design in silver, glass, pottery, wood, and textiles, many items designed on the premises. Good bargains in household items. There's also a self-service restaurant. The Parade (phone: 22118).

Marchioness Boutique – Women's clothing with a wide selection of Irish-made ready-to-wear, tweeds, handknits, etc. The Parade (phone: 65921).

Monster House – A solid, traditional department store selling woolens, tweeds, glass, and all the rest. High St. (phone: 22016).

P.T. Murphy – Just the spot to find a Claddagh ring, Tara brooch, or Celtic cross, as well as Irish silver, jewelry, Waterford crystal, and Royal Tara china. 84/85 High St. (phone: 21127).

Rothe Crafts – The merchant's shop at Rothe House is stocked with knits, tweeds, glassware, and souvenirs. Parliament St. (phone: 21066)

Weavers Craft Shop – This second-floor shop welcomes visitors to watch weaver Peter Mulhern at work on his double-length traditional Donegal hand-loom. Jackets, ties, suits, capes in tweed, alpaca, mohair, and brush wool fabrics are among the items found here. 92 High St. (phone: TK).

SPECIAL EVENTS: *Kilkenny Arts Week* is held every year in late August or early September (see *Extra Special*). Other events are: the *International Air Rally* (phone: 22036) at the Kilkenny airstrip, held annually during the third weekend in June; and *Genealogical Study Weekends,* with talks and tours, in mid-April and mid-October.

SPORTS: Bicycling – Bikes can be rented from *Bridge Bicycles,* 5 John St. (phone: 62037), and *J.J. Wall,* 88 Maudlin St. (phone: 21236).

Fishing – There is good trout fishing in the rivers Nore and Dinan north of Kilkenny. Consult J. J. Carrigan at the Sport Shop on High Street.

Golf – The *Kilkenny Golf Club* (phone: 22127) accepts guests at its pleasant 18-hole course about 1 mile from town.

Greyhound Racing – Races are held at St. James's Park every Wednesday and Friday evening (phone: 21214).

Hill Walking – Speaks for itself. Join the group that meets Sunday mornings, and wear sturdy hiking boots. Check local paper for time and venue, or Bobby Norwood, Tyndall Mountain Climbers (phone: 62024).

Horseback Riding – About 2 miles from the city is the *Warrington Stud Riding Centre,* with horses and ponies available for riding on its 200 acres of grass and woodland (phone: 22682). Other nearby stables are *Carrigbeg Riding Centre,* Bagenalstown, open all year, indoor and outdoor, plus cross-country (phone: 0503-21157), and *Thomastown Equitation Centre,* open April through August only (phone: 056-24112).

Horse Racing – The racecourse (phone: 26126) at lovely Gowran Park, 10 miles from the city, is the site of 8 meetings a year.

Hurling – Ireland's ancient stick and ball game is played most stylishly in Kilkenny. There is usually a game on Sunday afternoon at Nowlan Park.

 THEATER: The Kilkenny New Theatre group presents Summer Pub Theatre, a show of light plays, at the *Club House* hotel during the summer and at other times in *St. Kieran's College Theatre.* Other events occur in association with Kilkenny Arts Week.

 MUSIC: For traditional Irish music, try the *seisiún* presented by *Comhaltas Ceoiltóirí Eireann* once a week in July and August in Kilkenny Castle. In the summer months, the *Newpark* hotel also stages an "Irish Night" cabaret, usually on Wednesdays. Traditional music can be enjoyed throughout the year at the *Shamrock Bar,* 26 Parliament St., and at the Kilford Arms on John Street. *Kilkenny Arts Week* is the best source of information on classical music events; also check the newspapers.

 NIGHTCLUBS AND NIGHTLIFE: Pubs for the mature and discos for the young is the extent of the nightlife in Kilkenny as in most Irish towns. There's an Irish cabaret at the *Hotel Kilkenny* on Saturdays and Sundays and at the *Springhill Court* on Saturdays. The *Springhill Court* also presents *céilí* dancing on Wednesdays. The *Newpark Hotel* has dancing on Sunday and Tuesday nights.

 SINS: Repent for past sins or prepare for future ones. Dublin's Leeson Street is 75 miles away.

BEST IN TOWN

 CHECKING IN: Despite its obvious attractions, Kilkenny has not been much of a hotel town, at least until recently. The tourist circuit of Ireland tends to go clockwise around the coast, ignoring the interior, and only lately have hotels in midland towns roused themselves from a rather dull state of commercial plainness. There are exceptions, however, and on the whole, Kilkenny's hotels offer good value. Most make it into a moderate bracket of $50 to $75 per double room with breakfast; inexpensive ones cost $40 or less. Should you find it impossible to get into the hotel you select, the Tourist Information Office will be happy to help out. Your alternative may be a town or country home or farmhouse.

Club House – Almost 200 years old, this downtown hotel is full of atmosphere, with a cozy bar called the *Foxhounds Lounge,* a Georgian-style dining room, and a fine collection of turn-of-the-century magazine cartoons on the walls. 28 rooms, 16 with private bath/shower. Patrick St. (phone: 21994). Moderate.

Kilkenny – This is a Regency gem built as his own home by William Robertson, the architect who gave Kilkenny Castle its final Gothic trim. His touch here produced a fanciful structure in which the hotel's public rooms have retained some of their former domestic charm. The 60 bedrooms — ultramodern and spacious — are in a separate block. There's also an indoor swimming pool, sauna, hot tub, gym, and tennis courts. College Rd. (phone: 62000). Moderate.

Newpark – On the north edge of the city, this Victorian country house has been skillfully combined with modern extensions and converted into a comfortable hotel with 45 rooms (each with private bath and phone), in a peaceful garden setting. Facilities include a first rate dining room, a noon to midnight grillroom, Irish musical entertainment, and twice-weekly discos. The staff is efficient and enthusiastic. Castlecomer Rd. (phone: 22122). Moderate.

Springhill Court – Modern and of the motel type, this hotel provides 44 well-equipped rooms on the southern edge of the city. It is useful if you have a car. Phones in rooms. Waterford Rd. (phone: 21122). Moderate.

Lacken House – An old Georgian residence about a half mile east of Kilkenny, this lovely guesthouse has been renovated and updated by the McSweeney family to include nine rooms (seven with private bath) and a first-class restaurant in the basement. Open all year, except for a week at Christmas. Dublin Rd. (phone: 61085 or 65611). Inexpensive.

EATING OUT: In the past few years, Kilkenny and its environs have earned a reputation for fine food. Hotel dining rooms often rival local restaurants. As most likely you will be traveling by car, some worthwhile places in attractive spots at a distance have been included below. Expect dinner for two (without wine or tips) to cost from $30 to $45 in a restaurant listed as moderate; under $30 in an inexpensive one.

Damask – The dining room of the *Newpark* hotel, this elegant restaurant features piano music 6 nights a week. The menu ranges from coquilles St.-Jacques to châteaubriand, with some imaginative veal and chicken dishes, too. Castlecomer Rd. (phone: 22122). Moderate.

Kyteler's Inn – An inn since 1324, this restored medieval tavern has buffet lunches and full-menu dinners. Featured dishes include langoustines géante and veal Cordon Bleu, as well as local salmon and trout. Open daily year-round; in summer, a medieval banquet is held each Sunday evening. St. Kieran St. (phone: 21064). Moderate.

Lacken House – Chef Eugene McSweeney, formerly of the *Berkeley Court* in Dublin, is making his bid for haute cuisine immortality with this family operation. Fresh fish that comes from Dunmore East each day is the specialty. Dishes range from baked crab au gratin to paupiette of plaice with salmon stuffing, as well as filet of port or medallions of beef. Closed Sundays and Mondays. Phone for reservations. Dublin Rd. (phone: 65611). Moderate.

Lord Bagenal – You'll find this charming restaurant 15 miles from Kilkenny in a historic town at a crossing of the River Barrow. There is bar food throughout the day and a full restaurant menu in the evening, with a variety of dishes, from veal and mushroom pie to fillet of beef en croûte. Leighlinbridge (phone: 0503-21668). Moderate.

Maltings – About 10 miles south of Kilkenny, this family-run restaurant is situated right on the River Nore in the idyllic village of Inistioge. Specialties are Nore salmon, minted lamb, chicken bonne femme, and duckling with brandy. Open for dinner Tuesdays through Sundays in summer and Thursdays through Saturdays from mid-September to mid-May. Inistioge (phone: 29484). Moderate.

Step House – This fine Georgian house serves delicious French meals, including wood pigeon paté, avocado mousse with kilmore crab and wild duck from the Wexford marshlands (in season). Closed Sundays and Mondays and January through April. Reservations are recommended. Borris (phone: 0503-73209). Moderate.

Mulhall's – A digression off High Street through a small arcade and into a medieval lane leads to this airy, modern restaurant of wood and stone. Excellent coffee and pastries baked on the premises are on the menu all day; light or regular lunches are offered; and dinner is served on Thursdays, Fridays, and Saturdays only (until 9:45 PM). 6 High St. (phone: 21329). Inexpensive.

SHARING A PINT: Smithwicks, a medium-tart ale-type beer, has been the local brew for well over 200 years. You may get a free sample if you take the guided brewery tour (Parliament St.) at 3 PM daily, May through September. To try it elsewhere, take your pick of the pubs. They range from the dark and cozy but spartan to the modern, well-lighted plastic. A list of the best includes *Tynans Bar,* 2 Horseleap Slip, a turn-of-the-century pub that has survived with its fittings — brass scales, grocery drawers, beer pumps, gilt mirrors — miraculously intact. Locals and cosmopolitans share its great atmosphere and honest drink. The exterior of the *Marble City Bar,* 66 High St., is a museum piece; the interior is less authentic, but its character has not been overwhelmed by modernization. *Kyteler's Inn,* St. Kieran's St., was once the house of the redoubtable Dame Alice. It now has a friendly nest of bars. The *Club House Bar* is a quiet oasis in the hotel on Patrick St., with sporting prints, cartoons, and cast-iron bar tables. Also good for pub grub is *Langton's,* 69 John St., a lively, social pub favored by the young. Other pubs known for their food and convivial atmosphere are *Court Arms,* 9 Parliament St.; the *Thosel Bar,* 8 High St; *Jim Holland,* 60 Kieran St.; and *Castle Inn,* on Patrick St., facing Kilkenny Castle.

LIMERICK CITY

The fourth largest city in Ireland (population: 60,000) offers an appropriately engaging introduction to the country for those many, many visitors who begin journeys here after the short half-hour trip in from Shannon Airport. Limerick is a major port, an inevitable product of its enviable position on the River Shannon; and while the city has a reputation for industry, those it is most famous for are all amiably light: traditional Limerick lace, still produced here; wonderfully cured hams and bacon; salmon fishing; and flour milling.

Limerick is a city of narrow streets, handsome Georgian houses, and impressive public buildings such as the Custom House and the Town Hall. This gracious architecture hardly reflects its violent history. Invaded by the Danes in the early tenth century, the area suffered many long years of skirmishing, which ended only when the Vikings were finally crushed by the Irish chieftain, Brian Ború. He made Limerick (in Irish, *Luimneach*) the capital of Munster. In the twelfth century, the Anglo-Normans conquered the town, and settling on the island formed by the river Shannon and its tributary, the Abbey, they built stout walls to keep the natives at bay. This area became known as English Town, and the section across the river Irish Town.

Undeterred by walls, the Irish continued to make sallies into English Town, led by the king of Munster, Donal Mor O'Brien. Upon his death in 1194, however, the Normans consolidated their position, and in 1210 King John ordered a strong castle and fortified bridge built to control the crossing point of the River Shannon. In later years the city walls were extended for added security.

During the seventeenth century the city was torn between revolts by the Irish who seized the city and sieges by the English to bring them to their knees. The Treaty of Limerick in 1691 was to end hostilities and grant political and religious liberty to the Irish and the Catholics, but repeated violations of the treaty forced thousands into exile. Many of Limerick's most important landmarks — Thomond Bridge, the city walls, and St. Mary's Cathedral — have associations with these turbulent times.

But as befits a city that is the major western gateway to Ireland, contemporary Limerick has a great deal to offer besides its ancient history and sites. A roster of activities includes fishing, horseback riding, horse racing, golfing, and swimming and boating on the Shannon. The medieval banquets held at the nearby Bunratty and Knappogue castles, as well as the *céilís* at the Folk Park, offer a delightful — if somewhat rowdy — sampling of traditional Irish hospitality. The countryside surrounding Limerick has a quiet beauty, perfect for a peaceful day's rambling: Low hill ranges ruffle the plains; small towns rise here and there, each with its ruined castle, abbey, or bridge.

Unlike most Irish cities, Limerick does not have important literary connections. It is, however, the home of the limerick, that famous five-line rhyme derived from a round-game in which an individual extemporized a nonsense verse, followed by a chorus that included the words, "Will you come up to Limerick?" Over the years the term *limerick* became associated with the rhyme scheme *aabba,* devised by the nineteenth-century nonsense poet Edward Lear. A typical limerick might go like this:

> There was a fair Irish city,
> That lent its good name to a ditty;
> Though of dubious worth
> The verse caused great mirth,
> Now the limerick outshines Limerick City.

LIMERICK AT-A-GLANCE

SEEING THE CITY: For the best view of this rather flat city, climb to the top of King John's Castle; the key to the building is available from Mrs. Maloney, who lives at 5 Castle St., across from the main entrance to the castle. You can also view the city from the spire of St. Mary's Cathedral. Contact the caretaker to gain access to the tower.

SPECIAL PLACES: Limerick is very compact and most of the important sights are located in the same general area. As traffic is sometimes congested, the city is really best seen on foot.

CITY CENTER

Thomond Bridge – The present bridge, dating to 1840, was designed by Irish architect James Pain to replace the 13th-century structure erected by King John to defend the city. The original had a guard house and gate at the west end and a drawbridge at the east end near the castle. The Treaty Stone, on which the famous Treaty of Limerick was reputedly signed in 1691 after the Williamite Siege, is on the west side of the new bridge.

King John's Castle – This fortification at the east foot of Thomond Bridge was built in 1210 by King John to guard the city against invaders. It is one of the oldest examples of Norman architecture in Ireland, with rounded gate towers standing sentry over the curtain walls. In the 18th century a military barracks was installed within the walls, and, later, houses were built in the castle yard, some of which remain. The castle, in fairly good condition, is open to the public during the summer.

St. Mary's Cathedral – Established in 1172 by Donal Mor O'Brien, the last king of Munster, it has been restored and extended a number of times and combines features from many different centuries. Note especially the unusual (and unique in Ireland) 15th-century choir stalls whose misericords are carved with many medieval emblems, including those of Richard III. The cathedral is open daily in the summer, 9 AM to 1 PM and 2:30 to 5:30 PM; in the winter, 9 AM to 1 PM. Nicholas and Bridge sts.

Baal's Bridge – The original structure on this location linked the turf of the conquerers — English Town — with that of the natives — Irish Town. In Irish *Baal* means "bald," that is, the bridge had no battlements, but rather supported a row of houses. These disappeared in 1830 when the present bridge was constructed.

Limerick Walls – Forming a rough diamond shape, the Limerick walls run east and southeast from Ball's Bridge, along Old Clare Street and Lelia Street to the grounds of St. John's Hospital. There were four main gates: East Watergate, John's Gate, Mungret Gate, and West Watergate. The largest remaining portion of the walls is behind Lelia Street. Traces of the Black Battery (so called because it successfully resisted the Williamites) are found on the hospital grounds, while a badly deteriorated bit can be seen looking from Pike's Row toward High Street. There are two other sections — one forming part of the building housing Sinnotts Joinery Works and the other standing in the Charlotte Quay parking lot.

St. John's Cathedral – Originally intended as a parish church, this Gothic revival cathedral built in the 19th century eventually became the see of the diocese. It houses two of Ireland's most remarkable ecclesiastical treasures, the magnificently carved mitre and crozier made by Cornelius O'Dea, who was one of Limerick's bishops in the 15th century. At 280 feet, St. John's spire is the highest in Ireland; it's rather more ornate than the rest of the structure. The memorial to Patrick Sarsfield, hero of the 1690–91 sieges, which is located on the cathedral grounds, was rendered by John Lawlor of Dublin in 1881.

St. John's Square – A few steps from the cathedral, this square constructed around 1751 was once lined with fashionable stone houses owned by the local gentry. The square declined slowly over the years until the 20th century, when the houses were used less glamorously as offices, tenements, barracks, and a butcher shop. Eventually they fell into neglect and were abandoned, although interest in them has recently been revived and restoration undertaken.

Newtown Pery – Just 200 years old, this is the "new" part of Limerick — a grid of streets roughly extending between Sarsfield Street in the north and the Crescent on the south. Named after Edward Sexton Pery, a Speaker of the Irish House of Commons, under whose patronage the renovation was begun, the development was distinctly Georgian in character with town houses constructed of red brick. In the Crescent is a memorial to Daniel O'Connell, "the Liberator," rendered by Irish sculptor John Hogan in 1857. (O'Connell founded the movement for Catholic emancipation.)

Granary – Originally opened as a Georgian grain store in 1787, this old building was renovated in the early 1980s and has now become the social and commercial hub of Limerick life. Set among the quays near the River Shannon, it includes a tourist office, the city library, shops, restaurants, taverns, and a banquet and entertainment hall called *The Captain's Table* (open May to October). The *Granary* is open daily year-round. Charlotte Quay, Michael St.

ENVIRONS

Bunratty Castle and Folk Park – The original castle on this site was built in the 15th century by the McNamara family, but appropriated around 1500 by Conor O'Brien, earl of Thomond. Refurbished in the 1950s, it's now famous for the colorful medieval banquets presented in the great hall every evening (see *Nightlife*), but the castle also houses an incredible collection of European paintings, furniture, and tapestries dating from the 14th to 17th centuries. From the battlements, you have a splendid view — as did the Earl's warriors — of the surrounding countryside. Behind the castle is a model village, with cottages, workshops, and exhibits demonstrating how people in different regions of Ireland lived and labored years ago. The castle and Folk Park are both located on the main Ennis road. Across the street from them is the mustard-colored Bunratty Cottage, a shop noted for its clothing designed by the locally well-known Vonnie Reynolds.

Quin Abbey – Although the Franciscan friary, dating to 1402, is now roofless and in ruins, you can still see the tombs of the founding McNamara clan. Quin.

Craggaunowen – This project, like Bunratty, was developed to document life-styles in Ireland long ago. The complex has both a ring fort dating from early Christian times and a *crannóg,* or lake dwelling (stone hut situated on an island), typical of the Bronze Age. The castle on the grounds is an actual fortress built by the McNamara family in the 14th century. In the intervening years it suffered neglect, but it is now restored and contains many medieval artifacts. Open daily, April to October. Quin.

Ballycasey Craft Courtyard – The crafts workshops here encompass everything from basketry to leatherwork to pottery. Adjacent to the center stands *Balleycaseymore House,* a Georgian-style building that houses an international art gallery. Both attractions are open daily year-round. 10 miles west of Limerick in Shannon, about 3 miles from Shannon Airport.

Lough Gur – Around this lake are found a number of ancient ruins, including stone circles, cairns, dolmens, and crannógs. Human bones, weapons, and pottery have all been unearthed here and experts estimate earliest habitation of the site to be 2000 BC. A guide to the area (IR£2.15) and a self-guided walking-tour booklet (25p) can be obtained from the Limerick Tourist Office. Open daily, May to September. 12 miles south of Limerick on the Bruff road.

Hunt Museum – Donated by Celtic historian John Hunt, who also sponsored the Craggaunowen Project in Quin (see above), this is a collection of many artifacts found in Ireland dating to the Bronze and Early Iron ages. Open daily from May through September, 10 AM to 6 PM. Located 3 miles east of Limerick, at the National Institute for Higher Education, off the Dublin Road.

■ **EXTRA SPECIAL: Knappogue Castle** – Built in 1467 by the McNamara family, this castle was bought in 1966 by an American and restored to its original 15th-century elegance. Surrounded by lush green pastures and grazing cattle, Knappogue presents an imposing front. The interior is no less impressive, with its soaring ceilings and handsome antique furnishings. Ask to see the owners' magnificent private dining room. Open daily May to October. About 12 miles northwest of Limerick, near Quin (Shannon Castle Tours; phone: 061-61788).

SOURCES AND RESOURCES

TOURIST INFORMATION: For general information, brochures, and maps, visit the Tourist Information Office at The Granary, Michael St. (phone: 317522). The staff will advise you on any problems or answer any questions and can make hotel reservations anywhere in Ireland.

Guides to Limerick, as well as Clare and Tipperary (50p each), are available at the information office. *Historic Limerick* by Laurence Walsh (IR£1.95) will set you straight on the city's long history.

Local Coverage – The *Limerick Chronicle,* Ireland's oldest newspaper, is published once a week, as is the *Limerick Echo.* The *Limerick Leader* is published four times a week. The tourist board's weekly *What's On* guide gives entertainment schedules.

GETTING AROUND: Bus – Service between Dublin, Limerick, and Shannon Airport is frequent and convenient. The terminal, Colbert Station, is on Parnell St.; call 42433 for departure and arrival schedules.

Car Rental – All the major Irish and international firms are represented at Shannon Airport. In the Limerick area, you can rent a car from *Bunratty Car Hire,* Coonagh Motors, Coonagh Cross, Caherdavin, Limerick (phone: 51741); *Dan Dooley Rent-a-Car,* Knocklong (phone: 062-53103); *Hertz,* Glentworth St., Limerick (phone: 47017); or *Treaty Car Rental,* 37 William St., Limerick (phone: 46512).

Sightseeing – Day tours by bus are operated by *CIE Tours* from their railway stations in Limerick (phone: 061-42433) and Ennis (phone: 065-28038), and by *Gray Line Sightseeing* from the Granary (phone: 061-318519).

Taxi – There are cabstands on Thomas St., Cecil St., Bedford Row, and at Colbert Station. Or, you can order a taxi from one of the following: *Conway Cabs* (phone: 41149); *Express Taxies* (phone: 47777); *Limerick Taxi Co-op* (phone: 40011); *Speedi Cabs* (phone: 318844); *Star Cabs* (phone: 46111).

Walking Tours – Walking tours of Old Limerick are conducted from early June to mid-September; they leave at 3:30 PM from the Granary Courtyard. £1.50. Further information is available from the tourist office (phone: 317522).

 MUSEUMS: The *Limerick Art Gallery,* which exhibits modern Irish painting, is in People's Park on Pery Sq.; the *Limerick Civic Museum,* which documents local history, is at 1 St. John's Sq.

 SHOPPING: Along Limerick's main shopping street, O'Connell, are many knitwear, crystal, and crafts stores. If you're interested in antiques, you can find furniture, paintings, and prints in *George Stacpoole's* place at 35 Cecil St., and china and jewelry at *Once Upon a Time* at 17 Ellen St. To buy famous Limerick lace go to the *Good Shepherd Convent* on Clare St. (phone: 45178). For quality crafts, try the *Spinning Wheel,* 8 Rutland St. *White and Gold,* 34 O'Connell St., offers fine china, porcelain, and crystal. Limerick's major department store is *Todds,* on O'Connell St., where you can find Irish knits, tweeds, and woolens; Waterford crystal; linens; and more.

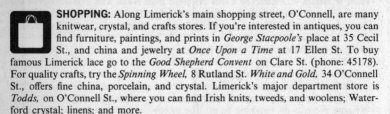 **SPECIAL EVENTS:** The most important event in this area is the annual *Limerick Civic Week* in late March, which features a St. Patrick's Day parade, a singing competition, a crafts exhibit, an international band competition, and a charity ball hosted by the mayor.

 SPORTS: Boating – In Killaloe, about 12 miles north of Limerick, are two companies that rent cabin boats for cruising the Shannon and neighboring lakes: *Atlantis Marine Ltd.* (phone: 76281); and *Derg Line Cruisers* (phone: 76364).

Cycling – You can rent a bike from *The Bike Shop,* O'Connell Ave. (phone: 315900); *Nestor Brothers Ltd.,* 28 O'Connell St. (phone: 44096); or *Limerick Sports Store,* 10 William St. (phone 45647). You pick up a bike at *Raleigh Rent-a-Bike,* then buy insurance and obtain touring maps of the area. (Contact Irish Raleigh, Broomhill Rd., Tallaght, County Dublin; phone 01-521888.)

Fishing – To fish for salmon in the Shannon or for trout and grilse in the Mulcair or Bunratty rivers, you must request a permit from the Shannon Fisheries, c/o ESB Showrooms, O'Connell St., Limerick City (phone: 45599).

Golf – Both the *Limerick Golf Club* at Ballyclough (phone: 44083) and the *Castletroy Golf Club* on the Dublin Road (335261) are open to the public; you can rent equipment and use the clubhouse.

Horseback Riding – You can hire horses at the following stables: *Ashroe House,* Newport; *Clarina Riding Centre,* Clarina; and *The Stables,* Rathkeale.

Hunting – Hiring a horse for a day will run about $60 and the cap fee about $80. To make arrangements to join a hunt, write in advance to hunt secretary Michael Binchy, *Limerick Harriers,* Fort George, Rathkeale (phone: 069-64163), or Bryan Murphy, *Foxhunting Centre of Ireland,* c/o Dunraven Arms Hotel, Adare (phone: 94209).

Tennis – Visitors are always welcome at *Limerick Lawn Tennis Club,* one of Ireland's oldest tennis centers, which has squash courts and a convivial bar as well. Ennis Rd. (phone: 52316).

NIGHTCLUBS AND NIGHTLIFE: The *Belltable Arts Centre,* 69 O'Connell St. (phone: 319866), has lunchtime and evening performances by local and touring companies. *Son et Lumiere,* a sound-and-light show portraying the history of Limerick, takes place inside 800-year-old St. Mary's Cathedral (near Thomond Bridge) at 9:15 nightly from mid-June to mid-September. For more information, contact Shannonside Tourism (phone: 317522). Also in summer, traditional music concerts, followed by *céilí* dancing with audience participation, are held at *Cois na hAbhna* (pronounced *Cushnahowna*), the Irish Traditional Cultural Center, Gort Rd., Ennis (phone: 065-27115). More formal, perhaps, is the *céilí* offered at Bunratty Folk Park, a program of singing, dancing, and storytelling accompanied by an Irish meal. In a similar vein are the banquets held at Bunratty and Knappogue castles — "medieval" feasts enlivened by traditional music and historical sketches. (Both located on the main Limerick/Ennis road; for reservations, call Shannon Castle Tours at 61788.) *The Captain's Table* in Limerick's *Granary* nightlife center offers seafaring music nightly. Irish cabaret, a dinner-plus-variety show, is offered by several hotels in the area, as are discos; check *What's On* for details. Finally, Limerick has many sing-along pubs, and local papers provide information on these.

SINS: In this part of horse-crazy Ireland, playing the ponies is a most fitting sin. Place your bet at one of Limerick City's many "turf accountant" offices or at the racetrack. Although the two main events, the Irish Derby and the Irish Grand National, are both held in County Kildare, the excitement is just as real at the smaller races held at Greenpark in the city's southwestern suburbs, and at Limerick Junction, about an hour's drive on Tipperary Road. At both courses you'll see 10 or 12 colorful "turf accountants" (bookies); lists of runners and the odds being offered are written on blackboards. "Punters" (gamblers) simply walk up to the bookie, hand him the money, name their choice of horse, and receive a betting slip with the man's name on it. If you win, return the slip to the bookie for your payoff — first allowing another race to lapse so that he can make up his cash.

BEST IN TOWN

CHECKING IN: Because of its proximity to Shannon Airport, the Limerick City hotel scene embraces part of County Clare (in which the airport is located). Hence, many of the hotels listed here are actually west of the city, between the environs of Shannon and downtown Limerick. Expect to pay $150 and up for a double in a hotel listed as very expensive; between $80 and $100 in expensive; and between $40 and $75 in moderate. In addition to the large hotels we mention, there are numerous small guesthouses for which you can make reservations at the local tourist board.

Dromoland Castle – Unadulterated luxury prevails at this renovated and regal former O'Brien stronghold. Besides 77 large, comfortable bedrooms, it offers 18 holes of golf, riding, tennis, fishing, and shooting within its spacious grounds. The dining room is formal, as befits a palace, and its cuisine is excellent. Lodgings are available April through October only. Newmarket-on-Fergus (phone: 71144). Very expensive.

Clare Inn – On the same grounds as *Dromoland Castle,* this contemporary inn shares the castle's sports amenities (golf, riding, tennis, fishing, shooting) and, unlike the castle, is open year-round. Its 120 rooms offer fine views of the countryside. Newmarket-on-Fergus (phone: 71161). Expensive.

Jurys – Just over the bridge from the city center, overlooking the River Shannon, this modern hotel offers efficient service and has 100 well-appointed rooms. Its restaurant, *The Copper Room,* is particularly good, and there is a new pub-like bar and coffee shop. Ennis Rd. (phone: 55266). Expensive.

Shannon Shamrock Inn – This Paddy Fitzpatrick hotel has 100 rooms, 10 river suites, a heated indoor pool, a sauna, a French/Irish restaurant, and a bar. It's next to Bunratty Castle and *Durty Nelly's* pub. Bunratty (phone: 61177). Expensive.

Limerick Inn – This is a modern, comfortable motel with 133 rooms, a Continental restaurant that's very good, and well above average service. Amenities include a new leisure center with a swimming pool and a gym, plus tennis courts and a putting green. Ennis Rd. (phone: 51544). Moderate.

Limerick Ryan – Part of the dependable Ryan Hotel Chain, it has 184 rooms, a restaurant, and a lively disco bar, *Magnums,* which features pub grub during the day. Ennis Rd. (phone: 53922). Moderate.

Two Mile Inn – Named for its location just outside of Limerick, this modern hotel (a Best Western affiliate) has a domed atrium, 125 rooms, and a restaurant serving such local specialties as Limerick ham, Burren lamb, and Shannon salmon. Ennis Rd. (phone: 53122). Moderate.

For an extra special treat, spend the night in a fully staffed, Georgian-style manor house on the grounds of *Dromoland Castle. Thomond House* is the private residence and seat of the Rt. Hon. Lord Inchiquin, Conor Myles John O'Brien, head of the O'Brien clan and the only man in Ireland to hold a British peerage and an Irish chieftaincy. He now welcomes visitors into his home as "private house guests." There are 5 deluxe bedrooms, each with private bath and views of the 900-acre estate. Lord Inchiquin, in grand fashion, presides over nightly dinners in the candlelit dining room. Minimum stay is three nights and rates start at about $850 per couple. Further information from Lord Inchiquin at Thomond House, Newmarket-on-Fergus (phone: 71304).

 **EATING OUT:** Although it's never been known for its wealth of restaurants, the Limerick-Shannon area has added some distinguished eateries, and you won't be disappointed with a meal at any of the places recommended below. Expect to pay $60 and up for dinner for two (not including wine) in places listed as expensive and between $30 and $55 in those mentioned as moderate.

Copper Room – The best in the downtown area, this rather small but attractive restaurant in *Jurys* hotel offers excellently prepared French cuisine. Service is efficient and friendly. Open for dinner only. Ennis Rd. (phone: 55266). Expensive.

MacCloskeys – Encompassing the former mews and wine cellars of Bunratty House, a restored 1804 mansion, this appealing candlelit restaurant is the creation of Gerry and Marie MacCloskey. They describe the cuisine as "French with an Irish flair," with such specialties as Dover sole, rack of lamb, pheasant, and lobster. Closed Sundays and Mondays; dinner only. Bunratty Folk Park, Bunratty (phone: 74082). Expensive.

Thisilldous – The name isn't as exotic as it sounds: One evening the McMahon family, searching for a place to open a restaurant, looked at their own living room and decided "This'll do us." Since then this bungalow bistro has gained a fine reputation for classic French cuisine. Among the dishes are coquilles St.-Jacques, veal Cordon Bleu, and sole stuffed with prawns. 10 Firgrove, Hurlers Cross, Bunratty (phone: 74758). Expensive.

Mustard Seed – In a historic Old World village setting, this recently renovated, thatched cottage restaurant is known for its beef Wellington as well as such innovative dishes as scallops and stir-fried vegetables, black grape sorbet, and Baileys and hazelnut ice cream. Dinner only. Adare (phone: 94451). Expensive to moderate.

Cronin's – An old house right in the middle of the village of Newmarket-on-Fergus is the setting for this combination restaurant/pub. At any time of day, Irish stew, soups, and snacks are available in the wood-paneled bar lounge, while the adjoining dining room makes an elegant setting to enjoy dinners of filet of beef en croute, *paupiettes* of trout with blue cheese sauce, or prawn tails thermidor. Main St., Newmarket-on-Fergus (phone: 71157). Moderate.

Mariner – Housed in a gracefully restored building that was once a grain store, it has vaulted ceilings, double arches, and original brickwork. Seafood is the specialty, but the meat and poultry dishes are also good. In the evenings there is lively piano or guitar music. The Granary, Charlotte Quay (phone: 47266). Moderate.

Barn – Part of the Ballycasey craft complex near Shannon Airport, this small restaurant is ideal for lunch or a light meal. The offerings include shepherd's pie, homemade scones and pastries, garden vegetable soups, salads, and seafood platters, as well as more predictable fare like pizza, lasagna, and quiche. Ballycasey Craft Centre, Shannon (phone: 62105 and 74115). Inexpensive.

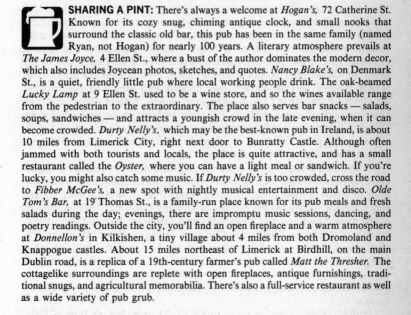

SHARING A PINT: There's always a welcome at *Hogan's,* 72 Catherine St. Known for its cozy snug, chiming antique clock, and small nooks that surround the classic old bar, this pub has been in the same family (named Ryan, not Hogan) for nearly 100 years. A literary atmosphere prevails at *The James Joyce,* 4 Ellen St., where a bust of the author dominates the modern decor, which also includes Joycean photos, sketches, and quotes. *Nancy Blake's,* on Denmark St., is a quiet, friendly little pub where local working people drink. The oak-beamed *Lucky Lamp* at 9 Ellen St. used to be a wine store, and so the wines available range from the pedestrian to the extraordinary. The place also serves bar snacks — salads, soups, sandwiches — and attracts a youngish crowd in the late evening, when it can become crowded. *Durty Nelly's,* which may be the best-known pub in Ireland, is about 10 miles from Limerick City, right next door to Bunratty Castle. Although often jammed with both tourists and locals, the place is quite attractive, and has a small restaurant called the *Oyster,* where you can have a light meal or sandwich. If you're lucky, you might also catch some music. If *Durty Nelly's* is too crowded, cross the road to *Fibber McGee's,* a new spot with nightly musical entertainment and disco. *Olde Tom's Bar,* at 19 Thomas St., is a family-run place known for its pub meals and fresh salads during the day; evenings, there are impromptu music sessions, dancing, and poetry readings. Outside the city, you'll find an open fireplace and a warm atmosphere at *Donnellon's* in Kilkishen, a tiny village about 4 miles from both Dromoland and Knappogue castles. About 15 miles northeast of Limerick at Birdhill, on the main Dublin road, is a replica of a 19th-century farmer's pub called *Matt the Thresher.* The cottagelike surroundings are replete with open fireplaces, antique furnishings, traditional snugs, and agricultural memorabilia. There's also a full-service restaurant as well as a wide variety of pub grub.

LONDON

British author and journalist V. S. Pritchett noted that the essence of London was contained in the very sound of its name: Lon-don, a weighty word, solid, monumental, dignified, even ponderous. London is a shapeless city without a center; it sprawls anarchically over 620 square miles and brims over with a variety of neighborhoods and people. One of its sharpest observers, Daniel Defoe, portrayed London in the eighteenth century much as it could be described today: "It is . . . stretched out in buildings, straggling, confused . . . out of all shape, uncompact and unequal; neither long nor broad, round or square."

London can best be understood not as one city but as a conglomeration of villages that were incorporated whole, one by one, as the monster expanded — Chelsea, Battersea, Paddington, and Hampstead are just a few. Fortunately, all of its important parks and squares have remained inviolate, but not without a struggle, for London's merchant class — its backbone and its pride — often resisted and defeated town planners, ever since Parliament turned down Sir Christopher Wren's splendid plan to rebuild after the fire of 1666. It was royalty and aristocracy that created and preserved the parks — St. James's Park, Hyde Park, Kensington Gardens, Regent's Park, and Kew Gardens were all royal parks — and their enthusiasm became contagious. The passionate regard of Londoners for their green spots has been one of the city's saving graces as it grew so helplessly and recklessly, more in the spirit of commerce than of urban planning.

Today's London — though marred by soulless high-rise intruders of glass and concrete — boasts more greenery than any metropolis could reasonably hope to retain in these philistine times. Aside from its many garden squares and the meticulously tended gardens of so many Londoners' homes, the city is punctuated by a series of large parks and commons; besides those already mentioned, there are Wimbledon Common, Highgate Wood, Primrose Hill, Hampstead Heath — the list goes on and on. And to make even more certain that citification does not intrude too far into London life, a green belt, almost 100 square miles of forest and grassland, virtually encircles the city and, to the chagrin and impatience of developers, is meticulously preserved by law.

London's other natural resource, the River Thames, has not been so fortunate. As any glance at a map will show, London follows the serpentine meanderings of the Thames, England's principal river. Nearly everything of interest in London is on or near the Thames, for London is London because it is a natural port. The river has always been London's mainstay, for centuries its only east-west road, and it has justifiably been said that "every drop of the Thames is liquid history." At the site of the Naval College in Greenwich, for example, there once stood a royal palace where Henry VIII and

Elizabeth I were born, and where tournaments, pageants, and banquets were held.

A great river port and a city of gardens, London is also a city of stately squares and monuments, of royalty with its pomp and ceremony, a cosmopolitan city of the first rank. Until World War II, it was the capital of the mammoth and far-flung British Empire upon which, it was said, the sun never set. For many centuries, a powerful Britannia ruled a considerable section of the globe — the largest since Roman times — and the English language spread from the inconsiderable British Isles to become the dominant language all over the world, from North America to India.

If the British Empire has contracted drastically, it has done so gracefully, among memories of its greatest days. And if once-subject peoples hated their oppressor, they still love London, and many have chosen to live there. London is still the center of the Commonwealth of independent nations that were once British colonies, and its cosmopolitan atmosphere owes a great deal to the ubiquity of former colonials. Their presence is felt in the substantial Indian-Pakistani community in the Southall district of West London; in the strong Caribbean flavor in Brixton; in Chinatown in and around Gerrard Street — a hop, skip, and a jump from Piccadilly Circus; in the Cypriot groceries and bakeries of Camden Town; and in the majestic mosque on the fringe of Regent's Park.

A tantalizing diversity of accents flavors the English language here — accents from Australia and Barbados, Bangladesh and Nigeria, Canada and Malaysia, Kenya and South Africa, Sri Lanka and Ireland, Hong Kong and the US. And then the various inflections of Britain itself are also to be heard in the streets of London — the lilt and rasp of cockney, Oxford, Somerset, Yorkshire, the Scottish Highlands, and the Welsh mining towns.

London's somewhat onomatopoeic name derives from the Celtic term *Llyn-din*, meaning "river place," but little is known of London before it was renamed *Londinium* by the Romans in AD 43. The rather fantastical twelfth-century historian Geoffrey of Monmouth may have originated the myth widespread in Shakespeare's day — that London was founded by Brute, a direct descendant of Aeneas in 1108 BC, who named it Troynovant, New Troy, or Trenovant. Even in medieval times, London had grandiose notions of its own importance — a prideful self-image that has been amply justified by history.

The city was sufficiently prominent for the Norman invader William the Conqueror to make it his capital in 1066. During the Middle Ages, the expansion of trade, population growth, and the energetic activities of its guilds of merchants and craftsmen promoted London's prosperity. Indisputably, London's golden age was the English Renaissance, the sixteenth century, the time of Queen Elizabeth I, Shakespeare, and Drake's defeat of the Spanish Armada. Most of the Tudor buildings of London were wiped out in the great fire of 1666. Christopher Wren, the architect of genius, undertook to rebuild many buildings and churches, the most outstanding of which is St. Paul's Cathedral. The eighteenth century, a highly sophisticated age, saw the building of noble homes and stately squares, of which only Bedford Square and Fitzroy remain complete. In the early nineteenth century, interest continued in homes and squares; and only in the Victorian age, the height of the Empire, were public buildings like the Houses of Parliament redesigned, this time in grand and fanciful neo-Gothic style.

London has seen whole catalogues of heroes and villains, crises and conflagrations, come and go, sometimes swallowed whole in the passage of time, sometimes leaving relics. Still on elegant display is stately Hampton Court Palace, the most magnificent of England's palaces, where Henry VIII lived now and again with five of his six wives. There is a spot downtown — in front of the Banqueting House on Whitehall — where another king, Charles I, was beheaded by his subjects, who were calmly committing dreaded regicide 150 years before the presumably more emotional and explosive French across the English Channel even contemplated such a gesture.

London has lived through the unbounded permissiveness of the flamboyantly royal Restoration period (1660–85), when even King Charles II frequented brothels and didn't care who knew it, and it has survived the stern moral puritanism of the Victorian era, when it was downright rude to refer to the *breast* of chicken or a piano *leg*. And most recently, London stood up with exemplary courage under the devastating effects of the Nazi bombings, which destroyed a great many buildings and killed thousands of people.

Many of our images of London, taken from old movies, actually mirror its realities: Big Ben rises above the Houses of Parliament, somberly striking the hour; ramrod-straight scarlet-uniformed soldiers half hide their faces in towering black bearskin hats; waiters at the Bank of England still sport the kinds of top hats and tailcoats their predecessors wore for a century; lawyers in court still don wigs and black robes. A few images, however, are outdated: The bowler hat has been slipping steadily out of fashion for years, and rigidly enforced environmental regulations have made London's once-famous pea soup fog a thing of the past.

London's nearly infinite variety of urban moods includes the sturdy edifices lining Whitehall, center of the British government, with Trafalgar Square at its head and Parliament at its foot; the elegant shopping areas of Knightsbridge, Bond Street, and the Burlington Arcade; suburban chic in Barnes and Blackheath; handsome squares in Bloomsbury; melancholy mystery in Victoria and Waterloo train stations with their spy-movie atmosphere; the vitality of East End street markets; and the riparian tranquillity of Thames-side towpaths in Putney and along Hammersmith Mall.

The British have a talent that amounts to a genius for government — for democracy and political tolerance — a talent that has been developing ever since the Magna Carta was signed in 1215 and one that makes London's ambience easy and relaxed for individualists of all sorts. It is no wonder that the eccentric and inveterate Londoner of the city's eighteenth-century heyday, Dr. Samuel Johnson, once declared, "When a man is tired of London, he is tired of life, for there is in London all that life can afford."

Johnson's opinion, though somewhat overblown, was essentially shared by one of several modern American writers who chose to live in London. Disillusioned with New York, Boston, and Paris, Henry James decided in favor of London in 1881. Somehow he concluded that London was a place eminently suited to human life: "It is not a pleasant place; it is not agreeable, or cheerful, or easy, or exempt from reproach. It is only magnificent. You can draw up a tremendous list of reasons why it should be unsupportable. The fogs, the smoke, the dirt, the darkness, the wet, the distances, the ugliness, the brutal size of the place, the horrible numerosity of society . . . but . . . London is on the whole the most possible form of life."

LONDON AT-A-GLANCE

SEEING THE CITY: London has, for the most part, resisted the temptation to build high. Aside from a handful of modest gestures toward skyscraping, there aren't many towering structures to obscure panoramic overviews of the city from its higher vantage points, which include:

London Hilton International – There were discreet noises of disapproval from Buckingham Palace when it was realized that the view from the roof bar of the *Hilton* included not only the palace grounds but, with high-powered binoculars, the inside of some of the royal chambers as well. In fact, the view over Mayfair, Hyde Park, and Westminster is breathtaking. Park La. (phone: 493-8000).

Westminster Cathedral – Not to be confused with Westminster Abbey. The top of the bell tower of London's Catholic cathedral looks down on a broad expanse of the inner city. An elevator takes visitors up for a token charge (from April to September only). Off Victoria St. near the station, at Ashley Pl. SW 1.

Hampstead Heath – Climb to the top of Parliament Hill, on the southern rim of this "wilderness" in north London. On a clear day, the view south from the Heath makes the city look like a vast village.

South Bank Arts Center – On the south bank of Waterloo Bridge, the bunkerlike complex of cultural buildings is an attraction in itself, including as it does Royal Festival Hall, the National Theatre, the National Film Theatre, the Hayward Gallery, and other cultural attractions. For a view of London, look across the Thames — upriver to the Houses of Parliament, downriver to St. Paul's Cathedral.

Tower Bridge Walkway – The upper part of one of London's famous landmarks is now open to visitors. In addition to the viewing gallery, there is an exhibition on the history of London's bridges and a museum that includes the bridge's Victorian steam pumping engines. Open daily. Admission charge.

St. Paul's Cathedral – The reward for climbing the 600 steps into the dome of this cathedral — the largest in the world after St. Peter's in Rome — is a panoramic view of London.

Docklands – A high-tech overhead train runs from Tower Hill to Greenwich, speeding over the city's fast-developing, and fascinating, docklands.

Walking Tours – A trained guide can show you Shakespeare's London or that of Dickens or Jack the Ripper — many different tours are offered. These reasonably priced tours last up to 2 hours, generally in the afternoon or evening. City information centers have lists of tour companies.

Bus Tours – *London Transport*'s 2-hour unconducted tour (the least expensive and most comprehensive tour of the city) leaves every hour from four sites: Marble Arch, Piccadilly Circus, Baker Street subway station, and Victoria St. (phone: 222-1234). Other guided bus tours include *American Express* (phone: 930-4411), *Frames* (phone: 837-6311), *Harrods* (phone: 581-3603), and *Thomas Cook* (phone: 499-4000).

Taxi Tours – Several firms and taxi drivers offer guided tours of London; details are available at information centers. You can arrange for the personal services of a member of London's Guild of Guides by phoning the London Visitor and Convention Bureau's Guide Dept. (phone: 730-3450).

Boat Excursions – See London from the Thames. Boats leave roughly every half-hour from Westminster Pier at the foot of Westminster Bridge and from Charing Cross Pier on Victoria Embankment; they sail (summers only) upriver to Kew or downriver to the Tower of London, Greenwich, and the massive Thames flood barrier. Also available is a journey along Regent's Canal through North London (summer only); *Jason's Trip,* opposite 60 Blomfield Rd., Little Venice W9 (phone: 286-3428). For further information about these and other boat trips, contact the London Visitor and Convention Bureau's River Boat Information Service (phone: 730-4812).

Helicopter Flights – See London from the air. Sightseeing tours, following the Thames from Battersea to Greenwich and back, are available for $54. Make a reservation with *UK Air Taxis,* Westland Heliport, Lombard Rd., SW11 (phone: 228-9114).

SPECIAL PLACES/ATTRACTIONS: Surveying London from the steps of St. Paul's Cathedral at the turn of the 19th century, a visiting Prussian general commented to his English host: "What a place to plunder!" Even those who are less rapacious will appreciate the extraordinary wealth of sights London displays for visitors to inspect. Though some are dispersed in various corners of this vast city, most are clustered reasonably close together in or near the inner districts of Westminster, the City, and Kensington.

WESTMINSTER

Changing of the Guard – An American who lived in London once said, "There's just no better way to convince yourself that you're in London!" This famous ceremony takes place daily from April to August (alternate days in winter) promptly at 11:30 AM in the Buckingham Palace forecourt, at 11:15 AM at St. James's Palace, and at 11:30 AM at the Tower of London. (In very wet weather, it may be canceled.)

Horse Guards – If you haven't had enough, you can see a new guard of 12 members of the Household Cavalry troop in with trumpet and standard, daily at 11 AM, 10 on Sundays. On the west side of Whitehall. Incidentally, they come from stables not far from Hyde Park and make a daily parade along the south roadway of Hyde Park, past Buckingham Palace, and then on to Trafalgar Square to turn into Whitehall. Their progress is as much fun to watch as the actual ceremony.

Buckingham Palace – The royal standard flies from the roof when the monarch is in residence at her London home. Although George III bought the palace in 1762, no sovereign lived here until 1837, when Queen Victoria moved in. The palace, unfortunately, is open only to invited guests. Its interior contains magnificently decorated apartments, a superb picture gallery, and a throne room (66 feet long), where foreign ambassadors are received and knights are knighted. The palace grounds contain the largest private garden in London (40 acres). And the gate that originally was built for the entrance, too narrow for the coaches of George IV, now marks an entrance to Hyde Park and is known as Marble Arch. Buckingham Palace Rd.

State Visits – If you aren't going to be in London for the Queen's official birthday in June, you might want to see her greet a foreign dignitary in full regalia. This happens quite frequently and is announced in the royal calendar in *The Times.* The Queen meets her guest at Victoria Station, and they ride to Buckingham Palace in a procession of horse-drawn coaches, followed by the colorful Horse Guards. Meanwhile, at Hyde Park Corner, the cannoneers on horseback perform elaborate maneuvers before their salute thunders through the whole city.

Queen's Gallery – Treasures from the royal art collection are on display in this room of the palace only. Exhibitions change about once a year. Closed Mondays. Admission charge. Buckingham Palace Rd. SW1.

Royal Mews – The mews is a palace alley where the magnificent state coaches and the horses that draw them are stabled. The public is admitted on Wednesdays and Thursdays from 2 to 4 PM. Buckingham Palace Rd. SW1.

St. James's Park – Parks are everywhere in London and Londoners love them. This is one of the nicest, where at lunch hour on a sunny day you can see the impeccably dressed London businessmen lounging on the grass, their shoes and shirts off. With its sizable lake inhabited by pelicans and other wild fowl, St. James's was originally a royal park, laid out by Henry VIII in 1532.

The Mall – The wide avenue parallel to Pall Mall and lined with lime trees and Regency buildings leads from Trafalgar Square to Buckingham Palace. This is the principal ceremonial route used by Queen Elizabeth and her escort of Household Cavalry for the State Opening of Parliament (October/November) and the Trooping of the Color (mid-June). It is closed to traffic on Sunday afternoons.

Trafalgar Square – One of London's most heavily trafficked squares is built around the towering Nelson's Column — a 145-foot monument that honors Lord Nelson, victor at the naval Battle of Trafalgar in 1805. At the base of the monument are four huge bronze lions and two fountains. Flanked by handsome buildings, including the National Gallery and the 18th-century church of St. Martin in the Fields, the square is a favorite gathering place for political demonstrations, tourists, and pigeons.

Piccadilly Circus – Downtown London finds its center here in the heart of the theater district and on the edge of Soho. This is the London equivalent of Times Square — lots of it is just as tacky — and at the center of the busy "circus," or traffic circle, is the restored statue of Eros (moved about 40 feet from its original perch), which actually was designed in 1893 as *The Angel of Christian Charity,* a memorial to the charitable earl of Shaftesbury — the archer and his bow were meant as a pun on his name. The Trocadero, a recently converted three-story shopping and entertainment complex featuring the *International Village Restaurants,* has lent Piccadilly a new level of bustle. Popular exhibitions include the *Guinness World Records* display, with re-creations of some dramatic entries in the best-selling book *The Light Fantastic Gallery of Holography,* and the London Experience, for a look at the city's history.

National Gallery – One of the world's great art museums, this is an inexhaustible feast for art lovers. In the vast collection on display are works by such masters as Uccello, Da Vinci, Titian, Rembrandt, Rubens, Cranach, Gainsborough, El Greco, Renoir, Cézanne, and Van Gogh. Open daily. Trafalgar Sq. WC2 (phone: 839-3321).

National Portrait Gallery – Right behind the National Gallery sits this delightful museum. Nearly every British celebrity you have ever heard about is pictured here, with the earliest personalities at the top and the 20th-century notables at the bottom. Open daily. 2 St. Martin's Pl. WC2 (phone: 930-1552).

Whitehall – A broad boulevard stretching from Trafalgar Square to Parliament Square, lined most of the way by government ministries and such historic buildings as the Banqueting House (completed in 1622, with a ceiling painted by Rubens) and the Horse Guards (whose central archway is ceremonially guarded by mounted troopers).

Detective novel fans may be interested to know that Scotland Yard once occupied a building at the Trafalgar end of Whitehall; it now houses offices for members of Parliament. The Yard has moved to Victoria Street near St. James's Park.

Downing Street – Off Whitehall, a street of small, unpretentious Georgian houses includes the official residences of the most important figures in the British government, the Prime Minister at No. 10 and the Chancellor of the Exchequer (Britain's secretary of the treasury) at No. 11.

Cabinet War Rooms – Constructed to resemble its wartime appearance, this under-ground complex of 20 rooms was Winston Churchill's auxiliary command post during World War II, which he used most often during the German Luftwaffe's blitz on London. Of special note are the map room, with maps pinpointing the positions of

Allied and German troops in the final stages of the war, and the cabinet room, where the prime minister met with his staff. Open daily. Admission charge. Beneath the government building on Great George St.

Westminster Abbey – It's easy to get lost among the endlessly fascinating tombs and plaques and not even notice the Abbey's splendid architecture, so do look at the structure itself and don't miss the cloisters, which display its Gothic design to advantage. Note also the fine Tudor chapel of Henry VII, with its tall windows and lovely fan-tracery vaulting, and the 13th-century chapel of St. Edward the Confessor, containing England's Coronation Chair.

Ever since William the Conqueror was crowned here in 1066, the Abbey has been the traditional place where English monarchs are crowned, married, and buried. You don't have to be an Anglophile to be moved by the numerous tombs and memorials with their fascinating inscriptions — here are honored (not necessarily buried) kings and queens, soldiers, statesmen, and many other prominent English men and women. Poets' Corner, in the south transept, contains the tombs of Chaucer, Ben Jonson, Tennyson, Browning, and many others — plus memorials to nearly every English poet of note and to some Americans, such as Longfellow and T. S. Eliot.

The Abbey is itself a lesson in English history. A church has stood on this site since at least AD 170; in the 8th century, it was a Benedictine monastery. The current early–English Gothic edifice, begun in the 13th century, took almost 300 years to build.

Guided tours are offered six times a day (phone: 222-5152). Broad Sanctuary SW1 between Victoria and Millbank.

Houses of Parliament – The imposing neo-Gothic, mid-19th-century buildings of the Palace of Westminster, as it is sometimes called, look especially splendid from the opposite side of the river. There are separate chambers for the House of Commons and the House of Lords, and visitors are admitted to the Strangers' Galleries of both houses by lining up at St. Stephen's Entrance, opposite Westminster Abbey. Big Ben, the world-famous 13½-ton bell in the clock tower of the palace, still strikes the hours. The buildings themselves are closed to the public. Westminster Hall, with its magnificent hammer-beam roof, and the gold and scarlet House of Lords are well worth seeing. St. Margaret St. SW1 (phone: 219-3000).

Tate Gallery – London's fine art museum includes an impressive collection of sculpture and art. It has recently been extended to include a permanent display of British modern art. Best of all are masterpieces by Turner, Hogarth, and Blake. The Turner collection is housed exclusively in the ultra-modern Clore Gallery extension. Millbank SW1 (phone: 821-7128).

Soho – This area of London is full of character; lively, bustling, and noisy by day; discreetly enticing by night. Its name comes from the ancient hunting cry used centuries ago when the area was parkland. The hunting, in a way, still goes on, but there's not much to shout about nowadays. Soho lacks the sophistication and glamour of its counterparts in Europe but it's not sleazy either. The striptease clubs vie for customers with numerous restaurants serving usually inexpensive (mostly Italian and Chinese) food. Soho offers a diversity of entertainments: Shaftesbury Avenue is lined with theaters and movie houses. Gerrard Street abounds with Chinese restaurants, and it is the place to go for Chinese New Year celebrations. London's liveliest fruit and vegetable market is on Berwick Street (if you shop here, never touch the produce as the vendors will get furious). Old Compton Street has several good delicatessens, perfect places to buy a picnic lunch to take to Soho Square.

Covent Garden – Tucked away behind The Strand, Covent Garden was the site of London's main fruit, vegetable, and flower market for over 300 years. The area was immortalized in Shaw's *Pygmalion* and the musical *My Fair Lady* by the scene in which young Eliza Doolittle sells flowers to the ladies and gents emerging from the Royal Opera House. The Opera House is still there, but the market moved out in 1974 and the Garden has since undergone extensive redevelopment. The central market building has been converted into London's first permanent late-night shopping center with emphasis on all-British goods. In the former flower market is the London Transport Museum, whose exhibits include a replica of the first horse-drawn bus and a steam locomotive built in 1866. Boutiques selling quality clothes for men and women are springing up all over, along with discos, wine bars, and brasserie-style restaurants. On weekends the whole area is packed with young people. One nice touch: Just to remind everyone of the Old Covent Garden, there are about 40 of the original wrought-iron trading stands from which the home-produced wares of English craftsmen and women are sold.

Bloomsbury – Well-designed squares — Bloomsbury Square, Bedford Square, Russell Square, and others — surrounded by pretty, terraced houses form this aristocratic district. Within its confines are the British Museum and the University of London, with its Courtauld Gallery, renowned for its Impressionist collection. The Bloomsbury group of writers and artists included Virginia Woolf, her husband Leonard Woolf, her sister Vanessa Bell and her husband Clive Bell, Lytton Strachey, E. M. Forster, Roger Fry, and John Maynard Keynes. Living nearby and peripheral to this central group were D. H. Lawrence, Bertrand Russell, and others. Unfortunately, none of the original buildings in Bloomsbury Square has survived, but the garden is still there, and nearby Bedford Square remains complete. Virginia Woolf lived at 46 Gordon Square before her marriage.

British Museum – One of the world's largest museums offers a dazzling array of permanent exhibitions — including the legendary Elgin Marbles (from the Parthenon) and the Rosetta Stone. In 1985 seven new sculpture galleries were opened, exhibiting some 1,500 Greek and Roman treasures. This magnificent collection includes two of the seven wonders of the ancient world and represents the bulk of the museum's Greek and Roman collection. There is an equally impressive parade of temporary displays. The Egyptian and Mesopotamian galleries are especially stunning. The manuscript room of the British Library, within the museum, displays the original Magna Carta, together with the signatures of a great many famous authors — Shakespeare, Dickens, and Joyce among them — and numerous original manuscripts, including *Alice in Wonderland.* Take a look at the remarkable, gigantic Reading Room where so many of the world's great books — Marx's *Das Kapital,* for example — were written (you must write to the library for tickets). Great Russell St. WC1 (phone: 636-1555).

Oxford and Regent Streets – London's main shopping streets include large department stores (*Selfridges, Debenhams, John Lewis, Liberty, D. H. Evans*), chain stores offering good value in clothes (*Marks and Spencer, C & A, British Home Stores, Littlewoods*), and scores of moderately priced clothing stores. The sidewalk has recently been widened, and one section of the road is open only to taxis and buses at certain times.

Burlington Arcade – A charming covered shopping promenade dating from the Regency period (early 19th century), the arcade contains elegant, expensive shops selling cashmere sweaters (we recently saw some here that were ten-ply!), antique jewelry, and other expensive items. One entrance is off Piccadilly (the street, not the circus), the other near Old Bond St. W1.

Hyde Park – London's most famous patch of greenery (361 acres) is particularly well known for its Speakers' Corner at Marble Arch, where crowds gather each Sunday afternoon to hear impromptu diatribes and debates. Among the park's other attractions are sculptures by Henry Moore; an extensive bridle path; a cycle path; the Serpentine lake, where boats for rowing and sailing can be rented and where there's swimming in the summer; a bird sanctuary; and vast expanses of lawn.

Madame Tussaud's – The popularity of this wax museum is undiminished by the persistent criticism that its effigies, besides being hideous, do not really resemble the illustrious personalities they are supposed to imitate. Moved to London from Paris in 1802, when Madame was 74, the current museum includes many modern and historical personalities and the gory Chamber of Horrors, with its murderers and hangmen. Open daily. Admission charge. Marylebone Rd. (phone: 935-6861).

THE CITY

The difference between London and the City of London can be confusing to a visitor. They are, in fact, two distinctly different entities, one within the other. The City of London, usually called only the City, covers the original Roman London. It is now the "square mile" financial and commercial center of the great metropolis. With a Lord Mayor (who only serves in a ceremonial capacity), a police force, and rapidly growing new developments, it is the core of Greater London. The latter, with its governing body, the Greater London Council, administers 32 boroughs including the City.

St. Paul's Cathedral – The cathedral church of the London Anglican diocese stands atop Ludgate Hill and is the largest church in London. This Renaissance masterpiece by Sir Christopher Wren took 35 years to build (1675-1710). Its domed exterior is majestic and its sparse decorations are gold and mosaic. The interior contains particularly splendid choir stalls, screens, and, inside the spectacular dome, the "whispering gallery," with its strange acoustics. Nelson and Wellington are buried below the main floor, and there is a fine statue of John Donne, metaphysical poet and dean of St. Paul's from 1621 to 1631 — he stands looking quite alive on an urn in an up-ended coffin which, typically, he bought during his lifetime and kept in his house. Wren himself was buried here in 1723, with his epitaph inscribed beneath the dome in Latin: "Reader, if you seek his monument, look around you."

A gorgeous monument it remains; though damaged by bombs during World War II, it became a rallying point for the flagging spirits of wartime Londoners. More recently, St. Paul's raised British spirits as the site for the royal wedding of Prince Charles and Lady Diana Spencer in July 1981. The Golden Gallery at the top of the dome, 542 steps from the ground, offers an excellent view of the city. St. Paul's Churchyard EC4.

Old Bailey – This is the colloquial name for London's Central Criminal Court, on the site of the notorious Newgate Prison. Visitors are admitted to the court, on a space-available basis, to audit the proceedings and to see lawyers and judges clad in wigs and robes. Old Bailey EC4 (phone: 248-3277).

Museum of London – Exhibits and displays depict London history from the Roman occupation to modern times. The museum is in the Barbican, the modern performing arts complex constructed in a section of the city turned to rubble by air raids during World War II. Closed Mondays. 150 London Wall EC2 (phone: 600-3699).

Bank of England – Banker to the British government, holder of the country's gold reserves in its vaults, controller of Britain's banking and monetary affairs, "the Old Lady of Threadneedle Street" is the most famous bank in the world. Bathed in tradition as well as the mechanics of modern high finance, its porters and messengers wear traditional livery. Visits by appointment only. Threadneedle St. EC2 (phone: 601-4444).

Mansion House – The official residence of the Lord Mayor of London, containing his private apartments, built in the 18th century in Renaissance style. Permission to view the house may be obtained by writing, well in advance of your visit, to the Public Relations Office, City of London, Guildhall, London EC2P 2EJ. Mansion House St. EC4 (phone: 626-2500).

Lloyd's – A new, strikingly dramatic, futuristic building now houses the world's most important seller of international maritime and high-risk insurance. The exhibition and gallery overlooking the trading floor is open to visitors (advance booking required for groups) on weekdays from 10 AM to 4 PM. Corner of Lime and Leadenhall sts. (phone: 623-7100, ext 3733).

Stock Exchange – The second largest exchange in the world can be seen from the viewing gallery on weekdays from 9:45 AM to 3:15 PM. Old Broad St. EC2 (phone: 588-2355).

The Monument – A fluted Doric column, topped by a flaming urn, was designed by Sir Christopher Wren to commemorate the Great Fire of London (1666) and stands 202 feet tall. (It was allegedly 202 feet from the bakery on Pudding Lane where the fire began.) The view from the top is partially obstructed by new buildings. Admission charge. Monument St. EC3 (phone: 626-2717).

Tower of London – The foundations of the infamous tower were built by William the Conqueror in the 11th century. Originally conceived as a fortress to keep "fierce" Londoners at bay and to guard the river approaches, it has served as a palace, a prison, a mint, and an observatory as well. Today the main points of interest are the Crown Jewels; the White Tower (the oldest building), with its exhibition of ancient arms, armor, and torture implements; St. John's Chapel, the oldest church in London; the Bloody Tower, where the two little princes were murdered in 1485 and Sir Walter Raleigh languished from 1603 to 1615; an exhibit of old military weapons; Tower Green, where two of Henry VIII's queens — and many others — were beheaded; and Traitors' Gate, through which boats bearing prisoners entered the castle. The yeoman warders still wear historic uniforms. They also give excellent recitals of that segment of English history that was played out within the tower walls. You can see the wonderful Ceremony of the Keys here every night at 9:30 PM; reserve tickets several months ahead. Send a stamped, self-addressed envelope to: Resident Governor Constable's Office, HM Tower of London EC3N 4AB (phone: 709-0765). Closed Sundays in winter. Admission charge.

Fleet Street – Most native and foreign newspapers and press associations once had offices here — in the center of London's active newspaper world — and many still do, despite the growing exodus to more technologically advanced plants elsewhere. The street also boasts two 17th-century pubs, the *Cheshire Cheese* (just off Fleet St. at 5 Little Essex St.) and the *Cock Tavern* (No. 22). The *Cheshire Cheese* is the tavern where Dr. Samuel Johnson held court for the literary giants of his day — Goldsmith, Boswell, and others.

Johnson's House – In nearby Gough Square is the house where Johnson wrote his famous *Dictionary;* the house is now a museum of Johnsoniana. Admission charge. 17 Gough Sq. EC4 (phone: 353-3745).

Inns of Court – Quaint and quiet precincts house the ancient buildings, grounds, and gardens that mark the traditional center of Britain's legal profession. Only the four Inns of Court have the right to call would-be barristers to the bar to practice law. Especially charming is the still-Dickensian Lincoln's Inn, where young Dickens worked as an office boy. In its great hall the writer later set his fictional case of Jarndyce v. Jarndyce in *Bleak House.* John Donne once preached in the Lincoln's Inn chapel, designed by Inigo Jones. Both hall and chapel can be seen on weekdays if you apply at the Gatehouse in Chancery Lane WC2 (phone: 405-1393). Also lovely are the gardens of Lincoln's Inn Fields, laid out in 1618 by Inigo Jones.

OTHER LONDON ATTRACTIONS

Regent's Park – The sprawling 472-acre park just north of the city center has beautiful gardens, vast lawns, a pond with paddleboats, and one of the finest zoos in the world (admission charge). Elegant crescents of terraced homes border the park.

Camden Passage – This quaint pedestrian alleyway lined with antiques and specialty shops has an open-air market — pushcarts selling curios and antiques — on Tuesdays, Wednesday mornings, and Saturdays. Islington, north of the city, N1.

Hampstead Heath – The North London bucolic paradise of wild heathland, meadows, and wooded dells is the highest point in London. Kenwood House, an 18th-century estate on the heath, is home to the Iveagh Bequest, a collection of art (Gainsborough, Rembrandt, Turner, and others) assembled by the first earl of Iveagh.

Kew Gardens – Here are the Royal Botanic Gardens, with tens of thousands of plants and trees. The gardens' primary purpose is to serve the science of botany by researching, cultivating, experimenting, and identifying plants. There are shaded walks, floral displays, and magnificent Victorian glass greenhouses — especially the Temperate House, with some 3,000 different plants, including a 60-foot Chilean wine palm.

Portobello Road – This area is famous for its antiques shops, junk shops, and outdoor pushcarts; it is one of the largest street markets in the world. The pushcarts are out only on Saturdays, which is the best and most crowded day for the market. Less well known is Bermondsey Market, Long Lane at Tower Bridge Rd. SE1, on Fridays from 7 AM on; this is where the antiques on Portobello Road or Camden Passage were probably purchased.

Victoria and Albert Museum – Born of the 1851 Exhibition, the museum contains a vast collection of fine and applied arts (probably the largest collection of the latter in the world) — an amalgam of the great, the odd, and the ugly. Especially delightful are the English period rooms. There are superb collections of paintings, prints, ceramics, metalwork, costumes, and armor in the museum, which also contains English miniatures and famous Raphael cartoons. The museum's new Henry Cole Wing (named after its founder) houses a broad selection of changing exhibitions as well as an interesting permanent display of printmaking techniques. Closed Fridays. Donation suggested. Cromwell Rd. SW7 (phone: 589-6371).

Greenwich – This Thames-side borough is traditionally associated with British seapower, especially when Britain "ruled the waves"; it includes such notable sights as the National Maritime Museum on Romney Rd. (phone: 858-4422), containing superb exhibits on Britain's illustrious nautical past; the Old Royal Observatory, with astronomical instruments; Cutty Sark, a superbly preserved 19th-century clipper ship that's open to visitors; Royal Naval College, with beautiful painted hall and chapel; and Greenwich Park, 200 acres of greenery sloping down toward the river.

Richmond Park – The largest urban park in Britain is one of the few with herds of deer roaming free. (Hunting them is illegal, though this was once a royal hunting preserve.) It also has large oaks and rhododendron gardens. From nearby Richmond Hill there is a magnificent view of the Thames Valley.

Manor Houses – Five beautifully maintained historic homes are in Greater London. Notable for their architecture, antiques, grounds, and, in the case of Kenwood, an 18th-century art collection, these homes are all accessible by bus and subway: Kenwood (Hampstead), Ham (Richmond), Chiswick (Turnham Green or Chiswick Park), Syon (Osterley), and Osterley (Gunnersbury).

Hampton Court – On the Thames, this sumptuous palace and gardens are in London's southwest corner. Begun by Cardinal Wolsey in 1515, the palace was appropriated by Henry VIII and was a royal residence for two centuries. Its attractions include a picture gallery, tapestries, state apartments, Tudor kitchens, the original tennis court, a moat, a great vine (two centuries old), gardens, and a maze. You can get there by bus, by train, or, best of all, in summer take the boat from Westminster Pier. Hampton, Middlesex (phone: 977-8441).

Freud Museum – This house was the North London home of the seminal psychiatrist after he left Vienna in 1938. His antiquities collection, library, desk, and famous couch are all on display. Open 10 AM to 5 PM daily, 1 to 5 PM Sundays. 20 Maresfield Gardens, NW3.

Highgate Cemetery – The awe-inspiring grave of Karl Marx in the new cemetery (open until 3:45 PM in winter, dusk in summer) attracts countless visitors, who can then stroll past the overgrown gravestones and catacombs of the not-so-famous in the old cemetery across the road (open until 3 PM in winter, dusk in summer). Entrance to the latter is by (hourly) guided tour only (free).

Thames Flood Barrier – A massive and intriguing defense structure across the river. Boats regularly leave Barrier Gardens Pier (or the riverside promenade nearby) for visits up close. Regular audiovisual displays at the Visitor Centre explain background and illustrate the risk to London of exceptionally high tides. Open weekdays, 10 AM to 5 PM; 10 AM to 5:30 PM weekends.

■**EXTRA SPECIAL:** *Windsor Castle* is the largest inhabited castle in the world. It is the queen's official residence and was built by William the Conqueror in 1066 after his victory at the Battle of Hastings. Windsor looks like a fairy tale castle in a child's picturebook: The huge Norman edifice looms majestically above the town; you feel awed and enchanted as you climb up the curving cobblestone street from the train station, past pubs and shops, toward Henry VIII's Gateway. The castle precincts are open daily and there's a regular changing of the guard. The State Apartments, which can be toured when they're not in use, are splendidly decorated with paintings, tapestries, furniture, and rugs. There is an exhibition of drawings by Leonardo da Vinci, Michelangelo, and Raphael, and a room displaying Queen Mary's dollhouse. Queen Victoria and her consort, Albert, are buried at Windsor. The castle is bordered by 4,800 acres of parkland on one side and the town on the other. While the town still has a certain charm, heavy tourism is beginning to have a deleterious effect. Across the river is *Eton* — considered by some to be the more attractive town — which is famous as home to the exclusive boy's school founded by Henry IV in 1440. Don't miss taking one of the many boat trips along the Thames to places like Marlow, Cookham, or Henley (where the first rowing regatta in the world was held in 1839). The *Royal Windsor Safari Park* is also southwest of London. Once a royal hunting ground, it's now a drive-through zoo, whose residents include baboons, camels, rhinos, cheetahs, and Bengal tigers. Be forewarned: In summer the park is very popular and traffic is bumper-to-bumper. An alternative would be to take the safari bus. Admission charge. A final attraction in the area, 5 miles to the southwest, is *Savill Garden* — 35 acres of flowering shrubs, rare flowers, and woodland. Open daily from March to October.

The train from Paddington stops right in the center of Windsor in 39 minutes, or there's a Green Line coach from Victoria (1½ hrs).

SOURCES AND RESOURCES

TOURIST INFORMATION: In the US, contact the British Tourist Authority, 40 W 57th St., New York, NY 10019 (phone: 212-581-4700). The London Visitor and Convention Bureau is the best source of information for attractions and events once you get to London. Its Tourist Information Centre on the forecourt of Victoria British Rail Station is open Mondays through Saturdays, 9 AM to 7 PM; Sundays, 9 AM to 5 PM. Many leaflets and brochures on the city's landmarks and events are available; people are also there to answer questions on what to do, how, and when. Other branches are at the tube station at Heathrow Airport Terminals 1, 2, and 3, *Harrods* and *Selfridges* stores, and the Tower of London (Easter to October only). A Telephone Information Service is offered daily except Sundays, 9 AM to 6 PM (phone: 730-3488).

The British Travel Centre books travel tickets, reserves accommodations and theater tickets, and sells guidebooks. It offers a free information service, including an information hotline covering the whole of Britain. Open 9 AM to 6:30 PM, daily except Sundays. 4 Lower Regent St. (phone: 730-3400).

Among the most comprehensive and useful guidebooks to London is the *Blue Guide to London* (Benn) and *Londonwalks* (Holt, Rinehart & Winston). The annual *Good Food Guide* ($16.95) and *Egon Ronay's* hotel and restaurant guide ($13.95) are available in most bookstores (prices slightly lower in Great Britain). For detailed information on 200 London museums, including maps, consult the *London Museums and Collections Guide* (CPC Guidebooks; $12).

London A-Z and *Nicholson's Street Finder,* inexpensive pocket-size books of street maps (available in bookstores and from most "newsagents"), are very useful for finding London addresses. Also helpful are maps of the subway system and bus routes and the *London Regional Transport Visitors Guide* — all available free from the London Transport information centers at several stations, including Victoria, Piccadilly, Charing Cross, Oxford Circus, and Heathrow Central, and at the ticket booths of many other stations (phone: 222-1234 for information). The US Embassy is at 24/31 Grosvenor Sq. W (phone: 499-9000).

Local Coverage – Of London's several newspapers, *The Times,* the *Observer,* and the *Daily Telegraph* are the most useful for visitors. Also helpful are the weekly magazines *What's On and Where To Go, City Limits, Time Out,* and *London Events and Entertainment.*

GETTING AROUND: Bus and Underground – The London public transport system gets sluggish now and then but is normally reasonably efficient. Its subway, called the underground or tube, and its bus lines cover the city pretty well, though buses suffer from traffic congestion, and the underground is notoriously thin south of the Thames. The tops of London's famous red double-decker buses do, however, offer some delightful views of the city and its people. The underground is easy to understand and to use, with clear directions and poster maps in all stations. Pick up free bus and underground maps from tourist offices or underground ticket booths. The fares on both trains and buses are set according to length of the journey. On most buses, conductors take payment after you tell them where you're going; some require that you pay as you enter. Underground tickets are bought on entering a station. Retain your ticket; you'll have to surrender it when you get off (or have to pay again), and bus inspectors make spot checks to see that no one's stealing a free ride. There are also Red Arrow express buses, but you'll have to check stops before you get on. With just a few exceptions, public transport comes to a halt around midnight; it varies according to underground line and bus route. If you're going to be traveling late, check available facilities.

A London Explorer ticket, which can be bought at any North American Britrail office, the London Visitor and Convention Bureau, or any underground station — at about £9 for 3 days, £11.50 for 4 days, and £16 for 7 — provides unlimited travel on bus and underground within a specified area.

The underground links Heathrow, London's main airport, with downtown. The Piccadilly Line zips from Piccadilly Circus to the airport in about 40 minutes. (The underground does not connect with Gatwick Airport, but there are trains to Victoria Station every 15 minutes from 6 AM to 10 PM during the day and hourly through the rest of the night. The journey takes about 30 minutes.) Buses also link Heathrow with the city. For bus and underground information, call 222-1234.

Thames Line runs a high-speed riverbus service linking East London to West, between Greenwich and Chelsea. It runs at approximately 15-minute intervals, 7 AM to 7 PM, calling at 8 piers. The service is expected to be fully operational by summer 1988.

From June through October, a Tourist Trail ticket serves the three daily coach routes from London to Edinburgh (via Oxford, Stratford, Chester, and Windemere), London to Edinburgh (via Cambridge, Lincoln, York, and Durham), and London to York (via Stratford and Lincoln). The ticket allows unlimited travel on the luxury coaches for 15 days and costs $115, with a discount for holders of Britexpress coach passes. Tickets are available at Victoria Coach Station (phone: 730-0202).

Taxi – Those fine old London cabs are gradually being replaced with more "practical" models. It is one of life's great tragedies. Taxi fares in London are increasingly expensive (we didn't mind the price so much when we could ride in the big, old, comfortable cabs), and a 15% tip is customary. Tell a London cabbie where you're going *before* entering the cab. When it rains or late at night, an empty cab (identifiable by its roof light being on) is often very difficult to find, so it is wise to carry the telephone number of one or more of the cab companies that respond to calls by phone. There are also many "minicab" companies that do not respond when hailed on the street, nor do they use meters. They operate on the basis of a fixed fare between their home base and your destination. Hotel porters or reception desks usually can make arrangements to have such a car pick you up at a specified time and place. Be aware that taxi rates are higher after 8 PM and on holidays.

Train – London has 11 principal train stations, each the starting point for trains to a particular region, with occasional overlapping of routes. The ones you are most likely to encounter include King's Cross (phone: 278-2477), the departure point for Northeast England and eastern Scotland, including Edinburgh; St. Pancras (phone: 387-8537), for trains going due north as far as Sheffield; Euston (phone: 387-7070), serving the Midlands, North Wales, including Holyhead and ferries for Dun Laoghaire, Ireland, Northwest England, and western Scotland, including Glasgow; Paddington (phone: 262-6767), for the West Country and South Wales, including Fishguard and ferries to Rosslare, Ireland; Victoria (phone: 928-5100), for Gatwick Airport and, along with Charing Cross Station (phone: 928-5100), for departures to Southeast England; and Liverpool St. Station (phone: 283-7171), for departures to East Anglia and to Harwich for ferries to the Continent and Scandinavia. All of these stations are connected via London's underground.

BritRail's Travelpak transportation program is intended for travelers who wish to venture out of London. It includes round-trip journeys from Gatwick or Heathrow airports to central London; the London Explorer (see "Bus and Subway"); and a 4-day BritRail pass for unlimited train travel within Britain. Maps and timetables are also included. BritRail Travelpaks must be obtained before leaving the US from any North American BritRail office. Write BritRail, 630 Third Ave., New York, NY 10017 (phone: 212-599-5400).

Car Rental – Several agencies, including *Hertz,* at 35 Edgware Rd. W2 (phone: 402-4242), and *Avis,* 35 Headford Pl. SW1 (phone: 245-9862), are represented in London. *Swan National,* 305 Chiswick High Rd. W4 (phone: 995-4665), is less expensive, or try *Guy Salmon Car Rentals,* 7-23 Bryanston St., Marble Arch (phone: 408-1255), or *Godfrey Davis,* Davis House, Wilton Rd. SW1 (phone: 834-8484). In addition, *Budget Rent-A-Car* has three reservation desks at Heathrow Airport terminals (phone: 726-8266). And for riding in style, call *Avis Luxury Car Services* (phone: 235-3235) for chauffeur-driven Rolls-Royces and Daimlers.

 SPECIAL EVENTS: Dates vary marginally from year to year and should be checked — together with details — with the London Visitor and Convention Bureau. In early June you can enjoy the annual *Trooping of the Color,* England's most elaborate display of pageantry — a Horse Guards' parade, with military music and much pomp and circumstance — all in celebration of the queen's official birthday. You can see some of the parade without a ticket, but for the ceremony you must book before March 1 by writing to the Brigade Major, Headquarters, Household Division, Horseguards, Whitehall SW1 (do not send money). Late June heralds the *Wimbledon Lawn Tennis Championship* — the world's most prestigious — complete with a member of the royal family presenting the prizes. The *Henley Royal Regatta*, in early July (at Henley-on-Thames, a 1-hour train ride from London), is an international rowing competition and one of the big social events of the year. Watch from the towpath (free) or from within the Regatta enclosure (£2 to £3). The *Royal Tournament*, a military pageant, takes place at Earls Court for 3 weeks in July. October or November is the time for the *State Opening of Parliament; Guy Fawkes Day* is on November 5, when fireworks and bonfires mark the anniversary of the plot to blow up both houses of Parliament and King James I in 1605; and on the second Saturday in November, an inaugural procession for the new Lord Mayor, who rides in a golden carriage, followed by floats and bands.

MUSEUMS: Many of London's museums are described in *Special Places*. Other noteworthy museums include:

Bethnal Green Museum of Childhood – Impressive collection of more than 4,000 toys, including dolls and dollhouses, games, and puppets. Cambridge Heath Rd. E2 (phone: 980-3204).

Courtauld Institute Galleries – A remarkable collection of French Impressionist paintings. Woburn Sq. WC1 (phone: 636-2095).

Dickens's House – 48 Doughty St. WC1 (phone: 405-2127).

Dulwich College Picture Gallery – Works by European masters in one of England's most beautiful art galleries. College Rd. SE21 (phone: 693-5254).

Institute of Contemporary Arts – 12 Carleton House Terrace SW1 (phone: 930-6393).

Jewish Museum – Woburn House, Upper Woburn Pl. WC1 (phone: 388-4525).

London Toy and Model Museum – October House, 23 Craven Hill W2.

Museum of Mankind – Ethnographic exhibitions. 6 Burlington Gardens W1 (phone: 437-2224).

Musical Museum – One of Europe's most comprehensive collections of pianos and mechanical musical instruments, all in good working condition. 368 High St., Brentford, Middlesex (phone: 560-8108).

Natural History Museum – Cromwell Rd. SW7 (phone: 589-6323).

Planetarium – Marylebone Rd. NW1 (phone: 486-1121).

Science Museum – Exhibition Rd. SW7 (phone: 589-3456).

Science Museum – Exhibition Rd. SW7 (phone: 589-3456).

Sir John Soane's Museum – Its collection includes Hogarth's series *The Rake's Progress*. 13 Lincoln's Inn Fields WC2 (phone: 405-2107).

Theatre Museum – Britain's newest collection of theatrical material: everything from circus to pop, grand opera to mime, straight theater to Punch and Judy and pantomime. 1E Tavistock St. WC2 (phone: 836-7891).

Wallace Collection – Sir Richard Wallace's fine collection of European paintings, sculpture, and armor. Hertford House, Manchester Sq. W1 (phone: 935-0687).

Whitechapel Art Gallery – An East End haven for modern art, including works by Moore, Hepworth, and Hockney. 80 Whitechapel High St. E7 (phone: 377-0107).

SHOPPING: Stores are generally open from 9 AM to 5:30 or 6 PM, daily except Sundays, but the shops in the West End stay open until about 7:30 PM on Thursdays. Although London is traditionally one of the most expensive cities in the world, savvy shoppers can still find good buys. The current lure, however, is more for fine British workmanship and style than very low prices.

The favorite items on any shopping list in London are cashmere and Shetland knitwear; fabric (tweeds, blends, men's suitings); riding gear; custom-made men's suits, shirts, shoes, and hats; shotguns; china and crystal; umbrellas; antiques; sporting goods; English food specialties (jams and marmalade, various blended teas, Stilton cheese, shortbread, and others). Books published by British houses, once a fine buy, are now far higher in price, and you probably will do better to buy the US editions.

Devoted bargain hunters recognize that the best time to buy British is during the semiannual sales that usually occur from Boxing Day (December 26) through the early part of the New Year and again in early July. The Christmas/New Year's sales offer by far the best bargains in the city, and the crowds can be the equal of the low prices. Many stores remain open on New Year's Day to accommodate the bargain hunters, and the best-publicized single sale is that offered at *Harrods* for three weeks beginning the first Friday in January. That opening day is an event in itself.

Be sure to take your passport when you shop, and always inquire about the VAT refund application forms when you make a purchase of over $25. The VAT (Value Added Tax) is a 15% surcharge payable at the sales counter, but foreign customers usually will be reimbursed for it at home. Though scattered about the city, the most appealing shops tend to center in the West End area, particularly along Bond, Oxford, South Moulton, Regent, and Jermyn streets and Piccadilly. Other good areas are Kings Road, Kensington High Street, and Kensington Church Street, along with Knightsbridge and Covent Garden.

This is a city of markets; we have already described Portobello Road and Camden Passage in *Special Places*. Also worthy of note are Camden Lock Market (Camden High St. NW1) on Saturdays and Sundays, for far-out clothes, leather items, antiques, and trinkets. Or get up early on a Sunday morning and head for the East End to sample a typically English transport café ("caff") breakfast at *Fred's* (40 Aberfeldy St. E1) before tackling the very famous Petticoat Lane for food, inexpensive clothes, crockery, and even the proverbial kitchen sink.

The following stores are only a sampling of London's treasure houses.

Anderson and Sheppard – A reputable "made-to-measure" tailor for men's clothes, 30 Savile Row W1.

Antiquarius – A good place for antiques. 135-141 King's Rd. SW3.

Aquascutum – Needs no introduction; famous for raincoats and jackets for men and women. 100 Regent St. W1.

Laura Ashley – A relatively inexpensive women's boutique specializing in romantic styled skirts, dresses, and blouses. 183 Sloane St. SW1; plus other branches on Regent St., Hampstead High St., Harriet St., and Fulham Raod.

Asprey & Company – Fine jewelry, silver, and luggage. 165-169 New Bond St. W1.

Bates – A gentlemen's hatter, and our favorite. Check out the eight-part caps. 21a Jermyn St. SW1.

W. Bill Ltd. – Shetland sweaters, knit ties, club mufflers, gloves. 28 Old Bond St. W1.

Body Shop – More than 150 different beauty products (perfumes, soaps, hair and skin care products), from the worldwide chain that started in Brighton. 32 Great Marlborough St., W1.

Browns – Beautiful but expensive women's clothes. 23-27 S Molton St. W1

Burberrys – Superb but expensive men's and women's raincoats and traditional clothes, and home of the now nearly ubiquitous plaid that began life as a raincoat lining, at 18 Haymarket SW1.

Cavendish Rare Books – Specializes in travel books and accounts from long, long ago. Princes Arcade W1.

Church & Co. – Superior men's shoes. 58-59 Burlington Arcade W1; Old Bond St.

Jasper Conran – Top British designer creations. 37 Beauchamp Pl. SW3.

Cordings – Specialists in outdoor and foul-weather gear. Oiled, bramble-proof jackets are especially great (how have you lived all these years without a grouse pocket?). 19 Piccadilly W1.

Crocodile – Chic and expensive women's clothes. 57 Beauchamp Pl. SW3.

Justin De Blank – Excellent specialty foods, especially cheese and take-out dishes. 42 Elizabeth St. SW1.

Dillon's – A good bookstore, London's most scholastic, partly owned by London University. 1 Malet St. WC1.

Emmanuel – Creative designers of Princess Diana's wedding dress and other clothing for members of the aristocracy. 10 Beauchamp Pl. SW3.

Feathers – French and Italian designer clothing for women. 40 Hans Crescent SWI.

Fenwick – Trendy, moderately priced women's clothes. 63 New Bond St. W1.

Fortnum and Mason – Boasts designer originals (usually of the rather dowdy variety), an appealing soda fountain-cum-restaurant, and one of the most elegant grocery departments in the world (where the staff wears striped trousers and swallow-tail morning coats). 181 Piccadilly W1.

Foyle's – London's largest bookstore. 119 Charing Cross Rd. WC2.

Gidden's of London – Riding gear. 15 Clifford St. W1.

Thomas Goode and Company – London's best china and glass shop first opened in 1827. Even if you don't plan to buy anything, you may want to look at their beautiful 1876 showroom. 19 S Audley St. W1.

Grays Market – The hundreds of stalls here and at the annex down the street sell everything from antique playing cards to 16th-century furniture. 1-7 Davies Mews W1 and 58 Davies St. W1.

Habitat – Up-to-the-minute designs with realistic prices for furniture and household goods. 156 Tottenham Court Rd., W1 and 206 King's Rd. SW3.

Halcyon Days – The best place to find authentic Battersea boxes — both antique and brand-new. 14 Brook St. W1.

Hamley's – The largest toy shop in the world. 200 Regent St. W1.

Harrods – The ultimate department store, although it does tend to be quite expensive. It has everything, even a mortuary and a bank, and what it doesn't stock it will get for you. The "food halls" particularly fascinate visitors, and traditional British merchandise is available in abundance. For those interested in trendy styles, it has the Way In boutique. Its annual January sale is legendary. 87-135 Brompton Rd., Knightsbridge SW1.

Harvie and Hudson – Men's shirts made to order. 77 Jermyn St. SW1.

Hatchards – Another excellent — perhaps the city's best — bookstore. 187 Piccadilly W1.

Douglas Hayward – A reputable made-to-order tailor. 95 Mount St. W1.

Heal's – Furniture and fabrics in the best modern designs. 196 Tottenham Court Rd. W1.

Jaeger – Tailored (and expensive) men's and women's clothes. 204 Regent St. W1.

Herbert Johnson – Men's hats. 13 Old Burlington St. W1.

Peter Jones – Another good, well-stocked department store, offering moderately priced, tasteful goods. Sloane Sq. SW1.

John Keil – Lovely, expensive antiques. 25 Mount St. W1.

Kent & Curwen – The place to buy authentic cricket caps, Henley club ties, and all sorts of similarly preppy raiment. 39 St. James's St. SW1 and 6 Royal Arcade W1.

John Lewis – Another good, moderately priced department store, particularly noted for its fabrics and household goods. 278 Oxford St. W1.

Liberty – Famous for print fabrics. Scarves and ties a specialty. 210 Regent St. W1.

Lillywhites – The whole gamut of sporting goods. Piccadilly Circus SW1.

John Lobb – World-famous for made-to-order shoes that will last ten years or more with proper care. 9 St. James's St. SW1.

James Lock and Company – The royal hatters. They fitted a crown for the queen's coronation and they'll fit you for your first bowler. 6 St. James's St. SW1.

Lord's – Tops in ties. 66/70 Burlington Arcade W1.

Marks and Spencer – Locally nicknamed "Marks and Sparks," this chain specializes in clothes for the whole family, made to high standards and sold at very reasonable prices. Its linens and sweaters (especially cashmere and Shetland) are among the best buys in Britain. 458 Oxford St. W1 (and many other outlets).

Moss Bros. – Men's formal attire (including dress tartans) and high-quality riding clothes. Bedford St. WC2.

Harvey Nichols – A luxury department store specializing in women's haute couture. Knightsbridge SW1.

Partridge Ltd. – Fine (but expensive) antiques. 144 New Bond St. W1.

James Purdey and Sons – The place to go for custom-made shotguns and other shooting gear. 57 S Audley St. W1.

Reject China Shop – Good buys in slightly (invisible) irregular, name-brand china. Glassware, crystal, and flatware, too. For a fee, the shop will ship your purchases back home. 33-35 Beauchamp Pl. SW3; also 134 Regent St. W1.

Peter Robinson Top Shop – Young, trendy, moderately priced women's clothing. 216 Oxford St. W1.

Scotch House – Famous for Scottish cashmeres, sweaters, tartans — a wide selection of well-known labels. 2 Brompton Rd. SW1 and many branches.

Selfridges – This famous department store offers somewhat less variety than *Harrods,* but it has just about everything too — only a little less expensive. The extensive china and crystal department carries most patterns available. Oxford St. W1.

David Shilling – His one-off (a tad eccentric) hat creations always create a stir at Ascot. 44 Chiltern St. W1.

Shirin – The best designer cashmeres in town. 51 Beauchamp Pl. SW3.

Simpson's – Elegant garments for men and women. 203 Eagle Place W1.

James Smith and Sons – The oldest umbrella shop in Europe. 53 New Oxford St. WC1.

Smythson of Bond Street – The world's best place to buy diaries, note pads, calendars, and exotic ledgers in which to record odd data. 54 New Bond St. W1.

Sotheby Parke Bernet – The world's oldest art auctioneer, interesting to look at even if you don't plan to buy. They auction books, porcelain, furniture, jewelry, and works of art; at times, even such odd items as vintage cars and wines. Viewing hours are between 9:30 AM and 4:30 PM on weekdays, at Bloomfield Pl. W1 (phone: 493-8080).

Swaine, Adeney, Brigg, and Sons – Riding gear and their famous pure silk umbrellas. 185 Piccadilly W1.

Turnbull and Asser – Men's shirts made to order. 71-72 Jermyn St. SW1.

Twinings – Tea — and nothing but — in bags, balls, and bulk. 216 Strand.

Wedgwood – Porcelain. 266 and 270 Regent St.

Westaway and Westaway – Cashmere and Shetland wool kilts, sweaters, scarves, and blankets. 65 Great Russell St. WC1 and 29 Bloomsbury WC1.

 SPORTS: Soccer (called football hereabouts) and cricket are the most popular spectator pastimes, but London offers a wide variety of other sports.

Cricket – The season runs from mid-April to early September. The best places to watch it are at Lord's Cricket Ground, St. John's Wood Rd. NW8 (phone: 289-1615), and The Oval, Kennington SE11 (phone: 582-6660).

Fishing – Several public ponds right in London are accessible to the angler. A permit is required from Royal Parks Department, the Storeyard, Hyde Park W2 (phone: 262-5484). The department can also provide information on where to fish.

Golf – Aside from private clubs, for which membership is required, there are several municipal courses, some of which rent clubs. Try *Pickett's Lock Center,* Pickett's Lock

La. N9 (phone: 803-3611), *Addington Court,* Featherbed La., Addington, Croydon (phone: 657-0281), and *Beckenham Place Park,* Beckenham, Kent (phone: 650-2292). *Wentworth,* Virginia Water, Surrey (phone: Wentworth 2201), and *Sunningdale,* Ridgemount Rd., Sunningdale, Berkshire (phone: Ascot 21681), are the best courses within driving distance of London, and a letter from your home club pro or president (plus a polite phone call) may gain access to their courses.

Greyhound Racing – Empire Stadium, Empire Way, Wembley (phone: 902-1234), and others. There are evening races, so check the afternoon newspapers for details.

Horse Racing – Nine major racecourses are within easy reach of London, including Epsom, where the Derby (pronounced Darby) is run, and Ascot, where the Royal Ascot takes place — both in June. The flat racing season is from March to November; steeple-chasing, August to June. Call the Jockey Club, 42 Portman Sq. W1 (phone: 486-4921) for information.

Horseback Riding – Try *Bathurst Riding Stables,* 63 Bathurst Mews W2 (phone: 723-2813), and *Ross Nye's Riding Establishment,* 8 Bathurst Mews W2 (phone: 262-3791).

Ice Skating – There is the *Queen's Ice Skating Club,* 17 Queensway W2 (phone: 229-0172), and *Silver Blades Ice Rink,* 386 Streatham High Rd. SW16 (phone: 769-7861). Skates are for rent at both rinks.

Rugby – An autumn-through-spring spectacle at Rugby Football Ground, Whitton Rd., Twickenham (phone: 892-8161).

Soccer – *The* big sport in Britain. The local football season is autumn to spring and the most popular clubs are *Arsenal,* Highbury Stadium, Avenell Rd. N5 (phone: 359-0131); *Chelsea,* Stamford Bridge, Fulham Rd. SW6 (phone: 381-0111); *West Ham United,* Boleyn Ground, Green St. E13 (phone: 470-1325).

Swimming – Several excellent indoor public pools include: *Swiss Cottage Center,* Adelaide Rd. NW3 (phone: 586-5989), *Putney Swimming Baths,* 376 Upper Richmond Rd. SW15 (phone: 789-1124), and *The Oasis,* 167 High Holborn, WC1 (phone: 836-9555). There is outdoor swimming in the Hyde Park Serpentine, and Hampstead Heath, in the summer.

Tennis – Aside from private clubs, more than 50 London public parks have tennis courts available to all. Get information from the London Visitor and Convention Bureau (phone: 730-3488).

 THEATER: London remains the theater capital of the world, with about 50 theaters regularly putting on plays in and around its West End theater district and a vigorous collection of "fringe" theaters in various parts of town. Best known, and most accomplished, are the two main repertory theater companies — the *National Theatre Company* at the National Theatre, South Bank SE1 (phone: 928-2252), and the *Royal Shakespeare Company* at the Barbican Centre, The Barbican EC2 (phone: 628-8795); both present dazzling productions of classics and new plays. Shakespearean plays are also performed in summer at the open-air theater in Regents Park NW1 (phone: 935-5756).

In the West End, presentations include both first-class and second-rate drama and comedy, a fair sprinkling of farce (for which the British have a particular fondness), and the best of imports from the American stage. Visitors from the US often find attending theater in London easier — and somewhat less expensive — than it is at home. Except for the small handful of runaway box office successes, tickets are usually available for all performances. In most cases, you can reserve by telephone, but tickets must be picked up well before curtain time. *The West End Theatre Society* operates a half-price ticket kiosk in Leicester Square. It posts a list of shows for which remaining seats may be purchased at half-price on the day of the performance. Ticket agencies that offer tickets to all shows, charging a small commission, include *Keith Prowse &*

Co. (phone: 437-8976), *Dial-A-Ticket* (phone: 930-8331/2), and *Ace Tickets* (phone: 223-8173).

The quality of London's fringe theater varies from accomplished and imaginative to amateurish. Theaters in pubs are at the *King's Head* in Islington, 115 Upper St. N1 (phone: 226-1916), and at the *Bush,* in the *Bush Hotel,* Shepherd's Bush Green (phone: 743-3388). The *Riverside Studios* in Hammersmith, Crisp Rd. W6 (phone: 748-3354), the *Tricycle Theatre* at 269 Kilburn High Rd. NW6 (phone: 328-8626), and the *New End Theatre* in Hampstead, 27 New End NW3 (phone: 435-6054), have established reputations for the excellence of their productions, which often move on to the West End and sometimes even directly to Broadway. Lunchtime fringe theater presentations offer an alternative to sightseeing on rainy days.

Check *Time Out* or *City Limits* for comprehensive lists, plot summaries, and theater phone numbers. Daily papers list West End performances. Theater tickets can also be purchased through a ticket broker, who will charge a fee for this service.

Show tours to London are very popular in season; see your travel agent for package deals. If you want to reserve specific tickets before you arrive in London, there are agencies in the US that keep a listing of what's on in London. For a service charge of about $5 per ticket, they will sell you the best seats only. Contact *Edwards & Edwards,* One Times Square Plaza, New York, NY 10036 (phone: 212-944-0290 or 800-223-6108) or *Keith Prowse & Co.,* 234 W 44th St., New York, NY 10036 (phone: 212-398-1430 or 800-223-4446).

MUSIC: Few cities offer a greater variety of musical performances — both classical music and the many varieties of popular music. For classical music, the focus of attention is the *South Banks Arts Center* with its three concert halls — Royal Festival Hall, Queen Elizabeth Hall, and the Purcell Room — (phone: 928-3191 for all three) the *Barbican Hall,* home of the London Symphony Orchestra (phone: 628-8795), and the *Royal Albert Hall,* Kensington Gore SW7 (phone: 589-8212). The latter is the home of the Henry Wood Promenade Concerts, or more simply, the Proms, an 8-week series of orchestral concerts that has been a popular feature of the London summer scene (July to September) for decades. Tickets are inexpensive, because the Proms came into being to give students and other people who are not affluent an opportunity to dress up and be part of a grand musical event. The performances are tops (some broadcast live by the BBC), and the SRO audience is large and enthusiastic. *Wigmore Hall,* Wigmore St. W1 (phone: 935-2141), is best known for recitals of chamber music and performances by some of the world's most accomplished instrumental and vocal soloists. Concerts are also often held in the dignified, splendid setting of St. John's Church, Smith Sq. SW1 (phone: 222-1061). The *London Symphony Orchestra* performs at Barbican Centre, The Barbican EC2. During the summer outdoor concerts are given at Kenwood, Crystal Palace, and Holland Park, and bands play in many of London's parks.

Operas at Covent Garden Royal Opera House, Floral St. WC2 (phone: 240-1066), are internationally famous. The *English National Opera Company* offers its performances at the London Coliseum, St. Martin's La. WC2 (phone: 836-3161). The best of London's ballet performances are presented at Covent Garden, the Coliseum and at Sadler's Wells, Roseberry Ave. EC1 (phone: 837-1672), as well as at *The Place,* 17 Duke Rd. WC1 (phone: 387-0161), home of the *London Contemporary Dance Theatre* and the *London School of Contemporary Dance.* Details about concert, recital, opera, and ballet performances are listed in the arts sections of the Sunday newspapers.

Although some superstar musicians and vocalists occasionally appear in the city's larger halls, good live popular music can be heard in London's music pubs. Among the best of them are the *Dublin Castle,* 94 Parkway NW1 (phone: 485-1773); *King's Head,* 4 Fulham High St. SW6 (phone: 736-1413); *Kensington,* 54 Russell Gardens, Holland

Rd. W14 (phone: 603-3245); and *Hope and Anchor,* 207 Upper St. N1 (phone: 359-4510).

 NIGHTCLUBS AND NIGHTLIFE: It used to be that they virtually rolled up the sidewalks in London at 11 PM. Now there's a very lively and often wild nightlife, including nightclubs, jazz clubs, historical feast entertainments, and gambling casinos. Some wind up around midnight; most go on until well into the early morning hours. In Covent Garden and still-trendy-after-all-these-years Chelsea, particularly along King's and Fulham roads, are fashionable pubs, wine bars, and restaurants. Two nightclubs with floor shows are the *London Room,* Drury La. (phone: 831-8863) and *Omar Khayyam,* 177 Regent St. W1 (phone: 734-7675). There is dancing at both. There's a show but no dancing at *Madisons,* Camden Lock, Chalk Farm Rd. NW1 (phone: 485-6044). The best jazz clubs are *Ronnie Scott's,* 47 Frith St. W1 (phone: 439-0747), and *The 100 Club,* 100 Oxford St. W1 (phone: 636-0933). For jazz and a slice, try *Pizza Express,* 10 Dean St. W1 (phone: 437-9595), with live music nightly except Mondays. *Dingwalls,* Camden Lock, Chalk Farm Rd. NW1 (phone: 267-4967) and the *Marquee,* 90 Wardour St. W1 (phone: 437-6603), have a continually changing program of much-acclaimed performers of rock music.

For a special treat, London offers the *medieval banquet,* complete with traditional meals served by costumed waiters and waitresses. Menus resemble those of traditional Elizabethan feasts, and there is period music, horseplay, occasional mock sword fights, Shakespearean playlets, and other light entertainment. Try *Tudor Rooms,* 17 Swallow St. W1 (phone: 240-3978); *Beefeater,* St. Katherine Dock E1 (phone: 408-1001); and *Shakespeare's Tavern,* Blackfriar's La. EC4 (phone: 408-1001).

As for discos, the scene is a rapidly changing one, and many places — such as expensive and exclusive *Annabel's,* 44 Berkeley Sq. (phone: 629-3558) — are open only to members. Clubs of the moment include: the *Hippodrome,* Charing Cross Rd. WC2 (phone: 437-4311); *Stringfellows,* 16-19 Upper St. Martin's La. WC2 (phone: 240-5534); *Legend's,* 29 Old Burlington St. (phone: 437-9933); *Crazy Larry's,* Lots Rds., SW10 (phone: 352-3518); *Xenon,* 196 Piccadilly W1 (phone: 734-9344); *Tramp,* 40 Jermyn St. SW1 (phone: 734-0565), where the chic social set meets to disco (members only), and Theatreland's newest, *Limelight,* at 136 Shaftesbury Ave. (phone: 434-0572). A smart addition to the West London night scene is *Broadway Boulevard* club in Ealing, particularly convenient for guests at the Heathrow hotels (phone: 840-0616).

Female impersonators regularly perform at the *Union Tavern,* 146 Camberwell New Rd. SE5 (phone: 735-3605), and *Black Cap,* 171 Camden High St. NW1 (phone: 485-1742). Phone for details.

Information on gay nightlife is published in the biweekly *Gay News,* sold at newsstands.

 SINS: London has a reputation for free and easy gambling, but over the last year or so the Gaming Laws have been enforced more rigorously and many clubs have had to shut down. It is best to check the current situation at your hotel desk when you arrive. Gambling club membership is usually available within 48 hours upon presentation of your passport. Card games, roulette, and dice are featured in most of the clubs.

By reputation, Soho is the sin center of London, but being ripped off is often the only sin visitors experience there. Soho striptease clubs usually give very little or no value for the money. Some of the worst are touted by street barkers or men who sidle up to passersby in the street, promising exotic and erotic pleasures. Exceptions, which try to redeem the good name of striptease, include *Raymond's Revue Bar,* 8 Brewer St. W1 (phone: 734-1593).

Soho does, however, boast a goodly number of prostitutes, some walking the street looking for customers, some advertising their services discreetly on nameplate cards in doorways — "Celeste, French lessons, second floor" — that sort of thing. Streetwalkers are also much in evidence in the Shepherd's Market district at night, and when the police aren't cracking down, on Park Lane, near the *London Hilton* and *Dorchester* hotels. Many of the "massage parlours" that have sprouted in various parts of town (there are several in Soho) offer clients more than a rubdown.

Blue movies are shown in many movie houses — advertisements for them appear in *What's On and Where To Go.* And the *Gay Switchboard* (phone: 837-7324) offers telephone information and advice to visiting gays of both sexes.

BEST IN TOWN

CHECKING IN: Visitors arriving in London between early spring and midautumn without hotel reservations are in for an unpleasant adventure. For many years now, there has been a glaring shortage of hotel rooms in the British capital during the prime tourist season, which each year seems to begin earlier and end later. (For a small fee, the Tourist Information Centre at Victoria Station Forecourt, or at the underground station in Heathrow, will try to help you locate a room.) This fact, plus years of general inflation and the difficulty of finding suitable hotel staff are largely responsible for often excessive hotel charges, generally out of keeping with other costs in Britain. As a rule, expensive hotels do not include any meals in their prices; moderate and inexpensive hotels generally include Continental breakfasts.

As an alternative to conventional hotel accommodations, it's easy to stay in one of 500 private homes and apartments through a program called Your Home in London. These vary from a single in a bed-and-breakfast establishment for $25 a night to a 2-bedroom apartment in central London for $120 a night. For information, in the US phone 212-688-2696.

Prices — with bath, English breakfast, VAT, and a 10% service charge sometimes included — are $110 to $160 and up for a double room in an expensive hotel; $65 to $100 is moderate; and $40 to $60 is inexpensive.

Berkeley – Remarkably understated, this 150-room hotel manages to preserve its impeccably high standards while keeping a low profile. Soft-spoken service complements the tastefully lavish, traditional English decor. Wilton Pl. SW1 (phone: 235-6000). Expensive.

Britannia – Mahogany furniture, velvet armchairs, rooms painted in colors you might choose at home — all very tasteful and solid, despite the anonymity of the spacious foyer with the pretentious chandeliers. This is where the American Embassy — also on the square — often puts up visiting middle-ranking State Department officials. Now part of the Inter-Continental chain. Grosvenor Sq. W1 (phone: 629-9400). Expensive.

Brown's – As English as you can get, retaining pleasing, quaint, Victorian charm, and not at all marred by heavy, sturdy furniture or the somewhat hushed atmosphere. Strong on service. If it's an English tea you're after, this is the place, though we were recently dismayed by the tie-and-jacket requirement at 4 PM. Dover St. W1 (phone: 493-6020). Expensive.

Cavendish – Immortalized as the *Bentinck*, the hotel run by Louisa Trotter (in real life, Rosa Lewis) in the TV series *The Duchess of Duke Street,* this modern replacement offers one of the most attractive locations in central London, near Piccadilly. Its 255 rooms are comfortable, though hardly elegant. Jermyn St. SW1 (phone: 930-2111). Expensive.

Chesterfield – In the heart of Mayfair and near Hyde Park, this small, recently rebuilt Georgian mansion has a certain exclusive elegance. Its 113 bedrooms are thoroughly modernized and well equipped. Amenities include a restaurant and a small bar that opens onto a flower-filled patio. 35 Charles St. W1 (phone: 491-2622). Expensive.

Churchill – A turn-of-the-century mood is reflected in the discreet decor. This is a well-run, efficient place, with a pleasant restaurant and a snack room that serves the best bacon and eggs in London. Very popular with Americans looking for accommodations somewhere between the old world and the new. Portman Sq. W1 (phone: 486-5800). Expensive.

Claridges – This plush outpost for visiting royalty, heads of state, and other distinguished and/or affluent foreigners is an Art Deco treasure. Somehow, even the dated decor is a delight. The line of chauffered limousines outside the main entrance sometimes makes traffic seem impenetrable. Wrought-iron balconies and a sweeping foyer staircase help provide a stately setting for one of London's most elegant hostelries. Liveried footmen serve afternoon tea. Brook St. W1 (phone: 629-8860). Expensive.

Connaught – A touch too sober for high livers; a trifle too formal for the rough-and-ready crowd. But there aren't many hotels left in the world that can rival this old London fixture in providing welcome, elegance, and comfort — particularly in its luxurious suites and its white tie and tail restaurant service. Carlos P1. W1 (phone: 499-7070). Expensive.

Dorchester – Directly on Park Lane, overlooking Hyde Park, this very luxurious hotel has a traditional British atmosphere, with Georgian and Regency furnishings and elegant service. Its *Terrace* restaurant serves fine food (recently awarded a Michelin star). Rooms are tastefully furnished, and 24-hour room service and central air conditioning are among the hotel's amenities. Recently sold to the Sultan of Brunei. Park La. W1 (phone: 629-8888). Expensive.

Dukes – Despite its modest size (only 36 rooms and 16 suites), this is an establishment where nobility and prestige shine through. It even extends to the rooms being named for former peers. A virtual total reconstruction has produced accommodations of great taste and warmth, and the snug location, down a quiet cul-de-sac, seems somehow uniquely British. 35 St. James's Pl. SW1 (phone: 491-4840). Expensive.

Grosvenor House – This 478-room grande dame facing Hyde Park has a health club, some interesting shops, the much-lauded *Pavilion* restaurant, the *Park Lounge,* which serves traditional afternoon teas, and the exclusive Crown Club on the top floor for members only — usually businesspeople who require special services — with rooms, suites, a lounge, and other complimentary extras. Park La. W1 (phone: 499-6363). Expensive.

Inn on the Park – Don't be deceived by the modern exterior; everything is traditional (and wonderful) within. A fine example of the superb service routinely offered by members of the Four Seasons chain, the rooms are comfortable, tastefully furnished, and commodious. The breakfast buffet is delightful; the *Four Seasons* restaurant is one of London's best. Hamilton Pl., Piccadilly W1 (phone: 499-0888). Expensive.

Inter-Continental – Smack-dab in the middle of the West End, right on Hyde Park Corner, with windows overlooking the route of the Royal Horse Guards as they go cantering off for the Changing of the Guard each morning. Its well-proportioned rooms are equipped with refrigerated bars. Modern and comfortable, particularly the Art Deco *Le Soufflé* restaurant, but the location's the main allure. 1 Hamilton Pl., Hyde Park Corner W1 (phone: 409-3131). Expensive.

London Hilton International – Well situated off Hyde Park Corner, near shopping and theater, this contemporary high-rise offers comfortable accommodations and spectacular views of the park and the city. Special attention to executives includes a multilingual switchboard, secretarial staff, office equipment, and private dining rooms. There's every conceivable service plus three restaurants — the *Roof,* with a view, the *Polynesian,* and the new *British Harvest,* serving organically grown traditional British produce — a disco, and snack bar. 22 Park La. W1 (phone: 493-8000). Expensive.

London Marriott – Close to the American Embassy and West End shopping, Marriott's recent refurbishment has transformed this modern hotel and increased the size of the rooms and suites. It's bright and busy, and it has everything — lounge, bar, two restaurants, shops, very comfortable rooms, and good service. Grosvenor Sq. W1 (phone: 493-1232). Expensive.

Londonderry – This deluxe hotel overlooks Hyde Park; it recently reopened after an extensive tasteful refurbishment. Its 3 penthouse suites and 150 rooms feature a French Mediterranean decor, a theme echoed in both the *Isle de France* restaurant and adjoining bar. Park La. W1 (phone: 493-7292). Expensive.

Mayfair Holiday Inn – Renovation hasn't damaged the hotel's all-pervading Regency style, unusual for this chain. Sitting in London's highly prestigious property belt, it has 192 rooms, the à la carte *Berkeley* restaurant, and an evening pianist in the *Dauphin* cocktail bar. 3 Berkeley St. W1 (phone: 493-8282). Expensive.

Meridien London – Formerly the *New Piccadilly,* located between the Royal Academy and Piccadilly Circus, this hotel has recently undergone a £16 million refurbishment, thought the rooms remain mostly modest in size and rather dark. A lofty, Edwardian marble entrance hall leads to the 296 rooms and 30 suites. The new *Terrace* restaurant, on the second floor, seats 140 under a glass roof, and the space beneath the hotel has been transformed into an extensive health club. There is also a less formal restaurant, a bar, and a cocktail lounge. Piccadilly W1 (phone: 734-8000). Expensive.

Montcalm – A smaller, elegant hotel with a lovely façade, a warm-toned and understated interior, and topnotch service. Its rooms have all the usual comforts, and many of its suites are especially luxurious. There's a bar, and in *Les Célébrités* restaurant, chef Gary Houiellbecq brings to bear all the skills he employed at the acclaimed *Compleat Angler* in Marlowe. Great Cumberland Pl. W1 (phone: 402-4288). Expensive.

Park Lane – If you don't mind the noise of the city streets, the site of this hotel, in the heart of the West End, is appealing. Some rooms have views of Green Park across the street. Piccadilly W1 (phone: 499-6321). Expensive.

Ritz – The fellow who was heard to mutter snootily "Nobody stays at the *Ritz* anymore" was off-base, especially since the recent renovation restored much of the old luster and certainly got the "bugs" out. It now ranks among London's finest stopping places. While the fare offered in the *Ritz* dining room is not quite the equal of the lush surroundings, the decor is especially splendid and the service impeccable. Piccadilly W1 (phone: 493-8181). Expensive.

Savoy – A favorite of film and theater performers, some of whom check in for months and have nothing but praise for the accommodations and service. Still one of London's top addresses, it's a 200-room hotel with armies of chambermaids and porters to keep things running, and the reputation of its famous *Savoy Grill* has been restored through a beautiful resuscitation of the decor and a revitalization of the kitchen. The Thames Suites are the most beautiful accommodations in the entire city. The Strand WC2 (phone: 836-4343). Expensive.

Selfridges – Just behind the department store of the same name, modern in both furnishings and tone, with a refreshing, unaffected courtesy that seems often to escape some of London's posher establishments. Convenient for shopping. Orchard St. W1 (phone: 408-2080). Expensive.

St. James's Club – For about $280 and an introduction by a member, you can join this exclusive residential club in the heart of London (though you don't need to bother for your first stay). Guests have full use of club suites. Some of the best food in the city is served in the downstairs dining room. 7 Park Pl. SW1 (phone: 629-7688). Expensive.

Stafford – In a surprisingly quiet side street close to the city center, this is where many American television and newspaper organizations often lodge visiting correspondents to give them efficient, friendly, British small-hotel management at its best. Many visitors think of it as their own personal secret. Recently purchased by Cunard, which has refurbished most of the 68 rooms. 16 St. James's Pl. SW1 (phone: 493-0111). Expensive.

Cadogan Thistle – Very comfortable, older, 69-room place, redolent of Edwardian England. Oscar Wilde was arrested here, and Lillie Langtry, who was having an affair with the Prince of Wales (later Edward VII), lived next door. The furniture and decor are original, but modern conveniences are offered as well — phone, TV, refrigerator in every room, bar, and restaurant. 75 Sloane St. SW1 (phone: 235-7141). Expensive to moderate.

Royal Court – Clean, comfortable, and recently refurbished, the hotel has a courteous, helpful staff, at the head of London's fashionable Chelsea shopping and residential district and within quick, easy reach of the rest of the action in town. Sloane Sq. SW1 (phone: 730-9191). Expensive to moderate.

Basil Street – A relic with a reputation for graceful, old-fashioned service and beautiful antique furnishings to match. It draws a faithful international clientele who, if they can get reservations, prefer staying here to patronizing any of the modern, impersonal, newer hotels. It has a women's health club and sits just down the street from *Harrods*. 8 Basil St. SW3 (phone: 581-3311). Moderate.

Drury Lane Moat House – Near the theater district and fashionable Covent Garden, this hotel is small and ultramodern with a cool, sophisticated decor. There's an elegant bar, and lunch is served on the terrace. 10 Drury La., High Holborn WC2 (phone: 836-6666). Moderate.

Durrants – This elegant Regency-style hotel has a splendid location behind the Wallace Collection and is only a few minutes' walk from the shopping on Oxford Street. It has been family-run for over 50 years and all the rooms have retained their character while being kept comfortably up to date. George St. W1 (phone: 935-8131). Moderate.

Ebury Court – A small hotel with smallish but cozy rooms and an intimate atmosphere (the owners dine with guests in the restaurant). Its faithful clientele testifies to its comfort, suitability, and "country house in London" touches. Hard to beat — all things considered — in a town where hotel prices tend to be unreasonable. 26 Ebury St. SW1 (phone: 730-8147). Moderate.

Embassy House – Over a million pounds has just been spent on renovating this Edwardian building on a wide tree-lined street in Kensington. It is very near the Albert Hall and all the main museums and an easy walk from *Harrods* and Hyde Park. Although the decor is modern, there are elaborate high ceilings and elegant staircases. There's also a restaurant and bar. 31 Queens Gate SW7 (phone: 584-7222). Moderate.

Gatwick Hilton International – Part of the airport's expansion program, this hotel provides much-needed accommodations for the ever-increasing number of visitors using the Gatwick gateway. Connected to the terminal by an enclosed walkway; amenities include many services for business travelers: bars, health club, 24-hour room service, and more. Gatwick Airport (phone: 0293-51-80-80). Moderate.

Kensington Hilton International – A bit out of the way, this modern hotel offers a great deal of comfort at prices below those of most Hiltons. Services include a restaurant, piano lounge, a Japanese restaurant, and a lavish brunch on Sundays.

Rooms are well designed and well maintained. 179-199 Holland Park Ave. (phone: 603-3355). Moderate.

Mountbatten – The life and times of Earl Mountbatten of Burma is the theme throughout this refurbished, wonderfully eccentric hotel's public rooms, all with exhibitions of various mementos from India. All 123 rooms feature Italian marble bathrooms, color satellite TV, and in-house movies, while 7 suites have whirlpool baths. Monmouth St., Covent Garden WC2 (phone: 836-4300). Moderate.

Royal Horseguards Thistle – This is one of the few London hostelries that overlooks the Thames with views of the South Bank. Recently modernized, it is a good base for those interested in the changing of the Buckingham Palace guard, Westminster Abbey, and the Houses of Parliament. Riverside rooms have balconies and there's a pleasant terrace. 2 Whitehall Ct. SW1 (phone: 839-3400). Moderate.

White House – A very big hotel, converted from apartments, in a quiet spot near Regents Park. Modernized and efficiently run, its facilities include a coffee shop and wine bar. Albany St. NW1 (phone: 387-1200). Moderate.

Harewood – This small modern hotel is well maintained by a pleasant and efficient staff. Some of its 93 rooms have private terraces. Restaurant and wine bar. Harewood Ave. NW1 (phone: 262-2707). Moderate to inexpensive.

Ramada Inn – Completely refurbished, redecorated, and generally upgraded, all 510 rooms have private bath and in-house movies. There's also a comfortable Victorian pub, *Duke of Wellington.* Lillie Rd. SW6 (phone: 385-1255). Moderate to inexpensive.

Pastoria – In the very center of the West End, near all theaters, this pleasant, comfortable little hotel has 52 rooms, most with baths and TV; it has a bar and a restaurant. St. Martin's St. WC2 (phone: 930-8641). Moderate to inexpensive.

YMCA – This relatively new "Y" could be the best and most comfortable low-cost hotel in the middle of London. Adequate, tidy rooms, complemented by a series of facilities not often found in hotels — including squash courts, a gym, billiard room, swimming pool, and sauna. Close to the British Museum and Oxford Street shopping district. Men and women of all ages are accepted, and triple rooms are available. 112 Great Russell St. WC1 (phone: 637-1333). Moderate to inexpensive.

Diplomat – Small, with no restaurant and only 26 rooms — all with baths — it is nonetheless comfortable, friendly, and affordable. In Belgravia at 2 Chesham St. SW1 (phone: 235-1544). Inexpensive.

 EATING OUT: Few London restaurants were ever known for the excellence of their cuisine — and some visitors of times past might call that a charitable understatement. But there's been a notable transformation in recent years. While restaurants offering really good English cooking — and not simply "chips with everything" — are still not easy to find (some are listed below), there has been a veritable explosion of good foreign restaurants in town (some of which are also noted below).

A meal for two will cost about $100 at a restaurant listed as expensive; $50 to $75 is moderate; and $30 and under inexpensive. Prices do not include wine, tips, or drinks. Most London restaurants have developed the Continental habit of automatically adding a service charge to the bill, so make certain you're not tipping twice. Reservations are necessary in all restaurants below.

Le Gavroche – Probably the best French restaurant in London and, according to *Guide Michelin,* one of the best in the entire country, with three stars to its credit (only one other establishment in Britain has received such a high rating). The cuisine is classic French; many of the dishes by those chefs extraordinaires, the Roux brothers, qualify as genuine masterpieces. Reserve well in advance, as there is great demand for tables. Closed weekends. 43 Upper Brook St. W1 (phone: 408-0881). Very expensive.

Capital Hotel Restaurant – The elegant, comfortable, small dining room in this hotel near *Harrods* offers well-chosen and richly prepared French dishes. It is considered by some discriminating Londoners to be the best place in town to eat. Avoids the aren't-you-lucky-to-get-a-table attitude flaunted by some other better London restaurants. 22-24 Basil St. SW3 (phone: 589-5171). Expensive.

Chez Nico – South of the river in dilapidated Battersea, Nico Ladenis set up what is now one of London's best restaurants. He had a reputation for perfection, and his shortage of patience with customers who expected anything less often reached the point of rudeness. But he now works almost exclusively in his second, Berkshire restaurant, leaving manager Phillip Britten in charge of *Chez Nico.* Reservations necessary. 129 Queenstown Rd. SW8 (phone: 720-6060). Expensive.

Connaught – Very dignified and very proper, this distinguished restaurant, with one Michelin star, has a fine reputation for both its cuisine and elegant service. Frankly, these guys carry stuffy to sometimes excessive lengths, but it's hard not to appreciate the masterful culinary performance. The setting — lots of rich paneling and crystal chandeliers — matches the distinction of the menu. Carlos Pl., W1 (phone: 499-7070). Expensive.

Guinea Grill – Down an alley off Berkeley Square, this unimposing restaurant serves the best beef in Britain. It also substitutes displays of its fresh food — steaks, chops, fresh vegetables — for a menu. It's as good as it looks, cooked with care. Closed Sundays. 30 Bruton Pl. W1 (phone: 629-5613). Expensive.

Leith's – A fine Continental restaurant in an out-of-the-way Victorian building northwest of Kensington Gardens, *Leith's* serves very good entrées, hors d'oeuvres, and desserts as part of a fine prix fixe dinner. Its wine selection is also very good. 92 Kensington Park Rd. W11 (phone: 229-4481). Expensive.

Lichfield's – Fish and game are the chef's specialties here: try ballantine of quail, for example, set on a bed of apples and bathed in Calvados sauce. As an alternative to the train, take a boat to Richmond from Westminster Pier, lunch at *Lichfield's,* and walk it off on Richmond Green. 13 Lichfield Terrace, Sheen Rd., Richmond (phone: 940-5236). Expensive.

Pavilion – A glittering restaurant in the *Grosvenor House* hotel which has been receiving more than its share of accolades recently — and justifiably so. The combination of cuisine, comfort, and calm is irresistible. The newest "must" meal on the London dining scene. Park Lane W1. (phone: 499-6363). Expensive.

Rue St. Jacques – Lavishly decorated with huge gold-framed mirrors. The food here is marked by rich cream sauces. Pricey, but well worth it. The formality stretches to jacket-and-tie requirement and a doorman who provides parking service. 5 Charlotte St. W1 (phone: 637-0222). Expensive.

Savoy Grill – Renowned as a celebrity-watching ground, but actually inhabited mostly by a male, business clientele. Although the menu features some classic French dishes, the English grills and roasts are its specialty. The lovely, newly restored decor resembles a luxurious ship's dining room (first class, natch) of 50 years ago. Perfect for after theater. At the *Savoy Hotel,* The Strand WC2 (phone: 836-4343). Expensive.

Tante Claire – Run by chef Pierre Koffman and his wife, Annie, this newly expanded establishment has been awarded two Michelin stars as well as many other honors. While fish dishes are the chef's specialty, everything — especially the duck, calves liver, and *Pied de Cochon farci aux Morilles* (pig's foot stuffed with foie gras and mushrooms) — is excellent. The prix fixe lunch is a remarkably good value at around $20. Closed weekends. 68 Royal Hospital Rd. SW3 (phone: 352-6045). Expensive.

Treasure of China – In a landmark Georgian building, this restaurant is a leader in original Peking and Szechwan cuisine. Owners Tony Low and Roger Norman offer a selective daily menu as well as superb banquets celebrating Chinese festivals. 10 Nelson Rd. SE10 (phone: 858-9884). Expensive.

Wilton's – Good food, skillfully prepared, elegantly served in a plush, rather formal Victorian setting. Game, fish, oxtail, steak and kidney pie — what the best of English cooking can be all about. Closed Sundays and 3 weeks in July/August. 55 Jermyn St. SW1 (phone: 629-9955). Expensive.

Langan's Brasserie – Still trendy after all these years, and still a popular haunt for celebrities. Ask for a downstairs table and take your time studying the lengthy menu. Reservations necessary. 1 Stratton St. W1 (493-6437). Expensive to moderate. *Langan's Bistro* serves slightly simpler and less expensive dishes prepared in the same style. 26 Devonshire St. W1 (phone: 935-4531). Moderate.

Poons – This Cantonese restaurant has built a reputation for good, authentic cooking and specializes in top-quality fish dishes and wind-dried food. You can even watch the chefs at work through a glass partition. Closed Sundays. 41 King St. WC2 (phone: 240-1743) and 4 Leicester St. WC2 (phone: 437-1528). Expensive to moderate.

L'Arlequin – A tiny establishment that offers unusual and innovative Gallic cooking by proprietor Christian Delteil, who reputedly makes the best sorbets in London. 123 Queenstown Rd. SW8 (phone: 622-0555). Moderate.

Au Bon Accueil – Over the years, this very busy (if somewhat cramped) French restaurant has kept up its reputation for good food and low prices. Efficient service in two small rooms plus a basement. Closed Saturday lunch and Sundays. 27 Elystan St. SW3 (phone: 589-3718). Moderate.

Bloom's – A large restaurant specializing in Jewish food, *Bloom's* has a bright and bustling atmosphere, a bit like the dining room of a large hotel, with waiters who almost — but not quite — throw the food at you. The popular take-out counter serves up the best hot salt beef (like corned beef) sandwiches in town. House wine is Israeli. Closed Friday evenings and Saturdays. 90 Whitechapel High St. E1 (phone: 247-6001). Moderate.

Bombay Brasserie – At lunchtime there is an Indian buffet; at dinner, classic cooking from the Bombay region. Parsi dishes, rarely found outside of India itself, are also included. And the setting is lovely, with lots of banana plants, wicker chairs, and ceiling fans. Courtfield Close, Courtfield Rd. SW7 (phone: 370-4040). Moderate.

Camden Brasserie – The daily specials are posted on a board outside this restaurant, found in an increasingly fashionable part of town. Among the selections are meat and fish grilled over an open fire. 216 Camden High St. NW1 (phone: 482-2114). Moderate.

Chuen Cheng Ku – At this huge restaurant in the heart of Chinatown, the overwhelming majority of the clientele is Chinese. The specialty here is dim sum, served every day until 6 PM. Also try the pork with chili and salt, duck webs, steamed lobster with ginger, and shark fin soup. 17 Wardour St. W1 (phone: 734-3281 or 437-1398). Moderate.

Gay Hussar – Among the best Hungarian restaurants this side of Budapest, its substantial menu offers a varied selection: chicken ragout soup, goulash, roast pork, and lots more. The food here is extremely filling as well as delicious. Informal atmosphere, with a regular clientele drawn from London's newspaper and publishing world. Closed Sundays. Make reservations early. 2 Greek St. W1 (phone: 437-0973). Moderate.

Hilaire – Thanks to chef Simon Hopkinson's superb French regional, classical, and nouvelle cuisine, this restaurant would not seem out of place in Paris, particularly as some of the waiters insist on speaking French exclusively. 68 Old Brompton Rd. (phone: 584-8993). Moderate.

Hungry Horse – This is the place to discover what a properly made English meat pie and Yorkshire pudding should taste like, as well as other English goodies. Don't be put off by having to pass under an archway and climb down a flight of stairs to get there — if anything, the inside looks a touch too tidy. 196 Fulham Rd. SW10 (phone: 352-7757). Moderate.

New Rasa Sayang – At this spacious, bilevel, Pan-Asian restaurant, Singaporean cuisine, based on various forms of coconut, is supplemented by Malaysian and Indonesian delicacies, which are often flavored with peanuts. Open daily. 3 Leicester Pl. W1 (phone: 437-4556). Moderate.

123 – One block away from the Japanese embassy, this is where the staff eats, a sure sign of quality. But be warned that there are two menus, one in English, the other in Japanese, and they are vastly different. The latter offers a far more extensive array of sashimi. Ask the waiter to translate. Closed Sundays. 27 Davies St. W1 (phone: 499-3911). Moderate.

Porters – A very English eatery in Covent Garden, famous for its home-cooked pies — steak, mushroom, and vegetable are a specialty. The kitchen, bar, and basement are even more spacious since the restaurant was completely redecorated. 17 Henrietta St. WC2 (phone: 836-6466). Moderate.

Le Routier – The English equivalent of a truck stop, with an interesting location overlooking the craft workshops and canal at Camden Lock. Inside you'll find a brasserie atmosphere, with specialties of the day chalked up on a blackboard. Very popular for lunch on weekends. Commercial Pl., Chalk Farm Rd. NW1 (phone: 485-0360). Moderate.

La Ruelle – Just off Kensington High Street, this small French restaurant recently introduced an imaginative selection of vegetarian dishes to its classic menu. 14 Wright's La. W8 (phone: 937-8525). Moderate.

Shezan – A quiet, brick and tile restaurant just below street level that prepares some very fine Pakistani food. Specialties include marinated-in-yogurt *murg tikka Lahori* (chicken cooked in *tandoori*, or clay ovens) and *kabab kabli* (minced spiced beef). An enthusiastic staff will explain the intricacies of tandoori cooking, help with your order, and lavish excellent service upon you. Closed Sundays. 16 Cheval Pl. SW7 (phone: 589-7918). Moderate.

Sweetings – A special London experience, this traditional fish restaurant is one of the great lunchtime attractions in London's financial district. You may have to sit at a counter with your lobster, brill, or haddock — but it will be fresh and perfectly prepared. Weekday lunchtime only; no reservations, so expect a wait. 39 Queen Victoria St. EC4 (phone: 248-3062). Moderate.

Tate Gallery Restaurant – Who would expect one of London's better restaurants to be in a fine art museum? But there it is — a genuine culinary outpost (leaning toward French cuisine) with a very good wine list. Not just another meal between the masterpieces. Lunch only. Closed Sundays. Tate Gallery. Millbank SW 1 (phone: 834-6754). Moderate.

La Trattoria dei Pescatori – A busy atmosphere pervades this restaurant, whose decor includes a boat, terra cotta tiles, copper pans, and chunky ceiling beams. The menu is enormous, with trout, halibut, salmon, shrimp, turbot, and lobster appearing in several guises. A typical specialty is *misto dei crostacei alla crema* — Mediterranean prawns, scallops, shrimp, and mussels sautéed with onions and herbs, simmered in fish stock and Asti, with a touch of cream. Closed Sundays. 57 Charlotte St. W1 (phone: 580-3289). Moderate.

Tuttons – One of the few restaurants in London that serves food all day, it's a very popular and lively brasserie in a former Covent Garden warehouse and a handy snack spot for theatergoers. Open from 9 to 12:30 AM daily; Sundays, noon to 11:30 PM. 11 Russell St. WC2 (phone: 836-1167). Moderate.

Wheeler's – One of the chain of London seafood restaurants with the same name, this is the original and the best of the lot. It's an old-fashioned, narrow establishment on three floors which specializes in the many ways of preparing Dover sole, most of them delicious. The oyster bar on the ground floor is our favorite perch. Closed Sundays. Duke of York St. at Apple Tree Yard (phone: 930-2460). Moderate.

Chiang Mai – Thai restaurants are a rarity in London. This one is easy to spot since it's the only eatery in Soho (and probably the whole of Britain) with a carved wooden elephant poised on the sidewalk. The menu offers such dishes as coconut chicken and galanga soup. Those unfamiliar with Thai cooking should inquire about the spiciness of individual dishes before ordering. Open daily. 48 Frith St. W1 (phone: 437-7444). Moderate to inexpensive.

HQ – An unusual (for London) Créole-style menu is the main attraction at this new restaurant/wine bar in trendy Camden Lock. Its location above the art and craft shops affords guests good views of the canal and weekend street performers. Commercial Pl. (phone: 485-6044). Moderate to inexpensive.

Khyber – A wide selection of Indian Punjabi specialties as well as tasty vegetarian dishes are served here. Try the *pannir,* mild cheese cooked with peas, meat, and spices, and the *aloa gobi,* a cauliflower dish. 56 Westbourne Grove W2 (phone: 727-4385). Moderate to inexpensive.

Last Days of the Raj – This popular restaurant on the eastern fringe of Covent Garden serves dishes from India's Punjabi region. Punjabi cuisine is rather mild, and one of its specialties is meat prepared *tandoori* style — marinated in yogurt and spices, then baked in a special tray oven. Some kind of tandoori cooking is usually on the menu in addition to other specials, which change every few months. The exotic mango-based cocktails are powerful, and the service is extremely friendly. Be sure to dine at the Drury Lane *Raj,* as other restaurants are now trading on the original restaurant's good name. Open daily. 22 Drury La. WC2 (phone: 836-1628). Moderate to inexpensive.

Smolensky's Balloon – This American-owned cocktail bar/restaurant with a 1930s piano-bar atmosphere is guaranteed to make you feel homesick. Steak and fries figure largely on the menu, offset by some interesting vegetarian dishes. Open daily, noon to 11:45 PM, Sundays noon to 10:30 PM. 1 Dover St. W1 (phone: 491-1199). Moderate to inexpensive.

Bangkok – Known for its *saté* — tender slices of beef marinated in a curry and soy sauce and served with a palate-destroying hot peanut sauce. From butcher block tables, diners can watch meals being prepared by chefs in the windowed kitchen. Closed Sundays. 9 Bute St. SW7 (phone: 584-8529). Inexpensive.

Café Maxim's – In the same building as *Maxim's de Paris,* it aims to combine the atmosphere of a brasserie with the already familiar Maxim's style. Live jazz in the evenings. Clareville House, Panton St. (phone: 839-4809). Inexpensive.

Calabash – West African cuisine gives this restaurant a unique position on London's restaurant map, especially since it's in the bubbling Covent Garden district. The service is accommodating and helpful and the food is both good and different. Closed Sundays. Downstairs at London's "Africa Center," 38 King St. WC2 (phone: 836-1976). Inexpensive.

La Capannina – Homemade pastas are offered by this unpretentious, friendly Italian restaurant, typical of those that flourish in Soho. Closed Saturday lunch and Sundays. 24 Romilly St. W1 (phone: 437-2473). Inexpensive.

Chicago Pizza Pie Factory – A little while ago, an American advertising executive turned his back on the ad world to bring London deep-dish pizza Windy City style, along with Budweiser beer and chocolate cheesecake. Londoners beat a path to his door and haven't yet stopped clamoring to get in. Open daily. 17 Hanover Sq. W1 (phone: 629-2669). Inexpensive.

Cosmoba – A small and friendly family-run Italian restaurant that is basic in every respect — except for its food. Tucked down a tiny alleyway and always packed with regulars. 9 Cosmo Pl. WC1 (phone: 837-0904). Inexpensive.

Cranks – There are three branches of this self-service vegetarian restaurant. All are popular and serve homemade desserts as well as salads, quiches, and other hot food. Drop in for coffee or afternoon tea. Closed Sundays. 8 Marshall St. W1 (phone: 437-9431; open for evening meals, Tuesdays through Saturdays); 11 The Market, Covent Garden WC1 (phone: 379-6508); Tottenham St. W1 (phone: 631-3912). Inexpensive.

Dumpling Inn – This Peking-style restaurant serves excellent Oriental dumplings, and most of the other dishes are equally good. Try the fried seaweed; it's got lots of vitamins and tastes terrific. The service, though efficient, is a little brisk. 15A Gerrard St. W1 (phone: 437-2567). Inexpensive.

Geales' – This place serves up truly English — and fresh — fish and chips in a setting that looks like a 1930s tearoom. Go early, because *Geales'* is no secret. Closed Sundays, Mondays, and the last 3 weeks in August. 2 Farmer St. W8 (phone: 727-7969). Inexpensive.

Hard Rock Café – This is the original. An American-style eating emporium with a loud jukebox and good burgers. It's always crowded, and the lines stretch well out into the street. As much a T-shirt vendor these days as a restaurant. 150 Old Park La. W1 (phone: 629-0382). Inexpensive.

Kalamaras Taverna – A small and friendly taverna with authentic Greek food prepared under the watchful eye of the Greek owner. The menu here is more varied than in most of the other Greek/Cypriot restaurants in London. Bouzouki music is sometimes played in the evenings. Closed Sundays. 66 and 76 Inverness Mews W2, off Queensway (phone: 727-5082 and 727-9122). Inexpensive.

My Old Dutch – This authentic Dutch pancake house serves endless varieties of sweet and savory pancakes on genuine blue Delft plates. Loud music. 132 High Holborn WC1 (phone: 242-5200). Inexpensive.

Oodles – A "country food" restaurant with branches on four of London's busiest streets. Wholesome quiches, spicy curries, and unusual salads are served under ceilings hung with (fake) country flowers and branches. Closed Sundays. 42 New Oxford St. WC1 (phone: 580-9521); 31 Cathedral Pl. EC1 (phone: 248-2550); 113 High Holborn WC1 (phone: 405-3838); and 128 Edgeware Rd. W2 (phone: 723-7548). Inexpensive.

Standard Indian – Possibly the best Indian restaurant value in London, so it tends to get crowded quickly. There are no reservations, so dine early to beat the rush. 23 Westbourne Grove W2 (phone: 727-4818). Inexpensive.

Widow Applebaum – Not an authentic New York Jewish delicatessen, but this place serves pretty good herring, cold cuts, chopped liver, potato salad, dill pickles, and apple pie. Closed Sundays. 46 S Molton St. W1 (phone: 629-4649). Inexpensive.

SHARING A PINT: There are several thousand pubs in London, the vast majority of which are owned by the six big brewers. Most of these pubs have two bars: the "public," which is for the working man who wants to get on with the business of drinking, and the "saloon" or "lounge," which makes an attempt at providing comfort and may serve good food and wine as well as beer. Liquor at the latter may cost more. Among the means by which pubs are appraised is the brand and variety of the draft brews that spew forth from its taps. The extraordinary variety can easily perplex the uninitiated. There's ale: bitter, mild, stout, and lager, whose varying tastes provide a perfect excuse to linger longer in pubs you find particuarly convivial. Eating in a crowded pub is not always easy because the limited number of tables are barely large enough to hold all the empty beer glasses, let alone food. Pub food is hearty but not especially imaginative: a ploughman's lunch, which is a hunk of bread and cheese plus pickle; cottage pie, which is ground meat with mashed potato on top baked in the oven; sausages; and sandwiches. The number (and quality) of pubs serving food should increase, since British law has recently expanded opening hours for pubs offering food.

Here are the names of pubs where we like to raise a pint or two: *Dirty Dick's,* 202 Bishopsgate EC 2, is offbeat but popular, with fake bats and spiders hanging from the ceilings, sawdust on the floor, and good bar snacks; *The Audley,* 41 Mount St. W1, is our favorite luncheon stop in the high-rent district, with fine sandwiches and salad plates in an atypically hygiene environment; *The Antelope,* 22 Eaton Terrace SW1, where the Bellamys (or even Hudson the butler) might have sipped a lager on the way home to nearby 165 Eaton Place; *The Grenadier,* 18 Wilton Row SW1, perhaps the poshest pub site in town, just off Belgravia Square; *Admiral Codrington,* 17 Mossop St. SW3, is large and Victorian, with brass beer pumps, engraved mirrors, and good food; *Dickens Inn* by the Tower, St. Katherine's Way E1, is a converted warehouse overlooking a colorful yacht marina and serving shellfish snacks; *George Inn,* 77 Borough High St. SE1, dates from 1676 and retains the original gallery for viewing Shakespearean plays in the summer; *The Flask,* 77 Highgate West Hill N6, serves drinks at three paneled bars and on its outside patio; *The Lamb,* 94 Lambs Conduit St. WC1, is also paneled and hung with photos of past music hall performers; *Museum Tavern,* 49 Great Russell St. WC1, is across the road from the British Museum and decorated with hanging flower baskets; *Princess Louise,* 208 High Holborn WC1, has live music, cabaret, and a wine bar upstairs with good food; *Salisbury,* 90 St. Martins La. WC2, is vintage late Victorian with ornate mirrors and a marble counter and has a gay clientele; *Bull and Bush,* North End Way NW3, dates to the 17th century and has a garden; *Prospect of Whitby,* 57 Wapping Wall E1, was once the haunt of thieves and smugglers, as the oldest riverside pub in London (now it draws jazz lovers); *Sherlock Holmes,* 10 Northumberland St. WC2, is dedicated to Holmesiana and excellent, made-to-order meat sandwiches; *Ye Olde Cheshire Cheese,* 5 Little Essex St. EC4 (just off Fleet St.), is a 17th-century pub with paneled walls and sawdust floors popular with the Fleet Street set.

 WINE BARS: An innovation on the London scene, they serve wine by the glass or bottle, accompanied by such light fare as quiche and salad, and occasionally full meals. You will find prices lower in wine bars than in restaurants and can often reserve tables in advance. Here's a selection of the finest: *Boos,* 1 Glentworth St. NW1, combines rustic decor with simple homemade food; *Cork and Bottle,* 44-46 Cranbourn St. WC2, is patronized by the London wine trade and has a classical guitarist providing background music; *Draycott's,* 114 Draycott Ave. SW3, has tables grouped outside on the pavement and is frequented by the smart London set; *Ebury Wine Bar,* 139 Ebury St. SW1, is in the heart of Belgravia and serves good food (try the English pudding), and offers live music nightly; *Le Bistroquet,* 273-275 Camden High St. NW1, is one of London's trendiest spots, popular with the city's yuppies; *Shampers,* 4 Kingly St. W1, is near the famous *Liberty* department store for shoppers and sometimes has a classical guitarist in the evenings; *Bar des Amis,* 11-14 Hanover Pl. WC2, is a crowded watering hole in fashionable Covent Garden; *Crawford's,* 10-11 Crawford St. W1, a lively basement bar serving full cold buffet lunches and suppers; *Penny's Place,* 6 King St. WC2 can be too crowded for comfort, but always has good wines, food, and music; *Julie's,* 137 Portland Rd. W11, has become a landmark for aging flower children of the 60s; *El Vino,* 47 Fleet St. EC4, is *the* haunt for journalists, and is most famous for refusing to serve women at the bar.

OXFORD

For 600 years, England had only two universities, and though more than 40 institutions of higher learning have opened their doors since the early nineteenth century, the two venerable ancients are still so embedded in the British psyche that they are often called by one name, Oxbridge, put asunder only by scholars debating questions of academic supremacy or by tourists comparing their visible merits. Although neither argument is likely to come to a conclusion soon, the casual visitor will notice a difference between Oxford and Cambridge. Whereas Cambridge, often described as a "city within a university," has the atmosphere of a small country town, Oxford is larger and bustling, not quite a metropolis, but transformed by a twentieth-century auto industry on its outskirts into a "university within a city."

Fortunately, Oxford University, though only part of present-day Oxford, remains its historic core, one of the great living architectural treasures of the world, where examples of every building style from the eleventh century on are preserved in less than one square mile. Oxford is Britain's oldest university, but age coupled with academe has not produced a dark, dreary collection of moss-covered monoliths. A much-quoted line by the nineteenth-century poet Matthew Arnold — "That sweet city with her dreaming spires" — aptly describes the university's towers, domes, and constant repetition of pinnacles when seen from afar or above. Close-up, as the visitor stands before a single façade of ribbed golden stone, limpid panes of glass, or alternating panels of the two, any sense of the laborious process of study fades and Oxford becomes the idea of learning incarnate, all light, clarity, and brilliance, even in the most inclement weather.

No one knows why scholars began to gather here. The city was probably in existence on the banks of the River Thames (called, in Oxford, the Isis) and its tributary, the Cherwell, long before the first reference to it appeared in the *Anglo-Saxon Chronicle* in 912. In 1121, the Priory of St. Frideswide was founded and it was possibly the presence of scholarly monks that drew English students to Oxford after a quarrel between Henry II and the French resulted in the closing of the Sorbonne to Englishmen in 1167. The university then developed quickly. By 1300, the first colleges had been established (University, Balliol, and Merton) and there were 1,500 students on hand.

Relations between town and gown were immediately antagonistic. Early students lived in lodging houses at the mercy of price-gouging townspeople; townspeople saw their city taken over by a young and boisterous occupying army. An outbreak of hostilities in 1209 caused some students to flee and set up a university at Cambridge. Even greater trouble in 1355, on St. Scholastica's Day, resulted in the death of 62 students and in the rest being driven from town. That the dispute was eventually resolved in favor of the university was a measure of its royal protection (because scholars became the basis of a king's loyal civil service, the gown-crown connection was strong). Thereafter, on every St. Scholastica's Day from 1357 to 1825, city dignitaries performed the humiliating penance of placing 62 pennies on the altar of the university church of St. Mary the Virgin and for nearly 500 years the university virtually ruled Oxford.

Rivalry between town and gown is now light-hearted, but the structure of the university has scarcely changed since the Middle Ages. By 1400, every student was required to be listed on the roll (matricula) of a master (or teacher — later to be called a don, from the Latin *dominus* for "master") responsible for him, and all were required to live in colleges or halls rather than in scattered lodging houses. The proliferating colleges became self-contained communities — behind the gates of each were living quarters, chapel, library, kitchen, dining hall, and even a brewery. This collegiate system in its modern guise continues to baffle visitors. Many an undergraduate popping out of Worcester or Wadham has been accosted by lost tourists looking for Oxford College, unaware that Oxford's colleges are part of Oxford University. Young men and women (the first of five women's colleges opened in 1878, and most of the colleges are now open to both sexes) seeking admission to the university have to be accepted, usually after an examination, by individual colleges, and live in them or in lodgings approved by them. But the university arranges academic curricula, administers financial aid from the government, and awards degrees.

This medieval organization also accounts for the type of sightseeing experience to be had in Oxford. More than 600 buildings in the city are considered of outstanding architectural merit and most belong to the university. Your time in Oxford will be spent wandering through gateways into "quadrangles," or courtyards (the students live up numbered staircases around the quads), discovering gardens, cloisters, and chapels, visiting the occasional open library or hall, following a passageway through still another arch and into one more quadrangle, often a spacious green lawn coaxed to perfection by centuries of loving care and hardly any pounding of feet — the sign will say who's allowed to walk on the grass and it's usually dons, sometimes postgraduates, occasionally undergraduates, never visitors.

Much of Oxford's history is brought to life by the anecdotes of local guides well versed in the city's folklore: How Dr. Johnson, a poor student at Pembroke College, was ashamed to walk into nearby Christ Church — always a grand college — because of his rundown shoes, yet threw away a pair of new ones left at his door by a rich scholar. Or how (the story everyone tells) one would-be undergraduate, up for an interview, was greeted superciliously by a don who turned from the awed youth, opened a copy of *The Times,* and said, "Right, impress me" — at which the boy took out a box of matches, set fire to the paper, and won a scholarship.

Oxford is primarily its students, and they do occasionally use humor to relieve the weight of tradition that is everywhere. At times, even on their backs. If exams are under way, visitors will see them going around in *subfusc* — dark suits or skirts with short black gowns on top, the age-old traditional dress for formal occasions. Some of the weightier traditions, in fact, seem actually born of silliness: "The Mallard Song," sometimes sung by the fellows of All Souls, celebrates a duck that flew out of a drain when the college was built. The Boar's Head Ceremony, held at Queen's College at Christmas, honors a legendary scholar who saved himself from a wild boar's attack by stuffing a Latin book down the animal's throat.

None of this, however, changes the fact that Oxford's stock-in-trade is the pursuit of knowledge, and of this visitors tiptoeing around quadrangles are constantly reminded by the firm signs asking them to be quiet. Such a polite command is not hard to obey, especially if it's all the better to hear the choristers of Christ Church singing in the cathedral. But even without the background sound, the sight of the sun glinting off the exalted architectural complex of Radcliffe Square, or of the progression of college façades on High Street coalescing to a magnificent skyline, is an inspiration.

OXFORD AT-A-GLANCE

SEEING THE CITY: An initial bird's-eye view of Oxford is absolutely essential so that you can get a clear idea of the layout of the colleges. Four of the best vantage points for such a perspective are the gallery near the top of the spire of St. Mary's Church, in High Street — colloquially known as "The High" — Carfax Tower in the very center of town (closed in winter), the cupola at the top of Christopher Wren's Sheldonian Theatre on Broad Street, and the tower of St. Michael at the North Gate. From St. Mary's you see much of High Street, with its gentle curve that is fancifully said to reflect most people's natural stroll: All Souls College; University College; and the Radcliffe "Camera," or Library. From the Sheldonian you look onto Broad Street (better known as "The Broad"); across The Broad to Balliol and Trinity colleges; closer by, down at Exeter College, the Bodleian Library, the Radcliffe Camera, and the Clarendon Building — once the home of the university printers, later to become the Oxford University Press. The view from South Park (east of Magdalen Bridge) of the "dreaming spires" set amid the trees is lauded in many a guidebook. For another traditional view of Oxford's spires, find the slightly unkempt piece of common land called Port Meadow, between the River Thames and the railway line. Or, closer and more congenial, though slightly less panoramic, Christ Church Meadow, near the southernmost point of the city, to the east of St. Aldate's.

SPECIAL PLACES: Ask any but the most disenchanted Oxford graduate about special places and he or she will answer "my college." Virtually all of them are worth a visit, but happily the most impressive are the most central. Not one is too distant from Carfax (from the French *quatre voies,* "four ways," or from the Latin *quadrifurcus,* "four-forked" — where the four main streets of Oxford met in Saxon times and still do) to be visited on foot.

THE HEART OF OXFORD

Magdalen College (pronounced Mawdlin) – Magdalen Tower, guarding the eastern end of High Street, was called by King James I, "the most absolute building in Oxford." An anthem is sung from the top of the tower at 6 AM every May Day morning. The college was established in 1458, by William of Waynflete, a bishop of Winchester, who was one of the first college founders to emphasize the importance of a chapel. There is a famous deer park, where the animals are fairly tame. Across High

Street from Magdalen, also on the banks of the River Cherwell, is the Botanic Garden, the oldest in Britain, laid out in 1621 with approximately £5,000 given by Henry Danvers, earl of Danby, primarily for the study of medicinal herbs. Open 2 to 6:15 PM daily. High St.

All Souls College – Founded 21 years before Magdalen by Henry Chichele, Archbishop of Canterbury, All Souls does not have undergraduates, only 60 fellows engaged in research and teaching. Because of its great academic distinction, it has been called "the most exclusive club in Britain." (A member of the college once remarked that he never needed an encyclopedia; if he wanted to know anything he just had to ask a colleague.) Behind All Souls' small 15th-century front quadrangle is the 18th-century great quadrangle, with twin towers and the magnificent Codlington Library whose central adornment is a sundial made by Christopher Wren. Open 2 to 5 PM daily. High St.

University College – Across High Street from All Souls, "Univ," as it is known, has the oldest building foundation in Oxford (1249). It used to be believed that it was founded by Alfred the Great, though the most telling comment on that occurred when one don — on being asked to a formal dinner to celebrate the millennium of Alfred's "foundation" — declined to come and sent two burned cakes instead. There's also a memorial to the poet Shelley (although he was expelled from the college). Open 10 AM to 6 PM summer; 10 AM to 5 PM winter. High St.

Church of St. Mary the Virgin – The oldest university building of all is part of St. Mary's; it looks like an aisle of the church, because in the 15th century it was remodeled. St. Mary's 14th-century spire is one of the dominant features of the Oxford skyline (climb to the tower at the top for a magnificent panorama of the city), and the church is a fine example of Perpendicular Gothic. At the northeast corner stands the old Congregation House built during the 1320s, which is the university's first building. High St.

Radcliffe Camera – This building commemorates Oxford's most generous 18th-century benefactor, Dr. John Radcliffe. It's such a distinctive building that when seen from miles away under the right conditions and from the right viewpoint, it has been compared as a landmark with Cambridge's King's College Chapel. Designed by James Gibbs — influenced by plans for a projected mausoleum for Charles I at Windsor — and completed in 1749, it was originally called the Radcliffe Library and is now a reading room for the Bodleian, the university library. Radcliffe Sq., behind St. Mary's.

Bodleian Library – Ball games are not allowed on the grass between the Radcliffe Camera and the Bodleian Library, and strollers are discouraged, because the earth here is only a thin crust: Below it are massive stores of books, and underground railways that bring books, on request by readers, from their shelves. The creation of the Bodleian Library was the outstanding achievement of 17th-century Oxford. Only a portion of the library — the Divinity School, with its magnificent carved ceiling — is open to visitors (9 AM to 5 PM, weekdays; 9 AM to 12:30 PM Saturdays). It was founded by Thomas Bodley, born in 1545 and a fellow of Merton at 19. It is one of the great libraries of the world, and has the right, like the British Museum Library and the Cambridge University Library, to a copy of every book published in the country. Across the road from the Sheldonian Theatre is an extension to the Bodleian, the New Bodleian, built in all its ugliness in the late 1930s. Radcliffe Sq.

Sheldonian Theatre – The degree-giving ceremony is held in the Sheldonian, which was designed by Christopher Wren in 1669, then professor of Astronomy at the university. Based on a classical amphitheater, it is enhanced by its own courtyard, entered from Broad Street, which it shares with the Clarendon Building. Its interior, also used for concerts, is magnificent. Its famous ceiling was the work of Robert Streeter, "Seargeant Painter" to King Charles II. You can climb a wide wooden stairway to the cupola for a partial view of central Oxford's spires and gargoyles. Open Monday through Saturday, 10 AM to 4:45 PM (to 3:45 PM November through February). Broad St.

New College – Its full name is St. Mary College of Winchester in Oxenford, but when it was completed in 1386, the full effect was so stunning that the college, founded by William of Wykeham, bishop of Winchester, has always been known as New College. The front quadrangle is the original one (the first quadrangle built as such in Oxford, following the example of Merton's Mob Quad, which became a quad a bit by bit), though the top story on three of its sides was added in the late 17th century. The other side is formed by the chapel, which should be seen inside, too, for various treasures including the bishop's crozier. New College's garden quad, also added in the late 17th century, incorporates a stretch of 13th- and 14th-century city wall. Open daily from 2 to 5 PM (termtime), and 11 AM to 5 PM (vacation). New College La.

Balliol College – Apart from All Souls, which does not admit undergraduates, Balliol is academically the most impressive college in the university, with a long list of distinguished graduates, particularly in the field of politics (Lord Curzon, Harold Macmillan, Edward Heath). The college originated in 1255 when the bishop of Durham levied a fine upon John de Balliol, a powerful landowner. He was to pay a sum of money for several years toward the support of poor Oxford scholars. After his death in 1269, his wife continued the project. Balliol, founded in approximately 1263, was actually a living quarters, not a college as we know it today. Outside Balliol, in the middle of Broad Street, a cross on the ground marks the spot where three Protestant martyrs, Thomas Cranmer, Nicholas Ridley, and Hugh Latimer, were burned at the stake during the reign of Mary Tudor in 1555. Open 10 AM to 6 PM daily. Broad St.

Exeter College – In the Fellow's Garden of Exeter is one of Oxford's most famous trees, a horse chestnut that reaches over the boundary wall toward Brasenose. It is said that when the branches of the tree *touch* Brasenose, Exeter will beat Brasenose on the river. The tradition is scoffed at, but Brasenose undergraduates are known to clip the branches just in case. The college is associated with the rise of the pre-Raphaelite movement: William Morris and Burne-Jones were fellow students and later close friends. There is a William Morris tapestry in the chapel. Open 2 to 5 PM (termtime) and 10AM to 5 PM (vacation). Broad St. at Turl St.

Christ Church – Lesson one: If you don't want to be taken for a complete country bumpkin, never say "Christ Church College," but simply "Christ Church." Lesson two (very subtle, this one): Contrary to usage at the other colleges, fellows, or dons, here are known as "students," but undergraduates never are. Christ Church was founded on the site of the Priory of St. Frideswide by Cardinal Wolsey in 1525, was refounded by Henry VIII in 1532 and 1546, and includes among its august alumni such names as Sir Philip Sidney, Richard Hakluyt, John Locke, John Wesley, John Ruskin, Lewis Carroll, W. H. Auden, and many others. Its exquisitely vaulted chapel is also Oxford's cathedral, one of the smallest cathedrals in England, while its 16th-century Great Quadrangle (or Tom Quad) is Oxford's largest. Great Tom, the imperious bell in Tom Tower, hangs right above the main Christ Church entrance and resounds 101 times at 9:05 each night, the original curfew time for the 101 undergraduates it summoned by its first peal. See, also, the paneled and gilded medieval dining hall and the 18th-century Palladian Peckwater Quad, behind Tom Quad. Open 9:30 AM to 4:30 PM weekdays; to 12:30 PM Saturdays. St. Aldate's.

Merton College – University College was founded in 1249, Balliol in 1263, but if it's a question of official papers, then Merton (founded in 1246, with final statutes dated 1274) can claim to be the oldest college in Oxford. It has, at any rate, Oxford's oldest quadrangle, Mob Quad (begun 1304), whose south and west sides are formed by England's oldest library — no lending library, some of the books are still chained to desks as they were for the early scholars. Merton also has Oxford's first collegiate chapel, containing original 13th-century stained glass. Intimate, quiet, and less neatly laid out than the other colleges, Merton's buildings only gradually assumed the familiar quadrangle form, but once this pattern was copied by New College, it was the model for all the colleges that followed. Open 2 to 5 PM weekdays, 10 AM to 5 PM weekends (closes 4 PM in winter). Merton St.

Ashmolean Museum – This collection of paintings, sculpture, musical instruments, artifacts of the Stone and Bronze ages, and other objets d'art originally belonged to John Tradescant (d. 1638), then his son, who in turn left it to Elias Ashmole, also a collector. Among the treasures you can see here are Michelangelo and Raphael drawings, and the Pomfret and Arundel marbles, Oliver Cromwell's death mask, and Guy Fawkes' lantern. Perhaps the most famous item in the whole museum is the exquisite Alfred Jewel, found in a field in 1693 and marked with an old English inscription "Alfred Had Me Made." The Ashmolean's wealth of rarities and curiosities outgrew its original building in the 19th century and moved to new premises. Closed Mondays. The Old Ashmolean, next to the Sheldonian Theatre on Broad Street, is now the Museum of the History of Science Open 9 AM to 5 PM Tuesday through Saturday; 10 AM to 4 PM Mondays; 2 to 4 PM Sundays. Beaumont St. (phone: 57522).

OFFBEAT OXFORD

Covered Market – Built in the 19th century, this is a busy and charming if down-to-earth street market. In its maze of tiny lanes crammed with tiny shops, the aroma of just-ground coffee and fresh fish mingles with that of ripe cheese and blood-stained sawdust from the butcher's shops. After a colorful morning's stroll, drop by at the rough-and-ready but locally popular *George's Cafe,* 77 The Market (phone: 249527). Downstairs is a basic coffee and tea shop, where you can buy pies, sandwiches, or cakes, while the upstairs caters to a health-conscious clientele with salads, homemade soups, cakes, and pies. Both claim a cult following among undergraduates. The tables may be covered in crumbs, the service off-hand, the floor unswept, the other customers morose or argumentative, but the place has style.

Blackwells Bookshop – Virtually an Aladdin's cave filled with books, *Blackwells* is where tourists buying paperback guides to the city rub shoulders with fellows of All Souls collecting esoteric tomes ordered on their behalf and undergraduates dutifully gathering up texts recommended by their tutors. Broad St., opposite the Sheldonian Theatre; other branches are on Hythe Bridge St., Leckford Rd., and (for music) Holywell St.

■**EXTRA SPECIAL:** Early summer sees Oxford at its best and brightest, and although most undergraduates have exams on their minds, that does not seem to obtrude — perhaps it even helps. Oxford has all kinds of activities and fetes during this season; check the *What's On* brochures as well as the college notice boards. There are open-air plays in college gardens; "commem" balls — grand, all-night black-tie affairs, to which you may have trouble obtaining tickets, especially for the more popular ones; picnics and madrigals on the river; garden parties; church festivals, and much more. Tickets are available from *Tickets in Oxford* (see *Sources and Resources,* below). (*A word of caution:* Because hotel rooms are at a premium at this time, be prepared to accept hotel accommodations some distance from the city center or even in the surrounding countryside. Woodstock and Weston-on-the-Green, for example, have good hotels.)

Visitors are welcome at services in the three college chapels which have resident choir schools — Magdalen, New College, and the Cathedral in Christ Church. Details are available at the Information Centre (phone: 726871).

SOURCES AND RESOURCES

 TOURIST INFORMATION: The City of Oxford Information Centre, St. Aldate's (opposite the Town Hall, about 100 yards from Carfax; phone: 726871), is excellent, and the staff is very helpful. It's open Mondays through Saturdays (and Sundays in summer), and stocks a massive amount of tourist literature, guides, maps, and *What's On* brochures. Very informative 2-hour guided walking tours depart from here daily. The cost is approximately £1.50 and includes the popular "American Roots in Oxford Tour." *Tickets in Oxford* (phone: 727855) is also based here, with tickets for plays and concerts in town as well as in London and Stratford-upon-Avon. The inexpensive *Oxford Guide* and the *Oxford Vade Mecum,* on sale in most bookstores, are both useful and detailed. The Information Centre and Thames and Chilterns Tourist Board, 8 The Market Pl., Abingdon, Oxfordshire, OX14 3UD (phone: 0235-22711), both have essential background information on the surrounding area.

Local Coverage – The *Oxford Mail* evening newspaper (whose editor, incidentally, is traditionally allowed to dine in All Souls when the mood takes him). Also available are the free information sheets *What's On* and *This Month in Oxford. Daily Information,* another city-published sheet, is available for reference from the Information Centre.

 GETTING AROUND: Except for the trip from the train station, for which you will need a taxi or a bus, and unless you choose a hotel out of the center, you will not need transport. Everyone goes on foot or by bicycle. In fact, guided walking tours of the city are popular and a good means of orientation. They are available in the morning and afternoon; the Information Centre has details.

Bus – The new, air-conditioned *Citylink 190* coaches run every half-hour from Oxford to London's Victoria Station. The *South Midlands Bus Company,* which provides very good service linking the city center with its outskirts, is located at 395 Cowley Rd. (phone: 711312).

Car Rental – You can rent a car from *Godfrey Davis Europcar,* Seacourt Tower, Botley Rd. (phone: 246373); *Hertz,* Woodstock Roundabout (phone: 50933); *Kenning,* Oxford TraveLodge on Woodstock Rd. (phone: 511232); *Motorlux, Ltd.,* 265 Iffley Rd. (phone: 240101) or *Swan National,* St. Clement's Garage, Dawson St. (phone: 240471). Others are listed at the Information Centre and in the yellow pages. Parking in Oxford is difficult to find, but day-trippers can take advantage of the "Park and Ride" scheme. Leave your car free of charge in the parking lots clearly marked as you enter Oxford, then take the blue and white buses that run frequently (from 7:30 AM to 6:30 PM weekdays; from 8:30 AM to 6:30 PM Saturdays) to the city center.

Taxi – Unfortunately, cabs in Oxford are expensive compared with most other cities. There are cabstands in several locations around the city; one convenient spot is the taxi rank near the Randolph Hotel. To order by phone, call *Radio Taxis* at 249743.

 MUSEUMS: In addition to those mentioned in Special Places, other museums of note are:

Bate Collection of Historical Instuments – A comprehensive collection of woodwind, brass, and percussion instruments. Free. Closed weekends. Faculty of Music, Floyds Row (phone: 247069).

Christ Church Picture Gallery – Old masters, glassware, antiques. In Canterbury Quad, Christ Church (phone: 242102).

OXFORD / Sources and Resources 393

Museum of Modern Art – Gallery, cinema, and bookshop. Closed Mondays. 30 Pembroke St. (phone: 722733).

Museum of Oxford – The history of the town from Norman times by means of photographs and models. Free. Closed Sundays and Mondays. St. Aldate's (phone: 815559).

Pitt Rivers Museum (access through the University Museum) – Ethnology, archaeology, musical instruments, weapons. Free. Closed Sundays (phone: 512541).

Rotunda Museum of Antique Dolls' Houses – A private collection featuring more than 40 historic dolls' houses, complete with period furniture and "inhabitants." Open Sundays, summer only. Grove House, Iffley Turn (phone: 777935).

University Museum – Mainly natural history, in what was once Oxford's most architecturally controversial building. Closed Sundays. Free. Parks Rd. (phone: 57529).

 SHOPPING: Inspired by the groves of academe, you will probably want to buy books, and possibly paintings or prints too. Besides *Blackwells,* there are several other bookstores on Broad St., but the city's largest secondhand bookstore, *Robin Waterfield's,* is at 36 Park End St. Along High St., you'll find many antique and picture shops; the *Oxford Gallery* sells as well as exhibits paintings (mostly contemporary). Also on High St. are *Reginald Davis* (No. 34), for silver and jewelry; *P. Audley-Miller* (No. 46), for antiques; *Magna Gallery* (No. 41), for old maps and prints; and *Shepherd and Woodward* (Nos. 109/114), for Oxford University paraphernalia (sweat shirts, scarves, ties, etc.). Just off High St., Turl St. has *Ducker & Son,* with top-quality shoes (No. 6 for men, No. 12 for women). Little Clarendon St., just north of the Ashmolean, has a couple of good crafts shops; two of these are *Gallery 57* (No. 29) and *Playhood Toyshop* (No. 22). Here you'll also find the well-known *Laura Ashley* (No. 27), along with *Sylvester* (No. 23), with a huge selection of interesting housewares, and the *Malvern Cheese Shop* (No. 32). For a picnic lunch visit the cheese shop, then pick up some other interesting comestibles at the *Covered Market,* off High St., or the Wednesday morning open market off St. George St. (near the bus station). A jug of wine to accompany that picnic can be found at *Oddbins,* 108 High St. Both the *Westgate Shopping Centre* and the new *Clarendon Centre* contain several well-known chain stores.

 SPECIAL EVENTS: Late May sees one of the biggest events of the Oxford calendar — *Eights Week,* when teams from the colleges compete for the coveted title of Head of the River. The annual *May Day Morning* is celebrated on May 1st, with traditional morris dancing and madrigal singing beginning at 6 AM. *Encaenia* takes place in the Sheldonian Theatre, most spectacularly at the end of the summer term, when honorary degrees are awarded to distinguished men and women. In late August the *Oxford Regatta* monopolizes the River Thames. Each September, the *St. Giles' Fair* is held in St. Giles', between the Randolph Hotel and the point at which the Woodstock and the Banbury roads fork off to the north. Traffic has to be diverted to accommodate this traditional, centuries-old fun fair.

 SPORTS: Biking – Bicycles can be rented from *Bee Line Bikes,* 14a Worcester St. (phone: 726643); *Denton's,* 294 Banbury Rd. (phone: 53859); *Penny Farthing,* 27 George St. (phone: 249368); *Reg Taylor's,* 285 Iffley Rd. (phone: 247040); or *Robinsons,* 46 Magdalen Rd. (phone: 249368). (Though biking around Oxford may seem romantic, it isn't very safe, so unless you're confident on two wheels, skip it.)

Boating – The sport most popularly associated with Oxford is rowing, especially in view of the Boat Race held every year against Cambridge. The river at Oxford is too narrow to accommodate teams racing side by side, so the colleges have devised "Bumps," (otherwise known as "Eights") or staged races in which crews try to bump each other's boats. But the best way for visitors to get properly acquainted with the river is to hire a punt at *Cherwell Boathouse,* Bardwell Rd. (phone: 55978), *C. Howard & Son,* Madgalen Bridge (phone: 61586), or *Hubbocks,* Folly Bridge (phone: 24435). Although unlikely, it is possible to fall into the river, and only competent swimmers are advised to venture out. Motorboats can also be rented for longer excursions from *Medley Boat Station,* Port Meadow (phone: 511660), or *Salters,* Folly Bridge (phone: 243421).

Golf – The *Southfield Golf Club* on Hilltop Rd., Headington (phone: 242158), welcomes visitors who are members of other golf clubs, weekdays only.

Ice Skating – The *Oxford Ice Rink* hires out skates. Oxpens Rd. (phone: 247676).

Swimming – Take a dip at the *Ferry Pool* (indoor and outdoor) near Ferry Centre, Summertown (phone: 50330). *Ferry Pool* also has squash courts, and rents racquets. *Temple Cowley Pool,* Cowley Rd. (phone: 716667), has the only ozone-sterilized pool in the area, as well as a sauna/solarium and fitness rooms.

THEATER: *The Playhouse,* Beaumont St. (phone: 247133), opposite the Ashmolean, is the university theater and features professionals on tour and amateurs from the university. The *Apollo,* George St. (phone: 244544), plays host to opera, ballet, pantomime, visiting pop groups, and jazz concerts. Production schedules for both are published in the *Oxford Mail,* and the whereabouts of theatrical productions, as well as movies, are posted on the notice board outside the Arts Centre on St. Georges St. *Tickets in Oxford* (phone: 727855), at the Information Centre, is the central booking agency.

MUSIC: Virtually all the colleges have a chapel of considerable architectural interest, and many of these showcase concerts and recitals. The best Oxford music is church music, and *Christ Church, Magdalen College,* and *New College* all have choir schools — so standards are very high. The *Holywell Music Rooms,* said to be the oldest of their kind in Europe, are a delightful setting for small concerts, as is the *Sheldonian Theatre.* Just watch for advertisements in the local newspapers or on college notice boards or ask at *Tickets in Oxford* at the Information Centre.

NIGHTCLUBS AND NIGHTLIFE: During the university term Oxford is a young city, so there's a lot going on. *The Boozer,* Frewin St., off Cornmarket, provides rock music on Saturdays and Sundays. Both *Boodles,* 34–35 Westgate (phone: 245136), which is fairly dressy, and *Bogarts,* the Plain (phone: 241047), are open 9 PM to 2 AM Tuesdays through Saturdays. *Cape of Good Hope,* the Plain, features disco groups. Non-members of clubs should try to arrive before 10:30 PM.

SINS: Despite the recent admission of women to the men's colleges and the presence of a few women's colleges, Oxford remains largely a male bastion. In such a setting, *lust* naturally flourishes. If *gluttony* is your secret vice, indulge in a meal and a bottle of claret at the highly regarded *Le Petit Blanc* restaurant in Summertown, *Le Manoir aux Quat' Saisons* in Great Milton near Oxford, or at the *Bear* in the nearby town of Woodstock.

BEST IN TOWN

 CHECKING IN: Perhaps it is because members of the university (which includes anyone who has graduated from it) can always get a room in their old college, or perhaps it is because during the vacation there are so many university landladies whose merits are passed by word of mouth — whatever the reason, Oxford is short of top-grade hotels, especially in the city center, and for the few that do exist, it's usually necessary to make reservations well ahead. You need never go without a bed however; if you are having trouble, consult the Information Centre in St. Aldate's (phone: 726871). Expect to pay $60 and up for a double room in a hotel listed as expensive; $40 to $60 for a moderate; and under $40 for inexpensive.

Le Manoir aux Quat' Saisons – At the top of the country house hotel league, this dining-and-lodging establishment, 15 minutes from Oxford, boasts two Michelin stars. The luxurious guestrooms feature half-testered beds and views overlooking nearly 30 acres of meadows and gardens. It is possible for two people to spend as much as $500 a night half board, but this discourages few, as booking months in advance is a necessity. See also *Rural Retreats* in DIVERSIONS. Church Rd., Great Milton (phone: 08446-8881). Very expensive.

Ladbroke Linton Lodge – A short bus or taxi ride from the city center, this modernized Edwardian townhouse has 70 bedrooms, including some "Gold Star" luxury rooms; an oak-paneled dining room with a traditional English menu; and pleasant, peaceful gardens. 13 Linton Rd. (phone: 53461). Expensive.

Oxford Moat House – This modern, recently renovated hotel plays host to many conventions. For the casual tourist, however, it also offers 155 sleek rooms and a convenient bistro-bar. This is a good starting point for a Cotswolds journey, as it is outside Oxford on the A40 Wolvercote Roundabout (phone: 59933). Expensive.

Randolph – The best in town, this is a Victorian Gothic monument with an efficient staff, and a very good location directly opposite the Ashmolean Museum and close to the Playhouse Theatre. Richly and elegantly furnished throughout, its 109 rooms are spacious and come with television sets and phones; other facilities include two luxury suites and the lofty *Spires* restaurant, which serves both à la carte and fixed price dinners; a coffee shop for quick meals; and a bar. Cream teas are served every afternoon in the lounge. Beaumont St. (phone: 247481). Expensive.

Eastgate – Not quite as luxurious as the first three, but newly refurbished, with an excellent location fairly near Magdalen College. Although the 35 rooms here are smallish, the staff is friendly. The High, entrance on Merton St. (phone: 248244). Expensive to moderate.

TraveLodge – It's one of those standardized, no-frills motels that offers efficient service, 24-hour snack service, outdoor pool, and a 24-hour gas station. Peartree Roundabout (phone: 54301). Moderate.

Westwood Country – Although its grounds are filled with all kinds of wildlife, like badgers and deer, this is still a peaceful 26-bedroom place just a few minutes from the city center. Four of the rooms have four-poster beds, and you can tone up in the multi-gym and wallow in a whirlpool before dinner. Price includes entry to the Cotswold Wildlife Park. Hinksey Hill Top (phone: 735408). Moderate.

Cumnor – In a hilltop-village setting on the edge of Oxford, this hotel has very comfortable surroundings and serves good, fresh food in its dining room. Six rooms. Off the A420 Swindon Rd. at 76 Abingdon Rd., Cumnor (phone: 862216). Moderate to inexpensive.

Old Parsonage – A kind of gem situated at the point where the main Banbury Road quiets down, this small, creeper-covered, former 13th-century hospital has a simple decor and tranquil atmosphere. Oscar Wilde was a frequent patron. 1–3 Banbury Rd. (phone: 54843). Inexpensive.

Turf Tavern Cottages – Well-known historic city-center pub close to the walls of New College, reached through a maze of pedestrian alleys. It's small (9 rooms), but has lots of atmosphere. 4–5 Bath Pl. (phone: 243235). Inexpensive.

EATING OUT: Oxford offers more in the way of restaurants than it does hotels. If you cannot secure an invitation to dine at High Table with a don in one of the colleges (gastronomically it may not be tops, but for atmosphere it's unbeatable), you can still eat very well indeed. This is, after all, a very sophisticated community, and fine food is much appreciated. On the other hand, it's also a youthful community and has lots of hamburger joints and pizza parlors. Expect to pay $55 and up for dinner for two, excluding wine and tips, in establishments listed as expensive; $25 to $35 in moderate establishments; and $25 and under in inexpensive places.

Le Manoir aux Quat' Saisons – In 1984, Oxford's best restaurant moved into a beautiful manor house hotel of the same name in Great Milton. Its menu is among the best in Britain featuring skillfully prepared haute cuisine and game in season, and there's an extensive wine list. Reservations necessary. Closed Sundays, Mondays, and at Christmas (phone: 08446-8881, 8883, 8884). Very expensive.

Le Petit Blanc – Owned by *Le Manoir* (above), *Le Petit* has recently moved to grander premises, complete with a *Le Manior* chef. This fine restaurant has a daily specialty, usually a fish dish. Closed Sundays and at lunchtime Mondays. 61a Banbury Rd. (phone: 53540). Expensive.

Elizabeth – Housed in one of Oxford's finest late-15th-century buildings, this chic little restaurant has a good location, where you can enjoy a fine meal as a fitting end to a day or weekend exploring Oxford. The sophisticated menu features French cooking; house specialties include trout stuffed with seafood, mousse, *suprême de volaille au vin blanc,* and *caneton aux abricots.* Reservations necessary. Open daily except Mondays, Christmas, and bank holidays. 84 St. Aldate's (phone: 242230). Expensive.

La Sorbonne – Occupying the second floor of a beautifully preserved half-timbered 17th-century house with overhanging eaves, this place offers classic French fare in a friendly, informal atmosphere. The wine list, as well as the service, is very good. Reservations necessary. Closed for ten days at Christmas. 130a High St. (phone: 241320). Expensive.

Michel's Brasserie – The owner is French, and he offers his native cuisine at this elegant restaurant in an up-and-coming part of town. Open daily. 10 Little Clarendon St. (phone: 52142). Expensive to moderate.

Saracen – Handily located (but easily overlooked) halfway between Oxford's Apollo and the Playhouse, this modern, white-walled French/Italian restaurant is popular with theatergoers, who pause here for a taste of the warm south — be it scampi, scaloppine, zabaglione, or anything else on the extensive menu. Closed Sundays. In the basement under the Jaeger's boutique at 15 Magdalen St. (phone: 249171). Expensive to moderate.

Cherwell Boathouse – Perched on the Cherwell, a tributary of the Thames, this restaurant is in a refurbished boathouse that rents punts and a gondola; they put out eight rooftop tables for summer dining. Two imaginative and set menus of three courses are offered daily — a recent example included hot vichyssoise, West Indian deep-dish meat pie, and Caribbean apple and grape dessert. Reservations necessary. Open daily for dinner except Sundays; also lunchtime buffets. Bardwell Rd. off Banbury Rd. (phone: 52746). Moderate.

Clements – Run by an Oxford alumnus, this double-fronted eatery offers carefully prepared food with a French accent. The ambience is relaxed and informal, but details such as candles and fresh flowers on the tables are not overlooked. Open daily for dinner; also lunch daily except Mondays. 35 St. Clements, near Magdalen College (phone: 241431). Moderate.

Head of the River – The ground floor of this converted wharf house is a pub, the second a bistro/cocktail bar, and the top a 40-seat restaurant overlooking the river. The whole is linked by a spiral staircase and decorated with Laura Ashley–style furnishings and an abundance of dried flower arrangements. 34 Park End St. (phone: 722433). Moderate.

Brown's – This sprawling row house restaurant decorated with lots of mirrors and hanging plants is a popular place in Oxford. It's always crowded so be prepared to wait in line and share tables. The entrées are wholesome and filling — spaghetti, steak and mushroom pie, hot sandwiches — and the desserts are homemade. String quartets accompany meals in the afternoons and there's usually live jazz late at night. No reservations. Open daily. 5–9 Woodstock Rd. (phone: 511995). Moderate to inexpensive.

Crypt – One of a new breed of wine bars in town, this is in the cellars of the Oxford Union Society. It has imaginative Anglo-French dishes such as the Mungo Bagger, steak wrapped around prawns, and scampi in white wine and Madeira. The wine list has 45 choices. Closed Sundays. Frewin Passage (phone: 251000). Moderate to inexpensive.

Bevers Wholefood – This small corner cafe serves salads, quiches, soups, and the like. All ingredients are organically grown and untouched by chemicals. Open daily. 36 St. Michael's St. (phone: 724241). Inexpensive.

Brewery and Bakehouse – There is a strong emphasis on food in this pub which brews its own beer and sells its own freshly baked bread and pizza. Live jazz is featured on Thursday nights and Sunday lunchtimes. 14 Gloucester St. (phone: 727265). Inexpensive.

Fasta Pasta – This tiny, American-run restaurant and shop perfectly captures the spirit of Italy. There's fettuccine and other fresh pasta, olive oil, wine, and salami to take away; or enjoy a plate of fresh pasta accompanied by a giant-size cappucino. 3 Little Clarendon St. (phone: 57349). Inexpensive.

Go Dutch – The pancakes served here are a meal in themselves — 12 inches in diameter and thick with a variety of fillings. Owner Rowena Greenwood recommends the bacon-and-apple. *Go Dutch* looks rather like Grandma's dining room, with heavy gate-leg furniture and plant-filled windows. No reservations on weekdays. Open daily. 18 Park End St. opposite the train station (phone: 240686). Inexpensive.

Heroes Sandwich Bar – Good sandwiches on whole wheat, rye, or pita are available here, as are picnic hampers for river or meadow outings. Ship St. (phone: 723459). Inexpensive.

Maxwell's – This faintly Art Deco, American-style diner is the place to go when you suffer a Big Mac attack. The menu features better-than-average burgers, milkshakes, and banana splits. There's also live music on Monday nights. Open daily. 35a Queen St. (phone: 242192). Inexpensive.

Nosebag – Oak-beamed ceilings, handmade pottery, and classical music make this eatery a pleasant respite in a busy sightseeing day. The soups, salads, and daily hot and cold specials are all very reasonably priced. No reservations at lunchtime, when it's very crowded; reservations recommended at dinner. Open daily. 6-8 St. Michael's St. (phone: 721033). Inexpensive.

SHARING A PINT: The *Turf Tavern,* 4–5 Bath Pl. (a narrow, cobblestone alleyway), is a great favorite, snuggled close to the walls of New College — it also serves coffee and tea; the 15th-century *Bear,* on Alfred St., close to Christ Church, was once a coaching inn and is full of atmosphere; the *Eagle and Child,* St. Giles, was frequented by literary lights such as J. R. R. Tolkien; the *White Horse,* in Broad St. next door to Blackwells, is handy and historic, despite the addition of electronic games; and the *King's Arms,* on the corner of Holywell St. and Parks Rd., close to Wadham, is a convenient spot for a little nip.

STRATFORD-UPON-AVON

Even without William Shakespeare's pervasive presence, Stratford-upon-Avon would be a very pleasant stopping point on a tour through the Warwickshire heart of England. It is a charming town, set congenially in the midst of peaceful green countryside, on a bend of the gentle River Avon. It is filled with the elegance of lovely, early-sixteenth-century half-timbered buildings. In its picture prettiness, swans glide by the spire of its riverside parish church, and trees, flowers, and gardens further soften its aspect. It is small enough to be seen in a day's stroll but large enough to have all the attributes of a busy market town — which it is and has been since receiving its first royal market charter in 1196, fully 368 years before William Shakespeare's birth ensured its enduring fame.

Stratford was first a Celtic settlement, then a small Roman town, its name — a mixture of the old Welsh for river and the Roman for street — meaning "the place where the street (or *straet*) fords the river (*afon*)." In the thirteenth century, the Guild of the Holy Cross, an Augustinian religious fraternity, was formed and it fostered the development of industries and crafts. It also maintained the grammar school and had almshouses and its own chapel, all of which were built by citizens of the town and are still among Stratford's most interesting buildings today.

The town has always been fortunate in the generosity of its citizens. John de Stratford, an Archbishop of Canterbury in the fourteenth century, is thought to have rebuilt Holy Trinity Church and to have established a college of priests to serve it. Later on, Hugh Clopton, who was to become Lord Mayor of London at the end of the fifteenth century, built the nave and tower of the Guild Chapel and the splendid 14-arch Clopton Bridge, which still takes the heavy traffic of the twentieth century into and out of town. More recent benefactors have been Charles Edward Flower, whose patronage made the first Shakespeare Memorial Theatre a reality in 1879, and his grandson Sir Archibald Flower, who was the major contributor to the present theater, opened in 1932.

Stratford's most illustrious citizen was undoubtedly William Shakespeare, son of John Shakespeare — "Gulielmus filius Johannes Shakespere" as the parish register puts it. Though he has been dead for more than three and a half centuries, his attraction is as strong as when he was a famous writer of plays in Elizabethan and Jacobean London. England's, and probably the world's, greatest playwright dominates the life of Stratford-upon-Avon: His houses and his children's houses are visited by hundreds of thousands of people every year; the big theater on the river, one of the world's most famous, bears his name and its actors perform his works; hotels and restaurants are named after him; and shopkeepers live on the sale of books, prints, portrait busts, trinkets, and souvenirs with a Shakespearean theme. The Shakespeare Connection is a lucrative one, and it is to the credit of Stratford's residents that they have not allowed it to overwhelm and cheapen their delightful town.

The Shakespeare Connection in a nutshell? Well, he was born here, on or about April 23, 1564, and he died here on April 23, 1616. In between, he grew up, went to school, moved to London to seek his fortune, and came back wealthy enough at 33 to buy a large house, New Place, in 1597, to which he retired in 1610, and where he died of a fever caused, it is said, by too strenuous an evening of eating, drinking, and being merry with friends a day or two beforehand.

Shakespeare's father was a glovemaker and his mother, Mary Arden, came from a respectable family of small landowners at Wilmcote, 3 miles from Stratford. The family house, from which John Shakespeare conducted his business, was on Henley Street, slightly to the north of the center of the busy little town. Young William went to school at the King Edward VI Grammar School on Church Street, and in 1582 married Anne Hathaway, a yeoman farmer's daughter 8 years older than himself. They had three children, Susanna and the twins, Judith and Hamnet (the latter died aged 11 in 1596). Then came the years of fame and glory in London, followed by a short period of happy retirement tending his garden in Stratford.

After his death, the town's interest in its brilliant native son subsided somewhat, though there was always a steady trickle of people to see his house and his garden with its famous mulberry tree. The turning point in the town's long-range fortunes came with David Garrick's Shakespeare Jubilee in 1769. The event could be called the original "Shakespeare Festival," and it grew out of Stratford's plans to decorate its rebuilt Town Hall.

Garrick was then England's foremost Shakespearean actor and as such was offered the honorary "Freedom" of the borough if he would provide a portrait or bust of Shakespeare to be hung in the Town Hall along with a portrait of himself. To no one's surprise, he accepted this opportunity to appear before an admiring posterity and organized his great jubilee — 3 days of celebration that, though marred by torrential rain, helped secure the future of Stratford as a great tourist attraction. The two portraits that were the occasion for the jubilee were both destroyed by fire in 1946, but a bust of Shakespeare that Garrick presented to Stratford can still be seen in the Town Hall.

The Shakespeare revival in Stratford grew apace during the nineteenth century, helped by interest from abroad and especially from the US. The first Shakespeare Memorial Theatre opened in 1879 to the sneers of the London theater establishment, but it was not long before they had to swallow their pride and take a serious interest in the little provincial theater, especially once the prominent producer Frank Benson began putting on Shakespeare there in 1886. His company remained for 30 years and established a performing tradition that became influential throughout the theater world.

Today Stratford-upon-Avon may be devoted to Shakespeare, but it has not been swamped by his cult. Its other side, its ancient existence as a very lively market town, continues unabated and almost undisturbed. Once a week, as has happened for centuries, Cotswold farmers bring their produce to market and shoppers come in from the surrounding villages. Branches of many of the large chain stores and a shopping mall blend with the Shakespearean sites, hotels, and restaurants. It's a comfortable mix of commerce and culture, of modern and medieval, that allows life to go on for its inhabitants while preserving for visitors the feel of countless generations that have gone before, and for the pilgrims who seek it, a shrine.

STRATFORD AT-A-GLANCE

 SEEING THE CITY: The towers of Holy Trinity Church and the Guild Chapel are not open to visitors and there are no tall modern buildings from which to get a bird's-eye view of the town, but the layout of the center of Stratford is simple. Most visitors start their tour at Shakespeare's Birthplace on Henley Street, which runs diagonally down to intersect Wood Street/Bridge Street, one of the four main thoroughfares that cut east-west across Stratford. The other three are Ely Street/Sheep Street, Scholars Lane/Chapel Lane, and Chestnut Walk/Old Town. Running north to south starting at the river are Waterside/Southern Lane, High Street/Chapel Street, and Rother Street/Windsor Street/Shakespeare Street.

SPECIAL PLACES: The Shakespeare Birthplace Trust is the official body that, on behalf of the nation, owns the five most important buildings connected with William Shakespeare. These are the Birthplace itself, New Place (with Nash's House), Hall's Croft, Anne Hathaway's Cottage, and Mary Arden's House. The Shakespeare Centre, the Trust's headquarters on Henley St., is also an academic center, opened in 1964, for anyone wishing to study its splendid collection of books and documents relating to Shakespeare, including translations of his plays in 67 languages. There is usually an exhibition in the front hall, where the engraved glass panels by John Hutton (depicting characters from the plays) are well worth a look. The Shakespeare Centre is open daily except Sundays; admission is free to the library and records office but there is a charge for the exhibitions. There is an individual admission fee for each of the Birthplace Trust buildings, but it's possible to lower the cost by buying an inclusive ticket for entrance to all five. The phone number for the Shakespeare Centre and all Trust buildings is 204016.

Most of Stratford's special places, including the ones without Shakespearean connections, are in the center of town within easy walking distance of each other. In the course of a day's stroll, you can see everything listed here (with the exception of Anne Hathaway's Cottage and Mary Arden's House), as well as experience the everyday workings of a typical English market town. Alternatively, you can take the *Guide Friday* "Open Top" Double Decker Bus Tour (see *Sources and Resources*), which runs every 30 minutes and links all the Shakespeare properties, including Mary Arden's House and Anne Hathaway's Cottage.

THE SHAKESPEARE BIRTHPLACE TRUST

Shakespeare's Birthplace – The spiritual center of Stratford-upon-Avon lies in this modest, half-timbered and gabled Tudor building where William Shakespeare was born on or about April 23, 1564. The house, visited by more than half a million people of all nationalities every year, is beautifully maintained and furnished with objects typical of Shakespeare's period. The bedroom in which the Bard is assumed to have been born is upstairs, its window scratched with the signatures of famous people who have visited it, including those of Sir Walter Scott, Alfred, Lord Tennyson, and the actress Ellen Terry. The Birthplace also houses a museum of relics and records of Shakespeare's day and a fine library as well as an exhibit of period costumes used in Shakespearean plays produced by BBC television. Don't miss the well-kept garden behind the house; in it grow many of the flowers, herbs, and plants Shakespeare knew. Open daily. Admission charge. Henley St. (phone: 204016).

New Place – Shakespeare's house stood on this site. The building passed out of the family's hands in 1670, and its last owner, constantly irritated by the numbers of admirers wanting to see it, demolished it in 1759. All you can see today are part of the foundations, and the once-extensive gardens. There is a replica of an Elizabethan knot garden — an elaborately laid-out formal garden typical of those times — and the Great Garden, which contains topiary work and a mulberry tree said to have been grown from a cutting from Shakespeare's original tree. The young mulberry in the center of the lawn was planted by Dame Peggy Ashcroft to mark the 200th anniversary of David Garrick's Jubilee. Nash's House, adjoining the gardens, was once owned by Thomas Nash, husband of Shakespeare's granddaughter Elizabeth Hall, and is furnished with items of their period. It also houses New Place Museum, devoted mainly to local archaeological material. Open daily. Admission charge. Chapel St. (phone: 292325).

Hall's Croft – A short walk from New Place to Old Town, a quietly elegant residential street, brings you to Hall's Croft. Shakespeare's elder daughter, Susanna, and her physician husband, Dr. John Hall, lived in this lovely house with its gabled front and overhanging upper floor from 1607 to 1616. Inside, it is the beautifully furnished house of a well-to-do Jacobean family, immaculately kept, with brass and copper glowing, and flowers in the living rooms. Don't miss the bedroom with its four-poster, and Dr. Hall's dispensary, stocked with pottery jars of herbs and potions, pestles and mortars, and surgical instruments. A large walled garden behind the house, again immaculate, provides an oasis of sweet-scented calm. Open daily. Admission charge. Old Town (phone: 292107).

Anne Hathaway's Cottage – So many hundreds of drawings, prints, engravings, and plaques portray this pretty, thatched house, that it is something of a surprise to come across the building itself on the outskirts of Stratford. It's about a 2-mile walk from the center of town (shorter by a footpath from Evesham Place) but it can also be reached by bus from Bridge Street, or even by bicycle. The trip is worth it, because Anne's cottage retains a charming English country air, with roses, jasmine, and other scented flowers in the garden, and Tudor furnishings in the house. Open daily. Admission charge. One mile from town in Shottery village (phone: 292100).

Mary Arden's House – Shakespeare's mother lived in this lovely gabled farmhouse in Wilmcote village before her marriage. The house is set in a garden, and the barns in back house a museum devoted to rural life and farming. About 3 miles from Stratford, Wilmcote can be reached by road, train, or even by boat along the canal. Open daily. Admission charge. Three miles from town in Wilmcote village (phone: 293455).

OTHER STRATFORD ATTRACTIONS

Holy Trinity Church – On the bank of the River Avon, this stately parish church dates from the 13th century. Shakespeare was baptized and buried here, and photocopies of the church register entries of both events are on display. On the north wall of the chancel is a bust of the poet carved by his contemporary Gerard Jannsen, a memorial erected by the Shakespeare family in 1623. Shakespeare's grave is below the bust, flanked by those of his wife and other members of his family. Open daily. Small admission charge to the chancel. Old Town.

Gower Memorial – An imaginative statue of William Shakespeare crowns this impressive memorial, which its creator, Lord Ronald Sutherland Gower, labored over for 12 years. Unveiled in 1888, it stands with its back to the Royal Shakespeare Theatre in Bancroft Gardens near Clopton Bridge. The four life-size bronzes at its base are of Hamlet, Lady Macbeth, Falstaff, and Prince Hal.

King Edward VI Grammar School – This half-timbered building on Church Street can trace its origins back to the 13th century and it was here that Shakespeare learned his Latin and Greek. Since it is still a school, it can only be visited by special arrangement, but don't walk by without pausing for a glimpse through the gateway or without noticing the ancient almshouses that border it (phone: 293351).

Guild Chapel – The beautiful, gray stone tower of the Guild Chapel is one of the finest landmarks in Stratford. It rises above the austerely elegant chapel, which was rebuilt by Hugh Clopton about 1496, on the site of a building dating from the mid-13th century. Today it is used by the grammar school, which holds a daily service there during the school term. Paintings that once covered the walls have mostly disappeared, except for one, *The Day of Judgment,* over the chancel arch. The Chapel adjoins the grammar school and almshouses on Church St. and is open daily.

Harvard House – The Stars and Stripes flying from a flagpole above the front door indicates the special importance of this old half-timbered building, dating from 1596. It was the home of a wealthy Stratford alderman, Thomas Rogers, whose daughter Katherine was the mother of John Harvard, the first benefactor of the university. The house now belongs to Harvard and is furnished in the style of the Elizabethan period. Open daily but closed Sundays through Wednesdays, November to March. Admission charge. High St.

Shrieve's House – Halfway down Sheep Street, stop for a moment outside this imposing late-16th-century private house with its great studded door and gateway. Shakespeare undoubtedly knew the owners of this Stratford townhouse, and may well have attended the wedding feast of their daughter there in 1613.

Stratford's Motor Museum – Nothing to do with Shakespeare at all, but it's worth a visit. The museum's specialty is cars from a bygone golden age, the 1920s. There are about 30 cars, and bicycles and motor bicycles as well. Open daily except Christmas. Admission charge. Shakespeare St. (phone: 69413).

Stratford Brass Rubbing Centre – Here is an opportunity to make your own souvenir of Stratford. The Centre has exact replicas of a large number of brasses, many from the Stratford area, and supplies paper and wax as part of the charge for doing a rubbing. Open daily. Royal Shakespeare Theatre Summer House, Avonbank Gardens (phone: 297671).

Stratford Butterfly Farm – A place that claims to be the most ambitious and revolutionary of its kind. They say that the world's largest spider lives here, too. Tramway Walk (phone: 299288).

Drinking Fountain and Clock – The ornate fountain and clock in the center of the Market Place was the gift of George W. Childs, a Philadelphian who presented it to the town in Queen Victoria's Jubilee year of 1887. It was unveiled by the famous actor Henry Irving.

Warwick Castle – Situated eight miles outside of Stratford, this is one of England's most visited stately homes. The grounds boast a re-created Victorian rose garden with more than 700 rose trees of at least 70 varieties. Open daily (phone: 0926-495421).

■ **EXTRA SPECIAL:** A visit to the *Royal Shakespeare Theatre* at its imposing riverside location is a major event for theater and Shakespeare lovers from all over the world. You can be sure that the production you'll see will have been thought out in meticulous, often controversial, detail and will be excitingly staged and beautifully acted by the Royal Shakespeare Company. The season, during which several Shakespeare plays are presented, generally runs from the end of March to January. Tickets should be bought as far in advance as possible from the box office, through Guide Friday (see *Sources and Resources*), or through a ticket agency. Tickets go on sale in early March, though it is often possible to buy them at the last minute. The theater holds back a few medium-priced tickets (maximum 2 per person) and some standing-room tickets for sale on the day of performance. Bona fide students (with identification to prove it) may chance upon an unsold ticket immediately before the performance. The theater has two restaurants, and a shop selling a good range of books and other items about the theater in general and Royal Shakespeare Company productions in particular. The attached Theatre Picture Gallery and Museum has interesting paintings, portraits, and relics of famous theater personalities. Backstage tours are also available daily except Sundays. The Royal Shakespeare Theatre, Stratford-upon-Avon, Warwickshire CV37 6BB (phone: 295623 for booking and for telephone credit card purchases; 69191 for 24-hour information on seat availability).

Next door along the river bank, the Bancroft Gardens contain the Shakespeare Memorial and lead to acres of open parkland and flowerbeds, popular with strolling theatergoers and picnickers.

SOURCES AND RESOURCES

TOURIST INFORMATION: The Tourist Information Centre at Judith Shakespeare's House, 1 High St. (phone: 293127), offers maps of the town, leaflets, accommodations advice, and guidebooks. Bookshops and newsagents are also well stocked with maps, guides, and other publications of interest to the visitor. The Stratford-upon-Avon Tourist (Telephone) Service (phone: 67522) gives prerecorded information such as opening times, telephone numbers, and other details of places of interest in and around the town. Short and long tours of the town and surrounding countryside are conducted daily by *Guide Friday Ltd.,* Civic Hall, Market Place, 14 Rother St. (phone: 294466). Most departures are from the company office, but car tours with a personal driver/guide can also be arranged. *Guide Friday* also operates a Tourism Centre at 14 Rother St. that provides visitors with town maps and area brochures.

Local Coverage – The *Stratford-upon-Avon Herald* is helpful, as is the free weekly publication called *Why?,* available at most hotels.

GETTING AROUND: The best way to see central Stratford-upon-Avon is on foot. Most of its important streets are laid out in a simple grid pattern, so it's not easy to get lost.

Bike – Stratford and its surrounding countryside are ideally suited to exploration by bike. *Knotts Cycles,* 15 Western Rd. (phone: 205149) rents bicycles. Along with renting bikes, *Pashley's,* Henley St. (phone: 297044), also provides guides and suggests routes.

Boat – Short trips for an hour or so or a holiday lasting several weeks are both possible on the Avon and the historic, early-19th-century Stratford Canal. Rowing boats, punts (propelled by poles), and canoes can be rented at *Rose's Boathouse,* Swan's West La. (phone: 67073). *Stratford-upon-Avon Marine Ltd.,* Clopton Bridge (phone: 69669), and *Western Cruisers Ltd.,* Western Rd. (phone: 69636), rent larger craft, including gaily decorated river barges.

Bus – *Midland Red (South) Ltd.,* Warwick Rd. (phone: 204181) serves Stratford and the surrounding villages. The bus departure point is on Bridge St. near Clopton Bridge.

Car Rental – Two local firms are *Arden Motors,* Arden St. (phone: 67446), and *Foster Motors,* Western Rd. (phone: 68913). *Guide Friday Ltd.,* Civic Hall, Market Place, 14 Rother St. (phone: 294466), will arrange rentals through the major national and international companies. The nearest *Hertz* and *Avis* locations are in Coventry.

Taxi – Taxis are relatively expensive, and can't be flagged down on the street. Go to the cab stand at the intersection of Rother and Wood sts. (the Market Place) or at Bridgefoot by the *Pen and Parchment* pub. Phone *Guide Friday* at 294466 or call 69999. Your hotel can also get you a taxi.

Tours – *Guide Friday,* Civic Hall, Market Place, 14 Rother St. (phone: 294466), runs tours via open-air, double-decker buses to the Shakespearean sites outside of town, saving a 13-mile walk. Buses depart during the summer every 30 minutes. Tours to Warwick Castle, the town of Warwick, and Charlecote Park leave every hour. Tours of the surrounding countryside, including the Cotswolds and Blenheim Palace, are also available.

 SHOPPING: Look for quality handicrafts — including pottery, stained glass, and carved woods — as well as English sheepskins, leather clothing, and china. Sheep Street has several elegant antique shops and an arcade with a dozen or so antique dealers' booths.

Campbell's Croft – Knitting, embroidery, and crafts materials, including the shop's own needlepoint canvas of Anne Hathaway's Cottage. 31 Henley St. (phone: 204428).

Peter Dingley – Good quality British-made crafts, including pottery and carved wood. 8 Chapel St. (phone: 205001).

Edinburgh Woollen Mill – A wide range of Scottish woolens and tweeds, usually at very reasonable prices. Bridge St. (phone: 205949).

Lamberts of Stratford – Comprehensive selection of English chinas and crystal. 1 Henley St. (phone: 293174).

Minories – It's a group of craft shops off Meer Street; be sure to stop in at *Purely Lace,* which specializes in English lace.

Sentre Arts – Another shop where everything is handmade. The stained glass is unusual and attractive. Centre Craft Yard, off Henley St. (phone: 68731).

Shakespeare Centre Bookshop – Specializes in Shakespearean books and other publications and sells gifts and souvenirs. Henley St. (phone: 204016).

Sheepskin Shop – Leather jackets, coats, children's toys, and other items. 33 Sheep St. (phone: 293810).

Staks China Centre – Glassware and china; some bargain seconds. 22 Henley St. (phone: 68758).

Tappit Hen – Broad range of English pewter. 57 Henley St. (phone: 69933).

Tradition of Wales – Welsh pottery, carvings, and woolen goods. 22 Henley St. (phone: 68758).

 SPECIAL EVENTS: Every spring, usually on the Saturday nearest April 23, Stratford and the world unite to honor Shakespeare. A procession that includes ambassadors from many countries walks from his Birthplace to Holy Trinity Church to lay floral tributes on his grave. Flags of the nations are unfurled in the center of town and there is a special performance at the Royal Shakespeare Theatre. The Boat Club holds its Regatta in June (heralded by a popular raft race), and a cultural festival featuring music, plays, and poetry readings, takes place during the last two weeks in July (for details contact the festival office at Civic Hall, Market Place, 14 Rother St.; phone: 67969). In October (usually on the 12th) there's the Mop Fair, when stalls, sideshows, and amusements take over the town center.

 SPORTS: Stratford has facilities for many kinds of sports; ask at the information center for a complete list.

Fishing – Go to 37 Greenhill St. for daily and season fishing tickets; you can get the necessary Fishery Board license there also.

Golf – Visitors pay greens fees to play on the 18-hole courses at the Stratford-upon-Avon Golf Club, Tiddington Rd. (phone: 205677), and the Welcombe Hotel, Warwick Rd. (phone: 295252).

Swimming – The District Council's modern pool at Bridgeway (which also has squash courts, sauna, and solarium) is open daily; there is a small admission charge (phone: 68826).

 THEATER: In addition to the main Royal Shakespeare Theatre along the river, the Royal Shakespeare Company runs another, smaller theater, The Other Place, on Southern Lane where it performs plays by Shakespeare and others, including modern playwrights. The season starts in late March. Information from the Royal Shakespeare Theatre (phone: 295623) or from The Other Place, Southern Lane, Stratford-upon-Avon CV37 6BB. The Heritage Theatre, Waterside (phone: 69190), is the home of "The World of Shakespeare," an entertainment of sound, music, and tableaux, with continuous performances daily. The new Swan Theatre, built within the shell of the old Memorial Theatre at the back of the Royal Shakespeare Theatre, features the works of Shakespeare's contemporaries, and the season lasts from April through January.

 MUSIC: Stratford's tradition is drama rather than music, but the town plays host to orchestras, bands, and soloists throughout the year. In July, in conjunction with the Stratford Festival, the Royal Shakespeare Theatre presents occasional concerts.

 NIGHTCLUBS AND NIGHTLIFE: Evenings are fairly quiet in Stratford; pubs close at 11 PM. The Toll House restaurant, Alcester Rd. (phone: 297812), has a disco on weekends that's popular with young people and stays open until the early hours. Christophi's, 21 Sheep St. (phone: 293546), is a Greek restaurant featuring a trio and belly dancer on Saturday nights. Along with Chinese food, *As You Like It,* 4/5 Henley St. (phone: 293022), has a large bar and dancing nightly.

 SINS: There is scope for indulging in a bit of *gluttony* in Stratford, which boasts a fine array of tea and cake shops. The well-stocked window of the *Cobweb,* 12 Sheep St. (phone: 292554), is a nearly irresistible display of breads, cakes, pies, and pastries. The *Welcombe* hotel, just outside town on Warwick Rd. (phone: 295252), is famous for its Saturday and Sunday afternoon cream teas, replete with hot scones, pancakes, and other goodies. And don't miss a visit to *Thornton's,* 15 Bridge St. (phone: 295251), famous for its handmade chocolates and toffee, or to *Sweet Indulgences,* Meer St., which also has a tempting array of sugary delights.

BEST IN TOWN

 CHECKING IN: If you intend staying in a modest bed-and-breakfast, there is no need to make reservations in advance; many of these worthy British establishments line the main roads leading into town. You should book ahead for a good hotel, however, especially at the height of the season, June to September. The Tourist Information Centre, 1 High St. (phone: 293127), supplies copies of the official *Accommodation Register* and can help you find somewhere to stay. For a small fee, *Guide Friday,* Civic Hall, Market Place, 14 Rother St. (phone: 294466), will also help you book a room.

A B&B offers a comfortable room (no private bath) and a good breakfast for about $13 to $16 per person a night. For the same thing in an inexpensive hotel, you will pay about $20 to $30 per person per night. Moderately priced hotels — which may not have private bathrooms with all rooms but will at least have hot and cold water in all rooms — run about $30 to $50 per person per night. And expect to pay from $50 to $85 per person in the large, expensive hotels. Smaller hotels may not accept credit cards, while the larger ones usually will.

Alveston Manor – Reputedly the setting for the first production of *A Midsummer Night's Dream,* this modernized Elizabethan manor with oak paneling and leaded windows is set on spacious grounds across the Avon from the theater and the center of town. There are 108 rooms, all with private bath, and a 9-hole golf course. Clopton Bridge (phone: 204581). Expensive.

Ettington Park – This newly converted Victorian Gothic building is considered *the* place to stay in Stratford — and retains many features redolent of 18th- and 19th-century gracious living. The 49 luxurious rooms and suites overlook the 40-acre Ettington Estate. Fresh herbs and salads from the garden are served at the imposing restaurant, and leisure activities include riding, tennis, and fishing, and swimming in the indoor pool. Alderminster, five miles from Stratford (phone: 0789-740740). Expensive.

Moat House International – Behind the somewhat pedestrian façade lie all the comforts and services expected of a major hotel chain. Color TV, individual climate control, and a mini-bar are in all 250 rooms; guests are permitted free use of an adjacent leisure center. It's a short walk to the Royal Shakespeare Theatre. Bridgefoot (phone: 67511). Expensive.

Shakespeare – A Stratford landmark, this gabled, timber-fronted 16th-century building is the place to stay if you want a taste of Elizabethan England. David Garrick stayed here in 1769, and since then most of its rooms have been named after Shakespeare's plays: You could find yourself sleeping in the *Midsummer Night's Dream* room and eating in the *As You Like It* restaurant. The 66-room hotel has been carefully modernized so that the authentic atmosphere endures. Chapel St. (phone: 294771). Expensive.

Welcombe – This elegant, 81-room hotel set in extensive parkland on the outskirts of Stratford was once a private mansion and retains the atmosphere of an English country house. The menu in its paneled restaurant is classic French. The park has room for an 18-hole golf course plus a heli-pad with connections to nearby Birmingham airport, and also offers coarse fishing and croquet; the hotel's garage has car-servicing facilities and gas. Warwick Rd., 1¼ miles from town center (phone: 295252). Expensive.

White Swan – One of the oldest inns in town, it dates back to the 15th century — beautifully evident from its medieval, gabled façade to the sturdy wood beams within. All 35 rooms have private bath. Rother St. (phone: 297022). Expensive to moderate.

Falcon – One of those stunning, half-timbered buildings that make Stratford so picturesque, the 73-room Falcon overlooks the gardens of New Place, Shakespeare's house. Inside, it is less elegant than the Shakespeare hotel, and all but 20 of the rooms are in the modern extension, but it has a charm of its own. Chapel St. (phone: 205777). Moderate.

Sequoia House – Situated across the river, opposite the Theatre, this 13-room Victorian hotel is only a five-minute stroll along the tramway from the town center. 51 Shipston Rd. (phone: 68852). Moderate.

Stratford House – Once a private Georgian home, this charming 9-room hotel has been recently modernized in delightful style, including the incorporation of the Shepherd's Garden restaurant. Sheep St. (phone: 68288). Moderate.

Grosvenor House – On the main Warwick Road, it's actually several large houses imaginatively linked into one big, comfortable hotel. Included are a sauna, fitness center, spa baths, and a beauty salon. Close to the center of town; restaurant and parking. 12 Warwick Rd. (phone: 69213). Moderate to inexpensive.

Coach House – On a main road out of town, this is a rambling hotel on several floors. Twelve bedrooms, pleasant dining room, and a friendly atmosphere. 17 Warwick Rd. (phone: 299468/204109). Inexpensive.

Glenavon Private – Just up the road from Holy Trinity Church and Hall's Croft, this is a congenial, family-style hotel in a quiet part of town. 6 Chestnut Walk (phone: 292588). Inexpensive.

Hardwick House – A cozy, family-run Victorian house in a quiet area, only a few minutes' walk from the town center and Shakespearean attractions. 1 Avenue Rd. (phone: 204307). Inexpensive.

Haytor – A smallish, family-run hotel with a quiet, friendly atmosphere and lovely private gardens. 18 rooms, almost all with bath. On the edge of town, a 10-minute walk from the center. Avenue Rd. (phone: 297799). Inexpensive.

Payton – Another well-maintained little hotel with a homelike atmosphere, it, too, is in a quiet part of town, though only a short walk from the back gate of Shakespeare's Birthplace. 6 John St. (phone: 66442). Inexpensive.

Salamander – Overlooking a small park about 10 minutes from the center of town, this Victorian guesthouse is pleasant and well run. 40 Grove Rd. (phone: 205728). Inexpensive.

 EATING OUT: With the help of a range of fast-food and snack restaurants, Stratford manages to feed its hundreds of thousands of visitors pretty well. Those arriving just for the day find that the coffee houses and tearooms are generally good, and many of them stay open long enough to provide an evening meal. Pizzas, hamburgers, and the glass-of-wine-with-food places have all found their way into town, and the sausage-egg-and-chip cafés offer good value for the money. At midday, there is the ploughman's lunch (bread, cheese, and pickle) to be sampled with a pint of beer in one of Stratford's typical pubs, many of which also offer an array of hot and cold food at the bar.

Those staying overnight can expect the full British breakfast — fruit juice, cereal, sausage, bacon and eggs, toast, and tea or coffee — in the morning, though a lighter Continental breakfast — usually fruit juice, croissants or toast, and coffee — is also available. Evening meals range from a standard "meat and three vegetables" to international cuisine. Prices for a three-course meal for two, without drinks but including VAT and service charge, work out at about $35 to $42 in the expensive category; $23 to $32 in the moderate category; and under $18 in the inexpensive category.

Da Giovanni – A discreetly curtained front and restrained gold lettering hide a plush restaurant very much in the Italian grand manner, complete with leather sofas and chairs, flocked wallpaper, and bronze statues. Delicious Italian cooking. Closed Sundays. 8 Ely St. (phone: 297999). Expensive.

Moat House International – The Warwick Grill was conceived on a luxury scale and has an impressive central buffet. Check the menu for re-creations of authentic Elizabethan dishes. Open daily. Bridgefoot (phone: 67511). Expensive.

Marlowe's – Approached down a narrow alley off the High Street, Marlowe's is in a house that dates back to Shakespeare's time. Once an inn, it's now a restaurant with a distinguished air, where oak paneling and wood fires in winter add to the atmosphere. The food is standard international cuisine, the wine list is good, and at its bar, *The Loose Box Tavern,* a meal can be had for about $5. Open daily. 18 High St. (phone: 20499). Expensive to moderate.

Arden – The restaurant here draws theatergoers (the Royal Shakespeare is just across the road), and both restaurant and bar are good places to celebrity-spot. The food is simple, based on the best available fresh ingredients. Open daily. 44 Waterside (phone: 294949). Moderate.

Christophi's – White stucco and blue awnings give this Greek restaurant an attractive air. For those whose tastes do not run to *taramasalata* or *moussaka,* there are more conventional grills, too. Dancing every evening, and a cabaret on Fridays and Saturdays. Open evenings only; closed Sundays. 21 Sheep St. (phone: 293546). Moderate.

Opposition – A bistro-style restaurant that has won a following for its imaginative and regularly changing menu. Closed on Sundays and Mondays for lunch. 13 Sheep St. (phone: 69980). Moderate.

Sorrento – Set in a beautiful, historic building, this Italian restaurant offers classical cuisine in an intimate atmosphere. 13–14 Meer St. (phone: 69304). Moderate.

Box Tree and River Terrace – Both are in the Royal Shakespeare Theatre building and are open to nonplaygoers — if you can't get tickets, at least you can say you've been there. The Box Tree is open for lunch on matinee days and Sundays, and every evening before and after performances except Sundays; the River Terrace, on the ground floor with a view of the river, is open from midmorning for snacks and light meals. Waterside (phone: 293226). Moderate to inexpensive.

Horseshoe Buttery – A favorite of locals — the best recommendation it could garner — the fare is good old-fashioned English, like steak and kidney pie, chops, and grills, all presented in a Tudoresque setting of wooden beams and brocaded furniture. Two B&B rooms available. 33-34 Greenhill St. (phone: 292246). Moderate to inexpensive.

Boat House – Set above Rose's Boathouse, this attractive wine bar and restaurant has splendid views of the river and theater gardens and offers a limited menu of entrées and salads. Open daily; the bar stays open late. Swan's Nest La., Bridgefoot (phone: 297733). Inexpensive.

Casa Bonita – Partly a shop that sells an interesting variety of gifts, this is also a small café that serves tasty sandwiches and other light snacks. In summer months there's outdoor dining on the patio. 59-60 Henley St. (phone: 205880). Inexpensive.

Centre Coffee House – A spotless coffee shop where the salads are fresh and the pâté homemade. Opposite Shakespeare's Birthplace. Open daily (except Mondays in winter). Henley St. (phone: 297490). Inexpensive.

Cobweb – Above a cake and confectionary shop, in a building so old that both the floors and the beamed ceilings have distinct slopes, this charming restaurant offers omelets, grills, and salads, as well as a typically English afternoon tea. Open daily. 12 Sheep St. (phone: 292554). Inexpensive.

Hills – Emulating a mini-theater, the tables are arranged in a pit and a balcony and, since it is open very late, this restaurant is popular with a post-theater crowd. The imaginative menu is prepared with all fresh produce. Closed Sundays. 3 Greenhill St. (phone: 293563). Inexpensive.

Old Tudor House – Your basic English sausage, eggs, and chips with everything, but nicely prepared and presented. A good family place — they will even provide a highchair for the baby. Open daily. High and Ely sts. (phone: 297140). Inexpensive.

SHARING A PINT: Among Stratford's array of pubs, two are particularly worth raising an elbow in. The *Garrick Inn,* next to Harvard House on High St., dates back to late Elizabethan times, but its ambience is delightfully Dickensian, with several small bars (phone: 292186). The *Black Swan* (commonly known as the *Dirty Duck)* is Stratford's theatrical pub, where actors and actresses come for their post-show pints and the atmosphere can become charged with the euphoria engendered by a good performance. Waterside (phone: 297312). *The Windmill*, on Church St., is one of Stratford's oldest pubs and serves good food and real ale. For something trendy, try the *Slug and Lettuce* (also a bistro), 38 Guild St. (phone: 299700).

WATERFORD

Waterford is a gentle city of Georgian doorways and back streets with names like Lady Lane. It stretches for a bit more than half a mile along the southern bank of the River Suir, well up a long inlet from the sea, and during the seventeenth century its harbor was one of the busiest in the country. Meat, fish, and corn were exported to the Continent and wine came back. Ships bound for America were provisioned here. Today, one of the principal exports from its still-busy quays is beef, though Waterford crystal is the most famous.

The old Waterford Glass Factory was founded in 1783, at a time when the city — originally a Viking settlement — was undergoing a burst of development and beginning to outgrow its medieval dimensions. Graceful Georgian homes belonging to the merchant class began to appear along The Mall, and John Roberts, an architect responsible for many of the city's elegant structures, was at work designing the public buildings and churches that are among the city's most prominent landmarks — City Hall and the Catholic and Protestant cathedrals are all his. The latter, which was erected between 1773 and 1779 on the site of a much earlier church, is a stately testimony to Waterford's rich Protestant families, some of whom were carried up the slight incline into Cathedral Square in sedan chairs.

Waterford's most famous landmark, however, is a remnant of Viking times. Sitric the Dane is credited with fortifying the site of the city in the ninth century, and Reginald the Dane, who was a descendant of Sitric, is believed to have strengthened the fortifications by erecting (in 1003) what has since become known as Reginald's Tower. Along with the city walls and two other towers, Reginald's Tower protected the city from invasion first by the Celts and later, when the Norsemen and Celts put aside their differences to join forces against a common enemy, from invasion by the Normans. You can still see part of the old city wall inside the Reginald Lounge, adjacent to the tower.

The Normans finally did take Waterford in 1170, in the person of Richard de Clare, an emissary of Henry II of England. De Clare was better known as Strongbow, for the sureness of his weapons and tactics, and his victory over the city's defenders was both an easy and far-reaching one. The capture of Waterford was the beginning of the Anglo-Norman domination of Ireland. Strongbow's marriage shortly thereafter to Eva, the daughter of Dermot MacMurrough, the Irish king of Leinster, consolidated the position of the conquering Normans. This fateful event, too, took place in Waterford, reputedly in Reginald's Tower (though the original Viking cathedral, predecessor of Christ Church Cathedral, may have been the actual site).

King John granted the city its first charter in 1205 (his sword and several of the city's subsequent charters are in the Reginald's Tower museum), and for several centuries to come, Waterford would be intensely loyal to the English crown. Henry VII gave it its motto, "Unconquered City," in the fifteenth century, in gratitude for its successful efforts in fighting off attacks by two pretenders to his throne. But loyalty to the English king in temporal matters did not extend to recognition of the crown's supremacy in religious matters. The city remained Catholic in the sixteenth century, and because of this, its charter was eventually withdrawn and its Catholic citizens suffered much in the Cromwellian sieges of the mid-seventeenth century. Their churches were closed and confiscated and many were sent as slaves to the West Indies.

Several abbeys flourished in Waterford. The ruins of the once-extensive thirteenth-century Dominican Friary can be seen. Another large abbey, the Holy Ghost Friary of the Franciscans, or, as it is known locally, the French Church, was built a little later in the same century and is also now in ruins. Both were suppressed by Henry VIII's Dissolution of the Monasteries, the Franciscan friary to become a hospital and then a home to a colony of French Huguenot refugees.

Most visitors come to Waterford to tour the glass factory and concentrate on the gift shops around the quays. But there are revealing detours from the beaten path. You can walk out to Ballybricken Green, one of the oldest sections.

When the Normans controlled Waterford proper, this is where the Irish lived, outside the Patrick Street gate of the city walls. And the side streets and back lanes of this city of 50,000 people are worth discovering for their quaint houses, historic churches, and unexpected finds such as the ancient carvings on the friary wall in Lady Lane. Not much of the great abbeys may remain, but in these narrow passageways, Waterford's medieval atmosphere seems trapped forever like snow in a glass paperweight.

WATERFORD AT-A-GLANCE

SEEING THE CITY: Ignatius Rice Bridge (formerly Redmond Bridge) spans the River Suir at the western end of the city. It can be a quiet spot from which to view the town, looking not unlike an 18th-century New England coastal village with its large buildings and many church spires. From its hilltop location across the river, the *Ardree* hotel also offers a panoramic view of Waterford.

SPECIAL PLACES: With the exception of the Waterford Glass Factory, about 1.5 miles from the center, most of the city's major points of interest are conveniently located in a central area between Ignatius Rice Bridge and Reginald's Tower, either along the quays or just a few blocks off them. Go to the glass factory by car, taxi, or bus; then see the rest of the sights on a walking tour to be taken at your own speed. You'll come across most of the city's shops, restaurants, pubs, and hotels in the same vicinity.

Waterford Glass Factory – It is said 3,000 people a week visit the Waterford Glass Factory to watch Ireland's most famous crystal being mixed, blown, and cut by hand from the raw ingredients of silica sand, potash, and red lead. Not only are the guided tours free, they are also interesting and enjoyable. The original plant opened in 1783 and continued in operation until 1851, when English law imposed heavy duties on the exported glass and made it an unprofitable operation. With the help of the Irish government, Waterford reopened on a small scale in 1947, and has since outgrown its buildings several times. The company now employs 2,700 people who cannot keep up with orders for their product, which is exported all over the world (the US is the biggest market). A Waterford chandelier hangs in Independence Hall in Philadelphia and 16 of them are in Westminster Abbey. The factory is closed on weekends and is usually closed for holidays during the first 3 weeks of August. Tours are given Mondays through Fridays at 10:15, 11, and 11:45 AM, and at 1:45 and 2:30 PM. You can check on the times and reserve in advance — highly advisable in summer — by calling 73311, or you can make arrangements through the tourist office. Showrooms are open Mondays through Saturdays, 9 AM to 5 PM. No crystal is sold at the factory. About 1.5 miles from the center of Waterford on Cork Rd.

St. Saviour's Dominican Church – This handsome church was built in 1874. The solemn interior features Corinthian columns and lovely frescoes over the altar. Corner of Bridge and O'Connell sts.

Chamber of Commerce – Architect John Roberts designed this aristocratic building of 1795 as a home for the Morris family, which was prominent in the shipping trade. It was purchased by the Chamber of Commerce in 1815. A large fanlight graces the entrance, and it is worth a look inside to see the beautiful plasterwork and splendid oval staircase. Open weekdays. Georges St.

Clock Tower – 19th-century sea captains relied on this landmark along the quays to keep their ships on schedule. It once had troughs of water at its base from which horses could drink and was thus known as the Fountain Clock. Built in 1861, the original clock was replaced in 1954. The Quay.

Cathedral of the Most Holy Trinity – After the confiscation of their churches in the mid-17th century, the Catholics of Waterford did not receive permission from the city's Protestant-controlled government to build another until 1792. Architect John Roberts designed it for them and it was completed in 1796. The cathedral has a beautifully carved oak pulpit. Barronstrand St.

Lady Lane – This little passage has been described as the best surviving example of a medieval street in Waterford. It is a charming lane with Georgian doorways on one side and two old stone carvings (one dated 1613) visible on the wall of the Franciscan Friary on the other side. Off upper Barronstrand St. (Broad St.).

Christ Church Cathedral – John Roberts also designed this Protestant church, which was completed in 1779 on the site of an earlier church erected by the Norsemen in 1050. The Norsemen had made Waterford a diocese of its own, and the old church grew in size and property through several centuries until Henry VIII's Dissolution of the Monasteries. Later, Cromwellian troops occupied the original church for a time. The present cathedral incorporates some monuments from the old church and a number of interesting tombs. Cathedral Sq.

French Church – Founded as a Franciscan abbey in 1240, this once included six chambers, a kitchen with four cellars, and stables, in addition to the church whose ruined nave, choir, and Lady Chapel still remain. After it was dissolved by Henry VIII, the former friary saw use as a hospital, a burial place for some of Waterford's prominent families, and as a parish church for French Huguenot refugees. Architect Roberts is among those buried here. You can visit the church by obtaining the key from the house across the road; a notice on the door gives the address. Bailey's New St.

Reginald's Tower – This 70-foot stone tower on the quays was built for defense purposes by Reginald the Dane in 1003. It was captured by Strongbow in 1170, and has had use as a mint, a military storehouse, and an air-raid shelter. It now houses a historical and maritime museum, which can be visited for a nominal fee. Open Mondays through Fridays from 10 AM to 12:30 PM and from 2 to 5 PM; and Saturdays, 10:30 AM to 12:30 PM, from April through September; closed in winter. Corner of The Quay and The Mall.

Father Luke Wadding and The Mall – This statue just across the street from

Reginald's Tower commemorates the birth in 1588 of one of Waterford's most distinguished sons. The Franciscan scholar was famous as a linguist and author of the annals of his order, and although he spent most of his life in Rome, he helped his Catholic countrymen both morally and financially in their attempts to establish their own constitution and government. The *Tower Hotel* on the left is on the site of the old bowling green. City Hall, completed in 1788 for the merchants of Waterford, now houses a museum (see *Museums*) and the Theatre Royal as well as administrative offices. Behind City Hall is the Bishop's Palace, designed in 1741 by Richard Castle, who also did Powerscourt, Westport House, and the Irish Parliament and the Rotunda Hospital in Dublin. It is now used by the city engineering staff.

■ **EXTRA SPECIAL:** *The Waterford International Festival of Light Opera* has been taking place every September for over 20 years. For 2 weeks, amateur companies from England, Wales, Scotland, Northern Ireland, and the Republic compete to give the best performance of an operetta or musical, and for 2 weeks visitors to Waterford have a chance to see and hear again such popular productions as *The Merry Widow, Oliver, South Pacific,* or the like. Fringe events include a ball, band concerts, bridge tournaments, sports competitions, and singing competitions in the pubs which, as is usual during a festival in Ireland, are open until late. Tickets are reasonably priced and can be obtained along with specific information on programs and dates by writing Billy Burke, Secretary of the Waterford Festival, New St., Waterford (phone: 74321).

SOURCES AND RESOURCES

TOURIST INFORMATION: The Tourist Information Office at 41 The Quay (phone: 75788) is open year-round. Hours from May through September are usually from 9 AM to 6 PM, Mondays through Saturdays; in winter it closes at 5:15 PM weekdays and 1 PM on Saturdays. One of the most helpful of the number of pamphlets and guides for sale is Patrick Mackey's *Selected Walks Through Old Waterford,* a handsomely illustrated paperback (IR£1), containing much information and history written in a style that is interesting and easy to follow. The tourist office also provides a free 12-page newspaper, *South East Tourist News.* The Tourist Information Office in nearby Tramore, the large seaside resort about 8 miles southwest of Waterford, is open during July and August in Railway Sq. (phone: 81572). The office puts out *All About Tramore,* an excellent guide to sports, entertainment, and restaurants in the area.

Local Coverage – The *Munster Express* published Thursdays and Fridays and the *Waterford News and Star* published every Thursday give specific information on entertainment and special events in the city and vicinity.

GETTING AROUND: Waterford can be a busy turnstile for traffic. Both the Dublin-Cork and Wexford-Tipperary roads pass through here, but much of the traffic avoids the narrow streets of the old city, traveling instead along the quays and then out along The Mall. The city is easily explored on foot, and for a change of pace, you can hop aboard one of the afternoon cruises of the River Suir and take your tea en route. (Cruises run from April through October; contact the tourist office for details.)

Bus and Train – Local buses leave from Plunkett Station, as do trains for Dublin, Limerick, and Rosslare Harbour (and intervening points); the station (phone: 73401) is located near Edmund Ignatius Rice Bridge on the north side of the River Suir. You can take a taxi into the city center for about $3, although it is a short walk if you are not burdened by luggage.

Car Rental – There are a number of car rental agencies in Waterford including *Boland's Car Hire,* Kilkenny Rd. (phone: 76558); and *Budget Rent a Car,* 41 The Quay (phone: 21556).

Ferry – Save an hour's driving time to Wexford by taking the lovely 10-minute-long car ferry from Passage East, south of Waterford. Fare per car is IR£3.50 round trip, or IR£2 one way; no reservations necessary (phone: 74730).

Taxi – Cabs wait at Plunkett Station and opposite the *Granville Hotel.* The tourist office will call a taxi for you, or you can call one yourself (phone: 75222). The minimum fare is about $3, with travel outside the city limits costing about 50¢ a mile.

Tours – Bus tours of Waterford and the surrounding area are operated by CIE from Plunkett Station during June, July, and August (phone: 73401).

 MUSEUMS: Besides Reginald's Tower (described in *Special Places*), the City Hall contains several items worthy of inspection. During normal business hours, you can visit the Council Chamber of this spacious building to view its beautiful glass chandelier, made at the original Waterford factory, a replica of which hangs in Philadelphia's Independence Hall. There is also a complete dinner service of old Waterford glass, and a flag from the Irish Brigade that fought on the Union side in the American Civil War. The Mall.

 SHOPPING: While Waterford is known for its crystal products, the city is also a source for a wide range of Irish-made gifts and souvenirs. You'll find most of the best shops along The Quay and on the long street that begins at Barronstrand. Smaller shops close on Thursdays and some shops stay open late on Friday evenings. Among the notable ones are:

Artwear Galleries – This gem of a shop features paintings and prints plus Irish-made jewelry, linens, and knits. 120 The Quay.

Book Centre – Large, and with a good selection of works by Irish authors. 9 Michael St.

George's Court Shopping Arcade – An attractive, skylit assemblage of late-model boutiques, food shops, and cookery and decor stores encircling a central café. Off George's St.

Handcrafts – Small shop specializing in made-to-order Aran knit sweaters; watch the work through the front window. 16 Michael St.

Hennebry Camera – All the basics and accessories plus kindly proprietors who will try to help when your shutter won't or the flash doesn't. 109 The Quay.

Joann's – A good place to buy brass, silver, crystal, and china. 30 Michael St.

Joseph Knox – This lovely store behind a Victorian shopfront is a major distributor of Waterford crystal and English bone china, and it's often crowded. If you do more than browse — there are many handsome pieces of porcelain and cut glass on display — you can arrange for your booty to be mailed. 3 and 4 Barronstrand St.

Kelly's – At this two-level department store you'll find crystal, china, linens, tweeds, silver, copper, coats of arms, and souvenir items from shillelaghs to shamrock seeds. 76 The Quay.

Midget, Ltd. – Stocked with stacks of appealing handcrafted baskets, crocks, stoneware, Kilkenny pottery, homespuns, and such. 85 The Quay.

Penrose – Although revived only in 1978, this locally made glassware dates back to 1786 and is well worth a look. Visitors are welcome to watch the craftsmen as they hand cut the floral motifs into the glass. John St.

Quay Antiques – A treasure trove of collectibles, posters, brass, etc. Near Reginald's Tower at 128 The Quay.

Shaw & Sons – A homey department store. It sells a broad range of goods, from Aran sweaters to silver. 53 The Quay.

Waterford Craft Centre – Prints of old Waterford, etched brass, heraldic crests, and ceramic jewelry are among this shop's wares. 28 Michael St.

Woolcraft – Established in 1887, specializing in Aran knit, mohair, Icelandic, and lamb's wool sweaters. Also tapestry jackets, gloves, tams, and scarves. 11 Michael St.

 SPECIAL EVENTS: The city's *International Festival of Light Opera,* which occurs every September, provides the excuse for a host of fringe events. (For details, see *Extra Special.*)

 SPORTS: Waterford has a variety of sports facilities both within and just outside the city, and the seaside resort of Tramore has a 50-acre amusement complex. During the summer, buses to Tramore leave on the half-hour from The Quay. You can check *All About Tramore* for information on the sports and entertainment activities going on there.

Golf – The 18-hole course of the *Waterford Golf Club* (phone: 74182) is open to the public. It's located in a scenic setting about 1.5 miles outside the city. Visitors are also welcome at the 18-hole course of the *Tramore Golf Club* (phone: 81247), a mile from Tramore.

Greyhound Racing – The dogs race at *Kilcohan Park* on Tuesdays and Saturdays in June, and daily for a week in August. For specific information, call the *Waterford Greyhound Track* (phone: 74531).

Horseback Riding – You can hire horses at *Melody's Riding Stables,* Ballmacarberry, near Clonmel, about 15 miles northwest of Waterford (phone: 052-36147); *Kilotteran Equitation Centre,* Kilotteran, about 3 miles southwest of Waterford (phone: 84158); and *Ballyglan Riding Centre,* Woodstown, about 5 miles southeast of Waterford (phone: 82133).

Polo – Europe's only residential polo vacation school is at *Whitfield Court* (phone: 84216) in Waterford, with 2 polo grounds, wooden horses, an enclosed riding school, video equipment, 20 polo ponies, a heated swimming pool, and a tennis court among its many facilities. One week sessions are offered from late April to mid-September; advance reservations are essential. For information, write to Major Hugh Dawny, Whitfield Court, Waterford.

Sailing – Details are available from the *Waterford Sailing Club* in Dunmore East, 9 miles southeast of the city (phone: 83230).

Squash – There are two courts at *Henry Downe's Pub,* 10 Thomas St. (phone: 74118). Other facilities are at the *Celtic Squash Club,* 71 Barrack St. (phone: 76541).

Swimming – The *Waterford Glass Swimming Pool* on the Cork Road is open to the public. You must arrive on the hour, and you may swim for a 45-minute session for a small fee. Hours vary, so it's probably a good idea to check in advance by calling the Pool Manager, Waterford Glass Ltd. (phone: 73311, ext. 266). Tramore has a 3-mile beach, with lifeguards on duty during the summer. Surfboards and deck chairs can be rented at the beach.

Tennis – *St. Anne's Lawn Tennis Club* on St. John's Hill has both grass and hard courts (phone: 74350).

 THEATER: Special productions take place during the summer at the *Theatre Royal,* housed in part of City Hall on The Mall (phone: 74402).

MUSIC: The high point of Waterford's musical season is the 2-week *International Festival of Light Opera* in the fall. In addition to the light opera on the program, there is also a singing pubs competition. (See *Extra Special.*) For traditional and folk music sessions, try *T. & H. Doolan's* pub on George's St.; you can hear traditional Irish music at any number of pubs; and there is jazz every Sunday at *Reginald's* on The Mall.

 NIGHTCLUBS AND NIGHTLIFE: There are often Saturday night dinner dances at the *Granville* hotel (phone: 55111) as well as frequent disco dances at the *Tower* hotel (phone: 75801), the *Ardree* (phone: 32111), and *Xanadu* in the *Bridge* hotel (phone: 77222). The *Stonecourt* (phone: 55089) — once a restaurant — now features an ever-changing agenda of cabaret, dancing, ballad, folk, and disco music Tuesdays through Sundays. Some pubs feature special appearances by singing groups, both popular and traditional. The best way to keep abreast of all evening festivities is to consult the tourist office and the local papers.

 SINS: Indulge yourself at the *Coffee and Cake Shop,* 47 Patrick St., where all the buttery cookies and pastries tempting you from behind the glass case are made on the premises.

BEST IN TOWN

 CHECKING IN: Waterford's hotels are convenient to the city center, and they offer the visitor a nice choice between the modern and the old. There are also a number of bed-and-breakfast houses in the area. If you wish to stay in this type of accommodation, the tourist office will help you find a vacancy in a house that meets their approval. Expect to pay from $70 to $80 for a double room in an expensive hotel, from $40 to $60 in a moderate one, and under $40 for inexpensive lodgings.

Ardree – In this modern hotel on a hill on the northern side of the River Suir, all 100 rooms have views that are especially striking at night when the lights of Waterford are twinkling. Amenities include private baths, air conditioning and central heating, a fine restaurant with panoramic city views, golf on an adjoining 18-hole course, and 38 acres of gardens. Ferrybank (phone: 32111). Expensive.

Bridge – This modern, 40-room (all with private bath/shower) hotel retains an Old World atmosphere, particularly in the *Timber Toes* lounge and the *Ignatius Rice* restaurant. 1 The Quay (phone: 77222). Expensive.

Granville – This Georgian mansion is probably Waterford's classiest hotel. It was once the home of Irish patriot Thomas Meagher. These days the hotel exudes an air of graciousness and respectability, with 55 rooms, recently and appealingly redone, and a fine looking paneled lounge bar, restaurant, and grill on the premises. The Quay (phone: 55111). Expensive.

Tower – Centrally located on The Mall near Reginald's Tower, this 100-room hotel has been tastefully refurbished, with an emphasis on brickwork, mirrors, and flowering plants in the public areas, and eclectic furnishings in the bedrooms. Waterford crystal chandeliers hang in the pink-toned dining room, known for such dishes as local river trout. The Mall (phone: 75801). Expensive.

Dooley's – This family-run hotel, formerly a coaching inn, was recently refurbished to offer 36 rooms, all with private baths. The restaurant is known for its special value tourist menus and a nice variety of bar food; a good place to meet the locals. The Quay (phone: 73531). Moderate.

Blenheim House – Located about three miles southeast of Waterford, overlooking the city and the River Suir, this gracious home was built in 1763. The current owners have restored it fully and have furnished it with their own antiques and dazzling collection of Waterford crystal. Each of the six guest bedrooms has its own private bath. Blenheim Heights, off the Passage East Rd. (phone: 74115). Inexpensive.

 EATING OUT: Waterford does not have a large selection of restaurants in town, but with the inclusion of a few hotel dining rooms, there are enough recommendable ones to keep visitors well fed. For anyone in a hurry or homesick for the US, there is *Chapman's Delicatessen* on the quays. Most pubs serve a lunch of soup and sandwiches or a special costing between $3 and $5. Dinner for two (wine not included) will cost under $20 in an inexpensive restaurant, between $20 and $45 in a moderate place, and $50 or more in an expensive one.

Granville – The cheerfully elegant Sword Room, handsomest in-town place for lunch or dinner, offers à la carte and table d'hôte choices, nicely priced chef's specials and "mini dinners" (three courses plus beverage), plus a candlelight dinner dance Saturday nights. The Quay (phone: 55111). Expensive to moderate.

Dooley's – This is an old hotel on the quays with a reputation for good lunches and dinners. The Quay (phone: 73531). Moderate.

Jade Palace – On the second floor of a charcoal steak house managed by the same people, the specialties at this elegant, award-winning Chinese restaurant include King Prawns and duck Cantonese, but you can also have steak, omelettes, and curry dishes. Dinner nightly; lunch Mondays through Fridays. 3 The Mall (phone: 55611). Moderate.

Manners – Found on the second floor of the trendy George's Court shopping arcade, this is a bright and airy restaurant filled with hanging plants and flowers. The menus for the daily lunches and the dinners served Monday through Saturday are eclectic, ranging from prime rib and rainbow trout to seafood paella and weight-watchers salads. George's Court and Barronstrand St. (phone: 78704). Moderate.

Oak Room – Housed in a 300-year-old building that's also home to the popular *Munster Bar,* this small oak-paneled gem of a restaurant is fairly new. Waterford crystal chandeliers and an open fireplace make dining on prime ribs and seafood even more enjoyable. During the daytime, the downstairs lounge serves some elegant pub grub, including hot prawns in Pernod or smoked mackerel salad. Factory La., off Bailey's New St. (phone: 74656). Moderate.

Reginald Grill – With a varied menu, this grill is quite handy because it's open continuously from lunch until 11 PM. Next to Reginald's Tower. The cocktail bar contains part of the city's 9th-century walls. The Mall (phone: 55611). Moderate.

Teaser's – An up-to-date, up-beat deli-café, pleasant for lunch, tea, snacks; also does Thursday, Friday, and Saturday dinners, with wine, from June to September. 124 The Quay (phone: 55908). Inexpensive.

Galley Cruising Restaurants – Dine as you cruise past the sylvan beauties of the River Barrow or Nore or down toward the sea (depending on the state of the tide and the inclination of the skipper). The 3-hour dinner trip is fun, and the food — fresh and all home cooked — unusually good for the size of the galley. Cruises depart from New Ross (15 miles northeast of Waterford). Dinner cruises are offered daily July through August and according to demand in April, May, and September; also 3 to 5 PM cruises from Waterford, and lunch and afternoon cruises from New Ross. Reservations are essential. New Ross (phone: 051-21723). Expensive, but the boat trip is included in the price of the meal.

SHARING A PINT: *Egans,* 36/37 Barronstrand St., is a Tudor-style bar with plenty of room to stretch. It's a convenient place to pause in shopping, enjoy a pint, and listen to the locals discuss the business of the day. *T. &H. Doolan's* in George St. is a small, old-fashioned gem. At the *Reginald Lounge,* on The Mall, there is usually a lovely peat fire, and old armaments hang on a wall that is really a restored section of the original city wall dating from the 12th century. If you like jazz, drop in on a Sunday afternoon when there's often a session by Waterford musicians. Whatever you do, don't leave town without looking in at *The Munster,* a 300-year-old inn, revived and added onto by the Fitzgerald family. The entrance to the mellowed though modern lounge, a favorite meeting and greeting spot for young Waterforders, is on The Mall; but walk around to the original Bailey's New St. door to see the men's bar on the right.

WEXFORD

You won't be long in Wexford Town before discovering that its people are its main attraction. Their Irishness is not of the mild, gentle folk strain. Here they are keen of mind and quick in discussion, and they often like their wit a bit on the saucy side. Spend a pleasant day browsing in the narrow-streeted and hilly town, then head for the nearest bar stool (an easy assignment as one local claims there are more than 50 pubs in Wexford), and you'll find that a friendly comment or two from you is likely to get things going, be it a recitation of the local history or a soliloquy on the praiseworthy local weather. If you happen to be a visiting Irish-American, expect a lively debate on the political fortunes of the Kennedy family, whose ancestors came from nearby Dunganstown in County Wexford.

It won't be difficult to engage the hardy ladies of the Country Market in conversation, either. They can tell you that from medieval times the market has been the heartbeat of the town, and that in the days of the schooners, the ships could dock quite close to unload their goods for sale. They'll also look you straight in the eye and tell you that long before the young people started their natural foods campaign, the wives of Wexford farmers knew the benefits of vegetables grown in chemical-free soil, and they never forsook their home-made breads and jams for commercial substitutes.

This boldness of spirit is not all talk. It produced such illustrious native sons as John Barry, regarded as the founder of the American navy, born 10 miles from Wexford at Ballysampson, and Sir Robert J. McClure, discoverer of the Northwest Passage. The boldest and proudest Wexford men of days gone by, however, were those who took part in the Rebellion of 1798. In that year, the United Irishmen were unsuccessful in planning a general uprising against the British, so Father John Murphy, a County Wexford priest, independently led his parishioners, armed with pitchforks, in revolt. The rebellion lasted a month before it was suppressed, but it has remained alive in folk memory through Irish ballads such as "The Wearing of the Green" and "The Boys of Wexford."

Wexford has a population of more than 15,300 people, with another several thousand living in the suburbs. Located where the River Slaney flows into the shallow Wexford Harbour, the town is old and has an impossibly narrow main street, a legacy of its Viking past. It is said that a settlement existed here as early as AD 150, but it was the Vikings who developed it, calling it *Waesfjord,* which means "harbor of mud flats." Initially, the Vikings used this as a base from which to plunder the countryside and later turned it into a major trading post.

The Anglo-Norman invasion led by Richard de Clare, earl of Pembroke, known as Strongbow, ousted the Vikings in 1169 and launched a new era of domination. The face of the town also changed. Selskar Abbey rose at its northwestern edge — Henry II came here in 1172 to do Lenten penance for the murder of Thomas à Becket and it was here that Strongbow's daughter was married — and Wexford soon became a walled town, with five fortified gateways and four castles. The only remains of these defenses are the West Gate, built in the fourteeneth century and used until the end of the sixteenth century, and a portion of wall nearby.

Norman nobles used one of the town's squares for the bloody sport of bull-baiting and to this day the square is called the Bull Ring. The name stuck, despite the fact that the worst of a much bloodier slaughter, the massacre of Wexford's citizenry by Oliver Cromwell in 1649, took place in the Bull Ring. The townspeople erected no monument to remind them of this deed, but in 1905, when they got around to commemorating the insurgency of 1798, they placed their statue of an Irish pikeman here, in a stroke of independent-mindedness. More of the same spirit lies behind the confusion of Wexford's street names. Many have two, one dating from the days of British rule, and the other from the founding of the Irish Republic in 1922, the latter likely to be the name of a rebel.

Wexford has not been immune to the recent recession, but the establish-ment of an industrial estate with German and American firms has brought needed jobs into the area in recent years. Lett & Company, which transplants small seed mussels into Wexford Harbour from less nourishing areas, is located in Wexford Town and is the biggest single employer in the Irish fishing industry.

Then there's the tourist industry, which Wexford comes by almost effort-lessly, given its location in the sunniest part of Ireland, near the 6-mile beach of Rosslare, which draws Irish holidaymakers unsolicited as honeybees to clover. Not entirely effortlessly, however, because the local energy that goes into putting on the yearly Wexford Opera Festival and all its accompanying fringe events, cannot be discounted. At opera time, nearly every family in town has at least one member backstage sewing costumes or painting props, or elsewhere hanging pictures for an exhibition or setting up chairs for a lecture.

That the festival exists at all is the result of another stroke of boldness on the part of Wexford's people. In 1951, a group of residents tired of listening to phonograph records and resolved to hear the real thing, even if they had to produce it themselves. The orchestra was hired, singers were engaged, other professionals were called in, and what eventually was to become an acclaimed event on the international opera calendar was off to a brave begin-ning.

WEXFORD AT-A-GLANCE

SEEING THE CITY: The best way to see Wexford is on foot. If you begin at the Tourist Office on Crescent Quay and walk in a northerly direction, you'll enjoy the harbor and the sea air. Any street off the quays leads to Main Street, which runs parallel to the harbor and is the central shopping area, but if you turn left at the Bank of Ireland onto Common Quay Street (also known as

O'Hanlon Walsh Street), you'll find yourself in a square known as the Bull Ring. This winds around to the right into the Cornmarket and Abbey Street, where you'll find *White's* hotel.

SPECIAL PLACES: Discovering Wexford on your own is not a fatiguing undertaking. The town's memorials, churches, and abbey are all within a 5-minute walk of Main Street.

John Barry Memorial – In 1956, the US presented Ireland with this handsome statue of the founder of the American navy, who was born in County Wexford in 1745. Commodore Barry stands on Crescent Quay where two former American presidents, Dwight D. Eisenhower and John F. Kennedy, both laid wreaths on separate occasions. The inscriptions on the monument list a few of Barry's accomplishments during the American War of Independence. Walk up the street behind the monument for a lifelike view of the commodore looking out to sea with his mighty cape blowing in the wind. Crescent Quay.

Maritime Museum – A retired lighthouse ship — the *Guillemot* — on the quays is home to a museum devoted to Wexford's seafaring days. When the ship's flag is flying, the museum is open. Summer only from 10 AM to 9 PM. There is a small admission fee. Custom House Quay.

Bull Ring – The medieval practice of bull-baiting — killing bulls for sport — once took place in this small, historic square. This is also the place where on October 1, 1649, Oliver Cromwell had 2,000 Irish men, women, and children slaughtered. A statue to a pikeman, done by Oliver Sheppard and erected in 1905, now dominates the square in tribute to the peasants who took part in what came to be known as the Rebellion of 1798. Oscar Wilde's mother lived in the house that is now Diana Donnelly's boutique (legend says she was born in room 10 of the *Old Wexford Coaching Inn*). At the east side of the ring on Tuesdays, Fridays, and Saturdays from 9:30 AM to 12:30 PM, you'll find a number of Wexford women selling their vegetables, baked goods, jams, jellies, and honey in buildings dating from 1871. Sometimes there are crafts for sale, too.

St. Iberius Church – A Georgian gem (Church of Ireland) built in 1760, on land occupied by other houses of worship dating back to earliest Norse days. Handsome interior and superb acoustics make it a favorite Festival concert hall. South of the Bull Ring on Main St.

Arts Center – Once the Market House, then Town Hall, recently restored as a cultural headquarters and special-events site. Its now-elegant second story boasts five Waterford chandeliers. Around the corner from the Bull Ring on the Corn Market.

Twin Churches – The Roman Catholic Churches of the Immaculate Conception on Rowe St. and the Assumption on Bride St., both designed by Robert Pierce, were inaugurated on the same day in 1858 when Wexford's original nine parishes became two, thanks to the unflagging efforts of Fr. James Roche, who is buried in the Bride St. church.

Selskar Abbey – It is a pity the town has not done more in restoring and promoting this 12th-century site. The abbey was once quite extensive although all that can be seen today are a 14th-century battlement tower and church. A long-covered passage runs underground to the far side of town. Tradition says Henry II did penance here for murdering Thomas à Becket, but historians now think St. Mary's, protected within the town walls, a more likely site for his acts of contrition. Some of the older people in town can remember when the church was still in use. You can explore the ruins by obtaining a key from a nearby house (there's a notice on the gate telling you where). Behind the abbey remain the old West Gate, the only one of Wexford's five original gateways still standing, and part of the town walls. Entrance at the intersection of Temperance Row, West Gate, and Slaney St.

Franciscan Friary – Built in the 17th century on the site of an earlier church destroyed during Cromwellian times, this was the parish church for Wexford Town until the twin churches of the Assumption and the Immaculate Conception were completed in 1858. The Franciscan Friary was extensively redecorated in the 19th century, when the vaulted ceiling, marbled columns, and organ were added. School St.

Johnstown Castle – This 19th-century turreted Gothic mansion incorporates an earlier castle and is the former home of the Esmonde, Grogan, and Fitzgerald families. It is now owned by the State Agricultural College, but you can visit the beautiful gardens, lakes, and nature trails that surround it. The grounds are open to the public without charge from 10 AM to 6 PM daily — take a picnic basket. Exhibits in the Irish Agricultural Museum in the castle's restored farm buildings include harness ware and antique farm machinery as well as a reconstructed farm kitchen and bedroom and a creamery. Open May through October, Mondays through Fridays from 9 AM to 12:30 PM and 1:30 to 5 PM, Sundays from 2 to 5 PM. Small admission fee. Off the Rosslare Harbour Rd., 2½ miles south of Wexford.

■ **EXTRA SPECIAL:** If you feel like time in the outdoors, spend a day roaming the Saltee Islands, Ireland's largest and most famous bird sanctuary. During spring and early summer, the Great Saltee (which is 1 mile in length) and the Little Saltee are home to over 3 million gulls, puffins, and other feathered creatures that delight bird-watchers. The islands are a 45-minute boat trip off the coast of Kilmore Quay, about 20 miles southwest of Wexford. You can arrange the trip by calling fisherman Willie Bates at 29644 or Tom O'Brien at 29727. Kilmore Quay itself is a quaint fishing village of thatched cottages and has the lovely, modern *Saltees* hotel (phone: 29601), where rooms are named after different species of birds found on the islands.

SOURCES AND RESOURCES

TOURIST INFORMATION: Wexford's Tourist Information Office on Crescent Quay is large and open all year, Mondays through Saturdays, from 9 AM to 12:45 PM and 2 to 6 PM (phone: 23111); winter hours may differ slightly. You can drop in for help or just to browse through the racks heavy with information on hotels and sights in the area. During the summer the Junior Chamber of Commerce puts out an excellent monthly guide that is available free from the tourist office as well as from most hotels. It contains names and phone numbers of doctors, dentists, and pharmacists as well as the timetable for buses and trains to Dublin and the ferries operating out of Rosslare Harbour. It also has two good maps of the town with a suggested walking tour. The Chamber of Commerce publishes a mini-brochure with some of the same information in a more condensed form along with a map.

Local Coverage – *The Wexford People,* the town's weekly newspaper, comes out on Thursdays with the news and an entertainment listing for the area.

GETTING AROUND: If you've come to Wexford by car, park it and see the town on foot. Among the dozen or so parking lots, there's a convenient one near the tourist office — turn left onto Custom House Quay if you're entering via the bridge and you'll find it on the right, just before the statue of John Barry. (For others, see the detailed town map in the monthly Junior Chamber of Commerce guide.) Consider tagging along on an Old Wexford Society walking tour.

Its members conduct them throughout the year at hours set to suit current visitor demand. Check starting times and places with your hotel or the tourist office.

Bicycle – *Hayes Cycle Shop,* 108 S Main St., *John Murphy,* 22A North Main St., and *The Bike Shop,* 9 Selskar St., have bikes for rent.

Bus and Train – There is no in-town bus service — it's not necessary. When you're ready to leave, however, you'll find the bus and railway terminals in Redmond Pl., near the quays just north of the bridge. CIE operates both buses and trains between Wexford and Dublin and between Wexford and Rosslare Harbour, 13 miles southeast (not to be confused with Rosslare, or Rosslare Strand, the seaside resort between Wexford and Rosslare Harbour). Ferries leave Rosslare Harbour regularly for Wales and for Le Havre and Cherbourg in France. Irish trains and buses are not known for adhering to timetables so check with CIE for delays (phone: 22522 from 6:30 AM to 6 PM). For information on ferries to Wales, call British Rail at 33115. For information on ferries to France, call Irish Continental Line (phone: 33158).

Car Rental – There are a number of car rental companies in Wexford and in nearby Rosslare Harbour, where some have dropping-off stations for their vehicles rented elsewhere. *Boland's Car Hire* has offices in both Wexford (phone: 23329) and Rosslare Harbour (phone: 33288). *Murrays Rent a Car* (phone: 22122) is located near the railway station and bus depot at the north end of town.

Taxi – Cabs are expensive, but sometimes they're the quickest and most convenient way of reaching your destination. Phone 22485, 23196, or 24056 to get one.

Tours – CIE operates afternoon bus tours of nearby scenic areas during July and August from Redmond Place (phone: 22522).

SHOPPING: The best guide to shopping in Wexford is to walk along Main Street and let yourself be tempted by the storefronts. Most stores are open from 9 AM to 5:30 PM, with slightly later hours on Fridays and Saturdays. During fall and winter, many are closed on Thursdays.

Barker's, Joyce's, and Martin's – All three have an extensive selection of Waterford crystal and Belleek and other chinas. S Main St.

Breen's – All types of Irish linens can be found here. S Main St.

Casket – A small shop with a big stock of Aran knit goods and handmade lace. 43 S Main St.

Martin Doyle – This tiny shop offers fine handwrought gold and silver jewelery. Lower Rowe St.

Hore's – Another good place for Irish linens. 31–37 S Main St.

Laurence's – A jewelry shop with attractive rings at reasonable prices, as well as crystal, china, silver, Lladros, and Hummels. 83 N Main St.

Lowney Antiques, Ltd. – Intriguing browsing, town's best selection of beautiful old things, large and small. Shipping arranged. S Main St.

Wexford Gallery – A showcase for local crafts, this shop sells paintings, pottery, knitwear, crochet work, hand-cut glass, enamels, and woodwork. Open 7 days. Crescent Quay.

Wool Shop – Offers a large choice of Aran sweaters, woven belts, and rugs, as well as local sheepskin and goatskin rugs. 39–41 S Main St.

SPECIAL EVENTS: Since 1951, the *Wexford Opera Festival* has brought singers from all over the world to present rarely performed operas, usually to sold-out audiences who've waited long and come from afar for the pleasure. The operas, three of them per festival, can be obscure works of the 17th, 18th, and 19th centuries, or even contemporary ones, and the performers may be equally unknown, though many are "discovered" here and go on to international careers. The 19th-century Theatre Royal on High Street is the Georgian setting of these

12 days of music that begin in late October, and since it seats only 446 opera lovers, early booking is necessary — bookings by mail open in June. Write to the Wexford Festival Opera, Theatre Royal, Wexford (phone: 22240), but if you don't get seats, don't despair. Many other events, from concerts, art exhibitions, and lectures, to street theater, fashion shows, and fishing contests, take place around the opera core and there is no doubt that this is the liveliest time of the year to be in Wexford under any pretext.

The *Wexford Mussel and Seafood Festival* is a popular annual affair, too. It is held in late August and features 3 days of fun, including the selection of a Wexford "mussel" man.

SPORTS: The monthly guide published by the Junior Chamber of Commerce has detailed information on recreational activities. The leisure center in the *Talbot Hotel* on the quays is open to nonresidents and has a number of facilities including a heated indoor swimming pool, squash courts, and saunas.

Golf – The *Wexford Golf Club* (phone: 42238) has a 9-hole course currently being expanded to 18 holes. *The Rosslare Golf Club* (phone: 32113) has an 18-hole course at Rosslare, 11 miles southeast of Wexford.

Horse Racing – Flat racing is held 5 times a year in the small-town atmosphere of Wexford's *Bettyville Racecourse.*

Riding – At *Horetown House,* the Young family offers daily rides, all levels of instruction, indoor ring, cross-country course for experienced riders on 17th-century manor grounds. Picnic rides, riding holiday packages, wonderful home-cooked food too. 12 miles west on L160 Rd. at Foulksmills (phone: 63633). You can also hire horses at *Mill Riding Centre,* Rathnure, Enniscorthy (phone: 054-55112), *Shemalier Riding Stables,* Forth Mountain, about 4 miles from town (phone: 053-39251), and *Slaney View Riding Centre,* Slaney View, Enniscorthy (phone: 054-34102).

Swimming – Southeast Ireland is known for its comparative abundance of sunshine, which can be enjoyed at a number of beaches around Wexford including Curracloe, Rosslare, Carne, and Kilmore Quay. Some hotels, such as the Talbot, Great Southern-Rosslare and Kelly's, also have indoor swimming pools for the use of guests.

Tennis – Visitors are welcome to use the all-weather courts at *Wexford Harbour Boat Club,* Redmond Rd. (phone: 22039 or 23672).

THEATER: During the summer season, there is Irish cabaret several nights a week at the *Talbot* hotel (phone: 22566). Special programs take place at the *Wexford Arts Centre,* located in the old Market House in the Cornmarket (phone: 23764).

MUSIC AND NIGHTLIFE: Wexford is a lively town at night with plenty of good singing pubs and cabaret and ballroom dancing at most of the larger hotels. If you're lucky, *Sonas,* a popular group of five young musicians, will be singing Irish ballads as well as a few humorous, modern tunes. There is Irish music most nights in the *Shemalier Bar* of *White's* hotel (phone: 22311) and in the *Tavern* of the *Talbot* hotel (phone: 22566). *McArthur Park* and *Eyecatchers* discos swing into action on Friday and Saturday nights at *White's* hotel, as does *Speakers Music Bar* next door. There is jazz on Sundays at the *Talbot. Kelly's Strand* hotel in Rosslare (phone: 32114) also has dancing and entertainment most evenings. Watch out for *Seisiún,* an evening — or session — of song and dance sponsored by Comhaltas Ceoltóirí Éireann, a national organization for the promotion of traditional Irish folk music. These very authentic sessions are held in some 30 cities and towns during the summer. In Wexford, they usually take place once a week in *White's* hotel and the *Talbot* hotel.

SINS: *Nangle's Coffee Shop,* 22 S Main St., serves some delicious pastry. For a less sinful treat, check out the treats at *A Humble Natural Food Shop* on Lower Rowe St.

BEST IN TOWN

CHECKING IN: Wexford is a very hospitable town. There are several fine hotels in the area and plenty of bed and breakfast houses. During the summer months, an expensive hotel room will cost about $75 and up, double (most hotels include breakfast in their rates), a moderate one, from $45 to $65, and an inexpensive one $40 or less. A single B&B room will cost about $15, and a double about $30. Rates are lower December through March, but about $10 higher per room on bank holidays and during Opera and Mussel festivals.

Talbot – This hotel overlooking Wexford Harbor along the quays has been totally refurbished and now has 104 rooms, all with bath/shower, and two fine restaurants. Its leisure center sports an indoor heated pool, gym, squash courts, saunas, and solarium. The *Tavern* offers live music, from traditional to jazz, and there's a weekly Irish cabaret in the summer. Trinity St. (phone: 22566). Expensive.

White's – Originally opened in 1779, it is now also known as the "new" *White's,* with 65 refurbished rooms, all with baths, and two restaurants and bars. Both taverns — the *Old Wexford* and the *Shemalier* — are popular for sing-along sessions. George's St. (phone: 22311). Expensive.

Kelly's Strand – This modern resort hotel on Rosslare Strand is usually booked well in advance. It is a popular weekend retreat for the Irish and is known for its good food and recreation facilities (tennis and squash courts, indoor and outdoor pools, saunas, beach). Closed from mid-December to mid-February. Rosslare (phone: 32114). Expensive to moderate.

Ferrycarrig – A modern family-run place, it has 40 rooms with bath, each with a view of the River Slaney. Its *Sandpiper* restaurant specializes in seafood. Closed November through March. Right outside of town at Ferrycarrig Bridge, Enniscorthy Rd. (phone: 22999). Moderate.

Great Southern – On a cliff overlooking Rosslare Harbor, this hotel has 100 rooms, all with private baths, plus an indoor heated swimming pool, a tennis court, saunas, and evening entertainment on summer weekends. Open April through October. Rosslare Harbor (phone: 33233). Moderate.

Kincone – New, comfortable, and much smaller than *White's, Kelly's,* or the *Talbot,* this 20-room motor hotel is just across the Wexford bridge from the town center. Dublin Rd. (phone: 23611). Moderate.

Whitford House – Follow the signposts two miles south of town and you'll find this modern guesthouse on its own grounds with countryside views from its wide windows. There are 23 cheery bedrooms, all with private bath, color TV, and telephone; guests also enjoy use of an on-premises heated indoor pool and tennis court. New Line Rd. (phone: 43444 or 24573). Moderate to inexpensive.

Killiane Castle – John Mernagh inherited this lovely 230-acre estate from his dad, and he and his wife, Kathleen, have converted it into a gracious guesthouse with 8 rooms of shared baths. They also have apartments to rent and hope to eventually restore the 17th-century tower on the grounds. Open March through October. Off the Rosslare Harbour Rd., Drinagh (phone: 22272). Inexpensive.

St. Aidan's Mews – This very old place near the Church of the Immaculate Conception is now a tidy guesthouse where you'll be tended to by Catherine and Martin

Redmond. All 7 rooms have hot and cold water. 25 Lower John's St. (phone: 22691). Inexpensive.

 EATING OUT: Whether you wish to dine by candlelight or to have a tasty salad in relaxed surroundings, you're likely to find a restaurant to suit your appetite and billfold in Wexford. Dinner for two in an expensive restaurant will set you back $45 or more. In a moderate one, you'll probably pay between $20 and $40, and in an inexpensive one, the bill will be under $20.

Captain White's – Comfortably stylish seafood restaurant with cozy cocktail bar; has made the Irish Tourist Board's top ten listing for several years. Only freshest fish, seafood done with great skill and respect. Chowder, mussels, scallops, pink trout with walnut stuffing are commendable; trust maître d's daily suggestions. There are some meat choices too. In White's Hotel on George's St. (phone: 22311). Expensive.

Kelly's Strand – The hotel has an elegant restaurant where you can dine on such tempting dishes as fresh scallops in season and apricot soufflé. There is often entertainment to round out the evening. Closed from mid-December to mid-February. Rosslare (phone: 32114). Expensive.

Guillemot – The main dining room of the *Talbot* hotel, this innovative restaurant has introduced a dual-menu concept to serve both expensive tastes and more moderate budgets. Seafood (especially local lobster, mussels, and pink trout) is a specialty on each menu. Extensive wine list. Trinity St. (phone: 22566). Expensive to moderate.

Cellar – The former wine cellar of a 300-year-old Georgian country house, this dining room is known for its carrot and verbena soup, steaks, seafood, and malt health bread. Closed January and February, and Sundays and Mondays except from June to August. Horetown House, Foulksmills, about 20 minutes west of Wexford Town. (phone: 63633 or 63706). Moderate.

Farmer's Kitchen – Informal atmosphere, friendly service, good local seafood, steaks. Bar lunches and restaurant dinners; open daily. On Rosslare Rd. (phone: 23295). Moderate.

Neptune Seafood – A recent arrival, it's set in a fishing village on the River Barrow estuary, about half an hour from Wexford town. Crab claws, prawns, mussels, and lobster are among the menu's bounty of seafood; other specialties include Hungarian goulash, T-bone steak, parsnip soup, vegetarian salads, and homemade ice creams. When weather permits, there's outdoor dining on the patio. Open daily April through October; weekends from November to March; lunches and dinners. Ballyhack Harbor (phone: 051-89284). Moderate.

Old Granary – Tables are in booths in this quiet, rustic restaurant with a beamed ceiling, wooden pillars, hanging plants, and copper kettles. The reputation for good food is well established and the menu ranges from veal à la creme, chicken flambé, and duck à l'orange to kebabs of pork and lasagna. Open 7 days for dinner, weekdays only for lunch. Westgate (phone: 23935). Moderate.

Michael's – This is pleasant and dimly lit, with aquariums and a nautical motif. The lunch and dinner menu ranges from steak to curry to pizza. 94 N Main St. (phone: 22196). Moderate to inexpensive.

Pike Room – The grillroom of the *Talbot* hotel, this is a good spot for steaks, chops, and seafood, all served in a setting full of historic mementos. Talbot Hotel, Trinity St. (phone: 22566). Moderate to inexpensive.

Tim's Tavern – Casual, folksy, recommended by locals for lunches, dinners, good steaks. 51 S Main St. (phone: 23861). Moderate to inexpensive.

Bohemian Girl – Homemade soups, salads, and appetizing specials make it a particularly good lunch stop. Kay and Seamus McMenamin run this colorful pub named after the opera by William Balfe, who lived in the corner building. N Main and Monck sts. (phone: 23596). Inexpensive.

SHARING A PINT: The *Crown Bar* on Monck St. is one of the oldest pubs in Ireland and has been held by the same family since 1841. Fiona Kelly and her mother, Mrs. Annie Kelly, open for business in the late afternoon and they can help you recall the past when the *Crown* was a stagecoach inn popular with traveling judges and their assistants. You'll see why the *Crown* is also one of Ireland's best-known pubs (it's been on television in various European countries) if you sip your drink in the cozy back rooms. They're filled with antique prints, military gear, swords, and other arms — including two guns from the famous Howth gun-running incident of 1914 — that the proprietor's father, the late Aidan Kelly, collected from all over the world. Another stop for a drink and a chat is the *Thomas Moore Tavern* in the Cornmarket. The poet's mother was born here. *Tim's Tavern,* S Main St., has thatching over the bar and good snacks, and *Andy Kinsellas,* also on S Main St., is a handsome old place and a quiet refuge from the shopping traffic. The *Westgate Bar,* near the old city walls, is also worth a visit. If you're looking for an unusual photo setting, Con Macken's "Bar and Undertaker" sign, near Bull Ring, is a classic.

YORK

"The history of York," according to King George VI, "is the history of England." In 1971, York celebrated its 1,900th birthday, and each successive epoch of the country's past is still legible in its ruin sites, buildings, and monuments. The Middle Ages are especially well represented, and for many visitors, it is this aspect of York that is the most interesting. Within the 3 miles of ancient defensive wall is perhaps the best-preserved medieval city in Great Britain, containing its largest medieval church, York Minster, and its best-preserved medieval street. The quirky, timbered, slightly akimbo buildings in the Shambles — once the butchers' quarters — may look like a stage set, but they are as authentic as the day they were built.

In AD 71, the Romans chose the meeting point of the rivers Ouse and Foss as the site of Eboracum, at first a temporary camp, then a permanent fort. From that it grew to become a major Roman city that the Emperor Hadrian (of Hadrian's Wall fame) used as a home base and where Constantine the Great was proclaimed Emperor. It flourished as a trade center at the hub of a network of roads and as a port for seagoing ships that navigated the 50-mile stretch up the River Ouse. The most inspiring physical legacy of those times is the surviving Multangular Tower in the museum gardens (though its upper stonework is "merely" medieval).

The Romans left to defend their own country in the early part of the fifth century and little is known of the next slice of history until the Saxons gained control of the city in the seventh century. They built a wooden church, the first York Minster, predecessor of the present building. The conquering Danes, arriving in the ninth century, further developed the city as an important port, called it Jorvik, and gave the name *gate,* Norse for "street," to several of its thoroughfares. Some of Jorvik's original Viking buildings have been excavated recently, superbly preserved in the peaty earth. The Normans' eleventh-century presence is recorded in today's landscape as two humps of earth on which William the Conqueror raised two wooden castles. One hump remains as Baile Hill; the other supports Clifford's Tower, a later structure in stone.

It was in the thirteenth century, however, that the city began to assume its familiar shape. Though it had earlier been surrounded by an earth mound and a wooden stockade, these were now replaced by the actual limestone walls, together with the four principal gateways (called bars, just to confuse matters): Monk Bar, Micklegate Bar, Walmgate Bar, and Bootham Bar. Within the boundaries, several churches, friaries, nunneries, and an abbey established York as a cradle of European Christianity and as the country's second city. The Minster, growing grander and grander over the 250 years of its construction, was finally completed in 1472, and has been York's crowning glory ever since.

Medieval city planners developed their roads along the main Roman streets. Stonegate was, for example, the Via Praetoria; Petergate, the Via Principalis; and Micklegate, meaning the Great Street, was the main route from London where the only bridge over the Ouse stood. The medievals then built connecting alleyways and the characteristic timber-framed buildings that overhang them, each story projecting farther than the one below. The Shambles is one such street; now restored not as a lifeless museum piece but as a still busy commercial artery.

The prosperity of medieval York stemmed from its thriving wool trade. With the slow decline of this industry, and in the wake of Henry VIII's purge against the power of the church, the city was doomed for some time to play only a minor role in English history until it became a fashionable social center in eighteenth-century Georgian Britain. The racecourse, Assembly Rooms, and many splendid townhouses belonging to large, landowning families were part of this scene. Because it was widely favored by wealthy northerners as a refuge from the grime of early industrialization, York remained relatively factory-free, with candy works a notable exception. It did, however, spawn George Hudson, a railway inventor and entrepreneur who was largely responsible for making the city a keystone in Britain's expanding railway network. Today you can see a plaque to his life and work outside the Railway King Hotel on George Hudson Street (the house of Joseph Hansom, inventor of the first horse-drawn cab, is in Micklegate).

To absorb York's antiquated atmosphere, simply wander around, particularly in the labyrinth of streets and alleyways in the shadow of the Minster. Stroll along the gates — the activities that once took place in them are evident in their names: Colliergate was the street of the charcoal dealers, Spurriergate belonged to the spurmakers, and Stonegate was the route used to carry building materials to the Minster. Whip-ma-whop-ma-gate is the longest name for the shortest street, one named after a whipping post where criminals were punished.

Everywhere there are curiosities of the past. In Deangate, for example, there is a working gas lamp in front of the Minster South Door. At nos. 5 and 7 Petergate, and at several other points in town, you can see the original firemark signs put there in Georgian days when each insurance company had its own fire engine that would only go to the rescue of its own blazing customers.

York does have its shabbier, modern appendages, though it has managed more successfully than most cities to conserve its age-old character. Whether it can continue to resist pressures to keep up-to-date by widening streets and building taller buildings, remains to be seen. In the meantime, it is not unusual for over 2 million visitors a year to step into York's time capsule to enjoy its ancient airs and graces. You will not be alone in admiring this most historic of cities.

YORK AT-A-GLANCE

SEEING THE CITY: For those who need an aerial perspective before tackling some of York's inner alleyways, the city walls offer a 2½-mile-long vantage point. The route along the crest of the barricades dates back to the 1200s and is still the traditional promenade for both natives and visitors. The path — 3 feet wide and often without handrails, so be careful — can be reached from the bars, or gateways, where the walls join the major roads (Bootham, Monk, Walmgate, Fishergate, Victoria, and Micklegate bars). The stretch between Bootham Bar and Monk Bar is particularly attractive and affords a good view of the spires and buttresses of York Minster. The walk, which is delightful in springtime when clouds of daffodils hug the grassy banks, is open daily from dawn till dusk.

SPECIAL PLACES: Nearly everything you'll want to see in York is in the medieval heart of the city. The only exception is the National Railway Museum on the west side of the Ouse near the railway station.

York Minster – York without the Minster's imposing skyline presence would be like Paris denied its Eiffel Tower. This grandiose church — the Cathedral of St. Peter — is the largest gothic cathedral north of the Alps. It was built over a period of 250 years, from 1220 to 1472, but even before that, there was a church on the spot, several in fact: The first was a wooden one built in the 7th century (the word *minster* is Anglo-Saxon for a mission from which the surrounding country was evangelized). York Minster contains the finest collection of medieval stained glass in England. Of the 130 windows (most removed at the outbreak of World War II and painstakingly put back together again), the 13th-century Five Sisters Window of delicate grisaille glass is the most famous, although the West Window with its heart-shaped tracery is perhaps the most beautiful. The Rose Window, commemorating the 15th-century War of the Roses, was badly damaged in the 1984 fire that swept through York Minster. However, an exhibition of its upcoming restoration is on display. Among the Minster's other proud features are the late-15th-century choir screen with its sculpted kings of England, and the Undercroft. The church was in danger of collapsing until desperately needed renovations were begun in 1967. During the course of the repairs, the foundations of an early Norman cathedral were revealed and it was discovered that the medieval church had been raised right above the city's Roman headquarters. There is now an Undercroft Museum where visitors can see the massive 20th-century concrete underpinnings as well as an exhibit on the history of the Minster and its site. The Minster is open daily from 7 AM, though sightseeing is restricted during services. It costs nothing to wander around the Minster itself, but there is an admission charge for the Undercroft Museum and Chapter House. Open weekdays and Sunday afternoons.

Jorvik Viking Centre – Small electric cars transport visitors underground to Jorvik — an old Viking city that's been uncovered by archaeologists. A bustling market, a busy wharf, houses with smoking chimneys, as well as reconstructions of the original excavation are on display; so are scores of objects — tools, kitchenware, shoes, and fragments of clothing — that have lain untouched since the Vikings lived here 1,000 years ago. Open daily; admission charge. Coppergate.

Treasurer's House – The official residence of the Treasurer of the Minster (until the post was abolished in 1547) is behind the Minster on the site of a Roman building. Though it dates back to the 13th century, most of what exists today is from the 17th century. The last owner, Frank Green, renovated the building and gave it to the National Trust in 1930. Visitors can walk around 20 rooms furnished with period pieces and take in a lively exhibition showing some of the personalities associated with the house. Open daily from April through October. Admission charge. On some summer evenings (contact the TIC for details) you can enjoy coffee by candlelight in the main hall and music in the drawing room. Chapter House St. (phone: 24247).

St. William's College – One of York's many picturesque half-timbered structures, this was built in 1453 to lodge the Minster's chantry priests and has been restored as a meeting place for church convocations. Its Tudor quadrangle is a particularly remarkable feature. Those interested in becoming more directly involved in the city's history, and possibly returning home with a 14th-century archbishop in tow, will find a wide selection of replicas in the York Brass Rubbing Centre here (phone: 52232), a few taken from original brasses found in local churches. Materials and advice, from £1. Open daily, when not being used for meetings. College St. (phone: 34830).

Shambles – Mentioned in the *Domesday Book,* this narrow cobble-stoned alleyway is one of the best-preserved medieval streets in Britain, if not in Europe. Originally it was a street of butcher shops, known as Fleshammels, but it is now lined with antique, craft, and gift shops (some still have the sloping wooden shelves in front that were used to display meat). People living in the upper stories of these typically medieval overhanging buildings can shake hands with their neighbors across the road if they lean out the windows far enough. The Shambles leads from King's Square (at the foot of Petergate) to The Pavement.

Castle Museum – The private collection of everyday "bygones" accumulated by a country doctor from Pickering, 25 miles northeast of York, and donated to the city in 1925, forms the basis of this museum which has become one of the most important folk museums in the country. Stars of the show are the reconstructed streets: a Victorian cobbled one complete with Hansom cab (the original taxi), candlemaker's, blacksmith's, and other shop fronts, and an Edwardian street with gaslighted pub. Among the other, diverse displays are a Victorian parlor, a Georgian dining room, snuffboxes, policemen's truncheons, old musical instruments, vintage candy bars that include sugar pigs and spice mice, firearms, and unintelligible tape recordings of the local Yorkshire dialect. All this is housed in a former 18th-century prison for women, with various craftsmen's workshops set up in the converted cells — except for one that remains untouched. In it Dick Turpin, the notorious highwayman who, legend has it, rode Black Bess and terrorized travelers in the early stagecoaches, was imprisoned before being executed in 1740. Open daily. Admission charge. Tower St. (phone: 53611).

Clifford's Tower – A confusing history is attached to this remnant of York Castle. William the Conqueror erected a wooden fortress on a manmade earth mound here in 1068. In 1190, a rioting anti-Jewish mob burned it down, killing 150 of the Jews of York who had taken refuge inside. The existing quatrefoil stone tower, actually the medieval keep of the castle, was built in the 13th century, gutted by fire in the 17th century, and later restored and named after a Roger de Clifford who had been executed here in 1596. In the 19th century, the tower was used as a prison. Open daily. Admission charge. Tower St.

National Railway Museum – One of the few national museums outside London, it is packed with reminders of the days of steam and appropriately housed in the old depot where the locomotives went for maintenance and repairs. The most famous items are the Pacific Mallard loco, which still holds the world's steam speed record at 126 mph, and Queen Victoria's luxuriously appointed Pullman carriage. Many of the locomotives and carriages on display stand on two giant turntables in the 2-acre Great Hall, and lots of other aspects of railway history are covered by the exhibits in the museum galleries. There is a shop and an upstairs restaurant overlooking the main London-Edinburgh line. Open Mondays through Saturdays from 10 AM to 6 PM; Sundays from 2:30 PM to 6 PM. Leeman Rd. (phone: 21261).

Yorkshire Museum and Botanical Gardens – The museum contains exhibits that date back 160 million years, but apart from the geological items, it is probably best known for its collection of archaeological remains, particularly finds from Roman York. The Roman Life galleries, opened in 1985, display relics — including a Roman kitchen, mosaics, and priceless gold and silver jewelry — from one of Britain's most fascinating periods. In the gardens are the ruins of St. Mary's Abbey (founded ca. 1080), once the most important Benedictine monastery in the north of England. (It was suppressed by Henry VIII's Dissolution of the Monasteries and thereafter lost many of its stones to local building projects.) The Multangular Tower and a section of the city walls, their lower portions Roman, are also in the gardens. Open daily. Admission charge for the museum. Museum St. (phone: 29745).

City Art Gallery – The collection includes minor old masters dating back to the 14th century, but works of 19th- and 20th-century European painters tend to be the specialty. The building itself is Victorian. Open daily. Admission charge. Exhibition Sq. (phone: 23839).

Assembly Rooms – Built in the 1730s, this was once the most fashionable social center in the north of England. It was *the* place to go in Georgian times to play cards and dice, drink tea, or attend a grand ball. Today dances are still held here, though exhibitions and conferences are more usual. The design of the building is Italian Palladian and the colonnaded Egyptian Hall is its chief interior feature. Open weekdays only, except when functions are taking place. Blake St. (phone: 59881).

Fairfax House – An 18th-century townhouse displaying the famous Terry collection of Georgian-era furniture and clocks. Now owned by the York Civic Trust, the house was used as a cinema and dance hall from 1920 to the mid-1960s. Today it contains the "Life in Georgian York" exhibit and is open daily. Castlegate (phone: 55543).

Holy Trinity Church – Completed before 1500, this picturesque church on a picturesque street contains a split-level pulpit, and 18th-century wooden box pews, each with its own door enabling it to be occupied by a single family. Goodramgate.

Merchant Adventurers' Hall – The wealthiest and most powerful of the city's trade guilds built this excellent example of a medieval guildhall in the 14th and 15th centuries. It has lovely timberwork inside and out. Open Mondays through Saturdays year-round, and most Sundays from April until the end of October. Fossgate (phone: 54818).

The York Story – York from pre-Roman times to the present day is the subject of exhibits in the city's heritage center, housed in the former St. Mary's Church. Lots of lavishly constructed models, a slide show, and audio presentations are included in the center, which was designed as York's contribution to European Architectural Heritage Year in 1975. See this before you explore the real thing. Open daily. Admission charge. Castlegate (phone: 28632). Joint tickets for the York Story and the Castle Museum are available from the latter for £2.50 (phone: 53611).

■**EXTRA SPECIAL:** The oldest inhabitants of York are its ghosts — the city is widely reckoned to be the most haunted in Europe. Monks, black cats, a duke, a 13th-century mayoress, the headless earl of Northumberland, and marching Roman soldiers have all been seen by upstanding and sober members of the community. Several buildings are steeped in ghostly tales. The modern Theatre Royal, for example, stands on the ruins of St. Leonard's Hospital whose medieval crypt is now a theater club room inhabited by the Grey Lady, the ghost of a young nun said to have been buried alive in the walls for having an affair with a monk. You can see for yourself: A 2-hour walking tour, led by an expert guide, leaves from outside the *Anglers Arms,* Goodramgate, at 8 PM Mondays through Fridays from Easter to the beginning of October in search of "haunted and historic York." The tour costs £1.20 and reservations are not required.

$$\boxed{\textbf{SOURCES AND RESOURCES}}$$

TOURIST INFORMATION: The Tourist Information Centre in the De Grey Rooms, Exhibition Sq. (phone: 21756/7), has lots of free or nominally priced pamphlets on the city and the surrounding area, including the *Official York Guide* (about 75p). A free 2-hour walking tour, led by members of the Association of Voluntary Guides, leaves here two or three times a day from Easter through October. The TIC is open daily in summer, closed Sundays in winter. Except for Venice and Florence, York has probably been the subject of more books and guides than any other single noncapital city in Europe. A broad selection is for sale at the York Minster Bookshop and at the bookstore in the Castle Museum. Among the shorter booklets worth reading are *The City of York and the Minster,* by A. L. Laishley; *Georgian Houses in York,* by the York Georgian Society; *Roman York from AD 71,* by the Yorkshire Architectural and York Archaeological societies; and *York Mystery Plays,* by Eileen White. The two historical works called simply *York* — one by George Benson, the other by Angela Fiddes — are meatier tomes.

Local Coverage – The *Yorkshire Evening Press* is the city's daily newspaper, on sale at various newsstands and from street-corner venders (whose cry doesn't sound anything like *"Yorkshire Evening Press"*).

GETTING AROUND: York is to be explored on foot, especially since parking is virtually impossible on the street and most of the major car parks are outside the walls, away from where you really want to be. Because it is a compact city, with all places of interest within strolling distance, you won't be logging mammoth mileages. There are guided walking tours and bus tours if you don't feel like going it alone, even 15-minute clip-clops around the town on a horse-drawn carriage, with en route commentary by the driver. They leave from opposite the front of the Minster and cost approximately £1 (phone: 769490). *Yorktour,* 12a Coney St. (phone: 641-737), offers a variety of tours — open-top bus tours, walking tours, double-decker boat tours. *Trevor Rooney's* nightly walking tours are led by Victorian-costumed guides who take visitors to several well-known haunted buildings. Cost: £2 (phone: 426767).

Bicycle – Not at all an unusual mode of transportation in York. You can rent one from *Cycle Scene,* 2 Ratcliffe St., Burten Stone Lane (phone: 53286), or the *York Cycleworks,* Lawrence St. (phone: 26664).

Boat – Several companies operate river tours. From mid-March through September, *Hills Boatyard,* Lendal Bridge (phone: 23752), has hour-long, 6-mile cruises up the Ouse to Bishopthorpe Palace, the 13th-century home of the Archbishop of York, and back. Times of the sailings are posted on the notice board by the boatyard gates. If you'd prefer to do it yourself, *York Cruiser Hire* rents out self-drive motorboats and rowboats by the hour, day, or week (phone: 0532-781622).

Bus – The railway station is really the hub of the bus network. The *West Yorkshire Bus Company* sells a 2-day tourist ticket allowing unlimited travel on any of its city bus routes for £3. Buy it from the driver on the city tour bus, from the company's head office on Rougier St. (phone: 24161), or from the British Rail inquiry desk in the station, where you can also pick up information on the company's city center coach tours, which depart daily from outside the *Royal York Hotel* (£1.75), and their morning "Super City" tours, which combine a walking tour with travel by bus (open-top double-decker on fine days) and riverboat (£3.50).

Car Rental – You won't need a car to see the city but they are available if you plan an excursion into the countryside. Major firms represented include *Godfrey Davis,* Station Garage, Leeman Rd. (phone: 20394); and *Kenning,* Micklegate Bar (phone: 59328).

Taxi – Centrally located cab stands are at St. Sampson's Sq. (phone: 22333), by the ABC Cinema on Piccadilly (phone: 54579), by the Odeon Cinema on Blossom St., next to the Windmill Hotel on Queen St., at the railway station, and at Bootham Bar.

MUSEUMS: In addition to the museums described in *Special Places,* you may want to visit *Impressions.* When it opened in 1972, it was the first photographic gallery outside London and there still aren't many others. Apart from its changing exhibitions, there are cards, prints, and specialist books on sale. Open Tuesdays through Saturdays, plus Mondays in August and December. 17 Colliergate (phone: 54724).

SHOPPING: York's Newgate marketplace has been the focal point of all trading activities since medieval times. The setting is beautiful and the variety of wares is bound to interest browsers of all dispositions. Among the stalls you'll find antiques, clothing, bric-a-brac, and homemade Yorkshire foods as well as fish, fowl, and vegetables. The market is in full swing every day except Sunday. More conventional shop premises range from Georgian frontages in the city's older thoroughfares to modern shopping center facilities. The new Coppergate pedestrian mall around St. Mary's Square contains shops, restaurants, branches of most chain stores, exclusive jewelers, and the Jarvik Viking Center.

Antique shops abound. Most carry a wide selection of pieces and periods, though they may be known for a specialty. Among them are *Greenwoods* in Stonegate (jewelry), *York House* in Petergate (furniture and paintings), *Trinity* in Goodramgate (dolls), *Morrison* in The Mount (furniture), *Donald Butler* in Goodramgate (fine china), and several others. There are lots of antiquarian bookshops, too, including *Spelman's* in Micklegate, *O'Flynn* in Bridge St., and *MacDowell and Stern* in Grapelane.

Some better stores are listed below. Not all of them may stock goods you'd care to buy, but they've been included as curiosities.

Cox – Sheepskin: Slippers, gloves, rugs, coats, hats, footmuffs, and powder puffs are among its variations on a theme. 19 The Shambles (phone: 24449).

Deco – Original pottery, jewelry, glass, and various decorative household items from the 1920s and 1930s. 39 Stonegate (phone: 31960).

Ralph Ellerker's – Famous since 1796, then as a saddler and harnessmaker, now as a store for the modern equestrian who rides for pleasure. Apart from its ancient beams and rich leathery fragrance, you'll also discover ropes and canvasses, a macrame or yachting enthusiast's dream. Lots of regular gift ideas, too. 25 Walmgate (phone: 54417).

Laura Ashley – A branch of one of Britain's best stores for women's ready-to-wear. Davygate (phone: 27707).

Liberty – The famous London store now has a branch in York, with printed fabrics and a variety of gifts. 15 Davygate (phone: 33093).

Little Gallery – "All gifts shipped to all countries" is the motto of this well-stocked souvenir emporium where solid English pewter, historical dolls, bone china, glass, copper, and brass are offered. 71–73 Low Petergate (phone: 23150).

Mulberry Hall – One of England's most respected porcelain shops. 17 Stonegate (phone: 20736).

Precious – A wonderful toy shop, the biggest in the city, and an exciting place to be for all children from 8 to 80. Lots of railway models. 87 Petergate (phone: 53751).

Preston's of Bolton – Established in 1869, this shop now calls itself "The Diamond Centre of the North," selling a wide range of watches and jewelry. Coppergate (phone: 34315).

Alan Stuttle Gallery – Original oils, watercolors, and limited-edition and other prints, including many of York. 42 Stonegate (phone: 24907).

Wooden Horse – An interesting collection of diverse ethnic items ranging from African tribal rugs to Nepalese clothing, Chinese kites, and Mexican silver. 9 Goodramgate (phone: 26012).

SPECIAL EVENTS: The *York Races,* run a few days each month from May through October (the most important race, the Ebor Handicap, takes place in August), are usually the biggest events on the calendar. They are regularly upstaged, however, by the *York Cycle of Mystery Plays,* a reenactment that traditionally takes place every fourth year. The 48 plays — first performed in the mid-14th century and repeated for about 200 years thereafter — tell the story of man from the Creation to the Last Judgment. Originally presented by the medieval guilds, each of which chose a Biblical story to illustrate, the revived plays are still performed by local citizens, 200 of them, along with a handful of professional actors. Most of the plays are set dramatically against the ruins of St Mary's Abbey, but some are presented on authentically built wagons drawn around the city as in medieval times. The performances (held every four years) go on for 3 weeks and coincide with the *York Festival* of symphony, chamber, opera, and choral music, dance, art exhibits, and other entertainment. The next festival will take place in 1988. For details, contact the York Festival Office, 1 Museum St., York Y01 2DT (phone: 26421).

SPORTS: Cricket – To see a first-class match, go to Leeds, 25 miles away. Yorkshiremen have always been fanatical cricketers and the *Yorkshire County Cricket Club* is based at the *Headingley Cricket Ground,* St. Michael's La., Leeds (phone: 52865). When Yorkshire meets Lancashire, it's the Wars of the Roses all over again — check local papers for the date of the annual "battle."

Fishing – Licenses to fish the River Ouse and others can be bought at *Hookes,* 28–30 Coppergate (phone: 55073), *G. E. Hill,* 40 Clarence St. (phone: 24561), or *Bulmers* at Monk's Bar (phone: 54070).

Golf – There are more than 60 courses within an hour's drive of York, but four within easy reach of the city center are the *Fulford Golf Club,* Heslington La. (phone: 412882), the *Heworth Golf Club,* Muncastergate, Malton Rd. (phone: 39100), the *Railway Institute,* Pike Hills, Tadcaster Rd. (708756), and the *York Golf Club,* 6 miles out of town at Strensall (phone: 490304). All allow temporary visitor membership. There is also a driving range at Wiggington Rd.; open daily from 10:30 AM (phone: 59421).

Horse Racing – The *York Racecourse* is the most important racetrack in northern England. Entrance to the grounds costs about £1, but if you don't want to take advantage of the facilities inside, you can watch from the common land around the track, even stroll almost to the winning post, without payment. The races begin in May and reoccur for a few days each month through October. Peak of the season is the running of the Ebor Handicap in August. On the Knavesmire, 1 mile south of the city (phone: 20911).

Swimming – The *Barbican Baths* are the city's most modern, with three separate pools. Admission charge. Paragon St. (phone: 30266).

Tennis – Courts are available at Rowntree Park, Hull Rd. Park, Glen Gardens, Scarcroft Rd., and at the university. Book at the courts.

THEATER: The *Theatre Royal,* St. Leonard's Pl., was built in 1740 and became one of the country's leading theaters in Georgian times. Rebuilt by the Victorians, it is still York's main theater, offering a range of dramatic performances by both local groups and leading actors and actresses. The box office is open from Monday through Saturday (phone: 23568), and most performances begin at 7:30 PM or 8 PM. The *Arts Centre,* housed in a converted medieval church in Micklegate, has much more varied entertainments — films, exhibitions, music, and other events — in addition to plays (phone: 27129).

MUSIC: With the exception of the University of York Music Department, which gives twice weekly concerts during term time in *Lyons Concert Hall,* York is a generally poor city for all kinds of music. A few pubs and restaurants have live folk or jazz performances, and there are several discos, but lovers of classical music will be extremely fortunate if they hear any during their stay. The *Theatre Royal* and the *Arts Centre* are the most likely settings for musical events and the tourist information office will know of any others.

NIGHTCLUBS AND NIGHTLIFE: York is not a night town. If you crave action in the wee hours, your best bet is to drive to Leeds, which thrives on things happening when most of its respectable citizens are tucked into their beds. However, York does have a few discos worth visiting. Most require jackets and ties; some allow informal attire other than jeans. Entrance charges vary according to the DJ and night of the week but generally they are inexpensive and membership, if necessary, is nominal for the transient visitor. The *Old World Club,* Stonegate (phone: 22904), has two dance floors, six bars, a beer garden, and light meals, all enjoyed by a predominantly young crowd. *Roxy Nightclub,* Bootham (phone: 27319), offers dinner and dancing in a Georgian house from 10 PM on Mondays through Saturdays. *Ziggy's,* 71 Micklegate (phone: 20602), has two bars and a disco; open 10 PM to 2 AM Mondays through Saturdays. *Oscar's Wine Bar and Bistro,* 8–10 Little Stonegate, provides jazz entertainment Mondays and contemporary music the rest of the week.

SINS: York isn't a sexy town. You won't be able to hear, see, or indulge in outlandish practices, and if you ask a local where the red-light district is, he'll probably point to the nearest set of traffic lights. York is famous for one vicelike indulgence, however — Yorkshire pudding. Despite its name, it isn't a dessert but a traditional accompaniment to roast beef served at Sunday lunch. The secret of a successful "pud" lies in its lightness and everyone seems to have his or her own secret recipe to achieve the same end. To make yours, whisk one egg, add a little milk, and gradually work in 3 ounces of flour, beating well. Add the rest of a half-pint of milk, leave it for an hour, then heat up some beef drippings in a baking tin. When very hot, pour in the batter and cook in a hot oven (around 425°) till the pudding rises and turns crispy brown at the edges.

BEST IN TOWN

CHECKING IN: August is a hopeless time to visit York if you want to stay in the city center. Not only is it the peak time for tourists, but their numbers are swelled by racegoers, here for the most important meeting on the calendar. Rather than try to squeeze into too few city beds, car drivers are advised to travel out and find smaller hotels in the Vale of York, the flat band of land to the north of the city, or even to go to Harrogate, a half-hour ride to the west where there's bound to be a room, even at the height of the summer. The Tourist Information Centre can give on-the-spot advice about room availability and operates a booking service for a fee, for those who apply in person. A double room with breakfast costs $70 and up at hotels listed as expensive; from $45 to $70 at moderate ones, and less than $45 at inexpensive ones.

Crest – A four-star haven of luxury in the city center that caters to business travelers. Features 128 superbly furnished bedrooms. Tower St. (phone: 648111). Expensive.

Judges Lodging – The stone head above the doorway represents Aesculapius, the Greek god of healing, because the building was once the town residence of a well-known physician. Later it was the residence of the Assize Court judges, hence the name. Built about 1710 in Georgian style and appointed with period furnishings and antiques. You'll find four-poster beds in 6 of the 13 lavishly decorated rooms. Cuisine is French and the wines are personally imported by the proprietor, who is also French. 9 Lendal (phone: 38733). Expensive.

Royal York – The place to go to experience Victorian period charm at its most overwhelming. This magnificent railway hotel has been in operation just over 100 years and although necessary steps toward modernization have been taken, the traditional air remains, especially at teatime in the high-ceilinged lounge. There is a fitness room and a putting green in the formal gardens. Naturally, it's convenient to the station. Station Rd. (phone: 53681). Expensive.

Viking – Large (187 rooms), centrally located (on the River Ouse), and with excellent service, the *Viking* is an expanse of Scandinavian modernity right down to the sauna and whirlpool bath. The restaurant specializes in local dishes, including apple pie and Wensleydale cheese, which you can consume with some Theakston's Old Peculier ale and round off with a taste of Brontë liqueur. North St. (phone: 59822). Expensive.

Ladbroke Abbey Park – A 5-minute wander away from the city center, the 84-room *Abbey Park* is a vintage Georgian brick building with updated bedrooms. The restaurant serves typical Yorkshire fare, including Yorkshire pudding and syllabub. The Mount (phone: 58301). Expensive to moderate.

Whitwell Hall Country House – This magnificent Tudor Gothic–style hotel is set amidst 18 acres of wooded garden. There's a log fire burning in the grand entrance hall, game in season, fresh garden herbs and salads, a heated indoor swimming pool, and a sauna. Pre-dinner drinks are served in the Orangery near the pool. Whitwell-on-the-Hill (phone: 065381). Expensive to moderate.

Abbots Mews – Located in a quiet cul-de-sac a few minutes' walk from the city center, this was a coachman's cottage in Victorian times which was extended to include the stable block. 6 Marygate La., Bootham (phone: 34866). Moderate.

Chase – The building is 19th century with later additions and it overlooks the Knavesmire racecourse. This is a pleasant, traditional sort of hostelry, about 1.5 miles from the center. Tadcaster Rd. (phone: 707171). Moderate.

Coach House – The 17th-century origins of this guesthouse are still much in evidence, with oak-beamed ceilings throughout. It's located in the same, traffic-free cul-de-sac as the *Abbots Mews Hotel.* There are 13 rooms, 2 with private bath. 20/22 Marygate, Bootham (phone: 52780). Moderate.

Hill – This Georgian establishment is family run, and since it has only 10 rooms (2 with four-poster beds), staying here is like staying in a private home — with private bath or shower, use of a delightful garden, and traditional cuisine. About 2 miles from city center. 60 York Rd., Acomb (phone: 790777). Moderate.

Hudson's – A large, four-story Victorian building just a few minutes' walk from the city center. All rooms have TV and private bath. Typical English fare is served in the downstairs restaurant amid Victorian-era kitchen decor. 60 Bootham (phone: 21268). Moderate.

Post House – Large, modern, and built close to the ground, this is about 1.5 miles south of the center of town. Part of it faces the racecourse; restaurant and other public rooms are arranged around a cedar of Lebanon tree planted in the garden of the manor house that used to occupy the site. There are 147 rooms. Tadcaster Rd. (phone: 707921). Moderate.

Ashcroft – The 2.5-acre setting with a view of the River Ouse compensates for this lovely Victorian hotel's distance from the city center (1 mile). All 15 rooms have private baths or showers. 294 Bishopthorpe Rd. (phone: 59286). Inexpensive.

Jorvik – Small and modest — most of the 18 rooms have private bath. The *Jorvik* faces the Abbey Gate and the 11th-century St. Olave's Church. 52 Marygate, Bootham (phone: 53511). Inexpensive.

Youth Hotel – Catering to the budget traveler, this unassuming place offers meals, bike rentals, and dormitory–style TV rooms at prices of £5 and up per night (bed only). 11/13 Bishopshill Senior (phone: 30613). Very inexpensive.

EATING OUT: Yorkshire's reputation for mountainous portions of everything is as apparent in its major city as anywhere else in the county, although the more cosmopolitan restaurants are less likely to plump you out of all proportion than those that pride themselves on real Yorkshire kitchens. The most renowned local specialty, of course, is roast beef with Yorkshire pudding (see *Sins*). And if you thought there was nothing as American as apple pie, be advised that — topped with a slice of Wensleydale cheese — this is just as much of an institution here as it is back home. Parkin, an oatmeal, molasses, and ginger-rich cake, is another Yorkshire institution, traditionally made for Guy Fawkes Day (see *Sharing a Pint*). From $7 to $13 per person will buy a full meal with coffee and dessert (but without wine) in a restaurant listed below as moderate. You'll pay less than $7 at those listed as inexpensive. In addition to its restaurants, several of York's pubs serve good quality bar snacks at lunchtime. The best of these are included in the listings.

Betty's Tea Room – There's nothing better than to come in from York's chilling winter air and wallow in the coziness of toasted, home-baked tea cakes and crumpets puddled in butter, Yorkshire parkin, Brontë-rich fruitcakes, and *Betty's* famous rarebit, made from farmhouse Cheddar and Yorkshire ale, grilled on toast, and all according to a secret recipe. Open for main meals, too, either in the licensed restaurant or the cafeteria. Closed from 5:30 PM and Sundays. St. Helen's Sq. (phone: 59142). Moderate.

Dominico's – Despite its name, this is a French restaurant with a small, discriminating menu that includes bouillabaisse and Normandy pheasant. 19 Grape La. (phone: 36366). Moderate.

Park – In the Coppergate pedestrian shopping area, with coffees, cocktails, salads, quiches, pastries, and roasts among its choices. Coppergate (phone: 647640). Moderate.

Plunkets – With some very tasty food, *Plunkets* has a friendly ambience, good music in the background, lots of plants, and quality hamburgers. 9 High Petergate (phone: 37722). Moderate.

Tanglewood Inn – "A haven for the hungry," located 5 miles from York on the Malton Road. The menu — served by a small, friendly staff — includes tanglewood pie, salads, and light lunches. Malton Rd. (phone: 86318). Moderate.

Thomas's Wine Bar – Pick your own salads from a wide selection, lunchtime or evenings. 3 Museum St. (phone: 54494). Moderate.

Cross Keys – One of the city's few authentically Edwardian pubs, this has one of the best shepherd's pies in town (ground beef crowned by mashed potato and lightly grilled). Goodramgate (phone: 59408). Inexpensive.

Danish Kitchen – Fittingly adjacent to the Viking Centre, this is the place for Danish-style open sandwiches as well as cakes and pastries. High Ousegate (phone: 37752). Inexpensive.

King's Manor – The historic Tudor setting of the York University refectory is open to the public for lunch from noon to 2 PM Mondays through Fridays. Both salads and hot meals are available. Exhibition Sq. (phone: 59861). Inexpensive.

Medio's Pizzeria – Enormous pizzas, baked in a brick oven, complete with pasta choices and a few other temptations besides. The atmosphere is lively. Open for lunch and dinner daily. 115 Micklegate (phone: 34765). Inexpensive.

Spud Murphy's and The Fillers – Spuds to go, baked and blessed with a variety of fillings including mussel salad, curried rice, coleslaw, and over two dozen others. Open daily in summer until 11:30 PM, shorter hours in winter. 33 Swinegate (phone: 36361). Inexpensive.

St. William's – Once a medieval house for chantry priests, the surroundings are monastic with a hint of luxury. A very popular luncheon spot for salads, quiche, teatime tea, and cakes. Stop in after visiting the nearby Minster or when you tire of brass rubbing. Enjoy a glass of elderflaver wine at one of the festive tables outside, during the summer. College St. (phone: 34830). Inexpensive.

York Wholefood – The emphasis here is on unprocessed, additive-free, natural ingredients done up in various vegetarian dishes. Open for lunch daily except Sundays and for dinner on Thursdays, Fridays, and Saturdays. 98 Micklegate (phone: 56804). Inexpensive.

SHARING A PINT: York has an embarrassment of riches when it comes to pubs. There are some 150 all told, quite a few of them crammed with character and characters. The drink is beer, especially beer from the local breweries and especially the famous Theakston's Old Peculier. *Ye Old Starre Inn,* easily located at 40 Stonegate by the gallows right across the road, is York's oldest alehouse. Its name was first recorded in 1644 and it has been a popular lodging house both for actors from the Theatre Royal and for church dignitaries visiting the Minster. Today's interior is Victorian. The *Bay Horse* pub, 55 Blossom St., where you can try the locally brewed John Smith beer, and the *Bootham Tavern,* Bootham, are other places to imbibe in a Victorian setting. The *King's Arms,* on King's Staith, is still sometimes flooded in winter with waters from the adjacent embankment — a board records the various flood levels. At the *Roman Bath,* St. Sampson's Sq., customers can view genuine Roman steam baths, or rather their 2,000-year-old remains. General Wolfe, who lost his life winning Québec for the British, spent part of his youth in the *Black Swan Inn,* his mother's home in Peasholme Green. It was built as a merchant's house in the 16th century, and a room upstairs was used for illegal cockfighting. *Young's* hotel, 25 High Petergate, is reputedly on the site of the birthplace of Guy Fawkes, the man who tried (unsuccessfully) to blow up the British Parliament in 1605, bequeathing to children all over England an annual (November 5) excuse to burn him in effigy to the accompaniment of firecrackers.

DIVERSIONS

For the Body

Great Golf

True golf devotees contend that the finest — and most authentic — golf courses in the world are found in Britain and Ireland. This is hardly surprising since the sandy land along their coasts was the terrain that spawned the game. It's hard to believe that less than a century ago golf was virtually unknown anywhere outside Scotland, though the Scots proved great apostles, spreading the word from Perth (where the first recognizable six-hole course is thought to have been constructed on the city's North Inch), St. Andrews, Prestwick, and Dornoch.

These are the icons of a game that has gripped the attention of an entire planet. At about the time golf leaped the Atlantic in the late 19th century, it also settled into the Irish Republic, an environment as congenial as Scotland's, and it grew along the same lines. Consequently, even now, the courses found in Scotland, England, Northern Ireland, and the Irish Republic provide a very different sense of the game than can be acquired anywhere else on earth. Nature was the architect of these courses. As a writer remarked in *The World Atlas of Golf,* "To this day nobody knows who laid [the courses] out . . . there were no fairways, no tees, and no greens, simply agreed starting and finishing points. The game had reached St. Andrews, Carnoustie, Leith, Dornoch, Montrose, North Berwick, and Musselburgh by the beginning of the 16th century. Golf thus became established on linksland . . . St. Andrews became — and still is — one long fairway, with nine holes out to a distant point, and nine holes back . . . designs incorporated stone walls, blind shots, hedges, irregularly-shaped mounds and greens in geometric shapes."

But it's more than history that lures generations of modern golfers to the game's breeding grounds. Particularly in Ireland, there's a friendliness to the sport; it's a community game, not cloistered and clubby. The intensity of the challenge found on these courses remains as vital as ever, and the chance to pit one's own skill against the achievements of golf's greatest historic figures is nearly irresistible. Not to play these courses at least once in a lifetime is not to know the real horizons of the game.

SUNNINGDALE, Sunningdale, Berkshire, England: While the Old Course is considered the championship layout here, the New is probably the harder of the two. When you play them, you will discover that the decision on difficulty is an arbitrary one at best. Fairways and greens are meticulously maintained, and this is perhaps the finest single brace of courses in England. Private but approachable. Details: Sunningdale Golf Club, Ridgemount Rd., Sunningdale, Berkshire SL5 9RW, England (phone: 0990-21681).

WENTWORTH, Virginia Water, Surrey, England: Generally considered the prettier of the layouts here, the East Course can do wonders for a shaky backswing. But it's the West Course, with its relatively narrow tree-lined fairways, that is sometimes not so affectionately called the "Burma Road." For a high-handicap player, the West is not unlike putting an innocent's head into the mouth of an unfriendly lion, and especially from the back tees, the cry of "You can't get there from here!" is continually heard. The World Match Play Championship has been held here every year since 1964. Again, it's a private club; access is available to traveling players on weekdays with prior notice — upon presentation of your own club membership card and, if possible, a letter from your club president. With its dozen tennis courts, its swimming pool, and its equally well-maintained nine-hole par-30 course, the Wentworth Golf Club is probably the nearest thing to an American country club in the south of England. Details: Wentworth Club, Virginia Water, Surrey GU25 4LS, England (phone: Wentworth 09904-2201).

ROYAL LIVERPOOL, Hoylake, Merseyside, England: This was the site of the first British amateur championship — which has been held here on 15 occasions since — and the first international golf competition (played between England and Scotland in 1902). In 1921, "Hoylake," as it's generally called, played host to the first international match between Great Britain and the U.S. which, the following year, was dubbed the Walker Cup. Today the course contains one controversial aspect: It's possible to be out-of-bounds and still lie within the course. That happens when a perfect long iron is hit directly at the heart of the seventh green and the ball hops over a bank to lie out of bounds, a scant few yards from the flag. Not for the faint of heart. Details: Royal Liverpool Golf Club, Meols Dr., Hoylake, Merseyside L47 4AL, England (phone: 051-632-3101).

ROYAL LYTHAM & ST. ANNES GOLF CLUB, Lytham St. Annes, Lancashire, England: Possessed of little visual splendor and set in an essentially urban setting, this course remains one of the most difficult of all the tracks in Britain and has maintained a special place on the British Open championship rota. Don't be deceived by the apparent tranquillity; the course is a test of golf that's among the finest in Britain, and nerve and subtlety are both required. Details: Royal Lytham & St. Annes Golf Club, Links Gate, Lytham St. Annes, Lancashire FY8 3LQ (phone: St. Annes 0253-724206).

ROYAL BIRKDALE GOLF CLUB, Southport, Merseyside, England: The site is one of England's most compelling, amid a stunning expanse of dunes on the Lancashire coast. This layout, one of surpassing challenge, has hosted many championships and international competitions, as many as any other course in Britain since the end of World War II. The final six holes cover almost 2.5 miles, and it takes supreme accuracy — rather than raw power — to avoid the fairway bunkers. Details: Royal Birkdale Golf Club, Waterloo Rd., Southport, Merseyside PR8 2LX, England (phone: Southport 0704-67920).

GANTON GOLF CLUB, Ganton, Yorkshire, England: The east coast of England is not well known for its golfing venues, but this Yorkshire course is one of Britain's finest inland layouts. The holes are positioned on open heathland. The prime hazards here are bunkers and gorse, especially those placed alongside and amid fairway landing areas. Straight hitting is a must. Perhaps the greatest lure here is the variety of challenge that requires accurate play and consummate concentration. Details: Ganton Golf Club, Ganton, North Yorkshire, England YO12 4PA (phone: 09444-70329).

ROYAL ST. GEORGE'S GOLF CLUB, Sandwich, Kent, England: This corner of Kent is rich in history and no course has a more constant involvement with the evolution of English championship golf. Often called "Sandwich," it was the site of the first Walker Cup matches ever held in England. It was also the scene of the first ever American victory in the British Amateur championship and in the British Open (by Walter Hagen). And it was here in 1949 that the Open saw the memorable tie between Henry Bradshaw and the South African Bobby Locke (who won the 36-hole playoff). This is a place where golf history buffs will want to make their mark. Details: Royal St. George's, Sandwich, Kent CT13 9PB England (phone: 0304-613090).

THE OLD COURSE, St. Andrews, Fife, Scotland: Dating at least from the 15th, but more likely from the late 14th, century, this is the sport's greatest magnet, drawing all of the world's golfers, and its aura is only slightly diminished by the bathers and strollers who occasionally cross the first and eighteenth fairways of the Old Course — it's the shortest route to the beach. Once on the course, its extreme difficulty and subtly careful layout becomes more apparent, but hardly surprising, since the course was fashioned by nature, with the help of the sheep and rabbits who created bunker locations when burrowing underground to escape the off-shore winds that blow year round. There are four other courses on the same site — the Balgove, Eden, Jubilee, and New (which was *opened* in 1894) — but it's the Old (the site of no less than two dozen British Opens, and now the permanent home of the Dunhill Nations Cup tournament held each October) that any dedicated golfer must play. Make plans carefully to be here on the right day (the Old Course is closed on Sunday), and confirm tee-off times well in advance — a year in advance is not too early. Details: Links Management Committee, Golf Pl., St. Andrews, Fife KY16 9JA Scotland (phone: 0334-75757).

GLENEAGLES, Auchterarder, Perthshire, Scotland: Visiting golfers looking for variety and adventure aren't likely to fall prey to the Scots' tendency toward denigratation of this superb quartet of courses due to the lack of conformity to the treasured linksland tradition. The Queen's Course was restored in 1983 to James Braid's original design, the King's Course is an absolute joy to play (in 1987 it became home to Bell's Scottish Open), and the Gleneagles links are also consistently in the best condition of any Scottish courses. But the extraordinary hotel here would alone be reason enough to visit. Details: Gleneagles Hotel Golf Course, Auchterarder, Perthshire PH3 1NF, Scotland (phone: 07646-3543).

CARNOUSTIE, Carnoustie, Tayside, Scotland: Just 5 miles from St. Andrews as the crow flies (or 25 miles by road) is this site of half a dozen British Open tournaments. If the Championship Course (the best of the trio of tracks here) is the least impressive of the championship Scottish courses at first glance, its true value is easily appreciated in a single round. It encompasses the very essence of what's best about playing golf in Scotland, and the back nine in particular — with the famous fourteenth hole, called "Spectacles" because of two yawning twin bunkers in mid-fairway — and the three backbreaking finishing holes offer lasting memories. Details: Carnoustie Golf Links, Links Parade, Carnoustie, Tayside DD7 7JE, Scotland (phone: starter, 0241-53249; secretary, 0241-53789).

THE HONOURABLE COMPANY OF EDINBURGH GOLFERS, Gullane, East Lothian, Scotland: The single best course in Scotland, this is home to the golf club with the longest continuous history in the world, one that has grown in status with each decade since its formal beginnings in 1744. Tucked along the south shore of the Firth of Forth, the course — most commonly called "Muirfield," — is totally challenging as well as beautifully simple. (For an idea of just how challenging it can be, know that the Committee recently imposed a maximum handicap of 18 for men and 24 for women because so many visitors, "unable to cope with the difficulty of the championship course," took 4½ hours or even longer to get around it.) Note that access is granted to nonmembers only by advance arrangement and only on Tuesdays, Thursdays, and Friday mornings. Still, getting to play at this wonderful place is considerably less problematic than it once was; when writing, include alternate playing dates. Details: The Honourable Company of Edinburgh Golfers, Muirfield, Gullane, East Lothian EH31 2EG, Scotland (phone: 0620-842123).

ROYAL DORNOCH, Dornoch, Highland, Scotland: No course in the world offers more wild beauty than this northernmost of the globe's great golf layouts. The course sweeps in a great curve along the shores of the Dornoch Firth, a site of splendid isolation that seldom fails to inspire a feeling of singular elation; many players echo the sentiments of Tom Watson, who remarked that the three rounds he played during one 24-hour visit were more fun than any other golfing experience of his life. Details: Royal Dornoch, Dornoch IV25 3LW, Highland, Scotland (phone: 086-281-219).

PRESTWICK, Prestwick, Strathclyde, Scotland: This famed course was the site of the first twelve Open Championships and another dozen in subsequent (but not consecutive) years. It has been taken off the Open rota because of its limited facilities for handling crowds, but it is still worth playing for its historic associations and for its challenges — long carries, deep bunkers, tough weather, rolling sand dunes, and the insidious Pow Burn, all nemeses for the inaccurate striker. However, on the admittedly rare occasions when the wind comes out of the east, you may need earplugs to drown out the din from neighboring Prestwick Airport, which can be seen across the railway line bordering the first hole. Bookings must be made well in advance. Details: Prestwick Golf Club, 2 Links Rd., Prestwick KA9 1QG, Ayrshire, Scotland (phone: 0292-77404).

ROYAL TROON, Troon, Ayrshire, Scotland: Laid out along the beach, with the outgoing nine heading virtually straight down the strand and the closing nine paralleling it only a few yards inland, the only distraction — aside from the view of the Firth of Clyde, the Isle of Arran, and the flaming sunsets — lies in the course's location directly below the flight path into Prestwick Airport. So it sometimes seems as though players are about to be sucked up into the jet wash. Another classic Open layout, it is one of the few important private clubs in Scotland open to visitors (although only to a very limited number), though playing privileges are usually open only to members of clubs in the US who can produce a respectable certificate of handicap and only on weekdays upon advance arrangement, which is essential. Ladies are allowed to play on the championship links only on Mondays, Wednesdays, and Fridays. The day-ticket greens fee also permits a round of play on the Portland, which some have pronounced even tougher than the Old Course. Details: Royal Troon Golf Club, Craigend Rd., Troon, Ayrshire KA10 6EP, Scotland (phone: 0292-311555).

TURNBERRY HOTEL GOLF COURSE, Turnberry, Strathclyde, Scotland: The two courses here, the Ailsa and the Arran, are quite close in quality, but it's the Ailsa on which the British Open was played in 1977 and 1986. The wind blows in from the sea, and it sometimes takes an act of courage just to stand up on the craggy tees and hit out into the teeth of what occasionally seems like a major gale. The beautiful *Turnberry* hotel — built at the turn of the century in the Edwardian style and now being completely refurbished — provides some respite from the elements. It has recently been sold to a Japanese investment group. But the golfing challenge is the real lure. Details: Turnberry Hotel Golf Courses, Turnberry, Strathclyde KA26 9LT, Scotland (phone: 0655-31000).

ROYAL PORTHCAWL, Porthcawl, Mid Glamorgan, Wales: Not a links course in the strictest sense, though there are occasional sandhills. The main hazards, however, are gorse, hummocks, heather, and deep bunkers. The good news is that the lay of the land permits players to look across Bristol Channel to the long dark line of the Somerset coast — and see the sea from any tee or green. Founded in 1891, the course combines links and heathland play, and there's a particularly high premium on a golfer's ability to place shots accurately against often furious natural elements. Just trying to find the fairway here can be a humbling experience. Details: Royal Porthcawl Golf Club, Porthcawl, Rest Bay, Mid Glamorgan CF36 3UW, Wales (phone: 065671-2251).

BALLYBUNION, Ballybunion, County Kerry, Irish Republic: The original course here is one of the two Irish tracks that Tom Watson plays every year or two just for fun (Lahinch, below, is the other), and no less an authority than Herbert Warren Wind calls the old course one of the ten toughest courses in the world. You will have no reason to disagree. The course is laid out at the point where the Shannon River estuary meets the Atlantic Ocean. Its fourteenth, seventeenth, and eighteenth holes are all roaring winds, and the out-of-bounds area beside the first hole is a graveyard. Welcome to Ireland. A second Robert Trent Jones 18-holer has recently been added. Details: Ballybunion Golf Club, County Kerry, Irish Republic (phone: 068-27146).

KILLARNEY GOLF AND FISHING CLUB, Killarney, County Kerry, Irish Republic: The scenery is lovely and dramatic in this fabled spot, and it may take an act of will to keep your head down while playing on one of the two championship courses, though it may not be worth the effort. The sight of the lakes framing the purple mountains is a once-in-a-lifetime experience. The older course presents the more taxing challenge. Details: Killarney Golf and Fishing Club, Mahoney's Point, Killarney, County Kerry, Irish Republic (phone: 064-31034).

PORTMARNOCK, Portmarnock, County Dublin, Irish Republic: This fabled layout (just outside Dublin) is perhaps the best single course in the Republic. The short flag sticks, which are set on springs to let them swing freely in the breeze, tell you something about the wind hazards here, and the last five holes are diabolically difficult. However, the quality of the course, especially the greens, is superb. Be prepared for the strong prevailing northeasterly wind, soaring scores — and a bracing outing. Details: Portmarnock Golf Club, Portmarnock, County Dublin, Irish Republic (phone: 323082).

ROYAL DUBLIN, Dollymount, County Dublin, Irish Republic: The "other" Dublin area golfing magnet that, though second to Portmarnock, still deserves a place among Europe's best. Again, the winds blow here and the rough grows to a size not normally known in the New World. Founded in 1885, the course is laid out remarkably like St. Andrews. The four famous short holes — the fourth, sixth, ninth, and twelfth — call for a keen eye and precision play; the demanding fifth hole, with its narrow valley of a fairway, prompted the late Danny Kaye to ask his caddy for a rifle. Details: Royal Dublin Golf Club, Dollymount, Dublin 3, Irish Republic (phone: 336-346).

LAHINCH, Lahinch, County Clare, Irish Republic: Created a century ago by some Irish merchants and a group of Scottish Black Watch regiment members stationed nearby, this extraordinary course has been known to inflict players with every conceivable plague, save famine and flood. The St. Andrews of Ireland — famous for its grazing goats — has one short par five that has been toughened a bit by putting something that looks like the Great Wall of China in the middle of the fairway, and to add a little extra spice to your round, there's a 145-yard par three that's completely blind. Would you like to guess how they managed that? And now they have added a second 18-hole course that is less demanding, but of championship standard nonetheless. Our pick for the best fun in the west of Ireland. Details: Lahinch Golf Club, Lahinch, County Clare, Irish Republic (phone: 065-81003).

COUNTY SLIGO GOLF CLUB, Rosses Point, County Sligo, Irish Republic: More popularly called "Rosses Point," this western Irish links maintains the conflict between golfer and the Atlantic ocean breezes. How you play here depends a lot on which way the prevailing hurricane happens to be blowing. Rosses Point is not quite as tight a course as the other Irish monsters, and some of its greens are even reachable by mere mortals in regulation figures. Chances are that this is the Irish golf course where your spirits (not your score) will soar. Details: County Sligo Golf Club, Rosses Point, County Sligo, Irish Republic (phone: 071-77186).

WATERVILLE GOLF CLUB, Waterville, County Kerry, Irish Republic: A modern resort hotel adjoins this championship course, but don't get the idea that this is a resort course, since the layout is as rugged as the surrounding countryside. This longest of Irish tracks (7,214 yards from the championship tees) plays between the Atlantic coast and an inland lake that's best known to trout and salmon fishermen. Though long teeing areas allow the course to be shortened to 6,024 yards (society tees), the brave playing from the back are in for a very exhilarating and challenging afternoon. Details: Waterville Golf Club, Waterville Lake Hotel, County Kerry, Irish Republic (phone: 021-775554; hotel 0667-4133).

ROYAL PORTRUSH, Portrush, County Antrim, Northern Ireland: Though the "troubles" in Northern Ireland persist, the golf remains above the internecine disputes. Of the two layouts here, the Dunluce Course — the only club in Ireland to host the British Open — is the championship one. It's named after the striking old castle that is perched on the white cliffs to the east of the course. The wind off the North Sea is usually intense and constant and no less than Pete Dye estimated not long ago that the course should be ranked eighth best in the world. Details: Royal Portrush Golf Club, Dunluce Rd., Portrush, County Antrim BT56 8JQ, Northern Ireland (phone: 0265-822311).

ROYAL COUNTY DOWN, Newcastle, County Down, Northern Ireland: This is "where the Mountains of Mourne sweep down to the sea." The British Amateur championship was played here a few years ago, and *Golf* magazine voted it the world's third best in 1983. So no one should be too surprised to find that there are hazards in certain places that can prove rather startling to weak-kneed players. The minutes of the founding club meeting in 1889 reported that "the Secretaries were empowered to employ Tom Morris to lay out the course at a cost not to exceed £4." God alone only knows how Old Tom hacked these holes out of the rough sandhills for that price, but he did make a beauty. Details: Royal County Down Golf Club, Newcastle, County Down BT30 0AN, Northern Ireland (phone: 23314).

Tennis

Britain practically closes down in late June and early July, the fortnight of the Wimbledon Lawn Tennis Championships. Ticket scalpers do a brisk trade at the queues outside the gate (and even advertise in the personal columns of the newspapers), and those who aren't lucky enough to secure tickets stay home and watch the competition on their televisions.

This passion has definitely had its effect on the number of participants in the sport, and the population of courts, players, clubs, and cute little robin's-egg blue outfits has soared in the last few years; although tennis still has a long way to go before it becomes the national mania in Britain and Ireland that it is in the US, there are now hundreds of thousands of players, and courts are seldom hard to find. While you still wouldn't come here to play tennis, you should be sure to pack your racquet and your tennis whites, since a tennis match is a fine, rapid way to get off the standard tourist circuit and into local life (which, in the case of British tennis clubs, is most often that of the upwardly mobile middle classes). In these circles, playing well is considered important — but playing as if you mean to win at all costs isn't the style. If you pass muster, you may end the match with at least an invitation to tea.

WHERE TO PLAY

Municipal courts abound in both Britain and Ireland; tourist literature can provide their locations in the towns you'll be visiting. In addition, many of the more luxurious hotels have their own courts. Your best sources of information:

Britain's Lawn Tennis Association, Queens Club, West Kensington, London W14 9EG, England (phone: 01-385-2366). Can supply information on tennis in Great Britain, including lists of affiliated private tennis clubs where visiting players may be able to get a game.

The Dublin Corporation, Community & Environment Department, Capel Buildings, 68-71 Great Strand St., Dublin 1 (phone: 01-786066). Can answer questions about playing on public courses around Dublin.

The Irish Lawn Tennis Association, 22 Upper Fitzwilliam St., Dublin 2, Irish Republic (phone: 01-606332). Can answer questions about playing around Ireland.

If you want to spend more than just a casual hour a day on the courts, you may want to plan your trip around stops at a handful of resorts, tennis schools, and other spots at which the game is given more than just a passing nod, such as the following:

Beaconsfield School of Lawn Tennis, Beaconsfield, Buckinghamshire HP9 2BY, England (phone: 0494-64744). Eastablished for 25 years, this school is open year round and offers individual and group courses at modest cost. Principal Suzan Livingston, who is also president of the British Women's Tennis Association and tournament administrator of the European Tennis Association, does not push a single style but works to encourage the skills of each individual player, whether beginner or pro. Lodging is in hotels or with local families; the setting is the rolling, wooded Chiltern Hills, only 30 minutes from Heathrow and 40 minutes by train or car from central London.

Fulcher School of Tennis, Thurleston Tennis Centre, Henley Rd., Ipswich, Suffolk IP1 6TD, England (phone: 0473-210-903). This center, one of England's most complete, sponsors summer tennis camps for adults and families nearby in Bildeston at Old Buckenham Hall, Brettenham Park. Three indoor and three outdoor courts are available, along with video replay equipment, ball machines, and the like.

Holbrook House, Holbrook, Wincanton, Somerset BA9 8BS, England (phone: 0963-32377). This is your chance to see how McEnroe feels when he plays on grass: This family-run hotel has a good grass court in addition to its all-weather court. Lodgings are in a former country house dating from 1530. No coaching is available.

Southampton School of Lawn Tennis Coaching and Europa Tennis Limited, 35 Cobden Ave., Bitterne Park, Southampton SO2 4FU, England (phone: 0703-556415). Residential junior and adult courses at every level on four indoor and four outdoor courts in the heart of the Hampshire countryside; videotapes record your efforts against ball machines.

Tennis Coaching International, Thurleigh Rd., Milton Ernest, near Bedford, Bedfordshire MK44 1RF, England (phone: 02302-2914). This leading tennis school, an hour from London in a pretty village alongside the River Ouse, offers an extensive program of courses at private and municipal clay, asphalt, and grass courts in the area. Instructors are picked for their patience, technical know-how, and teaching abilities; and videotape and ball machines and backboards are available, and adult and junior L.T.A. Tournament holidays are offered. Accommodations are in an evocative building that dates from 1694, in private apartments or hotels, or with English families.

Dublin Sport, Kilternan, County Dublin, Irish Republic. Set in the sylvan Dublin Mountains on two acres about 15 minutes south of Dublin city center, this leisure hotel complex includes an 18-hole golf course, horseback riding, an indoor heated swimming pool, a gym, saunas, and an artificial ski slope. It adjoins a new multi-million-dollar national tennis center, whose eight courts (four indoor, four outdoor) are open from early in the morning until midnight. Special tennis vacations are available through Carole Wright Haber, ILTA, 128 E 71st St., New York, NY 10021 (phone: 212-249-3869).

Kelly's Strand, Rosslare, County Wexford, Irish Republic (phone: 053-32114). Good tennis facilities, with outdoor and indoor courts, at a family-run hotel famous for its food.

Pontoon Bridge, Foxford, County Mayo, Irish Republic (phone: 094-56120/

56151). Another opportunity to test your skills on grass — there's a single grass court at this modern lakeside hotel.

WHERE TO WATCH

The big deal is unquestionably the *Wimbledon Lawn Tennis Championships,* which take place in late June or early July at the All England Lawn Tennis and Croquet Club. Still a magnet to players who compete for much bigger cash prizes elsewhere, this tourney is an experience even for those who have never held a racquet. Grass courts, strawberry teas, and the legendary Centre Court make for such a spectacle that visitors may find the world-class matches that are going on quietly on all the outlying lawns hardly more than a diversion. All public Centre Court seats and standing room space for the last four days of the competition are allocated by lottery. Ticket request forms should be submitted between October 1 and the end of December, and successful applicants will be notified and billed for their tickets by April. A limited number of tickets for Centre Court seats for the first 9 days of the matches, as well as tickets for seats at the Number One Court and at several other locations, may be purchased on the day of play. For details about these seats and the new ticket allocation procedure, contact the All England Lawn Tennis and Croquet Club, PO Box 98, Church Rd., Wimbledon, London SW19 5AE, England; a self-addressed envelope with the proper postage or international postage coupons should be included with any correspondence.

By far the most certain and efficient means of seeing the match of your choice is to purchase one of the many packages of Britain's *Keith Prowse & Co.,* 234 W 44th St., New York, NY 10036 (phone: 212-398-1430 and 800-992-9223), which offers a wide range of selection for first-week, second-week, and men's and women's finals play. Similar offerings with close-to-the-court grandstand seats are available for the Stella Artois (men's) championships at Queens Club, and for the Pilkington Glass Cup (women's) at Eastbourne.

In the Irish Republic, the *Irish Open* is the major event of the season. Although it's not now a major tournament, a number of up-and-coming players from the international circuit usually make the scene. For more information on other Irish tourneys, contact the Irish Lawn Tennis Association (above).

Horsing Around

Britain and Ireland are among the world's most horse-mad nations — as they have been practically ever since the Romans, and later the Normans, brought horses to Britain many centuries ago. There were races as early as the 12th century at London's Smithfield Market. Period romances speak of races between knights and noblemen. Later, Henry VIII and James I kept stables (the latter's at Newmarket), and from James II on down, English monarchs have been horse fanciers. Elizabeth II, who keeps a stable and rides regularly, can be at her most animated when urging on her horse. Princess Anne, who ranks in the international class in the demanding game of three-day eventing, competes in shows all over the country with her husband, Captain Mark Phillips. In Ireland, "The Race" is a national passion, and the horses and their trainers are legendary among horse lovers all around the globe. Millions of pounds worth of Irish-bred horses are exported every year.

For travelers, the ubiquity of the mania for horses means that equestrians will never want for a common ground for conversation in the village pubs around Britain and Ireland; and that horse-oriented vacations abound in both nations.

MEETS, SHOWS, AND RACES

You'll be meeting Britons and the Irish on their favorite turf when you take in one of the dozen international shows and hundreds of national events held in both Britain and Ireland every year. Britain alone has some 60 racecourses — 17 devoted solely to flat racing (whose season runs from the third week in March to the first week in November), 24 solely to National Hunt racing (or steeplechasing, whose season begins early in August and ends in June), and the rest with facilities for both. Major courses include *Ascot,* near Windsor in Berkshire (see below); *Doncaster's Town Moor* course, in South Yorkshire (the successor to two other courses that flourished in the area as early as 1595), home of the William Hill Futurity, the former Observer Gold Cup, a mile-long contest for 2-year-olds, and of the St. Leger Stakes, a September race for 3-year-old colts and fillies and the last classic of the flat racing season and the third in Britain's Triple Crown; *Epsom,* in Surrey (see below); the lovely *Goodwood,* situated in Sussex in the Duke of Richmond's Park, especially noted for the 1-mile Sussex Stakes, held in late July; *Newmarket,* the celebrated old course in Cambridgeshire, England's flat-racing headquarters; and *Sandown Park,* founded in 1875, now the home of the Eclipse Stakes, a 1¼-miler run every July since 1886 and named to honor the 18th-century nonpareil from whom all of the world's thoroughbred race horses are said to be descended. (This animal, who prompted his owner's now apocryphal remark "Eclipse first, the rest nowhere" didn't compete until he was five — but placed first in every race he entered.) The Triple Crown of the British racing season goes to the horse that wins Newmarket's Two Thousand Guineas, the Epsom Derby, and Doncaster's St. Leger. (Newmarket, the center of flat-track racing in England and the focal point of British training, is also the home of the new National Horseracing Museum, which tells the story of racing's development in England and shows videos of classic races. There are also a number of stud farms in the area, including the *National Stud,* open to the public on special days during August. *Tattersalls,* the celebrated English horse auctioneer founded in London in 1766, conducts a number of sales throughout the year, the most important being the two Yearling Sales held in fall.)

Tracks are always grass — rather than dirt or a synthetic surface as in many countries — so that meetings last only 4 or 5 days at a stretch (just 3 days in winter), and are spaced far enough apart to give the turf time to recover between meetings; the nationwide schedule is arranged so that there's always something going on in each region of the country. For dates and locations of upcoming weeks' fixtures (as racing events are called here), consult listings in newspapers such as *The Sporting Life.* A season-long fixtures calendar is available in booklet form from the Racecourse Publicity Agency, Winkfield Rd., Ascot, Berkshire SL5 7HX, England (phone: 0990-25912).

Ireland's fixtures calendar includes more than 250 race meetings at 28 racecourses, all of them wonderfully entertaining, with the brouhaha of bettors calling out the names of horses and "on course men" shouting the odds as they are posted on a board in the stands, wiped out, and reposted as the wagers are placed. At Fairyhouse and Punchestown, 14 and 20 miles from Dublin respectively, there are large enclosures where families picnic in the grass and watch the goings-on. At festival meetings in Punchestown in April or May, Killarney and Galway in July, Tramore in mid-August, Tralee in late August or early September, and Listowel in late September, all the inhabitants for miles around stop work to watch the races. Things are more informal — a bit more unbridled — in Ireland than on the other side of the Irish Sea. Ireland's Newmarket is the Curragh, where racing has been going on ever since the 3rd century AD; the main races nowadays are the Irish Derby, the Irish Oaks, the Irish St. Leger, and the One Thousand Guineas and the Two Thousand Guineas (nicknamed, respectively, the One and Two Thousand Guinnesses). At the *Irish National Stud,* adjacent to the Curragh, you can see some of the nation's greatest stallions and mares (small admission charge); the *Irish Horse Museum,* also on the grounds, has displays that tell about horses from prehistoric days, with good coverage of draft horses as well as racing, hunting, show jumping, and steeplechasing. (For details, contact the Tourist Manager, Irish National Stud, Tully, County Kildare, Irish Republic; phone: 045-21617.) For a calendar of all races, and for the latest dates of those described below, contact the Irish Racing Board, 9 Merrion Sq., Dublin 2, Irish Republic (phone: 761171).

GRAND NATIONAL, Aintree, near Liverpool, England: The grueling steeplechase described in Enid Bagnold's *National Velvet* — the most famous race of its kind and the premiere event of the steeplechase season subjects competitors to 4½ lung-tearing miles over wickedly mischievous banks and ditches and extremely high fences reputed to be bigger than those of any other steeplechase course in the world; it's so tough that only a small percentage of competitors even finish, and only a half-dozen horses have won the competition even twice in more than a century. Fences such as the Chair, grim and formidable, and Becher's Brook, named after the brilliant jockey who fell there during the first Liverpool steeplechase in 1839, make for the sort of race that warms even those who don't know a Totalisator from a tic-tac man. At least, it will help you understand the comment of the *Liverpool Courier:* "All men of ardent feelings love moderate danger for the very excitement it produces and the intrepidity it brings to action." On the night before, be sure to stop in at the cavernous cocktail lounge of the immense, Rococo *Adelphi Hotel* to see the jockeys who will prove the point on the morrow. The Grand National takes place annually at the end of March or early in April over a Thursday, Friday, and Saturday. (The main event is held on Saturday.) Details: Aintree Racecourse, Aintree, Liverpool L9 5AS, England (phone: 051-523-2600).

ROYAL ASCOT, Ascot, Berkshire, England: The June meeting at this racecourse on the southern edge of Windsor Great Park, 25 miles west of London, has enjoyed royal patronage ever since Queen Anne drove over to watch the first races on the Ascot Common in 1711 — and it is still considered a high point of the London social season. Ascot is where Eliza Doolittle (of George Bernard Shaw's *Pygmalion* and Lerner and Loewe's *My Fair Lady*) first encountered high society; things are as oh-so-social even today. In the Royal Enclosure — the pricey part of the seating area — men wear top hats and morning coats and women, their smartest dresses and hats. Models come here hoping to catch a photographer's eye and launch a career; while other females, including more than one dowager, show up in bonnets that some might call preposterous. The sovereign and members of the royal family drive in state carriages from Windsor Castle on each day of the 4-day meeting. The key race in the meeting is the Ascot Gold Cup — a 2½-mile race that ranks as one of the most important of British flat racing's season. The King George VI and the Queen Elizabeth Stakes, a 1½-miler first run in 1951, takes place each July. Packages that include admission to the Grandstand Enclosure and the Paddock for the Ascot Gold Cup are available from *Keith Prowse & Co.,* 234 W 44th St., New York, NY 10036 (phone: 212-398-1430 or 800-992-9223). Other details: Ascot Racecourse, Ascot, Berkshire SL5 7JN, England (phone: 0990-22211).

BADMINTON HORSE TRIALS, Badminton, Avon, England: Three-day eventing, Princess Anne's specialty, is one of the toughest tests that horse and rider can face; the trials held annually since 1949 at the Duke of Beaufort's lovely green park in Badminton — the small West Country village that has become something of a fox-hunting magnet because the Duke's world-famous pack of foxhounds make their home here — are so important that they're regularly televised, and in prime time no less: Certainly, the trials are the world's longest running and most famous. Competitors come from all over the world, and over 250,000 spectators attend. The first two days are devoted to dressage and the fourth to the jumping test, both in the main arena. But the main feature is the speed and endurance test, which takes place on Saturday. The cross-country section takes riders over about 30 terrifying obstacles of every description. They are fixed and can't be knocked down. And though there are always several brand-new fences to test competitors' courage, hardy annuals like the famous Jump into the Lake and the Quarry reappear frequently in different guises — and still manage to send riders' hearts into their throats. While the competitors are risking their necks, spectators can watch on closed-circuit televisions in several marquees, or follow the event's progress, fortified by visits to the several large refreshment tents around the course. It's also fun to see the Deer Park, full of red and fallow deer, and to browse through the veritable village of shops and exhibits that go up for the duration in the Badminton Park. The competition lasts 4 days and always takes place in April — the precise date depending on that of Easter. Ticket application forms are available in early January. Details: Badminton Horse Trials Office, Badminton, Avon GL9 1DF, England (phone: Badminton 045-421-272).

ROYAL INTERNATIONAL HORSE SHOW, Birmingham, England: Even those who sit in the stands and refer to the dressage display as "those circus horses who dance" — as more than one spectator has been known to do at this immensely popular June annual, over 70 years old and among the most prestigious shows in the international equestrian calendar — find that its magic wins their hearts in a twinkling. Dressage, Arabians, hackney ponies in single harness, pairs of ponies, weight-carrying cobs, heavy horse turnouts, and children's ponies ridden sidesaddle can all be seen, along with lightweight, middleweight, and heavyweight hunters, small and large hacks, ladies' hacks, and costers' turnouts. Jumping competitions keep spectators on the edge of their seats from start to finish: Sometimes the outcome is in doubt right up until the last sleek animal has taken the last fence. The site is Birmingham's National Exhibition Centre. Details: Royal International Horse Show, 35 Belgrave Sq., London SW1 8QB, England (phone: box office and tickets 021-780-4141; information 01-235-6431).

THE EVER READY DERBY STAKES, Epsom, Surrey, England: The race after which the Kentucky Derby was named, itself named for one of the men who founded it in 1780, the sporting twelfth Earl of Derby, is a carnival as much as a 1½-mile speed trial for 3-year-old fillies and colts. All kinds of people turn up: ancient Gypsy families come to settle debts and arrange marriages; the top-hatted and tail-coated with their Rolls-Royces and picnic hampers; families with children; Cockneys from the East End just out for a good time; fortunetellers; gaudy tipsters predicting the winners; bookies with bulging Gladstones stuffed with fivers quoting the odds; their helpers peering through binoculars to the other side of the course, where white-gloved tic-tac men are using age-old hand movements to signal how the money is going. The spectacle of this national festivity — the event that Benjamin Disraeli himself called the Blue Riband of the Turf — has hardly changed a bit since the 18th-century English painter George Stubbs memorialized it on canvas. Ever since Sir Charles Bunbury's horse Diomed won the first race in 1780, the Derby Stakes has had a history punctuated with colorful characters, among them the early-19th-century Jem Robinson, who won a thousand pounds on a bet that within a single week, he would win the Oaks and the Derby (the latter for a seventh time), and marry; and Miss Emily Davison, a suffragette who died in 1913 after hurling herself under the hoofs of King George V's Anmer. The meeting usually takes place during the first week in June; the Ever Ready Derby is staged on a Wednesday, and the Gold Seal Oaks — Epsom's other major contest, a 1½-miler for fillies named after the Earl of Derby's shooting box — 3 days later. Buy a grandstand ticket if you must, but it's more fun to watch the goings-on from the hill in the middle of the course. *Keith Prowse & Co.,* 234 W 44th St., New York, NY 10036 (phone: 212-398-1430 or 800-992-9223), has packages. Details: United Racecourses, Ltd., Racecourse Paddock, Epsom, Surrey KT18 5NJ, England (phone: 03727-26311).

THE SILK CUT DERBY, Hickstead, West Sussex, England: This August event at the All England Jumping Course ranks as the nation's premiere show-jumping event.

The fact that only eighteen horses have jumped clear rounds on the course since 1961 suggests its difficulty; the Derby Bank, one of several permanent obstacles in the International Arena here, is famous among horse folk. Novice jumping, showing classes, and driving take place in other arenas. The whole production is fast and easily understood. Details: The Secretary, All England Jumping Course, Hickstead, West Sussex RH17 5NU, England (phone: Hurstpierpoint 0273-834315).

HORSE OF THE YEAR SHOW, Wembley, near London, England: Hunters, hacks, and ponies show up in October for this important fixture of the British equestrian calendar. The Horse Personalities of the Year awards are always popular, but the whole event presents a wonderful display of horseflesh, an equine extravaganza if ever there was one. Details: Horse of the Year Show, Wembley Arena, Wembley, Middlesex HA9 ODW, England (phone: 01-902-1234).

CONNEMARA PONY SHOW, Clifden, County Galway, Irish Republic: These attractive native ponies, the focus of an increasing degree of attention over the last decade, make fine pets — and excellent jumpers, as evidenced at this lively, friendly, but very professionally run country show first organized over 60 years ago and now held annually on the third Thursday in August. Some 300 of the finest of Ireland's Connemaras are usually on hand; they are intelligent, full of stamina, versatile, and even-tempered. Details: Connemara Pony Breeders Society, 73 Dalysfort Rd., Salthill, Galway, County Galway, Irish Republic (phone: 091-22909).

DUBLIN HORSE SHOW, Dublin, Irish Republic: Whereas other cities wilt during the warm days of summer, Dublin is awhirl with activity from the first Tuesday in August through the following Saturday, as horse lovers from all over Ireland, Great Britain, and the Continent converge on the capital for this equestrian and social event. First held in 1868, it is one of the best shows of its kind in the world and, with its hunt balls and social and diplomatic parties, it is certainly the high point of the year for Dublin society. For Ladies' Day, the Thursday of Horse Show Week, citizens don their best bib and tucker, and a glittering automobile is presented to the most attractively dressed and suitably groomed lady at the show. The main show-jumping events, held on Friday and Saturday, are the Nations Cup for the Aga Khan Trophy and the Grand Prix of Ireland — the richest jumping competitions in the world. Grandstand tickets for these competitions, as well as for others held during the week, are quite difficult to come by, but standing room is always available. Hotel rooms are scarce as hen's teeth — so hard to find, in fact, that if you haven't booked well in advance, you may end up lodging with a family near the showgrounds. Details: Royal Dublin Society, PO Box 121, Ballsbridge, Dublin 4, Irish Republic (phone: 01-680645); or, for housing details, Dublin and Eastern Regional Tourist Information Office, 13-14 Upper O'Connell St., Dublin 1, Irish Republic (phone: 01-747733).

THE BUDWEISER IRISH DERBY, Kildare, County Kildare: Irish racing is world famous and Irish-bred horses regularly win the Continent's classic competitions; this event, a 1½-miler for 3-year-olds held at the Curragh annually in late June, is Ireland's star race. Among the other classic races that make this track so important are the Irish One Thousand Guineas (1 mile for 3-year-old fillies, in May); the Irish Two Thousand Guineas (1 mile for 3-year-olds, in May); the Irish Oaks (1½ miles for 3-year-old fillies, in July); and the Irish St. Leger (1¾ miles for 3-year-olds and up, in October). Details: Irish Racing Board, 9 Merrion Sq., Dublin 2, Irish Republic (phone: 01-761171).

TIPPERARY RACECOURSE, Tipperary Town, County Tipperary, Irish Republic: For those who are jaded by big meetings, this small racecourse named after the nearby railway station, 115 miles from Dublin, is ideal. In the heart of racing Ireland — not far from the home of none other than Vincent O'Brien, one of the world's leading buyers, breeders, and trainers of racehorses — this racecourse has events regularly from March through November, and draws a crowd that is at least as interesting as the horses. The equine aspect to the features of some of the onlookers is very real: That's what comes of generations of looking after horses. In its own small way, the Limerick

Junction course shows offer everything that is delightful about Irish racing — and Irish character. Details: Irish Racing Board (address above).

RIDING HOLIDAYS AND PONY TREKKING

The British and the Irish flock to horse holidays with exactly the same enthusiasm that Americans flock to dude ranches — except that they are more likely to wear jodhpurs than jeans, swing into saddles without horns as well as with, and do their riding at a stable that doesn't always have anything more than a casual arrangement with their lodging place. Top-notch horses, delightful scenery, and the chance to join the natives in one of their favorite pastimes are the main attractions.

When you do begin to look into the possibilities of an equestrian holiday, you may at first find the lingo bewildering. The term *riding holiday,* for instance, refers to not just any vacation spent on horseback, but specifically to one where you'll trot, canter, occasionally even take small jumps, and get basic instruction either by a full-fledged instructor accredited by the British Horse Society (a BHSI), a British Horse Society–designated assistant instructor (BHSAI), or, in smaller establishments, horse folk who instruct as a summer job. The organizations that sponsor such activities, called "riding holiday centres," may also arrange for guests to compete in local shows and contests — great fun — where they may find themselves making horse talk with anyone from a local farmer to the squire's lady. Some riding holiday centers — those termed residential — have accommodations on the premises; some arrange for lodging in nearby guesthouses, old coaching inns, quaint hotels, or with local families. Rank beginners and advanced equestrians alike can sign up for riding holidays, which are available year-round.

Pony trekking, on the other hand, involves day-long trips on the back of a sturdy native pony or cob (a stocky, short-legged horse), and has participants traveling mainly at a walk — partly because most are inexperienced riders, partly because the riding is across moors, through dense forests, and in steep mountain country mainly in Scotland, the Lake District, the north of England's Dales, and sections of Wales, along narrow trails and roads that don't lend themselves to a faster pace. Absolute novices may be provided with some instruction, but it will ordinarily be at a relatively elementary level. The season generally runs from mid-April until late September or early October. Note that Ponies of Britain, a nonprofit organization that inspects both trekking and riding holiday centers in Britain — an expert on the subjects — suggests that children under 12 will get tired and bored while pony trekking and are generally better off at a riding holiday center that specializes in youngsters. The real joy of pony trekking is the scenery en route, for on horseback, it's possible to cover great sweeps of terrain — forests, fields, and meadows full of ferns or bracken, or spotted here and there with a clump of rosy heather or purplish foxglove and thistle — that may not otherwise be accessible to any but the most intrepid of Wordsworthian walkers. With saddles squeaking, the horses' hooves pounding out a soothing rhythm, the smell of leather and sweat perfuming the sweet clean air, you'll pass through forest dells to wild clear streams with whitewater lacy as a Renaissance lady's collar; struggle up steep rocky hillsides; and then promenade across their flat summits, with the woods-and-farms countryside spread out like a piece of green velvet patchwork.

The following include some of the best of British and Irish centers offering riding holidays and pony trekking. A more comprehensive list of both types of establishments is available from Ponies of Britain Office, 56 Green End Road, Sawtry, Huntingdon, PE17 5UY (phone: Ramsey 0487-830278); send a stamped self-addressed envelope. Also useful is the Irish Tourist Board's *Guide for the Equestrian Visitor to Ireland.*

Crabbet Park Equitation Centre, Worth, near Crawley, West Sussex RH10 4ST, England (phone: 0293-882601). Associated with horses since Lady Anne Blunt founded the world-famous Crabbet Arabian Stud in the 1870s, this 60-acre complex offers courses for riders of all skills. Guests learn about jumping, equitation, horse ownership, training the young horse, dressage, sidesaddle, and an assortment of other subjects in the indoor and outdoor arenas, on the cross-country course, and in the stables and paddocks. The object is for the novice to acquire basic confidence in the saddle and to hone the skills of the more experienced rider.

Gooseham Barton Stables, Gooseham, Morwenstow, near Bude, Cornwall EX23 9PG, England (phone: 028-883204). Lovely riding through quiet, scenic countryside and forests, with a sandy beach nearby. Accommodation in a farmhouse or a self-catering five-berth trailer. For experienced riders and unaccompanied children aged 12 and older; beginners out of peak season only. The name derives from one Sir William de Gooseham, who is said to have owned the farmhouse around 1310.

Moat House, Benenden, Kent TN17 4EU, England (phone: 0580-240581), or, in the US, Patricia Grindle, 22 Pleasant St., South Natick, MA 01760 (phone: 617-655-7000). An English riding school in the traditional mold. Princess Anne took riding lessons here while a student at the Benenden School nearby.

North Wheddon Farm, Wheddon Cross, near Minehead, Somerset TA24 7EX, England (phone: 064-384-224). Riding at all paces is provided here on the wild moors of surrounding Exmoor National Park, which has been called "the riding playground of England." Lodging is in a fine, attractive, old Georgian farmhouse.

Porlock Vale Equitation Centre, Porlock, near Minehead, Somerset TA24 8NY, England (phone: 0643-862338). Courses are available in general equitation and dressage, and instruction covers all aspects of equitation, among them sidesaddle, stable management, the training of the young horse, and more. The object is to produce a thinking rider who can continue to progress on his own. The late Tony Collings trained Britain's Three-Day Event team here for the 1952 Helsinki Olympics. Facilities include two indoor schools, an outdoor manege, show jumps and jumping grids, permanent cross-country fences, and a lecture room. Location in the delightful country between the northern fringe of Exmoor and the Somerset coast, with paddocks running down to the sea, provides the opportunity to ride over nearly 100 square miles.

Shilstone Rocks Stud, Widecombe-in-the-Moor, Newton Abbot, Devon TQ13 7TF, England (phone: Widecombe 03642281). A riding and trekking center and stud on a Dartmoor farm with a history that goes back to 1244. Dartmoor, with its granite tors, deep bogs, and untamed ponies grazing on the open moorland, has a reputation for its wicked storms and thick, swirling mists, making it the perfect setting for Sir Arthur Conan Doyle to choose for his eerie novel, *The Hound of the Baskervilles.* It's one of Britain's greatest authentic wildernesses, a hill range of remarkable beauty.

Silverdown Riding School, Harwell, Didcot, Oxfordshire OX11 0LU England (phone: 0235-835377). Riding holidays, with dressage courses and gymkhanas in addition to the more usual instruction.

Blair Castle Trekking Centre, Blair Atholl, Pitlochry, Tayside PH18 5SH, Scotland (phone: 079-681263). Experienced guides lead hour-long, half-day, and day-long treks on sure-footed Garron ponies. Instruction is available. Open from April to mid-August.

Highland Riding Centre, Borlum Farm, Drumnadrochit, Highlands IV3 6XN, Scotland (phone: 045-62220). In one of the loveliest parts of Scotland, overlooking Loch Ness, this center is especially good for families. There are Shetland ponies for small children, and livelier mounts for the experienced. Instruction, which is available indoors as well as out, can be tailored to all levels. Disabled riders are welcome, and ramps and mounting facilities for guests in wheelchairs are available. And when chore time rolls around — grooming the ponies, cleaning tack, mucking out the stalls, helping the blacksmith, herding cows and calves, caring for lambs, searching for eggs, even making hay — guests are welcome to lend a hand. Long established and well run.

Cae Iago Trekking Centre, Farmers, Llanwrda, Dyfed SA19 8LZ, Wales (phone: 055-85303). Excellent trekking through beautiful wild country for all levels of riders and trail rides for the experienced.

Cwmyoy Pony Trekking Centre, Cornmill, Llanthony, Gwent NP7 7NN, Wales (phone: Crucorney 0873-890-565). Pony trekking through the heather-purpled Black Mountains and Brecon Beacons National Park. Near the ancient Llanthony Priory.

Golden Pheasant Riding Centre, Tal y Garth Farm, Glyn Ceiriog, near Llangollen, Clwyd LL20 7AB, Wales (phone: 069172-408). Accommodation is in a comfortable 18th-century stone farmhouse on 65 acres. Instruction is available in stable management as well as riding; there's an enclosed outdoor manège and a cross-country course. A swimming pool is available.

Greystones Equestrian Centre, Castle Leslie, Glaslough, County Monaghan, Irish Republic (phone: 047-88100). Riding lessons, with five separate cross-country courses full of prepared fences and all sorts of natural obstacles — rivers, ditches, fallen trees, log piles, stone walls, hedges, drops, and the like; the area was once called "the St. Moritz of equestrianism." Accommodation is provided in a Victorian country house and meals are typical Irish country fare.

Horetown House, Foulksmills, County Wexford, Irish Republic (phone: 051-63633). Week-long packages are available with trekking or riding lessons in dressage, show-jumping, and cross-country, with lodging in an 18th-century Georgian manor house. More than one guest has gone home applauding and agreeing with the Americans who called Horetown House "an authentic Irish country experience, with warm people, a cozy environment, and nourishing fires, food, and talk."

Kellett Riding School, Kill, Naas, County Kildare, Irish Republic (phone: 045-77208 or 045-77299). Training for equestrians of all levels under the supervision of internationally known horsewoman Iris Kellett and national dressage champion John Hall. Facilities include two indoor schools, a 200-by-200-foot outdoor sand arena, and a full cross-country course. Scenic trail rides can be arranged by appointment, and an equipment shop is available.

Whitfield Court Polo School, Waterford, County Waterford, Irish Republic (phone: 051-84216). Europe's only residential polo school. Beginners and advanced players alike have attended from more than 30 countries; some call their polo vacation the most memorable of their lives. Instruction is by Major Hugh Dawnay, who is assisted by a 5-goal Argentine player. April to mid-September.

Ashbrooke Riding School, Brookeborough, County Fermanagh, Northern Ireland (phone: Brookeborough 242). Instruction for riders of all levels; training includes dressage, show-jumping, and cross-country events. Restored housekeeping cottages available or you can stay with a family on the Viscount Brookeborough's estate.

POST TREKKING

There's nothing quite so delightful as seeing the country from the back of a horse or sure-footed native pony, heading from inn to inn along narrow trails, abandoned train beds, and down wide sandy beaches — and staying away from the trekking center for up to a week at a time. *Post trekking,* or *trail riding,* as this activity is called, is not widely available, and it is not generally recommended for riders without experience, as it usually involves good horses and a fast enough pace to cover about 25 miles a day. Usually a warm camaraderie develops en route, so that you become one of a cohesive band of pilgrims straight out of *Canterbury Tales* as you traverse the miles. That's one reason for going. Post trekking is also a practically worry-free holiday: There are guides to keep you going at a reasonable pace, to make sure you don't get lost, and to arrange for your luggage to be transported from one hostelry to the next. And at the end of each day, there's always a hot bath, a rustic feast, a good night's sleep in a clean-sheeted bed, and one of those massive breakfasts (the kind that make you feel as if it's going to take an Act of Parliament to get you into the saddle) before you hit the trail once again. Two excellent post treks are described below. For information about others, get a copy of the *Equestrian Guide* from the Irish Tourist Board and Ponies of Britain Office, 56 Green End Road, Sawtry, Huntingdon, PE17 5UY (phone: Ramsey 0487-830278).

CHEVIOT HILLS AND SCOTTISH BORDER COUNTRY, England: Superb riding country. In the flat-bottomed valleys, it's easy to work up a gallop. In higher areas, it's just as simple to slow down and take in the magnificent views over the wild countryside of sheep farms and tiny villages. Sometimes you may find yourself virtually alone with the rough grass and the sky, surrounded by ancient hill forts, cairns, standing stones, and other monuments of the ancient British tribes. Trips last 3 and 4 days and are available from mid-May to October. Some prior riding experience is essential. Details: Kidlandlee Riding Centre, Harbottle, Morpeth, Northumberland, England (phone: 0669-50254).

CONNEMARA TRAIL, Irish Republic: The particular attraction of this route, beyond the wonderful landscape that unfolds en route along pretty hill roads and tracks, are the lodgings in luxurious establishments such as Galway's *Great Southern* hotel, where the trip begins and ends. A highlight of the trip is the final day's romp down a glorious long beach. The mounts are hunters or half-bred horses. May through September. Details: William Leahy, The Connemara Trail, Aille Cross, Loughrea, County Galway, Irish Republic (phone: 091-41216).

DINGLE PENINSULA TRAIL, Irish Republic: This adventurous 10-day circle trip travels along beaches, out-of-the-way bridle paths through mountain defiles, and lovely stretches of sand in this sea-washed expanse of rugged hills where the film *Ryan's Daughter* was made. Accommodations en route are in good guesthouses or hotels — and the food is both good and plentiful. May to October. Details: William J. O'Connor Riding Stables, Ballyard, Tralee, County Kerry, Irish Republic (phone: 066-21840).

LOUGH DERG TRAIL, Cos. Clare, Tipperary, and Galway: The scenery on this trip is a special mix of mountains, rivers, forest, bog, farmland, and lakeshore — but few roads and little traffic — and the route jogs and bobs about to include such landmarks as the 300-year-old *BallycormacHouse* and the lakeshore Georgian country house hotel known as the *Gurtnaloughna House.* No more than 8 guests can be accommodated at a time. Details: Ballycormac House, Aglish, near Roscrea, County Tipperary, Irish Republic (phone: 067-21129).

ROB ROY COUNTRY, Scotland: This is post trekking at its best. After day-trekking in Queen Elizabeth Forest Park at Aberfoyle to check the compatibility of ponies and riders, participants travel through Duke's Pass to Loch Achray in the Trossachs, then by Loch Finglas, through Glen Mann to Balquhidder (where Rob Roy MacGregor is buried), over the Kirkton Pass and the eastern shoulder of Ben More to Killin, the spectacular falls of Dochar, then down through Glenogle to Lochearnhead and Bonnie Strathyre — returning to Aberfoyle via Brig-o'-Turk. The terrain is magnificent throughout, and the views are superb. Accommodations, in comfortable inns and hotels, are provided from Saturday to Saturday, with the post trek running from Sunday to Friday. May, September, and October. Details: Scott McGregor, Ballinton, Thornhill, by Stirling FK8 3QE, Scotland (phone: 0786-85-219).

CARAVANNING

Meandering along a narrow lane flanked by billowing meadows and fields, in a horse-drawn wagon, with grand vistas stretching off toward a purple-hazed horizon, is one of the most relaxed ways extant to spend a week — and Ireland is one of the few countries in the world where it's possible to see just why. Agencies in a number of regions rent out old-style gypsy wagons, bright-painted on the outside, fitted out with berths and cooking facilities inside; and the roads of the surrounding countryside are small and traffic-free — perfect for this kind of caravanning. Agents can suggest the most scenic routes; direct their guests to the beaches, overlooks, quaint old pubs, interesting restaurants, and historic sites in the areas they'll be passing through; and name the best overnighting spots, usually about 10 miles apart. The weekly cost for a caravan that will accommodate four is from IR£200 to IR£240, depending on the operator and the season. Principal operators include: *Dieter Clissmann Horse Caravans,* Carrigmore Farm, County Wicklow (phone: 0404-8188). *Ocean Breeze Horse Caravans,* Harbour View, Kilbrittain, County Cork (phone: 023-49731/49626). *Slattery's Travel Agency,* Tralee, 1 Russell St., County Kerry (phone: 066-21722).

HUNTING

In both Britain and Ireland, hunting — riding to the hounds (as distinct from shooting, which involves going after a quarry with firearms) — is an extremely popular pastime, and there are some 200 hunts each in Britain and Ireland meeting from November until spring. In Ireland alone, an ardent follower could hunt every day of the week with a pick of locations. The same situation prevails in Britain. And most hunts, on both sides of the Irish Sea, are delighted to receive guests.

Quite apart from the quality of the horses (and the half-thoroughbred Irish hunters command high prices all over Europe for their bred-in ability to take their fences), there is some stupendous scenery awaiting the visitor, and a rider may be forgiven for taking a tumble if distracted by the view — say, over the rolling farmlands of Leicestershire, England's best hunting country, or, in Ireland, across the miles and miles of hand-built loose gray limestone walls, which give the Galway landscape a gritty character — and which make for excellent hunting. Besides Galway, Ireland's best hunt country is in Clare, Limerick, Tipperary, and North Cork, and in the South — Limerick and Cork — there are great double banks, one or two yards high and as wide, made of clay and stone.

There are all sorts of hunting and all sorts of terrain in Ireland — and all sorts of people as well, since hunting is a very democratic sport here, with hunt memberships made up not only of the gentry, but also of priests and diplomats, innkeepers and farmers, and a variety of humbler horsemen; nonriders often follow the goings-on by bicycle, on foot, or in their cars and stand by for the chance to watch the hounds and the horses passing. From the stirrup cup that almost invariably precedes each meet to the rendezvous afterward in some favored hostelry, the atmosphere is at once efficient, orderly, friendly, and convivial; and the huntsman is judged not only on his skill in horsemanship but by his ability to mix with the hunt and share in the gaiety.

ENGLAND: The most favored hunt country centers on the town of Melton Mowbray in Leicestershire, which is renowned as much for its hunting as for its distinctive pork pies and well-known hunt cake, a rum-laced fruit mixture. The *Quorn, Cottesmore,* and

Belvoir hunts (this last named for the Duke of Rutland's splendid old castle nearby) are known throughout the country; to arrange for a hunt here, contact *Belvoir Vale Riding Centre, Ltd.,* Point Farm, Stathern, Melton Mowbray, Leicestershire, England. Catering to visitors' hunting holidays in Northumberland is the *Percy Arms* in Otter-burn, Northumberland NE19 1NR (phone: 0830-20261). *Best in Britain,* 48 Epple Rd., London SW6 4DH, England (phone: 01-731-1733) can also arrange for or advise you on hunting holidays. For advice on hunts in other parts of the country, contact *The Masters of Foxhounds Association,* Parsloes Cottage, Bagendon, Cirencester, Gloucestershire GL7 7DU, England (phone: North Cerny 470).

IRISH REPUBLIC: Dedicated hunters say that if you can hunt in only one place in Ireland, it should be around Galway, with one of the three Galway hunts:

The North Galway, which can be reached through Ms. Helen Howard Taylor, Grassendale Villa, Ballygaddy Rd., Tuam, County Galway (phone: 093-24843).

The County Galway ("The Galway Blazers"). Those wishing to participate in this hunt in unique stone-wall country must first apply to the Hon. Secretary, Mrs. J. Coveney, Ballygarriff, Craughwell, County Galway (phone: 091-96211).

The East Galway, which you can reach through its secretary, Mr. Joe McEvoy, Lawrencetown, County Galway (phone: 091-75141).

The *Great Southern,* Eyre Sq., Galway City (phone: 091-64041), is a comfortable hotel in which to stay during the Galway hunts.

A handful of other hunts are of special interest because of the variety of terrain and the availability of associated guesthouses and hotels.

The County Clare, c/o Mrs. Nally McCarthy, Cragwood, Quin, County Clare (phone: 065-25702). Hounds meet two days a week at a different venue on each occasion. Two establishments in the center of Clare cater to and organize hunting parties: the Georgian-style *Ballykilty Manor* hotel, Quin, County Clare, surrounded by a 50-acre park and until a few years ago the home of the Blood Family, one of whom stole the British Crown Jewels during the reign of Charles II (phone: 065-25627); and the handsome *Old Ground* hotel, Ennis, County Clare (phone: 065-28127). Flanking Clare are the great hunting counties of Galway and Limerick.

The County Limerick, c/o Lady Harrington, Greenmount, Patrickswell, County Limerick. The *Dunraven Arms,* Adare, County Limerick (phone: 061-86209), managed by a former amateur jockey, specializes in organizing hunting holidays and will book horses in advance to suit visitors' size and experience.

Duhallow, c/o Mr. Kevin Thompson, Brook Lodge, Mallow, County Cork (phone: 022-21114). Dates from somewhere before 1745.

A comfortable and warm guesthouse known as *Ballycormac House* (Aglish, near Roscrea, County Tipperary, Irish Republic; phone: 067-21129) can arrange for up to 8 guests to hunt with some of the most famous packs of hounds in the country, including the Ormond (the country's oldest), the Galway Blazers, the Bermingham, the East Galway, the Westmeath, and the Clare Hunt. Hire of horses is also arranged.

Most fox hunt clubs hold cub meets from September to November for training purposes; these workmanlike affairs, usually held early in the morning, are open to proficient riders by advance arrangement with the secretaries of the individual hunts.

Harrier hunting — the less glamorous sport of riding after the hare — is also done in Ireland at over 30 hunts. Near Dublin, there are two that are excellently run and take visitors by appointment:

The Bray Harriers, c/o C. J. Warren, 11 Whitethorn Rd., Dublin 14 (phone: 01-694403).

The Fingal Harriers, c/o Miss Patricia Murtagh, The Grange, Skerries, County Dublin (phone: 01-491467).

NORTHERN IRELAND: Among the 19 hunt and beagling clubs are the following:

The County Down Staghounds, c/o Mr. Nicholas S. Fenton, 54 Ballycrune Road, Hillsborough, County Down BT26 6NH (phone: Baillies Hills 697). The only pack of staghounds in Northern Ireland hunts the carted red deer from November to March and meets on Tuesdays and Saturdays.

The East Down Foxhounds, c/o Miss Diana Kirkpatrick, Church Hill, Newcastle, County Down (phone: Newcastle 23217). Meets on Tuesdays and Saturdays.

The Iveagh Harriers, c/o Mr. R. E. Boyd, 3 Mountainview Terr., Banbridge, County Down (phone: Banbridge 22468). Immensely popular.

Wonderful Waterways and Coastal Cruises

Whether you're dangling your hand from a dinghy or slicing through the waves underneath a billowing sail, being on a boat is something special. People wave and sing and talk to each other, the winds whip at your hair, the waves rock you like a baby in a cradle. The pace seems closer to man's own than that of the Concorde, slowing you down rather than speeding you up, and when your foot touches shore again, you can't help but feel supremely relaxed.

Britain and Ireland, with literally thousands of miles of shoreline and inland waterways, offer myriad opportunities for just that kind of refreshment. The British and Irish vacation on the water in droves — and support all manner of boat rental operations, sailing schools, and cruising establishments; you don't have to have your own craft to enjoy the nations' offshore pleasures.

SAILING

Many sailors do sail in the English Channel — and they savor the challenges posed by its changeable winds, fierce tides, heavy shipping traffic, and busy harbors. But both Britain and Ireland also offer more forgiving waters that don't, like these, require such stout seagoing yachts and solid sailing experience. In Britain, for instance, there are the sheltered bays along the notched Devon, Essex, and western Scotland coasts; the celebrated Solent, the 3-mile-wide arm of water between the north coast of the Isle of Wight and England's southern shore, south of Southampton, known as the cruising ground of the rich ever since the mid-19th century when Queen Victoria started summering there in a palace-sized "cottage" designed by her husband, Prince Albert; and the coastal waters of East Anglia, where splendid sprit-rigged sailing barges — Thames barges once used for cargo and now revamped to accommodate up to 12 passengers — are common sights. (The sailing barge *Victor,* built in 1895, rerigged in 1974, and refurbished every year, departs for cruises from Strood Pier out of the River Medway. Art and birding cruises are other possibilities. For details, contact Capt. Owen Emerson, the Ferry Boatyard, Dorothea Wharf, Lower Upnor, Rochester, Kent ME2 4XA; phone: 0634-723272 or 0636-253623.)

These popular cruising grounds' counterparts in Ireland are mainly on the east and southwest coasts. In the former area, the concentration of yachting clubs is high, particularly around Dublin and Belfast. Bray, Carlingford, Dun Laoghaire, Malahide, Skerries, Sutton, and Wexford are especially heavily used among small-boat sailors. The south and west coasts, the nation's prime yacht chartering area, offer both open water and sheltered bays and coves; dinghy sailors congregate around the ports of Ballycotton, Baltimore, Crosshaven, Dunmore East, Kinsale, Monkstown, and Youghal in the south, and Bantry, Dingle Bay, and Tralee Bay (Fenit) in the southwest. Cork City boasts one of the largest natural harbors in the world and provides excellent facilities for cruising and racing; the Royal Cork Yacht Club was founded in 1720.

For suggestions for sailing in any given area, the best sources are always local yacht clubs and harbormasters. In Britain, another must is whichever pub is patronized by the local branch of the Royal National Lifeboat Institution's members, who are apt to be experienced watermen whose families have fished in the area for hundreds of years; their advice will come salted with tales of shipwrecks, which can be contemplated over a pint of beer.

SAILBOAT CHARTERS: These are widely available in resort centers of the most popular sailing areas; experienced sailors can charter bareboats for cruises, while novices can hire their craft with crew. Information regarding charters can be obtained from the following:

Irish Tourist Board's Information Sheet, "Sailing and Coastal Cruising." For Irish charters.

Scotland Afloat, Box NT, Marine Parade, Dundee DD1 3JD (phone: 0382-21555). Provides information on bareboat and crewed charters, sailing schools, and water sports centers all over Scotland and Orkney.

Yacht Charter Association, 60 Silverdale, New Milton, Hampshire BH25 7DE (phone: 0245-619004). Gives details on member charter operators in Britain who offer insured craft meeting Association standards. Since no registration exists in the United Kingdom, and charter yachts are not required to carry any specific safety equipment — not even a compass — it is highly advisable to charter only from Y.C.A. members, who acheive such membership by meeting its safety standards.

SAILING SCHOOLS: Week-long sailing courses in dinghies and cruisers, for novices and more advanced sailors alike, are available at dozens of sailing schools and clubs in Great Britain and Ireland. Three organizations that set minimum safety standards and levels of instruction are, in Britain, the *Royal Yachting Association,* Victoria Way, Woking, Surrey GU21 1EQ (phone: 04862-5022); and in Ireland, the *Irish Association for Sail Training,* c/o the Irish Federation of Marine Industries, Confederation House, Kildare St., Dublin 2, Irish Republic (phone: 01-779801), and the *Irish Yachting Association,* 4 Haddington Terr., Dun Laoghaire, County Dublin, Irish Republic (phone: 01-800239). The *RYA* and *IYA* will send complete lists of recognized schools on request.

Among the noteworthy schools are the following:

Dolphin Sailing School, The Foreshore, Woodside, Wootton, Isle of Wight PO33 4JR, England (phone: 0983-882-246). Dinghy sailing in the scenic Solent for beginners and for more seasoned sailors, with all equipment and training meeting Royal Yachting Association standards. Lodging is in the *Foreshore,* a century-old former boathouse, situated between the woods and the water, with lawns running down to the sea.

Fowey Cruising School, 32 Fore St., Fowey, Cornwall PL23 1AQ, England (phone: 072-683-2129). Courses in theory and practice are taught year-round, with cruising venues ranging from the coasts of lush Devon and Dorset and the Scilly and Channel Isles to the mysterious coves of Cornwall. Quayside accommodation dates back to the 15th century.

Hayling Sailing School and Windsurfing Centre, Northney Marina, Hayling Island, Hampshire PO11 0NH, England (phone: Hayling Island 070-16-67334).

Island Cruising Club, 10 Island St., Salcombe, Devon TQ8 8DR, England (phone:

054-884-3481). Courses in handling cruisers, keelboats, and dinghies, with lodgings aboard the club's own floating hotel, a converted Mersey ferry.

Jersey Cruising School, PO Box 531, Jersey, Channel Islands (phone: 0534-78522). Sailing an Anglo-French cruising ground with the third-highest tidal range in the world — a rise and fall of 30 to 36 feet every 6 hours. Bareboat and skippered charters are also available.

John Sharp Sailing, Brockles Quay, St. Veep, Lostwithiel, Cornwall PL22 0NT, England (phone: Bodmin 0208-872470).

Ocean Youth Club, Ltd., The Bus Station, South St., Gosport, Hampshire PO12 1EP, England (phone: 0705-528421/2). Some of Britain's finest sailing in twelve 50- to 76-foot vessels; mainly for young people aged 12 to 24 (though some programs exist for older vacationers). Cruising grounds include the coast of Britain and Continental waters.

Lochearnhead Water Sports Centre, Lochearnhead, Perthshire FK19 8NS, Scotland (phone: Lochearnhead 05673-330). Week-long courses in dinghy sailing, windsurfing, water skiing, and canoeing on an inland loch. Within 60 miles of Glasgow, Edinburgh, Perth, and Dundee in the heart of Scotland.

Tighnabruaich Sailing School, Tighnabruaich, Argyll, Strathclyde PA21 2BD, Scotland (phone: Tighnabruaich 0700-811396). This large sailing school specializes in dinghy sailing and offers courses for novices and experienced sailors alike, along with programs in windsurfing and coastal cruising. The scenery is nothing short of magnificent.

Baltimore Sailing School, The Pier, Baltimore, County Cork, Irish Republic (phone: 028-20141). Sailing instruction using traditional craft and modern dinghies and cruisers in Carbery's Hundred Isles and around Baltimore, Crookhaven, and Cork.

Dun Laoghaire Sailing School, 115 Lower Georges St., Dun Laoghaire, County Dublin, Irish Republic (phone: 01-806654). Three-hour courses in dinghies and dayboats, plus cruising in the Irish Sea to Wales and the Isle of Man.

Fingall Sailing School, Upper Strand Rd., Broadmeadow Estuary, Malahide, County Dublin, Irish Republic (phone: 01-451979). Sailing and windsurfing instruction on the safe Broadmeadow Estuary, in Malahide inlet, and along the coast from Howth to Skerries.

Glenan's Irish Sailing Club, 28 Merrion Sq., Dublin 2, Irish Republic (phone: 01-611481). An international sailing club that originated in France in 1947, it has three centers in Ireland (two in West Cork; one in County Mayo). Courses cover the basics of sailing and board sailing for beginners, dinghy handling, racing techniques, navigation, and more. Coastal and offshore cruises are available. Three-quarters of the students are French.

International Sailing Centre, 5 East Beach, Cobh, County Cork, Irish Republic (phone: 021-811237). Many Americans' ancestors bade farewell to the Emerald Isle from Cobh, whose seafaring tradition goes back centuries. Nowadays, *International Sailing Centre* programs visit hidden creeks and wooden coves once frequented by topsail schooners. Sailing, windsurfing, and cruising holidays are available, and lodging ranges from simple bunkhouses to comfortable hotels.

Craigavon Water Sports Centre Sailing School, Craigavon Lakes, Portadown, Craigavon, County Armagh BT64 1AL, Northern Ireland (phone: Craigavon 42669). Tuition on manmade, 170-acre Craigavon Lake, not far from several bird sanctuaries and 153-square-mile Lough Neagh, the largest lake in Britain and Ireland.

Strangford Sailing School, Sketrick Island, County Down, Northern Ireland (phone: Killinchy 0238-541592). All courses on sheltered Strangford Lough.

EVENTS: Not only do all the sailing craft look postcard perfect against the blue sky and the blue water on a breezy summer's day, but the well-tanned yachting folk striding around in Topsiders, toasting their victories at the local pub, also make for an entertaining spectacle. One of the biggest of the British events is *Cowes Week,* which takes place in the Solent. It is sponsored by the Cowes sailing clubs — among them the Royal Yacht Squadron, an organization so exclusive that even royalty has been barred from membership. True, you don't see the 300-foot spectator craft — floating hotels, really — that once appeared at Cowes every year in August, or the grandiose racing yachts that used to accompany them; and the days are gone that you might see four bearded gentlemen promenading along the waterfront and later learn that all of them were kings, as in Edwardian days. But the event still brings literally millions of pounds' worth of yachts to the area, along with an equally high sum's worth of somebodies' rich uncles. The goings-on are as toney as ever, and the race is remarkably easy to see from shore, especially around the Royal Yacht Squadron's esplanade (best for viewing the start) and Egypt Point, where the racers nearly touch land. The tough *Fastnet Race,* held every other year, is also important.

In Ireland, where the racing is in full swing from May to October, one of the major events is the *Round Ireland Race,* which takes place biennially in June; the Royal Cork Yacht Club's *Sailing Race Week,* held in July in even-numbered years, is also important.

CRUISING THE INLAND WATERWAYS

Salt air isn't the only tonic that will make a vacation lively: While thousands of Britons and Irish descend on the coast, just as many more head for waters inland, and spend their holidays floating down narrow canals or streams, or navigating lakes and broads such as those described below. This extensive system of waterways, some 2,200 miles in England alone, takes in the most wonderful scenery — castles of kings and queens, universities renowned around the globe, exquisite gardens manicured to perfection, nature preserves, and tranquil lakes and fens. While many of the noteworthy streams of other countries carry too much ship traffic to be enjoyable for pleasure boaters, most of Britain's canals are free of commercial craft and ideal for recreation.

There are three ways to go — by self-skippered boat, on chartered cruises, or on fully catered hotel boats. The self-skippered arrangements work like this: You hire a craft, a cabin cruiser or a steel-hulled narrowboat (so-called because they are only about 7 feet wide, and even then they must squeeze through the locks, which are self-operated). Someone shows you how to work the thing and tells you whom to call if you need any help. You buy a pile of groceries, some fishing tackle, and a book of folk songs — and cast off for a floating holiday that will take you along as many miles of waterways as you choose, at the rate of about 15 to 20 miles per day. There are plenty of places to moor, to walk and bicycle in the countryside, and to buy fresh supplies. If you fear you'll feel as if you're driving at Indy after only an hour of Driver's Ed., you can sometimes hire a skipper to do the piloting. And if you don't feel like cooking, you can stop in restaurants and pubs along the way. Alternatively, you can join a group on one of the so-called hotelboats that cruise some of the waterways. The cruising life is simple, idyllic, and restorative, any way you slice it. And everyone who does it goes home talking about next year. The British Waterways Board (Melbury House, Melbury Ter., London NW1 6JX, England; phone: 01-262-6711) can supply a great deal of general information about the cruising possibilities in Britain, as can the Irish Tourist Board and the Northern Ireland Tourist Board for opportunities across the Irish Sea. Bookings for a variety of types of craft on a wide assortment of British waterways can be arranged through the following:

Blakes Holidays, Wroxham, Norwich, Norfolk NR12 8DH, England (phone: 06053-3221/3).

Blakes Vacations, 4939 Dempster St., Skokie, Illinois 60077 (phone: 312-539-1010). Agents for Blakes Holidays.

Boat Enquiries Ltd., 43 Botley Rd., Oxford OX2 0PT, England (phone: 0865-727288).

Dial Travel, PO Box 1034, Hunt Valley, MD 21030 (phone: in Maryland, 301-683-4310; elsewhere, 800-424-9822). Agents for UK Waterways Holidays.

Hoseasons Holidays Ltd., Sunway House, Lowestoft, Suffolk NR32 3LT, England (phone: 0502-64991).

Skipper Travel Services, 210 California Ave., PO Box 60309, Palo Alto, CA 94306 (phone: 415-321-5658). Agents for Hoseasons Holidays Ltd. and UK Waterways Holidays.

UK Waterways Holidays Ltd., Penn Pl., Rickmansworth, Hertfordshire WD3 1EU, England (phone: 0923-770040). This firm, which is jointly owned by the British Waterways Board and the Association of Pleasure Craft Operators, has a special information service to help make its clients' visits to the UK more enjoyable.

Be sure to review sales material thoroughly to determine what exactly is included: Some firms offer a discount for two consecutive weekly bookings, and some include linen, fuel, car parking, and VAT, for which others may charge, in their rates. Also find out if there is a cancellation penalty.

NORFOLK BROADS, England: Described in a 1965 Nature Conservancy Report as "an extensive system of marshland, interconnected waterways and shallow lakes or Broads lying in the valleys of the rivers Bure, Yare, and Waveney and their tributaries," this area — formed as a result of medieval peat digging — was discovered by vacationers at the end of the 19th century, and has been booming as a recreational center ever since. The villages are full of establishments where you can park your car, have a meal and a good night's sleep, and rent or moor a boat. Thousands of British families do just that every summer; along with fishing, boating is the prime recreational activity in the Broads. They are the finest inland sailing waters in Europe with the exception of Holland; and the rivers and lakes teem with cruisers chugging along at about 5 miles an hour. When dusk falls, boats are tied up in force along the riverbanks, the pubs do a booming business as vacationers come in off the water for a pint and some talk, and the moorings take on an eerie blue glow as those who have stayed aboard switch on their televisions for another sort of evening's relaxation. Certainly, most Broads cruisers don't come here to get away from the crowds but to join them. But the months of April, May, June, September, and October are peaceful throughout the area; and even in season, there are a number of areas in this lacework of dykes and rivers where you can get off to yourself for a bit among the reedy swamps, scrubland, and occasional bits of forest; in all there are some 140 miles of navigable waterways. Acle, Potter Heigham, Horning, Stalham, Norwich, and Wroxham are the centers for most commercial facilities. Most boats are floating bungalows, complete with television, showers, cooking facilities, and central heating; prices vary according to the time of year and the size of the boat. For more information, contact the two major area liveries, *Blakes Holidays* or *Hoseasons Holidays Ltd.* (addresses above).

ENGLISH RIVERS: Of all the nation's rivers, three warrant special attention because of their navigability and accessibility. The Thames, which stretches across the breadth of the southern part of the country and is navigable for about 125 miles, twists and winds its long way through pastoral green landscapes punctuated by villages so quaint you'll think you've stepped into a photograph from *National Geographic;* there are lovely estates, grand old houses, medieval churches, marvelously well-tended gardens — and even a few gray cities where the unceasing roar of traffic may blot out the memory of the birdsongs that accompany you the rest of your trip. As John Burns once commented, "Every drop of the Thames is liquid history." Commercial traffic along most of the Thames's navigable length is light, and the current is almost nonexistent in most seasons.

Also delightful is the River Avon between Stratford and Tewkesbury, which meanders through a string of delicious 16th-century villages and towns (including none other than Stratford-upon-Avon, where it's possible to take in performances of the *Royal Shakespeare Company*); the river proper is linked to a system of narrow canals that give the option of making loop cruises. The Severn, England's longest river, travels through towns like Worcester, noted for its splendid cathedral and its porcelain manufactory, and Upton-upon-Severn, a market town full of houses dating to the Georgian era and earlier, as it meanders for 42 navigable miles from Stourport to ancient Gloucester. *UK Waterways Holidays Ltd., Hoseasons Holidays, Blakes Holidays,* and *Boat Enquiries Ltd.* (addresses above) hire craft here. Also consult the Upper Avon Navigation Trust, Avon House, Harvington, Evesham, Worcestershire, England (regarding the River Avon between Stratford-upon-Avon and Evesham; phone: Evesham 870526); the Lower Avon Navigation Trust, Ltd., Mill Wharf, Mill Lane, Wyre Piddle, Pershore, Worcestershire WR10 2JF, England (for information about the Avon between Evesham and Tewkesbury; phone: 0386-552517); and the Thames Water Authority, Nugent House, Vastern Rd., Reading, Berkshire RG1 8DB, England (regarding the Thames above Tedington; phone: 0734-593777).

BRITAIN'S CANALS: The Industrial Revolution brought many changes to Britain, not the least of them being the lacing together of the country by literally hundreds of miles of canals — waterways abandoned not long afterward when the railroads began to prove their greater speed. Many of the canals continued to be used for freight — but it has been only recently that they have seen anything approaching the traffic they did at first. Boats that now thread the waters transport holidaymakers, and their primary function is not commerce but leisurely pleasure in the now-pastoral scene along the route. Some cruisers take bikes along on the cabin tops for cycling into villages along the way for a drink in a pub or a foray to the local greengrocer's. Children work the locks by which the craft sail uphill. All along the route are old buildings whose impressive size or construction testify to the canals' former importance. Some have been converted to contemporary uses: The canal-side granary on the Grand Union Canal at Stoke Bruerne in Northamptonshire now houses the Waterways Museum, with exhibits relating to the canals' heyday. Good publications to take along on any canal crawl is the British Waterways Board's *Canal Architecture in Britain,* or their new book *Inland Waterways Architecture and the Environment.* To order copies, and for more information about planning a cruise, contact the British Waterways Board; or write to UK Waterways Holidays for a copy of their brochure (addresses above).

CALEDONIAN CANAL, Scotland: This 60-mile-long waterway, one of the grandest in Britain, joins the east and west coasts of Scotland and links Loch Ness, Loch Lochy, and Loch Oich through the heart of the Great Glen, a valley rich in history and wildlife, lands once occupied by clans like the MacDonalds, the Camerons, and the Stewarts. In the pretty, loch-side communities, villagers sell crafts and restaurants purvey venison, salmon, pheasant, and other local specialties. The pubs serve single malt whiskies. Will Nessie make an appearance? You may develop your own theory about who she really is. It's a beautiful trip, whether you come for the vivid greens and brilliant yellows of spring, the wildflowers and heather purpling the mountainsides in summer, or the splashes of color in autumn, when you'll appreciate the heating in your boat. The cabin cruisers in which most people make the trip can be hired from *UK Waterways Holidays.*

RIVER SHANNON, Irish Republic: In a country where the rivers and canals are delightfully pollution free as well as relatively uncrowded even in summer, this stream stands out. The longest river in Ireland, it is navigable for about 140 miles, from its headwaters in Derrylahan in County Cavan southward and slightly west to near

Killaloe, with only six locks along the way, and no commercial traffic. It's possible to cruise the stream in its entirety, beginning around Carrick-on-Shannon, and, en route, take in giant loughs Derg and Ree — broad places in the river, which are really inland seas and so susceptible to storms and heavy waves that boaters are advised never to cross them alone. Or tackle a trip across Ireland, beginning in Dublin on the Grand Canal, heading due west through its 44 locks, and then covering only the lower portion of the Shannon from near Portumna to the Atlantic. Alternatively, you could begin on the Grand Canal at Dublin and turn southward near Robertstown to explore the River Barrow, which flows into the sea near Waterford. At every turn, there are lovely waterside villages, fascinating small towns, and unspoiled pastoral countryside littered with abbeys, castles, and old fortifications. Amateur botanists, ornithologists, and peripatetic archaeologists alike should have a field day; photographers call these landscapes paradise. A good guide to the waters is the *Inland Waterways Association of Ireland Guide to the Grand Canal and Barrow River* (IR£5), available from Eason & Son, Ltd., 40–42 Lower O'Connell St., Dublin 1, Irish Republic (phone: 01-733811). Details: The Irish Tourist Board and, for information about luxury hotelboat cruises, Horizon Cruises, 16000 Ventura Blvd., Suite 200, Encino, CA 91436 (phone: 818-906-8086), or Shannon River Floatels, Ltd., Killaloe, County Clare, Irish Republic (phone: 061-76205).

ERNE WATERWAY, Northern Ireland: Two huge island-studded lakes joined by narrows at the ancient island town of Enniskillen, the Erne Waterway in County Fermanagh is a paradise for birds, wildflowers, and anglers. Seven miles wide at one point, and running 54 miles to the Atlantic, the loughs Erne have 280 islands where you can land to visit old churches, castles, caves, and a ruined monastery — plus dozens of coves and inlets, good hotels and tackle shops, and seven hire-cruiser operators. Boating on the labyrinthine Upper Lough Erne can be a challenge because of the many islands, though navigation charts are widely available; on Lower Lough Erne, waves can build to open-sea size when the winds pick up. Below the lake, passing the little village of Belleek, where the world-famous lustrous Belleek pottery is made, the Erne river at last plunges into a gorge to meet the ocean. To find out more, contact the Erne Charter Boat Association, Lakeland Visitor Centre, Enniskillen, County Fermanagh, Northern Ireland (phone: Enniskillen 0365-23110). Request the free booklet *Holidays Afloat and Ashore on the Erne Waterway,* which lists all the association's members and their facilities. The Northern Ireland Tourist Board, 48 High St., Belfast BT1 2DS (phone: 0232-246609), also keeps copies of this booklet and can provide details of day cruises on Lough Erne and on Neagh, the biggest lake in Britain and Ireland.

Gone Fishing

 It's not hard to understand the overwhelming popularity of Izaak Walton's sport when you consider just how much water there is on the islands, how pretty most of the angling hot spots are, and how good the fishing is. Though the day is long past that a monster 72-pound, 8-ounce salmon can be caught in the London section of the Thames — as it was in the early part of the 19th century — most of the streams and lakes in Britain are remarkably pollution-free; and conditions in a number of those which used to be, like England's Thames, are improving. The game fishing — that is, for salmon, sea trout, and brown trout — is some of the best in the world, and the sea fishing and coarse fishing — for bream, carp, chub, dace, perch, pike, roach, tench, eel, and other species — are excellent.

Each section of Britain and Ireland offers a different proportion of these three types of angling, and where you go will depend on what you're looking for. In Scotland and

Wales, the rivers are thought of entirely as game fishing streams. Scottish rivers are world famous for their salmon (though other game species are taken), particularly because of the consistent excellence of the fishery; Britain's record salmon, a 64-pounder bagged in 1922, was caught in Scotland's Tay. In Wales, salmon, and to an almost equal extent sea trout (which the Welsh call sewin), are the big deal. English streams stand out for the sheer variety of angling offered: Some streams are consecrated primarily to game fishing; some entirely to coarse fishing; and some are mixed fisheries, offering both coarse and game species. There are many reservoirs, and many waters are stocked. The rivers of Northern Ireland are particularly productive — both for game fish and coarse fish; it's almost a situation of an embarrassment of riches, and a few streams seldom see an angler. This is even more true in the Irish Republic.

Game fishing is the glamour sport on the local angling scene, and while many vacationers do some coarse fishing or some sea angling as a sidelight to a sightseeing vacation, game fishing is something to plan a trip around. In Britain, that's all the more true because of the existence of many quaint and comfortable old fishing hotels, the perfect answer to one pressing problem encountered by most avid fishermen hankering for an exciting angling vacation — that of the fed-up fishing widow. Attractively situated within a short drive of all the shops, ruins, and cathedrals an inveterate sightseer could desire, the best of these hostelries offer spacious chambers with high ceilings, French doors, balconies entwined with wisteria, or similar features. Cucumber sandwiches and currant scones, fruitcakes and jam tarts, may be standard fare at tea; and at dinner, guests discuss not just the best flies of the day but also where to get the best buy on a pair of sheepskin gloves or a handmade tapestry.

For details about fishing in England, Scotland, Wales, and Northern Ireland, consult the excellent *Where to Fish* (£11.95 from Thomas Harmsworth Publishing, 13 Nicosia Rd., London SW18, England). Published biannually, its 470 pages contain thousands of entries with information supplied by hoteliers, tackle dealers, club secretaries, and other on-the-spot sources. The Promotions Department of the Irish Tourist Board can send information about accommodations throughout that country, and a number of publications covering angling in various regions of England are also available, among them *Fishing in the North West* (available for 85p from the North West Water Authority, Dawson House, Great Sankey, Warrington, Cheshire WA5 3LW, England; phone: 092572-4321) and the *Northumbrian Angling Guide* (available for 20p from Northumbrian Water, Northumbria House, Regent Centre, Gosforth, Newcastle upon Tyne NE3 3PX; phone: 091-284-3151). For Northern Ireland, the *Angling Guide* gives fairly comprehensive information about all kinds of angling (available from the Fisheries Division, Department of Agriculture, Hut 5, Castle Grounds, Stormont, Belfast BT4 3TA, Northern Ireland; phone: 0232-63939).

GAME FISHING

At their best, Britain and Ireland can provide such good fishing for salmon, trout, and sea trout that it can make anglers sound as if they're telling fish stories when they talk about it back home. However, nearly all game fishing waters in England, Wales, and Scotland are private, with the fishing rights controlled by clubs and associations. Some permit no outsiders at all; some charge a fee high enough to implement the same situation; and some sell day tickets, weekly tickets, or short-term memberships at prices rising — usually with the quality of the fishing — from the nominal to the expensive-but-still-not-exorbitant range. These are generally available through the association's office in advance, or on the spot through hotels, pubs, and tackle shops.

In addition to permission, you also usually need, for salmon, sea trout, and brown trout, Water Authority–issued rod licenses, available through fishing hotels, post offices, pubs, and tackle shops. (You won't need a rod license to fish for any game fish in Scotland, or for brown trout in the Irish Republic.) When you purchase your license, inquire about local rules governing such matters as closed seasons, minimum sizes for each species, bait and tackle permitted, and Sunday fishing.

ENGLAND: Hatchery-raised trout can be found almost everywhere in the country except the east coast — in lakes, reservoirs, and a variety of rivers. Native brown trout proliferate in the famous chalk streams of the southeast — fast, clear-flowing, highly alkaline, and generally ideal for nurturing big ones that rise freely even when they reach 4 pounds or more; these streams offer some of the world's best dry-fly trout fishing.

It's usually necessary to wait a decade for your turn to fish more famous rivers like the Itchen and the Test. But *The Orvis Co., Inc.* (The Mill, Nether Wallop, Stockbridge, Hampshire SO20 8ES, England; phone: 0264-781212) offers exceptional, though inevitably expensive, fishing with guides (unusual for trout rivers in England) to an international clientele on private stretches of these two legendary streams, which flow practically in the shadow of Winchester Cathedral, Izaak Walton's burial place. Orvis waters include a short stretch on the celebrated Itchen, which produces extra-wily wild trout, and several on the Test, including one that ranks among the best free-rising stretches in the country, good for large and exceptionally active trophy fish.

Other well-known area streams include the Derwent, an important and especially scenic tributary of the immense Trent; the Dove, where Walton fished, though it's generally not the stream it once was; the Eden, famous for its January-to-May salmon run; the Kennet; the Lune; the Ribble, especially in the middle reaches; and the Wharfe. The Camel and the Fowey are two of Cornwall's important sea trout rivers, and some hotels have good water on the Tamar, among southwest England's most important game fisheries; the Taw, a game river known for a March-to-May spring salmon run, with good sea trout action beginning in July, with some roach and dace downstream; and the Torridge, where the same salmon-in-spring, sea-trout-in-July patterns prevail. In the northeast, the Coquet and the Tweed are the best-known salmon streams.

To find out who owns the fishing rights to any given stretch of stream in England, contact the local Water Authority.

WALES: Here, the Wye is justly famous for salmon, and several hotels have water on the main river and on its tributaries. The Dee, which yields good-sized salmon and smaller browns and sea trout, and the swift Usk, which has produced some 800 salmon usually averaging 10 pounds and more every season for the last eight decades, are Wales's other important salmon rivers. The prolific Towy, and the Dovey and the Conwy, both of which hold numerous records, are the counterparts of the Dee and the Usk for sea trout sport. Offering good opportunities for both sea trout and salmon action, there's the Clwyd; the Glaslyn, which rises in Snowdon; the Mawddach; the Taf, which has its source on Mynydd Prescelly; and the important Teifi, which claims some of the Principality's top trout fly fishing.

SCOTLAND: Exclusiveness is the hallmark of the very finest Scottish angling — some streams are so closed that even rich folk and VIPs may find the door barred — but it does not prevail along all of the Tay, the king of Scotland's salmon rivers, or along the entire length of its rivals, the Aberdeenshire Dee, noted by some fly fishermen as Britain's best major salmon stream; the fast-flowing Spey, Scotland's most thrilling fishery; and the prolific Tweed. Also good are the aptly named Awe; the Don, superb for dry-fly trouting; the Northern Esk, which produces abundant numbers of medium-sized salmon; the Findhorn, among the more outstanding of the smaller Scottish salmon streams, with brown trout sport rivaling that of the nearby Spey and good sea trouting in summer; the fairly exclusive, fly-only Helmsdale; the good-quality Naver, especially for salmon and sea trout; and the 30-mile-long Ythan, an excellent sea trout fishery.

District Fishing Boards, addresses of which can be obtained from local tackle shops, can provide information about who owns fishing rights for given stretches of water; contact the BTA for assistance.

IRISH REPUBLIC: The angling here is excellent for wild brown trout — which are not found in Britain except in streams like the Itchen and the Test, where rights are privately controlled and waiting lists for fishing holidays stretch years into the future. There is also good salmon fishing here. As in Scotland, this depends to a great extent on spate rivers — which can offer fine sport when a stretch of rainy weather produces the proper conditions; but, with the exception of the river Moy, the celebrated Blackwater, and the rivers Slaney, Nore, Barrow, Bundrowes, and Laune, Ireland lacks the mighty streams that do not depend on precipitation to assure good fishing, and so the quality of the angling experience can be less predictable than in Scotland waters. However, the overall catch in Ireland is often larger than in Scotland, and an angling vacation here will also be less expensive and more accessible.

Angling for both salmon and sea trout (which make up an important part of the Irish Republic's fishing) can be done from the banks of rivers or from a boat drifting on one of the many large lakes. Generally speaking, the best salmon and sea trout fishing is on the south and west coasts. But there's good fishing in the River Slaney, which goes into the sea at Wexford, on the east coast. Scenic Lough Currane, near the resort town of Waterville, County Kerry, has the distinction of having free salmon and trout fishing with the largest and earliest run of sea trout in Ireland. Near the village of Killorglin, County Kerry, Caragh Lake and its rivers — the Meelagh, Brida, Owenroe, and Caragh — have good fishing, good hotels, and good pubs. Even those who do not fish will enjoy the salmon at Galway City; the spectacle of the salmon nudging their way upstream from the Weir Bridge on the River Corrib, which drains loughs Corrib and Mask, is one of the city's more remarkable sights. In Connemara, the Ballynahinch system (on which there are at least six fisheries) and the Erriff stand out as salmon and sea trout waters. The famed Costello fishery, with its many scenic lakes, the Inver fishery, the Gowla, and the Screebe are the pick of the greats for sea trout. The River Moy vies with the Blackwater for the title of Ireland's premier salmon fishery. Brown trout are everywhere in Ireland, and any time during the open season, most anglers see enough action to keep them happy. There are small browns in the tiny lakes and rivers from Cork north to Donegal, larger ones in the great lakes of Mayo and Galway — loughs Corrib, Carra, Conn, and Mask — and fish that are bigger yet again in the midland lakes of Arrow, Derravaragh, Owel, and Sheelin. The River Laune and the beautiful Killarney lakes are also good.

The season generally runs from February 15 to the end of September, but April and September stand out — as does the period from mid-May to mid-June, during the mayfly hatch, when the fish rise high and fast, and many anglers call the action the season's best. Loughs Mask, Conn, and Carra in County Mayo and Lough Corrib in Galway are widely considered the best lakes for mayfly fishing. At any rate, wet-fly fishing on these lakes at that time of year is usually excellent.

For information about the Irish Republic's trout waters and their seasons, contact the Irish Tourist Board.

NORTHERN IRELAND: Anglers will find an abundance of sea trout near the mouth of the Lower Bann (also good for salmon) and plenty of brown trout in the Upper Bann, the Ballinderry, the Moyola, the Maine (also good for salmon and a local species of very large trout known as the dollaghan), and the Blackwater (which produces salmon in the upper reaches and big catches of coarse fish lower down), all rivers that feed giant 153-square-mile Lough Neagh, the island's largest expanse of still water, itself seldom fished with rod and line because the angling is so good on the feeder streams. The rivers in the narrow, picturesque valleys known as the Glens of Antrim — among them the Glenshesk in County Antrim — have good runs of sea trout, as well as salmon, in July and August. On the north coast, the River Bush is world famous and the Foyle and its tributaries — the Derg, Finn, the Mourne, and the Strule — form one of the best mixed game and coarse fishing areas. Lough Melvin, in the west, which has a spectacular run of spring salmon, is worth a special visit since it also contains three unique trout species — the sonaghan, the gillaroo, and the ferox — and an Ice Age predecessor of the trout — the char.

A detailed look at fishing in all of these areas is provided by *Game Fishing Waters,* published by the Northern Ireland Tourist Board (free). To find out who owns the rights to privately owned stretches of water in Northern Ireland, contact the Tourist Board (48 High St., Belfast BT1 2DS; phone: 0232-246609), the Department of Agriculture (Fisheries Division, Stormont, Belfast BT4 3PW; phone: 0232-63939), and the Fisheries Conservancy Board (1 Mahon Rd., Portadown, County Armagh BT62 3EE, Northern Ireland; phone: 0762-334666).

COARSE FISHING

All the fish in freshwater rivers and lakes that are not trout or salmon — bream, carp, chub, dace, perch, pike, roach, rudd, eel, and tench — go by the name of coarse fish, and there are millions of anglers who have made this quarry their specialty. The almost total absence of coarse fish in the streams and still waters of Scotland and Wales is compensated for by the abundance in England and Northern Ireland.

ENGLAND: There is an enormous range of possibilities for coarse fishing here, particularly in the eastern and central regions: the giant and sluggish Great Ouse, where you'll find almost every species (although some stretches boast larger populations of a given species than others), with the town of Huntingdon among the most favored angling centers; the Nene, also primarily for bream and roach; the Norfolk Broads and the Broadland rivers like the Bure, the Waveney, the Yare, and their tributaries (except during the daytime in summer, when boat traffic makes the angling fairly slow), especially for bream and roach; and the Welland, another big important stream.

Refer to *Where to Fish* (listed above) for more information.

IRISH REPUBLIC: Since the waters are freer from pollution here than almost anywhere else in Europe, the coarse fishing can be exceptional; in fact, most waters are greatly underfished. Recently, more and more anglers from abroad have discovered the joys of Ireland's long, slow, and deep rivers, its half-dozen great lakes up to 30 miles long, and its thousands of lesser lakes. Not many Irish fish, of course, are as heavy as the 42-pound pike caught in the river Barrow or the 38-pounder caught in Lough Corrib a few years back, but most Irishmen believe that plenty of far bigger fish, particularly pike, lurk in the depths of the rivers.

The River Erne, which runs into Northern Ireland, offers great coarse fishing, with the major centers to be found at lovely Lough Gowna, the source of the Erne, and the area near Belturbet, County Cavan, between the two lakes; at nearby Foley's Bridge and Drumlane Lake, the action is so lively that some locals will swear that everyone catches a fish. The River Barrow, flanked by the kind of supremely pastoral countryside that you expect when you go to Ireland, has its best fishing at Graiguenamanagh, County Kilkenny, an attractive village in the shadow of Mount Leinster, once a great monastic center. Best of all is the lordly River Shannon, with its three great lakes — lovely 25-mile Lough Derg, 17-mile Lough Ree, and 7-mile Lough Allen. Some of the best centers are at Mohill, County Leitrim, well-organized Carrick-on-Shannon, and Lanesborough, County Longford, in a famous "hot water" stretch, where catches running into the hundreds of pounds have been made.

No rod license is required in the Irish Republic, and there is no closed season. For an abundance of detail about these streams and others and the rules that govern them, get a copy of the Irish Tourist Board's *Coarse Angling.*

NORTHERN IRELAND: Though still best known for its game fishing, Northern Ireland offers some of Europe's finest coarse fishing as well. On the Upper Bann, the section above Lough Neagh is a standout, and individual anglers regularly catch more than 100 pounds of bream and roach in 5-hour matches. The Lower Bann, north of Lough Neagh, also has fine coarse angling, especially for perch. Also superb is Lough Erne, with its two gigantic loughs; the area around Enniskillen, where the world 5-hour match record is regularly broken, still holds the record of 258 pounds, 9½ ounces — which exceeded the previous record by more than 50 pounds. The Fairy Water, a tributary of the Foyle via the Strule, was the first of Northern Ireland's coarse fisheries to come into the public eye, and it still yields roach in immense quantities. Lough Creeve has proved to have a perch growth rate exceeding all other Irish waters. And the Quoile, which flows south from its source not far from Ballynahinch, has made a big splash with its rudd production. Pike fishing, another of the province's attractions, is found at its best in both Lough Ernes, and the two Lough Macneans and in Lough Beg at the mouth of Lough Neagh.

In Northern Ireland you need a rod license (issued by the Fisheries Conservancy Board) for everywhere except the Foyle system. A coarse fishing permit is also required for waters controlled by the Department of Agriculture. There is no closed season. *On Coarse in Northern Ireland,* published by the Northern Ireland Tourist Board, gives details (free).

SEA ANGLING

Britain has hundreds of miles of ragged coastline where anglers reel in anything from half-pound flounders off a sandy bottom to giant mako sharks in deep waters, or wrasse, pollack, and mackerel from the rocks. No license is necessary, and few advance arrangements are required; tackle can usually be hired; and the chefs in most hotels will cook a guest's prize on request. For trips out over the wrecks and sunken reefs where some of the bigger fish lurk, boats and professional skippers are readily available, and a day out with a group in a boat with a local who can rendezvous with fish on request can be a most rewarding (and reasonably priced) experience. All that's required is a stomach strong enough to hold up through a day on the short choppy seas. Shore fishing for sea bass with a powerful rod and reel requires a little more equipment — namely good oilskins — since these delicious creatures favor "storm beaches" and the best fishing is done when there's a strong onshore wind that will drench an angler to the skin with salt spray.

ENGLAND, SCOTLAND, AND WALES: In England, the best areas include the Channel ports of Dover and Deal, in Kent; the small resorts of New Haven and Littlehampton, in Sussex; Salcombe, set in a many-branched estuary with wooded hills in rolling Devon; Fowey and Looe, among the rocky cliffs of Cornwall; and the mountainous Isle of Man in the middle of the Irish Sea between England and Ireland.

The potential of the fishing in Scotland is largely unexploited. Shetland and Orkney have Britain's best common skate action, and the Pentland Firth, which separates Orkney and the mainland, produces large halibut. In the southeast, there's plenty of good shore fishing from the rocks and beaches.

In Wales, the best shore fishing is found west of Cardiff, and the fishing offshore in the south can be superb. In the north and west, boat fishing is quite good.

For more information, consult *Sea Angler* and *Sea Angling Weekly,* available at newsstands. The National Federation of Sea Anglers (26 Downsview Crescent, Uckfield, Sussex TN22 1UB; phone: 0825-3589) organizes over 100 competitions annually, to which visitors are welcome, and will answer questions about them.

IRISH REPUBLIC: In the Irish Republic, though sea angling has been organized only for the last quarter century, there are about 150 clubs that sponsor dozens of fishing competitions throughout the year. The big quarry include shark and skate — blue shark, which can weigh in at over 200 pounds and come in season around the south and west coast from mid-June to mid-October; porbeagle shark, of which the Irish record 365-pound specimen was caught off the Mayo coast; the tough-fighting, hard-to-catch mako shark, which visits the south coast in summer; the common skate, a worthy adversary at its most plentiful around the south and west coasts in deep water from April to early October, growing to over 200 pounds; and the somewhat smaller white skate, which favors the western seaboard. Flatfish, halibut, conger, monkfish, mackerel, ling, cod, red sea bream, pollack, ray, turbot, plaice, brill, and flounder can be found around the coast. (Note that there is a conservation order on the common skate, and in order to preserve the species, anglers are asked to return to the water any skate caught alive.)

Centers like Youghal, Kinsale, Crosshaven, Baltimore, and Courtmacsherry rank among the best places to fish in the country. In Kinsale, particularly, the angling is well organized, the town is pretty, and there are numerous good lodging places and fine restaurants. Blue shark, skate, and conger are the quarry.

Also good is Fenit, in County Kerry, where monkfish, ray, conger, and skate can be caught right from the ocean pier; boats take anglers out into the even more productive waters of Tralee Bay for larger specimens.

The surf fishing for bass and the flatfishing northward along the delightfully scenic Clare coast road is good (although dwindling bass stocks have prompted authorities to encourage anglers to return smaller bass to the sea). Green Island at the south of Liscannor Bay is renowned for its rock fishing; porbeagle sharks of around 150 pounds have been landed here. Ballyvaughan and Liscannor (birthplace of the inventor of the submarine), further up the coast, have boats and tackle for hire.

In County Mayo, there are many major sea-angling centers. Clew Bay, with its 365 islands in the shadow of Ireland's holy Croagh Patrick, has fast tides that give splendid opportunities for shore fishing, while Westport boasts a number of excellent charter boats that go out for the renowned shark and skate fishing; many Europeans come here. Lovely Achill Island, once so favored by English anglers that the coastline resounded with their clipped accents, still has superb deep-sea fishing, and past creels have included a number of record-sized shark; the main centers are Purteen Harbour and Darby's Point. Belmullet, the peninsula on the northwest coast, is also famous for its deep-sea action and shore fishing, as are Newport and Killala.

Sea Angling, published by the Irish Tourist Board, provides details about what can be caught where and with what, and when and from what. The Irish Federation of Sea Anglers (c/o Mr. Hugh O'Rourke, 67 Windsor Dr., Monkstown, County Dublin) administers local competitions and can provide details.

NORTHERN IRELAND: In Northern Ireland, good bass and sea trout action can be found at Portrush in County Antrim and at Portstewart in County Londonderry. An Irish record hake was caught in Belfast Lough, and Carlingford Lough in County Antrim has produced a national record tope (66 pounds, 8 ounces). Off Ballintoy, also in County Antrim, there is the very unusual fishing for herring on rods with feathered lures, done at dusk and dawn in May and June. Wreck fishing from Portaferry at the mouth of Strangford Lough always guarantees good cod, ling, and conger. But almost everywhere along the coast, there's an abundance of rocky points, piers, estuaries, and storm beaches that don't get nearly the attention the good sea angling — among Britain's best — certainly warrants.

The Northern Ireland Tourist Board publishes *Sea Fishing* and *Fishing from the Seashore* (free), good guides to the possibilities.

FISHING SCHOOLS

CHARLES BINGHAM FISHING, LTD., Coryton, near Okehampton, Devon, England: Mr. Bingham, who has landed more than 200 salmon on the fly from some of England's most famous rivers, has held salmon, trout, and sea trout permits on many miles of the River Dart and its tributaries on Dartmoor for 30 years, so he knows the waters very well. The school, which emphasizes fly fishing, concentrates on teaching beginners the basics, but also provides good refresher courses for experienced anglers. Since classes are limited to three or four students, each participant gets plenty of personal attention. February to October is the season. Lodging is in the Fisherman's Wing of the comfortable family country house, and waders may be rented. Details: Charles Bingham Fishing, Ltd., The Rod Room, Broad Park, Coryton, near Okehampton, Devon EX20 4AA, England (phone: 082286-281).

ARUNDELL ARMS, Lifton, Devon, England: This traditional West Country hotel pioneered fishing courses many years ago and now offers them for beginning, intermediate, and advanced anglers. Courses are taught by a Cornish champion tournament caster who is reckoned to be one of the best fly-fishing instructors in the country and, as lecturer, the *Times*'s fishing correspondent, Conrad Voss-Bark, who is married to the proprietor (herself a passionate fly-fisher and an author of books on the waters of the area). All of the courses, which are run on the inn's extensive river, mix fly-fishing theory with a great deal of on-the-water experience. In addition, there are always two bailiffs on the property to advise visiting fishermen. Weekend fly-tying courses are available in winter. Details: Arundell Arms Hotel, Lifton, Devon PL16 0AA, England (phone: 0566-84666).

OSPREY, Aviemore, Highland, Scotland: Introductory fly fishing courses, weekend-long crash courses in fly fishing, and salmon fishing courses are available, along with game fishing holiday packages, at this Scottish Highlands fishing school presided over by one Jim Cornfoot, an amiable Scotsman who has been fishing these waters since he was 10 — nearly 30 years. Participants learn casting, watercraft, fly tying, spinning, knots, entomology, rod, reel, and line construction, how to choose the right tackle and equipment for their needs, how to use a landing net; there's plenty of casting practice, both on the waters adjacent to the school and on the wide, shallow River Spey, and there's plenty of time to wash down a dram or two of famous Grouse whisky with a pint of good beer — the favored local method of raising good cheer. Details: Osprey Fishing School, The Fishing Centre at the Aviemore Centre, Aviemore, Highlands PH22 1QP, Scotland (phone: 0479-810911 or 0479-810132).

PEEBLES, Peebles, Borders, Scotland: This small county town in the beautiful rolling Border area is just 25 miles from Edinburgh. A popular center for fishing on the river Tweed, it offers Friday-through-Sunday trout fishing courses presided over by former British Open casting champion Andy Dickison, Tweed Valley born and bred, in April and May. There are also Sunday-to-Sunday salmon week courses in November, when the large salmon, usually weighing in between 10 and 30 pounds, are running. Private instruction in both bait and fly casting techniques is also available, and Melrose Abbey (for more about which, see *Ancient Monuments and Ruins*) and Abbotsford, the former home of novelist Sir Walter Scott, are nearby. Accommodation is at the *Tontine Hotel,* a three-star Trusthouse Forte establishment. Details: Peebles Angling School, 8 Chambers St., Innerleithen, Peeblesshire EH44 6JY, Scotland (phone: 0896-830178).

GAME FISHING HOTELS

The complicated process of arranging to fish in areas where the angling rights are privately held — particularly in Britain — can be much simplified when you base yourself at a special fishing hotel, which may either control a stretch of a nearby stream or be able to carry out the necessary negotiations with owners of local estates. Most of the following establishments are country house hotels, in attractive settings; waters to which they control rights are indicated. Hotels mentioned in areas where fishing is free are conveniently located with respect to the best local waters — and, like the rights-owning establishments, are exceptionally hospitable to anglers: When you want to haul out your tales of that day's triumphs, you'll be sure to find a willing ear.

CAVENDISH, Baslow, Derbyshire, England: The angling available on the rivers Derwent and Wye, by courtesy of the Duke of Devonshire, provides only part of the charm at this establishment, where diners eat off Wedgwood china with Sheffield silver and rest up from a day on the stream in lounges with open fires, oak beams, fresh flowers, and fine views of the adjacent Chatsworth estate. Local fishing celebrity Arnold Mosley is available for coaching by prior arrangement, and fishing tackle may be borrowed if you forget your own. The hotel itself was restored and decorated by the Duchess of Devonshire and has 23 superbly furnished rooms. The setting is Chatsworth, described in *Stately Homes and Great Gardens,* and the magnificent Derbyshire Peak District. Details: Cavendish Hotel, Baslow, Derbyshire DE4 1SP, England (phone: 024688-2311).

TILLMOUTH PARK, Cornhill-on-Tweed, Northumberland, England: This Victorian mansion-turned-inn occupies over 1,000 acres of rolling Northumberland border countryside — and boasts 9 miles of water on the rivers Till and Tweed. Details: Tillmouth Park Hotel, Cornhill-on-Tweed, Northumberland TD12 4UU, England (phone: 0890-2255).

IZAAK WALTON, Dovedale, Derbyshire, England: This comfortable hotel in the heart of the Peak District National Park started its life in the 17th century as a farmhouse. It offers 3 miles on the River Dove. Details: Izaak Walton Hotel, Dovedale, Derbyshire, England (phone: 033529-555).

CARNARVON ARMS, Dulverton, Somerset, England: This fine English country sporting hotel, built in 1873 by the fourth Earl of Carnarvon at one of the entrances to the Exmoor National Park, occupies 50 acres along the banks of the River Barle, and the hotel has some 7 miles of bank on that stream and along the rivers Exe and Haddeo for its guests. Set in the heart of Negley Farson country, these typical moorland rivers run clear, bright, and shallow between pools. The wild brownies are small but excellent fighters; late May, June, and early July are the best months. Salmon, whose numbers are currently increasing, range from 5 pound grilse to 8 to 12 pounds for spring and autumn fish. The hotel itself — a warm and friendly family-run establishment for nearly three decades — has spacious lounges with open log fires and is furnished with comfortable armchairs and fine antiques with accents of gleaming copper and brass. There's also an outdoor swimming pool and a handsome full-size billiard table. Details: Carnarvon Arms Hotel, Dulverton, Somerset TA22 9AE, England (phone: 0398-23302).

HACKNESS GRANGE, Hackness, near Scarborough, Yorkshire, England: With 11 miles on the River Derwent in North York Moors National Park, this peaceful hotel occupies a stately limestone residence built in the mid-19th century, and its additions. Details: Hackness Grange Hotel, Hackness, near Scarborough, Yorkshire, England (phone: 0723-369966).

HOLNE CHASE, Holne Ashburton, Devon, England: Surrounded by woodlands laid out in the 19th century and by the Dartmoor National Park, this singularly secluded and romantic hotel on an 11th-century hunting estate has about a mile of salmon fishing on the River Dart, whose valley the principal rooms overlook. Sea trout in the 1½- to 4½-pound range, as well as a number of other types of fish weighing from 10 to 15 pounds, have been taken in the last couple of years. The season is April to

September. Details: Holne Chase, Holne Ashburton, Devon TQ13 7NS, England (phone: 03643-471).

DEER PARK, Honiton, Devon, England: This family-run country house hotel in a 17th-century hillside manor is set on 30 acres of Devonshire countryside overlooking the valley of the River Otter. It offers 5 miles of private fishing for brown and rainbow trout on that stream as well as on a small lake. Details: Deer Park Hotel, Honiton, Devon EX14 0PG, England (phone: 0404-2064).

ARUNDELL ARMS, Lifton, Devon, England: Some 20 miles of private salmon, sea trout, and brown trout fishing on the River Tamar and its tributaries, and a 3-acre lake stocked with rainbow and brown trout. Details: Arundell Arms, Lifton, Devon PL16 0AA, England (phone: 0566-84666). See also *Rural Retreats.*

WHITTON FARM HOUSE, Rothbury, Northumberland, England: This charming country hotel, which occupies a converted farm, has a mile-long beat on the Coquet and, by special arrangement with the Northumberland Angler's Federation, access to some of the river's lower stretches (described by *Trout and Salmon* magazine as some of the top club-owned waters in Britain and Ireland). When you've had your fill of fishing, you can have a drink in the former calf house, eat dinner in the former milking parlor, and then go to bed in a converted stable. There are beamed ceilings, stone walls, and polished pine floors throughout. Details: Whitton Farm House, Rothbury, Northumberland NE65 7RL, England (phone: 0669-208-11).

ANGLERS ARMS, Weldon Bridge, Morpeth, Northumberland, England: A mile of water for trout and salmon on the River Coquet. The hotel, in an 18th-century building, has five simple rooms, one with a four-poster bed, plus a restaurant that serves the native specialties of the establishment's Portuguese owners. Half of the restaurant occupies a converted Pullman car reminiscent of the Orient Express, and train noises are piped in over the PA system. Four luxurious cottages are also available. Details: Anglers Arms Hotel, Weldon Bridge, Morpeth, Northumberland NE65 8AX, England (phone: 066570-271 and 655).

HALF MOON INN, Sheepwash, Devon, England: This quaint, friendly, and comfortable village inn has 9 miles of privately owned salmon and trout fishing on the River Torridge, a small river renowned for its spring run of salmon, its dry-fly fishing in May and June, and its excellent run of sea trout in July and August. Details: Half Moon Inn, Sheepwash, Beaworthy, Devon EX21 5NE, England (phone: 040923-376).

RISING SUN, Umberleigh, Devon, England: The 13th-century *Rising Sun,* a personable cottage-style fishing hotel, has 3½ miles of salmon, sea trout, and brown trout fishing on the River Taw — the first waters above the tides. The salmon action is liveliest from March through May; average catch weighs in at 10 to 12 pounds. Large sea trout averaging 4 or 5 pounds run in mid-April; small sea trout of 1½ pounds are running from the third week in June until late September. Grilse run at the end of July and summer salmon in August and September. Details: Rising Sun, Umberleigh, Devon EX37 9DU, England (phone: 0769-60447).

KENMORE, Kenmore, by Aberfeldy, Perthshire, Scotland: Handsomely situated in one of Scotland's prettiest villages and surrounded by pristine countryside, this 39-room hotel, established in 1572 (Scotland's oldest) on the banks of the River Tay in an area of tremendous natural beauty, stands out for more than its setting. It offers 4 miles of private salmon fishing on the River Tay and has rights for salmon and brown and rainbow trout for the entire 16 miles of Loch Tay. Salmon season runs from mid-January through mid-October (and is best from April through June and in September and October); brown trout may be taken from mid-March through mid-October. An 18-hole golf course is also on the property. Details: Kenmore Hotel, The Square, Kenmore, by Aberfeldy, Perthshire PH15 2NU, Scotland (phone: Kenmore 08873-205).

ALTNAHARRA, Altnaharra, by Lairg, Sutherland, Scotland: One of the country's most celebrated angling hotels, this 20-room establishment has been welcoming anglers since 1887 to the tiny hamlet of Altnaharra and the superb private fishing on 4 miles of the rivers Mudale and Mallart. Salmon and brown trout are the quarry here. There are also private beats on several nearby lochs, where sea trout may be taken in addition. Best times are late June through late September for sea trout, late May into September for brown trout, and April through June and September for salmon. Details: Altnaharra Hotel, Altnaharra, by Lairg, Sutherland IV27 4UE, Scotland (phone: Altnaharra 054981-222).

BANCHORY LODGE, Banchory, Grampian, Scotland: Fishing at this 24-room country house hotel full of Georgian charm is on the River Dee, one of the world's most celebrated salmon rivers, and anglers come from the far corners of the earth to experience the salmon season here, from the first of February through the end of September; only fly fishing is permitted after April. The dining room and lounges of the hotel itself are furnished in period style, have open log fireplaces, and overlook the river, as do many of the bedrooms (some of which have four-poster beds). Details: Banchory Lodge, Banchory, Grampian AB3 3HS, Scotland (phone: 03302-2625).

TULCHAN LODGE, Grantown-on-Spey, Morayshire, Scotland: Edward VII used to come here to shoot and fish. Recently refurbished, this Scottish country house hotel, overlooking the Spey Valley in the midst of Highland malt whiskey distilling country, is as delightful as it was then, with its magnificent paintings, paneled hall and library, and elegant drawing and billiard rooms. There are 11 rooms and 8 miles of private fishing for salmon and sea trout on the River Spey. Seasons run from mid-February through September; it's best from April to August for salmon, in June and July for sea trout. Details: Tulchan Lodge, Grantown-on-Spey, Morayshire PH26 3PW (phone: 08075-200).

EDNAM HOUSE, Kelso, Borders, Scotland: This stately 33-room establishment built in 1761 has a high percentage of repeat business, thanks to the excellent sport in the River Tweed, which flows just outside (so that all the bars and public rooms and half of the guest quarters have river views). Most anglers come for the salmon fishing in spring and fall; however, rights are privately owned and difficult to negotiate. For trout, 8 miles of the Tweed and the Teviot and numerous other small streams in the district are available to hotel guests at a nominal sum; best sport is in May and June. Details: Ednam House Hotel, Kelso, Borders TD5 7HT, Scotland (phone: 0573-24168).

INVERESHIE HOUSE, Kincraig, Highland, Scotland: Occupying a lovely Georgian building at the foot of the Caringorm mountains overlooking Loch Insh and the River Spey, this establishment offers angling on both bodies of water, as well as the Lower Feshie, for salmon, sea trout, brown trout, and Arctic char. Instruction is available. Details: Invereshie House, Kincraig, Kingussie, Inverness-shire PH21 1NA, Scotland (phone: 05404-332).

CROOK INN, Tweedsmuir, by Biggar, Lanarkshire, Scotland: This 16th-century coaching inn, set on 5½ acres of the border hills, was where the Scottish poet Robbie Burns wrote "Willie Wastle." Now it has 8 rooms and 8 miles of private fishing on the River Tweed for salmon and sea trout. It also makes available an additional 30 miles of association and club brown trout waters. November is the best month for salmon and sea trout; May through July is tops for brown trout. Details: The Crook Inn, Tweedsmuir, by Biggar, Lanarkshire ML12 6QN, Scotland (phone: Tweedsmuir 08997-272).

TWEED VALLEY, Walkerburn, Borders, Scotland: Traditional Scottish food is one of the major attractions of this former Edwardian country house — along with salmon and trout fishing on the River Tweed, which is regarded as one of the foremost salmon rivers in Scotland. Private salmon beats are also available and guests may purchase permits to fish for brown trout and grayling on more than 30 miles of the river and its tributaries. Best times are from February through May, with peak runs of sea trout and salmon in late September, October, and November. Guides, lessons in both fly and bait casting, and tackle hire are available to guests. Details: Tweed Valley Hotel, Walkerburn, Peeblesshire EH43 6AA, Scotland (phone: 089687-220).

GLIFFAES COUNTRY HOUSE, near Crickhowell, Powys, Wales: The River Usk, celebrated for its wild brown trout season, is a prime attraction of this stately, late-19th-century private-home-turned-inn. The average brown trout catch is 10 ounces, but there are three good stretches of salmon water as well, with average annual catches at around 25 to 30 fish. Eight reservoirs stocked by the Welsh Water Authority lie within a 15-mile radius. Details: Gliffaes Country House Hotel, near Crickhowell, Powys NP8 1RH, Wales (phone: 0874-730371).

THE LAKE, Llangammarch Wells, Powys, Wales: Set on 50 acres of sweeping lawns and thick woods, this 29-room country house offers a 3-acre trout lake and 5½ miles on the rivers Wye and Irfon, two of the best salmon streams in Wales; the latter passes within 100 yards of the hotel. Salmon fishing comes into its own in the latter part of the season, which runs from late January to late October on both streams. The spring fish are very powerful and can occasionally run over 30 pounds. Trout — mostly wild local fish weighing up to 34 pounds — can also be taken on the Irfon. Those on the smaller Chewfru also provide interesting sport, while the Wye provides specimens of 1 pound and more. The largest salmon ever caught on hotel waters weighed in at a whopping 28 pounds, 8 ounces. Details: The Lake Hotel, Llangammarch Wells, Powys LD4 4BS, Wales (phone: 05912-202).

LAKE VYRNWY, via Oswestry, Powys, Wales: Fishing on Lake Vyrnwy, which is best in May, brings some guests to this 28-room establishment, while others are drawn by the very fine Bechstein grand piano, the unusual fishing and working holidays, and other special programs such as bird-watching weekends, clay pigeon shoots, and the like. The atmosphere is old-fashioned and unpretentious; one American visitor implored his hosts, "For heaven's sake, don't modernize the place! It's perfect!" Details: Lake Vyrnwy Hotel, via Oswestry, Powys SY10 0LY, Wales (phone: 069173-244).

TYN-Y-CORNEL, Talyllyn Tywyn, Gwynedd, Wales: Angling on Tal-y-llyn Lake, on the shore of which sits this hotel, is the prime attraction here. The lake is owned by the hotel and contains wild brown trout as well as hatchery-bred fish. The hotel has been in the same family since 1924, and parts of the building date back to the 1500s, but the plumbing is strictly 20th century. Details: Tyn-y-Cornel, Talyllyn Tywyn, Gwynedd LL36 9AJ, Wales (phone: 065477-282).

MOUNT FALCON CASTLE, Ballina, County Mayo, Irish Republic: This elegant home stands in a 100-acre park near the River Moy, Ireland's most prolific salmon river, and it owns and leases four beats on 7½ miles of the stream for the use of its guests. The river's massive run of grilse (averaging 5 pounds) is famous; they run from May until mid-August and peak from early June to mid-July. Spring salmon averaging 10 pounds can be taken in April and May. However, there are runs throughout the season since the loughs Conn and Cullin, of whose system the Moy is a part, provide a good supply of water most of the time. Good creels of wild brown trout are also taken, particularly during the mayfly hatch around the first week of June. Details: Mount Falcon Castle Hotel, Ballina, County Mayo, Irish Republic (phone: 096-21172).

ZETLAND, Cashel Bay, County Galway, Irish Republic: This panoramic hotel established in 1850 overlooking Cashel Bay ranks among the country's most comfortable fishing hotels; the chef is *Ritz* (Paris) trained John Prendergast. Certainly, with its traditional turf fires, magnificent views, extensive gardens and lawns, and ambitious kitchen, it does not want for charm. Anglers go for its sea trout fishery, one of the best in the country, on the Gowla fishery's several lakes and rivers. Details: Zetland Hotel, Cashel Bay, County Galway, Irish Republic (phone: Cashel 8).

ASHFORD CASTLE, Cong, County Mayo, Irish Republic: Wonderfully luxurious. Details: Ashford Castle Hotel, Cong, County Mayo, Irish Republic (phone: 094-46003). See also *Rural Retreats*.

PONTOON BRIDGE, Foxford, County Mayo, Irish Republic: Salmon and trout fishing in Lough Conn (famous for its mayfly, grasshopper, and daddy longlegs dapping periods) and Lough Cullin, home cooking, peace and quiet, and fantastic scenery are the attractions in this comfortable, modern establishment. Details: Pontoon Bridge Hotel, Foxford, County Mayo, Irish Republic (phone: 094-56120/56151).

DUNLOE CASTLE, Gap of Dunloe, County Kerry, Irish Republic: On the grounds of a castle that — with its historic park and gardens — dates to the 15th century, this luxurious hotel offers elegant decor with splendid period furnishings and amenities, such as a heated swimming pool, sauna, tennis courts, and restaurants. To anglers, the prime interest is the River Laune, which flows across the grounds. Salmon season is from mid-January to mid-October; the best times are from mid-February to the end of July and from mid-August to the close of the season. Trout may be taken from mid-February to mid-October; best months are from March to July and in September and October. Details: Dunloe Castle Hotel, Gap of Dunloe, County Kerry, Irish Republic (phone: 064-44111).

GLENCAR, Glencar, County Kerry, Irish Republic: Salmon, grilse, and brook and brown trout are the sport in the small rocky rivers and rugged mountain lakes in this area in southwestern Ireland. The establishment — which has been one of the country's premier angling hotels for the last century — is a snug, homey place, with plain guest quarters and public rooms a-jumble with photos of guests and their catch, antlers, oil paintings in gold frames, and antique furniture from the time of Thomas Sheraton through Queen Victoria as well as more modern fittings. The best time for salmon fishing is from February to June; for sea trout from June to September. Details: Glencar Hotel, Glencar, County Kerry, Irish Republic (phone: 066-60102).

KYLEMORE PASS, Kylemore, County Galway, Irish Republic: The hotel sits atop one of the Twelve Bens overlooking Kylemore Lake, and the scenery is magnificent. So is the traditional music you can hear regularly in the hotel's bar. So is the friendly atmosphere. And so is the fishing (for sea, river, and lake trout, as well as salmon — and for the free brown trout in the hotel's own lake). Details: Kylemore Pass Hotel, Kylemore, County Galway, Irish Republic (phone: 095-41141).

SHEELIN SHAMROCK, Mountnugent, County Cavan, Irish Republic: Lough Sheelin, on whose shores this luxurious 20-room hotel is situated, is widely known as one of the best brown trout lakes in Europe, and the hotel has its own fleet of motorboats for its guests' free use. Coarse fishing for pike and perch is available on another lake 2 miles away. Details: Sheelin Shamrock Hotel, Mountnugent, County Cavan, Irish Republic (phone: 049-40113 or 40101).

NEWPORT HOUSE, Newport, County Mayo, Irish Republic: This handsome country house, the home of the historic O'Donnels, offers good fishing on private waters on the Newport River and Lough Beltra and sea fishing on the tidal river from the quay facing the estate. A member of the Relais et Châteaux organization. Details: Newport House Hotel, Newport, County Mayo, Irish Republic (phone: 098-41222).

DROMOLAND CASTLE, Newmarket-on-Fergus, County Clare, Irish Republic: Eight miles from Shannon Airport, with coarse fishing on a lake and trout and late salmon fishing in a small river in the 400-acre park. The hotel also makes a good base for fishing Lough Derg when the Mayfly is up. Details: Dromoland Castle, Newmarket-on-Fergus, County Clare, Irish Republic (phone: 061-71144). See also *Rural Retreats.*

CORRIB, Oughterard, County Galway: The proximity of Corrib Lake and the Connemara fisheries — which are good for salmon, sea trout, brook trout, brown trout, and pike — makes this town a popular destination for fishermen. May and June, the so-called dapping period, are regarded by most local anglers as the best brown trout fishing months. Details: Corrib Hotel, Oughterard, County Galway, Irish Republic (phone: 091-82329).

EGAN'S LAKE, Oughterard, County Galway, Irish Republic: Located in one of the prettiest villages in the West of Ireland, on the shores of 68-square-mile Lough

Corrib, the largest free-fishing lake in the British Isles. The mid-May mayfly dapping period produces tremendous creels of salmon and sea trout. Grilse run in mid-June. And pike can be taken year-round; July is prime time. In addition, this family-run hotel — the longest-established in town — can reserve rods on nearby rivers and streams. Details: Egan's Lake Hotel, Oughterard, County Galway, Irish Republic (phone: 091-82275).

SWEENEY'S OUGHTERARD HOUSE, Oughterard, County Galway, Irish Republic: Owned by the same family since 1913, the hotel occupies a structure dating (in part) from the 18th century. This establishment boasts extensive gardens and a knot of ancient beeches facing the wooded banks of the Owenriff River. There are log and turf fires in the fireplaces and Irish and classic French cuisine is served in the dining room. Many guests come to angle for free trout, salmon, pike, and perch in Connemara's huge Lough Corrib. Details: Sweeney's Oughterard House Hotel, Oughterard, County Galway, Irish Republic (phone: 091-82207).

BLACKWATER LODGE, Upper Ballyduff, County Waterford, Irish Republic: The lodge, now owned by an avid Welsh angler, has been renovated and reorganized to cater to the game angler. It controls seventeen of the best beats on the 30-odd miles of high-record salmon waters between Lismore and Mallow on the celebrated Blackwater River; guests' total catch usually amounts to 350 to 400 salmon per season — 1986 having been a record year with some 750 salmon brought in. There is also excellent fishing for grilse, backend, and sea trout (as well as for wild brown trout, which can range up to 3 pounds, from March on). Details: Blackwater Lodge Hotel, Upper Ballyduff, County Waterford, Irish Republic (phone: 058-60235).

BUTLER ARMS, Waterville, County Kerry, Irish Republic: This homey, 36-room hotel has been considered one of the country's best fishing hotels almost since it opened more than a century ago; it was a favorite of Charlie Chaplin, who returned annually with his family from the early 1960s into the '70s. The free salmon and sea trout fishing on Lough Currane — the attraction here — is considered by some anglers to be Western Europe's best; optimal periods are from the beginning of the season until July; there are sea trout from early May until mid-October. And there's also salmon fishing on the Inny, a spate river, when conditions are right. Details: Butler Arms, Waterville, County Kerry, Irish Republic (phone: 0667-4144).

CORRALEA LODGE, Belcoo, County Fermanagh, Northern Ireland: Anglers who come for the action in Upper Lough McNean and nearby Lough Erne — many of them German and French — stay in the luxurious guesthouse or in six self-catering chalets. The fishing is mainly for pike, though there are also perch, breem, roach, and trout. Details: Corralea Lodge, Belcoo, County Fermanagh BT74 6DX, Northern Ireland (phone: 0365-86325).

MAHON'S, Irvinestown, County Fermanagh, Northern Ireland: Fishing on Lough Erne, known for having some of the best coarse fishing in Europe, has been a prime drawing card of this antique-filled family-owned establishment since it was founded in 1883. Details: Mahon's Hotel, Irvinestown, County Fermanagh BT74 9XX, Northern Ireland (phone: 036-5621656).

MANVILLE HOUSE, Aughnablaney, County Fermanagh, Northern Ireland: Loughs Melvin and Erne and the River Bundrawes. Best fishing is from March through May and in August and September. Private instruction is available, and accommodations are in a house about 100 yards from shore, with lovely views from every window. Details: Manville House, Aughnablaney, Letter, County Fermanagh, Northern Ireland (phone: Kesh 31668).

EVERGLADES, Londonderry, County Londonderry, Northern Ireland: For fishing on the River Foyle. Details: Everglades Hotel, Prehen Rd., Londonderry, County Londonderry BT47 2PA, Northern Ireland (phone: 0504-46722).

BEACH, Portballintrae, County Antrim, Northern Ireland: With fishing on the

River Bush, this establishment is now run by the third generation of Maclaines, who bought it more than six decades ago. Details: Beach Hotel, Portballintrae, County Antrim BT57 8RT, Northern Ireland (phone: Bushmills 31214).

Freewheeling by Two-Wheeler

 The landscapes you see from the roads of Britain and Ireland unfold with such endless diversity at every bend and turn that traveling through quickly in a car seems a real shame: The villages full of ancient half-timbered houses, the heather-clad plateau country with its deep valleys and minuscule settlements, the rolling hills, the quaint seacoast towns, and the regions of moors and mountains all beg to be explored at bicycle speed — that is, fast enough to cover a fair amount of terrain, but slow enough to stop to inspect a wildflower or admire a view. It's lovely to be able to pull over to the side of the road, or pop into a tea shop with a minimum of fuss or bother. Cycling provides all that. There's something quite special about the rhythm of your days on the road — the slow but steady ticking away of the miles, the lure of the unknown just over the next hill, the ready meetings with fellow cyclists on the road or at pubs and hostels, and the special camaraderie that prevails.

The fact that Britain and Ireland offer not only a great variety of scenery in a relatively compact area, but also an abundance of well-surfaced, little-trafficked secondary roads, as well as many facilities for rental and repair and hundreds of small restaurants and informal hotels that are no less than delighted to welcome bedraggled pedalers, makes the countries well-nigh perfect candidates for cycling vacations — for beginning tourers and experts alike. Even those who are not particularly experienced and postpone their planning until the last minute can still enjoy a two-wheeling vacation here: Just travel light, start out slowly, and don't give up just because of saddle-soreness and tender muscles.

Rentals are widely available in both Britain and Ireland. In Ireland, *TI Irish Raleigh Limited* (Broomhill Rd., Tallaght, Dublin 24, County Dublin, Irish Republic; phone: 01-521888) oversees a rental service involving some 100 dealers throughout the country who provide men's and women's 3-speeds, 5-speeds, and mountain bikes and publishes good *Cycle Route Maps*. For names of cycle hire firms in Britain, contact the BTA. Rental rates vary (as do the quality of the bikes available and the standard of maintenance), but they average $27 to $30 for a week's rental, or slightly more if insurance, panniers, lights, and the like are also included. Broader selections are generally available at large companies, usually based in cities — though basic machines can be had in rural towns for as little as $7 a day.

However, since the amount of pleasure at least partially depends on the bike, you may well want to bring your own. Airlines will generally transport bikes as part of passengers' personal baggage, but may insist that the whole machine be crated. At any rate, be sure to check your insurance coverage before you leave home. If you have none, consider joining the *Cyclists' Touring Club* (Cotterell House, 69 Meadrow, Godalming, Surrey GU7 3HS, England; phone: 04868-7217), which has a plan for its members. You will also need to bring a basic set of tools and spares, including tire pump, puncture repair kit, tire levers, spanners/wrench, spoke key, chain rivet extractor, chain links, inner brake cables, pliers, odd nuts and bolts, brake blocks, oil can, batteries and bulbs, freewheel block remover, rag, extra spokes, inner tubes and outer tires, and a small file for honing spokes. British law requires cycles to have two independent brakes, and a red rear light and reflector as well as a white light in the front for night riding; since riding is on the left here, it's a good idea to fix the front light onto the right-hand side. Not required by law — but certainly eminently practical — are a padlock and chain, though theft is not the problem in rural areas that it is in centers such as Birmingham, Glasgow, Liverpool, Manchester, Sheffield, and, of course, London.

To get out of these cities without battling the traffic is a relatively simple matter, since bikes are allowed to accompany passengers on the train at no extra charge. The procedure is simple: Buy your ticket, take your bike onto the platform, and ask the guard's permission to put your bicycle in the luggage van — a request usually refused only when the car is full of other goods. There are a few exceptions, and they change occasionally, so check with British Rail for specifics. And always label your bike with your name, address, and the station of origin and destination.

BEST CYCLING AREAS

The touring possibilities are extensive. In England, for instance, any number of "B" and unclassified roads connect nearly every community in the country. In Wales, only the trunk routes in the southeast are too busy for cycling. In Scotland, their counterparts in the south are generally busy. In summer, Scotland's "A" routes in the north can be congested, more because of their narrow and winding nature than because of the quantity of traffic they carry, as can the north and west coast routes and some of the interior highways in Wales. Nearly all the roads in both Northern Ireland and the Republic (with the exception of trunk routes between the larger cities) offer cyclists not only smooth surfaces but also little traffic. In addition, both nations have unsurfaced tracks, cattle drovers' routes, bridleways, and woodland paths that lend themselves to two-wheeling (though the going can be a bit rough). Britain has, for instance, hundreds of miles of towing paths along the canals that ribbon the countryside, waterways constructed during the Industrial Revolution and now largely deserted by commercial transport. Some are available for cycling; for information about necessary permits, contact the Information Centre and Canal Shop, British Waterways Board, Melbury House, Melbury Ter., London NW1 6JX (phone: 01-262-6711.)

Here are some of the best cycling areas in Britain and Ireland. Bike rentals, routes, lodgings and camping, and repairs for most of these are covered by the invaluable publications of *Cycling World* magazine (£1.80, from Andrew House, 2a Granville Rd., Sidcup, Kent DA14 4BN, England).

LONDON, England: Bicycling may not be everyone's idea of the best transportation here, and in fact, it can prove a nightmare to newcomers not forewarned about patterns of flow and congestion. But it's also true that there's no better way of seeing the real London — away from the main thoroughfares used by most buses and taxicabs. Traveling by bike, more than any other mode of transport, will provide a good feel for the way London's villages all fit together. The London Cycling Campaign's excellent booklet *On Your Bike* (£1.80, including postage) is full of maps of central London on which are designated streets good for bicycling, as well as the official cycle routes through London. Though aimed at Londoners who use their bikes as transportation, it can be useful to sightseers as well — and serves as an excellent primer on English laws pertaining to cyclists, and cycling safety, maintenance, and repairs. Cycling shops are also listed. The Campaign's bimonthly newsletter is also available providing up-to-date information on cycling in London as well as a listing of shops where L.C.C. members can get a 10% discount. Fold-out cycling route maps of south, east, and northwest London (£1 each) are also available. Details: London Cycling Campaign, Tress House, Stamford St., London SE1, England (phone: 01-928-7220).

EAST ANGLIA, England: The generally low-lying terrain of Suffolk and Norfolk, which, along with parts of neighboring counties, used to be an old Saxon kingdom, seems custom-made for cycling — though there are enough gentle hills to keep the horizons constantly changing. East Anglia is a land of farms, isolated villages full of thatched houses, grand mansions, and inspiring Gothic churches. Where these flatlands slip gently into the sea, there are salt marshes and sand dunes teeming with birds, deserted beaches, and The Broads. Details: East Anglia Tourist Board, Toppesfield Hall, Hadleigh, Suffolk IP7 5DN, England (phone: 0473-822922).

COTSWOLDS AND THE HEART OF ENGLAND: This region shows a number of faces to the world: There are the chalk hills known as the Chilterns, billowing up out of the valley of the Thames; the jagged blue-hazed Malvern Hills; the Avon valley, with Stratford, the Bard's hometown, and nearby villages full of thatched-roof cottages — not to mention the Cotswolds, where you'll roll past dotted pastures and shallow trout streams that look like ribbons of silver when you see them from on high, through placid hamlets (some almost *too* picture-postcard pretty), and alongside occasional fuzzy patches of beech trees that shimmer in the sunshine. Everywhere there is the limestone characteristic of the area — intricately fitted as cottage walls and stone fences, and colored the mellow hues of cream and honey and slate so that the structures seem to grow out of the earth itself. There are ups and downs enough that beginners may find themselves stretched to the limits; intermediate pedalers should find the challenges just about right. Details: Heart of England Tourist Board, PO Box 15, Worcester WR1 2JT, England (phone: 0905-29512); and the Thames & Chilterns Tourist Board, 8 The Market Pl., Abingdon, Oxon OX14 3UD, England (phone: 0235-22711).

NORTH YORK MOORS, England: This roughly oval moorland plateau, barren-looking until summer blossoming of heather makes it glow purple and blue, is broken up by inviting dales where cozy accommodations can be found. A 553-square-mile national park, bounded on the east by the North Sea, it is generally a country of sheep-dotted, stream-crossed pastures, with fine views in the uplands, and tiny villages. National park information centers are at Danby Lodge, not far from Grosmont; in the market town of Pickering, the site of ruined Pickering Castle, and at Sutton Bank, on the western edge of the park, with magnificent views of the Vale of York. The roads between Pickering and Whitby and Whitby and Scarborough can be busy in summer, but most other north-south routes over the moors are quiet enough, and dead-end valley lanes are idyllic. Details: Yorkshire & Humberside Tourist Board, 312 Tadcaster Rd., York YO2 2HF, England (phone: 0904-707961).

PEAK DISTRICT, England: The Pennine Hills, England's great backbone, begin in this wild upland practically within shouting distance of the great industrial centers of the Midlands. The more southerly area offers steep-sided valleys; in the north, the characteristic formations are the sharp-edged gritstone cliffs that inspired Daniel Defoe to dub them the nation's Andes. Farther north, the Pennines become wilder, more remote, and harder to cycle. Details: East Midlands Tourist Board, Exchequergate, Lincoln, Lincolnshire LN2 1PZ, England (phone: 052231521).

SOUTHEAST, England: Even as close as this area is to London, the countryside is still given over to orchards and hop fields, woods, and farmlands green and fertile enough to warrant the nickname the "Garden of England." Most cycling is on roads and country lanes through the ranges of low chalk hills known as the North and South Downs, which stretch eastward to the high cliffs on the shores of the English Channel, and are separated by The Weald — the farm- and village-dotted remains of a once-large regional forest. At practically every turn, the land is fine for beginning cyclists. Much of the area has been designated an "Area of Outstanding Natural Beauty"; Canterbury, Chichester, Guildford, and Rochester Cathedrals, the area associated with the Norman invasion and the Battle of Hastings, and a number of seacoast castles and fortifications are among the points of interest. Details: South East England Tourist Board, 1 Warwick Pk., Tunbridge Wells, Kent TN2 5TA, England (phone: 0892-40766).

LAKE DISTRICT, England: Unquestionably one of England's grandest regions, this mountain mass, its valleys bejeweled with lakes, is a favorite among Britain's national parks — and with reason: The ravines and their sapphire tarns, and the volcanic peaks, stark and jagged, sometimes rising abruptly from just above sea level so that they seem even bigger than they really are, make for an effect of striking grandeur. Considering the manmade landscape as well — the velvety pastures laced with lichen-splotched drystone walls, the antique farmhouses, and the lovely villages — it's not hard to see why William Wordsworth, a native son whose various cottages are preserved and open for tours, was so inspired (as were countless other poets and artists down through the years). The hills can be steep — but then, some of those whistle-fast descents from the tops rank among the country's most exhilarating. Despite the area's popularity, there are still plenty of quiet roads. To detour farther from the beaten path, a good bet is the Cumbria Cycle Way, wending along the Smugglers' Coast and through the secluded hamlets of the Eden Valley. There are information offices throughout Cumbria. Details: Cumbria Tourist Board, Ashleigh, Holly Road, Windermere, Cumbria LA23 2AQ, England (phone: 09662-4444).

SOUTHWEST, England: From the cathedral cities and Stonehenge, on the Salisbury Plain, to the New Forest, through the peaceful towns of Dorset (Thomas Hardy's Wessex), and on to the Somerset and Devon uplands — among them Exmoor and Dartmoor — and rugged Cornwall, the southwest of England will challenge even expert cyclists, though less so along the coast than throughout the hilly inland areas. But toward Land's End the scenery rewards cyclists amply for their efforts. The villages are lovely, the vistas unfailingly grand or pastoral, the traditional cream teas scrumptious, and the seacoast wonderfully varied. There are desolate moors, medieval churches, and the prehistoric ruins described in *Ancient Monuments and Ruins*). Details: West Country Tourist Board, Trinity Ct., 37 Southernhay E, Exeter, Devon EX1 1QS, England (phone: 0392-76351).

YORKSHIRE DALES, England: Rivers flowing down from high in the Pennine Hills have cut out a wondrous landscape of steep mountains and deep valleys whose finer points are not well known even in Britain. Like Teesdale, the northernmost of the dales, most boast impressive waterfalls. Swaledale is generally ranked as one of the lovelier dales, but the others have their particular charms as well: Wensleydale, its local cheese; austere, lonely-looking Wharfedale; Nidderdale, with its impressive How Stean gorge; Airedale, with its spectacular Craven Country, Malham Cove's gigantic limestone bluffs, and the heavily visited Gordale Scar gorge; and not too well known Ribblesdale, in the center of the Pennines, where there are abundant potholes and waterfalls — to name only a few. Nearly 700 square miles of this water-carved wonderland have been designated as a national park. Details: Yorkshire & Humberside Tourist Board, 312 Tadcaster Rd., York YO2 2HF, England (phone: 0904-707961).

NORTHEAST, England: Apart from a few urban areas near the coast, this is a quiet, sparsely populated region that boasts more ancient remains and medieval castles than any other part of Britain; Hadrian's Wall, Bamburgh Castle, Alnwick Castle, Dunstanbugh Castle, Lindisfarne Priory, Durham Cathedral, the 8th-century churches at Hexham and Jarrow, and Scotland's Melrose, Jedburgh, and Kelso abbeys (described in *Ancient Monuments and Ruins*) are among the notable sites. Roads through the grass-covered Cheviot Hills offer particularly challenging cycling; the rest of the area, mainly given over to forests, farms, and beaches, is more rolling. Details: Northumbria Tourist Board, Aykley Heads, Durham DH1 5UX, England (phone: 0385-46905 or 091-384-6905).

WELSH MARCHES, England: In this area between Chepstow, on the Bristol Channel to the south, and Liverpool Bay, just north of Chester, the green and gentle hills of the valley of the meandering Wye and the country north of that offer some pleasant cycling. There's the Forest of Dean, the wild woods between the rivers Severn and Wye; Hay-on-Wye, a town full of secondhand bookshops, including "the world's largest"; the Shropshire Hills; and historical towns like the ancient religious center of Hereford, picturesque Ludlow, and Shrewsbury, full of half-timbered houses. Castles and abbeys are abundant. In few places in England will you find so little motor traffic. Details: Heart of England Tourist Board, PO Box 15, Worcester WR1 2JT, England (phone: 0905-29512).

HIGHLANDS, Scotland: This region of ridges and glens, many loch-filled, are really restricted to cyclists with plenty of pedal power and a love of wilderness wandering: There are relatively few major roads (though hundreds of miles of narrow lanes), particularly in the west, and these get somewhat more crowded during the summer; and outside the main towns, there are few bicycle shops, so it's necessary to carry all spares. The rewards are many, however: the northwest coast, looking much like Norway with its fjords; the vistas of snow-capped peaks; the islands, where it is flatter, less crowded, and even wilder; ancestral castles with long histories of the Scottish clans; and vast blue lakes like Loch Ness, Loch Long, and Loch Lochy, to name only a few. Details and advice: Hi-Line, Bridgend Rd., Dingwall, Ross-shire IV15 9SL, Scotland (phone: 44-349-63434).

NORTH, Wales: Apart from the highway along the north coast, the roads here — as elsewhere in the country — are not at all heavily trafficked as they twist and climb into wild, mysterious mountains that are some of the most beautiful in all of Britain — slate brown, full of foaming rivers, huge smooth lakes, castles, and prehistoric sites. The Isle of Anglesey, across a narrow channel to the north, is more rural than rugged, making for a pleasant contrast. Details: North Wales Regional Office, Wales Tourist Board, 77 Conwy Rd., Colwyn Bay, Clwyd LL29 7LN, Wales (phone: 0492-531731 or 0492-534626 for lodging reservations).

MID AND SOUTH WALES: Inland, the terrain is peaceful. Farms are interspersed with patches of woods. Rolling hills climb out of pastoral valleys. The neat hamlets scattered here and there are laced together by country lanes and "rough stuff" tracks — unsurfaced but bikeable by the adventurous. But in the south, the countryside is dramatic. There are the mountains of the Brecon Beacons, with their thundering cascades, lakes, forests, moorlands, passes, deeply incised valleys with their rich industrial and cultural heritage; and the Pembrokeshire coast, where mountains plunge to the sea and rocky headlands are interspersed with delightful sandy beaches and punctuated by ancient towns such as Cardigan, Pembroke and its castle, St. Davids with its historic cathedral, and delightful Terby. For intermediate cyclists, this is Wales's must — an experience of a lifetime, to boot. Worth a look is the new National Mountain Bike Centre at Llanwrtyd Wells, which stages a number of "fat tyre" competitions in season. Details: Mid Wales Regional Office, Wales Tourist Board, Canolfan Owain Glyndwr, Machynlleth, Powys SY20 8EE, Wales (phone: 0654-2653), and the South Wales Regional Office, Wales Tourist Board, Ty Croeso, Gloucester Pl., Abertawe/Swansea SA1 1TY, Wales (phone: 0792-465204).

DUBLIN ENVIRONS, Irish Republic: The wonderful thing about Ireland is that only about 20 miles outside Dublin — or 10 miles from Cork, Derry, Galway, Limerick, or Waterford — the roads are virtually traffic-free. In County Meath, the doorstep of Dublin Airport is the departure point for nearly ideal runs through villages like Ballyboghil and Naul, on to Duleek, and to the remarkable Boyne Valley and the Hill of Tara (whose sites are described in *Ancient Monuments and Ruins*). Don't miss the monastic remains at Slane and Navan. South of Dublin, those who like hill climbing can take the road from suburban Rathfarnham to the Sally Gap and Devil's Glen and, within a half an hour, find themselves out of sight of human habitation, in lovely countryside where the lark rising is the only sound to be heard. The small but lovely Wicklow Mountains, which extend from around Dublin in the north to as far south as Arklow, and inland for about 25 miles from the sandy shores of the Irish Sea, make for excellent cycling; the wide, long, dune-backed strand at Brittas Bay is one of the best places for a swim here, and Glendalough (described in *Ancient Monuments and*

Ruins) is a sightseeing must. Details: Dublin and Eastern Regional Tourism Organisation, 13-14 Upper O'Connell St., Dublin 1, Irish Republic (phone: 01-747733).

MIDWEST, Irish Republic: The 700-foot Cliffs of Moher, which plunge into the foaming sea near the fishing village of Liscannor, the spa town of Lisdoonvarna, the village of Doolin (a home of traditional Irish music), and the Burren — bare and almost lunar in appearance — are some of the notable sites in County Clare, while in more-frequented County Galway, the place to explore is rocky, boggy, lake-studded, and partially Gaelic-speaking Connemara, with the Twelve Bens presiding over flatlands speckled with ruined rock-walled cottages. There are good beaches — and they're seldom busy; loughs Corrib and Mask (see *Gone Fishing*) are not too far distant. Still farther north, small roads meander through pretty quiet villages scattered around the tranquil heather and rhododendron country of less-populated Mayo or hug a coastline as wild and lonesome as those tired of city life could ever desire. The routes from Newport and Mulrany by Lough Furnace, over the bridge at Achill Sound to Achill Island, and then around Achill Island, are pleasant. Details: Shannonside Tourism, The Granary, Michael St., Limerick, Irish Republic (phone: 061-317522) and Ireland-West Tourism, Áras Fáilte, Victoria Pl., Galway, Irish Republic (phone: 091-63081).

SOUTHWEST, Irish Republic: Outside busy Cork City, counties Cork, Kerry, and Limerick are quite rural. There are mountains and steep gradients, but gently rolling hills and flat valleys are part of the cycling picture as well. Most dramatic scenery is along the coast, where lovely deep bays are interspersed with cave-pocked cliffs and promontories. Blarney Castle is here, along with the Fota House near Cork City, the fishing town of Youghal, the pretty port of Kinsale and Cobh on Cork Harbour, the remote district around Allihies on the coast, Georgian-era Bantry House, Killarney, *Durty Nelly's Inn* (see *Pub Crawling*), Ross Castle and the ruined remains of Muckross and Innisfallen Abbey, and the spectacular Gap of Dunloe that slashes through the countryside between Macgillycuddy's Reeks and the Purple Mountains. The Ring of Kerry and the Dingle Peninsula are particular standouts. Details: Cork/Kerry Region Tourism Organisation, PO Box 44, Tourist House, Grand Parade, Cork, Irish Republic (phone: 021-273251).

NORTHERN IRELAND: Ulster's 5,500 square miles encompass some of the most spectacular and varied scenery that one could imagine. Blue mountains and sandy beaches, open moorlands and clear lakes, small towns hidden away in the green places of the countryside, and fishing villages strung out along the rocky shores — and you are never more than an hour from the sea. The only heavy traffic on the excellent network of small, well-signposted roads is the occasional tractor, and the only traffic jams are caused by sheep and cattle changing fields. Perhaps the most rewarding outing for the cyclist is to take the 60-mile coast road from Larne up around the northeast corner of County Antrim to the resort of Portrush. The celebrated Antrim coast road, which passes countless villages, ruined Norman castles, and the nine green Glens of Antrim, is reminiscent of California Highway 1 south of Carmel. Ancient rocks jut out as cliffs in all their brilliant colors — bright red sandstones, white chalk, black basalt, and blue clays. The beckoning hills of Scotland can be seen along part of the route. Stop off at Ballycastle and take a boat across to Rathlin Island, where Robert the Bruce once found sanctuary. There's a guesthouse and a licensed restaurant on the island, and you can walk or cycle across to the bird sanctuary on the west side and explore the cliffs and caves. Once back on the mainland, pedal on to the strange and remarkable rock formation called the Giant's Causeway, an astonishing complex of basalt columns packed tightly together; the tops of the columns — 38,000 of them — form stepping-stones leading from the cliff foot and disappearing under the sea. Details: Northern Ireland Tourist Board.

HOW TO PLAN A TOUR

After picking a region to explore, it's a fairly easy matter to sketch out an itinerary. First decide on exactly what to see and do. For ideas, consult local tourist literature; articles about touring in bicycling magazines such as the Cyclists' Touring Club's bimonthly *CycleTouring* (available from the club; address above) or *Cycling World* (published by Stone Industrial Publications, Ltd., 2a Granville Rd., Sidcup, Kent DA14 4BN, England; phone: 01-302-6150 or 01-302-6069), both widely available from newsstands as well as from the publishers at £1 per copy; and specialized bikers' books such as the *Cyclists' Touring Club's Route Guide to Cycling in Britain and Ireland* by Christa Gausden and Nicholas Crane (£8.95 from the Oxford Illustrated Press, The Gables, Newington, Oxford OX9 8AH, England; phone: Oxford 890026), which lists 365 connecting routes based on minor roads and lanes throughout Britain, suitable for tours lasting anywhere from a single day to several months. *Cycling World* magazine also publishes a Bed & Breakfast Series outlining routes and facilities for lodging, camping, and cycle rental (£2 each).

Once you have a general idea of where you want to go, plot out your tour on a large-scale highway map of the country — the sort of map supplied by a national tourist office. Base your daily mileage on what you usually cover on the road at home, but be sure to allot time for en-route dawdling — chatting with the locals, long stops for admiring the panoramas from a picnic spot, walks through ruined abbeys, and the like.

Then tackle detailed route finding with small-scale topographical maps that will not only tell you about the smallest country lanes, but also alert you to the contours of the land and the steepness of the hills throughout the area you've chosen to cover. The 1:100,000-scale National Map Series (£2.50 from John Bartholomew & Son, Duncan St., Edinburgh EH9 1TA, Scotland; phone: 031-667-9341), key contours to colors and are excellent; they can be ordered directly from the company or from the Cyclists' Touring Club (address above). These can be used in conjunction with lodging guides such as the BTA publications *Britain: Stay on a Farm, Britain: Stay at an Inn,* and *Cycling,* as well as the CTC's annual handbook for members, which lists not only some 3,000 inexpensive hotels and B&Bs that extend particularly warm welcomes to cyclists but also bicycle repair shops throughout the country. The CTC Touring Department also provides its members with excellent help in planning trips.

CYCLING HOLIDAYS

Although there are no organized bike trips in the Irish Republic, there are several cycling holidays available in Britain and Northern Ireland. Among them are:

Freewheeling Holidays, 9 Kandahar, Aldbourne, Marlborough, Wiltshire SN8 2EE, England (phone: 0672-40069). Custom-tailored cycling tours for groups large and small in the Cotswolds, Wessex, Dorset, the Isle of Wight, the Mendips — or just about any other destination you can name. Individual tours arranged.

Bike Tours, PO Box 75, Bath, Avon BA1 1BX, England (phone: 0225-310859). Tours in various parts of England and France — different destinations every year, plus a 2- or 3-week, camping-based "Great British Bike Ride," from John O'Groats to Land's End — all with mechanics, guides, and sag wagons.

Cyclists' Touring Club, Cotterell House, 69 Meadrow, Godalming, Surrey GU7 3H7, England (phone: 04868-7217). Tours organized by club members.

Cyclorama Holidays, The *Grange* hotel, Grange-over-Sands, Cumbria LA11 6EJ, England (phone: 04484-3666). Cycle tours through the Lakeland with accommodations in guesthouses and hotels and a sag wagon to transfer your gear between overnight stops. You get a choice of routes with distances that suit your abilities. Cycles can be supplied, or you can bring your own. Holidays for cyclists are usually 7 or 8 days long.

Youth Hostels Association, Trevelyan House, 8 St. Stephen's Hill, St. Albans, Hertfordshire AL1 2DY, England (phone: 0727-55215). Group trips to favored biking destinations in England and Wales.

Peninsula Bike Tours and Expeditions, Church View Cottage, Church Rd., Bebington, Wirral, Cheshire L63 3DY, England (phone: 051-645-3927). Cycling holidays in Cheshire, North Wales, and Snowdonia.

East Anglia Cycling Holidays, Ballintuim Post Office, Blairgowrie, Perthshire PH10 7NJ, Scotland (phone: 025086-201). East Anglia in southeast England is ideal cycling country with a network of quiet byroads and easy cycling in unspoilt country and along the coast. Self-led inclusive tours with accommodations in pubs, inns, or guesthouses. Cycles and all gear can also be supplied.

Scottish Cycling Holidays, Ballintuim Post Office, Blairgowrie, Perthshire PH10 7NJ, Scotland (phone: 025086-201). Inclusive self-led cycling tours throughout Scotland, with multi-speed touring cycles specially geared for the terrain supplied, along with all gear. Accommodations in hotel of any standard, guesthouse, or youth hostel, with routes planned accordingly. Cyclists can be picked up at Glasgow or Edinburgh airports.

Stalking and Shooting

Men have been making sport of their search for game, both large and small, since the time of the Pharaohs (who were so enamored of the activity that they looked forward to continuing it in the afterlife) — and the sport's devotees in Britain and Northern Ireland are no less enthusiastic. In fact, the Glorious Twelfth, which marks the opening of the shooting season for grouse, is something of a national day of festivity in Britain.

But grouse are only one quarry. In both Britain and Ireland, you can go for a variety of game, from rabbits to pigeons to wildfowl to pheasants (which were first brought to Britain by the Romans). Scotland and Northern England are known all over the world for their red grouse shooting, and sportsmen from the far corners of the globe come here to participate in shoots at which teams of beaters drive the birds over a line of concealed guns, or to flush them out with the aid of dogs — pointers, setters, Labradors, or springer spaniels. Woodcock, some of them resident in Britain and others that overfly the islands during their fall migrations, are another favorite target, challenging because of their predilection for flying erratically between trees. Except in Ireland, capercaillie, which inhabit pine and fir forests, are also sought after, as are snipe, which fly fast and unpredictably. Cock pheasant and wild duck are plentiful in the Irish Republic. So are snipe, which favor marshy areas; these are also numerous in the boggy country of Wales, Norfolk, Scotland's Western Islands, the Irish Republic, and Northern Ireland.

Pheasant shooting is of excellent quality and good value, often with the possibility of guaranteed bags. For a party of six to nine guns, 100- to 250-bird days are typical. These are usually driven out of woodland to the standing guns, and bookings are generally made with a bag expectancy in mind.

Shoreline duck and goose hunting is a chancy affair, and access is fairly heavily restricted throughout most of Britain. However, there are good areas for duck and goose hunting inland, particularly in Scotland for geese.

In Scotland, you can also stalk deer, taking advantage of all available cover as you creep up on the animal — often over a period of several hours and a distance of several miles, until you get within 120 to 180 yards of it. Though this can be a very expensive proposition, it is one of the most exciting sports that the United Kingdom has to offer, and even though the red deer trophies taken here are not generally as large as those you might get on the Continent, many a sportsman prizes his Scottish trophies far more than larger ones taken more easily. Roe buck and Sika stag trophies are often far superior to Continental Europe's because of more selective shooting over the years. And the delights afforded by the scenery — everything from flat heather moors to mountainous rocky countryside and wooded farmland — may even outweigh the pleasures of the sport.

For hunting in England, Scotland, Wales, and Northern Ireland, firearms certificates must be obtained by visitors from overseas; arrangements can be made through reputable agents, such as a holiday tour organizer, with a minimum of a month's notice. Game licenses, available from all main and branch post offices, are also required.

In the Irish Republic, all visitors wishing to shoot wild birds must have a current Irish firearm certificate and an Irish hunting license as authorization to hunt game species during open seasons. Here, too, you must apply at least a month in advance. All shooting is done on private land, on estates managed specifically with the shooting in mind. On sections of all grouse moors, for instance, the heather is burned at certain seasons, and in others the moorland is left to grow to protect the birds at various stages in their development. Keepers and farm managers patrol to prevent poaching and to control predators. Many of these estates are run in concert with a hotel or booking agency specializing in shooting holidays, and when you begin to plan a shooting holiday, these are your best contacts.

BOOKING AGENCIES: These organizations can send the particulars describing several estates, including the details of the shooting and fairly complete descriptions of available accommodations. Most shoots are organized for groups of six to eight, and it's common for friends to get together to form a shoot; if you can't make up a party on your own, the agents can usually fit you into someone else's. (Though, quite naturally, most groups are wary of having an inexperienced sportsman in their midst because of the danger of injury.) The organizers can advise you in advance about open seasons and license requirements. In the Irish Republic, several estates are available directly to the public.

Best in Britain, 48 Epple Rd., London SW6 4DH, England (phone: 01-731-1733).

John Birth Sporting Organisation, Greenlawalls Lodge, Duddo, Berwick-on-Tweed, Northumberland TD15 2PR, England (phone: 0289-082-261).

Macsport Ltd., Macsport House, Ballater Rd., Aboyne, Aberdeenshire AB3 5HT, Scotland (phone: 0339-2896).

Major Neil Ramsay & Co., Farleyer, Aberfeldy, Perthshire PH15 2JE, Scotland (phone: 0887-20523 or 20540).

Peter Readman Sporting Agent, Hirsel Law, Coldstream, Berwickshire TD12 4NY, Scotland (phone: 0890-2139).

Sport in Scotland, Ltd., 22 Market Brae, Inverness, Highland IV2 3AB, Scotland (phone: Inverness 222757).

Tours and Travel Promotions, 25 Brunstane Dr., Edinburgh EH15 2NF, Scotland (phone: 031-669-5344).

Travel Scotland, 10 Rutland Sq., Edinburgh EH1 2AS, Scotland (phone: 031-229-7366).

Alpine Club Shoot, Inniscrone, County Sligo, Irish Republic (phone: 096-36252). This 100,000-acre estate attached to the *Alpine Hotel* specializes in snipe and woodcock shoots but also offers duck flighting and rough shooting.

Ballyarthur Estate Shoot, Arklow, County Wicklow, Irish Republic (phone: 0402-

5100). Known for its very high birds, this driven shoot — involving dog handlers as well as some 20 beaters in the woods — bags between 300 and 400 birds per shoot out of the 8,000-odd reared and turned out each year. Driven birds are very different from those encountered while walking up, so that considerable experience is required for the best results. Very strict rules apply regarding insurance, and there is a 10-gun-per-day limit.

Donegal Highlands Game Shoot, c/o Gilbert McCool, 20 The Willows, Glasnevin Rd., Dublin 11, Irish Republic (phone: 01-305530). Has 250,000 acres stocked with duck, pigeon, grouse, pheasant, snipe, woodstock, and the like in County Donegal.

Shelton Shoot, c/o Miniphoto Limited, Coolock Industrial Estate, Coolock, Dublin 5, Irish Republic (phone: 476877). Adjoins the *Ballyarthur Estate Shoot* and resembles it in size and terrain.

Forest Service, Department of Agriculture, Belfast BT4 38B, County Antrim, Northern Ireland (phone: 0232-650111). A wide range of game shooting and stalking, both for deer and goat, is available on a daily permit basis. The northwestern forests' natural stock of home-bred woodcock is augmented each fall by migrants from Scandinavia. This is regarded as a windfall by hunters, and charges are made only for pheasants cropped during a hunt.

Game Services, Pinetree House, 32 Aghnatrisk Rd., Hillsborough, County Down BT26 6JJ, Northern Ireland (phone: Hillsborough 682172).

Irish Tourist Handling, Ltd., 13 Moss Rd., Banbridge, County Down BT32 5EF, Northern Ireland (phone: 082-065-208).

HOTELS FOR SHOOTING HOLIDAYS: A number of hotels located in the richest shooting areas can also organize shooting holidays for their guests, among them:

Arundell Arms, Lifton, Devon PL16 0AA (phone: 0566-84666). The well-organized program at this sportsman's hotel includes 4-day shoots for driven snipe, as well as driven pheasant shoots, duck flighting, rough and woodcock shooting, and red and roe deer stalking. See also *Rural Retreats.*

Craig-y-Dderwen Country House, Betws-y-Coed, Gwynedd LL24 0AS, Wales (phone: 069-02-293).

Golden Pheasant, Glynceiriog, near Chirk, Llangollen, Clwyd LL20 7BB, Wales (phone: 069-172-281). Situated in the Berwyn Mountains, one of the finest areas in Wales for shooting high and fast pheasant. Blackcock is also an area specialty. The sport is also for grouse, partridge, and duck from August to November. To arrange for shooting, contact Geoff T. Turner, Aelybryn, Dolywern, near Llangollen, Clwyd LL20 7BB, Wales (phone: 069-172630).

Kenloch House, Crossmichael, near Castle Douglas, Kirkcudbrightshire, Scotland (phone: 055667-452). A small guesthouse in an old manse in a beautiful part of Scotland that provides fine shooting for duck and geese.

Invereshie House, Kincraig, Kingussie, Inverness-shire PH21 1NA, Scotland (phone: 05404-332). Occupying a lovely Georgian building at the foot of the Caringorm mountains overlooking Loch Insh and the River Spey, this establishment was built as a shooting lodge in the 1690s, and there is still an abundance of game for shooting and stalking — primarily the magnificent red deer in autumn.

Tweed Valley, Walkerburn, Borders EH43 6AA, Scotland (phone: 089687-220). This former Edwardian country house with beautiful views overlooking the River Tweed and its valley can arrange for grouse, pheasant, and mixed shooting as well as roe and sika deer stalking.

Ashford Castle, Cong, County Mayo, Irish Republic (phone: 092-46003). One of the most luxurious establishments in the country; a sportsman's paradise, offering some of Ireland's best woodcock shooting.

Blackwater Lodge, Upper Ballyduff, County Waterford, Irish Republic (phone: 058-60235). This hotel, which is famous for its high-record salmon fishing on the Blackwater River, can also arrange for rough shooting over many nearby farms and along the riverside.

Great Southern, Parknasilla, County Kerry, Irish Republic (phone: 064-45122). Miles of shooting over some outstandingly beautiful country. See also *Rural Retreats.*

Pontoon Bridge, Foxford, County Mayo, Irish Republic (phone: 094-56120/ 56151). Offers 5,000 acres of rough shooting for woodcock, snipe, grouse, duck, pheasant, and geese in autumn and winter.

Carlton, Belleek, County Fermanagh, Northern Ireland (phone: 036-565-282).

Lakeland, Bellanaleck Quay, Enniskillen, County Fermanagh, Northern Ireland (phone: 036-582-301). Shooting for mallards, widgeons, and teal ducks on the Lough Erne system; walk-up rough shooting for pheasant, snipe, and woodcock; and driven shoots by prior arrangement.

GENERAL INFORMATION: There are a number of sources a sports-minded visitor should contact for more details about shooting-oriented holidays. These include the following:

British Field Sports Society, 59 Kennington Rd., London SE1 7PZ, England (phone: 01-928-4742). A membership organization devoted to hunting, shooting, and fishing, the Society can provide lists of shooting agents in the United Kingdom.

Clay Pigeon Shooting Association, 107 Epping New Rd., Buckhurst Hill, Essex IG9 5TQ, England (phone: 01-505-62212). Governs and provides information about the sport in England.

Scottish Clay Pigeon Association, 2 Greengill, Gilcrux, Aspatria, Carlisle, Cumbria CA5 2RA, England (phone: 0965-21600). Scotland's sister organization to the above.

Scottish Sporting Gazette, 22 Market Brae, Inverness, Scotland IV2 3AB (phone: Inverness 222757). A glossy 88-page annual ($5) filled with articles on all aspects of Scottish sport; advertisements for private hunting estates, country hotels, gunshops, and the like complete the coverage.

Forest and Wildlife Service, Leeson La., Dublin 2, Irish Republic (phone: 01-600444). Has details on obtaining hunting licenses, firearm certificates, and hunting regulations.

Bord Fáilte (Irish Tourist Board), Baggot Street Bridge, Dublin 2, Irish Republic (phone: 01-765871).

Government Publications Sale Office, Sun Alliance House, Molesworth St., Dublin 2, Irish Republic (phone: 01-710309). Write for a copy of *Wildlife and the Law* (90p).

Forest Service, c/o Chief Wildlife Officer, Department of Agriculture, Belfast BT4 38B, Northern Ireland (phone: 0232-650111). Provides information on stalking and shooting in Northern Ireland.

Great Walks and
Mountain Rambles

Almost any walker will tell you that it is the footpaths of a country — not its roadways — that show off the landscape to best advantage. You're closer to earth than you are when driving or even biking, and you notice details that might not otherwise come to your attention: incredibly tiny wildflowers blossoming cheerfully in a crack between limestone boulders, for instance, or a fox lurking in the shadows of the woods at dawn. And the scenery moves by you at a relatively slow speed: Hedgerows, fences, and the green velvet pastures can be contemplated at leisure. Churches and barns, old windmills and lichen-crusted stone walls, and farms and villages are seldom far out of sight as you follow in the footsteps of Neolithic man or Bronze Age gold traders, travel along Roman ways, or follow tracks first defined by smugglers, cattle drovers, abbots, or coffin carriers, whose ways would often be marked at the tops of passes by the stone piles where they rested their load. Many paths were literally walked into existence by generations of country folk traveling to work, market, church, or the ale house, and in all, over 100,000 miles of public footpaths have been recorded and mapped (a number that swells still further when you consider those in Scotland, where the laws do not require that they be mapped and measured).

In England and Wales, many footpaths are in the 10 national parks and 36 Areas of Outstanding Natural Beauty (AONB). The national parks, which cover some 5,256 square miles, about 9% of the total acreage of England and Wales, contain some of their most spectacular scenery, a blend of mountain and moor, down and heathland, cliffs and seashore, and all offering plenty of relatively wild mileage for the pedestrian. The land is not owned by the state, as in some countries, but remains in private hands, so that you must stick to the public rights-of-way unless a so-called access agreement exists, permitting you to do otherwise (as in over half of Dartmoor and the Lake District, for example). Local planning authorities, responsible for the parks' administration, protect their landscape, clear away eyesores, keep footpaths passable, regulate vehicular traffic, appoint wardens, and alert the public to their recreational potential. AONBs enjoy a looser measure of legal protection. The Countryside Commission, the body responsible for designating these especially scenic areas, has also created several official long-distance trails by negotiating new rights-of-way and linking them to established footpaths. Each of these trails is highlighted by *signposts* (which announce its beginning and its direction) and by *waymarkings* (acorn symbols placed at potentially confusing junctures).

In Scotland, you won't be walking in national parks as in England, because there are none, despite the fact that the scenery is some of Britain's loveliest and most varied — mountains and moors, lochs, grassy hills, forests and glens, cliffs and sandy beaches, and very few people. The law regarding rights-of-way is complex — and in principle you can't walk just anywhere. But in practice, you can roam more or less freely as long as you respect the obviously off-limits, and keep off the moors during the early August through late October grouse-shooting and deer-stalking season.

In the Irish Republic and Northern Ireland, the situation is similar. Though some hundred-odd forest parks — as well as national parks such as Killarney's Muckross Estate and Donegal's tranquil Glenveagh — exist throughout the country, the walks here are mainly short and relatively easy. For longer tramps, you've got to head into the wild high country, mainly along the coast, where tracks are rare and ill defined and you will generally be crossing pathless hills and where (as in Scotland) map and compass are essential companions. With summits that seldom rise above 3,000 feet, these mountains are no giants. But because the way up begins in valleys that are usually near sea level, the hikes turn out to be a good deal more demanding than you might at first expect. Your rewards are abundant, however: The sea-and-mountain views that keep you company as you go are awash in incredible blues and intense greens (thanks to the abundant rainfall). And chance encounters en route with fellow ramblers, or with tweed-hatted shepherds and their collies, can be a lot of fun.

That's true even when the weather turns rainy, as it may well do even at the height of the British summer (which King Charles II once gloomily described as "three fine days followed by a thunderstorm") — providing you come prepared. Stout walking shoes or boots are essential, as is a good rain parka, with leggings. And in addition to

the usual walker's gear, you always need a spare sweater, even on a day hike —
especially on the British hills, where conditions can turn literally arctic within a matter
of hours. Both hiking and backpacking equipment are best bought in the US, where
the selection is greater and prices are lower.

WHERE TO WALK

You don't have to dismiss the idea of walking in Britain just because you're not a
hotshot mountaineer at home. Even novices can share the delights: Just find a hotel
in the heart of good walking country, and use it as home base for daily expeditions;
at the end of each day, you'll come back to a hot bath and a hearty meal.

Areas that offer these experiences are delightfully abundant. Among Areas of Outstanding Natural Beauty, a number are really good for walking: the path-crossed,
beechwoods-dotted chalk uplands known as the Chilterns, which roll through parts of
Bedfordshire, Buckinghamshire, Hertfordshire, and Oxfordshire (for details, contact
the Thames & Chilterns Tourist Board, 8 The Market Pl., Abingdon, Oxfordshire
OX14 3UD, England; phone: 0235-22711); the 582 square miles of the oh-so-English
Cotswolds, full of cozy villages, extending through the counties of Avon, Gloucester
shire, Hereford and Worcester, Oxfordshire, and Wiltshire (Heart of England Tourist
Board, PO Box 15, Worcester WR1 2JT, England; phone: 0905-29512); rolling Dorset,
with the "far from the madding crowd" scenery of novelist Thomas Hardy, and its fine
seaside scenery (West Country Tourist Board, Trinity Ct., 37 Southernhay East, Exeter, Devon EX1 1QS, England; phone: 0392-76351); the distinctive Norfolk Coast, a
delight to those whose souls resonate to its moody expanses of salt marshes and tidal
creeks (East Anglia Tourist Board, Toppesfield Hall, Hadleigh, Suffolk IP7 5DN,
England; phone: 0473-822922); the meandering Wye Valley and the Forest of Dean,
where you can explore woodlands and the lovely cliffs and gorges along the river (Heart
of England Tourist Board, above). The Wye Valley continues through Wales, the
country which is home to the breezy Gower Peninsula, where you can tramp through
the coastal dunes and beach country or head inland up into the hills (South Wales
Regional Office, Wales Tourist Board, Ty Croeso, Gloucester Pl., Swansea SA1 1TY,
Wales; phone: 0792-465204).

National parks offer still better walking — and public transportation is good enough
that you don't have to plan all your trips to end back at your starting point.

Ireland's mountain areas open up still further options. In the area around Clonmel
alone, there are the Galtees, the location of one of Ireland's highest inland peaks
— 3,018-foot Galtymore; the Comeraghs, with their flat summits and beautiful corries
(blunt, cliff-backed valley ends known elsewhere as cirques); and the less-demanding
Knockmealdowns to the west. You can hike around 1,730-foot Ben Bulben, in County
Sligo, storied in the lore of the poet William Butler Yeats, who is buried not far away;
or tackle County Mayo's isolated Nephins, with distances between possible overnight
stops substantial enough to keep beginners away — and views, solitude, and scenery
(magnificent moors and cliff-girt coastline) plentiful enough to make them a favorite
among enthusiasts. Achill Island, off the coast, offers more of the same. In mountainous
Donegal, both the rough Derryveagh Mountains in the north, and, in the south, the
Slieve League's high cliffs near Carrick and the Blue Stack Mountains are also popular.
For guidebooks covering these walks, contact Jean Boydell, Federation of Mountain-
eering Clubs of Ireland (FMCI), 56a Rockville Dr., Blackrock, County Dublin, Irish
Republic.

Some of Britain and Ireland's most interesting walking country is detailed below:

LAKE DISTRICT NATIONAL PARK, Cumbria, England: This 880-square-mile
area, within the county of Cumbria, is the largest of all the national parks. It is also
one of the most beautiful, with jewellike lakes and steep mountains rising precipitously

from close to sea level so that they seem even higher than they actually are; and its dazzling colors, a function of the seasonal changes in vegetation. Poets and writers — among them Coleridge and Ruskin, Hugh Walpole and Beatrix Potter — have been inspired by the landscape for centuries; the area's fame has grown to such proportions that you can no longer expect to "wander lonely as a cloud" just everywhere — as did the 19th-century romantic poet William Wordsworth. To experience the real beauties of the Lake District, you must steer clear of the larger tourist centers such as Ambleside, Keswick, and Windermere; avoid weekends and public holidays; or go just a bit farther afield than everyone else — something that is not too difficult since there are hundreds of miles of footpaths here, ranging from nature trails and level walks along the lakeshore and in the valleys to the strenuous routes that cross the mountains from valley to valley. By tradition, visitors can go almost anywhere on the open high land, and with care, anyone can reach the summits of 3,206-foot Scafell, 3,054-foot Skiddaw, and 3,116-foot Helvellyn — three of the park's more noteworthy peaks. A number of leaflets describing walks from various starting points are available from the park's information office, and guided walks are also available. The best general guidebooks to the area are the *A.A. Ordnance Survey Leisure Guide to the Lake District* (£6.95, available from Lake District National Park Visitor Centre, address below), and W. H. Pearsall's *The Lake District National Park* (unfortunately out of print); the best footpath guides, which describe your way in delightful illustrated commentary, are in Alfred Wainwright's seven-volume *A Pictorial Guide to the Lakeland Fells* (£6 per volume, from Westmorland Gazette, 22 Stricklandgate, Kendal, Westmorland LA9 4NE, England; phone: 0539-20555). For general area information, contact the Lake District National Park Visitor Centre, Brockhole, Windermere, Cumbria LA23 1LJ, England (phone: 09662-6602); and the Cumbria Tourist Board, Ashleigh, Windermere, Cumbria LA23 2AQ, England (phone: 09662-4444).

NORTH YORK MOORS NATIONAL PARK, North Yorkshire, England: The site of the largest expanse of heather-covered moorland in England and Wales, this 553-square-mile park is a walker's paradise with its 1,130 miles of public footpaths and overall scenic splendor — rolling heather moors, which flower to even higher glory in August, as well as placid, rich green dales, and vale plains full of market towns, villages, rows of cottages, and a peppering of distinctive farmhouses built of light gray or honey-colored stone, capped by red pantile or gray slate roofs and looking as solid as fortresses — in all, a naturally beautiful landscape that man's additions have only enhanced. Considering the additional visual rewards offered by the dramatic, cliff-lined coastline that edges the park on the east, it's not hard to understand why, each year, the area attracts some 137,000 visitors on an average summer Sunday. But once on the moors, except at Easter and during the summer, only the occasional sheep staring contentedly through the mists is to be seen. The Cleveland Way, a walk that consists of nearly 100 miles skirting the coast and the park's inland boundaries on its way around most of the circumference of the park, and the Esk Valley Walk, which follows the River Esk for 30 miles from its source on the high moors to the sea at Whitby, are among the longer footpaths; but there are many others. Details about the park and leaflets describing area long-distance walks are available from the park's Information Service, North York Moors National Park, The Old Vicarage, Bondgate, Helmsley, Yorkshire YO6 5BP, England (phone: 0439-70657).

NORTHUMBERLAND NATIONAL PARK, Northumberland, England: This long, narrow 398-square-mile region, one of England's least populated, extends southward from the Scottish border, through the lonely sheep-spotted Cheviot Hills and the heather- and bracken-clad Simonside Hills, to Hadrian's Wall — the most spectacular legacy of Britain's 400-year Roman occupation, and one of the world's most important archaeological remains outside Greece and Italy (see *Ancient Ruins and Monuments*). The diversity of landscape results from a lively geological history whose players include the ancient volcano that created the Cheviots, the sea (which subsequently inundated the land), the monumental up-thrusting forces that created the highlands, and the glaciers that carved the terrain into an approximation of its present shape. The Pennine Way, one of the most difficult of England's long-distance footpaths (described below), is among the especially scenic trails in the park. Details: Northumberland National Park Information Service, Eastburn, South Park, Hexham, Northumberland NE46 1BS, England (phone: 0434-605555).

SNOWDONIA NATIONAL PARK, Gwynedd, Wales: Bordered on the west by the beaches and sand dunes of Cardigan Bay, this 838-square-mile expanse of mountains, glacier-scoured passes and valleys, lovely lakes, and white-foaming waterfalls is by no means the exclusive territory of climbers — who come here by the score to tackle 3,560-foot Snowdon (the loftiest summit in England and Wales) and the other 14 peaks over 3,000 feet in the still-wild Snowdon range. It is also a hiker's paradise, and there are guided walks, nature trails, and scores of footpaths. Details: Snowdonia National Park Information Service, Penrhyndeudraeth, Gwynedd LL48 6LF, Wales (phone: 0766-770274), and, for lodging, the North Wales Tourism Marketing Bureau, 77 Conwy Rd., Colwyn Bay, Clwyd LL29 7LN, Wales (phone: 0492-531731), and the Mid Wales Regional Office, Wales Tourist Board, Canolfan Owain Glyndwr, Machynlleth, Powys SY20 8EE, Wales (phone: 0654-2653).

KERRY AND WEST CORK, Irish Republic: The Republic's choice offering for walkers and scramblers, this region of relatively unexplored red sandstone country is known, first and foremost, for the Macgillycuddy's Reeks, the high peaks that form the roof of Ireland; the main peak, 3,414-foot Carrauntoohil, can provide a good day's workout with fine views as your reward; local guides are available. But the whole of the Iveragh Peninsula, the largest of Kerry's trio of peninsulas, whose eastern end the Reeks occupy, boasts enough equally good walking to keep you occupied for more than one vacation. East of the Reeks, and east of the Gap of Dunloe, there's 2,739-foot Purple Mountain; to the south, there's 2,756-foot Mangerton, whose summit is accessible via the deep lake known as the Devil's Punch Bowl. And in addition to the walks on the Iveragh Peninsula, there are those on the more southerly Beara Peninsula, backboned by the Caha Mountains, where you can climb 1,887-foot Sugarloaf and 2,251-foot Hungry Hill, or explore the deep valleys, as well as the treks on the Dingle Peninsula, the most northerly peninsula of the three, where the standout peak is 3,127-foot Brandon, a giant that drops almost straight into the sea on the north. For general information, consult the Irish Tourist Board; for the details, see the *The Irish Walk Guide: South-West* by Sean O'Suilleabhain, and J. C. Coleman's *Mountains of Killarney* (IR£1.25 and 65p respectively, from Jean Boydell, FMCI, 56a Rockville Dr., Blackrock, County Dublin, Irish Republic).

WICKLOW MOUNTAINS, Counties Wicklow and Dublin, Irish Republic: Reaching southward from Dublin City, these thousand-odd square miles of granite domes and the deep valleys between them — including Glencree, Glendalough, and Glenmalure — offer some pleasant day hikes. The 1,654-foot summit of Sugarloaf Mountain, which is easily accessible by bus, stands out as just one example: In the center of an area where the mountains close in on small patches of rolling farmland, it offers fine views, at first out over the sea not far away, and beyond that, on a clear day, all the way to the Welsh mountains; the ascent begins near Rocky Valley, off the main Dublin-Glendalough Road, and the descent takes you through the wooded Glen of the Downs — a steep-banked, 800-foot-deep ravine that the novelist Sir Walter Scott once termed "the most beautiful view" he had ever seen. The Irish Tourist Board can provide general information; for particulars, consult *The Irish Walk Guide: East,* edited by D. Herman, and *Dublin and Wicklow Mountains,* a detailed account of how to get up into these hills, edited by members of the Irish Ramblers' Club (IR£1.25 and IR£1.50 respectively, from Jean Boydell, address above).

CONNEMARA, County Galway, Irish Republic: One of Ireland's most scenic and unspoiled regions, Connemara offers its share of the country's best walking. The quartzite pyramids known as the Twelve Bens, which are the most widely known of the peaks here and look like nothing more than minor hills, provide the quality of experience afforded by real mountains, because of their cliffbound ridges and slopes of bare rock and scree. (In fact, the north face of 2,336-foot Bencorr offers some of the country's longest rock climbs.) The highest, 2,395-foot Benbaun, provides solid footing and fine views out over some of the other good Connemara hiking country — most notably the northwest-to-southeast running range known as the Maumturks, to the east; and, to the north, the Mweelrea, rising impressively out of the northern rim of Killary Harbour. Still farther north, not far from the southern shore of Clew Bay, Ireland's holy mountain, 2,510-foot Croagh Patrick, affords yet another good climb — among Ireland's more popular, and, consequently, well worn and easier to follow than most here (but still a challenge because of the loose shale at the top). Tens of thousands climb "the Reek," as the mountain is called, on the last Sunday in July as part of a great national pilgrimage; even out of season, there are plenty of hikers, since the view from the top out over island-strewn Clew Bay — boasting as many shades of blue as the Bahamian seacoast, and littered with landfalls — is worth gawking at any time of year. For further general information, contact the Irish Tourist Board; details are contained in *The Irish Walk Guide: West* by Tony Whilde (IR£1.25) and *The Twelve Bens* by Joss Lynam (IR£1.50), both available from Jean Boydell (address above).

MOURNE MOUNTAINS, County Down, Northern Ireland: This granite range in the northeastern section of the island south of Belfast is not very large, but the scenery is especially lovely, with good views, sapphire lakes, and rugged gray rocks. The principal peak of the group, 2,796-foot Slieve Donard, stands out as one particularly good climb — both relatively easy and especially attractive when approached from the town of Newcastle; on fine clear days, it's possible to see the Isle of Man, the peaks of the English Lake District, the mountains of Wales, and Scotland's islands. Those with a full day to spare should walk along the ridge to 2,448-foot Slieve Binnian, to see the aptly named Silent Valley and its reservoir, and, beyond it, the lonely little Lough Shannagh. Other good hikes include the ascents of 2,394-foot Slieve Bernagh and of 2,512-foot Slieve Commedagh. Details: J. S. Doran's *Hill Walks in the Mournes,* which describes 21 good hikes (£2.50 from Mourne Observer Press, Castlewellan Rd., Newcastle, County Down BT33 0JX, Northern Ireland), and *The Irish Walk Guide: North East* by R. Rogers (IR£1.25, available from Jean Boydell at the address above). On the spot, the personnel at the various mountaineering club huts can be helpful; for hut locations, ask locally before heading out.

STAR TREKS

If day-tripping seems a bit tame, consider a walking tour along one of several long-distance footpaths in England and Wales. Thirteen of them have already been created by the Countryside Commission and others are being planned. They are created by establishing new rights-of-way to link previously existing trails to form continuous, multimile stretches of public footpath; each is signposted and, at shifts in directions and other potentially confusing points, waymarked with acorn symbols. In addition, there are over 70 other recreational walks devised by local county councils, rambling groups, and even individual enthusiasts eager to share their love of a particular corner of the English landscape, sometimes their own rural backyard. The number of these long-distance delights, both officially and informally arranged, is steadily increasing all the time.

In Ireland, hiking groups are also at work on long-distance footpaths, and three have been officially opened. The Wicklow Way, the oldest and longest, is described below. The approximately 58 miles of the South Leinster Way switch back in a roughly southwesterly course from Kildavin, County Carlow, to Carrick-on-Suir, County Tipperary, along old sheep tracks, forest firebreaks, and old byroads; much of the route is in high country with capricious weather conditions. The 37.2-mile Kerry Way encircles the Iveragh Peninsula on unsurfaced and surfaced roads, old droving paths, and various routes used since the earliest days of Christianity in Ireland — some call it a journey through time. And though it is at a relatively lower altitude than the South Leinster Way, it's higher than present-day roads and therefore more panoramic. A number of other proposed footpaths are developing quite quickly.

One of the pleasures of traversing these routes is that, while they cover some of the nation's loveliest countryside, they're close enough to civilization that it's possible to stay overnight en route at small hotels, B&Bs, or huts and mountaineering hostels — or camp out with tent, sleeping bag, and cookstove. (The Ramblers' Association, 1/5 Wandworth Rd., London SW8 2LJ, England, phone 01-582-6878, publishes an annually updated *Ramblers' and Cyclists' Bed and Breakfast Guide,* which lists 2,300 B&Bs convenient to long-distance footpaths; £1.75.) Camping is permitted, though it's essential to ask permission of the landowner before pitching a tent for the night, particularly where the surrounding land is cultivated — not only to avoid problems but also to make friends: More than one farmer has been known to show up in the morning bearing a pint of fresh milk for visiting campers to pour over their morning granola. For a free leaflet on long-distance footpaths, contact the Countryside Commission (Publications Despatch Department, 19 Albert Rd., Manchester M19 2EQ, England; phone: 061 224-6287). Also contact the Ramblers' Association (address above). An excellent guidebook series on long-distance routes in both England and Scotland, published on behalf of the Countryside Commission by Her Majesty's Stationery Office, contains all necessary maps and local information. The series is available from the HMSO (PO Box 276, London SW8 5DT, England, and in the US, HMSO Books Bernan-Unipub, 4611-F Assembly Dr., Lanham, MD 20706-4391; phone 301-459-7666).

For information about other long-distance footpaths in other parts of the country, consult the following:

> *Across Northern Hills: Long-Distance Footpaths in the North of England* by Geoffrey Berry (£6 from the Westmorland Gazette, 22 Stricklandgate, Kendal, Westmorland LA9 4NE, England (phone: 0539-20555).
>
> *Scottish Hill Tracks: Southern Scotland* by D. G. Moir (£2 from John Bartholomew & Son, 12 Duncan St., Edinburgh EH9 1TA, Scotland). Describes short paths that can be hiked in sequence over long distances.
>
> *Backpacking in Wales* by Showell Styles (£7.50 from Robert Hale, Ltd., Clerkenwell House, 45-47 Clerkenwell Green, London EC1R 0HT, England; phone: 01-251-2661).
>
> *The Sports Council for Northern Ireland,* House of Sport, Upper Malone Rd., Belfast BT9 5LA, Northern Ireland (phone: 0232-661222).

CLEVELAND WAY, from Helmsley to Filey, North Yorkshire, England: This horseshoe-shaped, 100-mile footpath bobs along over moors and down dales, then sweeps along the tops of the cliffs of the county's stunning coastline. The going, while not particularly rough, does demand more than either the North and South Downs trails or the Ridgeway (all described below), and, though rain is not a problem in this relatively dry corner of the nation, occasional chilly spells require warm clothing. For details, consult Alan Falconer's *The Cleveland Way* (£3.95 from HMSO, address above).

COTSWOLD WAY, from Chipping Campden, Gloucestershire, to Bath, Avon, England: The attractions of this route along the crest of a limestone escarpment

— one of those outside the purview of the Countryside Commission — include ever-changing skies, the panoramic views out over the wooded valleys and lush green fields, and frequent calls at the delightfully mellow yellow villages scattered here and there along the way. The pathway ends at the Roman baths themselves. *The Cotswold Way* by Mark B. Richards (£1.50; Thornhill Press, 24 Moorend Rd., Cheltenham, Gloucestershire GL53 0EU, England; phone: 0242-519137) describes the route.

DALES WAY, from Ilkley, West Yorkshire, to Bowness-on-Windermere, Cumbria, England: Apart from a climb up and over the Pennines' watershed (where only fate determines whether a raindrop finds its way to the North Sea instead of the Irish), this 81-mile-long hike involves low-lying country along the banks of lovely clear rivers. For details see Colin Speakman's *The Dales Way* (new edition to cost approximately £2.25; Dalesman Publishing, Ltd., Clapham, Lancaster LA2 8EB, England; phone: 046-85225).

LONDON COUNTRYWAY, around London, England: Even the metropolis has its rural back door: This 200-mile circle shows it off. For details, see Keith Chesterton's *The London Countryway* (£5.95; Constable & Co., 10 Orange St., Leicester Sq., London WC2H 7EG, England).

NORTH DOWNS WAY, from Farnham, Surrey, to Dover, Kent, England: This 141-mile-long footpath travels through the rolling Surrey Hills and Kent Downs, along the crest of the North Downs, and across several rivers and highways to its end at Shakespeare Cliff, where the panorama is of the celebrated English Channel. In parts, the footpath follows the medieval Pilgrims' Way. The North Downs Way is similar to its cousin, the South Downs Way (described below), but with more nooks and crannies and fewer grand, obstacle-free stretches in which to develop a steady stride. But the going is relatively easy, as is access to London via train and bus. For details, consult Christopher John Wright's *A Guide to the Pilgrims' Way and the North Downs Way* (£5.95; from Constable at the address above), and *North Downs Way* by Denis Herbstein (£3.95 from HMSO, address above).

PENNINE WAY, from Edale, Derbyshire, England, to Kirk Yetholm, Borders, Scotland: The first of the official trails to be designated, "expressly for those who seek the call of the hills and the lonely places," this track takes in 270 demanding, often extremely boggy miles, up the backbone of England to a point just north of the Scottish border, traversing the Pennines, the Peak District National Park, and the Cheviots; and traveling through eerie forests and over high peaks; down old pack horse and shepherds' tracks and old Roman roads; across several rivers; and along well-preserved portions of Hadrian's Wall to a point not far from the impressive fort at Housesteads. Waterfalls and peat bogs, fine views, limestone cliffs, ruined mines, and other landmarks all add still more variety to the pathway. But it's not for everyone: In all, more altitude is gained than climbing Everest, and the weather can be terrible (dangerous, at this latitude, at these altitudes). In addition, while B&Bs are plentiful along some of the route, they are scarce enough along other sections to make it essential to plan stops carefully — or carry camping gear. But for experienced walkers, this famous footpath is a delight. Of the plethora of publications covering the route, one of the best is Alfred Wainwright's *A Pennine Way Companion* (£6; Westmorland Gazette, address above); also consult Tom Stephenson's *The Pennine Way* (£3.95; from HMSO, address above).

RIDGEWAY, from Overton Hill, near Avebury, Wiltshire, to Ivinghoe Beacon, Buckinghamshire, England: This 85-mile-long footpath follows the ancient Icknield Way and the Great Ridgeway, first trod by Neolithic man; and, consequently, ancient burial places, religious monuments, Iron Age hill forts, and other evidences of bygone days, are abundant along the route as it traverses farms, beech woods, and downlands. The section from Overton Hill to Goring has been designated a bridleway — and so can be used by cyclists and horseback riders as well as hikers; but at no point is the going particularly difficult. For details, consult Sean Jennett's *The Ridgeway Path*

(£3.95; from HMSO, address above) or H. D. Westacott's *The Ridgeway Path* (£1.95; Penguin Books, Bath Rd., Harmondsworth, Middlesex, England).

SOUTH DOWNS WAY, from Eastbourne, Sussex, to Harting, near Petersfield, Hampshire, England: It's true enough that in his *Natural History of Selbourne* Gilbert White referred to the South Downs as "majestic mountains"; and, indeed, when standing on high and looking southward toward the sea, or in the opposite direction, across the partly wooded Weald (the remains of an ancient forest), toward the North Downs, most hikers do feel themselves at the top of the world. Nonetheless, the 80-mile route through the range of chalk hills known as the South Downs offers relatively gentle walking. And there's no shortage of places to stay along the way. This is the country's only long-distance bridleway — cyclists and horseback riders share the path. For details, consult Sean Jennett's *South Downs Way* (£4.95 from HMSO, address above), or the Society of Sussex Downsmen's *Along the South Downs Way,* which describes the route in both directions and on to Winchester (£2 plus postage; Society of Sussex Downsmen, 254 Victoria Dr., Eastbourne, East Sussex BN20 8QT, England; phone: 0323-32227).

SOUTHWEST WAY, from Studland, Dorset, to Minehead, Somerset, England: For lovers of hours spent with the sea as a constant companion, this 567-mile track is not only England's longest long-distance footpath, but also its best — and, except for its considerable number of ups and downs, the walking is not difficult. There now are five sections: the Dorset Coast Path, noted for its special quiet loveliness; the South Devon Coast Path, much of it through the South Devon and East Devon Areas of Outstanding Natural Beauty, full of stunning headlands, broad rivers, busy resort towns, quiet bays, and lush greenery; the Cornwall Coast Path, which leads around Land's End, past spectacular cliffs, lighthouses, stone circles, and more resorts; and the Somerset and North Devon Coast Path, which travels from Exmoor National Park into the North Devon Area of Outstanding Natural Beauty — abounding in stony beaches and high beautiful cliffs. With the recent addition of the Trans Cornwall Heritage Path from Padstow to Fowey (named The Saints' Way), walkers can now complete a circular Cornish peninsula walk that is some 220 miles in length. Along the length of the path, accommodations and campsites are easy to find (but since this is a resort area, it's necessary to reserve ahead for visits during school holidays). For more information, consult the Sou'West Way Association's *Complete Guide to the Coastal Path* (£1.95 from the Sou'West Way Association, 1 Orchard Dr., Kingskerswell, Newton Abbot, Devon TQ12 5DG, England; phone: 08047-3061); H. D. Westacott's *The Devon South Coast Path* (£1.95) and *The Dorset Coast Path* (£1.95), both from Penguin Books at the address above; *Cornwall Coast Path* by Edward Pyatt (£3.95, from HMSO); Brian Le Messurier's *South Devon Coast Path* (£3.95 from HMSO); *Dorset Coast Path* by Brian Jackman (£3.95 from HMSO); and *Somerset and North Devon Coast Path* by Clive Gunnell (£3.95 from HMSO).

WOLDS WAY, from Filey, North Yorkshire, to North Ferriby, Humberside, England: This long-distance footpath traverses considerable agricultural land and follows the chalk hills and pretty valleys of the Yorkshire Wolds for 71 miles, from the eastern terminus of the Cleveland Way to the banks of the River Humber to the south. For details, consult David Rubinstein's *The Wolds Way* (£1.95; Dalesman, address above), or Roger Ratcliffe's *Wolds Way* (£3.95; HMSO, address above).

OFFA'S DYKE PATH, from near Chepstow, Gwent, to Prestatyn, Clwyd, Wales: For 60 out of its total 168 miles, this Welsh track follows the distinctive earthwork built by King Offa of Mercia in the 8th century as a frontier between England and Wales. It meanders through the Shropshire Hills and Wye Valley Areas of Outstanding Natural Beauty; climbs up into the imposing Black Mountains; visits Hay-on-Wye, the town of books (see *Shopping*); and eventually takes you along a high ridge through the Clwydian Hills. The walking can be demanding in spots; the terrain is wonderfully varied, taking in everything from wild hills to wooded valleys and peaceful lowlands. For details, consult Christopher John Wright's *A Guide to Offa's Dyke Path* (£5.95; Constable, address above); Mark Richard's *Through the Welsh Borders Country Following the Offa's Dyke Path* (£4.50; Thornhill Press, address above); and John B. Jones's *Offa's Dyke Path* (£3.95; HMSO, at the address above). For more information on the South Wales region bordered by the path, contact the South Wales Regional Office, Wales Tourist Board, Ty Croeso, Gloucester Pl., Swansea SA1 1TY, Wales (phone: 0792-465204).

PEMBROKESHIRE COAST PATH, from St. Dogmaels to Amroth, Dyfed, Wales: Despite the beauty of the wild seascapes of this southwestern part of the country, the area has remained unspoiled by visitors, and often it's possible to walk for many hours along this 180-mile-long footpath without meeting a soul. That is only one of its special offerings, however: It also provides wonderful scenery — limestone and sandstone cliffs, windswept headlands, jagged inlets and coves, splendid beaches, and blue water (warm in summer, icy the rest of the year). The walking varies from the easy to the occasionally strenuous. For details, consult John Barrett's *The Pembrokeshire Coast Path* (£3.95 from HMSO, at the address above); and the National Park (address below) publishes a series of ten Coast Path cards, a mileage chart, and other informational pieces. Also: Pembrokeshire Coast National Park, County Offices, Haverfordwest, Dyfed SA61 1QZ, Wales (phone: 0437-4591).

WICKLOW WAY, from near Rathfarnham, County Dublin, to Clonegall, County Carlow, Irish Republic: This footpath is nearly 100 miles long, and it is worth noting for its proximity to Dublin — and for the sheer beauty and wildness: Though never more than a couple of miles from a road, hikers are always out of calling distance from the settled lowlands, and when drastic weather changes occur, as they sometimes do, those who are not prepared can find themselves in serious trouble. The rewards are ample, especially in terms of views — which by turns take in the high Powerscourt Waterfall, the mountains of Wales, the Irish Sea, the Mourne range, and more. For general information, see *The Wicklow Way*, available from the Irish Tourist Board, and the Irish Ramblers' Club's *Dublin and Wicklow Mountains* (IR£1.50), or the *Irish Walk Guide: East* (IR£1.25), both available from Jean Boydell, at the address above.

ULSTER WAY, around Northern Ireland: A 500-mile circle of Ulster, now practically completed, takes in some of Ireland's finest scenery — including the coast and glens of County Antrim with the magnificent Atlantic coast cliffs and bays, the Giants Causeway, the Sperrin Mountains, the County Fermanagh Lake District, and the Mountains of Mourne and St. Patricks Country, rich in legend and antiquities. From Belfast, the route winds through the quiet wooded valley of the River Lagan. A 30-mile spur route extends into County Donegal in the Irish Republic. Details: Sports Council of Northern Ireland, House of Sport, Upper Malone Rd., Belfast BT9 5LA, Northern Ireland (phone: 0232-661222).

MAPS AND MORE INFORMATION

When Daniel Boone was once asked whether he had ever been lost, he replied, "Nope, but I was a mite confused once for three days." To avoid that fate, and to help plan a trip, it's essential to have the proper maps and guidebooks.

Some of the most beautiful areas of Britain are covered by 1-inch-to-1-mile Tourist maps and by 1:25,000-scale Outdoor Leisure maps. These are the best choice for those regions for which they exist. Elsewhere, consult the relevant 1:50,000 Ordnance Survey maps. Rights-of-way are indicated by red lines (the dotted lines referring to footpaths, the dashes to bridleways). These symbols and the many others are explained in an elaborate key, a brief study of which will have anyone with even a little aptitude reading these British plans as well as, if not better than, the far less colorful US Geological Survey maps.

In addition, virtually every defined trail in Britain is also covered by one or more step-by-step guidebooks. To find out exactly what's available and what you need, contact the Ramblers' Association (1/5 Wandsworth Rd., London SW8 2LJ, England; phone: 01-582-6878) for copies of county Fact Sheets (75p each, postpaid), which list relevant guidebooks and maps for the main walking areas of the country; be sure to tell the association which area is of interest. Authoritative general books on walking in Britain such as H. D. Westacott's *The Walker's Handbook* (£2.50; Penguin, address above) provide the same sort of information for footpaths, AONBs, and national parks throughout England, Scotland, and Wales; this publication also contains useful information about techniques and equipment that will come in handy when planning a walking trip in Britain.

A good magazine for the hiking enthusiast is *The Great Outdoors,* published monthly by Holmes McDougall, Ltd., Ravenseft House, 302-304 St. Vincent St., Glasgow G2 5NL, Scotland (phone: 041-221-7000), and available by direct subscription and from most major newsstands and outdoor equipment shops; in addition to both informative and descriptive articles on hiking, backpacking, and cycling, each issue includes a useful directory that lists stores specializing in outdoor equipment; reviews of equipment, maps, local guidebooks, and other books; and advertisements for equipment rental agencies and organizations that sponsor walking tours.

As background reading, try to locate a copy of John Hillaby's *A Walk through Britain* (Houghton Mifflin Co.; now out of print).

Many useful hiking publications can be bought at *Stanford's* (12 Long Acre, London WC2E 9LP, England; phone: 836-1321).

Irish Peaks, edited by Joss Lynam and published by Constable at the address above (£5.95), describes routes up the 50 best mountains in Ireland. For the Wicklow Way, it's possible to buy 1-inch or 1:50,000 Ordnance Survey maps; for the rest of the Republic, ½-inch maps are available. All series are essentially accurate, but since the scale is too small to show even some large physical features such as cliffs, it's a good idea to check out routes locally before heading for the hills. To get maps, contact the Ordnance Survey Office, Phoenix Park, Dublin, Irish Republic (phone: 01-213171), or the Government Publications Sale Office, Sun Alliance House, Molesworth St., Dublin 2, Irish Republic (phone: 01-710309). *Eason's* bookstore (O'Connell St., Dublin 1) stocks a good selection. Joss Lynam's *Irish Peaks* (IR£7.25 from Jean Boydell at the address above) covers mountain areas in Ireland, detailing huts and hostels among other things. *Irish Walk Guides* (IR£1.25 each), a few of which have been referred to in the preceding pages, are also available for the the northwest, the east, and the southeast, and may be ordered from Jean Boydell. Maps are included, but the paper quality is poor, and dedicated hill climbers will want to supplement them with the OS maps.

In Northern Ireland, the Mournes are now covered by an outdoor pursuits map called Mourne Country, scaled to a generous 2½ inches per mile. The Ordnance Survey of Northern Ireland, which produced it, has also issued a series of excellent 1:50,000 maps. To obtain copies, contact the organization at Colby House, Stranmillis Court, Belfast BT9 5BJ. Be sure to check your route locally before setting out.

GROUP TRIPS

If you don't want to go it alone — or do all the requisite planning — contact the following organizations about group treks:

Countrywide Holidays Association, Cromwell Range, Manchester M14 6HU, England (phone: 061-225-1000). Founded in 1893, this is Britain's first outdoor and recreational holiday organization, and it owns and operates 14 country houses and coastal hotels in prime walking areas throughout the UK. In addition to long-distance walks, packages include accommodations at one of a number of unusual centers and day trips into the surrounding countryside with an experienced guide.

Dales Centre, Grassington, near Skipton, North Yorkshire BD23 5AU, England (phone: 0756-752757), and c/o Reg Pickett, 3387 Lubich Dr., Mountain View, CA 94040 (phone: 800-443-8550). Leisurely 1- to 2-week vacations in the Yorkshire Dales and the Lake District. Specialties coast to coast with the best of walks featuring the Cotswalds, Wales, and Scotland; hotel and inn accommodations.

English Wanderer, 13 Wellington Ct., Spencers Wood, Reading RG7 1BN, England (phone: 44734-882515). Guided walking through the hills of England, including the Yorkshire Dales, the Lakes District, and the Cotswalds. An easy Cornwall and Somerset walking tour is called "In Search of King Arthur." For the Highlands, there is the Scottish Wanderer; the Irish Roamer takes in County Kerry, and Crwydryn Cymreig explores Wales. Accommodations are in small hotels and inns along the way.

Lord Winston's Walking Tours, East Wing, The Manor, Moreton Pinkney, Daventry NN11 6SJ, England. These easy to moderately difficult walks around Land's End, Exmoor, the Lake District, the Cotswalds, and other picturesque destinations are personally guided by the very personable and highly efficient Ken Ward. Accommodations range from simple farmhouses to three-star hotels, and the trek vehicle carries all baggage between overnight stops. For those who prefer to be their own guide, Lord Winston's also produces guide books to walking in the United Kingdom.

Mountain Goat Holidays, Victoria St., Windermere, Cumbria LA23 1AD, England (phone: 09662-5161). Guided rambles through the Lake District with hotel and guesthouse accommodations. Weekly holidays of both low- and high-level walking are based in Windermere and Keswick.

Ramblers Association Services, Ltd., 13 Longcroft House, Fretherne Rd., Welwyn Garden City, Hertfordshire AL8 6PQ, England (phone: 0707-331133). Over a hundred guided walking trips in Britain and Europe, ranging from easy to very tough, are offered to small parties of 8 to 20.

Wayfarers, Chepynge House, 22 Maltravers St., Arundel, West Sussex BN18 9BU, England (phone: 0903-882925), and c/o Mary McCarty, 307 E 91st St., Apt. 4R, New York, NY 10128 (phone: 212-369-4322). Guided walks through Thomas Hardy's Dorset, James Herriot's Yorkshire, Wordsworth's Lake District, the Cotswolds, the border castle country of Wales, the Devon Coast, and Dartmoor, with cozy lodging in inns, taverns, hotels, and private homes.

YHA Travel Adventure Holidays, 14 Southampton St., London WC2E 7HY, England (phone: 01-836-8541).

Earthwalk, Newtown, Powys SY16 4AB, Wales (phone: 0686-28282). Six-day guided walks between exclusive hilltop campsites in the little-known hills of Mid Wales; the organization provides the equipment — and the vehicles to carry it — plus good home cooking.

Head for the Hills, The Recreation Hall, Garth, Builth, Powys LD4 4AT, Wales (phone: 05912-388). The 12-person walks arranged by this organization travel along an ancient and often obscure network of paths and tracks of the remoter parts of the countryside, in an attempt to introduce participants to an experience of the landscape that travelers might have had in ages past. Areas explored include Dorset, Dartmoor, Exmoor, Cornwall, Avebury and Glastonbury, Derbyshire, Shropshire, Yorkshire, and the Lake District, as well as parts of Wales.

Camping equipment — and belongings — travel ahead in the organization Land Rover and a trailer. Cuisine is vegetarian. Enclose International Postal Reply Coupons when requesting information.

Association for Adventure Sports (AFAS), c/o Tiglin Adventure Centre, Ashford, County Wicklow, Irish Republic (phone: 0404-40169). Mountaineering training courses, walking tours, and adventure holidays in County Wicklow.

Little Killary Adventure Centre, Salruck, Renvyle, County Galway, Irish Republic (phone: 095-43411). Week-long holidays among the high peaks of Connemara — including Croagh Patrick, the Sheffrys, Mweelrea, the Maamturks, and the Twelve Bens. Overnights are either at the center, or one or two nights are spent under canvas in the hills. All camping equipment and personal belongings are transported to the sites.

For the Mind

Marvelous Museums

 It may be true, as people often say, that in 1649 when King Charles I died and the Parliamentarians auctioned off his collection of paintings and other treasures, Britain lost a heritage. But the growth of the great national collections beginning as early as the 17th century with the founding of Oxford's Ashmolean Museum, and the collecting mania of the 18th and 19th centuries — when the rich were really rich and gentlemen made careers of their hobbies, accumulating not only the fine art of Western Europe, but also trifles and prizes from the farthest corners of the empire — more than made amends. As a result, Britain is home to a staggering agglomeration of works of art from all over the world. And although some small percentage of this remains in private hands, the better portion is on display in the nation's great museums, not to mention hundreds of country houses that are as noteworthy for the collections housed within as for their often stunning architecture. (England's estimable National Portrait Gallery, for instance, maintains two collections outside London at Montacute, Somerset, and at Beningbrough, North Yorkshire.) The furnishings in such homes are often in mint condition, and seeing them displayed along with porcelain, silver, and tapestries is indeed a pleasure. You'd need a lifetime to go around to all these stately pleasure domes.

As for Britain's museums themselves, they are usually well conceived and designed so there's no problem seeing the pictures because of improper lighting or accumulated filth. And despite recent cutbacks in government support of the arts, most museums are free, and open every day except on principal holidays. Special lecture programs are usually offered as well, and they are designed as much for experts in the fields as for beginners seeking a greater appreciation of what they've seen and admired. Check the newspapers or a museum's events calendar for notices.

In Ireland, the picture is not so rosy. While the collections themselves were amassed much like England's, the institutions that house them have been continually plagued by shortages of funds, and for many decades, Ireland's antiquities have not been kept in a manner to match their worth. But there are signs that the situation is improving. More money is being spent and many regional museums have been set up with some good results; the Monaghan County Museum, which won a Council of Europe prize in 1980, is but one example. While it will always be important for scholars and researchers to have exhibits in one central place, facsimiles as well as material of local interest may eventually help enlarge these few and currently tiny regional museums — and certainly, this is a step in the right direction.

In any event, a museum visit can be a great deal more pleasurable if a few simple guidelines are kept in mind. First, make several short visits to a large museum rather than one long one. Stay just an hour, and take in no more than a dozen really fine works. There's no fatigue quite like aching, yawny museum fatigue — once described as the dread "museum foot" — and when it has set in, merely sitting for 3 minutes in front of a Rubens won't cure it. So plan to visit important collections when you're fresh

— preferably as soon as the museum opens, before the crowds have arrived. If possible, know what you want to see before beginning your rounds, so as not to clutter the experience with too many bleeding saints and blustery seascapes; most museums publish excellent pamphlets or booklets to steer visitors to the more noted works in their collections, and it's a good idea to buy a copy. At the very least, stop at the museum shop on your way *in* to thumb through the catalogue or look at the postcards to get an idea of what there is to see and where it's to be found.

And visit a gallery or an auction house occasionally — just to remind yourself that once it was *all* for sale.

AMERICAN MUSEUM IN BRITAIN, Bath, Avon, England: Oddly enough, this elegant and very English town is home to the country's best collection of things American — Hopi kachina dolls and Shaker furniture, patchwork quilts and Pueblo pots, and even a teepee and a Conestoga wagon. While British visitors (particularly children) are marveling at these oddments, munching gingerbread baked in a historic oven on the spot, and otherwise pondering how their colonies were getting along before the big revolt, Americans admire the quality of the items on display and the thoughtful manner in which the several period rooms are put together. Claverton Manor, the Greek Revival mansion housing these exhibits, is where Sir Winston Churchill delivered his first political speech in 1897. Details: American Museum, Claverton Manor, Bath, Avon BA2 7BD, England (phone: 0225-60503).

CECIL HIGGINS ART GALLERY AND MUSEUM, Bedford, Bedfordshire, England: Installed in the fine old Victorian structure that was once the home of a local brewer and art lover named Cecil Higgins and in an adjacent annex built in 1974, this lively and especially hospitable museum boasts a distinguished collection of English and Continental porcelain and glass, watercolors by artists such as Constable, Cotman, Gainsborough, and Turner, and prints by Dürer, Picasso, Rembrandt, the Impressionists, and others; these last are displayed in a succession of changing exhibitions in the new building. The Victorian Mansion is set up to show you how a family might have kept house about a century ago and has a homey, lived-in look. A fire winks on the hearth, clocks ticktock faithfully away, children's toys litter the floor next to a dollhouse, a letter lies half written on the desk, and a woolly shawl hangs from the hatstand, just waiting for a Victorian lady to throw it on her shoulders and leave the house for a walk. Upstairs, a newly opened nursery with glowing fire, clothes on the fender, and toys on the floor provides a convincing look at childhood at the turn of the century; a guest bedroom is awry with the recent arrival of a Victorian lady, her baby, and her luggage; and the William Burges room illustrates the eccentricity of the man's work, from its dark green star-studded ceiling to its rich colors and decoration. Throughout, the captioning helps visitors understand what they are seeing. Details: Cecil Higgins Art Gallery and Museum, Castle Close, Bedford, Bedfordshire MK40 3NY, England (phone: 0234-211222).

BIRMINGHAM MUSEUM AND ART GALLERY, Birmingham, West Midlands, England: Boasting one of the nation's most important art collections outside London, with good representations from the 17th through 19th centuries, this institution provides an exceptionally good look at the work of the Pre-Raphaelites, in an assemblage that is well nigh without equal; English watercolorists from the 18th century onward are thoroughly represented, and there is a handsomely refurbished gallery containing fine examples of such applied arts as jewelry, metalwork, stained glass, costume design, and ceramics. In addition, the Department of Archaeology and Ethnography presents objects from cultures around the world, the Department of Local History exhibits items from the Birmingham of bygone days, and the Department of Natural History displays, among other things, a life-size replica tyrannosaurus rex and Britain's finest fossilized triceratops skull. Also featured are shops and an Edwardian Tea Room, and facilities for the disabled are available. The associated Museum of Science and Industry in Newhall Street offers old steam engines, aircraft, cars, machine tools, scientific instruments, and the like — a large number of them actually in working order. They can be seen in action at the Steam Weekends held in March and October, at the Traction Engine Rally in May, and at the Stationary Engine Rally in September. Details: Birmingham Museums and Art Gallery, Chamberlain Sq., Birmingham, West Midlands B3 3DH, England (phone: 021-235-2834).

BRIGHTON MUSEUM AND ART GALLERY, Brighton, East Sussex, England: Installed in the former stables and coach houses of the Prince Regent's fantastic "Eastern" palace (now one of the world's great showpieces), the Museum and Art Gallery houses fine collections of Old Masters, watercolors, furniture, musical instruments, costumes, and English pottery and porcelain, as well as of archaeological and ethnographic items and displays relating to Brighton history; the collections of applied art of the Art Nouveau and Art Deco periods — in which the museum specializes — and the new Fashion Gallery are particularly interesting. The Hove Amber Cup, found in 1857 in Hove, in a Bronze Age barrow carbon-dated to about 1500 BC, is another treasure. As part of the museum's lively exhibition program, shows on the Jazz Age, the British in India, the inspiration of Egypt, the Gothic, Vanity, fairies, and other such subjects have been mounted; check in advance to see what's on. Details: Royal Pavilion, Art Gallery and Museums, Brighton, East Sussex BN1 1UE, England (phone: 0273-603005).

FITZWILLIAM MUSEUM, University of Cambridge, Cambridgeshire, England: One of the nation's greatest and oldest public museums, the Fitzwilliam was founded in 1816 when Richard, the 7th Viscount Fitzwilliam of Merrion, left his superb collections, his library, and a good endowment to his alma mater, the University of Cambridge. The collections — not to mention the stature of the museum — have been growing ever since. Thanks to the innovative spirit of Sir Sydney Cockerell, the museum's fourth director, it is also especially charming and a good deal less chilly and solemn (though every bit as grand) as its peers. Cockerell instituted the then-revolutionary policy of enlivening the picture galleries with Oriental rugs, sculpture, period furniture, and even flowers. Pick up a copy of the museum's brochure-guide to lead you through the extensive collections of coins and medals, European applied arts, Islamic and Far Eastern treasures, manuscripts, paintings and drawings, portrait miniatures, prints, and West Asiatic, Egyptian, Greek, and Roman antiquities. Be sure to note the lovely Roman mosaic fountain niche from 1st-century Baiae, the extensively illuminated 13th-century Peterborough Psalter, Frans Hals's *Portrait of a Man,* Delacroix's *Odalisque,* Renoir's *Coup de Vent* and *La Place Clichy,* Stubbs's *Gimcrack,* and masterpieces by the greatest Venetian painters of the 16th century — Palma Vecchio, Titian, Tintoretto, Veronese, and Jacopo Bassano. The music collection, which includes autograph scores of Handel, Bach, Chopin, Britten, and Elgar, is one of Britain's finest, and the holdings of works by Blake and the members of his circle are without peer. Details: Fitzwilliam Museum, Trumpington St., Cambridge, Cambridgeshire CB2 1RB, England (phone: 0223-332900).

BRITISH MUSEUM, London, England: Founded in 1753 around the lifetime accumulations of Sir Hans Sloane, one of the earliest physicians to use the smallpox vaccine, this vast institution remains Britain's largest and most celebrated, and trying to knock it off in a single visit is like trying to master nuclear physics while in a barber's chair. The crown jewels of the collection, consecrated to the whole of human history, are the renowned Elgin Marbles, the massive sculpture and reliefs that once adorned the ruined Parthenon, bought by Lord Elgin from the Turkish sultan and carted off to safe, civilized England, where they were purchased by the government for £35,000 and presented to the museum. But there's also the Rosetta Stone, the black basalt tablet that provided the key to Egyptian hieroglyphs; the Royal Gold Cup; the deep blue and white cameo-cut Portland Vase, a great marvel of the glassmaker's art dating from Roman times; the gold and silver treasures from the Sutton Hoo Burial Ship, found at an East Suffolk archaeological excavation; the Tomb of Mausolus from Halicarnassus, which brought the word *mausoleum* to the English language; the Temple of Diana from Ephesus; many mummies, among them the one that is widely (and erroneously) believed to have occasioned the legends of the curse of the mummy's tomb; and much more. Seven sculpture galleries were just opened, exhibiting some 1,500 Greek and Roman treasures, including 2 of the 7 wonders of the ancient world. It represents the bulk of the museum's Greek and Roman collection. Man Before Metals provides an enthralling look at the art and technology of the Stone Age. The departments of Western Asiatic Antiquities and Oriental Antiquities are quite simply magnificent. The Magna Carta is on view in the Manuscript Saloon of the British Library (a separate institution since 1973, though still housed in the British Museum), and the King's Library houses a Gutenberg Bible. Depending on what is on display at the time, glimpses may be had of such wonders as the sketchbooks of Dürer or Leonardo da Vinci, manuscripts of famous composers' famous works and of *Alice in Wonderland,* or the signatures of Shakespeare, Dickens, and Joyce. The British Library Reading Room, where Karl Marx wrote *Das Kapital,* is accessible only to those who come well recommended (preferably by a scholar of some note) and apply in advance for a ticket, or who pay £10 and join the National Art Collections Fund; but visitors may view the Reading Room on the hour when it's open. The rest of the museum can be overwhelming; guidebooks to various parts of the collections, for sale in the main lobby, are good investments as are detailed guides to single aspects of the offerings. Details: British Museum, Great Russell St., London WC1B 3DG, England (phone: 01-636-1555; for the library, 01-636-1544).

COURTAULD INSTITUTE GALLERIES, London, England: When you learn that this institution was established in 1932 to teach art history to University of London students, you might not expect anything very special. Yet, like a good many museums of its type, this one is approachable and enjoyable in ways that its far larger and more widely known confreres can never be. The setting, replete with Oriental rugs and handsome furnishings, is lovely; beyond that are the collections, made up of the art bequests of industrialist Samuel Courtauld (whose generosity also benefited the Tate Gallery) as well as Lord Lee of Fareham and art critic Roger Fry (who organized London's first post-Impressionist exhibition in 1910). The excellent assemblage of Impressionist and post-Impressionist works includes Manet's *Bar at the Folies-Bergère* and *Le Déjeuner sur l'Herbe;* van Gogh's the *Artist with His Ear Cut Off* and *Peach Trees in Blossom;* Cézanne's *Lake of Annecy* and one rendering of the easily recognizable *Card Players;* Tahitian scenes by Gauguin; and wonderful works by Bonnard, Renoir, and Seurat. (A word of warning, however: Since the Courtauld has graciously permitted much of its Impressionist and post-Impressionist collection to tour in an American exhibition, they won't be on view here again until June 1988.) In addition, there are early Italian paintings from the Gambier-Parry Bequest and the superb Princes Gate Collection of Flemish and Italian Old Masters. Details: Courtauld Institute Galleries, University of London, Woburn Sq., London WC1H 0AA, England (phone: 01-580-1015).

DULWICH PICTURE GALLERY, Dulwich, London, England: Tucked away in a quiet, leafy, almost rural (but easily accessible) suburb of southeast London, this gallery — recently redecorated and rehung in the best Regency manner — boasts a collection of old masters well worthy of a capital city anywhere. The nation's oldest public picture gallery, it contains works bequeathed by the great Shakespearean actor-manager Edward Alleyn, the founder of Dulwich College, plus nearly 400 others from the collection of the French-born art dealer Noël Joseph Desenfans; many of these had been collected at the behest of Poland's King Stanislas, who abdicated before they could be delivered (or paid for). There are works by such Dutch painters as Rembrandt, Cuyp, and Hobbema; by 17th- and 18th-century British portraitists such as Gainsborough and Reynolds; by the Flemish painters Rubens and Van Dyck; by Claude, Poussin, Watteau, and Charles LeBrun — all Frenchmen; and by Italians such as Raphael, Veronese, Tiepolo, and Canaletto, among others. The austerely neoclassical building that houses the collection was built in 1811 and is often considered to be the masterpiece of its designer, Sir John Soane. Details: Dulwich Picture Gallery, College Rd., London SE21 7AD, England (phone: 01-693-5254).

IVEAGH BEQUEST, London, England: The collection here, assembled by the first Earl of Iveagh, includes works by Cuyp, Gainsborough, Hals, Rembrandt, Reynolds, Romney, Turner, Vermeer, and others, and would stand out in itself; what makes this institution particularly interesting is its setting, a late-17th-century house remodeled beginning in 1764 by the Scottish architect Robert Adam, a marvelously stately neoclassical villa that was scheduled for demolition until it was rescued in 1925 by the first earl of Iveagh, who then presented the house together with the better part of his own collection to the nation. The mood is of an 18th-century English country house; the chamber recitals, poetry readings, and open-air concerts held here frequently in summer complete the effect. Details: The Iveagh Bequest, Kenwood, Hampstead La., London NW3 7JR, England (phone: 01-348-1286).

MUSEUM OF MANKIND, London, England: Only the collections of Berlin's Ethnographic Museum can rival those of the British Museum, which are housed in this structure next to the Burlington Arcade in Piccadilly. By far the largest part of its holdings of items relating to African, American, Asian, and Pacific cultures is brought out of the relative limbo of the reserve areas only for special theme exhibitions. However, a selection of the greatest treasures is normally on display: items such as bronzes from Nigeria, Maori jade ornaments, and a crystal skull probably made by the Aztecs. Details: Museum of Mankind, Burlington Gardens, London W1X 2EX, England (phone: 01-437-2224).

NATIONAL GALLERY, London, England: Among the greatest art museums on earth, this was instituted in 1824 when the connoisseur Sir George Beaumont convinced the government to buy the three dozen–plus paintings put up for sale after the death of the wealthy Russian-born merchant-collector John Julius Angerstein — among them Rembrandt's *The Woman Taken in Adultery* and *The Adoration of the Shepherds,* Rubens's *The Rape of the Sabine Women,* and Titian's *Venus and Adonis.* Subsequent gifts and acquisitions have endowed it with a collection that is remarkably balanced, showing off a cross section of the chief schools of Western European art from Giotto to Picasso. Leonardo da Vinci's great cartoon *The Virgin and Child with St. Anne and St. John the Baptist* has a dimly lit room all its own; and here and there masterpieces such as Botticelli's *Venus and Mars,* Holbein's *The Ambassadors,* Breughel's *The Adoration of the Kings,* van Eyck's *Arnolfini Marriage,* and Rubens's *Samson and Delilah* — over 2,000 jewels in all — glow at visitors from the walls. As the holdings are highly selective rather than comprehensive, the museum is not huge (though nearly every item it owns is on view at any given time), and seems especially inviting as a result. Homan Potterton's *A Guide to the National Gallery* (available at the gallery shop) makes an erudite — and delightful — companion to a visit. Information: National Gallery, Trafalgar Sq., London WC2N 5DN, England (phone: 01-839-3321).

NATIONAL MARITIME MUSEUM, Greenwich, London, England: In a Royal Park by the Thames and partially in the Queen's House, England's first Palladian building, a beautifully proportioned white structure designed in 1616 by Inigo Jones for James I's consort, Anne of Denmark, this institution tells the story of Britain's long involvement with the sea — a matter of no mean historical importance. There are pictures and silver, porcelain and uniforms, swords and medals, ship models and dioramas, by the score. New galleries in the West Wing explore "Discovery and

Seapower" and the "Development of the Warship." Neptune Hall in the West Wing is the home of the world's largest ship in a bottle. There, too, is to be seen the steam paddle tug *Reliant,* which rests after a career on the Manchester Ship Canal; the *Donola,* a 60-foot steam launch; and the smaller *Waterlily.* Next door in the Barge House, Prince Frederick's Barge glitters in golden livery. Another must: the uniform that Lord Nelson wore when he was shot at the Battle of Trafalgar in 1805, complete with bullet hole and blood stains. Finally, the Old Royal Observatory — the home of the Greenwich Meridian, which divides the western hemisphere from the eastern — is centered around Sir Christopher Wren's 1675 Flamsteed House, and has exhibits that illustrate the history of nautical astronomy, timekeeping, and Greenwich mean time. The refracting telescope located here is the largest in the United Kingdom and is open to visitors. Also in Greenwich, don't miss the *Cutty Sark,* once the fastest clipper in existence; and the *Gipsy Moth IV,* the 53-foot ketch which, in 1966–67, bore Sir Francis Chichester — solo — around the world. Details: National Maritime Museum, Romney Rd., Greenwich, London SE10 9NF, England (phone: 01-858-4422).

NATIONAL PORTRAIT GALLERY, London, England: Established in 1856, this gallery is devoted to the portraits of the most important figures in British arts, letters, history and politics, military life, science, and assorted other fields; and in all, over 9,000 of their likenesses, arranged chronologically, stare down at visitors from the walls. Elizabeth I is there as a young woman and a dowager, not far from Shakespeare, Mary Queen of Scots, Thomas More, Cardinal Wolsey, Essex, Leicester, and Raleigh. The list of authors portrayed reads like the table of contents in a literature text — Pepys, Milton, Dryden, Pope, Swift, Boswell, Johnson, Tennyson, Dickens, the Brontë sisters, Wilde, Auden, Shaw, and more. Especially since the 1984 opening of a series of galleries devoted to post–World War I portraiture, there's far too much to see in one visit — but it's difficult not to want to give it a try. Special exhibits on historical themes or individual artists are frequently mounted as well. Details: National Portrait Gallery, St. Martin's Pl., London WC2H 0HE, England (phone: 01-930-1552).

QUEEN'S GALLERY, London, England: The British Royal Collection — one of the world's greatest — remained outside the experience of the common man until 1962, when this gallery was created at Buckingham Palace, and even now, only a fraction is on view at any one time. But the exhibitions that are mounted here never fail to impress, whether they are devoted to a subject such as royal children, animal paintings, or British soldiers; to single artists — da Vinci or Gainsborough or Canaletto or Holbein, to name a quartet of past shows; or to groups of painters — the Italians or the Dutch, for instance. Exhibitions change about once a year. Details: Queen's Gallery, c/o the Lord Chamberlain's Office, St. James's Palace, London SW1, England (phone: 01-930-3007).

SIR JOHN SOANE'S MUSEUM, London, England: Located on the north side of central London's largest square (a haunt of lawyers since the 16th century), in two houses designed by the great architect Sir John Soane (1753–1837), this is a remarkable survival of an early museum. The rooms are ingeniously designed, have curious lighting effects, and are packed with objects which were arranged in a very personal manner by Soane himself. The place is full of surprises that the plain and fairly straightforward exterior does not foretell. In the Library, for instance, the spaces behind the flying arches are mirrored, so that a visitor is left with the impression of more space than there actually is. The Monk's Yard, a "Gothick fantasy," is concocted of bits of masonry from the old Palace of Westminster; the Monk's Parlour houses Flemish woodcarvings, casts from medieval sculptures and buildings, and models for architectural features for some of Soane's own designs; the Sepulchral Chamber contains the alabaster sarcophagus discovered in the tomb of Seti I (d. 1290 BC) by G. B. Belzoni in 1817, purchased by Soane for £2,000 after British Museum authorities decided they could not afford it, having just bought the Elgin Marbles; and the shallow-domed Breakfast Room displays ingenious use of mirrors and indirect lighting. All in all, the place is a hodgepodge — but who ever said a house had to be otherwise? Don't miss Hogarth's famous series *The Rake's Progress,* recounting the life and hard times of one Tom Rakewell, and his four-part political satire *The Election,* both installed in an amazing small gallery with hinged walls. The Library contains the world's greatest collection of 17th- and 18th-century architectural drawings — works by Sir Christopher Wren, Robert Adam, George Dance, Soane himself, and many others. There is also a Model Room, open by request, that houses Soane's collection of cork, plaster, and wooden architectural models. (Students wishing to visit the Library, Drawings Collection, and Model Room are advised to make an appointment.) Details: Sir John Soane's Museum, 13 Lincoln's Inn Fields, London WC2A 3BP, England (phone: 01-405-2107).

TATE GALLERY, London, England: Built in 1897 on the site of Millbank Prison, the gift of the sugar broker and art collector Sir Henry Tate, this national collection of British painting and 20th-century painting and sculpture came into being less than half a century after the National Gallery, when bequests had swelled the size of the latter's collection to an extent that there was no longer room to house all the paintings — 282 oils and 19,000 watercolors by Turner, among them. Tate bequeathed his own collection plus £80,000 to house it, art dealer Sir Joseph Duveen gave additional funds, and the Gallery was on its way. A major extension of the Gallery opened in 1979 and increased exhibition space by half. An even newer wing — the magnificent Clore Gallery, designed by James Stirling — houses the Turner Collection. During the summer of 1988, a northern branch of the Tate Gallery is due to open in Liverpool's Albert Dock. Often overlooked is the fact that the Tate also houses one of the world's best collections of French post-Impressionist works; the sculpture collection offers excellent examples of the artistry of Rodin, Maillol, Mestrovic, Moore, and Epstein. The British Collection contains the world's most representative collection of works by Blake as well as works by Hogarth, George Stubbs, John Constable, and the Pre-Raphaelites. The Modern Collection includes works of conceptual, minimal, optical, kinetic, British figurative, pop, and abstract art; it incorporates the most extensive survey of British art of its period in any public collection, including selected examples of very recent art. Rothko, Nevelson, Bacon, Ernst, and Picasso are all represented. Rex Whistler, the noted *trompe l'oeil* painter, is responsible for the decor of the excellent restaurant. Details: Tate Gallery, Millbank, London SW1P 4RG, England (phone: 01-821-1313; 01-821-7128 for recorded information).

VICTORIA AND ALBERT MUSEUM, London, England: An offspring of that celebration of the progress of human knowledge known as the Great Exhibition of 1851, this museum originally came into being in a roundabout fashion as a repository of the finest in craftsmanship from around the world, from ancient times onward, to lend inspiration to leatherworkers and ceramicists, furniture makers and woodcarvers, architects and dressmakers, silver- and goldsmiths, and other artisans working in the applied arts in the 19th century. The original function has not been abandoned even today, though the collections are a bit more wide-ranging than perhaps was originally intended, encompassing as they do not only textiles and furniture but also watercolors and paintings — among them John Constable's *Salisbury Cathedral from the Bishop's Grounds;* the collections of British art (which include the Constable Collection, presented to the museum by the artist's daughter) stand out for their scope and comprehensiveness. Of particular interest are the Raphael cartoons (designs for tapestries for the Sistine Chapel), the period rooms, Queen Elizabeth I's virginals, the world's first teapot, and the intricately carved, abundantly graffiti'd Great Bed of Ware, which Shakespeare's Sir Toby Belch mentioned in *Twelfth Night* and (measuring about 11 feet square) was said to be big enough to sleep a dozen couples, half of them at the head, the other half at the foot. The Chippendale furniture once owned by David Garrick, pieces by designer William Morris and his followers, Marie-Antoinette's music stand,

Russian imperial jewels, patchwork quilts, medieval hangings, and tiles and stained glass are also on exhibit. The museum's Henry Cole Wing (named after its founder) houses a broad selection of changing exhibitions as well as an interesting permanent display of printmaking techniques. Details: Victoria and Albert Museum, Cromwell Rd., London SW7 2RL, England (phone: 01-589-6371).

WALLACE COLLECTION, London, England: The fourth marquess of Hertford, who died in 1870 after living most of his life in Paris, had one major criterion in collecting: "I only like pleasing paintings," he claimed. But what he called "pleasing" included works of many types — Italian, Dutch, French, Flemish, and Spanish, as well as British — as you'll see when you visit Hertford House, his former town house off Oxford Street, which now contains the collection he amassed and added to that was first put together by his great-grandfather in the 18th century and enlarged in the two succeeding generations. The museum's French furniture from the 17th and 18th centuries is very fine, as are the considerable numbers of 18th-century French clocks and the collections of miniatures, gold boxes, and Sèvres porcelain. Painters whose works are represented include Boucher, Canaletto, Fragonard, Gainsborough, Guardi, Hals, Rembrandt, Reynolds, Rubens, Titian, Van Dyck, Velázquez, and Watteau. The famous collection of oriental and European armor was formed principally by Sir Richard Wallace, the illegitimate son of the fourth marquess of Hertford. His widow, Lady Wallace, bequeathed the vast collection to the nation in 1897. Details: Wallace Collection, Hertford House, Manchester Sq., London W1M 6BN, England (phone: 01-935-0687).

ASHMOLEAN MUSEUM, Oxford, Oxfordshire, England: As Oxford's Bodleian was Britain's first truly public library, so is the Ashmolean — opened in 1683 — its first public museum (possibly the first in Europe as well); it celebrated its tercentenary in May 1983. Even today a visitor will find many of the same scenes enjoyed by Oxford scholars over the years — among them, examples of items from Tradescant's Ark, the "closet of rarities" assembled by John Tradescant the Elder (d. 1638), which formed the nucleus of the collection, as well as odd lots such as Guy Fawkes's lantern, Powhatan's mantle, and the armor-plated hat that belonged to William Bradshaw, who was president of the court that passed sentence on Charles I. Medieval pieces, bronzes (Chinese, Indian, Greek, Roman, Etruscan, Italian Renaissance, later European), ceramics (Chinese, Islamic, Japanese, English, and European), clocks and watches, coins and medals, antiquities (Cretan, Cypriot, Egyptian, Etruscan, Greek, Near Eastern, and Tibetan), paintings (Dutch, English, Flemish, French, Impressionist, Italian, Venetian), and weapons are all represented in this *omnium gatherum* of a museum: There's something for everyone. Details: Ashmolean Museum, Beaumont St., Oxford, Oxfordshire OX1 2PH, England (phone: 0865-278000).

NATIONAL GALLERY OF SCOTLAND, Edinburgh, Scotland: One of a trio of National Galleries of Scotland within walking distance of one another, this one, situated on a manmade embankment known as the Mound at the center of Princes Street Gardens, has a small but vital collection of European paintings, prints, and drawings that includes works by Verrocchio (*Madonna and Child*), Domenichino (*Adoration of the Shepherds*), Claude (*Landscape with Apollo and the Muses*), Poussin (*Mystic Marriage of St. Catherine*), Gauguin (*Vision of the Sermon*), Andrea del Sarto (*Self-Portrait*), Velázquez (*Old Woman Cooking Eggs*), Rembrandt (*Woman in Bed*), Vermeer (*Christ in the House of Martha and Mary*), Watteau (*Fêtes Vénitiennes*), Degas (*Diego Martelli*), van Gogh, Renoir, Cézanne, Monet, Goya, Gainsborough, Reynolds, Constable, Millais, Turner, and others. The collection of works by Scottish artists is particularly good; don't miss Henry Raeburn's *Rev. Robert Walker,* ice skating through a scene that looks almost luminous. Details: National Gallery of Scotland, The Mound, Edinburgh EH2 2EL, Scotland (phone: 031-556-8921).

ART GALLERY AND MUSEUM, Glasgow, Scotland: One of Britain's finest civic art collections, this one installed in a fine red sandstone building near the banks of the River Kelvin in Kelvingrove Park includes a variety of works from many European schools (though the collections of Dutch art of the 17th century, French of the 19th and early 20th centuries, and of Scottish works are particularly strong); Corot, Degas, Monet, Millet, Raeburn, Turner, van Gogh, and Whistler are among those represented. Don't miss Rubens's *Nature Adorned by the Graces,* Giorgione's *The Woman Taken in Adultery,* Rembrandt's *A Man in Armour,* and Salvador Dali's *Christ of St. John of the Cross.* The Glasgow Style gallery houses the work of the architect and designer Charles Rennie Mackintosh and his contemporaries. In addition, the building houses galleries devoted to natural history (and to British birds and geology in particular), and to Scottish prehistory and history, ethnographical materials from as far away as Africa and Polynesia, decorative arts from Western Europe, and more. The collection of European arms and armor, housed in a striking glass-roofed hall, is particularly fine. Details: Glasgow Museums & Art Galleries, Kelvingrove, Glasgow G3 8AG, Scotland (phone: 041-357-3929).

BURRELL COLLECTION, Glasgow, Scotland: Built in 1983 in Pollok Country Park to house the collection given to the city by Sir William and Lady Burrell in 1944, this rich and varied assemblage of art and artifacts reflects the wide-ranging tastes of its collector. Paintings by Cézanne, Rembrandt, and Hals, as well as fine examples of the arts of Egypt, Iraq, Iran, Greece, and Rome highlight the 8,000-piece collection. Pieces of medieval stonework are built into the fabric of the building — the intention of Sir William when he acquired them — and three of the rooms from his home at Hutton Castle, Berwickshire, have been reproduced and are grouped around the courtyard. Details: Glasgow Museums & Art Galleries, Kelvingrove, Glasgow G3 8AG, Scotland (phone: 041-357-3929).

NATIONAL MUSEUM OF WALES, The Main Building, Cardiff, Wales: One of the largest museums in Britain, this institution, opened to the public in 1927, concentrates on things Welsh — its plants and animals, its industry past and present, its history and prehistory, its rocks and minerals, and its fine and applied arts. A Coal Mining Gallery illustrates mining techniques, an Iron and Steel Gallery treats the manufacture of tinplate, iron, and steel during the last three centuries, and a Shipping Gallery shows models of lighthouses and ships, plus figureheads. Among archaeological exhibits, the Caergwrle Bowl, noteworthy for its abundant gold embellishments, and the collection of stone monuments and casts thereof, representing the 5th through the 9th centuries, are particularly interesting. The collection of wax models of plants in the botany section ranks among the world's finest; and the displays of the Welsh countryside and the animal kingdom are also musts. The fine arts galleries include many paintings from the rest of Europe as well — including an impressive collection of Impressionist and post-Impressionist works by Cézanne, Corot, Degas, Monet, Pissarro, and Renoir; Welsh painting is represented by the 18th-century landscape artist Richard Wilson and the 20th-century painters Augustus John, Gwen John, J. D. Innes, Frank Brangwyn, and David Jones. Antiques buffs should be sure to explore the China Room, which contains good examples of Swansea and Nantgarw china and porcelain. Apart from the Main Building in Cardiff's civic center, the National Museum of Wales comprises the Welsh Folk Museum at St. Fagan's and the Welsh Industrial and Maritime Museum in Cardiff's docklands, as well as seven other branches scattered throughout the country. Details: National Museum of Wales, Cardiff, South Glamorgan CF1 3NP, Wales (phone: 0222-397951).

CHESTER BEATTY LIBRARY, Dublin, Irish Republic: The collection that copper millionaire Chester Beatty bequeathed to the Irish nation in 1968, housed near the Royal Dublin Society building in plush, embassy-belt Ballsbridge, evokes one superlative after another. The collection of Islamic art and manuscripts, among the finest in the world, includes more than 250 Korans; Persian, Turkish, and Indian painting are also extensively covered. The collection of Chinese jade books is unique. The Chinese snuffbox collection numbers 900 pieces, and that of rhinoceros horn cups includes some 220 items. The collection of Japanese illuminated manuscripts (*nara-e*) ranks with the foremost in Europe, as does the collection of Japanese woodblock prints (*surimono*). The superb group of Western manuscripts includes illuminated Books of Hours and a volume of Gospels from Stavelot Abbey, executed in Flanders in about AD 1000. The important biblical Papyri, 11 manuscript volumes of the Bible dating from the early 2nd to the 4th century, are also in the library's possession. Naturally, it is only possible to display a tiny fraction of the library's holdings at a time, but the permanent exhibitions do present a representative sampling, and there are major shows a few times a year. Details: Chester Beatty Library, 20 Shrewsbury Rd., Dublin 4, Irish Republic (phone: 692386).

NATIONAL MUSEUM, Dublin, Irish Republic: The massive Thomas Deane building on Kildare Street into which the old Royal Dublin Society moved its collection in 1890 and the antiquities from the Royal Irish Academy a short time later has lost some of its territory over the years; its display space is inadequate, and many items are not exhibited to their best advantage. All the same, the museum should not be missed. It has priceless collections of prehistoric gold artifacts, such as solid gold dress fasteners, torques, and lunulae made by the skilled craftsmen of the Bronze and Iron ages. A recently opened exhibition area called "The Treasury" highlights the museum's important collection of Early Christian metalwork including the Ardagh Chalice and the Cross of Cong. The Georgian silver, Waterford crystal, and Belleek pottery on display is equally captivating. And look for the collection of Irish harps and uilleann pipes and other musical instruments, and for the Derrynaflan chalice, paten, and strainer, found in March 1980 at Killenaule in Tipperary. Finds from the site of Viking Dublin are on display in the museum's new exhibition center at nearby Merrion Row. Details: The National Museum, Kildare St., Dublin 2, Irish Republic (phone: 765521).

NATURAL HISTORY MUSEUM, Dublin, Irish Republic: Much loved for its refusal to change even one iota over the course of the past century, this museum, originally among the three major Royal Dublin Society collections, was moved over a century ago to a building designed by Thomas Clarendon and constructed on the south side of Leinster Lawn, with an entrance on Merrion Square. The first sight to greet a visitor's eye is that old favorite, the Basking Shark, ever popular with school parties, who also have soft spots for the Giant Irish Deer and the fine display of birds. On the ground floor, the Irish Room shows off Irish fauna and a new exhibition of Irish insects. The galleries on the upper floor have a late Victorian ambiance, and an impressive collection of big game heads and antlers from India and Africa hang on pillars and walls — bison, panda, giraffe, okapi, rhinos, hippos, elephants, and gorillas. On the next floor are exotic shells, butterflies, birds — plus skeletons of the extinct Dodo, Solitaire, and Giant Bird of Madagascar, with its 11.7-inch egg. A priceless assemblage of glass models of the invertebrates, which dates back to the museum's earliest days, is also well worth seeing. Suspended from the roof are the huge skeletons of humpback whales. From the museum's last period of vigorous acquisition — the 1880s to 1914, when deep sea explorations generated additions to the marine biology and zoology sections — to very recently, there was little activity in the museum. The impressive geological collection has long languished unseen for want of a proper home. Recently, a staff has been appointed to the geological section and a small exhibition of Irish rocks and minerals has been set up; the fossils remain interspersed with the zoological collections. The museum has also expanded its activities in the field of entomology and marine invertebrates. This evidence of an upsurge of interest is most welcome, as is the ecology-conscious generation's increasing use of the museum as a research tool and archive. Details: Natural History Museum, Merrion St., Dublin 2, Irish Republic (phone: 765521).

WEXFORD COUNTY MUSEUM, Enniscorthy, County Wexford, Irish Republic:
A medieval air hangs over this town, with its narrow streets winding down to the River Slaney on one side, and Vinegar Hill, where the Irish rebels were defeated in 1798, rising on the other. The museum, housed in a 13th-century Norman castle on which the Elizabethan poet Edmund Spenser once held a lease (one of the few Irish castles not in ruins), contains muskets, pikes, and other relics of the battle, as well as objects from the 1916 Rising (during which this town was the last in the country to surrender). But the museum's contents are not restricted to military impedimenta: A kitchen at the back of the castle and a dairy show off traditional cooking utensils and tools, including churns used in the old days for making butter and cheese. There are also striking displays of figureheads salvaged from ships wrecked off the coast, a stone covered with Ogham script, ships' anchors, stone crosses, and chalices dating from the 17th century. A recently added feature is a sports collection, housed in a hitherto unused tower of the castle, and the view from the castle roof alone is worth the visit. Details: Wexford County Museum, Castle Hill, Enniscorthy, County Wexford, Irish Republic.

MONAGHAN COUNTY MUSEUM, Monaghan, County Monaghan, Irish Republic: One of the Republic's first county museums, this institution — formerly situated in a bleak old court house with huge Doric columns that must have put the fear of God into prisoners during the last century — has a stunning and eclectic collection ranging from Neolithic relics to folk items. And it now has a home of its own that allows it to show them off. The place is stuffed with china dinner sets, lace made in nearby Carrickmacross, the cotton crochet known as Clones lace; there's the Cross of Clogher, which dates to the early 15th century; a cauldron (ca. 800 BC), found in a bog in 1854; old photographs; and, in an open-access exhibition area, a collection of querns (hand mills), milk churns, and milestones from the now-unused Ulster Canal. Certainly, this award-winning museum is one of Ireland's most progressive, and the collections are constantly improving. Details: Monaghan County Museum, 1-2 Hill St., Monoghan, Irish Republic (phone: 047-82928).

MUCKROSS HOUSE FOLK MUSEUM, Muckross, Killarney, County Kerry, Irish Republic: Emphasis at this museum, another among the Republic's most forward-looking, is as much on making the objects on show interesting to visitors as on preserving them, and a great deal of thought and effort has been put into every display. In addition, potters and weavers can be seen at work, while other artisans toil in the book bindery, blacksmith's forge, and harness-making workshop, producing the kind of items displayed in the museum proper. When you've had your fill of these, you can go out for a stroll on one of the nature trails that meander across the vast grounds (which, together with the early-19th-century house where exhibits are set up, were presented to the nation in 1932). The footpaths alone might warrant a visit here, encircling as they do, two of the lakes of Killarney; you'll also find a superb natural rock garden and an abundance of free-roaming red deer and rare flora. Details: Muckross House Folk Museum, Muckross, Killarney, County Kerry, Irish Republic (phone: 06431440).

IRISH AGRICULTURAL MUSEUM, Wexford, County Wexford, Irish Republic:
This museum in the restored 19th-century farm buildings of Victorian Gothic Johnstown Castle, 4 miles southwest of Wexford town, gives an excellent picture of just how much Irish farming has changed in the last 50 years. Its display of old farming and rural craft items, the country's largest, includes the hand flails, the pitchers, turnip pulpers, butter-making instruments, ploughs, harrows, sowers, mowing machines, harnesses, and carts and traps that were once among every Irish farmer's most important tools. A complete model of an old kitchen is on exhibit, along with a laundry, a creamery, a laborer's bedroom, a stable, and displays on coopering, blacksmithing, wheelwrighting, harness making, and traditional Irish country furniture. The castle's 50-acre ornamental grounds — with meandering pathways, artificial lakes, and interesting shrubs and flowers — are also a delight, and from June through August a tea room is open

at the museum. The castle and surrounding farm are used for soils research by the Agricultural Institute. Details: Irish Agricultural Museum, Johnstown Castle, Wexford, County Wexford, Irish Republic (phone: 053-42888).

ULSTER MUSEUM, Belfast, Northern Ireland: Housed in a Neoclassical 1920s building with a well-designed modern addition, in the city's delightful Botanic Gardens with their great Palm House and Tropical Ravine, the collections shown here are broad-ranging. There's an old and functioning water wheel (in the Industrial Archaeology section); a collection of contemporary painting and sculpture unrivaled in Ireland (in the Art Galleries); interesting prehistoric collections that include the only surviving pair of late Bronze Age trumpets that can still be played; a display of minerals and gemstones unique in the country (including the biggest group of quartz crystals in Britain and Ireland, an attractive display of fluorescent and phosphorescent minerals in a darkened central vault, and a full-size cave); and, adding a touch of glitter, the fabulous collection of jewelry, coins, and other items recovered from the *Girona,* a galleass of the Spanish Armada, which went down off the Antrim coast in 1588. The Living Sea surrounds visitors with realistic models of marine creatures. The Dinosaur Show is a new gallery, designed with children in mind, which includes a near-complete skeleton of *Anatosaurus annecteus,* and in the old entrance hall there's an enormous, now extinct coelacanth. The museum store sells copies of the gold *No tengo mas que dar te* ring, the original of which was worn by a Spanish sailor as he went to his watery grave, mindful, no doubt, of the sweetheart who gave it to him. Details: The Ulster Museum, Botanic Gardens, Belfast BT9 5AB, Northern Ireland (phone: 0232-668251).

ULSTER FOLK AND TRANSPORT MUSEUM, Holywood, County Down, Northern Ireland: This is the place to see how Ulster folk lived back at the turn of the century. Terraces of townhouses, as well as farmhouses, mills, a church, and schools, have been moved here brick by brick, stone by stone; then furnished with the everyday objects of the appropriate period, and landscaped as they might have been originally. A farm from mid-Antrim has been reconstructed right down to the stone walls, hedges, and ditches around the fields. And, in addition, there's an assortment of galleries filled with domestic and agricultural artifacts and vehicles used in Irish transport over the ages — rail, road, air, and sea. In fact, the museum is the home of the finest and most comprehensive such display in Ireland. There are wheel-less sledges, elegant horse-drawn carriages, automobiles, and even a vertical take-off plane; railway rolling stock is kept in Belfast in Witham Street, off the Lower Newtownards Road. Throughout the year there are demonstrations of seasonal crafts. Details: Ulster Folk and Transport Museum, Cultra Manor, Holywood, County Down BT18 0EU, Northern Ireland (phone: Belfast 0232-428428).

The Performing Arts

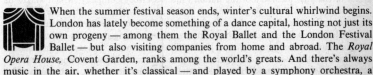 When the summer festival season ends, winter's cultural whirlwind begins. London has lately become something of a dance capital, hosting not just its own progeny — among them the Royal Ballet and the London Festival Ballet — but also visiting companies from home and abroad. The *Royal Opera House,* Covent Garden, ranks among the world's greats. And there's always music in the air, whether it's classical — and played by a symphony orchestra, a chamber group, or a soloist — jazz, or the most traditional folk work. And the theatrical tradition both in Britain and in Ireland runs deep and strong. London, for instance, is a hotbed of dramatic affairs, with literally hundreds of offerings in hundreds of playhouses. The dozens of theaters in the West End (London's answer to Broadway) regularly mount ostensibly commercial productions (although many, as a result of

British theater's fondness for the experimental, have a long way to go before they make money), and the fare swings wildly: The tiny *Duchess,* for example, for years the host of *Oh! Calcutta,* gave itself over to a glistening *Private Lives* in 1980, and by now may be playing *Hamlet* for all one can forecast. The same tradition of eclecticism and experimentation has put the English theater — and great actors and actresses like Sir John Gielgud, Lord Olivier, Dame Edith Evans, and so many others — at the forefront of world drama.

The Irish, for their part, tend to agree with theater critic Kenneth Tynan, who once noted "Ireland's sacred duty to send over, every few years, a playwright to save the English theatre from inarticulate glumness" — but the attitude cannot be blamed on sour grapes, because the contribution of this nation's writers is equally outstanding and all out of proportion to the island's small population. The names Sheridan, Goldsmith, Wilde, Shaw, Synge, O'Casey, Behan, and Beckett, for instance, inevitably crop up wherever great drama is under discussion — and with them, the names of actors and actresses such as Siobhan McKenna and Barry Fitzgerald. A current feature of the Irish theater scene is the colorful show of song, dance, and story at Galway's all-Irish *Taibhdhearc na Gaillimhe* (Middle St., Galway; phone: 091-62024).

With all this going on, settling on an evening's entertainment (or an afternoon's — or even a morning's, for that matter) can pose some problems. When it comes to theater, one man's meat is another's moan, so before settling on a play, ask a friend or check newspapers — in London, for instance, the *Sunday Observer* or well-regarded tourist magazines such as *What's On and Where to Go* or the BTA's monthly theater guide, the *London Planner.* Information about what's playing in Ireland can be found in the daily papers in Dublin, Cork, and Belfast; in Galway's *Connacht Tribune;* in the fortnightly events guide *In Dublin;* and in the monthly guide *In Belfast.*

But throughout Britain and Ireland, some theaters reliably turn out productions and concerts that are more interesting or wonderful than others, and some are worth a visit in their own right — either because they are particularly beautiful or unusually historic. A few are quite small, so that even the most remote corner (or "gods," as the heights of the balconies are called) affords a fine view of the activities on stage — and the prices are usually relatively low by stateside standards.

We've given a sampling of halls worth going out of your way to experience. It's possible to order tickets in advance of arrival in Britain directly through the individual box offices and through *Keith Prowse & Co.,* 234 W 44th St., New York, NY 10036 (phone: 212-398-1430 and 800-223-4446). This organization, the world's largest entertainment ticket agency, sells some 53,000 tickets per week, and its allocations range from a fifth to nearly half of all the seats for London theaters. Tickets to major festival events can also be booked in advance through Edwards & Edwards, One Times Square Plaza, New York, NY 10036 (phone: 212-944-0290 and 800-223-6108).

BIRMINGHAM REPERTORY THEATRE, Birmingham, West Midlands, England: A list of the past members of the nation's first repertory company, which makes its home here, reads like a *Who's Who* of British theater. Richard Chamberlain, Julie Christie, and Albert Finney played here; and so did Laurence Olivier, Paul Scofield, Ralph Richardson, and Edith Evans, among others, during the years after Sir Barry Jackson founded the organization in 1913 with his own money "to serve an art instead of making that art serve a commercial purpose." In addition to earning fame for its actors, the Rep also became known for its attention to modern work, particularly plays by George Bernard Shaw, back when Shaw was considered a contemporary; for its successes in London; for Jackson's involvement with the origins of the *Malvern Festival* (described in *Feis and Fleadh: The Best Festivals*); and for its modern-dress productions of Shakespeare — all of whose works the company has performed at least once, in one form or another, over the years. Now in a spiffy new home, the Rep performs a season of plays that include the classics, musicals, and premieres in an 899-seat Main House cunningly designed on a steep tilt so that no one ever sits more than 65 feet from the stage; and assorted new works and innovative restagings of golden oldies in the more flexible 50-by-30 Studio Theatre. At Christmastime, there's always a special show. (*The Wizard of Oz, Treasure Island,* and *Pinocchio* are past successes.) And every year, when the company is not in residence, the main house hosts a visit by the Ballet Rambert. The new Young Company, a resident group of young actors selected from the best young talent in British theater, has brought zest and style to a varied season of plays in the Main House, the Studio, and on tour. Details: Birmingham Repertory Theatre, Broad St., Birmingham, West Midlands B1 2EP, England (phone: 021-236-4455).

THEATRE ROYAL, Bristol, Avon, England: Peter O'Toole, Barbara Leigh-Hunt, Jeremy Irons, Jane Lapotaire, Greta Scacchi, and many other well-known British actors have started out on the boards of this splendid 18th-century playhouse, the oldest continuously active theater in Britain, and one of a pair that serve as home to the respected Bristol Old Vic Company. (The remaining theater is the New Vic, which opened in 1972 and is used for smaller productions.) Either one delivers a thrilling evening, whether the fare is one of the classics to which the Theatre Royal is so well suited, or a contemporary piece. Details: Theatre Royal, King St., Bristol, Avon BS1 4ED, England (phone: 0272-264388).

BARBICAN CENTRE, London, England: An apparent tribute to modern architecture, this 1982 structure looks like a maze of concrete towers and corridors from the outside. Once inside, it's impossible not to be overwhelmed by the lavish decor, the complex design, the exciting potential of the building, and the breadth of artistic activity generated within by day as well as by night. The Royal Shakespeare Company performs here, as does the London Symphony Orchestra. There are two theaters, cinemas, an art gallery, and a concert hall that holds regular performances of classical music, opera, and more. The Waterside Café, where you can have a snack by the fountains in summer, Wine on Six (the Barbican's wine bar), and the more luxurious Cut-Above Carvery all make for a delightful interlude as well. Details: Barbican Centre, Silk St., London EC2Y 8DS (phone: 01-638-8891 and -8795).

LONDON COLISEUM, London, England: There's a sense of occasion surrounding any visit to this floridly Edwardian, 2,358-seat theater, London's largest, at the foot of St. Martin's Lane not far from St. Martin-in-the-Fields and the National Gallery. The interiors are all alabaster and marble, bronze and splendid gleaming mahogany, as posh as those of the ships that crisscrossed the Atlantic during the years around 1904, when the theater was opened. Diaghilev's Ballet Russe performed here, as did Sarah Bernhardt, Mrs. Patrick Campbell, Ellen Terry, and a child star named Noel Coward; the impresario who conceived the place even staged tennis matches and rodeos to keep it filled. Since 1968, the English National Opera Company, which stages classic and contemporary operas in English, has called it home, and is in residence during an August-to-June season. Details: English National Opera, London Coliseum, St. Martin's La., London WC2N 4ES, England (phone: 01-836-3161 or 01-240-5258).

NATIONAL THEATRE, London, England: Anyone who visits this trio of houses in a handsome, large, Thames-side drama complex is sure to have plenty to talk about — even if the fare is not to his taste. That, however, is unlikely, for Albert Finney, John Gielgud, Ian McKellen, Ralph Richardson, Peggy Ashcroft, and Paul Scofield have all appeared here; and plenty of breath-stopping acting takes place, in parts ranging from the soul-stretching to the small, in a selection of plays that embraces the classics; translations of works by European dramatists such as Schnitzler, Horvath, Feydeau, or Brecht; revivals of contemporary plays; new pieces by living playwrights like Pinter, Stoppard, Brenton, Storey, or Bolt; and adaptations of such books as *Lark Rise* or *The World Turned Upside Down.*

The building itself is wonderful, with an interior that feels like a walk-through sculpture, a huge foyer with bars that seems to be London's answer to Paris's sidewalk cafés, and all manner of walks, terraces, restaurants with fine views of Somerset House and the river curving off toward St. Paul's.

Before performances ensembles and soloists play for free in the foyers, and it's possible to browse through art exhibitions while listening. There are also almost always so-called platform performances — brief plays, readings, poetry, music, and mime — in all three theaters: 400-seat Cottesloe, which is otherwise mainly used for works requiring small-scale staging, the 890-seat proscenium-arch Lyttelton, and the 1,160-seat open-stage Olivier. The latter two feel almost as intimate as the Cottesloe, thanks to their excellent design. Details: National Theatre, South Bank, London SE1 9PX, England (phone: 01-928-2252).

OLD VIC, London, England: Architects, bombs, and ill-advised alterations had left the Old Vic nothing short of a mishmash when a Canadian named "Big" Ed Mirvish bought it sight unseen a few years ago and commenced transforming it into one of the most elegant, attractive, and comfortable theaters in central London. The façade was returned to its 1818 incarnation, complete with brick arches, and the interior was restored to a semblance of its 1880s self. Boxes, ceiling, proscenium arch, and tier fronts were elaborately painted in shades of ivory, apricot, coral, pewter, and gold and silver. House curtains made of velvet were installed. And the entire auditorium was decked out with wallpaper and carpeting with a period flavor. The house now produces its own subscription season and, beginning in 1988, Jonathan Miller takes over as Artistic Director, which should ensure much interesting — if controversial — theater. And the remarkable restoration alone makes a visit worthwhile. Details: The Old Vic, Waterloo Rd., London SE1 8NB, England (phone: 01-928-7616).

OPEN AIR THEATRE (REGENT'S PARK), London, England: It's hard to find a more pleasant way to spend a summer evening in London than to take in a performance of Shakespeare (or a musical) in this lovely amphitheater in the woods near Queen Mary's Rose Garden. Established in 1932, it quickly became an institution among London theatergoers, and actors from Vivien Leigh and Deborah Kerr to Jack Hawkins and Jeremy Irons have played here. Since 1962, the New Shakespeare Company has made its home here and offers three plays, two by Shakespeare, every summer. The new auditorium, which opened in 1975, provides plenty of space for a bar, a visit to which is an integral part of any experience here; Puck's Fizz and mulled wine, barbecue and the cold buffet are the favorites. Details: Open Air Theatre Regent's Park, London NW1 4NP, England (phone: 01-486-2431).

ROYAL ALBERT HALL, London, England: Designed in the Italian Renaissance style and opened by Queen Victoria in 1871, this round house is truly splendid — a quarter of a mile around, and domed, with red brick and terra-cotta façades, an immense Great Organ, and three tiers of boxes with seats for thousands. All manner of musical concerts, from a Bach B Minor Mass to a spine-tingling, cannon-throttled "1812" Overture, will fill it up. Particularly special are the Henry Wood Promenade Concerts ("The Proms," in local parlance), which attract hordes every year from July to September. Concerts feature the BBC Symphony Orchestra and visiting orchestras from Britain and the rest of the world in programs of music from all eras; some pieces are specially commissioned for the occasion. Traditionally, the final concert closes with a program of British music that includes Elgar's "Pomp and Circumstance March." For this, and for other programs, prices are remarkably low. The hall has also hosted such well-known performers as Paul Simon, Eric Clapton, and Frank Sinatra, and has been the sight of international-caliber tennis matches and grand balls. A recent addition is the Royal Albert Hall Tour & Exhibition, which permits the visitor to get a behind-the-scenes look at the history and operation of the hall. Details: Royal Albert Hall, Kensington Gore, London SW7 2AP, England (phone: 01-589-8212; tour coordinator: 01-589-3202).

ROYAL COURT THEATRE, London, England: One of the most famous of London's small theaters, this one has made theatrical history more than once — first in about 1904 with Harley Granville Barker's stagings of Arthur Pinero farces and George Bernard Shaw plays, and again in the late 1950s when George Devine's English Stage Company presented John Osborne's *Look Back in Anger.* Even today, the theater is associated with the contemporary, and works of new writers such as Caryl Churchill, Edward Bond, and Snoo Wilson can often be seen. And, though chronic shortages of money are a fact of life, standards are always high. The Royal Court is a great place for spotting talent, and the audience is lively. *Top Girls* started here before heading for the West End and New York (as did Ron Hutchinson's *Rat in the Skull,* Michael Hastings's *Tom and Viv,* and Wallace Shawn's *Aunt Dan and Lemon*), and the latest *Hamlet* was pronounced revolutionary. Never a dull moment. Details: The Royal Court, Sloane Sq., London SW1W 8AS, England (phone: 01-730-1745).

ROYAL FESTIVAL HALL, London, England: Opened in 1951 and seating 3,000, London's premiere concert hall is part of the South Bank Centre (which also includes the nearby National Theatre, the National Film Theatre, the Hayward Gallery, and two smaller halls, the 1,150-seat Queen Elizabeth Hall and the 370-seat Purcell Room). In addition to an annual program of 1,200 events that feature most major performers on the international music and the lyric arts scene, there are free foyer exhibitions and lunchtime concerts, and shops and catering facilities are open all day. Details: Royal Festival Hall, South Bank, London SE1 8XX, England (phone: 01-928-3002).

ROYAL OPERA HOUSE, COVENT GARDEN, London, England: Worth a look for its grandeur alone, this jewel of a 2,000-seat opera house, the third on the site, is splendidly Victorian, with its red plush, its shaded lights, its scarlet and gold tiers, its domed turquoise ceiling, and its sweeping horseshoe-shaped balconies. But the play's the thing, and some of the best singers in the world have performed here — among them Dame Nellie Melba, Dame Joan Sutherland, Kirsten Flagstad, and Maria Callas. The traditions of excellence continue unabated, so that now the hall ranks among the world's half-dozen true greats of its kind, and newcomers believe that success here gives their careers the stamp of international greatness. The Royal Opera shares the house with the Royal Ballet, which, under noted choreographers such as Sir Frederick Ashton and Sir Kenneth MacMillan, with dancers like Antoinette Sibley and Dame Margot Fonteyn, Rudolf Nureyev and Anthony Dowell, has become one of the world's most noted companies. Nearby, a silver casket on the south wall of St. Paul's, Covent Garden, contains the ashes of Ellen Terry, the famous actress who died in 1928. Details: The Royal Opera House, Covent Garden, London WC2E 9DD, England (phone: 01-240-1066 and -1911).

SADLER'S WELLS THEATRE, London, England: Built on the site of a pair of mineral springs discovered in 1683 by one Richard Sadler, this member of the trio of the capital's oldest more or less continuously operating halls has seen its jugglers and clowns, rope-dancers and performing animals, plays and pantomimes, and even roller-skaters and boxers; reopened after a brief closing during the war, it hosted the world premiere of Benjamin Britten's *Peter Grimes,* and, in its time, it has also been home to the Royal Ballet and the English National Opera. Today, it hosts touring opera and dance companies from all over the world — among them Merce Cunningham, Twyla Tharp, Pilobolus, the Central Ballet of China, the Sydney Dance Theatre, the Cologne Opera, and others. The London seasons of the country's leading dance companies, including Ballet Rambert, the London Contemporary Dance Theatre, and the Sadler's Wells Royal Ballet, are also here. The exterior, foyer, and performance areas have been beautifully redecorated, and the young and with-it audience and the onstage goings-on make a stop here well worthwhile. Details: Sadler's Wells Theatre, Rosebery Ave., London EC1R 4TN, England (phone: 01-278-6563; box office, 01-278-8916).

THEATRE ROYAL (DRURY LANE), London, England: The productions may not be London's most innovative, but this 2,283-seat theater, with its beautiful symmetrical staircase and domed entranceway — "a tradition, national treasure" and "not just a theater" in the words of one past showman — is unarguably one of London's most historic. The fourth playhouse on the site, it was preceded by a theater where Charles II met Nell Gwyn, who once sold oranges at the entrance; by another designed by Christopher Wren, with John Dryden as chief playwright, and as manager, David Garrick and Richard Sheridan, whose 1777 *School for Scandal* was written upstairs while actors rehearsed completed sections below. The present house, designed by Benjamin Wyatt in 1812, has seen opera and drama, pantomime and film, and even musicals. Edmund Kean, whom many believe to be the greatest tragedian of all time, played here in 1814, and so did Sir Henry Irving, Ellen Terry, Sir John Gielgud, and other famous actors. The theater has its tradition — the cutting of the so-called Baddeley Cake (named after the actor whose will supplied the funds) in the Grand Saloon after the performance every January 6 — and its ghost, a gray-cloaked, high-booted bewigged fellow who haunts the upper circle — in the daytime only, however. For a splurge, hire the Royal Box or the Prince of Wales Box, which come complete with seating for six and tiny Regency or Adamesque retiring rooms. Drury Lane Theatre Tours are available by arrangement with the theater's historian, Mr. George Hoare. Details: Theatre Royal (Drury Lane), Catherine St., London WC2B 5JF, England (phone: 01-836-3352).

THEATRE ROYAL (HAYMARKET), London, England: Architect John Nash, who designed this small modish theater, gave it a wonderful Corinthian portico, which looks all the grander when floodlit, as it often is at night. Henry Fielding managed a predecessor on the site around 1737, and the present hall, built in 1821, has been the setting for plays by everyone from Ibsen to Wilde, T. S. Eliot and Tennessee Williams to Noel Coward, Barrie, and Rattigan; Sir Beerbohm Tree played here in the late 19th century. The hall itself, renovated at the beginning of this century, is all white, rich blue, and gold leaf; there's a wonderfully crafted royal arms above the stage. Details: Theatre Royal (Haymarket), Haymarket, London SW1Y 4HT, England (phone: 01-930-9832).

WIGMORE HALL, London, England: One of Europe's most elegant and intimate concert halls, this fine example of the art nouveau style — full of alabaster, marble, polished mahogany, and brass — was created in 1901 by Carl Bechstein (of piano fame) and is famous for its nearly perfect acoustics. A delight for recitals and chamber music, it has hosted debuts by Elisabeth Schwarzkopf (in 1948), and Daniel Barenboim (in 1958); and recitals by Julian Bream, Peter Pears, Andrés Segovia, and many others. Arthur Rubinstein not only made his debut here (in 1912) but also his last public appearance (in 1976). These days, the hall attracts artists such as Dame Janet Baker, Shura Cherkassy, and the Beaux Arts Trio, and has a regular series of celebrity and early music concerts, as well as a very popular series of Sunday Morning Coffee Concerts. Details: Wigmore Hall, 36 Wigmore St., London W1H 9DF, England (phone: 01-935-2141).

YOUNG VIC THEATRE, London, England: The theater, founded more than 15 years ago, is relatively new by London standards, but the spirit of experimentation and the *joie de jouer* that go into the productions are as much a tradition in the British theater as is the Bard himself. Founder Frank Dunlop's adaptation of a Molière work went to Broadway as *Scapino!,* and the production of Tom Stoppard's satire *Rosencrantz and Guildenstern Are Dead* made theater history. Productions of classical and modern established authors such as William Shakespeare, David Edgar, Tom Kempinski, Willy Russell, Arthur Miller, and David Holman are typical fare, and it's a lively place, quite different architecturally from most theaters. Children's pieces and the avant-garde are standard in a small studio theater. Details: The Young Vic, 66 The Cut, London SE1 8LZ, England (phone: 01-928-6363).

ROYAL EXCHANGE THEATRE, Manchester, England: Installed in a former cotton exchange, the Royal Exchange Theatre Company, whose roots go back to 1959 and a group of actors who had trained at the Old Vic Theatre School, performs Shakespeare, Marlowe, Sheridan, Chekhov, Coward, Ibsen, and a variety of other works old and new, including an occasional world premiere. Several productions — including *The Dresser* — have gone on to London or Broadway, and audiences usually pack the unusual theater-in-the-round, Europe's largest, to 90% capacity. Concerts of classical and folk music and jazz are also held here, along with a host of other activities. Details: Royal Exchange Theatre, St. Ann's Sq., Manchester M2 7DH, England (phone: 061-833-9333).

THEATRE ROYAL, Norfolk, Norwich, England: Considering only its atmosphere, the sleek Theatre Royal, a 1970 update of a structure put up in 1935 in the theater and cinema style of the day (the fourth theater on the site), doesn't hold a candle to the grander London halls. Yet, as Europe's most successful provincial theater, it is that remarkable thing, an arts institution that manages to be totally self-supporting. Current management keeps things hopping with a continual and very lively procession of circus, grand opera, ice shows, ballet, pantomime, variety shows, vaudeville, classical music concerts, and programs from the touring companies of the National Theatre Company, Sadler's Wells Royal Ballet, the Glyndebourne Opera, the London Festival Ballet, and foreign dance companies. Charlie Chaplin, as the Lancashire Lad, performed in a previous theater on the site, back in 1904 when it was called the Norwich Hippodrome. Open every day except Christmas, and a visit is not to be missed. Details: Theatre Royal, Theatre St., Norfolk, Norwich, NR2 1RL, England (phone: 0603-628205).

ROYAL SHAKESPEARE THEATRE, Stratford-upon-Avon, Warwickshire, England: The senior of the United Kingdom's two national theaters, under the patronage of Her Majesty the Queen, this 1,500-seat hall opened on April 23, 1932, on the Bard's own birthday — appropriately enough, since it's Shakespeare that you'll see on these boards throughout the season, from late March through January. The immense Royal Shakespeare Company — the association of actors, directors, and designers who name the place as one of their principal homes — has numbered almost all the greats of British theater among its members in the course of the last century, and the quality of the work is at least professional if not superb, and often innovative (witness one season's *Taming of the Shrew* with motorcycles). The Other Place, a small theater seating between 150 and 200, houses the company's small-scale productions of new British writings and classical works. The new Swan Theatre, built within the shell of the old Memorial Theatre, has a horseshoe-shaped auditorium that closely resembles those of 16th-century playhouses, and has been earmarked for performances of popular plays of Shakespeare's contemporaries — Jonson, Marlowe, Kyd, and Tourneur. And in London, where the 1,000-seat Aldwych and the smaller Warehouse theaters have been the group's longtime bases, the RSC moved to a new theater (the Barbican) and attached studio space (the Pit) in the Barbican Arts Centre, described above, in late 1982; the almost-continuous season includes a mix of Shakespeare (transferred from the previous Stratford season) and new productions of modern and classical works. Details: Royal Shakespeare Theatre, Waterside, Stratford-upon-Avon, Warwickshire CV37 6BB, England (phone: 0789-295623), or the Royal Shakespeare Company, Barbican Theatre, Barbican, London EC2Y 8BQ, England (phone: 01-628-8795).

CITIZENS' THEATRE, Glasgow, Scotland: The *Times* called it Britain's "most challenging theater," the *Observer* characterized it as "the most unusual and individual theater in the land," the *Daily Mail* noted that it "puts the West End in the shade," and the US's *After Dark* commented on its "outrageously adventurous nature" and its "perverse and avant-garde flair": The accolades for this first-rate regional theater just don't stop. The century-old playhouse-with-a-past has recently been renovated, and the house is now a stunning example of a traditional proscenium-arch Victorian theater. The company has performed over 140 British and foreign classics since its formation, and has acquired a reputation around the world; most of the actors have worked with the company for over a decade, and all are paid the same salary. During the summer months, when the company is not in residence, visiting troupes can be seen. Details: Citizens' Theatre, Gorbals, Glasgow G5 9DS, Scotland (phone: 041-429-5561).

THEATRE ROYAL, Glasgow, Scotland: Those who think that Edinburgh is home to anything cultural in Scotland are overlooking the fact that it is Glasgow that is home to the Scottish Opera, the Scottish National Orchestra, and the Scottish Ballet; and that Scotland's only opera house is here. The Theatre Royal, which lays claim to that distinction, is without question one of the more gorgeous relics of Victorian days in Britain. Now owned by the Scottish Opera, it has been recently and ingeniously restored — so that the most modern theatrical equipment is available but mainly hidden; there is marvelous plasterwork ornamenting the swooping balconies and the domed ceilings, an overwhelming sumptuousness in the scheme of things. Unlike many refurbished opera houses, this one is not done in red and gold, but in various shades of cream and brown, highlighted here and there with blue and orange. The Scottish Opera subscription season runs from September through May; when the opera is not in residence, the hall welcomes performances by many other companies including the Scottish Ballet, Sadler's Wells Royal Ballet, Ballet Rambert, the Royal Shakespeare Company, the National Theatre, the Scottish Theatre Company, and others. Details: Theatre Royal, 282 Hope St., Glasgow G2 3QA, Scotland (phone: 041-331-1234).

IRISH NATIONAL BALLET, Cork, County Cork, Irish Republic: In 1945, when Joan Denise Moriarty returned to Cork from her dance studies abroad and began her long battle for a national ballet company, she was condemned from the pulpit. No doubt, it was suspected that anything more sensual than the rigid, arms-at-the-sides traditional dancing, with its concentration on footwork to the exclusion of any other movement, would lead to dreadful depravities in theaters throughout the land. But Ms. Moriarty persevered, founding the amateur Cork Ballet Company in 1945, and was rewarded in 1973 when Ireland finally acquired its own national ballet, the state-subsidized and fully professional Irish National Ballet. In addition to performing many of the standards from the classical repertoire, Ms. Moriarty and the company's artistic adviser, Domy Reiter-Soffer (who has also worked with the Bat Dor Company of Israel and American Ballet Theatre), have created many new works in contemporary styles. The company has also developed a unique blend of Irish traditional dancing and ballet that mixes the detailed steps of the former with the latter's physical expressiveness to produce a highly original form that reaches its peak in a version of John Millington Synge's *The Playboy of the Western World,* which was presented very successfully in both London and New York with the renowned Chieftains supplying the music. Much of the company's time is devoted to touring Ireland; they're at the Cork Opera House in February and August and at Dublin's Abbey Theatre in June. With the 1986 appointment of a new artistic director — the Finnish Anneli Vuorenjuuri-Robinson — the company continues to explore new directions. Details: Irish National Ballet, 1b Emmet Pl., Cork, County Cork, Irish Republic (phone: 021-270112).

ABBEY THEATRE, Dublin, Irish Republic: The fine collection of portraits, including likenesses of W. B. Yeats, Lady Gregory, John Millington Synge, and Sean O'Casey, which graces the foyer of the Abbey Theatre — the country's National Theatre — is a vivid reminder of those heady days when the premieres of O'Casey's *The Plough and the Stars* and Synge's *The Playboy of the Western World* were greeted by riot and disorder. Though audiences are less boisterous now and the company is less likely to be arrested, as in Philadelphia in 1912, for performing "immoral and indecent" plays, the Abbey still presents the best of contemporary Irish playwriting, including productions of works by Brian Friel, Hugh Leonard, and Thomas Murphy, among others, as well as revivals of the classics that made the 85-year-old Abbey Players famous to begin with. Work of a more experimental nature is presented downstairs, in the Peacock; the opportunity to visit this wonderfully intimate auditorium should not be missed. After the show, slip across the road for a drink in *The Plough,* full of posters of past Abbey successes, or *The Flowing Tide,* where you can admire the stained-glass panels set into the walls — and mingle with the actors whose efforts you have just applauded. Details: Abbey Theatre, Lower Abbey St., Dublin 1, Irish Republic (phone: 01-744505 or 01-787179).

FOCUS THEATRE, Dublin, Irish Republic: Dublin's smallest theater is also one of its most exciting. In 1963, when Deirdre O'Connell returned to Ireland after studying in New York at Lee Strasberg's Actors' Studio, she began to train some Dublin actors in Stanislavskian technique, and, by 1967, had formed the nucleus of a company and moved into a converted garage in a lane off Pembroke Street. An evening in this tiny, 72-seat auditorium is never disappointing, whether the play is a classic by Chekhov or the latest offering of a young Irish writer. Besides the resident Focus Company, there is a Studio Company of young actors-in-training who occasionally present their own improvised and very original adaptations of Irish legends and literature. It is no exaggeration to say that, along with some of the finest actors in Dublin (including Ms. O'Connell herself), Focus theatergoers glimpse the stars of tomorrow. Details: Focus Theatre, 6 Pembroke Pl., Dublin 2, Irish Republic (phone: 01-763071).

GAIETY THEATRE, Dublin, Irish Republic: The Gaiety is where many a Dublin child brought for a special occasion to a pantomime, perhaps, or a Gilbert and Sullivan musical, gets a first taste of the magic of theater. It was founded in 1871 by Michael Gunn and his brother John (a bust of whom can be seen on the staircase that leads to the Circle) and, although the original gallery, or "gods," was removed when the theater was renovated in 1955, the theater remains a very fine example of the typical late Victorian playhouse — marvelously opulent with its red carpets, dark pillars, golden draperies, and ornate pink cream plasterwork; the orchestra pit's brass surround adds its gleam to the total effect, and, when you sit in a private box, you feel like no less than visiting royalty. The Letters Patent issued at the theater's founding allows for the production of "any interlude, tragedy, comedy, prelude, opera, burletta, play, farce or pantomime," and today's repertoire remains just that broad. As a result, the list of the famous who have played at the Gaiety is formidable, including as it does, Lily Langtry, the D'Oyly Carte Opera Company, Burgess Meredith, Siobhán McKenna, Paulette Goddard, the Bolshoi Ballet, Peter O'Toole — and Dublin's own Jimmy O'Dea, who for nearly 30 years appeared in pantomime and musical and, in the character of Biddy Mulligan, captured the true spirit of the city. His delightful successor today is the diminutive and exuberant Maureen Potter. Details: Gaiety Theatre, South King St., Dublin 2, Irish Republic (phone: Dublin 771717).

GATE THEATRE, Dublin, County Dublin, Irish Republic: The name of the Gate Theatre is synonymous with those of the late Michael MacLiammoir and Hilton Edwards, who organized the company in 1928 to present plays of unusual interest, regardless of nationality or period, at a time when the Abbey devoted itself entirely to Irish work. The founders' tradition continues under the direction of Michael Colgan, and theatergoers here are as likely to find a play by Tennessee Williams as one by Brian Friel or a young unknown. The visual emphasis is strong, and the theater has received awards for its stage designs. The auditorium is quite small and, as might be expected from the Gate's reputation for stage design, beautifully decorated so that it feels less like a modern playhouse than an 18th-century aristocrat's court theater. The young Orson Welles was once employed by the Gate, after exaggerating his previous experience — but proved his talents there as, subsequently, elsewhere. James Mason and Geraldine FitzGerald also began their careers here. Details: Gate Theatre, Cavendish Row, Dublin 1, Irish Republic (phone: 01-744045 or 01-743722).

OLYMPIA THEATRE, Dublin, Irish Republic: The Olympia occupies a very special place in the hearts of Dubliners, perhaps because of its connection with music hall, always the most popular form of theater here. Patrons on the 1879 opening night at Dan Lowrey's Star of Erin (as the playhouse was then called) enjoyed such wonders as Mademoiselle Miaco, the Boneless Wonder, and Signor Zula, who swung from a high trapeze by his feet, with weights suspended from his teeth. Part of the Olympia's charm may be gauged from the fact that the smaller stalls bar is named, not for some famous performer or patron, but for Kathleen Kelly, who served wit and kindness as well as drink from behind the counter for many decades. The Olympia is the only theater in Dublin that still retains its gallery, or gods, from whose dizzying heights one can see the tops of the performers' heads far below. Also notable are the Waterford cut-glass chandeliers and the two huge mirrors on either side of the circle in which the spectators can monitor their own reactions while watching the performance. And, though television has meant the end of theatrical variety, the Olympia still presents concerts and pantomimes as well as plays, both Irish and foreign, and hosts visiting performers such as mime king Marcel Marceau. After each show, the bars remain open for half an hour; the actors congregate in Kelly's to drink to the memory of days gone by. Details: Olympia Theatre, Dame St., Dublin 2, Irish Republic (phone: 01-778962).

ROYAL DUBLIN SOCIETY CONCERT HALL, Dublin, Irish Republic: While most people think of traditional Irish music when they think of Dublin, it's also true that high-quality classical music can be found here. This is at least in part thanks to the Royal Dublin Society, which stages recitals from November to March in its 1,206-seat Members' Hall, also known as the RDS Concert Hall. Although the acoustics are not all that one might desire for small chamber ensembles and soloists, the attractive book-lined walls add a touch of intimacy that is not often encountered in concert halls nowadays. And a great many distinguished musicians have played at the RDS in recent years — among them the Smetana String Quartet, Isaac Stern, Julian Lloyd Webber, and others. Details: Royal Dublin Society, Ballsbridge, Dublin 4, Irish Republic (phone: 01-680645).

DRUID LANE THEATRE, Galway, County Galway, Irish Republic: Installed in a former grocery warehouse in the oldest part of the city, near the Spanish Arch, the quays, and the old city walls, the home of the Druid Theatre Company is perhaps the most attractive small theater in Ireland, its intimacy enhanced by the way in which the seating surrounds the stage on three sides. The company was founded in 1975 by Garry Hynes, still the artistic director, and in a short time has become renowned for its productions of Irish classics such as Boucicault's *The Colleen Bawn* and Molloy's *Wood of Whispering,* as well as contemporary Irish plays (in particular, those by Tom Murphy) and works from abroad. Upon its recent restaging of Synge's *Playboy of the Western World,* the Druid players were described as "the most consistently original and dynamic theatre company in Ireland." There's good reason to believe that the lane on which the theater is built is haunted by the ghost of a nun who walks slowly through the street at night. But don't let this get in the way of an evening with this exciting young group. Details: Druid Lane Theatre, Druid La. (also known as Chapel La.), Galway, County Galway, Irish Republic (phone: 091-68-617).

SIAMSA TÍRE, THE NATIONAL FOLK THEATRE OF IRELAND, Tralee, County Kerry, Irish Republic: In the evenings of the days before television, the country people of Ireland would gather around a turf fire to play music, sing songs, tell stories, and just recount the day's activities. Such an occasion was called a *siamsa* (pronounced *shee-am-sah*) and down in "The Kingdom," as Kerry is called, Siamsa Tíre has taken the spirit of those days of neighborly entertainment and translated it into a stage show that has been received with delight not only abroad but, proof of its faithfulness to tradition, in Ireland itself. The show *Siamsa,* which critic Clive Barnes acclaimed as "absolutely superb," is a whirlwind of song, dance, and music in three acts that recreates a time when life was simpler, certainly harder, but perhaps more rewarding in its closeness to nature. Watching it in Siamsa Tíre's fine new theater in Tralee seems like sitting in a country kitchen long ago. *Siamsa* is not only a recreation of the past, but also a proof of the liveliness of those traditions. June through September. Information: Siamsa Tíre Theatre, Godfrey Pl., Tralee, County Kerry, Irish Republic (phone: 066-23055).

GRAND OPERA HOUSE, Belfast, Northern Ireland: When architect Robert McKinstry first went into the deserted building of Belfast's Grand Opera House and Cirque in the summer of 1975, he found the house manager's black jacket still hanging on the back of his office door. Crates of bottled beer stood unopened behind the bar where 4 years of dust topped the dour liquids in the half-empty glasses. An upturned chair floated in the orchestra pit. The ashtrays on the backs of the seats in the circle were stuffed with the detritus of chocolate box wrappings and butts of now unfashionable local cigarette brands. In a drawer in the projection room lay a single copy of a pamphlet entitled *How to Emigrate.* But now the Opera House has come back to life. The brass rails that once reflected the footlights that illuminated Pavlova and the "Divine Sarah" (Bernhardt) glisten again, and the turn-of-the-century theater has been restored to its full plush and stucco glory. Christmas pantomimes share the bill with drama companies from all over Britain and Ireland, international opera and ballet companies, and major popular entertainers — among them the likes of the National Theatre, the Royal Flanders Ballet, the Centaur Theatre of Montreal, the Berlin Chamber Orchestra, Carlo Bergonzi, the Scottish Ballet, Tom Paxton, the Moscow Balalaika Orchestra, a harp ensemble from Japan, the Peking Opera, James Galway, the Chieftains, and modern dancers from New York. Note that in July and early August, the house is usually dark. Details: Grand Opera House, Great Victoria St., Belfast BT2 7HR, Northern Ireland (phone: 0232-249129 for recorded information; 0232-241919 for advance booking).

TRADITIONAL IRISH MUSIC

Though there are more concerts, folk festivals, folk clubs, and informal sessions of music-making in Ireland than ever before, those magical nights of wild sweet music and hilarity are still as elusive as the rainbow's end. You might hit upon the right pub on the wrong night, or settle yourself down beside a stack of musicians only to find that they're more of a mind to chat with each other than lash out the reels. Before you set out to fill your ears with concertinas and flutes, it's useful to have a pretty good idea about where you might expect to find them.

For Dublin, you'll find a thorough listing of the traditional goings-on in the fortnightly magazine *In Dublin,* the monthly *What's On In Dublin* guide from the local tourist office, and in the ads in the evening newspapers. Some of the best choices in the capital are the famous *O'Donoghue's* at 15 Merrion Row; its neighbor at 1 Merrion Row, *Foley's;* atmospheric *Kitty O'Shea's* at 23/25 Upper Grand Canal Rd.; the *Abbey Tavern* in the seaside village of Howth north of the city, heavily beamed and warmed by turf fires; and the creaking old *Brazen Head,* said to be the city's oldest pub and located at the end of a cobblestone courtyard near the Liffey at 20 Lower Bridge St.

For information about concerts, folk clubs, and festivals around the country, see the Folk Column in Friday's *Evening Press.* Also, before leaving Dublin, stop in at the elegant Belgrave Square, Monkstown, headquarters of the Comhaltas Ceoltóirí Éireann (phone: 01-800295) where there is entertainment nightly. The CCÉ has traditional music concerts, shows, and informal sessions nightly from May through September and on Friday and Saturday nights the year round; it also sponsors the All-Ireland Festival every year on the fourth weekend in August, a Mardi Gras of Irish traditional music that attracts up to 100,000 people. The office can provide the particulars and can tell you where to find traditional music "down the country."

The mountainous area of County Kerry known as Sliabh Luachra, with its bordering county of North Cork, the land of melodeons, polkas, and slides, is one of the few places in Ireland where people still dance to the music; for as long as anyone can remember, traditional music and dancing have thrived here, and today many an Irish traditional music lover will tell you that there are more active musicians and dancers per acre than in any other Irish country district. In tiny Knocknagree, in northwest Cork, the locals — including more than one sprightly octogenarian — have been tripping it out every Friday and Sunday night for a couple of decades at *Dan O'Connell's,* to the accordion music of Johnny O'Leary, widely reckoned among the most original masters of the squeezebox in Britain and Ireland; he founded the sessions with the late Denis Murphy, one of the best pupils of that great fiddle master Padraig O'Keeffe. Rathmore is known for its music pubs, as are Newmarket, Kenmare, Scartlaglen, Ballydesmond, and Kanturk, birthplace of the accordionist Jackie Daly, who used to play with the group De Danann. Traveling west through Kerry, there's traditional music in various pubs in Tralee and in Irish-speaking Dingle. In the *Great Southern Hotel* in Killarney and at the National Folk Theatre of Ireland in nearby Tralee, you can experience the "Siamsa Tíre," described above. During July and August, similar sessions take place weekly at Finuge, 3 miles from Listowel, and Carraig, 6 miles from Dingle. *Ceolann* — in the village of Lixnaw, between Tralee and Listowel — provides periodic concerts and *ceili* dances; an *oiche cheoil,* or Irish Night, is held the first Friday of the month, and all these festivities give the visitor a chance to enjoy and join in the musicmaking and dancing.

Killarney is also known for its organized pub music sessions — you'll find them at *The Danny Mann* on New Street and *The Laurels* on Main Street. Spontaneous strains can be heard issuing from the *Dunloe Lodge* on Plunkett Street. In northern Kerry, on the border of County Limerick, the tiny town of Glin is famous for its storybook castle and for the music sessions at *O'Shaughnessy's Pub* on the main square. A *bodhrán,* fiddle, and accordian are a permanent part of the decor here, even when no one is playing them at the regular daytime gatherings. (Note: This pub closes at 7 PM.)

The Dingle Peninsula is also known for traditional music. Venues include *An Bóthar* at Brandon Creek, Ballydavid; *Tigh Ui Murchu (Murphy's Bar)* at Ballyferriter; the *Ventry Inn* at Ventry; *Garvey's, O'Flaherty's,* and *Murphy's* of Dingle Town; *Duchas House* at Tralee; and *Kruger's* of Dunquin, named after the Boer War leader Paul Kruger who is described in a locally famous poem of Brendan Behan's.

In Clare, which locals deem the home of the very best Irish music, the community of Miltown Malbay hosts the week-long *Scoil Samraidh Willie Clancy,* a traditional music school that draws the county's finest musicians for nonstop music sessions — in the pubs and hotels, on street corners, and in tents and under open skies all day and all night during the first week in July. In Ennis, often regarded as the center of Irish traditional music, *Kelly's* pub on Carmody Street has good weekend sessions, while out on the Galway Road, the new cultural auditorium, the *Cois na hAbhna,* has programs from Wednesdays through Saturdays during the winter months for those who want to learn the steps of Irish set dancing. Mondays, Thursdays, and Saturdays in July and August are also lively, with tea and scones and a show served to visitors along with songs and dances and chat. The *Fleadh Nua,* a late-May weekend of music and dancing in Ennis, is definitely worth planning for. Kilmihil, Mullagh, Feakle, and Tulla (home of the Tulla Céilí Band, still going strong now after some four decades) are good bets throughout the year. At *Gus O'Connor's,* a homey pub in Doolin with lobster pots hanging from the ceiling and photos of local musicians on the walls (and a menu of pub grub available in a new restaurant on the premises), Micho Russell can often be found playing his tin whistle in the simple, centuries-old style he learned over 50 years ago. The place itself was established in 1832 and has been owned by the same family for six generations. Other Clare towns that are favorites with traditional musicians are

Kilrush (home of *Crotty's*) and Ballyvaughan (home of *The Inn* and *Monk's Harbour Bar*).

In neighboring County Cork, best-known spots include the *Folk House,* the *Spaniard,* and the *Shanakee* in Kinsale; *Craigie's* at Castletownbere; and the *Clock House Bar* in Mallow. In Cork City, the best are *An Bodhrán, DeLacy House,* and the *Courthouse Tavern.*

Galway City is known for its swans, the soft speech of its natives, and *Cullens,* in whose cozy rooms musicians can be found just about any night of the week — and sometimes during the day as well. The *Quays, Flanagan's,* and the *Crane* also have music; the latter has established itself as the city's leading traditional music pub over the past few years and offers sessions not only every night but also on Sunday mornings, with some of the finest musicians in the country. Another favorite is the *King's Head* on High Street, where traditional music is performed nightly in the back room. In Salthill, within walking distance of the city center, the *Cottage Bar* and *Faherty's* pub occasionally resound to a few fiddles and banjos (the former on almost any night of the week). Galway is also the gateway to rocky, desertlike, Irish-speaking Connemara, where the musical emphasis is not so much on instruments as on songs, which are sung in the *sean nós* style — solo, heavily ornamented, unaccompanied, and in Irish. Look for music at *An Droighnean Donn* and *Hughes* pubs, in the town of An Spideal and at *Teach Furbo,* farther into the country. in tiny Cleggan, 10 miles from Clifden, Connemara's capital, there are sessions at the *Pier Bar* on Fridays. Some nights on Inishbofin Island, musicians blast away at *Day's* pub until long after licensing hours — since no *gardai* live on the island, its pubs never have to close. With any luck, you should also find good music in East Galway, around Ballinakill, Woodford, and Loughrea, where Moylan's has a long-standing Saturday night session.

Donegal is fiddle country and it's scarcely possible to pass through it without hearing about the Fiddler King, Johnny Doherty, born in Fintown in 1895 into a family of traveling musicians and tinsmiths; until his recent death, this little town drew many musicians and listeners who came to hear him play. Now a noteworthy spot for great bowing (nightly), *Teach Hiudai Bhig* in Bunbeg also has the traditional after-Mass get-together on Sunday mornings. *Teach Leo,* in the village of Crolly, is also a good bet for music, particularly when the local group Clannad, now internationally known, is at home. In Donegal Town, it's at the *Talk of the Town* where musicians gather for a song or two. The island of Arranmore — only a 70p ferry ride from Burtonport — exists in another time and another world, and the sessions go on into the wee hours at Bernadette and Tony Cox's Plohogue pub (tucked away at the less frequented top end of the island). Musicians come from the mainland and from Belfast. In August, don't miss the Festival of International Folk Music in Letterkenny.

In County Mayo, musicians gather on summer evenings at the *Asgard Tavern* on the Quay in Westport.

Also, the area of South Sligo and North Roscommon is great flute and fiddle country. The local newspapers will note who is playing and where — usually on weekends around Ballymote, Gurteen, and Boyle. Pubs in this area known for their traditional music sessions include *Ellen's* at Maugherow, one of the last of the old Irish thatch-roofed establishments; *The Thatch* at Ballisodare; *Laura's* at Carney; and *McLynn's* and the *Yeats Tavern* in Sligo Town.

As for the cities, in Limerick, the venue of choice is the *Lucky Lamp;* in Wexford, *Tim's Tavern;* and in Waterford, the *Munster Bar* and *T. & H. Doolan.*

Northern Ireland has a music all its own — a plaintive, almost eerie blend of fiddles and flutes, with long spare notes and little ornamentation — closer to that of the Shetland Islands or Sweden than to Kerry's frolicsome polkas and slides. They are all performed with great verve in many parts, nowhere more so than in Belfast, which has seen a remarkable resurgence of nightlife of late. There are informal traditional Irish music sessions in a number of Docks area pubs such as *Pat's Bar* at 109 Princes Dock and the *Rotterdam* in Pilot Street, which have sessions on most nights, and at hotels in the downtown area. At *Harper's Bar* in the *Europa* hotel, Friday is the night when the rafters ring with traditional Irish music.

Belfast's folk club scene is also good. Try the *Sunflower Bar* in Corporation Street on Friday nights (where a mid-September folk festival is presented annually), or the *Errigle Inn* in Ormeau Road on Tuesdays. The *Errigle* on Ormeau Road has folk music on Mondays, while the atmospheric *Blackthorn Bar* on Church Street is a good pub in which to hear the more traditional types of Irish music on Tuesdays and Saturdays. For a similar type of musical offering, *Fealty's* on High Street in Bangor, County Down, is particularly lively on Wednesday, Friday, and Saturday nights. *Grace Neill's* at Donaghadee, County Down, is very spontaneous, though Friday and Saturday nights tend to be liveliest; and *Balloo House* in Killinchy, County Down, is a good bet for a more folky type of music on Tuesdays.

In County Antrim, Irish music is played enthusiastically, especially in and around the Glens, and the town of Portglenone is noted for its fine sessions. Also highly recommended is the beautiful thatched-roof *Crosskeys Inn* off the main Randalstown–Portglenone Road outside Toomebridge, where, on a Saturday night, you might find four sessions at once and turf fires warming the old kitchen, one of the loveliest sections of the premises.

In County Fermanagh, *Blakes of the Hollow* in Enniskillen turns musical on Friday and Saturday nights. See *Pub Crawling* for more information about this handsome spot.

Feis and Fleadh: The Best Festivals

 With their wealth of talents in so many fields it's hardly surprising that Britain and Ireland should be blossoming with festivals. What is surprising is that, not depending for a moment on the possibility of the summer being warm and sunny, they take place virtually year-round and last anywhere from a day or a week to a month or even a whole summer. Some are oddball festivals devoted to snuff-taking or pancake-racing; some are rooted in centuries-old tradition, with plenty of Morris dancing, craft displays, and brass band music. The British Tourist Authority publishes *Customs and Pageantry,* which describes a number of these.

In Ireland, all during the summer, when the evenings are long and the weather is warm, there are rallies and angling competitions, horse shows and country fairs, and people stand around in their town's main square listening to bands and ballad singers, meeting neighbors they mightn't have had a proper chance to speak to since the previous year's event. There is a very good reason for this abundance of festivals: During festival times, the draconian Irish licensing laws ease up a bit, and all bars are allowed to stay open a bit later than usual (though in the cities, late night drinking — that great source of Irish joy — is confined to a single appointed place). Consequently, the atmosphere is usually jolly, and there is generally a feeling that something is actually happening.

Music festivals are increasingly abundant. In Ireland, for instance, Cork holds an International Jazz Festival annually in late October, and Dublin holds a Festival of Music in Great Irish Houses every June. Also, the number of Woodstock-style music festivals, with acres of tents and dozens of superstars, is growing. These are held mainly in June and July and can, if the weather is good, be very enjoyable. The same goes for the kind of event known in Ireland as a *fleadh cheoil* ("festival of music"), which can be found almost every weekend in summer all over Ireland. The festivals manage an extraordinary combination of sixties bonhomie and the long-standing Irish tradition of playing music at fairs. Whether you take in the biggest of the breed, the All-Ireland Festival (the *Fleadh Cheoil na hEireann*), which generally takes place the fourth weekend in August, or one of the smaller affairs, the experience is usually fairly unbelievable. Thousands of people, young and old, take over the host town. Guest-houses and hotels don't have a bed to spare, ordinary homes turn into lodging places, and the young put up tents. People drink in the streets and day and night the music continues on and on. Many of the best interpreters of Irish traditional music and dance show up for performances and competitions alike (so it is not all just drinking and carousing). The size of the throngs who come to listen and take part demonstrates once again how Irish traditional music has grown in importance and popularity over the last decade. For dates, contact the central organizers in Dublin. Comhaltas Ceoltóirí Éireann, 32 Belgrave Sq., Monkstown, County Dublin (phone: 800295).

At the larger events of all types — in addition to all the listed offerings — visitors will still get, like a plum in a pie, the "fringe." The one at the Edinburgh Festival is world-famous (and, to be truthful, sometimes more interesting than the main show, though director Frank Dunlop is bringing a whole new air of excitement to Edinburgh's annual junketings). Add to that the fact that host towns are often *en fête,* too, with floral displays everywhere, and the fact that standards of British catering have been creeping upward enough that there are almost always one or two good restaurants for that all-important socializing over a meal or a drink before and after events — and you've got the makings of a fine vacation. Check also with bodies such as the National Trust, the various Garden Schemes, and local tourist boards as to other area events. If you get hooked on vacationing at such goings-on, you may want to acquire specialized volumes such as Carol Rabin's *Music Festivals in Europe and Britain* ($8.95 postpaid from the Berkshire Traveler Press, Stockbridge, MA 01262; phone: 413-298-3636).

In any event, remember that even though festivals may be full of Serious Events they are also, in a word, fun — and the opportunity to meet and talk with local people who are delighted to welcome foreign visitors is part of the experience. Therein lies a good deal of the charm and pleasure of a country festival, and the memories that go with it. The various tourist boards can provide listings of festivals of all types. Meanwhile, here are some notes on a few of the best.

WORTH A LONG DETOUR

ALDEBURGH FESTIVAL, Aldeburgh, Suffolk, England: Beloved by musicians the world over for its warmth, intimacy, and exceptionally fine acoustics, the remarkable concert hall established by composer Benjamin Britten and tenor Peter Pears is the focal point for this quaint little sea town's annual mid-June festival. A platform for recent developments in British and American music, it also honors the anniversaries of the classical masters. The main concert hall is situated 6 miles from Aldeburgh in Snape; nearby churches and stately homes are also used for the events. The town also holds a Rostropovich Festival in August, with the maestro lending great warmth and charisma; it has also established a reputation for a high standard of music-making. The Britten-Pears School for Advanced Musical Studies, also at Snape, participates in both festivals. Details: Aldeburgh Foundation, High Street, Aldeburgh, Suffolk IP15 5AX, England (phone: 072-885-2935).

ARUNDEL FESTIVAL, Arundel, West Sussex, England: Held annually for 13 days in August, this festival is held in a charming South Downs resort dominated by a Norman castle owned by the premier duke of Great Britain; its panoramic tilting yard is used as an open-air theater for the festival goings-on — performances by the New Shakespeare Company and, each year, special emphasis on one other aspect of the arts.

And there are many other events, ranging from concerts of classical music to gym-khanas. Details: Festival Office, The Mary Gate, Arundel, West Sussex BN18 9AT, England (phone: 0903-883690).

BATH INTERNATIONAL FESTIVAL OF MUSIC, Bath, Avon, England: For 17 days in late May and early June, this magnificent city, famous for its Roman baths and outstanding Georgian architecture, annually offers a catholic choice of concerts by top musicians of all persuasions, from medieval to jazz; informative tours and lectures in historic buildings, houses, and gardens; performances of opera and dance by leading companies; literary events and lectures; films; many art exhibitions, including Britain's only contemporary art fair; relaxed late-night musical shows; and a candlelight procession through the handsome streets. What sets this event apart are the concerts' settings. The performances of choral works and the organ recitals are presented in Bath Abbey or nearby Wells Cathedral, while there are also concerts and operas in handsome halls that date from the late 18th or early 19th century — an *opera buffa,* for instance, in the city's Theatre Royal, an intimate hall refurbished not long ago to its early-19th-century splendor, or a recital or chamber music concert in the elegant Bath Assembly Rooms (ca. 1771), the largest of which, the eggshell blue and gray Ball Room, is illuminated by no less than five 200-year-old chandeliers. During intermissions, visitors promenade through similarly stately, classically proportioned halls; and the route to their hotel leads through streets that seem equally removed from the modern. The spell doesn't let up for a minute. Details: Bath Festival Office, Linley House, 1 Pierrepont Pl., Bath, Avon BA1 1JY, England (phone: 0225-62231).

BRIGHTON FESTIVAL, Brighton, East Sussex, England: Brighton, that strange mixture of the beautiful, with its Regency buildings, and the raffishness typical of a popular seaside resort, is always a joy to visit — but never more than during the 3 weeks in May when the Brighton Festival fills the town with music, both classical and popular, in recitals, chamber and orchestral concerts, and operas, as well as programs of jazz and rock, dance and drama, art exhibitions, and seminars and workshops. There's also a dramatic fireworks display, some sheepdog trials and guided walks, a bric-a-brac market, and open house at local artists' studios, plus a grand procession by the light of hundreds of real torches. Details: Festival Office, Marlborough House, 54 Old Steine, Brighton, East Sussex BN1 1EQ, England (phone: 0273-26894).

BUXTON FESTIVAL, Buxton, Derbyshire, England: The plays, operas, films, and lectures presented in this attractive Georgian spa town's elegant Edwardian opera house and its fine concert hall as part of this young and still rapidly developing 3-week midsummer event focus on a figure from the world of literature, such as King Arthur or Shakespeare, and his or her influence on the arts. Buxton's productions of lesser-known operas have put it on the map alongside such events as those in Bayreuth and Glyndebourne. The town nestles amid the rugged hills of central England's Derbyshire Peak District and is easily accessible from Manchester. Details: Festival Office, Hall Bank, Buxton, Derbyshire SK17 6EN, England (phone: 0298-70395).

CHELTENHAM INTERNATIONAL FESTIVAL OF MUSIC, Cheltenham, Gloucestershire, England: This delightful Regency spa town's annual July festival (held for 2 weeks in some very historic places in the Cotswolds vicinity) presents a wide range of music, with a bias toward the contemporary and the British; some works are commissioned especially for the event. There are master classes, recitals, chamber music and orchestral programs, opera, ballet, and more. The Cheltenham Festival of Literature, which runs for a fortnight in October, is the biggest of its kind in the country, with lectures and readings by major authors, poets, and other literary figures, plays and dramatic presentations, and a large book exhibition. Also offered are a program of events for children and a book fair. Details: Town Hall, Cheltenham, Gloucestershire GL50 1QA, England (phone: 0242-521621).

CHICHESTER FESTIVAL THEATRE, Chichester, West Sussex, England: The repertory for this extremely popular theater festival, which runs from May through

September, includes a mixture of the old and the new: The emphasis is on entertaining rather than experimenting, and the most successful plays usually end up in London. During its nearly 30 years of existence, the roster of performers has grown into a veritable *Who's Who* of the English-speaking theater, and the festival has come to be the most important annual theatrical event outside London, Edinburgh, and Stratford. The theater that houses the goings-on is attractively modern, hexagonally shaped, and set in a lovely parkland; every seat is a good one. Other pluses: the new alternative productions of The Studio Company, and Chichester itself, a magical place in some of the most enchanting country in Sussex, sophisticated enough that restaurants keep late hours and chefs serve lobster thermidor as well as steak and kidney pie. Details: Chichester Festival Theatre, Oaklands Park, Chichester, West Sussex PO19 4AP, England (phone: 0243-781312).

THREE CHOIRS FESTIVAL, Gloucester, Gloucestershire, and Hereford and Worcester, Herefordshire and Worcestershire, England: This August annual, the oldest music festival in Europe, highlights the great English tradition of choral singing. The three cathedral choirs join forces with each other and with world-class artists, orchestras, and ensembles from around the world to provide a week of splendid music-making that ranges from the 16th century to the present. A few works are commissioned especially for the occasion, and there's a varied fringe program. The surrounding countryside — the Cotswolds and the Malvern Hills — is wonderfully scenic and full of beautiful old buildings. Details: Festival Office, Community House, College Green, Gloucester GL1 2LX, England.

GLYNDEBOURNE FESTIVAL OPERA, Glyndebourne, East Sussex, England: Founded in 1934 by John Christie and his wife, the singer Audrey Mildmay, and held on their ancient Sussex country estate some 50 miles south of London, this festival now runs from the third week in May to late August. It is top-drawer musically — with artists coming from all over the world — and socially as well: The splendid program of opera (6 productions each summer) is garnished with a 75-minute supper interval — perfect for a meal in one of the restaurants, or for champagne picnics in the gardens and on the velvety English lawns. Details: Glyndebourne Festival, Lewes, East Sussex BN8 5UU, England (phone: 0273-812321).

HAXEY HOOD GAME, Haxey, Humberside, England: One of dozens of English festivals rooted in age-old tradition, this one got started some 600 years ago when Lady Mowbray lost her hood to a sudden gust of wind, and thanked the 13 men who strove gallantly to rescue it by instituting an annual reenactment of the occasion. Thought by some to have been the origin of rugby, the game is played today — on January 6 — by the descendants of those men and their neighbors. The contest involves a Lord, 13 Boggins, a Fool, a bonfire, a no-holds-barred free-for-all in which writhing and grunting masses of humanity struggle for long hours over a piece of leather stuffed with straw, coins, and other fillings, and equally drawn-out victory celebrations in the local pubs. Details: Tourist Information Centre, Doncaster Central Library, Waterdale, Doncaster, South Yorkshire DN1 3JE, England (phone: 0302-734306).

GREENWICH FESTIVAL, London, England: The events of this annual 2-week-long June festival include operas; mime and dance performances; poetry readings; concerts of rock, reggae, jazz, classical, and folk music; as well as many children's events. Internationally known artists such as Janet Baker, Claudio Arrau, James Galway, Alfred Brendel, and others perform alongside amateurs and local groups: The Greenwich Festival began as a purely community-oriented affair. Greenwich itself is a historic town on the banks of the Thames, and the magnificence and variety of its concert locations make its festival very special indeed. Details: Greenwich Festival Office, 25 Woolwich New Rd., London SE18 6EU, England (phone: 01-317-8687).

ANNUAL BOTTLE KICKING AND HARE PIE SCRAMBLE, Hallaton, Leicestershire, England: When the *Guardian* described this small village's 700-year-old Easter Monday event, the high point on the village calendar, as being "unsurpassed for sheer animal ferocity," it wasn't far from wrong. As the opposing two teams from neighboring villages scramble to maneuver two out of three small wooden beer kegs across a goal line, the field is sheer anarchy — a situation that may have something to do with the fact that every now and again each player drops out to have another pint. Details: East Midlands Tourist Board, Exchequergate, Lincoln, Lincolnshire LN2 1PZ, England (phone: 0522-31521).

HARROGATE INTERNATIONAL FESTIVAL, Harrogate, North Yorkshire, England: Elegant buildings stand beside modern facilities in this Victorian spa town. The new Harrogate Spring Music festival in early May features some of the world's greatest artists performing music in an informal atmosphere. The 2-week festival in July and August embraces all the arts and, from time to time, the sciences as well. In the various halls and churches used during the event, among them the 9th-century Ripon Cathedral, a visitor will encounter orchestral and chamber music, celebrity recitals, plays, late night shows, literary events, and programs for children. Details: Festival Office, Royal Baths, Harrogate, North Yorkshire HG1 2RR, England (phone: 0423-62303).

CITY OF LONDON FESTIVAL, London, England: London's own festival, held for 3 weeks in July within the old city's square mile, takes advantage of the area's many fine halls and churches — including the Tower of London, Guildhall, the Barbican Centre, and St. Paul's itself — for concerts of serious music, featuring choirs, orchestras, chamber groups, and leading soloists of international repute. Running concurrently is a popular program of jazz, cabaret, poetry, dance, and a wide range of exhibitions. Details: City of London Festival Box Office, St. Paul's Churchyard, London EC4M 8BU (01-236-2801).

LONDON-TO-BRIGHTON VETERAN CAR RUN, London, England: Until 1896, one now-amusing British law prohibited the operation of a car unless it was preceded by a man on foot carrying a red flag (so as not to scare horses). Its repeal is the *raison d'être* for this 50-mile drive full of shiny antique autos, held annually on the first Sunday in November. Details: RAC Motor Sports Division, Ltd., 31 Belgrave Sq., London SW1X 8QH, England (phone: 01-235-8601).

LORD MAYOR'S PROCESSION, London, England: For this event, held annually on the second Saturday in November, the newly inaugurated Lord Mayor and the profession that he is leaving for the duration of his term are honored. The Lord Mayor is transported in an 18th-century gold State coach drawn by six gray horses. Leaving Guildhall, the destination is the Royal Court of Justice, where the oath of office is administered. The Lord Mayor inaugurated in 1988 will be the 660th to hold the position since it was established in 1189. Wonderfully colorful. Details: City of London Public Relations Office, Guildhall, London EC2P 2EJ, England (phone: 01-606-3030, ext. 1450 to 1455).

MALVERN FESTIVAL, Malvern, Worcestershire, England: In 1929, Sir Barry Jackson directed the first Malvern Festival, George Bernard Shaw wrote plays especially for it, and Edward Elgar conducted his own compositions at it. The Malvern Festival provides an environment in which new works can be presented, new composers heard, and new drama productions introduced. The Fringe is the largest in Britain outside Edinburgh. Of course, Elgar and Shaw still play a part. The picturesque Malvern Hills are within easy reach of the Cotswolds and Wales. Details: Malvern Festival Promotions, Malvern, Worcestershire WR14 3HB, England (phone: 06845-2700).

KING'S LYNN FESTIVAL, King's Lynn, Norfolk, England: The Queen Mother is the patron of this late July week of art exhibitions and classical music, both serious and light, plus jazz, puppetry, children's programs, theater, film, talks, and late night shows — and she usually attends. Street shows and fireworks are part of a fringe that rounds out the program. The site, an ancient market town riddled with quaint streets, curious churches, and historic buildings, is also a delight. Details: King's Lynn Festival, 27 King St., King's Lynn, Norfolk PE30 1HA, England (phone: 0553-773578).

HOBBY HORSE CELEBRATIONS, Padstow, Cornwall, England: Among Europe's oldest festivals, this annual May Day event brings this sleepy seaport town to life. Caroling and carousing go on all night, but the real highlight of the affair is a long parade in which the Hobby Horse — a fabulous creature with a fierce-looking cone-shaped head protruding through a black, sailcloth-covered hoop — acts out a skit in which he dies and is revived over and over, then, at day's end, prances around a Maypole. Details: West Country Tourist Board, Trinity Ct., 37 Southernhay E, Exeter, Devon EX1 1QS, England (phone: 0392-76351).

SALISBURY FESTIVAL, Salisbury, Wiltshire, England: This 2-week-long September event, one of the leading cultural affairs in the South of England, includes lovely concerts by candlelight in the cathedral, operas and plays, a variety of late evening shows, and assorted outdoor events. There are many points of interest in the region — mysterious prehistoric Stonehenge and the charming Wilton House among them — and Salisbury itself is a fine ancient town. Details: Salisbury Festival, The King's House, 65 The Close, Salisbury, Wiltshire SP1 2EN, England (phone: 0722-23883).

YORK EARLY MUSIC FESTIVAL, York, North Yorkshire, England: Ancient York is the ideal setting for this July annual, one of the world's leading festivals devoted to music from medieval to classical. Concert venues are historic — public buildings and country houses. Early dance workshops, medieval drama productions, talks, and exhibitions round out the program of concerts. Details: York Early Music Festival, 1 Museum St., York YO1 2DT (phone: 0904-58338).

YORK FESTIVAL AND MYSTERY PLAYS, York, North Yorkshire, England: Every four years, during June and July, this historic city gives itself over to one of the country's largest festivals. The focal point is the cycle of mystery plays that take place outdoors nightly in the magnificent ruined St. Mary's Abbey, but there are also concerts in the minster and in historic churches throughout the city, as well as plays and other sport and outdoor entertainments, which are held in pubs, clubs, streets, and various community venues of modern York. In intervening years, the city hosts the York Early Music Festival, described above. Details: York Festival Office, De Grey Rooms, Exhibition Square, York, North Yorkshire YO1 2DT, England (phone: 0904-610266).

EDINBURGH FESTIVAL, Edinburgh, Scotland: During its 3-week run in late August, this grande dame of festivals offers a cornucopia of activities. Most of the city's bigger public buildings, as well as many smaller ones, are taken over for exhibitions, performances, lectures, conferences, master classes, and other cultural affairs of global significance or for nearly 960 more presentations of the Festival Fringe, which the *Guinness Book of World Records* lists as the largest arts festival in the world. The Fringe, nowadays more straightforward than experimental, gives particular encouragement to comics; past performers have included Dudley Moore as well as Michael Palin and Terry Jones, later of the Monty Python team. There, as at the festival proper, patrons also find music, dance, theater, opera, and the visual arts represented; there are many world premieres. The artists are the best in the world, and the audiences are big and international. The colorful Tattoo that takes place at the castle every night is almost as popular as the musical goings-on. A book festival, a film festival, and a jazz festival run concurrently. Details: Festival Society, 21 Market St., Edinburgh EH1 1BW, Scotland (phone: 031-226-4001), and the Festival Fringe Society, 170 High St., Edinburgh EH1 1QS, Scotland (phone: 031-226-5257 or 031-226-5259).

UP-HELLY-AA, Lerwick, Shetland Isles, Scotland: This traditional annual ceremony takes place toward the end of January to celebrate the end of the winter solstice. Dating back to times when the islanders were compelled by their rulers to embrace Christian beliefs, but were indeed holding on to their pagan Norse ways, this celebration was their way of marking the ending of the Christian holy days of Christmas. Each year a Viking galley is built and transported in torchlight procession by the up to 900 Shetlanders dressed in Viking or fancy dress costume to the park where the torches are put to use as fire starters for the ship. After the blaze has reached the skies, the "guizers" visit each of several halls open to invited guests, where they perform a sketch inspired by their garb, then dance the night away. Details: Shetland Tourist Organisation, Market Cross, Lerwick, Shetland ZEI 0LU, Scotland (phone: 0595-3434).

FISHGUARD MUSIC FESTIVAL, Fishguard, Dyfed, Wales: The renowned Welsh choral tradition has generated this week-long July annual. The music is mainly classical, but new works are commissioned for performance by visiting musicians from home and abroad; and there's also jazz, poetry, film, and art. The festival often ends with the presentation of a large choral work. Many concerts take place in ancient St. David's Cathedral and in Fishguard. The setting for the 1971 filming of Dylan Thomas's *Under Milk Wood* starring Richard Burton, this town on the edge of Pembrokeshire National Park is beautiful — backed by cliffs and partially edged by a shingled beach. Details: Fishguard Music Festival Office, Fishguard, Pembrokeshire, Dyfed SA65 9BJ, Wales (phone: 0348-873612).

INTERNATIONAL MUSICAL EISTEDDFOD, Llangollen, Clwyd, Wales: Music and friendship abound here for a week in July as over 10,000 competitors from 30 countries from Hungary and Bulgaria to Norway, Italy, South Africa, the US, and others compete in folk song and dance competitions and choir contests. Evening concerts are given by choirs, dance groups, and renowned singers and instrumentalists. The colors, costumes, and sounds are dazzling, and there's always a special moment — as when an American choir and a Russian chorus got together and sang the Welsh national anthem, in Welsh, or when a group of Zulu dancers swept onstage, interrupting the national anthems, to present the festival's music director with their tribe's highest honor. In 1987, the Choir of the World competition was instituted in which this title is bestowed on the men's, women's, and mixed choirs deemed best in each category. Details: Eisteddfod Office, Llangollen, Clwyd LL20 8NG, Wales (phone: 0978-860236).

ST. PATRICK'S WEEK, countrywide, Irish Republic: Irishmen from around the world come to the Auld Sod to celebrate the feast day of the nation's patron saint. In Dublin, the week beforehand means concerts of music and dancing on St. Stephen's Green, Gaelic football and hurling, and horse racing; and there's a mammoth parade, with military bands, accordion bands, fife and drum bands, flute bands, marching bands, pipe bands, and show bands from all over the world, not to mention enormous crowds. It goes without saying that all the pubs and cabarets are jammed (though there's none of the green beer so beloved in stateside bars). The citizens of other Irish cities are almost as wild. Details: Irish Tourist Board, 757 Third Ave., New York, NY 10017 (phone: 212-418-0800).

DUBLIN THEATRE FESTIVAL, Dublin, Irish Republic: For the last week in September and the first in October, the Irish theater goes mad. Plays open daily — new plays by contemporary Irish authors, high classics by late Irish playwrights, productions by visiting theater companies, late night revues, mime shows. Actors get work, directors get work, would-be theater critics get work. Theater people are all very happy. And so are visitors. Those who like light comedies will be as gleeful as those who swear by experimental theater. Anyone with stamina and eclectic tastes could spend both weeks watching plays and then rounding off each night in a special Festival Club where all the casts usually congregate, along with directors and critics. Increasingly, especially since the introduction of the Irish Plays weekend, the festival seems to be functioning as a showcase for new works by Irishmen like Tom Murphy, Hugh Leonard, Stewart Parker, Brian Friel, and J. Graham Reid. Visitors are generally surprised by the quality of the productions. Details: Dublin Theatre Festival, 47 Nassau St., Dublin 2, Irish Republic (phone: 01-778439).

DUN LAOGHAIRE SUMMER FESTIVAL, Dun Laoghaire, County Dublin, Irish Republic: During the last week in June, this old, prosperous, well-kept borough 6 miles from Dublin, which, although increasingly a bedroom community, continues to retain its own essentially Victorian style, goes culture-mad. There are exhibits of old photographs and paintings, art shows and musical soirées in the Maritime Institute on High Street, tours of the area and trips to pretty Dalkey Island, balls, a regatta, lectures, air-sea rescue demonstrations, parades, athletics, concerts of all types and descriptions featuring everything from light classical fare to sea chanteys and other traditional music, and, for children, afternoon Punch and Judy shows, theater workshops, and windsurfing exhibitions — in short, a little something for everyone. Dun Laoghaire also has a good harbor, which on fine summer days fills up with lovely boats and yachts, and favorite swimming holes like Killiney, Seapoint, and the Forty-Foot are just down the road. Details: Festival Director, Marina Rd., Dun Laoghaire, County Dublin, Irish Republic (phone: 01-742740).

GALWAY INTERNATIONAL OYSTER FESTIVAL, Galway, County Galway, Irish Republic: This city on Ireland's western seaboard, colonized in the 16th century by Elizabethan planters, and the surrounding bays have always been famous for their oysters and scallops. In recent years local agencies and fishing cooperatives have actually farmed them. So it's only appropriate that the big annual wingding here, traditionally held during the last weekend in September just as the shellfish come back into season after a succession of R-less months, is devoted to the succulent creature; after all the cultural festivals, this is the place to come and relax. The festival begins with the Irish Oyster-Opening Championship; people come from around the globe to take part in the World Oyster-Opening Championship that takes place a couple of days later; and, throughout the festival, there are yacht races, golf competitions, and other festivities. After all these activities, head for the pubs of Clarenbridge, where many a tasty bivalve slips down an eager throat on a stream of foaming stout. Or take a boat or plane to the Aran Islands. Or explore the city: Tudor doorways and coats of arms are still visible in Shop Street. Details: Áras Fáilte, Victoria Pl., Galway, Irish Republic (phone: 091-63081).

GOREY ARTS FESTIVAL, Gorey, County Wexford, Irish Republic: For the first 2 weeks in August anything can happen in Gorey. One night there's jazz, the next a puppet show or a performance by Ireland's newest rock band (U2 got its start here) or perhaps mainstream theater. When the major exhibitions of painting and photography that take place at the same time are included, not to mention the readings, the writing workshops, and the master classes in both classical and Irish traditional music, it seems that there is, literally, something for everyone. Paul Funge, the Irish painter who designed and built the exhibition area and theater where most of these events take place, is, in the words of Irish art critic Adrian Dunne, "the mercurial superstar of the Irish art scene." Though Funge is still only in his midthirties, what happens in Gorey is a reflection of his many talents. And as he moves toward the avant-garde and the experimental, so do the goings-on. The festival, and indeed the town, are served by two wonderful hostelries — friendly, efficient, and cavernlike *French's Bar* on Main Street, and across the road, the *Railway* hotel, which, since nothing has been touched for years, has the feeling of the Ireland of 40 years ago. To take a break, there are always the beaches at nearby Courtown and Ardamine. Details: Gorey Arts Festival, Rafter St., Gorey, County Wexford, Irish Republic (phone: 055-21470).

KILKENNY ARTS WEEK, Kilkenny, County Kilkenny, Irish Republic: Established enough to have acquired a fringe, this event held at the end of August or the beginning of September benefits greatly from being held in one of the most pleasant and prosperous of Irish towns, not to mention from the presence there of a group of very comfortable hotels, and a location which makes it feasible to drive down from Dublin (a matter of a couple of hours), have a drink in *The Marble City* or *Tynan's Bar,* catch a lunchtime concert, browse through the arts and crafts exhibitions, see the city's many interesting sights, attend an evening concert in acoustically excellent St. Canice's Cathedral, stop in at the Arts Week Club to make merry until all hours of the night

— and then, for those who are still not worn out, drive back to Dublin. Many writers — poets Robert Lowell and Ted Hughes among them — have read their work here; but music is the main thing, and many of the performers are internationally known. Traditional music and folk songs are on the program along with classical works. Details: Kilkenny Arts Week, Butler House, Patrick St., Kilkenny, County Kilkenny, Irish Republic (phone: 056-21667).

LISTOWEL WRITERS' WEEK, Listowel, County Kerry, Irish Republic: Listowel is the chief town and center of an area distinguished by its writers, among them playwright John B. Keane, who runs a pub here, the short story writer Brian MacMahon, and the poets Brendan Kennally and Gabriel Fitzmaurice, who are the presiding spirits of this increasingly popular and enjoyable festival usually held during early June. They hold workshops in drama, poetry, fiction, and other literary disciplines for aspiring writers; produce plays by young and established Irish writers alike; launch books; stage lectures on many aspects of contemporary Irish writing; and host readings from their own work and that of other writers, Irish and otherwise. Yet the atmosphere is anything but academic. There are musical concerts and art exhibitions, and people are interested in enjoying themselves — and have been known to go on doing so all night. There may be plenty of shop talk, but equal time is apt to be given to the upcoming tennis matches at Wimbledon, or to the previous night's hoopla. The pubs are very friendly, and often, a musician in the crowd will suddenly bring out his instrument for a round of something traditional and Irish. There's also an official club where a band plays dance music, and the assembled writers, aspiring writers, and other attendant festive spirits — when not drinking — leap about the floor. Details: The Secretary, Listowel Writers' Week, St. Patrick's Hall, Listowel, County Kerry, Irish Republic (phone: 068-21074).

ROSE OF TRALEE INTERNATIONAL FESTIVAL, Tralee, County Kerry, Irish Republic: Nowadays, nobody takes the competitive element of this beauty-contest-with-a-difference too seriously. But girls still come from all over the world at the end of August or the first of September to vie for a Waterford crystal trophy and the title "Rose of Tralee," first made famous by tenor John McCormack: "She was lovely and fair/Like a Rose of the summer/Yet it was not her beauty alone that won me/O no it was the truth in her eyes ever dawning/That made me love Mary, the Rose of Tralee." But this 6-day event goes beyond McCormack and, as a sort of Irish Mardi Gras, provides an extraordinary range of entertainment, from donkey and greyhound races and tugs-of-war to fireworks, brass band concerts, performances of traditional music, cabarets, and much more. At any given moment it might be possible to find four or five acts going on in different parts of the town, and people roam the streets from early morning until late at night. There's always something happening, and most of it is free. Nearly 100,000 attend. Details: Festival of Kerry, 5 Lower Castle St., Tralee, County Kerry, Irish Republic (phone: 066-21322).

NATIONAL PILGRIMAGE TO CROAGH PATRICK, Westport, County Mayo, Irish Republic: Annually on the last Sunday in July, hundreds of pilgrims follow in the footsteps of Patrick, the good saint who had what some might call a masochist's knack for concocting ways of doing penance. Barefooted, sometimes crawling on his knees, he would make his way over thorns and jagged rocks, through mud and water, to the summit of this mountain. As he did then, his followers do today — and, once at the top, celebrate Mass in a little oratory. Details: Tourist Office, The Mall, Westport, County Mayo, Irish Republic (phone: 098-25711).

WEXFORD FESTIVAL OPERA, Wexford, County Wexford, Irish Republic: In the latter half of October when the nights get long and cold, this harbor town comes alive with an event that, from a social point of view alone, is probably one of the most enjoyable in Ireland, and the town's narrow winding streets fill with opera lovers from all over the world. The festival's long drawing card is the opera — usually two seldom-performed works by well-known composers and one contemporary opus. Ticket prices are low even by European standards, and performance quality is very high, as it has been since the festival's inception in 1951. Talented newcomers often use Wexford to launch their careers, and many well-known singers (among them Frederica von Stade) have sung there. Much of the backstage work, the ushering, and ticket selling is done by volunteers, and at least one member of most local families is directly involved in the festival — as a result, this otherwise very elite event has become very public and popular. What makes it really special is the productions' setting — a tiny opera house that seats only 446, situated down a capillary of a side street — plus a general feeling of style and opulence. The events roster also includes concerts and recitals, and exhibitions and readings at the local arts center. All of Wexford's public buildings — several of which were designed by Pugin — are floodlit for the duration. Details: Theatre Royal, Wexford, County Wexford, Irish Republic (phone: 053-22240).

BELFAST FESTIVAL AT QUEEN'S, Belfast, Northern Ireland: One of the three biggest arts festivals in Britain and Ireland, this November event has, since its beginnings in the early 1960s, created excitement on the cultural scene that even "the troubles" have not been able to undermine. Although it covers the entire spectrum of the arts, there traditionally has been an emphasis on classical music. But the jazz and film programs are excellent; folk and popular music are well represented, as is a spectrum of drama, opera, and ballet, with visiting companies from the Republic and the rest of Europe. Superstars like Cleo Laine and Dame Janet Baker, James Galway and Yehudi Menuhin, and Billy Connolly and Michael Palin have performed here. The setting is the Victorian campus of Queen's University; concerts are also presented in the Grand Opera House, the Ulster Hall, and the Arts, Lyric, and Group Theatres. Details: Festival House, 8 Malone Rd., Belfast BT9 5BN, Northern Ireland (phone: 0232-667687).

IF YOU'RE NEARBY

WINDSOR FESTIVAL, Windsor Castle, Berkshire, England: Concerts, dance programs, readings, lectures, walks, and exhibitions that take place in or near Windsor Castle and Eton College occupy this community annually for two weeks in September or October. Details: Dial House, Englefield Green, Surrey TW20 0DU, England (phone: 0784-32618).

MINIATURE EXHIBITION AND FAIR, Birmingham, West Midlands, England: The country's best craftsmen and artisans in the field of miniatures are featured at this event — a must for enthusiasts. Details: ICTS, Inc., 4133 Taylor St., San Diego, CA 92110 (phone: 619-299-4217 and 800-428-7462; 800-457-9515 in California).

CAMDEN FESTIVAL, London, England: Progressive opera, new music, and performers from the Third World are featured in the historic buildings, concert halls, churches, and playhouses of this London borough every year in early spring. The Jazz Week is one of Britain's best known. Details: Camden Festival, 100 Euston Rd., London NW1 2AJ, England (phone: 01-388-1394).

EDINBURGH INTERNATIONAL FOLK FESTIVAL, Edinburgh, Scotland: Folk music, dance, drama, a crafts fair, children's events, lectures, courses on traditional instruments, *ceilidhs,* workshops, and an Oral History Conference are the heart of this festival, which takes place over the ten days that lead up to Easter weekend in March/April. The Edinburgh Harp Festival is an integral part of the event, and in 1987 the Festival of European Piping was incorporated as well. Details: Edinburgh International Folk Festival, Shillinghill, Temple, Midlothian EH23 4SH, Scotland (phone: 031-087530).

PITLOCHRY FESTIVAL, Pitlochry, Perthshire, Scotland: Plays in repertory, celebrity concerts, and art exhibitions are presented in Scotland's Theatre in the Hills from May through October. Details: Pitlochry Festival Theatre, Pitlochry, Perthshire PH16 5DR, Scotland (phone: 0796-2680).

NORTH WALES MUSIC FESTIVAL, St. Asaph, Clwyd, Wales: New and old music is presented in this quiet town's 6th-century cathedral, the smallest in England and Wales, annually for a week in late September. Details: North Wales Music Festival, High St., St. Asaph, Clywd, Wales (phone: 0745-584508).

ST. DAVID'S CATHEDRAL BACH FESTIVAL, St. David's, Dyfed, Wales: Her Majesty the Queen is the patron of this festival held during the last week in May in Wales's largest cathedral, the shrine of the nation's patron saint, St. David. The building comes as a surprise, because the surrounding area, within the Pembrokeshire Coast National Park, is rural and isolated. But so will its interior, which is far more ornate than the rather plain exterior, and the quality of the music — not only traditional music but also newly commissioned pieces. Details: John Mogford, c/o St. David's Cathedral, St. David's, Haverfordwest, Dyfed SA62, Wales.

SWANSEA FESTIVAL, Swansea, West Glamorgan, Wales: Annually for 3 weeks in October, Wales's most important arts festival is held here, in the area where Dylan Thomas grew up and wrote *Under Milk Wood.* There's ballet, drama, poetry, art, and a week of opera featuring the Welsh National Opera Company. But orchestral music is the main feature, and in a quantity second only to that of the Edinburgh Festival. There's always an orchestra from London, another from the Continent, and another from Wales, and past soloists have included Ashkenazy and Abbado. Details: Swansea Festival, The Guildhall, Swansea, West Glamorgan SA1 4PA, Wales (phone: 0792-50821).

CORK INTERNATIONAL CHORAL AND FOLK DANCE FESTIVAL, Cork, County Cork, Irish Republic: This event takes place annually at the beginning of May. Choirs and folk dance teams from all over the world participate, and each year a number of choral works are commissioned from distinguished composers. Details: Cork International Choral and Folk Dance Festival, PO Box 68, Cork, County Cork, Irish Republic (phone: 021-312296).

Antiques and Auctions

Perhaps no nations take better care of their past than Britain and Ireland. From the top of the Tower of London to the most remote County Donegal crypt, tradition is a cherished possession. And if you're one of those people who are driven to possess a chunk of history, not simply observe it, and would rather own a coal scuttle than just ogle the Crown Jewels, gather up your checkbook and head for these isles. You'll have the chance to outbid a London dealer at a rural Ayrshire auction, blow dust off a first edition of Dickens at an Aberdeen antiquarian's, and haggle for a special price at the Faversham flea market — if you decide to take *both* the Georgian silver salver *and* the yeoman's crossbow. There's no time like the past — and no time like the present for enjoying it.

A REPERTOIRE OF ANTIQUES SOURCES

There are four distinctly different types of dealers in Britain and Ireland. At the low end of the scale are the flea markets. True bargains are often available — to those willing to sift through piles of not always interesting miscellanea. Auction houses can often yield a find, under the right circumstances — to those able to visit the pre-sale exhibition before bidding. Antiques shops offer convenience. A dealer has made the rounds of the markets and has purchased the pick of the auction houses for you

— and you pay the price for his time and trouble. Fairs often bring many dealers — and many wares — together in one place. The quality may be high, with prices to match, but the selection can't be beat. In short, your repertoire of sources for antiques is not so different than that in the US, Canada, and many other countries. What *is* notable is the selection of these fairs, auction houses, shops, and markets. Below we describe a few of the very best.

SHOPS AND ANTIQUES CENTERS: From Abbotsbury to Zither-on-Thames, there are some six thousand "olde curiosity shoppes" dappling the landscape of Britain and Ireland. Whether your quarry is barometers or bond certificates, tools or toy soldiers, you'll find a shop catering exclusively to your collecting passion. The antiques trade in Britain and Ireland has developed great sophistication in many specialties over the centuries.

Ethical standards are generally high, and you shouldn't be surprised if dealers spontaneously divulge all the defects of an item you are considering for purchase. A number are members of recognized, reputable national guilds, with clear and rigorous codes in matters of authenticity and quality. But if the caveats aren't offered unsolicited, be sure to question the dealer about what is original, what has been restored or retouched, and what has simply been replaced. If you are spending any significant sum, have the qualifications put in writing.

For advice about purchasing and shipping and customs regulations, you can contact one of the following dealers' associations:

> *British Antique Dealers' Association,* 20 Rutland Gate, London SW1 1BD, England (phone: 01-589-4128).
> *Cotswold Antique Dealers' Association,* High St., Blockley, Gloucestershire GL56 9ET, England (phone: 0386-700280).
> *London and Provincial Antique Dealers' Association,* 3 Cheval Pl., London SW7 1 EW, England (phone: 01-584-7911).
> *Irish Antique Dealers' Association,* 16 Kildare St., Dublin 2, Irish Republic (phone: 01-762614).

These organizations can send lists of their members, who adhere to association standards. In addition, a comprehensive list of dealers in Britain can be found in two marvelous and exhaustive books, both revised annually and available at fine bookstores in London:

> *British Art and Antiques Directory,* available from National Magazine House, 72 Broadwick St., London W1V 2BP (phone: 01-439-7144). Offers a comprehensive listing of dealers, restorers, shippers, auction houses, courses in fine and decorative arts and restoration, and various antiques-related businesses throughout Britain and Ireland — everything cross-referenced by specialty.
> *Guide to the Antique Shops of Britain,* £7.95 from the Antique Collectors Club, 5 Church St., Woodbridge, Suffolk IP12 1DS, England (phone: 0394-385501). Contains more than 6,000 entries that outline the type of stock, size of showrooms, years in business, hours, and much more.

Note that if you're heading for a small shop in a small town, it's wise to phone ahead. Most dealers will see visitors by appointment, even outside normal shopping hours. You'll also avoid the frustration of finding the maddening "Back in ten minutes" sign on the door. Even in punctual Britain, that can mean a long wait.

A recent trend has been the gathering of many small shops into antiques centers — something like toney shopping centers or indoor markets with all the stalls under one roof. These intriguing places to spend a rainy hour are also superb for giving you a quick overview of the local market, and there's no greater pressure to buy than in a department store. You'll see hundreds of interesting items that rarely make it across the Atlantic.

London, England – There are several antiques centers in London.

Camden Passage Antiques Centre An 18th-century, traffic-free pedestrian walk that houses 350 dealers. In Islington, north of the city, in Camden Passage, N1. Antiques market days are Wednesdays and Saturdays; book market day is Thursday.

Grays Antique Market, installed in a beautiful terra cotta Victorian structure, houses dozens of stands, and its dealers are more selective than not. Antique jewelry is notable for its selection, but there are also antiquarian books, maps, and prints, arms and armour, lace, scientific instruments, and thimbles. Around the corner, *Grays In The Mews* has Victorian and Edwardian toys, paintings and prints, and orientalia. 58 Davies St., W1 (phone: 01-629-7034).

Chenil Galleries is increasingly important as a center for Art Deco and Art Nouveau objects. But dealers' specialties range from Gothic furniture, tapestries and textiles, to 18th-century paintings, scientific instruments, and fine porcelain. 181-183 King's Rd., SW3 (phone: 01-351-5353).

Alfie's Antique Market is housed in what was once a Victorian department store. This warren of 300 stalls, showrooms, and workshops is the biggest covered antique market in London — and likely the least expensive, since it is where the dealers come to buy. 13-25 Church St., NW8 (phone: 01-723-6066).

Bath, Avon, England – There are some 50 antiques shops in this charming spa town, and more than 70 stallholders in the *Great Western Antique Centre,* where dealers purvey everything from antique beds to cameras. It's the largest and most comprehensive antiques center under one roof outside London. Just across the street is the *Bartlett Street Antique Market.* Bartlett St.

Bristol, Avon, England – In this busy city, once a booming port, the 60 dealers at the suburban *Clifton Antiques Market* offer a wide selection at prices that range from the ridiculous to the sublime. 26-28 The Mall, Clifton (phone: 0272-741627).

Woburn Abbey, Bedfordshire, England – The *Woburn Abbey Antiques Centre* is another good bet. Housed in an old stable behind façades rescued from demolition, restored, and then re-erected, are collectibles ranging from oak furniture to paintings and prints, silver and glassware — everything dating from before 1870 (phone: 05252-5350).

Brighton, East Sussex, England – In this old fishing town, a famous resort since the days of the Prince Regent, the 22 stalls at the *Brighton Antiques Gallery* sell a wide variety of wares ranging from Georgian and Victorian silver and jewelry to ceramics, small furniture, antique glass, and other collectors' items. 41 Meeting House La. (phone: 0273-21059).

Edinburgh, Scotland – The Scottish capital bustles with the antiques trade and has its share of shops. The antiques center that stands out is the *Ingliston Market* on the city's outskirts (Sundays only).

Glasgow, Scotland – At the *Victorian Village,* there are more than two dozen dealers — and roomfuls of antiques, ornaments, and old lace, with Beethoven melodies wafting through the corridors while you browse. Its home is Castle Chambers, a building listed for its historical and architectural interest. 53-63 W Regent St. (phone: 041-332-4033).

Dublin, Irish Republic – The capital is the true center for the Irish antiques trade, and the restoration of Lord Powerscourt's town house — itself a magnificent structure, with fine plasterwork ceilings among its many fine features — is the standout, on South William and Clarendon streets. Most of the city's best dealers have an outlet here.

FAIRS: There are dozens of fairs in all sizes and qualities. Whether they last 2 days or 10, they attract dealers from all over the region, the country, and Europe. Many dealers make the rounds of these events, beginning in January and continuing through the year. A complete list of the leading pre-1890 dateline shows outside London and their exact dates can be found in a little publication called *Antiques in Britain Fairs,* available for $1 including postage from Toni Keniston, Hopton Castle, Craven Arms, Salop SY7 OQJ, England (phone: 05474-356).

The most prestigious fairs by far are the *Burlington House Fair,* held in March at the Royal Academy, and the *Grosvenor House Antiques Fair,* held in June at Grosvenor House in Park Lane. But there are dozens of others, among them:

British International Antique Dealers' Fair, Birmingham, England. To some minds, the country's most important provincial fair. April.

Buxton Antiques Fair, Pavilion Gardens, Buxton, Derbyshire, England. Early May. One of the largest vetted antiques fairs in the North of England.

Kensington Antiques Fair, New Town Hall, Kensington W8, England. Early November.

Surrey Antiques Fair, Civic Hall, Guildford, Surrey, England. Early October. A popular annual event for the serious furniture buyer.

Edinburgh Annual Antiques Fair, Roxburghe Hotel in Charlotte Sq., Edinburgh, Scotland. Late July.

Scottish Antiques Fair, same location as the above. April.

Welsh Annual Antiques Fair, Castle Hotel, Brecon, Wales. Mid-September.

Fine Art and Antiques Fair, Culloden Hotel, Bangor Rd., Craigavad, Holywood, County Down, Northern Ireland. First week in November.

Irish Antiques Fair, Mansion House, Dublin, Irish Republic. The main Irish event of its type, it derives a bit more gloss from its timing at the height of Dublin's biggest social season, the week around the Dublin Horse Show. August.

FLEA MARKETS AND OTHER WEEKLY SPECTACLES: That heady mixture of rubbish and relic known as the flea market is the ultimate paradise for the collector. It offers the chance to find that special, unrecognized rarity, the eye-catching castoff whose true value only *you* perceive — say, a yak saddle from the Indian Mutiny, a left-handed pewter monocle, or a chipped 78 rpm recording of Edward VII's abdication speech. If you dream of snapping up a precious item before the professionals send it successively to auction, fair, and trendy shop (at prices that spiral ever upward), you must frequent the weekly markets, especially those that flourish outside London.

Your best allies in this odyssey are bad weather and early arrival. If you're a serious buyer, get to the market at dawn and pray for torrential rain. If it's the spectacle that intrigues you, then hope for a sunny morning. Fine days provide such good theater — at such moderate cost — that you won't even mind trudging home empty-handed. Though the civilized British have managed to get many of their markets under a roof, thereby sacrificing local color to comforts, the bargains are still there. Try your luck at the following:

Bath, Avon, England – This city is the antiques center of the west of England, and on Wednesdays, over 300 dealers trade in its quartet of markets.

Great Western Antique Center has a Wednesday market that boosts the already estimable number of dealers at this location. Bartlett St.

Guinea Lane Antique Market is run by the largest group of dealers in the West Country. Its 100 stalls are packed with the rare, the quaint, the beautiful. Wednesdays.

Bath Saturday Antiques Market features more than 50 stalls. Walcot St.

Paragon Antiques Market also attracts dealers from all over the country every Wednesday. Small, easily-carried items are the specialty. 3 Bladud Buildings.

Birmingham, West Midlands, England – At the *Birmingham Thursday Antique Market,* some 30 dealers sell general antiques, furniture, clocks, and small objects ranging from porcelain to Victoriana every Thursday. 141 Bromsgrove St. (phone: 021-622-2145).

Dorchester, Dorset, England – The *Dorchester Antique Market* holds forth one Wednesday each month; call ahead for the date. Town Hall, Corn Exchange (phone: 0963-62478).

London, England – Open-air markets flourish all over the city, and for ferreting out curios, they can't be beat.

Jubilee Market at Covent Garden, WC2, is a good bet on Mondays.

Bermondsey–New Caledonian Market complex, where several dealers hold forth every Friday in a good-sized open space at the end of Long Lane and in an erstwhile factory nearby, is known for being a dealers' market. Fresh shipments from the country go on sale here first (and, in fact, many of the goods you see in Portobello Road were purchased here). If you arrive after 9 AM, the best will be long gone; regulars try to arrive not much after 5 AM — and bring flashlights if necessary. Tower Bridge Rd., SE1.

Greenwich Antiques Market is a less frenetic place to be on Saturdays (and on Sundays in summer). Greenwich High Rd., SE10.

Portobello Road is famous for antiques shops, junk shops, outdoor pushcarts, and legions of antiques lovers from all over the world trying to buy up bits and pieces of England. The activity is astonishing — but by the same token, don't expect to turn up a treasure at a good price except occasionally in winter, when the weather is so blustery that only the most intrepid antiques hounds venture outside. There are fleas on both Friday and Saturday; on Saturday, you'll also find antiques. W11.

Orsett, Essex, England – The *Orsett Antiques Fair* is open the second Sunday of each month. Orsett Hall, Prince Charles Ave. (phone: 0702-714649 or 0268-774977).

Westcliff-on-Sea, Essex, England – The *Boston Hall Antiques Fair* is a fixture of the last Sunday of each month. Boston Hall Hotel, the Leas (phone: 0702-714649 or 0168-774977).

Edinburgh, Scotland – The major market here is the *Ingliston Market,* which takes place on Sundays on the city's outskirts at Ingliston. Don't expect acres full of exquisite antiques; this is a true flea market, with goods ranging from fresh food and clothing to china and toys. The average weekly attendance often tops 25,000.

Glasgow, Scotland – A weekend fixture here since Victorian times, the *Barrows* is one of the most colorful flea markets in Britain and Ireland, bar none. It takes up a square mile and it's packed with stalls, up to a thousand of them, almost as colorful as their proprietors. Small wonder that the BBC called it Europe's bargain basement. Saturdays and Sundays. 244 Gallowgate.

Cardiff, Wales – *Jacobs Antique Market* is open on Thursdays and Saturdays. West Canal Wharf.

Cork, County Cork, Irish Republic – The *Cork Antique Market* is a must if you're here on Thursday, Friday, or Saturday. 7 Tuckey St.

AUCTIONS: An auction, as any addict knows, is a mixture of stock market, gambling, casino, and living theater. It's the perfect answer to rainy day blues.

Auctiongoers should attend to these notes:

Don't expect to make a killing. But your chances are better at smaller country auctions. Look carefully at mixed lots, and always venture out in filthy weather. Every so often someone picks up a golden goblet for 10p at a Girl Guide (the British version of a Girl Scout) auction and then resells it for £9,000. In any event, expect to save about 30% on the shop price of a comparable item.

Buy the catalogue before bidding. Catalogues often include a list of estimated prices. Those prices are not a contractual commitment — but they do act as a guide for prospective buyers. An elaborate stylistic code hints at the conviction the house may have about the age and authenticity of an item. The use of capital letters, of artists' full names, and of words like *fine, rare,* and *important* all carry positive connotations. The use of a last name only and of words like *style* and *attributed* should serve as flashing red warning lights.

Visit the pre-sale exhibition carefully, lengthily, and even repeatedly. There is the pleasure of browsing in a store without a hovering clerk. Even more important is the chance to see what you're going to buy. *Caveat emptor* is the prevailing rule at an auction. No one but you will be held accountable for any mistakes you commit. So make a pest of yourself: have high paintings taken down from the wall and ask to handle objects under lock and key. If you can't be at the sale, you can leave a commission bid with the auctioneer or even place a bid by telephone — but if you can't be at the exhibition, don't buy.

Decide on your top bid before the auction begins, and don't go beyond it. The bidding has its own rhythm and tension. The auctioneer becomes a Pied Piper, with the buyers winking, blinking, and nodding in time to his music. This situation arouses unusual behavior in some people. Suddenly their self-worth is at stake, and they'll bid far beyond what the item is worth — or even what they can afford. If you do make a bid you regret, promptly call out "Withdrawn." *Note:* In determining your top price, remember to add the house commission, which can be up to 20%, and any Value Added Tax. Fingers rise and hammers fall all over Britain and Ireland — but the following spots warrant prime attention:

London, England – London is still the auction capital of the world, and the market price of a work of art or an antique generally refers to the price items of its genre have fetched in the London salerooms. Of the auction houses in London, three stand out as the most important.

Christie's was founded in 1766. The fortunes of England's great families can be read in Christie's records, and an object's whole lineage can often be traced through its appearances in two centuries of Christie's sales. No wonder the mother house is something of a national landmark. There are auctions daily, and the exhibition rooms are a constantly changing museum. Andrea Mantegna's *The Adoration of the Magi* was on view here (before fetching a record £8,100,000 in April 1985). So was a bottle of Chateau Lafite 1787 bearing the initials *Th.J.,* for Thomas Jefferson (which later brought £105,000 on the block). Don't be put off by furred ladies, pin-striped Rembrandt hunters, or the bespectacled experts from US museums. Ordinary Londoners do their Christmas shopping here, especially at the South Kensington saleroom, which handles items of recent vintage and generally lower value — toys, telescopes, top hats, and the like. 8 King St., St. James's, SW1 (phone: 01-839-9060). The South Kensington branch is at 85 Old Brompton Rd., SW1.

Sotheby's is the world's oldest auction house. The little white building in which it is discreetly housed, on the most elegant street in England, is a kind of nerve center of the art world. Its roster of experts in every field rivals the British Museum's. An important sale of Old Masters or Impressionists, with hundreds of thousands of dollars riding on every twitch, beats an evening at the National Theatre, as its chandeliers glitter next to a computer board that translates bids into dollars, yen, marks, lire, and Swiss and French francs. In its surprisingly large complex of salerooms, auctions of every kind of work of art, including books, manuscripts, coins, medals, and jewelry, take place regularly throughout the year. 34-35 New Bond St., W1 (phone: 01-493-8080).

Phillips is number three and it's trying harder and harder. This house does a large number of estate sales, held on the owners' premises in fine English country houses. Since they are often sparsely attended by the general public, there's a fair chance of encountering dealer-level prices. The house does a large volume in modestly priced lots, and the staff is extremely helpful to auction novices. 7 Blenheim St., W1 (phone: 01-629-6602).

Bath, Avon, England – *Aldridges Auction Galleries* holds sales on Tuesdays, with viewing on Saturday mornings and Mondays through early evening. 130-132 Walcot St. (phone: 0225-62830).

Leicester, Leicestershire, England – *Heathcote Ball and Company Castle Auction Rooms* is the prime source of auction action. A restoration and advisory service is also available. 78 St. Nicholas Circle (phone: 0533-536789); also at Northampton (phone: 0604-22735).

Norwich, Norfolk, England – *Aylsham Salerooms* have regular sales of furniture, silver, porcelain and glass, collectibles, and books, and bimonthly sales of paintings, watercolors, and prints. G. A. Key, 8 Market Pl., Aylsham (phone: 0263-733195).

Penzance, Cornwall, England – *W. H. Lane and Son* has about a dozen general sales annually of antiques and objets d'art. In addition, there are a number of specialist sales devoted to antique books, coins, medals, stamps, and pictures; occasionally there are also treasure trove sales in which pieces of eight and other finds from old wrecks are put on the block. 64 Morrab Rd. (phone: 0736-61447).

Edinburgh, Scotland – *Phillips Scotland* has monthly sales of oil paintings, furniture, Oriental rugs, clocks, bronzes, silver, and other works of art; European ceramics and glass, orientalia, jewelry, and watercolors are auctioned bimonthly; books, postcards, and maps are offered in eight sales annually, and four annual sales are devoted to dolls, costumes, and textiles. Viewing is usually two days prior; on Wednesdays and Thursdays, there's always something to be seen, not least of which is one of the best panoramic views of Edinburgh from its fifth floor. 65 George St. (phone: 031-225-2266).

Glasgow, Scotland – *Christie's Scotland,* Christie's Scottish saleroom, has weekly auctions of jewelry, silver, objets d'art, and furniture, and regular sales of items of specialist interest — including Scottish silver, collectors' items, and paintings. 164-166 Bath St. (phone: 041-332-8134).

Phillips Scotland holds auctions of furniture, paintings, ceramics, silver, and jewelry every Tuesday; annually they have two special sales of fine jewelry, and four of collectors' items. 207 Bath St. (phone: 041-221-8377).

Dublin, Irish Republic – *James Adam and Sons,* founded in 1887, is the country's major auction house, with regular sales of objects of fine and decorative arts. St. Stephen's Green (phone: 01-760261).

Cork, County Cork, Irish Republic – Since *Joseph Woodward & Sons* is the only antiques and fine art auction house in the city, there tends to be a very good selection at each of the monthly sales. The house, whose chairman is a direct descendant of the original owner, celebrated its centenary in 1983. Cook St. (phone: 021-273327).

ANTIQUES PEAKS ON THE BRITISH AND IRISH LANDSCAPE

There are a handful of cities and towns in Britain and Ireland that stand out for their selection of shops, antiques centers, flea markets, and auction houses. These are the places that savvy antiques dealers from the Continent visit when they're on the prowl for newly fashionable 19th-century English furniture and objets d'art — and they are a must on any antiques lover's tour of Britain and Ireland.

BATH, Avon, England: Bath is the antiques center of the west of England. Its elegant 18th-century squares and crescents are the natural setting for dozens of intriguing antiques shops, and over 300 dealers trade in four antiques markets every Wednesday. Some of your best bets for antiques hunting here include the following:

The Great Western Antique Centre adds to your selection. Open 6 days a week, it's a busy bazaar devoted to the old. Bartlett St.

The Guinea Lane Antique Market is a must if you're in town on a Wednesday. Guinea La., Paragon.

Paragon Antiques Market is another fixture of the devoted antiques hunters Wednesday itinerary. 3 Bladud Buildings, Paragon.

The Bath Saturday Antique Market is also worth a look. Walcot St.

Aldridges Auction Galleries has Tuesday sales, with viewings on Saturday mornings and on Mondays through the early evening. 130 and 132 Walcot St. (phone: 0225-62830).

The West of England Antiques Fair is an event of regional importance. Early May.

BRISTOL, Avon, England: In addition to dozens of antiques shops, this busy, commercial city has an antiques and crafts market in the Exchange. More than 50 stalls there offer a wide selection of glass, china, jewelry, and bric-a-brac. It's open on Thursdays and Fridays.

The Clifton Antiques Market in the charming suburb of Clifton is well worth visiting. In a handsome Georgian building near the famous Clifton suspension bridge at 26-28 The Mall (phone: 0272-741627).

The Bristol Antiques and Collectors Fair takes place annually at the Bristol Exhibition Centre on the first day of January, and on variable dates during spring, summer, and fall. More than 100 dealers exhibit annually. Bristol Exhibition Centre, 2 Canons Road (phone: 0272-215206).

CANTERBURY, Kent, England: The compact size of this famous city makes antiques hunting especially pleasant, and the prime destination is Palace Street, not far from the Christ Church Gate of the cathedral, where there are 15 antique shops alone. Good shops here include:

Five Centuries Antiques, at No. 18.

The Aristocrat, at No. 19. Small and family-run, with a specialty of engraved glass and collectors' items.

Parker-Williams Antiques, at No. 22. 17th- to 19th-century English antiques.

CHESTER, Cheshire, England: The Rows, the centuries-old aboveground network of walkways for which the city is famous, are blessed with some of England's most abundant antiques hunting. Watergate Street Row, which is the most redolent of the past of all the Rows, offers particularly numerous shops. Good shops along the street include the following:

Erica and Hugo Harper, at No. 27 (phone: Chester 23004). The city's best junk shop, with masses of bric-a-brac, clocks, and furniture in several rooms and prices ranging from the small to the mighty.

Chester Antiques, at No. 49. Stocks a large selection of 18th-century grandfather clocks and Victorian clocks as well as Victorian dolls, rosewood furniture, fine English china, barometers, and weapons.

Goss Street (off Watergate Street) was also the site of the Assay Office, where the city's own hallmark (three wheat sheaves) was stamped on the handiwork of Chester's celebrated silversmiths. Today, fine quality work is available from such specialists as:

Boodle and Dunthorne, next door to the Grosvenor Hotel. Established in 1798 and still thriving. Eastgate St. (phone: Chester 25850).

Lowe's, founded 28 years before *Boodle and Dunthorne,* is the oldest silversmith in Chester and offers the county's largest collection of estate jewelry and silver. 11 Bridge St. Row (phone: Chester 25850).

Brown's, the oldest jeweler in the city, owned by the same family since 1848. It focuses on unique items with investment value. 2 Eastgate Row (phone: Chester 24357).

There's also the *Chester Antiques Hypermarket,* which boasts more than three dozen dealers. 41 Lower Bridge St.

COTSWOLDS, England: The most romantic antiques hunting in Britain and Ireland is to be found in the Cotswolds, about 100 miles west of London. The area's charming, unspoiled towns, its quaint stone cottages, and its oh-so-English countryside make it very popular with visitors, so you can't expect bargains. But the antiques shops are so close to one another that you can visit quite a few without racking up excessive mileage. You will also find an expert shipping service for furniture and other large items.

The most important towns for antiquing include Stow-on-the-Wold, a hilltop community whose low houses huddle around a handsome market square (its selection of furniture is so enormous that locals joke that an American who'd just finished a spending spree had labeled his purchases for shipping with "Stow In The Hold"). Nearby Tetbury, home of the Prince and Princess of Wales, has at least a half-dozen good shops. Other good bets are Moreton-in-the-Marsh (particularly High Street); Chipping Norton; Burford (especially on High Street and The Hill); Cirencester; and Cheltenham, a genteel spa with spacious gardens, perfectly preserved Regency buildings, and over 60 shops plus the *Cheltenham Antique Market* at 54 Suffolk Rd.

Some well-known dealers in these very special towns and others include:

Peter Stroud Antiques, for 18th- and 19th-century English and French furniture. Station Yard Industrial Estate, Chipping Norton (phone: 0608-41651).

Rankine Taylor Antiques, for 16th-, 17th-, and 19th-century furniture and objets d'art from France, Italy, and America as well as England, Scotland, Ireland, and Wales displayed in a series of eclectic room settings that show off the proprietor's eye for the decorative and the unusual; the atmosphere is reminiscent of some 18th-century grande dame's drawing room. A 1961 Silver Cloud II Rolls Royce in Racing Green, won by the proprietor in a raffle in 1975, can be viewed in her back yard. 34 Dollar St., Cirencester (phone: Gloucester 2529).

Christopher Clarke Antiques, for furniture, pictures, pottery, and other works of art dating from the 17th to the 19th centuries. The Fosse Way, Stow-on-the-Wold.

EAST ANGLIA, England: This bulge of coastline to the northeast of London is off the beaten track and little frequented by overseas visitors. But it's rich territory for the antiques collector nonetheless. The Essex towns of Battlesbridge, Coggeshalle, Colchester, Stansted Mount Fitchett, and Kelvedon (especially High Street) make for especially happy hunting, as does Cambridge (especially the Trumpington Street area near Fitzwilliam and Kings Colleges).

The Antiques Centre in Coggeshall has 10 dealers stocking items both large and small, and several others have shops nearby. Open Mondays through Saturdays. The Market Place.

There is also a series of antiques fairs worth attending. Bury St. Edmunds has fairs in March and September as well as one-day events that take place monthly. Cambridge has a major event in July. Ely has a one-day fair every month. There is also a well-established fair at Snape in July.

Norwich has a weekly market on Wednesdays at St. Andrew's Hall as well as longer events in early January, at Easter, and during July. It also has a sizable antiques center at The Quayside.

LONDON, England: For centuries, London represented a safe haven for things of value. Consequently, it became the unquestioned center of the world's antiques trade. Anything can be bought here, and everything has a market value and instant liquidity.

Best Antiquing Streets – Shops are in greatest numbers along Bond Street, Brompton Road, Fulham Road, Jermyn Street, Kensington Church Street, King's Road, and Mount Street.

Antiques Centers – In addition to the enormous variety of flea markets, there are also excellent markets that you can visit almost any day of the week:

Antiquarius Antique Market. 200 vendors with specialties ranging from theatrical items and delft to faïence and items from the fifties. 135-141 King's Rd., SW3 (phone: 01-351-5353).

Bond Street Antique Centre. A source for finely worked antique jewelry, watches, portrait miniatures, silver, porcelain, and other objets d'art. 124 New Bond St., W1 (phone: 01-351-5353).

Chelsea Antique Market. The original indoor antiques market, and still one of the best. 253 King's Rd., SW3.

Gray's Antique Market. Davies Mews and 58 Davies St., W1 (phone: 01-629-7034).

Street Markets – London is unique in its great variety of street markets, and each one has its own flavor and appeal.

Petticoat Lane, London's largest Sunday market, has a special antiques section in Goulston Street. This is known as the New Cutler Street Market and is best known for the sale of scrap gold and silver, as well as coins, stamps, and medals. Open until 1 PM.

The *Jubilee* antiques market, Mondays in Covent Garden, W2, has a good selection of small items such as silver and glassware.

Camden Passage in Islington, N1, is not a market for bargains but offers good-quality porcelain, clocks, prints, and silver. Some of the 350 dealers and 150 stalls packed into this mere 200-yard passageway are indoors in *The Georgian Village* while others are in *The Mall.* Wednesdays and Saturdays are the days to browse; there's little to see at other times.

The Bermondsey–New Caledonian Market is Friday, and dealing starts — briskly — at dawn or before. It's a market for the dedicated and the knowledgeable and is frequented primarily by dealers. Flashlights are essential in the wee hours. Note that there is some activity throughout the week in furniture warehouses of the area. Bermondsey Sq. and Tower Bridge Rd., SE1.

Portobello Road often turns up merchandise that you could have had for less at the Bermondsey–New Caledonian Market the day before. W11.

Shops – London is not only auction action and wearying market mobs. It is also the cushioning courtesy of some of the world's most distinguished antiques shops. Visit their carpeted serenity and examine some of the world's best wares:

Alexander Juran, a continuation of a business started in Prague during the reign of Emperor Franz Josef II. The showrooms are small and shabby, but the textiles, rugs, and carpets on offer can be exceptional, and the attitude is one of uniform helpfulness. 74 New Bond St., W1 (phone: 01-493-4484).

Antique Porcelain Company Ltd., for 18th-century English and Continental porcelain. 149 New Bond St., W1 (phone: 01-629-1254).

Grosvenor Prints, resembles a great aunt's attic with more than 100,000 prints, on all subjects. There are also four annual exhibitions covering dogs 1660–1940 (February), portraits (April), mixed subjects (June), and London (November). 28-32 Shelton St., Covent Garden, WC2 (phone: 01-836-1979).

London Silver Vaults, for silver. An underground warren of dealers of fine china, objets d'art, and silver (new, old, secondhand), in the strongrooms of the original Chancery Lane Safe Deposit Company, which opened its doors in 1885 and started serving as a secure base for silver vendors during World War II. 53-65 Chancery La., WC2 (phone: 01-242-3844).

Mallett and Son, specializing in the finest English antique furniture, but for almost all things antique — every item chosen with consummate taste. A miniature museum displaying wares ranging from the late 17th century to the early 19th. 40 New Bond St., W1 (phone: 01-499-7411). For French and continental furniture and a large, eclectic stock of works of art and decorative items, visit their shop at Bourdon House, 2 Davies St., W1 (phone: 01-629-7411).

Pickering and Chatto, for antiquarian books in English literature of the 17th and 18th centuries, economics, science, and medicine. 17 Pall Mall, SW1 (phone: 01-930-2515).

S. J. Phillips, for silver jewelry and objets d'art ranging from the 16th to the early 19th centuries. 139 New Bond St. (phone: 01-629-6261).

Temple Gallery, for Byzantine, Greek, and early Russian icons. 4 Yeoman's Row, Brompton Rd., SW3 (phone: 01-589-6622).

Vigo-Sternberg Galleries, for tapestries. 37 S. Audley St., W1 (phone: 01-629-8307).

Incidentally, if you've bought — or taken on approval — something you'd like an expert to examine, try the British Museum, where you'll never be quoted a value, or *Sotheby's,* where you'll be reminded that the house will be happy to sell it for you.

At Auction – The great auction houses, *Christie's* (8 King St., SW1; phone: 01-839-9060) and *Sotheby's* (34-35 New Bond St., W1; phone: 01-493-8080), are instrumental in setting market prices; they're superb places to develop a feel for the market.

At the Fair – The *Grosvenor House Antiques Fair,* held for 10 days every June, is a sun in the antiques dealer's solar system; you'll find everything from Etruscan heads to Victorian bustles, and every piece has been authenticated by independent experts.

OXFORD, Oxfordshire, England: Some of England's happiest antiques hunting is found in this ancient university town along High Street. A number of the shops offer paintings as well as furniture, porcelain, silver, and the like.

YORK, Yorkshire, England: It's perhaps the best-preserved medieval city in England and the site of the nation's largest medieval church, York Minster. And the curiosities of the past that you'll find in York are not restricted to unusual street names like Whip-ma-whop-ma-gate or to the museums. Antiques shops stocking a selection of pieces from all periods can be found in abundance as well — though the concentration is slowly moving from Goodramgate (and its rising rents) to Micklegate. Among the city's more noteworthy are the following:

MacDowell, for antiquarian books. 56 Micklegate.

Robert Morrison and Son Antiques, for furniture. Its 18th- and 19th-century rosewood, mahogany, and oak pieces — together with its case clocks and decorative items — are in immaculate condition, restored as necessary before going on sale. Trentholme House, 131 The Mount (phone: York 55394).

O'Flynn, for York's biggest stock of antique maps and prints of York, Britain, and the world. There are also manuscripts dating from the 15th century and a broad selection of antiquarian books. 35 Micklegate (phone: 0904-641404).

Spelman's, for antiquarian books. Fifty thousand of them occupy the handsome oak breakfront shelving. A coal fire warms visitors in season. 70 Micklegate (phone: 0904-624414).

Trinity, for dolls, jewelry, clocks, watches, etc. Now trading along with nearly three dozen other dealers at the *York Antiques Centre* at 2 Lendal (phone: 0904-641445).

EDINBURGH, Scotland: Stark yet startlingly beautiful, Edinburgh is a seductive site for antiques shopping. Its dour custodian, Edinburgh Castle, sets such a sober tone as it looms over the city that all things light and modern seem trivial, and the mood is just right for buying solid old objects of silver and pewter, dueling pistols, and the like. Edinburgh is also Britain's second city when it comes to the antiquarian book trade.

Best Antiquing Streets – Dundas, Grassmarket, Randolph Place, St. Stephen's, Thistle, and West Bow are full of antiques shops offering everything from furniture and Sheffield plate to Scottish paintings and leatherbound books.

Antiques Centers and Markets – These are the locales to scour for bargains:

Ingliston Market, a Sunday experience. On the city's outskirts at Ingliston.

Shops – There are dozens in the city, but there are a few of particular interest. These include the following:

Joseph H. Bonnar, jewelry. 72 Thistle St. (phone: 031-226-2811).

Eric Davidson, period furniture, ceramics, paintings, and clocks. 4 Grassmarket (phone: 031-225-5815).

John R. Martin, an eclectic assortment of wares that has included gold thimbles and stuffed elephant alongside the more usual breakfronts. Sells largely to the trade. 96 West Bow (phone: 031-226-7190).

The Scottish Gallery, 20th-century Scottish works of art. 94 George St. (phone: 031-225-5955).

At Auction – There are regular sales at several houses:

Lyon and Turnbull is based locally. 51 George St.

Phillips has weekly sales. 65 George St. (phone: 031-225-2266).

At the Fair – The major annual events are held in the *Roxburghe Hotel* in Charlotte Square.

The Edinburgh Annual Antiques Fair. Late July.

The Scottish Antiques Fair. April and November.

DUBLIN, Irish Republic: Compact, low key, and relaxed, Dublin is full of appeal for the antiques seeker. It is also the true center for the Irish antiques trade.

Antiques Centers – The Powerscourt Town House Centre is not devoted exclusively to antiques, but it's a lovely place and it does offer the convenience of several dealers under one roof. S William St. and Clarendon St.

Best Antiquing Streets – Grafton and Dawson streets are chockablock with antiques stores. The quays along the Liffey, a hunting ground where it was once possible to turn up treasures for shillings, are less polished. But dealers still trade there, and Liffey Street, Bachelor's Walk, and Ormond Quay all make for a pleasant morning's browse thanks to the evocative panoramas of those reddish façades with their faded lettering and the odd assortment of dusty prints and used furniture in the shops.

Shops – The selection of antiques shops in Dublin is very broad. Any roster of the best has to include the following:

Hyman Danker, for silver and jewelry. This is a real family business, and if you don't see what you're looking for, be sure to ask, since the Danker brothers and their daughters, who run the place, can be extremely helpful. 10 S Anne St. (phone: 01-774009).

Ronald McDonnell, for just about everything — his very beautiful old Georgian house makes a wonderful setting for the furniture, paintings, glass, and silver that he sells. 16 Kildare St. (phone: 01-762614).

Rembrandt Antiques, for porcelain. Proprietor Phyllis Jackson, one of Ireland's experts in the field, has crammed every corner of her shop with silver, jewelry, brassware, glass and more from all periods. 24 S Anne St.

At Auction – There are salerooms for all purses in Dublin:

James Adam and Sons, for select goods. St. Stephen's Green (phone: 01-760261).

Allen and Townsend, for its monthly 3-day-long sales at the Mansion House that include quality Belleek; Georgian, Victorian, and modern jewelry; silver and plate; and Georgian and Victorian furniture and oils. 10 St. Stephen's Green (phone: 01-710033).

Tormey Brothers, for household items and the occasional surprising find. Tuesdays. 26-27 Lower Ormond Quay (phone: 01-748002).

At the Fair – The *Irish Antiques Fair* coincides with the Dublin Horse Show, a major social event on the Irish calendar, held during the first full week of August. At the Mansion House.

BELFAST, Northern Ireland: Antiques shopping is an important part of Belfast's shopping scene, and the selection is tantalizing in Donegall Pass, Arthur Street, and Bradbury Place.

RULES OF THE ROAD FOR YOUR ODYSSEY OF THE OLD

Buy for sheer pleasure and not for investment. Forget about the carrot of supposed resale value that dealers habitually dangle in front of amateur clients. If you love an object, you'll never part with it. If you don't love it, let someone else adopt it.

Don't be timid about haggling. That's as true at a Bond Street jeweler's as at the most colorful flea market. You'll be surprised at how much is negotiable — and the higher the price, the farther it has to fall.

Buy the finest example you can afford of any item, in as close to mint condition as possible. Chipped or tarnished "bargains" will haunt you later with their shabbiness.

Train your eye in museums. Museums that specialize in items you collect are the best of all, though they may break your heart. See the coins and medals of the Fitzwilliam in Cambridge; the furniture and clocks of London's Wallace Collection; the Persian and Chinese antiquities at the Chester Beatty Library in Dublin. They'll all help you set impeccable standards against which to measure your purchase. Also, investigate the special tours of Historic Homes of Britain (described in *Stately Homes and Great Gardens,* DIVERSIONS).

Peruse British art books and periodicals. Among the best are the following:

> *The Antique Collector,* available from National Magazine Company, 72 Broadwick St., London W1V 2BP (phone: 01-439-7144) and on newsstands. Parent publication to *The British Art and Antiques Directory* (listed below), this is the leading British monthly for the antiques collector.
>
> *The Antique Dealer and Collector's Guide,* available from King's Reach Tower, Stamford St., London SE1 9LS, England (phone: 01-261-6894) and from larger newsagents.
>
> *The Antiques Trade Gazette,* available from 17 Whitcomb St., London WC2H 7PL, England (phone: 01-930-4957). A weekly newspaper listing and reporting on auctions and shows in Britain and on the Continent. Available at the newsstand adjoining *Sotheby's* in Bond St. and at other antiques centers.
>
> *Apollo,* an international magazine of arts and antiques available on newsstands or from 22 Davies St., London W1Y 1LH, England.
>
> *The British Arts and Antiques Directory,* available from National Magazine House, 72 Broadwick St., London W1V 2BP, England (phone: 01-437-7833).
>
> *The Burlington Magazine,* available on newsstands.
>
> *Buying Antiques in Britain,* published by the London and Provincial Antique Dealers' Association, 3 Cheval Pl., London SW7 1EW, England (phone: 01-584-7911). Lists 680 UK antiques and fine arts dealers. Free in return for valid antiques business card, or for £2 (surface) or £8 (airmail).
>
> *The International Herald Tribune* art pages, particularly on Saturday.

Get advice from a specialist when contemplating a major acquisition. The various dealers' guilds can be helpful. Major auction houses like *Sotheby's* and *Christie's* have fleets of resident specialists who can be consulted. So does the British Museum. Or you might enroll in a special instructional program to become an expert in your own right. The *Christie's Fine Arts Course* (63 Old Brompton Rd., London SW7 3JS; phone: 01-581-3933) is the Harvard of such endeavors. These two intensive year-long courses cover Greek and Roman antiquity to 1450 AD, and 1450 AD to the present day respectively. Evening courses are also available in specialized subjects, including wine. *Sotheby's Works of Art Courses,* can be found at 30 Oxford St., London W1R 1RE (phone: 01-408-1100). The British Tourist Authority can send you a list of special interest holidays that includes several others.

Ancient Monuments and Ruins

Britain and Ireland have been inhabited for thousands of years, and scarcely a single one of the population groups who have settled here has disappeared without leaving a trace. The countryside is littered with their remains: stone walls, tombs and burial chambers, barrows and henges, hilltop forts, castles, abbeys, crosses, churches, and towers. Ruined and crumbling, they stand as reminders to a turbulent and fascinating past.

Prehistoric monuments are fairly evenly distributed throughout the area, although the Irish Republic has the richest group of early Christian monuments, round towers, and high crosses. Romanesque and Gothic cathedrals are particularly well represented in England, and to a certain extent in Scotland and Wales.

The most comprehensive book now in print on these historic places is the *Guide to the National Monuments in the Republic of Ireland* by Peter Harbison (£7.95; Gill and Macmillan Ltd., Goldenbridge, Inchicore, Dublin 8, Irish Republic.) Also good is *Early Ireland: A Field Guide* by Anthony Weir (Blackstaff Press, Belfast), which you may be able to find in libraries.

AVEBURY STONE CIRCLE, Avebury, Wiltshire, England: Eighteen miles from Stonehenge, the map explodes with prehistory. Not only is the area the site of Silbury Hill (Europe's most massive artificial earth mound), but there is also an abundance of long barrows, standing stones, and stone circles — among them, just off the A4 between Marlborough and Calne, the Avebury stone circle. One of the largest in the world, and certainly the greatest among Britain's some 900 megalithic rings, it encloses approximately 28 acres, at the center of which are traces of two smaller stone circles; the whole is ringed by an earthen bank that stands 20 feet high in spots, and, abutting it, a ditch up to 30 feet deep. About 200,000 tons of earth were moved to create the ditch and bank; some of the heaviest of the 25 stones that remain from the group of 100 that once completed the ring weigh over 40 tons and would have required about 200 people to raise. It has been estimated that if 750 people worked here for 10 hours a day for 2 months of every year (after the harvest was in), then the enclosure would have taken about 4 years to complete. And this was during the second millennium BC, a time when the population of the surrounding region, according to some estimates, numbered only about 1,500. Why such a whole society of small farmers was prepared to take time off to create such a place in an age when merely subsisting was a struggle is not known; nor is the nature of the ceremonies that took place there, or the type of beliefs that governed them, or even the ring's exact function, though speculation suggests that it was probably used as a meeting place or a temple, or to fulfill some astronomical function. As is the case with most stone circles, there is no evidence of human sacrifice. Yet Christians who sought to eliminate all records of their pagan past attempted in the 14th century to break up and bury many of the stones (and at least one of their number, a man whose trade as a barber was identified by a pair of scissors found alongside him, was crushed to death in the effort, when a pillar toppled over on him). More early efforts at destroying the great stone circle never entirely succeeded, and, though it probably ceased to serve its original purpose in the first millennium BC, the tradition of its importance persisted, and it continued in use as late as the 19th century, when maypoles were erected within the circle and children frolicked there, waiting for the midsummer sun to appear, as their ancestors might possibly have done. The stones here are smaller than those at Stonehenge and natural rather than hewn; Avebury exceeds the more widely known circle, in the words of one 17th-century observer, "as a cathedral doeth a parish church." For information about the region, contact the West Country Tourist Board, Trinity Ct., 37 Southernhay E, Exeter, Devon EX1 1QS, England (phone: 0392-76351).

GLASTONBURY ABBEY, Glastonbury, Somerset, England: Romance and tradition cling to this historic site like ivy to the walls of a Harvard dormitory. The site itself was probably sacred in pre-Christian days; later, progressively larger churches were built as the abbey became increasingly wealthier. At one point, one of Britain's more irreverent observers noted that the first son born of a marriage between the abbot of Glastonbury and the abbess of Shaftesbury would own more land than the king. Under Dunstan, who introduced the Benedictine rule after he was chosen as abbot in the year

940, the abbey became a center of learning, producing many great ecclesiastics; and for many years, England's premier abbot was Glastonbury's. Its greatness endured for centuries afterward, and its importance diminished only with the Dissolution of the Monasteries in 1539 under Henry VIII, when Thomas Cromwell (later executed at the Tower of London) ordered the elderly abbot Richard Whiting, the sixtieth abbot of Glastonbury, hanged on the Tor. In the words of the 18th-century writer William Stukely: "For every week a pillar or buttress, a window jamb or an angle of fine hewn stone is sold to the best bidder . . . they were excoriating St. Joseph's Chapel for that purpose, and the squared stones were laid up by lots in the Abbot's Kitchen; the rest goes to paving yards and stalls for cattle, or to the highway." Lead stripped from the roofs was melted down in fires fueled by priceless manuscripts and carved wooden screens that were antique even then.

Legend has elaborately embellished the known history of the millennium before this debacle. One story says that Christ came here as a child in the company of Joseph of Arimathea, the wealthy trader in whose garden tomb Christ's body was placed when it was taken from the cross. According to another story, Joseph of Arimathea came alone; landing here in the winter, and, wearily, planting his staff into the ground, he saw it sending up leaves and blossoms. It was he who, as legend would have it, brought to England the Holy Grail, which Arthur's knights sought so avidly in later years. Traditions also record that King Arthur was buried at Glastonbury; and it is widely told that toward the end of the 12th century, when Henry II had excavations made here, monks found a stone inlaid with a leaden cross that had been inscribed according to Gerald the Welshman, "Here lies buried the renowned King Arthur in the isle of Avalon with Guinevere his second wife"; there were two skeletons, one of a man of gigantic size, and one of a woman with a bit of golden hair that crumbled at the touch. The bones were reburied at Glastonbury's high altar, but the tomb was broken up at the dissolution and the bones were dispersed; the leaden cross no longer exists, but a drawing made at the beginning of the 17th century does. As to the ultimate truth of the whole story, no one can say. But Cadbury Castle, believed to be Arthur's Camelot, is not far away; and roads can still be traced between the two sites. As historians keep speculating, the impressively large ruins of the abbey, surrounded by manicured lawns ringed by a stone wall, are open to visitors; they can walk down into an ancient crypt, take in a performance of a play or pageant (in summer), climb the 525-foot Tor for a view out over Wiltshire Downs and the Mendips all the way to Bristol (on a clear day), poke around at the Chalice Well where the Holy Grail is supposed to be lost, and see a thorn tree grown from a cutting of the one that sprouted from Joseph of Arimathea's staff. Glastonbury proper is not too exciting a town, filled as it is (like Stratford-upon-Avon and other towns-with-a-past) with souvenir shops; but the Glastonbury Thorn still flowers in the mid-winter. The abbey now belongs to the Church of England, the Tor to the National Trust. The Abbey Barn, which contains a Rural Life Museum, and the historic *George and Pilgrim's Inn,* which opened in 1475, are nearby. Details: West Country Tourist Board (address above) or the Custodian, The Abbey Gatehouse, Glastonbury, Somerset BA6 9EL, England.

TOWER OF LONDON, London, England: The Tower — known in some quarters as the world's most famous castle — is actually a complex of buildings. Begun during the days of William the Conquerer and expanded many times over the years, it has figured in British history for a millennium as palace, fortress, treasury, mint, bank, arsenal, munitions factory, garrison, library, museum, observatory, and even zoo. Its most famous function, however, has been that of prison, and many came through the so-called Traitor's Gate hoping to be ransomed or pardoned and thereby avoid the fate — endless incarceration or death — of those who had passed that way before them. Many hoped in vain. The stories of the executions, murders, and suicides within these walls are legion. Henry VI, imprisoned during the Wars of the Roses, was stabbed to death during his prayers, allegedly on the order of Richard, Duke of Gloucester, the "usurper of the realm" who became Richard III after the murder of the about-to-be-crowned Edward V and his brother the Duke of York. (The youngsters disappeared from public view in 1483 while lodged in the Tower; the next trace of them was two sets of bones found under a staircase in Charles II's time.) Henry VIII hustled wives, dissidents, and possible claimants to the throne into the Tower, the first step in the journey that usually ended at the executioner's block. Among those who made that journey were Anne Boleyn and Catherine Howard, the monarch's second and fifth wives, who were executed on the Tower Green and buried in the chapel of St. Peter ad Vincula; Sir Thomas More ("the king's good servant but God's first"), who met his end after rejecting his sovereign's claim to the leadership of the English church; and Thomas Cromwell, the not-always-so-jolly king's chief administrator. Later, Lady Jane Grey was beheaded on Tower Green after the Duke of Northumberland, the father of her husband, Lord Guilford Dudley, persuaded her young cousin Edward VI to pass his crown to the 17-year-old Jane rather than to Elizabeth's half-sister Mary, the rightful heir to the throne; she reigned for 9 days, beginning on July 10, 1553, until the English rallied around Mary I. In the days of Elizabeth I (who herself had been imprisoned in the Tower on the orders of her half-sister Mary), the Earl of Essex was executed at the age of 34 after the discovery of a plot to kidnap the aging queen he had courted. James I dispatched Sir Walter Raleigh to the Tower in 1603; Raleigh passed the time of day writing *A History of the World* until 1616, and his stay in the Tower ended in 1618, when the monarch finally had him beheaded. In modern times, German spies were executed in the courtyards during the two world wars, and in 1941, Rudolf Hess, Hitler's deputy, was imprisoned there for a few days. Such colorful episodes of the Tower's history are hard to imagine when you're confronted with the multitudes of tourists and guides milling about, as they do most of the year; it's most atmospheric when other people don't go — on a rainy day, for instance, or at night for the Ceremony of the Keys. (Book ahead by writing to the Resident Governor, Queen's House, HM Tower of London EC3N 4AB. Enclose the appropriate international postage coupons.) Rapiers, clubs, maces and flails, long-bows and cross-bows, cannon and muskets, shields, daggers, and all manner of other weapons, as well as glittering armor displayed in the White Tower, the 92-foot-high structure begun by William the Conqueror in 1078 as his palace and fortress, and renamed in the mid-13th century when Henry III had the structure whitewashed; the collections are among the finest of their kind in the world. In the Jewel House, a later addition to the complex (closed annually in February), visitors see the Crown Jewels — the splendid St. Edward's crown worn only during coronations; the Imperial State, which contains over 3,500 precious stones, including four large pearls that probably belonged to Elizabeth I; the ancient Black Prince's Ruby, which Henry V wore at Agincourt; the Stuart Sapphire; and the 317-carat Second Star of Africa, the second largest of the nine major stones cut from the 3,106-carat Cullinan. The largest Star, a 530-carat, pear-shaped bit of glitter, which is not only the world's biggest cut diamond but also, according to some experts, its most perfect, embellishes the Royal Sceptre, which is also in the Jewel House, along with countless swords, bracelets, ewers, dishes, and their dazzling company. Don't fail to look for the Tower's group of ravens, whose eventual demise, legend has it, means that the Tower will fall.

HADRIAN'S WALL, near Newcastle-upon-Tyne, Tyne & Wear, England: Take any road west of this Northumberland shipbuilding city, and you're in the country of Hadrian's Wall, that phenomenal fortification put up by the Romans in the 2nd century AD as the northern limits of the Roman Empire to protect the legions from the northern barbarians. A standout even in an empire full of impressive fortifications, whose construction required 16,000 men to quarry and cart to the site over a million cubic yards of stone, it stretched over 70 miles across the neck of England, from what is now

Bowness-on-Solway, on Solway Firth, in the west, to Wallsend, near the mouth of the River Tyne, in the east; it consisted of a broad V-shaped ditch (the vallum) and a stone barrier 15 feet high, up to 9 feet thick (enough to drive a chariot along), and punctuated at third-mile intervals by so many guard towers, massive forts, and "milecastles" that some 5,500 cavalry and over half that many infantry were required to man it. Surprisingly enough, considering the wars and skirmishes that have taken place on and around it in the centuries since the Romans abandoned the country, many of these fortifications are still standing. The ditch is almost entirely intact; the wall itself can be seen from the Military Road, and the remains are particularly extensive in the area between Housesteads and Greenhead (where the wall runs along the border of Northumberland National Park for some 15 miles). There are fine views into the hills, and, at Housesteads, site of the most impressive remains of the 17 forts that once punctuated the wall, there are the remainders of the barracks, the commandant's offices, the granaries, hospital, and a latrine. Similarly well preserved are the remains west of Housesteads at Peel Crag and Walltown Crags. At Vindolanda, near Bardon Mill, and farther west near Greenhead, there are two fine museums that depict life on Hadrian's Wall during the Roman Army's occupation; Roman artifacts are on display alongside the Roman fort at Corbridge. As an introduction to what you'll see on the wall itself, the scale models and exhibits at Newcastle University's Museum of Antiquities at Newcastle-upon-Tyne are a must. Details: Northumbria Tourist Board, Aykley Heads, Durham City DH1 5UX, England (phone: 0385-46905).

CADBURY CASTLE, South Cadbury, Somerset, England: A century ago, when a party of Oxford archaeologists climbed the hill above this village 2 miles from the Wincanton-to-Ilchester A303, an old man met them at its foot and asked tearfully whether they had come to take the old king away. He was referring to Arthur. For this hill fort, one of the many occupied by a farming community since the 8th century BC and stormed by Vespasian, is thought by some to have been Camelot. Fortified for over five centuries, it was defended on the eve of the Roman invasion by four massive earth banks that the Romans partially dismantled before slaughtering the inhabitants and leaving the settlement to lie derelict for the next 200 years. Then, in the late third or early 4th century, activity here — perhaps in the form of pilgrimages — resumed, and, toward the end of the 5th century, the innermost of the four ancient banks was greatly strengthened by the addition of a new rampart held together with timber framing, a new gateway was built, and a small wooden tower was created above it, in building styles that reflected the manners of the Celts and the Romans. When men moved back into the old forts, it was usually to take advantage of the abandoned defenses to provide themselves with an attack-proof homestead. But the prehistoric ramparts here enclose some 18 acres — enough space, suggests archaeologist Leslie Alcock, to have accommodated an army as large as Arthur's. If he was truly the military leader for several small kingdoms, as some historians have surmised, this isolated hill near South Cadbury would have made an ideal base, situated as it was high enough to send signals by lantern to distant Glastonbury, where allies could then, in turn, summon armored horsemen from the hill forts of South Wales. Even the traditions of the Round Table find their corroboration at South Cadbury, with the excavation of a great hall, 63 feet by 34 feet, wooden and thatched. During the digging, fragments of imported pottery and broken wine pitchers were found, and it's easy to imagine these early Britons carousing in the days of darkness brought down around them during these years of warfare. For local tourist information, contact the West Country Tourist Board (address above).

STONEHENGE, Wiltshire, England: It's hard to appreciate this fantastic monument, not far from magnificently spired, equally celebrated Salisbury Cathedral, surrounded as it is by fences and gates — and all the more so when tour buses are disgorging masses of tourists on day trips from London, a common sight. Yet the mysterious pull exerted by England's most famous prehistoric monument — two concentric circles of stones, some over 20 feet high, ringed by a ditch 300 feet in diameter — is so strong that it's hard not to sense the rightness of myths that explain its origins in terms of Merlin and magic: Certainly the fiction is only a little stranger than the fact — that it was constructed in stages beginning in about 2750 BC, with stones that were rafted and dragged for many long miles (some from as far away as southwestern Wales), and then raised with wooden levers and rollers and ropes made of leather thongs. Its function is similarly unknown; some archaeologists — remarking on the way in which various stones are aligned with midsummer sunrise and midwinter moonrise — point out the possibility that it served as a sort of vast open-air observatory. Or perhaps that it was used for worship. Today, in midsummer, English druids still come here to celebrate their antique rites. Dressed in hooded white robes and carrying mistletoe and holly and banners emblazoned with mystical signs, they sing their hymns and chant strange runes as they march in procession amongst the megaliths and so await the coming of the dawn. For details about the region, contact the West Country Tourist Board (address above).

GLENELG BROCHS, Glenelg, Highland, Scotland: The fact that the name of this hamlet-by-the-sea is a palindrome ranks with the lovely rocky mountain scenery as one of its more fascinating aspects. Archaeologists and lovers of antiquities, however, are most drawn by the presence of two of the best preserved of Scotland's defensive stone towers known as brochs. Many now are little more than piles of rubble; the ones at Glenelg are not too much different than they were when the Picts built them all over the country during the Iron Age, with their 30-foot-high dry stone inner and outer walls, hollow between; their stone lintels; and their center courtyard. Nearby Dun Grugaig, another broch, occupies a lovely site close by a roiling cascade and fine views southward toward Ben Sgriol. For local information, contact the Highlands and Islands Development Board, Bridge House, 27 Bank St., Inverness IV1 1QR, Scotland (phone: 0463-234171).

MELROSE ABBEY, Melrose, Borders, Scotland: "If thou would see fair Melrose aright/Go visit it by the pale moonlight," wrote Sir Walter Scott in his *Lay of the Last Minstrel* about the ruins here. Among the finest and best preserved in Scotland, they move present-day visitors just as they did that celebrated 19th-century Scottish poet, who spent the last two decades of his life at nearby Abbotsford in a turreted, baronial sort of manse that is open to the public for tours. Melrose Abbey, one of four Border abbeys founded for a group of Cistercian monks by David I in 1136 just after the return of Roman Christianity to Scotland, was destroyed during English raids in 1322, restored by Robert Bruce in 1326, battered again in 1385, and ultimately destroyed in invasions in 1543 and 1544 — that is, all but the few sections that stand today in mute testimony to its past beauty. Particularly lovely is the reddish stonework in parts of the nave: the large five-light window in the south transept, the elaborately carved foliage embellishing the capitals nearby, the flying buttresses, and the porcine gargoyle playing bagpipes on the roof. According to tradition, the heart of Robert Bruce — which Sir James Douglas was taking to the Holy Land when he was killed — was buried under the east window, and Tom Purdie, the forester for Scott's estate, and Peter Matheson, the writer's coachman, are interred in the abbey cemetery. The choir is believed to be the resting place of Douglas himself as well as Alexander II and Michael Scott, the wizard of the *Lay of the Last Minstrel.* Melrose town, described as Kennaquhair in Scott's *Monastery* and *The Abbot,* is at one corner of what is widely known as the Scott Country, whose boundaries are also delimited by the towns of Galashiels, Selkirk, and Dryburgh. The latter is the site of Dryburgh Abbey, where Sir Walter Scott, Earl Haig (commander-in-chief of the British Army during World War I), and members of their families are buried. The ruins of its cloister are remarkably preserved — far better than those at the ruins of the remaining pair of David I's Border abbeys, not-far-distant

Kelso and Jedburgh. Both of these are also worth visiting; at Jedburgh, you can tour the house where Queen Mary stayed for a short while and visit imposing, 19th-century Jedburgh Castle, which now houses a museum devoted to the penal system of the period. Details: Scottish Border Tourist Board, Municipal Buildings, Selkirk, Borders TD7 4JX, Scotland (phone: 0750-20555).

SKARA BRAE and MAES HOWE, Mainland, Orkney, Scotland: This 70-island group across the Pentland Firth from John O'Groats on the Scottish mainland has Britain's densest concentration of prehistoric monuments — an average of about three recorded sites of archaeological note per square mile; those on the large island known as Mainland are particularly notable. Maes Howe (or "greatest mound"), for instance, is Europe's best example of a Stone Age circular chambered cairn — and it has no rival on mainland Britain. Constructed as the tomb of a very important chieftain and measuring over 110 feet across and over 300 feet around, this hollow 24-foot-high mound of rock and clay is entered through a low stone passageway, which gives access to a vaulted chamber 14 feet square flanked by a trio of burial niches walled and paved in huge single stones embellished in what some authorities believe to be the single richest collection of Runic inscriptions to be found in any one place in the world. The carvings, left by Norsemen who raided the grave in the 12th century, describe how the contents were spirited away by night, hint of a hiding place nearby, and tell of the problems that resulted when two members of a band that had sought refuge here during a storm went crazy. You can see the kind of village where the Stone Age men, whose deaths are so widely memorialized, lived at Skara Brae, which was constructed at about the same time as Maes Howe, lived in for perhaps six centuries, and then inexplicably buried with sand for the almost four millennia that followed, until unearthed by another storm around 1850. Most of the pottery, beads, tools, and implements found on the site are now displayed in the National Museum of Antiquities in Edinburgh; but the site as you see it today — a group of small squared lane-linked huts clustered around a central courtyard in a field just about 20 feet above sea level — is impressive enough. The flagstone blocks with which the structures were built, the slate shale with which they were paved, the shelves and built-in boxes and cubbyholes, stone beds, drains, and other impedimenta of the life of the three dozen souls who called this home so long ago are still remarkably well preserved. Other major sites are nearby: the four remaining Standing Stones of Stenness, a henge dating from about 2300 BC; the great Ring of Brodgar, where more than two dozen stones can be seen inside a ditch on a 2.5-acre site; the Broch of Gurness, Orkney Mainland's best representation of this type of structure, situated amidst a group of other stone buildings of assorted ages; the Onstan Chambered Cairn, dated about 2500 BC; and many more — on this island and on the others. Cliffbound Hoy, for instance, boasts two martello towers constructed as defenses against American privateers. The islands are particularly lovely during the twilight nights of late summer, when the sun never quite rests. Not all archaeological sites can be seen at all times, and some are relatively inaccessible; so it's wise to plan your visit well before you arrive. For details, contact the Orkney Tourist Board, Kirkwall, Orkney KW15 1NX, Scotland (phone: 0856-2856).

CAERNARFON, Gwynedd, Wales: Though little remains of this castle save its walls, it is easy to imagine the grandeur that Edward I planned when he began construction in the late 13th and early 14th centuries. He was building not only a military fortress, but also a symbol of his sovereignty over Wales and, accordingly, he had it executed very much in the style of the Romans who had ruled Wales centuries earlier from this site on the Menai Strait, with stonework much like that of the 5th-century Roman wall at Constantinople. The cost of such monumentality was immense — the equivalent of nearly £15 million by today's standards. There were shooting galleries both high and low, courtyards and drawbridges, portcullises, arrow loops and spyholes — many of which, or remnants thereof, can still be seen. With the turrets and towers to explore, vaulted chambers to poke around in, walls and lawns to walk upon, a museum to visit, and a film on the castle's history to view, this is understandably a popular destination in Wales. Dr. Samuel Johnson, on visiting the castle two centuries ago, allowed as how he had not thought that there had been such buildings, that it surpassed all his ideas. You may well agree. The future Edward VIII was invested here in 1911, and the present Prince Charles in 1969 — only appropriate since Edward I's son, the first Prince of Wales, was born here. For more information about the area, contact the Northern Regional Office, Wales Tourist Board, 77 Conwy Rd., Colwyn Bay, Clwyd LL29 7LN, Wales (phone: 0492-531731).

CONWY CASTLE, Conwy, Gwynedd, Wales: Counted among Europe's greatest fortresses when taken together with the town's walls, and once one of its most powerful fortifications, this magnificent piece of medieval architecture, one of ten castles built by Edward I as his headquarters in his efforts to control the Welsh, must have been all the more striking in its early years when its walls — whitewashed at the time — gleamed brightly from afar. But even now the structure is altogether impressive. Built in the main between 1283 and 1287 after designs by the king's castle engineer, one James of St. George, it required the work of some 1,500 men and the expenditure of some £15,000 before its completion. The eight towers, each with walls 15 feet thick, rise to a height of 70 feet; they are not, as they seem, perpendicular to the ground, but instead taper gradually toward the top. The Northwest Tower has a fine view over the river, and the Prison Tower has a concealed dungeon as fearsomely dark and close as the imposing 38-by-125-foot Great Hall just above is spacious and airy, with its grand north- and east-facing windows. In the part of the castle known as the Inner Bailey, which lies to the east of the Great Hall, you can view the elegantly detailed Queen Eleanor's Chapel, the best-preserved part of the structure; the name is merely traditional because the castle wasn't finished during her lifetime. The most important battle fought within the castle's walls took place in 1294, during a rebellion led by Prince Madog ap Llywelyn; Edward I took refuge there and, when trapped without proper food and water by the rising tide of the river, was almost beaten. The castle's subsequent history was marked by a visit by Richard II at the end of the 14th century (he was captured by the duke of Northumberland and Archbishop Arundel for Henry Bolingbroke, later Henry IV); by occupation by Royalist forces during the 17th century; and by plundering, dismantling, and damage during the 19th century. For more information, contact the Wales Tourist Board's Northern Regional Office (address above).

BALLINTUBBER ABBEY, Ballintubber, County Mayo, Irish Republic: The site of this Augustinian community has long been an important one; tradition tells us that St. Patrick baptized local peasants with water from its well. Later, the monastery became the departure point for pilgrimages to Croagh Patrick. Now it is noted for the fact that Mass has been said in its church ever since the community's founding by Cathal Crovdearg O'Conor, the king of Connacht, for the Canons Regular of St. Augustine in 1216 — despite the suppression of the abbey under Henry VIII and the depredations of the Cromwellians in 1653. The fact that there has been no interruption in religious rites for over 760 years makes the church unique in the English-speaking world. It is an exceptionally handsome structure. Thanks to sensitive restoration work begun on the initiative of a former priest, Father Egan, finished in 1966, a new wooden roof was constructed for the nave and the interior walls whitewashed in the ancient fashion, so that the church looks much as it must have upon its completion. The carving around the three lancet windows in the gable and on the capitals of the chancel exemplifies the best work of a school of talented late Romanesque carvers who worked in the province of Connacht in the early 13th century after the rest of the country had gone over to the Gothic style; the Augustinians, who were more permissive in their rules than some other orders, allowed the artists more latitude in their designs — which the results reflect. The wonderfully monstrous snakes twined around each other on the capitals between the triple round-headed window in the front of the church (which you'll be able to see in those distant gloomy recesses only if you've brought along field glasses) and the grotesque creatures creeping along the corbels that uphold the chancel's ribbed vaulting are just two examples. Nearby, you can see the well where St. Patrick did his baptizing and the attractive cloisters, reconstructed from the ruins of the 15th-century originals with the aid of fragments that came to light in the course of archaeological excavations in the 1960s. For local information, contact Westport Tourist Office, The Mall, Westport, County Mayo, Irish Republic (phone: 098-25711).

ROCK OF CASHEL, Cashel, County Tipperary, Irish Republic: Even in Ireland's earliest days, before any fortresses or cathedrals or castles were built atop this chunk of carboniferous limestone, the Rock must have looked a bit unreal, rising precipitously, as it does — a block of slate gray — above the rock-studded green plains all around; now, capped by the spare and broken remains of structures once frequented by saints, kings, and bishops, the Rock provides a visual experience that is, quite simply, one of Ireland's most stupendous. The longtime capital of the kings of Munster, the Rock was visited in 450 by St. Patrick, who baptized King Aengus and his brothers. (During the baptism ceremony, St. Patrick accidentally put the point of his crozier through the king's foot; the king, thinking the action part of the ceremony, bore the pain with fortitude.) Later, Brian Ború, who defeated the Norsemen in the battle of Clontarf near Dublin in the 10th century, was crowned king here, and, though it stayed in the hands of his descendants, its importance declined; in 1101, it was presented by Brian's grandson, King Muirchertach, to the church, which is responsible for most of the buildings in the tightly grouped complex you see on the Rock today. These are as impressive when you see them at close range as they are from afar. Dominating the scene is the cathedral, begun in the 13th century and abandoned in 1749 when the archbishop (too laggardly, perhaps, to trek to his church) removed the lead roof; the central tower offers fine views into the distant mountains and to the Devil's Bit — the mountain pass said to have been created when the Dark Angel took a large bite. (The size of the Rock is said to match the void in the mountain exactly.) A very well preserved round tower, probably 12th century, stands at the corner of the cathedral's north transept; and the massive rectangular, three-storied archbishop's palace, honeycombed with passageways to explore, adjoins the west end of the cathedral's nave, which was never completed. The newly restored 15th-century Hall of the Vicars Choral, used to house laymen who participated in the chanting of the cathedral's services, is nearby; the 12th-century Cross of St. Patrick was recently transferred to this site. Tiny Cormac's Chapel, wedged into a corner between the cathedral's choir and its south transept, is especially interesting. Built in 1134 by Cormac MacCarthy, the bishop of Cashel and the king of Desmond (in the realm created after a defeat by the king of Connaught divided Munster in half), it is well known as the nation's best example of the Irish Romanesque style; volumes have been written tracing its origins. You will probably be most impressed by the elaborate carvings, the ribbed vaulting, twisted capitals, and richly embellished blind arcades; the tympana (the surfaces between the arch and the lintels) surmounting the south door by which you enter today, and the far grander north door, through which worshipers gained access to the nave until the construction of the cathedral, are beautiful. The lions and centaurs you see here are even more exotic than the human heads that peer out at you from around the chancel. After you've completed your tour, don't fail to see some of the older structures in Cashel proper — among them the 15th-century Quirke's Castle and the 18th-century Palace of Protestant Archbishops — both now used as hotels. Also worth noting are the ruins of the 13th-century Dominican monastery close to the center of town, and the 18th-century Church of Ireland St. John the Baptist Cathedral. For local information, contact the South Eastern Region Tourist Information Office, 41 The Quay, Waterford, County Waterford, Irish Republic (phone: 051-75823).

GLENDALOUGH, County Wicklow, Irish Republic: Nestled in a valley deep in the Wicklow Mountains about 30 miles south of Dublin, this "valley of the two lakes" is the most beautifully situated of Ireland's important early Christian monasteries, particularly when the gorse blooms in May. This monastery grew up around the site where St. Kevin settled to renounce human love and live as a hermit during the 6th century, and like many other Irish monasteries, was pillaged and sacked many times by the Vikings and assorted other marauders; like Clonmacnoise, it was particularly vulnerable because of its fame as a seat of learning. And, as at Clonmacnoise, the ruins are extensive: better than half a dozen churches, crosses, grave slabs, a priest's house, a round tower, and old wells. The stone of which most are constructed, granite and mica-schist, has chipped and crumbled over the centuries, giving the walls a rough texture and providing a fine medium for the growth of the pale soft local lichen; the buildings at Glendalough have that particularly antique look that you may imagine all ruins will have until you find out otherwise. It's certainly pleasant to spend a day here, poking around among the broken walls, wandering along the pathways between them, and admiring the glass-smooth waters of Upper and Lower lakes. Especially noteworthy are the 7th-century cathedral, Ireland's largest pre-Romanesque church; St. Kevin's Church (generally known as St. Kevin's Kitchen) with its round-tower-like belfry rising up above a stone roof; the small, 12th-century Priest's House, perhaps originally a mortuary chapel or even the saint's shrine; the Reefert Church, around whose walls sleep many Leinster kings; and, farther down the valley, accessible via a narrow sylvan path, St. Saviour's Monastery, a 12th-century church probably built by Laurence O'Toole, former abbot of Glendalough, archbishop of Dublin, and Ireland's first canonized saint. There are especially fine walks around the Upper Lake, which is picturesquely backed by the steep cliffs of Camaderry and Lugduff mountains, ribboned by the rushing Glenealo Stream and a waterfall; the stand of firs on the north side is quite lovely. Information: Eastern Region Tourism Organisation, St. Michael's Wharf, Dun Laoghaire, County Dublin, Irish Republic (phone: 01-806984).

GRIANÁN OF AILEACH, Burt, County Donegal, Irish Republic: Ulster cannot boast megalithic monuments of the scope of Leinster's Boyne Valley cemeteries (although there do exist several structures with elaborate entranceways that have earned them the name "court graves," as well as standing stones and stone circles and dolmens). Here, however, the most characteristic and striking ruins are those of circle-shaped ring forts, which protected farmhouses up until AD 1000 (and which you'll find today scattered here and there by the thousands throughout Ulster's fields), and, even more striking, stone *cashels* (a circular wall enclosing a group of ecclesiastical buildings). The Grianán of Aileach (the sunny place in the territory of Aileach), one of the most important antiquities in the northern part of the island, is among the most striking. Situated atop 800-foot Grianán Mountain not far from Londonderry, this fortification measures about 77 feet across; the 13-foot-thick walls, restored in the 1870s by the bishop of Derry to their original height of 17 feet, contain galleries and guard chambers, and enclose a series of stairway-connected terraces. The views afforded by the topmost of these, out over the blue reaches of Loughs Foyle and Swilly, are glorious — fully worthy of the O'Neills, the kings of Ulster, whose northern branch made this fortification its base from approximately the 5th century AD through the twelfth, when Muirchertach O'Brien, the king of Munster, avenging the pillaging of his own residence, completed the destruction of this structure, which had already been badly battered during a 676 attack by the southern O'Neills under Finechta the Festive: The Munster king instructed each of his men to carry away a single stone of the fort. The exact date of construction is unknown, since no excavations have been made here; in their Annals of the Kingdom of Ireland, the Four Masters put its origins back in the Iron Age, while other scholars suggest that it was probably built within a few centuries either way of the lifetime of St. Patrick — that is, in the 5th century AD. The round shape has inspired the church nestling at the foot of the mountain at Burt, one of Ireland's most interesting modern structures. It was built in 1967 after designs by Liam MacCormick and Una Madden. Similar, and equally impressive, fortifications include Dun Aengus on the Aran Islands, and Staigue Fort in County Kerry. Details about the area are available from the Donegal/Leitrim/Sligo Region Tourist Information Office, Temple St., Sligo, County Sligo, Irish Republic (phone: 071-61201).

HILL OF TARA, near Navan, County Meath, Irish Republic: Little but legend and a handful of earthworks and stones remains of the glories of Tara — but of legend and conjecture there is plenty, and this 512-foot hill about 25 miles from Dublin, commanding a fine view of a vast expanse of lush meadows, is well worth a visit. Already a significant burial place two millennia before Christ (as revealed by the excavation of one of the site's most notable monuments, the Mound of the Hostages), it ranked among Ireland's most important political and religious sites for almost 2,000 years all told; it became the center of priestly rulers even before St. Patrick came to Ireland in the 5th century, and long served as a residence for anyone strong enough to make himself at least nominally high king of Ireland. One of Tara's most glorious periods came in the first centuries after Christ, when the celebrated Cormac the Wise constructed the wooden palaces that you can read about in some of Ireland's early literature. (It was his daughter who, though betrothed to Finn MacCool, eloped with Diarmuid O'Duibhne, and gave rise to the wonderful stories about the lovers' flight from one end of Ireland to the other.) Later, after St. Patrick triumphed in a contest of feats with the druids of High King Laoghaire, whose authority the saint had challenged, the king allowed his subjects to be converted to Christianity (although he himself remained a pagan until his death). Tara's importance declined until its abandonment in 1022. Relics of all of these eras can be seen today. The Mound of the Hostages (*Dunha na nGiall*), an early passage grave (ca. 1800 BC) with a 17-foot-long corridor, covered by a mound that measures 72 feet in diameter, is at one edge of the large circular Iron Age ring fort called the Royal Enclosure (*Rath na Ríogh*), at whose center are two other earthworks — the Royal Seat (*Forradh*) and Cormac's House (*Teach Cormaic*), where you'll see a modern statue of St. Patrick and the 5-foot-long chunk of granite known as the Stone of Destiny (*Lia Fáil*), which, according to tradition, would roar when the king being crowned upon it was acceptable. Just south of the Royal Enclosure is *Rath Laoghaire*, which is said to be near the above-mentioned king's burial place. To the north, you'll find the Rath of the Synods (*Rath na Seanad*), an erstwhile fortress and burial place; the Banquet Hall (*Teach Miodchuarta*), where festivities are reported in the 12th-century *Book of Leinster,* and where each class of society had its own compartment; the circular *Rath Gráinne,* named for the fugitive king's daughter; and the odd-shaped Sloping Trenches (*Claoin Fhearta*), which probably had a ceremonial function of some sort. Also interesting is Adamnán's Stone, a 6-foot-high chunk of sandstone bearing the incised likeness of a human figure — perhaps the horned Celtic Cernunnos or a type of fertility figure known as a *sheila-na-gig.* For local information, contact the Eastern Region Tourism Organisation (address above).

NEWGRANGE, Newgrange, County Meath, Irish Republic: Very few relics of the daily life of the people of the Neolithic Age (ca. 3700–2000 BC) survive in Ireland today; it seems as if all the creative energies of the communities of this period were directed toward the construction not of homes for the living, but of monumental repositories for the remains of the dead, and the whole valley of the river Boyne, about 30 miles north of Dublin, is scattered with cairns, standing stones, and earthworks both large and small. Of these, Newgrange is the most impressive by far. In fact, this so-called passage grave ranks among the most important of its type in Europe, and scholars have spent centuries studying it. Literature of the ancient Irish links it to a mysterious personage who is sometimes called Oengus an Brogha (Oengus of the Palace) and sometimes dubbed Oengus mac an Dagda (Oengus son of the good god); some archaeologists have suggested that Newgrange and similar tombs on the Continent were constructed for the important personages in groups of traders and prospectors who first migrated from Spain or Portugal around 4000 BC. Certainly, they had a civilization far more highly organized than the widespread belief in our "primitive ancestors" credits them — at least if they are to be judged from the sophistication of the building and decorative techniques evidenced here. The earth mound that is the most immediately obvious feature of Newgrange, entirely man-made using alternate layers of turf and stones, is unusually large — 40 feet high and 300 feet in diameter; estimates put the quantity of stones required for the whole undertaking at 180,000 tons. Now covered with grass, the mound was originally paved with white quartz pebbles so that it glistened brightly enough in the sun to be seen from afar (as indeed it does now, thanks to a careful restoration in the 1960s). Inside, leading into the depth of the hill from the entrance on the southeastern frontage, is a 62-foot-long, yard-wide passage. High enough to let you walk upright and lined with a series of orthostats, or upright stones, 5 to 8 feet high, it ends at a generally circular burial chamber, whose notable features include its beehive-shaped ceiling paved with overlapping stones (following a method of construction found over and over again at Irish ruins of this period), and, adjoining the main chamber — and giving the tomb's interior a roughly cruciform shape — three recesses contain stone troughs or basins probably once used to contain the ashes of the dead. On the morning of the shortest day of the year, rays of sun shine directly up the passageway to the center of the burial chamber — a design that required some sort of calendar to calculate. The decoration throughout further confirms that sophisticated minds were at work. The ceiling of the north recess, covered with carved spirals, lozenges, triangles, zigzags, diamonds, and other shapes, is particularly noteworthy, as are the gigantic threshold stone, at the entrance to the tomb, and many of the orthostats. Similar motifs appear on many other megalithic stones (and on Mycenean tombs as well); it's thought that far from being mere ornament, the designs, probably rooted in the pre-Mycenean civilization of the third millennium BC, are magnificent abstract representations of gods, goddesses, and human beings. A museum and tourist information office at Newgrange can give you details about Newgrange as well as about nearby Dowth and Knowth, the two other major monuments in this area, which is often called Brugh na Boinne (Bend of the Boyne). Note that access to the Newgrange site is available only on the excellent guided tours provided by the National Parks and Monuments Branch of the Office of Public Works, Dublin 2, Irish Republic. Details: Eastern Region Tourism Organisation (address above).

CARRICKFERGUS CASTLE, County Antrim, Northern Ireland: Along with Trim Castle in County Meath, Carrickfergus Castle remains the mightiest symbol of the presence of the Normans in Ireland after the invasion of 1169. Situated strategically on the shores of Belfast Lough, it is one of Ireland's strongest castles, and its story continues through a number of important eras in Irish history. Founded in 1180 by John de Courcy, the first Norman Lord of Ulster, it was besieged in 1210 by King John of England, who feared the rising independence of his Norman barons. After some resistance, the castle fell to Robert Bruce, whose brother Edward had invaded Ireland from Scotland in 1315. In 1690, William of Orange landed here during his campaign to defeat the Stuart kings and to take possession of Ireland; some 70 years later, it was taken by a French expeditionary force. The American John Paul Jones, captaining the *Ranger,* defeated the HMS *Drake,* which was moored beneath the castle, in 1778; and in the 18th century, the castle was used as a prison for United Irishmen and others. You enter the impressive structure through a gate flanked by two rounded towers, then proceed through the Outer Ward past a handful of 16th-century storehouses into the Middle Ward; the Inner Ward, which is adjacent, is dominated by the squarish Keep — five stories or about 90 feet high, 56 feet across, and 58 feet deep. A stairway, which climbs inside the 8-foot-thick walls, takes you upward from the ground level (where you'll see an early-20th-century steam engine and an antique wooden dugout canoe) to a group of military exhibits on the floor above, and into the Great Chamber, a spacious room with good-sized windows. The walled town's handsome late-18th-century Town Hall, and its Church of St. Nicholas, which dates from the 12th and 17th centuries, are also worth visiting; don't miss the monument there to Sir Arthur Chichester, who built the town walls and figured importantly in the establishment of the Ulster we know today. For details of the medieval fairs and banquets held at the castle during the summer, phone 09603-63604; for other information, contact the Northern Ireland Tourist Board.

For the Experience

Pub Crawling

Everywhere in Britain and Ireland there's a pub, and in most places there are many pubs. In Ireland there are 11,000 licenses to sell intoxicating liquor, and even if every eligible adult were a drinker, there would still be more pubs per head than any place else on earth; towns like Listowel seem to have more pubs than dwelling houses. In Britain, London alone has 5,000 pubs; in the country, there are so many that during World War II, when road signs were removed, people could give directions in terms of the local watering hole: "Turn left at the *Dog and Duck,* go for half a mile as far as the *King's Arms,* then . . ." Those English villages that have lost their last remaining pub have won some degree of celebrity as a result, being very unusual indeed. There are pubs in the city and in the country, pubs in the theater district, pubs patronized heavily by journalists, pubs with gardens, and pubs where you can listen to music or catch a striptease show.

Yet only a fraction of them have the kind of decor and atmosphere that would measure up to most Americans' idea of what British and Irish pubs are like. Dark paneling, a long mahogany bar, and an abundance of engraved glass mirrors and gleaming brass fittings are occasionally to be found — but they're the exception rather than the rule.

In Ireland, for instance, there are hundreds of pubs which, though reasonably well run, are functional, unpretentious — and instantly forgotten; there are thousands of "lounge bars," where you will find soft seats, soft lighting, soft Muzak, and soft carpets — just like home; and there are the so-called singing pubs, which are well advertised and known to all taxi drivers. (Contrary to popular belief, singing is greatly discouraged in most Irish pubs, particularly in the cities, and only in the singing pubs is one guaranteed music — but even then, the quality is variable, the crowds enormous, and the comfort minimal.) Then there are a few pubs like the city-center establishment in the west of Ireland, where there are flush toilets for men but none at all for women; where the glasses seem to be doused only infrequently in cold water; and where the only ice is in the voice of the owner at closing time. The Guinness draft is a danger to public health; there are few stools and only one table; and the fire, when lit, is carefully covered in case the habitués might derive a jot of warmth from it. The most timorous suggestion that there might be room for improvement causes the proprietor to purse his lips in profound disapproval: Any improvement would "spoil the place." As for the above-noted west of Ireland pub, the reader should know that in this pub, and *only* in this pub, is he likely to hear a heady discourse on the relative merits of Eliot, Pound, and Auden intermingled with passionate discussion of the forthcoming All-Ireland Hurling Final and the chronically bad state of the country's industrial relations while he sips 15-year-old whiskey from the barrel and listens to music, which comes from an ancient wireless and is usually classical. To round off the picture, one corner of the bar is gay.

Character is the word that the Irish use to describe premises like these, and it doesn't have anything to do with whether the walls are paneled in mahogany and polished or plastered and badly in need of a paint job. The true joy of Irish pubs is chat, banter, repartee. The physical shortcomings of the premises are more often than not made up for by the spiritual and mental experiences that are to be enjoyed.

The average British pub, while far less primitive, may be no more wonderful to look at: Though some of the worse abuses of the recent past — the superabundance of Formica and other plastics, loud juke boxes, the battery of electronic games that bleep and squeal above whatever noises of good cheer a draft from the pressurized aluminum keg has managed to encourage — have begun to disappear in pubs in London and the South, the garden variety British pub generally reflects many of the more obnoxious intrusions of 20th-century civilization.

Yet, paradoxically enough, it doesn't seem to matter. Just as an American neighborhood tavern can manage to entertain even when the floor is ugly green tile, its bar stools covered plastic, and its lighting murky, the pub is a centerpiece of social life here. (In Ireland, in fact, the melancholy truth is that very few people choose a pub for comfort. Masochism being a national malaise, the more stuffy, smoky, noisy, pokey, and uncomfortable a pub is, the more likely people are to say how much they are enjoying it.)

Before setting off on that most convivial of pleasures, the pub crawl, there are a number of facts a visitor should keep in mind:

Pubs are also for eating in, but they provide light fare only. Anyone who asks for a full meal will receive looks of horrified incredulity: "Pub grub" has traditionally been fairly simple fare: In Britain, the choices most often are sandwiches; a ploughman's lunch, a hunk of bread and cheese plus pickle; or cottage pie, ground meat topped with mashed potato and baked in the oven. In London and the South, pub grub has begun to be somewhat more ambitious, and often includes a couple of hot dishes and a salad. In Ireland, the selection consists mostly of soup or sandwiches (although delicious exceptions such as those noted below do exist). Often, food is available only at lunchtime — though in London, many pubs serve food into the evenings.

Pub crowds vary. British pubs usually attract a motley crowd of all ages — silver-haired ladies clutching shopping bags and bolting shots of gin; workmen in stained overalls arguing politics and draining pints of beer; tourists juggling plates of Scotch eggs and pints of lager. In Ireland, until recently it was not only considered improper for ladies to drink in bars, but they would often be refused a pint. Although the clientele in countryside pubs tends to be mostly male, those in the city draw an equal number of women. And the snugs, cubicles traditionally reserved for genteel ladies, may now be occupied by men seeking quiet amid the clamor.

Pub hours differ widely from area to area and occasionally also from pub to pub. Most pubs in England, Scotland, and Wales open in the late morning, do a booming business through the lunch hour, shut down for the afternoon, then start serving again at the end of the working day or around the dinner hour; closing is generally around 10:30 or 11 PM on Sundays. However, a recent amendment of the regulations relating to "opening hours" in England eliminated the afternoon closing, but *only* for those establishments in which a "real" meal is available and on the table with your beer mug during that period. It's too early to appraise how the broad range of pub owners will adopt this change, since the meal specified under the new rules must be one that is eaten with a knife and fork. Normal "pub grub" munchies — sandwiches, or finger foods such as Scotch eggs, for example — don't qualify. And to confuse matters even more, local variations are legion. Pubs in some market areas may begin business with the sun; pubs in Edinburgh and Glasgow are generally open throughout the day — in fact, licensing laws in Scotland as a whole are more liberal than in England. Pubs in other parts of the country, particularly Northern Ireland, the islands, and certain corners of Wales, are generally closed all day Sunday.

In Ireland, all pubs open at 11:30 AM and close at 11 PM on weekdays. On Sundays, pubs in Northern Ireland are closed (though hotels and licensed restaurants are open).

In Dublin, the pubs close from 2:30 to 3:30 PM for a hiatus known to all as the "holy hour." In the Republic, pubs are open from 12:30 to 2 PM and again from 4 to 10 PM. Pubs in the countryside are usually quiet during the day, since people still eat a noon dinner at home; anyone interested in catching these bars at their liveliest should visit in the evening. Pubs in the cities do a bustling day-long business, as people flock in at lunchtime for a snack and perhaps in the late afternoon for a drink.

Beer is not the name of the brew. The sheer variety of drafts can perplex newcomers. Britons and the Irish talk of lagers and of ales and their subtypes rather than "beer." Lager is made from a yeast that sinks to the bottom of the brewing tank during fermentation (rather than rising to the top, as does the yeast used in traditional ales). It is also activated at a lower temperature, so the product stays clear instead of turning cloudy when cooled. Typically, lagers are also lighter in color and body, fizzier, and drier, and taste more of malt than hops. But there are exceptions, because many lagers are made to taste like ales and vice versa.

Ales fall into several distinct categories. Bitter, usually served on draft, has a good strong brown color, a frothy head, and a taste that tends toward the sharp or the earthy (thanks to a large proportion of hops in the brew). The terms "special" and "best," applied to bitters, refer not to quality but to strength. So-called pale and light ales are the bottled versions of bitter; pale is apt to be the stronger. Mild is yet a different brew, made from a recipe that calls for more sugar and less hops. Served on draft, it is usually sweeter in taste, and (except in the Midlands, where the milds look almost like bitter) usually dark brown to black. Brown ale is like a bottled version of mild. Stouts — brews made of a well-roasted, unmalted barley — are all very dark and sometimes sweet; Guinness, Ireland's most famous drink, is thick and rich like all stout, but not at all sweet. Guinness, particularly, seems to be an acquired taste. (To sample it at its best, stop in at the factory on the shores of the River Liffey at St. James Gate, the world's largest stout-producing brewery; after a visit to the Guinness Museum and a viewing of films describing the brewing process in the newly restored *Guinness Hop Store,* visitors can sip a glass or two — delicious.)

At one time, it was common for pubs in Britain to serve only keg beers, which have been filtered and pasteurized at the brewery and packed under pressure. But because of the "real ale" movement of the last few years, most pubs now also serve brews that are still fermenting when they are delivered to the pub. Unlike keg beers, which have been filtered and even pasteurized at the brewery and then packed under pressure, real ales require careful handling — but the taste warrants the effort.

The best guide to pubs is the *Good Beer Guide,* published under the aegis of the active Campaign for Real Ale (CAMRA) and available for £5.95 from its offices at 34 Alma Rd., St. Albans, Hertfordshire AL1 3BW, England (published in the US under the title *The Best Pubs of Great Britain,* by Globe Pequot Press, Old Chester Rd., Chester, CT 06412 for $9.95). This guide lists over 5,000 pubs that serve the better brews. We also like the annually revised *Good Pubs Guide,* published by Consumers' Association and Hodder & Stoughton (£7.95), and for an extra fillip with your topping, check out *Haunted Pubs in Britain and Ireland* by Marc Alexander (£2.95; Sphere Books Limited).

The following selection, which includes some of the very best, most unusual, and those with the most atmosphere, shows off the variety of pubs you'll turn up when you prowl farther afield.

MINER'S INN, Acomb, Northumberland, England: Only 2 miles from Hexham, a busy but largely unspoiled market town with a beautiful ancient abbey, this cozy 18th-century coaching inn, comfortable if a bit garish in its plushness, has thick walls, immense and impressive original oak beams, brass ornaments that suggest antiquity, a garden, and — perhaps best of all — a pleasantly mixed clientele that includes not only locals but also bankers and plastics manufacturers who drive out from 20-mile-distant Newcastle, long-distance hikers heading for the Northumbria National Park, and campers. Steak, trout, and duck are among the dishes available in the restaurant at moderate prices. Phone: 0434-603909.

EAGLE, Cambridge, Cambridgeshire, England: One of the oldest of dozens of pubs in this ancient university city, this former coaching inn in sequestered Eagle Yard, near King's College Chapel and just off Bene't Street, is a favorite among undergraduates — but there's generally an agreeable assortment of young townspeople on hand as well; the excellent lunchtime salad buffet is popular with both groups. Architecturally important, and therefore "listed" so that the building can't be tampered with, the Eagle has been little altered over the years — and certainly not prettified — since it was used by stagecoaches on the route between Huntingdon, Hertford, and London; and both of its wood paneled bars, one much larger than the other, are fairly spartan, with bare floors and uncushioned seating, but they're rich in atmosphere as a result. Outside the windows of the upper story, the keen of eye should be able to see an old gallery, which, in the absence of interior passages to connect the upstairs rooms, once performed the function corridors do today. Phone: 0223-353782.

ROYAL OAK, King's Bromley, Staffordshire, England: The public bar section of this half-timbered erstwhile farmhouse, originally part of a big estate, is basic if congenial; but the lounge is wonderfully comfortable with its red carpet, button-backed plush seats, and open fires: It's just the place to while away a long winter's eve. The dining room is just as attractive. The long oak beams there and in the bars — said to have come from early-17th-century sailing ships — give the place an old world look; there's no question but that the place really does date from 1610, as local historians assert. The venison and omelettes are worth a detour, and the scenery in the surrounding country is exceptionally pretty in places, and highly underrated. Burton-on-Trent is the nearest town of any size. Phone: Yoxall 472289.

ANGEL, Lavenham, Suffolk, England: Even in a superbly preserved medieval town like Lavenham, where scarcely a dwelling seems less than a few centuries old, this inn on the marketplace overlooking the historic gray-and-white half-timbered guildhall — itself barely changed for hundreds of years — is very old, dating in part from the 15th century and built atop the much older remains of a dormitory for a religious order. There are now two bars — one, the public, catering to the needs of locals; the other, oak-beamed and thickly carpeted, more attuned to the requirements of the many tourists who flock to Lavenham and, after much rubbernecking around the rural corners of Suffolk, want to put their feet up. At midday and in the evening, excellent home-cooked meals and snacks are always available. Phone: 0787-247388.

ANTELOPE, London, England: If you've ever wondered where the Bellamies (or Hudson) might have lifted a stein of lager when they ventured from their home at nearby 19 Eaton Square, this probably would have been it. You can almost imagine the head of the *Upstairs, Downstairs* household at this 18th-century pub at the edge of regal Belgravia, barely a block from Sloane Square, and on the periphery of the punk precincts of the King's Road. Indeed, this is a place where the posh people of London's most luxurious lanes meet both crass commercial types and denizens of London's drop-out world. Though the main saloon is very unprepossessing — wooden tables surrounded by unmatched chairs — the crowd is mostly chic and stylish. The food counter here is a fine place to sample your first ploughman's lunch or shepherd's pie. Phone: 01-730-7781.

AUDLEY, London, England: Found in London's higher rent Mayfair district, this large establishment sits on the corner of South Audley Street, barely a block from the American Embassy at Grosvenor Square. Its cleanliness makes it a major luncheon favorite, and sitting on one of the stools at the lunch counter here is a special treat. The large, recently remodeled bar and cold carvery offer first-class sandwiches, and a slab of Stilton served for dessert is fresh and feisty. A smaller lounge bar, complete with roaring fire in winter, is the place to find the majority of London patrons, who visit the *Audley* more often to drink than eat. The conversation varies substantially from room to room, and it's fun to move between the two very different groups of customers. But regardless of which part of the premises you choose to inhabit, the Victorian decor, with its garish ornamentation, provides a very pleasant environment. This is one of the places where you're most likely to run into a friendly accent from home. Phone: 499-1843.

DIRTY DICKS, London, England: Abandoned by his fiancée on the eve of his wedding day, the Dirty Dick in question, one Nathaniel Bentley, went into seclusion and lived out his life in isolation and ever-increasing squalor in the apartments that now make up the downstairs section of this pub at 202 Bishopsgate. The spiders and bats that used to swing from the walls and ceiling in the downstairs bar as reminders of the weird, Dickensian story have been relegated to a small museum area — but the place is a pleasant enough spot to begin an evening. The area above, rebuilt in 1870, lends itself to other functions. Galleried and spacious, with wood everywhere and sawdust on the floors, it's plain rather than plush (much like the East End surrounding it), and, in its dark and clubby way, it's a supremely restful place to quench a thirst after a hectic Sunday morning's bargaining along nearby Petticoat Lane. Phone: 01-283-5888.

EL VINO, London, England: Though a wine bar rather than a pub, this establishment at 47 Fleet Street deserves special mention as a bastion of City tradition. From its earliest years, for purely chivalrous reasons, women were not allowed to stand at the bar (though a recent High Court action funded by the Equal Opportunities Commission has changed all that). Men must wear collar, tie, and jacket, and women must wear skirts or dresses (never trousers). Considering also the magnificently polished Victorian setting, it's scarcely possible to imagine a more Dickensian scene. Savoring the varied offerings of wine — both plain and fortified — is a tony Fleet Street crowd, not so much the hard-working newsmongers but the publishers, editors, and feature writers, plus an occasional lawyer. Phone: 01-353-6786.

GRENADIER, London, England: A very special stopping place in a most unlikely location, since it's necessary to ignore a barrier and coachman, who present a very forbidding obstacle. The fact is they're there to keep cars (not you) out of this very narrow mews-style residential street, just off Wilton Crescent, only a block up from Belgravia Square. There's a tiny bar at the front, with a rare pewter-topped counter, and the military moniker derives from the time when this was the Officers' Mess for the Duke of Wellington's soldiers. The exterior is chauvinistically red, white, and blue, featuring a bright sentry box, and access from the north is via narrow Old Barracks Yard. Being an ideal place to stop for lunch after a hegira to Harrod's or a boutique browse up the Brompton Road, the clientele is unceasingly posh. The two back rooms serve as an intimate candlelit restaurant. The place is reportedly haunted by a ghost who seems to make his presence known especially during September. The resident spectre is purported to be a young officer who was caught cheating at cards and was ruthlessly beaten by his fellow officers. But he's apparently a relatively stable spirit and seldom disturbs drinkers or diners. Phone: 235-3074.

OLDE CHESHIRE CHEESE, London, England: Here's the perfect place to stop and rest from a tour of the nearby Inns of Court, made familiar in those murky scenes on PBS's presentation of Dickens's *Bleak House*. This makes the nip down the narrow alley (beside 145 Fleet Street) to the pub door all the more evocative; it's easy to imagine a London of a century or so ago. The character of the pub has remained remarkably intact, despite its place on many tourist itineraries. The wooden stairs are narrow and the downstairs bar always several drinkers deep, but somehow the bumping and squeezing past is part of the fun here. On a very cold winter's afternoon, a bowl of beef barley soup can be a special saviour and the warmth of the roaring fire upstairs a consummate joy. Those interested in unusual beer brands should try a pint of Marston's Pedigree or a mug of Merrie Monk. Phone: 481-1533.

SHERLOCK HOLMES, London, England: Forget about Baker Street; this Northumberland Street pub, which Conan Doyle used to frequent when it was called the Northumberland Arms (and which he mentioned in his *Hound of the Baskervilles*), is the nearest most people will ever come to the great man. Drawings and photographs of actors playing Holmes and of scenes from Holmes and all manner of other Holmesiana adorn the downstairs bar; upstairs, on the way to a first-floor restaurant, there's a replica of Holmes's Baker Street study, cleverly walled off by glass. The collection of memorabilia was assembled in 1951 by the Sherlock Holmes Society of London for the Festival of Britain, and this smart and congenial pub — whose clientele, appropriately enough, includes policemen from nearby Scotland Yard — provides it with an excellent home. Phone: 01-930-2644.

PIKE AND EEL, Needingworth, Cambridgeshire, England: Pubs where fishermen congregate tend to be clubby places, however humble, and ordinary visitors may not feel welcome. This establishment, built of brick in the 16th century and much extended during Oliver Cromwell's time, is an exception — yet there's no mistaking where its loyalties lie: In front, a large garden, with lawns and umbrella-shaded tables, runs down to the river Ouse, where yachts and cabin cruisers are moored in summer. And inside, glass cases show off stuffed pike and eels (not particularly agreeable to look at, but a favorite quarry of nighttime fishermen hereabouts). The flat, windswept, and mysterious fens that surround this low-ceilinged, oak-beamed pub make it all the cozier, and it's pleasant to spend the night in one of the handful of rooms available to overnight lodgers. The restaurant has a fine local reputation, particularly for Dover sole and halibut dishes; bar snacks are also good. Needingworth is not far from St. Ives. Phone: 0736-63336.

PLOUGH AND SAIL, Paglesham, Essex, England: This clapboard-walled pub is better known by yachtsmen than by passing motorists: The location — not far from the town of Rochford, near the Essex marshes within sniffing distance of the North Sea — is wonderfully remote, and cars just do not pass. Yet the pub itself is remarkably lively thanks to the vivacious family of broad-speaking former East Enders who run the place. It is also quite comfortable, but charming and very much of the period. Summer weekends bring crowds; at other times, things are quieter, and in chilly weather, there's always a log fire crackling on the hearth. Phone: 3706-242.

BLACK SWAN, Stratford-upon-Avon, Warwickshire, England: Sir Laurence Olivier, Sir John Gielgud, Albert Finney, Peter O'Toole, and Glenda Jackson have all frequented this place at one time or another: The "Dirty Duck," as it's informally known, is very much the actors' hangout. That is due in part to a location conveniently down the street from Stratford's Royal Shakespeare Theatre, but in equal part, perhaps, to a certain attitude on the part of the management that rates the comforts of its thespian patrons as a high priority. No matter that less illustrious visitors may have to try a little harder to order some of that wonderful steak-and-kidney pie — there's always someone interesting to look at while waiting. The pub also boasts a first-class restaurant that stays open for after-theater suppers. Phone: 0789-297312.

ROSE AND CROWN, Tewin, Hertfordshire, England: Overlooking the village green, in a part of the Home Counties whose peaceful aspect belies its relative nearness to London (about 25 miles) and its even greater proximity to the new town of Welwyn Garden City, the Rose and Crown is a typical country local, with a mixed clientele — deadly serious darts players, who monopolize the boards in the public bar for matches with representatives from neighboring towns' watering spots; village elders, playing cribbage or dominoes; children, who frolic out in the garden in summer; and stylish young people, who favor the comfortable pile-carpeted lounge. The bar snacks are good, and the warm, candlelit restaurant serves up traditional English food like roast beef, steak-and-kidney pie, and jugged hare. Phone: 43871-7257.

HOLE IN THE WALL, Tunbridge Wells, Kent, England: From the mid-17th century until the early 1970s, this red brick structure known in Victorian times as the Central Smoking Divan and believed to date back to the Restoration housed a tobacconist's shop; the snug in the rear was virtually unknown. The establishment that now occupies the premises at 9 High Street is another kind of place altogether, and it has been almost totally transformed. The interior space has been divided into two tiers, one overlooking the other; and both areas are full of red flocked wallpaper and comfortable furniture with upholstery to match. There's a separate restaurant, but the homemade pies and pasties and assorted other bar snacks served in the single bar are quite tasty. The *Hole in the Wall* is known for the variety of beer available; this is a so-called free house — not owned by a brewery like most in England. Phone: 0892-26550.

ROYAL OAK, Winsford, Somerset, England: There are other pubs that claim to be 300 years older than this archetypically pretty West Country village inn, adorned outside by hanging flower baskets. But, as it dates from the 14th century, it still ranks among the nation's oldest, and it is certainly one of the most imposing properties in the area, with its whitewashed stone walls, its thick thatched roof, and its interesting sign — an oak surrounding the head of Charles I. (Such a tree, which supposedly sheltered the king during his flight from Cromwellian troops, functions in English lore much like the beds in which George Washington slept: There are whole galaxies of communities which, in search of a claim to fame, have managed to come up with one.) The *Royal Oak,* which is popular with passing tourists, has two bars, both heavily beamed — a traditional public, with a dart board, and a comfortable lounge. Good snacks are served, including a fine steak-and-kidney pie. Minehead is the closest good-size town. Phone: Winsford 064385.

GLOBE INN, Dumfries, Dumfries and Galloway, Scotland: To Scots, the poet Robert Burns is Shakespeare, Tolstoy, Mozart, and Beethoven all rolled into one; and so, the fact that this pub on a narrow alley near 56 High Street was his "favourite howff" makes it very important indeed — even though it was old even before he knew it, and even though only one room of the building where Burns lodged is really part of today's Globe. Certainly, it's an exceptionally charming place — and would be even if it weren't possible to see the verses that the poet inscribed onto glass with a diamond stylus, sleep in the room where Burns slept (albeit on rare occasions), and sit in his favorite chair. The Globe has as its signpost not a globe, but Burns's head. Meals served at lunchtime — soups, roast beef, fish, and sweets — are good and inexpensive. Phone: 0387-52335.

TILTED WIG, Edinburgh, Scotland: This locally famous city pub at 1 Cumberland Street, in elegant, classically inspired New Town, names among its distinctions a garden where, in summer, it's possible to sit under umbrellas and order from a waitress; a good selection of beers (real ale among them); and a clientele that, as the name suggests, includes a disproportionate number of lawyers and solicitors, especially at lunchtime. A casual visitor might easily think he had walked in on some private club: The walls are hung with all manner of etchings and engravings on juridical subjects, elegant French wallpaper adorns the ceiling, and there's oak paneling to complete the cozy effect. Haggis is among the assortment of good bar snacks. Phone: 031-556-9409.

OWAIN GLYNDWR, Corwen, Clwyd, Wales: Here's a place with real local character. Used by townspeople more often than by tourists, this establishment on the town square occupies a plaster-over-stone building that was partly built in the 13th century, used to be a monastery's outbuilding, and is said to be haunted by the ghost of the 15th-century Welsh freedom fighter Owen Glendower. There are three bars — among them an unpretentious old-style public bar with a dart board and a jukebox; another

— rather plush and cozy with its red carpet, original oak beams, decorative horse brasses, and old saddles; and yet another, a small one attached to the restaurant. And on tap, a thirsty visitor won't find the aerated (and even gassy) pressurized brews, but instead a good range of real ales. Bar snacks like scampi or steak and chips are provided as well as complete meals. Phone: 0490-2115.

GROES INN, Ty'n-y-Groes, near Conwy, Gwynedd, North Wales: The oldest pub in Wales, as many believe, is installed in a building that was already old when the license was issued in 1573. Whitewashed and pleasantly tree-shaded, with thick walls constructed from locally quarried Conwy stone, which may date from an Ice Age, the pub is full of charming antique settles — the kind of high-backed wooden benches traditionally used for sitting in front of the fire on a cold night because of the protection they afforded from drafts. Here, the fireplace conceals a locally famous "priest hole," the hideaway for many a devout Roman Catholic during Elizabeth I's reign. The views — out over the Conwy valley and distant Snowdon, Wales's highest mountain — are outstanding, and the food is well worth waiting for. Phone: Ty'n-y-Groes 545.

DURTY NELLY'S, Bunratty, County Clare, Irish Republic: In the opinion of some experts, this is the finest pub in Ireland. Situated on the main road within 10 miles of Limerick City and Shannon Airport, it is next door to Bunratty Castle, where the buses disgorge great clumps of tourists bound for the medieval banquets (see *Mead and Meat Pies: Historical Banquets*); and so the pub is never without its share of rubberneckers, mostly American. Nonetheless, the large majority of people in the vast and almost always crowded premises are Irish — and very intent on enjoying themselves in the lounge, where the tourists go; in the local bar, where they do not; or in the piano room, separating the two, from which the highest volume of music comes. Upstairs is what the management terms the "quiet bar"; and sure enough, it's an oasis of stillness, where the murmuring of the two dozen white doves kept by owner Humphrey O'Connor is about the only sound. The *Oyster,* the restaurant on the premises, which has a small stand-up bar, is also pleasant; visitors are permitted to sit at the tables only when ordering a meal. The fare is good, the prices reasonable, and the restaurant is popular with locals on a night out. Hearty sandwiches are available in the bars. Music and song may erupt at any time; it's welcomed and even encouraged by the enlightened management. Phone: 061-74861 or 061-74072.

HENCHY'S, Cork, County Cork, Irish Republic: Cork City is a kind of independent nation within the Republic, and the rest of the Irish are often made to feel that they should show their passports when they enter the environs. This has much to do with the distinctive singsong local accent, whose subtle variations may be heard at the century-old Henchy's — at least by those with an ear fine-tuned to linguistic distinctions. If yours isn't, you'll enjoy the spectacle anyway. All levels of Cork society are represented — even to the odd poet, a regular, who is very odd indeed. The pub, a night place if ever there was one with a fine snug, is owned by Micheal Henchy and his mother, Catherine. You'll find it at 40 St. Luke's. Phone: 021-501115.

OYSTER TAVERN, Cork, County Cork, Irish Republic: While *Henchy's* is splendid for *drinking* and listening, this not-to-be-missed wonder, tucked away off Patrick Street opposite *Bolger's,* is delightful for *eating* and listening. The food, particularly the fish, is fine: The whitebait is delicious enough, and the portion generous enough, to make a main dish in itself when it's on the menu. But the real joy is hearing the maître d' sing out, "Your table will be ready in five more minutes, *Professor*" (or "*Doctor,*" or even, bless the mark, "*Surgeon,*" as the case may be — Cork people are very high on titles). Phone: 021-272716/272635.

BAILEY OF DUKE STREET, Dublin, Irish Republic: The watering place for generations of Dublin's writers and artists directly across the street from *Davy Byrne's* (below) has been preempted by ubiquitous youth, and the clientele is now what can only be described as androgynous; at night, it's definitely for the young and pretty of all sexes.

But at other times, there is peace, and time to admire the handsome iron and marble tables. And many young artists, some writers, and some musicians are still among the crowds. The best way to use the pub is to meet for drinks at noon, and, at about 1 AM (having reserved a table), climb the stairs to the restaurant overhead, where the food is quite good and the service faultless; on the way up or down, be sure to study the original door of Bloom's house at 7 Eccles Street, lovingly preserved by the Bailey's former owner, artist and patron John Ryan. Phone: 01-773055/770600.

BRAZEN HEAD, Dublin, Irish Republic: Here, legend has it, the winsome Robert Emmet plotted the ragged and abortive little rebellion of 1803. Although only a few hundred yards from *Guinness's* famous brewery, the *Brazenhead* hubristically disdains to serve draft stout. It is a dark and very intimate place, with hallways leading off in all directions, one of them into the little room where the poetry and music sessions are held. The poetry readings have a charmingly inverted nature: One gets the impression that the people are listening to poetry while drinking, rather than the opposite. Outside on the quays and not too far away is the church immortalized by James Joyce in the opening line of *Finnegans Wake:* "riverrun, past Eve and Adam's, from swerve of shore to bend of bay, brings us by a commodious vicus of recirculation back to Howth Castle and environs." You may pause a while and watch the seagulls swoop and screech above Anna Livia Plurabella. This 17th-century "hotel" at 20 Lower Bridge Street is not easily found; better ask a taxi driver. Phone: 01-779549.

DAVY BYRNE'S OF DUKE STREET, Dublin, Irish Republic: This, the "moral pub" in which Leopold Bloom had Gorgonzola cheese and his glass of Burgundy on June 16, 1904, may not bring to mind the place Joyce was visualizing when he wrote of Bloom's visit in *Ulysses.* Having undergone much updating, the pub still features murals by Cecil Salkeld (father-in-law of the late Brendan Behan) which depict famous Irish literary and artistic personalities of the early 20th century. And one of the three bars still bears the name of the novel in which it was immortalized. Situated at the hub of the main shopping and business district of Dublin, it is frequented by a predictably varied clientele. Food is served all day, with salads and sandwiches made with fresh or smoked salmon being the specialty — except on June 16, when Gorgonzola and Burgundy may take precedence for some. Phone: 01-775217.

DOHENY & NESBITT'S, Dublin, Irish Republic: Owned and run by Ned Doheny and Tom Nesbitt, this Lower Baggot Street establishment is very small, and late at night, especially on weekends, it's almost impossible to breathe for the heaving mass of trainee architects, students, and tired political pundits taking time off from reporting the proceedings in the Dail (parliament) around the corner. So come early, or, better still, sidle in at noontime, when there is breathing space as well as an opportunity to munch on hot beef sandwiches, medium, well-done, or (rare treat in Ireland) rare. Close to the National Museum, National Library, National Gallery of Art, and St. Stephen's Green, that wonderful city-center oasis of quietude, ponds, and trees. Phone: 01-762945.

MULLIGAN'S OF POOLBEG STREET, Dublin, Irish Republic: This very old pub, which has been in existence since the 1750s, serves nothing but plain drink. But what it does, it does well, and the Guinness draft offered here is probably the most consistently good, if not the best, in the country. (A constant flow throughout the day is the secret.) The curates — that is to say, the barkeeps — have abandoned their charming aprons, but it is still possible to visualize what it was like to drink here a century ago. There are three rooms in constant use, and, since the pub is situated between the harbor, the *Irish Press,* and Trinity College, the patrons include journalists, dockworkers, and students. In these frantically egalitarian days, part of the fun of drinking in Mulligan's is guessing whether that long-haired melancholic in the corner is a longshoreman, a music critic, or an aspiring Lionel Trilling. Phone: 01-775582.

NEARY'S OF CHATHAM STREET, Dublin, Irish Republic: The back door of this pub opens directly opposite the stage door of the *Gaiety,* the capital's principal variety theater, so the noises here are made mostly by actors, musicians, and the sort of pallid cohorts that these two professions attract. Visiting celebrities from both professions drop in here from time to time, so you may find yourself rubbing shoulders with the great. When this happens, the place is full and there is little comfort, but at lunchtime, it's easy to find consolation in the sandwiches, or, in season, fresh oysters. Four beautiful gas lamps stand on the marble counter, the seating is plush and bouncy, and there is usually a young "lounge boy" running his feet off trying to serve everybody at once. Phone: 01-778596.

STAG'S HEAD, Dublin, Irish Republic: Nowadays, this classic at 1 Dame Court (off Dame St.), gorgeously turned out right down to its stained-glass windows, generally draws a clientele from all strata of society, but at lunchtime on weekdays the observant will note a preponderance of the pinstripe vests, fob watches, and cold noses of members of the legal profession as they dig into their hot meat-and-two-veg meals. The exact make-up of the crowd is anybody's guess, because the pub is awkward to get to. But the conservationists who yelped with dismay at a recent threat to pull it down are seldom moved to actually visit the place. Phone: 01-779307.

MORAN'S OYSTER COTTAGE, The Weir, Kilcolgan, County Galway, Irish Republic: A family-run, thatch-roofed pub over 200 years old, hard by the tidal river, Moran's, which started serving oysters and crab in a small way back in the 1960s, is now a thriving and much-extended bar and seafood restaurant. If you are a party of four, six, or eight, this is the perfect place for a lunch in one of the comfortable snugs or, if the weather is fine, outside in the sunshine, at the tables in front of the pub. Galway oysters are served with homemade brown bread — which sends most Americans into a swoon — butter, and Guinness. Or there's smoked salmon, dressed crab, or any of a number of soups. The choice is never immense, but what there is is always delicious, and the wine list is adequate to the fare. Moran's is an important part of the Galway Oyster Festival (see *Festivals*), a jolly gathering much beloved of Ireland's nouveau riche, which descends on the town in force every year in mid-September. Phone: 091-96113.

SEAGAN UA NEACHTÁIN, TABHARNEOIR, Galway, County Galway, Irish Republic: Ireland's western capital has a number of comfortable and well-run pubs, but none as authentic and little changed as this house at the corner of Cross and Quay streets which has recently come under new ownership (and acquired a cozy upstairs restaurant as well). In the old days, the main door of the pub (above which the name of the original owner is still written out in Irish) would not open, and visitors had to go around to the side door (on Quay St.), and give a knock. They were then quietly ushered into a small room, the pub's one and only, where someone would be singing a lament or playing a tune on the tin whistle. If they made too much noise, they were shushed. The pub is the antithesis of *Durty Nelly's:* Voices are never raised, Irish is often spoken, and potential patrons are carefully screened. Phone: 091-66816.

TOWERS, Glenbeigh, County Kerry, Irish Republic: Hotel bars are much of a muchness — with a few noble exceptions — among them the *Horseshoe Bar* of Dublin's *Shelbourne* and this one, which is really an annex to a justly famous seafood restaurant. The *Towers* is famous for being famous, and dozens of international celebrities have stayed here — understandably, since Glenbeigh is the perfect base for exploring the Ring of Kerry. There is music here every night, much of it of the inspired amateur variety and some of it even very enjoyable. Phone: 066-68212.

AHERNE'S PUB & SEAFOOD BAR, Youghal, County Cork, Irish Republic: For complex historical reasons, the Irish are, at best, indifferent to fish and only very gradually is the prejudice (ludicrous in an island people) being abandoned; this North Main Street establishment owned and managed by former army captain Gerry Fitzgibbon, his wife, Betty, and their family — perhaps the best and most unpretentious pub restaurant in the south — is in the vanguard of the movement to dissipate it. In the bar, there's smoked mackerel, smoked salmon, oysters, and dressed crab in addition to chicken liver pâté, vegetarian salad, and all kinds of succulent sandwiches; and in the restaurant, lobster, scallops, prawns, mussels, black sole, fresh trout, and salmon from the River Blackwater, which enters the sea here, are served, as well as a number of nonpiscine dishes. Youghal (pronounced *yawl*) is worth visiting anyway: An attractive Victorian seaside resort, this is the spot where, legend has it, Sir Walter Raleigh grew the first potatoes in Europe. The bar food at Aherne's is available all day, but it is advisable to call for reservations to eat in the restaurant. Phone: 024-92424.

CROWN SALOON, Belfast, Northern Ireland: This venerable establishment on Great Victoria Street, opposite the *Forum Hotel,* has recently been marked for preservation by the National Trust — as it well deserves. The windows are stained glass, the floor is of mosaic tiles, and all around are little intricacies of Victorian fancy — woodcarvings, glass mosaics, intricate plasterwork, painted mirrors, and so much more that every nook and cranny seems filled with delightful ornamental details. As for the snugs — where serious drinkers can hoist their pints in contented privacy — they are in the same good condition as when the place was built back in Victorian days. Next door, and notable, is *Robinson's,* which has ornate papered walls, a mahogany bar, polished wooden snugs, and a men's room dubbed "AdamAnt." Phone: 084-249476.

BLAKE'S OF THE HOLLOW, Enniskillen, County Fermanagh, Northern Ireland: Noted for its handmade lace, its attractive knit sweaters, and its Belleek china, Enniskillen is also home to this handsome old pub, tucked away in a rabbit's warren of streets and alleys not far from St. Macartan's Cathedral. Lamentably, the stock of rare Old Dublin Potstill Whiskey, an Irishman's collector's item that was once among the alcoholic specialties of the house, has been depleted. But otherwise things are much the same as they were when the bar was last refurbished in 1887 (particularly the long marble-topped mahogany bar and the pine snugs, attractive enough to warrant praise from Ulster Heritage Societies publications and a government preservation listing). As for the mood, it is always subdued, and television intrudes on the drinkers' solitude only for major sporting events. The entrance on Church Street is easiest to find. Phone: 0365-22143.

Rural Retreats

 To travelers from abroad, the most striking features of the British and Irish countrysides are the absence of billboards, the almost total lack of motels — and the abundance of homey inns, guesthouses, and country manors turned hotels. The tradition of innkeeping, particularly in England, goes back for centuries, and that's easy enough to see: Wooden stair treads are worn to concavity by the footsteps of travelers down over the ages; and walls are half-timbered, ceilings beamed. In northern England, the lodging places tend toward the rickety and quaint; in the South, there is an excellent assortment of charming, country house hotels. Ireland, which for a long time demonstrated a notable lack of hostelries with personality, has been catching up fast.

As for the food, establishments in both Britain and Ireland are in varying states of emergence from the age of soggy sprouts and overcooked plaice, meat roasted to a fare-thee-well, and vegetables that would make the army's steamtable offerings look crisp. A whole generation of young Irish chefs, trained on the Continent and, in a surprising number of cases, at the hotel school at Shannon, have brought the kind of new look to the nation's menus that England, Scotland, and Wales began to see a few years ago. This means a respect for the freshness of ingredients so intense that some masters of the new cuisine don't just go out and buy the best that the local market has to offer, they also work with local farmers to have vegetables planted and grown to their specifications. The undeniably positive by-products are no longer destroyed through overcooking. And unlike some of the practitioners of the nouvelle cuisine in France, the new chefs here are delightfully straightforward and unpretentious about their presentations.

In both Britain and Ireland, some of these special establishments are more noteworthy than others — either because of their decor, the friendliness of their management (more often than not a whole family), or their setting or food. Here is an assortment of some of the best castle-hotels, inns, country houses, and restaurants the rural region has to offer. Some warrant a stop when you're in the area; a handful of others, perhaps a shade more wonderful on one or more counts, are worth planning a whole holiday around.

WORTH A LONG DETOUR

ELMS, Abberley, near Worcester, Hereford and Worcester, England: Built primarily during the early 18th century after designs by a student of Sir Christopher Wren, then added to during a neoclassical 1927, this grand country house has a magnificent tree-lined drive and gardens as clipped and formal as they come; the scene suggests morning suits and garden party hats, white gloves and flouncy dresses. The interiors are just as elegant, from the sumptuously carpeted oak staircase to the public rooms full of tufted settees and velvet chairs and the fine Library Bar, still boasting its original mahogany bookcases; the guestrooms boast oil paintings, interesting knick-knacks, spacious bathrooms, antique furnishings (one room is graced by a four-poster bed), and — not the least important — fine views over the surrounding park. But despite the luxury of the setting, the *Elms* is never stuffy, and it's easy to spend days on end strolling across the grounds, batting tennis balls on the hotel's courts, and practicing your putting on its green. Details: The Elms Hotel, Abberley, Hereford and Worcester WR6 6AT, England (phone: 029921-666).

EASTWELL MANOR, Ashford, Kent, England: Set in some 3,000 acres of parkland picturesquely speckled with fluffy white sheep, this elegant, rambling stone country house was opened as a hotel just in 1980, but, though the present house was rebuilt in 1926, its history can be traced back to the Norman Conquest; over the years it has had 20 owners, and Queen Victoria once made a visit here. (You can see a picture of her, seated in a chair on the manor's frozen lake, surrounded by the other members of her skating party, when you arrive for a stay.) Purchased in November 1982 by a Canadian family and renovated not long before, the manor has been earning hearty kudos ever since, for a lavish use of space and splendid service that reminds guests of an earlier, grander age: One visitor called it "the world's best 24-room hotel." Though the rooms are absolutely huge, they are so cleverly decorated with sitting areas, soft colors, and pretty fabrics, that they seem positively inviting; all of the bathrooms are vast, and some are sumptuous as well. Among public rooms, there's an oak-paneled bar to lure guests down for drinks before dinner, which is served in a baronial dining room. The menu is English, but draws on the best concepts of both classical French and nouvelle cuisine. Vegetables are cooked so as to retain their natural crispness, and meats are left pink as a matter of policy. You'll find such delicacies as sliced breast of duck laid on a lemon sauce and garnished with glazed raspberries, or salmon steak lightly poached in butter, served on a fresh tomato and dill purée and topped with a sauce of dry vermouth and cream. The young English chef selects game, lamb, and beef from the Eastwell estate and purchases other ingredients from London and Paris markets. A very extensive wine list, which includes three English wines, complements the offerings. Details: Eastwell Manor, Eastwell Park, Ashford, Kent TN25 4HR, England (phone: 0233-35751).

BELL INN, Aston Clinton, Buckinghamshire, England: Once a favorite of Evelyn Waugh, this former coaching post has been welcoming guests since about 1650. But seldom during the last three centuries has it looked quite as lovely as it does today, with its cozy bar — the ceiling beamed, the floor paved in flagstones, the air warmed by the fire blazing away on the hearth — and its scattering of antiques. Fresh flowers are a common sight, both in the public rooms and in the guest quarters, which are located in former stables and malt houses ranged around a small, cobbled courtyard. Bath salts, bathroom scales, thick terry robes, refrigerators stocked to answer post-midnight thirsts, and other amenities complete the picture. The setting, on A41 a few miles east of Aylesbury and not far distant from Heathrow, is not the nation's most pastoral, but when one is cosseted in that fashion, it almost doesn't matter. And the food is good enough to warrant a special mention. While there's plenty of traditional English fare such as the famous Bell Inn smokies, tipsy cake, and poached salmon, it's also possible to savor wondrous French specialties such as *caneton ballottine,* a savory, crisp-skinned boned duckling; since the restaurant is near Aylesbury, famous as the home of the Aylesbury duck, this fowl is always on the menu. The wine list is especially fine. Details: Bell Inn, Aston Clinton, Buckinghamshire HP22 5HP, England (phone: 0296-630252).

WATERSIDE INN, Bray-on-Thames, Berkshire, England: Multiple Michelin stars are still not all that common in England. Yet this establishment's claim to being one of the honorees is only part of the reason to make a detour to the village of Bray, not far from Windsor and 27 miles west of London. Brothers Albert and Michel Roux (French chefs with embassy experience and service for the best private families before they opened London's renowned *Le Gavroche*) chose to open their Thames-side country restaurant in a setting that provides a feast for the eyes before the feast for the palate begins. In spring, enormous red tulips are in bloom all around, flowering cherry trees line the river, and swans circle past almost as though summoned by a magic wand. In summer, apéritifs are served on the terrace and in two delightful summer houses, and the sight of weeping willows and boats on the water may distract a diner — momentarily — from the extraordinary menu. The Roux brothers are ceaselessly inventive. Among their enduring specialties are a chicken mousse with Roquefort cheese and walnuts inside, served on a bed of apple sticks and topped with a mousseline sauce; warm oysters served in a puff pastry case, garnished with sprouts, a raspberry vinegar butter sauce, and fresh raspberries; a medium rare roast duckling pierced with cloves and served with a sauce flavored with honey; and a Grand Marnier–touched soufflé laid on a Melba sauce and garnished with orange segments. The wine list, which counts no less than 350 bin numbers, is first rate, and some of the restaurant's personal touches are charming — for example, the small hot tomato hors d'oeuvres served with cocktails and billed as "tiny pizzas." The cost of all this is "rather dear," as the British would say, but less than its equivalent in Paris and well worth it for a memorable occasion. Closed Mondays, Tuesday lunches, Sunday dinners from October through Easter, and for about five weeks from December 25. No rooms. Details: Waterside Inn, Bray-on-Thames, Berkshire SL6 2AT, England (phone: 0628-20691/22941).

LYGON ARMS, Broadway, Hereford and Worcester, England: The Lygon Arms wasn't founded nearly as long ago as some buildings in the Cotswolds, but 1532 seems a respectable enough birth date; that makes it old enough to have frequently welcomed Charles I as a guest and to have harbored Oliver Cromwell on the eve of the battle of Worcester. But there are indications that the building itself is much older. A stone fireplace set into one 4-foot-thick wall, for instance, appears to have been crafted in the 14th century; and the rear courtyard door dates from the 15th century and the front door from the early 16th. All of the rooms are furnished with antiques of similar vintage, and a few pieces are of quality substantial enough to be illustrated in *The Dictionary of English Furniture.* The nine rooms in what is called the old wing are a study in Tudor, with beams, charmingly tilted oak floors, and dozens of blue Spode dishes on the fireplace mantels; the Great Chamber — one of the hotel's most famous rooms, for its vaulted timber-crossed ceiling and its massive canopied bed — is number 20. The rooms in the new wing boast more dependable plumbing — and equivalent charm, thanks to a vigorous refurbishing program. All this is as might be expected in the inn that is probably Britain's most photographed. What may be a surprise is the quality of the service. For example, if you ordered Foster's Lager on your previous visit, and you arrive late on a hot, sunny afternoon, along with your tea will be a Foster's. As for meals, they are as elegant as the setting — the Great Hall, with its barrel-vaulted ceiling, great fireplace, and fine wood paneling. The candlelit after-theater suppers — smoked salmon, cold chicken, roast beef, salad, and fresh strawberries in season — can be a joy, as are the game dishes (served when available). The wide, mile-long street on which the inn fronts is almost as pretty as the cream-colored stone hotel itself, and Stratford-upon-Avon is just 20 miles away. Details: The Lygon Arms, Broadway, Hereford and Worcester WR12 7DU, England (phone: 0386-852255).

GRAVETYE MANOR, near East Grinstead, West Sussex, England: Located about halfway between London and Brighton, at the end of a meandering country road some 5 miles from East Grinstead, this ivy-covered Elizabethan manor house, built by one Roger Infield for his bride, Katherine Compton, in 1598 and enlarged in the same style over the centuries since, has become one of rural England's most impressive hostelries since it was converted to use as a hotel in 1958; it's now internationally known. One point of fame is its gardens, created by Gravetye's most famous owner, the great English horticulturalist William Robinson, who eschewed the formalized style that had been favored until then for a more natural look. In the years after his death in 1935, the gardens suffered badly, and it was left to the present owners to restore them to their former glory; whether you see them during a stroll along the garden paths, or through your mullioned windows, they never cease to give pleasure. Robinson's influence is felt inside as well. The rooms are paneled with the estate's oak, bouquets of flowers he planted brighten the corners of all the rooms, and the 14 guestrooms are named for English trees such as bay, holly, beech, and ash. Many of these rooms have fireplaces; all have thick carpets, soothing decor, and such extras as a fruit basket, an ice water thermos, books, a hair dryer, and a special red telephone for emergencies. Touches like these have earned the hotel its membership in the prestigious Relais et Châteaux group. Its restaurant's Michelin star is equally well deserved. Current owner Peter Herbert takes justifiable pride in his wine list, one of the most extensive in the country, and in his menu, which changes with the season. Among the highlights: a velvety chicken liver pâté, *sole de Douvre Victoria* (grilled Dover sole garnished with langoustine, avocado, and tomato), the tenderest Scotch beef, and a selection of fresh vegetables from the kitchen garden, cooked to crisp perfection. A separate dessert menu lists some 20 sweets (including homemade sorbets and ice creams) plus savories and cheeses. There are ways to work off a bit of excess: playing croquet on the lawn, fishing in the well-stocked trout pond, or sightseeing in the neighborhood, where there are several other gardens of note. Details: Gravetye Manor, East Grinstead, West Sussex RH19 4LJ, England (phone: 0342-810567).

COMBE HOUSE, Gittisham, near Honiton, Devon, England: It takes a long time to wend your way up the winding drive to Combe House, a cream-colored Elizabethan mansion that dates back to the 14th century; but it doesn't particularly matter because the lush emerald parkland that rolls around you on all sides, studded with rhododendrons, magnolias, and cedars, is so lovely. The mansion, owned by a descendant of Dr. Johnson's biographer James Boswell, is roomy, elegant, and furnished throughout with antiques, but not too formal; and almost every room has something that catches your eye: the ornate plaster ceiling and gleaming paneling in the main hall, full of squashy chintz-covered chairs, for instance; or the pink dining room's rococo fireplace, attributed to Chippendale, depicting the fable of the fox and the crow; or the bar (the kind of place solitary travelers might enter and find friendly and gregarious faces), hung with old hunting and coaching prints and photographs of the owner's horse-racing triumphs. Most guestrooms are exceptionally large and — a rare and therefore notable bonus — very quiet. And the food is good, thanks to Cordon Bleu–trained co-owner Therese Boswell and her team of young chefs. The hotel has fishing rights to 1.5 miles of the south bank of the River Otter, which can produce some good creels of brown trout, and the establishment makes an excellent base for tours of East Devon, and for visits to nearby golf courses or to the ocean only 7 miles away. Closed the last half of January and all of February. Details: Combe House Hotel, Gittisham, near Honiton, Devon EX14 OAD, England (phone: 0404-2756).

LE MANOIR AUX QUAT' SAISONS, Great Milton, Oxfordshire, England: Fifteen minutes from Oxford, this establishment earned two Michelin stars even before it opened in 1984 and is now one of the country's most talked about dining and lodging retreats. Housed in an old, golden-hued, Cotswold stone structure, it has mullioned windows, thick stone walls, and molded cornices that are Tudor to the core. Yet the decor — part of the $1.5 million restoration that it underwent before its debut — is relaxed and airy, and the 17th- and 18th-century French furniture adds a note of elegance and grace. Bedrooms all have half-testered beds and fine views of the surrounding 27 acres of meadow and garden, and the management omits no small touches: After checking in, guests find fresh flowers, decanters of Madeira, and bowls of fresh figs in their quarters. In the tranquil pink and gray dining room, the best available ingredients go into every dish (the poultry comes from France), and lightness is the operative word. Sample the soufflés aux framboises, or, as did *Le Gavroche* chef-proprietor Albert Roux not long ago, try the wild salmon tartare with sour cream and caviar or the pigeon baked in a salt crust and served with a truffle fumet. Closed Sundays, Mondays, and a month at Christmas. Details: Le Manoir aux Quat' Saisons, Church Rd., Great Milton, Oxfordshire OX9 7PD, England (phone: 8446-8881).

BOX TREE, Ilkley, West Yorkshire, England: This small restaurant may just be the chief industry of the small town of Ilkley, 16 miles northwest of Leeds. When Englishmen Malcolm Reid and Colin Long opened it in a 300-year-old cottage some 25 years ago, they served afternoon teas only, because they were entirely unschooled in the gastronomic arts and the operation of a restaurant. Over the years, as they taught themselves and business grew, they graduated from teas to lunches to dinners, and finally to a two-star rating by the august *Michelin Guide,* an honor shared by only a few other restaurants in their native land. This extraordinary increase in stature, however, has not been accompanied by a comparable increase in size. The establishment still seats about 50 diners and, given its reputation, it's essential to reserve in advance. Even then, before being seated it's sometimes necessary to spend a bit of time in the cocktail bar, a room attractively stocked with the owners' collection of antique English porcelain and oil paintings. The rest of the restaurant is decorated with more antiques and genuine objets d'art, replacements for the reproductions that were good enough for tea but not for grand cuisine. The menu is not overly long, though there is certainly enough to choose from. The *coquilles St.-Jacques* and the *dariole de champignons et truffes,* for starters, have been praised in the past; the *marquise au chocolat et cognac* is a popular dessert. In between, any number of entrées are worthy and the wine list is weighty — some 200 selections, including "native" wines. Open for dinner Tuesdays through Saturdays, on Sundays for prix fixe lunch; closed Mondays. Details: Box Tree, Church St., Ilkley, West Yorkshire LS29 9DR, England (phone: 0943-608484).

ARUNDELL ARMS, Lifton, Devon, England: This former coaching inn covered with Virginia creeper would be pleasant enough by anyone's standards: Log fires blaze away on the hearths downstairs, the floors are laid with locally quarried dark blue slate, and the culinary offerings of the young French-trained chef (which include an excellent Tamar salmon served with a champagne sauce) are of international standard. But it really stands out for its fishing; for half a century now, it has owned the fishing rights on 20 miles of the Tamar, the stream that forms the boundary with Cornwall and ranks as the best of the West Country salmon streams, and four of its tributaries, so-called spate rivers, which rise on the moors and deepen and widen as they come down through woods and farming country into the valleys. Some of the smaller streams run knee-deep over pebbly beds, down long riffles of rough white water, sometimes forming deep pools that are especially lovely when dappled with sun and shadow from the leaves of the alder trees whose branches meet overhead. In the course of the last decade or so, the season's salmon take has averaged around 80, and there's an abundance of beautifully colored, wild and wily brown trout — small, but scrappy enough to take a dry or wet fly with a great slash and then fight like tigers. Also worth noting is the big run of salmon and sea trout for which the Tamar is famous; the first spring salmon usually have entered Arundell Arms waters by mid-May, and the fishing for them, mostly by fly only, runs right through to mid-October. Sea trout fishing runs from late June to early September, by fly only, and since the best of the sea trout are taken at night, guests usually go out for them after dinner and fish until midnight or after, sometimes all night. Details: Arundell Arms Hotel, Lifton, Devon PL16 OAA, England (phone: 0566-84666).

COTTAGE IN THE WOOD, Malvern Wells, Malvern, Worcestershire, England: Much more than a cottage, this Georgian mansion — rambling but beautifully proportioned — occupies 7 acres of its own woodlands, and enjoys wonderful views over the Severn Valley. The style is very English and very traditional; both in the main building and in the more modern coach house, the rooms are superbly appointed, and the level of maintenance is high. Three of the 20 guestrooms boast four-posters. The cozy and intimate restaurant is ideal for special meals; English dishes predominate, and the wine list is excellent. Note that Malvern Wells is distinct from the larger, better known former spa town just to the north, Great Malvern. But both places are famed for mineral water, and during a stay, a visitor should be sure to try a bottle of the locally produced Malvern Water — sold in London in the 1780s for a princely shilling a bottle. Details: Cottage in the Wood, Holywell Rd., Malvern Wells, Malvern, Worcestershire WR14 4LG, England (phone: 06845-3487); US agent: Josephine Barr (phone: 800-323-5463).

CHEWTON GLEN, New Milton, Hampshire, England: The New Forest, which William the Conqueror claimed as a royal hunting ground in 1079, was already old when this brick mansion went up on 30 acres of peaceful parkland near its fringes. It must have looked a bit raw in contrast at first, but the years have mellowed it and it now seems almost as old as the forest. Since 1967, managing director Martin Skan has renovated the rooms, built new kitchens, completed a modern wing, converted the coach barn and the stable into suites, added a swimming pool, a tennis court, and a 9-hole golf course, installed a new driveway with a long approach through fields and woods, adorned the lovely courtyard with an antique fountain, and, along the way, won an Egon Ronay Hotel of the Year award, a Michelin star (albeit only one), and membership in the exclusive Leading Hotels of the World and Relais et Châteaux associations. That those kudos were well deserved is immediately evident when you see the rooms. Named for characters from *The Children of the New Forest,* whose author, Captain Frederick Marryat, spent some time in the house during the 19th century, they are done up with pretty flowered fabrics that are constantly replaced to keep things looking fresh, and the color televisions have been equipped to show a feature film every evening; a bottle of sherry is set out to greet arriving guests; and the bathrooms come furnished with fragrant bars of Crabtree & Evelyn soaps and bubble bath. The same perfectionism pervades the hotel's restaurant, the *Marryat Room,* from the fresh bouquets of flowers and the coral and green color scheme to the Villeroy & Boch dinner plates and the exquisite food produced by a young French chef and his staff. Though the raw materials are English, the cooking is nouvelle, with sublime specialties such as *coquilles St.-Jacques au gingembre;* fresh salmon marinated in olive oil, coriander, and lemon juice; *canard aux framboises;* roast rib of Scotch filet stuffed with foie gras, baked in pastry, and served with a Périgordine sauce; chicken cooked in a mint-flavored cream sauce; and more. The wine list offers nearly 200 selections, ranging from an inexpensive Moselle to a Château Lafite-Rothschild 1952. You'll appreciate *Chewton Glen* the most if you recognize high standards and are irritated by equally expensive establishments that don't quite measure up. Details: Chewton Glen Hotel, New Milton, Hampshire BH25 6QS, England (phone: 04252-5341).

HAMBLETON HALL, Hambleton, Leicester, England: Set on a peninsula jutting into Rutland Water, this restored inn offers lovely views over the lake as well as fishing, horseback riding, and bicycling. The restaurant, under chef Brian Baker, is one of only a dozen outside London to have earned a Michelin rosette. Tennis is on the premises. A Relais et Châteaux establishment. Details: Hambleton Hall, Hambleton, Oakham, Rutland LE15 8TH, England (phone: 0572-56991).

DUCK INN, Pett Bottom, Kent, England: Housed in an unpretentious little 16th-century country cottage and patronized by minor royalty and West End stars, this is widely regarded as the best and most exclusive restaurant in southeastern England. Fine French cuisine is painstakingly prepared; try the *brandade parisienne* (a fresh fish pâté). The place is not easy to find, but well worth the effort; it's about 5 miles outside Canterbury, near the village of Bridge on the road to Dover. Closed Mondays; the restaurant is closed Sunday evening. Details: Duck Inn, Pett Bottom, Kent CT4 5PB, England (phone: 0227-830354).

SHARROW BAY, Pooley Bridge, Cumbria, England: For over three decades, Francis Coulson has been cooking up some of Great Britain's best food for guests at this lakeshore establishment, a member of the Relais et Châteaux group in a late-17th-century house that had been enlarged over the years to a comfortable size in a quartet of other buildings nearby. A diner might order avocado mousse topped with tiny cooked prawns and unsweetened whipped cream; roast pork loin with fresh rosemary, stuffed with sage and onion dressing, and served with apple sauce and cracklings; and an egg custard flan and a coffee soufflé, served with petits fours. Or end with sticky toffee sponge, or almond meringue *gâteau dacquoise* with strawberries, or lemon flummery, or any number of other equally wonderful sweets; the *gâteau Alcazar,* a cake made with almonds and kirsch, is a standout. Considering the mouthwatering menu, it's not surprising that some people motor up from London, 300 miles distant, just for lunch. What makes the establishment particularly wonderful, however, is that the care that makes every meal such a treat also is accorded the workings of the hotel. The guestrooms are beautifully decorated in the English style, furnished with antiques here and there, plus books and parlor games to amuse. Thick carpets make for a quiet more intense than even the country setting alone could provide, and the efficient central heating system keeps the old house beautifully warm when the weather is chill. Proprietors Francis Coulson and Brian Sack (who joined forces in 1952) try to welcome all their guests personally, and the feeling is very much of visiting someone's very elegant country home. There are 30 rooms and suites altogether, including 26 with private bathrooms or showers; just under half are in the main house, with the others scattered among a cottage and a gatehouse on the grounds, a converted farmhouse a mile away, and a 17th-century cottage in the village of Tirril 4 miles distant. Closed December through February. Details: Sharrow Bay Hotel, Lake Ullswater, Penrith, Cumbria CA10 2LZ, England (phone: 08536-301/483).

KING'S HEAD, Richmond, Yorkshire, England: This 29-room establishment on the edge of the impressive cobbled marketplace has hardly changed at all since the 18th century — at least on the outside. Inside, however, it's plush, warm, and welcoming. The wide main staircase, the sort that ladies *glide* down on their way to the bar, makes it a real pleasure to travel to and fro from the guestrooms, which are full of 18th-century features — sash windows, elaborate moldings, high ceilings, decorative paneled doors — and carpeted with red or rich patterns to set off the white or cream walls. The restaurant is comfortable and the service solicitous; the best tables overlook the market-place. Details: King's Head Hotel, Richmond, Yorkshire DL1O 4HS, England (phone: 0748-2311).

GEORGE OF STAMFORD, Stamford, Lincolnshire, England: It is believed that a hostelry in some form has been situated here for 900 years, but most of the present building wasn't erected until Lord Burghley, High Treasurer to Elizabeth I, got around to doing so. The gallows sign originally put up to scare away highwaymen still hangs in front of the inn, and you can almost hear the London and York stagecoaches clattering to a stop when you have a drink in the still-preserved cobbled courtyard behind the hotel. The entranceway has floors of stone, the ceiling in the bar is beamed, and you'll find paneling and rough stone walls throughout. It's very comfortable, with good food available both in the restaurant and the bar. All 47 rooms have baths and have just been refurbished; the ones in the front can be a bit noisy because of the passing traffic. Stamford itself, a study in gray stone, is a gem. Details: The George, St. Martin's High St., Stamford, Lincolnshire PE9 2LB, England (phone: 0780-55171).

ALVESTON MANOR, Stratford-upon-Avon, Warwickshire, England: Whether or not *Midsummer Night's Dream* actually received its first performance here, as some longtime Stratford residents like to suggest, the *Alveston* fairly oozes with the English atmosphere that most people travel to England to find. From the warm oak-paneled entryway to the fine lounge, it is the kind of place most people feel they could stay for hours. The atmospheric Manor Bar is remarkable for its attractive paneling and beamed ceiling. Of the 108 guestrooms, those in the main building are the most interesting; those in the new wing tend toward the standard British modern. Best of all, the *Alveston Manor* is a mere 5-minute walk from the theater. Details: The Alveston Manor, Clopton Bridge, Stratford-upon-Avon, Warwickshire CV37 7HP, England (phone: 0789-204581).

HORSTED PLACE, Uckfield, East Sussex, England: A stately Victorian mansion built in 1850 and, until recently, the home of the late Sir Rupert Neville, treasurer to Prince Philip. It has 17 suites, a heated swimming pool, tennis court, croquet lawn, and 23 acres of magnificent gardens. Furnished with beautiful antiques, the house has been made bright and cheery with chintz. Afternoon tea is served in the large, multi-windowed living room, and there is an impressive library, complete with fireplace, overlooking the garden. As if all this weren't enough to satisfy the most demanding of guests, the dining room dispenses remarkable food — not what might be expected in an English hotel, but very French and very fine. Unfortunately, there are only a few tables, and so it is limited to registered guests. *Horsted Place* offers the kind of comforta-ble country elegance that travelers go to England specifically to find. Only 90 minutes south of London, near Glyndebourne. Details: Abercrombie & Kent International, 1420 Kensington Rd., Oak Brook, IL (phone: 312-954-2922; in Illinois: 800-323-3602).

MILLER HOWE, Windermere, Cumbria, England: If you tire of looking at the ever-changing light and shade over Lake Windermere in this lovely Wordsworth coun-try hotel, you can play Scrabble, read a book from your private bookshelf, listen to one of the cassettes on the stereo equipment in the room, or just browse through the knickknacks in your bedroom. There is something very personal about the rooms here, as though you have borrowed someone else's private domain for a day or two. If you want, you can wander into the kitchen to watch the friendly cooks prepare roast loin of lamb with five fresh herbs; pea, pear, and watercress soup; or any number of other goodies that appear on the interesting menu. These eventually wind up on your table in the charmingly autumnal yellow and brown dining room that looks out on to a beautiful flagstone terrace and flower-bordered lawns, which in turn slope gently to the lake. The bathrooms here are basically sybaritic. Step out from your scented shower and you will find morning tea waiting for you in pretty floral pots with lemon biscuits to satisfy hunger pangs before a substantial breakfast downstairs. Dinner specialties include loin of Lakeland lamb and smoked salmon and avocado roulade. Details: Miller Howe, Windermere, Cumbria LA23 1EY, England (phone: 09662-2536).

GLENEAGLES, Auchterarder, Perthshire, Scotland: *"Heich abune the heich"* — better than the best — might seem a grandiose claim to make about a hotel. But once you've experienced Britain's finest luxury resort — the Scottish Versailles of hotels — you will agree with the decades of hoteliers who have believed their boast, from the early days when a chief point of pride was the fact that every room had its own bath, on through the years, as crowned heads, aristocrats, and millionaires flocked to the establishment by the score. *Gleneagles* has just had a £9 million refurbishing, including the upgrading of kitchen facilities, the building of a complete country club, and the addition of a new floor, bringing the room total to 254, 20 of which are suites. Most guests rave about the four golf courses. But nongolfers will never be bored: On the 750-acre grounds, there are facilities for fishing, clay pigeon shooting, croquet, lawn bowling, miniature golf, Ping-Pong, all-weather tennis, squash, dancing, billiards; plus a sauna and Turkish baths, hairdressing salons, Jacuzzi, swimming pool, and gymnasium. The gardens alone, spotted with bright-colored flowers, are a joy. The high-ceilinged rooms are spacious enough that you don't trip over each other when room service sets up tea; the windows provide an eyeful of the lonely Scottish hills beyond the gardens; and the service can't be faulted, thanks to a better than one-to-one staff-guest ratio. When pipe bands set up on the velvety lawns, you may get goose bumps. Details: Gleneagles Hotel, Auchterarder, Perthshire PH3 1NF, Scotland (phone: 07646-2231).

INVERLOCHY CASTLE, near Fort William, Highland, Scotland: When Queen Victoria came to visit this baronial granite mansion a decade after Lord Abinger built it in 1863, she noted in her diary that she had never seen "a lovelier or more romantic spot." She wasn't the only visitor to express those sentiments. Outside there are the terraced gardens, the rhododendron bushes bigger than a child's playhouse, the emerald lawns, and, beyond them, the great mass of Ben Nevis and the Western Highlands rising in the distance; inside, there are antiques enough to do justice to a museum — carved mahogany sideboards, gleaming oak chests, portraits by Sir Benjamin West, and such — and wonderful carved paneling, elaborate moldings, frescoes: Almost everyone who comes for just a night regrets not having planned to stay longer. The 16 guestrooms are spacious and quiet. Dinner, always at 8, consists of regional game and fish, and the wine list is outstanding. Closed November through March. Details: Inverlochy Castle, Fort William, Highland PH33 6SN, Scotland (phone: 0397-2177).

SKEABOST HOUSE, Skeabost Bridge, Isle of Skye, Scotland: Built in Victorian times, and beautifully situated at the southernmost tip of a sea loch, this 22-room hostelry — one of the finest hotels on "the islands" (as Scotland's Inner and Outer Hebrides are widely known) — incorporates all that is best in Scottish country hotels, without being exorbitantly expensive. Particularly in the old part of the hotel, the ceilings are high, the furniture old-fashioned or antique, and the armchairs and sofas plush and comfortable; when it's cool, log fires blaze on the hearth. The restaurant is perhaps more functional than might be expected, but a genuine attempt is made to serve interesting local dishes, and at relatively modest prices. Closed mid-October to mid-April. Details: Skeabost House Hotel, Skeabost Bridge, Isle of Skye IV51 9NP, Scotland (phone: 047-032-202).

PORTMEIRION, Portmeirion, Gwynedd, Wales: The only lodging place in the bizarre Italianate village created between 1925 and 1975 by the late and celebrated architect Clough Williams-Ellis, this out-of-the-ordinary establishment, the setting for the 1960s TV series *The Prisoner,* proves its creator's contention that a naturally beautiful site like Portmeirion's could be developed without defiling it. The main building has a superb view over a river estuary and houses the restaurant and a number of public rooms; the fire of a couple of years ago is now nearly forgotten. Guests stay in rooms there and in a scattering of cottages around the pastel, ornately decorated, and altogether fantastic village; some are set in exotic woodland on a promontory overlooking Cardigan Bay, some atop a hill above it all. Open late March to early November. Details: Portmeirion Hotel, Box 50, Portmeirion, near Penrhyndeudraeth, Gwynedd LL48 6ER, Wales (phone: 0766-770228).

PADDY BURKE'S, Clarenbridge, County Galway, Irish Republic: Burke's was strictly a pub until the bar food got so good that it started winning awards. Now locals still gather at dusk for a "jar" at the bar, but the large room to the left has been turned into a proper restaurant with tapestried chairs and all that. The bar food is still exemplary (big Galway oysters in season, smoked salmon, the rich fish pâté, huge juicy mussels); it's ideal for a drop-in lunch. The dining room food is excellent too. Don't miss Paddy Burke's salmon soup, the baked sea trout, the foil-baked fresh fish, or the luscious fried scallops; try the fresh strawberry cheesecake for dessert. There's draft beer and Guinness. Details: Paddy Burke's, Clarenbridge, County Galway, Irish Republic (phone: 091-96107).

ASHFORD CASTLE, Cong, County Mayo, Irish Republic: It looks like an extended Magic Kingdom lining the shore of Lough Corrib, complete with green demesne and velvet lawns, drawbridge and portcullis, Gothic-arched entry and an oak-paneled great hall handsomer in reality than anything a Disney architect could dream up. In fact, although *Ashford* is often called a "fantasy" place, in its ramble of buildings the present hotel incorporates not one, but three castles: the ruins of the de Burgos's 13th-century stronghold, the original Ashford House (an 18th-century French château), and Sir Benjamin Guinness's splendid 19th-century Victorian addition — all so deftly linked to later guest wings that you can scarcely tell where one ends and the next begins. A hotel since 1939 and unstintingly refurbished in recent years by its Irish-American owner, John Mulcahy, *Ashford* has a genuine luxury: Fine paintings, sculpture, and antique armor are artfully deployed around its public rooms; gilt mirrors reflect the sparkle of its Waterford chandeliers; thick Oriental-toned carpeting hushes footsteps in salons and corridors. And at least one real king has stayed and played here: Edward VII of England, for whom, they say, the billiard room was built. The fishing (salmon, trout, pike, and perch) and shooting (pheasant, woodcock, snipe, and duck) attract sportsmen from all over the world; there is also a 9-hole golf course, tennis, croquet, boating, picnicking on the Lough's wooded islets; and miles of walks wander through the rose gardens and into the trees. The original dining room serves unremarkable lunches, but the dinners are expertly done with matching wines from an extensive cellar; the addition of a new restaurant, which specializes in seafood, has added to the variety available. Ashford has recently undergone some major refurbishment and all 83 guestrooms are poshly furnished, all having bathrooms with showers. A game room has also been added, and the Castle is now open year round. Information: Ashford Castle, Cong, County Mayo, Irish Republic (phone: 092-46003).

ARBUTUS LODGE, Cork, County Cork, Irish Republic: Next to the *Mirabeau,* it's Ireland's most talked-about restaurant, having garnered two Egon Ronay stars (plus an "Outstanding" for its cellar) and a Gault Millau toque. Declan Ryan's apprenticeships in the Isles and on the Continent included stints with the *frères* Troisgros at Roanne, with whom his kitchen still makes an informal exchange (a Troisgros *fils* recently served as his sauce chef). Now elegantly established in the ballroom of his family's small hotel in suburban Montenotte, he offers a menu of classic and "sensibly nouvelle" French cuisine based on the best of regional foods ("no flying stuff halfway round the world"). The emphasis is on style with integrity ("if you doll a dish up to the point where you don't know what it is, you've made a mistake"); case in point: his *mosaique des légumes* — an intricate terrine of vegetables in ham aspic in which each ingredient maintains its own bright identity. Also notable: the sea bass with fresh ginger, escalope of salmon in sorrel sauce, breast of pheasant with three purées, a most interesting board of local cheeses. The seven-course Tasters Menu is an excellent introduction. Closed a week at Christmas and on Sundays to nonresidents. Details: Arbutus Lodge, Cork, County Cork, Irish Republic (phone: 021-501237).

DOYLE'S SEAFOOD BAR, Dingle, County Kerry, Irish Republic: Tucked away in a narrow old house at the back of town, John and Stella Doyle's place has a scrubbed, rustic look (butcher block tables, rush-seated chairs, flagstone floor) and a menu that's gathered all sorts of stars. You can lunch from the bar's blackboard (a Saturday choice included kedgeree, quiche, open smoked salmon sandwiches on Stella's crusty brown bread, and house salad, nicely dressed). Or step to the rear and order something more substantial: Don't miss the smoked mackerel pâté, piquant crab bisque, scallop and chicken pie (steeped in wine, wrapped in puff pastry). Or indulge in crayfish served with pots of garlic butter, then almond meringue or kiwi fruit for a light, happy ending. Closed Sundays and November through February. In the works — with opening pro- jected for the 1988 season — is the addition of 8 bedroom suites in the house next door. With this come breakfasts featuring homemade jams, breads, sausages, and puddings that draw upon the best of local farm and sea produce. Details: Doyle's Seafood Bar, Dingle, County Kerry, Irish Republic (phone: 066-51174).

GREAT SOUTHERN, Parknasilla, County Kerry, Irish Republic: Most people wouldn't regard George Bernard Shaw as a tropical type, yet he loved this warm-weather resort with its fuchsia hedges and lush, palm-dotted gardens enough to write much of *St. Joan* here and return again and again. So the great granite mansion boasts a *Pygmalion Restaurant* (dressy, with French-accented cuisine) and a *Dolittle Bar,* an affable spot to relax in after a sports-filled day. And sports there are: tennis and golf on a private 9-hole course, sailing, water skiing, speedboating, windsurfing on Kenmare Bay, horseback riding, and pony trekking through the neighboring countryside. Plus a heated indoor pool, sauna, sun lounge, and sun terrace overlooking the water. Fishing and shooting can also be arranged. There's nightly entertainment during the season. But activity notwithstanding, there's the grace of another time about resort life here; the 60 rooms all have a nice old-fashioned elegance about them. Open Easter through October, and Christmas and New Year's. Details: Great Southern Hotel, Parknasilla, County Kerry, Irish Republic (phone: 064-45122).

VINTAGE, Kinsale, County Cork, Irish Republic: The plastic grapes, the brown cloths, and the flickering red candles are gone (thanks to a much-needed overhaul), and the decor can now be described as cozy/romantic and as delightful as the food, which has always been outstanding. Every evening, in a kitchen that is minuscule by restau-rant standards, master chef Michael Riese, who was formerly head chef at the *Four Seasons Hotel* in his native Hamburg, conjures up a menu remarkable for its freshness of ingredients and approach. As much as possible, he uses local foodstuffs — organi-cally grown vegetables, eggs from free-range chickens, seafood caught just offshore, and free-range goose, duckling, and rabbits, as well as pheasant, quail, pigeon, and venison in season. His Kinsale hot smoked salmon steak in a Charlesfort sauce and his *sole véronique* — fillets stuffed with fresh prawns and sauced with grape-studded dry white wine and cream — are superb. The menu is complemented by an excellent wine list. Closed Sundays, except during holiday weekends. Details: The Vintage, Kinsale, County Cork, Irish Republic (phone: 021-772502).

LONGUEVILLE HOUSE AND PRESIDENTS' RESTAURANT, Mallow, County Cork, Irish Republic: There's a lovely formality about this cream-white Georgian manor house on a hill and its fine interior detail (inlaid mahogany doors, a marble Adam fireplace, Italian plasterwork ceilings). There's also inviting color and clutter: bowls of flowers, chairs to sink into, paintings, a Victorian whirligig stand stacked with paperbacks as well as room-high shelves of rare editions. In the valley of the Blackwater River below, the massive ruins of Dromineen attest to the fact that this has been O'Callaghan soil since the start of Irish time. The castle was tumbled and the land commandeered by Cromwellian forces in the 1640s. A full 300 years later, it is back in family hands. Now Michael O'Callaghan and his wife, Jane, are hosts in a handsome, Relais et Châteaux establishment famous for its food. On any given evening, the gooseberry chutney, the cream of tomato and vegetable soups, the chicken, the lamb, and the pink trout are lovingly home-cooked with sophisticated simplicity and consummate skill by Jane. The sweets — soufflé cake, fresh fruit tarts, homemade ice cream — are good enough to swoon over. The O'Callaghans care a lot — enough to spend their "off" months (from mid-October to Easter) "refreshing" — Jane at London's Cordon Bleu or with one of France's great chefs, Michael traveling in search of wines for his impressive cellar. (They now boast Ireland's only vineyard, consisting of three acres planted to Rickensteiner grapes.) Between meals, guests lodged in *Longueville*'s 20 pretty rooms fish in the Blackwater's pools, play the Mallow golf course, or sun in the palm-lined Victorian conservatory. Outside guests are welcome for dinner only. Details: Longueville House and Presidents' Restaurant, Mallow, County Cork, Irish Republic (phone: 022-47156 or 47306).

BALLYMALOE HOUSE, Shanagarry, Midleton, County Cork, Irish Republic: Ballymaloe House dates from the 17th century with extensions and a chunky stone keep that survives from a 14th-century castle of the Fitzgeralds. It beckons across grassy lawns where plump sheep crop away. You park under the big chestnut tree by the flagstone terrace with its tubs of flowers. A breeze ruffles the ivy walls, the door swings open, and you're home — even if it's your first visit. As the Allens, Ivan and Myrtle, whose 400-acre farm this is, put it, *Ballymaloe* is an "old family home, with the family still in it, children and grandchildren come and go, guests become friends." There are usually children around, but they don't get underfoot and there's plenty for them to do: swim; play croquet; create mountains, cities, and rivers in the sandpit. Children's meals are served early, while the adults play at the pool, on the tennis court, the 7-hole golf course, or at the trout pond. A cooking school has recently been added. Everyone gathers in the lounge to wait for Myrtle's meals, famed through all Ireland. The food is simple and marvelous — even at breakfast: "muisli" cereal is grated apple, oatmeal, honey, a squeeze of lemon; the marmalade is homemade. But then almost everything is; and, with rare exceptions, everything is grown on the family farm as well. Lunch is a cold buffet; the dinner menu is short, straightforward: perhaps crudités with garlic mayonnaise (so perfectly fresh that a cucumber wedge is like nothing you've ever tasted) or watercress soup to start; then locally smoked mackerel, "little pots of hot mussels," or homemade Danish pâté; summer turkey baked in butter and fresh herbs, roast rib of beef with three sauces, or French casserole of roast pork with Normandy mustard sauce; and the board of local cheeses, fruit tarts, cake, and — finally — coffee with Ballymaloe chocolates. Of 30 guestrooms, those in the main house are most comfortable; the recently upgraded courtyard rooms are just as good, if not better. Alternative gatehouse, gate lodge, and cottages at son Timothy's farm home are also available. Outside guests are welcome for lunch or dinner. Details: Ballymaloe House, Shanagarry, Midleton, County Cork, Irish Republic (phone: 021-652531).

DROMOLAND CASTLE, Newmarket-on-Fergus, County Clare, Irish Republic: It sits, gray and graceful, turreted and towered, in the heart of a 450-acre park whose green velvet lawns roll away into dark green woods. Ireland's banner flies from the battlements mirrored in the small lake. And if Dromoland looks like a fantasy come true, it's because it is — for guests who roam its garden, golf on its golf course (now a full 18 holes), fish and boat on its lake and streams, ride horseback over neighboring hills, and call it temporary home. It was once the real home of Bernard McDonough, a West Virginia gentleman who'd always wanted a castle to call his own and finally realized his impossible dream when he bought this 16th-century seat of the bold O'Briens and restored it as a hotel. A regal job he's done too. Inside, antique O'Brien portraits line halls that glow with rich wood paneling, silken fabrics, and sunlight. Through the tall dining room windows, you can watch deer on the distant morning grass (the breakfast buffet is piled with fresh fruits, croissants, fresh-baked pastries); at night its damask walls and polished silver gleam in the chandelier light, and the food is very good. Its 77 rooms — all with bath — are airy and bright with flowered papers and flower colors. The occasional Irish purist harumphs and finds it "all a bit too grand." But its many repeat guests wouldn't have it any other way. Details: Dromoland Castle, Newmarket-on-Fergus, County Clare, Irish Republic (phone: 061-71144).

IF YOU'RE NEARBY

CAVENDISH, Baslow, Derbyshire, England: Set on the Chatsworth estate, described in *Stately Homes and Great Gardens,* this 18th-century inn restored in 1975 was expanded in 1984 with an annex whose architecture — and whose charm — matches the original. The builders even searched out secondhand stone to match the original. Recently completed is a renovation that makes the kitchen so fine that a dining table for guests' use has been installed along with the fixtures. The rooms are impeccably elegant and splendidly appointed. Details: Cavendish Hotel, Baslow, Derbyshire DE4 1SP, England (phone: 024688-2311).

CLIVEDON, Taplow, Buckinghamshire, England: One of England's great country estates, *Clivedon* stands majestically on 400 wooded acres by the River Thames. Long the property of the most powerful of the English nobility, it is now managed by Blakeney Hotels (also the proprietors of the sumptuous *Royal Crescent* in Bath), who have preserved and classically redecorated the original rooms of the 17th-century mansion, retaining the works of art that reflect the lives of its previous owners. The incomparable grounds, which once received the attention of as many as 50 gardeners, include a sweeping pasture, dazzling flower borders, hanging woods, exquisite pavilions, temples, sculptures, 2,000-year-old Roman sarcophagi, and an amphitheater where *Rule Britannia* was first performed in 1740. In addition to beautiful walks, guests enjoy boat trips on the Thames, tennis (on both indoor and outdoor courts), swimming, squash, fishing, horse racing, polo, golf, and rowing. Details: Clivedon, Taplow, Buckinghamshire (phone: 06286).

PRIORY, Bath, Avon, England: This handsome Georgian home built of Bath stone in the Gothic style, now converted to a small hotel, ranks among the best country hotels in England. The atmosphere is tranquil, the furnishings antique and well-kept, the swimming pool in the two-acre English garden heated, the dining room's cuisine French and highly praised. All 21 rooms have private baths or showers, and 6 deluxe rooms were recently added along with an Orangery-style restaurant. A Relais et Châteaux establishment. Closed the first two weeks in January. Details: The Priory, Weston Rd., Bath, Avon BA1 2XT, England (phone: 0225-331922).

ROYAL CRESCENT: Forming the impressive center of the famous Royal Crescent, this elegant and historical Georgian hotel is part of Bath's architectural heritage. With commanding views, it is within walking distance of the Assembly Rooms, the Roman baths, the Pump Room, and the abbey. It has 36 super-deluxe rooms and some extra-special apartments. The Sir Perry Blakeney Suite, for example, has a 17th-century canopied bed, pale blue sofas, an Oriental carpet, and a white and gold ceiling of intricate gesso swirls. There are magnificent Georgian public rooms, a good restaurant, and attractive gardens. Details: Royal Crescent Hotel, 16 Royal Crescent, Bath, Avon BA1 2LS, England (phone: 319090).

GARDEN HOUSE, Cambridge, Cambridgeshire, England: The lawn of this modern, luxurious hotel stretches to the edge of the River Cam, and every morning the waiters put out bread for the duck colony that inhabits its peaceful waters. Most of the 117 rooms have balconies overlooking the riverside; all have private baths and showers. Details: Garden House Hotel, Granta Pl., Mill La., Cambridge, Cambridgeshire CB2 1RT, England (phone: 0223-63421).

THE CASTLE, Taunton, Somerset, England: This erstwhile Norman fortress, now covered with wisteria, has won acclaim from all corners for its peaceful garden and its polished English manner. The 35 bedrooms are especially luxurious; each has its own style (mahogany, walnut, yew, painted bamboo, pickled pine). The fine dining room, which received a Michelin star in 1984, is frosting on the cake. Details: Castle Hotel, Castle Green, Taunton, Somerset TA1 1NF (phone: 0823-272671).

THE CLOSE, Tetbury, Gloucestershire, England: This former 16th-century wool merchant's home of Cotswold stone offers a dozen beamed bedrooms fitted out with antiques (one with a four-poster bed), a walled garden with a lily pond, croquet, and a dining room known for its new English cookery and extensive wine list. All rooms have baths or showers. Details: The Close, 8 Long St., Tetbury, Gloucestershire GL8 8AQ, England (phone: 0666-52272; in the US, 800-243-9420).

ISLAND, Tresco, Isles of Scilly, Cornwall, England: Old and new architecture keep company in this resort hotel on a secluded, car-free island; private beach, heated outdoor pool. Fishing, sailing, and rowing can be arranged. Of the 24 rooms and 6 suites, all but 2 have private baths. The Tresco Abbey Gardens are world-famous for their subtropical vegetation. Closed mid-October through February. Details: Island Hotel, Tresco, Isles of Scilly, Cornwall TR24 0PU, England (phone: 0720-22883).

WENSLEYDALE HEIFER, West Witton, Leyburn, North Yorkshire: In the heart of James Herriot Country, equidistant from the Lake District, the Scottish border, and the North York Moors, not far from the sparkling river Ure, this picturesque 17th-century coaching inn is full of nice touches like canopy beds, beamed ceilings, and huge old fireplaces where fires blaze merrily in winter. Accommodations are in the main building and several equally charming adjacent structures. The traditional Yorkshire Sunday lunches are well known. Details: The Wensleydale Heifer, West Witton, near Leyburn, North Yorkshire DL8 4LS (phone: 0969-22322).

CULLODEN HOUSE, Inverness, Highland, Scotland: The guestrooms and public rooms of this 18th-century mansion are stuffed with antiques; the dining room is by Adam, and the former dungeons now house a sauna. All of the 21 rooms have baths and showers. Prince Charles visited here a few years ago; a photograph hangs in the hallway underneath a painting of Bonnie Prince Charlie, who stepped outside one morning in 1746 to fight his last battle. Details: Culloden House, Inverness, Highland IV1 2NZ, Scotland (phone: 0463-790461).

RUTHIN CASTLE, Ruthin, Clwyd, Wales: This hotel occupies a former mansion dating from the 19th century, and some of the public rooms are impressive — witness the hotel bar, situated in the former library. The establishment is well known for its medieval banquets, Welsh-style. All 64 rooms have baths or showers; one of the largest has a four-poster bed that has been used by two Princes of Wales. On the extensive grounds are the ruins of the original castle, which was built in 1282; you can see the whipping pit, the drowning pool, and the dungeon, all of which bear battle scars from the time of Oliver Cromwell. Details: Ruthin Castle, Ruthin, Clwyd LL15 2NU, Wales (phone: 08242-2664).

BALLYLICKEY HOUSE, Ballylickey, County Cork, Irish Republic: The former hunting lodge with the Bantry Bay view that you may have found here a few years ago burned in 1983. But the new *Ballylickey* may be even better than the old — more personal and very carefully tailored to the management's ambitions to offer only the best. The main house has been rebuilt on the plans of the original, but with two wings of suites provide true seclusion. There are also a number of cottages. Its handsome lawns, gardens, and parkland bordering the Ouvane River and its heated outdoor swimming pool and stables make this Relais et Châteaux establishment a lovely base for tours of Cork and Kerry. Closed November to mid-March. Details: Ballylickey House, Bantry Bay, County Cork, Irish Republic (phone: 027-50071).

CASHEL HOUSE, Cashel, County Galway, Irish Republic: This gracious mansion-turned-hotel has been welcoming guests to its quiet, Relais et Châteaux comforts since 1968. The 50 acres of landscaped grounds offer fine views over Cashel Bay, and the area is full of beaches, horseback riding, golf, and fishing for salmon and sea trout. The hotel has 17 bedrooms, 13 mini-suites, and its own hard tennis court. Details: Cashel House Hotel, Cashel, County Galway, Irish Republic (phone: 095-31001; in US: 800-223-6764).

DUNDRUM HOUSE, Dundrum, County Tipperary, Irish Republic: This gracious country manor, built in 1730 on 2,400 acres, has been extensively renovated since its purchase by its present owners, Austin and Mary Crowe, and the high ceilings, the ornate plasterwork, the carved mantlepieces, and the fine views over the tree-studded grounds make it a delightful place to stay when visiting the Rock of Cashel (see *Ancient Monuments and Ruins*). Details: Dundrum House Hotel, Dundrum, County Tipperary, Irish Republic (phone: 062-71116).

MARLFIELD HOUSE, Gorey, County Wexford, Irish Republic: The former dower house of the Courtown Estate, later the principal Irish residence of the Earl of Courtown, offers guestrooms with canopied and half-testered beds, drawing rooms full of antiques and beautiful oil paintings, a curvilinear Victorian cast-iron conservatory, a tennis court and croquet lawn. Surrounding you are acres of beautiful woodlands and gardens. Everything has been restored to its original Regency splendor. A Relais et Châteaux establishment. Closed at Christmastime. Details: Marlfield House Hotel, Gorey, County Wexford, Irish Republic (phone: 055-21124).

CAHERNANE, Killarney, County Kerry, Irish Republic: This former Victorian home occupies a peaceful 100-acre estate; parklands, pastures, lakes, and mountains are its backdrop. The high-ceilinged, antique-furnished bedrooms in the original mansion are more romantic than those in the modern annex. All 52 rooms have baths. On-site sports facilities include private river fishing, hard-court tennis, 9-hole mini-golf, and croquet. Open Easter to December. Details: Cahernane Hotel, Muckross Rd., Killarney, County Kerry, Irish Republic (phone: 064-31895).

CROCNARAW COUNTRY HOUSE, Moyard, County Galway, Irish Republic: An inviting and homey Georgian house with lovely gardens on 20 acres on the shores of Ballinakill Bay 6 miles from Clifden. The dining room serves tasty meals with fish, fresh seafood, garden vegetables, dairy products. Of the 10 rooms, 6 have baths. April to October. Details: Crocnaraw Country House, Moyard, County Galway, Irish Republic (phone: 095-41068).

RATHMULLAN HOUSE, Rathmullan, County Donegal, Irish Republic: This late-18th-century country house resort is as snug as it can be. Log and turf fires burn in the drawing room and library; the assorted rooms and cottages are stylishly scattered with antiques; and the conservatory-style dining room, with its tented ceiling, makes guests feel that they are dining in a garden. Outside the scenery is magnificent — from the tree-lined shore of Lough Swilly (on whose banks the hostelry sits) to the wildly grand coast and mountains to the west. The gardens are stunning and have won several awards. On its 50 acres of grounds, the hotel also has its own grass tennis court, a croquet lawn, and a putting green. A Relais et Châteaux establishment. Open Easter to October. Details: Rathmullan House, Rathmullan, County Donegal, Irish Republic (phone: 074-58188).

LISS ARD HOUSE, Skibbereen, County Cork, Irish Republic: This impressive 150-year-old manor house has been converted with a fine sense of style and color and has been fitted out with handsome antiques. A worthy bar, good Irish food, country riding (with instruction), and jaunting car rides are all features; other sports can be arranged. Of the 10 rooms, 5 have baths. Details: Liss Ard House, Skibbereen, County Cork, Irish Republic (phone: 028-21109).

LONDONDERRY ARMS, Carnlough, County Antrim, Northern Ireland: An old coaching inn built in 1848 by the Marchioness of Londonderry and inherited by his great-grandson Sir Winston Churchill in 1921, this family-run hostelry is full of unusual pieces of carved furniture, Ulster artists' paintings, early Irish maps, and open fires. It also boasts a fine garden that runs down to the sea. The home-cooked meals are made with seasonal local produce. Rooms are comfortably furnished, and all have private baths. Details: Londonderry Arms, Carnlough, County Antrim, Northern Ireland (phone: 0574-85255).

CULLODEN HOTEL, Craigavad, Holywood, County Down, Northern Ireland: This splendid Scottish baronial structure on 12 acres of secluded gardens and woodlands, a former bishop's palace, is possibly the most luxurious hotel in Northern Ireland. Its 80 handsomely decorated rooms are full of velvets and silks, and the lovely dining room and public areas are embellished with fine plasterwork ceilings, Louis XV chandeliers, handsome paintings, and other beautiful antiques. The former bishop's chapel is now the bar. All 80 rooms have baths. Amenities include a pair of squash courts, Ping-Pong, tennis, and croquet. Details: Culloden Hotel, Cragavad, Holywood, County Down, Northern Ireland (phone: Holywood 5223).

Stately Homes and Great Gardens

Many Britons bemoan their nation's penchant for demolition, and there is always a great outcry among preservationists each time Britain's death duties, rising maintenance costs, or a personal financial crisis forces an owner of one of the nation's great stately homes (one that may have been in the family for centuries) to sell out. Over 600 of these structures met the wrecker's ball between the end of World War II and the mid-1970s. Yet the fact is that in England, Scotland, Wales, and Northern Ireland, the number of such unhappy events has dwindled to a fraction of what it was during that period. Whereas approximately twenty per year were destroyed then, only around two or three are lost annually nowadays. And while even that small number may be too many, it is also true that what remains is a number of fine castles, mansions, and country homes that travelers can scarcely believe.

This is in part thanks to organizations like the National Trust, the National Trust of Scotland, and the National Trust of Northern Ireland, which have been able to accept great houses and estates in settlement of taxes, and the National Heritage Fund, which may supply endowments for those that the trusts might not be able to take over for want of the monies to maintain them. But the longevity of these stately homes through the centuries also resulted from the fact that England, at least, has never been physically invaded, and its society has remained relatively stable down through the years. The system of primogeniture, which allowed the eldest son to inherit the whole of a property, also kept estates together. Since the houses were year-round homes and usually not mere refuges from the hot summers of the city, there developed a devotion for ancestral dwelling places akin to that which citizens of other nations extend only to their children. To see these grand homes, standing regally at the end of tree-lined lanes, surrounded by beautiful parks and gardens full of fountains and miniature temples, enormous trees, and fine hedges, is to understand why.

Many of the finest stately homes on view today date back to the very beginning of the great period of English domestic architecture, in the 15th century, when, following the Dissolution of the Monasteries, the estimated one-third of the kingdom that had been cloistral land suddenly became available to the laity. These, like others that came later, seldom remained untouched by the fickle hand of fashion, as wealthy landowners strove to keep up with the latest styles. In the 18th century, the symmetrical Palladian style (named for the 16th-century Venetian Andrea Palladio) became the rage, together with the work of that Scottish master designer Robert Adam, who began executing his gracefully articulated designs at Hatchlands, now a National Trust Home in East Clandon, Surrey. In the latter, the ceilings were covered with ornate plaster relief work, often painted many colors, and the floors were patterned. But there was a grace and a lightness to it all, and Adam interiors made perfect settings for glittering society in their bright silks and satins. In succeeding years, energetic invention and tireless adaptations of the architectural styles of Italy and France began to appear.

Examples of houses of all of these eras are currently open to the public — sometimes at no charge, sometimes for a fee — in England, Scotland, Wales, Northern Ireland, and the Irish Republic, in such numbers that it would be easy to construct a whole vacation around stately home tours. *Historic Homes of Britain* (21 Pembroke Sq., London W8 6PB, England; phone: 01-937-2402) designs tours for 2 or more people which may include meals or overnight stays in privately owned historic and stately homes. Tours can be arranged to cater to visitors' special interests like gardens, art, or antiques buying, and often feature lectures by specialists in the specific fields.

For the most copious listing of all visitable country homes, a representative selection of which follows, consult the following publications:

> *The AA Guide to Stately Homes, Museums, Castles and Gardens in Britain* (£5.95 from the Automobile Association, Fanum House, Basingstoke, Hampshire RG21 2EA, England; available in the US for $14.75 postpaid from the British Travel Bookshop, 40 W 57th St., New York, NY 10019; phone: 212-765-0898). It gives capsule histories, entrance fees, and hours, which vary wildly and unpredictably from one home to the next.
>
> *The Intelligent Traveller's Guide to Historic Britain,* by Philip A. Crowl ($19.95; Congdon & Weed, 298 Fifth Ave., New York, NY 10001). Thorough descriptions. An excellent companion to the above.
>
> *The National Trust Guide to England, Wales and Northern Ireland, 3rd edition,* edited by Robin Fedden and Rosemary Joekes ($24.95; W. W. Norton, 500 Fifth Ave., New York, NY 10110). Interesting discussions of the National Trust properties.

Admission fees can add up for those who want to see many of the homes, so travelers in England should consider purchasing an Open to View ticket from British Rail ($29 from BritRail at 630 Third Ave., New York, NY 10017; phone: 212-599-5400). These month-long passes allow access to all ancient monuments under the wing of the Department of the Environment, every National Trust property, and to more than four dozen other sites.

CHATSWORTH, near Bakewell, Derbyshire, England: Mary, Queen of Scots, stayed at this home on the banks of the River Derwent (now in the Peak District National Park) when in the custody of Lord Shrewsbury, the fourth husband of the redoubtable Bess of Hardwick, who began building the place with her second husband, Sir William Cavendish, in 1552. But the quarters in which the unfortunate queen lodged on and off between 1569 and 1584 were rendered unrecognizable in about 1686, when the fourth earl of Devonshire (a descendant of Sir William's second son, the first earl) spent two decades renovating it into one of the finest houses in the nation and among the most beautiful in Europe. The façade is stately, Corinthian-pilastered and strictly classical, and the interiors are insistently baroque, with a splendid ornate silver chandelier, wall coverings of oak, silk, and gilt leather (among other resplendent materials), dizzying paintings by Laguerre, Verrio, and Thornhill on the walls and ceilings, and elaborate woodcarvings that for many years passed as the work of Grinling Gibbons (but were actually executed by a local artisan). Those, together with the *trompe l'oeil* violin painted on an inner door of the State Music Room, may be the most immediately memorable sights in Chatsworth. But the collection of furniture by William Kent, the first English architect to attempt to integrate furniture and architectural ornamentation, is one of the finest extant. Also on display is a grand collection of works by Hals, Reynolds, Landseer, Lely, Rembrandt, Sargent, and Van Dyck. Travelers have been marveling at all of this for centuries, and considering that there are 175 rooms (of which 51 are "very big indeed," according to the Duchess of Devonshire, who lives there), it's not hard to understand the nature of the wonderment, even before a stroll in the 105-acre gardens and the 1,100-acre park, which are no trifles either. A most delightful aspect of a Chatsworth visit, the garden was one of several English preserves formally planted in the 17th century by George London and Henry Wise. It was reconstructed a century later, much to the dismay of 20th-century critics, by the ubiquitous Lancelot "Capability" Brown, who — even in a day of formal architectural styles — espoused naturalistic landscape design. (The gentleman's nickname derived from his habit of referring to the capabilities of any tract he had been called upon to improve.) The Water Garden, which features a great, glittering staircase of water known as the Grand Cascade, constitutes most of the original design. Also worth noting is the Emperor Fountain, a single powerful jet of water capable of shooting 267 feet into the air. Its designer, Joseph Paxton (1803–65), spent 32 years as Chatsworth's chief gardener; he left the estate blessed with greenhouses that were the forerunners of the Great Exhibition of 1851's Crystal Palace, which earned him not only celebrity but also a knighthood. Sadly, the major greenhouses were pulled down long ago, but giant rockeries remain as evidence of Paxton's prodigious imagination and industry. Details: Comptroller, Chatsworth, Bakewell, Derbyshire DE4 1PP, England (phone: 024-688-2204).

BOUGHTON HOUSE, near Kettering, Northamptonshire, England: In the late 17th century, Englishmen were building grand homes as testimony to their great faith in the future and the increase of their prosperity — and borrowing architectural styles from the Continent with aplomb. The starting point for the great extension to Boughton House, a prime example of French influence, was one Ralph, Earl of Montagu, who served Charles II as ambassador to France beginning in 1669 (and made such a favorable impression there that Louis XIV himself ordered the Versailles fountains to be played on his every visit). Ralph Montagu laid out new gardens with lakes, fountains, and avenues, and added a château-style front wing. Today, several remodelings beyond its 15th-century beginnings as a monastery, Boughton is an enormous place, boasting a courtyard for every day of the week, a chimney for every week of the year, and a window for every day of the year. The furniture and the porcelain, which the house has in abundance, are mostly French, as are the paintings on the ceilings by the Huguenot Louis Cheron, and the floors on a stairway landing and in a state room, made of *parquet de Versailles;* the art collection, which includes paintings by El Greco, Gainsborough, Gheeraerts, Kneller, Lely, and Van Dyck, are particularly notable. As for the Earl of Montagu, it has been said that he was "too ambitious and in the end too successful to avoid envy, and too overtly pro-French . . . to be trusted in his own time." Embroiled in the intrigues concerning the succession of Charles II after his return from the French court, he was forced to live in exile from 1679 to 1685. When the Catholic James II snubbed him when he did hazard a return, he repaired to Boughton and began building the great château-like addition. His marriage to the wealthy widow Elizabeth Wriothesley, daughter of the Earl of Southampton, greatly facilitated his patronage of the arts and of the Huguenot craftsmen whose works adorn Boughton today. Finally, with Protestants back on the throne, he was made a duke. The property passed through the marriage of his great-granddaughter to the Scottish Duke of Buccleuch, in whose descendants' care Boughton House remains today. Details: Boughton House, Geddington, Kettering NN14 1BJ, England (phone: 0536-82248).

HAREWOOD HOUSE, near Leeds, West Yorkshire, England: Robert Adam was only in his early thirties when he was invited to begin work on the interiors of Harewood House, designed by the York architect John Carr for one Edwin Lascelles, but the interiors that resulted, full of delicately fluted Ionic columns, beautifully molded plaster ceilings, and classical fireplaces, confirm his great talent (even though his brother joked that he had only "tickled it up so as to dazzle the eyes of the squire"). And despite exterior renovations since then, this remains a stunning house for its fine Chippendale furniture, made after Adam's designs; its collection of paintings by Bellini, El Greco, Gainsborough, Reynolds, Tintoretto, Titian, Turner, Veronese; and the collections of Sèvres and Chinese porcelain. The grounds were designed by the prolific Capability Brown beginning in 1772, a year after the house was finished; the resulting landscape, meant to look as natural as nature's own, was substantially unchanged except for the 19th-century addition of the terraces near the house — until 1962, when a furious storm smashed some 20,000 trees. There is also a fine Bird Garden, where rare and endangered species are bred in cooperation with zoos and gardens around the world; the penguins are particularly beloved. The estate is currently the home of the seventh earl of Harewood, whose mother was Mary, Princess Royal, the daughter of George V. Details: Harewood House and Bird Garden, Estate Office, Harewood, Leeds LS17 9LQ, England (phone: 0532-886225).

BEAULIEU ABBEY AND PALACE HOUSE, near Lyndhurst, Hampshire, England: The wars and other extravagances of Henry VIII had left the king in less than ideal financial straits, and Parliament was in no hurry to levy new taxes so he could pay his bills. Thus it happened that the Cistercian monastery on the Beaulieu River close to the Solent coastline, for which King John had ceded the lands in 1204, came into the hands of Thomas Wriothesley, who served as secretary of state and lord chancellor to Henry VIII and later became the earl of Southampton. Working with his minister Thomas Cromwell, the king had cajoled Parliament into dissolving the smaller monasteries and confiscating their lands and their fortunes in plate and jewels, tapestries and statuary, and other portable items. Their sale meant an overflowing treasury for Henry, and for England a legacy of not only stark ruins but also of stately homes built on the grounds of former religious houses. In the case of Beaulieu Abbey — one of a number of lands granted to Wriothesley at the time of the Dissolution — its Palace House occupies the former 13th-century cloistral gatehouse; its great interest lies in how this two-storied structure has changed through the years. Originally converted after the Dissolution in 1538, it was remodeled beginning around 1870, but many of the original Tudor elements — among them the drawing room, the private dining room, the reception hall, and the gables — can still be seen. A new building has been constructed on the property to house a collection of 250 vintage automobiles, one of the best in England. In passing, it's interesting to note that scholarly conjecture has it that Wriothesley's grandson, known for being Shakespeare's patron, was also the Friend described in the sonnets. Palace House is presently the home of Lord Montagu. Details: Palace House, John Montagu Building, Beaulieu, Hampshire S042 7ZN, England (phone: 0590-612345).

CASTLE HOWARD, near Malton, North Yorkshire, England: The socialite Sir John Vanbrugh served in the army, spent two years in a French prison on espionage charges, and wrote plays for the theater, such as *The Provoked Wife.* But he is perhaps best known for his work as an architect, and his most famous creation, especially since the TV version of Evelyn Waugh's novel *Brideshead Revisited* was filmed there a few years ago, is the palatial home known as Castle Howard. He had met Charles Howard, the third earl of Carlisle, during his playwriting days, and when the Howard family home was destroyed by fire in 1693, Vanbrugh won the commission. Executed with the help of Nicholas Hawksmoor, who had worked with the great Christopher Wren, it has been earning paeans from travelers ever since. Horace Walpole, after a visit there two centuries ago, noted that he had expected to see one of the finest places in Yorkshire. "But nobody had informed me that I should at one view see a palace, a town, a fortified city, temples on high places, woods worthy of being each a metropolis of the Druids, vales connected to hills by other woods, the noblest lawn in the world, fenced by half the horizon, and a mausoleum that would tempt one to be buried alive. In short, I have seen gigantic places before but never a sublime one." Aside from its lovely site on a plateau north of the River Derwent between York and Malton, its sheer immensity is one of its most overwhelming features. Inside the 323-foot-long, cupola-topped south front and the mammoth wings on either side, there are endless rooms and corridors packed with paintings and porcelains by the score, not to mention bronzes, sculptures, gleaming antique furniture, and impressive architectural features, such as the multiwindowed dome that lights the vast marble entrance hall. Visitors must also consider the 1,000 acres of grounds — with a splendid, dramatic fountain and formal gardens surrounding the house, the preserve of the Castle Howard peacocks; the broad terrace of grass beyond; and the fine outbuildings meant to add interest to the landscape, including the Temple of the Four Winds, which Vanbrugh designed, and Hawksmoor's mausoleum for the Howard family, which inspired Walpole's comment about burial alive. The elegant stables, designed by the same John Carr of York who worked on Harewood House, now contain tableaux featuring selections from a collection of some 12,000 costumes and accessories spanning three centuries; the workmanship of the lavish embroideries in silk thread and silver tinsel and other rich materials call to mind Beatrix Potter's comment that the stitches "looked as if they had been made by little mice." It is not hard to see why the third earl, whose descendants still own and occupy the place, ran out of money before its completion. Details: Castle Howard, York Y06 7BZ, England (phone: 065384-333).

ALTHORP, near Northampton, Northamptonshire, England: This wonderful home had long been known as one of England's greatest country houses at the time the youngest daughter of the present owner, the eighth Earl Spencer, was married to the eldest son of Queen Elizabeth II. The estate was created by one John Spencer, who made a fortune through perseverance, hard work, and good business sense, then cemented his family's place in society by alliances with the wealthy. Almost every successive generation has added to its beauties. Robert Spencer bought pictures when he served three successive kings in Paris and Madrid. The first Earl Spencer commissioned a series of portraits from his friend Sir Joshua Reynolds. The house, an early Tudor structure remodeled in the 17th century, was redone in the classical style beginning around 1790 by the architect Henry Holland, who resurfaced the walls with a grayish-white tile that was popular at the time and added Ionic decorations to the rooms inside on a commission from the second Earl Spencer, a passionate bibliophile whose collections once filled the Long Library, the family's main sitting room. And the entire home is filled with great works of art by Gainsborough, Kneller, Lely, Reynolds, Rubens, Sargent, and Van Dyck; fine furniture by Saunier, Vardy, Seddon, and others; china from Sèvres, Chelsea, and Bow; and 18th-century armorial porcelain from China. The high-ceilinged entrance hall, one of the rooms seen on guided tours, has been characterized as "the noblest Georgian room in the country." Details: The Countess Spencer, Althorp, Northampton NN7 4HG, England (phone: 0604-69368).

BURGHLEY HOUSE, near Stamford, Lincolnshire, England: Queen Elizabeth I last visited this house in the closing years of the 16th century, when its creator and owner, William Cecil, Lord Burghley — her secretary of state for four decades, the grandson of an obscure Welshman named Seissylit — was on his deathbed, and its exterior now exhibits the same Italianate columns and the same bristle of domes and clustered chimneys that it did then. The design of this assemblage suffers, said one critic, from the loss of the restraints of medieval architectural rules: "Nothing as yet had appeared to take their place, so that the architects, with a number of new processes at their disposal, were at a complete loss as to how best to apply them." But most others who have visited this splendid place, which was built lavishly enough for entertaining a queen and has served as the home of the Cecils and the Exeters for four centuries since, agree that not only is it the nation's largest Elizabethan home, but also one of its grandest and most beautiful. A 17th-century remodeling eradicated most of the original Tudor design, but the years since William Cecil's day have also been marked by the acquisition of vast art collections. Together with the second Lord Sunderland of Althorp, the fifth Lord Exeter ranked among the most discriminating collectors of the Restoration era; few besides Charles I himself, who accumulated nearly 1,400 paintings (most returned to the Continent after a Commonwealth sale), owned as many works of art. The magnificent stone staircase and the great hall (both from Tudor days), the room in which Elizabeth I passed the night (where the bed in which she slept and all its coverings are intact), and the aptly named Heaven Room, where Verrio frescoed the ceiling with his interpretation of the hereafter, are particularly memorable. Guided tours are mandatory. As for the huge park, it was landscaped in the 18th century by Capability Brown. Details: Burghley House, near Stamford, Lincolnshire PE9 3JY (phone: 0780-52451).

BLENHEIM PALACE, near Woodstock, Oxfordshire, England: Britons come in droves, it sometimes seems, to see the bedroom where Sir Winston Churchill was born. But that is certainly not all they see in this giant of a house. Built essentially as a monument to England, with funds supplied by Parliament on direction from Queen Anne, as thanks to the duke of Marlborough for his 1704 victory over the French at Blenheim, the structure was designed by Sir John Vanbrugh with the assistance of Nicholas Hawksmoor, as at Castle Howard. Sarah, duchess of Marlborough, never wanted anything more than "a clean sweet house and garden be it ever so small"; the battles she had with the architect as some 1,500 artisans were laboring on the job and the cost of construction climbed toward the final £250,000 have become legendary. "I made Mr. Vanbrugh my enemy by the constant disputes I had with him to prevent his extravagance," she said at the time; it is reported that she even refused to let him enter her home after its completion. Whether or not viewers agree with Voltaire's pronouncement that it was "a great mass of stone, unattractive and tasteless," it is impossible to dispute the grandeur of the place. The structure measures 850 feet from end to end, and there are Tuscan colonnades galore, not to mention a vast Corinthian portico, a balustraded roof bristling with statues and towers, and more. From the great state rooms and the library to the saloon, the rooms dwarf mere mortals, and the assemblage brings to mind the rhyme of Alexander Pope: "Thanks sir, cried I, 'tis very fine,/But where d'ye sleep, or where d'ye dine?" The art collections are every bit as dazzling as their setting. The 18th-century gardens, revised in the 1760s by Capability Brown, were restored and expanded by the ninth duke two centuries later. Details: Administrator's Office, Blenheim Palace, Woodstock, Oxfordshire OX7 1PX (phone: 0993-811325).

CRATHES CASTLE, Banchory, Grampian, Scotland: In Scotland, the wealthy built not houses but castles, right up until the time of Cromwell. Nonetheless, through the years, the importance of matters of defense in the layout of domestic structures did dwindle considerably, and as part of a growing concern with design, erstwhile defensive features were exaggerated and used as decorative elements. Thus Scotland developed an indigenous domestic architecture unique in all of Europe. With Fyvie and Craigievar castles, Crathes Castle offers a prime example of this style. Like its fellows, Crathes is built of stone — the nation had almost no trees until the mid-18th century — in a configuration that is more vertical than horizontal so as to cram the most living space possible under the least amount of roof. And, because of the established traffic between Scotland, Scandinavia, and the Benelux countries, it exhibits the national taste for brightly colored designs painted on the ceilings. Crathes Castle is not dreary inside, as a reader of *Macbeth* might surmise, but is surprisingly cheerful, and the procession of gables and turrets is almost as fascinating as the rumor of a female ghost with a child in her arms, or the gardens outdoors, a series of small plantings separated by gigantic yew hedges, which rank among the finest in the country. On the 595-acre estate, there are also some fine specimen trees and 15 miles of nature trails. A visitor center presents exhibitions concerning the natural history of the area as well as the history of the family who owned the castle — the Burnetts. Details: The Administrator, Crathes Castle, Banchory, Aberdeenshire AB3 3QJ (phone: 0330-44525).

ERDDIG HOUSE, near Wrexham, Clwyd, Wales: It's not possible to view all of these fine old homes without wondering about everyday life — cooking meals and changing sheets and other such homely chores. Unfortunately, the quarters of the servants to whom these task fell are seldom on view. Not so at Erddig. In this 17th-century country home, occupied by generations of the Yorke family until a decade ago, though there are fine pieces of furniture in abundance (many with original upholstery) and many stately chambers, the most riveting area is "downstairs," where some 45 staff members labored: the laundry, where clothing was boiled in copper cauldrons, wrung out on rollers, dried on racks, and then ironed; the joiners' shop, where furniture and fences and other wooden items were mended, and which is still operational; and the new kitchen, detached from the house as a precaution against fire during the 18th century, where three kitchen maids and a cook toiled over the meals. The gallery of staff portraits with clever rhymes penned below and the display of photographs are particularly intriguing. All of this is the more impressive for the fact that until 1973, when the National Trust acquired and restored it, the house was in equally noteworthy disrepair: Philip Yorke III lived in two unheated, unelectrified rooms, and he would often be seen picking up scraps of paper off the floor. "I wish nothing should be parted with," wrote the first Philip Yorke of Erddig in 1771. Consequently, every bicycle, every automobile, and reams of receipts and letters were saved; what the master of it all was salvaging from the floor were bits of priceless hand-painted Chinese wallpaper that had peeled off the walls. Details: Erddig, Wrexham, Clwyd, North Wales LL13 0YT (phone: 0978-355314).

MALAHIDE CASTLE, Malahide, County Dublin, Irish Republic: "As in France," says Desmond Guinness in his treatise on Irish houses and castles, "where the word *château* so conveniently means both house and castle, so in Ireland *castle* can have the double meaning." Accordingly, this 12th-century structure, one of the oldest homes in the nation, looks like every fairy tale reader's idea of a castle on the outside, yet inside it appears more dwelling than battle station. Certain sections — the west drawing rooms, for example — date from Georgian times, as do the characteristic round turrets that look so old, while others are medieval but were given a veneer of civilization during a 19th-century restoration. The castle boasts one of the finest paneled rooms in Ireland, the Oak Room, which dates from the 16th century. And its great hall is unique in still being used in the manner for which it was built — that is, as a banqueting hall. Malahide was the home of the Talbot de Malahide family for over 800 years until 1973, when Lord Talbot died and the Castle was purchased by the Dublin County Council. It now houses one of the finest collections of Irish period furniture and a substantial display of Irish historical portraits and other works of art. Thanks to the enthusiasm of Lord Talbot, the gardens are exceptional as well. Details: Malahide Castle, Malahide, County Dublin, Irish Republic (phone: 452655).

Tea Shops and Tea Gardens

That great British institution, afternoon tea, had been given up for lost a few years ago: The cost of the ingredients and the extensive labor required had soared, just as weightwatchers had begun to question the healthfulness of the scones and pastries habit that their parents and grandparents always took for granted. But like that other great British institution, fish and chips — which was also, for a brief moment, put down as a thing of the past — afternoon tea has survived and has actually enjoyed something of a resurgence in popularity as harried Londoners have given up the rat race, moved to the country, and converted cow barns and old cottages into quainter-than-quaint tea shops where you can get the kind of set teas that dreams are made of — those archetypically wonderful teas whose passing was so vigorously lamented until just recently.

The reasons for the revival of interest in the institution are hard to gauge. Simple economy may be among them: As the prices of full meals climb, tea becomes increasingly attractive since most vacationers know that they can get by on nothing more than a full breakfast in their hotels and a relatively inexpensive tea in some country café. But nostalgia, in the form of a stubborn refusal to abandon tradition even in the face of stern realities, may also figure. Tea as an afternoon meal, first served in the late 18th century by the duchess of Bedford to entertain her guests between the early lunches and late dinners at her house parties, soon became an integral part of everybody's everyday life. A whole industry grew up around the manufacture of teacups and saucers, cake stands, tea forks for the cakes, silver teapots, sugar bowls and tiny silver tongs, linens, and the like. Less aristocratic families developed elaborate teatime rituals around the new meal in Victorian days; at a time when, it sometimes appeared, Britons lived to eat rather than the other way around, it seemed quite natural to nosh away the otherwise gustatorily empty late afternoon hours. "Everything stops for tea" became an English saying, and the World War I poet Rupert Brooke wrote about it in a poem, referring to a tea garden at Grantchester, near Cambridge (which still exists after all these years, in a sun-dappled meadow close to where the undergraduates leave their punts).

In days gone by, beginning around the turn of the century when one Miss Cranston established the nation's first tea room in Sauchiehall Street, Glasgow, running such tea gardens and tea shops was considered one respectable occupation for spinsters, and the foods you find at tea still reflect their genteel touch. Honey and country preserves, particularly strawberry jam, show up on the tea tables, along with biscuitlike scones. In Devon and Cornwall, thick clotted cream — too stiff for pouring — invariably accompanies the cakes; strawberry teas, a summertime specialty, include a bowl of the luscious red fruit. In country districts, especially in the Midlands and the North of England, you'll often encounter "farm teas," made up of enough salad, ham, fish, and other fairly substantial edibles that you can skip your evening meal and still not go to bed with a rumbling stomach. During afternoon tea, as served in its most elaborate form at some London hotels — the *Ritz* among them — it may take you a couple of hours or more to make your way through the endless procession of comestibles — thin sandwiches filled with cucumbers, watercress, or smoked salmon, and delicate pastries; not to mention the good selections of fine China and India brews. High teas such as the Scots love so well — still found in many seaside cafés around Britain — consist of a salad or "something on toast" in addition to the usual spread of buns and cakes. That may include, depending on where you are and when, Victoria spongecakes, gâteaux (cream cakes), rock cakes, fairy cakes, Battenberg and Madeira cakes, buns, scones, flans and egg dishes, savouries (meat pies), Bakewell puddings, meringues, cheesecakes, lemon meringue pies, lemon curd tarts, and more. In Scotland, fruitcakes, soda bread, and tea breads (a sort of cake and bread hybrid) show up on the tea table. In Wales, you can expect bacon, fish, pancakes, and Bara Brith (speckled bread). Many of the food specialties of the South appear most frequently at teatime: brandy snaps doused with fresh cream, custard tarts smoothed with red currant jelly and slathered with more cream, Chelsea buns, and above all, crumpets — a wintertime delight that resembles American English muffins, but with holes.

The settings for tea are as varied as the food. In Scotland, with few exceptions, you'll have to take your chances in big hotels. And in Wales, except in a few towns that are more frequented by tourists, it's in a café that you'll find the best teas. In England, tea shops are most numerous in the south and the west; cream teas, originally a West Country specialty, have become equally popular in other areas. You might pause for one in some unpretentious shop — or you might find yourself pouring your Earl Grey in the orangery, the dairy, or the stable of one of England's stately homes (especially if the house is owned and run by the National Trust). You can munch your teacakes in a battlefield, old almshouses, a castle, Sally Lunn's original shop, or the Pump Room in Bath. Or in the shop where the lace for Queen Victoria's wedding dress was made (*The Old Lace Shop,* Fore St., Beer, Devon). Or in a thatched cottage half covered in creepers and rambling roses (*Dunnose Cottage,* Luccombe Chine) — on the Isle of Wight, an exceptionally good location for summertime tea seekers. Local tourist offices can generally tell you what's good when you arrive in their area.

Here, then, a representative sampling:

WORTH A LONG DETOUR

SHIP'S LIGHTS, near Bridport, Dorset: Eype, a pretty hamlet a mile or so southwest of Bridport and only about 5 minutes' walk from the sea, is so tiny that you might not expect to find anything in the way of a tea shop amongst its handful of little houses — but there it is, in one of those archetypically whitewashed two-story cottages that are scattered so picturesquely along the winding lanes of this part of England. Inside, there's a little parlor where you can sit when the weather is poor. But the best thing about this establishment is the garden, a glorious flagstone enclosure that in summer fills up with emerald green and scarlet, brilliant yellow and orange — and, next to an old stone wall, there really is an old ship's light. You can take tea here, and savor scones slathered with clotted cream and jams as sweet and full of fruit as any you'll ever taste; and if you're really hungry, you can sample some of the establishment's own pastries or fancy cakes and sandwiches — all the tastier for the fresh sea air that comes with the package. Lunches available in summer. Open Easter through September. Phone: 0308-25656.

OLD FIRE ENGINE HOUSE, Ely, Cambridgeshire: If you have ever been to a first-class restaurant, got as far as dessert, and wished you could come back the next day for that, then you'll like this well-established restaurant, not far from Ely's lovely, stark, and cool cathedral, a landmark in this flat, low-lying part of eastern England. Some of the gâteaux, pastries, and flans served here are worthy of any groaning sweets trolley. Scones are served warm, if you wish, and there's local honey and homemade shortbread. *The Old Fire Engine House* is a good example of the kind of place best known as a restaurant but also operating, on a more modest and certainly more inexpensive scale, as a tea shop. It's especially handsome with its shady, well-tended garden, large windows and chintz curtains, warm-looking flagstone floor, and solid wooden furniture. Phone: 0353-2582.

GATEWAY CAKESHOP, Evesham, Worcestershire: Aside from the fairly uninspiring snack bars and plastic and functional establishments run by chains, it's increasingly difficult to find a pleasant spot for tea in a town; most tea shops are such small operations that rising rents have been lethal to them. But every country market town has its cake shop, and many of them serve tea on the side. The *Gateway,* installed in a pretty Tudor townhouse, is a good example. Dark and cozy and full of plain old-fashioned furniture, with ancient oak beams overhead, and round panes of Georgian bottle glass in many of the windows, the establishment is great for afternoon teas (and it's for these that the place is locally best known — even though morning coffee and cakes and light lunches are also served). John and James Miller, who do the baking, are famous for their fruit pies and gooey cream and liqueur cake. People in the town swear by their bread — and it makes an exceptionally fine addition to any picnic. 7 Market Pl., in the oldest part of this historic town. Phone: Evesham 2249.

SETTLE, Frome, Somerset: Situated in the most charming part of the oldest corner of this old town, an area of cobbled streets and half-timbered houses, this small Cheap Street establishment is warm and homey looking with its warm brick walls and black and white paintwork. Inside, there are vases of flowers to brighten the windowsills, and pressed wild flowers to decorate the menus; and an autumnal color scheme — all russets, grays, and golds — makes things more appealing still. Best of all is the immense variety of imaginative yet inexpensive food: English breakfasts of omelettes, a wide selection of homemade scones, cakes, and toasted cheese muffins; traditional lunches featuring such delights as Grannie's old-fashioned cheese puddings, Settle vegetarian bobbins, Priddy Oggies, game casserole, or Elizabethan pork, followed by hedgerow pudding, or the specialty — Frome bobbins, a delicious confection of apricots and sultanas steeped in local cider. Phone: Frome 65975.

KEEPERS, Haworth, West Yorkshire: The Brontë sisters' hometown, which is generally overrun by visitors, suffers no shortage of places to eat. But at this restaurant/ tea shop off High Street in a tiny cul-de-sac near the top of the hill, the proprietors have not let the regular supply of transient customers make them complacent. The mid-18th-century building in which the establishment was installed in the early 1970s is exceptionally comfortable and attractive with its wallpaper, the wooden or plush seats, and wallfulls of prints and paintings (not, alas, for sale); white tablecloths give the place a Victorian flavor. Homemade cakes and scones and cream teas are always available at teatime, as are sugary homemade meringues and a rich chocolate brandy cake; and curries are a specialty at lunch. Phone: 0535-42919.

ORIGINAL MAIDS OF HONOUR, Kew Gardens, Surrey: Directly opposite outer London's most famous public garden, the 18th-century Royal Botanic Gardens at Kew, and so busy during the tourist season that it's necessary to go early to enjoy your tea in a leisurely fashion, this shop has been serving up Maids of Honour (a curd tartlike sweet first mentioned in a 15th-century manuscript and said to have been enjoyed by Henry VIII) for over a century now — and it's as pretty as ever, part whitewashed, with a handsome brick and tile roof and broad eaves. The impression of *rus in urbe* is enhanced by the wrought ironwork and Victorian lampposts outside and an old-fashioned interior. The waitresses are as attentive as they can be, and, with the help of a handful of young girls, fuss over orders of pots of tea and toast, scones and fancy cakes, like so many English nannies. Open Tuesday through Saturday. 288 Kew Rd. Phone: 01-940-2752.

BARN, Sidmouth, Devon: Installed in a 15th-century cottage, this pretty stucco establishment looks almost like an antiques and bric-a-brac shop, with its walls hung with old agricultural implements and pictures by local artists, its pretty cupboard-like Welsh dresser, its shelves chock-a-block with old cottage china, vases, miniatures, and assorted other fascinating bygones. You sit at rustic old tables, set with vases of flowers from the garden, and enjoy such fare as homemade cakes, farmhouse cream teas, etc. Things are very chic here, and friendly besides. Lunches are served as well as teas, and accommodation, with home-cooked evening meals, is sometimes available. Phone: Sidmouth 3613).

IF YOU'RE NEARBY

OLD ORIGINAL BAKEWELL PUDDING, Bakewell, Derbyshire: Bakewell puddings are said to have been invented here by mistake in 1860 when an original recipe was misunderstood and a cook who had been asked to make a strawberry tart spread a custard mixture on top of the jam instead of stirring the two ingredients together. One Mrs. Wilson, a tallow chandler's wife who lived nearby, saw possibilities in making the popular sweet for sale and commenced a business of her own, and the house where she made them, a late-17th-century structure owned by the Duke of Rutland until 1921, has become a draw in its own right. There is now an 85-seat restaurant above the shop. On the square. Phone: 062-981-2193.

OLD LACE, Beer, Devon: The lace for Queen Victoria's wedding dress was made here, on these fairly unpretentious premises, now a quaint 17th-century village tea shop notable for its old oak tables, its fine collection of lace samples, and its location in a deep, narrow glen on a small creek that runs out to the sea. Evening meals are available as well as cream teas featuring homemade tea cakes, gâteaux, and plenty of scones still warm from the oven, ready to be slathered with clotted cream and strawberry jam. Fore St. Phone: 0297-22056.

ROSE OF TORRIDGE, Bideford, Devon: Once a hotel (Charles Kingsley wrote part of *Westward Ho!* here), this old-fashioned establishment now serves good cream teas as well as lunches and dinners.

BANTAM, Chipping Campden, Gloucestershire: An extra-friendly staff serves homemade cakes, buttery shortbread, nutty florentines, and sherry truffles, plus light salads and hot dishes in a 300-year-old High Street structure built of honey-colored Cotswold stone, superbly located in the middle of this exquisite and, though much visited, unspoiled Cotswold village. Hanging baskets of flowers welcome visitors in summer; log fires roar on the hearth come winter. Phone: 0386-840386.

HORSE WITH THE RED UMBRELLA, Dorchester, Dorset: This establishment at 10 High West St., in an erstwhile theater, offers a very good selection of cakes, pastries, and savouries, not to mention the largest selection of fresh cream cakes for miles around — many of which are baked by the owners' friends and neighbors. It's a great place to stock up for a picnic. Phone: 0305-62019.

ANGLER'S REST, Fingle Bridge, near Drewsteignton, Devon: For over 90 years, traditional cream teas — scones, strawberry jam, thick clotted cream, and a pot of perfumed brew — have been served at this delightful family restaurant in the cool green depths of the gorge at Fingle Bridge.

STONE CROSS COTTAGE, Godshill, Isle of Wight: A Gypsy caravan that used to stand outside the 17th-century thatch-roofed cottage, in the tea garden, collapsed a few years ago, but the home-baked scones, cakes, the local strawberries and farm cream are as good as ever. Open Whitsun through mid-September; closed on rainy days. Phone: 0983-840680.

DUNNOSE COTTAGE, Luccombe Chine, Shanklin, Isle of Wight: Tucked away in a thatched cottage half covered in creepers and rambling roses, this bright and sunny tea room serves lovely homemade cakes and gâteaux, and, on Sundays, a fine hearty roast for lunch. In fine weather, tea may now be taken in the gardens as well. The proprietors are among the rare species who serve clotted cream and eschew tea bags in favor of loose tea leaves. They've earned a reputation for their scones and are esteemed by some as the best tea shop on the island. Phone: 0983-862585.

EDITH'S, Marlborough, Wiltshire: Installed in three old cottages on London Rd., these tea rooms have a far-flung reputation for their delicious pots of freshly brewed tea, scones served with jam and cream, light and delicate spongecakes and other cakes, shortbreads, flapjacks, and hot savouries. The energetic Edith Coplestone also makes 35 varieties of jams and marmalades and 30 different chutneys and pickles that are tasty enough that more than one visitor ends up taking home a jar or two. And don't miss her fudge, rum truffles, and peppermint creams. Phone: 092-52405.

STABLE DOOR, Middleham, North Yorkshire: Light lunches are available, but this Market Place establishment, installed in a former tavern built in 1682, is best known around this famous racehorse training center for its wonderful cream teas and delicious fat scones and English muffins. The service is friendly and the atmosphere is a pleasure, thanks to old oak beams overhead, whitewashed walls, old-fashioned tables, and a handsome bay window. Phone: 0969-23568.

WHEATSHEAF, Morpeth, Northumberland: This establishment has a really fine sandwich bar, as well as good whole wheat bread and an interesting range of sweets. 1 Newgate St., Wheatsheaf Yard. Phone: 0670-519414.

ASSEMBLY HOUSE, Norwich, Norfolk: The 18th-century building in whose former banquet hall this restaurant makes its home is as elegant as can be; its homemade scones and cakes are as delicious as its hot entrées, salad specialties, and supper dishes. Theatre St. Phone: 0603-627526.

SUTHERLAND HOUSE, Southwold, Suffolk: In an offbeat little seaside holiday town, this well-established and slightly genteel place, installed in the former home of a prosperous Elizabethan merchant and full of fine plastered ceilings that date from the Armada years, is a good bet for hot meals as well as scones and pastries. 56 High St. Phone: 0502-722260.

BAY TREE, Stamford, Lincolnshire: In one of England's loveliest and most historic market towns, this tiny tea room at 10 St. Paul's St. maintains a strong reputation for top-quality gâteaux and lunchtime snacks. Phone: 0780-51219.

COTTAGE, Tintagel, Cornwall: The homemade bread and cakes and the toasted tea cakes here draw constant crowds to this 500-year-old cottage with beamed walls hung with brass ornaments and prints. Cornish cream teas, the specialty, are served on handsome china; light meals have been added to the establishment's offerings. Seating is inside and outside in the garden. Bed and breakfast accommodation is also available. Phone: 0840-770639.

OLD BAKERY, Woolpit, Bury St. Edmonds, Suffolk: This bakery and tea shop off the busy Midlands-to-Felixstowe A45 trunk road occupies a 16th-century building with oak beams, a quarry tile floor, and pine tables and offers many treats like honey-roast Suffolk ham, pizza, pâtés, cabbage and apple soup, and zucchini au gratin, not to mention sweets like treacle tarts and German apple pies. Phone: Elmswell 40255.

COFFEE SHOP, Yarm, Cleveland: Savouries like quiches and homemade soups and lasagna, chessey prawns, and mushroom provençal are all available, and they're all made on the premises, eschewing unnatural additives of any sort. And then there are the sweets: Bakewell tarte, apple pie so full of apples the proprietors say "It will never make us rich," ice cream made right here, and Yorkshire curd cake. All this is served in the back of a family-run gift shop, inside a Victorian building that most people call genteel and old-fashioned, with seating in old pine church pews and oak chairs. The high ceilings and big sash windows add another graceful note. 44 High St. Phone: 0642-782017 or 782101.

Mead and Meat Pies:
Historical Banquets

It would be hard to find a more touristy way to pass an evening than by partaking of one of the period banquets held in some six dozen hotels, castles, and other historic buildings throughout England, Wales, Scotland, and, to a lesser degree, Ireland. Yet, like a good Gothic novel, these entertainments are a painless way to absorb a bit of history, and the chance they give you to slurp down a five-course feast in the best Tom Jones fashion — that is, with a knife as your only utensil — can be a lot of fun besides. Knights and ladies in satins and velvets, jesters, and maybe a king or queen, provide entertainment as you sup, while a Henry VIII, a Queen Bess, a William Shakespeare, or some other figure out of the distant past acts as master of the ceremonies.

These usually begin in a foyer where a bit of bread is served with salt "to ward away evil spirits" and your health is toasted with mead — a heady concoction of fermented honey, apples, and spices, "to be drunk for virility and fertility," as your hosts tell you by way of explaining the origins of the word *honeymoon,* "one month, or moon, after a wedding" — and then continue, after the mead has taken effect, in a banqueting hall full of long oak trestle tables set with pewter plates, mugs, and the knife with which you're to shovel in your supper. (Most people find this progressively less difficult as the evening wears on — perhaps thanks to the copious quantities of wine and beer that are poured with each remove, as banqueting parlance names your courses.) Serving wenches keep the food coming, and between removes, the singers and jesters and harpists keep you smiling — or at least they try, and actually succeed with some people (and not always the same ones who have swallowed wine and beer enough to put Henry VIII himself under the table). You may or may not find the entertainers appealing, depending on your tolerance for the occasionally forgettable. What you find does depend on where you go: In the country, the music can be sublime by any lights; city banquet leaders' proclivity for *Oklahoma* and other all-American favorites meant to please the bus groups may drive you to fury. As for the food, it varies too. Along with reminders to "Belch . . . near no man's face with corrupt fumosity," your menu will list a number of removes in appropriate lingo. There is "Ye Potted Spiced Mete," for example, the making of which is also described: "Take: Item — Finest Gammons and choicest parts. Boyle them until ye mete so tendre leaves ye bones. Ye whole pounded in a marble mortar to smoothest paste. Strewe over it: Item — Freshly ground Herbes and Spices and Item — Liquor from ye hocks — Then when perfectly mixed, set all into Potting pans." The idea is nice, but in practice, the meat may taste like nothing more nor less than your local deli's second-best corned beef — and if you're in an urban area, you're doing well if it's even that good. Often, you will be glad for the distractions of the entertainment and the palate-numbing effects of the wine or beer; sometimes even the terminally hungry traveler may find himself picking at the plain roast chicken.

But on the other hand, it's seldom that you're served something that's totally inedible, and there's usually no shortage of food. Moreover, times will come when you'll toss down the food with the relish of the famous Tudor himself; sometimes you'll find yourself belly-laughing at one of the jester's corny jokes; and sometimes, too, a song will turn out to be so beautiful that it brings tears unbidden to your eyes. The best banquets — a few of which are listed here — may surprise you in just that way.

Some operate nightly, others only on weekends, and still others on a seasonal basis. Reservations are required, and most banquet managers demand a deposit when the booking is made (usually about $4.50) and full payment of the fee, usually from about $15 in more remote areas, to about $25 in a city, no later than a month in advance. For listings of other feasts, some of them from periods other than the medieval, contact the British Tourist Authority and the Irish Tourist Board.

COOMBE ABBEY, near Coventry, West Midlands, England: Medieval banquets are staged throughout the year in the splendor of a candlelit hall in this ancient abbey. The full evening of entertainment includes songs from the Ladies of the Courte, and there's plenty of mead and wine to consume during the four-course meal, which is presided over by the baron and baroness in person. Advance bookings are essential. Details: Coombe Abbey, Brinklow Rd., Binley, Coventry, West Midlands CV3 2AB, England (phone: 0203-452406).

BEEFEATER BY THE TOWER OF LONDON, London, England: In the historic vaults of a former ivory warehouse, within cannon shot of the Tower in picturesque St. Katherine's Dock, Henry VIII lords over a crowd that can number 550. The entertainment by the jesters, magicians, sword swallowers, and fighting knights borders on the vaudevillian; the atmosphere is lively and bawdy, and the setting impressive. The fare includes pâté, leek soup, smoked mackerel, chicken, and spare ribs. Details: Beefeater by the Tower of London, Ivory House, St. Katharine's Dock, London El, England (phone: 01-408-1001).

SHAKESPEARE'S TAVERN AND PLAYHOUSE, London, England: In the 16th century, the area known as Blackfriars played a large part in Shakespeare's life, being both his home and place of work. Today, a former wine cellar here is the setting for an Elizabethan banquet whose creators have paid homage to the Bard by hanging up murals that depict scenes from his plays and by filling up the "Bill of Fayre" with dishes like "Puck's Pâté." There are puppet and magic shows, jugglers and jesters, and a fight scene from *Macbeth;* the audience is invited to jig to Scottish reels — a good way to work off the five removes. You can't help but wonder what Will would have made of it. The food is a cut above the *Beefeater's.* Open nightly. Details: London Entertain, 6 Hanover St., London W1R 9HH, England (phone: 01-408-1001).

COCKNEY CLUB, London, England: Pearl kings and queens, buskers, flower girls, and assorted soloists entertain cabaret-style as guests put away a four-course dinner with unlimited wine and beer. Details: The Cockney Club, 18 Charing Cross Rd., London WC2, England (phone: 01-408-1001).

ADAMTON COURTE, Monkton (near Prestwick), Ayrshire, Scotland: There's a corny quip to the effect that the haggis is a three-legged beastie that hops around the mountaintops; in reality it's a delectable concoction of not-so-sweet-sounding sheep's pluck, and at this true north-of-the-border Jacobite banquet, held in the dungeons of Adamton Courte near Prestwick Airport in "Rabbie Burns Country," the haggis is played in by bagpipers and served, as custom goes, with potatoes and turnips, locally called "champit tatties and neeps." A traditional Scottish broth, freshly baked bread, Ayrshire chicken seasoned with basil and oregano and honey and mead, and Scottish country cheeses and oat cakes round out the feast. Wine and mead are included and there's entertainment throughout the evening. Details: Adamton Courte, Monkton, Ayrshire, KA9 2SQ, Scotland (phone: 0292-70678).

HWYRNOS, Swansea, West Glamorgan, Wales: The entertainment presented in a historic building in the center of this city in South Wales is not so much a medieval banquet as a Welsh evening or *hwyrnos* (literally "late night"). It's informal, not touristy, and reminiscent of the days before electricity and easy transportation, when rural people used to gather at their neighbor's place to sing along to melodies of the sweet Welsh harp, and to dance, play games, tell stories, and recite poems. The meal is as hearty as they come, with fare like roast leg of lamb and the traditional Welsh stew known as cawl, followed by a traditional pudding with fresh cream. Inevitably, all the other banquets are attempting to show off the 20th century's idea of life in a previous historical period — but because the Welsh commonly enjoyed just such evenings as this one until very recently, it has an extra bit of authenticity and that much more immediacy. Open most evenings in summer and at Christmas, several times weekly in spring and fall, and on most weekends in January and February. The same management also offers a smaller *Hwyrnos* in the country at Dolgellau, Gwynedd. Details: Hwyrnos, Green Dragon La., Swansea SA1 1DG, Wales (phone: 0792-41437).

RUTHIN CASTLE, Ruthin, Clwyd, Wales: Although history says that Ruthin Castle came to be in 1282, when Reginald de Grey enlarged the original wood-and-stone fortress on the site, legend has it that the castle was created by two giants throwing stones at each other from opposite mountaintops. True or not, the castle's subsequent stormy history — full of changes of ownership, and death and destruction that left the castle a near-total ruin more than once — needs no embellishment. Today's offerings are equally wonderful, from the food — among the best in Britain and certainly the best of the banquets' — to the entertainment, which features a jester who is actually funny and minstrels (local housewives rather than the usual moonlighting pros) who sing their beautiful Welsh ballads to the accompaniment of harps, like angels. And the setting, in a wonderfully pastoral corner of northern Wales, full of rolling hills dotted with peaceful cattle and scattered here and there with quaint old farmhouses and pretty villages, can't be beat. Details: Ruthin Castle, Ruthin, Clywd LL15 2NU, Wales (phone: 08242-2664).

BUNRATTY CASTLE, Bunratty, County Clare, Irish Republic: After you climb the narrow circular stone stairway to the dining hall and quaff your first goblet of mead, you can stroll around for a close look at this 15th-century castle's remarkable collection of art and antiques; traditional songs and harp music sustain a pleasantly medieval mood during the banquet. Details: Shannon Tourist Office, Shannon International Free Airport, County Clare, Irish Republic (phone: 061-61664).

GRANARY TAVERN, Limerick City, Irish Republic: Presented in a restored 18th-century structure once used to store grain, now part of a complex that also includes craft and antiques shops and an exhibition area, this entertainment sketches the history of the town of Limerick through ballads, sea chanties, and other music and dance. May through October. Details: The Granary, Charlotte Quay, Limerick City, Irish Republic (phone: 061-47266).

KNAPPOGUE CASTLE, Quin, County Clare, Irish Republic: Served in a huge stone dining hall lit by candles and hung with tapestries, the banquet here is very hearty, if not especially medieval: salad, soup, chicken, vegetables, cheese, and fruit. The evening's program features snippets of Irish history and some very fine music performed on the harp and sung by the "ladies of the castle." The castle itself, one of 42 massive structures built by the McNamara tribe that ruled the territory of Clancullen from the 5th to the mid-15th centuries, deserves a daytime visit as well so that you can explore its several elegantly furnished rooms and walk around its verdant and undulating grounds. Its excellent state of preservation is due to the cooperation of its owners, a Houston couple, with the Shannon Free Airport Development Company and the Irish Tourist Board. Details: Shannon Tourist Office, Shannon International Free Airport, County Clare, Irish Republic (phone: 061-61664).

SHANNON CEILI, Bunratty Folk Park, County Clare, Irish Republic: The music and song at this evening of Irish merriment are purely traditional; there are flutes and fiddles, *bodhráns* and spoons, an accordionist and singers. The meal is equally traditional: Irish stew, soda bread, apple pie doused with fresh cream, and tea and wine. Open mid-May through September. Details: Shannon Castle Tours, Shannon International Airport, County Clare, Irish Republic (phone: 061-61788), or in the US, BMIT, 149 Main St., Medway, MA 02053 (phone: 617-982-2299 from Massachusetts, 800-343-6472 outside Massachusetts).

Shopping Spree

No matter where the dollar stands relative to the pound (British or Irish), the lure of shopping in Britain and Ireland is irresistible. London and Dublin, in particular, seem to awaken the dormant consumer in even the most monastic visitor. Sooner or later, he finds himself walking around with a bulging carrier bag, rummaging feverishly through the sale sweaters at Liberty's or Switzer's, or shuffling past the bric-a-brac stalls on Portobello Road or beside the Liffey. Shopping has become such an institution among travelers here that the English word for it has found its way into the other European languages. Oxford Street on a Saturday is the West's most teeming bazaar.

Quality, durability, and what the natives are fond of calling "value for money" are the norm. And the best buys are still those articles in which craftsmanship counts: riding equipment, humidors, umbrellas, china, crystal, fireplace tongs, and other items of the sort essential to every well-equipped Victorian household. When it comes to clothing, the rule is the same; a purchase made in Britain and Ireland will more than likely last for years and never go out of style — partly because it was never that much in style to begin with (although this is changing somewhat today).

WHERE TO SHOP

One can find good buys all over Britain and Ireland, provided you know where to look.

CHAIN STORES: Some of the great British chain stores are as dedicated to quality as their Bond Street betters. *Marks and Spencer,* for clothing, is a prime example of attractive prices and vast selection. The linens and sweaters, especially those in cashmere, lamb's wool, and Shetland wool, are among Britain's best buys. (But get there early before the aisles become impassable with the day's blizzard of buyers.) Also note *Boots,* for cosmetics, pharmaceuticals, and sundries; *Sainsbury's* for food products; and *W. H. Smith's* for books and stationery supplies.

POST-CHRISTMAS AND JULY SALES: These British events have the stature of Wimbledon or a Royal Family christening. Travel agents are now packaging tours to the sales with the promise that participants' savings in discounts will cover the cost of the trip. The sale at Harrods that begins the first Friday in January is a ritual no devout shopper can afford to miss, and values can be breathtaking. Some stores stay open on New Year's Day to accommodate the throngs. But beware of smaller stores that stock their racks with cut-rate merchandise specially acquired for a sale event.

OPEN MARKETS: Never pass a chance to wander through one of Britain's buzzing, bustling open markets. They're a cross section of local life and a glorious experience for all the senses. The stalls are a riot of colors — scarlets and yellows and bright blues. Oranges and tomatoes keep company with spinach and celery and garish crockery. The calls and clatter of startling accents delight the ear. The smells of the flowers and the cheeses and the fish, one aroma blending with the next, assail the nose.

London, England – The Berwick Street market in Soho, W1, has been bustling with fruit and vegetable hawkers for over a century now. Never touch the goods or the vendors will get furious. Open Mondays through Saturdays, with an early closing on Thursdays.

The Electric Avenue market in Brixton, SW 9, is chock-a-block with exotic foodstuffs and secondhand clothes. The atmosphere is straight from the West Indies. Open Mondays through Saturdays, a half day only on Wednesdays.

The Camden Lock Market off Chalk Farm Road, NW1, purveys high-quality crafts and bric-a-brac of all descriptions on Saturdays and Sundays.

The Kensington Market off Kensington High Street, W8, sells clothing, jewelry, and antiques Mondays through Saturdays.

Petticoat Lane, which radiates from Middlesex Street, E1, overflows with fruit, vegetables, clothes and crockery. It's mostly rubbish, but the browsing is always fun. And you never know what you'll find. Sunday mornings.

The Earls Court Exhibition Center Sunday Market, which is entered from Lillie Road, SW5, is a source of knickknacks and low-priced clothing every Sunday morning and early afternoon.

Bristol, Avon – The St. Nicholas markets sell fruit and vegetables, fish, flowers, and even the occasional parakeet Monday through Saturday. Off Baldwin and Corn sts.

Cambridge, Cambridgeshire – There has been a market in Market Square since medieval times. Today, you'll find fruit, vegetables, fish, cheese, fresh flowers, records, books, and inexpensive clothing piled high under brightly colored canopies every day but Sunday.

Oxford, Oxfordshire – Built in 1774, this covered market off High Street is open daily except Thursday afternoons and Sunday; at this gourmet's paradise, you can pick up game, fresh fish, cheese, bread and cakes, and vegetables, as well as the fixings for a picnic.

York, Yorkshire – Beautifully situated Newgate Marketplace, the center of local trading since the Middle Ages, sells clothing, bric-a-brac, and foodstuffs from Yorkshire and beyond on Mondays through Saturdays.

Glasgow, Scotland – Glasgow's answer to Petticoat Lane is The Barrows (known in Scotland as "the Barras"), the area on either side of Gallowgate that has been holding forth on Saturdays and Sundays since Victorian times, when people with weekday jobs elsewhere in the community would set up stalls to sell whatever they could to bring in extra cash. Today, this square mile of the city, which the BBC called Europe's bargain basement, is packed with stalls, up to a thousand of them — all manned by colorful characters who seem by turns intriguing, exciting, and occasionally ungracious. Don't fail to stop at one of the convivial pubs in the area.

Cardiff, Wales – Welsh lamb, the fruit bread known as *bara brith,* and the local delicacy known as *laverbread* are only a few of the culinary delights to be found in this bustling market, entered in St. Mary Street or the Hayes. Open Mondays through Saturdays.

DEPARTMENT STORES: You'll find some of Europe's greatest department store shopping in Britain and Ireland. The multitude of stores, the quality of the goods, and the wide price range all make for unparalleled shopping fun.

London, England – For department store shopping, there's no place like London. First, it's the home of *Harrods,* whose motto is *Omnia, Omnibus, Ubique* (Everyone, Everything, Everywhere). This giant among emporiums can offer everything from pianos to straight pins. It has a butcher, a bank, a library, a kennel, and even a funeral service (for clients who prefer to deal with the store from birth to death); and whatever it doesn't have it will order. (Consider the joke about the man who went in requesting an elephant — only to be asked whether he preferred African or Indian — or the story about a crowd-loathing sheik who asked to have the store opened at an unusual hour for his private shopping.) The January and July sales are world-famous. Brompton Rd., Knightsbridge SW1 (phone: 01-730-1234).

Selfridges claims "all the needs of civilized life under one roof." The variety is somewhat smaller than at its Knightsbridge competitor's, but the prices are generally lower. The china and crystal department is extensive and the Miss Selfridge department particularly lively. 400 Oxford St., W1 (phone: 01-629-1234).

Fortnum and Mason, which was founded by a footman and a greengrocer from the 18th-century court of Queen Anne, makes high art of selling fashions, fragrances, fine tableware, clothing, and groceries. Jams and preserves, tea, crocks of Stilton cheese — all sold on the ground floor by salesmen in swallowtail coats — are specialties. 181 Piccadilly, W1 (phone: 01-734-8040).

Edinburgh, Scotland – *Jenner's* stands out for its superb stocks of bone china and Scottish crystal. Princes and St. David's sts. (phone: 031-225-2442).

Glasgow, Scotland – Four-tiered, balconied *Fraser's,* a department store of the Victorian vintage, is built around a central court, with a glass-paneled ceiling and a beautiful crystal chandelier. It's a treat, if only for the surroundings. The wares include a good selection of Edinburgh crystal and food delicacies as well as English bone china, clothes, and linens. 21 Buchanan St., G1 3HR (phone: 041-221-3880).

Dublin, Irish Republic – *Brown Thomas* and *Switzer's* are the two principal department stores. They're both large, lively, and full of good merchandise — *Switzer's,* in fact, is owned by Harrod's. Both department stores stock Aran Island sweaters. Grafton St., across from one another.

SPECIAL SHOPPING STREETS AND DISTRICTS: Endowed with special character and verve, some streets invite you to linger as you browse. These areas may be brassy, quaint, or even supremely grand. But when you stroll along them, you enjoy a real spectacle made up partly of the stores, partly of your fellow shoppers. Whether you're buying or just looking, these streets are worth a walk.

Brighton, East Sussex, England – Occupying roughly a square mile, the maze of alleyways, byways, and passages known as the Lanes in the Old Town is hard to beat for character. The shops are weighted toward book and antique dealers, but there's no dearth of other stores as well. Entrances off East, North, Ship, and Middle sts.

Another good bet is Western Road, which runs into North Street. Together they offer almost 2 miles of continual shopping with all manner of odd and unusual stores. And the North Laine area, between North Street and the Railway Station, has a multitude of little bric-a-brac and junk shops as well as some unusual specialty shops.

Chester, Cheshire, England – The Rows, an aboveground network of walk-ways that originated centuries ago, carry everything from antiques to expensive fashions.

London, England – There's are so many tempting things to buy on so many streets here that it's hard to point a finger at only a few. But certain streets stand out.

New Bond and Old Bond streets, laid out by Sir Thomas Bond in 1686, would leave even an oil sheik yearning for more of the kinds of luxury items that these places make their specialty. The area was fashionable as early as the Regency days of Beau Brummel and friends; back then, there was an establishment that offered lessons in tying cravats to aspiring dandies.

Regent Street, which runs parallel to Bond Street between Oxford and Piccadilly circuses, is as elegant as its shops' façades. It was originally planned as a grand processional between Regent's Park and the Regent's palace, to divide Mayfair from Soho. *Liberty & Co.* is just one of its retail landmarks.

Crowded Oxford Street has department stores — *Selfridges, John Lewis* ("never knowingly undersold"), *Debenham's,* and *Marks and Spencer* among others.

Special fun are the pedestrian streets. Carnaby Street, which made its name in the sixties, and Rupert Street are lively, though tacky. South Molton Street, off Oxford Street, has become a trendy center; chairs and umbrellas preside over much of the sidewalk in the summer.

Covent Garden, London's longtime vegetable market district, has undergone tremendous redevelopment, and the central market building concentrates on wares from Britain and stays open late. The whole area is crammed with trendy boutiques stocked with clothing for men and women, not to mention wine bars, restaurants, discos, and the like.

The Burlington Arcade, a charming covered Regency shopping promenade, is another must. It dates from the early 19th century and is crammed with shops piled elegantly with cashmeres, antiques, and other costly wares. Off Piccadilly near Old Bond St., W1.

Edinburgh, Scotland – Princes Street, Edinburgh's Fifth Avenue, is the best place in the country to get a good overview of things Scottish, and it's the home of the *Scotch House, Marks and Spencer's, Jenner's,* and *Debenham's,* among other emporia. Lush gardens full of flowers and Edinburgh Castle flank the south side to make the shopping experience all the more pleasant.

Dublin, Irish Republic – Grafton Street and the lanes leading away from it constitute Dublin's most elegant shopping precinct. Keeping company with *Brown Thomas* and *Switzer's,* Powerscourt House Centre is just a few yards off Grafton. Installed in the glass-roofed courtyard of an elegant Dublin townhouse, it is crammed with fashion, antiques, and craft shops whose numbers are growing all the time.

Cork, Irish Republic – There are two unique shopping malls here: *Queen's Old Castle,* an erstwhile department store, now houses many shops plus cafés for shoppers' refreshment. Grand Parade.

In addition, there's the *Savoy Center,* with shops and cafés in the attractive Art Deco setting of a former movie theater. Patrick St. (also the center for department stores in Cork); and the new *City Car Park* shopping center. Paul St..

BEST BUYS

Britain and Ireland may be the last holdouts against synthetic everything. Some of the products and shops are of a superior quality, which puts them on the road to obsolescence, like the great ocean liners. So let yourself be tempted by the classic adornments — the finest china, the softest cashmere, the sturdiest shoes, while you can still get them. Britain and Ireland are the perfect places to indulge yourself.

BAGPIPES: You may spend the rest of your life learning to play them, but you'll never forget the day you bought them.

Edinburgh, Scotland – *Hugh Macpherson (Scotland) Ltd.* is a three-generation family business that sells, in addition to bagpipes, Highland costumes handmade by local women. To go with your bagpipes you might buy a pipe band uniform, or order a tartan skirt or a kilt made-to-measure, or buy Highland and country dance supplies. 17 West Maitland St. (phone: 031-225-4008).

Dublin, Ireland – *Waltons Musical Instrument Galleries* stocks not only bagpipes but also Irish harps, tin whistles, old violins, and traditional goatskin drums known as the *bodhrán.* Records are also available. 2-5 N Frederick St. (phone: 01-747805); and Dun Laoghaire Shopping Centre (phone: 01-807352).

BASKETS: Traditional baskets known as trugs are the specialty in Herstmonceux, East Sussex. They're shallow and made of bent willow, and they come in seven different types of varying size at the workshop of *Thomas Smith,* established over 150 years ago. Each one is fully handcrafted, individually finished, and made from locally grown woods — pliable sweet chestnut for the rims and handles and split-resistant willow for the body — to produce a product that is lightweight and incredibly durable. The wide, shallow flower trugs and the strong, deep fireside log trugs are particularly handsome. Smith was the trug manufacturer to Queen Victoria. Phone: 0323-832137.

BOOKS: Don't leave Great Britain without buying at least one book. Rare and secondhand volumes are well priced and available. Addicted browsers will have to be dragged out of the following haunts:

Cambridge, England – *Heffer's* and *Sherratt & Hughes* are both on Trinity St. — the latter for four centuries now, although under different names during that time (phone: 0223-358351 and 0223-311243 respectively).

G. David is a Cambridge institution as well and is now owned by the great-grandson of founder Gustave David. 3 and 16 St. Edward's Passage (phone: 0223-354619).

London, England – *Foyle's* is the largest general bookstore in the world — and it's enormous. 119 Charing Cross Rd. (phone: 01-439-8501).

Cavendish Rare Books holds a treasure trove of antique travel guides and fine bindings, including first-hand accounts of voyages by some of the great travelers of the past. Prince's Arcade, off Piccadilly (phone: 01-734-3840).

Just next door, the narrow and utterly classic *Hatchard's,* founded in 1797, is London's oldest bookseller — and one of its most civilized. It currently stocks more than 250,000 titles on its four floors. 187 Piccadilly (phone: 01-439-9921) .

Oxford, England – An Aladdin's cave among bookshops, *Blackwells* offers everything from the paperback guidebooks snapped up by tourists to the arcane tomes purchased by undergraduates on the recommendations of their tutors. It also boasts that its Norrington Room is the largest single room of books in the world. 8 Broad St. (phone: 0865-249111).

Stratford-upon-Avon, England – There are gifts and souvenirs at the *Shakespeare Centre Bookshop,* but the specialty is things Shakespearean, particularly books and publications on all aspects of his life, works, and times, as well as those dealing with the interpretation of his works on stage. This is the place to obtain anything you need to help learn about Will. 39 Henley St. (phone: 0789-204016).

Hay-on-Wye, Powys, Wales – Hay-on-Wye has become the town of secondhand books. *Richard Booth (Bookseller) Ltd.* on Lion Street (phone: 0497-820322), listed in *The Guinness Book of Records* as the largest secondhand bookshop on earth, displays about a million books on nearly 11 miles of shelves. A dozen more competitors line the streets. A must for passionate readers.

CHINA: The world's best pottery and porcelain has been produced in England since the 18th century, and many of the factories whose names are synonymous with elegance and quality can be found in and near the town of Stoke-on-Trent in Staffordshire. Royal Doulton, Spode, Minton, and Wedgwood all originate here. Visit the factories and the exhibitions, and immerse yourself in a manufacturing tradition over 200 years old. Only the most resolute will leave without a souvenir. Contact the British Tourist Authority for its booklet *Fine English Glass and China,* which provides complete information about factory visits.

Derby, England – *Royal Crown Derby Porcelain* has been "royal" since the days of Queen Victoria. Factory tours are available and a museum established by the duchess of Devonshire in 1969 is on the premises. Osmaston Rd. (phone: 0332-47051).

London, England – *Thomas Goode and Company* occupies a showroom built in 1845, a half century after the store first opened, and when you behold the lavishly set tables that fill it from wall to elegant wall, visions of pheasant, champagne, and brilliant conversation will dance in your head. All the most famous names in china and crystal will be found here, under one imposing roof. It's London's best china and glass shop. 19 S Audley St. (phone: 01-499-2823).

The Reject China Shops offer slightly irregular brand-name china on the premises at such reduced prices that you'll call them a bargain even when shipping charges are included. First-quality china, crystal, and gifts from makers as diverse as Coalport and Aynsley, Spode and Baccarat, Waterford and Lalique are also available at good prices. 134 Regent St., Beauchamp Pl., W1, and other locations in London, Windsor, Bath, Oxford, Chester, and York (phone: 01-749-9191).

Stoke-on-Trent, Staffordshire – The following illustrious firms all offer tours of their premises. Be sure to call ahead:

Coalport, Park St., Fenton (phone: Stoke-on-Trent 45274). Factory tours provide an opportunity to see the production of figurines, florals, and collages. The factory shop has a good selection of slightly imperfect china for sale.

Minton, London Rd., Stoke (phone: 0782-49171). The factory of this company founded in 1793 and patronized by Queen Victoria welcomes visitors. The museum's exhibits date back to the 1790s.

Royal Doulton, Nile St., Burslem (phone: 0782-85747). The Sir Henry Doulton Gallery tells the story of the Doulton tradition that its namesake, who did the work that earned the company the right to call itself "Royal," established here. The company's historical figure collection is also on display at the gallery. At the factory, you can see the production of tableware and figurines, from the automatic platemaking to the hand-painting of limited edition pieces.

Spode Works, Church St. (phone: 0782-744011). Bone china was developed on this site in the last years of the 18th century and is still made here by the original processes, as visitors can see while touring the factory. Recently added is a connoisseurs' tour — two hours during which rooms not normally open to the public are on view, including the superb Blue Room.

Wedgwood, Barlaston (phone: 078139-4141). A visitors center offers a craft manufacturing hall, a film, and a new living museum that houses the world's most comprehensive collection of Wedgwood ware in period settings, such as Josiah Wedgwood's Etrusia workshops and the 18th-century London showrooms.

Wedgwood and *Spode* sell seconds, china with slight imperfections, at half the normal retail price. The latter usually has a good selection in the popular Christmas tree pattern. An excellent selection of first-quality goods is also available.

Just outside Stoke-on-Trent in Longton, tour the *John Beswick Studios,* where the Royal Doulton Bunnykins and Brambly Hedge collections as well as a variety of toby jugs and animal figurines are made. Gold St. (phone: 0782-313041.)

Belleek, County Fermanagh, Northern Ireland – Creamy, wafer-thin Belleek Parian china is made here in the famous *Belleek Pottery.* Tours of the pottery are given daily from March through October, and the visitors center has the full line along with some antique pieces on display. Phone: Belleek 501..

CHOCOLATE: The English have long been famous for what's known as confectionery — creams, marzipan, truffles, fudge, and other such irresistible trifles. Don't deny yourself a Mocha Baton, said to be Prince Philip's favorite, at *Charbonnel et Walker* in London. This establishment, founded in 1875 and a Royal Warrant holder, "enrobes" their creations' interiors with dark chocolate (bittersweet plain) and white chocolate — you won't find anything so humdrum as milk chocolate. The round white *boîtes blanches* (white boxes) traditionally hold gold foil-covered chocolates emblazoned with letters and numbers; purchasers make a selection to spell out a message. 28 Old Bond St., W1 (phone: 01-629-4396).

Prestat is a center for the richest of truffles. Paddington Bear figurines in white, milk, and dark chocolate are an exclusive. 40 S Molton St., W1 (phone: 01-629-4838).

CRYSTAL AND GLASS: The manufacturing of crystal in the UK takes place mainly in England's West Midlands, in Waterford, Galway, and County Cavan in the Irish Republic, Tyrone in Northern Ireland, and at Penicuik near Edinburgh in Scotland. But outstanding items can be purchased all over both islands.

Bristol, Avon, England – The *City Museum and Art Gallery Shop* stocks among its wares handmade reproductions of the blue glass for which the town's glassmakers were once famous, and which is not available anywhere else in the world. Queens Rd. (phone: 0272-299771).

Cambridge, Cambridgeshire – *The Friar's House* has been described as "a collector's treasure house" and it is crammed with fine crystal and porcelain, not to mention a selection of paperweights to delight collectors. 1 Free School La. (phone: 0223-60275).

Barretts, established in 1782, stocks Waterford, Stuart, Webb, and Edinburgh crystal in addition to a selection of china. 2 St. Mary's Passage (phone: 0223-66711).

London, England – *Thomas Goode and Company,* described above, sells the best crystal as well as the best china. 19 S Audley St. (phone: 01-499-2823).

Kilkenny has uncut handblown crystal, as well as Waterford crystal, in addition to all sorts of wonderful Irish products.

Stourbridge, West Midlands, England – Many manufacturers of fine crystal offer tours of their premises and a good selection of their wares for sale in their factory shops. Among them:

Royal Doulton Crystal Webb Corbett Studio, Amblecote (phone: 0384-395281). On weekday mornings, factory tours are available in which all stages of the manufacture of full lead English crystal are shown.

Stuart and Sons Ltd., the Redhouse Glassworks, Stourbridge (phone: 0384-71161). The Redhouse Cone Museum is the historic home of Stuart crystal, and here visitors can tour the works to see how modern technology and ancient skills are blended to produce fine crystal.

Tudor Crystal, Junction Rd., Stourbridge (phone: 0384-393325). Visitors may purchase fine Tudor crystal at the shop or take a tour of the factory.

Thomas Webb, King William St. (phone: 0384-392521). Dennis Hall, Thomas Webb's Georgian red brick mansion, houses a museum chock-a-block with crystal, documents, and photographs. After touring the factory, you can stop at its shop, which stocks the company's crystal and other products of sister companies — including Denby ware.

Aberbargoed, Mid-Glamorgan, Wales – At *Stuart and Sons Ltd.,* visitors can see every aspect of glassmaking and glass-cutting in a tour of the factory — and then purchase the output in the factory shop. Angel La. (phone: 0443-832705).

Waterford, County Waterford, Irish Republic – You can see Ireland's most prestigious product, Waterford crystal, being produced here in the world's largest hand-made full-lead crystal factory. The dramatic process yields stunning goblets and gift items. Factory closed weekends and the first three weeks in August (phone 051-73311 for reservations). The new shop and showroom are open year-round.

Joseph Knox, installed behind a handsome Victorian shopfront, is the place to buy the beautiful pieces (for there are no sales at the factory). Or just spend a few moments browsing along with the rest of summer's throngs. 3 and 4 Barronstrand St. (phone: 051-75307).

CURIOSITY SHOPS: England, particularly London, is a wonderful source for eccentric items you might never even have imagined.

Anything Left-Handed offers tools designed specifically for the left-handed person — can openers, over 30 types of scissors, potato peelers, special mugs, pens (including Italic and calligraphy writing sets), knitting guides, corkscrews, bread knives, and boomerangs, among other items. 68 Beak St., London W1 (phone: 01-437-3910).

Nail-O-Mania has as its motto, "Look at your nails. Everyone else does." If the fancy strikes you, you can have this visible part of your body painted in stripes or emblazoned with words or initials. Straightforward manicures, pedicures, hand massages, and natural-looking tips are also available. 1 Hinde St., London (phone: 01-486-8079).

Naturally British will make you feel as if you've traveled all over the country, even if you never leave London. Its stock includes dolls from Dorset, glass from the Lake District, woolen shirts from Wales, hand-knits from Scotland, and many wooden items such as rocking horses and traditional pub games. 13 New Row, Covent Garden, London WC2 (phone: 01-240-0551).

Norfolk Lavender, England's largest growers of lavender, has plants to suit gardens of all sizes; it's a fragrant marvel, especially in late spring and throughout the summer. On guided tours, you can learn how lavender oil is extracted, buy some to take home, and top off your visit with a cream tea or a light lunch. Caley Mill, Heacham (phone: 0485-70384).

Sitting Pretty specializes in antique and reproduction wood lavatory seats and other antique bathroom paraphernalia from brass taps to marble basins. And by appointment you can view dozens of old cast-iron roll-top baths ranging in size from 4 to over 6 feet in the firm's workshops just outside London. 131 Dawes Rd. London SW6 (phone: 01-381-0049).

DESIGN: The best of British craft and design is available in a pair of London shops.

The Lock Shop in Camden Lock carries mobiles, lampstands, ceramics, designer knitwear, jewelry, and many unusual gifts — all original and tempting, the latest from art colleges and craft fairs all over the country. Collections for cat lovers (ceramic cat plaques, cat jerseys, cat clocks) and for lovers of frogs, pigs, and penguins stand out. Commercial Pl., Chalk Farm Rd., NW1 (phone: 01-485-3450).

The Design Centre offers elegantly functional and very modern British-made housewares and souvenirs. 28 Haymarket, SW1 (phone: 01-839-8000).

DESIGNER CLOTHING: Britain and Ireland offer the ultimate in things traditional — and the fantastic.

London, England – At *Bellville Sassoon,* the client list reads like a chapter from Debrett's, and the Princess of Wales is a loyal customer — choosing a saucy sailor dress for her first official picture with the Queen. The specialty is glamorous eveningwear in fabrics and prints specifically designed for the shop. 73 Pavilion Rd., SW1 (phone: 01-235-3087).

Zandra Rhodes, a fearlessly original designer, makes garments that are elaborate and intricate, made of hand-printed or hand-embroidered silk chiffon or organza and full of hand-pleating or ruffles with unusual details and extravagant shapes. The prices are even more extravagant. Beaded stoles, beaded sweatshirts, and stockings are also available. 14a Grafton St., W1 (phone: 01-499-6695).

Dublin, Irish Republic – Romantic ball gowns made with finely pleated Irish linen are only one of the exceptional productions of Ireland's reigning couturière, *Sybil Connolly.* The adjacent boutique handles ready-to-wear and accessories. 71 Merrion Sq. (phone: 01-767281).

Paul Costelloe designs stylish ready-to-wear for women. 42 Drury St. (phone: 01-711598).

FABRICS: The yard goods to be found in both Britain and Ireland will bring out the seamstress in even the least handy traveler. From luscious woolens in the colors of an Irish landscape to fine lawn reminiscent of an English meadow in springtime, you'll find it all. *Laura Ashley* has cloth steeped in the English country look; there are stores in both London (256-258 Regent St., Oxford Circus, W1) and Dublin, among many other locations.

London, England – *Liberty*'s name is synonymous with printed fabrics in cotton, wool, and silk. The scarves and ties are beautiful, and the façade of the store — romantic and half-timbered — is equally appealing. 210 Regent St. (phone: 01-734-1234).

Bianchini Ferier offers pure silk crêpe de chine, jacquards, and other fine silks at wholesale prices. Discounts on last year's designer fabrics are available. Ties and scarves are also for sale. Broadbent House, 65 Grosvenor St., W1 (phone: 01-499-5767).

FOODSTUFFS AND LIQUOR: Jams and marmalades, blended teas, Stilton cheese, shortbreads, and other edibles for sale throughout Britain and Ireland make wonderful souvenirs — for yourself or to give as a present.

London, England – At old-fashioned, wood-paneled *Ferns,* the carved mahogany shelves are chock-a-block with teas, tea caddies, and more, and the drawers are packed with beans of all types. Since many of these are roasted on the premises, you can smell the wares from several doors down. 27 Rathbone Pl., W1 (phone: 01-636-2237).

Fortnum and Mason is the British Empire's most elegant grocery store: The staff wear trousers and swallowtail morning coats. The wine department is noteworthy for its breadth and for the rarity of its selections. 181 Piccadilly, W1 (phone: 01-734-8040).

Harrods is a must, if only for the experience. The gigantic Food Halls, reminiscent of a late Victorian cathedral, will leave you salivating. From poultry to pâtés, from plum pudding to pork (the pigs raised to the store butchers' own standards), Harrods has it all. The wine selection, one of London's largest, offers bottles ranging from the insignificant and inexpensive to the superb and very costly. There are also dozens of pure single-malt Scotch whiskies. Brompton Rd., Knightsbridge, SW3 (phone: 01-730-1234).

Justin De Blank sells specialty foods of excellent quality, including whole-grain bread baked in century-old ovens on the premises and a wide array of cheeses, among them Brie and Camembert. 42 Elizabeth St., SW1 (phone: 01-730-0605).

Paxton and Whitfield, a pungent paean to cheese housed in a little black-beamed building built in 1674, shows cheeses the way some shops display jewelry. There are cones and cubes large and small, pepper-covered logs of goat cheese, cakes with rinds of gray and tan, huge wheels of snowy Brie, light-gold cheddar, peach-colored Cheshires, deep gold Derbies, and more — all of it superb. Established in 1797, the firm has held the Royal Warrant since 1973. 93 Jermyn St., SW1 (phone: 01-930-0250).

Norwich, Norfolk – In this cathedral town, *Colmans* has been milling mustard for over 160 years. The firm's shop offers unusual varieties not often found elsewhere, along with reproductions of Colman posters, tea towels, aprons, and the like. 3 Bridewell Alley (phone: 0603-627889).

Cork, Irish Republic – *Barry's Tea,* a superb provision shop, stocks exquisite freshly packed teas and preserves. But the unique offering here is a Hadji Bey Turkish Delight made in Cork itself. Princes St. (phone: 021-20995).

Dublin and Shannon, Irish Republic – Behind its beautiful stained glass windows, *Bewley's Cafés Ltd.* roasts and packs coffee it has imported itself. Its chocolates, fudge, Barm Bracks, and rich, small Mary cakes are famous. 78-79 Grafton St. (phone: 01-776761).

And don't forget to pick up a side of Irish smoked salmon, one of the world's great indulgences, before leaving for home. They're available at prices that are positively reasonable in airport duty-free shops, and will be packed properly for travel on the spot. Also good bets and widely available are heather honey from the Boyne Valley, Molly O'Rourke's fruitcakes, W. H. Mosse mix for Irish brown soda bread, and Bewley's cakes and coffees. Also be on the lookout for Irish whiskeys, which come in a selection wider than you find readily at home: Power, Jameson, Paddy, and Tullamore Dew are a few of the better known brands. Look for special offers at supermarkets and wine shops or purchase them in the duty-free shops.

Throughout Scotland – Don't fail to bring home a bottle of Scotch whisky. More than 200 brands are produced here. And while it's not inexpensive, it comes in a selection you won't find at home.

GUNS: London is the source for precision arms. At *Holland and Holland,* the making of a gun is high art, and many of the customers choose their weapons with more care than they would choose a home. Peek in, if only to inspect the binoculars, the folding earmuffs, or other appurtenances of hunting and shooting. You'll see the England that used to be — and obviously still is, for some. 33 Bruton St., W1 (phone: 01-499-4411).

James Purdey and Sons, distinguished gunmakers who have been in business for over a century, have served royalty. Prince Philip and Prince Charles are both supplied from these quiet and dignified premises. Owning one of the house's beautifully worked metal-and-walnut creations is the dream of many a sporting shot. 57 S Audley St., W1 (phone: 01-499-1801).

HANDICRAFTS: Especially in Scotland, Wales, and Ireland, you'll find hand-wovens, hand-spuns, hand-throwns, and hand-knits galore.

England – Handicrafts centers can be found throughout the country.

The one in Bristol, the *Bristol Craft Centre,* is typical. A collection of workshops, at any given time there may be jewelers, potters, weavers, leatherworkers, and others. 6 Leonard La., beside 31 Corn St. (phone: 0272-297890).

Wellow Crafts in Bath offers knitwear, patchwork quilts, hand-smocked Liberty print dresses for little girls, basketwork, and some 30 types of other traditional craft items from nearly 200 artisans. Kingsmead Sq. (phone: 0225-64358).

The Minories in Stratford-upon-Avon is typical of a number of English craft clusters where several craft workers products are available under one roof. Meer St.

Scotland – Potters, weavers, and knitters predominate among the artisans who run more than 1,000 crafts workshops here. Jewelers make wonderful pieces using Celtic motifs. For a list of those that welcome visitors, order the *Visitor's Guide to Scottish Craft Workshops,* available at no charge from the Scottish Tourist Board.

If you're not planning a drive around the countryside, you can visit the *Scottish Craft Centre* in Edinburgh to inspect the selection of handmade glasswares, jewelry, woolen goods, and pottery. Acheson House, Canongate.

Wales – The national traditions of weaving, pottery, wood, and leatherworking are still flourishing. The Wales Tourist Board (Brunel House, 2 Fitzalan Rd., Cardiff CF2 1UY) can help with information on current goings-on and the whereabouts of craft enterprises you can visit.

Things Welsh in Cardiff offers homey, rural crafts all in one place. Duke St. Arcade (phone: 0222-33445).

Also in Cardiff is *Castle Welsh Crafts & Woollens,* which sells designer fashions in Welsh wool as well as traditional quality woolens. 1 Castle St. (phone: 0222-43038).

Irish Republic – This nation escaped the worst of the Industrial Revolution, so many traditional crafts never died out; the last few years' surge of interest has meant that many are flourishing as never before. Emigrés from the rest of Europe have brought new ideas and increased sophistication to rural craftsmen and craft shops. Workshops and stores throughout the country now stock handmade goods in both traditional and contemporary styles. Shillelaghs and blackthorn walking sticks are still to be found, and briar pipes are world famous. There are hand-turned tableware and platters, salt and pepper shakers, and tables and chairs with rustic-looking seats made of twisted hay or straw. Pottery is being produced in studios all over the island in simple sculptural shapes and earthy colors. Metalsmiths produce bowls and bracelets, chains and ear-rings, pendants and rings, and tea and coffee sets in silver, gold, and copper. Sometimes jewelry is set with semiprecious stones or half-moons of Connemara marble; sometimes the designs derive from the Book of Kells.

Fine cotton Irish lace, the crafting of which was introduced during the 1840s famine, can make an everyday wearable fit for a special occasion, and there are dozens of patterns.

Basketmakers turn the rushes and sallies that grow along the country's slow-flowing rivers and lakes into sturdy shallow baskets, shopping baskets, table mats, St. Brigid crosses, harvest knots, and other items.

Stained glass, patchwork quilts, cut stones, candles, handmade carpets and rugs, and soft toys and quaint rag dolls can also be found.

Every county has its specialty and its assortment of little shops, some of which keep company with workshops in craft centers ("craft clusters" in the local parlance) where you can watch the artisan at work.

The *Kilkenny Design Workshops* are worth mentioning in particular. The Kilkenny headquarters is in a cupola-crowned group of buildings that used to be the stables of imposing Kilkenny Castle; it became the center for the government-sponsored design workshops in 1963. While the designers and some artisans work undisturbed in back, the store up front sells wares ranging from the very traditional hand-crafted items to the utterly contemporary, machine-made items; there's glass, silver, ceramics, rugs, knitwear, and more (phone: 056-22118). And the presence of the workshops has brought a number of other craft workers to town. You can shop for their wares in their studios. The organization also has outlets in Dublin on Nassau Street, and in London at 150 New Bond St.

Tower Design Craft Centre, a former sugar refinery, is another good bet in Dublin. Newly renovated, it now houses 30 innovative craftspeople working with heraldic jewelry, woodcarving, weaving, pottery, silks, crystal, heraldry, knitwear, and more. At the Tower, one has the opportunity to watch the wares being created and to discuss the work with the makers. Pearse St. (phone: 01-775655).

H. Johnston in Dublin has traditional blackthorn walking sticks. 11 Wicklow St. (phone: 01-771249).

Northern Ireland – *A Guide to Northern Ireland Crafts and Craftsmen* (available from the Local Enterprises Development Unit, 19 Linenhall St., Belfast BT2 8B5) provides an overview of the craft activities here.

But the area is famous for its lace and linen, and the best of that is available in a couple of stores in Belfast — *Hall's Linen and Traditional Irish Crafts* (23 Queen's Arcade) and *Simpson Brothers Ltd.* (14 Callendar St.).

HATS: The traditional cool, damp weather has led to the evolution of a number of distinctive kinds of headgear in Britain and Ireland.

London, England – *James Lock and Company,* an institution since 1759, are the royal purveyors. They fitted a crown for the queen's coronation — and they'll fit you for your first bowler. Bankers, tycoons, politicians, actors, horse owners and trainers have all been hatted here. 6 St. James's St., SW1 (phone: 01-930-5849).

Bates, founded by George Bates just after the turn of the century and still in the family, is the destination whether you fancy a tweed cap or a black topper to protect you from the London weather. Presiding over the premises — in top hat, of course — is Binks, a huge tabby cat who resided here from 1921–26 and was preserved on his demise by a first-class taxidermist. 21A Jermyn St., SW1 (phone: 01-734-2722).

The Hat Shop sells balaclavas, berets, cloches, deerstalkers, fedoras, flying caps, panamas, pillboxes, tam o'shanters, and even baseball caps with earflaps. Women's hats are made-to-measure in the color or fabric of a special outfit for occasions such as weddings and the Ascot races. 58 Neal St., in Covent Garden, WC2 (phone: 01-836-6718).

Clifden, County Galway, Irish Republic – *Millars* makes a famous hat known as the Original Irish Country Hat, the Irish Walking Hat, and the Fishing Hat. As they tell it, the only place you might not wear it is to bed. It's made from wool purchased from local farmers and processed in a mill that incorporates part of the town's old railway station, and it's an essential part of every sportsman's wardrobe.

JEWELRY: Beautiful jewelry is available all over Britain and Ireland. There is jewelry in nearly every antiques shop, for instance. And craft workers in increasing numbers are using silver and gold, both in Ireland and England. In Scotland, look for Luckenbooth brooches representing two entwined hearts surmounted by a crown as well as clan brooches and kilt pins and other treasures set with quartz, amethyst, cairngorm stones, and other semiprecious jewels. Distinctive local pieces are available in three locations:

Castleton, Derbyshire, England – Blue John, the semiprecious yellow and blue decorative stone found in ancient mines of the Peak District, is made into jewelry and sold at the entrances to the mines and in local shops.

Southwold, Suffolk, England – Amber, a fossilized resin common in Suffolk, is carved or made up into jewelry here. Visit *The Amber Shop,* where colors range from pale opaque yellows to reds and prices from £4 to £400. Various nuggets are on display in their unworked states along with other pieces made into jewelry; the rarest is a necklet reportedly found in Tutankhamen's tomb in 1923. 15 Market Pl. (phone: Southwold 723394).

St. Andrews Fife, Scotland – *The Iona Shop* specializes in Celtic jewelry, including pieces that are handmade in silver and studded with burnished Scottish stones. Scottish craft products in hornware and silverplate and a line of Art Nouveau–inspired boxes and frames are also available. 7 Bell St. (phone: St. Andrews 73102).

Perth, Tayside, Scotland – Rare freshwater Scottish pearls from mussels that live in the River Tay are luminous and beautiful with a lovely untouched quality. At *A. and G. Cairncross,* they're used in settings of great delicacy that reflect the mountain stream settings in which they're found. 18 St. John St. (phone: 0738-24367).

MAPS AND PRINTS: A map of an area you've just visited makes a fine and eminently packable souvenir. And antique maps are a specialty at many stores. A beautiful print can bring many hours of enjoyment at home — all the better if it's an old one.

London, England – *Colnaghi* is a respected specialist in Old Master prints as well as drawings and paintings, with prices commensurate to the quality. 14 Old Bond St., W1 (phone: 01-491-7408).

Craddock and Barnard. Generations of students have leafed through its boxes. An excellent source for prints for all collectors. 32 Museum St., WC1 (phone: 01-636-3937).

Stanford's is the principal destination for maps, whether you want a topographic of the mountains you've just walked, a yachting chart for an area you want to cruise, or a road map of the byways you've just cycled. Landsat pictures, world maps, atlases, and globes are all available. It may well be, as the proprietors contend, the world's largest map shop. 12 Long Acre, WC2 (phone: 01-836-1321).

Dublin, Irish Republic – *Eason & Son,* the capital's best bookstore, is also the best spot to buy maps. 40-42 Lower O'Connell St. (phone: 01-733811).

MENSWEAR: What Paris is to clothing for women, London is to men, and you'll find the finest of everything. Herewith, a few of our selections.

Anderson and Sheppard is just one of the city's celebrated made-to-measure tailors. 30 Savile Row, W1 (phone: 01-734-1420).

Harvie and Hudson offers men's shirts made to order, not to mention a selection of all-silk ties designed and colored to coordinate with the shirts. 77 and 97 Jermyn St., SW1 (phone: 01-930-3949).

Douglas Hayward, one of the most distinctive tailors in London, makes bespoke suits for an exclusive clientele. A boutique stocks knitwear, luggage, accessories. 95 Mount St., W1 (phone: 01-499-5574).

Simpson's wares are very solid, very English, and utterly classic. The large shop also stocks clothing and accessories for women. 203 Piccadilly, W1 (phone: 01-734-2002).

Turnbull and Asser makes the Rolls-Royce of shirts to order; it provides a shirttail long enough to reach to midthigh so that it stays tucked in even after many hours at a desk. Prince Charles is a customer. 71 Jermyn St., SW1 (phone: 01-930-0502).

MUSIC: *Chappell* in London is the city's largest supplier of sheet music, from Bach to rock. Pianos, electronic keyboards, guitars, and metronomes are also available. 50 New Bond St., W1 (phone: 01-491-2777).

PAPER GOODS: England is the source of some of the most beautiful stationery anywhere, and London is its headquarters.

Paperchase, a delightful shop, deals in beautiful wrapping paper, unique greeting cards, posters, prints, kites and mobiles, toys and games, hand-marbled papers, and more. 213 Tottenham Court Rd., W1, and 167 Fulham Rd., SW3 (phone: 01-580-8496).

Smythson of Bond Street has personalized writing paper and visiting cards, sealing wax, diaries, calendars, and leather-bound pocket notebooks specially designed for wine connoisseurs, golfers, fishermen, gardeners, travelers, etc. The selection of address books is vast, and each of the nearly two dozen desktop accessory items is available in 10 colors. Everything is in exquisite taste. The Queen patronizes the firm. 54 New Bond St., W1 (phone: 01-629-8558).

PERFUMES: France may be more famous for its scents, but the English have a nose for them as well, and the fragrances are equally subtle, equally appealing. And they all make light, inexpensive gifts for men and women alike. In London, visit the following shops:

Floris has been blending flower-based perfumes since 1730 when Jermyn Street was a cobbled, unlit byway and the young Spaniard Juan Famenias Floris sailed to England from Minorca. The shop, which holds two Royal Warrants, now sells delicious-smelling powders in boxes and tins, potpourris, toilet waters and perfumes, bath essences and soaps. 89 Jermyn St., SW1 (phone: 01-930-2885).

Penhaligon's Victorian shops offer an extensive range of classical scents, toilet waters, soaps and bath oils for ladies and gentlemen — along with antique scent bottles and old English silver for the dressing table. They hold Prince Philip's Royal Warrant. 41 Wellington St., WC2, and three other locations (phone: 01-836-2150).

Taylor of London, founded in 1887, offers English floral fragrances not only as perfumes and toilet waters but also as scented sachets, soaps, pomanders, and potpourris. 186 Sloane St., SW1 (phone: 01-235-4653).

RAINWEAR: The best quality rainwear in the world can be found in London. The umbrellas, particularly, are durable and distinguished. These are the shrines of the rainy day:

Aquascutum, established in 1851, is famous for its tailored raincoats and classic English woolens. 100 Regent St., W1 (phone: 01-734-6090).

Burberrys is the home of the superb but expensive men's, women's, and children's raincoats with the omnipresent and often imitated beige and red plaid linings. 18-22 Haymarket, SW1 (phone: 01-930-3343).

James Smith and Sons is Europe's oldest purveyor of umbrellas and a variety of equipment that might pass for an umbrella. (Walking sticks are among the wares.) And if you don't like anything you see, the company will make something up to your specifications. 53 New Oxford St., WC1 (phone: 01-836-4731).

Swaine, Adeney, Brigg, and Sons is one of the last firms extant to make umbrellas in pure silk. Sword umbrellas, walking sticks that convert to .410 shotguns, are also available, along with riding gear and what's probably London's largest selection of attaché cases. 185 Piccadilly, W1 (phone: 01-734-4277).

RIDING EQUIPMENT: Horse-mad countries that they are, England and its neighbors offer some of the best riding equipment on earth.

London, England – *Gidden's of London,* founded in 1804, sells saddles and other riding equipment to the Queen. On three floors, near New Bond St. at 15d Clifford St., W1 (phone: 01-734-2788).

York, North Yorkshire, England – *Ralph Ellerker's,* established in 1795, is dusty, smells of leather and rope, and offers sherry on cold winter mornings in the back room. It's a pleasure just to inhale the scents and to experience the treasury of textures, rough and smooth. You can buy the famous hand-crafted all-leather Ellerker Dealer Boot, usually worn by market men, gypsies, and horse traders — but there are also coils of rope, string of all sizes and types, canvas tarpaulin sheets, and many other items, from waterproof suits to leather palms for leather work. Country clothing, boots, and shoes are now part of the stock. 25 Walmgate (phone: 0904-54417).

Kilcullen, County Kildare, Irish Republic – *Berney Brothers* makes fine saddles of all types — and you can watch them being produced on the premises (phone: 045-81228).

SHOES: In England you can still have a pair of shoes made to order — providing you're patient, since the labor can take months. For people with time to wait, there's an embarrassment of choice of wonderfully high quality footgear.

London, England – *John Lobb* will custom-make both men's and women's shoes (for an average of $900 a pair) that will likely last longer than you, with proper care. Still in the family that founded it in 1849, the rich scent of the leathers, the superb workmanship that is everywhere evident, and the opportunity to view Queen Victoria's own lasts make a visit well worth your while, even if you buy nothing more than a tin of the shop's celebrated shoe cream. 9 St. James's St., SW1 (phone: 01-930-3664).

Church's, over a century old, manufactures footwear with consummate care — and the results are fabulous. 58–59 Burlington Arcade, W1, and New Bond St., W1 (phone: 01-493-8307).

Street, Somerset, England – *Clarks* was founded here 150 years ago and is still going strong. You can find low-priced seconds and visit a fascinating museum that displays the queer-looking footgear of ages past.

SHEEPSKINS: Warm and nearly indestructible, sheepskin makes up into a winter coat that is close to ideal, and England and Scotland are one of the principal sources.

Bungay, Suffolk, England – *Nursey's* keeps on making and selling increasingly lighter and more colorful sheepskin coats, hats, gloves, rugs, and other items. The firm is now nearly 200 years old. Bungay is packed with antiques shops and historical buildings. 12 Upper Olland St. (phone: 0986-2821).

Loch Lomond, Strathclyde, Scotland – *The Antartex Factory Shop* offers top-quality sheepskin goods at factory prices, only about a half hour's drive from Glasgow. The company, which has supplied sheepskins to British Antarctic expeditions since 1955, has recently broadened its line to include sheepskin accessories, rugs, fashion leathers, and knitwear. Lomond Industrial Estate, Alexandria (phone: 0389-52393).

SPORTING GOODS: The great outdoors figures so strongly in the leisure activities of British and Irish citizens that it's not surprising to find an abundance of excellent equipment for the sportsman's pleasure.

London, England – *Lillywhites* has equipment for some three dozen sports, from cricket (the avocation of its mid-19th-century founder, James Lillywhite) to Ping-Pong to polo, on a half-dozen floors. It's the largest store of its kind in the country and has held a Royal Warrant since 1955. Piccadilly Circus, SW1 (phone: 01-930-3181).

TOBACCO: The Englishman's grasp of the world of tobacco is immediately evident at two London shops:

Alfred Dunhill offers the best in precision lighters, pipes, tobacco, and cigars. Claiming to provide almost anything that a man can carry or wear, their offerings include luxury leather accessories, watches, writing instruments, and classically styled casual clothes. With its thick carpeting, gleaming paneling, and many fragrances of sweetly scented tobacco, this is another of those stores that is a destination in its own right. 32 St. James's St., SW1 (phone: 01-499-9566).

James Fox specializes in cigars. They come from around the world, including Havana, and most brands are represented. Another draw for the connoisseur is the use of climate-controlled conditioning rooms for bringing the cigars to peak condition. 2 Burlington Gardens, W1 (phone: 01-493-9009).

TOYS: The first stop in London for parents and other doters is *Hamleys,* whose 7 floors make it one of the world's largest toy shops. There are magicians doing tricks, demonstration models whizzing, dolls walking and talking, teddy bears 6 inches to 6 feet begging to be cuddled, electronic games blipping and bleeping, and trains of every gauge whistling along their tracks. (No less than six on the ground floor encircle the escalators and stop at famous London landmarks.) *Young Hamleys* specializes in playthings for youngsters under six. Elsewhere there are board games, computers, and a Model Centre that offers scaled-down versions of practically anything. The selection is astonishing, to say the least. 188 Regent St., W1 (phone: 01-734-3161).

Pollock's Toy Museum may have a museum upstairs — but downstairs there are miniatures, little theaters in the Victorian style to cut out, and all manner of teddy bears and reproduction toys from Victorian and Edwardian times. 44 The Market, Covent Garden, WC2 (phone: 01-379-7866), and 1 Scala St., W1 (phone: 01-636-3452).

WOOLENS: The tweeds and plaids and knits of Britain and Ireland are justly famous, and they're to be found in nearly every shop and department store. Wool is a way of life as well as an attraction for tourists.

Scotland is best known for its subtly patterned and colored Harris tweeds, woven by hand in the Outer Hebrides. Shetland and Fair Isle sweaters are Scottish products, along with most of the world's best lamb's wool and cashmere pullovers and cardigans. Tartans are Scottish, and there are more than 500 patterns, most of which can be purchased by the yard or stitched up into a kilt (or a "kilted skirt" for women).

In the Irish Republic, weavers no longer give the world the kind of homespun, handwoven tweeds that differed from one part of the country to the next because of regional variations in the wool and dyes — but tweed from Donegal, which comes from Ireland's northwest coast in varying weights, is still one of the country's best buys, as are the items made from it.

Equally renowned are fishermen's sweaters hand-knit from heavily oiled or scoured off-white wool in the tree of life, crooked road, tobacco, carrageen moss, castle, and popcorn-like bobaleen stitches, combined in almost sculptural patterns that sometimes resemble the carvings on Celtic crosses. There's a special meaning to each pattern. Originally, they were made on the Aran Islands, but cottage knitters throughout the west and north now produce them for sale across the nation and around the world. Since no two are quite alike, it's best to shop where the selection is largest — nowadays in Dublin and Galway — and keep looking until you find one you can't resist.

St. Helier, Jersey, Channel Islands, England – There used to be plenty of craftswomen on Jersey who spent their time knitting the island's distinctive navy blue, oiled wool pullovers, and on neighboring Guernsey, women's organizations used to turn out similar models in white as well. Now, they only finish by hand what machines have made and their products come in all colors. You can buy the product at shops in town. (The cabbage walking sticks that are made and sold here also make unusual mementos.)

London, England – *Kilkenny* sells Irish fashions for men and women, Donegal tweeds, thick Aran sweaters, and vividly colored shawls to travelers who won't be proceeding on to the Emerald Isle. 150 New Bond St., W1 (phone: 01-493-5455 or 5456).

The Scotch House, founded in 1834, has not only plaids but also lamb's wool, Shetland pullovers, classic cashmeres, and 57 styles of cashmere, as well as 350 different tartans in pure wool. This may be the best single source for woolen items in London. 3 Brompton Rd., Knightsbridge, SW1 (phone: 01-581-2151).

Westaway and Westaway has traditional pullovers in cashmere and lamb's wool. Some are hand-knit. And there's not a synthetic thread in the place. A new shop at 92 Great Russell Street specializes in hand-knits and designer knits and adjacent premises are devoted entirely to woolens made in the Shetland Isles. 65 Great Russell St., WC1, and 92-93 Great Russell St., WC1 (phone: 01-405-4479).

Edinburgh, Scotland – Tartans seem to line the streets here.

Kinloch Anderson is the Kilt Maker for the Royal Family. Kilts and kilted skirts can be purchased either ready-made or made to order in some 400 of the tartans in existence, from the Abercrombie, Black Watch, Bruce, and Culloden patterns to the Urquhart and Wallace. Sporrans, tweed jackets to match the plaids, ties, stockings, garters, and other accessories to complement the outfit are all available. What you can't buy here is the Balmoral tartan; though Kinloch Anderson stocks it exclusively, it is held on behalf of the royal household and is not for sale to the public. 45 High St. (phone: 031-556-6961).

The James Pringle Woollen Mill has a comprehensive range of things woolen at mill prices, plus a Clan Tartan Centre that offers an audio-visual presentation covering the history of the tartan from its beginnings. 70–74 Bangor Rd., Leith (phone: 031-553-5161).

Pitlochry Knitwear offers excellent prices in Scottish goods, particularly sweaters, kilts, and women's suits. 28 N Bridge St. and 50 other locations in England, Scotland, and Wales (phone: 03552-43901).

The Scotch House is the best place in the city for classy, expensive woolens — kilts, sweaters, tweeds, scarves, shawls, and mohairs. 60 Princes St. (phone: 031-226-5271).

The Woollen Mill provides a good inexpensive alternative to the Scotch House. Outlets are at 453 Lawnmarket (phone: 031-225-1525) and 51 High St. (phone: 031-556-9786).

Galashiels and Hawick, Borders, Scotland – Both towns are well known for knitwear and woolens. The former is the site of the Scottish College of Textiles, which offers summer courses in techniques. It is also the home of the *Peter Anderson* factory, where you can see 670 different tartans and tour the factory from April to October. Nether Mill (phone: 0896-2091).

Nearby shops sell tweeds, mohairs, and cashmere items plus knitting yarn.

Hawick, the largest of the Scottish Border towns, has two major weaving mills,

Teviotex and *Trowmill,* where visitors can view the manufacture of tweeds. And some of the most famous knitwear producers also make their home here; they do not have mill shops, but a wide range of local shops stock their goods.

There are also factories in Innerleithen and at Walkerburn, the site of the Scottish Museum of Woollen Textiles, a sheep auction mart in Hawick, and annual ram sales at Kelso. Jedburgh and Kelso also have a good selection of knitwear and tweed shops. *Scotland: Borders Woollen Trail,* a brochure that gives background on the industry and highlights the area mills, museums, and shops, is available from the Scottish Borders Tourist Board, Municipal Buildings, High St., Selkirk TD7 4JX (phone: 0750-20555).

Glasgow, Scotland – *Lawrie's,* established in 1881, has a worldwide reputation for its knowledge of Highland dress in all its nuances. Kilts, skirts, jackets, tweeds, mohairs, and all manner of accessories and souvenirs are available. 110 Buchanan St. (phone: 041-221-0217) and 38 Renfield St. (phone: 041-221-9047).

Inverness, Highland, Scotland – *James Pringle,* who sells possibly the world's best cashmere sweaters, also manufactures cloth and has a factory and shop where you can buy it made up into skirts, sports jackets, and the like, as well as cashmere, lamb's wool, and Shetland knitwear. Holm Woolen Mills, Dores Rd. (phone: 0463-223311).

Outer Hebrides, Western Isles, Scotland – The wool cloth bearing the distinctive trademark of Harris tweed, a circle and a Celtic cross, is hand-woven by islanders following age-old methods; the yard goods are for sale in shops throughout the islands. Stornoway, the largest town of the Lewis-Harris landmass, has a mill that sells tweeds at competitive prices. Sweaters knit from Harris wool are available at all the local craft shops. On Eriskay, island women produce distinctively patterned fisherman's sweaters.

St. Andrews, Fife, Scotland – One of the biggest and best outlets for knitted and woven woolens and cashmeres is the *St. Andrews Woollen Mill,* In its former golf club factory, you'll find first-quality goods, seconds, discontinued lines, and remnants. The Golf Links (phone: 0334-72366).

Dublin, Irish Republic – *Irish Cottage Industries* stocks sweaters, tweeds, and anything else you can imagine that's been knit, crocheted, braided, or woven by hand, as well as a line of womens' clothing tailored from the company's own tweeds. 44 Dawson St. (phone: 01-713039).

Cleo Ltd. offers an exceptional variety of hand-woven and hand-knit sweaters, capes, scarves, and other garments, in wool and linen. The quality of the knitting is exceptional, and sweaters in traditional Aran patterns are available in an array of colors reminiscent of an Irish landscape — misty violets and smoky blues, soft greens by turns mossy or gray, and pungent scarlets, russets, and oranges. 18 Kildare St. (phone: 01-761421) and 2 Shelbourne St., Kenmare, County Kerry.

Ardara, County Donegal, Irish Republic – Donegal is the birthplace of the tweeds for which Ireland is so famous and it still does a thriving business in woolens colored like Ireland's bluebells and gorse and its hawthorn and heather — all woven in wonderful herringbones and houndstooth checks and other patterns. In this town, though synthetic dyes can occasionally be found, vegetable matter is still the coloring material that gives such a subtle and luscious array of hues to wares found in establishments like the *John Molloy Ltd. Factory Shop.* A hand-weaver can be viewed on the premises. Killybegs Rd. (phone: 075-41133).

DIRECTIONS

Great Britain

Southeast England

For better or worse, geography conspired to make Kent and Sussex — the broad heel of land that opens out below London to form the bluff-lined and beach-speckled coast of southeast England — the only welcoming mat England has ever extended to the Continent. It is country suited to landing parties: Kent's rich orchards, hop fields, thatched barns, and high-hedged roads giving way to Sussex's high South Downs, from which one can see for miles in all directions. To the north is the wide estuary of the Thames; to the south, the English Channel; and to the east, where England and France are only some 20 miles apart, the Straits of Dover.

Such an invitation has been hard for European warlords to resist, and for 2,000 years attempts have been made to enter England through the southeast. Some have been successful. The Romans established an administrative center in London, and the Normans conquered all of England after their decisive victory at the Battle of Hastings in 1066, a date no English schoolchild ever forgets. Other attempts have failed. From August to October 1940, Britain stood virtually alone against the full weight of the Nazi war machine as the Battle of Britain raged over Kent. But each of these efforts has left some mark on this extraordinarily rich part of England. Kent, the Garden of England, nurtures as much history as fruit and hops in its fertile countryside.

Much of the southeast is dominated and influenced by London. Hundreds of thousands of those who live in this region commute daily to and from the capital. The region, too, is London's principal playground, and on good summer weekends its beaches and country resorts fill with hosts of fugitives from town. But the countryside and the coast have proved surprisingly tenacious despite their proximity to a city of 8 million inhabitants. Once you realize that this area, and especially the northern part of Kent, is Britain's main thoroughfare to Europe, and that it is one of the most densely populated parts of the country, you will be prepared not to find vast tracts of it in virgin condition. But having said that, you will be surprised at how much of it is unspoiled and rarely visited and at how well it has held on to its past.

Along the south shore of the Thames as far as Gravesend, major industries dominate the waterfront before the Kent countryside comes into view and Thameside busyness gives way to the first of several holiday resorts that round the northeast coast of the county. Below the river and the coast, parallel to them, lie the North Downs, a range of low chalkland hills that run east from Surrey to meet the sea spectacularly as the white cliffs of Dover. Impossible to cultivate, they are either forested or left to grazing. Still farther south lies the Weald, the central region of the southeast. The Weald takes its name from the Anglo-Saxon *Wold,* meaning "a wood." Throughout the later Middle Ages, the woods of this region were cleared, and the fertile soil turned to agricultural use. The result was a prosperous area of substantial villages and market towns, and to this day it is quite possible to find them still full of sixteenth- and seventeenth-century houses and farms, and to sense in them a strong continuity with their isolated past.

Up and over the South Downs that run through Sussex and Hampshire below the Weald, you come to a coast given over largely to pleasure. Like the Kent coast, the Sussex coast abounds with resorts. They are a little less fashionable now than in their Victorian and Edwardian heydays, but perhaps more attractive for that very reason. In the little ones especially, you will find clear signs of the elegance that transformed these watering places from the fishing villages that they once were.

The major sights of England's southeast — Canterbury, Dover, Hastings and Battle, Arundel, and Brighton — can all be visited on day trips from London. Travelers with little time should certainly choose the most appealing destinations and make the journey by car or, even more simply, by train. But more rewarding is a perambulation through the countryside, following the coast as a rough guide, and taking in both the large, obviously popular spots along the beaten path and the smaller, quieter places off it.

The route outlined below begins in Rochester, familiar to readers of Charles Dickens, then takes the less traveled road to Canterbury through hop-growing country, the town of Faversham, and the old-fashioned seaside resorts of Whitstable and Herne Bay. From Canterbury the route returns to the coast at Sandwich, one of the five Cinque Ports that banded together in the Middle Ages to furnish ships to a previously nonexistent English navy. Next along the coast is the historic port of Deal; Dover and Hythe, two more of the Cinque Ports, are a short drive farther south. The route then crosses the Romney Marsh — a bleak peninsula once known to smugglers, now livened by a string of tiny, traditional beach towns — on its way to Rye and Winchelsea and to Hastings and Battle, where a new era began for England. Next comes a fork in the road: You can detour into the Kent and Sussex Weald, where the essential character of this part of England can still be felt, or you can head straight for the hurly-burly of Brighton. The route ends in Southampton, but not before visits to Arundel and Chichester and, if you wish, a sojourn on the Isle of Wight.

The southeastern region is a very popular vacation spot, so make hotel reservations far in advance. Expect to pay around $60 and up for a double in those places listed as expensive; from $40 to $60 in moderate; and under $40 in inexpensive. A meal for two, excluding wine, tips, or drinks, will run to $50 and up in places listed as expensive; $25 to $50 in moderate; and under $25 in inexpensive.

ROCHESTER: The River Medway forms a natural barrier between London and the Channel, neatly dividing Kent in two, and Rochester is primarily a bridge town for the river. It can be easily overlooked now that the M2 motorway from London to Dover rushes by it 2 miles upriver, but if you take the turning before the Medway bridge, you will soon find yourself in the center of the city. The Romans recognized Rochester's strategic importance early and built a bridge (the London to Dover extension of Watling Street, England's ancient Roman highway, crossed the river here), and after they left, a succession of bridges followed. The Normans, too, saw the importance of the crossing and late in the 11th century began a magnificent castle to defend it. The enormous square keep, 120 feet high with 12-foot-thick walls, was built in the 12th century and is still standing, open to adventurous visitors prepared to climb its steep spiral staircases and be rewarded by a marvelous view of the Medway estuary, the North Downs, and, best of all, Rochester Cathedral. Next to the castle, the cathedral is set on a 7th-century foundation, with a plain Norman nave and many features gradually added from the 12th to the 14th century. The Norman doorway at the west entrance, the walled choir, and many of the tombs are noteworthy.

Castle and cathedral share the summit of Boley Hill, the center of the old city and an area that boasts many ancient and interesting buildings. They catch the rare flavor of a Victorian city, a flavor enhanced by their close associations with Charles Dickens, who lived in nearby Chatham as a boy and came back near the end of his life to Gad's Hill, 3 miles west. Many scenes in his novels take place in Rochester and the surrounding countryside, and each year, in late May and early June, the city stages a rich festival in his honor. Dickens's favorite inn, *The Leather Bottle* (in Cobham, 5 miles west), figures in the *Pickwick Papers* and still dispenses food, drink, and atmosphere. The *Royal Victoria and Bull* hotel, on High Street near the bridge and Boley Hill, is both the Bull Inn of the same novel and the Blue Boar Inn of *Great Expectations,* and many of the shops around it are readily identifiable as Dickensian settings. The 16th-century Restoration House on Maidstone Road is Miss Havisham's Satis House in *Great Expectations* (not open to the public), and about 6 miles north, in the village of Cooling, there's the original setting of Joe Gargery's forge and the graveyard where Pip first met Magwitch. Both are on the edge of an alluringly bleak marshland. Thinly disguised, Rochester is also the Cloisterham of Dickens's last, unfinished, work, *The Mystery of Edwin Drood.* This strange novel gives a good picture of Victorian Rochester, but much can also be seen in the marvelous Dickens Centre in Eastgate House on High Street (open daily). The house itself is Elizabethan and appears in *Edwin Drood* as the Nuns' House. Dickens's Gad's Hill home is not open to the public, but the Swiss chalet in which he wrote has now been moved to the garden of Eastgate House.

CHECKING IN: *Royal Victoria and Bull* – In fact, a 400-year-old coach house and the fictitious scene of Dickensian revels — the novelist thought it was a "good house" with "nice beds." The food is plain English fare, well cooked and well served. 16-18 High St., Rochester (phone: 0634-46266). Moderate.

En Route from Rochester – Before proceeding to Faversham, you may want to make an 8-mile detour to Maidstone, the bustling agricultural center of Kent, with a long history in the brewing industry. Many old buildings line its streets, several of which have been closed to traffic to preserve these fine examples of early architecture. Near the town's 14th-century Church of All Saints is a medieval building with an Elizabethan front, the Archbishop's Palace. What may have been the palace stable or a tithe barn now houses the Tyrwhitt Drake Museum of Carriages, a collection of ornate, horse-drawn vehicles (closed Sundays in winter). Chillington Manor, an Elizabethan mansion on St. Faith's Street, is the home of the Museum and Art Gallery, which contains the memorabilia of essayist William Hazlitt, a native of Maidstone (closed Sundays). Leeds Castle, built in the middle of a lake in the 1200s, is 4 miles east of Maidstone. This former residence of Henry VIII and Lord Culpepper (governor of Virginia, 1680-83) is often the focus of a day trip from London.

Returning to Rochester, you'll find Allington Castle, an imposing, moated, 13th-century castle, and the Carmelite retreat, Aylesford Priory, both off Route A229. The Order controls the structures, which are both open to visitors daily.

FAVERSHAM: If you are in a hurry or the weather is dull, the motorway will whisk you from Rochester to Faversham in half an hour. The old main road (A2), however, winds through Gillingham, then Sittingbourne, where there is a museum of sailing barges at the Dolphin Yard (open Sundays, Easter through October, and public holidays), and some Kent countryside that is especially lovely when the apple blossoms are out or the hops are fully grown. Faversham is at the center of hop-growing country, and the conical structures seen frequently in this region, called oasthouses, are used to dry the hops. Most people bypass the town, a pity that perhaps adds to its attractions for those who do stop. Another Roman site, it received its first charter in 811 and developed after that into a fine medieval city, not least because it was once a small port on the quiet River Swale, which divides the Isle of Sheppey from the Kent mainland. The whole town is beautifully redolent of a thriving brewing industry: Tours of Shepherd Neame Ltd., which has been brewing ale here since the late 16th century, can be arranged, but only with a month's written notice.

The best place to sample Faversham's past is on Preston Street in the Fleur de Lis Heritage Centre, a well-illustrated guide to the town's thousand years of history housed in a converted 15th-century inn (closed Sundays and Thursday afternoons). In the Market Place at the center of town, where three of its oldest streets meet, is the Guildhall, a 19th-century rebuilding of a 16th-century market hall, raised on pillars. At the north end of the Market Place is Court Street, with many 17th- and 18th-century houses. Joining it is Market Street where, at No. 12, James II was held prisoner by local fishermen as he tried to escape to the Continent. The many 16th- and 17th-century houses jostling together on West Street, however, make it the loveliest street of all. Faversham Creek, about 3 miles north of town, has medieval warehouses and a delightful pub, the *Coal Exchange Inn,* while the little harbor of Conyer Creek, a few miles west, is a favorite spot for artists and sailors. None of these places is much known except by natives, who understandably have kept them to themselves.

 CHECKING IN: *Ship –* In an 18th-century coaching house with many Tudor features, it's the perfect place in which to get the feel of this pleasant town. West St., Faversham (phone: 0795-532179). Moderate.

WHITSTABLE AND HERNE BAY: From Faversham, the direct route into Canterbury follows the M2 motorway, but a slower, winding route along the Thames estuary coast will bring you, after about 10 miles, to the small seaside towns of Whitstable and Herne Bay. Like Faversham and Rochester, these places are usually bypassed by overseas visitors, although they are quite popular with the English holidaymakers who have had the luck to discover their quiet charms. For centuries, Whitstable thrived as a fishing port involved principally in the production of oysters, the famous "Whitstable Natives." But by the 1950s, the Thames had become so polluted that the trade declined almost to nothing. The good news for both environmentalists and gourmets is that the river is now so much cleaner than before that the oysters have returned, and so have the restaurants selling them. (For two especially good ones, see *Eating Out.*) The nicest part of the old town still clusters around the old harbor. Here weatherboarded houses perch right on the edge of the shingle beach, and in the narrow streets you'll find a host of small pubs selling local ale and offering a very friendly welcome to the visitor. Another of Whitstable's attractions is the huge number of secondhand or "junk" shops, more per hundred yards than in almost any other town in the southeast. Stroll along High Street from the harbor to the town center and you'll find books, old clothes, antiques, and all sorts of bric-a-brac every few steps of the way. The prices aren't London prices, so you could pass a whole day in these shops, looking for bargains.

Herne Bay, the small town next to Whitstable, could be the nearest thing to a Victorian seaside resort in England. Primarily a retirement town with a predominantly elderly population, it has a general air of sedateness that is very attractive. Like its saltier neighbor, however, it abounds in friendly pubs and in good secondhand shops, too. The holiday resorts of Margate, Broadstairs, and Ramsgate lie along the coast beyond Herne Bay, but our route takes us south along the pleasant country road leading from Whitstable directly into Canterbury.

EATING OUT: *La Chandelle* – Robin and Susan Gundry serve tasty French fare, such as *suprême de faisan forestière* (pheasant with mushrooms, bacon, and potatoes) and *boeuf bourguignon.* Closed Sundays and Mondays. Charles St., Whitstable (phone: 02273-61126). Moderate.

Pearson's Oyster Bar – Don't leave Whitstable without sampling the locally caught seafood at Pearson's on the seafront, or the strong local Fremlin's ale. From the restaurant above the bar you can see out over the Thames estuary to the Isle of Sheppey. Sunsets there are so spectacular that the painter Turner used to sketch them for future use. Horsebridge, Whitstable (phone: 0227-272005). Moderate.

CANTERBURY: This is the spiritual center of the Anglican faith and Britain's cathedral city par excellence. It was from Canterbury that St. Augustine converted the English to Christianity, founding both an abbey and a church in AD 602. St. Augustine's Abbey survives in ruins, but the first cathedral was lost to fire and replaced by the massive 11th-century masterpiece that today dominates the red-roofed, still medieval town around it. The murder of Archbishop Thomas à Becket in 1170 and his canonization two years later elevated the cathedral to its status as a shrine; ever since Canterbury has been the goal of pilgrims, including Chaucer's group, who wended their way to the scene of Becket's martyrdom telling tales. Visitors should allow plenty of time to explore the cathedral — it's marked in every nook and corner with nine centuries of English history — and the many other ancient buildings nearby. Afterward, you'll find several inns, such as the 16th-century *White Hart* near Canterbury East Station, the half-timbered *Seven Stars* on Orange Street, or the bow-windowed *Olive Branch* on Burgate Street, all inviting places to stop and rest. For a full report on the city's sights, hotels, and restaurants, see *Canterbury,* THE CITIES.

En Route from Canterbury – Part of Canterbury's prosperity grew from its role as a market center for the many villages and agricultural communities of East Kent, and it still serves the same purpose for the region. If you have time, these small villages are well worth visiting. Particularly nice ones are Chilham, 10 miles to the southwest, which has the magnificent Chilham Castle (open to the public only when Elizabethan banquets are held in the Gothic Hall, although its gardens are open from late March to October, and, at various times of the year, jousting and falconry displays are held); Barham, which nestles below the Downs just off the Dover Road, 5 miles southeast of Canterbury; and Westbere, tucked away off the main Margate Road, 3 miles northeast of the city. Westbere has kept its almost medieval character intact, and in the middle of the village is the *Yew Tree,* a delightful inn in a medieval house.

EATING OUT: *Wife of Bath* – Five miles south of Chilham is Wye, a village that would escape notice altogether if it weren't for this very fine restaurant with English and French cuisine. Weekly menus change with the season to ensure as much absolutely fresh food as possible. Closed Sundays and Mondays. Make reservations. 4 Upper Bridge St., Wye (phone: 0233-812540). Moderate.

SANDWICH: Route A257 leads due east from Canterbury to the medieval port of Sandwich, one of the original five Cinque Ports (see *En Route* after Deal). As Sandwich's harbor became clogged with silt in the 16th century, the city lost importance and it is now 2 miles from the sea. Sandwich gained lasting fame, however, when the fourth earl of Sandwich invented the world's most popular and enduring meal. According to legend, the earl was loath to leave the gaming tables to eat and asked that a concoction of bread and meat be made for him. Since he was a dissolute man — and infamous for having been in charge of the admiralty when Britain lost its North American colony — the story has something of the ring of truth about it. Two inns, the *Bell* and the *King's Arms,* will be glad to provide a sample of this handy bar snack and something with which to wash it down. Richborough Castle, just off Route A257 a mile and a half outside of Sandwich, was established by the Romans in about AD 43 and added to by the Saxons during the 3rd century. Route A258 leads to Deal, about 6 miles south along the coast.

 CHECKING IN: *Fleur De Lis* – This small (5-bedroom) house is in the center of Sandwich. Its oak-paneled restaurant was converted from the old Corn Exchange. Delf St., Sandwich (phone: 0304-611131). Inexpensive.

DEAL: Deal was an important shipping center through the early 19th century. Under Henry VIII, three castles were erected here: Deal Castle, designed in the shape of a six-petaled rosette (open daily); Walmer Castle, more like a four-leaf clover and a mile south of the city (open daily); and Sandown Castle, since washed away and nothing more than a pile of stones at the northern end of the seafront. There is a good possibility that Caesar's forces landed along this shore when the Romans invaded Britain, and Henry VIII feared a repeat Roman invasion, this time in the form of a Holy War that the pope might launch against him as the self-proclaimed head of the Church of England. Off the coast of Deal are the Goodwin Sands, a dangerous and complicated series of sandbanks that are exposed at low tide. Lighthouses and lightships illuminate the area after dark, but maritime accidents persist even though Deal is no longer the swaggering seaport it once was. Before the coming of steamships, the narrow stretch of shallow water between Goodwin Sands and the shore, popularly known as the Downs and not the safest anchorage, was filled with cargo vessels and men-of-war. The Time Ball Tower on the seafront, a late-18th-century structure, used to give the correct Greenwich time to ships in the Downs (the ball dropped every day at 1 PM).

 CHECKING IN: *Royal* – The best features of this comfortable hotel are the balconies of the rooms facing the English Channel. The hotel is decorated with Georgian antiques, and its restaurant serves quite good fresh fish. Beach St., Deal (phone: 0304-375555). Expensive.

En Route from Deal – Traveling south on A258 toward the busy port of Dover, Walmer Castle is only 1 mile from Deal. Built as a fortress by Henry VIII, the castle became the official residence of the Lord Warden of the Cinque Ports in the mid-1700s. This association of seaports began in the 11th century, when five principal ports (Hastings, Romney — now New Romney — Hythe, Dover, and Sandwich) banded together to provide England with a makeshift navy. Later this was formalized by a charter that granted certain privileges in exchange for the pledge of supplying ships and men for the country's defense. Other ports along the southeast foot of England, the part closest to France, became involved in this arrangement during the dangerous period from the 13th to the 16th century. Following the establishment of the Royal Navy, the importance of the association and the post of its highest officer, the Lord Warden, declined drastically, and though there is still such a title today, it is largely without power. Two of the most prominent Lord Wardens to live in the castle have been William Pitt the Younger and the first duke of Wellington. The castle is open to visitors except when the present Lord Warden is in residence (usually in August). Dover, the Gateway of England, is only 7 miles farther south on A258.

DOVER: The chalky white cliffs of Dover have been a strategic landmark ever since the early Iron Age, when a settlement was established here. Roman invaders quickly erected a fortress and an octagonal lighthouse, or pharos, and an extension of the ancient Roman roadway called Watling Street ran between Dover and London via Canterbury. The Romans' pharos still stands within the walls of the more recent Dover Castle, an imposing Norman stronghold on the eastern cliffs of the city. Its huge, square keep was built by Henry II in the 1180s around a 240-foot-deep well — the keep had a lead-piped water supply, a surprising amenity for so old a structure. You can easily spend several hours wandering throughout the towers, gateways, and chambers, outer bailey, inner bailey, and keep of the enormous fortification, and even the underground works, where passages lead into the cliffs, are open to the public. On clear days, France is easily visible across the Straits of Dover, roughly 20 miles away, and the view from the battlements of Dover Castle atop the 400-foot bluff overlooking the city and sea is magnificent. Dover is one of Britain's main embarkation points for ferries to France (Calais and Boulogne) and Belgium (Oostende and Zeebrugge), and talk of a channel tunnel has yet to threaten its activity.

During both world wars, Dover again rose to prominence as a point of departure for troops bound for the Continent and as the goal of planes straggling back from the fighting. The city was pounded by long-range artillery during World War II, and the thick castle walls sheltered the population through the 4-year bombardment.

CHECKING IN: *Queen's Moat House* – This hotel is large, luxurious, and convenient to the ferry terminals, so it's popular with overnighters on their way to and from the Continent. It has a restaurant and a heated indoor swimming pool. Townwall St., Dover (phone: 0304-203270). Expensive.

En Route from Dover – The famous cliffs extend southwest toward Folkestone, neatly trimming the coastline with a tall white chalk seawall for almost 7 miles. Beyond this point the cliffs fall away, exposing the shore. Stretching westward is a line of defenses constructed in the early 19th century against the threat of an invasion by Napoleon: a series of 74 small coastal fortresses — circular martello towers from Folkestone around Beachy Head to Seaford. The towers are reinforced a short distance inland by the Royal Military Canal, dug in the same period, from Hythe to Rye. Additional defenses were erected in 1940 when Hitler massed his forces along the French coast. Take Route A20 southwest along the coast from Dover to Folkestone before picking up Route A259 for the additional 4 miles to Hythe.

If you're favored with good weather in Folkestone, take a stroll on the Leas — a broad, mile-long, grassy walkway on the crest of the cliffs just west of the harbor. From here the coast of France unfolds in a beautiful panorama 22 miles distant. On the east side of the harbor is the Warren, where a section of the chalk cliff has crumbled and fallen on the beach — a great hunting ground for fossils. Folkestone has a plentiful supply of good, reasonably priced family hotels, many of them on the seafront.

CHECKING IN: *Eastwell Manor* – Set in some 3,000 acres of private parkland, this elegant mansion was rebuilt as recently as 1926, though its history dates from the Norman Conquest. Huge rooms are cleverly decorated to make them inviting and some of the bathrooms are positively sumptuous. There is an oak paneled bar and a baronial dining room. The menu makes extensive use of local produce, as well as more exotic ingredients. Eastwell Park, Ashford (phone: 0233-35751). Expensive.

HYTHE: Three martello towers still guard the former Cinque Port of Hythe, although the harbor has long since silted up and the sea receded. There are also fortifications from other periods, including the ruins of a Roman castrum, Stutfall Castle, about 2½ miles west of Hythe along the banks of the Royal Military Canal that bisects the city. Above Stutfall is Lympne Castle (pronounced Lim), a home of the archdeacons of Canterbury until the mid-1800s. It incorporates a square 12th-century Norman tower into its otherwise 14th- and 15th-century construction, and though it is not impressively fortresslike, its sweeping views as far as the sea would have satisfied any ancient watchman (open daily, May to September). Hythe itself is a pleasant seaside town, a mixture of old houses, inns, and antique shops on narrow streets. The presence of over 1,500 human skulls in the medieval church has never been satisfactorily explained. Hythe is also the place to catch a ride on the Romney, Hythe, and Dymchurch Light Railway (open Easter and during the summer months). Miniature engines hauling real passengers for modest fares puff back and forth along the sea edge of Romney Marsh, the remote, sparsely populated lowland stretching southwest of Hythe. Port Lympne Zoo Park and Garden, with its herds of rare horses, deer, antelope, gazelle, rhinos, and other beasts, is nearby (phone: 0303-60618).

En Route from Hythe – Route A259 takes you into Romney Marsh, first following both the coast and the railway as far as New Romney (like Hythe, also a closed port, having lost its harbor in the 13th century), then bearing inland toward the ancient towns of Rye and Winchelsea. If you stopped for the view from Lympne Castle, you will have seen a great deal of this flat, sometimes bleak expanse of low-lying fields and marsh grass full of grazing Romney Marsh sheep and full of memories of the old smuggling days when untaxed (and often illegal) cargoes were unloaded here. In deep winter, the marsh can seem utterly detached from the present century. In summer, however, there are many attractions. The coast is flat, sandy, and ideal for bathing. If you want to see the English doing all the traditional seaside things, then Dymchurch, St. Mary's Bay, or Littlestone-on-Sea, New Romney's seaside suburb, are the places to go. Dymchurch, a popular weekend resort with a 5-mile beach, lies in the shelter of a 3-mile fortified seawall built by the Romans to prevent the marshes from flooding. The wall has been continuously improved, and the fortifications were added in 1940. Inland, the hamlets and villages of Romney Marsh proper are less frequented than the coastal towns and well worth seeing. These are quiet spots with ancient and historic churches — some of which, at some period in their past, served as caches for smugglers' contraband. Burmarsh, Newchurch, St. Mary in the Marsh, Ivychurch, Snargate, and Fairfield (all off Route A259), and Old Romney, Brenzett, and Brookland (on A259) are all typical. After Brookland, Route A259 crosses the border of Kent and heads into Rye (21 miles from Hythe) in neighboring East Sussex.

CHECKING IN: *Chantry* – This friendly half-timbered hotel is next to fine sandy beaches. Sycamore Gardens, Dymchurch (phone: 0303-873137). Moderate.

Red Tiles – A pleasant country hotel, it sits amid 2 acres of lawns and gardens only half a mile from good beaches. Warren Rd., Littlestone-on-Sea, New Romney (phone: 0679-62155). Moderate.

RYE: Along with Winchelsea, Rye is one of the two "Ancient Towns" added to the original Cinque Ports, though the receding sea and centuries of silt buildup have obstructed its port, limiting traffic to small coastal vessels and fishing boats. Now the harbor is no more than a narrow creek winding its way to town and Rye, essentially a medieval seaport stranded 2 miles inland, combines the flavor of a large fishing village with that of a remote country settlement. The effect is an alluring one that draws nearly as many visitors as Canterbury. Rye stands on an almost conical sandstone hill, its red roofs piled up to the point of the parish church on top, the whole fairy tale conception circled by a crumbling 14th-century wall. The town was razed by the French in 1377 and again in 1448, destroying the most historic buildings, but many of the houses erected during the late 15th century still grace the narrow, cobblestone streets. Gabled and half-timbered, Rye is quite simply a lovely town, and it retains the atmosphere of medieval times along with a measure of its former bustling activity.

Both the *Mermaid Inn,* rebuilt during the 15th century and rumored to have been a smugglers' rendezvous, and the timbered *Flushing Inn* (15th century) are excellent haunts for travelers. The works of the great clock (ca. 1560) in the 12th-century Church of St. Mary are thought to be among the oldest still functioning in England. Lamb House, a Georgian building on West Street, was the residence of novelist Henry James from 1898 until his death in 1916 (open Wednesday and Saturday afternoons, April to October). Fletcher's House, now a tea shop near Lion and Market streets, is thought to be the birthplace of the 16th-century dramatist John Fletcher. The 13th-century Ypres Tower (here pronounced Wipers) was purchased by the de Ypres family in the early 14th century; it is now a museum with exhibitions pertinent to the Cinque Ports and some local pottery. Rye specializes in pottery, and it's easy to pick up some good bargains in the many shops and workshops just off the High Street area.

Winchelsea, also added to the Cinque Ports alliance before the changing coastline ruined its harbor, was completely relocated to its present site in 1283 by Edward I. The church, begun soon afterward, is dedicated to St. Thomas à Becket. Parts of William Thackeray's *Denis Duval* are set in the two towns.

CHECKING IN: *George* – The tiled façade is a Georgian addition, but behind that is a 400-year-old Tudor inn, with oak beams and fireplaces. Centrally located. High St., Rye (phone: 0797-222114). Expensive.

***Mariners'* –** The reception and service are exceptionally warm in this lovely 17th-century house, now a 14-room hotel with restaurant. 15 High St., Rye (phone: 0797-223480). Expensive.

***Mermaid Inn* –** When Queen Elizabeth visited Rye in 1573, she stayed here. Even older than the George, this beautifully preserved inn was rebuilt in 1420 and is one of the most charming old hotels in England. Its walls still conceal the priest holes and secret staircase used to avoid arrest in the old days of pirates and smugglers. Mermaid St., Rye (phone: 0797-223065). Moderate.

EATING OUT: *Flackley Ash* – This cozy hotel, 4 miles from Rye, has a well-deserved reputation for its food prepared by owner-chef Clive Bennett, who also holds several "jazz weekends" during the year. London Rd., Peasmarsh (phone: 0797-21381). Moderate.

HASTINGS (ST. LEONARDS and BATTLE): Nine miles from Rye, Route A259 meets the coast at Hastings and adjoining St. Leonards. The small town of Battle is 6 miles inland. This area is of immense strategic and psychological importance to England, as becomes clear when its history is reviewed: It was here that the last successful invasion of the British Isles began.

Following the death of Edward the Confessor in January 1066, Harold of Wessex, the son of Edward's adviser, ascended to the throne of England. His claim to the monarchy was weak, however, and Duke William of Normandy felt his own to be more justified, since Edward had been a distant cousin and Harold himself, he said, had previously sworn to support his right to wear the crown on Edward's death.

It was just a few miles west of Hastings, at Pevensey Bay, that William landed his forces on September 28, 1066.

King Harold and his men were busy fighting his brother Tostig and the invading king of Norway (another claimant to the throne) in the north, and after defeating them at the Battle of Stamford Bridge, Harold and his tired army marched southward. They gathered support en route but it was not until the morning of October 14 that Harold's men, perhaps 10,000 ax- and spear-carrying foot soldiers, formed a shield wall along a ridge just north of Hastings. William's force was composed of a few thousand archers and several thousand mounted knights and armed men. Norman arrows rained on the defenders, and cavalry charges broke on the wall of spears and shields. In the late afternoon William faked a retreat, drawing many of the inexperienced English militiamen from their positions, and decimated them with his cavalry. King Harold and the remainder of his army were soon slaughtered. On the spot where Harold planted the Royal Standard, where he and his closest followers actually died, William the Conquerer erected Battle Abbey. By Christmas, William was crowned king of England in Westminster Abbey.

Hastings today is a popular resort much loved by the British for its wonderful setting between the hilly South Downs and the Channel coast. The original Cinque Port city stagnated after the harbor became clogged with silt during the late 12th century, and the 600-year sleep that followed kept the Old Town beautifully intact. This is at the east end of Hastings, where the town began as a fishing village. Narrow streets and age-old houses characterize this area, and two medieval churches survive, the 14th-century St. Clement's and the 15th-century All Saints'. Even the tall, skinny, tarred-wood sheds, or "net shops," built in the 16th century and used to store fishermen's nets, have survived along a part of the beach called the Stade. Near them, the Fishermen's Church is now a museum (open from the end of May through September; closed Fridays). The ruins of Hastings Castle, erected around the time of William's invasion, overlook the 3-mile beach area. The magnificent homes in this section of town reflect the resurgence of Hastings as a resort during the late 18th and 19th centuries when sea bathing became popular among the English. Eventually, the town grew westward to meet St. Leonards, a planned Regency "new" town laid out and developed by architects James and Decimus Burton in the 1830s. By the 1870s, the two had coalesced into one resort, with St. Leonards as its stylish western end. Hastings has all the usual seaside entertainments, and an amusement pier and pavilions plus a model railway add to the gaiety of its beachfront. The most beautiful aspect of the town, however, is natural — St. Clement's Caves (below the castle), once used by smugglers, and the cliffwalks to the east of Hastings.

The nearby small town of Battle, which derives its name from the famous Battle of Hastings, includes the abbey founded by William the Conquerer. The battle site, from the ridge where Harold formed his lines to the heights of Senlac and Telham on the far side of the valley, where William's forces gathered, is just southwest of the town. The abbey gatehouse is on Market Square, and the ruins of the abbey church (destroyed in about 1540) center on the spot where Harold fell. Those sections of the abbey that survived intact and those added in later years are now used as a school. (The Abbey ruins are open daily excluding Sunday mornings from October to March.)

CHECKING IN: *Beauport Park* – Set off in a beautiful park area, this stately Georgian hotel has a formal garden to add to the timeless atmosphere. The service is in keeping with that feeling of another age, and the heated outdoor pool is a bonus during the summer. Battle Rd., Hastings (phone: 0424-51222). Expensive.

En Route from Hastings – Route A259 continues along the coast and rounds Beachy Head, 20 miles westward and just beyond the seaside town of Eastbourne. This chalk headland is one of the highest coastal peaks in Sussex, 575 feet above the Channel, and the views out to sea or back over the South Downs make it a favorite lookout point. The coastal road then continues to the large and busy resort of Brighton, another 20 miles or so away. In summer, however, the coastal road is often clogged with traffic, and to avoid it you may want to forgo Beachy Head and take the inland route to Brighton, A27, which veers off from A259 at Pevensey. If time permits, you may even want to leave the sea and salt air behind temporarily and detour inland directly from Hastings to visit the Weald, the prosperous band of farmland that stretches between the North and South Downs as far west as Hampshire.

THE WEALD: Hawkhurst, reached from Hastings via A21, then A229, is not only a splendid and typical large village in the Weald but also an excellent base from which to explore the countryside. Hawkhurst grew in association with ancient iron and cloth industries, the wealth of which, together with agriculture, fashioned an elegant village of many weatherboarded, substantial houses. In the early 18th century, the town was also famous as the home of the notorious Hawkhurst Gang of smugglers who terrorized the region — their delinquent faces were well known at the *Mermaid Inn* in Rye where they would sit quaffing ale and smoking their pipes with loaded pistols on the tables, secure in the knowledge that no magistrate dared challenge them.

There are several places of interest, each within 15 miles of town. Northeast (along A229 as far as Sissinghurst) is Sissinghurst Castle, a beautiful Tudor house once owned by writers Victoria Sackville-West and Harold Nicolson, who laid out some of the loveliest formal gardens in the country, all within the red brick walls and open to the public from April to mid-October. Bodiam Castle, southeast of Hawkhurst (off A229), is a spectacular moated ruin, one of the best examples of medieval military architecture in Britain (closed Sundays from October to March). Southwest (along A265, outside the town of Burwash) is Bateman's, a 17th-century stone ironmaster's house that became the home of Rudyard Kipling and now is a museum of his life and work (open Saturdays through Wednesdays, April through October). Heathfield, west of Burwash, is a small country town where an interesting market is held on Sunday mornings. Northwest (follow the A268 out of Hawkhurst, then the A21) is Scotney Castle, a mile southeast of the village of Lamberhurst. This is a particularly romantic ruin, part 14th and part 17th century, surrounded by a moat and a picturesque garden (open afternoons except Mondays and Tuesdays, April through October). Two miles west of Lamberhurst is Bayham Abbey, one of the finest monastic ruins in the southeast.

Bayham Abbey is just north of B2169, 4 miles east of Royal Tunbridge Wells, the health resort that has been extremely popular since the discovery of the "healing powers" of its mineral waters in 1606. A promenade called The Pantiles, designed as a shopping and visitor area in 1638, is just as popular today. The mineral waters can be sampled from the springs at the far end of the walkway, and the *Duke of York* pub serves those looking for something a little stronger at tables outside its Victorian building on the promenade. Royal Tunbridge Wells, a relatively new town for this region, was at the height of its glory in the 18th century, until sniffing sea air and bathing in saltwater became the socially and physiologically proper thing to do and the smart set transferred its allegiance to the upstart Brighton on the coast. Queen Victoria spent time here as a princess and because of this and other royal visits the town — once simply Tunbridge Wells — was permitted by Edward VII to add "Royal" to its name in 1909.

Royal Tunbridge Wells is only 36 miles from London and if you decide to cut short your tour of southeast England and return to the capital, you can easily do so by taking Route A21, which passes just east of town. A slight detour along the way would allow you to visit Knole, one of the largest and most magnificent baronial mansions in England, outside the village of Sevenoaks on Route A225. The building, referred to by Virginia Woolf as "a town rather than a house" in her novel *Orlando,* sprawls over 3 acres and includes (according to legend) 7 courtyards corresponding to the days of the week, 52 staircases for the weeks, and 365 rooms — one for each day in the year. The house was begun in the mid-15th century by an archbishop of Canterbury, then belonged in turn to Henry VIII and Queen Elizabeth I, who gave it to the Sackville-West family. The state rooms contain a fine collection of portraits, including works by Reynolds and Gainsborough, silver, tapestries, and hangings. The furnishings are virtually as they were in Elizabethan times (open Wednesdays through Sundays, April through October).

The southeast route continues with a visit to Brighton. To get back to the coast from Royal Tunbridge Wells, take Route A267 to the quiet B2192, which wanders through woods down to Lewes. From there, A27 crosses the South Downs to the seaside city.

CHECKING IN: *Gravetye Manor* – Just west of Royal Tunbridge Wells is this ivy-covered Elizabethan manor house surrounded by glorious gardens. One of England's most impressive hostelries, its rooms are paneled with the estate's oak and brightened by bouquets of flowers. The restaurant's Michelin star is well deserved. 4 miles from East Grinstead (phone: Sharpthorne 0342-810567). Expensive.

Calverley – An elegant 18th-century stone mansion set in a delightful garden, the hotel overlooks the lower town. There are antiques throughout, but the chintz coverings detract more from the style than they add to the countrified atmosphere. Crescent Rd., Royal Tunbridge Wells (phone: 0892-26455). Moderate.

Royal Oak – This small, 18th-century weatherboarded inn has 12 rooms. The food is good (the restaurant is open to nonguests Saturday evenings and Sundays at lunch) and accommodations are very reasonable. Rye Rd., Hawkhurst (phone: 05805-2184). Inexpensive.

BRIGHTON: The popularity of England's most famous resort began in the late 18th century and developed hugely during the early 19th century, leaving a wonderful architectural legacy for the modern visitor. Chief among the attractions — the heirloom, you might say — is the Royal Pavilion, the seaside home of the eccentric Prince Regent who became King George IV. The Pavilion was begun in 1786, then transformed between 1815 and 1821 into the exotic Mogul palace that exists today. Inside, its rooms are crammed with gorgeous chinoiserie and fully furnished in the original grand style. Brighton's seafront — King's Road — is chockablock with fish and chip cafés, cotton candy stalls, and amusement arcades, and the Victorian Palace Pier adds to the carnival atmosphere. Another attraction is the Old Town, known as the Lanes, a picturesque area of narrow, brick-paved alleyways full of good tea shops, pubs, and antique shops. It's traffic-free and it will give you an idea of what Brighton was like before the fairy godmother touched her magic wand and turned the fishing village of Brighthelmstone first fashionable, then flossy. For a full report on the sights, hotels, and restaurants of this seaside resort, see *Brighton,* THE CITIES.

ARUNDEL: From Brighton, Route A27 hurries through a not particularly pleasing bit of coast, but the reward for the 20-mile drive is this small, medieval-looking town on the River Arun, spectacularly dominated by its massive castle and an equally large cathedral. The castle, family seat of the dukes of Norfolk, dates from the 11th century, though most of what is seen today — except for the Norman keep — was rebuilt in the old style in the 18th and 19th centuries. The picture gallery contains the dukes' collection, including paintings by Van Dyck, Gainsborough, and Reynolds, and on the grounds is the Roman Catholic Fitzalan Chapel, occupying a quarter of the town's 14th-century Anglican parish Church of St. Nicholas. The dual allegiance is explained by the fact that the dukes of Norfolk, who own the chapel, are Catholic — in the 1880s the fifteenth duke had a wall built to divide chapel from church and they still have separate entrances. The same duke had previously built the imposing, Gothic, Roman Catholic cathedral Church of St. Philip Neri. Around these two monoliths of castle and cathedral are many old houses and small inns, Potter's Museum of Curiosity (containing the work of a Victorian taxidermist and naturalist who set animals in nursery rhyme tableaux), and a cheerful Saturday morning market.

Less than a mile to the north is the 55-acre Wildfowl Trust, where you can watch a sampling of the world's waterfowl from observation hides. North again, in a 19th-century quarry and limeworks, is the Chalk Pits Museum at Amberley. On display in this large outdoor museum of industrial history are the original lime kilns, plus a blacksmith's shop, locomotive shed, a narrow-gauge railway, and much more.

CHICHESTER: The cathedral city of Chichester is 10 miles from Arundel. The original town was Roman and walled, and the city plan still reflects Roman beginnings in the two long, straight main streets that intersect at right angles at the 16th-century Market Cross. Portions of the walls, both Roman and medieval ones, remain, but Chichester today is predominantly a Georgian market town with many quiet corners and the lovely cathedral at its heart. The cathedral spire, visible from a distance, is a Victorian replacement of one that collapsed over a century ago, but the rest of the cathedral, built between 1091 and 1199, is largely Norman. The 15th-century bell tower is the only example of a detached belfry still surviving in England. The most attractive buildings of Georgian Chichester are close by on North Street and in an area called the Pallant, a city-within-a-city southeast of Market Cross, while the best of Roman Chichester is 1½ miles west of town. In 1960, workmen laying a water pipe at Fishbourne discovered the remains of a magnificent Roman palace built in AD 70. When fully excavated, it turned out to be the largest Roman palace yet found in Britain. Twelve of the mosaic floors can be seen and there is a museum telling the history of the site up to AD 280 (open year-round). In mid-July, Chichester stages the Chichester Festivities, a varied festival of the arts, which includes concerts in the cathedral. Better known is the top-flight Chichester Festival Theatre season, four plays running from May through September at a strikingly modern theater in the middle of a 40-acre parkland.

The nearby harbor is one of Britain's prettiest — it's a natural center for sailors with small boats. On its far shores, small resorts such as Bosham, West Itchenor, Emsworth, and Hayling Island are all quietly attractive. Goodwood House, 3 miles north on A286, is the historic home of the dukes of Richmond (open Sundays and Mondays, May through October; also open Tuesdays, Thursdays, and Sundays in August), and the park around it is the site of the racecourse where the "glorious" Goodwood Week of racing takes place at the beginning of August. Six miles north of the city, at Singleton, the Weald and Downland Open Air Museum, high on the South Downs, is especially worth a visit. Typical old buildings have been saved from destruction elsewhere in southeast England and transferred here, among them a 14th-century Kentish farmhouse, a 15th-century Wealdan hall house, and others (open daily April through October; open Sundays, Wednesdays, and bank holidays only November through March).

En Route from Chichester – Route A27 continues west to the bustling naval town of Portsmouth where you can board a car or passenger ferry that will cross the Spithead — a body of water no more than 4 miles wide — and deposit you 30 to 45 minutes later at Ryde or Fishbourne on the holiday Isle of Wight. The hovercraft from Southsea, a residential suburb of Portsmouth, makes the trip even faster — in 10 minutes. Farther west, other ferry, hydrofoil, and hovercraft services leave from Southampton and Lymington and cross the Solent, again a maximum 4 miles wide, to arrive on the island at Cowes or Yarmouth.

 CHECKING IN: *Ship* – This was originally a private house, built in 1790 for George Murray, one of Nelson's admirals. It is large and wonderfully old-fashioned in the Georgian manner. In April 1944, General Eisenhower dined here prior to D-day. North St., Chichester (phone: 0243-782028). Mod-erate.

Ship Inn – Very small (7 rooms) and friendly, it overlooks the harbor. West Itchenor (phone: 0243-512284). Moderate.

 EATING OUT: *Hole in the Wall* – This informal pub-restaurant is popular with Festival theatergoers. 1 St. Martin's St., Chichester (phone: 0243-782555). Inexpensive.

ISLE OF WIGHT: Though it was once part of the mainland, it's a mistake to think of the Isle of Wight as a small (23 by 13 miles) piece of England cast adrift in the Channel; it has a flavor of its own, at once pastoral and nautical. The island's northern end is flat, but its steep cliffs to the south are spectacular and draw the majority of visitors. Besides the seaside activity, walking is a major pastime here, and a network of footpaths leads nearly everywhere, including the circumference of the entire island. For most visitors, Ryde, one of the major resort towns, is the gateway to the Isle of Wight. On the southeast coast, Sandown, Shanklin, and Ventnor are strictly resorts, busy and particularly sunny ones, and they clearly reflect the Victorian popularity that established and expanded them. Of the three, Ventnor, terraced up to the highest point of the island, is the oldest and perhaps the most interesting. Inland, there are many small villages, doubly remote for their island setting: Godshill has many thatched cottages; Calbourne, too, has thatched cottages and one of the country's finest examples of an early-17th-century water mill, still in working order. Newport, in the center on the River Medina, is the capital, and it's strangely the least hurried town on the island. A mile southwest, Charles I was once held prisoner in Carisbrooke Castle, which is reputedly built on the site of a Roman fort; parts of it date back to the 12th century (open daily). On the north coast, Yarmouth is an ancient town and an important yachting center, but Cowes, divided in two by the Medina, is the headquarters of British yachting, internationally famous. The highlight of the regatta season is Cowes Week, the first week in August, when ocean racers from all over the world compete in the blue Solent. Cowes is not all ocean yachting, however — there are plenty of facilities for smaller boats. Osborne House, Queen Victoria's palatial Italianate retreat (she used it for over 50 years and died here in 1901), is just outside of Cowes. The perfectly preserved state apartments and a museum are open to the public from April to mid-October.

 CHECKING IN: *Winterbourne* – Charles Dickens, who lived here in 1849, called it "the prettiest place I ever saw in my life, at home or abroad." Today the hotel has magnificent sea views, fine cuisine, and an outdoor pool. Closed mid-November to mid-January. Bonchurch, near Ventnor (phone: 0983-852535). Moderate.

Farringford – Another "famous" Isle of Wight property, this once belonged to Alfred Lord Tennyson. In addition to 20 bedrooms, the hotel offers a number of cottages with fully equipped kitchens. Croquet, a 9-hole golf course, and an outdoor pool contribute to the country house atmosphere. Freshwater (phone: 0983-752500). Moderate.

En Route from the Isle of Wight – Sealink operates frequent car ferries between Portsmouth and Fishbourne and between Lymington and Yarmouth. There is a foot-passenger ferry from Portsmouth to Ryde and hovercraft service between Southsea and Ryde. Car ferries and hydrofoils depart daily year-round from Cowes to Southampton. The city suffered heavy damage during World War II, and as a result it is largely modern, though there are some medieval remains, including parts of the ancient walls and the Bargate, once the north gate of the old town. Southampton was already an important port in the Middle Ages, trading with Venice up to the early 16th century, but a setback in its fortunes came when the port of Bristol captured the tobacco and sugar trade with the New World — and the black slave trade. Thousands of early American settlers sailed from Bristol, but Southampton has the honor of having waved good-bye to the *Mayflower* in 1620, and there is a Pilgrim Fathers' Memorial commemorating that voyage near the Royal Pier. When the day of the large transatlantic liners dawned, Southampton became Britain's chief port for the Atlantic crossing, bar none. Today, the last luxury liner making anything resembling a regularly scheduled transatlantic run is the *Queen Elizabeth 2,* and its home port is Southampton. Southampton is also an important embarkation point for cross-Channel ferries to Cherbourg and Le Havre, in France.

The cathedral city of Winchester, the starting point of our *Southwest England* route, is only 12 miles north of Southampton via Route A33. If you won't be touring Wiltshire, Devon, and Cornwall, you can visit Winchester, then proceed out of town on the A33, which meets the M3 motorway some 10 miles north and will speed you back to London. The distance from Winchester to London is 66 miles.

Channel Islands

Geographically the Channel Islands, lying as little as 8 miles off the coastline of Normandy and Brittany, are part of France. But historically the islands — Jersey, Guernsey, Alderney, Sark, Herm, Jethou, and a smattering of islets — have been connected with the British Crown for more than a thousand years. They were part of the Duchy of Normandy when William the Conqueror invaded England in 1066 and became its king, and they remained part of Britain when Normandy was subsequently reunited with the rest of France.

This heritage has given the Channel Islands a curiously mixed identity — they are a sort of halfway house between England and France stuck out in the English Channel. Partly self-governing, and with a hodgepodge of English and French laws, they retain French as their official language yet universally speak English. They issue their own banknotes, coinage, and stamps, yet British currency is accepted. The food is French, but habits and manners are English.

The Channel Islands attract upward of 2 million tourists every year. Their popularity is partly due to the feeling of being "abroad" that the blend of cultures gives to both British and French visitors, partly due to their enviable sunshine record (about 100 miles south of the English mainland, they get the best of the weather), and partly because no two of the islands are the same and so offer visitors the opportunity to have one or several kinds of holiday. Jersey, the most southerly of the islands and also the largest (although it only measures 9 by 5 miles), has a reputation as a "swinging" holiday resort with a wide choice of hotels, restaurants, and entertainments. Quieter, centrally situated Guernsey, the other main island, is only now turning from agriculture to tourism as its principal livelihood. And on the smaller islands there is little to do except eat, sleep, walk, and admire some stunning seascapes and cliff scenery.

The islanders have been molded both by history and by the surroundings in which they live. Calm, unhurried, contemplative, yet with a sharp sense of humor, they also have remarkably sophisticated taste when it comes to food and wine — the development of smart restaurants on wealthy Jersey or even the smuggling of fine wines and spirits, which is still said to flourish, may be due to the close proximity of France.

They couple this with an enthusiasm for their own dialect — a Norman-French patois that differs from island to island and can still be heard in the countryside and markets — and with an equal enthusiasm for their ancient traditions, the most famous of which is a legal oddity dating from the Norman period and is known as the *Clameur de Haro*. There's no need to call an attorney if you feel that you are being legally wronged in Jersey or Guernsey

— you just drop to your knees and shout: *"Haro! Haro! Haro! à l'aide, mon Prince, on me fait tort."* ("Help, my Prince, they are wronging me.") This has the same effect as a court injunction, but nowadays it is only used in cases of interference with real property. The penalties for ridiculing or abusing this ancient law are heavy.

Other island oddities include the ormer, a rubbery-fleshed shellfish related to the abalone but unique to the Channel Islands, which has a particularly attractive mother-of-pearl-like shell; and giant cabbages with stalks so long that walking sticks can be made from them. More practically, for souvenir hunters, there are the heavy-knit oiled wool sweaters known as "jerseys" and "guernseys," which have given their names to knitwear all over the world.

In recent years, Jersey and Guernsey have both made strenuous attempts to extend their tourist seasons. Both offer discounted, inclusive winter holidays at major hotels, and provide entertainment that often comes up to London standards. This trend is likely to continue because, as the islanders point out, the climate is similar to that of Bermuda and thus offers an escape from British winters.

Prospective visitors should also note, however, that because the islands are exposed to the Atlantic, the sea is colder than you might expect, and swimming is comfortable only between late April and late September. The islands are also subject to occasional dense sea mists that can disrupt air traffic. Such disadvantages, however, are easily outweighed by the exceptionally clean air.

Jersey has led the way in introducing new attractions such as a spring festival and an annual *Good Food Festival,* which encourages island restaurants to submit their culinary delights to be judged by both French and English gourmets. But the most popular carnival on both Jersey and Guernsey dates back to the 1902 coronation, the annual Battle of Flowers. This colorful and picturesque event, involving processions of floats decorated with flowers as well as other, less formal, celebrations, takes place in August and is the high spot of any visit.

Hotel prices for a double room throughout the Channel Islands range from $80 in places noted as expensive to $50 to $80, moderate. Lodging costing less than $50 is considered inexpensive. A expensive dinner for two, without wine, drinks, or tips, begins at $30. A moderately priced meal will be in the $15 to $30 range, and anything below $15 is inexpensive.

JERSEY

Jersey, the largest of the Channel Islands, got its name from the Normans, who called it Gersey ("the grassy isle"). Between the two world wars it acquired the nickname of "the honeymoon isle" because of its popularity with newlyweds holidaying there from the mainland. (Traditionally, March was the most popular time for honeymooning because couples who married at the end of the fiscal year could claim full tax allowances for the preceding year. Now, however, honeymooning is a year-round activity, and newlyweds even get a small gift from the local tourism department!)

It was in this interwar period that Jersey began the transition from isolated farming community to modern holiday resort. The main attraction then was the big, safe, sandy beaches, and the inexpensive accommodations. Today the beaches are unchanged, but now the island also boasts a sparkling nightlife as well as many fine shops, hotels, and restaurants. It also manages to pack into its tiny land area some glorious woodland walks, lots of quiet countryside where Jersey cattle graze, historic castles, and interesting sightseeing trips.

The island's capital is the south coast port of St. Helier, which contains about half of Jersey's population. It is built around the rather ugly, though recently improved, harbor, and is divided by a massive rock on which stands the Napoleonic Fort Regent — now converted into a comprehensive, all-weather entertainment, leisure, and sports complex complemented by a new marina frequented by visiting yachts. The town itself is a maze of narrow streets, some of them for pedestrians only and many having French names, with a big range of shops specializing in low-duty luxury goods.

St. Helier is on one of Jersey's best beaches, St. Aubin's Bay, and out in the bay stands Elizabeth Castle, built on rocks in the sixteenth century and named after Queen Elizabeth I by Sir Walter Raleigh when he was governor of the island. At low tide the castle can be reached on foot by causeway, but there are boat services at other times. It is attractively floodlit on summer nights.

There is another fine castle 5 miles out of St. Helier on the east coast at Gorey: Mont Orgueil Castle. Built to defend Jersey against attacks from neighboring France from the twelfth to the fifteenth century, it is beautifully preserved and, again, floodlit. Below the castle, the tiny fishing village of Gorey is worth exploring, and is a good place to stop and eat. Pub lunches are popular, and are an excellent value.

The north coast of the island is composed mostly of cliffs, which hide many small, sheltered beaches and tiny harbors. You'll do some excellent walking here, since there are fine views of the other islands as well as of France.

The west coast of the rectangular island consists almost entirely of one huge bay, St. Ouen's Bay, backed by sand dunes. Winter seas here, rolling in from the Atlantic, can be awesome, but in summer St. Ouen's is a popular beach too large to ever get crowded.

In addition to St. Aubin's Bay, the south coast has the island's most attractive bay, St. Brelade's, which has good recreational facilities as well as miles of sand. The nearby Portelet Bay is also popular, and is very sheltered. Those who tire of the beach will find an interesting little structure hidden beside St. Brelade's Church called the Fishermen's Chapel; it is an ancient monastic chapel dating back in parts to the sixth century, and has some recently discovered fourteenth-century murals on the walls (they are seen at their best in damp weather).

Visits to the island's chapels, old Norman churches, and more modern churches (the "glass church," at Millbrook, is lavishly decorated with glass by the Parisian artist René Lalique) are free. But even the island's organized excursions are relatively inexpensive, and three of them are particularly worthwhile.

The first of these is to St. Peter's Bunker, in the center of the island. This museum of the German occupation of the Channel Islands during World War

II is housed in a seven-room German bunker. It provides a fascinating insight into how both occupiers and occupied lived during the war years.

Far more ancient history is to be found at La Hougue Bie, one of Jersey's two best-preserved Neolithic tombs. Visitors to the site, at Grouville, can creep down the 33-foot-long tunnel entrance to the tomb itself, where the temperature remains constant whatever the weather. The tomb is covered by a 40-foot-high mound on which two medieval chapels were constructed under a single roof. There are other historical displays on the grounds as well.

Finally, one of Europe's most interesting zoos has been set up in the grounds of Les Augrés Manor in the northeast of the island by author and naturalist Gerald Durrell. Jersey Zoo is not dedicated to the display of animals, or to entertainment, but to the preservation and rearing of some of the world's rarer species. Watch for the families of lowland gorillas, orangutans, Tibetan white-eared pheasants, and Egyptian bare-faced ibis, all very rare.

Jersey has direct airline links with most British airports, and there are daily services to and from London — Heathrow and Gatwick — taking only 45 minutes. There is also air transportation from France. Sealink car ferries connect Jersey both with France and with the British ports of Weymouth and Portsmouth (Sealink, Continental Ticket and Information Office, PO Box 29, Victoria Station, London SW1V 1JX), and Channel Island Ferries has service from Portsmouth to both Jersey and Guersey (Channel Island Ferries, Wharf Rd., Portsmouth PO2 8RU). A number of firms specialize in inclusive holidays to the Channel Islands from Britain; these include Preston Travel (4 Dollis Park, London N3) and Modernline Travel (Kingsgate House, Kingsgate Pl., London NW6 4HG).

 CHECKING IN: *Longueville Manor* – A magnificently restored 33-room manor house, with elegant furnishings throughout. There is also a heated outdoor pool and riding stables on its 15 acres. St. Helier (phone: 0534-25501). Expensive.

***L'Horizon* –** Nestled in St. Brelade's Bay, considered one of Europe's finest beaches, this 106-room hotel has its own indoor pool. St. Brelade's Bay (phone: 0534-43101). Expensive.

***Water's Edge* –** At the bottom of a steep hill, beside the sea on the north coast, this handsome 56-room hotel is well away from the crowds and has a swimming pool. Bouley Bay (phone: 0534-62777). Moderate.

 EATING OUT: *Victoria's* – A mock-Victorian restaurant in one of Jersey's period hotels, the *Grand,* overlooking the seafront. French nouvelle cuisine recommended by Egon Ronay. Esplanade, St. Helier (phone: 0534-72255). Expensive to moderate.

***La Capannina* –** Much favored by residents, this place specializes in Italian dishes. Halkett Pl., St. Helier (phone: 0534-34602). Moderate.

GUERNSEY

The second largest of the Channel Islands, Guernsey is roughly triangular; its 5-mile-long east coast contains its two towns: the industrial port of St. Sampson, and the island's capital of St. Peter Port. The latter is a pretty town, built on a hillside overlooking the large harbor and the smaller islands of Sark,

Herm, and Jethou. Like the other islands, Guernsey enjoys tax advantages, which makes shopping in the narrow, winding streets of St. Peter Port doubly appealing.

St. Peter Port is dominated by the town church, a granite building known as "the Cathedral of the Channel Islands," and by the medieval fortress of Castle Cornet, which overlooks the harbor. Castle Cornet saw action in the English Civil War, when the Royalist governor held it throughout a 9-year siege against a predominantly Cromwellian populace (the castle finally fell to the Parliamentary forces in 1651).

In addition to the castle and the church, St. Peter Port's most interesting building is Hauteville House, the nineteenth-century home of the French writer Victor Hugo who lived in exile in Guernsey from 1855 to 1870; it now belongs to the City of Paris, and is furnished and maintained just as it was in the eccentric Hugo's day. Hugo chose the house because of its fine views of the French coast.

With beaches on all three of its coasts, Guernsey can provide a sheltered bay whatever the direction of the wind. In good weather, the big, sandy beaches of the west coast are the best, particularly Cobo and Vazon, although swimmers should beware of the strong currents in places marked with danger flags. Children will like Portelet, a little harbor forming a tiny beach of its own within Rocquaine Bay. Lihou, a tiny islet, is offshore, as are the dangerous rocks of the Hanois, marked with a tall lighthouse.

There are several lovely walks along the picturesque south coast, which has a number of rocky headlands, towering cliffs, and good, sandy beaches — of these, Moulin Huet, Petit Bôt, Petit Port, and Saints Bay are the most popular. Visitors can stroll down to the beach along wooded paths beside streams known as "douits."

Although it's the beaches and cliffs that draw tourists, this is still predominantly a horticultural island, and much of the interior is given over to greenhouses in which early tomatoes and flowers are cultivated.

Many of the islanders' houses are notable for having "kitchen stones" sticking out from their chimneys. Guernsey was at one time a superstitious island, and legend says that passing witches will not curse a house if they can stop and warm themselves by the chimney.

Some of the parish churches on the island are Norman in origin. The sloping aisle of one of these, St. Pierre du Bois (St. Peter-in-the-Wood), has lead to a popular local joke that any bridegroom leaving the church after a wedding is already going downhill. Outside St. Martin's Church stands Guernsey's most famous resident, a prehistoric stone figure known as La Grandmère de Chimquiere or, more simply, La Grandmère. Locals do not pass La Grandmère without saying good morning to her.

Excursions on Guernsey are varied, and a circular coach tour of the island is interesting. You can get anywhere on the bus services radiating from St. Peter Port. But do not miss seeing the grim German Underground Hospital, a relic of the World War II occupation, or the shell-dotted Little Chapel at Les Vauxbelets, an 18-by-10-foot model of Our Lady of Lourdes shrine in France — big enough only for a priest and a congregation of two.

Guernsey has direct airline links with most British airports, and there are daily services to and from London (Heathrow and Gatwick) and Southampton. The islands' own Aurigny Airlines (based at Alderney Airport on Alderney island) provides a regular inter-island service as well as connections to Southampton and France. Car ferries run between Weymouth, Portsmouth, and Guernsey (Sealink, British Ferries, and Channel Island Ferries). For package tours to Guernsey, contact the firms listed for Jersey.

CHECKING IN: *St. Pierre Park* – Fast becoming the island's best, this smoothly run modern hotel has tennis courts, swimming pool, sauna, solarium, and a host of other facilities. It's popular with business travelers as well as tourists. St. Peter Port (phone: 0481-24921). Expensive.

Old Government House – Once the town's principal hotel, it is still striving to retain that position by combining old-fashioned courtesy with 68 modern rooms and a pool. Anne's Pl., St. Peter Port (phone: 0481-24921). Expensive to moderate.

Les Douvres – This restored 15th-century manor house on the south coast is within easy reach of St. Peter Port. There are 18 guestrooms and a heated swimming pool. St. Martins (phone: 0481-38731). Expensive to moderate.

La Frégate – This restored 18th-century manor house on a hill above the harbor has a good restaurant (French, natch) and 13 modern rooms, most of which overlook the sea and the other Channel Islands. Les Cotils, St. Peter Port (phone: 0481-24624). Moderate.

Le Chalet – A mile outside St. Peter Port, above a sheltered but stony beach, Le Chalet offers a peaceful atmosphere, fine sea views, and a good restaurant. 51 rooms. Closed in winter. Fermain Bay (phone: 0481-35716). Moderate.

Cobo Bay – This modern hotel on the west coast overlooks the beach and has 29 rooms. Cobo Bay (phone: 0481-57102). Moderate.

EATING OUT: *Steak and Stilton* – A popular seafront lunch spot, it's also nice in the evenings. The menu combines local fish dishes with those suggested by its name. Esplanade, St. Peter Port (phone: 0481-23080). Moderate.

ALDERNEY

Besides being the most northerly and the most barren of the Channel Islands, Alderney is often ignored by tourists. It's only about 4 miles long and a mile wide, and although it has a massive breakwater built as part of a Napoleonic military harbor, the port itself is a tiny one. Most of the population of only 1,700 live in or around the centrally situated town of St. Anne.

Hotel accommodation is usually available in all but the peak months, but can be expensive for what you get. For diversion there is sailing, windsurfing, tennis, squash, or simply walking alongside or swimming in one of the safe and sandy south coast bays. It's also possible to take a scenic ride on the Channel Island's only working railway.

Aurigny Airlines provides several flights a day from and to Southampton, and has frequent interisland flights from Guernsey and Jersey. There are also flights and a summer hydrofoil service to France, 8 miles away. There are no interisland boats; you have to hire a fishing boat.

SARK

An unspoiled atmosphere and an extraordinary individuality are the hallmarks of the feudal island of Sark — a rocky plateau of an island 9 miles off the coast of Guernsey. Its constitution dates back to Elizabethan times, and it still has a hereditary ruler, called the Seigneur, who today is Mr. Michael

Beaumont, son of the famous Dame of Sark and her American husband. Cars, divorce, adoption, and income tax are banned on the island, and the Seigneur retains such ancient feudal rights as that of being the only person on Sark who may keep pigeons (a rule designed to protect seed corn).

Sark is, in fact, the smallest state in Europe, which no doubt adds to its attraction for visitors. Several small bays and coves are good for swimming and sunbathing; Grande Grave is one of the most popular. There is no actual town and most tourists travel around by horse-drawn carriage (expensive) or hired bicycle (inexpensive), and visit tiny Creux Harbour; the sixteenth-century Seigneurie with its walled gardens; the two-man prison, Sark's only other noteworthy building; and the precipitous path known as La Coupée, where only 10 feet of soft rock and clay stops Sark from dividing itself into two islands.

There is frequent ferry service from Guernsey, weather permitting, and summer excursions also run from Jersey.

HERM

The attractive little island of Herm, 3 miles off Guernsey's capital of St. Peter Port, belongs to "King" Peter Wood, an ex-Army officer who leases and farms it. Roughly 1½ miles long and ½ mile wide, it is a Channel Island in miniature, with cliffs on its northern tip and long, sandy beaches to the south.

It's a very popular destination for day-trippers from Guernsey, but some visitors like to stay overnight because of the island's solitude. A pub, some shops, and the island's only hotel cluster around the harbor, and footpaths lead from there to the common, the beaches (Belvoir Bay, on the east coast, is the best), and the farm. Shell Beach, also on the east coast, is the most famous beach in the Channel Islands: Instead of sand, it is made up of millions of tiny shells washed up by the Gulf Stream — many of them originating in the Caribbean.

A frequent launch service operates from St. Peter Port, Guernsey, in summer; winter visitors are met by arrangement.

 CHECKING IN: *White House* – An unpretentious yet comfortable hotel (the only one on the island), offering an unexpectedly high standard of service for so small an island. Several of its 32 rooms feature superb views and were so much in demand that 20 more were added in 3 cottages on the grounds. Closed November through April 24 (phone: Guernsey 22159). Moderate.

JETHOU

This island, once the home of the English writer Sir Compton Mackenzie, is privately owned and cannot be visited.

Southwest England

That the legendary Arthur should spring from this distant corner of England isn't surprising. For here, where the island narrows down to a horny point separating the English Channel from the Atlantic, the boundaries between the natural and supernatural are very indistinct. It doesn't take long to notice it — a constant tug on your imagination, the sense that the low green hills and languorous rivers simmer with an animation barely and only intermittently apparent to human senses. This, after all, is a land where walking sticks sprout into flowering hawthorns, where dancing maidens turn to stone, and where a baby delivered to an old magician on the crest of a fiery wave becomes a warrior, a king, a superhuman mortal who unites and gives identity to the English people. Even today, when modern sensibilities are so ruthlessly rational, there are quite sane folk who claim that fairies dance on the Dorset coast and pixies bedevil Dartmoor travelers.

The land itself conspires to enchant. To the east, Dorset's rich dairyland folds and unfolds in a continuous succession of hills and vales, while Somerset's miles of meadows and orchards are cradled in a basin protected on all sides by hills and the sea. In the heart of Devon, the county occupying the broad square of the peninsula, is Dartmoor, a solitary and taciturn landscape of bare hills bristling with strange winds. Beyond, and to the end of England, lie the neat, stone-walled fields and lanes of Cornwall. But nowhere does the magic seduce as powerfully as where land meets the sea, and the southwest has more miles of coastline than any other part of England. Here are long strands of beach that disappear with the tide, steep coves nearly obscured by their dense foliage, headlands shrouded in mist, and towering black cliffs that meet the crashing sea in an Olympian test of wills.

For all its wildness, though, the southwest is essentially a human landscape. Thousands of years of habitation by man has shaped the countryside as surely and as gradually as the elements. The soft, sculpted shape of the hills is the result of centuries of plowing and grazing, and the high-hedged roads that have carried countless generations from village to village are etched deeply on the land. It's the cluster of thatched cottages covered with primroses, the isolated church standing on an open knoll above the sea, that please the eye as much as the grandeur of the setting.

Everywhere are reminders of the successive occupants of the land, from paleolithic drawings in the Mendip caves to a deserted World War II air force base near Bodmin Moor. Bronze Age circles, Iron Age villages, Celtic hill towns, Roman roads, Saxon farms, Norman churches and cathedrals, Tudor coastal fortifications, grand Georgian mansions, and Victorian resorts all combine to make this part of the country a visible record of English history. Some sites, like Stonehenge or the Normans' magnificent cathedrals, are well known, but others, perhaps the most rewarding, are those you come across yourself — an enigmatic formation of stones in the middle of a sheep pasture, or a fanciful church carving done by a nameless artisan of the Middle Ages.

The southwest is hardly an undiscovered paradise. Britons come by the droves to enjoy Cornwall's and Devon's fine beaches and warm weather. But apart from tourism, people make their livings much as they have for centuries, by sheep herding, dairy farming, fishing, and sea trade. There is now a good deal of mining for china clay around St. Austell, but tin mining, which for many hundreds of years brought wealth to Cornwall (or at least to some of its families), is almost a thing of the past. Plymouth and Exeter, both ports, are the only cities of any size that Devon and Cornwall can claim, and although the population in resort towns swells with summer visitors, the rest of the year you'd have to search a bit to find a crowd.

The route we suggest starts in Winchester and heads west to Sherborne — two Saxon towns that have arrived at the twentieth century with their vitality and charm intact — before plunging south through Dorset's rolling green countryside, then following the Dorset coast to Exeter, the gateway to Devon and Cornwall. The route then meanders through Dartmoor and heads back to the coast at the south Devon sea towns of Dartmouth and Plymouth. Crossing the River Tamar into Cornwall, the route hugs the coast all the way to the Lizard and Land's End before turning north. Then it climbs up the spectacular west coast of Cornwall, makes a loop through Bodmin Moor, and returns to the coast to stop at Tintagel, the legendary birthplace of Arthur. From here the route follows the steep and wooded north coast of Devon, passes into Somerset and Exmoor Forest, then cuts across the Somerset levels to the historic town of Glastonbury and the Cheddar Caves.

Take your time through this country. Much of its beauty and charm is to be found down exasperatingly narrow lanes that can't be taken at more than 20 miles an hour or along public footpaths that link village to village. There is also an extensive system of splendid coastal footpaths that even at the height of the tourist season are quiet, private retreats. (The National Trust, which maintains some of these paths, along with scores of historic sites, isn't supported by government funds, as most people think. So don't pass up its contribution boxes without expressing — in cash, that is — your appreciation for the fine job it does.) One last tip: Most towns and villages with tourist attractions have large car parks (parking lots) near the center of town. Do use them. You'll save yourself the aggravation of trying to park on streets built for foot traffic — and possibly a dented fender.

There are so many excellent small hotels in this neck of the woods that you'll be tempted to extend your stay just to sample them all. Most are also well known for their food and open their restaurants to nonresidents. These hotels aren't inexpensive, but they are good value for the money. For a double room with breakfast, expect to pay between $80 and $110 at places we list as expensive; $45 to $80 for those in the moderate range; and between $25 and $45 for those listed as inexpensive. Restaurants listed as expensive will charge $40 and up for a meal for two excluding wine; moderate ones will cost between $20 and $40; and the inexpensive ones, less than $20.

WINCHESTER: Although Winchester lies slightly to the east of the center of England, it is, nonetheless, an excellent place to start a tour of the southwest. Here one meets the various people who overran, then settled, that part of England: Celts founded the town, Romans took it over, Saxons made it their capital, Danes besieged it, and Normans built the cathedral that presides majestically over it.

Sheltered between the green hills of the Hampshire downs and fed by the gentle River Itchen, Winchester takes its physical character primarily from the 18th century — Great Minster Street near the cathedral is a charming example of the graceful architecture that period produced. But it is the harmonious mix of buildings from every era, including low brick structures from the last few decades, and the welcome lack of quaint trappings that give Winchester its air of vitality.

The main tourist area, also the town's business and shopping district, runs along High Street, from the statue of Alfred the Great, the Saxon king who in 871 made this the capital of Wessex, at the east end, to Westgate, one of two gates remaining from the old city walls, at the west end. Westgate, which from the 16th century on was the town's prison (Charles I was among its inmates), is now a small museum. Prisoners' graffiti cover the walls and floors, and among the artifacts on display is the City Coffer, a 16th-century oak- and iron-bound casket at least 6 feet long, 4 feet wide, and 3 feet deep, a relic from the days when a city's coffer was something more substantial than the bottom line of an annual report. (Open daily; admission charge.)

Just south of Westgate, and adjacent to the new Crown Court building, is the Great Hall, all that remains of the Norman castle that was a royal residence until destroyed by Oliver Cromwell's Parliamentarians in 1645 and considered to be one of the finest examples of a medieval hall in England. The Great Hall's most famous possession is King Arthur's Round Table. No one claims this great oak table 18 feet in diameter is *the* legendary table of Arthur's court, since it dates from only the 14th century. But such was the continuing power of Arthur's legend that nearly a thousand years after his death, a shrewd King Henry VIII, wanting to strengthen his family's fairly recent claim to the throne, had the table painted with Arthur seated above a Tudor rose (open daily).

At the center of Winchester, physically and spiritually, stands its magnificent cathedral. The massive transepts are Norman, but the long nave, with its intricate web of fan vaulting, is the work of William of Wykeham, a 14th-century bishop who also founded Winchester College (southeast of the cathedral), one of the oldest schools in England (open daily). The *Wessex* hotel, whose dining room faces the cathedral across the green expanse of the close, is a perfect place for afternoon tea. If time permits, take a walk along the Weirs, which follow the Itchen through town, past lovely gardens and the ruins of the Bishop's Castle (also a victim of the Civil War). Continue on the footpath beside the river for another mile or so and you'll come to the Hospital of St. Cross, founded in the early 12th century for indigent men (open weekdays).

CHECKING IN: *Fifehead Manor* – On the site of Saxon Earl Harold's and Lady Godiva's estate, this small hotel offers large, comfortably furnished rooms and a warm country ambience. The mullioned-windowed and oak-paneled dining room is especially pleasant. Closed 2 weeks at Christmas. Middle Wallop, Stockbridge, about 15 miles west of Winchester (phone: 0264-781565). Expensive to moderate.

Lainston House – This Georgian mansion, surrounded by 60 acres of parkland, offers an authentic taste of English country living. The restaurant serves Swiss-influenced cuisine. Two miles from Winchester on A272 to Stockbridge. Sparsholt (phone: 0962-63588). Expensive.

SALISBURY: Compared to Winchester, Salisbury is a mere pup of a city. It wasn't until the 13th century that the church, exasperated by constant quarrels with its military neighbors and tired of the harsh weather it suffered from its exposed position on top of the hill at Old Sarum, decided to move the cathedral to the low-lying meadows beside the River Avon. The very elegant cathedral is crowned by the highest spire (404 feet) and houses the oldest clock (c. 1386) in the country. Many other buildings in town present fine examples of medieval and Georgian architecture: Mompesson House, built in 1701, retains much of its original plasterwork and paneling; part of Malmesbury House dates from the 14th century (visits by appointment only). A colorful market has been held in Salisbury every Tuesday since 1227. Now held Saturdays as well.

About 10 miles north, standing silently on the bleak Salisbury Plain, is Stonehenge, a wonder of the world that attracts about three quarters of a million visitors a year. The site (about 100 feet in diameter) consists of several earthen banks and barrows (burial mounds); concentric circles of standing stones, some capped in pairs with lintels; and an avenue leading away from the site (originally toward the River Avon). Erected in three stages, beginning in about 3000 BC, some of the stones are aligned with astronomical events (the position of the sun at summer solstice, for example). As a result, it is thought that the site may have had some primitive religious significance. Although the area is surrounded by wire fencing to deter latter-day druids from performing occult rituals, there is none of the usual touristy clutter and the surrounding rolling, grassy countryside is devoid of 20th-century intrusions. (For more about Stonehenge, see *Ancient Monuments and Ruins,* DIVERSIONS.)

The broad plain north of Salisbury probably contains more prehistoric monuments per square mile than any other part of England. There are literally dozens of other relics left behind by men and women who worked the plain as early as 6,000 years ago. Woodhenge, a few miles to the northeast of Stonehenge, consists of six concentric rings of post holes whose timbers probably supported a circular temple. Durrington Walls, a 30-acre earthwork with a circular structure near the town of Durrington, is probably another temple. Then there are the numerous barrows: long barrows, round barrows, bowl-shaped, disk-shaped, and bell-shaped barrows. The *Official Guide to Stonehenge* by the Department of the Environment shows the location of many of the barrows and temples near Stonehenge.

 CHECKING IN: *Rose and Crown* – Right on the bank of the Avon, it's a happy amalgam of half-timbered ancient inn and comfortable modern hotel. Harnham Rd., Harnham, near Salisbury (phone: 0722-27908). Expensive.

White Hart – A city landmark near the cathedral with a Georgian, pillared portico and rooms in traditional style stocked with plenty of comforts. 1 St. John St., Salisbury (phone: 0722-27476). Moderate.

 EATING OUT: Salisbury's bustling downtown is full of pubs, and you could hardly go wrong stopping at any for a tasty pub lunch. If you're not deterred by convivial lunchtime crowds, try the *Haunch of Venison,* a venerable old pub smack in the center of things with a reputation for good food, or the *New Inn,* a cozy 15th-century pub near the cathedral.

Harper's – The place for nouvelle English cuisine, with excellent, home-cooked, well-flavored dishes chalked up on a blackboard, and imaginative ways of treating old favorites — lamb with apricot and cider sauce, for example — and traditional desserts. 7 Ox Row, The Market Square, Salisbury (phone: 0722-333118). Moderate.

Mayor Ivie – This small, pleasant restaurant is one of a growing number devoted to old English cuisine. Stilton cheese and apple turnovers, spiced pork, and homemade breads are some of its specialties; the menu changes every 3 months. Dinner only; closed Sundays. 2-4 Ivy St., Salisbury (phone: 0722-333948). Moderate.

En Route from Salisbury – The A3094 follows the River Avon, but at a safe distance, out of Salisbury to Wilton, passing through the pretty little village of Netherhampton. Wilton was once the capital of King Egbert's Wessex and Kent, and for many years its abbey was Salisbury's ecclesiastical rival. The abbey was dissolved by Henry VIII and the land given to the Earl of Pembroke. The opulent Wilton House that now stands on the abbey grounds was designed by Inigo Jones and contains a superb collection of art and furnishings, and enough gilt to blind (open Tuesdays through Saturdays and Sunday afternoons from April to mid-October; admission charge). Wilton also boasts what is probably the only Italianate basilica in the neighborhood and is the home of Wilton Carpets, which has been turning out fine wool carpets since the 17th century (factory tours weekdays year-round).

Although in this countryside of tidy villages tucked in the folds of green hills it is usually advisable to stick to secondary roads, take the main road, A30, from Wilton to Sherborne. After you pass the town of Shaftesbury, one of the wealthiest cities in England until its powerful abbey was destroyed by Henry VIII, there's a stretch of road that affords some of the most scenic driving in the country. To your left, a 15-mile-long escarpment rises dramatically over the gentle rolling pastures of Blackmoor Vale. Objectively, it's not very high, perhaps 400 to 500 feet. But it comes on so suddenly that Thomas Hardy described it as the "green sea of Blackmoor Vale washing up to the foot of the bare chalk uplands." For Hardy fans, there is an obligatory stop nearby. About 5 miles outside Shaftesbury, turn left onto B3092 for another 5 miles to the pretty, prosperous village of Marnhull, transformed by Hardy into Marlott, the birthplace of the fictional Tess of the d'Urbervilles. Tess Cottage, supposedly the cottage Hardy had in mind when creating the Derbyfields, stands about a mile from the village church. It's a private residence, but can be viewed from the road. Head back to A30 via Fifehead Magdalen, the location of which above the Stour River is as pretty as its name is melodious.

SHERBORNE: Even before you reach Sherborne, you catch a glimpse of its powerful past. Standing on a knoll to the southeast of town are the ruins of Sherborne Castle, a magnificent fortified palace built in the early 12th century by Roger de Caen, bishop of Sarum and, at his height, second in power only to Henry I. Even the remains are impressive: A grassy moat 30 feet deep encircles the site, and the thick walls and gracefully vaulted hallways still standing catch the late afternoon sun with a special brilliance. The castle passed back and forth between the monarchy and the church, and then to Sir Walter Raleigh (open daily). Eventually it was razed by Parliamentarian troops in the Civil War. From the southeast corner of the castle keep you can see "new" Sherborne Castle, an Elizabethan house built by Raleigh after he despaired of ever modernizing Bishop Roger's castle. In the Digby family since 1617, the house contains an impressive collection of paintings, furniture, and porcelain. Sherborne Castle and its grounds, landscaped by Capability Brown, are open Thursdays, weekends, and bank holidays, Easter through September; admission charge.

Like Winchester, Sherborne was a power long before the Normans came. It was chosen as one of two cathedral cities in Wessex in 707, and for the next 400 years the Saxon bishop-warriors consolidated the city's power and prestige. When the Normans moved the See to Sarum in the 11th century, the church became an abbey, and when Henry VIII dissolved the monasteries, the townsfolk bought it for £300 and made it their parish church. Much of the splendid Norman church, built of golden-colored Ham Hill stone, remains, and there's even a door on the west front that dates from the Saxon cathedral.

Sherborne has long since passed into graceful old age. It's a charming town, compact and self-possessed, with an attractive high street. Its main industry these days is education. There are ten private schools in Sherborne (a town of 9,000 people), and on weekday afternoons the streets are awash with blue-uniformed schoolchildren. The *Three Wishes* restaurant, on Cheap St., does a delicious tea of clotted cream, scones, and jam.

CHECKING IN: *Eastbury* – For a taste of seclusion in the town center, try this traditional townhouse hotel sitting in its own acre of walled garden. It has a large library of antiquarian books, and all bedrooms, newly decorated, are named after English garden flowers. Long St., Sherborne (phone: 0935-813131). Expensive.

En Route from Sherborne – Quiet, agricultural Dorset is a collection of villages, each prettier than the next, linked together by fields, hills and valleys, rivers, and spring-fed meadows of unparalleled beauty. While you can shoot straight down to Dorchester on A37 (pick it up at Yeovil, 5 miles west of Sherborne), you'd be missing the best of this county. Here's a route that will take you through a handful of Dorset villages and some of the loveliest countryside. The roads are sometimes little more than cowpaths, so don't expect to make time.

Start at Melbury Osmond, about 6 miles south of Yeovil, just off A37, a village of stone houses jumbled together in some of the greenest hills man ever laid eyes on. From here there's a public footpath (a little over a mile long) through Melbury Park, a lovely and peaceful private estate, to Evershot, a perfect gem of a village — one street long, one street wide — that looks like Melbury Osmond would if its cottages were laid side by side. (You can also reach Evershot by road.) The cottage just beyond Evershot's parish church is supposedly Hardy's model for the one where Tess rested on her travels.

From Evershot, take an unnumbered road to Minterne Magna, which will take you along the top of Batcombe Hill. It is hard to imagine a more beautiful drive. From the ridge of the escarpment, the land falls away to soft green pastures, hedged fields, and houses and farm buildings built of mellowed Ham Hill stone. This is a human landscape, sculpted by centuries of man's careful and continuous husbandry. It's a short stretch of road — perhaps 5 miles — but you'll be tempted to make it last much longer.

When this road runs into A352, turn south and proceed to Cerne Abbas. Once an abbey and market town, Cerne Abbas is now a pretty triangle of pubs, inns, and handsome merchant houses sitting in a little valley among the rolling upland hills of Dorset. Cerne's other claim to fame is the Cerne Giant, a 180-foot-tall man with prominently exposed genitalia carved into the chalk hillside overlooking the old abbey. There's some disagreement over the identity of the original sculptors, although it's safe to say the giant dates back to at least the Romans.

Pick up B3143 at Piddletrenthide and follow the road through the other Piddle River villages to Puddletown, which for many years also took its name from the river until delicate Victorian tastes demanded the name be changed.

You're in the heart of Thomas Hardy country now. So many of his fictional characters crisscross this corner of Dorset that there is hardly a village, manor house, farm, or hill that doesn't have literary associations. Hardy himself was born a few miles west of Puddletown (Weatherbury in *Far from the Madding Crowd*) at Higher Bockhampton, on the edge of what he calls Edgon Heath, the brooding backdrop for *The Return of the Native*. His cottage is now in the hands of the National Trust and can be visited by prior appointment with the occupant (phone: 03056-2366), although the gardens are open daily from April to October. A mile or so east of Puddletown is Athelhampton, which Hardy calls Athel Hall, a 15th-century Tudor manor house with a remarkably well preserved dovecote from the same period. Athelhampton is a private home, but is open on Wednesdays, Thursdays, and Sundays from April to October, and Sundays through Thursdays in August; admission charge.

CHECKING IN: *Plumber Manor* – A small jewel set in four acres of gardens in the Dorset countryside, it's best — and deservedly — known for its food, which is elegantly and imaginatively English. But its 12 attractive rooms are easily equal to the food. Closed the last 2 weeks of January and the month of February. Sturminster Newton (phone: 0258-72507). Moderate.

Summer Lodge – Also small, and everything about this Georgian hotel speaks of care and thoughtfulness: bouquets of flowers everywhere; homemade shortbread on the tea tray; the quiet, good taste of the decor. The food — traditional English fare cooked with a French feeling for sauces and an oriental respect for vegetables — is excellent. Heated outdoor pool and 10 rooms. Summer La., Evershot (phone: 093583-424). Moderate to inexpensive.

DORCHESTER: Dorchester is Thomas Hardy's town. He lived here, wrote here, and made it live for all the readers who have never set eyes on its ancient cobbled streets or dour stone and brick façades. There's an excellent collection of Hardy material at the Dorset County Museum on High West St., which includes the original manuscript of *The Mayor of Casterbridge* (Hardy's name for Dorchester) and a reconstruction of the author's study. There are also Roman mosaics and other artifacts from when the town was known as Durnovaria. The Roman city boundaries are still visible in the Walks that ring the city center.

There's a relic of even older inhabitants just a mile or so southwest of town. Maiden Castle, an earth fort believed to be about 4,000 years old, is an astounding piece of work. Sprawling over 120 acres, wave after wave of earth ramparts lap up to an elevated enclosure that could hold 5,000 people. The last occupants of Maiden Castle were forcibly evicted by the vastly superior army of the Romans, who then abandoned the site for Dorchester (open all year).

CHECKING IN: *Casterbridge* – This beautifully furnished Georgian guesthouse has no restaurant, but it does have a small bar and a lovely conservatory where tea is served on summer afternoons. Some of the bedrooms are on the small side, but this flaw is generously compensated by immense breakfasts. 49 High St., Dorchester (phone: 0305-64043). Moderate to inexpensive.

ABBOTSBURY: The straightest shot from Dorchester to the seaside village of Abbotsbury also happens to be the most scenic. Head out of Dorchester west on A35. About a mile from town turn left on an unnumbered road to Winterborne Martinstowe, then follow signs to through Portesham to Abbotsbury, and for the next 6 miles watch the green Dorset hills tumble down to the coast. (Hardy Monument, about midway to your left, commemorates Thomas Masterman Hardy, a captain who served under Nelson at Trafalgar, not the novelist.) Abbotsbury is an exquisite village of thatch and stone cottages lining a single winding street. All that remains of the 11th-century Benedictine Abbey is the tithe barn, although the abbey has survived, in a manner of speaking, since much of it was used to build many of the village's cottages. The Abbotsbury Swannery, a large breeding ground on the edge of the Fleet freshwater lagoon, shelters many species of wild fowl (open from mid-May to mid-September; admission charge), while a subtropical garden, open from late March to September, flourishes in a coombe east of the village. Just outside Abbotsbury, southwest on B3157, stop for a lofty look at Chesil Beach, an 18-mile-long, 600-foot-wide stretch of pebble beach that separates the Fleet lagoon from Lyme Bay. The church standing lonely on a hill in the middle distance is St. Catherine's Church, the parish church of Abbotsbury.

En Route from Abbotsbury – Take the B3157 along the coast to Bridport, a small market town that was thriving when the Domesday Book was written and that has fortunately looked after its heritage of medieval buildings. Probably the town's greatest event happened in 1651, during the English Civil War, when the fugitive Charles II, fleeing Cromwellian troops after the battle of Worcester, came here in disguise hoping to escape by sea. But his identity was soon uncovered, and he was chased out of town. Had he made his escape, it would have been from the little harbor at West Bay, 1½ miles to the south. Bridport's broad sidewalks, originally rope walks, date from a time when local rope manufacturers stretched their famous products along them to dry.

The main A35 winds along the coast to Lyme Regis.

LYME REGIS: Lyme Regis is probably best known for the Cobb, "a long claw of old gray wall that flexes itself against the sea," as the town's most famous citizen, John Fowles, describes it. (It was from the Cobb that Fowles's heroine, Sarah, the French lieutenant's woman, stared for sad hours at the sea.) Built over 700 years ago to create an artificial harbor, it has probably cost the good folk of Lyme Regis more to repair than it ever brought in in trade. Still, the attachment to it is long and unshakable, and today it harbors scores of pleasure craft and lobster boats.

This is the quintessential seaside town — whitewashed and salty, built up the steep hillsides over the harbor. In summer, Lyme Regis is a very popular resort, but at any other time of year, the seagulls make the most racket. Fossil hunting in the sheer sea cliffs near town is a local sport, but there is also a collection of fossils at the Lyme Regis Museum for those who aren't paleontologically adventurous (open April to September; closed Sundays; admission charge).

CHECKING IN: *Combe House* – A slight detour inland from Lyme Regis will bring you to this cream-colored Elizabethan mansion run by John Boswell, a descendant of Dr. Johnson's biographer. It's an elegant and roomy hotel, furnished throughout with antiques but retaining an air of informality. And the food is good thanks to Cordon Bleu–trained Therese Boswell. Closed from mid-January through February. Gittisham, near Honiton (phone: Honiton 0404-2756). Expensive.

EXETER: In 1282, Isabella de Fortibus, countess of Devon, in a fit of pique with the citizens of Exeter, built a dam across the River Exe below the city in order to deprive it of its access to the sea and the rich trade it brought to Exeter's doorstep. The townsfolk were furious and vowed to undo the countess's work. They did — by building a canal to circumvent the Wear (called Countess Wear in its builder's honor) — and if it took 300 years to accomplish, it's just an indication of Exeter's determination to remain the preeminent city in the region. Exeter is still a thriving commercial center. But it is also a cathedral and university city, a government center, and the gateway to Devon and Cornwall for thousands of vacationers.

At the center of the city sits its grand cathedral, a Norman and Gothic work of great beauty. The cathedral is exceptionally rich in carvings, although you need binoculars to really enjoy the often fanciful creatures carved on the roof bosses. The Minstrels' Gallery on the north side, which shows an entire angel orchestra, is utterly charming.

Not far from the cathedral is *Mol's Coffee House,* a 16th-century inn, now a gold- and silversmith's shop. Across High Street from the cathedral close is the Guildhall, a municipal building built between 1330 and 1593 and in continuous use since then (closed Sundays). North of the Guildhall is the ruins of Rougemont Castle, a Norman fortification, and to the south is St. Nicholas Priory, a restored monastic house with a cavernous 11th-century wine cellar that is the envy of all oenophiles (open Tuesdays through Saturdays; admission charge). No boating enthusiast should miss the Maritime Museum on the Quay. With over 100 vessels from around the world, this is considered to be one of the finest collections extant (open daily; admission charge).

Five miles north of Exeter is Killerton, an 18th-century mansion housing a fascinating collection of costumes displayed in rooms decorated in different periods. Killerton's superb garden, with rhododendrons, azaleas, magnolias, and stately oak and beech trees, is a beautiful spot, and near here, at Killerton Clump, herons nest from March to July. Killerton House, a National Trust property, is open daily from April to October, and the garden is open all year; admission charge.

CHECKING IN: *Woodhayes* – A small, peaceful Georgian house set in its own secluded grounds 8 miles northeast of Exeter. Antiques and oil paintings decorate the hotel, and among the refined touches in the half dozen or so bedrooms are novels on the table and bottles of spring water. The restaurant's reputation for fine English cooking goes far before it. Whimple (phone: 0404-822237). Moderate.

DARTMOOR: Such is its reputation, Dartmoor's name alone evokes a vivid description: treeless brown hills covered with heather and gorse and pockmarked with treacherous boggy pits, a place where shaggy ponies run wild and the black hounds of hell collect the souls of the damned, a spot so godforsaken and bleak that even desperate prisoners prefer the dank gloom of their cells to the inhospitable hills outside. And, in fact, the moors are startlingly severe, especially after the cultivated beauty of most English countryside. The B3212 road from Exeter to Plymouth will speed you through this wild landscape, but that would be a pity, since Dartmoor is far more than the barren, though incontestably beautiful, face it shows the passer-through. More than a dozen rivers rise in the upland moors, and as they make their way to the sea, they carve lush deep wooded valleys. Chagford, a picture-perfect village near the River Teign, has for years attracted artists, writers, and fashionable folk, as has Moretonhampstead, the village at the junction of B3212 and A382. Castle Drogo, strategically set on a granite bluff above the Teign northeast of Chagford, may look like a medieval fortress, but it was actually built between 1910 and 1930 by a businessman with the means to indulge a romantic fantasy and make his home his castle. Now a National Trust property (open daily from April through October; admission charge), it is probably the last private house built on such a scale in Britain.

Scattered throughout Dartmoor are tors, rocky hills as high as 2,000 feet, that offer superb views of the surrounding countryside. One especially accessible tor is Haytor, not far from Widecombe-in-the-Moor, one of the most picturesque villages in England and also, in summer, one of the most crowded. There are also numerous relics from prehistoric times — hill forts, stone circles, and barrows. Grimspound, about 3 miles from Manaton, is a Bronze Age settlement consisting of 24 hut circles and a stone enclosure that was probably used for livestock. And everywhere are the sheep, black-faced and woolly, pursuing scrubby moor grasses up steep hillsides, crowding onto narrow Devon roads through a break in the hedge.

Dartmoor is marvelous hiking country. Before you set out, stop at the National Park Information Center at Postbridge (much of Dartmoor is now national park land) to pick up maps and advice. Although the days when the moors seemed to mysteriously swallow up hapless travelers are gone, it would be foolhardy to misjudge them.

CHECKING IN: *Gidleigh Park* – Take 30 acres of secluded Devon woodlands, add a turn-of-the-century mansion built for comfort and elegance, furnish it in impeccable good taste, and you have Gidleigh Park. And as if that isn't enough, there's the food, nouvelle cuisine, certainly deserving of its Michelin star, and the wine list, mostly Californian and distinguished. Chagford (phone: 06473-2367). Expensive.

Holne Chase – It used to be a Victorian hunting lodge. Now it's a charming retreat with 12 simple rooms overlooking the valley of the River Dart (where salmon fishing can be arranged on a private mile-long stretch) and one self-catering cottage on the grounds. Holne Ashburton (phone: 03643-471). Moderate.

Teignworth – This beautiful stone house, in a miniscule hamlet near Chagford, is an oasis of peace and quiet in the very heart of the national park. Excellent food and wine are guaranteed — it's also one of the best hotels in England in terms of access to footpaths. Frenchbeer (phone: 06473-3355). Moderate.

En Route from Dartmoor – Leave the area by way of the B3357 southeast to Buckfastleigh. Since it was founded in the late 1800s, monks at Buckfast Abbey have prepared Buckfast Tonic Wine (exported all over the world) and also tended one of the largest honey industries in the country. All the products of this hard work are available at the abbey shop (open daily year round). The abbey church and an exhibition of the site's history are also open year round, except during services. Continue, via A364, to Totnes.

TOTNES: Totnes looks every bit as medieval as its name suggests. Its steep narrow streets curl up and around themselves, and the timbered and slate-shingled buildings that overhang the main street lean and sag like clowns in a Shakespearean comedy. If you climb the narrow passageway to the church and guildhall, a wonderful old building with columned porch and frightfully low oak doors, you'll find yourself peering down on the roofs of buildings. Totnes Castle, one of the first to be erected by the conquering Normans, stands near the center of town (open daily March to October; Saturdays through Wednesdays only the rest of the year), and Totnes Museum, in one of the Elizabethan merchant houses, has an interesting collection of local costumes and household goods (open March to October; closed Sundays; admission charge).

DARTMOUTH: In 1147, 164 ships sailed from here on the Second Crusade. Some 800 years later, a fleet of 485 American ships left Dartmouth's snug harbor on another crusade, this time to the beaches of Normandy. Between the two events the town grew and prospered, first from the wine trade with Burgundy, later from cod fishing off the coast of Newfoundland, and whenever it could, from piracy and privateering.

It was the Elizabethans who really left their stamp on this thoroughly and wonderfully nautical town on the estuary of the Dart River. The crooked, elaborately decorated half-timbered buildings in the harbor area make Dartmouth look much the way it must have when Sir Walter Raleigh brought his royally sanctioned booty here. Occupying a commanding position above the harbor is the Royal Naval College, Britain's main naval training center since 1905, while right on the town quay is the Royal Avenue Gardens, a charming reminder of the town's present popularity as a resort. Its amusement park entrance, a blue and white iron gate strung with colored lights and topped with a crown done in lights, doesn't lead you to expect the beautifully kept garden where primroses, crocuses, and daffodils bloom as early as March. Just outside town is Dartmouth Castle, one of Henry VIII's many coastal fortifications (open daily). Not much is left of its twin across the mouth of the river, Kingswear Castle (a private residence).

EATING OUT: *Carved Angel* – The seafood in this bright and airy restaurant on the quay is outstanding, and no one has been heard to complain about the other dishes on its imaginatively French menu. Closed January. 2 South Embankment, Dartmouth (phone: 08043-2465). Expensive.

En Route from Dartmouth – Slapton Sands, about 5 miles south on A379, is where American troops practiced for the invasion of Normandy. In the middle of the 5-mile-long stretch of sand is a monument erected by the US government, thanking the local people for the use of their beach.

PLYMOUTH: Driving into Plymouth from the east, you come across a curious sight — the ruins of a church in the middle of a traffic roundabout. Charles Church was destroyed during a Nazi raid on the city during the spring of 1941. Over 1,000 people died, 70,000 were left homeless, and most of the city center was devastated in the attack. The shell of the church was left as a memorial to those who lost their lives, and if at first it seems irreverent to surround a memorial with traffic, on second thought it seems entirely appropriate to see it part of the daily flow of life.

The raid irrevocably changed the face of this vigorous old port, the second largest city in Britain's southwest (Bristol is first). The postwar center is an excellent shopping area that draws people from all over the region, although, unfortunately, it isn't very handsome. But a lot of Plymouth was miraculously spared damage. The Barbican, on an indent of the sea called Sutton Harbor, is where rich Elizabethan merchants built their houses and is now a lively spot full of antiques shops, art galleries, restaurants, and pubs. Elizabethan House, on New St., has fine furnishings from that period (closed Sundays in winter and open daily in summer; admission charge). Nearby, too, is Mayflower Steps, a monument commemorating the sailing of the *Mayflower* in 1620. At the edge of the Barbican is Prysten House, a 15th-century priory that survived both

Henry's purge of the monasteries and Hitler's terrible assault (closed Sundays; admission charge).

In contrast to the amiable bustle of the Barbican, the face Plymouth shows the sea is a formidable one. The Citadel, a low gray stone fortress built in the late 1600s by Charles II and still used by the military, sits brooding on the high ground above the Plymouth Sound. Its strength has never been tested, perhaps because the sight of it alone is enough to deter any would-be invaders. Sharing the commanding position over the Sound is Plymouth's famous Hoe, the broad green where Sir Francis Drake unhurriedly finished his game of bowls before dealing an ignominious defeat to the Spanish Armada. There's a statue of Sir Francis near the bowling green. At the center of the Hoe is another monument, this one to the thousands of sailors, British and Commonwealth, who were killed in the two world wars. It's a moving tribute, especially apt in this city whose namesakes in the far flung reaches of the Empire number no fewer than 40. Before leaving the Hoe, walk to the edge of the seaward side. Built into the rocky cliffs of the headland is a series of steps and platforms that lead down to an open-air bathing pool jutting out into the sound, a surprising retreat hidden away from the city that buzzes above it.

En Route from Plymouth – There are a wealth of historic homes nearby. Just outside the city to the east is Saltram, a classic Georgian mansion containing Chippendale furniture, portraits by Sir Joshua Reynolds, and interiors by Robert Adam. (The house is open Tuesdays to Sundays and some bank holidays from April to October; the gardens are open all year; admission charge.) About 10 miles north of Plymouth on high ground with a clear view of distant Plymouth Harbor is Buckland Abbey, Sir Francis Drake's house. It contains plenty of Drake memorabilia, as well as a Naval and Devon Folk Museum. (Open Wednesdays and weekends in winter; daily Easter to September.)

Across the Tamar River (the border between Cornwall and Devon) and a bit to the north of Buckland Abbey is Cotehele, an especially fine gray granite house, built between 1485 and 1627, in an exquisite setting of wildflowers and meadows on the river bank. Inside are beautiful furnishings, tapestries, needlework, and armor, and there's also a working 18th-century watermill on the grounds (open daily, April to October; admission charge). Also across the Tamar, but just outside Plymouth, is Antony House, a graceful Queen Anne mansion long — and still — the home of the powerful Carew family (open Tuesdays to Thursdays and some bank holidays, April to October; admission charge). As you cross the Tamar to Saltash, look to your left for the Royal Albert Bridge, one of the engineering masterpieces by Isambard Kingdom Brunel.

ST. MAWES: Its mild climate isn't all that prompts comparisons between St. Mawes and the French Riviera. It has the same easygoing charm and the same air of a perpetual party. Sitting on the tip of a peninsula in a large sheltered bay, St. Mawes is a perfect yachting and fishing town. Add to this, stunning coast walks, secluded beaches, and subtropical gardens where, as one long-time resident says, "there's nothing as *common* as a palm tree," and it is easy to understand why the mood is so buoyant. Don't look for countrified charm here, although charm exists by the bushel in this village of whitewashed cottages ranging along the town quay. Well-to-do Britons with a yen for the sea and soft climate make St. Mawes a sophisticated outpost: Good food and gracious hotels are expected, not just hoped for.

Across the Carrick Roads, as the wide estuary of the Fal River is known, and linked by a pedestrian ferry to St. Mawes is Falmouth, once a port and now also a resort town. From here you can take a steamer up the Fal to the ancient high tide port of Truro, Cornwall's cathedral city, or south, down along the coast, then up the Helford River. Falmouth and St. Mawes share a pair of Henry VIII castles. St. Mawes Castle, its central tower surrounded by three battlemented semicircles, sits prettily on a knoll outside the village. Unlike Pendennis, its twin at Falmouth, which held out against Parliamentarian troops for 5 months, St. Mawes was never the site of any action and thus is in near-perfect repair. The view from Pendennis Castle, built by Henry VIII as protection against Spanish attacks, is one of the best — one side overlooks the beach, the other the docks and town. (Both castles are open daily all year.)

The gardens that flourish around the Carrick Roads are so wildly exotic partly because the climate is mild but also because Falmouth was the first port of call for water for English ships returning from long voyages, and for hundreds of years sailors brought back plants from the farthest flung reaches of the world. When the English turned their considerable gardening talents to these rare plants, they developed a dizzying number of subspecies. The church grounds of St. Just in Roseland, 4 miles outside St. Mawes and linked by coastal and inland footpaths, is a splendid garden where date palms, bamboo, camellias, rhododendrons, azaleas, Chilian fire bushes, and magnolias flourish alongside England's own bluebells, snowdrops, and primroses. North of St. Mawes is Trelissick Gardens, a beautifully tended woodland on the River Fal (open daily, March to October); to the west is Penjerrick Gardens (open Wednesdays and Sundays from March to September) and Glendurgan, on the Helford River (open Mondays, Wednesdays, and Fridays, March to October), each with enough varieties of subtropical and indigenous plants to satisfy the most avid gardener.

CHECKING IN: *Rising Sun* – It's hard to imagine a quainter, cosier, more gracious hotel than this one. The front terrace, which fills with the overflow of its congenial pub in warm weather, faces the town quay, and a guest in a room in the front will go to sleep to the sound of the tide slapping against the harbor wall. From the justly renowned kitchen comes a fine *crème brûlée*, a creamy custardy confection that to have once is to yearn for forever. St. Mawes (phone: 0326-270233). Expensive.

Tresanton – This lovably overgrown, white vine-covered cottage combines the sophistication and the country charm of St. Mawes in one delightful package. On the coastal road, it has subtropical gardens spilling down its hillside toward the bay and a private beach. Sailing and water skiing are possible. All the 21 bedrooms have private baths; breakfast and dinner are included in the room price; and the food is delicious. Closed mid-November to late March. St. Mawes (phone: 0326-270544). Expensive.

THE LIZARD AND WEST PENWITH: It takes a jaded traveler indeed to resist the urge to travel to the ends of the earth, and in England the earth ends most spectacularly at the tips of a broad stirrup of land called the Lizard and West Penwith. Despite the summer crowds that converge on these popular spots, they are, nonetheless, impressive examples of nature's handiwork. The Lizard ends in cliffs of brilliant serpentine — olive green rock veined with red and purple and polished by the sea and wind — while Land's End meets the sea with granite cliffs and a wash of shiny black boulders. Go early in the morning or at sunset to avoid the crowds. Or better yet, park your car a mile or so away and approach the spots on foot via one of the coastal paths.

Just 10 miles from the cliffs of Lizard Point in the northern part of the peninsula is scenery of a different, but equally pleasing, order — wooded coves leading down to the Helford River. Helford village is a completely charming place on one of these sylvan inlets. The *Shipwrights Inn,* a pretty pub with sunny terraces jutting out over a brook, is a perfect spot to while away a summer afternoon.

On the main road from the Lizard to West Penwith, A394, is Helston, a pleasant market town best known for its Flora Day celebration, when the whole town turns out, flower bedecked and beribboned, to "furry" dance through the streets to a 1,500-year-old processional tune. The date, in early May, is well before the annual influx of vacationers, so the holiday is still mostly an event for townsfolk. Also, 3 miles north of Helston on the B3297 is the Poldark Mine, an old tin mine that has been converted into an industrial museum (open April through October; admission charge).

Midway between the two peninsulas is Godolphin House, built in the 16th century by one of the most powerful families in England whose fortune came from the rich tin veins in Cornwall (open Thursdays from May to June, Tuesdays and Thursdays from July to September). The castle that seems to rise out of the water like a vision as you approach West Penwith is real enough. It's St. Michael's Mount, once a monastery, later a fortress, and for the last 300 years the home of the St Aubyn family. It's now owned by the National Trust and can be visited on Mondays, Wednesdays, and Fridays all year, and also on Tuesdays from June to October.

Land's End and the splendor of the Cornish coast is only part of West Penwith's attraction. This westernmost nub of England is an open-air museum of ancient Britons. There are dozens of stone circles (most, for some arcane reason, having nine or nineteen stones), hut circles, and burial mounds. Near Lamorna is a fascinating formation called the Pipers and the Merry Maidens — two tall upright stones and a circle of nineteen stones. Local legend has it that the village girls were caught dancing on the Sabbath, and they and their musicians were turned to stone as a punishment. Carn Euny, near Crows an Wra (Witches' Cross), and Chysauster, 5 miles from Penzance, are two well-preserved Iron Age villages.

If you want to see the source of much Cornish wealth, head for Pendeen, on the west coast, where you can visit Geevor Mine, a working tin mine that gives guided tours. You can also get a look at Cornwall's other mainstay — fishing — at Mousehole, a granity fishing village about 5 miles south of Penzance, or at Newlyn, once a Victorian artists colony and now the largest fishing port in the southwest. Much of the delicious fish you get in this part of the country comes from there. A bit farther down the coast is Minack Theatre, an amphitheater built into the granite cliffs overlooking the sea. The season, which runs from June to September, includes a variety of theater productions — from Gilbert and Sullivan to Maxim Gorki — by different repertory groups. The setting is nothing short of spectacular, but be sure to wear warm clothes.

Penzance and St. Ives guard West Penwith like a pair of Henry's castles. Both are near excellent broad swaths of beach, and for that reason are crammed with the less appealing sights of tourism — drab hotels and tacky souvenir shops. The Barbara Hepworth museum at the artist's home in St. Ives is, however, well worth a visit (open Mondays and Saturdays, September to June; daily in July and August).

CHECKING IN: *Lamorna Cove* – This hotel takes its name from the tranquil wooded cove over which it perches. Although the modern additions don't do justice to the original granite house or the setting, the hotel is very comfortable. Fresh fish, of which there is an unending supply from nearby Newlyn, is a specialty. Lamorna (phone: 0736-731411). Moderate.

ISLES OF SCILLY: The often rough 2½-hour boat passage from Penzance to the Isles of Scilly prompted one wag to describe the islands as paradise which can only be reached through purgatory. Now, thanks to the 20-minute helicopter flight, you can go straight to heaven, in this case a group of 150-plus islands 30 miles off the Cornish coast. Connected by shallow straits treacherously studded with outcroppings of rock and reef, the islands have a schizophrenic nature. The northwestern side of the islands is usually bleak, windswept plains of gorse and heather. But the sheltered southern side supports vast fields of flowers — daffodils, jonquils, narcissus, anemones, iris, tulips, and lilies. Flowers are the main business of the 2,000 people who live in the Isles of Scilly: more than 1,000 tons of cut flowers are exported from here every year.

Only five of the islands are inhabited by man. The rest are inhabited by seals, puffins, gannets, kittiwakes, and other ocean birds. (The rent for the entire island chain in the 15th century was six and eightpence — or 50 puffins.) Their quiet sandy beaches are perfect for picnicking or sunbathing. No wonder former Prime Minister Harold Wilson chose these islands as a refuge from the political hurly-burly of 10 Downing Street.

St. Mary's is the largest island in the chain and has the distinction of having what is probably the least expensive and most quickly constructed castle in Britain — Star Castle, built by Sir Francis Godolphin in 1593 for under £1,000. The island of Tresco draws the most visitors. If you stop for a pint of beer at the island's *New Inn*, take a look at the wall chart showing how the savagery of the surrounding seas have, over the years, been the graveyard of some 2,000 ships: vessels with salt from Spain, silks from Italy, rice from Rangoon, elephant tusks from Africa, cotton from Galveston, hides from Argentina, and tea from Fuchow. The gardens at Tresco Abbey contain a staggering variety of plants — between 3,000 and 4,000 — the lifetime achievement of botanical zealot Augustus Smith, whose descendants still hold the lease of the island (open daily). Also on Tresco is the Valhalla Maritime Museum (open daily), which has a fascinating collection of figureheads from shipwrecks, relics of the days when Scilly islanders made their living scavenging from the many ships that went aground on Scilly's dangerous reefs. To absorb some of the islands' character, visit Longstone Centre on St. Mary's, with its garden of Scillonian flora, an exhibition on the history of the daffodil, a butterfly house, and a farm trail (open mid-April to November; phone: 0720-22924).

En Route from the Isles of Scilly – It's best to meander up the rocky north coast of Cornwall. No single road follows the coastline, but there are secondary roads that loop off the main road (the A30, which runs about 5 miles inland) to hug the coast for 5 to 10 miles before rejoining it. Just past Newquay, a popular and congested summer resort with a fine stretch of beach, take B3276 to Bedruthan Steps. Here, mammoth chunks of the cliff have tumbled onto the wide strand of beach below, forming steps for the Cornish giant, Bedruthan. When the tide is in, Bedruthan's Steps jut out from the white agitation of the sea like bits of black coral strung on a necklace, but when the tide is out, you can explore the rock pools and caverns cut into the cliffs by the sea. Continue on B3276 another 8 miles to Padstow.

PADSTOW: From June to September, Padstow, with its compact horseshoe of a harbor and pleasant tangle of streets, rings with the holiday fun of summer folk who come to fish, swim, and sail in the waters of the north Cornish coast and the Camel River. But on May 1, before the season gets under way, the town holds its own celebration, the Hobby Horse or, as it is locally known, 'Obby 'Oss, a day when a huge, fierce hobby horse prances through the streets in the midst of singing and dancing villagers. According to one story, the 'Obby 'Oss started when the village women, whose husbands were off fighting the French in one of the numerous wars between the English and their channel neighbors, fashioned an enormous stallion to scare away enemy raiders. However, most think the raucous celebration has its roots in earlier pagan times. Clearly, there is a strain of unrepentant wit — pagan or otherwise — in Padstow: One of the bench ends in the 13th- and 14th-century church shows the devil disguised as a fox, preaching to a flock of geese.

En Route from Padstow – A few miles south of the town of Bodmin on B3268 is Lanhydrock, a grandiose Tudor house built in the late 1800s and set in meticulously tended grounds and rolling parkland. Never were the fruits of the Empire more impressively displayed. The elaborate kitchens — with numerous larders — and lavish baths are especially fascinating insights into that incredibly wealthy time. The house is open daily from April to October and the gardens daily year-round; admission charge.

BODMIN MOOR: Bodmin Moor reverberates with almost as many legends as the more famous moor in neighboring Devon. Dozmary Pool, a shallow tarn nearly dead center of Bodmin Moor, is supposedly the pool (one of three) into which Arthur flung Excalibur. Nearby at Bolventor is Jamaica Inn, the scene of Daphne du Maurier's tale of smugglers and pirates. And there are holy wells — at St. Neot on the southern edge, and, on the northern edge, at St. Clether and Altarnun, whose well is reputed to cure madness by the near drowning of the sufferer.

Driving across the bare brown hills broken only by tors, it is easy to see how legends attach themselves to these spots. There are a few minor roads that penetrate the southeast corner of the moor, but to get to Rough Tor (pronounce Rough to rhyme with now) and Brown Willy, where the best views can be had, you have to circle the moor and come up behind it at Camelford, on its northwestern edge. From here you can drive to a car park at the foot of Rough Tor and climb up or hike on to Brown Willy, a mile away. There's a turnoff to the left just before you get to Rough Tor that takes you to an eerie relic of modern times — the ruins of a World War II Royal Air Force base at Davidstow. It could be a scene straight out of any number of contemporary doomsday stories: abandoned runways, control towers, all the paraphernalia of modern technology left to decay along with the crude barrows and hut circles of ancient Britons. Just to balance the vision of life left by the opulence of Lanhydrock, stop in at the North Cornwall Museum at Camelford, which has a reconstruction of a Cornish cottage (closed Sundays, April to September).

 CHECKING IN: *Arundell Arms* – This former coaching inn covered with Virginia creeper is well worth a slight detour (about 4 miles east of Launceston via A30): Log fires blaze away, the floors are laid with dark blue slate, and the culinary offerings are of international standard. But it really stands out for its salmon fishing, since it owns the fishing rights to 20 miles of the Tamar River. Lifton (phone: 0566-84666). Moderate.

NORTH CORNWALL COAST: It would be a Herculean task to find any part of the Cornish coast not worth seeing. But there is a stretch of coast north of the Camel River that in 20 miles contains dramatic cliffs, surfing beaches, sand dunes, historic spots, and exquisite villages.

From Wadebridge, at the mouth of the Camel River estuary, take B3314 about 2 miles till you see a turnoff to Rock. Another 3 miles along this unnumbered road will take you past this not terribly attractive resort town to a car park at Daymer Bay. The dunes here are marvelous, covered with clumps of coarse grass and just the place to find dog-walkers and families on weekend outings. There is a golf course along the coast, and in the middle of one of the fairways stands St. Enodoc Church, less curious now, even given its fairly odd surroundings, than it was 100 years ago when it was half buried in sand and the vicar was forced to crawl in through the roof to deliver the sermon. It is hard to imagine who was there to hear it.

Stick to the unnumbered coast road by following signs to Trebetherick, Polzeath (a surfing beach), Pentireglaze, and Port Quin. According to local lore, all the men of Port Quin were lost at sea in one accident, and shortly after the women mysteriously disappeared as well. The abandoned village — four stone cottages that sit precariously over the water at the end of a steep cove and an old stone barn next to a tumbling stream — is now in the hands of the National Trust and is a lovely, quiet spot.

Just a few miles from Port Quin is Port Isaac, an old corn port and modern-day fishing village that you literally descend into. The streets tumble down to a postage stamp of a beach where visitors pay to leave their cars in the summer (the only tidal car park in Britain, and hence only for those with an accurate sense of timing). The color-washed houses seem to be piled one on top of the other in the narrow "coombe" or valley. One of the streets is called "Sqeezibelly Alley" because a mere 18 inches separates one wall from the other. In the very center is the Birdcage, a delightful high, narrow house, part of the National Trust. The *Golden Lion* pub sits right on the harbor wall and is a congenial spot from which to watch the tide slowly creep up the harbor. At the end of another steep valley about 10 miles up the coast is Trebarwith Strand, where massive fingers of sculpted black rock, pink-veined and highly polished, lead down to a broad swath of beach that in high tide is completely covered.

From here it is just a mile or so to Tintagel, possibly the most visited spot in Cornwall. The town itself is unlovely and crowded most of the year. What draws such crowds is Tintagel Castle, the ruins of a 12th-century castle and 6th-century monastery where, according to some folk, King Arthur, who has fascinated and inspired the English soul for fourteen centuries, was born. Even if you don't subscribe to that story, Tintagel is well worth a stop. Right on the edge of a rocky promontory, the castle ruins are dramatically beautiful. Follow the causeway to the castle and stand on the ramparts looking out to sea.

What Tintagel town lacks in charm, Boscastle, just 3 miles on, offers in spades. Boscastle is a cozy village sheltered in a deep valley that you enter from a ridge running along the valley wall. The dark stone buildings and the snug harbor give the village a serious, settled mien, not likely to be altered by the excesses of tourism. And as a conservation area, Boscastle will probably remain that way.

CHECKING IN: *Tredethy Country* – In a spacious manor house facing an expansive patchwork of fields, sheep pastures, and woods, this friendly hotel has large, pleasant rooms and 9 acres of grounds — including a swimming pool and redwood solarium — in which to wander. Helland Bridge, near Bodmin (phone: 020884-262). Moderate.

Port Gaverne – Tucked into a tiny inlet of the same name, only a few yards from the sea, this peaceful, restored 17th-century inn sports a traditional pub setting. It's owned by an American, Fred Ross. Closed February. Near Port Isaac (phone: 0208-80244). Moderate.

Bridge House – This 17th-century stone house on Boscastle Harbor offers small attractive rooms, a cheerful ambience, and a most charming location. Bed and breakfast only. Boscastle (phone: 08405-477). Inexpensive.

CLOVELLY: Clovelly is so perfectly picturesque — an unbroken line of shuttered and flower-bedecked cottages down a steep, cobbled street to the harbor — you can't quite believe anything so quaint and charming isn't contrived. But Clovelly isn't, though it is on the map for every tourist bus coming to the Devon coast (the Cornwall-Devon border is less than 10 miles south). It is probably best to avoid it during the day in July and August; but if you go in the early morning or evening, you'll find simply a beautiful village going about its business. No cars are allowed in Clovelly; visitors and villagers alike have to leave them at a car park at the top of the hill. You might enjoy a stop at *Gladys Friend's* tearoom. The main activity in Clovelly is strolling down to the quay and making the arduous climb — for it is steep; be sure to wear flat shoes — back up.

NORTH DEVON COAST: Start a tour of the North Devon coast at Ilfracombe, long a port and shipyard, now a popular resort. With its ranks upon ranks of small hotels all with similar sounding names — Golden Sands, Sandy Cove, Cove Haven — and imposing Victorian hotels daringly perched on the city's magnificent cliffs, Ilfracombe has a certain period charm.

Leaving Ilfracombe, take A399 east, a road that for about 8 miles follows a beautiful stretch of coast. Just past Combe Martin, a not very pretty resort town, take an unnumbered road to *Hunter's Inn* and Trentishoe. The variety of landscapes this road covers in a few short miles will make your head spin. First it follows a ridge above gentle green downs dotted with prosperous-looking farms. Then, suddenly, you're on the loneliest coast road in the world — wild moorland, raw to the sea wind, stretches on either side of you. Press on, for within another mile or so, the road runs along the top of a deep, wooded combe. When you reach the bottom of this serene valley, you'll be at the door of *Hunter's Inn,* a gabled and Alpinesque inn popular with tourists and a gathering spot for the hunt. Nonetheless, the spot is unarguably beautiful and a cool beer on the inn's terrace, in the company of the resident peacocks, is almost mandatory.

Lynmouth, about 5 miles on, is a pretty resort village hedged in by the sheer cliffs of the Lyn River Valley. You need steady nerves and reliable brakes on your car to take the direct road from Lynton, a larger town which literally hovers 500 feet above Lynmouth. It is a vertiginous drop, and the three sand-filled offshoots along the road — escape roads for runaway cars — probably see their share of business. Percy Bysshe Shelley lived here for a while, although his cottage no longer exists.

There are two spectacular drives out of Lynmouth. One is along B3223 inland into Exmoor, which follows the high curving ridge of the East Lyn River Valley to Watersmeet, where the East Lyn and the Hoar Oak Water meet. Much of this land is owned by the National Trust, which has marked several nature trails through the dense woods of the valleys. The other drive is along the coast on A39, up Countisbury Hill (as demanding of your car's engine as the road into Lynton was of its brakes). Superlatives only suffice to describe the view. Bracken- and gorse-covered hills break suddenly at black cliffs, and in the distance looms Foreland Point, at 900 feet the tallest cliffs in England.

Porlock, about 12 miles east of Lynmouth on the A39 and across the Somerset border, is utterly unlike most southwest sea towns that either cling to the edge of cliffs or shelter in narrow coves. Occupying a broad, sea level plain that opens up in the Exmoor Hills, it's a sweet little place with a sleepy, satisfied air. Porlock Weir, about 2½ miles from town, is a pretty collection of hotels and harbor buildings, and a long curve of white beach that looks positively Caribbean.

 CHECKING IN: *Yeoldon House* – This rambling Victorian house on the edge of Bideford has been very ably converted to an attractive hotel. The rooms are bright and comfortable, and the English and Continental cooking do justice to local produce and fresh fish. Durrant La., Northam, near Bideford (phone: 02372-74400). Expensive to moderate.

***Heddon's Gate* –** Perfectly poised close to the sea in the midst of the national park, this large country house has a well-deserved reputation for good food and lodging and is popular with wildlife lovers. Closed from the second week of November through Easter. Heddon's Mouth, Parracombe (phone: 05983-313). Moderate.

EXMOOR FOREST: Anyone expecting dense woods is likely to be disappointed by Exmoor Forest, as the parcel of hills in northeast Devon and west Somerset is known. It is a forest in the ancient English sense — land owned by the king and subject to his hunting laws. In fact, at one time early in the 19th century, a royal commission found only 37 trees in all of Exmoor. There are more trees than that now, but Exmoor is still more moor than forest, full of ancient relics, tors, wild red deer, and its famous ponies. Exford, at the center of Exmoor, is a pretty spot and a good center for fishing, hiking, or horseback riding. Oare, near the Somerset-Devon border, is at the head of Doone Valley, the setting for R. D. Blackmore's story, *Lorna Doone.* Doone Valley and the surrounding area are indeed lovely, but, sadly, have been commercialized.

 CHECKING IN: *Simonsbath House* – In a sheltered valley in the heart of Exmoor, this 17th-century house has eight pretty bedrooms and a well-regarded menu featuring early English recipes (phone: 064383-259). Moderate.

En Route from Exmoor Forest – Around the town of Dunster, the moors give way to soft green meadows backed by even softer hills where clusters of houses linked by ivy-draped walls smugly sit. Dunster itself is a lovely town in a peerless setting, but it is very crowded in summer and is best seen off season. Dunster Castle, occupying a knoll on the edge of town, has been the home of the Luttrell family for 600 years and was the object of both Royalist and Parliamentarian attacks in the Civil War (open Saturdays through Wednesdays from April to October).

Five miles east of Dunster on A39 in a tranquil setting called Flowery Valley is Cleeve Abbey, built by Cistercian monks in the 12th century. It was spared the full wrath of Henry VIII at the Dissolution of the Monasteries, and although the church no longer exists, the gatehouse, refectory, and dormitory are beautifully intact (open daily). Continue on A39 another 10 miles or so to Nether Stowey, a village nestling on the eastern slopes of the Quantock Hills, where Samuel Taylor Coleridge wrote *The Rime of the Ancient Mariner.* (For a time William Wordsworth and his sister Dorothy lived about 4 miles away at Holford.) Coleridge's cottage, now owned by the National Trust, opens its parlor doors Tuesdays through Thursdays and Sundays from April to September.

The A39 cuts across a broad basin of land between the Quantock and Mendip hills called the Somerset levels, low marshy land reclaimed from the sea over the centuries. Somerton and Glastonbury, about 15 miles inland, were, until the 17th century, islands, and the sea, at high wind and high tide, can still flood these towns. Indeed, it's thought that Somerset takes its name — summer settlers or settlers by the sea lakes — from this region. For during this season the lagoons would dry up, leaving behind fertile tidal land for grazing. Early inhabitants would drive cattle and sheep down to the plain in summer and then return to the hills when winter brought more flooding.

GLASTONBURY: About 20 miles east of Nether Stowey is Glastonbury, fabled island of Avalon where the strands of early Christianity and English national identity meet and intertwine. Christ himself is said to have built the church that later became the most powerful abbey in the country, and it was to this sacred spot that Arthur and Queen Guinevere were brought to be buried. The long and rich history of Glastonbury and nearby South Cadbury, thought to be Arthur's Camelot, is discussed in *Ancient Monuments and Ruins,* DIVERSIONS.

 CHECKING IN: *George and Pilgrims* – Many a pilgrim has bedded down for the night at this venerable old hotel, and although it hasn't lost an ounce of the character it has acquired over the years, it has managed to incorporate all the comforts a modern traveler demands. For a real treat, ask for a room with a four-poster bed. 1 High St., Glastonbury (phone: 0458-31146). Moderate.

WELLS: What makes this little town basking on the sunny side of the Mendip Hills a city is its cathedral, an early-English-style church whose elaborately carved west front has been awing visitors for centuries. Inside, of less divine purpose perhaps but of spirited inspiration, is the Wells Clock, an enchanting timepiece made by a Glastonbury monk, Peter Lightfoot, in the 14th century. A carved figure of a man announces the quarter hour by kicking his heels against two bells, and four mounted knights, who charge out and knock each other off their steeds, bring in the hour.

CHEDDAR CAVES: Under the Mendip Hills that tower over the Somerset levels is a labyrinth of caves eaten out of the soft limestone hills by constant flooding. For thousands of years, and until as late as the mid-19th century, many of these caves were inhabited by people. Adventurous spelunkers still explore the underground streams and roads, and thousands of tourists visit the larger caves, Cheddar Caves, near Cheddar, and Wookey Hole, near Wells. Cheddar Gorge, a deep limestone cleft through the Mendips, makes for a scenic drive, but is terribly congested in July and August. The town of Cheddar, home of the most famous English cheese, more recently has become the center of a thriving industry growing strawberries and anemones, which flourish on the sunny sheltered slopes of the Mendips.

From the Cheddar Caves, it's just a short ride to Bristol. (For a complete description of the city, its sights, hotels, and restaurants, see *Bristol,* THE CITIES.)

The Cotswolds

Less than 100 miles west of London is the region known as the Cotswolds. It encompasses about 450 square miles of rolling limestone upland of the Cotswold Hills, punctuated by charming, carefully preserved medieval towns and villages built from the honey-colored stone, quarried from the hills, which gives the region its character. The Cotswolds themselves stretch northeast in a curving 60-mile arc from Bath to the vicinity of Stratford-upon-Avon. Along their western edge they form a steep ridge of solid limestone, and their crest is the Thames-Severn watershed. But the overall character of the countryside is tranquil and picturesque, like a rich tapestry. Much of this land is a great, sweeping pasture for the famous Cotswold sheep, with their heavy ringlets of fleece that once upon a time brought wealth to the area.

This is the England of the imagination: rolling hills covered by copses of ancient oak and surviving elm, a landscape scaled to size for country walks and bird-watching. Towns are tied to one another by twisting country lanes that carry a constant commerce of farmers and shepherds, postmen, parsons, and pubgoers. The vista from any hill is as apt to include the square tower of a Norman church as a far field of cropping sheep, and any church is likely to be surrounded by the stone tile roofs of a tiny village, now no longer populated by farm workers but by retired folk, weekenders, and commuters to the larger towns. Village cemeteries are shaded by yews and village streams guarded by weeping willows. Nothing is very far from anything else, but privacy and protective isolation are accentuated by the quiet and country peace that settles over all. Village names are remnants of an earlier language and a younger England: Wyck Rissington, Upper and Lower Slaughter, Oddington, Guiting Power, Clapton-on-Hill, Bourton-on-the-Water, Moreton-in-Marsh.

The Cotswolds provided a rich agricultural center for the Romans until the fifth century, and the Roman presence is still visible in many places, such as the roads out of Cirencester and the baths in Bath. The Saxons routed the Romans; the Normans routed the Saxons; and they all left their mark. But when the Cotswold sheep began to pay off, it was the wool merchants of the Middle Ages who built the enduring symbols of the area — magnificent churches like the fifteenth-century one at Northleach and the fourteenth-century one to St. John the Baptist at Cirencester.

Our route through the Cotswolds is long, lazy, and serpentine. We begin in Oxford and end in Bath, both important and fascinating cities that border the Cotswolds area. In between we savor most of those golden towns that are quintessentially Cotswold in flavor: Northleach, Chedworth, Burford, Bourton-on-the-Water, Stow-on-the-Wold, Moreton-in-Marsh, Chipping Campden, Broadway, Winchcombe, Cheltenham, Cirencester, and Malmesbury.

An eminently English way to see the Cotswolds is to take to shank's pony and walk all or part of the 100-mile Cotswold Way, a trail that links a series of well-marked and easily negotiated paths that follow the crests of the Cotswold hills from Bath to Chipping Campden in the north. These ancient routes, first used by Neolithic travelers 3,000 years ago, were well worn by medieval pilgrims and traders moving from village to village, the same villages that dot the course today. One need not be an accomplished hiker to follow the Way for a distance, and the weak of spirit can take heart from the thought that village and pub are never far apart. The benefits are multiple: Immersed in the countryside, you have a walking-pace view of the villages, buildings, cottages, churches, Roman ruins, and barrows — Stone Age burial mounds — that dot the region (the barrow at Belas Knap, between Cheltenham and Winchcombe, is thought to be the most impressive specimen in England). The Way is maintained by the Gloucestershire County Council, which marks its course with large yellow arrows to make hiking easier. Thornhill Press publishes *The Cotswold Way,* an excellent guide by Mark Richards, available throughout the area.

A detailed guidebook, *The Cotswolds and Shakespeare's Country,* is available from the Heart of England Tourist Board, PO Box 15, Worcester WR1 2JT (phone: 0905-29512).

OXFORD: A visit to this beautiful city is the perfect start to a tour of the Cotswolds. For a detailed report on the city, its sights, hotels, and restaurants, see *Oxford,* THE CITIES.

To begin the Cotswold tour, take the A40 west from Oxford to Northleach.

NORTHLEACH: In the 15th century Northleach was one of the busiest wool towns in the Cotswolds. During this period prosperous wool traders built the church of St. Peter and St. Paul, which is designed in the Perpendicular style and constructed of local stone. Note especially how the South Porch is richly decorated with statuary and carved stone. It is perhaps best known, however, for its numerous brasses representing the wool merchants. The church has undergone and survived much recent restoration, including work by Sir Basil Spence, architect of Coventry Cathedral.

Because the River Leach did not provide sufficient power to drive the watermills that were speeding up the manufacturing process in other parts of the region, the wool trade declined after the 16th century and Northleach suffered. But the town came into its own again when stagecoaches began to run between London and Gloucester, and several coaching inns opened their doors to travelers.

Take the A429 south from Northleach and follow signs for Chedworth.

CHEDWORTH: This quiet town has a fine Norman church worth a look inside for its carved stone pulpit. About 2 miles outside Chedworth in a pretty wooded part of the Coln Valley is a partly reconstructed Roman villa. Here you can see some very well preserved examples of Roman mosaic floors and bathhouses.

BIBURY: This picturesque village, through which the River Coln flows, is one of Britain's most photographed. The avid shutterbug will find yet another perfect composition everywhere he looks: Bibury's partly 13th-century church contains many of the earlier Saxon features as well as some Norman additions. Then there's Arlington Row, a group of early-17th-century stone cottages huddled together on a terraced hillside near the Coln, and Arlington Mill, a former 17th-century corn mill, which houses a country craft museum.

En Route from Bibury – An interesting side trip would be to Quenington and Fairford; to reach these towns follow an unclassified road toward Coln St. Aldwyne.

At roughly the southernmost extreme of the Cotswolds proper, Quenington, in the Coln Valley, is notable for its well-restored 17th-century buildings, some of which open their gardens to the public in the summer. The best house is Quenington House, a 19th-century building on the site of what was a Preceptory, or lesser and subsidiary property, of the Knights Hospitalers, dating from about 1190. But the best gardens are probably those of Barnsley House. The Norman church was built in about 1170 and later restored in 1882 by the architect of Gloucester Cathedral. It's particularly famous for the stone carvings around the north and south doors.

Fairford, a little town perched on the edge of the Cotswolds, boasts a jewel of a parish church — built in the Perpendicular style by 15th-century wool merchants and lit by 28 brilliant stained-glass windows. As was then the custom, the windows were not simply decorative but also educational — they illustrated Bible stories for parishioners who couldn't read.

The English poet and clergyman John Keble was born in Fairford in 1792. He was one of the leaders of the Oxford Movement, which among other things made church services more formal and sought to reduce secular power over the church. Keble College, Oxford, was founded in his memory, partly with money left over from sales of Keble's poetical bestseller, *The Christian Year,* which went into no fewer than 92 editions.

Fairford's main square, the Market Place, is lined with ancient trees and stone houses; there are several inviting old pubs, the best of which are probably *The Bull* and *The George.*

CHECKING IN: *Swan* – Crouched low by the River Coln (where you can cast a line for trout), this creeper-covered 17th-century coaching inn has just 23 rooms. On A433 (phone: 028574-204). Expensive.

Bibury Court – Run by the Collier family, this rambling Tudor and Jacobean manor, set in 6 acres of gardens, is furnished in antiques; trout fishing is available. Off A433 (phone: 028574-337). Moderate.

BURFORD: From Bibury, take the A433 to Burford. Although on the edge of the Cotswolds, Burford is a typical Cotswold community — its steep main street, stippled with ancient stone houses and shops, rolls down a hill to meet the River Windrush. In the 18th century, Burford was an important coaching stop. Now, in the 20th century, it's an antiquer's delight; Burford is full of antique shops — some of the most expensive in the country.

A number of Burford's buildings are antiques themselves, notably the almshouses built in 1457; the Grammar School for Boys founded in 1571; the Priory, an Elizabethan house; the Great House, built in 1690; and the Tolsey (or Toll House), now a town museum. The spired church is Perpendicular in style and has an old Norman tower. One of the houses in Sheep Street is known as "Kit's Quarry," built by Christopher Kempster, who was the master mason commissioned by Christopher Wren to provide stone from local quarries for St. Paul's Cathedral. Tours of Burford take place every Sunday afternoon in summer, conducted by members of the Burford and District Society.

Drive from Burford to Great Barrington, turning left on to an unclassified road just north of the bridge over the Windrush (approximately 4 miles).

THE BARRINGTONS AND WINDRUSH: From the 14th to the 19th century, the quarries of Great Barrington and Little Barrington produced some of the best Cotswold stone. Many of England's more impressive buildings were constructed using the stone, including sections of St. Paul's Cathedral in London and several Oxford colleges.

Great Barrington consists mainly of a double row of cottages partly surrounded by a country estate called Barrington Park. The centerpiece of the estate is a Palladian mansion which dates from 1736–38. Close to the house is a mostly Norman church that underwent complete restoration in 1815.

Little Barrington, across the River Windrush (which meanders rather than rushes), is the prettier of the two villages; it is centered around a triangular green, which was supposedly built over old quarry workings. The pub now called the *Inn for All Seasons* was popular with quarrymen, and it is said that its cellars are on the same level and have access to the quarry's underground passages. Little Barrington's houses are of different shapes, sizes, and periods and present a varied but harmonious composition.

The village of Windrush is also on this side of the river. From the pleasant shaded lane that links it with Little Barrington there are lovely views across to Great Barrington. But the real reason for stopping in Windrush is to visit St. Peter's Church, a Norman building decorated with much fine carving, especially around the south doorway.

 CHECKING IN: *Bay Tree* – This 16th-century mansion down a quiet side street has retained its cozy, antique and fireplace-lit atmosphere despite recent updating — 16 new rooms in adjacent cottages have been added to the original 24. Sheep St. (phone: 099382-3137). Moderate.

Bull – History is in every nook and cranny of this 14th-century coaching inn on one of England's most famous and prettiest High Streets. There are 14 rooms, peacefully decorated with modern touches, a bar, and a restaurant. High St., Burford (phone: 099382-2220). Moderate.

Lamb Inn – Built of Cotswold stone and dating from the 15th century, this hotel also has a restaurant and a garden. Sheep St. (phone: 099382-3155). Moderate.

BOURTON-ON-THE-WATER: This village is very pretty, with the River Windrush running right through it, crossed by unusual and attractive stone bridges that link rows of shops and small hotels set back behind greenswards where people picnic and children play. Be sure to visit St. Lawrence Church, which has a late-18th-century spire and a 14th-century chancel; it was heavily restored in Victorian times — although more successfully than many. Next to the *Old New Inn* on High St. is a famous model village of Bourton; across the river on A429 is Birdland Zoo Gardens, a 4-acre preserve where many species of exotic birds reside. Also in town is the Cotswold Perfumery where visitors can sample perfumes manufactured on the premises (open daily). *Note:* Almost too popular, Bourton has allowed itself to become very commercial and is jammed with tourists in the summer.

En Route from Bourton – Stow-on-the-Wold is about 4 miles north via A429; a pleasant detour would be a left turn toward the Slaughters. This lane leads first to Lower Slaughter, named after the Norman De Sclotre family; it's a rather self-consciously pretty village as yet unspoiled by tourist traffic. You may see artists at work on the green banks of the river. Upper Slaughter is on higher ground, as the name suggests, and is reached by winding leafy lanes. This village is more interesting than its sister. The *Lords of the Manor* hotel at Upper Slaughter was originally the village rectory, and it was enlarged by one incumbent, the Reverend F. E. Witts, also known as the author of the *Diary of a Cotswold Parson.* Upper Slaughter also boasts the oldest and most impressive dovecote in Gloucestershire, dating from the 16th century. Also of note is *The Manor House,* an interesting Elizabethan building that incorporates the remains of a 15th-century priory and has an outstanding Jacobean porch. Open afternoons from May through September. And so strong is local pride that even some of the council houses (subsidized low-income homes) are roofed in Cotswold stone slates.

CHECKING IN: *Lords of the Manor* – If Upper Slaughter didn't have a beautifully preserved 17th-century manor house and surrounding grounds as a hostelry for visitors, it would be necessary to build one. Luckily it was done some 300 years ago, and we need only call for reservations (phone: 0451-20243). Expensive.

STOW-ON-THE-WOLD: This town sits squarely on the Fosse Way, one of the Roman trunk routes that cuts a swathe through southern Britain. (The name is not Roman but Saxon; and the road was used later by Normans as well.) Stow was another important wool market town in medieval times; there were two annual fairs, with merchants dickering over the sale of thousands of sheep. Many hotels, shops, and restaurants sprang up around the famous Market Square designed by the lord of the manor, the abbot of Evesham, in the 11th century. The *King's Arms,* an old inn on the square, was once a lodging house for household servants of Edward VI, son of Henry VIII; in late March 1646, after what was to be the last battle of the Civil War, Cromwell incarcerated Royalist troops in the church that stands on one corner of the square.

CHECKING IN: *Fosse Manor* – This ivy-covered manor house has 22 spacious rooms and a restaurant. Fosse Way, Stow (phone: 0451-30354). Moderate.

King's Arms – This 500-year-old inn offers simple lodgings and a hearty breakfast. Market Sq., Stow (phone: 0451-30364). Inexpensive.

En Route from Stow-on-the-Wold – It's about a mile to Upper Swell via the B4077; Lower Swell lies on the A436.

Upper Swell is a charming 18th-century village known for its handsome early-17th-century manor house, arched stone bridge over the River Dikler, and early-19th-century watermill capped with a Welsh slate roof. Stop for a moment at the parish church for a look at its exceptional Perpendicular font. Close to the village is the Donnington Brewery, once a corn mill, and now one of the last privately owned breweries. It's been producing beer since about 1865.

A mineral spring was discovered in Lower Swell in 1807, and for a while it was thought that the Swells might develop into another Cheltenham. All that remains of those fine dreams today, however, is a row of curiously decorated and rather exotic houses optimistically known as the "Spa Cottages." Despite this setback, Lower Swell regained its reputation with the success of another kind of watering hole — the *Golden Ball Inn,* which has for many years greeted travelers with food, drink (including Donnington beer), and a warm welcome. Treat yourself to lunch here.

Another sidetrip from Stow-on-the-Wold is in the opposite direction, to Chipping Norton, about 9 miles via A436 and A44.

"Chipping" may be a corruption of "cheapening," meaning "market." Chipping Norton, perched high on a hill near the Evenlode, was a busy market town for centuries. Today its wide streets are no longer filled with medieval wool merchants and its imposing Victorian tweed mill has been closed down. Instead, the market square now bustles with tourists sampling Chipping Norton's many cafés, pubs, restaurants, and hotels. The parish church, built in the Perpendicular style by wool merchants in the 14th and 15th centuries, is one of the largest in Oxfordshire and is especially noteworthy for its several fine medieval brasses.

Four miles north of Chipping Norton off A34 are the Rollright Stones, a circle of about 70 stones that date from between 1800 and 500 BC. To one side stand 5 other stones, said to represent a king and his knights. The name of these stones derives, it is believed, from *Rollanriht,* or "the jurisdiction of Roland the Brave." The name appears in the Domesday Book as *Rollandri.*

MORETON-IN-MARSH: This town lies on the railway, and therefore has a more workaday atmosphere than most other Cotswold communities. It is another old market town that can be fun to explore on foot. Main Street, which follows the route of the Fosse Way, is unusually wide and contains many antique shops. On High Street is the Market Hall, built in Victorian Tudor style in 1887. Note the Curfew Tower on Oxford Street; it dates from the 17th century and its bell was rung daily until the 19th century. About a mile west of town is the Batsford Park Arboretum, with 50 acres of rare trees (open daily, April to October).

 CHECKING IN: *White Hart Royal* – If you stay here, you will have shared a place with royalty — Charles I spent the night in this half-timbered posting inn in 1644. Cobbles more than 300 years old have been carefully preserved, and old hunting trophies and weapons adorn the Cotswold stone bar. The hotel has 27 rooms and a small timbered dining room. High St. (phone: 0608-50731). Moderate.

En Route from Moreton-in-Marsh – A worthwhile side trip is to Chastleton House; take A44 to the southeast, then turn right onto an unclassified road for Chastleton (approximately 5 miles). Chastleton House was built in 1603 by Walter Jones, a Witney wool merchant who bought the land from one of the Gunpowder Plot conspirators. Jones spent half his fortune improving the house in 1603, and the other half — unfortunately for him — on the Royalist cause during the Civil War. He was a man of taste, as is shown by the richly carved paneling and the furniture. Among the items in the house are Charles I's Bible, which he used on the morning of his execution, valuable tapestries; and rare china. The topiary garden is one of the best in Britain: There are good views of it from the windows of the Long Gallery in the house. The idea of such gardens was imported from the Continent by William of Orange, and although the representation of birds and animals has altered over the years, the layout has remained the same. The house and gardens are open year-round; closed Wednesdays.

From Moreton-in-Marsh, take the A44 west for about 6 miles, then turn right onto the B4081 for Chipping Campden.

CHIPPING CAMPDEN: This town was restored carefully by the Campden Trust, a group of people mindful of the past; as a result, it is remarkably well preserved. If you can ignore the traffic — mostly visitors looking for somewhere to park — the main street looks just as it did hundreds of years ago. And Chipping Campden's many fine old buildings are a delight. The church, though heavily restored by the Victorians, is one of the best in the Cotswolds. Built in the Perpendicular style by the town's wool merchants in the 15th century, it is unusually large and contains several fine brasses. Near the church are almshouses dating to 1612. All along High Street, you'll see many houses built with warm Cotswold stone; also stop at the handsome bow-windowed Grevel House (the former home of a wealthy woolman) on Church Street. Across the way is Woolstapler's Hall, a 14th-century house where wool merchants traded; it's now a museum of the town's history and a tourist information center. The Market Hall, a solid yet graceful structure composed of fourteen stone arches built in 1627, was where the area's farmers sold their dairy products.

CHECKING IN: *Cottage in the Wood* – Roughly 30 miles off the driving route but worthy of a detour. Much more than a cottage, this mansion occupies 7 acres of woodlands and has wonderful views of the fertile Vale of Evesham.

The style is very English and very traditional and the guestrooms are superbly appointed. The intimate restaurant features English dishes and has an excellent wine list. Holywell Rd., Malvern Wells, Malvern (phone: 06845-3487). Expensive.

King's Arms – These two converted 17th- and 18th-century stone houses have a total of 14 rooms, a good restaurant, quiet gardens, and a good deal of character. The Square (phone: 0386-840256). Moderate.

Noel Arms – A pub-like atmosphere prevails at this 14th-century coaching inn — lots of oak beams, armor-hung walls, and a cheering fireplace. Some of the 19 rooms sport four-poster beds. High St., Chipping Campden (phone: 0386-840317). Moderate.

EATING OUT: *Bantam Tea Rooms* – This cozy, traditional tearoom is the perfect spot for a cup. High St., Chipping Campden. Inexpensive.

En Route from Chipping Campden – Take the B4081 north to Mickleton, then follow signs for Hidcote Manor Gardens, opposite which are Kitesgate Court Gardens. (Note that while Hidcote Gardens are open daily except Tuesdays and Fridays from April to October, Kitesgate Gardens are open only twice a week.) Hidcote Manor Gardens are formal, with impressive and varied hedges, rare trees, and shrubs. The gardens were laid out in the first few years of this century by Laurence Johnston, and it was here that he originated the mixed or "harlequin" hedge. There are small individual gardens with pools, rare plants, and gazebos. As the poet Vita Sackville-West said of Major Johnston, "He spilled his cornucopia everywhere." Kitesgate Court Gardens are steeper, less formal, and, like Hidcote, are enhanced by the presence of an impressive house, Mickleton Manor.

Pick up the A46 and proceed south to Broadway.

BROADWAY: Henry James once described Broadway thus: "The place has so much character that it rubs off on the visitor . . . it is delicious to be at Broadway." Many people would agree with James, judging from the traffic and numbers of tourists who throng here to shop for antiques and to stroll among the 17th- and 18th-century golden Cotswold stone houses. (Partly due to heavy tourism and partly just to preserve the old stone — which is highly vulnerable to even the comparatively mild Cotswold weather — there has recently been some renovation and new building. But it has been done well, and stone facing rather than complete razing is the general rule.)

The *Lygon Arms* is probably Broadway's main attraction; the hotel's elegance is only exceeded by its history. The main building dates from 1530, though parts of it are more than 600 years old. It was frequented by Charles I and Oliver Cromwell, and rooms named after each have been carefully preserved or restored.

Some of Broadway's other notable structures include Middle Hill, the estate of Sir Thomas Phillips, the eccentric and wealthy book collector; St. Eadburgha's, a Norman church; and Broadway Beacon, an 18th-century, 65-foot-high, stern stone edifice on Broadway Hill, all of which are within Broadway Tower Country Park. You can climb the tower for a view of the countryside, spread your picnic lunch in one of the designated areas, or visit the 150-year-old barn that houses an exhibit on the geology of the hill.

CHECKING IN: *Lygon Arms* – Both Charles I and Oliver Cromwell slept in this elegant, 16th-century, ivy-covered inn, now a staple in international hotel rankings. There are 70 antique-furnished rooms, 4 with four-poster beds, and an award-winning dining room. High St., Broadway (phone: 0386-852255). Expensive.

EATING OUT: *Dormy House* – Built on an escarpment of galloping Cotswolds above the village of Broadway, *Dormy* began life as a 16th-century farmhouse. Ancient beams and exposed stone walls prove the historic pedigree, but open fires, a cheery staff, and French-inspired cuisine provide the contemporary touch. There are 50 elegantly furnished rooms, and one of the friendliest staffs around. Willersey Hill, Broadway (phone: 0386-852711). Expensive.

En Route from Broadway – Near the western end of Broadway, *before* you reach the A46 to Winchcombe, turn left for Snowshill Manor — about 3 miles. The manor house, a fine example of Tudor and Georgian architecture, was part of Catherine Parr's dowry (she was Henry VIII's last wife). It contains an eclectic collection of antiques and trivia accumulated by Charles Wade, who subsidized his mania with an income from West Indian sugar plantations. He was so devoted to his collection that he actually lived in the adjoining cottage in order to give it more space. Both are open to the public.

Another interesting sidetrip is to the Cotswold Farm Park, a survival center for rare breeds of British farm animals, including shire horses; Soay and Orkney sheep (the former originally from St. Kilda, a now uninhabited Scottish island far off the mainland in the Atlantic); and examples of the breed of sheep upon which the medieval wool trade depended (the "Cotswold Lions"). To get here, follow the unclassified road from Snowshill toward Bourton-on-the-Water, which joins the B4077 directly east of Temple Guiting. The park is just before that junction.

You must get back on the A46 to drive south to Winchcombe.

WINCHCOMBE: Though it suffers a little from through traffic, not all of Winchcombe is on the main road, and it is a good example of a genuine Cotswold town going about its business as it has done for several hundred years. Before the Norman Conquest this was the capital of Winchcombeshire, and here you will see half-timbering among the stone houses. For example, the *George Inn,* which once provided lodgings for pilgrims visiting nearby Hailes Abbey, has a half-timbered coaching yard. Hailes Abbey was built between 1245 and 1253 and prospered for some 300 years before Henry VIII's Dissolution of the Monasteries, at which time it was razed. (The order to surrender was actually given on Christmas Eve 1539.) Now only the ruins remain. The site is 3 miles northeast of Winchcombe, clearly signed off the A46. Winchcombe's 19th-century town hall, which contains the original stocks, now houses a folk museum. The parish church is mainly remarkable for the gargoyles that decorate its exterior — at least 40 of them; inside there is an altarcloth believed to have been woven by Catherine of Aragon, Henry VIII's first queen.

Half a mile southeast of the town center, clearly signed, lies Sudeley Castle, open to the public during the summer. Now the private home of Lord and Lady Ashcombe, its interior is quite labyrinthine. The castle has been the home of several of England's queens: Anne Boleyn and Elizabeth I spent time here, and it was the final home and final resting place of Catherine Parr, the only wife to outlive Henry VIII. During the Civil War that affected so much of this now tranquil part of England, Sudeley Castle was extensively damaged, and it was virtually abandoned for nearly 200 years. But with the help of Sir George Gilbert Scott, responsible for, among other things, London's Albert Memorial, the castle was restored. The restoration work went on until the 1930s; tantalizing traces remain of the original buildings, including a few dating to the 15th century, and some very old stained glass. The castle now houses an important collection of art treasures, including works by Constable, Turner, Rubens, and Van Dyck.

From Winchcombe follow the A46 to Cheltenham.

CHELTENHAM: Popularly regarded as a genteel place largely inhabited by geriatrics, Cheltenham is more lively than many think. For example, it's practically impossible to find accommodations within a 30-mile radius during Cheltenham Gold Cup Week, a national horse race held every March. (For information, write to Racing Information Bureau, 42 Portman Sq., London W1.) In addition, there is the Festival of Music and Drama in May, the International Festival of Music in July, and the Festival of Literature in October (for information, write Town Hall Box Office, Imperial Sq., Cheltenham, Gloucestershire). While here, try the waters that made Cheltenham famous — either at the town hall or the Pittville Pump Room (named after local MP Joseph Pitt, who served in the House of Commons from 1825 to 1830). The medicinal properties of these waters are said to derive from the magnesium and sodium sulphates and the sodium bicarbonate they contain. When your thirst is slaked, visit the Gallery of Fashion in the same building, or stroll to the Gustav Holst Birthplace Museum in the Regency House. Open Tuesdays through Fridays, noon to 5:30 PM; Saturdays, 11 AM to 5:30 PM (phone: 24846). Before you leave Cheltenham, be sure to take a stroll along the famous Promenade, made lovely by its rows of great horse chestnut trees. Along one side are first-class shops, similar to those found in Cheltenham's Regent Arcade and Montpellier area; along the other side stand beautifully preserved Regency terraced buildings. The town also has many spacious and colorful gardens, the best of which is the Imperial Gardens, adjoining the town hall on Imperial Sq.

The A435 will take you from Cheltenham to Cirencester.

 CHECKING IN: *Hotel de la Bere and Country Club* – A lovely mock-Tudor mansion (built in this century) with 42 guestrooms and very good sports facilities including tennis, squash, horseback riding, and swimming as well as a sauna and solarium. Southam (phone: 0242-37771). Expensive to moderate.

***Queens* –** A colonnaded hotel overlooking Imperial Gardens which has graced the Promenade since the 19th century. Grand and lofty layouts, with 77 bedrooms, elegantly furnished and beautifully equipped. The Promenade (phone: 514724). Expensive to moderate.

 EATING OUT: *Forrest's Wine House* – Hearty German cuisine and wines are the specialty here. Imperial La., Cheltenham (phone: 0242-38001). Inexpensive.

***That Sandwich Place* –** Stop here for a tasty lunch of salad or sandwiches. 69 Regent St., Cheltenham (phone: 0242-29575). Inexpensive.

CIRENCESTER: Established by the Romans at the junction at which their vital trunk route Fosse Way met five other roads, Cirencester (or Corinium) was a strategic link in their defenses. As a result, Corinium grew to be second in size only to London. In the 6th century it was destroyed by the invading Saxons, so little of the Roman occupation remains in the town itself. However, mosaic floors, sculpture, and pottery recovered from excavations now form the extensive collection of Roman relics in the Corinium Museum on Park St. You can also see the ruins of a Roman amphitheater on Cotswold Ave. Periods of English history seem piled one atop another by a profligate hand in Cirencester. The parish church, St. John the Baptist, built by wool merchants in the 14th century, is a fine example of the Perpendicular style. One of the largest churches in England, it is not to be missed for its rich stone carvings, magnificent array of medieval stained glass, and many fine brasses. On Stroud Rd. is Cirencester Park, the 3,000-acre estate of the earl of Bathurst; although the house is not open to the public, the grounds are. Also interesting are the Cirencester Workshops in the center of town. The craft gallery and workshops are open daily except Sundays.

Take the A423 from Cirencester to Malmesbury.

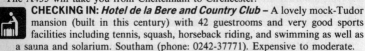 **CHECKING IN: *Fleece* –** Outside is a handsome black and white half-timbered façade; inside are Cotswold stone walls, fine open fireplaces, and low-beamed ceilings. Gastronomic festivals are a regular attraction of the hotel restaurant, which specializes in nouvelle cuisine and real ales — try the Three B's Ale, the local brew. Market Pl., Cirencester (phone: 0285-68507). Moderate.

King's Head – Opposite the famous parish church, this 14th-century coaching inn with 70 rooms has been completely modernized without destroying its charm, although the presence of tour parties can sometimes be overwhelming.. Market Pl., Cirencester (phone: 0285-3322). Moderate.

MALMESBURY: This pleasant little town high above the Wiltshire Avon is the site of a magnificent Norman abbey with a most unusual history: During the Dissolution under King Henry VIII in the 16th century, the building was sold to a clothier for £1,500. The man promptly brought in his weaving machinery and converted it into a factory. It was not until 1823 that a restoration effort was begun. Despite the many years of decay, the restoration was eminently successful, and today the abbey is considered one of the finest examples of Norman building remaining in Britain. The richly carved south porch and the musicians' gallery are especially impressive.

The town has two special connections with aviation. The first was established at Malmesbury Abbey in the 11th century, when Brother Oliver attempted to defy gravity by leaping from the tower wearing a pair of homemade wings. He survived the leap but was lame ever after. And at Kemble, 6 miles north of Malmesbury, the Royal Air Force aerobatic team, the Red Arrows, practice their aerial formations.

Malmesbury is one of the oldest boroughs in England and a very well planned medieval city; it was already an important town before the Norman invasion. Some medieval remains are still extant, including fragments of walls and ruins of a 12th-century castle that can be seen today at the *Old Bell* hotel. Six bridges lead to the Market Square, at whose center is an impressive octagonal Tudor market cross. There are several lovely 17th- and 18th-century houses built by rich weavers on the adjoining streets. George Washington's ancestors appear to have come from the region, since at least five Washington predecessors are buried in a churchyard in Garsdon, 2 miles east of Malmesbury.

En Route from Malmesbury – Going southwest, there are several noteworthy stops: Badminton House, off the B4040; Dodington House, off the A46; and Dyrham Park, farther south and also off the A46.

The Badminton estate has been in the same family, the Beauforts, for over 300 years, and is the magnificent setting each April of the Badminton Horse Trials, an international competition. For information, write: Box Office, Badminton Horse Trials, Badminton, Avon, G19 1DF. The house itself is open only on rare occasions during the summer months. (A note of fascinating trivia: the game of badminton was invented here by house guests in the 1860s.)

Dodington House is an impressive Neoclassical structure built between 1796 and 1817 for Sir Christopher Codrington, the wealthy owner of a West Indian sugar plantation. In the stable wing of the house is a carriage museum with hansom cabs, a pony phaeton, a funeral hearse, and a Black Maria.

Stop for tea served in the orangery of the elegant, low-lying mansion in Dyrham Park. Afterward, stroll around; the house, built between 1692 and 1704, shows considerable Dutch influence, perhaps because its owner, William Blathwayt, was a representative at the Hague.

Follow the A46 to Bath.

CHECKING IN: *Old Bell* – This is a fabulous old inn, a wisteria-clad gabled building on the site of 12th-century Malmesbury Castle. It still retains a medieval spiral staircase, part of the castle wall, and a huge fireplace (recently revealed in all its former glory) in the entrance hall. There are 19 rooms, a garden, a good restaurant, and the charming *Castle Bar.* Abbey Row (phone: 06662-2344). Expensive.

BATH: This city was once one of Europe's greatest spas. Originally founded by the Romans, who in AD 54 built an elaborate system of baths, it was named Aquae Sulis, after Sulis Minerva, a Roman goddess. In succeeding centuries Bath lost and regained its reputation; at one point in the 17th century, it became so popular with royalty and gentry that diarist Samuel Pepys wondered how the water could be sanitary with so many bodies jammed into it. For a detailed report on the city, its sights, hotels, and restaurants, see *Bath,* THE CITIES.

The Lake District

The most efficient bridging of the gap between London and Scotland passes perforce through the western Midlands, an area whose concentration of heavy-duty industrial cities is particularly high and whose interest to visitors is, consequently, supposedly low. Stoke-on-Trent, Sheffield, Manchester, Liverpool — these names reverberate with the crash of the steel mill and the roar of the factory. Well-meaning Londoners will most likely urge you to stay steadfastly to the east, ensuring that you encounter the bucolic pleasures of Cambridge, Lincoln, York, and Durham. Indeed, so splendid are those towns and the country around them that it is hard to argue with such advice unless you are fortified by a familiarity with the less obvious satisfactions to be had in the birthplace of the Industrial Revolution. Or unless bearing east means forgoing forever that crumpled, rumpled, well-watered mountain country known as the Lake District.

Only 30 miles across in any direction, there is a special intensity in the beauty of the Lake District — tarn, mere, beck, and fell, scoured and sculpted by the Ice Age and squeezed into the small county of Cumbria; just an hour or so north of Manchester. It is as though nature were offering a consolation for the sprawling rigors of the industrial belt, much too near-at-hand. No part of England is so universally loved by Britons — for the purity of its clear mountain lakes (meres); its almost vertical fields filled with grazing sheep, each field carefully delineated by painstakingly maintained stone walls; its sharp rocky peaks; and the thousands of tiny lakes (tarns) fed year in and year out by innumerable waterfalls and streams (becks). Its traditional industry has always been hill farming, which gives a steady rhythm to the lakeland year from lambing time onward, but increasingly the area's livelihood is tourism. Since 1951 the Lake District has been a national park, and visitors — hill walkers, rock climbers, historians, artists, ornithologists, and those seeking simply a bit of peace and quiet — number in the millions annually.

What is earth-loving and ancient in the English spirit is drawn irresistibly to the Lake District's uncompromising beauty. Small wonder that J. M. W. Turner, the famous English landscape painter, spent time here sketching it. The Lake District is primarily associated, however, with a group of his contemporaries, poets of the late eighteenth and early nineteenth centuries who not only celebrated the beauty of the region in words, but discovered here values to stand against the encroaching horrors of the industrial age. Chief among them was William Wordsworth, who lived here for most of his life, but others are equally well known: Robert Southey, Samuel Taylor Coleridge, and the writers John Ruskin and Thomas De Quincey. Much of what you see and do in the region is associated with the Lake Poets.

One of the most surprising things about the Lake District is how small this famous area really is. You can drive right through it in less than an hour and yet spend a month without ever seeing half of what time and nature have created here. Looking at a map, you see that the principal lakes — Derwentwater, Ullswater, Windermere, wild Wastwater, Buttermere, Crummock Water, Grasmere, and Rydal Water — radiate from the central mass of the Cumbrian Mountains like the spokes of a wheel. A few of them, such as Thirlmere and Haweswater, are reservoirs slaking the thirst and industry of northern cities, but the living lakes are busy with sails and some of them with stately steamers. The distances between these postcard-perfect bodies of water are short, but each of the larger lakes provides a good base for exploring the neighboring area. Allowing time for some hiking as well as exploration of towns and villages, you could easily spend 2 days around each major lake — Windermere, Derwentwater, and Ullswater especially — before moving on.

The route described below begins in the southeastern corner of the Lake District at the town of Kendal, takes the back road to Lake Windermere, and crosses the water on the ferry to Near Sawrey, Hawkshead, and Coniston. The next leg of the trip, north from Windermere, crosses the paths of the Lake Poets. For the last 37 years of his life Wordsworth lived at Rydal Mount, just a few miles from Ambleside. Dove Cottage, the home he had occupied previously, is a few miles farther north, at Grasmere. Thomas De Quincey, author of *Confessions of an English Opium-Eater,* took over the cottage after Wordsworth left for Rydal Mount. The route then proceeds north from Grasmere and passes Thirlmere from where there is easy access to the challenging 3,118-foot mountain peak, Helvellyn. At the end of this leg is Derwentwater — perhaps the most beautiful of all the lakes. Robert Southey made his home here, in the town of Keswick, where he frequently was joined by Percy Bysshe Shelley and Coleridge. The twins, Buttermere and Crummock Water, are just a short drive southwest of Keswick, and beyond them, in the northwest corner of the Lake District, is Cockermouth. Wordsworth and his sister Dorothy were both born and raised in Cockermouth, and the family home and nearby fields became part of the joyous imagery of the poetry that introduced this area to readers everywhere. From Cockermouth, two choices present themselves. One possibility is to follow the western boundary of the Lake District, heading south, from where numerous small roads lead into the heart of the mountains and the area's best climbing, a prospect particularly appealing for experienced and properly equipped backpackers and hill walkers. Another is to return to Keswick, drop south off the main road for a visit to the lovely lake of Ullswater, and complete the tour at Penrith, which is conveniently at the northeastern flank of the Lake District at the intersection of several main north-south and east-west routes.

The Lake District offers a wide range of accommodations — from small but comfortable inns to some of the best hotels in the country, and plenty of guesthouses offering bed and breakfast *and* an evening meal for as little as $20 per person. Expect to pay between $60 and $120 for a double in those places listed as expensive; from \$40 to \$60 in moderate; and under \$40 in inexpensive. A meal for two, excluding wine, tips, or drinks, will run about \$35 to \$50 in places listed as expensive; \$25 to \$35 in moderate; and under \$20 in inexpensive.

KENDAL: Holiday traffic threads constantly through the one-way streets of this old market town, the gateway to the southern part of the Lake District. Because it is busily engaged in the manufacture of shoes, snuff, and Kendal mint cake (after six centuries in the wool industry), the town pays less attention to visitors than many another place in Cumbria. Visitors, in turn, in a headlong dash to begin lakeside vacations, often give short shrift to everything but the large shopping center. But the old part of this town on the River Kent is an attractive huddle of slate-roofed buildings separated by small alleyways, yards, and courts, and there are several buildings of particular interest. The ruined Kendal Castle, on a hill east of town, dates back to Norman times and was later the birthplace of Catherine Parr, the last of King Henry VIII's six wives. The 13th-century parish church near the center of town is unusual for its five aisles and its brasses. Abbot Hall, a Georgian house beside the river, is now an art gallery with modern collections and 18th-century period rooms displaying furniture and paintings, including one by Turner and one by the famous portrait artist George Romney, who spent his youth in Kendal. The Museum of Lakeland Life and Industry, installed in what was once the stables of Abbot Hall, and voted British Museum of the Year in 1986, gives an interesting backward look at the social and economic life of the area. Its World Wildlife Gallery devotes a large section to local creatures and their habitats. The Tourist Information Centre in Kendal's town hall has a mass of leaflets and hotel lists for the southern Lake District.

The main road west out of town climbs a long hill and, after about 2 miles, comes to a large traffic circle. Turn off the A591 here and head down the B5284 through countryside typical of the edge of the Lake District: neat fields, thick woodland, and a landscape that is all mounds and hummocks building up to the larger hills beyond. The village of Crook is along the way 5 miles from Kendal, and after another 5 miles the route crosses two roads skirting the eastern side of Lake Windermere and comes to a stop at the terminal of the car ferry. Bowness-on-Windermere and Windermere itself are a mile or so north of the terminal.

 CHECKING IN: *Wild Boar* – This pleasant country hotel in a converted 17th-century house is a quiet, comfortable staging post. Gardens outside and a beamed bar and fireplaces inside add to its charm. The dining room is highly rated. Crook (phone: 09662-5225). Expensive to moderate.

***Natland Mill Beck Farm* –** An extremely warm atmosphere at this 17th-century farmhouse with sturdy beams, pine doors, ancient oak cupboards, and 4-foot-thick walls. Kendal (phone: 0539-21122). Inexpensive.

WINDERMERE AND BOWNESS: These adjoining resort areas on Lake Windermere make up one town that is the focal point of tourism in the Lake District. Bowness is the actual port on the water and Windermere is just above Bowness, inland from the lake. Between the two, virtually every recreational activity is available.

It is difficult to actually see Lake Windermere or the surrounding mountains from the town, but a 20-minute walk up Orrest Head hill (to the north of the railroad station) reveals all in a good view of the lake and the hills beyond. Scenic outlooks are a particular attraction of the Windermere countryside and some other notable ones include Queen Adelaide's Hill, an ideal picnic spot between Bowness and the main Ambleside Road; Millerground, a little farther along the same footpath; Biskey Howe, reached from Helm Road, Bowness; and School Knott, which has an easy, winding path to its summit east of Windermere. The information centers at Windermere and Bowness have details of these and other walks.

Lake Windermere, the largest of the lakes in the district (10½ miles long), has a much softer aspect than most, the happy product of its luxuriantly wooded banks, filled with rhododendrons that burst into flaming color each June. The waterfront of Bowness has been attractively developed with restaurants overlooking the lake, chandleries, and shops. During the holiday season (May through October) pleasure cruises operate from the pier nearby along the length of Windermere between Lakeside at its southern end, Bowness, and Waterhead at its northern end. These services connect with the Lakeside and Haverthwaite Steam Railway, a private line running 3½ miles south of Lakeside through the attractive valley of the River Leven. There are several small islands in the lake, and on one of them, Belle Isle, stands an 18th-century mansion that was the first completely round house built in England. It is one of the more unusual stately homes in the Lake District, and among its contents are portraits by Romney and lake views by the French landscape painter, Philippe de Loutherbourg (open May through September; ferry from Bowness). The Windermere Steamboat Museum just north of Bowness has a wonderful collection of Victorian and Edwardian steam launches, including *Dolly,* the oldest mechanically propelled boat in the world, built in 1850 (open Easter through September). The museum pieces are afloat and in working order and you may occasionally see them steaming about on the lake. Races are held on the lake on summer weekends, and the biggest, the annual power boat Grand Prix and Record Attempts Week, takes place in October. In late summer there is the Windermere Swim, when well-greased long-distance swimmers brave the chill length of the lake.

Midway between Windermere and Ambleside off the A591 is the Brockhole National Park Centre, a country house set in beautiful gardens and grounds that reach down to the lake. The center (phone: 09662-2231) has a constant program of lectures, films, and exhibitions covering crafts, natural history, farming, industrial archaeology, the ubiquitous Wordsworths, and other aspects of past and present life in the Lake District, and is open daily from 10 AM, late March to early November.

CHECKING IN: *Belsfield* – This magnificent Georgian house overlooking Lake Windermere is decorated with an interesting blend of period pieces and modern furnishings. A new wing (in the garden) has been added, making a total of 66 rooms, and there's a ready-made jogging track that winds through 6 acres of grounds. Bowness-on-Windermere (phone: 09662-2448). Expensive.

Miller Howe – Is it the beautiful view of the placid, tree-lined lake that makes this 13-room hotel seem such a bastion of calm, or is it the impeccable service? In either case, there is hardly a better headquarters for touring the area, and the restaurant is excellent, too. Closed mid-December through February. Rayrigg Rd., Windermere (phone: 09662-2536). Expensive.

Quarry Garth – Built with stone quarried from its beautifully landscaped grounds, this mansion is typical of scores of private summer retreats built in the lakes by wealthy industrialists. Although there are just 7 guestrooms, the place is run with great professionalism by owner Rudi Shaefer. Ambleside Rd., Windermere (phone: 09662-3761). Moderate to inexpensive.

NEAR SAWREY: The ferry to the other side of Lake Windermere deposits travelers on a road leading to the village of Far Sawrey, then on to the village of Near Sawrey, the site of a literary connection more important to children than to adults. This is Hill Top Farm, the home of a Mrs. Heelis, better known as the author Beatrix Potter, whose Peter Rabbit classics, illustrated with drawings and watercolors of the hills and lakes around the village, have been staple reading for generations of youngsters. The quaint 17th-century farmhouse she lived in is open to the public (April through October);

while you are admiring the drawings on display, there may well be some small child searching earnestly through the garden for a glimpse of Peter, Jemima Puddleduck, Tom Kitten, or other old friends. When Mrs. Heelis died in 1943, she left the whole of her property, including 4,000 acres of land, to Britain's National Trust, a bequest that has done much to preserve the surrounding countryside.

HAWKSHEAD: Just beyond the head of Esthwaite Water, a small lake about 2 miles long, the road threads its way through a picturesque row of buildings. This is the quiet little village of Hawkshead, and it offers an introductory course in Lake District life that begins at the 17th-century *Queen's Head Inn,* where you can get a pint of ale to fortify you for a stroll through the stone cottages of the town. Start at the Hawkshead Grammar School, founded in 1585 by native son Edwin Sandys, archbishop of York, and attended by Wordsworth between 1779 and 1783. He left a lasting impression by carving his name in one of the original desks. While a student, Wordsworth may have lodged at Ann Tyson's cottage, on a lane off Red Lion Square, before moving to Green End Cottage in the hamlet of Colthouse, east of Hawkshead. Years later, he recalled the Esthwaite area where he spent his schooldays as "that belovèd Vale."

From Hawkshead, follow the signs over Hawkshead Hill directly to Coniston or detour via a steep byroad that leads to Tarn Hows, a small fir-fringed lake high in the hills that has the best views of the surrounding countryside, especially of Coniston Water to the south and of the mountain called the "Old Man of Coniston," which lords it over the lake.

CONISTON: Approaching from Hawkshead, Coniston is about half a mile around the northwest tip of Coniston Water. It is another charming village with strong artistic associations. A Turner masterpiece, now hanging in the Tate Gallery in London, was based on studies done at dawn from the crags above the village. Wordsworth wrote lovingly of the place and Alfred Lord Tennyson spent his honeymoon at Tent Lodge at the head of the lake. John Ruskin, the writer, painter, critic, social reformer, and scientist, moved here in 1871, producing some of his finest work at his home, Brantwood (open Easter to mid-October), on the lake's eastern shore. He is buried in the Coniston churchyard and there is a Ruskin Museum (open all year) in the village. It was on Coniston Water that Sir Malcolm Campbell set a world water-speed record of 141 mph in his boat *Bluebird* in 1939, and his son, Donald, later set four world records here. The local history section of the Ruskin Museum has photographs of the younger Campbell's last (and fatal) attempt, in 1967, to set a new speedboat record on Coniston Water. To explore in less hair-raising style, take the renovated Victorian steam yacht *Gondola,* which tours the lake 4 or 5 times a day from April through November (phone: 05394-41288).

En Route from Coniston – The A593 winds north into the junction of the Great Langdale and Little Langdale valleys. A side trip due west from this point follows a narrow road over two high passes in the mountains. The first, Wrynose Pass, is a long but straightforward climb. The second, Hard Knott Pass, is reckoned to be the toughest in Britain, a tortuous snake of a road climbing the fellside by hairpin curves and descending in the same style into Eskdale, the valley of the River Esk. The reward of the route is a series of wonderful views, but unless you're ready for some rigorous, adventurous driving, ignore the turnoff and follow the main road to Ambleside, Rydal, and Grasmere. Another alternative would be to take the cutoff to Elterwater, which has an excellent hotel, the *Britannia Inn,* then proceed directly and spectacularly into Grasmere via the narrow road over High Close, dropping steeply into Grasmere down a hill called Red Bank.

AMBLESIDE: Just less than a mile from the north end of Lake Windermere, Ambleside is an excellent touring base for climbers eager to explore lakeland's hills and forests. Wordsworth's famed Scafell Pike (3,210 feet, the highest peak in England) is a considerable hike from Ambleside, but other peaks are more accessible. Be sure to obtain detailed maps of trails and to make proper arrangements before starting any trek. The local information center is in Ambleside's old Court House in Market Square. A short distance away, up the lane past the *Royal Yachtsman* hotel, is Stockghyll Force, a beautiful waterfall cascading 70 feet to rocks below. St. Mary's Church, erected in 1854 by Sir Gilbert Scott, has a memorial to Wordsworth and a mural of the village's rush-bearing festival, when flowers and rushes are carried through the streets to the church. The festival is thought to descend from a Roman harvest ceremony and is still held yearly on the first Saturday in July. Waterhead, the northern terminus of the Lake Windermere pleasure cruises (they can also be boarded at Bowness and at Lakeside) is just south of Ambleside on A591. Just 2 miles north is Rydal.

 CHECKING IN: *Rothay Manor –* Near Ambleside at the head of Lake Windermere, this small, elegant hotel has its own croquet lawn. The country house feeling extends to the restaurant with its traditional cuisine. Closed early January to mid-February (phone: 0966-33605). Expensive.

RYDAL: William Wordsworth, with his wife, three children, sister, and sister-in-law, moved to this village in 1813 and lived here until his death 37 years later. His home, Rydal Mount, is an interesting, rambling old house, open to visitors from March to mid-January. It contains a large collection of memorabilia, including several portraits of his family and friends, and his personal library. His love of nature is reflected in the 4.5-acre garden he grew around Rydal Mount, as attentively cared for today as by the poet himself. Wordsworth drew heavily on the surrounding countryside for inspiration and poetic images, and the mute crags and flowered hillsides around his home appear repeatedly in his work. But the golden daffodils in Dora's Field, a plot of land below the garden, are not the descendants of the golden host he came upon unexpectedly while wandering "lonely as a cloud." The lake referred to in that poem is Ullswater and the poem predates Wordsworth's move to Rydal.

Just a short distance up the road is Nab Cottage, occupied briefly by Thomas De Quincey (1806) and later by Samuel Taylor Coleridge's eldest son, Hartley. The roadway continues to the village of Grasmere along the north bank of Rydal Water, which is one of the smallest lakes in the district and which, together with the River Rothay, links Lake Windermere to Grasmere Lake.

GRASMERE: The main route north from Rydal Water skirts Grasmere Lake, just a mile long and half as wide and, with an emerald green island in its center, almost too perfect for words. Farther on, off the highway to the right, is Dove Cottage, another of Wordsworth's homes, perhaps the one where his finest work was written. Then, at the heart of the Lake District, lies the beautiful and easily accessible village of Grasmere set against a backdrop of high hills. The road winds through town, its path dictated by the haphazard scattering of houses of somber, blue-green lakeland stone.

Wordsworth and his sister Dorothy lived at Dove Cottage from 1799 until 1808. Before their arrival, the house had been a small inn called the Dove and Olive Branch. While they lived there, it became a frequent stop for a stream of eminent literary figures such as Coleridge, William Hazlitt, Charles Lamb, and Sir Walter Scott. After Wordsworth married (and fathered three children), he and his family moved, turning the cottage over to their friends Thomas De Quincey and his wife. A new Wordsworth exhibition building has been constructed in the Dove Cottage complex to replace the former museum, just across the road. It contains manuscripts of letters and poems and a remarkable collection of portraits on loan from the National Portrait Gallery. Both the museum and the cottage are open to the public from Easter through September. Wordsworth lived in two more houses in Grasmere, first at Allan Bank where Coleridge was his house guest, then at the old rectory, before moving to Rydal Mount where he spent the rest of his life. Now the squat, foursquare walls of the Church of St. Oswald (parts of which may be 13th century) preside over his grave and those of his wife, his sister, and Hartley Coleridge, buried in a corner of the churchyard within earshot of the River Rothay.

Although August is the most crowded month in which to visit the Lake District, it is also the month of the Grasmere Sports, usually held on the third Thursday of the month. Begun in the mid-1800s to encourage Cumberland and Westmorland wrestling, the event now includes other traditional lakeland sports such as fell running and hound trailing. Until Cumberland and Westmorland were combined into Cumbria County (1974), competition between these rivals was intense, and the administrative alteration hasn't changed anything. The wrestling, especially, is a curious sport to watch. Competitors stand chest to chest and grasp one another by locking arms behind each other's back. The aim of this subtle combat is to throw the opponent to the ground and toward this goal the weighty and well-balanced wrestlers may struggle all day while other events take place elsewhere. Fell running or racing, an all-out dash to the top of the nearest mountain and back, is another spectacle at the Grasmere games. The Guides' Race directly up the steep sides of Butter Crags is undertaken by lean, narrow-chested athletes who move with astonishing speed up the fell to the turning point and then bound back down again with the agility of mountain goats. Other events are the hound trail competitions, which reflect the Lake District's importance as a center for fox hunting, done here on foot with packs of hardy hounds that ripple across the fells after their prey. (Caldbeck, in the far north of the Lake District, was the home of the celebrated huntsman John Peel, about whom John Woodcock Graves wrote the song "D'ye ken John Peel?" that practically became the Cumbrian anthem.)

Grasmere, like Ambleside, also has an annual rush-bearing ceremony, held on the Saturday nearest August 5, St. Oswald's Day. If you want to sample the tasty gingerbread that is distributed to the bearers, stop by the *Old Gingerbread Shop* — the local specialty will make a great snack while driving the rest of the route. There are some other distinctive shops in town, among them *English Lakes Perfumes,* offering such fragrances as Grasmere Rose and Keswick Gardenia, and the *Studio,* with the work of W. Heaton Cooper, best known of the Lake District watercolor artists. The sound of industrious clattering comes from the shop of *Chris Reekie,* weaver, who has a nice display of woolen wear, some of it produced on the original loom on which he served his apprenticeship in Scotland.

CHECKING IN: *Michaels Nook* – A charming Victorian country home furnished by the proprietor, Reginald Gifford, with many beautiful antiques. Reservations are necessary for the very fine restaurant. Guests may use the pool, sauna, and solarium at the nearby *Wordsworth* hotel, also owned by Gifford. Grasmere (phone: 09665-496). Expensive.

***Red Lion* –** This old coaching inn is in the center of the village. Closed December through February. Grasmere (phone: 09665-456). Expensive.

***White Moss House* –** Originally three separate cottages, owned by Wordsworth's family until the 1930's. The current owners have made this 7-room hotel into a pleasant place to stay. It overlooks Rydal Water, and there's usually a roaring fire to welcome hikers in from the dampness. No choice of entrees in the dining room where some uncommon English dishes are served and reservations are essential. Closed from early November to mid-March. Rydal Water (phone: 09665-295). Expensive.

***Swan* –** Centuries ago, Wordsworth brought Sir Walter Scott and other friends to enjoy a dram or two at this old coaching inn. Today it's a friendly 41-room hotel with a good restaurant that features vegetarian dishes. Grasmere (phone: 09665-551). Moderate.

En Route from Grasmere – Continuing north on A591, the road climbs Dunmail Raise. Over the summit, Thirlmere comes into view, a long, lifeless-looking lake from which water runs helped only by gravity to the taps and factories of Manchester, 100 miles to the south. In 1876, the lake level was raised artificially by the construction of a 100-foot-high dam intended to meet the needs of the Industrial Revolution in urban Lancashire. The unintended result was one of the earliest environmental battles in Britain and because of it, seeds were sown that eventually brought about the National Trust and, ultimately, the national parks. The village of Wythburn, at the foot of the lake, was lost in the flooding that occurred in the creation of Manchester's reservoir, but the tiny 17th-century chapel at Wythburn was on high enough ground to survive. It's worth a visit and its parking lot is the starting point of a climbing trail to the peak of Helvellyn, the 3,118-foot mountain that rises to the right of A591. Helvellyn offers spectacular views and can be climbed easily from the Thirlmere side. But the climb is more interesting from the east side where long, lateral ridges fall into Patterdale, a village near Ullswater. There are few more exhilarating scrambles in the whole of Britain than along Striding Edge to Helvellyn summit and back to Patterdale via Swirral Edge.

Keswick, 13 miles from Grasmere, is just a few miles beyond the north end of Thirlmere. You'll get an excellent view of the area from the crest of Castlerigg, and a road on the right leads to the prehistoric Castlerigg Stone Circle.

KESWICK: Sheltered by the towering Skiddaw (3,053 feet), this ancient and prosperous market town sits close to the north shore of Derwentwater, 3 miles long and a mile wide, surrounded by a delightful mixture of bare rock, grassy banks, and forested glens. It is one of the loveliest (some say *the* loveliest) of lakeland's lakes, and there are rowboats and cruising craft that can be rented to explore its variety, troll for trout and pike, or visit some of the many tiny islands that dot its surface. The remains of a 7th-century retreat are on the island of St. Herbert.

Many poets, including Shelley, Southey, Wordsworth, and Coleridge, were drawn to this area and Keswick's Fitz Park Museum displays some of their manuscripts, letters, and personal effects (open daily, Easter through October). Hugh Walpole, who lived on the shore of Derwentwater and set his powerful "Herries" series of novels in this valley, is also represented in the collection. Wordsworth's memory slips in again at Old Windebrowe, a 16th-century farmhouse lent to the poet and his sister in 1794. The kitchen and parlor are restored to their early condition and an exhibition illustrates the house's links to a number of other leading literary figures. Southey's home, Greta Hall (Coleridge lived in it for 3 years before the Southey family took over), has become Keswick School, and his body lies in the Crosthwaite churchyard. Southey, Wordsworth, and Coleridge all patronized the bar at the *George Hotel,* which claims to be the oldest structure in town. Judging by the crude stone masonry and faded walls, it may well be. Walpole is buried in St. John's churchyard.

Keswick earns its living from visitors and caters to them with a long list of hotels and boarding houses; the ubiquitous bed-and-breakfast sign is nowhere more evident than here. The information center, in Moot Hall, Market Sq., during the summer (its winter address is Council Offices, Main St.), can advise you on accommodations, walks, and current happenings.

Two of the best points for viewing Derwentwater and its environs are at Castle Head (529 feet), just south of Keswick, and at Friar's Crag, a rocky headland on the lake. John Ruskin was particularly enamored of the latter, and there is a memorial to him here. Southey favored the view from the hill near Greta Bridge.

CHECKING IN: *Lodore Swiss* – On the edge of Derwentwater, 3 miles south of Keswick, with glorious views of the lake and Lodore Falls. Though the building is fairly large (72 rooms) and very grand in appearance, it is run by a Swiss family (the Englands!) and their high standards are readily apparent. The restaurant features international, including Swiss, dishes. Facilities expand annually and include indoor and outdoor pools, sauna, massage, tennis, squash, and boat trips on Derwentwater. Closed November through March. Borrowdale (phone: 059684-285). Expensive.

Mary Mount Country House – Also on the shores of Derwentwater and owned by the Englands, this cozy 15-room hotel is set in beautiful woodlands. Paneled bar. Guests have access to the facilities of the *Lodore Swiss.* Closed in December. Borrowdale (phone: 059684-223). Expensive to moderate.

Royal Oak – This famous lakeland inn is old, rambling, and comfortable, and it's in the center of town. Keswick (phone: 0596-72965). Moderate.

En Route from Keswick – Drive south on B5289 to the quite beautiful Borrowdale valley. The road runs between the east shore of Derwentwater and high gray cliffs that are immensely popular with climbers. Before the village of Rosthwaite, the Bowder Stone, a huge boulder that tumbled from some nearby height, stands precariously on edge near Castle Crag, a 900-foot-high rock cone that can be climbed without too much effort in under half an hour. Great Gable, a little farther along the route, is a more challenging target — 2,949 feet of tough climbing. It takes about 3 hours to ascend this monster, but the view is well worth the effort: The entire area from Skiddaw to Windermere, and even the Isle of Man are visible from the crest.

Continue on B5289, crossing over Honister Pass, which rises well over 1,000 feet. From the summit there is an impressive view toward Buttermere Lake, with Fleetwith Pike and the steep face of Honister Crag dominating the road. A quarry operated by the Buttermere and Westmorland Green Slate Company is near the youth hostel here and visitors are welcome to watch the splitters (called "rivers") and dressers at work preparing the attractive olive-green slate for export all over the world. Beyond the pass, the road drops through rough territory before reaching Gatesgarth farm at the foot of the long, winding descent. The farm specializes in raising Herdwick sheep, a tough breed that is able to survive the often harsh conditions of the Lake District fells. They are thought to be either the original native sheep of Britain or to have been introduced by enterprising Norsemen who settled in this region a thousand years ago. (At the well-known Lakeland Sheepskin stores in Bowness, Ambleside, Kendal, and Keswick, you can buy clothing made from Herdwick wool.)

The placid waters of Buttermere come into view as the roadway curves in a giant U, first west and then north. Buttermere's twin, Crummock Water, lies just beyond to the northwest. The flat mile of valley floor separating the two lakes suggests that they were once one, but each now has its own distinct character. In olden days, the village of Loweswater, off the north end of Crummock Water, was the metropolis of these parts and the pretty village of Buttermere lay tucked between the two lakes, nothing more than a huddle of houses and a small click-mill to grind rye and oats. The local balance shifted with the coming of the road across Honister Pass. The Lake Poets discovered and wrote about Buttermere and its charms, Turner painted the lake and Honister Crag, and gradually the number of visitors increased. Today the village has more than one hotel, including the *Fish* hotel, a typical lakeland inn whose name reflects Buttermere's appeal to trout fishermen, particularly in April, May, and September. The village is also another popular base for climbers, and not far from it is Scale Force, a lively waterfall with a drop of over 120 feet, the object of a short, muddy excursion. The easiest access is by crossing the stream between the two lakes and following the path on the far side, but do wear boots or hiking shoes.

A few miles farther north, B5289 intersects B5292; you can either take B5292 east over Whinlatter Pass (not as steep as Honister Pass) toward A66, Keswick, and Penrith, or extend your trip by heading northwest toward Cockermouth.

COCKERMOUTH: An attractive market town with a number of good antique shops, Cockermouth is famous as Wordsworth's birthplace (1770). It is strategically placed at the junction of the Cocker and Derwent rivers and, though its origins date to pre-Roman times, little remains from its earliest period. Even its 12th-century castle was destroyed during the Civil War violence of the mid-1600s. Wordsworth House (open daily from April to October except Sundays and Thursday afternoons) was built in 1745. This house, in which Dorothy and William were born and grew up, is a fairly simple, countrified example of Georgian architecture that has survived intact. The furnishings used by the Wordsworth family, however, are long gone. William's father is buried in the churchyard. Fletcher Christian, leader of the mutiny on the *Bounty*, was born in 1764 at Moorland Close, a nearby farmhouse.

CHECKING IN: *Pheasant Inn* – This 16th-century coaching inn, with 20 rooms, huge log fires, and a traditional atmosphere, is on Bassenthwaite Lake near Thornthwaite Forest. Views of the lake are, unfortunately, blocked by a hill. Food in the pub restaurant is simple and English. Bassenthwaite Lake, off A66, near Cockermouth (phone: 059681-234). Moderate.

En Route from Cockermouth – Take the A5086 south, explore the western fringe of the Lake District, and leave the area the same way you came in, via Kendal. Or return east through Keswick, detour from the main road onto A5091 to the shore of Ullswater, and leave the district via its northern gateway, Penrith.

If you choose A5086 south, Ennerdale Water, perhaps the least visited of the larger lakes, lies about 10 miles away, on a secondary roadway to the east. A similar turnoff about 10 miles beyond leads to Wastwater, the deepest of the lakes, set among stern and savage-faced mountains in marked contrast to the gentle placement of Windermere. The village of Wasdale Head, a mile beyond the lake, is an excellent climbing center, but these mountains are strictly for experts. Return to the main road (A5086 becomes A595 near Ennerdale Water) and drive to Ravenglass, a port at the mouth of the River Esk about 25 miles from Cockermouth. The Eskdale valley can be explored either by road or on the narrow-gauge, steam-powered Ravenglass and Eskdale Railway (narrow is an understatement — 15 inches make it positively skinny), which runs between Ravenglass and Dalegarth Station near the village of Boot year-round, although there's limited service in winter. Just beyond Ravenglass, Muncaster Castle, the seat of the Pennington family for 700 years, overlooks the Esk (open Easter to September, Tuesdays to Sundays; and bank holiday Mondays). Farther on, at Broughton, another secondary road (A593) leads up toward Coniston. Just east of Broughton, A595 bears south along the coast, and A5092 continues east toward A590, A6, the market town of Kendal, and the M6 motorway.

If you choose to visit Ullswater, return to Keswick (either on the main A66 road or on B5292 across Whinlatter Pass). Follow the main road east out of town for 9 miles, then turn south onto A5091, which leads to the second largest of the region's lakes, a lovely winding stretch of water cradled by high fells. The best way to explore Ullswater is to set out on it. Boats are for hire and cruises start at Glenridding pier at the head of the lake, and at its northern end, Pooley Bridge, with a pier to match, is another place to arrange a day's outing. The lake is only 7½ miles long (and an average ½ mile wide) but the distance between the two towns by road is 13 miles, along a stretch of A592 that skirts the northern bank of Ullswater, bypassing Gowbarrow Park. This grassy fell comes alive with daffodils each year and traveling poets can, as Wordsworth did, pause beneath the trees to write about the yellow blooms that may be "fluttering and dancing in the breeze" just as they were when he saw them. On the lake's western shore, the pretty Aira Force waterfall is a pleasant place to stop. A worthwhile diversion from Pooley Bridge is the secondary road along the southern shore of the lake past the *Sharrow Bay Hotel,* which surveys the most scenic views in the district; the road leads ultimately to the peaceful valley of Martindale.

Route A592 continues northeast of Ullswater toward Penrith. (South of Glenridding at the opposite end of the lake it heads toward Windermere, crossing the Helvellyn mountain range through Kirkstone Pass, at the summit of which is the *Kirkstone Pass Inn,* one of the highest taverns in England. On the far side of the pass are the Troutbeck Valley, the village of Troutbeck, and the 17th-century Townend House, once the residence of a yeoman's family. The interior, furnishings, and timbered barn remain intact and can be visited daily except Mondays and Saturdays, from April to October.)

CHECKING IN: *Leeming House* – Commanding fine views over Ullswater, this is a gracious, porticoed Georgian country house sitting on 20 acres of landscaped gardens on the northern shore of the lake, not far from the site of the famous daffodils. Lake swimming and fishing during the summer. The restaurant is rather grand. Closed January to mid-March. Watermillock (phone: 08536-622). Expensive.

Sharrow Bay – Partners Francis Coulson and Brian Sack have spent years making this spot one of the most respected and attractive hotels in the area. This stone country house is on the southern shore of Ullswater, about 2 miles from Pooley Bridge, and rooms in a farmhouse addition are another mile down the road. The restaurant's dinners are a pleasure. Closed November to early April. Pooley Bridge (phone: 08536-301). Expensive.

Old Church – About 400 yards of Ullswater lap the front lawn of this 18th-century house. Owners Kevin and Maureen Whitemore will arrange all manner of sporting activities. Watermillock (phone: 08536-204). Moderate.

PENRITH: This charming town was burned twice during the 14th century by bands of marauding Scots from across the border, but since then it has withstood time and the onslaught of travelers comfortably. Its oldest section grew up around the 13th-century Church of St. Andrew (rebuilt in the 1700s) and the nearby 16th-century schoolhouse. Several conflicting legends surround the presence of the two stone formations on the church grounds, known as Giant's Grave and Giant's Thumb: One version holds that this is the burial place of an ancient king. The ruins of Penrith Castle are now a town park, but two fine 16th-century inns, the *Gloucester Arms* and the *Two Lions,* are still thriving.

Penrith is at the convergence of several main roads. From here you can take the M6 just west of town, pick up the A74, and follow the A75 into Dumfries to connect with the *Scottish Lowlands* route.

Scottish Lowlands

No tourist should tread the hallowed ground of the Lowlands without first learning a few rudiments of the history of Scottish Presbyterianism. Here's an emergency grab bag of key religious events from the sixteenth century to the present as well as brief profiles of the two major players:

John Knox, a brilliant and incendiary preacher fired by the theology of John Calvin, came to St. Giles's Cathedral, Edinburgh, in 1559. Many of the Norman-blooded Scottish nobility, looking to siphon off riches like those enjoyed by their counterparts in England under Henry VIII's Dissolution of the Monasteries, hopped on Knox's bandwagon against a corrupt Catholic Church and the Catholic Royal House of Stuart. This was the takeoff point for the Protestant Reformation in Scotland. With fifteen 4-hour sermons a week on the democratization of Christian worship rumbling from his pulpit, Knox soon gathered the rabble to his bosom. His reforms were implemented in every corner of the Lowlands amid the wrecking of church interiors and ravaging of altars. Yet, contrary to generations of popular opinion, Knox was no puritan; he could enjoy a good belly laugh and freely sanctioned his fellow citizens to drink, dance, and be merry. Social restraints closed in on the Presbyterian faith much later, in the wake of royal persecution from London.

Charles II, successor in 1660 to a disagreeable Cromwellian interlude (which had however allowed Presbyterianism to flourish), continued his executed father's bad habit of ramming Episcopacy down Scotland's throat, backed by an obsequious and dissolute Scottish Parliament. Groups of worshipers called Covenanters (because of two written oaths they had signed, some in blood, proclaiming their inalienable anti-Episcopal beliefs) gathered on open hillsides, away from the churches, flouting a Parliamentary Act. Charles's troops zeroed in for a series of massacres. The Lowlands are full of interesting old churches and Covenanting martyrs' graves.

In 1712 a new act was passed by England's and Scotland's now unified Parliaments, which instituted lay patronage; this was a system revoking the right of congregations to choose their own ministers, and granting the task instead to each parish's local "laird" (lord or resident aristocrat). Often tyrannical, these handpicked ministers tightly controlled life in the Lowland towns and villages, banning music, dancing, theatrical performances, and country walks on Sundays. Scotland's national bard, Robert Burns, was one of many who were forced at the hands of church elders to appease God's wrath by standing publicly in a wooden dock protractedly confessing to fornication.

With the coming of the Industrial Revolution, economic and social conditions in the Lowlands, especially Glasgow and Edinburgh, became appalling. In comparison to their working-class congregations, men of the cloth were fat cats. In 1843, 450 ministers with sorely tried consciences walked bravely out of their manses, their livings, and the annual General Assembly of the Church of Scotland to form a new movement, the Free Presbyterian Church. This breach was not healed until 1929, after lay patronage had been abolished within the Kirk (as the established Presbyterian Church was — and still is — called). Attendant upon the tireless and dedicated slum-based social work of the new Free Church was a harsh (but possibly necessary) list of "don'ts" for its followers: no uncleanliness; no laziness; no bankruptcy; no "Sabbath breaking"; no drinking and gambling; no loud, indelicate behavior. As you'll quickly discover, these cast-iron virtues are tightly woven into the fabric of Scottish life today, especially on Sundays, when the world stops. The only noticeable shift from the old ways in the last decade — other than a greater availability of intoxicating beverages — has been the Scots' increasing willingness to admit that Christmas is not simply an unnecessarily flamboyant papish holiday, to be eschewed in favor of New Year. Both holidays are now celebrated for days on end. On January 2, when Americans go back to work, most Scots are in bed recovering.

The language spoken by Lowlanders derives from "La'lands," an old form of Norman-infused Anglo-Saxon once known as "Inglis." It's full of dialect words, rolled r's, and unexpected pronunciations: *guid* for "good," *doon* for "down," *fitba* for "football." La'lands is sometimes droll, often pithy, and — with the help of great poets like William Dunbar, Robert Burns, or Hugh MacDiarmid — sweepingly majestic. Dunbar is unfathomable at first, like Chaucer, but it's worth reading a bit of Burns or MacDiarmid to get a sense of Lowland Scotland's people, speech, and concept of nationhood.

Have a look also at the English-language Lowland poetry of Sir Walter Scott, who set *Marmion* and *The Lay of the Last Minstrel* among the Border Country's rolling, variegated, green and brown brackeny hills. The Borders, Scott's home for many years, are the Lowlands' most intriguing district: It's a moorish land interspersed with lush farms and prosperous mill-spangled towns. Ruined abbeys sit like sad marooned kings above gladed loops in the River Tweed. Picturesque villages dot its valleys. Its folklore is widely known, especially its ballads, from *Thomas the Rhymer and the Queen of Elfland* (on which the English poet John Keats may have based *La Belle Dame Sans Merci*), to narrative poetry that recounts the dramatic cattle-rustling Border Raids of the fourteenth, fifteenth, and sixteenth centuries. Under this Scottish version of the chivalric code, knights called "mosstroopers" or "reivers" gathered their families and retainers and forayed into each other's territory, burying their differences only when England's marauders posed a greater threat. The former British prime minister Sir Alec Douglas-Home is descended from at least two of these families. "The Riding of the Marches," an ancient way of delineating jealously guarded boundaries by tracing them in assembled companies on horseback, is ritually practiced on a festival day every summer by each of the main Border towns. Catch one if you can.

The Lowlands route begins at Edinburgh and runs east along the Firth of Forth, dips south into the Borders, veers southwest to the southern shore, then returns north to Glasgow via Galloway Forest Park and the Atlantic coast. The entire distance is about 335 miles. Be sure to buy the Scottish Tourist Board's kit called *Enjoy Scotland* (£4.80), which includes a very detailed touring map and a booklet of 1001 things to see. Keep scones (biscuits) or sandwiches, bought from bakeries in the towns, in your car for when lunchtime rolls around and you find you're still in the wilds. Don't pass a gas station assuming you'll see another one. If you're traveling in the Lowlands from May through September, you must book your hotels in advance.

The price categories for the hotels listed in this route are expensive, $85 and up for two for bed and breakfast; moderate, $55 to $85; and inexpensive, $40 to $55. Dinner for two in an expensive restaurant will run $50 and up; in moderate, $35 to $55; and in inexpensive, under $35.

EDINBURGH: For a detailed report on the city, its sights, hotels, and restaurants, see *Edinburgh*, THE CITIES.

En Route from Edinburgh – On the B1348 is the Prestongrange Mining Museum, one of only two former mines open to the public. It features a visitor center, a massive five-story beam pump dating from 1874, 3 steam locomotives, a steam navvy (shovel), and a winding engine. Open weekdays, 10 AM to 4 PM, weekends noon to 5 PM (phone: 661-2718).

GULLANE: Despite strong winds in winter, rich Edinburghers maintain a posh suburban existence here. Gullane gets more sun than anywhere else in Scotland. Tourists throng here in late spring and summer because of its four incomparable golf courses. Muirfield, the finest (the site of the 1987 Open Championship), is the home of the Honourable Company of Edinburgh Golfers; to play, a letter of introduction from your home club secretary is necessary, as is a request with alternate playing dates, sent well in advance. Do not bother to apply if your handicap is higher than 18. Muirfield is open to guests on Tuesdays, Thursdays, and Friday mornings only and costs £20 a round. Gullane also has wide, luxurious sandy beaches.

 CHECKING IN: *Greywalls* – Gullane's most exclusive place to stay is this lavishly appointed, 23-room golfers' retreat. Just beside Muirfield Golf Course, Gullane (phone: 0620-842144). Expensive.

 EATING OUT: *La Potinière* – The French cooking at this small and unassuming restaurant is so good that one of its recipes — *soufflé aux courgettes* — appears in the Good Food Guide's *Second Dinner Party Book.* Reservations a must. Lunches only, except Saturday, when there is only dinner. Closed Wednesdays, part of February, and October. On the main route through Gullane (phone: 0620-843214). Moderate.

DIRLETON: This charming little village, with its spectacular castle and busy yew-encircled bowling green, is reputedly the prettiest in Scotland. The castle, entered dramatically by a long ramp leading sharply upward to a gate in its stark and stony heights, was built in 1225. Additions were made in the 15th and 17th centuries, but the whole was sacked by Oliver Cromwell's troops in 1650. The castle shares with clusters of 17th- and 18th-century cottages the borders of the Village Common. If you feel like taking a walk, trees and springy turf line the lovely Yellowcraig Nature Trail for 2 miles from Dirleton to the sea. Otherwise, continue on the A198 to North Berwick.

 CHECKING IN/EATING OUT: *Open Arms* – A country-style, 7-room hostelry famed for its restaurant, which is included on the Scottish Tourist Board's Taste of Scotland roster. Decorated in soft pink and lilac, its candlelit tables are graced by such delicacies as salmon, venison, and Cranachan pudding — cream, toasted oatmeal, and rum, topped with fresh berries! On the main route through Dirleton (phone: 85241). Moderate.

NORTH BERWICK: The farming folk who inhabit the surrounding countryside habitually converge on this holiday spot, making the most of its sands, shops, and two fine golf courses. North Berwick has the kind of natural topography that proves God must be British: The middle-class beach is divided from the lower-class beach by the harbor, and each looks onto its own separate bay. The sun at east coast resorts like this one has a striking, harsh brilliance, unbroken by the soft air and purple-hilled isles that characterize the Atlantic coast to the west. You may offend the natives' old-fashioned priorities if you venture onto the middle-class beach without a hat!

A mile or so south of the center of town is North Berwick Law, a grassy rise decked with a whalebone arch, from which to enjoy a magnificent view. Motorboat trips from North Berwick go to the nearby island of Fidra in summer, and also to fascinating Bass Rock, to which every Edinburgh schoolchild is whisked off by at least one teacher in the course of his or her career. The rock's steep, straight sides make it look much higher than its 350 feet. It's part of a chain of volcanic masses, made of especially hard stone, that withstood glacial pressure in the last Ice Age (the Castle Rock, which Edinburgh

Castle sits on, is another). The Bass Rock is totally inaccessible except at one point, which made it irresistible to hermits in early Christian times; to prison wardens detaining Covenanting ministers at the time of King Charles II; and to soldiers rallying round the flag of the exiled Stuarts who needed a safe fortress in the reign of William of Orange. Today the Bass Rock is "held," as is Fidra, by the keepers of its lighthouse and scores of swirling silvery gannets. For boat trips, contact Fred Marr, 24 Victoria Rd. (phone: 2838).

 EATING OUT: *Marine* – A hot and cold smorgasbord lunch — savory pies, lasagna, puddings — is served, as are evening meals. North Berwick (phone: 2406). Inexpensive.

En Route from North Berwick – About 3 miles farther on the A198 is Tantallon Castle, on a cliff overlooking the North Sea. An extensive rose-colored ruin that once was a stronghold of the famous Border family named Douglas, it has captured the Scottish popular imagination and worked its way into the native patois. Any feat of the impossible is said to be as hard as to "ding doon" Tantallon Castle. You can go inside during daylight hours only (except Sunday mornings); closed Wednesday and Thursday mornings in winter.

DUNBAR: The Great North Road, A1, leads to this quiet town, in sailing ship days the only safe port between Edinburgh and the English city of Berwick, and now a golfing and sailing haven for vacationers seeking a rest. But it wasn't always restful. The earl of Hertford attacked it by land in 1544, during the so-called Rough Wooing by which King Henry VIII tried to force Scotland to bind the young Mary Queen of Scots to his son Edward in a treaty of marriage. Years later Mary stayed in Dunbar Castle (today a mere shred) with her husband and cousin Lord Darnley, and again with her lover Lord Bothwell who carried her off there, fairy tale style, after the murder of Lord Darnley. Cromwell laid waste the town in 1650. The Castle was destroyed in 1567, after Mary and Bothwell had fled for their lives.

Something very dear to many American visitors had its roots in Dunbar. The building at the north end of High Street is the birthplace of John Muir, the man responsible for the US National Park system. A pioneer geologist, explorer, and naturalist, Muir spent the first 11 years of his life in the top apartment with his family (six brothers and sisters) until emigrating to the US in 1849. The flat is appropriately furnished, and one room is reserved for audio-visual presentations on his life and work. Open late May through September, except Wednesdays and Sundays. For more details contact the tourist information center, also on High St. (phone: 0368-63353).

Sadly, apart from fast-food eateries, Dunbar has lost most of its elegant restaurants since the influx of workers building the nearby Atomic Energy station.

 CHECKING IN/EATING OUT: *Battleblent* – Looking somewhat like a small castle — with a turreted roof and sitting atop a hill — this recently modernized family-run hostelry features 7 guestrooms, a dining room specializing in seafood, and two bars. 1 mile east of Dunbar, West Barns (phone: 0368-62234). Moderate.

Bayview – The 6 rooms here (sharing one shower!) are graced by sea views and the sparkling *Klownz* restaurant, with white walls, white tablecloths, pine chairs, and toy clowns for decoration. The meals are either British or Italian. 3 Bayswell Rd. (phone: 0368-62778). Inexpensive.

En Route from Dunbar – Continue 11 miles on the A1 before bearing onto the A1107 along the coast. Before crossing from East Lothian into the Borders, a mile north of Cockburnspath, you will pass the entrance to Dunglass Collegiate Church (follow the turn-off sign for Bilsdean), founded in 1450. The nave, choir, transepts, sacristy, and central tower are all still intact. The church was used as a barn after sackings during the Reformation; today it stands empty. The interior stonework is especially arresting. Also at Cockburnspath is the eastern entrance to the Southern Upland Way, a coast-to-coast footpath across the Border hills that takes experienced hikers 15 days.

Four miles farther along the A1107 is the signposted approach to the ruins of Fast Castle, an ancient Home stronghold spectacularly poised on a cliff. At Coldingham is a small 13th-century Benedictine priory. Reformation zealots wrecked most of it, but the choir and sanctuary, with later additions, are now the Coldingham parish church. Legend has it that the stones here glow rose red in a supernatural manner.

COLDSTREAM: You now reach (not for the last time) the trout-laden waters of the River Tweed. The 300-foot Tweed Bridge across the river into England was built in 1776, after which it rapidly became notorious for heavy traffic in eloping couples heading for the Old Marriage House beside its northern entrance. (Scotland's relatively lax marriage laws made Coldstream the British equivalent of Maryland.) The town is famous too as the starting point of the 1660 march of the Coldstream Guards to London, where they effected the restoration of Charles II. Their original headquarters is on the north side of the main square.

En Route from Coldstream – About 2 miles northwest on the A697 is Hirsel, Sir Alec Douglas-Home's ancestral home and where he resides today. The house itself is closed to the public, but the magnificent gardens are open and include rhododendrons, woodlands, and a small lake chockablock with wildfowl. BBC Radio at its most precious has been known to fill an idle minute or two with live choruses of Hirsel birdsong. Return to A698 and continue to Kelso.

KELSO: Site of one of the four Border Abbeys of the incomparable Scott Country, this small bastion of what could almost be French civilization (its center looks like an enormous *grande place*) is nonetheless your first taste of the netherworld between past and present, legend and reality, which suffuses this part of Scotland. The town, like the abbey, is situated on the rivers Tweed and Teviot. Its five-arched bridge, begun in 1800, was an exact model for the later Waterloo Bridge across the Thames, demolished in 1934. The lamp standards, visible at the bridge's south end, were salvaged and brought here from London after the demolition.

Kelso Abbey, founded in 1128 by King David I (son of the King Malcolm who succeeded Macbeth, and ancestor of King Robert the Bruce) was destroyed by the earl of Hertford in 1545. What remains of it shows a Norman-Transitional style unique in Scotland. In the main Kelso car park behind the abbey is *Kelso Pottery,* where you can watch the making and glazing of stoneware and buy some of the products (phone in advance: 24027). The mid-September Kelso Ram Sales in Springwood Park are a fascinating event indigenous to Border life; Civic Week, the third in July, is full of colorful equestrian pageants; and in May, gaily costumed local bargemen compete in the Great Tweed Raft Race.

En Route from Kelso – Some 2 miles northwest on the B6089 is Floors Castle, seat of the dukes of Roxburgh, said to be the largest inhabited mansion in Britain. It has 365 windows, one for every day in the year. Built by William Adam in 1721, it underwent various additions and remodelings until it became spectacularly grandiose — a kind of fantastic Brobdingnag dollhouse, with its battlements, water spouts, and pepper-pot towers, its amphitheater, and its golden gates. The furniture, porcelain, tapestries, and paintings are all superb. The fine grounds include a holly tree supposedly marking the spot where King James II (of Scotland) was killed in 1460 firing one of his own cannons. An adjoining veranda restaurant serves food from the castle kitchen. Open May through September; closed Saturdays during July and August. Pipe band displays on certain days in summer.

A 20-mile detour north to Hume Castle, Mellerstain House, and Smailholm Tower is a must (these places are clearly marked on your *Enjoy Scotland* touring map: the route between them from Kelso and back — the B6364, some unnumbered roads, and then the B6397 — forms the shape of a fan). Thirteenth-century Hume Castle preceded Hirsel as seat of the earls of Home. Cromwell wrecked it in 1651. The view from its parapets (these were reconstructed in the 18th century) is glorious. The castle key is available on request at The Smiddy, Hume village.

Mellerstain House is, architecturally speaking, an Adam pie — begun in 1725 by William and finished in 1778 by his famous son, Robert. Despite this, it is proportionally perfect. No finer meringue exists anywhere than the plasterwork ceilings inside; Mellerstain is one of the great Georgian houses of Scotland. There are outstanding collections of 18th-century furniture too, and paintings by old masters (open May through September; closed Saturdays). Mellerstain House takes part in an annual Borders springtime rally, mounting an exhibition of its vintage car collection.

Sir Walter Scott used to sit like a medieval princess in the top of Smailholm Tower concocting romantic novels. The best extant example of a 16th-century Border keep, its 57-foot summit overlooks vast expanses of country, English and Scottish, that sweeps your breath away! Strategically placed stone fortresses like Smailholm, into which Border reivers herded women, children, and cattle as enemies approached, had roofs fitted out with pans of pitch and peat for kindling; on a clear night it was said to take only two minutes for a chain of danger signals to reach Edinburgh Castle from the English borderline.

Return to A698 and continue to Jedburgh.

CHECKING IN: *Sunlaws House* – This appealing Georgian hotel is owned by the duke of Roxburgh and draws guests who enjoy fishing and shooting. Its 21 rooms contain modern amenities, and its restaurant specializes in local game and salmon pulled from the River Tweed. Heighton (phone: 05735-331). Expensive.

Marlefield Country House – Set in a 12th-century fortified manor, this historic stone building is long on character and charm. There are 7 guestrooms and a restaurant featuring international cuisine. Morebattle, south of Kelso (phone: 05734-205). Expensive to moderate.

Cross Keys – This 25-room, newly renovated old inn has Taste of Scotland cooking and a charming bar decorated with horse and wagon motifs. The Square (phone: 23303). Moderate.

Ednam House – Built in 1761 as the abode of a prominent Kelso merchant, this historic, 32-room hotel has an arresting façade and its original Italian ceilings. Bridge St., Kelso (phone: 24168). Moderate.

Queens Head – This family-run old coaching inn is short on one or two amenities, but long on friendliness and architectural fascination. The close-up view of the Abbey out its back door is priceless. 24 Bridge St. (phone: 24636). Inexpensive.

JEDBURGH: Although the priory section of Jedburgh Abbey was leveled during the Rough Wooing, the church is amazingly well preserved. The elegant rose window is nicknamed St. Catherine's Wheel (a Catherine Wheel is a circular-acting firework). There was a church here as early as the 9th century, but the abbey dates from 1138, when David I brought Augustinians to Scotland from Beauvais in France. It enjoys a lovely setting above Jed Water, a tributary of the Teviot. In certain evening lights it appears to be made of solid gold (closed Thursday afternoons and Fridays, October through March).

The great and wise King Alexander III, the first king of a truly unified Scotland, was married in Jedburgh in 1285 to a young and beautiful second wife. His love for her seems to have spurred him to foolish and hotheaded passion: It is said that the spectral figure of Death was seen among the dancing guests at the wedding reception in Jedburgh Castle, now the site of the Jail Museum — and sure enough, Alexander was killed when his horse fell over a cliff as he rode out 6 months later on a stormy night, against the advice of all his aides, from Edinburgh Castle to join his bride in Dunfermline. The museum, in the Castlegate, is as it was in 1823 when erected as an experimental "modern" jail (closed Sunday mornings).

Jedburgh was once surrounded for protection by a series of "bastel houses," one of which, on Queen St., was a residence of Mary Queen of Scots. Today it is open to the public (Easter through October) and is fascinating chiefly for the number of portraits it contains of that enigmatic lady, each looking less like the next than the last. In the unlikely event you are in Jedburgh in mid-February, you can enter the spirit of Mary's troubled times by watching the annual Ba' Game, played in the 16th century with Jedburgh citizens' slain enemies' heads! The "Uppies" (those born above the Mercat Cross) and the "Doonies" (those born below) have to get a ball into its goal (the goals are the Jail Museum grounds and the Townfoot) by fair means or foul in 2 hours.

The Friday after the second Saturday in July sees the start of the 3-day Jethart Callants' Festival, in which the Riding of the Marches takes the form of mounted ceremonial dashes to historically important places, the Jedburgh flag to the fore. A "callant" is a gallant, or youngblood. Also part of the festival are the Jedburgh Border Games, held on the Saturday in Riverside Park from 10 AM to teatime.

 CHECKING IN: _Glenbank Country House_ – A short walk from town, this pretty, 9-room Georgian house has home cooking, which it serves with tea on the lawn. Castlegate (phone: Jedburgh 62258). Moderate.

En Route from Jedburgh – Halfway to Hawick on the A698 is charming Denholm, with its 18th-century cottages and expansive village green. John Leyden, a shepherd's son who was a minor poet and friend of Sir Walter Scott, and who left Scotland eventually to become Commissioner of the Calcutta Mint, was born here in 1775. A few miles south of Denholm is Trow Mill, an 18th-century grain mill that became a woolen mill around 1800 and today is completely modernized. They have factory tours, their own shop, and free coffee for visitors (no advance warning necessary).

HAWICK: Pronounced "Hoyk," this largest of the Border burghs, a busy farm market and knitwear and electronics capital, rings the junction of the Teviot and Slitrig rivers. Its citizens are inveterate rugby nuts, and it has contributed many a famous player to internationally known rugby teams. Its home team, the Greens, plays Saturdays at Mansfield Park.

In the leafy shades of the 107-acre municipal Wilton Lodge Park is Hawick Museum and Art Gallery, bursting with Border relics. The Riding of the Marches is at its most full-blooded in Hawick, where it is called the Common Riding and takes place around the second week in June. It is led by an unmarried callant elected months in advance, the Cornet, who trains his men beforehand in a series of death-defying cavalry charges, culminating in their promotion to the Ancient Order of Mosstroopers. Three days of festivities include the Mosstroopers' all-important private performance at breakfast of ancient druidical rites in preparation for the Riding; the thrilling equestrian chases that constitute the Riding; additional horse races (at which you can place official bets) on Hawick Moor; athletic matches in Volunteer Park between top British professionals; all-night dinners and dances; and the singing, on the town heights at dawn, of the Hawick battle song "Teribus," which begins in Latin, lurches into Old Norse, and then plunges into Scots. The whole experience is the ultimate in Scottish machismo, if you can stay the course!

SELKIRK: To get here drive north on the A7 from Hawick to the Ettrick Water. Halliwell's House, in the main square, is an interesting museum of local history (open April through October; closed Sunday mornings). Sir Walter Scott was sheriff of Selkirkshire from 1799 to 1832; the courthouse, on High Street, displays some of his letters. At teatime, the *Court House Coffee Shop* on High Street is a good place to try a slice of Selkirk bannock, the richest raisin bread in the world. Or buy a whole loaf at *Houston Bakers* (where it was invented) across the square.

En Route from Selkirk – A 20-mile circular detour via the A699, A68, A6091, B6360, and A7 takes in Dryburgh Abbey, Melrose Abbey, and Abbotsford House.

On the Tweed near the village of St. Boswell's is majestic Dryburgh Abbey. Many think its setting the most beautiful of all. It, too, was founded in the reign of David I and later sacked by English raiders. Only the transepts remain of the church, but the cloister is nearly complete. Sir Walter Scott is buried here, as is Earl Haig, Britain's chief World War I general.

Another of David I's now ruined monasteries, Melrose Abbey graces the central square of the lovely little town of Melrose. Notice that the abbey's exquisite 15th-century traceried stonework features a pig on the roof playing bagpipes! According to legend the heart of Robert the Bruce is buried in the abbey; another legend has it that the Eildon Hills, which loom to the southeast, are shaped as they are (two pointed, one shorter and flat-topped) because the devil was so piqued by the dawn chanting of the abbey monks that he thrust three mountains between them and the rising sun — but dropped and broke one mountain in transit. Sir Walter Scott used to gaze across the Tweed at the Eildon Hills from a point above Melrose now known as Scott's View. (It's on the B6356 a couple of miles east of town; see your *Enjoy Scotland* touring map.)

If you'd like to go riding or pony trekking in the Eildon Hills, contact Elspeth McDonald at the *Ellwyn Glen Riding Centre,* Eildon Estate, Melrose (phone: 2908). Hikers can do the Eildon Walk, with the aid of nature trail leaflets available (free) at the tourist information bureau next to Melrose Abbey.

Built to Sir Walter Scott's own specifications in 1812–24, his fascinating country home, Abbotsford House, broods in stately somnolence by the Tweed. A trip here gives a vivid picture of Scott's personality. He could carry his starry-eyed antiquarianism to laughable lengths, as when he made off with the door to Edinburgh's just-razed, 15th-century "Heart of Midlothian" (the county jail) and had it installed in a wall at Abbotsford. He later wrote a not-so-laughable book about the Heart of Midlothian. There are historic relics he carefully collected, impressive armories, a 9,000-volume library, and the study in which he wrote the Waverley novels trying to reduce a £117,000 debt. The effort eventually killed him; he died at the age of 61. Open daily, except Sunday mornings, from the last week in March through October.

Returning to Selkirk and proceeding 3 miles to the west on A708, you'll find Philiphaugh, the field where the army of the noble Scottish Cavalier and poet-soldier the Marquis of Montrose lost a key battle to Puritan forces in 1645. Near the Yarrow Water is Bowhill, home of the dukes of Buccleuch and Queensberry (one dukedom), another of the Borders' ancestral palaces. This one has early-19th-century silk brocades and hand-painted Chinese wallpapers, sumptuous art treasures, lush woods and gardens, an elaborately inventive jungle-playground-type Tarzan complex for kids, and pony trekking. Open afternoons except Fridays from July through mid-August; grounds open afternoons daily except Fridays from May through August. Pony trekking center open daily except Mondays from 10 AM (phone: Selkirk 20192). Adjacent to Bowhill is Newark Castle, a five-story oblong towerhouse where the "Last Minstrel" recited his "Lay" to the duchess of Buccleuch. It was a royal hunting seat for the Forest of Ettrick in the Middle Ages. Another 4 miles along is picturesque Yarrow Kirk, dating from 1640.

Continuing along the Yarrow, you reach the wild, godforsaken country over which the merlinhawks fly. These small, ferocious birds are said to embody by magic the spirit of Merlin the wizard. Near desolate St. Mary's Loch and its sibling, the Loch of the Lowes, are two historic inns where Scott met literary friends — the *Gordon Arms* and *Tibbie Shiels* (both are on the *Enjoy Scotland* touring map, albeit in tiny print). Across the main road from St. Mary's Loch are the remains of Dryhope Tower, which, like Smailholm, is a medieval watch or "peel" tower.

Stay on the A708. On the right, about 8 miles before Moffat, is the Grey Mare's Tail, a magnificent 200-foot waterfall formed as the Tail Burn drops from Loch Skeen to meet the Moffat Water (you lose the Yarrow at St. Mary's Loch). The whole area is resplendent with wildflowers. Covenanters used to hide out here. The hollow below the falls is the "Giant's Grave," which figures in Scott's poem *Marmion.*

CHECKING IN: *Dryburgh Abbey* – A good place to leave your car while you cross the Tweed by foot on pilgrimage to Dryburgh Abbey, this 19th-century house in the baronial mode has all the swagger of the horse and hound set that patronizes it. It has 29 rooms, serves elegant afternoon teas, and its restaurant is the last word in traditional Scottish cooking. On the banks of the Tweed (phone: St. Bowells 22261). Expensive.

***Phillipburn House* –** Families are positively coddled in this slickly modernized old house overlooking the famous battlefield of Philiphaugh. There are 17 rooms, gardens and woodlands, a heated swimming pool, a well-equipped playground, riding and fishing facilities, and real log fires. On the A708, 2½ miles west of Selkirk (phone: Selkirk 20747). Expensive.

***Burt's* –** In addition to full-fledged restaurant meals, this bustling 22-room hostelry provides substantial and delicious bar snacks. Gleaming everywhere under its wooden roofbeams are pieces of copper and brass. Market Sq., Melrose (phone: 2285). Moderate.

EATING OUT: *Queenshead* – Robert Burns once slept in this friendly coaching inn during a stint as an exciseman. Although no lodging is available today, the bar has tasty food including homemade soups. West Port, Selkirk (phone: 21782). Inexpensive.

MOFFAT: The pride of the town is Colvin Fountain, erected in 1875; the huge bronze ram on top symbolizes the importance of sheep farming in the surrounding districts. Moffat was for two centuries also a fashionable spa, and among the 18th-century greats to case the place were James Boswell, Robert Burns, and the James Macpherson of *Ossianic Ballads.* Today it's a touring base, flush with hotels and Italian cafés. But it retains a days-gone-by image and seems unlikely ever to shed its air of pleasant pokiness.

A good pottery with a retail showroom is the *Moffat Pottery,* Ladyknowe (in the town center beside the telephone exchange). Also at Ladyknowe are the *Moffat Weavers,* who display antique looms as well as demonstrate the art of skirtmaking. They keep a shop with a wide choice of Scottish products, including their own.

A detour 6 miles north on the A701 brings you to the Devil's Beef Tub, famous in literature and lore. An astonishing feature of Dumfriesshire's natural geography, its vast, smooth, basinlike recess has a rotund regularity more believable in classical art than in nature. As its name suggests, Border reivers herded pilfered steers into the Devil's Beef Tub to conceal them. If your family name is Armstrong or Douglas, your ancestors were the scourge of this part of Scotland.

CHECKING IN/EATING OUT: *Beechwood Country House* – A comfortable haven on a Moffat hill, this 8-room home-away-from-home sets a tempting Taste of Scotland table, including beetroot soup, venison casserole, and the best Orkney cheeses. Restaurant reservations necessary on weekends and for dinner. Harthope Pl., Moffat (phone: 20210). Moderate.

DUMFRIES: The A701 brings you to this quaint but sonorous symphony in red sandstone. Although its written history began in 1186 with its legal recognition by King William the Lion, it is in fact much older; excavations have yielded Bronze Age relics. In Dumfries you are out of the bewitched furze-ridden Borders; here in the gentle dale of the River Nith you'll find, as all over the surrounding area of Galloway, hillocked meadows flecked with buttercups, peacefully grazing cattle, and grass as green as any in Ireland. Spring comes earlier to Dumfries and Galloway than elsewhere in Scotland and the climate stays comparatively warm.

In summer Dumfries is a-bubble with Burns freaks visiting Burns House on Mill Vennel (now called Burns St.), where he died in 1796. His tomb in nearby St. Michael's Churchyard is augmented by an unintentionally humorous sculpture showing him at his plough (Scotland knows him as "the Ploughman Poet") somewhat hampered by Coila, the muse of Scottish poetry, who flings o'er his shoulders a voluminous mantle as cumbersome as a tent. The *Globe Inn,* Burns's "favourite howff" in a narrow alley off High Street, is exactly as it was in his day, furnishings and all, and is still in the bartending business. Then there is Ellisland Farm, 6½ miles north of Dumfries on the A76. Here Burns lived from 1788 to 1791, trying to make a living by the new agricultural methods (such as drainage) being introduced then. He failed, partly because he was also at the time a Dumfries exciseman traveling on horseback up to 200 miles a week. Several of his poems were written at Ellisland; these are commemorated by plaques at points where inspiration came to him.

A saunter through Dumfries takes you past some other not-to-be-missed high spots: Greyfriars Church on High St., whose monastery (now a supermarket) was the scene in 1306 of the murder by Robert the Bruce of his cousin and heir to the Scottish throne, John "the Red" Comyn; the Burns Statue opposite this church; the Mid Steeple of 1707, which is the remains of the central square's old Town Hall; and Dumfries Academy on Academy St., where a pupil named J. M. Barrie first conceived the characters Peter Pan and Wendy while exploring the garden of the Moat Brae Nursing Home in the lane behind. The River Nith is spanned by the six-arched Devorguilla's Bridge, a 13th-century gift from Devorguilla Balliol, founder of Balliol College at Oxford (and ancestral cousin-in-law of the Bruce and the Red Comyn). The expansive "caul," or weir, by the bridge is a salmon leap and was once the power supply for the town's many grain mills. The path through the 2-mile wood along the Nith bank is Burns's Walk.

T. C. Farries (Irongray Rd., Lochside Industrial Estate) is considered by many the best bookseller north of Oxford (it's off A76 by New Bridge). A delectable trove of antiques has filtered into Dumfries's multitudinous curiosity shops. A side step down Friars' Vennel to Whitesands by the Nith brings you to an interesting market, held Wednesdays on a former site of horse and hiring fairs.

The Burgh Museum, Observatory Rd., housed in an 18th-century windmill, has local archaeological and other exhibits and a camera obscura (closed Tuesdays and Sundays, October through March). There's also a folk museum, in Old Bridge House, Mill Rd., adjacent to Devorguilla's Bridge. Dumfries has an excellent municipal indoor swimming pool on Greensands by the Nith, and boats are available for hire along the quays.

The Theatre Royal on Shakespeare St. bolsters its usual pop-vein fripperies with occasional plays by the likes of Ibsen and Coward. Gracefield Arts Centre, 28 Edinburgh Rd., is a showcase for works by Scottish artists; it also sponsors the Dumfries and Galloway Arts Festival every year around the last week in May, providing military, rock, and folk bands, a serious guest orchestra, puppet shows, and exhibitions. *Guid Nychburris (Good Neighbors) Week,* in late June, offers concerts, parades, baby and beauty shows, the cavalcaded "stobbing and nogging" of Dumfries's boundaries, and the "kirking" (public promenading to church) of a newly elected Cornet, or chief eligible bachelor.

Worth a jaunt into the countryside are Shambellie House, at the village of New Abbey, 7 miles south of Dumfries on the A710, and 12th-century Caerlaverock Castle, 9 miles south of Dumfries on the B725. Shambellie House, approached through an avenue of tall gracious pines, opened in 1982 for the first time as Scotland's foremost museum of costumes (closed Tuesdays, Wednesdays, and Sunday mornings). Caerlaverock Castle is a striking triangular ruin with round turrets and a real moat. Try to visit it at sunset. The castle was a prime target in the 14th century for Edward I's wars against Scotland and its weak king, John Balliol (Devorguilla's son, known to his subjects as Toom Tabard, which means "empty coat"). Next to the castle is Caerlaverock National Nature Reserve, on the Nith estuary and the Solway Firth: Here you can see the exhilarating spectacle of 9,000 barnacle geese in open flight (East Park observation towers open mid-September through April). Also at New Abbey near Shambellie House is Sweetheart Abbey, built in 1273, the last pre-Reformation Cistercian foundation in Scotland and one of the nation's most beautiful. Devorguilla, who established it, is buried here; her husband's heart, encased in an ivory casket, sits in the tomb upon her bosom — hence the abbey's name.

 CHECKING IN: *Cairndale* – This rouge-hued stone inn is what passes in these parts for a *bon viveur*'s retreat. Its 60-car parking lot is handy (there are only 45 rooms) and its food — fresh local produce — is excellent. English St., Dumfries (phone: 0387-54111). Inexpensive.

Station – Owned by one of Dumfriesshire's dairy magnates, this overblown chocolate box with Hansel and Gretel portals has 30 rooms, a hearty array of Taste of Scotland delights, and two bars offering more than just milk. 49 Lovers Walk, Dumfries (phone: 0387-54316). Inexpensive.

 EATING OUT: *Bruno's* – In this ritzy Italian sanctum thoughts of salmons and haggises vanish at the flick of a cannellone. The red plush banquettes have at one time or another seated most of the posteriors in Caledonian gourmetdom. Dinner only; closed Tuesdays. 3 Balmoral Rd., Dumfries (phone: 0387-55757). Expensive.)

En Route from Dumfries – Follow the A75 southwest to Castle Douglas, an unassuming little town with an idyllic setting on Carlingwark Loch, a-sprinkle with brightly painted boats. *Galloway Gems* at Carlingwark St. sells handmade silver jewelry, set with Galloway stones.

KIRKCUDBRIGHT: Pronounced Ker-coo-bree. About 6 miles south on the A711, this town, long famous as an artists' haunt, was used by the late-19th-century Glasgow School as a base from which to work on their characteristic "kailyard" (farmyard) scenes of the surrounding countryside. Its flowery lanes, elm-lined streets, and enchanting knots of whitewashed 18th-century cottages appeal no less to today's palettes; all summer the place supports a steady stream of painters, pupils, and patrons. Broughton House on High Street was once the home of A. E. Hornel and contains many of his canvases. Adjacent to the much-photographed picturesque harbor is an exhibition gallery.

Dominating the harbor is jagged MacLellan's Castle, built in 1582. The town's impressive Mercat Cross dates from 1610 and the late-16th- or early-17th-century tollbooth once imprisoned the American naval hero John Paul Jones. The Stewartry

Museum on St. Mary Street houses, among other features of Kirkcudbright history, a John Paul Jones display (open Easter to October; closed Sundays).

The fascinating process of copperwheel engraving on glass can be viewed at *David Gulland's,* 6 Barrhill Rd. (phone first: 31072).

 CHECKING IN: *Selkirk Arms* – A charming, comfortable 27-room place where Robert Burns wrote the popular "Selkirk Grace." Some of its paneled walls are inscribed with Burns's verses. Old High St., Kirkcudbright (phone: 0557-30402). Inexpensive.

 EATING OUT: *Coffee Pot* – A cheerful bow-windowed snuggery across from the castle caters to everybody from snackers to three-course gorgers with its Scots-French cuisine. Open in summer only. 5 Castle St., Kirkcudbright (phone: 30569). Inexpensive.

En Route from Kirkcudbright – Follow the A755 west to rejoin the A75. Gatehouse-of-Fleet is a scenic spot renowned for its archaeological remains and its forest trails leading to lovely little Fleet Bay. Among the ancient sites in the district are Anworth Church on Gatehouse-of-Fleet's northwest outskirts, which contains a Dark Ages' cross; Palace Yard at Enrick, which is a medieval moated manor with the foundations of a palace of the Bishops of Galloway destroyed in the Reformation; and a 1st-century Roman fort just north of town beside the Water-of-Fleet. Relics of the not-so-distant past are the disused early-19th-century cotton mill covered in ivy above Fleet Bridge and the soaring 75-foot castellated clock tower (ca. 1871) in mid-village. As in Kirkcudbright, artists of all kinds live in Gatehouse-of-Fleet.

The road from Gatehouse-of-Fleet to Creetown is full of delightful picnic places and the views along this stretch are terrific; you follow the eastern shore of Wigtown Bay to the Cree River estuary, looking across to the Wigtown peninsula. Cardoness Castle, a mile after Gatehouse-of-Fleet, is a well-preserved 15th-century stronghold with an original staircase. Carsluith Castle, 6 miles from Cardoness Castle, is a roofless 16th-century structure in the shape of an "L." Between the two is Dirk Hatteraick's Cave (see the *Enjoy Scotland* touring map), a voracious crevice in the rocks where pigeonholes were cut to hide that dashing bandit's smuggled brandy. Kirkdale, a wooded glen near the cave, is the entrance to Cairn Holy, a Neolithic graveyard.

The Gemrock Museum on the main road here in Creetown, with its fine collection of rocks, minerals, and semiprecious stones from all over the world, testifies to Galloway's preeminence in stone-building and jewelry-making. The Mersey Docks and part of the Thames Embankment are made of Creetown granite. *John Prince,* jeweler and silversmith, is well worth a look-in at 93 St. John St. Jewelry and silversmith courses are also available. (phone first: 067182-396).

GALLOWAY FOREST PARK: A glorious, gargantuan green space entered off the A714 a few miles north of Newton Stewart, this majestic wilderness's chief fascinations are detailed on the *Enjoy Scotland* touring map. Rocky glens and mountain lakes have won it the title "The Highlands of the Lowlands."

Bruce's Stone on Loch Trool records an important victory there of Robert the Bruce over England in 1307, which helped secure Scotland's independence. A short walk away the Galloway Deer Museum has a tank full of live trout as well as other exhibitions about indigenous Galloway species (open April through October only). But you don't need a museum to take in the native wildlife: red deer, roe deer, foxes, otters, red squirrels, and wild goats abound on the park's many miles of secluded woodland footpaths, and the wild geese and ducks, pheasants and grouse, falcons, owls, ravens, and golden eagles are an ornithologist's orgy.

En Route from Galloway Forest Park – Pick up the B734 at Barr, off the northwest tip of the park. This takes you to the Atlantic coast, where you can gaze at the regal heights of Ailsa Craig, rearing up out of the sea. Stay on the coast road until you reach Turnberry, the site of the internationally famous Ailsa championship golf course. You can visit Turnberry Lighthouse next to "Bruce's Castle" (the ninth hole); get there between 2 PM and 1 hour before sunset (phone the lightkeeper first: 225). Nearby Turnberry Castle is the real Bruce's Castle, said to be the birthplace of Robert the Bruce in 1274 (you'll have to look closely to spy its scant remains).

CHECKING IN: *Turnberry* – Site of the Ailsa championship golf course, this 120-room, Edwardian resort looks a little like a landlocked ocean liner. It has a tennis court and indoor swimming pool and offers reduced greens fees for guests playing on the Ailsa course, as well as its other 18-hole course, the Arran. Just recently sold to Japanese investors. South of Ayr, off the A719 or the A77 (phone: Turnberry 202). Expensive.

CULZEAN CASTLE: About 12 miles south of Ayr is Scotland's most visited castle, Culzean (pronounced Koo-lane), situated within a remarkable 560-acre country park. Designed around an ancient tower of the Kennedy family (the earls of Cassilis) by Robert Adam in 1777, its turrets flank the Atlantic. General Dwight D. Eisenhower became its chief denizen in 1946, using it as a golfing base on frequent trips to Scotland. Note the drum-shaped drawing rooms in which even the fireplaces curve. Go in the morning to avoid the tourist buses that pour in after lunch, and ask for the head guide, Mr. McBain, a foremost authority on Culzean's contents and history.

The castle grounds include a walled garden, aviary, swan pond, camellia house, and orangery. There are palm trees everywhere, picnic tables, a seashore trail, and a tearoom. Farm buildings also designed by Robert Adam are now a lecture and exhibition theater and are (in summer) the starting point for conducted nature walks. The park grounds are always open; the castle, exhibition theater, and tearoom are open April through October only.

En Route from Culzean Castle – On the road beyond Culzean you'll see a sign marking the Croy Brae, also called "Electric Brae" because when its fantastic properties first became apparent, Ayrshiremen thought the cause could only be electricity. Now they think it's optical illusion: Switch off your motor and you'll coast uphill! (That however is nothing compared to your descent down the brae's other side, when you can coast uphill backward.) Along this route are some of the most beautiful views imaginable, often augmented by extraordinary weather effects creating ethereal lights. The shoreline gleams with watery inlets and wild red poppies, and the ghostly shell of Danure Castle, standing like a stony wraith against the sky, assails you as you start around the Heads of Ayr to meet the Firth of Clyde.

AYR: Ayrshire is Burns country the way the Borders are Scott country — a focal point for adulation. But where it's often foreigners who adulate Scott, it's the Scots themselves who revel in "Rabbie." Burns Night, every January 25, is a nationally observed occasion for dusk-to-dawn rituals of a kind that must have Scotland's Presbyterian forefathers bucketing up and down in their graves.

Burns was born in 1759 in the "auld clay biggin" built by his father, which is now the Burns Cottage Museum at Alloway, 2 miles south of Ayr on the B7024. Also on the site are the Land O' Burns Centre with its audiovisual program, book and crafts shop, cafeteria, and picnic tables; the Burns Monument, a rococo stone folly on a leafy hill; and the 700-year-old Brig O' Doon, where the witch in Burns's famous narrative poem, *Tam O' Shanter*, catches hold of Tam's mare's tail. Spooky-looking Auld Alloway Kirk, a ruin even in Burns's day, has an empty window through which Tam sees "Warlocks and Witches in a dance." Burns's father lies in Auld Alloway Kirkyard.

The Land O' Burns Centre has leaflets about a Burns Heritage Trail you can follow through two counties. A week-long Robert Burns Festival held every June in the

Ayrshire district is administered from Alloway and includes music, poetry, exhibitions, dinners, and dances.

Back in Ayr, the Tam O' Shanter Museum on High St. was once a brewery to which Douglas Graham of Shanter (the real-life Tam) supplied the malted grain. Also to be seen in this busy dairy farmers' town are its large harbor; the 13th-century Tower of St. John at Citadel Place; the 15th-century Auld Brig over the River Ayr; the 16th-century Loudon Hall, house of the hereditary sheriffs of Ayrshire, in Boat Vennel; and the 17th-century Auld Kirk built by Cromwell, where Burns was baptized, just off the High St. Ayr is celebrated too for its racetrack on Whitletts Rd., and its panoramic beach with a view of the Isle of Arran. Belleisle Park on the south side has a zoo, nature trail, lush gardens, and a championship golf course.

CHECKING IN: *Pickwick* – One of the best of a seafront string of Victorian villas specializing in pure malt whiskies and Scottish foods. Each of the 15 rooms has a bath. 19 Racecourse Rd., Ayr (phone: 0292-260111). Moderate.

Marine Court – After a refurbishment, this seaside hotel now has 30 comfortable rooms and a restaurant with a varied menu. 12 Fairfield Rd., Ayr (phone: 0292-267461). Moderate.

Belleisle House – Once an aristocrat's home, this delightful 18-room hotel retains such personal embellishments as engraved fireplaces. Elegant traditional dishes are served in one of two dining rooms, done up in Marie Antoinette style. Inside Belleisle Park grounds on Doonfoot Rd., Ayr (phone: 0292-42331). Moderate to inexpensive.

En Route from Ayr – Actually a continuation of Ayr, Prestwick is Scotland's main transatlantic airport. It also has a fine beach and a rather whimsical championship golf course, where the first-ever Open was played in 1860. *Adamton Courte,* an 18th-century castle of modest size, offers medieval banquets on weekends. It's off the main road around Monkton, just north of Prestwick (phone: 0292-70678; moderate).

Take the A77 from Monkton to Kilmarnock, a city in the heart of industrial West Scotland; from here to Glasgow are factories and smelting works, coalfields, and railroads. Burns's first poems were published in Kilmarnock; a Burns monument in Kay Park has good views of the surrounding countryside, and the Burns Museum has stacks of important Burnsiana including a large library. Museum can be visited by appointment only (phone: 0563-26401). Also in Kilmarnock are Dean Castle, on Dean Rd., containing a fine collection of European arms and armor, as well as early musical instruments (open mid-May to mid-September); and the Dick Institute, on Elmbank Ave., with archaeological exhibits, including fossils of international importance (closed Sundays).

CHECKING IN: *Chapeltoun House* – A small but posh early-20th-century mansion, with a new antique-style cocktail bar that matches the original paneling. Wonderful food is produced by the marriage (literally) of the chefs, who met in France at a Cordon Bleu cookery course. On the A735 through Stewarton, 8 miles north of Kilmarnock (phone: 0560-82696). Expensive.

Scottish Highlands

The Highlands of Scotland: The very words evoke romantic visions of hill and glen, bagpipe and drum, purple heather and curling mist. But behind the picture-postcard Highlands of every visitor from Queen Victoria to Pope John Paul II is a real Highlands that, though scenically among the most glorious places on earth, was for centuries a land of harsh living conditions, brutal internecine clan warfare, and rank exploitation by aristocratic power. It is a kind of divine wilderness suffering from depopulation even today.

That however only makes it more attractive to travelers, who can still steal a march on Paradise for two weeks or three in a Highland hotel away from the grime and confusion of modern city life. Just driving through the mountains, with their ancient Gaelic names (*Beinn Nevis, Beinn Bheag, Beinn à Chrulaiste*) and their plethora of interlinking waterways, is a soul-binding experience. Even better is to get out and walk — hillwalking, as it's called (it's really mountain climbing) is one of the great Scots pastimes; or just stroll down the glens and look up! If you do climb make sure you have a compass, warm clothes, and the right sort of boots. (You'll have a foot in everything from bogs to "scree," that is, loose slaty rubble.) And beware of hidden treacheries: A hike to a seemingly low peak from a warm sunlit valley could precipitate you suddenly into snow, thick fog, and a loss of your sense of direction. Every year people die on Scottish mountains from lack of knowledge, equipment, and judgment.

Historically, where the Lowlands came under English, French, Norman, and Scandinavian influence, the Highlands were dominated by the Irish, so that a true Highlander, one with Celtic blood, is very like his cousins in the Emerald Isle (always excepting Dublin). He is socially conservative, community conscious, and hostile to cosmopolitan ideas. He is courteously hospitable and as a rule no longer speaks Gaelic, but an English of old-fashioned phrasing. While Lowlanders got on with the business of urbanization, farming, trading, and general moneymaking in the seventeenth and eighteenth centuries, Highlanders remained cut off, nomadic, warlike, and idealistic. Loyalty to clan chiefs held good almost to a man. Cattle rustling, raiding, and feuds were rife. A Highlander's home, a bleakly appointed thatch-roofed stone cottage called a "black house," contained only one room — with a smoky fire on an earthen floor in its middle and wooden shelves for beds — and one stable, joined to family quarters by a large and gaping doorway.

Religion in the Highlands was, as the historian and essayist T. B. Macaulay put it, "a rude mixture of Popery and paganism." But after the Glorious Revolution of 1688–89 (by which the Roman Catholic James II was deposed from the British throne in favor of Protestants William and Mary), Episcopalianism and Presbyterianism both began to penetrate behind the Plaid Curtain. The powerful Clan Campbell, dukes of Argyll, became Presbyterians and others followed, especially during the late eighteenth century, when Episcopalianism in its turn declined. For three centuries from 1700 a series of schisms rocked Presbyterian Highland Scotland, throwing up movements faster than people could count them and leaving large parts of the West Highlands today under the rod of the archaic sect, the "Wee Frees." A Wee Free Sabbath makes an ordinary Lowland Sunday look like a chapter in the life of Sodom and Gomorrah, so if you're anywhere west of Inverness on the Day of Rest, don't try to buy anything, including gasoline. Nor will it do you any harm to walk funereally, wear black, and make sure the proprietor of your chosen hotel sees you in church.

Not only religious but social shake-ups in the Highlands occurred on a massive scale. The late eighteenth and early nineteenth centuries saw the Clearances, the cruelly inhuman spectacle of landowners driving tenants from their homes in order to replace them with sheep, financially a more profitable venture. Thousands of Highlanders teemed south into Glasgow's slums and points more distant, never to return. Next came the era of the deer park, when a coterie of London-based aristocrats, the 7% of the Scottish population who owned 84% of the land, evicted another wave of Highlanders in order to create holiday playgrounds in the shape of private shooting and fishing preserves. Queen Victoria's love affair with her Highland castle at Balmoral inadvertently provided these plunderers with a fashionable impetus. Now the Highlands are undergoing another change: The Highlands and Islands Development Board, seeking to lure tourists and to take advantage of the North Sea oil boom that began in the early 1970s, has aided new wealth in parts of the Highlands but has increased the isolation of other parts, especially where fishing has suffered from oil operations or railway lines have been cut.

Customs and preoccupations that would long ago have vanished in less remote districts continue in the Highlands and form no small part of Scotland's tourist delights. Apart from obvious examples such as kiltwearing, bagpiping, and the drinking of pure malt whiskies tasting of smoked peat (*never* water them!), there are Highland games (contests of strength featuring such marathon events as "tossing the caber" — a full-grown de-branched tree); the National Mod (Scotland's peripatetic annual orgy of Gaeldom in which Gaelic singers and reciters compete for prizes — the Scottish Eisteddfod) and other folk and musical happenings; and "Nessie-Watching" (a sport begun by St. Columba of Iona, the sixth-century Christianizer of Scotland, who sighted a prehistoric monster in Loch Ness's mysterious deep).

Battlefields, too, are a big draw, not only for tourists but for legions of Scots as well. Culloden Moor, near Inverness, is thus a focal point. Here Jacobitism, primarily a Highland movement seeking to restore the Stuart descendants of King James VI and I to the British throne, met a dire end in 1746 at the hands of the duke of Cumberland, second son of the Hanoverian king George II. Whole clans were wiped out under the inadequate generalship of "Bonnie" Prince Charles Edward Stuart, the Jacobite royal heir, who fled in defeat to France whence he had come. All signs of Highland culture, including the kilt and the Gaelic language, were proscribed for a long time afterward, and the Culloden legend swelled the characteristic ethereal glooms of Celtic composers and poets in both Scotland and Ireland for generations.

This tour route begins at Stirling, "Gateway to the Highlands," and leads north through Glencoe, Fort William, and the "Great Glen" by Loch Ness to Inverness, a distance of some 160 miles. Two outings from Inverness are also suggested: one to Gairloch on the Wester Ross Atlantic seaboard, one to Balmoral at Braemar along Royal Deeside. As when touring the Lowlands, book hotels in advance from May through September; keep sandwiches in your car and be opportunistic about petrol pumps, which are harder to find than Brigadoon! Remote areas have paved cattle tracks as roads — if you meet a vehicle head on, you'll have to back into one of the lay-bys provided at several-hundred-yard intervals. An alternative to driving yourself is *Travelpass,* which, for a flat fee, provides 7 to 14 days' unlimited travel through the

Highlands and Scottish Islands by train, bus, and ferry. For more information contact Pickfords Travel, 25 Queensgate, Inverness (phone: 232134), or Britrail Travel International, 630 Third Ave., New York, NY 10017 (phone: 212 599-5400). Carry the Scottish Tourist Board's *Enjoy Scotland* road map, which shows information centers, picnic tables, and woodland and nature trails in abundance. Also helpful are their publications *Walks and Trails* (£1.50) and *Hillwalking* (£1.75). Hotels listed as expensive will charge $85 and up for bed and breakfast for two; moderate ones, from $55 to $80; and inexpensive ones, from $35 to $50. Unless otherwise stated, all hotel rooms provide TV and private bath. A meal for two in an expensive restaurant will cost $50 or more; in a moderate one, $35 to $50; in an inexpensive one, less than $35.

STIRLING: Like Edinburgh, Stirling began on an exalted crag and spread out downward; unlike Edinburgh, it failed to develop points of interest outside its ancient zones. You should zero in on Stirling Hill where you'll find Stirling Castle, garnished by a subsidiary handful of aged buildings and intriguing ruins. The castle is the most famous in Scottish history, not only for its dramatic 250-foot drop to Stirling Plain and its eye-boggling view, but also for its strategic position controlling lands to the north during the Middle Ages, its associations with Robert the Bruce and his predecessor, William Wallace, and its magnificent Renaissance architecture, lavishly elaborated during its heyday as one of the four royal residences of the Stuart kings. Representations of Baccanalian-looking characters such as Love and Lust on the façade, the work of stonemasons from France employed by Mary of Guise, wife of James V, have been confused (but not obliterated) by centuries of irate Presbyterian rains. A guidebook bought at the castle entrance will heighten your enjoyment of the towers built by James III, the fine 15th-century hall, James V's palace, the Parliament Hall, and the Chapel Royal of 1594. The Castle Visitor Centre on the esplanade revives Stirling's past through an imaginative picture gallery and multiscreen show (there's a bookshop, crafts shop, and tea garden, too); joint admission charge to Castle and Centre.

Mar's Wark, beside the castle, was built in about 1570 by the first earl of Mar, Regent of Scotland, and was the home of his descendants until 1715, when the sixth earl had to flee the country after leading an unsuccessful major Jacobite rebellion. It became a barracks, then a workhouse (hence its name). Bonnie Prince Charlie's army sacked and ruined it in 1746, but some of its exquisite embellishments remain. Also by the castle are the still-used Church of the Holy Rude, dating from 1414, where John Knox preached the sermon when James VI, aged 13 months, was crowned (open daily, May through September); the Guildhall, south of the church, founded in 1639 by the then Dean of Guild for the support of twelve "decayed Guild Breithers"; and the impressive 17th-century townhouse, Argyll's Lodging, now a youth hostel but once the residence of Sir William Alexander of Menstrie, the founder of Nova Scotia. An exhibition displaying the coats of arms of 107 Nova Scotian baronetcies is at 16th-century Menstrie Castle, Sir William's birthplace 5 miles to the east on the A91 (open 2:30 to 5 PM Wednesdays and weekends, May through September). Cambuskenneth Abbey, on the River Forth a mile northeast of Stirling, was founded in the 12th century by the Scottish king David I, and was the scene in 1326 of King Robert the Bruce's first formal Parliament. The church and conventual buildings are rubble but a detached 67-foot 13th-century bell tower survives intact.

The Scottish Wars of Independence, which took place around the turn of the 13th century, were distinguished for the valor not only of the aristocrat King Robert the Bruce ("Robert de Brus" in his native Norman tongue) but also of William Wallace, the People's Hero, who drove back an English army in 1297 at the Battle of Stirling Bridge, a mile north of the castle. Wallace's control over Scotland was short-lived — he was defeated at Falkirk in 1298 by a massive avenging force, imprisoned in London, and hacked limb from limb in 1305 — but his memory is sacred in Scottish hearts. The grandly towering Wallace Monument near the site of his triumph (off Hillfoots Rd., 1½ miles north-northeast of town) is a famous landmark, erected in 1861. Inside, the Stirling District Council offers an audio-visual historical crash course. Views are heavenly from its 220-foot top.

Bannockburn, off the M80 just south of Stirling, is a must. Beside the Battlefield is a film theater where you can catch up with the full story of the Wars of Independence (open daily, March through October). Bruce was not eager to fight the English at the time and place now so famous for his victory, but his hand had been forced by his brother, who made a deal in 1313 with the governor of Stirling Castle — in English hands since soon after the defeat of Wallace — securing the castle's return to Scotland if the English did not relieve it by St. John the Baptist's Day (Midsummer Day) of the following year (the Bruces had the castle under siege). On Midsummer Day, 1314, 20,000 English troops, commanded by King Edward II himself, marched on the castle. Bruce's tactics were brilliant: He let the English come within 2 hair-raising miles of the target and then attacked — on the only piece of ground in the English route north where his mere 5,500 spearmen could hope to hold out — at first light, before the king's cavalry could see to charge. Finding themselves cut off to left and right by unexpected and treacherous marshes, Edward's stalwarts fell back in confusion and flight. A magnificent 20-foot equestrian statue of Robert the Bruce in shining armor, unveiled by Queen Elizabeth II on the battle's 650th anniversary, stands today on the spot reputed to have been the Scottish royal headquarters during the fighting.

Also to be seen in Stirling are its old Mercat Cross and its 18th-century tollbooth, on Broad St.; the bastion, or jail, within the original fortified town wall, just inside the Port St. entrance to the Thistle Shopping Centre; the 15th-century Auld Brig still used by pedestrians at Stirling Bridge (north of city center off the A9); and the Smith Art Gallery and Museum on Albert Pl., housing, among other treasures, objects from early local history (closed Mondays and Tuesdays). The MacRobert Arts Centre, one of Scotland's foremost music, film, and theater venues, is on the grounds of Stirling University off the A9, 2 miles north of town. During the Stirling District Festival, held around the last week of July and first week of August, the center hosts Scottish dancing and other events.

 CHECKING IN: *Dunblane Hydro* – Set in a 60-acre park, this is the largest hotel in the area and a holiday center in itself. Along with 188 well-equipped rooms and two restaurants serving traditional Scottish cuisine, the hotel has a heated indoor swimming pool, tennis courts, sports hall, Jacuzzi, and more. 3 miles from Stirling in Dunblane (phone: 0786-822551). Expensive to moderate.

Royal – Robert Louis Stevenson stayed in this impressive 32-room mansion house as a boy, when his family visited the nearby spa. Its Taste of Scotland menu is much in local demand. Henderson St., in Bridge of Allan, 4 miles north of Stirling (phone: 0786-832284). Moderate.

Portcullis – Built in 1472 as a school for the children of Scottish noblemen — and reputedly where James VI of Scotland (later James I of England) was taught — this attractive, historic building is now a hospitable 6-room hotel. The restaurant offers Scottish fare, and there's also a bar and beer garden. Castle Wynd (phone: 0786-72290). Moderate to inexpensive.

Golden Lion – Though now clinging for dear life to its immaculate historic pedigree, this 75-room hotel is nonetheless the best of Stirling's lately rather dubious center-city bets. Robert Burns, the royal family, Billy Graham, and a host of film stars have all been guests. 8 King St., Stirling (phone: 0786-75351). Inexpensive.

King's Gate – Decorated like a house, the pleasant, down-to-earth atmosphere of this individualistic 15-room establishment takes its cue from the mounted zebra skins brought from East Africa by the proprietors. The food is good and inexpensive. 5 King St., Stirling (phone: 0786-73944). Inexpensive.

 EATING OUT: *Cross Keys Inn* – Dinner at this little English pub with a restaurant and 3 rooms is worth the 10-mile run from town. In Kippen village, via A811 west from Stirling (phone: 07867-293). Inexpensive.

En Route from Stirling – Take the A84 northwest. Between Stirling and Doune is *Scotland's Safari Park,* full of free-roaming wild animals. Performing seals, parrots, or dolphins are an added attraction in summer (open from around mid-March to the third week of October; £2.40 per adult, £1.90 per child).

DOUNE: The dark fastnesses of 14th-century Doune Castle, ancestral seat of the earls of Moray, have lasted unscathed. Not so some of its owners: the "Bonnie Earl" of Moray, who was the "Queen's love" in the famous murder ballad (actually he was her nephew; the queen was Mary Queen of Scots), was killed by the earl of Huntly in a clan feud in 1592. Doune Castle is beautifully set in a wooded clearing at the junction of the Teith and Ardoch rivers, approached just south of Doune village by a side road off the A84 (open April through October). Monty Python's Flying Circus filmed *The Holy Grail* here.

Doune village has a 16th-century bridge, built originally by James IV's tailor to spite a ferryman who had refused him passage. A mile north of the village is the Doune Motor Museum, showing off the present earl of Moray's collection of vintage cars (open April through October).

CALLANDER: A very long street with mountains to either side, this bustling gateway to Sir Walter Scott's beloved Trossachs, the "bristly country," just misses being a typical Highland town — the Teith flows through it too complacently for that, and its fields are too prosperously green. In former times it was a cattle drovers' stop. If you give a day's notice to John Virando, proprietor of the *Callander Pottery,* 120 Main St. (phone: 0877-30487), you can watch him throw pots and decorate them.

CHECKING IN: *Cromlix House* – This lovely mansion set on 5,000 acres has recently been converted to a hotel. All 14 rooms have private bath, and some have sitting rooms. Shooting, riding, tennis, and fishing for brown trout are some of the activities here; this is also the perfect headquarters for golfers since many of Scotland's finest courses are within an easy drive. Edinburgh and Glasgow are less than an hour away as well. Dunblane (phone: 0786-822125). Expensive.

Roman Camp – Lawns sweeping down to the River Teith and lordly Old World hospitality are the keynotes here. There are 11 guestrooms, and the excellent traditional dishes include beef, salmon, and venison. Closed December through February. Off Main St., Callander (phone: 0877-30003). Expensive to moderate.

Auchendoune – A lovely, antique-filled private home with a breathtaking view of Doune Castle and the Doune valley. Your hosts will make you feel like one of the family, serving American waffles for breakfast. On A84 at Doune's southern boundary — look for the Scottish flag flying from the roof (phone: 0786841-217). Inexpensive.)

Dalgair House – A distinguished, family-run townhouse, with 10 rooms, traditional Scottish home cooking, and a wide selection of wines and whiskies. 113/115 Main St., Callander (phone: 0877-30283). Inexpensive.

En Route from Callander – The A84 leads north through the Pass of Leny, noted for its waterfall, dwarfed oaks, and wild primroses. Four miles north of town, 2,875-foot

Ben Ledi (Hill of God), overlooking Loch Lubnaig, is an easily manageable, highly rewarding 3.5-hour climb on foot. The A84 skirts the edge of the lake to the picturesque hamlet of Strathyre, once a crofting settlement. Rob Roy's Grave is along an unnamed side road turning west 2 miles farther north. The fabled outlaw lies in a setting of seraphic peace in the Macgregor family plot in Balquhidder Churchyard, beneath the lovely Braes of Balquhidder at the head of Loch Voil. The church itself contains an 8th-century carved tombstone and some old Gaelic Bibles.

LOCHEARNHEAD: Famous throughout Scotland for its water skiing facilities, this resort on the west shore of Loch Earn is also an excellent spot for boating. *Lochearnhead Water Sports Centre* and *Clachan Cottage Marina,* beside the lake on the A85, will cater to your sporting needs. The road around Loch Earn makes a pleasant 10-mile detour, including views of two fairy tale mansions owned by aristocrats on the south shore. In July, Lochearnhead hosts the Balquhidder-Lochearnhead-Strathyre Highland Games.

CHECKING IN: *Clachan Cottage* – This row of 250-year-old white one-story cottages — with 25 rooms all told — winks at Loch Earn with its prettily lamplit windows. On the A85 along the loch's north shore (phone: 05673-247). Inexpensive.

***Kingshouse* –** Once the hunting abode of the "Bonnie Earl" of Moray, this small white edifice with 9 rooms is decorated with tartans and oil paintings in traditional Highland style. The bar attracts "shepherds and gamekeepers" and there's a crafts shop in the byre. On the A84, 2 miles north of Strathyre (phone: 08774-646). Inexpensive.

EATING OUT: *Ledcreich* – Much patronized by surrounding districts, this captivating 4-room country lodge is famous for its dinners, served en casserole in the manner of the provincial French. The restaurant, converted from a stable, has candlelight, red Regency chairs, and old wooden ceiling beams. Reservations. On the north side of Loch Voil, 2 miles west of Balquhidder village (phone: 08774-230). Expensive.

En Route from Lochearnhead – Glen Ogle, on the A85 immediately to the north, is a gloomy mountain pass with towering rock masses to left and right. It leads to Glen Dochart, once a place of ruthless bloodletting among the clans Campbell, Macnab, Macgregor, and Maclaren. Crianlarich, in a pretty, tree-speckled hollow in an otherwise austere territory, is more a crossroads than a village: It fuses two routes north, one from Stirling and one from Loch Lomond. The road above it leading to Tyndrum (the A82) is the King's Road of 200 years ago — widened and paved — linking Stirling Castle and Fort William. It was at Tyndrum that Robert the Bruce barely escaped with his life 8 years before the Battle of Bannockburn when he was ambushed by his enemies, the Clan Macdougall. (The Macdougalls still have the pearl and crystal brooch he lost in the struggle.) Tyndrum is also worth a visit for the popular *Clifton Coffee House,* which serves fine Scottish food and has a gift shop with an extensive selection of Scotch whiskies and souvenirs. North of Tyndrum, in the vicinity of Bridge of Orchy, the cone-shaped wonder on your right is Beinn Dorain, a subject of praise in Gaelic poetry. Just to the north on the shore of Loch Tulla is a smattering of ancient trees, once part of the medieval Caledonian Forest. The road hits the barren edge of Rannoch Moor before bearing west to Glencoe.

GLENCOE: More famous than any city, town, or village for miles around, this most portentous and claustrophobic of glens was the scene, in 1692, of the massacre of the Clan Macdonald by the Clan Campbell. The Campbells were guests of the Macdonalds and murdered their hosts — on orders from King William III, to whom the Macdonalds had failed to pledge allegiance — in their beds. The horrible double-dealing nature of the deed has set it apart from the run-of-the-mill massacres, and if your name is Campbell, you'd better sign into Glencoe hotels under a false one, or you may be tarred, feathered, and run out of town on a *skean dhu* (the dagger a Highlander wears in the top of his sock).

Bald mountains on both sides of the glen make modern Glencoe a haunt of hillwalkers and skiers. The view from the top of the ski runs (there's a chair lift) is terrific — in spring anyway, when the clouds that usually sulk over the scenery disperse (skiing is available on weekends, Easter, and Mondays February to May only). Popular foot trails and climbs — some too tough for amateurs — encompass topographical features such as Ossian's Cave, the Devil's Staircase, and Signal Rock (from which went forth the signal for the massacre). Wildcats, golden eagles, deer, and ptarmigans patrol the upper reaches of Glencoe's pinnacled heights. A visitor center giving geographical information is on the A82 (open early April to mid-October) and the Glencoe and North Lorn Folk Museum, containing historic relics and antique local domestic implements, is at the end of the glen beside Loch Leven (open May through September).

CHECKING IN: *Clachaig Inn* – Dramatically set in a deep rocky gorge is this 10-room climbers' retreat, long a Glencoe landmark. Its friendly, colossal public bar is a garrulous sea of beards and boots. On the unmarked road north of the River Coe near Signal Rock (phone: 08552-252). Inexpensive.

King's House – A medieval hunting lodge that became a barracks and later a staging post, this venerable octopus with sprawling public rooms and 22 bedchambers today harbors skiers (the Glencoe chair lift is just across the road). On the A82 at Glencoe's east head (phone: 08556-259). Inexpensive.

En Route from Glencoe – Until recently, the small village of Ballachulish at the west head of Glencoe was a port for ferries crossing Loch Leven to North Ballachulish. It now boasts a bridge which, like the ferry, saves travelers bound for Fort William the long detour around the lake. At Onich, views across Loch Linnhe, a sea arm of the Firth of Lorn, are exceptionally stunning — Loch Linnhe stretches 32½ miles from Fort William south to the Sound of Mull, encompassing the Hebridean island of Lismore. From Ballachulish and Onich northward, the route follows the Great Glen, an extraordinary 66-mile geographical fault that slices Scotland diagonally in two and leads all the way to Inverness.

FORT WILLIAM: A stone fort erected to quell unrest among turbulent Highlanders marked this site from the time of William of Orange until 1864. Then the fort was demolished to make way for a railroad, and the town you see here mushroomed up around the newly laid tracks. Fort William today is a hub not only for tourists but for campers, youth hostelers, conference-goers, and climbers. Snow-trimmed Ben Nevis (4,408 feet), Scotland's highest mountain, looms nearby looking (somewhat disappointingly) like a megalithic iced bun. Below it is the glen of the same name — narrow, lush, overpowered by the rocky monarchs of the mighty Mamore range.

The West Highland Museum in Cameron Square stockpiles objects that once belonged to Bonnie Prince Charlie, including his breeks and a lock of his hair. There's an antique "secret portrait" in which a smeared half-moon of paint turns into his likeness when viewed through a special cylinder (closed Sundays). The A82 just north of Fort William brings you to Old Inverlochy Castle, a 13th-century ruin with soaring circular towers. Also just above town, on the A830, the eight locks of Neptune's Staircase are a remarkable feat of engineering. Constructed between 1805 and 1822, they raise barges a total of 64 feet at the entrance to Thomas Telford's famed Caledonian Canal linking Loch Linnhe, Loch Lochy, Loch Oich, and Loch Ness.

For the most fun of all, take "Concrete Bob" McAlpine's 42-mile scenic railway (84 miles round-trip), parallel to the "Road to the Isles" (the A830, which you can also do — as a detour — by car) between Fort William and the Atlantic port of Mallaig opposite the Isle of Skye. The route, administered by British Rail ("Concrete Bob" was its builder), crosses the Caledonian Canal by a swing bridge, passes Loch Eil buttressed by 17 sea walls, and swoops above the Glenfinnan Monument at the head of Loch Shiel on a curving white viaduct of 21 pillared arches 100 feet high! The Glenfinnan Monument stands where Bonnie Prince Charlie unfurled the Jacobite flag to a roll of drums in 1745. If you have your own transportation, you can catch up on the Bonnie Prince's career at the Glenfinnan Monument Visitor Centre, open mid-April to mid-October. The famous sands at Morar just before you reach Mallaig are so silvery they look as if they've been lifted wholesale from beside the Indian Ocean.

CHECKING IN: *Alexandra* – An attractive alternative to Fort William's chronic chromium blight with 92 rooms, red carpets, an open fire in the drawing room, and plain beige walls hung with paintings. The dining room is known for its English breakfasts. Opposite the station, Fort William (phone: 0397-2241). Inexpensive.

Moorings – A delightful stone dwelling on Loch Eil near the tiny papermill town of Corpach (which has the best view of Ben Nevis). It has 16 rooms and good Taste of Scotland home cooking by resident proprietors. On the B8004 off the A830 near Neptune's Staircase (phone: 0397-550). Inexpensive.

EATING OUT: *Inverlochy Castle* – Thought by many to contain the finest restaurant in Britain, this opulently furnished 19th-century mansion has 13 rooms, castellated wings and turrets, painted ceilings, and vulcanic blazes in huge marble fireplaces. Delicacies such as game pâté and spinach soup are exquisite curtain raisers for the ravishing entrées. Closed November to Easter. Reservations suggested. On the A82 just north of Fort William (phone: 0397-2177). Expensive.

Stag's Head – Bar lunches here are a knockout; for a few pounds you can get roast haunch of venison in port sauce or fresh salmon salad. There's a restaurant, too, with elegant dark oak furniture, and a drying room for rain-drenched climbers' gear. Guestrooms total 48. Closed November through March. High St., Fort William (phone: 0397-4144). Inexpensive.

En Route from Fort William – Spean Bridge is 10 miles northeast on the A82. An impressive Commando Memorial, erected in 1952 just north of the bridge over the cauldronlike River Spean, honors World War II commandos who trained in this area. A 9-mile detour east (18 miles round-trip) by the A86 and then the first left takes you to that geologists' dream, the Parallel Roads, a group of evenly graduated earthen terraces marking levels of lakes dammed by Ice Age glaciers. There's nothing quite like them in all of Europe. Return to the A82 and continue north through Invergarry, where the River Garry meets Loch Oich and where *Garry Crafts* produces and sells handmade gifts (open daily Easter through October, with 1-hour courses in hand-spinning and "flower"-making). A 20-mile civilization-haters' detour (40 miles round trip) at Invergarry — onto the A87 followed by the unmarked road to your left — fetches you up on the wildest, most untrammeled corner of Scotland, the shores of Loch Hourn (Lake of Hell), along a road thick with wild deer.

CHECKING IN: *Inn on the Garry* – The pretty parlors and cheerful log fires at this stunning 10-room inn are widely renowned. Newly culled local produce graces its tables. On the A82, Invergarry (phone: 0893-206). Inexpensive.

FORT AUGUSTUS: This fishermen's paradise at the base of Loch Ness will give you your first glimpse of the world famous 22-mile waterway; the Great Glen Exhibition, a museum by the Caledonian Canal in the center of town, has an audiovisual historical show to acquaint you with the monster (open April through October). The fort that gave rise to the town was established (1730) on the site of a barracks set up after the 1715 Jacobite rising and was named after William Augustus, the son of King George II, who later erased Jacobitism forever at Culloden. Ironically, one of the fort's Protestant walls eventually became part of Fort Augustus Abbey, a lavishly designed Benedictine priory and school (on the main road) begun in 1876. The present community of monks gives guided tours of the abbey three times a day.

DRUMNADROCHIT: The A82 continues north along the edge of Loch Ness to this attractive hamlet at the head of Glen Urquhart. The ruins of pre-14th-century Urquhart Castle, one of the largest in Scotland until it was blown up by Williamite forces in 1692, can be seen jutting into the water just south of the village. This is the point from which "Nessie" has most often been seen: Waters here are deeper than the North Sea and perfect for prehistoric inhabitors, but hunts by midget submarine, tungsten TV lamp, strobe light, time-lapse camera, and SX70 Polaroid have so far proven nothing. Nonetheless, there is a Loch Ness Monster exhibition center in Drumnadrochit village.

Pony trekkers at Drumnadrochit should apply to the *Highland Riding Centre,* Borlum Farm (phone: 04562-220); there's a plethora of beautiful glens nearby to be explored, gentler than the ones farther south. Glen Urquhart holds Corrimony Cairn, a Neolithic structure with a circle of standing stones. The glens can be toured by car, too — consult the *Enjoy Scotland* map, which prints their names next to the roads that serve them.

 CHECKING IN: *Polmaily House* – An Edwardian country house on its own grounds, with 11 rooms and delicious local food. Glen Urquhart (phone: 04562-343). Moderate to inexpensive.

Drumnadrochit – With an imposing view overlooking Drumnadrochit village, this 30-room hotel is comfortable and reasonably priced. Its restaurant has a varied menu (phone: 04562-218). Moderate to inexpensive.

Inchnacardoch Lodge – Fishing, sailing, and water skiing are organized from this charming 17-room country mansion house still retaining its original paneling. The tasty cooking is unwaveringly Scottish. On Loch Ness off the A82 a mile north of Fort Augustus (phone: 04562-6258). Inexpensive.

INVERNESS: Despite its flat location — a shock after previous scenic grandeurs — and the Plain Jane look of its streets, the "Capital of the Highlands" is an exhilarating place to be. It has a population of 40,000, which swells to 100,000 during the summer as visitors pack its hotels, and is the commercial and administrative hub of a vast surrounding region, overseen by the Highlands and Islands Development Board, which is stationed here. The River Ness winds a courtly path through the city's center beside high-spired churches, and the sun never quite goes down in midsummer, but bathes the shining water in an exquisitely lyric gold half-light.

Civilization is very old at Inverness, dating from at least as far back as the 4th century BC. Pictish kings ruled from here; it was for here that St. Columba of Iona was making, to convert King Brudei, when in 565 AD he spied the Loch Ness Monster. In the 12th century, Inverness became a Royal Burgh under the patronage of King David I, who erected a castle on Castlehill. Jacobites sacked this castle in 1745 but it was eventually replaced by the present lovely pink one, housing the Inverness Sheriff Court.

Not much remains of the Inverness of yore, though an amble down Church Street takes you past Dunbar's Hospital of 1668, the Old High Church of 1772 (it has an earlier tower and spire), and the Steeple of 1791. A clock tower on Ness bank is all that's left of Oliver Cromwell's "Pentagon" (a 5-sided fort blown up at the time of the Restoration); but the Gothic Town House on High St. where Lloyd George and his cabinet met to discuss the 1921 Irish Treaty is alive and well. A minor nugget of preserved Victoriana is the area comprising Union Street, Queensgate, Station Square, and the adjacent part of Academy St. Tomnahurich Cemetery, on a cyprus ridge above the river, has a delightful view that contributes to its fame as the handsomest graveyard in Scotland.

But Inverness's best sights aren't urban. Culloden Battlefield, with its clan graves, Well of the Dead, Memorial Cairn, and Old Leanach Farmhouse (a small war museum), lies 5 miles outside town on the B9006. Bonnie Prince Charlie's mournful fiasco here in 1746 was the last land battle on British soil. For information about Culloden Battlefield film shows, call the Visitor Centre (phone: 790607), open April through mid-October. Near Culloden are the Clava Cairns, an extensive group of Bronze Age standing stones and burial chambers. Cawdor Castle, the seat of the Thanes of Cawdor for 600 years, is 13 miles northeast of Inverness on the B9090. Within its walls, according to Shakespeare, Macbeth stabbed King Duncan. The castle has everything: a drawbridge, a tower built around a tree, a freshwater well inside the house; gardens, nature trails, a pitch-and-putt course; a picnic area, snack bar, licensed restaurant, and gift shop (castle and grounds open May through September; phone: 066-77615). Nearby on the B9039 (turn off the A96 at Gollanfield) is Fort George, begun in 1748 to prevent another Jacobite rebellion. It's one of the finest late artillery bastions in Europe. Adjacent is the Regimental Museum of the Queen's Own Highlanders (closed Saturdays all year and Sundays October through March). The 7-foot Boar Stone at Knocknagael, 2 miles south of Inverness on the B861, is a striking, Pictish carved slab dating from around 300 AD; equally hoary is the vitrified fort along the Craig Phadrick Forest Trail off the A9 to Inverness's west.

Throughout the year the Inverness Museum and Gallery in Castle Wynd mounts a dazzling barrage of learned lectures and special exhibitions; it also has a permanent display of Highland silver from the 17th century on, and a large natural history wing (open Mondays through Saturdays). Of utmost importance to local cultural life is the Eden Court Theatre on Bishop's Rd., opened in 1976. Designed with contemporary panache around part of a medieval bishop's palace, its glass-gabled anterooms look out on the river while its high-walled auditorium features everything from ballet, opera, symphonic recitals, drama, films, art exhibitions, and pop and rock concerts to *ceilidhs*.

Bught Park, off Glenurquhart Rd., is the rendezvous in summer for colorful Highland playoffs such as the Highland Shinty Cup Final and the Inverness Highland Games. Northern Meeting Park on Ardross St. is the scene of summer tattoos, tartan shows for tourists, and piping competitions. From mid-May to mid-September a "Welcome Piper" struts his stuff on Castlehill, and to top all this there's a Music Festival and a Folk Festival in spring. You can pick up a comprehensive activities sheet at the tourist board office on Church St. during the summer.

Cruises down Loch Ness on the MV *Scott II* (phone: 233140) operate from mid-April to September; and the breathtaking 3-hour train trip from Inverness south to Kyle of Lochalsh has been on BBC Television's *Great Railway Journeys of the World.* Another fine cruise, offered by *Jacobite Cruises* (phone: 241730), runs to Loch Ness and Urquhart daily. *Holm Woollen Mills,* 2 miles outside town on Dores Rd., is owned by the famous Pringle Company and has tours as well as extensive showrooms.

 CHECKING IN: *Culloden House* – Residents feel like kings in the light, spacious rooms of this beautiful 18th-century palace full of ornate plasterwork and priceless antique furniture. There are 20 bedchambers, carpets in the bathrooms, extensive park grounds, enchanting views, and a sauna. On Culloden Moor (phone: Inverness 790461). Expensive.

Kingsmills – A 10-minute walk from downtown, the *Kingsmills* is a striking, white 200-year-old time capsule, with its front door in an architraved turret; it has 54 rooms (some in recently built extensions), private squash courts, and 4 acres of gardens. Culcabock Rd., Inverness (phone: 237166). Expensive in summer, moderate in winter.

Station – The comfortably plush Victorian grandeur of this central 66-room relic has been heightened by the recent refurbishment of its public rooms. The restaurant has good Taste of Scotland fare. Academy St., Inverness (phone: 231926). Expensive to moderate.

Beaufort – Half of Inverness is laid out before you at this glorious 25-room hilltop mansion in a first-class residential area. All the charms of the past combine with private showers and color TVs. Enormous steaks are the chef's specialty. 11 Culduthel Rd., Inverness (phone: 222897). Moderate.

Caledonian – This popular modern riverfront all-rounder zings inside with decorator colors. It has a bouncy local clientele, convivial staff, 120 rooms, a Laundromat, cabarets, and dancing. Church St., Inverness (phone: 235181). Moderate.

Cummings – The complete ordinariness of this 38-room rectangle somehow manages to be endearing. Nightly Scottish cabarets here have been wowing audiences April through September for years. Church St., Inverness (phone: 232531). Moderate to inexpensive.

Redcliffe – This friendly, family-run establishment with 6 guestrooms and big, bright windows has a bar that is home to many Castle Hill residents. Its location affords a lovely elevated view of the river, despite its proximity to the town center. 1 Gordon Terrace, Inverness (phone: 232767). Inexpensive.

EATING OUT: Dunain Park – Guests of this family-owned country house are treated to sumptuous breakfasts, snack lunches in the garden, teas with homemade jams, and outstanding, imaginatively prepared dinners. Nonresidents with the necessary reservation may partake of the latter — and if you insist on risking gout in this oasis with a hint of sniffy respectability, spend the week in one of its 6 rooms. Open year-round. On the A82, 2½ miles south of Inverness (phone: 230512). Expensive.

Dickens – The decor in this fashionable midcity restaurant — a classic medley of browns and whites — is glossily smart. Its Chinese proprietors are equally adept at Chinese and European cooking, including vegetarian selections. 77-79 Church St., Inverness (phone: 224450). Inexpensive.

En Route from Inverness – Two possible small tours will give you a taste of the amazing variations in typical Highland scenery — from the wild, rocky splendors and salty sea lochs of regions in the west to the heather-covered braes (hills), freshwater streams, and gentle pine forests of the Grampian Mountains in the east. Each is an approximately 150-mile round-trip.

For the first, start out on the A862 west, switching to the A832 at Muir of Ord. This crossroads is at the southwest tip of Black Isle, a verdant peninsula full of whitewashed crofters' cottages between the Moray and Cromarty firths. Farther west, a detour via the A834 will take you to Strathpeffer, at its height as a fashionable spa in the late Victorian era. (The wedding cake architecture in the central square alone is worth the 6-mile round trip.) The A832 parallels the Inverness–Kyle of Lochalsh railway as far as Achnasheen, and a few miles beyond this romantic outpost is a sudden, spectacular view of Loch Maree, thought by many to be Scotland's loveliest lake. You'll skirt part of it later, just before the journey west ends at Gairloch in a triumph of scenic majesty opposite the Torridon peaks and the Outer Hebrides. Gair Loch, the sea inlet on which the village of Gairloch stands, is famous for sailing, deep-sea fishing and diving, and heavenly sand beaches. Six miles northeast, Poolewe is renowned throughout Britain for Inverewe Gardens, a sheltered subtropical spot where heather blooms with Himalayan lilies and huge South Pacific forget-me-nots. Flowers that survive only under glass at Kew Gardens in London grow here in the open air! There's an Inverewe Gardens Visitor Centre (open April to mid-October).

The second small tour sets out on the A9 eastward, with the first stop at Tomatin by the River Findhorn for a demonstration of the process through which *Uisge Beatha,* "The Water of Life," comes into existence. Tours of the Tomatin Distillery are given weekdays at 3 PM (phone them at 234 before you go; closed October through May). Continue to the fun-loving Spey Valley town of Carrbridge (on A938, just off A9), a microcosm of Scotland at leisure, bursting with anglers, skiers, climbers, ponytrekkers, and folk singers. The nearby Spey is one of Scotland's best salmon rivers, and the *Carrbridge Ski School* is a Strathspey legend. Do not, under any circumstances, bypass the Landmark Visitor Centre at Carrbridge. It has a multiscreen theater, bookshop, crafts shop, bar, restaurant, nature trail, sculpture park, and picnic tables in a pine wood. Displays evoking Spey Valley through the ages are whimsically intriguing; they include the sound of artificial arctic winds, a hand quern in which you can grind your own oatmeal, and more.

Boat of Garten, where a ferry once whisked travelers across the River Spey, has considerable popularity with fishermen and an 18-hole golf course said to be a miniature Gleneagles. The Strathspey Railway offers a 6½-mile journey to Aviemore (13 miles round-trip) on a genuine Victorian steam train on weekends from mid-May to mid-October and Mondays through Wednesdays during July and August. (The holiday complex at Aviemore is a major winter sports center, with skating and curling rinks and several buses daily taking skiers to the nearby Cairngorm Mountain slopes during the November through April season.) Leaving Boat of Garten, an access road from the B970 carries you into Loch Garten Nature Reserve where you can watch those lordly fishhawks, the ospreys, back in Scotland after a long extinction. On the B970 beyond Nethybridge is 13th-century Castle Roy, a massive red ruin said to be the oldest castle in the country; an unclassified road east of Nethybridge eventually joins the A939 and leads on to Tomintoul, the highest village (1,160 feet) in the Highlands. Regally set on a ridge overlooking the glen of the River Avon and the vale of the Water of Conglass, Tomintoul has only one long street, but Scotland's largest collection of whiskies is in its shops. Between Tomintoul and Cock Bridge, the Lecht Pass road climbs to a height of over 2,000 feet across a seemingly trackless waste that looks like the surface of the moon.

The junction of the A939 with the A93 at Bridge of Gairn brings you finally to Royal Deeside, that magic valley of laughing water and soughing birch and pine, cosseted by blue hills. A few miles to the west is Crathie Church — a major sight — where the royal family worships when staying at Balmoral Castle just across the River Dee. The 11,000-acre Balmoral estate was bought by Prince Albert in 1852 and its existing castle was then widened for Queen Victoria to its present leviathan proportions. You can visit the castle ballroom (unless the queen is in residence) daily except Sundays from May through July. A little farther along the A93 is Braemar, where Robert Louis Stevenson wrote *Treasure Island,* and another castle, Braemar Castle, a turreted 17th-century stronghold. *The* time of the year to drop into the festive little pocket of Braemar is the first Saturday in September, when the queen and 20,000 other people attend the 900-year-old Royal Highland Gathering (or Games) in the Princess Royal and Duke of Fife Memorial Park at Invercauld. Massed piped bands at the Braemer Games are the most sensational in all Scotland, and the number of local aristocratic mansions that disgorge their owners for the event — plus an international audience bent on wining and dining, mirth, and song — make it truly a Scottish day of days. Advance booking, a necessity, is possible from March 20. Write to W. A. Meston, Bookings Secretary, Balcriech, Ballater, Grampian, Scotland.

Scottish Islands

Scotland has 787 islands, including uninhabited stone dollops like Ailsa Craig and the Bass Rock (see the *Lowlands* route). These vary in size, topography, history, climate, racial mix, and ethos. Of the ones included here, however — Orkney and Shetland plus the Hebridean Arran, Skye, Harris, and Lewis — there are common denominators. All have a remote otherworldliness, a sense of infinite time; all but Arran reflect antiquity both in archaeological riches and in the natives' ardent stubborn tribalisms; all have vivid, unusual flora and fauna, colonies of seals, seabirds, and wildlife; all possess multicolored skies and magic, luminous air. All are sparsely populated. Winds can be incredible (a gale is recorded at the Butt of Lewis one day in every six) and on Shetland, Orkney, Harris, and Lewis there are almost no trees. Skye, Orkney, Arran, and Harris have fantastic gnomic rock formations, whipped perhaps from briny deeps by the gnarled wand of some primeval wizard. All but Arran and Orkney live by fishing and crofting, and all but Orkney and Shetland show a dangerous dependence on Highlands and Islands Development Board projects, and on tourism. So far tourists continue to roll in.

And not just tourists! Also drawn to the Islands are artists, craftsmen, poets, scholars, and dreamers, who set up shop in deserted thatched-roofed cottages and hag peat, write books, throw pots, and weave caftans. You'll have access to the wares of this entrepreneurial yeomanry as well as to Shetland sweaters and Harris tweeds. Don't miss reading the fascinating *West Highland Free Press,* a radical weekly published Thursdays by immigrant intellectuals from an old schoolhouse on Skye. Hugh MacDiarmid, the greatest Scottish poet of the twentieth century, lived for a time in Shetland; the composer Peter Maxwell Davies finds inspiration in the sounds around his Orkney home; Sorley Maclean, chief among contemporary bards of the Gaelic tongue, dwells in Skye. In addition to works by giants like these you should try a page or two by Orkney's delightful favorite sons, George Mackay Brown and Eric Linklater, and the Outer Hebrides's Compton Mackenzie (Mackenzie's novel *Whisky Galore* is especially delicious).

Two centuries of Viking invasions, from 800 to 1000, left all the islands under Norse control, linked with the also-vanquished city of Dublin and Isle of Man. In the Hebrides, Scottish Gaelic leadership gradually reemerged though the Gaelic Lordship of the Isles was not absorbed into the Scottish crown until the reign of James IV. But Orkney and Shetland continued under Scandinavian occupation through the end of the Middle Ages. Their inhabitants today are still primarily Nordic; they keep up special friendship societies with Iceland and the Faroes, and surnames — a break from Scandinavian custom — have existed in Shetland only for the last 100 years. Orcadians and Shetlanders are a down-to-earth, straightforward people — Celtic Twilights and such mystiques have no place among them. Until recently they spoke Norn, a Viking dialect that has fostered a pleasing singsong quality in their English. Shetland fisherfolk employ many "haaf" words from Norn even now (there's a handy selection of 10 different nouns for "wind" and 19 for "sea").

The Western Isles preserve both the Highland culture now lost on the mainland (Gaelic is still spoken in parts of Harris, Lewis, and Skye) and the old Presbyterianism gone from the Lowlands. Many guesthouse owners eschew cooking, watching TV, etc., on the Sabbath, so mind when you wash your socks. A duality of the public and private man exists in the Hebrides, epitomized by areas that vote themselves dry before dotting the moors with illegal makeshift drinking *bothans* ("cabins"). The satiric tradition of the ancient Gaelic bards — in which verses were thought to wield witch-doctor-style curses — may have reinforced in Hebrideans their unquenchable love of invective; their mellifluous lilts promise Paradise but shoot wide of the mark, delivering the sentiments of hexmen in accents of angels.

Despite drawbacks like high prices, frequent wet weather, summer midges, and occasional roadside views of gargantuan rubbish dumps, the Scottish Islands are unsurpassed as holiday spots. Their romance is legendary. It's said there are peat fires in Hebridean houses alight continuously for over a hundred years, and that you can spy faeries in Skye's unearthly kaleidoscopes of sunbeams, mists, and rainbows. In Orkney and Shetland, where the land is so flat it scarcely breaks the sky's endless embrace, the moon, stars, and aurora borealis are dazzling. Fiddling and dancing swell all the village halls. Even the food tastes different; for example "bere bannocks" are made from a grain grown only in Orkney, and lamb in Harris and Lewis has a special sweetness caused by the heather in the sheepfeed. Best of all are the island people, who welcome you into their lives unquestioningly.

Airports in Lewis, Skye, Orkney, and Shetland are a thrill to set down at because of the comprehensive overviews you get of famous landscapes. Rentable cars get snapped up fast, so make sure you book yours before touchdown. Or, for a flat fee, you can buy a *Travelpass,* providing 7 days' or 14 days' unlimited travel through the Scottish Islands and Highlands by train, bus, and ferry. For more information contact Hi-Line Holiday Lodge, Bridgend, Dingwall, Ross-shire (phone: 63434) or Britrail Travel International, 630 Third Ave., New York, NY 10017 (phone: 212-599-5400). Sea and air links are detailed below for each island individually under the name of the island. So are addresses of main tourist offices, where you should go for additional sightseeing advice. Hotels listed as expensive will charge $80 to $85 and up for bed and breakfast for two; moderate ones, from $60 to $80; and inexpensive ones, from $45 to $60. A meal for two in an expensive restaurant will cost $50 or more; in a moderate one, $30 to $50; in an inexpensive one, less than $30.

ARRAN

Just 1¼ miles off Ayrshire's shore, Arran has 14 charming villages, no towns, and only 3 roads, one of which skirts in a circle a ravishing 60-mile coastline. A schizophrenic terrain, full of craggy Highland hills in the north but lush lowland farms and winsome little resorts in the south, makes the island a miniature Scotland. Arran's climate is comparatively dry and warm (here and there palm trees kiss the breeze) and every summer families arrive for idyllic low-key holidays. Jukeboxes, casinos, and chromium chip shops are rare; 2-year-olds on beaches with buckets and spades are prolific.

The chief villages, all by the sea, are Whiting Bay, Lamlash, Corrie, Lochranza, and Brodick. From Whiting Bay you can walk inland to the beautiful 140-foot Glenashdale Falls. Lamlash was a naval base till World War I and is now an educational and administrative center. Corrie with its adorable dinky harbor is the prettiest hamlet on Arran, while northerly Lochranza, dwarfed by a semicircle of most of Arran's spectacular over-2,000-foot peaks, is dramatically stark. Brodick is the island's main port and biggest tourist haunt; it's guarded by the soaring presence of Mt. Goatfell and has an entrancing *cladach* (old fishing wharf).

Brodick Castle and Gardens are owned by the National Trust for Scotland, which also owns 7,000 acres nearby, including the lovely Glen Rosa. The castle is an ancestral seat of the dukes of Hamilton and contains fine silver, porcelain, pictures, and trophies. The duchess of Montrose founded its opulent rhododendron garden in 1923 and its formal garden dates from 1710 (1½ miles north of Brodick Pier; open afternoons May through September, plus some in April). Lochranza Castle in Lochranza is a picturesque sixteenth-century ruin with two square towers (the key is with the custodian at his house, Croft Bank). Lochranza is only one of three places on Arran visited by Robert the Bruce — the others are King's Cross by Whiting Bay, where he embarked for the mainland in 1307 on the slow boat to Scottish independence, and King's Cave, 2 miles north of Blackwaterfoot on the west coast (you have to walk it), a possible site of the legendary spider incident.

Isle of Arran Heritage Museum, in an eighteenth-century croft on Brodick's northern edge, includes a smithy that occasionally demonstrates the art of horseshoeing (in summer). Near Kilmory village on the south coast are the Neolithic Kilmory Cairns, while the Standing Stones of Machrie Moor, a complex of six 15-foot Bronze Age megalithic circles, rise skyward on Moss Farm Road just south of westerly Machrie Bay; try to see them at sunset. Folklore maintains they supported the giant Fingal's cooking pot.

Details of fishing, sailing, deep-sea diving, golf, swimming, pony trekking, hiking, and hill-walking are available from the Tourist Information Centre on Brodick Pier (phone: 0770-2401). The center also issues a comprehensive guide to Arran's crafts shops. Boat trips to Holy Island across Lamlash Bay (daily, Easter through October) give you a gander at a twelfth-century fort, St. Molios's Well (St. Molios was an Irish missionary), and a pleasant nature reserve. You can buy locally produced mustard at the Arran Mustard factory shop in Lamlash from Easter through October (phone: 07706-370).

Festivals are Arran's long suit: there's a Music Festival (in February/ March), a Sea Angling Festival (in May), the Goatfell Race (May) and Fiddlers' Rally (June), a steady stream of assorted small festivals at Brodick Castle all summer long, the Brodick Sheepdog Trials (June), the Heather Queen Gala (in July), the Arran Riding Club Horse Show (July or August), Lamlash Laughabout Week (July), Whiting Bay Fun Week (July), the Lamlash Horticultural and Agricultural Shows (in August), the Corrie Capers, with family events like puppet and dog shows (August), and the Brodick Highland Games (August).

Several car ferries go daily from Ardrossan on the mainland to Brodick; space should be reserved on summer weekends. During the tourist season, there's a route (about eight sailings a day) from Claonaig on Kintyre to Lochranza. For further information, contact Caledonian MacBrayne Ltd., Ferry Terminal, Gourock, Scotland (phone: Gourock 34531). Ask about their special deals called Hebridean Drive-Away, Island Hopscotch, and Car Rover Tickets; these could save you money.

CHECKING IN: *Glenisle* – Opened in December 1986, the motto of this family-run establishment is, "we treat people as we would expect to be treated ourselves." A wide choice of Scottish/European–style food is served in a traditional dining room (with open hearth fire). It has earned a good reputation in a short time. Lamlash (phone: 07706-258). Moderate.

Lagg – The setting here is lovely, with gardens, a secluded beach, and a river full of salmon. Regional specialties, including fresh salmon and venison, are served in the restaurant. On the south end of Arran at Lagg (phone: 077087-255). Moderate.

Kingsley – Real beer in the bar makes this modest 29-room seafront affair a worthy bet. Taste of Scotland menu. Brodick (phone: 0770-2226). Inexpensive.

EATING OUT: *Hind* – Part of the Glen Cloy Farm Guest House in Brodick, this recently opened restaurant already has a following for its wide variety of local fresh food. For the romantically inclined, dinner is served by candlelight, in traditional surroundings. Brodick (phone: 07702-351). Expensive to moderate.

Carraig Mhor Eating House – A popular bayside restaurant with a homey air, converted from a dwelling. Omelettes and seafood at lunch, full dinners at night. Lamlash (phone: 07706-453). Moderate.

SKYE

Skye is a large island with 6 peninsulas, a coastline of sparkling sea lochs, and countless fabulous panoramas. Traditionally it has belonged to the clans Macdonald and Macleod. Set very close to the most isolated parts of the West Highlands (herdsmen used to swim cattle across the narrow strait of Kyle Rhea from Skye to the mainland at low tide), it has a population of only 7,000.

On Skye's south shore are the legendary, oft-climbed Cuillins, a high mountain range whose tops Sorley Maclean described rhapsodically as "exact and serrated blue ramparts." In some lights they look black — like the teeth of a black saw blade. Their strange shape is the result of basalt dykes seeping into a hard underlayer of gabbro. Just west of the Cuillins is the lovely lochside campsite Glen Brittle; northeast is Glen Sligachan, whose inn was visited in 1773 by James Boswell and Samuel Johnson (see *Checking In*). Bonnie Prince Charlie had popularized Skye by fleeing to it after Culloden in company with Flora Macdonald, a brave Skye native, disguised as Flora's maid; Boswell and Johnson met Flora 27 years later and wrote a tribute to her, enshrined today on a Celtic cross in Kilmuir Churchyard near the island's north tip.

Oak, birch, willow, and hazel grace most of Sleat, Skye's southernmost peninsula. The Aird of Sleat, below the village of Ardvasar, is barren, but its view across Sleat Sound to Mallaig is a wow! Lava flows and landslips have caused the phantasmagoric moss-dappled marvels on the basaltic northern peninsula of Trotternish, including the Old Man of Storr, a 160-foot obelisk well over 2,000 feet above the sea (a 3-to-4-hour climb from your car); the Kilt Rock; and the weird, pinnacled Quirang. Don't miss traveling the small corkscrew road from the Quirang to the Trotternish west coast.

Give equal time to castles and villages: Knock Castle on Sleat, with a vista across Knock Bay to the mainland territory of Knoydart, is a ruined Macdonald stronghold; so is Dunsgiath Castle at blissful Tokavaig on Sleat's opposite side, and Duntulm Castle near the tip of Trotternish. Castle Maoil ("The Roofless Castle"), a welcoming beacon for voyagers by ferry to the Skye pier at Kyleakin, was a keep of the Mackinnon Clan. Armadale Castle, north of Ardvasar, was a nineteenth-century Gothic mansion and family seat of the Macdonald chiefs, Lords of the Isles; nowadays, in summer it's a clan Donald museum, congenial tearoom, and bookshop loaded with stuff about Skye. Dunvegan Castle, on northwesterly Loch Dunvegan, is the island's only remaining stately home, the 700-year-old abode of the Macleods (open April through October; see the castle guidebook for the story of the "fairy flag"). Villages to see are Portree, Skye's harbor and capital, where you can shop and mail postcards (have a bun in *Mackenzie's Bakery* in the main square, too); Stein, a dreamy shell of an eighteenth-century fishing settlement on the Vaternish peninsula beside lavish fields of sweet wild orchids; Carbost, fermenting ground of the incomparable Talisker whisky, on a forgotten corner of the Minginish peninsula; and Broadford and Elgol, at opposite ends of the majestic A881 past the Red Hills and Mt. Blaven on the island's lower wing. Beautiful Elgol, from which Bonnie Prince Charlie left Scotland forever, has boat trips across Loch Scavaig into Loch Coruisk, a favorite subject of Romantic painters, hemmed in like a mighty well by the Cuillins.

Kilmuir Croft Museum near Kilmuir Churchyard is one of three folk museums on Skye (open Easter through October); another is the Skye Water Mill and Black House on Loch Dunvegan (open Easter through September). Glendale, not far from the Black House, has a tempting lineup of crafts shops. There's a permanent display on the history of the bagpipes at Boreraig, also on Loch Dunvegan.

Tourist Board offices in Broadford (phone: 04712-361) and Meall House, Portree (phone: 0478-2137) have information about climbing and hiking, swimming, fishing, golf, pony trekking, bird-watching, sailing, cruising, and dinghy excursions. En route to the neighboring island of Raasay you can see seals, porpoises, and (with luck) bottle-nosed whales. The Portree Highland Games and Dunvegan Piping Competition both take place in August.

Ferries leave the mainland for Skye from Mallaig, from near Glenelg (in summer), and from Kyle of Lochalsh. Details from Caledonian MacBrayne (except for the Glenelg run, owned by M. A. Mackenzie; phone: Glenelg 059-982-224). Loganair operates flights from Glasgow to Broadford (phone for details: Glasgow 889-3181, or call Glasgow Airport at 887-1111).

 CHECKING IN: *Coolin Hills* – Situated on its own grounds and overlooking Portree Bay, this old Victorian mansion used to be a hunting-lodge of the Macdonald clan. All its 26 rooms have the facilities of a first-class hotel. Portree (phone: 0478-2003). Moderate.

Kinloch Lodge – A most exuberant welcome awaits visitors to the lovely home of

Lord and Lady Macdonald (who will immediately insist that you call them Godfrey and Claire). From the cheery, individually decorated guestrooms to the excellent homecooked meals to the relaxed conversation with other guests before a crackling fire, a stay here is supremely pleasant. Sleat, Isle of Ornsay (phone: 04713-333). Moderate to inexpensive.

Sligachan – Travelers, aristocrats, painters, anglers, and climbers have been packing out this famous 23-room landmark for over 200 years. A fascinating logbook documenting first ascents of the Cuillins is on show. Closed November through April. Junction of the A850 and A863 at Glen Sligachan (phone: 047852-204). Moderate to inexpensive.

Broadford – Also in business over 200 years, the dining room at this serviceable old 28-room favorite exhibits a 4-foot Drambuie bottle honoring a past chef who invented the stuff for the Bonnie Prince. Closed November through March. Broadford (phone: 04712-205). Moderate to inexpensive.

Skeabost House – Built in Victorian times, and beautifully set at the southernmost tip of a sea loch, this 27-room hostelry is one of the finest on Scotland's islands. The furniture is antique, log fires blaze on the hearth, and the restaurant serves interesting local dishes. Closed mid-October to April. Skeabost Bridge (phone: Skeabost Bridge 202). Moderate to inexpensive.

Tigh Osda Eilean Iarmain – Unique in its Gaelic-ness — there's a Gaelic-speaking staff, and Gaelic menus — this 13-room hotel, owned and run by an Edinburgh banker who has also established on Skye a thriving Gaelic college, makes its own whisky, *Té Bheag*. Guests are allowed both to speak English and to sample the whisky. Isle of Ornsay (phone: 04713-332). Moderate to inexpensive.

Rosedale – The only hotel in Portree situated on the waterfront. The building is an amalgamation of 3 fishermen's houses dating from the 1830s. It makes an attractive setting for a visit. There are 23 rooms, each with a private bath. Portree (phone: 0478-2531). Inexpensive.

Stein Inn – Right by Loch Bay, this quaint and beckoning 6-room edifice at the outer edge of civilization is one of the most romantic hostelries on Skye. Stein, on the Waternish peninsula (phone: 047083-208). Inexpensive.

EATING OUT: Glenview Inn – This traditional Scottish-French restaurant has won the Taste of Scotland award for the excellence of its fresh Scottish cuisine. On Staffin Road, 13 miles north of Portree (phone: 047062-248). Moderate.

Three Chimneys – Scallops, crab, salmon, and trout are specialties at this white-washed cottage restaurant decorated with propped-up wagon wheels. Colbost, beside the Black House Museum (phone: 047081-258). Moderate.

Three Rowans – Also a candlemaker's shop, this inviting hilltop dining-cum-tearoom has a native Skye cook (an increasing rarity in Skye) and three aged rowans outside to ward off evil (planted in the days when rowan trees had magic powers). Kildonan, near Edinbane on the Portree-Dunvegan road (phone: 047082-286). Inexpensive.

HARRIS

So unspoiled and deserted is Harris, 40 miles off Scotland's northwest coast, that the Scottish Tourist Board lists only one Harris entry in its booklet *Scotland: 1001 Things to See.* That entry is St. Clement's Church, a cruciform building dating from about 1500 (restored in 1873) at Rodel on the island's southern tip. The exquisite carved stonework behind a Macleod chief's tomb shows the Twelve Apostles, a stag hunt, and an angel and devil weighing souls of the dead. The *Rodel* hotel (closed temporarily) has the key. Rodel itself is a tiny hamlet with clean-looking cottages and a pond ringed by slopes of mushrooms and wild blue irises.

North Harris is full of mountains, 8 of which exceed 2,000 feet; according to geologists these peaks are so old they antedate the separation of the continental land mass from Britain and Ireland and make parvenus of the Alps. Also on Harris are gleaming beaches, green seas, and, on lucky days, a still, clear air bright with the songs of birds. There are ranging moors with no roads; the whole atmosphere is primitive; the only real village — a one-streeter — is Tarbert. On the east coast are rocky shores verdant with "lazy beds," thin half-arable plots once tilled by crofters driven off richer lands in the west. The west coast has the almost Mediterranean sands of Luskentyre and Hushinish.

Your Harris survival kit should contain ordnance maps, sandwiches, dubbined boots, midge repellent, whisky, binoculars, and your own angling equipment if you fish (fishing tackle is hard to come by on Harris). Bathing suits will be useful only if you like swimming in temperatures not usually exceeding 55°.

Tarbert is a picturebook townlet with general stores, a harbor, and a vast public vegetable patch full of strutting roosters. The Harris tourist office is in Tarbert (phone: 0859-2011). Harris Tweed jackets for sale dangle from hangers on the outer walls of brightly painted corrugated-iron Tarbert sheds (you can also buy Harris Tweeds in Stornoway, or by the yard — about £4 per yard — from the weavers themselves in Drinishader on the coast farther south). Hard-wearing, made from the wool of Harris sheep, this world-famous fabric was, until recently, hand-spun, hand-dyed, and handwoven on antiquated looms producing only an old-fashioned, narrow cloth length. Today, a Miss Campbell of Plockropool (the village above Drinishader) is the only Harris native who still spins and dyes by hand, though handweaving continues apace.

Toe Head, the outermost point of the small peninsula northwest of Rodel (served by a sand track), is a wilderness full of golden eagles, sheep, and the distinctive and beautiful *machair,* a beach grass vibrant with a species of pale wildflower found only on Hebridean dunes. The trail from the B887 past Mt. Uisgnaval More to Loch Voshimid, about 12 miles round-trip, is in some weathers very eerie: it's the setting for J. M. Barrie's play *Mary Rose,* about a mysterious, mist-enshrouded, disappearing maid.

Ferries dock at Tarbert from Skye's port of Uig. Details from Caledonian MacBrayne.

 CHECKING IN: *Scarista House* – Once a manse, this delightful 7-room hotel, near Scarista beach, still has a fine library that's open to residents. Although there's no bar, liquor can be served at the table. 15 miles southwest of Tarbert on the A859 (phone: 085985-238). Moderate.

Harris – This faithful 26-room standby lacks the refinement of *Scarista House* but is a reasonable (and more accessible) eatery, drinkery, and sleepery. Tarbert (phone: 0859-2154). Inexpensive.

Rodel – Unchanged since the 17th century (there are fascinating antiques everywhere including, in the boudoirs, wee wooden washbasins), this former great house has passed from an aristocratic family to Jock McCallum, host extraordinaire and distiller of Royal Household, the smooth-as-silk house whisky. Jock has recently handed the business down to his son, who has closed it for modernization. Check before you visit. Rodel (phone: 210). Inexpensive.

LEWIS

Lewis adjoins Harris, making the combined island 95 miles in length. Lewis is the upper partner. It consists of marshy peat bogs and a coastline dappled with 25 beaches.

Its center is Stornoway, the only actual town in the Outer Isles. Stornoway has a charming landlocked harbor with a large, tame colony of inquisitive gray seals — you can watch them from the pier along with the nostalgic spectacle of colorful homeward-bound fishing boats. Churches are everywhere, as befits a locale so Sabbath-conscious you can't even buy cigarettes from a machine on Sundays; neither shall ye drink in hotels ye aren't staying at. There's a pleasant square with an attractive town hall and a huddle of gracious houses on a hill. The *Stornoway Gazette,* with news of local events, comes out on Thursdays. Key shops are *Loch Erisort Woollens* on Cromwell St., *Lewis Crofters* (for outdoor gear), and *The Corner Shop* (a delicatessen) on Kenneth St.

The A858 west from Stornoway has Lewis's main attractions including the Standing Stones of Callanish, an elaborate setting of megaliths, unique in Scotland, running Stonehenge a close second; Dun Carloway Broch, a well-preserved 30-foot Iron Age tower; the Shawbost Museum and Mill illustrating old Lewis folkways (open April through November; closed Sundays); and the Lewis Black House, a clachan, or adjoining series of traditional thatched-roofed huts, now operated as a tourism gimmick — these were inhabited till 1960! Lews Castle Gardens on the west side of Stornoway Harbor are worth a visit; so is St. Moluag's, a restored twelfth-century Episcopal church with regular Sunday services at the village of Eoropie, near the Butt of Lewis, the island's north tip (apply to McLeod's in the village for the key). On the Eye Peninsula to Stornoway's east is Ui Chapel, a picturesque ruin of a former priory in the burying ground of the Lewis Mcleod chiefs.

The Lewis tourist office is at 4 South Beach St., Stornoway (phone: 0851-3088); here you can get advice on sailing, fishing, golf, hiking (the remote western parish of Uig is a good place), and bird-watching (Tiumpan Head on the Eye Peninsula has a burgeoning rabble of petrels and kittiwakes). The tourist office has a leaflet detailing Hebridean crafts and craftshops: consider buying a handmade set of Lewis Chessmen, modeled on four ancient sets discovered under Uig sands in 1831. Scandinavian in design, carved from walrus tusks and stained red on one side, the originals are thought to have been buried in the twelfth century by a shepherd after he murdered a merchant sailor whose ship, carrying the chessmen, ran aground. Museums in London and Edinburgh have the originals today.

Sea-angling competitions are a highlight of Stornoway summers, with the Western Isles and the Highlands and Islands Open Boat Championships in July or August.

Ferries to Stornoway are from Ullapool on the northwest Scottish mainland: for further information contact Caledonian MacBrayne (don't forget you can drive right into Lewis from Harris). British Airways flies to Stornoway from Glasgow and Inverness.

 CHECKING IN: *Crown* – Hospitality is an important feature of this fine hotel overlooking the harbor and the pier. Each of the 15 rooms has a private bath. Stornoway (phone: 0851-3181). Moderate.

Caberfeidh – Stornoway's finest, this custom-built haunt of tourists and business travelers on the edge of town has a garden, attractive tartan and mock Viking furnishings, frequent *ceilidhs,* 2 bars, and 38 rooms. The dining room specializes in seafood. Percival Rd. South, Stornoway (phone: 0851-2604). Moderate to inexpensive.

County – A warm welcome is assured in this centrally located, family-run hotel with traditional pine-paneled interior design and 11 rooms. Stornoway (phone: 0851-3250). Inexpensive.

Seaforth – A 75-room downtown establishment with nightly entertainment — movie, disco, cabaret. James St., Stornoway (phone: 0851-2740). Inexpensive.

ORKNEY

Orkney comprises 68 islands, some 29 of which are inhabited. Throughout the whole cluster lie chambered cairns, traces of 78 brochs, rings of standing stones, and vestiges of prehistoric villages. Many are extensive survivals, making Orkney the archaeological treasure house of Great Britain.

Several pre-Pictish peoples lived on Orkney, then Picts, then Vikings. Strangely none of the races they conquered are mentioned by the Vikings in their remarkable medieval epic and folk history, the *Orkneyinga Saga,* a product of Orkney's Golden Age. A fine long literary tradition of which the *Saga* is part stretches even to America: Washington Irving's father was an Orkney sailor and James Russell Lowell's forebears included two Orcadian clans.

More sunshine bathes Orkney (and Shetland) than almost anywhere else in Britain, and there are bright-hued farmhouses, green fields, primroses, violets, golden sands, and clifftop sea-pinks. Fulmars, cormorants, Manx shearwaters, petrels, gulls, kittiwakes, guillemots, puffins, and gannets abound. On country strolls watch out for bulls. Hotels should be booked several months in advance; so far Orkney seems oblivious to the lucrative potential of tourism, and accommodations are few.

Orkney's two centers of civilization are Stromness and Kirkwall on the largest island, the so-called Mainland. Stromness, in the west (Kirkwall is in the east), is a small eighteenth-century port that hasn't changed since its founding; it's full of charm and has a main street that snakes along the sea. The Pier Arts Center on Victoria St. in Stromness contains an internationally famous display of works by Ben Nicolson and Barbara Hepworth (closed Mondays); the Stromness Museum, 52 Alfred St., has a curio collection from local history. *Stromness Books and Prints* on Graham Place is well worth a browse.

Kirkwall is Orkney's capital, site of St. Magnus Cathedral, Orkney's pride. The cathedral is an impressive twelfth-century pink sandstone Norman building still in use, the burial place of St. Magnus, Orkney's patron saint. Take it easy in Kirkwall's ancient streets, which wind narrowly and look illusively like pedestrian precincts — till cars belt down them full throttle! A thriving stone-built town with crow-stepped gabled houses and magnificently old-fashioned shops painted berry and peach, Kirkwall also encompasses Earl Patrick's Palace, the imposing remains of an accomplished piece of Renaissance architecture belonging originally to a wicked Stewart earl, a nephew of Mary Queen of Scots; the Bishop's Palace, a thirteenth-century ruin with an ascendable sixteenth-century round tower; Tankerness House, a sixteenth-century merchant-laird's mansion and museum — sometimes with guest exhibitions — of 4,000 years of Orkney life; the Highland Park Distillery, which has recently opened a visitors' center, gives year-round tours of its nearly 200-year-old special processes (and free sips of its whisky); and *Robert Towers's Workshop* at Rosegarth, St. Ola (phone: 3521), a manufactory of traditional Orcadian tall-backed, straw-weave chairs. Behind Kirkwall on Wideford Hill the view is a superb pastiche of bays and islets.

In a knot in mid-Mainland near the Harray and Stenness lochs are three venerable marvels, Maeshowe, the Standing Stones of Stenness, and the Ring of Brodgar. Maeshowe, the finest chambered cairn in western Europe, was constructed around 1800 BC, and is entered on hands and knees by a narrow downward-sloping tunnel. Viking marauders wrote the runic inscriptions in the cells. In midwinter, dusk's last shaft of sunlight strikes one of the dark entombing walls, as it has done for untold centuries, a deeply moving sight with a mystic suggestion of resurrection. The Standing Stones of Stenness — four are still upright — are part of a circle of 3000 BC; the Ring of Brodgar, 340 feet in diameter, boasts 36 stones of its original 60. Also on the Mainland are: Skara Brae, a Neolithic complex with a paved courtyard, covered passages, and 10 one-room houses full of "built-in" stone furniture (life here came to an end when a sandstorm blanketed all, sometime after 4500 BC); Gurness Broch, over 10 feet high, surrounded by stone huts and inhabited well into Viking times; Click Mill, the only operative example of old-style horizontal-wheeled Orkney water power (wear rubber boots, it's in a bog); Corrigall Farm Museum showing old Orkney folkways (open April through September); and Birsay, a quaint village with another ruined palace of the Stewart earls. Opposite Birsay is the Brough of Birsay, an adorable island and beachcombers' delight accessible only at low tide, where you'll find the remains of a Romanesque church and of Pictish and Nordic settlements.

Hoy, Orkney's most romantic island, is famous for its strange offshore rock formation, the Old Man of Hoy, a supreme test for rockclimbers. Hoy has hills, gaunt high cliffs, and wild unpopulated valleys. There's only one road, along the east coast, passing the martello towers built in 1812 against attack by American ships. Attainable by tramping inland is panoramic Ward Hill, Orkney's highest point at 1,565 feet, near the site of a supposedly haunted Neolithic sepulcher called the Dwarfie Stone — this overlooks the beautiful half-deserted hamlet of Rackwick, Peter Maxwell Davies's home. If you go to Hoy, take a picnic; there's almost nowhere to buy food.

The island of South Ronaldsay is another good place to go, completely different from Hoy; you can drive to it from near Kirkwall via the island-hopping Churchill Causeway, erected in 1939-40 to protect the adjacent waterway of Scapa Flow, then a naval base. En route at the island of Lamb Holm is the lovely Italian Chapel, built in ornate Italianate style from a mere Nissen hut by Italian World War II prisoners and affectionately preserved to this day by admiring Orcadians. It was in Scapa Flow in 1916 that Lord Kitchener's ship, the *Hampshire,* was blown up with him on board, and there 3 years later that the German Fleet of World War I heroically scuttled itself. Hoxa Head, the entrance to Scapa Flow, is a fascinating surreal jumble of half-sunk hulks and wartime concrete barriers. Also on South Ronaldsay is St. Margaret's Hope, an idyllic coastal settlement popular with artists and craftsmen, an excellent place to shop for handmade goods.

Other islands are alluring, too: northerly Westray has Noltland Castle, a prepossessing sixteenth-century relic; Wyre near the Mainland has twelfth-century Cobbie Row's Castle, the earliest authenticated castle in Scotland (it's mentioned in the *Orkneyinga Saga*), and nearby St. Mary's Chapel of the same date; ruin-rich Rousay, the "Egypt of the North" beyond Wyre, has bicycles for hire and boat trips to Egilsay, another island, where St. Magnus was murdered (there's part of a fine medieval church on Egilsay). Sanday, well north of the Mainland near Westray, is seal country, a beachy place to take kids and has sellouts in *The Wool Hall* (every other Wednesday evening) of goods made by the Sanday Knitters, a women's cooperative. The goods can also be seen and purchased by appointment; call Mrs. Sinclair (phone: 367).

Tourist Board offices in Broad St., Kirkwall (phone: 2856) and the Ferry Terminal Building, Stromness (phone: 850716) have data on the rest of Orkney's islands and archaeology and on interesting natural features you can explore — most of the latter have intriguing names (Yesnaby Cliffs, Brinkie's Brae, St. John's Head, the Gloup of Deerness, the Barrel of Butter). Also available are tips on fishing, golf, deep-sea diving, crafts (potters are plentiful), walks, sailing, swimming, and bird-watching. Many British seafowl nest in Orkney (the season is May-July); their favorite places include the deserted islands of Copinsay and Eynhallow, the Mainland cliffs at Marwick, and the bird reserve on Westray at Noup Head. Information about local events is in the *Orcadian,* published Thursdays. The tourist offices give advice on getting from island to island.

Twice a winter Kirkwall's annual Ba' Games are played (they're just like the Jedburgh ones — see the *Lowlands* route). Other orgies are the internationally important St. Magnus Festival of the Arts in June; Kirkwall's County Show, a major agricultural fair in August; the Orkney Folk Festival in late May; and Stromness Shopping Week in July, when all Orkney comes to Stromness for 7 days of fêtes, dances, and general merriment.

A 2-hour ferry route links Stromness with Scrabster, near Thurso on the Scottish mainland. For details: P&O Ferries Terminal, Pierhead, Stromness (phone: 850655); or P&O Ferries Terminal, Jamieson's Quay, Aberdeen (phone: 572615). As well as regular services, P&O offers a special 4-day motorists' package tour. British Airways flies every day but Sunday from Aberdeen to Kirkwall; details of other flights, including inter-island Orcadian puddle-jumps, are at Kirkwall Airport (phone: 2233). Summer coach tours of major Orkney sights are organized by James Peace, Junction Rd., Kirkwall (phone: 2866). Since opening in 1982, a new tour company called Go Orkney has been wowing visitors and locals alike with its upbeat style (6 Old Scapa Rd.; phone: Kirkwall 4260).

CHECKING IN: *Balfour Castle* – The Zawadzki family welcome paying guests in their late-19th-century fantasy. All the trimmings of Victorian romanticism are here — dark paneling, a huge staircase, big rooms with gold-etched period floral wallpapers, intriguing outbuildings, and an island setting by a storm-lashed sea. A real find. On Shapinsay across Shapinsay Sound from the Orkney mainland (phone: 085671-282). Expensive.

Foveran – A comfortable, modern 8-room oasis near Kirkwall, famous for its cuisine. St. Ola, overlooking Scapa Flow (phone: 2389). Inexpensive.

EATING OUT: *Hamnavoe* – An extensive variety of international cuisine can be found at this recently opened spot. It has already found its way into various good food guides. Stromness (phone: 0856-750606). Expensive.

Creel – An award-winning establishment (the BTA's Best Scottish Restaurant for 1986), the dining room here overlooks the harbor and the open coal fire provides a cozy, intimate atmosphere. A wide choice of seafood, roasts, and venison is served. St. Margaret's Hope, south of Kirkwall (phone: 0856-850606). Moderate.

Binnacle – You guessed it, the theme here is nautical. *Binnacle,* in the *Commodore* hotel, serves a good selection of locally caught seafood and produce. Its steaks are notable, too. St. Mary's on Holm, south of Kirkwall (phone: 0856-78319). Inexpensive.

SHETLAND

"Ultima Thule" sounds like the name of a fashionable debutante, but in fact it's what the Romans called Shetland. Nothing lies between Shetland and the Arctic Circle. Lerwick, Shetland's capital, is much farther from Edinburgh than Edinburgh is from London; it's breached even from Kirkwall by a distance of over 60 miles. The famous north Shetland outpost, the Muckle Flugga Lighthouse, a remarkable feat of engineering poised on faces of sheer, almost vertical rock, is Britain's last window on the world (alas, it's not open to the public, but you get a good view of it from the coast).

Shetland's 100 islands (only 3 are of any size) are chilly even in summer. Winters are very dark but May, June, and July nights are aglow with the "simmer dim," a beautiful horizontal twilight lasting several hours, the next thing to a midnight sun — everything under its luminous rays looks phosphorescent. There are no rivers on Shetland, but sparkling streamlets, lily-bright lochans, and bays jeweled with waving sea-pinks. The sea is inescapable, for you can always see or hear it; Lerwick rises right out of it as if in a fairy tale — houses, stone steps, ramp-shaped flagstone alleys, and all; nets and fishing boats are everywhere and the raucous cry of seabirds splits the air (300 bird species nest in Shetland, lining up colony by colony on rock cliff shelves in a surreal cross between a supermarket and an aviary).

Traditionally it's said that an Orcadian is a farmer with a boat, whereas a Shetlander is a fisherman with a croft. This is still true, but North Sea oil has given Shetland an added dimension: coffers are bulging, Portakabin villages full of roustabouts have sprung up overnight, and there are symptoms of boomtown-ism like prostitution and black-marketeering. Sullom Voe, a waterway along the north Mainland (as in Orkney, the chief island is called the Mainland) serves a massive oil terminal covering a whole neck of land from sea to sea; helicopters carrying shiftmen whiz back and forth between offshore sites and Sumburgh Airport; tourists must battle riggers for rooms in Shetland's precious few hotels (reservations are vital). But around all this, life on the islands goes on as it has for generations, with great tracts of land given over to grazing the special small sheep that provide the wool for Shetlanders' famous sweaters.

Vikings dominated Shetland as long as thirteen centuries ago, though other settlers were on the scene 1,000 years before that, as you'll see on the Mainland's south tip at Jarlshof, a fascinating sunken city with overlayers from three prehistoric civilizations. Orkney's archaeological treasures are older, but it's Shetland that clings to primitive forms: Shetland ponies are still reared on common landholdings, and Lerwick is in a way another Jarlshof with its arrow-thin streets, enclosing wharves, and snuggling clusters of stone homes and warehouses. Commercial Street, Lerwick's main thoroughfare, is anything but a boulevard — yet it has its own glamour.

In pre-Victorian days when half the fishing fleet of Holland put in at Shetland after sailing the North Sea, Lerwick was a smugglers' nest and an almost European city. Explore Shetland's history at the Shetland Museum, Lower Hillhead, Lerwick (the exhibits cover prehistory to the present). Other Lerwick attractions are Fort Charlotte, built in 1665 to protect the Sound of Bressay from the Dutch; the Lerwick Town Hall, a Scots-baronial building with stained-glass windows and a climbable tower; and Clickhimin Broch, an ancient 17-foot stronghold within the remains of an Iron Age stone fort. *The Shetland Workshop Gallery,* 4-6 Burns La., Lerwick, has native crafts for sale: sealskin handbags, silver and polished stone jewelry, sweaters, and Shetland shawls (the last, though large, warm, and sturdy, are so fine they can be drawn through a wedding ring). *John Tulloch (Shetland Products) Ltd.,* Market Cross, Lerwick (phone: 3150), sells wool garments at cut-rate prices.

Yell and Unst are the next biggest islands after the Mainland; they continue north from the Mainland in that order and are easily accessible. On Unst is Mu Ness Castle, constructed from rubble in the sixteenth century with an amazing eye for architectural detail. The prettiest Shetland islands are Bressay, Whalsay, Noss, Fetlar, Foula, the Out Skerries and Muckle Roe. Foula, 30 miles west of the Mainland, is the most isolated and therefore perhaps most exciting — it's served by a regular passenger line (no cars). But close your eyes, touch your map, and go where your finger falls! The islands are *all* pretty and there's no place you can't get by hiring a boatman, unless the weather's too rough — ask at the Lerwick tourist office, Market Cross (phone: 3434), or in outlying coastal pubs.

The tiny seal-haunted island of Mousa opposite Sandwick on the east Mainland (7 miles south of Lerwick) holds Mousa Broch, a princely 40 feet high, some say the best broch in Britain. St. Ninian's Isle, not an island but a small south Mainland peninsula, is famous for white sands and the priceless fifth-century silver plate unearthed there on a Dark Age church site in 1958. Other Mainland must-sees are the Croft Museum of nineteenth-century Shetland life on the A970 at South Voe (open May through September; closed

Mondays); the Tingwall Valley Agricultural Museum of crofters' tools and implements, on the same road 5 miles north of Lerwick (open Tuesdays, Thursdays, and Saturdays, May through September); the Ness of Burgi, an Iron Age defensive stone structure near the southern town of Sumburgh; and Stanleydale, a Neolithic heel-shaped edifice containing an oval chamber, at the western hamlet of Walls. Ruined Scalloway Castle, a building dating from 1600 in a flamboyant corbel-turreted medieval style, overlooks Scalloway, the unbelievably picturesque west coast Mainland fishing village that once was Shetland's capital (the castle belonged at that time to the wicked Stewart earls prominent also in Orkney).

Geological wonders of Shetland, visitable by boat, include "Orkneymen's caves," narrow of entrance but inside grand like cathedrals (the best is the stalactited Cave of Bressay, and there are lots along the coast of the island of Papa Stour); the sea-filled, once natural-bridged Holes of Scrada on the Mainland's northwesterly Esha Ness peninsula (you view these on foot); the Grind of the Navir, also at Esha Ness, where waves have ripped off huge cubic rock hunks and carried them 180 feet; and the Bressay Giant's Leg (his other leg is said to be in Orkney and his body above you somewhere midway).

The Shetland tourist office (the one in Lerwick) has information on fishing, golf, deep-sea diving, hiking, crafts, and bird-watching. Unst is a good place to see Icelandic owls. Fetlar is now a 1,400-acre Statutory Bird Reserve; other ornithological havens are the islands of Foula, Noss, and Haaf Gruney, the Pool of Virkie on the Mainland's south tip, and Hermaness on Unst opposite the Muckle Flugga Lighthouse.

"Up Helly Aa," a dramatic boat-burning ceremony celebrating the return of the sun, dates from pagan times and is still performed in Shetland every January using traditional Viking costumes and boats; the Viking International Festival at Lerwick in September is a major sea-angling competition; a Shetland Folk Festival in late April or early May gives full rein to Shetland fiddlers, a breed admired and envied by all of musical Scotland; and the Lerwick Midsummer Carnival in mid-June features a parade of floats and dancing in the streets. The *Shetland Times,* published Fridays, has news of other events.

P&O Ferries runs an overnight route from Aberdeen directly to Lerwick, weekdays; on weekends it makes a stop at Orkney. Details from P&O. Viking Island Ferries (phone: Orkney 74-351) operates a Kirkwall-Westray-Scalloway run twice weekly in summer. Flights into Shetland are frequent; British Airways goes from the major Scottish airports (there are at least four flights every weekday from Aberdeen alone) and from Kirkwall, and Loganair zooms direct to a small landing strip at Tingwall from Edinburgh.

 CHECKING IN: *Shetland* – Situated directly opposite the ferry docks is Shetland's largest hotel, with 64 rooms. It contains all the facilities of a modern hotel, including a swimming pool, fitness center, solarium, and sauna. Lerwick (phone: 0595-5515). Expensive to moderate.

***Busta House* –** This hotel's specialty is traditional Scottish food, but its location — in a splendid 400-year-old country house overlooking the picturesque Busta Voe fjord and harbor — is also special. It has the full range of private facilities in its 21 rooms. Brae (phone: 0806-22506). Moderate.

Grand – This recently modernized, historic old building stands at the center of Lerwick. The 24 rooms contain private facilities. The hotel has a nightclub and a beauty salon. Lerwick (phone: 0595-2826). Moderate.

Queen's – This property has two things in common with the *Grand:* a central location and its phone number (the latter similarity seems to cause no problems). *Queen's* is an old-fashioned, comfortably appointed hotel. The sea washes against the building on two sides. Most of its 33 rooms overlook the Island of Bressay and have the full range of private facilities. Lerwick (phone: 0595-2826). Moderate.

St. Magnus – Another fine example of Shetland's many picturesque hotels. Built with pine and spruce in a traditional Scandinavian style, it overlooks St. Magnus Bay on one side and West Beach Bay on the other. Its 26 rooms have all the private facilities. *St. Magnus* has won several awards for its outstanding Scottish cuisine. Hillswick (phone: 0806-23372). Moderate.

Sumburgh – Conveniently located near Sumburgh airport, this hotel is next to 2 sandy beaches and it boasts its own birdwatching sanctuary. The 30 rooms all have standard private facilities, and the dining room specializes in seafood. Sumburgh (phone: 9590-60201). Moderate.

Baltasound – A 10-room hybrid that is, on the whole, more modern extension than grand old Victorian abode. There's a big bar with attractive local posters. Baltasound, Unst (phone: 095781-334). Inexpensive.

Westings – Another contemporary hostelry based on an old building but with a distinctly Scandinavian appeal, it has 6 rooms and a large new bar. The service is friendly, the food good, and the proprietors organize pony treks. Wormadale, near Whiteness, Mainland (phone: 059584-242). Inexpensive.

EATING OUT: Burrastow House – Situated in a renovated building dating back to 1759, this excellent inn has a distinguished reputation for its traditional British cuisine: game, roasts, seafood, and vegetarian dishes. Walls (phone: 059571-307). Moderate.

Wales

It doesn't take long to understand why Wales is to many Welshmen a song and an inspiration. It has been so for many centuries. From the earliest times — and Welsh has been written since the seventh century AD — bards have expressed their love of their land. And what an enchanting and enthralling land it is.

Wales is small. So you can get to know quite a lot of it even in a short time. It is just over 8,000 square miles, about half the size of Switzerland, has about 2.8 million people — and about 6 million sheep. It is about 200 miles in length and it takes about 4½ hours to travel from north to south in a car in normal conditions. But don't: It would be like bolting down a gourmet meal.

Wales is special. From its seabird-haunted islets and seal-sentried rocks reaching out into the Irish Sea, to its mountains where Everest teams train, Wales mixes sudden drama with soft stillness. There is a grandeur about it, a sense of stubbornness. It is brightly pastoral, offset here and there with dark smudges of industry.

While Cardiff, the capital, can be reached by the new 125-mph supertrains in less than 2 hours from London, there is a sense in which Wales remains England's unknown neighbor. It is, as it has always been, a mountainous stronghold in the west. The land and the original Celtic people somehow keep their separate character. And a fifth of the people still use the Welsh language, rich in literature and color, older than English, the tongue of the original Britons. It is therefore a great vehicle for legends: Perhaps the legendary King Arthur himself roamed the hills of Wales in noble defiance of the encroaching Saxons.

Indeed, it was the Saxons who gave Wales its name. They called the fiercely defiant people who lived there the *wealas*, meaning "foreigners." The Welsh, however, gave their land a different name: Cymru (pronounced Kum-ree), "the land of brothers." You'll see the word on the signs as you cross the border: "Croeso i Gymru — Welcome to Wales." (Don't be worried that Cymru changes to Gymru. Welsh is a language in which certain initial letters change, depending on the words preceding them.)

Bear in mind, as you travel around, that the story of the language is a considerable part of the story of Wales. It is one of the oldest languages and literatures in Europe. It is flowing and musical. And lovely Welsh first (given) names remain very popular. Females have names like Lowri, Menna, Megan, and Rhiannon. Males are called Idris, Owen, and Rhys.

In the sixth and seventh centuries Wales became a largely Christian country through the work of St. David and his followers. And St. David, the patron saint, is one of the prime figures of Welsh history. Between the sixth and thirteenth century Wales was divided into kingdoms and princedoms. The rulers sometimes fought among themselves as well as battling the English on the border. But there were exceptions, like the tenth-century King Hywel Dda (Hywel the Good), who framed laws for an orderly way of life. Hywel was not blind to human problems: He was a pioneer supporter of women's equality and decreed that a woman could get a divorce if her husband were impotent and had halitosis! Under men like Hywel, culture flourished and the *eisteddfod* (pronounced eye-steth-vod), a competitive festival of poetry and song, became part of the Welsh tradition. There are numerous *eisteddfodau* in Wales today, and the biggest is the National Eisteddfod held in the first week of August, which attracts huge crowds. This festival is traditionally a nomadic one, held alternately in north and south Wales. In 1988 it is scheduled to take place in the town of Newport in Gwent. The bardic ceremonies, held on Tuesdays and Thursdays, were invented in the last century to provide pageantry (but no one takes them *too* seriously), and the winning poets are treated like pop stars, feted by crowds, blinking in the TV lights. What other country has, as national hero and king-for-a-day, a poet?

During the twelfth and thirteenth centuries the rulers of England sought to bring the troublesome Welsh under their control. The most striking reminders of this period are the great castles that dot the land. There are scores of them, many of them the finest in Europe, majestic residue of war and conquest. They look splendid against their backdrops of coast or mountains and reflect the wild land they were built to defend and subdue. Among the best are the eight built by King Edward I of England to complete and sustain his conquest. Hugely expensive, they brought the king to fiscal crisis. But warrior Edward was determined to defeat Llywelyn, the last native Prince of Wales, and bring the country to heel. Llywelyn's head ended up on a pike in London, and Wales came under English control.

In 1536, during the reign of King Henry VIII, Wales and England were formally joined together and made equal under the law. In the same century the Bible was translated into Welsh, the most single important influence on the language's survival. It made the Welsh a literate people in their own language. And in the nineteenth century, when Wales embraced the nonconformist form of worship, the Welsh Bible was a keystone of education. During this century the Welsh language has declined in numerical strength. Some fear that it will eventually die out, and there have been many campaigns to strengthen it. Threatened as it is, it nevertheless remains strong and lively in certain respects. It is the domestic language of many people (there are more than half a million who speak it) and it lives in books, songs, comics, radio, and television.

Much of Wales is rural. It is a farming country. In the mountains you can see the tough little hill farms and hear shepherds whistling for their scruffy, intelligent, black and white dogs. A good Welsh sheepdog is worth hundreds of pounds.

The southeast of the country is heavily industrial (coal mining, steel making, and manufacturing), and this is where most people live. The coal-mining belt stretches from Ebbw Vale in the east to Ammanford in the west, an area known as The Valleys. The narrow and tortuous valleys were once peaceful and wooded gorges, but the coal age changed everything. South Wales became an industrial powerhouse, one of the keys to British economic expansion. A century ago this part of Wales was the most intensively mined area of the world, and during the coal rush thousands of workers poured in from rural Wales, England, Ireland, Italy, Greece, and Spain. They made an exciting mixture, creating a varied and fascinating community, renowned for its spirit, its politics, and its culture. Coal's heyday has passed, but the valley towns, with their neat rows of houses slotted into the steep hillsides and the huge chapels standing guard, remain alluring.

While Welsh coal was warming the world, Welsh slate was roofing it. The great slate quarries and caverns of north Wales were the heart of a big industry. But that industry has shrunk dramatically and vast heaps of slate waste are monuments to an epoch.

Thus Wales is a place of contrasts. You don't have to be there long before you realize how it is weathered by history's storms. Its patches of industrial ugliness are honorable scars. And it has some of the loveliest scenery you are ever likely to see. As for the people, they are proud of their land, aware of its difference, and immensely hospitable. Their accents are distinctive (you will soon tell a South Welshman from a North Welshman) and their humor is delightful.

It is no wonder that Wales intrigues. It has a certain magic about it, an intangible something in the Celtic air.

Our route gives travelers the essential flavor, starting in the southeast and traversing the Brecon Beacons to lovely Carmarthen. It is all dramatic hills, soft pools, rushing waterfalls, and stately rivers. The route heads northwest across old Cardiganshire and to the pleasant and softer land of mid-Wales. Farther on it forges into sublime Snowdonia with its darkly handsome peaks and robust and defiant cottages and farms. It will be hard to resist the temptation to take diversions from the route. Why resist? Off the beaten track are many small pubs, guesthouses, farmhouses, and restaurants where you can get a night's stay and a decent meal for a very reasonable price.

Expect to pay $60 and up for a double room in those places we've listed as expensive; $40 to $60 in the moderate category; and under $40 in the inexpensive range. You'll find that a good majority of the hotels we list in the Welsh countryside are inexpensive — usually small inns with few rooms and delightful surroundings. But even expensive Welsh hotels aren't *too* expensive considering the experience that awaits. No matter where you stay, and even if it's off-season, book your room well in advance. This is especially crucial in summer months when the national music festivals are held throughout the country. Over the last few years, there has been an increase in the number and quality of restaurants in Wales. Witness the *Walnut Tree Inn* near Abergavenny (see below), which was nominated by Egon Ronay as the Best Restaurant in Britain in 1987. This recent example notwithstanding, the best are still found in the better hotels.

MONMOUTH: The Romans saw at once that this site had an important strategic position at the junction of the rivers Monnow and Wye and built a fort here that they called Blestium. There is not much left of the later Norman fortifications except the remarkable bridge and gate house over the Monnow, dating from the 13th century. And, almost nothing remains of the castle where King Henry V was born. Today, Monmouth is an easygoing market town content with its role. There is an 18th-century shire hall in Agincourt Square with statues of Henry V and Charles Rolls, founder of Rolls-Royce, who was born nearby. The bottom of the hall is now a cluster of market stalls and parts of the interior, though not original, are interesting and attractive, especially the staircase and dome. Behind the hall is the Nelson Museum with some of the sea hero's memorabilia.

The countryside surrounding Monmouth is delightful, particularly the Wye valley. And you can take a meandering side trip to Tintern by driving 7 miles south on the A466 road. The abbey, a lovely 13th- and 14th-century ruin in a tranquil setting beside the River Wye, was founded by a Baron Walter de Clare in 1131. The building fell victim to Henry VIII's Dissolution of the Monasteries in 1539. But though roofless and ruined, it's still romantic and inspiring. William Wordsworth, who wrote the famous poem about the abbey, commented, "No poem of mine was composed under circumstances more pleasant than this."

CHECKING IN: *King's Head* – King Charles I of England, beheaded at the end of England's 17th-century civil war, is said to have stayed in this handsome place, and there is a fine plaster cast of him to ponder. A bar, a restaurant, and 28 comfortable rooms, each with a private bath. Agincourt Sq., Monmouth (phone: 0600-2177). Moderate.

Stowe Court – Just over the English border, this small country house has only 3 double rooms, each with either bath or shower. Book ahead if you'd like a four-course dinner in addition to bed and breakfast. The owners run an antiques shop on the premises and conduct antique-oriented tours of Wye Valley, the Forest of Dean, Bath, Bristol, Cheltenham, and Cardiff. St. Briavels, Lydney (phone: 0594-530214). Moderate.

En Route from Monmouth – In Gwent, 8 miles on the main A40, is Raglan Castle, built in the 1430s. It's the central feature of the little town and one of the best examples of late medieval castles. Henry VII was imprisoned here, and Charles I stayed at the castle after his army lost the battle of Naseby in the civil war. Note especially the large hall, the six-sided keep, and the long, surrounding wall.

Six miles south of Raglan, off the A449 road to Newport, is the meadowy little borough of Usk built on the bank of the river from which it derives its name. Taste Usk salmon while you're here; it's justly famous. The history-minded will enjoy the 13th-century Church of St. Mary's and the ruins of the castle dating from the days when barons ruled the border country in the 12th century.

The A40 west from Raglan will take you to Abergavenny.

ABERGAVENNY: Gateway to the Brecon Beacons National Park, bustling market town, soaked in history, Abergavenny stands beside the River Usk guarded by four mountains: Sugar Loaf, Blorenge, Skirrid, and Little Skirrid. The streets of Abergavenny are lined with Tudor, Georgian, and Victorian buildings, and canny trading takes place in the marketplace, where weatherbeaten farmers sell their sheep, pigs, cattle, and horses. Romans and Normans occupied the site of the town because of its strategic location, and the frontier Clan De Braose made it their base in the battles against the Welsh. Tough William De Braose invited Welsh chiefs to a Christmas dinner at Abergavenny castle in the 12th century and had them murdered while they supped. The treacherous baron had his comeuppance years later: The king stripped his lands from him and William died a beggar. The castle ruins are worth exploring and from here you can get a great view over the rolling hills. Inside the castle is the Abergavenny and District Museum. Abergavenny is a good center for tourists: Hill-walking, fishing, and pony trekking are excellent and you can rent canal cruisers on the west side of town. Red Line Boats (Goytre Wharf, Llanover; phone: 0873-880516) has full-day rentals (£24) and also provides cruisers by the week (from £180). Road House Holiday Hire (Main Rd., Gilwern, Gwent; phone: Gilwern 830240) rents narrowboats (traditional canal boats never more than 6 feet 10 inches wide) on a weekly basis only. Rates fluctuate between £120 and £320, depending on the time of year. Beacon Park Boats (Llangattock Park House, Crickhowell (phone: 0873-810240) offers half- and full-day rentals and provides weekly cruises from £63 to £90 per person. There is a tourist information center on Monk Street with an exhibition on Brecon Beacons National Park.

CHECKING IN: *Angel* – This handsome old coaching inn, with 29 comfortable rooms and a restaurant, is in the center of town, convenient to the many attractions in the area. Cross St., Abergavenny (phone: 0873-7121). Moderate.

EATING OUT: *Walnut Tree Inn* – Advance booking is essential here, especially since it won the Egon Ronay Best Restaurant in Britain award for 1987. Fish dishes, which change daily, predominate, but patrons will also find more elaborate creations, such as guinea fowl with port and truffles. Llandewi Skirrid, 2 miles north of Abergavenny (phone: 0873-2797). Expensive.

En Route from Abergavenny – The A40 toward Brecon is a delightful stretch through the Usk valley, with the Black Mountains to the right and the outriders of the Brecon Beacons to the left. There are pubs and small cottages, and little towns like Crickhowell that welcome fishermen and pony trekkers. Many travelers speak highly of the *Nant-y-ffin Cider Mill* in Crickhowell where you can get hearty homemade food — terrines, pies, cheesecake, and (in season) local salmon. All along this road are interesting narrow lanes turning off into the hills and anyone with the time and inclination to roam is advised to do just that: Turn off and explore. For example, at Llansantffraid you can turn left toward Talybont and drive for 9 miles through forest and hills to Talybont and Taf Fechan reservoirs: This is lovely walking and picnicking country. Another pleasant diversion on the road from Abergavenny to Brecon is to Hay-on-Wye — although you will need the best part of a day to enjoy it. Turn right onto the A479 just after Crickhowell, coast through the hills for about 20 miles to Talgarth, and pick up the A438 north to the B4350 to Hay-on-Wye. Hay is a picturesque little border town, whose main industry is secondhand books; it is absolutely bulging with books, a paradise for bibliophiles, and is reckoned to be the world's largest secondhand bookshop. From here, get back on the A438 southwest to Brecon.

BRECON: The district is still called by the old name of Brecknock, as you will see on some maps, while the town of Brecon is known in the Welsh language as *Aberhonddu.* Its English name is derived from *Brychan,* the vigorous Celtic chieftain (sire of 36 children, the story goes) who ruled this region in the 5th century. The Welsh name is taken from the River Honddu which runs into the Usk. Brecon has narrow streets, a cathedral, a busy livestock market, good shops and pubs, and a peaceful air. It's also a convenient home base for exploring Brecon Beacons National Park. The 13th-century cathedral, built first as a fortified priory, overlooks the River Honddu. The town's castle, built by the half-brother of William the Conqueror, was dismantled by the townsfolk during the 17th-century civil war in an attempt to avoid the bloodshed necessary to defend it. The remaining parts of the castle are now in the garden of the *Castle of Brecon* hotel,

The Brecknock Museum, in the old County Hall in Glamorgan Street, displays interesting examples of Welsh folk art and local crafts, such as the hand-carved wooden "lovespoons" young Welshmen used in bygone days to plight their troth.

CHECKING IN: *Miskin Manor* – This stone manor house, set on 20 acres of Wye Valley parkland, was glorious in its 1920s heyday (when the Prince of Wales paid a visit). It deteriorated over the years, but has been restored to its former glory. Miskin, Mid Glamorgan (phone: 0443-224204). Expensive.

Nythfa House – Another Georgian house nicely set on 4 acres, it has 16 guestrooms, squash, and sauna (phone: 0874-4287). Moderate.

Wellington – This old, established centerpiece of Brecon Beacons National Park has 20 comfortable, recently refurbished rooms, a restaurant, and two bars that serve a good variety of beers. The Bulwark (phone: 0874-5225). Moderate.

Bishops Meadow – Most people stay here for the great views of the Beacons. It's a modern motel with 24 rooms, bar, cafeteria, and gas station. On the B438, also called Hay Rd. (phone: 0874-2051). Moderate to inexpensive.

George – A small, straightforward place in the center of town, perfect for one-night stopovers. All 7 rooms come with private baths. Brecon (phone: 0874-3422). Inexpensive.

Landsdowne – In this handsome Georgian building are 12 pleasant rooms and a good restaurant. The Watton (phone: 0874-3321). Inexpensive.

En Route from Brecon – Take A470 south toward Merthyr Tydfil, for grand views of the Beacons' red sandstone peaks. Turn right after Libanus along A4215 to Defynnog and you will soon pick up signs directing you to the Mountain Centre of Brecon Beacons National Park. The park covers 519 square miles, running east to west, in the heart of the mountains of South Wales. The center is out in the wilds and a friendly, informal place where the park's staff is keen to help in your exploration of the mountains. You can use the center as a base for walking, for picnicking, for light meals, or for just sitting and staring (highly recommended). Join up with the A40 trunk road at Sennybridge, a pleasant town, and head west for Trecastle, with its engaging landscape. It used to be an important stop in the old coaching days, and its coaching inns deserve a visit. It is worth pausing here, anyway, to decide on your route to Llandeilo. You can continue on the A40 road, through the village of Halfway, and then go on to Llandovery — in Welsh *Llanymddyfri* ("the church among the waters"). Llandovery is a pleasant town where you can eat well and stay comfortably. It stands by the Tywi

(Towy) river, the longest of Welsh rivers and famous for its salmon. The alternative route to Llandeilo needs more careful navigation. From Trecastle, turn left along a little-used country road toward Llanddeusant and thread your way through Twynllanan and up the A4069 to Llangadog, a quiet market town. The attractive, quiet village of Bethlehem, off the A4069, is also worth a visit.

LLANDEILO: Near this small riverside town are several interesting castles. Dinefwr Castle was built in AD 876 by Rhodri the Great, who divided the kingdom of Wales among his three sons so as to strengthen its defenses against invaders. Dinefwr — given to son Cadell — was the stronghold of South Wales. The castle also featured in the wars between the Welsh and the English in medieval times, and was improved by members of the great Rhys family. After the English conquest, Dryslwyn Castle was the center of a Welsh uprising led by Lord Rhys in 1287. It failed, and Lord Rhys was beheaded. Carreg Cennen Castle stands atop a cliff, naturally fortified and a hard nut for those warring medieval chiefs to crack. Dating from about the 13th century, it commands a marvelous view of the Black Mountain. Caerphilly, 8 miles north of Cardiff, is famous as the home of one of Europe's largest castles; the castle's leaning tower (a result of Civil War blasting) features an exhibition recounting the complete history of castle building in Wales.

CHECKING IN: *Cawdor Arms* – In the center of town with 17 rooms, it's a convenient base for touring West Wales. Rhosmaen St., Llandeilo (phone: 0558-823500). Moderate.

EATING OUT: *Angel Inn* – This small place is memorable for its home cooking, especially the dessert trolley. Salem (phone: 0558-823394). Inexpensive.

CARMARTHEN: King Arthur's magician, Merlin, was said to have been born hereabouts and that's how this most pleasant of towns gets its name. In Welsh it is called *Caerfyrddin,* or "Merlin's City." In ancient times, as now, it occupied an important and strategic position above the Tywi (Towy) River. The Romans had a base here, as the deteriorated amphitheater testifies, and the ruins of the Norman castle can still be seen. During the early part of the 12th century, monks collected and wrote poems in the *Black Book of Carmarthen,* the oldest known Welsh manuscript, which can be seen in the National Library of Wales in Aberystwyth on the west coast.

Carmarthen is also the administrative hub of the southwestern corner of Wales. Its large covered market draws crowds every Wednesday and Saturday, and behind it the cattle market holds sales each Monday, Wednesday, and Thursday.

In Nott Square stands a monument to Dr. Robert Ferrar, bishop of St. David's, who was burned at the stake on this site in 1555. Also of interest is the museum housed in what was the Bishop's Palace at Abergwili, on the outskirts of town. Merlin's Oak, formerly on Priory Street, has been moved to the museum's grounds. Legend says that when the oak falls, so will the town; to make sure it does not topple, the townspeople have propped it up with concrete.

An interesting 13-mile side trip from Carmarthen is to Laugharne (pronounced Larn), where the Welsh poet Dylan Thomas lived and wrote many of his famous works. You can visit his home, called the Boathouse (now a Dylan Thomas museum); *Brown's* hotel, where he drank; and the churchyard where he is buried. Laugharne is reached by driving along the A48 to St. Clear's and turning left onto the A4066. Six miles farther is Pendine with its romantic stretch of sands, on which 1930s heroes smashed world speed records in their roaring cars.

CHECKING IN: *Ivy Bush Royal* – With 80 rooms, this is certainly one of the best hotels in rural west Wales in terms of atmosphere, design, service, and cuisine. Spilman St., Carmarthen (phone: 0267-235111). Moderate.

Waungron Farm – A comfortable, family-run hotel. Its 14 rooms have four-poster beds and private bath/showers. Good local produce on the restaurant menu. Waungron Isaf, Whitland, Dyfed (phone: 0994-240682). Moderate.

En Route from Carmarthen – The A484 winds for 5 miles through pleasant wooded country to little Cynwyl Elfed with its white- and color-washed cottages, a genuine piece of old Carmarthenshire calm and beauty. Seven miles north of here the road branches northwest to Cenarth, noted for its waterfalls and the last of the coracle men on this stretch of River Teifi. A *coracle* is a little basket-shaped boat made from tarred cloth stretched over a frail wooden frame, and it's been used in Wales for 2,000 years. Coracle fishermen work in pairs, drifting down the river with a net suspended between their boats to catch salmon and sewin, a delicious sea trout. After drifting for a while, the fishermen climb onto the riverbank, hump their coracles onto their backs and, looking rather like upright turtles, walk back up the river to start all over again. During the 19th century, there were thousands of coracles on Welsh rivers, but laws framed to conserve fish and protect the sport of salmon fishing steadily squeezed the coracle men out. Today there are only about a dozen left, and most are on the rivers Teifi and Tywi around Carmarthen. But if you branch right, on the A486, you will soon be in charming Llandysul, with its late Norman church and bridge spanning the river rapids. Here you can pick up the A475 to Lampeter. If you have time, however, pick your way through the lanes and little roads to Llanybydder, a Teifi-side market town with a continuing tradition of weaving. Factories such as the Siwan Woollen Mills (Llansawel Rd.; phone: 0570-480722) welcome visitors. Try to be in town on the last Thursday of any month for the horse fairs, which attract buyers the world over. From Llanybydder it is only 7 miles into Lampeter.

LAMPETER: Lampeter in Welsh is *Llanbedr Pont Steffan.* It's a busy place, where farming folk meet, set in the lush land of the upper Teifi valley. The most famous landmark is St. David's College, part of the University of Wales since 1971, but founded in 1822. Its buildings are open to visitors.

CHECKING IN: ***Black Lion Royal*** – This hostelry has 17 comfortable rooms, 8 with bath, and a restaurant. High St., Lampeter (phone: 0570-422172). Moderate to inexpensive.

En Route from Lampeter – You have a choice of roads to Tregaron: The main A485 is quicker, but the B4343 on the eastern side of the Teifi is more attractive. The latter passes through Llanfair Clydogau, where the Romans mined silver, no doubt with the labor of indigenous slaves. The lure of Welsh gold and silver was one reason why the Romans conquered and colonized Britain. The 2,000-year-old gold mines in the hills at Dolaucothi are now open for guided tours. Four miles on is Llanddewi Brefi, where St. David, patron saint of Wales, preached in 519. Stop for a look at the 13th-century church, supposedly built on the spot where David delivered an inspirational sermon.

Tregaron is 3 miles from Llanddewi Brefi. It's a friendly market town with craft workshops and welcoming inns. In the square is a statue of the town's most famous son, Henry Richards (1812-88), dubbed the Apostle of Peace for his espousal of international arbitration and founding of the Peace Union, a forerunner of the United Nations. Twm Shon Catti, a 16th-century Robin Hood–like character, rogue, and poet, was born and roamed near here. Just north of the town is the 4-mile-long Bog of Tregaron, said to be the largest peat bog in Britain and now the Cors Tregaron Nature Reserve. Tregaron earns part of its living as a pony trekking holiday center, and the land here is just right for riding: wild and remote. The central agency to contact for information on pony trekking is the Tregaron Pony Trekking Association, Tregaron (phone: 09744-364). It will cost about £10 for a full day of riding.

Not many people know the road from Tregaron to Llanwrtyd Wells (20 miles away;

known locally as the Abergweryn Pass), but it is a thrilling journey over a narrow and winding mountain pass. Once in Llanwrtyd, you can pay a visit to the Cambrian Woollen Factory where yarn, spun from locally made wool, is sold. Our main route, however, continues up the B4343 to Pontrhydfendigaid and the abbey at Strata Florida, known in Welsh as *Ystrad Fflur,* or "Valley of the Flowers." The abbey, built by Cistercian monks in the 12th and 13th centuries, is ruined now. It suffered in the fighting between the Welsh and English in medieval days, and received a final blow when Henry VIII ordered the destruction of monasteries. Although crumbled, it's worth a look. Legend has it that beneath a yew is the grave of Dafydd ap Gwilym, one of the leading medieval poets of Europe, who divided his time between making verse and love.

In this district of old Cardiganshire there were once many lead mines, and the narrow-gauge steam railway, which runs from Devil's Bridge to Aberystwyth on the coast, started life as an ore-carrying line. It's a romantic ride today.

ABERYSTWYTH: A popular seaside resort with both sand and pebble bathing beaches, Aberystwyth is also the seat of the University of Wales and the administrative center for Cardigan Bay. Its lively seafront promenade is lined with hotels and has a bandstand and the ruins of a castle, which stand sentinel on the headland.

History is carefully preserved at the National Museum of Wales (Penglais Hill), which houses some of the earliest Welsh manuscripts; and the past is still alive at the station where British Railways' last steam-powered service departs for the spectacular falls at Devil's Bridge, high in the Vale of Rheidol, which according to legend was built by the devil himself. Closer to home, the town's cliff railway carries visitors to the peak of Constitution Hill, where they have a splendid view of the bay and town.

Concerts and evening shows are regular features along the promenade. The Arts Centre holds frequent exhibitions and the University Theatre presents a summer season of plays. Nearby is the Nanteos Stately Home, a Georgian mansion with an imposing oak staircase, some fine plasterwork, and Italian marble.

CHECKING IN: *Belle Vue Royal* – This seafront hotel overlooking Cardigan Bay has a large restaurant, 42 comfortable rooms, and an 18-hole golf course nearby where guests can play without charge on weekdays. Marine Terr., Aberystwyth (phone: 0970-617558). Moderate.

Bay – Also facing the sea, this hotel has 32 rooms and a restaurant. Marine Terr., Aberystwyth (phone: 0970-617356). Moderate to inexpensive.

Marine – On the seafront, it has 24 rooms, 3 bars, a restaurant, and lounges. Marine Terr., Aberystwyth (phone: 0970-612444). Moderate to inexpensive.

University College of Wales – For something rather different, you can stay in one of the more than 1,200 rooms when students are away. The college is near Cardigan Bay and guests can take advantage of campus sports facilities. For information, write to the Conference Office, Penbryn, Penglais, Aberystwyth SY23 3BY (phone: 0970-3702). Inexpensive.

EATING OUT: *Julia's* – There have been many good reports about this pleasant bistro; soups (especially the chilled sort), pâté, and syllabub are specialties. 17 Bridge St., Aberystwyth (phone: 0970-617090). Expensive.

Gannets – Everything on the very reasonable menu is homemade, from the quiches and casseroles to the treacle tart. 7 St. James Sq., Aberystwyth (phone: 617164). Moderate to inexpensive.

Blue Bell Inn – On the A44 to Aberystwyth, in Llangurig village by the River Wye, is this attractive 16th-century country inn with good, reasonably priced meals and accommodations (phone: 05515-254). Inexpensive.

DEVIL'S BRIDGE: Monks built the first bridge over the Mynach River ravine, but two modern bridges have been built above the original. It is an attractive spot, and for a small fee you can take the steps down into the gorge and walk the winding paths to admire the river's waterfalls.

 CHECKING IN: *Devil's Bridge* – Built in 1787 as a hunting lodge, the hotel has an unusual Swiss appearance. There are 22 rooms and a restaurant. Devil's Bridge (phone: 097085-232). Moderate to inexpensive.

Woodlands – This attractive stone house above the gorge at Devil's Bridge has 8 cozy bedrooms as well as a relaxing sitting room with fireplace and a good restaurant. Devil's Bridge (phone: 097085-666). Inexpensive.

En Route from Devil's Bridge – By now you will have decided whether to go to Aberystwyth and the coast. Our route branches inland on the A44 from Ponterwyd. On the right you'll see the sweep of the Ystwyth forest and on the left the rolling hills of the Plynlimon range, where the Wye and Severn rivers rise. It is worth penetrating this area on foot if you can. It's wild and haunting, with rushing streams, old caved-in farmhouses, and a few birds circling overhead. The road goes on to Llangurig, which has a handful of inns and shops. The A470 forks toward Llanidloes.

LLANIDLOES: The central feature of the town, and you have to drive slowly to negotiate it, is the half-timbered market hall built in 1609. Llanidloes has a long tradition of wool weaving and trade, but the town was not always as calm as it looks today. In the 1830s the Chartist workmen's reform movement (a political organization popular in Britain then) began to have some impact on Llanidloes's discontented weavers, resulting in the Chartist riots of 1839. The museum in the market hall has some exhibits devoted to this episode in the town's history.

From Llanidloes, you can take several pleasant side trips into the country lanes of the district. One in particular starts on the eastern edge of the town, on the B4518, and leads out to Staylittle and Llanbrynmair. Six miles out from Llanidloes you'll come upon a lovely view over Llyn Clywedog reservoir.

 CHECKING IN: *Angel* – Congenial and very small with only 2 rooms. High St., Llanidloes (phone: 05512-2381). Inexpensive.

Severn View Guest House – This pleasant inn has a friendly atmosphere and 16 comfortable rooms. China St., Llanidloes (phone: 05512-2207). Inexpensive.

Trewythen Arms – An attractive Georgian house with 12 rooms, 2 bars, and a dining room that offers good country cooking. Great Oak St., Llanidloes (phone: 05512-2214). Inexpensive.

En Route from Llanidloes – The A470 follows the Severn River northeast and passes through Llandinam. Near the bridge you'll see a statue of the village's most famous son, Lord David Davies, the civil engineer, railroad builder, and developer of coal mining in the Rhondda valleys of South Wales. The town of Caersws above Llandinam is typical of the small settlements in this area, planted in the green and open land. It is worth making an 8-mile diversion here along the A492 east to Newtown, a busy and growing place with a mixture of many old and new architectural styles. Newtown is a hub of economic growth in this part of rural Wales, and industrial development here is designed to stop the drift of young people out of the countryside into the bigger towns of England. Newtown's past prominence as a weaving industry giant is chronicled at the Textile Museum. There is also a museum devoted to Robert Owen, the social philosopher, who was born and buried in Newtown. Owen's many theories finally resulted in an experiment in communal living at New Harmony, Indiana.

The route from Caersws, slightly northwest of Llandinam, goes through Clatter and Carno (headquarters of the Laura Ashley textile manufacturing empire), Commins Coch, and Cemmas Road along A470. From here you can take a 6-mile side trip down the A489 to Machynlleth, a market town with a tall clock tower as its signature, standing on the Dovey (Dyfi) River. The Welsh hero Owain Glyndwr, who fought a doomed war of independence against the English in the years around 1400, chose Machynlleth for his capital and he was proclaimed king of Wales. Machynlleth is a busy meeting and trading place, and a good town for strolling.

The main route winds through the Dovey valley by way of the A470 to Mallwyd and Dinas Mawddwy, set in alpine countryside.

DINAS MAWDDWY: It looks hard to say, but pluck up some courage and say Deenass Mouth-oo-ee. It's a rather special place. The landscape is singular, with steeply sloped hills, and the soaring peaks of the Arans close by, to the north. The people here were once known for their red hair and independent nature. And 400-odd years ago travelers feared a gang of them known as the Red Brigands. They ambushed and killed a judge during Henry VIII's reign and for that they were finally hunted down and dispersed. Even today you might see flame-haired people in Dinas Mawddwy. But the visitors today need not worry that the spirit of the Red Brigands lives on: Dinas people are as friendly as the little town they inhabit. It is a restful place, with good fishing for salmon and trout or just for walking. The weaving industry has been revived with some success; the Meirion Mill is open to visitors and wools are available for purchase. You can also take a most enjoyable side trip for 15 miles or so along the narrow road to Llanymawddwy and up to Llanuwchllyn, an off-the-beaten-track ride leading to Bala Lake. The largest natural lake in Wales — almost 4 miles long — Bala is the home of the little gwyniad, a fish found nowhere in the world but here. The lake is also a center for sailing, canoeing, and swimming, and the Bala Lake narrow gauge railway runs alongside it. The town, at the lake's eastern end, has plenty of places to eat, drink, and stay. The whole area makes a worthwhile day out from Dinas Mawddwy.

CHECKING IN: *Pale Hall* – A country house with its own park, built in 1870 and visited by Queen Victoria in 1889. *Pale Hall*'s modern conveniences include sauna and indoor plunge pool, clay pigeon–shooting facilities on the grounds, and nearby sailing, white-water canoeing, and fishing in Lake Bala. Llanderfel, Bala (phone: 06783-285). Expensive.

Brigands Inn – A 15th-century coaching inn in the Dovey Valley steeped in history and character, it has roaring fires and 14 cozy rooms. Salmon and sea trout fishing are nearby. Mallwyd, Machynlleth, Powys (phone: 06504-208). Moderate.

White Lion Royal – A large and charming old post house, it's right in the center of town with a good restaurant and 22 rooms. High St., Bala (phone: 0678-520314). Moderate to inexpensive.

Buckley Pines – The amenities here include 14 comfortable rooms, 5 with private bath; a restaurant; and parking facilities. Dinas Mawddwy (phone: 06504-261). Inexpensive.

Plas Coch – This comfortable, centrally located hotel has a restaurant and 10 rooms. High St., Bala (phone: 0678-520309). Inexpensive.

Red Lion – A bit smaller but just as cozy as the *Buckley,* it has 8 rooms, all sharing a common bath, as well as parking and a restaurant. Dinas Mawddwy (phone: 06504-247). Inexpensive.

DOLGELLAU: Pronounced Doll-geth-lay, this is the chief town of the old shire of Merioneth, now incorporated into the county of Gwynedd, which also includes Caernarfonshire and the island of Anglesey. Dolgellau is solidly built in dark, local stone and is a sturdy, foursquare town perfectly in tune with its surroundings. It lies under the bulk of Cader Idris mountain (the name means "Idris's Chair") and is an important marketplace for the many small mountain villages in the vicinity. It has ancient origins: The Romans were here, as were Cistercian monks who left Cymer Abbey, founded in

1199. The church, built in 1726, has an interesting barrel roof, and its graveyard has a fascinating mixture of tombstones with Welsh and English inscriptions. The Welsh *er cof* means "in memory." Dolgellau's bridge, built in 1638, is now protected as a historical structure and an old tollhouse also remains.

In the midst of Snowdonia National Park, Dolgellau is naturally an excellent place for touring by foot. Several paths lead up the slopes of Cader Idris ranging from easy walks to hard climbs. Two miles out of town, on the A494 Bala road, there is a turnoff to the left clearly signposted Precipice Walk. This is a scenic walk, not difficult, and takes about 2 hours. Information on all trails winding up to the summit of Cader Idris is available from the park information office at Maentwrog (phone: 0766-770274).

The Snowdon Sherpa bus service is an efficient way to get to and around Snowdonia National Park. You catch the bus at designated pick-up points in the area and it drops you off at major walking and hiking paths and trails leading to Mt. Snowdon. A brochure with a map of the bus route is available from the BTA.

Gold found at Llanelltyd and nearby Bontddu transformed Dolgellau into a gold rush town for the last part of the 19th century. Traditionally, Welsh gold has been used for royal wedding rings, and you can see some displayed in the little jewelry shop in Dolgellau Square. Although the gold rush days are gone, gold mining is again becoming a lucrative local industry.

CHECKING IN: *Borthwnog Hall* – A beautiful country house on 75 acres along the banks of the Mawddach estuary, with a restaurant. Bontddu (phone: 0341-49271). Moderate.

***George III* –** Gerard Manley Hopkins once wrote a poem telling those "who pine for peace and pleasure" to "taste the treats of Penmaenpool." And many say he was referring to this 300-year-old hotel and restaurant delightfully situated at the head of the Mawddach estuary. Freshly caught fish is the specialty in summer, and in winter the menu turns to local game. Six of the 13 guestrooms are in a lodge on the grounds, and all have views of the Mawddach estuary and the mountains. Just out of town on the A493 in Penmaenpool (phone: 0341-422525). Moderate.

***Golden Lion Royal* –** The decor here ranges from casual to formal, with 28 comfortable, antique-furnished rooms. Lion St., Dolgellau (phone: 0341-422579). Moderate.

***Dolserau Hall* –** A warm welcome, 12 lovely rooms, and a good restaurant await you here. Just outside Dolgellau on the Bala road (phone: 0341-422522). Moderate to inexpensive.

***Cross Foxes Inn* –** Snug, small, and in Snowdonia National Park, with 4 rooms. Dolgellau, at the crossroads of A487 and A470 (phone: 0341-422487). Inexpensive.

***Gwernan Lake* –** On the sweeping slopes of Cader Idris, this hotel has 9 simple, attractive rooms. There's also a bar with lakeside view and a restaurant. Cader Idris Rd., Gwernan Lake (phone: 0341-422488). Inexpensive.

En Route from Dolgellau – An English poet once mused that there was only one thing better than going from Dolgellau to Barmouth, and that was going from Barmouth to Dolgellau. This route follows the estuary of the River Mawddach, with its fine scenery. You can go direct by the A496, or go to Penmaenpool on the A493 and cross the river by the narrow wooden toll bridges. It is a drive worth doing at an easy pace so you can enjoy the grand views.

And just around the corner, so to speak, is jolly little Barmouth, a resort tucked in under the mountainside and edging the waters of the Mawddach estuary. It is a good stopping place with beaches and a variety of sports and entertainment. For a few pence, you can walk across the rail and footbridge that spans the Mawddach. The view is sublime: sands, sea, and mountains. For more active outings, Barmouth has swimming, golf, climbing, fishing, and rough shooting. And, as you would expect in a seaside town like this, there are numerous hotels, guesthouses, and restaurants. It's ideal for those on a modest budget.

The A496 road runs northward to Llanbedr. On the left is the haunting stretch of dunes and marsh known as Morfa Dyffryn and to the right are the rather fearsome mountains called the Rhinogs, said to have been created by God while in a bad temper. Llanbedr is a quiet village and nearby is Mochras Island, or Shell Island, a shingly peninsula famed for the variety of shells on its shores. If you press inland from Llanbedr you will pick up the signs to Cwm Bychan, a remote and peaceful valley.

A few miles north of Llanbedr on the A496 is Harlech, one of the romantic names of Wales. Still a small village, Harlech's historic heart and motif is the castle, standing high upon the rocks and defying all who come. It's one of the most photogenic of Welsh castles, and provided the inspiration for "Men of Harlech," one of the best-known traditional Welsh songs. Completed in 1289, the castle was one of the many fortifications built by King Edward I during his campaign to subdue the Welsh in the 13th century. The rebel Owain Glyndwr (freedom fighter for the Welsh) captured it in 1404, but his war of independence came to an end shortly after the castle was stormed and taken by Henry of Monmouth. In 1468, Harlech was the last castle to fall to the Yorkists in the Wars of the Roses. It was also the last castle to hold out on the Royalist side in the 17th-century civil war. Thus, Harlech has its battle scars. Those with no fear of heights can walk all around the castle on its unfenced, 10-foot-thick walls and climb the 143 steps to the top of its gate house. Look toward the sea, half a mile away, and recall that when the castle was built it actually stood on the shore. Since that time, however, the sea has receded.

From here the road winds toward Talsarnau. On your left there is a good view of Tremadog Bay and the glistening Glaslyn estuary. Follow the signs to Penrhyndeudraeth and cross the river by toll bridge. The town's name is a mouthful, it's actually Welsh shorthand for "peninsula with two stretches of sand." A solid and amiable village, it has lots of ships and pubs. But no doubt it is rather overshadowed by Portmeirion, just up the road on the A487.

PORTMEIRION: This is an enchanting corner of Wales, a village and hotel created by the distinguished, lovable, and fun-loving architect Sir Clough Williams-Ellis. Begun in the 1920s, today it is an established, picturesque, and rather Italianate waterside village with views of the mountains, the sea, and the river and accents of rhododendron, shrubs, trees, and flowers. It has been called the Welsh Xanadu. There is a campanile, a dome and a town hall, pools, and statuary. Of course, its character and vistas have made it ideal for film settings, and it was used as the set for the television series *The Prisoner.* The lovely *Portmeirion* hotel (phone: 0766-770228) has just undergone an extensive renovation following a tragic fire and now features 20 rooms, each with private bath. Accommodations are also available in cottages in the village. There is an entrance fee for day visitors.

En Route from Portmeirion – Just outside town, on the main road, is the hamlet of Minffordd, where the philosopher Bertrand Russell lived for some years. He loved this part of Wales, and was one of his pleasures in his declining years was to lie in bed and watch the sun go down over Tremadog Bay. The A487 leads westward into Porthmadog, often rendered as Portmadoc, which is reached by crossing a causeway for a small toll. The causeway is part of the harbor construction planned by William Madocks in the 1820s, which led to the town's economic success as a port. Madocks also built the town of Tremadog (*tre* means town) nearby, one of the first planned towns in Britain and the birthplace of Lawrence of Arabia. Porthmadog is a busy holiday and business center, a good base for sailing and for exploring the local countryside.

Leaving Porthmadog, take the main road (A487) to Tremadog and turn right onto the Beddgelert road (A498). After 3 miles, turn right to Garreg and Tanybwlch. Incidentally, an interesting and rather spectacular side trip is to Tanybwlch by train, on the narrow-gauge railway from Porthmadog. This is a former slate railway that used to bring the stone down from Blaenau Ffestiniog for shipping from Porthmadog quay. It fell into disrepair, but has been successfully restored. Its gleaming steam engines are an impressive and picturesque sight as they wind through the gorges of Snowdonia. The railroad has been restored and again runs all the way to Blaenau. Near the village of Beddgelert, at Sygun, is an old copper mine that was abandoned in the 19th century; now restored, the mine has tours of the workings and rock formations.

Back on the road, join the A487 near Maentwrog and from here go through Ffestiniog and pick up the A470 north to Blaenau Ffestiniog, 3 miles farther on. Blaenau, one of the great old slate towns, seems to be entirely grayish blue, since buildings, roofs, garden fences, and other items are made from the slate that made Blaenau. The vast slate mines are today a kind of monument to the heyday that straddled the 19th and 20th centuries. Slate is still worked on a smaller scale, and you can visit the enormous caverns hollowed out of the mountains at the Llechwedd Slate Cavern and Deep Mine here. It is worth doing, for slate has a fascinating history, which is related as you explore the underground maze of mines. They are open daily from 10 AM to 5:15 PM (April through October), but we recommend getting there early since there are attractions aboveground as well: the Slate Heritage Theatre, which presents a short narrative on slate's importance to Wales; the craft shop where you can see workers carve souvenirs from slate and a gift shop where you can buy them; and a tramway exhibit of the old carriers that transported the slate from the mines. Llechwedd Slate Cavern and Deep Mine is popular so it's a good idea to reserve tickets at least a day ahead (phone: 0766-830306). You can also stop at the Gloddfa Ganol Slate Mine, the world's largest, which is open from Easter to October.

The landscape is dramatic in this area and remains so all along the A470 north to Betws-y-Coed. It is a noted beauty spot, resting in a narrow valley, and its famous Swallow Falls are close by, to the north, and worth seeing.

BETWS-Y-COED: Pronounce it Betoosy-Coyd to please those who have gamely suffered the mangling of their town's name. Because it is at a major crossroads with easy access to Snowdonia National Park and Gwydir Forest, there are crowds here during the height of summer, especially on weekends, so a midweek visit would be more enjoyable then. The town has ancient origins and a very old church with parts dating from the 12th to 16th centuries. Its gray stone buildings are typical of this region. There are a number of craft shops; Welsh woolens are of high quality and Betws has a large selection. The *Anna Davies Welsh Wool Shop* (phone: 06902-292) sells tapestry garments, wools, tweeds, quilts, rugs, pottery, sheepskin, perfume, and knitwear (open daily except Sundays in January and February).

CHECKING IN: *Park Hill* – With 11 rooms (8 with private bath) high above Conwy Valley and the golf course, this inn is renowned for its cuisine. Llanrwst Rd., Betws-y-Coed (phone: 06902-540). Moderate.

Craig-y-Dderwen Country House – Snuggled in a cluster of trees right on the banks of the River Conwy, the hotel has 22 rooms, 16 with private bath. Reduced charges for all local golf. Betws-y-Coed (phone: 06902-293). Moderate to inexpensive.

Royal Oak – Huddled in Snowdonia National Park and set beside the River Llugwy, the hotel has been completely refurbished but still retains its old-fashioned charm. The food is good and the service dependable. Holyhead Rd., Betws-y-Coed (phone: 06902-219). Moderate to inexpensive.

Waterloo – More modern in design than the other hotels mentioned, the *Waterloo* has three bars and 28 rooms, all with private bath; there's also a restaurant for leisurely meals. Betws-y-Coed (phone: 06902-411). Moderate to inexpensive.

Fairy Glen – This 17th-century house — more of a B&B than a hotel — is near the entrance of Snowdonia National Park and the Lledr Valley and also overlooks the River Conwy. Some of the 10 rooms have private baths and there is central heating. A bar is available to guests; beef, trout cooked in butter with almonds, and roast duckling are the chef's best for dinner. Dolgellau Rd., Betws-y-Coed (phone: 06902-269). Inexpensive.

EATING OUT: *Plas Bodegroes* – A Georgian country house newly opened as a restaurant with rooms. The owner and chef, Chris Chown, offers fine cuisine based on area freshwater fish and local produce. Pwllheli, Gwynedd (phone: 0758-612363). Moderate.

En Route from Betws-y-Coed – At this point you may choose either of two side trips depending on how much time you have. First, you can make an expedition into deeper Snowdonia (known in Welsh as *Eryri,* "the land of eagles"). Contact Guides (Plas y Brenin, Capel Curig; phone: 06904-214) provides reliable guides through the Snowdonia area. Or head westward to Capel Curig, Llanberis, Caernarvon, and the Isle of Anglesey.

It is a nice 8-mile drive along the A5 from Betws-y-Coed to Capel Curig, and you can circle Mt. Snowdon itself by going 5 miles down to Pen-y-Gwryd and continuing on the A4086 to Llyn Peris and Llyn Padarn (two pretty lakes), passing through Llanberis, a Snowdonia town of mountains and quarries. The Welsh Slate Museum, near Llanberis, is worth seeing and gives a good insight into the slate industry, once the great industry of this region. The Llanberis Lake Railway (1 ft. 11½ in. in gauge) runs alongside Lake Padarn for 2 miles from Padarn Park to Penllyn. The original railway transported slate from the Dinorwic quarries (the world's largest) to Port Dinorwic on the Menai Strait.

From Llanberis, it's a short trip to Caernarvon and the Isle of Anglesey — a trip worth considering. From Llanberis, take the A4086 to Caernarvon.

CAERNARVON: Rendered in Welsh as Caernarfon (there's no *v* in the Welsh language and *f* is pronounced like *v*), the town's magnificence lies in its castle and its setting. Caernarvon Castle is one of Europe's greatest, built in the late 13th and early 14th centuries. Like some other grand castles in Wales, its construction was ordered by King Edward I of England as part of his successful effort to keep the rebellious Welsh in order. From this strategic site on the Menai Strait, beside the River Seiont, the English could control a huge stretch of the Snowdonia wilds.

Although the castle's interior was never fully completed, there are still many turreted towers and narrow passageways to explore. The Queens Tower holds the Museum of the Royal Welsh Fusiliers with a collection of regimental memorabilia; the Northeast Tower has an exhibit on the Prince of Wales investiture ceremony (Prince Charles was invested here in 1969); and the Eagle Tower has a display of medieval armor. The latter gets its name from three statuettes of eagles that were once perched on the tower's turrets; today, only one is left guarding it. Caernarvon Castle is open almost daily all year (for a small admission charge), and the staff is a jolly lot who are delighted to answer questions.

From the castle's ramparts, you can see the town walls. Built at the same time as the castle, the walls still surround the oldest section of the city. Inside the walls are fascinating narrow streets with little pubs and shops. In the main square (Castle Square) there is a statue of David Lloyd George, who rose from humble beginnings in the tiny village of Llanystumdwy, near Criccieth, to become MP for Caernarvon Boroughs, prime minister of Britain, and one of the 20th century's greatest statesmen.

The shopping in Caernarvon includes crafts, and there is a branch of the Craftcentre Cymru group that sells tweeds, woolens, pottery, and items made from metal and wood. In addition, there's a market on Saturdays in Castle Square. For sporting activities,

Caernarvon boasts two yacht clubs, tennis, and golf facilities, and good river and sea fishing.

Near town is the Roman fort of Segontium, a military center founded in AD 78. Some buildings date only from the 2nd century and some were rebuilt in the 4th century. Although there aren't a great many ruins left to explore, the museum here has interesting exhibits on the history of the Roman takeover of Wales, archaeological finds from the period, and displays on the Roman military system and culture.

 CHECKING IN/EATING OUT: *Chocolate House* – There are 7 private studio cottages around the courtyard here, offering full hotel facilities, and the restaurant specializes in chocolate desserts. Plas Treflan, Caeathro (phone: 0286-4872). Moderate.

Royal – A modernized coaching inn with 58 rooms and a well-regarded restaurant that uses fresh local produce. North Rd., Caernarvon (phone: 0286-3184). Moderate.

Black Boy Inn – Dating from the 14th century and inside the old walled section of Caernarvon, this inn has charming wood beams, crooked floors, and low ceilings. Good breakfasts, lunches, and dinners are served in the attractive restaurant, and colorful locals frequent the bar. North Gate St., Caernarvon (phone: 0286-3604). Inexpensive.

ISLE OF ANGLESEY: From Caernarvon, it's about 10 miles along the A487 road to Bangor, where you take a bridge over to the Isle of Anglesey. A lovely stone suspension bridge built in 1826 by Thomas Telford (a Scottish engineer) spans the Menai Strait. The bridge is not only handsome, but a tribute to its designer's skill, since it has no problem coping with the traffic loads of the present century. However, to alleviate congestion, the new Brittania Road Bridge has recently been opened.

These bridges cross over the swirling strait to the island of Anglesey, a corner of Wales that doesn't see many overseas travelers because it's rather off the beaten track. But it repays the trouble. Anglesey is a place for quiet, personal discoveries: a place to wander down narrow side roads and find charming, unspoiled hamlets and pubs.

You can cut diagonally across the island on the A5 to Holyhead, a distance of about 20 miles; or northeast to Beaumaris, a 9-mile drive; or, if you have the time, it's very rewarding to drive all the way around the island via the A5025 and the A4080.

Holyhead and nearby Trearddur Bay bustle with a number of hotels, small restaurants, and pubs. Most likely, the reason for the bustle is the ferry service between here and Dun Laoghaire, Ireland, 3¼ hours away.

The cliff scenery around Holyhead is striking. South Stack, a tiny, rocky island brightened by a lighthouse, is justly famous for its pounding surf, shrieking seabirds, and strong sea breezes.

If you decide to cover the entire coast of Anglesey, there are all sorts of delightful, relaxing places with good beaches: Red Wharf Bay, Moelfre, Amlwch, Bull Bay, Cemaes Bay, and Rhosneigr. Sailing, fishing, walking, swimming, and sunbathing are the order of the day, and you can surf at Rhosneigr.

If you can't travel all the way to Holyhead, you can take the short drive (from the bridge) out to Beaumaris.

BEAUMARIS: The town of Beaumaris (pronounced Bew-marris) proudly harbors the last castle Edward I built in Wales, and many say he saved the best for last. Built at the end of the 13th century, the moated castle guards the entrance to the Menai Strait, and looks particularly fine against a backdrop of sea and mountains. Its beauty, however, is secondary to its strength: It has impenetrable fortifications. The castle was simply a milestone in medieval fortress building. The ingenious design includes two defense walls encircling the castle. The inner wall is square, while the outer wall seems square but actually has bowed sides. This roundedness permitted virtually no corner to go unseen by the castle's keepers. Also interesting is the angle at which the entryways meet the gate houses. Instead of a direct alignment, they're off-center to force a slanted approach by aggressors, making them almost certainly visible to the heavily armed guards. Beaumaris Gaol is also an interesting stop. It has remained virtually unaltered since it was built in 1829. The prison cells, a unique treadwheel, and the condemned prisoner's walk to the scaffold all serve as grim reminders of harsh times. Open June to September.

Back on the main route, from Betws-y-Coed, the A470 winds attractively through the Conwy valley north to Llanrwst, a picturesque little market town beside the river with an interesting church and a most striking bridge across the Conwy, built in 1636, thought to have been the work of the noted architect Inigo Jones. From Llanrwst, take the A548 and watch, after about 5 miles, for signs pointing to Llansannan on your right. The road winds through wild and spacious country — hills, moors, and river valleys. From Llansannan, turn southeast onto A544 to Bylchau and look for signs for the A543 to Denbigh. It's a lovely run over the moors.

CHECKING IN: *Henllys Hall* – A former Franciscan monastery, set on forested acreage with superb Snowdonian views, it has tennis facilities, a heated outdoor pool, sauna, solarium, Jacuzzi, a good restaurant, and 25 rooms, as well as 2 cottages, 7 apartments, 2 bungalows, and a farmhouse. Beaumaris (phone: 0248-810412). Expensive to moderate.

***Ye Old Bulls Head* –** This establishment has been around since 1472, which makes it something of a historical landmark. Copper ornaments dangling from ceiling beams and snapping fires in the hearths warm up the place and the mood quite a bit. There are 17 pleasant rooms, some with private bath. Castle St., Beaumaris (phone: 0248-810329). Moderate.

DENBIGH: Called *Dinbych* in Welsh, this town looks out over the Vale of Clwyd, the river that gives the county its name. This is true border country, so it has seen its share of battle-axing, swordplay, and the zizz of arrows. The castle, which stands on a hill, was first built by William the Conqueror as part of his effort to annex this region. It was greatly extended and improved during King Edward I's reign, and along with Edward's other castles — Harlech, Beaumaris, Conwy, Caernarvon, and Criccieth — it played a large part in bringing the Welsh under the king's rule in the 13th century. Later, the castle was sold by Queen Elizabeth I to Robert Dudley, her favorite courtier. And it was a focal point of the great civil war in the following century. Action against King Charles's supporters was directed from Denbigh and Sir John Owen, leader of a determined Royalist army, was captured and kept in the castle. It is worth visiting: Note its unusual octagonal towers. The Elizabethan town hall is just one of many interesting corners of Denbigh. The steep streets make for some memorable snapshots. Perhaps Denbigh's most famous son was H. M. Stanley, the poor local boy who made good; he emigrated to the US, became a newspaper man, explored Africa, and found Dr. Livingstone, he presumed.

CHECKING IN: *Bryn Morfydd* – Set on 40 acres, this hotel has 23 comfortable rooms with private bath and great views, tennis court, golf course, and a swimming pool. 3 miles south of Denbigh on A525 in Llanrhaeadr (phone: Llanynys 074578-280). Expensive to moderate.

En Route from Denbigh – Eight miles south on the A525 lies Ruthin (pronounced Rithin), a handsome town whose market square is fringed by 16th- and 17th-century houses. It was once a wool trade center, but its history goes much farther back. It was here that Owain Glyndwr started his uprising against English rule in 1400. Glyndwr and his men burned the town but failed to capture the castle. The medieval castle is now a ruin, but the big mansion on the site is a fine hotel, expensive as Welsh hostelries go, but with good facilities and fine dining. It is called, naturally enough, the *Ruthin Castle,* and you cannot mistake its imposing redstone appearance. The castle offers medieval banquets with ale, mead, roasts and the like done in what is thought to be a medieval style. It makes a jolly evening and you need to go with an empty stomach.

The route from Ruthin winds across the Vale of Clwyd and across the Clwydian range of mountains by way of the A494. But a side trip 15 miles along the A525 to the A542 to Llangollen is well worth any effort. It stands beside the rushing River Dee, and words simply cannot do it justice. The four-arched bridge across the Dee is traditionally one of the seven wonders of Wales and was built in the 12th century. Later, it was widened. Llangollen is deeply embedded in the history and lore of Wales, and the town is featured in many legends of love, jealousy, rivalry, and blood and thunder. It takes its name from Collen, a saint of the ancient Celtic church. The Valle Crucis Abbey, 2 miles out along the canal, was ruined on Henry VIII's orders when he was stamping out monasteries, but it is still imposing. Any visit to this town must include the home of the "Ladies of Llangollen," two eccentric women who played host to such literary lights as Wordsworth, Browning, Hazlitt, and Sir Walter Scott. The house, Plas Newydd, is open to visitors.

Nearby, on the Corwen road, is Plas-yn-Ial. This is the ancient seat of the Ial family, whose name, pronounced "Yal," was corrupted to "Yale," and one of whose sons founded the American university. Llangollen is abundantly endowed with pubs, hotels, and cafés, and every July it rings to the sound of music, when the International Musical Eisteddfod, founded to bring the world's people together in peace, has the town bulging. People come from all over the world to compete in song and dance and instrument-playing, so that the town is a mass of color and a happy babble of tongues. Evening concerts are given by renowned singers and instrumentalists. Information: Eisteddfod Office, Llangollen, Clwyd, North Wales LL20 8NG (phone: 0978-860236).

Northern Ireland

Antrim Coast

In many ways reminiscent of the California coast as seen from Highway 1, the stretch of coastline between Larne and Portrush is exceptionally beautiful, offering spectacular views of the sea at every twist and turn. And along the eastern part of the Antrim Coast, as far as Ballycastle, drivers will be tempted to turn inland and explore the Glens of Antrim, a series of nine lovely valleys formed some 20,000 years ago by retreating glaciers. Of great interest to scientists, the coastline is a veritable textbook illustration of the geological history of the earth, with its rock layers of red sandstone, white chalk, black basalt, and blue clay jutting out from beneath ancient lava flows.

Antrim has been inhabited for at least 5,000 years and probably for a great deal longer than that. In Glenballyeamon, near Cushendall, stone "axe factories" dating from the Neolithic period have been discovered, and it is known that some of the tools made here of the local stone, diorite, were "exported" to countries outside Ireland. A Harvard University archaeological expedition has uncovered several layers of flint tools in a cliff face at Cushendun; they think this may be the key to the Irish Stone Age. So many ancient artifacts have been found near the ruins of Olderfleet Castle in Larne that fragments from Ireland's Stone Age are termed "Larnian." And Danish archaeologists believe this area to be a prime example of the development of post–Ice Age society.

Although not part of the Roman Empire, Antrim was visited by the Romans from time to time and some trade developed with Britannia. Upon the decline of the empire and the weakening of its defense, Irish kings launched raiding parties to steal booty and capture slaves. One of the most famous slaves, Patrick, spent 6 years as a shepherd, then escaped to Gaul. Here he underwent monastic training and (legend says) had a holy vision recalling him to Ireland to convert the country to Christianity. He returned in AD 432 and proselytized from then until his death in about 457; he was later canonized. Throughout this region you'll hear lots of anecdotes about the saint's activities, and for centuries Slemish Mountain (1,437 feet) has been a place of pilgrimage on St. Patrick's Day.

Many Irish missionaries who set out to convert Europe to Christianity hailed from the north of Ireland, most notably St. Columbanus and St. Gall, who went to Germany, Switzerland, and Italy, and St. Columcille (or Columba), who went to Scotland. Because of the proximity of Ireland and Scotland, there has always been much traffic between the two countries.

Besides Christianity, Ireland gave Scotland its Gaelic language (which replaced Pictish from the fifth century onward); shared the game of hurling (called shinny or shinty in Scotland); and even sent over the famous bagpipes (there's a joke hereabouts that the Irish exported the bagpipes to Scotland and the Scots haven't seen the joke yet!).

The patriarch of the Scottish Royal House, Fergus, was Irish and the town of Carrickfergus is named in his honor. Two Scotsmen, Robert the Bruce and his brother Edward, who had freed their country from English rule, attempted to do the same for Ireland, but succeeded only briefly — Edward was declared king of Ireland in 1316, but his death 2 years later threw Ireland back into its feud with the English crown. The wars continued until the end of the sixteenth century, culminating in the conquest of the north by the soldiers of Queen Elizabeth I. To tighten English control, a new policy — the "plantation of Ireland" — was devised; this was a plan for introducing Scottish and English Protestant settlers into the area. The scheme was quite effective. Many plantation manor houses still exist today and can be seen along this route in Ballygally, on Rathlin Island, and other places.

Whatever their roots, the people in the Antrim area are exceptionally friendly. In the countryside visitors will be bidden the time of day and perhaps engaged in a conversation, for as the Irish are fond of saying, "When God made time, he made plenty of it."

Our Antrim Coast route starts at Carrickfergus on the east coast, about 9 miles above Belfast, tracing the northeastern shore of Ireland. The road from Larne to Cushendall (25 miles), mostly at the foot of the cliffs, was a great engineering feat when it was constructed in the 1830s. Its magnificent east coast curves around the base of steep headlands between which the beautiful nine glens of Antrim open to the sea. Almost every bay along the coast is a link in a chain of attractive holiday resorts. Near the northeasternmost point, Torr Head is only 12 miles from Scotland. Near the northern tip of mainland Northern Ireland's Antrim coast is the Giant's Causeway, a curious basalt rock formation that is Ireland's most celebrated natural wonder. Portrush forms the Western boundary of the Antrim Coast and Antrim County. The tour ends in the ancient walled city of Londonderry.

Generally speaking, hotels in Northern Ireland are not first class by international standards, but they are always clean and usually reasonably priced. Most hotels have a dining room, where the food served is fresh and hearty, if not haute cuisine. The hotels mentioned in this chapter are all moderate, which means that a double room with bath and full breakfast will run between $40 and $55.

CARRICKFERGUS: Said to be one of the oldest towns in Northern Ireland, Carrickfergus was the north's main port and principal town until Belfast began to expand in the 17th century. Its proud history is personified by the grand castle built on a spit of basaltic rock and standing watch over the harbor. Northern Ireland's largest and best-preserved Norman castle, it has been carefully restored. Note especially the 14th-century portcullis and the machinery that operates it. Sections of the castle were begun by John de Courcey, earl of Ulster, in about 1180 and it was completed by his successor, Hugh de Lacy, by about 1205, although renovations were made as late as the 17th century to accommodate newly developed artillery. The stronghold's central feature is the rectangular keep. Some 90 feet high and 60 feet square, its five stories are linked by a spiral stone staircase that winds up to the roof and ramparts. From here sentries could survey the sea for hostile ships and troops could defend the fortress.

Carrickfergus has seen many aggressors: King John in 1210, who attempted to subordinate the earl of Ulster; Robert the Bruce of Scotland and his brother Edward in 1315, who took the castle (in an unsuccessful attempt to drive the English from Ireland); and the French under General Thurst in 1710, who merely wanted to steal food and money. For seven and a half centuries, Carrickfergus was continually garrisoned; then, in 1928, it became a museum. Visitors can inspect the 40-square-foot banqueting hall, view the old castle well, and sneak down into the impressive dungeon. The castle also houses the Regimental Museum, which features armor, artillery, cavalry uniforms, and displays on the history of the Inniskilling Dragoons, Irish Hussars, and North Irish Horse. Open daily; nominal charge (phone: Carrickfergus 62273).

St. Nicholas Church, first built in 1185, retains some of the original 12th-century arcades and other features added in the 14th century, but most of the present structure dates from the 17th and 18th. The chancel, renovated in 1305, has just one original window, and the spire was only recently built in 1778. The church has a memorial to Sir Arthur Chichester, first English governor of Ulster and earl of Belfast. The four stained-glass windows were designed by Irish artists.

Sections of Carrickfergus's town wall remain, particularly the North Gate, which was the strongest due to restoration work in 1911. The four walls of the old County Antrim Courthouse on High St., which date from 1613, are now the exterior walls of the town hall. Also on High Street are some attractive 18th-century houses.

For those who wish to retrace the footsteps of the famous, Carrickfergus offers two interesting possibilities: Just east of town is Boneybefore, where the grandparents of Andrew Jackson (seventh president of the US) lived. A monument marks the site of their home, while a reconstruction of their thatched house, which contains period furnishings, stands nearby. Two miles along the coast road toward Larne, a right turn will lead you to Kilroot and the ruins of the church where Jonathan Swift began his clerical career. It was in Kilroot that he wrote *Tale of a Tub.* (An aside to Swift fans: Cave Hill, near Belfast, which resembles a giant human profile, and supposedly inspired Swift to write *Gulliver's Travels.*)

LARNE: Second only to Belfast in its importance as a port, Larne is the closest point in Ireland to Britain, and the ferry trip to Stranaer, Scotland, takes just a bit over two hours. Huge freight ships as well as smaller pleasure craft rock in her harbor.

A 95-foot tower is Larne's landmark. Modeled after the traditional Irish round tower, it was built to honor James Claine, a member of Parliament who so loved the harbor's view that he was buried upright so he "would never lose sight of it." Nearby you'll find lots of recreation facilities: You can swim in the pool, lie on the beach, take a boat ride, or play tennis. But if you'd like to tap Larne's historical vein, start with the Curran, a curved strip of land in the harbor and site of much excavation. At the end of the Curran are the ruins of Olderfleet Castle, where many flint implements were unearthed. So many ancient artifacts have been found around here that fragments from Ireland's Stone Age are termed "Larnian." This is also where Edward the Bruce landed in 1315 with hopes of becoming king of Ireland. (He stayed only 2 years, then was killed near Dundalk.) St. Cedma's parish church is also worth a stop for its stained-glass windows executed by Irish artist Wilhemina Geddes.

Island Magee, only a short ferry ride from Larne, is actually a peninsula. Most of its acreage is given over to farming, but there are plenty of spots for exploring and picnicking. The 250-foot basaltic cliffs on the eastern coast of the island are called "The Gobbins" and are inhabited by flocks of singing seabirds. (Be careful on the cliffside walkways; they can be dangerous.) At Portmuck, north of the Gobbins, are the ruins of a castle believed to have been the home of a Scottish family, the Magees, from whom the snip of land takes its name. On the island's northern tip, near Brown's Bay is the 9-hole Island Magee Golf Course.

En Route from Larne – On the way to Ballygally you'll pass Ballygally Head, a cluster of irregular rock pillars formed by lava that burbled to the surface in the Cenozoic era. *Ballygally Castle,* really a plantation manor house, was built in 1625 by a Scottish landowner, James Shaw. Although occupied by the Shaw family until the early 19th century, it was turned into a luxury hotel by Major Ian Gordon in 1948. It's a fine place to stop for dinner.

A bit farther up the road is Glenarm Castle, set near a forest park and glen. Built for Sir Randal MacDonnell, the first earl of Antrim, in 1636, it's been altered and added to over the years and is now largely 18th century in appearance, with minarets, Tudor windows, and cupolas. Near St. Patrick's Church is the grave of Shane O'Neill, leader of the 16th-century Irish revolt against the English. He was decapitated by the Mac-Donnells in Cushendun in 1567, and his head sent to Dublin where it was put on macabre display.

Just a few miles past Glenarm you'll come upon Carnlough, an old limestone quarrying town that's now a summer vacation spot. You're now entering Glencloy (one of the nine glens of Antrim), a valley crosscut by streams and splashed by numerous waterfalls. About 5 miles farther is Garron Point, a hub of land jutting into the North Channel presided over by Garron Tower. Originally a mansion and now a school, it was built by Lady Londonderry between 1848 and 1850; visits are by appointment only.

Continuing on from Garron Point, you'll soon see Red Bay, which takes its name from the red sandstone cliffs that slope into it and which lies at the foot of one of the most scenic of Antrim glens, Glenariff. The cliffs are punctured in two places by tunnels through which the road passes. (The sandstone cut from the cliff was used to build Cushendall's courthouse.)

 CHECKING IN: *Ballygally Castle* – This hotel — a 17th-century manor house with a 20th-century addition — has lovely views of Ballygally Bay and 30 modern, comfortable bedrooms. The sleek, picture-windowed dining room serves fine fresh fish. 274 Coast Rd., Ballygally (phone: Ballygally 83212). Moderate.

CUSHENDALL/CUSHENDUN: Cushendall is a bustling town whose streets are lined with stately Georgian and Regency houses. In the village center is a structure called Curfew Tower, a sort of jail built by Frances Turnley in 1809. Cushendall is a holiday center, and you could stop here to do some swimming, boating, or fishing.

A few miles west of Cushendall you'll see signs for Ossian's Grave, a court cairn or burial mound made of stones. The Ossian in question was a poet warrior in the 3rd century AD and supposedly the son of that mythological Irish hero, Finn MacCool. Be warned that it's not an easy climb up the lower slopes of Tievebulliagh Hill to the grave.

Cushendun is regarded by some as one of the most attractive Irish villages; threaded by the Glendun River, it occupies a lovely sandy crescent of shore washed by the bay and anchored by sandstone cliffs at either end. The Cornish-style cottages on the north side of the river were designed by Clough William Ellis, an imaginative and innovative architect whose most famous work is at Portmeirion in Wales. The whitewashed stone cottages and the surrounding countryside are now maintained by the National Trust. This area has been much painted by artists, and during the summer you'll often see them there busy at work. Cushendun is a pleasant spot for a sojourn. Despite some traffic, the village is delightfully tranquil; boats are available for hire; and you can explore the many caves in the sandstone cliffs. One of these is 20 miles deep and leads to Cave House, once the vacation home of the poet John Masefield, which is now owned by the Catholic Church. The famous Irish chieftain Shane O'Neill (Shane the Proud), an opponent of Queen Elizabeth and a leader of an Ulster revolt against England, was decapitated in Cushendun in 1567.

En route from Cushendun – For a pleasant side trip take the A2 slightly east, then north, over the Glendun Viaduct, an 82-foot-high bridge that crosses the Glendun river and offers an impressive panorama of the area. Across the bridge the road continues to Loughareema, called locally the "vanishing lake": When there is a downpour, the lake can rise and fall dramatically because of the permeable chalk bed underneath it. Near Loughareema is Balleypatrick Forest with a 4½-mile scenic drive. It's also a good spot for picnicking, pony trekking, or for just walking along the Corratary River.

Returning to Cushendall, take the cross-country Torr Road along the coast up to Fair Head.

FAIR HEAD: This impressive 636-foot-high cliff rising from huge sandstone blocks and towering over Murlough Bay. The terrain across the mouth of the bay and opposite the head is gentler, with lush green vegetation carpeting the slope right down to the sandy beach. This area was much loved by Roger Casement, the Irish patriot and international philanthropist, and there's a monument to him here. The descent to Murlough Bay is steep, although the road is in good condition. Be sure to sound your horn on blind curves.

BALLYCASTLE: At the mouth of the Glenshesk River and overlooked by the 1,696-foot-high Knocklayd Hill, Ballycastle is actually two towns linked together by Quay Road, a pretty avenue lined with trees and Georgian and Victorian homes. Lower Town is a seaside resort with facilities for swimming, tennis, boating, golf, and fishing. Upper Town, the older of the two, has restaurants, shops, and many fine houses. The center of upper town is called the Diamond; here you'll find the Greek-style Holy Trinity Church, built in 1756, as well as a memorial to George O'Connor, one of the town's patrons. The Diamond is also the scene of the annual Ould Lammas Fair, a kind of flea market where all manner of new and used articles are sold. Along the sidestreets leading from the Diamond are a few shops, such as *D. Donnelly & Co.*, which feature paintings by local artists.

On the outskirts of town is the Franciscan Bonamargy Friary, founded by the MacQuillan family in 1500. Damaged by fire in 1589, it was refurbished and occupied until 1642, after which it gradually went into decay; in 1931 the friary underwent final restoration. Note the earls of Antrim (MacDonnell) family tomb.

The town has mythological as well as religious associations, for it was in the nearby Sea of Moyle that the tragic Children of Lir, who were changed into swans by their jealous stepmother, had to spend 300 of their 900 years' transmutation.

Before you leave Ballycastle, be sure to visit Ballycastle Forest Park and Knocklayd Hill, where there are camping sites and picnic grounds. Several scenic walks are also signposted in the Glenshesk valley, near the park.

RATHLIN ISLAND: A visit to Rathlin can be a delightful interlude in your driving journey, for you must leave your car behind and explore the island on foot. The 6-mile crossing takes 50 minutes by motorboat and should be undertaken only in good weather, as the Rathlin Sound can be treacherous when rough. (Long ago the sound was called the "Cauldron of Brecain" because it was in these stormy waters that Brecain — grandson of the legendary king of Ireland, Niall of the Nine Hostages — perished with his fleet.)

As you approach the harbor in Church Bay, you'll get a good view of Rathlin's steep, 200-foot-high white limestone cliffs that surround almost all of the island. Fishing is the main occupation on the island; lobster, conger eel, and many varieties of fish are all found in Church Bay; if you want to go fishing, talk to one of the local fishermen about arranging an outing.

With a population of only about 100 — down from 1,000 a century and a half ago — people are a minority here. The island is really owned and occupied by the thousands of seabirds that nest on Rathlin's crags and cliffs. The best vantage point for bird-watching is West Lighthouse, on the western end of the island. And the nearby vicinity of Kebble is a breeding ground for the island's puffin, guillemot, and razorbill population.

Although tiny, Rathlin has seen much history. The island's most famous landmark is Bruce's Cave, on the eastern end, to which Robert the Bruce retreated in 1306 after he was outlawed in Scotland. At Knockans are the ruins of an Irish sweathouse, a primitive version of the sauna, for which steam was produced by pouring water on heated stones. (Remember Tomas Larkin purging his soul — and sweating off a drunk — in *Trinity?*) In the center of the island, Brockley is the site of a Stone Age "ax factory," and slightly north, Doonmore once was the site of an ancient hill fort. Near the harbor is an 18th-century manor house built by Viscount Gage.

 CHECKING IN: *Rathlin Guest House* – Down on the harbor a few minutes' walk from Tony McCuaig's pub is a small (5 rooms, none with private bath) guesthouse with a reputation for hearty breakfasts. Snacks, soups, sandwiches, high tea, and dinner are available by arrangement. The Quay (phone: Rathlin 63917). Inexpensive.

GIANT'S CAUSEWAY: Most people would disagree with English writer Samuel Johnson's opinion that the Giant's Causeway is "worth seeing but not going to see." In fact, the rock formation is so remarkable that it's often called the eighth wonder of the world. Legend has it that Finn MacCool threw the polygonal rocks to the ground to begin a road of conquest to Scotland. The more prosaic explanation for the causeway's existence is that it was formed by the quick-cooling lava that burst to the earth's surface in the Cenozoic era about 70 million years ago. Altogether there are about 40,000 basaltic columns packed together in a shape so regular they seem manmade. Some sections of the lava were naturally molded into unique designs that have been nicknamed Lady's Fan, Lord Antrim's Parlour, the Giant's Horseshoe, and the Giant's Coffin. Another, called the Giant's Organ, is an astonishing 60-yard series of pillars of incredible regularity. Providing a backdrop to the causeway are large basalt pillars called "The Chimney Tops"; in 1588, the retreating Spanish Armada aimed an attack on these columns, thinking they were part of Dunluce Castle. Past these stacks is Port Na Spania Bay, where one of the Spanish galleons, the *Girona,* was destroyed. In recent years, the wreckage of the sunken ship was explored, and the items that were recovered are on display at Ulster Museum in Belfast. The collection consists of Renaissance jewelry, including a Cross of the Knight of Malta belonging to Captain Fabricio Spinola, some tableware, and artillery.

The adventurous can hire a boat and a boatman to wander through the nearby caves of the Causeway; one called the Runkerry is 700 feet long.

En route from the Giant's Causeway – Bushmills, a pleasant hamlet slightly southwest, is the home of the well-known Old Bushmills Distillery Company, the oldest licensed distillery in the world, established by Thomas Phillips in 1608 and still in operation. Visitors are welcome from 10 to 11:45 AM and 2 to 3:45 PM Mondays through Thursdays, and Friday mornings. The tour takes about an hour and, since the company is small, appointments are suggested (one day's notice is sufficient; phone: Bushmills 31521).

A few miles past Bushmills is Dunluce Castle, built by Richard de Burgh, earl of Ulster, in about 1300. Awesomely placed on a basaltic rock jutting from the sea, the structure is reached by a wooden walkway and has five towers linked by a curtain wall. Since its builders thought — with some justification — the fortress was impregnable, the castle is odd in that it doesn't have a keep. Dunluce was held for centuries by the de Mandevilles (also called the MacQuillans), but was taken from them by the MacDonnells during the 16th century, and they occupied it for the next hundred years. In 1639 the castle kitchen collapsed into the sea, killing eight servants; the buildings on the mainland, adjacent to the castle, are thought to be the rebuilt and safer kitchen and servant quarters.

PORTRUSH: This resort town has long sandy beaches and facilities for tennis, boating, and fishing. It's most famous, however, for the outstanding course at Royal Portrush Golf Club, the only Irish club to host the British Open (in 1951). Royal Portrush's two 18-hole courses and one 9-hole course are located on 480 acres of wildflowered dunes, which are among the natural hazards that rule out the need for many bunkers. The scenic Dunluce is the championship 18. Guests welcome. (For more about the Royal Portrush Golf Club, see *Great Golf,* DIVERSIONS.)

For the first time along this route, we veer inland from Portrush to Coleraine via the A29.

 CHECKING IN: *Bayview* – Small (16 rooms, each with a private bath) and comfortable, it's in a fishing village about 10 miles east of Portrush. Portballintrae (phone: 02657-31453). Moderate.

COLERAINE: A 17th-century plantation town at the head of the River Bann estuary, Coleraine was established by the London Company on land granted by James I in 1613. Since then Coleraine has become a bustling industrial center engaged in the distilling of whiskey and the linen trade; it is a good regional shopping center. Some say that Coleraine's roots stretch far beyond the 17th century to prehistoric times, and, indeed, nearby archaeological excavations have indicated that there were settlements here as early as about 7000 BC.

Whatever Coleraine's ancient origins, you'll notice that most of its architecture is fairly recent. This is because many of the earlier structures were either washed away, burned out, pillaged, or rebuilt. Of the town's churches, St. Patrick's is most noteworthy despite changes and additions to its old framework and interior. First built in the 17th century, it was almost completely reconstructed in 1883 and bears little resemblance to the original. Aside from the church, Coleraine's most interesting structure is Charles Lanyon's stucco railway station, built in the mid-19th century. The newest addition to the town's architectural face is the modern concrete and brick buildings of the University of Ulster, a few miles north off Portrush Road.

A mile south of Coleraine, on the east bank of the Bann, is Mountsandel, the ruin of a fort once held by an early king of Ulster and later by the de Courceys. This is also where the Mesolithic artifacts thought to be the earliest traces of civilization in Ireland were discovered.

From Coleraine, take the coast road to Limavady; the signposts leading to this road are marked Downhill.

 CHECKING IN/EATING OUT: *Macduff's* – About 6 miles south of Coleraine, this charming Georgian establishment serves Continental dinners (game, fresh salmon, vegetables) Wednesdays through Saturdays, 7:30 to 9:30 PM. All 6 Georgian period bedrooms have private bath. 112 Killeague Rd., Blackhill, Aghadowey (phone: Aghadowey 433). Moderate.

DOWNHILL: From Coleraine, take the A2 northwest to Downhill. Most historians consider Downhill the private domain of the colorful — and eccentric — Bishop Frederick Augustus Hervey, fourth earl of Bristol who in 1779 began his reign in Derry, the second wealthiest of Ireland's church districts. Hervey was a man of extremes: He lived extravagantly, collected art avidly, and traveled extensively. Hervey always took a large group of attendants on his journeys and hotel owners were so anxious for his business that they sometimes named their establishments in his honor — hence, the many Bristol Hotels throughout Europe. Hervey's ostentatious lifestyle even included running horse races for the pleasure of his clergymen at Magilligan Strand, the 6-mile-long beach below the castle. Hervey, however, was not all frivolity. His more serious accomplishments include putting into practice the Catholic Relief Act of 1791; leading a private army on horseback to the Volunteer Convention in Dublin; and supporting demands and rallies for an Irish Parliament.

No fewer than four different architects were employed in designing the bishop's splendid estate. The castle's interior was destroyed by fire in 1851 and refurbished in 1876, but the restoration bore little resemblance to the original. Parts of the estate still standing are: the Bishop's Gate, an arched portal with Doric columns; the Lion Gate, a sandstone structure carved with the two animals that are on the Bristol coat-of-arms; and the Mussenden Temple, a circular, Corinthian-columned structure built by Michael Shanahan and modeled after the Italian temples of Vesta. Established as a memorial to Hervey's cousin — some say mistress — the temple was also used as the bishop's library. It's now open to visitors in the afternoons. At Magilligan Point (the west end of Magilligan Strand), there is a martello tower, one of the many early-19th-century fortresses built in response to Napoleonic invasions. From Magilligan Point it 1 mile across the mouth of Lough Foyle to Donegal.

En Route from Downhill – Take the Bishop's Road (yet another creation of Frederick Hervey's), a pretty jaunt through Eagle Hill and Binevenagh. Here you can stop to enjoy lovely vistas of Scotland and the mountains across Lough Foyle. Continuing along you'll see Hell's Hole, deep gorges that were carved into the cliffs by glaciers centuries ago.

LIMAVADY: This delightful old Georgian town set in the valley of the River Roe is perhaps best known as the place where William Thackeray wrote the poem "Sweet Peg of Limavady"; he met his muse, a barmaid, at an inn on Ballyclose Street (the inn is now a private home). It's also in Limavady that Miss Jane Ross heard and transcribed in 1851 that traditional Irish song "Londonderry Air" (popularly known as "Danny Boy") as it was played by a wandering fiddler named MacCormick. (The original composer is believed to have been Rory O'Caghan, a blind 16th-century harpist.)

When you visit Limavady's parish church, note its finely crafted woodwork and tapestried kneelers. Each of the latter has a different design, all were rendered by local women.

Limavady actually means "dog's leap" and refers to the legendary dog who leaped over a wide crevice to deliver an important message to the chieftain of North Derry, Rory Dall O'Caghan. The parish church contains a carving of the "Dog of Limavady," and a spot in Roe Valley Country Park is designated Dog's Leap in commemoration. Also in the park are picnic and camp sites, walking trails, and a memorial called O'Caghan's Rock, which marks the site where O'Caghan's castle once stood.

In 1896 some valuable Celtic gold objects were found in the marsh area near Limavady called Broighter. Although it is thought that these items — a miniature boat and pieces of jewelry — date from early Christian times, no one has ever determined to whom they belonged or whether they were hidden or lost. They are now on display at the National Museum in Dublin.

En Route from Limavady – On the way to Londonderry is Ballykelly Forest. Sometimes called Walworth Wood, it was planted in the 17th century to honor Sir

William Walworth, head of the London Fishmongers' Company in the late 14th century. Walworth House, also part of the grounds, is now in ruins except for a few of its towers.

Continue along the A2 to Londonderry.

LONDONDERRY: Most often bypassed by travelers en route to Donegal or Belfast, this hardworking city (also called Derry) astride the River Foyle deserves a visit as well. It's quite compact, and the major sites can be easily covered in a day's walk. Most of the special places are on the west side of the river within and just outside the old walls. For the official guide to Derry, contact the Tourist Information Centre on Foyle St., across from the bus station (phone: 269501).

Derived from the Irish word *doire,* the city's name means "oak grove." The site was a densely wooded hilltop when St. Columcille (Columba) arrived in AD 546 to establish a monastery, and in the ensuing centuries the religious settlement became known as "Derry Columcille." The abbey was burned down by piratical Danes in 1812 — the first of a succession of invasions Derry was to endure. The city, however, continued to grow in size and importance, and in about 1164 the famous church Templemore was built.

Like other Irish cities, Derry came under English control when King Henry II claimed Ireland in the 12th century. The skirmishes that ensued did not seriously damage the city until the rebellion in 1566 led by Ulster chieftain Shane O'Neill, during which Templemore was destroyed. Queen Elizabeth I sent a small army to fortify Derry, but it failed and withdrew. In 1600 an English army led by Sir Henry Dowcra besieged and took possession of the city.

Dowcra called for the erection of huge earthen bullwarks to protect Derry against further invasions, but in 1608 another Irish chieftain, Cahir O'Doherty, raided the city and once again it was ruthlessly sacked. O'Doherty was later killed and his lands confiscated. With the accession of James I to the English throne in 1603, Derry was made a satellite of the City of London. As a result, its name was changed to Londonderry and, more important, it fell subject to the new policy of "plantation." The lands forfeited by vanquished Irish leaders were distributed among English and Scottish colonists. Estates went for a nickel an acre, and the newly created hereditary title of baronet sold for $2,500.

Between 1617 and 1619 the city was rebuilt and stone walls constructed in place of the earthworks. Derry successfully withstood three more sieges: In 1641 the Irish rose yet again against the English, and in 1648, during the English Civil War, Derry underwent a 4-month attack by Royalist forces. But it is the third siege that is most memorable.

In April 1689, in an attempt to gain a foothold in Ireland from which to resume the English throne, the deposed Catholic King James II marched on Londonderry. His troops shelled the city and blockaded the River Foyle to thwart rescue and to starve its citizens into submission. The garrison's commander, Colonel Lundy, something of a traitor, advised surrender and fled. A Reverend George Walker was then elected governor, and under his leadership Derry's population of 30,000 held out for 105 days until the relief ship *Mountjoy* broke through the barrier. Two days after the siege was over, James was defeated by "King Billy" (William III) at the Battle of the Boyne.

Though battered by these sieges, Derry's walls remain intact; they're about 1 mile in circumference and between 14 to 30 feet thick and 20 to 25 feet high. The four original gates — Shipquay, Butcher's, Bishop's, and Ferryquay — have all been restored. Guarding the walls is the famous "Roaring Meg," a cannon named for the thunder and fear it created in the Great Siege of 1689; you might also take a look at the flintstone watchtowers at Church Bastion and New Gate. (The former is better preserved.) The memorial to Reverend George Walker at Lord Dowcra's Bastion was damaged by a bomb in 1972.

From on top of the old city walls, you get a fine view of all Derry: Inside the walls are St. Columb's Cathedral and the Court House; to the northeast is the Guildhall; to the east drifts the languid River Foyle; to the south is Columba's Church; and to the northwest is St. Eugene's Cathedral. The city within the walls retains its original 17th-century layout, with four main streets leading from the central square (called the Diamond) to the gates. Guided tours of the city walls leave from the information center on Foyle St. four times daily on weekends.

Construction of St. Columb's — the Church of Ireland cathedral on London St. — was begun in 1628 and finished in 1633; since then it has undergone much restoration and alteration, although its façade remains basically austere "Planter's Gothic" in appearance. The original spire was built in 1778 by Frederick Hervey, bishop of Derry; the present 171-foot spire was added in the early 19th century. Its porch bears the telling inscription, "If stones could speak then London's prayse should sounde./Who built this church and cittie from the grounde," and its 18th-century chapter house displays the locks and keys to the original Derry gates.

The nearby Greek Revival courthouse (Bishop St.) is presided over by statues of Justice and Peace, sculpted by Edward Smyth, who also worked on the Four Courts of Justice in Dublin. Its handsome colonnade resembles the Temple of Erechtheus in Athens.

Follow Bishop Street to the Diamond, then pick up Shipquay. Leading down to Derry Quay, it is the main street of Derry, and in some stretches where the modern macadam paving is worn thin, the original cobblestones show through. (Often referred to as the steepest street in Ireland, Shipquay can be treacherous to walk down in leather-soled shoes on a damp or drizzly day.) Note the original red brick 18th-century Custom House at #33, a well-preserved example of Georgian design.

Just outside the gate at the foot of Shipquay Street, the fussy yet impressive Guildhall — with pinnacles, spire, and clock — was built in 1890 of Antrim red sandstone. It houses the sword said to have belonged to the Irish chieftain Cahir O'Doherty, who led an attack on Derry in 1608. Concerts and plays are sometimes held in the main hall.

From the Guildhall, you can proceed either north along Strand Road toward St. Eugene's or south along Foyle, Orchard, and Fountain streets toward St. Columba's Church.

St. Eugene's, a Catholic cathedral begun in 1851 and finished in 1873, was built in the Gothic Revival style — tall and airy in proportion, yet unadorned except for its fine stained-glass windows depicting the Crucifixion. In the Catholic district called the Bogside, it is reached from Strand Road along Great St. James Street.

In striking contrast to St. Eugene's is St. Columba's, the many-gabled and marble-columned church built on the site of the original 10th-century church. It is sometimes called the Long Tower Church, in reference to the cylindrical shape typical of Irish fortresses built in the medieval period. Long Tower St.

Derry's location on the doorstep of Donegal means that the famous tweeds are in plentiful supply; try the *Donegal Shop,* 8 Shipquay St.; *Austin's,* a department store on the Diamond; and *Hill's,* Spencer Rd. If you're interested in pottery, stop at the *Ulster Ceramics* factory outlet at the Springtown Industrial Estate. For information about other handcrafts, ask for the free booklet *A Guide to Northern Ireland Crafts and Craftsmen,* which gives the names, addresses, and specialties of Irish artisans in the Derry area. Contact: Local Enterprise Development Unit, 17 Linenhall St., Belfast (phone: 242582).

The Derry area has several "leisure centers" that are open to the public and have pool, squash courts, sauna, and other facilities. Contact the Tourist Information Centre for details. The fishing in the River Foyle and its tributaries is legendary; you can buy a license from the Foyle Fisheries Commission at 8 Victoria Rd. (phone: 42100). The

City of Derry Golf Club, an 18-hole golf course at Prehen, 2 miles south on Strabane Rd., is open to the public (phone: 42610).

Derry offers little in the way of nightlife, although a pleasant evening might be spent at the *Chariot Inn,* 17 Butcher St. (phone: 261319), *The Venue,* 122 Northland Rd. (phone: 266080), or *Inn at the Cross,* 171 Glenshane Rd. (phone: Cross 480). The *Gweedore Bar* on Waterloo St. has traditional Irish music Wednesday through Saturday nights, and the *Andy Cole,* 135 Strand Rd. (phone: 267123) — the oldest pub in Derry — holds sessions every other Tuesday and most Saturdays. There is no established theater, but concerts are often given in the Guildhall on Shipquay Pl. (phone: 265151) and plays staged in the Little Theatre on Orchard St. (phone: 262880).

CHECKING IN: *Everglades* – Set amid landscaped gardens 2 miles south of the city, this 60-bedroom, modern, two-story hotel is the best place to stay near Londonderry. Recently renovated, it offers 24-hour room service, elegant dining, a bar-lounge, nightly piano music, and other amenities. Prehen Rd., across the Foyle (phone: 0504-46722). Moderate.

Glen House – On the tree-lined main street of a pretty village — founded by the Grocers' Company during the Plantation era — this full-service, 16-room hotel retains an English appearance. In a rural setting 9 miles northeast of Londonderry, on the road to Limavady. 9 Main St., Eglinton (phone: Eglinton 810527). Moderate.

White Horse Inn – A modern hotel built around an old pub, the inn was completely refurbished and squash courts added in 1986. The *Grille Bar* restaurant is a local favorite. 68 Clooney Rd., Campsie, northeast of Londonderry, on the road to Limavady (phone: 0504-860606). Inexpensive.

EATING OUT: Regional food specialties include Foyle salmon, Donegal lobster, locally cured Londonderry ham and bacon, and Ballarena smoked fish. *Bells* – Open daily for lunch and dinner. Just past the City of Derry Golf Club. 60 Victoria St. (phone: Waterside 41078).

Brown's – Nice decor, in an old railway station, at the far side of the Craigavon Bridge. Open daily for lunch and dinner. 1 Victoria Rd. (phone: Waterside 45180).

Embassy Court Steak House – European cuisine, dancing facilities. Open for lunch and dinner, daily except Sundays. 3 Strand Road (phone: 265861).

Happy Landing – Pub-style lunches and dinners Monday to Saturday. 4 Main St., Eglinton (phone: Eglinton 810206).

India House – Indian menu and a favorite locally. Lunch and dinner Monday to Saturday; dinner only Sunday. 51 Carlisle Rd. (phone: 260531).

Irish Republic

Southeast Ireland: Dublin to New Ross

This route will take you through only three Irish counties — Dublin, Wicklow, and Wexford — and it will keep you close to shore most of the time, yet the changing mood and character of the land along the way will still surprise you. It may seem impossible, but a mere half-hour's drive from the city center of Dublin brings you to the splendid isolation of the Wicklow Mountains. Here, great valleys with melodious names such as Glendalough, Clara, and Avoca wind through the hills, and uncrowded roads pass unforgettable sights — a high waterfall, an ancient monastic settlement, a proud estate. Several miles out of Glencree, the boggy terrain, flaked with granite and crusted in late summer with purple heather, seems primitive, still awaiting the arrival of man, whereas the wooded glens met later seem more soothing in their ageless beauty, not quite as lonely.

To the south lies the friendlier, less dramatic landscape of County Wexford, where fertile farmland is served by picturesque villages and the historic town of Wexford itself. The coast is lined with inviting beaches — if you are ever going to enjoy one in Ireland, it will probably be here in this sunniest, driest corner of the country. You'll find busy seaside resorts with shooting galleries, amusement rides, and golf courses, but you'll also find the secluded and tiny fishing village of Kilmore Quay, its traditional thatch cottages all freshly painted and still very much occupied.

En route, you'll come across urban exiles who have fled the congestion and pace of London and Dublin for the tranquillity of the Wicklow Mountains, weavers and potters with skilled hands musing away in modern bungalows and old cottages, and families cutting and collecting peat throughout the summer along the Military Road through Sally Gap. You'll meet the people of Wexford in singing pubs and good restaurants, while outside the town, time will seem to recede with the sight of older men in black suits rambling down country lanes, the postman delivering his parcels by bicycle, or women placing statues wrapped in rosary beads at the pilgrim shrines of Lady's Island.

The route heads south through the suburbs of Dublin to the residential and resort town of Dun Laoghaire and keeps to the coast as far as Bray. It then turns inland to the village of Enniskerry and Powerscourt Estate, continues west to Glencree, and turns south again over the Military Road to Laragh, the gateway to the monastic site of Glendalough. The route next passes through the vales of Clara and Avoca and returns to the coast at Arklow, where a succession of smaller and larger beachside resorts and villages leads south and then west to Kilmore Quay, interrupted only by the county town of Wexford on Wexford Harbour. At Kilmore Quay, it is possible to backtrack to Rosslare Harbour (a terminus for ferries to Wales and France) or to proceed to New Ross, from which neither Kilkenny nor Waterford is very distant.

A hotel listed as expensive will cost $80 or more for a double room; a moderate one, from $50 to $75; an inexpensive one, less than $40. Dinner for two without wine or tips will come to $50 or more in an expensive restaurant; $30 to $45 in moderate, under $30 in inexpensive.

DUBLIN: For a full report on the city, its sights, restaurants, and hotels, see *Dublin,* THE CITIES.

En Route from Dublin – Go south on O'Connell Street and turn left onto Nassau Street just after Trinity College. Follow the signs to Ballsbridge, passing Merrion Square with its Georgian houses, the American Embassy, and the grounds of the Royal Dublin Society (where the famous horse show is held every August), and continue until Dublin Bay is visible on the left. This coastal road will take you by the Booterstown Bird Sanctuary and through the small towns of Blackrock and Monkstown, and then, 7 miles south of Dublin, into Dun Laoghaire. Craft enthusiasts will enjoy a stop in Blackrock to see the factory and shop of *Dublin Crystal* on Carysfort Ave., about a mile off Main St. This enterprise, begun in 1968, carries on glass-making traditions that thrived in Dublin from 1764 to 1800 (phone: 887932).

DUN LAOGHAIRE: As the terminus of the cross-Channel ferry route from Holyhead, Wales, this busy residential town, holiday resort, and yachting center is one of the main gateways into Ireland. It has grown considerably as a suburb of Dublin in recent years and has innumerable hotels and restaurants, but it still has Victorian charm below its modern surface, and you could as easily stay a few days as a few hours. Dun Laoghaire (pronounced Dun Leary) was named after a 5th-century Irish king (O'Leary in English) who established a fort, or *dún,* here to protect the lands of the High Kings of Tara from their rivals. In the 16th century, the area figured in the fighting between the English, who had their main port at neighboring Dalkey, and the Irish, who opposed the English from the nearby Wicklow Mountains. (Traces of the ditch marking the Pale, that area under English control, can still be found around Booterstown.) Dun Laoghaire remained primarily a small fishing village until the present harbor was built in 1817, opening the way for mailboat and ferry services with Wales. George IV came to christen the harbor in 1821 (after which the town was renamed Kingston and known thus for the next 99 years), the railway line from Dublin arrived in 1834, and the town rapidly became a fashionable resort for the wealthy — many of the streets with their big Victorian houses are named after English royalty.

If you are just passing through town, head down to the harbor and walk the mile-long east pier, with Howth Head stretching in the distance. In summer, band concerts are sometimes held here, and not too long ago people brought chairs to sit and watch the sunset. On a nice night, much of the town with spouses, children, and dogs in tow still parades the pier to watch the departure of the evening ferry. Nearby People's Park, which has swings and lovely flowers landscaped beneath shady trees, is the place to see next, perhaps after a stop for an ice cream cone at *Teddy's.* George's Street is the main shopping area, and at the corner of Royal Marine Road is one of the most modern shopping malls in Ireland, with three floors of boutiques and gift shops and a tempting delicatessen in the basement. Across the way, St. Michael's Church is worth a visit. Its striking modern design incorporates a 19th-century bell tower from an earlier church destroyed by fire. Farther down Royal Marine Road are the Post Office and Town Hall, built in 1878. If you want to pause in your sightseeing, *Ann's Hot Bread Shop,* where the apple squares sell out quickly, is on George's Street just around the corner from St. Michael's. Or walk up Patrick Street and try the *Cake Shop,* where the sandwiches are fresh and the coffee strong. *Ursula's Place* in Moran Park, down on the waterfront, is also good for homemade food. For healthful fare, such as salads, oat flakes, and carrot cake, don't miss *Earthworks,* at 96 Lower George's Sq.; or pick up fresh fruits and vegetables at *Pick of the Crop,* an open-air stand across the street.

An enjoyable evening can be spent near Dun Laoghaire at Culturlann na hÉireann, the headquarters of the national organization for the promotion of traditional Irish music, song, and dance known as Comhaltas Ceoltóirí Éireann. The same group that sponsors sessions of authentic music and dance (*seisiún*) throughout the country during the summer has here converted a large house into a cultural center, transforming the basement into an Irish kitchen complete with peat fire. There is something going on most evenings from early June to early September: either *seisiún; céilí* dancing; *fonntrai,* a show spotlighting Irish traditions; or informal sessions of music and talk. Admission is charged, there is a nice bar area with tables for socializing, and there are off-season programs, too. The building is at 32 Belgrave Sq., Monkstown (phone: 800295), about 20 minutes on foot from Dun Laoghaire or a short drive by car (it's off the main road, so ask directions to Belgrave Square).

 CHECKING IN: *Court* – Set on 4 acres overlooking Killiney Bay, with a private garden walk to the beach, this converted residence has 34 rooms, all with bath and a view of the bay, and a fine French-Irish restaurant. A DART station, adjacent to the hotel grounds, makes downtown Dublin a 15-minute ride away. On Killiney Bay (phone: 851622). Expensive.

***Fitzpatrick's Castle* –** Two generations of Fitzpatricks oversee the operation of Dublin's only castle-hotel. It has 100 rooms and suites (many with four-poster beds), suites in the castle's turrets, a fine dining room (*Truffles*), grill room, bar, indoor heated pool, saunas, squash and tennis courts, and 9 acres of grounds with gardens and views of Killiney Bay. Courtesy coach service to the city center and airport is provided. Killiney Hill Rd., Killiney (phone: 851533). Expensive.

***Royal Marine* –** This elegant, older hotel set back from the waterfront by a gracious lawn and gardens is a lovely setting for a drink and dinner followed by a romantic stroll down to the harbor. Amenities for guests include 90 recently renovated rooms with bath, sauna baths, a beauty salon, and a large parking lot just behind the shopping mall on George's Street. Royal Marine Rd., Dun Laoghaire (phone: 801911). Expensive.

***Scarsdale* –** A cheery bed-and-breakfast inn within walking distance of Dun Laoghaire's waterfront, it's run by Doris Pittman, who lived for several years in Scarsdale, New York. Four of the 5 bedrooms have hot and cold running water; the other, a full private bath. Tivoli Rd., Dun Laoghaire (phone: 806258). Inexpensive.

 EATING OUT: *Digby's* – On the seafront, this is an elegant place with a reputation for fine food. The menu usually changes with the seasons to take advantage of whatever's freshest — perhaps wild sea trout, venison, teal, brace of quail, pigeon, or rack of lamb — and there's also a long list of wines. Open for dinner daily. Windsor Terr., Dun Laoghaire (phone: 804600). Expensive.

***Guinea Pig* –** Former Dalkey town mayor Mervyn Stewart is the chef-owner, and seafood is the specialty, including scallops with crab claws and "symphonie de la mer" — monkfish, salmon, sole, and shellfish simmered in herbs, garlic, butter, and lemon. 17 Railway Rd., Dalkey (phone: 859055). Expensive.

***na Mara* –** This Dublin Bay restaurant in a former train station is known for its good seafood, especially prawns flame-cooked in Pernod, smoked fish pâté, and lobster. 1 Harbour Rd., Dun Laoghaire (phone: 806767). Expensive.

Salty Dog – This pleasant restaurant is filled with Persian rugs and wall hangings a roaming salty dog might have brought home from his travels. The daily menu features dishes such as boneless stuffed duckling, while on Sundays, you can partake of the special Indonesian rice table of 18 different dishes including deep fried chicken and spiced lamb. 3A Haddington Terr., Dun Laoghaire (phone: 808015). Expensive.

Baroque – The atmosphere is Old World; the menu includes lobster thermidor, rack of lamb, and boneless stuffed duck. Main St., Dalkey (phone: 851017). Expensive to moderate.

Steers – Steaks — 17-ounce sirloins — are the big attraction at this restaurant on the waterfront, which also serves seafood. Windsor Terr., Seafront (phone: 806535). Moderate.

Heroes – A trendy wine bar decorated with old movie posters. The light cuisine on the menu includes casseroles and salads, all served to the beat of popular music from the last 3 decades. 66a Upper George's St. (phone: 800875). Inexpensive.

Wishbone – Right over *The Eagle* pub, this place is popular for steaks, burgers, fresh fish, and crêpes. Open daily for lunch and dinner. Sandycove, Dun Laoghaire (phone: 808021). Inexpensive.

Dun Laoghaire has become a center for Oriental cuisine — in fact, a section of Upper George's Street is now known as Chinatown. The following restaurants are open daily and are considered moderate to inexpensive: *Joyous,* 69a Upper George's St. (phone: 858719); *Lotus House,* 54 Upper George's St. (phone: 804103); *Taipan,* 66b Upper George's St. (phone: 803205); and *Mr. Wong,* 51 Upper George's St. (phone: 807007).

En Route from Dun Laoghaire – The coastal road southeast of town leads to a district known as Sandycove, the site of a martello tower built as protection against a possible Napoleonic invasion and now a museum dedicated to James Joyce. The author lived in the tower briefly with Oliver St. John Gogarty, and in the opening scene of *Ulysses,* the character Stephen Dedalus lives there with Buck Mulligan. The museum, which currently has a small collection of Joyce's letters, books, and other memorabilia, is the starting point of many a Bloomsday tour taken by Joyce fans every June 16, the day in 1904 on which the events of *Ulysses* take place. There is a small admission fee and visitors can climb to the top of the handsomely restored tower for a great view of the harbor and the Irish Sea as Joyce saw it. The museum is open May through September, by appointment at other times (phone: 808571).

A short distance down the coastal road is Bullock Castle, at one time a powerful abbey and inn run by Cistercian monks who exacted tolls from ships entering Bullock Harbour and now owned by American Carmelite nuns who staff the adjoining nursing home. The castle has been restored, and the tiny prayer cells of the monks and the large dining hall make it an interesting stop. (Note the carved head on the corner of the western wall, which dates the castle at about 1160.) It is open May through September and by appointment at other times. Bullock Castle is at the northern approach to the small resort village of Dalkey. A major port when Dublin was yet developing, it was once guarded by no fewer than seven castles, two of which remain on Castle Street (one has been rebuilt as the Town Hall). Continue following signs for the Coast Road, which will take you around Sorrento Point and then, via the Vico Road, high over Killiney Hill for a view of Killiney Bay. A local saying, "See Killiney Bay and die," compares the view to that of the Bay of Naples. You can judge for yourself by parking your car and enjoying the beautiful stretch of ocean as far as Bray Head to the south and Dalkey

Island to the north — the tiny flecks of black against the blue-gray surface of the water are fishing boats. At the end of Vico Road, follow the signs to Bray, in County Wicklow, a short 12 miles from Dublin and one of Ireland's most popular seaside resorts. Bray has a mile-long beach (a shingly one, compared to those farther south along the coast), with a mile-long esplanade running its length to Bray Head. This nearly 800-foot cliff rises sheer from the sea at the end of the esplanade.

After Bray, turn inland and drive the short 3 miles to Enniskerry.

ENNISKERRY: Though this tiny village is very pretty, its main attraction is the 14,000-acre Powerscourt Estate on its southern outskirts. A fire in 1974 destroyed the interior of the lovely 18th-century mansion, whose substantial skeleton still attests to its grandness, but the wonderful formal terraced gardens with pebble-paved ramps, statuary, and ironwork are still intact in a heady location looking out over the Wicklow hills to Sugar Loaf Mountain. There are also pleasant Japanese gardens on the grounds as well as a 400-foot waterfall, the highest in Great Britain and Ireland. The gardens are open from Easter through October; the waterfall area is open year-round. You can also browse through the two shops on the estate's grounds.

En Route from Enniskerry – Head west, following signposts for Glencree. The road now climbs into the splendid Wicklow Mountains on a winding course hugged by trees that now and again give way to views of white cottages planted in the midst of brown fields. At Glencree, follow the signs south to Sally Gap over the Military Road, so called because it was built by the British after the rebellion of 1798 and used to flush out Irish rebels hiding in the glens of the Wicklows. This stretch of the route is a winding one, too, passing peat bogs, glacial lakes, and a landscape somber and unyielding in its flatness till it reaches the crossroads of Sally Gap (1,631 feet) and begins to descend toward Laragh through the valley of Glenmacnass. At the northern end of the glen, where the road joins the course of the Glenmacnass River, there is a parking lot. Be sure to stop and walk down to the waterfall, pristine and powerful in its simple beauty as it tumbles over silent slabs of stone into the deep valley below. At the southern end, where the Glenmacnass River meets the Avonmore, there is the village of Laragh. Browse for a while in the *Glendalough Craft Center,* a transformed farmhouse where weavings and jewelry are made on the premises, and the wares include sheepskins, woodcarvings, hand-woven clothing, and pottery. Then drive the mile west to the entrance to Glendalough.

GLENDALOUGH: This deep glen, set between two lakes amid the towering wooded slopes and granite hills of the Wicklow Mountains, is at once a place of great natural beauty and immense historical interest. Glendalough means "the valley of the two lakes," and in the 6th century, when St. Kevin came to Wicklow in search of tranquillity, he found it here. But the hermit's sanctity attracted so many disciples that, almost unwittingly, he founded a great monastery that eventually became one of the most renowned centers of learning in Europe. It was sacked by the Danes in the 9th and 10th centuries, and later (1398) by the English, although some of the buildings remained in use until Henry VIII dissolved the monasteries in the 16th century. Today the ruins of the monastic city are scattered over 1½ miles of a valley that insulates visitors from the present the minute they step through the aged arched gateway at its entrance. It was in the solitude of the Upper Lake at the base of 2,296-foot Camaderry and 2,154-foot Lugduff that St. Kevin first prayed in his stone beehive hut. In the same area, with its gravestones and crosses, is Reefert Church, which was the burial ground of the O'Tooles and other local chiefs. You can walk (or drive) to the Upper Lake, use the picnic grounds, and (for a small fee) hire a boat to take you out for some splendid views of the valley and a closer look at St. Kevin's Bed, an excavation in the cliff-face about 25 feet above the water level, said to have been used as a retreat by the saint. As it grew, the settlement spread toward the Lower Lake and the entrance, and the ruins in this area include the Cathedral, the largest church on the site; St. Kevin's Church, with its sturdy stone ceiling; and the much-photographed Round Tower, over 100 feet high. Built in the 9th century, this was probably a bell tower, lookout point, and place of refuge all in one; the only door is fully 10 feet above the ground. Glendalough's walks and ruins are marked by plaques for easy exploration, and after steeping themselves in this ancient beauty made mellow by human habitation, visitors can stop at one of the many tea shops in the vicinity.

 CHECKING IN: *Royal* – Offers 17 recently renovated bedrooms (all but 4 with private baths), a dining room with views of the river and mountains beyond, and a bar with snacks. Glendalough (phone: 0404-5135). Moderate.

En Route from Laragh – Leaving by the road to Arklow (T61), the route once again parallels the course of a river, this time the Avonmore, and passes through the wooded Vale of Clara before reaching the town of Rathdrum, 8 miles south of Laragh. Here it is possible to interrupt the route for an interesting diversion at the nearby Clara-Lara Fun Park, an outdoor amusement center offering row boats, rides, and a trout farm where you pay IR£2 for every pound of fish you catch (full barbecue facilities are available on the premises). Admission charge to the park includes fishing pole rental. Open April through October.

About 1½ miles southeast of Rathdrum is Avondale, the lovely birthplace and home of the Irish patriot Charles Stewart Parnell, a member of a Protestant land-owning family who became a leader in the fight for Catholic emancipation and land reform in the 19th century. The house was built in 1777 by Parnell's cousin, Samuel Hayes, who was much interested in forestation and wrote the first book on tree-planting in Ireland in 1794. Now the 530-acre estate that the Parnell family inherited from Hayes in 1795 belongs to the Forest and Wildlife Service and is used as a forestry school. The guidebook on sale at the estate discusses the wildlife and trees found on the grounds as well as the recommended walks, but for the tourist budgeting time the house, with its lovely furnishings and moldings, is the main interest. Note the poster from the day Parnell addressed the US House of Representatives in 1880 (Parnell's mother was American, the daughter of Admiral Charles Stewart who fought the British in the War of 1812). The house is open Fridays through Mondays from 2 to 6 PM, from May to the end of September; a nature trail on the grounds is open year-round.

From Avondale, return to Rathdrum and pick up the main road (T7) south toward Woodenbridge. The approximately 8-mile distance between the two towns is known as the Vale of Avoca, a beauty spot immortalized in verse ("There is not in this wide world a valley so sweet/As that vale in whose bosom the bright waters meet") by Ireland's national poet, Thomas Moore. The Meeting of the Waters, where the rivers Avonmore and Avonbeg join to form the River Avoca, is about 3½ miles south of Rathdrum, and the tree under which Moore is supposed to have sat to contemplate the beauty he saw is marked by a plaque. *The Meetings,* a combination pub, restaurant, nightclub, and crafts shop, overlooks this pastoral junction, standing on the site of a cottage where Moore once lived. (You can have an Irish coffee here and listen to the hearty publican, an amateur Moore scholar, discuss the poet's works; he owns an 1889 edition of the poems with the noted tribute to the vale on page 200.) If time permits, visit the Motte Stone, signposted near the meeting. The large boulder marks the halfway point between Dublin and Wexford, and you can sit on its top and enjoy a fine view of the countryside. Legend has it that the boulder was the hurling stone of the giant Finn MacCool.

You can stop and watch the weaving process at *Avoca Handweavers,* in the small but friendly village of Avoca, about 3 miles south of the Meeting of the Waters (turn left at the sign for Avoca on the main road, and then left again after the bridge). The operation, in a cluster of stone buildings that was once a corn mill, employs about 30 people who prepare, roll, and weave the wool, about 75% of it for export. The remainder, as capes, ponchos, suits, vests, bedspreads, scarves, and so on, can be bought in the mill shop. Besides the handweavers, Avoca has a short main street that seems like a stage set with its three or four buildings, a few of them pubs, and several B&Bs on the main road near the bridge, including *Riverview,* a lovely one run by May Byrne, a retired schoolteacher and fluent speaker of Irish.

About 2 miles south of Avoca, the Aughrim and Avoca rivers form a second "meeting of the waters" at Woodenbridge, and though no poets have sung its praises, many travelers find it more beautiful than the first. The main road then bears eastward toward the coast and in 5 miles arrives at Arklow.

ARKLOW: This busy town at the mouth of the River Avoca has long been a fishing and shipping port and a boatbuilding center: *Gipsy Moth IV,* the yacht that took Sir Francis Chichester around the world, was built in an Arklow shipyard. The town is also a popular seaside resort, with beaches to the north and south of it, and it is the home of *Arklow Pottery,* the largest pottery manufacturer in Ireland. Arklow was founded by the Norsemen, and when they gave way to the Normans, it became the property of the Fitzwalters, ancestors of the Butlers, one of the most powerful families in Irish history. The decisive battle of the Wexford Rebellion of 1798 was fought here; the insurgent leader, Father Michael Murphy (not the same Father Murphy who led the pikemen in Wexford), lost his life in the battle and a statue of him, the 1798 Memorial, now commemorates his bravery.

Arklow Pottery, now part of the Japanese china company Noritake, employs over 200 people and has been making domestic earthenware since 1934. Though the plant is open to visitors by appointment only, there is a shop on the premises that's open daily, where you can buy seconds at discount prices. Golf, tennis, fishing, and boating are all possible in the Arklow vicinity, but the major attraction outside of town is about 10 miles north, at Brittas Bay. The 3-mile stretch of silver strand and sand dunes can be crowded with picnickers and bathers from Dublin on sunny weekends, but normally there's only a modest crowd.

 CHECKING IN: *Marfield House* – This 18th-century mansion was once part of the extensive Courtown estate and has been handsomely restored by owners Raymond and Mary Bowe. Some of the furniture belonged to the original estate, and the 12 bedrooms are elegantly decorated. There are beautiful staircases, marble fireplaces, and long windows that look out onto the spacious grounds and award-winning gardens. Vegetables and herbs grown on the premises appear in the dining room where the dinner menu can include such fare as crab salad, beef Wellington, and chocolate whiskey cake. On the Gorey to Courtown road, Gorey (phone: 055-21124). Expensive.

Tinakilly House – Once the home of Captain Charles Halpin, who laid the first successful cable connecting Europe with America, it is filled with seafaring memorabilia and paintings, family silver, and other precious heirlooms. Now run by the Power family, this house overlooking the Irish Sea has been completely refurbished. All 14 rooms have private baths, and most have marble fireplaces, needlepoint chairs, wood paneling, and antique Victorian furnishings. There's also a restaurant with three dining rooms, tennis courts, a sitting room with piano, and open fireplaces in all the public rooms. And all of it is set on 7 acres with gardens. About 2 miles south of Rathnew, right off the main Dublin road (phone: 0404-9274). Expensive.

Hunters – This 200-year-old coaching inn is now in the hands of the Gelletlie family's fifth generation. Flowering gardens along the banks of the River Vartry, part of the extensive grounds, also supply the inn's restaurant with fresh vegetables. 17 rooms, 10 with bath. Newrath Bridge, Rathnew (phone: 0404-4106). Moderate.

EATING OUT: *Singing Kettle* – Just 200 yards from the beach at Courtown, this lovely candlelight restaurant is run by the McGuinness family. Lunch and dinner daily, June through September; dinner only on Saturdays and Sundays the rest of the year. Ardamine, Courtown, about 10 miles south of Arklow (phone: 055-25151). Moderate.

Woodenbridge – Attached to one of Ireland's oldest hotels (c. 1601), this Tudor restaurant has a warm Old World atmosphere and features local produce and freshwater trout. Open for lunch and dinner; dancing, entertainment on weekends. Woodenbridge, near Arklow (phone: 0402-5146). Moderate.

En Route from Arklow – While the main road south follows the railway line to Wexford, the coastal road, a pleasant, quiet drive of about 40 miles, runs along a succession of sandy beaches in the sunniest and driest part of Ireland. Courtown is a lively resort during the summer; besides its 2 miles of beach, it has an 18-hole golf course, typical seaside amusements, and entertainment — Irish nights, *seisiún,* and disco dancing — at the *Sands* hotel. In August, the nearby town of Gorey, 3½ miles inland, hosts an arts festival that includes art exhibits, films, theater, and a variety of music from traditional Irish to jazz and rock. (The Church of St. Michael and Christ Church are among the things to see at other times of the year.) Farther south along the coast, the beaches continue almost uninterruptedly to Wexford, including especially good ones at Cahore, Kilmuckridge, Blackwater, and Curracloe, all backed by picturesque villages. South of Curracloe, where the River Slaney runs out to sea, the road crosses the bridge into Wexford.

WEXFORD: This town combines city sophistication with village warmth. Built on the River Slaney, its narrow streets date from medieval times, so leave your car outside the town proper or in the parking lot on the quays near the tourist office. Wexford was founded by the Vikings, taken by the Normans, suffered terrible destruction at the hands of Oliver Cromwell, then rose up in the Rebellion of 1798, when a local priest led his parishioners against the English armed only with pikes. Wexford has good singing pubs, restaurants, and hotels, but it is best known for its annual Wexford Opera Festival. For 12 days every October, rarely performed operas, new and old, are performed in the restored 19th-century Theatre Royal, sung by highly regarded, though not yet famous, opera singers from around the world. Wexford's normal population of 15,000 swells by about 6,000 at this time, and the whole town celebrates: There are singing pubs competitions, theater presentations, and other festival events. Be sure to have a drink at the intriguing *Crown Bar* on Monck Street, and at the *Thomas Moore Tavern* (the poet's mother was born in this house) in the Cornmarket. The *Bohemian Girl* at North Main and Monck streets is a good spot for lunch or an Irish coffee. For a full report on Wexford, its sights, restaurants, and hotels, see *Wexford,* THE CITIES.

En Route from Wexford – If you wish to visit Johnstown Castle, a 19th-century Gothic mansion now owned by the State Agricultural College, proceed south for about 3 miles via a country road. The grounds have lovely ornamental gardens, walks around artificial lakes, a picnic area, and the Irish Agricultural Museum, an interesting exhibition on farming and rural life. If not, start out on the road to Rosslare Harbour (T8 or N25). On a fine summer's day, this area southeast of Wexford is the stuff of poetry: Clean sea air sweeps over green hedges and down country roads little changed by the 20th century. Turn left at Killinick and head for Rosslare (branching left when the T8 bears right for Rosslare Harbour). Rosslare, or Rosslare Strand, is a seaside resort in the middle of a wonderful 6-mile beach, which is not its only attraction. Besides the beach, there are public tennis courts, an 18-hole golf course, a playground, fishing and boating, and *Kelly's Strand* hotel, which is a center of activity and a popular year-round retreat for the Irish.

The road south from Rosslare leads to the village of Tagoat and two possibilities. A left turn onto the T8 will take you to a selection of good hotels and restaurants in Rosslare Harbour, the departure point for ferries to Fishguard, Wales, and Le Havre and Cherbourg, France (but don't follow the road to the end, since it leads directly onto the boats). Go straight through Tagoat, and you will come to the tiny village of Broadway, with an enormous tavern and thatch cottages. Broadway is at the head of Lady's Island Lake, actually a sea inlet, and Lady's Island is in the lake, connected to land by a causeway. The ruins of an Augustinian priory dedicated to the Virgin Mary and a Norman castle with a curiously leaning limestone tower are on the island, which has been the object of pilgrimages for centuries and still is in August and September.

From Lady's Island, you can continue east to Carne Harbour, where there is more beach and a very good seafood restaurant, the *Bakehouse,* or return to Broadway and turn left for Kilmore Quay, one of the most delightful villages in Ireland. Kilmore Quay is a fishing village whose main street is no more than a cozy row of thatch cottages with a fisherman's cooperative at one end. You can hire a boat here to visit the great bird sanctuary of the Saltee Islands (phone Willie Bates at 29644), a 45-minute trip off the south coast of County Wexford. Bird-watchers should note that about three quarters of the total Irish bird species have been seen in the county, and most of these frequent either Great or Little Saltee, where they rub feathers with many rare migrant birds. Great Saltee (only a mile in length) was once inhabited and caves in its rugged, rocky cliffs were used as hideaways by insurgents after the Rebellion of 1798 was crushed. If you want to stay in the area, the small, modern *Hotel Saltees* in Kilmore Quay (phone: 053-29601, 29602) has a restaurant and pleasant accommodations, with rooms named after the various species of birds found on the Saltees.

Less than 20 miles northwest of Kilmore Quay is the town of New Ross, built on a steep hill of the River Barrow. You can spend an enjoyable 3 hours dining on the water aboard the *Galley Cruising Restaurants* (phone: 051-21723) whose dinner cruises depart from New Ross at 7 PM daily during the summer and according to demand in April, May, and September. Five miles south of New Ross, on L159, is the John Fitzgerald Kennedy Memorial Park, a splendid 480-acre arboretum commemorating President Kennedy, whose ancestors came from nearby Dunganstown. The park covers the lower slopes of Slieve Coillte, and if you drive to the top on a nice day, you'll see much of the counties of Wexford and Waterford. The city of Waterford is 15 miles southwest of New Ross and Kilkenny is 26 miles northwest.

South-Central Ireland

Despite the recent influx of industry and factories, Ireland is still very much a rural and agricultural country, and this journey will take you through some of the island's best farmland. Tipperary Town is in the midst of the Golden Vale, fertile acreage extending from the valley of the River Suir, east of town, across the border into County Limerick, west of town. The rich pastureland rolls down to Mitchelstown, County Cork, where the vast creamery of the Mitchelstown Cooperative Agricultural Society gathers in its bounty, and then on to the valley of the River Blackwater, no less known for bounty of another sort. The Blackwater, which cuts across County Cork on its way into the Celtic Sea, is popular with sportsmen, especially fishermen keen on the trout, perch, roach, dace, rudd, and, above all, salmon, in it and its tributaries.

Mountain scenery is not missing: South of Tipperary Town, the Glen of Aherlow is a romantic drive through the mighty Galtee Mountains — you might meet a donkey cart or two along the road. Farther south, two other ranges, the Knockmealdowns and the Comeraghs, become a palette of greens in the afternoon light. The route goes around these two, but a detour, a hairpin scenic drive called "The Vee," will take you through the former if you have the time. Nor is seascape missing: The route also leads along the Celtic Sea from Cobh, where the great passenger liners once docked, into Youghal, where a version of *Moby Dick* was filmed, past cliffs and miles of beach into quaint Annestown, the seaside resort of Tramore, and, finally, Waterford. The route turns inland again after Waterford to enter a landscape where historic castles guarding river banks are commonplace, then terminates at Cashel, one of Ireland's greatest historic sites. If you're lucky, you'll have bad weather for your explorations here. A little fog and mist add a dimension of mystery to the imposing Rock of Cashel, and you will almost be able to hear the old heroes of Erin clanging their armor as you pass through the ruins.

The south-central route forms a triangular loop that begins in Tipperary, goes south to the sea at Cobh, up the seacoast to Waterford, and then inland almost back to Tipperary, but turns north for Cashel at the town of Cahir. There are areas along the way where few tourists tread and hence they pro-vide a glimpse of Ireland without makeup — raw and beautiful. These quiet stretches are interspersed with the liveliness of good pubs, restaurants, and lodgings that are plentiful from Tipperary right back around to Cashel. The shingles of artists and craftsmen working at studios and kilns in tiny villages will suggest impromptu breaks in the itinerary from time to time, and the organized tour of the Waterford Glass Factory, where you'll see how the classic crystal is made, should not be missed. You'll visit a remote Irish-speaking area, one of the few pockets of Irish not on the west coast, and you'll see a castle you've probably seen before — in film. The route is one that blends the pleasure and hospitality of Ireland with the tranquillity and beauty that once made it the land of saints and scholars.

Hotels listed as expensive will cost $80 or more for a double; those listed as moderate will range from $50 to $75; and inexpensive ones will be $40 and under — well under in the case of the bed-and-breakfast houses included. Dinner for two (without wine) will cost $50 and up in an expensive restaurant; from $30 to $45 in a moderate one; and less than $30 in an inexpensive one.

TIPPERARY: "It's a long way to Tipperary" goes the famous World War I song, but this cozy town in the Golden Vale has developed a personality and prosperity that makes the journey worth the distance. Viewed from the footpaths of the hills just outside town, "Tip," as it is called by the locals, resembles a quiet New England village bordered by the green back of the Slievenamuck Mountains. But Main Street is a busy place lined with pleasant shops, entertaining pubs, and good restaurants. This is prime farmland, and many in the area are employed in the Tipperary Cooperative Creamery at the end of Bridge Street. Fenian leader John O'Leary was born in Tipperary, and the town was famous during the Land League Plan of Campaign of the 1880s, when residents refused to pay property rents to landlord Smith Barry and established a "New Tipperary" just outside the town borders. The shops and timber houses of Emmet and Dillon streets are still inhabited, although the plan eventually failed, especially when

Smith Barry discovered he owned the land on which a new butter market had been erected by the rebels and tore it down. Kiely's Breads now stands on the site of the butter market, near the town well. Tipperary has had a long history (it grew around a castle built here by King John in the late 12th century), but one that contrived to leave it with few very ancient or notable buildings (it was laid waste during the course of the Desmond Wars in the late 16th century). It is a friendly place, however, and to sample its hospitality stop at the *Irish House* on Main Street. Once a millinery, later a technical school, it has now been converted by Noel and Alice McInerney into a small shopping mall with a wine bar. The mall contains a large crafts shop and a hair salon, among other things, but the pride of *Irish House* is its self-service coffee shop, which resembles the inside of a spacious, old-fashioned farmhouse. The tables are student desks, lantern-shaped lights by local craftsman James McEvoy hang overhead; blackened kettles swing from the crane in the fireplace, and antiques line the mantel. The sandwiches and pastries are made by Mrs. McInerney, who also makes a first-rate Irish stew. Have a look at the guestbook, which includes the signatures of World War I veterans, lured to Tipperary by the Pied Piperish sound of its name. Elsewhere in town you can sip a pint of beer underneath a thatched roof in the *Kingswell* across the street, or have a quiet drink at *Sloane's* near the Maid of Aran statue at the end of Main Street. *Captain Sensibles,* a "supper-disco" within the nightclub *Dobbyns* on Main Street, is open until 2 AM every Saturday.

 CHECKING IN: *Glen* – This inviting 24-room hotel is on the drive through the Glen of Aherlow a few miles outside Tipperary. Glen of Aherlow, Tipperary (phone: 062-56146). Moderate.

Royal – Right off Main Street, this older hotel has 20 rooms, only two with private bath. Bridge St., Tipperary (phone: 062-51204). Inexpensive.

Clonmore – Many visitors come back a second time to this popular bed-and-breakfast house in an attractive bungalow run by Mary Quinn. Four rooms with hot and cold running water and regular B&B rates. Open April through October. Cork-Galbally Rd., Tipperary (phone: 062-51637). Inexpensive.

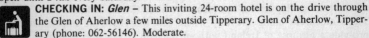 **EATING OUT:** *Brown Trout* – Long established and known for its inexpensive but good fare, ranging from sole on the bone to grilled trout. The *Brown Trout* is light on atmosphere but generous with portions. Bridge St., Tipperary (phone: 062-51912). Inexpensive.

En Route from Tipperary – Leave by Bridge Street and follow the signs south for the "Glen of Aherlow," a lovely valley between the Slievenamuck Hills and the Galtee Mountains, and a wending, scenic drive. Stop at the car park before the statue of Christ the King, from where there is a vast view of the valley into which time does not seem to have intruded. Two-story farmhouses are more common than modern bungalows, and donkey carts pulling containers of milk still travel the roads. Follow the signs to Galbally and then on to Mitchelstown, just over the County Cork border.

MITCHELSTOWN: This butter- and cheese-producing town is an interesting mixture of the old and the new. The Catholic Church of the Blessed Virgin Mary with its window-slashed brick interior overlooks Mitchelstown from Convent Hill and was opened in 1980. In contrast, Kingston College was erected in 1761 by the earl of Kingston, whose family laid out much of the town. The establishment is a collection of attached stone houses that open onto College Square. Originally built as almshouses for "decayed gentlefolk" as well as some of the families who worked for the Kingstons, it is now the home of about 30 retired couples. Each of the Georgian houses has a back garden and one house is set aside for community affairs, although daily life at the Kingston College once had its unharmonious moments. The houses used to share common entrances, but this gave way long ago to individual doorways so that feuding families would not have to meet. The extensive creamery run by the Mitchelstown Cooperative Agricultural Society can be toured (stop in at the communications office in New Square). The society, which began in 1917 and grew as small cooperatives merged with it, employs about 2,300 people and has 4,500 shareholders, all of whom are farmers. Before leaving Mitchelstown, try the pastries at *The Torten* on Cork Street or stop for a pint at one of the pubs, known for their evocative names — like *The Cave, Hunter's Rest,* and *The Blackthorn.* Mitchelstown Caves, two long, complex caves with large halls and interesting formations that can be visited with a guide, are 6 miles northeast, off the Cahir Road.

En Route from Mitchelstown – Drive due south 10 miles to Fermoy, a fairly large and busy town that was once prosperous as a garrison for the British Army and is now popular with sport fishermen. The town straddles the River Blackwater, one of the better-known salmon-fishing rivers in Ireland. The Blackwater rises on the Cork/Kerry border and flows 85 miles out to sea at Youghal, and the stretch of the river around Fermoy is the part that is best for salmon. The river is also coarse fishing competition water, with Fermoy as the fishing center that has hosted most of the championships. The tourist office (4 Patrick St., near The Square; phone: 025-3110) is run by genial Jack O'Sullivan, who will inform you about other activities in the area; there are numerous sports associations, including five hunt clubs. Castle Hyde House, the beautiful Georgian home of Douglas Hyde, the first president of Ireland, is just outside town, but it is privately owned and not open to the public. About 3 miles northwest of town (off the Glanworth Road) and worth a visit is Labbacallee or the Hag's Bed, one of the largest wedge-shaped gallery graves in the country. It looks like a pile of stones from the roadside, but closer inspection (climb over the steps in the stone wall at the side) reveals the massive shape of the two burial chambers covered by three immense capstones. It is guarded by several standing stones and dates from about 1500 BC.

From Fermoy, head south to Midleton and turn west onto the T12 (N25), dropping down to the T12A at the turnoff for Cobh. The route leads across a strip of water to Great Island (approximately 17 miles by 2 miles) and curves down and around its southern side to where Cobh (pronounced Cove) stands facing the greater part of Cork Harbour.

COBH: One of the nicest times of the year to enjoy this former port of call for the great transatlantic passenger liners is during the annual International Folk Dance Festival, a week of dancing, concerts, fireworks, and parades each July. The blue haze of a summer's evening settles over the harbor and the graceful tower of St. Colman's Cathedral high on the hill above gives it a medieval character that is heightened by the presence of European dancers mingled on the waterfront in traditional costume, singing Irish songs in foreign accents, and waving the flags of their country. The cathedral, though not medieval (it was built between 1868 and 1915), is Cobh's most striking feature. It tops off the hill of old houses built shoulder to shoulder in ascending height and, from the harbor, looks like a guardian angel hovering over so many members of a family posing for their picture. During the famine years, the harbor at Cobh was the last image of Ireland impressed on the minds of many thousands of Irish emigrants leaving their native soil on ships that all too often were not seaworthy enough to carry them to their destinations. The view then was without the cathedral, but those who survived the "coffin ships" to do well in the New World sent back money to help build this crowning touch to the town's skyline. Its exterior of Dublin granite is covered with statues and gargoyles, its interior features stained-glass windows and a 43-foot-high marble altar alive with carvings, and there are weekly concerts on the 47-bell carillon.

Until the 18th century, Cobh was a small fishing village accessible only by ferry and known simply as the Cove of Cork. In medieval times, it had belonged to an Irish chieftain whose son fought with Brian Ború against the Danes in the Battle of Clontarf (1014). Later, it became the home of Anglo-Irish families such as the Barrys, the Hodnetts, and the Roches, one of whose castles (the 14th-century Belvelly Castle) can be seen near the bridge on the way into town. The British began to develop the fishing village as a strategic naval base during the war with the American colonies. They erected a military barracks on the site of an ancient monastery across from Cobh on Spike Island (later used as a prison for Irish rebels and now an Irish army coastal defense station), and a naval station west of Spike Island on Haulbowline Island (now the site of a huge steel complex and headquarters of the Irish navy). Many of the town's streets were laid out during the 1800s, as Georgian and Victorian homes for British officers rose along Harbour Row. In 1838, the first transatlantic steamship sailed from Cobh, initiating an era of prominence for the town as an international passenger port, and in 1849, the Cove of Cork became Queenstown, renamed in commemoration of a visit by Queen Victoria. During World War I, both the British and the Americans used Queenstown's port facilities; when a German submarine sank the *Lusitania* off Kinsale in May 1915, it was from here that ships sailed to rescue the survivors.

Today, with its own name, Cobh is a holiday resort focused on its attractive harbor. The International Sailing Center, based near the town hall in an old house where equipment lies in colorful disarray, offers courses in sailing. Sea angling can be arranged through the Cobh Sea Angling Club. The Royal Cork Yacht Club across the harbor at Crosshaven dates from 1720 and is the oldest in the world. The Lusitania Memorial is in Roger Casement Square, where there are also some restored Italianate shops. A local museum is housed in a converted church on High Road. The rest of Great Island can be explored. Victims of the *Lusitania* disaster are buried in the Old Church Cemetery, about a mile north. Nearby at Carrigtwohill is Fota Island, an estate once owned by the Smith-Berry family and now in the care of University College Cork. The family home, built in the 1820s, is a splendid example of Regency architecture. Displayed inside is a private collection of Irish landscape paintings from the 1750s to the 1870s. (Open April through September, Mondays through Saturdays, 11 AM to 6 PM, Sundays, 2 to 6 PM; the rest of the year, Sundays and holidays only.) Also on the grounds are a wildlife center and an arboretum open to the public.

CHECKING IN: *Commodore* – This veteran hotel overlooks the waterfront. It has an Old World atmosphere, modernized facilities (about 33 of the 39 rooms have private baths), a lovely dining room serving excellent meals, and a heated indoor swimming pool, squash court, and sauna. Deep-sea fishing trips can be arranged. Cobh (phone: 021-811277). Moderate.

Rinn Ronain – Picturesquely set on the River Lee, this cozy hotel was once the home of J. P. Ronayne, a 19th-century Irish patriot. It has a picture-window restaurant and 21 rooms, newly renovated with private baths. Open year-round. Rushbrooke, Cobh (phone: 021-812242). Moderate.

En Route from Cobh – The main Cork-Waterford road (N25) leads east to Youghal. But there are several reasons to turn off the road at Castlemartyr and follow the signs to Ballycotton, stopping 3 miles short of the coast at the tiny village of Shanagarry. One is a meal or an overnight stay at *Ballymaloe House,* a small guesthouse and family-run restaurant that is one of Ireland's most delightful country hotels. Another is a stop and perhaps some shopping at the pottery studios of Stephen Pearce and his father, Philip. Stephen Pearce, whose brown pottery with frosty white glaze is his trademark, built a studio for himself deep in the Shanagarry woodland a few years ago and has ever since been turning out a distinctive line sold in stores around the world. Philip Pearce, working in a complex of farmhouses known as *Shanagarry Pottery,* turns out pottery in handsome blacks and whites. Before leaving the area, drive down to the cliffs at Ballycotton for a breath of sea air, then return to the main road for the drive east into Youghal.

CHECKING IN: *Ballymaloe House* – Myrtle and Ivan Allen opened a restaurant in their stone farmhouse in 1964, and a year later began taking overnight guests. Now travelers from all over the world have stayed at this 400-acre rural retreat, an experience something like paying a visit to country cousins. The high ceilings and spacious rooms of the farmhouse, actually part of an old Geraldine castle, have been handsomely renovated, and other buildings such as the gatehouse and lodge have been modernized to make a total of 30 rooms, all with private bath/shower. Facilities include a heated swimming pool, tennis courts, 9-hole golf, horseback riding, deep-sea fishing (at nearby Ballycotton), and a craft shop well stocked with local wares. Myrtle Allen's award-winning *Yeats Room* restaurant, and her cookbook, have spread the Ballymaloe reputation for fine food worldwide. The dining rooms are open daily, with a cold buffet on Sundays (reservations recommended). The Allens also run a year-round cooking school, with courses lasting from a weekend to 12-week intensive sessions. Shanagarry, Midleton (phone: 021-652531). Expensive.

YOUGHAL: Pronounced "yawl," this pleasant resort town has an old quarter and a 5-mile beach where the River Blackwater pours into Youghal Bay. The tourist office on South Main Street in the 18th-century Clock Gate (which once served as a prison where inmates were flogged and often hung from the windows for their rebellious plots) can give you a *Tourist Trail* booklet describing a signposted walking tour of the town. The trail will take you up (Youghal is built on a hill) and around the old town walls, which date from the 15th century and are among the best preserved in Ireland. St. Mary's Collegiate Church, dating from the 13th century, was damaged in 1579 when the town was sacked during the Desmond Rebellion, but it has been restored and is still in use. Nearby Myrtle Grove, an Elizabethan mansion (not open to the public but visible from the church), belonged to Sir Walter Raleigh, who helped put down the rebellion and was granted Irish lands by Elizabeth I for his effort. Raleigh, fresh from Virginia, is supposed to have planted Ireland's first potatoes on the property (and to have smoked the country's first pipe of tobacco here, too), but he probably never lived in the house, though he was the mayor, or warden, of Youghal for a time in 1588 and 1589. He sold the estate to Sir Richard Boyle, who rose from poverty to great wealth during Elizabeth's reign and became the first earl of Cork; a monument to him and his family is in St. Mary's. The tourist trail leads past the remains of Tynte's Castle, a tower house built by the English in the 15th century, and by the Benedictine Priory, which was Oliver Cromwell's headquarters during his Munster campaign of 1649 and is now partly converted into a tea shop. Stop for a rest here or have a drink in the *Moby Dick* lounge around the corner from the Clock Gate. The lounge gets its name from the film, starring Gregory Peck, made in Youghal some years back, and it is appropriately decorated. Other pubs worth a visit are the *Clock Tower,* the *Castle Tower Bar,* and *Harbour Lights.*

CHECKING IN: *Devonshire Arms* – This is a friendly, older hotel convenient to town; all 10 rooms have private bath. Open year-round. Youghal (phone: 024-92827). Moderate.

Hilltop – This modern hotel, just outside town, has a stone ice house from the 1800s on its grounds, as well as an outdoor swimming pool. All 50 rooms have private bath. Closed November through March. Youghal (phone: 024-92911). Moderate.

Monatrea House – Surrounded by farmland and overlooking Youghal Bay, this Georgian country house has 14 rooms (8 with baths), a first-rate dining room, outdoor seawater pool, tennis, sea and river fishing, and horses and ponies for riding. Closed November through mid-March. Ferry Point, Youghal (phone: 024-94293). Moderate.

EATING OUT: *Aherne's* – The best of the local catch is always on the menu here, including lobsters and oysters from the tank as well as succulent crab claws and giant prawns. Lunchtime bar food is plentiful. Open year-round; closed Mondays in winter. 162/163 N Main St., Youghal (phone: 024-92424). Expensive to moderate.

Salmon Cellar – In the cellar of the *Youghal Inn* and known for its seafood. Open May through September. Youghal (phone: 024-92592). Moderate.

Clancy's – Near the old train station by the bay, this restaurant/pub features a railway theme with hot bar lunches during the day and a seafood/steak menu for dinner. Open all year. Strand Buildings, Youghal (phone: 024-92615). Moderate to inexpensive.

En Route from Youghal – Waterford is 48 miles via the main (N25) route, but if you have time, explore some of the side roads along the way. Just north of Youghal, the road crosses the line into County Waterford, and a few miles farther along you'll come to a turnoff for Ardmore, a quaint village with impressive cliffs on Ardmore Bay (Ardmore means "the great height") and the site of many a shipwreck. There used to be an Irish college here whose students included Eamon de Valera and Maud Gonne MacBride. Ardmore is famous for the ruins of a monastery founded by St. Declan in the 7th century, though the buildings that remain are not quite that old. The 12th-century round tower is one of the tallest and best-preserved examples of this type of structure in Ireland. Near it is St. Declan's Church (or Cathedral), Romanesque style, also of the 12th century. St. Declan's Oratory (or Tomb) is a small church traditionally held to be the saint's grave.

Return to the main route and continue north toward Dungarvan, but turn off again before you get there and drive down to Ring, near Helvick Head. This is an especially beautiful spot in the evening, when you can sit on benches in the tall grass along the elevated waterfront and watch the sun set slowly behind the mountains as golden washes of light linger on Dungarvan Bay. Ring is a fishing village in the midst of the Waterford Gaeltacht, one of the few — and scattered — Irish-speaking areas left in Ireland. The Irish college here is half a century old and in the summer it is full of students learning the language and studying traditional music and dance. All signs in the area are in Irish, including the stop signs, which read "Stad." You might like to pause for a drink at *Mooney's,* a flagstone bar with a front deck overlooking the water, at the turn in the road leading toward Helvic Head.

Ring is only 5 miles south of Dungarvan, an administrative center for part of County Waterford and a town that comes alive with a market on Thursdays. North of Dungarvan, leave the main route again and take the coastal route, following signs for Stradbally. The road goes inland for a distance and then follows the seacoast through a somewhat isolated region where the wind sweeps over grassy cliffs. Just before Annestown, stop at *Waterford Woodcraft,* a woodworking studio turning out functional and ornamental pieces in native woods including yew, gathered in the nearby Comeragh Mountains. Annestown has a small beach and the distinction of being just about the only village in Ireland without a pub. Its name comes from Anna De La Pore, a Catholic relation of Lord Waterford, who is said to have given Cromwell only buttermilk to drink when he sought accommodation for the night. The coastal route leads next to Tramore, a lively seaside resort whose population nearly doubles in July and August. Tramore has a 3-mile beach with lifeguards on duty in summer (you can rent surfboards on the beach), a 50-acre amusement park, 18-hole golf course, horse racing (the most important meeting is in August), and many hotels. The tourist office in Railway Square (open July and August) is well stocked with literature about sports, entertainment, and restaurants in town. From Tramore, it is only 8 miles north on the T63 to Waterford.

◙ EATING OUT: *Seanachie* – The name of this thatch cottage pub/restaurant is Irish for "storyteller." Brother and sister Michael and Laurann Casey, he with an interest in Irish culture, she a graduate of Cordon Bleu in London, have converted old farm buildings into an intimate dining room and a rustic bar where locals lift a few jars while raising their voices in ballads. The barnyard is now a courtyard for dancing. Open for lunch and dinner, and the food is varied. 5 miles south of Dungarvan on the main road, Dungarvan (phone: 058-46285). Moderate.

WATERFORD: Ireland's fourth largest city is a busy port on the banks of the River Suir. Reginald's Tower, built by Reginald the Dane in 1003, protected the small Viking settlement from invasion for a time, but in 1170, the Normans captured Waterford anyway, and the centuries of Anglo-Norman domination in Ireland began. The tower, now a museum, is Waterford's most prominent landmark, but the city also has several 18th-century churches and public buildings and the remains of once-extensive medieval abbeys. Waterford is best known, however, for the crystal that bears its name, and you can watch it being blown and cut as you tour the Waterford Glass Factory, about 1½ miles from the center of town on the Cork Road. Tours take place on weekdays, except for the first 3 weeks in August. No crystal is sold at the factory, but you can buy it in town. For more information on the city's sights, accommodations, restaurants, and entertainment, see *Waterford,* THE CITIES.

En Route from Waterford – The town of Carrick-on-Suir is 17 miles northwest via the T13 (N24). On both sides of the river, partly in County Waterford and partly in County Tipperary, the town was another of the seats of the Butler family of Kilkenny Castle. The Elizabethan manor house built (around 1600) by "Black Tom Butler," the tenth earl of Ormonde, is in a style uncommon in Ireland, probably because Black Tom had spent time in England and built it hoping to entice his cousin, Queen Elizabeth I, for a visit. What remains of a 15th-century Butler castle, much damaged by Cromwell, is behind the manor house. Be sure to stop at *Shanahan Willow Crafts* on Chapel Street in Carrick-on-Suir. John Shanahan learned to make baskets from his father, who learned it from his father, who opened the shop in 1886. The nimble fingers of John and his brother, Michael, have woven some most unusual things — 10-foot goal posts for polo games and passenger baskets for hot air balloons — but their most popular items these days are shopping baskets and baby cradles, and the prices are quite low for such skillfully crafted, handmade goods. After Carrick-on-Suir, continue on the T13 to Clonmel, another 13 miles.

CLONMEL: According to legend, ancient settlers were led to this town — "meadow of honey" in Irish — by a swarm of bees. It is the chief town of County Tipperary, an administrative, horse-breeding, and cider-making center. St. Patrick is said to have visited the area, which eventually passed into the hands of the powerful Anglo-Norman Butler family. In 1650, the town fell to Cromwell, but only after a very stiff resistance led by Hugh Dubh O'Neill. Clonmel runs along the River Suir, with wide O'Connell Street as its major thoroughfare. The Main Guard, a 17th-century building at the eastern end of the street, is said to have been designed by Christopher Wren and has been used as a courthouse, prison, and military headquarters. At the other end is West Gate, a 19th-century rebuilding of one of the town's original gates (you can see a portion of the old 14th-century town wall in the graveyard of St. Mary's Church of Ireland on Mary Street). A plaque on one side of West Gate commemorates Laurence Sterne, author of *Tristram Shandy* and a native of

Clonmel. Be sure to stop by the 19th-century St. Mary's Catholic Church on O'Connell Street to see the ceiling and the ornate altar with statues; the latter is supposed to have been made for a church in Rome but mysteriously ended up here. The Franciscan Friary on Abbey Street has a 13th-century choir wall, a 15th-century tower, and a tiny chapel to St. Francis that is a beauty when the sun shines through the reds and oranges of its modern stained-glass windows. Near the entrance is a tomb of the Butler family. (Press the light switch on the wall at the side for a better look at the knight and lady carved on it.) The library on Parnell Street houses a museum of local interest. Also on Parnell Street is *Hearn's* hotel, which at one time was the base of operations for the first Irish passenger transport system. In 1815, Charles Bianconi, an Italian-born resident of Clonmel, sent a horse-drawn carriage to Cahir. The number of vehicles and his network grew, and until the coming of the railways, "Bianconi cars" carried people all over the south of Ireland.

Clonmel has regular horse-racing meetings, weekly greyhound racing, good fishing in the Suir, and pony trekking into the Comeragh Mountains from Ballymacarbry (about 9 miles south of Clonmel). If time permits a detour, there is a magnificently scenic drive through the Knockmealdown Mountains southwest of town. Take the road to Ardfinnan and then on to Clogheen, where a left turn leads to a height of 1,700 feet and the hairpin curve known as "The Vee." The descent brings you into Lismore, a town on the River Blackwater, and the site of Lismore Castle. Built in the 12th century and remodeled in the last century, it is not open to the public though its gardens are. (The castle itself can be rented by the week; for reservations, call 058-54424 several months in advance.) The village of Cappoquin is 4 miles east of Lismore, also on the river, and the stretch of valley between the two is especially beautiful. From Cappoquin, you can return to the route by following the main Dungarvan road (T30) east as far as the turnoff to the T27, then driving the 20 miles north to Clonmel. Slievenamon, the "mountain of the women," rises to a height of 2,368 feet northeast of Clonmel; it is said the legendary giant Finn MacCool watched while girls raced up to its summit to win him as a husband.

CHECKING IN: *Clonmel Arms* – This comfortable and nicely furnished hotel in town has an elegant dining room. All 35 newly decorated guestrooms have private bath. Sarsfield St., Clonmel (phone: 052-21233). Moderate.

***Hearn's* –** The starting point of Charles Bianconi's transport system still has the clock he used to keep the cars on schedule. This pleasant establishment has 25 rooms, more than half with bath. Parnell St., Clonmel (phone: 052-21611). Moderate.

EATING OUT: *La Scala* – In an old limestone building with original rustic log wood and red brick decor, this restaurant's menu includes beef fondue, stroganoff, chicken vol au vent, crêpes del mar, lasagna, and flambée desserts. Market St., Clonmel (phone: 052-24147). Moderate.

En Route from Clonmel – Take the N24 west for 10 miles to Cahir. The lands of the Butlers also extended to Cahir (meaning "stone fort" and pronounced Care), where the family served as the earls of Glengall. Richard, the second earl of Glengall, helped plan much of the town, somewhat to his financial ruin. He commissioned John Nash to design the local Church of Ireland (1817) and also the Swiss Cottage Fishing Lodge in Cahir Park. The wallpaper, which can still be seen on the cottage walls, was imported from Paris. The town is small but pleasant and it prospers from what seems to be an annual influx of film makers to Cahir Castle, one of the largest and most splendid medieval castles in Ireland. Parts of *Barry Lyndon* were made here, as were scenes of several other recent films. Built on a rocky inlet in the River Suir where an ancient ring-fort may once have stood, the castle dates mainly from the 15th century. It was thought to be impregnable, but it was captured by Robert Devereux, earl of Essex and

Queen Elizabeth's favorite, in 1599, and by Cromwell in 1650, though each time it returned to the hands of the Butlers. It is now restored and open to the public year-round. Cashel is 11 miles north of Cahir via the N8.

CHECKING IN: *Kilcoran Lodge* – A few miles outside Cahir, on the right side of the Mitchelstown Road, this former shooting lodge is a charming country hotel on the slope of the Galtee Mountains. Recently renovated, it now has 15 spacious rooms, all with private bath. The cuisine in the airy dining room is good. Cahir (phone: 052-41288). Moderate.

Carrigeen Castle – If you're up for a night in a cell, stop by this unusual bed-and-breakfast house run by Peggy Butler on the road to Cork. Built solidly in stone, complete with turrets, it used to be a jail and Peggy and her husband have turned the seven cells into four cozy guestrooms decorated with antiques. Hot and cold running water in all rooms; bed-and-breakfast rates. Cork Rd., Cahir (phone: 052-41370). Inexpensive.

EATING OUT: *Earl of Glengall* – This restaurant serves tasty pub lunches, including Irish stew and steak and kidney pie, at very reasonable prices. Castle St., Cahir (phone: 052-41115). Moderate.

Crock of Gold – The restaurant on the upper level of this little shop serves light meals daily from 9 AM to 9 PM. Castle St., Cahir (phone: 052-41951). Inexpensive.

CASHEL: Dominating the market town that bears its name is the Rock of Cashel — Cashel of the Kings — the history of which spans sixteen centuries. From the 4th century, the kings of the province of Munster were crowned on this limestone rock rising proudly from the surrounding plain and they had their palace here. St. Patrick preached Christianity on the site in the 5th century and Brian Ború was crowned here in the 10th century. In 1101, his grandson, King Muirchertach O'Brien, gave the Rock to the Church and a period of great ecclesiastical building began. Even the roofless buildings retain their grandeur, but tiny Cormac's Chapel, still roofed, is a gem of Irish Romanesque architecture. Built between 1127 and 1134 by Cormac MacCarthy, both a king and a bishop, it is now wedged into an angle formed by the choir and the south transept of the sprawling cruciform cathedral, the largest building on the Rock, added in the 13th century. The three-story archbishop's castle, actually a fortified residential palace, was added to the western end of the cathedral in the 14th or early 15th century. The oldest structure on the Rock is the 12th-century round tower outside the north transept of the cathedral (as is usual for these watch towers, storehouses, and refuges in time of danger, the door is well above the ground). One of the first monuments to greet the visitor entering the top of the Rock is the 12th-century Cross of St. Patrick. Its base is traditionally said to have been the seat of the king whom St. Patrick baptized here. Also in the grouping is the 15th-century Hall of the Vicars Choral, which housed laymen who participated in the cathedral services. The Rock is floodlit at night in the summer — an impressive sight, and there are guided tours, after which you can explore the town itself. On John Street, the Cathedral of St. John the Baptist, Church of Ireland, is a fine 18th-century classical building, which became the cathedral when the one on the Rock was abandoned. The building adjacent to it houses the Diocesan Library, an extensive collection of 16th- and 17th-century books. *Grant's* hotel on Main Street was formerly Quirke's Palace, and parts of it date from the 15th century. The *Cashel Palace* hotel, also on Main Street, was the palace of the Protestant archbishops when it was built in the 18th century in lovely Queen Anne style. Cashel Folk Park, between the hotel and the path up to the Rock, has a museum, dairy kitchen, forge, and craft shop; frequently, there are Irish dancing demonstrations and folk music. The ruins of a medieval Dominican Priory are also near the center of town. Before you leave, be sure to visit some of Cashel's craft shops: *Rossa Studio Pottery* and *Shanagarry Weavers* are two good ones on Cahir Road.

CHECKING IN: *Cashel Palace* – Edward Lovett Pearce, who designed the Parliament House in Dublin, designed this red brick building (c. 1730) as a residence for Protestant archbishops. It sits back off Main Street and has lovely gardens behind. Paneling, columns, and handsome marble fireplaces grace its interior. Its 20 rooms have private baths. Of the 2 restaurants, the *Bishop's Buttery* features light meals all day long, while the *Four Seasons* is the dinner venue. Cashel (phone: 062-61411). Expensive.

***Dundrum House* –** Built in 1730 as a private residence and later used as a convent school, this Georgian country manor was completely renovated in the 1970s to become a gracious hotel. It has since been expanded to 50 rooms, all with private bath. Other features include a fine restaurant, stained glass in the lounge, tennis, horses, plus 100 acres of gardens and a trout-filled river. Dundrum, Cashel (phone: 062-71116). Expensive.

***Rectory House* –** Ancient trees and flowering bushes line the driveway to this 19th-century house, which once belonged to a Church of Ireland rector. Now a 10-room (all with private bath) hotel run by Stephanie and Paul Deegan, it has a very good dining room with candlelight and a homey lounge bar where residents gather around the open fireplace. Dundrum, Cashel (phone: 062-71115). Moderate.

EATING OUT: *Chez Hans* – This excellent restaurant, in a small Gothic chapel at the foot of the Rock of Cashel, has lots of atmosphere. Dining is by candlelight, and the chef-owner is skillful with veal, beef, and seafood. Rockside, Cashel (phone: 062-61177). Expensive.

***Pepper's* –** Tom Egan's restaurant has been growing in popularity since it opened in 1980. Steaks are the specialty. The building itself, one of the oldest in Cashel, dates from the 17th century and was once a blacksmith's shop. It's now painted forest green and is open for lunch and dinner as well as tea. 23 Main St., Cashel. Moderate.

West Cork

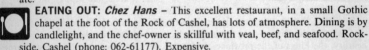

Although often overlooked in favor of its more famous neighbor, Kerry, West Cork is a very special part of Ireland. Here the landscape is a palette of infinitely changing colors, and the terrain varies from the soft shoulders of the inland Shehy Mountains to the sandy coves along the southern coast. Around Bantry Bay — an area kissed by the warm and gentle Gulf Stream current — you'll see lush palm trees and much other subtropical foliage. Pointing to several soaring 80-foot eucalyptus trees, one Corkman boasted: "The trees in this part of Ireland grow as tall as those in Disney cartoons!"

But scenic beauty is by no means Cork's sole attraction. Its fine bathing strands, climbable peaks, excellent fishing waters, and busy marinas make the area a paradise for sports lovers. In addition, there are many lively, cheerful villages where pub regulars have formed singing groups; small mountain towns where the lilt of the ancient Irish tongue is still heard; remote and lovely places where time has stood still. Even on the road, visitors will feel warmly welcomed. Everybody waves: The child on a bicycle beams; the farmer in the field looks up to lift an arm in salute, and conversations at cottage gates pause as heads turn and a chorus of hands are raised in greeting.

Our route, which begins and ends in Cork City, traces a leisurely circuit around West Cork. First stops are the towns of Macroom and Irish-speaking Ballingeary, and next is the historic, lovely lake of Gougane Barra. We continue west to balmy Bantry Bay, then south and east to the picturesque villages of Skibbereen, Clonakilty, and Kinsale. The entire route is about 130 miles and can be covered easily in 2 days.

Except perhaps in high season, it's fairly safe to ramble along without reservations, although many places are open only from May to October. A wide selection of accommodations is possible, from bed and breakfast in a simple bungalow to a fine meal and elegant room in a former mansion. Expect to pay around $80 and up per night for a double in those places listed as expensive; from $50 to $75 in moderate; and under $40 in inexpensive. A meal for two will cost about $50 and up in a restaurant listed as expensive; between $30 and $45 in moderate; and under $30 in inexpensive. Prices don't include wine, tips, or drinks.

CORK: For a detailed report on the city, its sights, hotels, and restaurants, see *Cork,* THE CITIES.

En Route from Cork – Route T29 takes you along the north bank of the River Lee and passes through the charming villages of Dripsey, with its woolen mills, and Coachford.

MACROOM: At the center of town stands Macroom Castle, granted to Admiral William Penn by Oliver Cromwell in 1654. (Penn, once governor of Kinsale, was the father of William Penn, founder of Pennsylvania; the younger Penn also spent several years in Ireland handling the family estates.) Over the years the castle underwent much strife and was burned for the final time in the Irish Civil War in the early 1920s. The ruins have been declared a monument and partly restored. There's a 9-hole golf course nearby on a steep slope overlooking the Sullane River.

Macroom owes its existence to its location near the confluence of three rivers — Lee, Laney, and Sullane — where people have gathered to barter and swap food and produce for centuries. It's still a thriving market town, with an annual agricultural show in summer. Posters for this show advertise competitions for "horses, cakes, sheep, and honey" — a compelling collage of images and flavors!

En Route from Macroom – Go back 1 mile on the Cork road and turn south onto R584 for Inchigeelagh. Past Inchigeelagh the road hugs the north bank of the long and lovely Lough Allua. But the minor road along the south bank is even more beautiful, so that's the one you should take.

BALLINGEARY: This village is in the heart of the Gaeltacht — an Irish-speaking district — in West Cork, and every summer young people flock here from all over the country to study in school-sponsored Irish language programs. Villagers, however, will greet you in a perfect and often mellifluous English. There's a very good craft shop in the village, run by the Quill family, which produces and sells handsome garments made from the skins of sheep and goats. Just two doors from this shop is the birthplace of Cardinal Manning, the archbishop of Los Angeles.

Make a right turn 3¾ miles beyond Ballingeary, where the sign reads Gougane Barra. The fork in the road is marked by a large crucifixion tableau and a memorial to local poet Máire Bhuí Ní Laoghaire.

GOUGANE BARRA: The mountain-encircled lake of Gougane Barra, source of the River Lee, is where St. Finbar, the founder of Cork, had his hermitage in the 6th century. Joined to the lakeshore by a causeway is an island with a modern Irish Romanesque chapel. The isolation and serenity of the place makes it immediately apparent why this valley was chosen for monastic contemplation. The surrounding area is a beautiful forest park with picnic areas and hiking trails. Fishing is free, although you may not catch anything; as one local put it, "St. Finbarre let everybody fish free, and that was about a thousand years ago, so I don't expect there's much left to catch."

Return to R584. Continue southwest as the road descends via Keimaneigh Pass and the Ouvane Valley to Ballylickey and Bantry.

 CHECKING IN: *Gougane Barra* – The dining room at this 34-room hotel has lovely views of the lake and hills. If given notice, the owner will lend you a boat. Open April to October. Gougane Barra (phone: Ballingeary 026-47069). Inexpensive.

BANTRY: This is the home of the spectacular, mostly Georgian-style Bantry House. Once the seat of the earls of Bantry, the mansion is furnished with antiques, tapestries, and paintings chosen by the second earl of Bantry during his travels in Europe in the 18th century (open daily, 10 AM to 6 PM; admission charge). It is surrounded by elegant terraces and gardens and looks out over beautiful Bantry Bay.

Bantry is the perfect base for those interested in water sports; there's a fine beach and facilities for skin diving and water skiing (check at the Tourist Office on New St.; phone: 027-50229).

 CHECKING IN: *Ballylickey House* – This lovely Georgian mansion was gutted by fire in 1983, but its cottages and a couple of apartments in the main house reopened the next year. The gardens and grounds were unharmed and remain as beautiful as ever. Amenities include an outdoor swimming pool and poolside restaurant. Open mid-March to mid-October. Ballylickey (phone: 027-50071). Expensive to moderate.

Sea View House – A cheery and colorful country house full of family heirlooms, the pride and joy of owner Kathleen O'Sullivan. Amenities include extensive gardens, outdoor deck/patio, panoramic views of Bantry Bay, and a very good restaurant as well as 13 rooms, 7 with private bath. Open March through October. Ballylickey (phone: 027-50073). Moderate.

Westlodge – A modern, 104-room hotel, surrounded by mountains on one side and Bantry Bay on the other. There's a restaurant–grill room, tavern, indoor pool, sauna, all-weather tennis court, squash courts, and jogging trail. About 1 mile outside Bantry on the N71 coastal road (phone: 027-50360). Moderate.

Shangri-La – A modern, private residence with hotel-type comforts (6 rooms, 5 with private bath, wine license restaurant, and car park), it overlooks Bantry Bay just outside the village. Open all year. Bantry (phone: 027-50244). Inexpensive.

EATING OUT: *Blair's Cove* – On a country lane southwest of Bantry overlookng Dunmanus Bay, in a renovated stone barn with a 250-year-old Georgian courtyard. Specialties include seafood, beef, and lamb grilled on an oak fireplace, a buffet of help-yourself appetizers, and a grand piano that doubles as a dessert trolley. Open Easter to mid-October; dinner only except Sundays and Mondays; open weekends except January and February. Durrus/Barley Cove Rd. (phone: 027-61127). Expensive.

En Route from Bantry – Continue along the eastern shore of Bantry Bay; soon the road leaves the sea, and the landscape becomes a great patchwork of farm fields, with colors changing every mile. This region has enjoyed a great surge of affluence in the past decade and the prosperity is reflected in freshly painted farmhouses and neatly kept yards. In West Cork, as elsewhere in Ireland, cattle are the mainstay of the economy. (The human population of the entire Republic is just over 3 million; the cattle population often reaches 9 million.) On the road, you will often have to stop your car to give way to lumbering herds, although the Cork farmer may not be leading his cattle on foot, but instead nudging them along with his Mercedes-Benz. One local wit remarked, "Americans can grumble all they like about oil sheiks, but here in Ireland we have milk sheiks!"

From Ballydehob you can drive directly to Skibbereen or try a scenic side trip westward on the road down the peninsula. First on the detour is Schull, a little village popular with fishermen and sailors; a deep-sea angling competition is held here in July and a regatta in August. Follow the road to Goleen, where you can sunbathe on the fine strand, then press on to Crookhaven, a pretty harbor town with some small beaches. A few miles farther are the dramatic cliffs of Mizenhead, the southernmost point in Ireland. Instead of backtracking, you can go back to Schull and Ballydehob via the northern route across the peninsula, which passes Mt. Gabriel (1,339 feet) and the well-preserved castle of Dunmanus, one of the many 15th- and 16th-century strongholds that dot this part of the country.

CHECKING IN: *Ard Na Greine* – On its own secluded grounds just a mile outside the village and harbor of Schull, this 18th-century farmhouse became a country inn during the 1970s. With 7 rooms, all with private bath, it's a delightful retreat with a seafood restaurant, fully licensed pub, and extensive gardens. Open April through September. Schull (phone: 028-28181). Expensive to moderate.

Barleycove Beach – On a cliff overlooking the Atlantic, this complex includes 50 rooms and chalets (all with private bath), indoor heated pool, tennis court, fishing, and a 9-hole golf course. Barley Cove, near Goleen (phone: 028-35234). Moderate.

SKIBBEREEN: This town offers some very good fishing in the nearby Shepperton, Ballinlough, Lissard, and Ballyalla lakes (tackle and boats may be rented). It's also a convenient jumping-off point for exploring the shores and islands of the quaintly named Roaring Water Bay. Eight miles to the southwest, the little town of Baltimore has been for hundreds of years one of Ireland's more popular ports of call due to its sheltered harbor. You can go fishing and boating here or take the Cape Clear Island ferry over to this Irish-speaking island, with its megalithic stones, ancient church, bird observatory, and youth hostel. There's also a ferry to Sherkin Island, with its ruins of a Franciscan friary and an Outdoor Pursuits Centre, with facilities for hiking, skin diving, riding, and boating.

CHECKING IN: *Ardnavaha House* – About 5 miles from Clonakilty, with 40 acres of woods, meadows, and gardens, this renovated Georgian manor house has a modern extension of 36 rooms, all with private bath and balcony or terrace. Restaurant, heated outdoor pool, sauna, tennis court, horses and riding stables with arena. Open Easter to October. Ballinascarthy (phone: 023-49135). Moderate.

Liss Ard House – Only the freshest vegetables, meat, and fish are served in the dining room of this recently renovated Georgian mansion surrounded by its own lovely estate. The 10 luxurious rooms, half of which have private bath, are furnished with antiques. There's also a weekly session of traditional Irish music. Skibbereen (phone: 028-21109 or 21511). Moderate.

En Route from Skibbereen – It's a very pretty and relaxing drive along the coast road to Kinsale; each small town is worth a look for its particular attraction. There's a ruined castle and prehistoric stone fort at Castletownshend; Glandore offers good fishing; Rosscarbery is the site of a monastery established by St. Fachtna in the 6th century; Clonakilty, close to many fine beaches, is also the home of the West Cork Regional Museum; and the Franciscan abbey in Timoleague dates from the 14th century.

KINSALE: Clinging to a hill overlooking the Bandon River estuary, Kinsale is an appealing little town (pop. 2,000) whose tall, whitewashed houses huddle together along narrow, twisting lanes. A morning's stroll along the signposted walking tour will take you through the town's most charming streets and past St. Multose Church, an impressive stone structure dating from the 13th century. The wide and sheltered harbor at Kinsale is one of the most scenic in Ireland, and since the building of a modern marina in 1979, it has become a favorite port with British and European yachtsmen. Deep-sea fishing, off the Old Head of Kinsale, can be arranged — try the Kinsale Angling Centre, c/o *Blue Haven* hotel (phone: 021-772209), or the Trident Hotel Angling Centre (phone: 021-772301) — and the swimming and sunning are very fine on the neighboring strands at Sandy Cove and James Fort. Another — but no less essential — attraction is the town's growing reputation as the "culinary capital of Ireland." There is, for the town's size, an extraordinary range of really top-class restaurants whose proprietors sponsor an annual Gourmet Festival in October; they are all members of the Kinsale Gourmet Food Circle.

Kinsale is also an important footnote in Irish history, for it was here in 1601 that the Irish forces, led by the chieftains Hugh O'Neill and Hugh O'Donnell, suffered their final defeat at the hands of Queen Elizabeth I's army, led by the English Lord Mountjoy.

From Kinsale, it's just 18 miles back to Cork city.

CHECKING IN: *Acton's* – This member of the Trusthouse Forte hotel chain has a terrific location facing the harbor, extensive rose gardens, a seafood restaurant, and a nautical tavern. There are 58 rooms, 41 with private bath. Closed January and February. The Waterfront, Kinsale (phone: 021-772135). Expensive.

Blue Haven – In the middle of the village, this small, cozy hotel has 10 individually decorated rooms, 7 with bath. But the star attraction here is the dining room's platters of local crab, mussels, and lobster and its fish casseroles, veal Cordon Bleu, and duck baked in brandy. The paneled bar has log fires, seafood soups, and sandwiches. Open year-round. Pearse St., Kinsale (phone: 021-772209). Moderate.

Perryville House – A Regency building, this small hotel offers 10 rooms with bath, a pleasant restaurant and bar, views of the harbor, and an edge-of-town location. Open April through October. Long Quay, Kinsale (phone: 021-772731). Moderate.

EATING OUT: *Cottage Loft* – About a mile outside town on the James Fort road and right on the water, this converted cottage is almost alpine in design, but with all the warmth of an Irish hearth. Featuring a range of dishes from seafood kebab and sole on the bone to Peking pork and duck in black cherry sauce. Castlepark, Kinsale (phone: 021-772803). Expensive to moderate.

Coyle's – This small, intimate reataurant specializes in seafood and seasonal dishes such as sea trout *en papillote,* black sole with oysters, brace of quail with bacon, and rack of lamb. Fisher St., off Lower O'Connell St., Kinsale (phone: 021-772664). Expensive to moderate.

Man Friday – Beautifully situated in its own garden, this friendly restaurant has a rustic decor and a menu ranging from prawns Napolean and Polynesian chicken to shellfish nouvelle. Scilly, Kinsale (phone: 021-772260). Expensive to moderate.

Vintage – This vine-covered, beamed little restaurant stands in a winding street near the harbor. The cooking is imaginative, with particular emphasis on local produce. Choices include noisettes of lamb, free-range duckling, medallions of monkfish, and *wiener schnitzel*. Main St., Kinsale (phone: 021-772502). Expensive to moderate.

Bernard's – The emphasis is on new Irish cuisine in a modern bistro setting, with entrées ranging from wild rabbit in cider and chicken stuffed with oysters to a medley of salmon and sole or Kinsale seafood bouillabaisse. Milk Market, Kinsale (phone: 021-772233). Moderate.

Max's Wine Bar – This tiny but busy bistro serves simple meals — salads, soups, oysters, and slices of lasagne. Main St., Kinsale (phone: 021-772443). Inexpensive.

Kinsale is also famous for its assortment of lively public houses. Try the *Greyhound* or the *Anchor* for pub grub, or the *Dock* for memorable views of Kinsale's inner harbor. Pubs known for their music and entertainment include the *Spaniard, Shanakee,* and *Folk House.* Other pubs as intriguing as their names are the *White House, Hole in the Wall, Silver Salmon,* and *Lord Kingsale.*

En Route from Kinsale – From Kinsale, it's just 18 miles back to Cork City. Any of several routes will get you there; R600 passes by Cork Airport.

The Ring of Kerry and the Beara Peninsula

Artists and writers have for centuries celebrated the beauty of the Kingdom of Kerry, where the majesty of Ireland's highest mountains contrasts starkly with romantic glens, and the splendor of the rugged coastline gives way to glorious lakes and luxurious forests. It is a landscape of great variety, with the sea and ever-changing patterns in the sky as much a part of it as the primordial shapes of solid ground or the seasonal come-and-go of blossoming bushes and trees or the green ground cover. A good portion of this southwestern county is made up of three peninsulas that constitute Kerry at its picturesque best: Dingle, Iveragh, and Beara, the latter shared with County Cork.

The best known of these mountainous projections into the Atlantic is the middlemost one, the Iveragh Peninsula, circled by a famed scenic route known as the Ring of Kerry. Browse through a brochure of bus tours of the Emerald Isle and a day trip around the Ring will rarely be missing. Nor will a stop in Killarney, both the gateway to the Iveragh Peninsula and the focal point of an enchanting district of mountains, lakes, and valleys that would put it on the map even if the Ring happened to be nowhere handy. Because Killarney is definitely on the beaten path and takes advantage of it, the town has its detractors who will point out that it is more of a tourist center than a representative Irish city and none the prettier for this transformation. Its fans will answer that Killarney has long been a tourist attraction and that there is no denying the beauty of the surroundings that made it so.

In truth, Killarney has relied heavily on tourism since the mid-eighteenth century when the local magnate, Lord Kenmare, developed the trade and four major roads were opened to the outside world. In the nineteenth century, Victorian travelers became the most enthusiastic of visitors. Killarney's purple glens, silent glades, ruined castles, and fairy isles afloat on misty lakes appealed to the Victorian imagination, and the journals of their travels are breathless with wonderment at what they saw and replete with apologies for their inability to convey its magic on their pages. Twentieth-century visitors can take heart. The enthralling scenery around Killarney hasn't changed at all, and if the parking lots of the town's hotels are filled with tour buses, its streets are also lined with pony traps and jaunting cars. Just as the Victorians would be swaddled in lap robes and stashed in the back of a horse-drawn carriage, so, too, will today's jet-age traveler be tucked in and trotted out of town in the turf-scented morning, off to affront the Gap of Dunloe.

Even back then there was disdain for the traveler on too tight a schedule. William Makepiece Thackeray, in his *Irish Sketch Book* of 1843, had little good to say of the "man coming from his desk in London or Dublin and seeing 'the whole lakes in a day.' " But many visitors today choose to do just that, to have time to push farther west to more open vistas on the wilder peninsulas. Out on the edge of Europe, these provide unforgettable sights of mountains and bare headlands meeting water in a splash of surf, of sandy coves, of offshore islands spotting the distant sea.

The Iveragh Peninsula is the most traveled, but an air of remoteness clings to it still in tiny fishing villages where Irish is spoken and in ancient stones left behind by forgotten peoples. Ascetic monks who withdrew as far as they could from the world built their retreat on Skellig Michael, and the deserted site can be visited today. According to George Bernard Shaw, "No experience that the conventional tourist travel can bring you will stick in your memory so strangely; for Skellig Michael is not after the fashion of this world."

This route begins in Killarney and explores the lakes around it, then proceeds around the Ring of Kerry in a counterclockwise direction from Killorglin to Kenmare. From Kenmare, it turns south to Glengarriff (a fair number of palm trees will linger in your mind along with pictures of peat bogs; the warm Gulf Stream causes Mediterranean flora to prosper in this corner of Ireland with the conviction of converts). Glengarriff is the starting point for a loop around the least traveled peninsula, Beara. (Dingle, the most northerly of the three Kerry peninsulas, is treated in a separate tour route.) Hotels encountered along the way are rated as in the rest of our Irish listings: $80 and up for a double room in an expensive hotel; from $50 to $75 in a moderate one; and under $40 in an inexpensive one. A meal for two in a moderate restaurant will range from $30 to $45 without wine, while prices in expensive and inexpensive restaurants will naturally fall above and below that.

KILLARNEY: This lively marketing town is on the itinerary of almost every visitor to Ireland not so much for itself as for what lies around it. The lakes of Killarney and the mountains that hold them are in a boulder- and rock-strewn location of unrivaled natural beauty sculpted by the Ice Age and trimmed with woods of oak, cedar, mountain ash, juniper, holly, hawthorn, and the arbutus — or strawberry tree — the special botanic glory of the area recognizable by its small, glossy dark green leaves, white flowers in spring, and brilliant red berries in autumn and winter.

The three main lakes stretch through a valley in the mountains south of the town, with Killarney located on the largest, the Lower Lake, or Lough Leane. The Muckross peninsula separates the Lower Lake from the Middle Lake (also known as Muckross

Lake), which is in turn connected to the Upper Lake by a narrow strait called the Long Range. The district includes the 11,000-acre Bourne Vincent Memorial Park, once a private estate whose owners presented it to the Irish government, which promptly turned it into a national park. Do not miss Muckross House, the focal point of the park, 3½ miles from Killarney on the road to Kenmare (open daily Easter through October; closed Mondays the rest of the year). The 19th-century manor house of the estate contains furnished period rooms upstairs and a folk museum in the basement where a working weaver, potter, and blacksmith bring the display to life. Around the house, Muckross Gardens are especially glorious in May and June when the azaleas are in bloom and giant clumps of rhododendrons are ablaze with color.

Killarney's scenic mountains and lakes can be explored by car, taxi, bicycle, boat, pony, or on foot, but the most traditional way is by jaunting car — a horse-drawn wagon on which you and your companions sit back to back behind the driver and face the roadside. Visitors with the time for a leisurely exploration will not be at a loss to fill it, but those without that luxury will find that the standard tour routes set up by jaunting car and taxi drivers (at set rates; check with your hotel or at the tourist office) do cover the highlights.

The first, most comprehensive, and most spectacular route (a full-day tour available from May to October) is the trip through the Gap of Dunloe, a 4-mile long gorge between Macgillycuddy's Reeks and Purple and Tomies mountains, southwest of Killarney. You'll leave town by the Killorglin Road, passing the ruins of Dunloe Castle perched on a bend of the River Laune. Dating from 1207, the castle was a Gaelic stronghold for 400 years until temporarily rendered uninhabitable by Cromwellian forces. In the 18th century one Donal O'Mahony, although a Catholic, maintained a feudal state here with a private militia of 4,000 men, and as far as Dublin Castle was concerned, he was as ungovernable as any medieval baron. At *Kate Kearney's Cottage,* a former coaching inn turned snack bar, pub, and souvenir shop at the entrance to the Gap of Dunloe, you'll transfer to the back of a pony or to a pony and trap (another of the traditional carts carrying visitors through the lake area) for the trip through the gap itself. (If you've driven your own car, you can park it here, but you'll have to come back for it later by taxi or jaunting car, which you might want to do anyway. *Gap of Dunloe Industries,* run by Michael Moriarity, is just about 100 yards short of the cottage, and is a good place to shop for jackets, capes, sweaters, scarves, blankets, and other Irish goods you might not want to take with you on horseback.) For the next 4 miles, you'll pass through an extraordinarily remote and gloomy scene, with massive rocks on either side and an accompanying narrow stream widening here and there into sullen lakes. One of them — Black Lough, or Serpent Lake — is where St. Patrick is supposed to have drowned the last snake in Ireland, and to this day it is without fish. Emerging from the gap, the wooded Upper Lake, still 3 miles away, comes into view and Black Valley stretches off in the distance to the right. You'll stop for a picnic lunch (or bring your own) when you reach Brandon's Cottage near the lake shore, then board a boat for the trip down the lakes: From the Upper Lake, considered to be the most beautiful of the three, the boat turns into the Long Range, which grows progressively swifter until the boatman "shoots the rapids" at the Old Weir Bridge into a beautiful calm spot called the Meeting of the Waters. After a look at Dinis Island, rife with shrubs and arbutus, you'll cross the Middle Lake (the mountain rising steeply above is Torc Mountain and it will be covered with rhododendrons in late spring) and row under Brickeen Bridge into the Lower Lake. Among its 30 islands, the most noteworthy is Innisfallen Island, with remains of a small church and an Augustinian priory of the 11th and 12th centuries. Innisfallen was the site of a monastery and important educational center for 1,000 years beginning in the 7th century — one of its students may have been Brian Ború himself. A major Irish historical source, the *Annals of Innisfallen,* compiled here from the 10th to the 14th century, is now in the Bodleian Library in

Oxford. The tour ends at the ruined 15th-century Ross Castle, the last stronghold in Ireland to stand against Cromwell's troops. From here, a jaunting car returns visitors to town. Note that it is possible to drive through the Gap of Dunloe, but if you do, the recommended route is in the opposite direction, coming down from Moll's Gap, and then not until the late afternoon when the last of the ponies will have gone by.

The second standard itinerary is the half-day jaunting car tour of the Muckross estate to Muckross Abbey, Muckross House, and the Torc Waterfall. The entrance to Bourne Vincent Memorial Park is 3 miles from Killarney, and once inside, it is another ½-mile trot through the greenery and past herds of grazing Kerry cattle, an old Irish breed, to the remarkably well-preserved Muckross Abbey. Founded in 1448 by the Irish chieftain MacCarthy Mor and completed 50 years later, the abbey is mainly, but not entirely, Gothic, as is evident from the cloister: Two sides have pointed arches and two have rounded arches, indicating a change in style during the course of its construction. See the yew tree in the middle of the cloister (it is supposed to be as old as the abbey, but probably isn't), then go upstairs to see where the friars lived until the abbey was suppressed by the Cromwellians in 1652. The tour next takes in Muckross House and Gardens and then proceeds to Dinis Island and to the Torc Waterfall, where the waters of the Devil's Punch Bowl fall 60 feet into a leafy glen and a winding path leads above the fall for a view over the lakes. Motorists can do this route, too, by following the Kenmare Road, though some walking will be necessary to see Muckross Abbey, since only pedestrians, bicycles, and jaunting cars are allowed into the section of the park near it. Muckross House has its own entrance farther along the Kenmare Road, where cars may drive in as far as the parking lot.

The third standard jaunting car itinerary, the half-day trip to Aghadoe Hill, can also be done by car. Start out on the Tralee Road, following the signs for Aghadoe, which may have been a pagan religious site prior to becoming a Christian settlement even before the time of St. Patrick. The ruins here include the stump of an 11th-century round tower, a stone church of the same period, and a later, much truncated castle, but it is the Viewing Point just beyond the *Aghadoe Heights* hotel that is the main attraction. The entire Killarney area, from the spire of Killarney Cathedral on the left, clear across to Macgillycuddy's Reeks and the Iveragh Mountains beyond, is visible in one sweeping panorama.

Killarney town has hotels, restaurants, lively singing pubs (try *The Laurels* on Main Street), a racecourse, two beautifully situated golf courses, and ample opportunity for fishing — the catch is trout or salmon and you'll see fishing boats tucked away everywhere around the lakes. Few buildings have architectural merit, though St. Mary's Cathedral on New Street, designed by Pugin and built between 1842 and 1914, is ranked among the finest examples of the Gothic Revival in Ireland. Killarney also hosts Pan Celtic Week in May, a week of song, dance, and sport by gathered Celts from Scotland, Wales, Cornwall, Brittany, the Isle of Man, and, of course, Ireland.

CHECKING IN: *Europe* – It has a marvelous location on the shore of the Lower Lake as well as a heated indoor pool, sauna, horseback riding, fishing, bicycling, and billiards. The 168 rooms vary in size and degree of luxury; many have balconies. There are two restaurants: The main dining room and a more intimate second room are good but not wildly exciting. Closed December, January, and February. Fossa, Killarney (phone: 064-31900). Expensive.

Killarney Great Southern – Most of the 180 rooms (all with bath/shower) of this 1850s ivy-covered hotel have recently been refurbished and 10 new deluxe suites have been added. The public areas have also been revitalized, though there is still a roaring fire glowing in the lobby as you enter this "grand dame" of Killarney hotels, and the Waterford crystal chandeliers remain. The elegant dining room is as large as a ballroom; for a haute cuisine meal, try the adjoining *Malton Room,* an intimate à la carte restaurant. Indoor heated pool, saunas, tennis; golf and fishing nearby. In the summer there is entertainment four nights a week by the National Folk Theatre of Ireland. Killarney (phone: 064-31262). Expensive.

Dunloe Castle – This is not an old Irish fortress but a modern, German-owned hotel near the Gap of Dunloe. (The actual Dunloe Castle is on its grounds, however.) All 140 rooms have private bath, and other amenities include a heated indoor pool, sauna, tennis, and croquet. Open May to October. Beaufort, Killarney (phone: 064-44111). Expensive to moderate.

Aghadoe Heights – This modern hotel is small — 55 rooms that are less than luxurious but make up for it with fine, panoramic views of the lakes. The service is friendly and the rooftop restaurant is quite good. Closed December to March. Aghadoe, Killarney (phone: 064-31766). Moderate.

Castlerosse – Also beautifully situated, this is a low, motel-style hotel adjoining one of Killarney's championship golf courses. It has 40 rooms with bath. Closed November to mid-March. Killarney (phone: 064-31144). Moderate.

Ross – In the town center, this hotel is warm, friendly, and family owned and run. The restaurant is simple but tasteful, with very good service. There are 40 rooms, all with bath, plus self-catering apartments. Killarney (phone: 064-31855). Inexpensive.

EATING OUT: Dingle's – The decor of this basement bistro is a blend of old church pews, arched ceilings, and cozy alcoves. The menu includes chicken curry, chili con carne, beef Stroganoff, and Irish stew as well as some exceptional seafood dishes. Closed Mondays through Wednesdays in winter; open nightly the rest of the year. 40 New St., Killarney (phone: 064-31079). Moderate.

Foley's – A delightful Georgian place, decked out with flowers, candlelight, and a fireplace, it offers seafood specialties — mussel soup, Dingle Bay scallops and salmon — as well as steaks. The brown bread scones are home-baked. On weekends a tuxedo-clad pianist plays traditional Irish tunes and classical and contemporary music. 23 High St., Killarney (phone: 064-31217). Moderate.

Gaby's – The Flemish couple who run this good seafood restaurant also offer some cooking from their homeland. The atmosphere is bright and nautical with light knotty pine wood and blue-and-white- and red-and-white-checked tablecloths; there's a lobster tank at the entrance where you can pick your own. Closed Sundays and December to March. 17 High St., Killarney (phone: 064-32519). Moderate.

En Route from Killarney – The coastal road around the Iveragh Peninsula, known as the Ring of Kerry, is one of Ireland's most famous scenic drives. The complete circuit of the peninsula — which extends nearly 40 miles southwest of Killarney and has an average breadth of 15 miles — is an approximately 110-mile round trip that will take most of one day to see in a leisurely way. It is possible to do it counterclockwise as described below (from Killarney to Killorglin and around) or clockwise (from Killarney to Kenmare and around), but the former route is suggested because some of the scenery is seen to best advantage in that direction. (Tour buses take the same route, but they do it to be on the inside of the sharp curves in the often narrow road.) Do not attempt this scenic run if there is a sea mist, because you will see little, or during heavy and continuous rain — though the latter seldom lasts more than half a day. If in doubt, you should be able to get a weather report by phoning the Valentia Meteorological Station (phone: Cahirciveen 27).

From Killarney, take R562 for Killorglin. The jagged mountains to the left of the road are Macgillycuddy's Reeks, reduced to stumps by 200 million years of ruthless erosion but crowned, nonetheless, by the highest peak in Ireland, Carrantuohill (3,414 feet). Eight miles from Killarney, take the signposted turn left for Ballymalis Castle, on the banks of the Laune. This is one of a line of castles originally built by the

Anglo-Normans when they overran the area in the early 13th century. The present castle — recently partly restored — is a typical 16th-century tower house of four stories: the ground floor for storage; the second for defense; the third for sleeping; and the top, a single, splendid living room. Return to the road and continue the remaining 5 miles into Killorglin.

KILLORGLIN: The presence of another Anglo-Norman castle, now almost totally ruined, gave rise to this small town on the River Laune. Killorglin is famous for its Puck Fair, actually a 3-day horse, sheep, and cattle sale accompanied by unrestricted merrymaking. Held every year from the 10th to the 12th of August, it is the area's greatest festival and draws people from all over County Kerry. On the first day, called Gathering Day, men of the town go into the mountains and capture the "puck," or wild male goat, who is then decorated with ribbons and enthroned on a platform above the town square from where he presides over the festivities until Scattering Day, the end of the fair. In the meantime, shops are open day and night. The Puck Fair has been going on for a long time but its origins are uncertain. It may date from the worship of the Celtic god Lúg or it may be an upstart from the 17th century, when a herd of wild goats stampeded the town ahead of approaching Cromwellian soldiers and thereby saved many lives.

En Route from Killorglin – Continue southwest on N70 for the 9 miles to Glenbeigh. Along the way, you will pass Caragh Lake inland on the left, and if you detour to it, you will find it surrounded by magnificent scenery (the parking place up the rough road is one viewing point and another is at the end of the path leading to the top of the hill).

GLENBEIGH: This tiny holiday and fishing resort is situated at the foot of Seefin Mountain (1,621 feet), not far from where the River Behy flows out into Dingle Bay. The Glenbeigh Horseshow, a semicircle of hills from Seefin to Drung Hill, is known to nature lovers as one of the county's most scenic mountain walks. At the end of the village are the gaunt — and burnt — ruins of Glenbeigh Towers, built by the local landlord, Lord Headley, in the 1870s. His architect was an Englishman who kept the famous actress, Ellen Terry, as a mistress during the years of construction, and had the bailiffs as constant visitors after Lord Headley took local action against him for cost overruns, leaking walls, and a leaking roof. A right turn onto an unclassified road beyond Glenbeigh leads, in 1½ miles, to Rossbeigh Strand, a long spit of land reaching into Dingle Bay to nearly meet its counterpart, Inch Strand, coming across the water from the Dingle Peninsula. The 2 miles of sand beach are backed by dunes and at the end of the spit is a 19th-century stone tower built to guide ships into Castlemaine Harbour. In the 18th century, many transatlantic ships, driven by terrifying southwest storms, met their end at Rossbeigh, sometimes helped, it is said, by shipwreckers greedy for their cargo. Also remembered in the area are some much more remote incidents that occurred here — those connected with the Fenian cycle of Irish legends. Ossian, the son of Finn MacCool (who was the leader of the Fianna, a sort of standing army of the Iron Age), had met the beautiful, golden-haired Niamh, who persuaded him to return with her to her own kingdom. Together the pair mounted the girl's white horse and galloped out along the Rossbeigh spit into the western ocean to the paradisal Land of Youth. Ossian came back 300 years later, but once off the horse he immediately turned into a very old man. Another famous story is that of Diarmuid and Grainne, daughter of the king of Ireland, who was betrothed to Finn, whom she found too old. Instead, she forced Diarmuid, a handsome young Kerryman, to elope with her. With a gang of murderous desperadoes (hired by Finn) in hot pursuit, they fled — first to a cave at Glenbeigh. The chase lasted 7 years and eventually Diarmuid was killed (by a magic boar) and Grainne did marry Finn, but in popular speech, many Irish prehistoric tombs are still called "beds of Diarmuid and Grainne."

CHECKING IN: *Ard na Sidhe* – Elegant, quiet, and beautifully secluded in the forest at Caragh Lake, this was once a private home. All 20 rooms have private bath. To find *Ard na Sidhe,* "hill of the fairies" in Irish, look for the signs on Route N70 between Killorglin and Glenbeigh. Open May through August. Killorglin (phone: 066-69105). Moderate.

***Glenbeigh* –** Here the beauty is in the gardens. There are 18 old-fashioned rooms, 11 with bath, and the restaurant is good. Glenbeigh (phone: 066-68204). Inexpensive.

EATING OUT: *Towers* – This hotel restaurant specializes in seafood at night and hearty pub lunches during the day; the hotel has 22 modernized rooms, all with bath. Closed November to March. Glenbeigh (phone: 066-68212). Moderate.

En Route from Glenbeigh – The main road to Cahirciveen, a distance of 17 miles, encompasses some of the most memorable scenery of the Ring of Kerry. The road rises to Mountain Stage, so called because it was once a station for stagecoaches, and hugs the side of Drung Hill (2,104 feet), providing wonderful views of Dingle Bay and the mountains of the Dingle Peninsula beyond. A cairn near the top of Drung Hill is reputed to be the grave of St. Finian, a major leader of the great religious movement of the 6th and 7th centuries. The road continues high over the sea to Kells, a small resort on Kells Bay, where it descends to a broad valley running on to Cahirciveen. A mile short of the town, just beyond the sharp turn left indicated by a series of striking yellow arrows, the ruins of Carhan House can be seen. Daniel O'Connell, the national leader — known as the Liberator — who achieved emancipation for Irish Catholics, was born here in 1775.

CAHIRCIVEEN: Set on the Valentia River at the head of Valentia Harbour, Cahirciveen grew up in the early 19th century. Its most notable building is the O'Connell Memorial Church on Main Street, meant to honor the centenary of Daniel O'Connell's birth in 1875, but only begun in 1888 when the cornerstone, sent by Pope Leo XIII from the catacombs in Rome, was laid. Across the bridge, about 2½ miles northwest of town, are the remains of Ballycarbery Castle, which had been, in the 15th century, the magnificent castle of MacCarthy Mor, guarded by the old Gaelic O'Connell family as seneschals. Cromwell's forces destroyed the castle in 1652 and drove the O'Connells to County Clare, though they later returned to the area (a junior member eventually moved to Derrynane). The ruins of an ancient stone fort, Cahergal, are nearby, and another, Leacanabuaile, is a few hundred yards away. The latter, dating to the 9th or 10th century, is one of very few of these stone forts to have been excavated. Inside, the remains of three stone beehive houses, once occupied by a very poor farming community, were found, along with a square house apparently added later. Note the souterrain, originally an escape hatch, a place of refuge, and also a place for storage.

Valentia Harbour (you'll get a good view of it at the bridge) was well known in the 18th century as a smuggling port and hiding place for privateers. British naval vessels often anchored here, too, but the smugglers earned their tolerance with judicious gifts of brandy. Valentia Island, 7 miles by 2 miles, is in the harbor, joined to the mainland by a bridge at Portmagee. Its inhabitants live by fishing, farming, and some tourism — the sea fishing is especially good and so are the views from its steep cliffs. The island is one of the most westerly points in Europe, and the first transatlantic telegraph cable, which came to Valentia in 1866, was in use for 100 years.

En Route from Cahirciveen – The Ring of Kerry route (N70) turns inland across the tip of the Iveragh Peninsula to Waterville, 11 miles away. Three detours along the way are possible, however: to Valentia Island (where there's good deep-sea fishing), to the offshore monastic site of Skellig Michael, and to the tiny village of Ballinskelligs on Ballinskelligs Bay. The turnoff for Portmagee and the bridge to Valentia Island is 4 miles southwest of Cahirciveen on N70 and the turnoff for Ballinskelligs is 2 miles beyond that, also on N70. Skellig Michael, one of the Skellig Rocks, can be reached by boat from Portmagee or Valentia Island, but only when the weather permits.

VALENTIA ISLAND: Seven miles long and 2 to 3 miles wide, this tiny island is now connected to the mainland by a newly constructed bridge. Knightstown, at Valencia's eastern end, consists of one main street, a lovely harbor and waterfront, and is a popular holiday resort renowned for its deep-sea fishing. Also in Knightstown is the old Western Union cable office, the receiving station for the first messages sent across the Atlantic in 1858.

SKELLIG ROCKS: These two small islands, pyramids of rock actually, are 7 and 8½ miles off the coast of Bolus Head. Little Skellig (445 feet high), the smaller of the two and all but inaccessible by boat, is a bird sanctuary with thousands of seabirds, especially gannets, nesting on its precipitous stone peaks. Bird life — puffins, razorbills, kittiwakes, gannets, and more — is abundant on Great Skellig (714 feet), or Skellig Michael, as well, but this island is better known for the remains of the simple monastic settlement that existed here for six centuries. Founded, according to tradition, by St. Finian and occupied by hermit monks between the 6th and 12th century, the monastery has survived in almost perfect condition, probably because of the absence of frost in this mild westerly climate. Six beehive huts, intact and of advanced construction; two oratories evolving into the boat-shaped style that would be used at Gallarus on the Dingle Peninsula; a ruined medieval church; crosses and graves; even tiny patches of imported earth behind retaining walls where the monks may have attempted to grow something to vary their diet of seaweed, birds, and fish, are located on a rock shelf 550 feet above the sea. Three steep stone stairways, corresponding to the three separate landing places whose use once varied according to weather conditions, lead to the settlement. Boats for Skellig Michael leave only if the weather is suitable — a calm day when the wind is not coming from the east. The trip takes 1.5 hours one way from Portmagee, the point of departure closest to the island (the trip can also be made from Knightstown on Valentia Island and from Bunavalla, below Coomakista, farther along the Ring of Kerry). Allow at least 3 hours for exploration. The climb to the monastery by the most commonly used route consists of more than 600 steps, but once there, the site — which must have been terrifying in fierce Atlantic storms — is extraordinarily evocative and beautiful.

BALLINSKELLIGS: The blessing of a 4-mile beach along the western shore of Ballinskelligs Bay has made this tiny, partly Irish-speaking village a seaside resort. It is part of the Kerry Gaeltacht and in the summer a language school for children is conducted here. The ruins of a 16th-century MacCarthy castle are west of town, not far from the remains of an Augustinian monastery that was probably founded in the 12th or 13th century by monks returning from the monastic settlement of Skellig Michael. The ruins date from the 15th century and are much eroded by the sea.

From Ballinskelligs, follow the signposts for Waterville; when you turn right onto the main route 6 miles northeast of Ballinskelligs, you'll be just above the bridge over the River Inny, 2 miles north of Waterville.

WATERVILLE: This small unspoiled village lies on a strip of land between the Atlantic Ocean and beautiful Lough Currane, on the eastern shore of Ballinskelligs Bay. Mountains rise from the east and south of the lake, several islands float in it, and in addition to Lough Currane, there are many smaller lakes in the vicinity. With all this water, Waterville is a famous angling center almost by default. Fishing for salmon, sea trout, and brown trout is free on Lough Currane and some of the smaller lakes, and by permit (available from hotels) on still others and the River Inny. No aquatic pursuit is ignored: There is boating, bathing from the fine sandy beach on the bay shore, and, for resolute landlubbers, golfing on a championship course. Many early Christian remains — stone forts, religious settlements, beehive huts, and old roadways — are scattered around Lough Currane and the ruins of a 12th-century Romanesque church are on a small island, Church Island, in the lake (you can hire a boat in Waterville if you wish to make the excursion). Waterville and Ballinskelligs Bay figure in many legends. According to one, Noah's son and granddaughter landed here after having been excluded from the Ark. According to another, the alignment of four stones on the skyline to the left of the road 1 mile south of town is the burial place of Scéné, wife of one of the eight leaders of the Milesians in the last, and greatest, of the legendary invasions of Ireland.

CHECKING IN: *Waterville Lake* – This deluxe resort is just south of Waterville in a setting of unparalleled beauty on the shores of lovely Lough Currane, within a stone's throw of the sea, and it makes the most of the panorama around it. Sports facilities include an 18-hole championship golf course (the first in Ireland to have electric golf carts), heated indoor pool, thermal spa pool, sauna, and solarium. Open May through September. Waterville (phone: 0667-4133). Expensive.

***Butler Arms* –** A well-known fishing hotel in town, this rambling, crenellated white house has been run by the same family for three generations and was a favorite haunt of Charlie Chaplin. Its restaurant, specializing in shellfish, is quite good. The 37 rooms, 27 with bath, are open May through mid-October. Waterville (phone: 0667-4144). Moderate.

EATING OUT: *Huntsman* – Furnished with dark oak priory tables and chairs, wrought iron fixtures, and colorful hanging plants, this chef-owned restaurant provides lovely waterside views with its seafood delights. Open for lunch, dinner, and light snacks from noon to 10 PM daily; closed November through March. Waterville (phone: 0667-4124). Expensive to moderate.

***Smuggler's* –** A renovated farmhouse with a nautical decor and panoramic views all round, this, too, is chef-owned. Seafood specialties such as lobster Newburg, meat and poultry dishes, and selections from an extensive bar menu are offered daily, noon to 11:30 PM. Closed November through February. Cliff Rd., Waterville (phone: 0667-4330). Expensive to moderate.

En Route from Waterville – Traveling south on Route N70, the road winds up to a height of 700 feet at the pass of Coomakista and offers superb views. While the inland mountains rise sharply — to 1,600 feet — on one side, the lonely Skellig Rocks can be seen beyond the mouth of the bay on the other side, out in the open Atlantic. The road descends in the direction of Derrynane Bay, separated from Ballinskelligs Bay by a point of land called Hog's Head, and from the Kenmare River (even though this arm of the sea extending inland as far as Kenmare is in places as much as 5 and 6 miles wide, you'll only occasionally see it called Kenmare Bay) by another point called Lamb's Head. Before the village of Caherdaniel, a signposted road to the right leads to Derrynane House, ancestral home of the O'Connell family, with a magnificent beach to the front of it and a more sheltered one at the side. The O'Connells were a shrewd

Irish family who lived by smuggling, importing embargoed goods, and exporting young Catholic Irishmen to European educations and jobs denied them at home. Daniel O'Connell, the first Irish Catholic member of Britain's Parliament, inherited the Derrynane property from an uncle and lived here during his political life, often holding consultations on the lawn with troubled constituents who would gather from miles around to speak to him. The house has now been restored and is open daily year-round as a museum with O'Connell's personal possessions and furniture. It is part of Derrynane National Historic Park, which also includes a nature trail through lovely scenery.

Next along the route, Caherdaniel, near the shore of Derrynane Bay, takes its name from a stone fort or *caher,* possibly of the 6th century, a short distance outside the village. Near it are the ruins of a much older fort and what would seem to be an ancient road system used some 4,000 years ago to link copper mines in the mountains above with the harbor at Derrynane. The route then continues along the coast toward the small resort of Castlecove. Just short of the village a signposted left turn points the way to Staigue Fort, 2½ miles off the main road, beautifully positioned at the top of a valley that stretches to the sea.

STAIGUE FORT: Nothing is known of the history of this circular stone fort, which could date as far back as 1000 BC. Though such forts are plentiful in the area, Staigue is one of the largest and most sophisticated, a masterly example of drystone construction (without use of mortar). It is also one of the best preserved of all ancient Irish structures. Little has been lost of the wall, which is up to 18 feet high on the north and west sides, 13 feet thick at the base, and is scaled by sets of steps up to a long-gone rampart. The area enclosed is 90 feet in diameter, but contains no signs of houses, as at Leacanabuaile, leading to speculation that the fort — which has yet to be excavated — may have been occupied by nobility. In Iron Age times, the poor lived in stone houses; royalty and aristocracy rated perishable wooden ones. Admire the quality of the fort's stonework, the sloping back of the walls, the massive lintels, and, especially, the architectural flourish of the steps inside; and on your way back to Castlecove, look for a stone bridge with two spans on the left — apparently in a field going nowhere — part of an old road system. Close by is an exposed rock with copperworkers' scribings.

En Route from Staigue Fort – About half a mile beyond Castlecove village, a road branches off the main route to White Strand, a particularly pleasant beach with beautiful views and good bathing. The route then bends inland to Sneem, 13 miles from Caherdaniel, climbing through a low pass where there is a fine panorama of the Sneem valley with its great backdrop of mountains stretching as far — just dimly to be seen — as Macgillycuddy's Reeks beside Killarney. The glacial basins or corries in the mountains on the left were scooped out by the Ice Age, and antiquities of the Bronze and Iron ages — old fields, roads, settlements, standing and scribed stones — are scattered around them.

SNEEM: With its pink, green, bright red, robin's-egg blue, and even checked houses freshly painted each year, this is a very colorful and pretty village at the head of the Sneem River estuary. The town is divided in two by the river and it has two village greens. Just before the narrow bridge between them, note the tiny Protestant church on the left, with its curiously Elizabethan air, a piece of 18th-century antiquarianism. Because Sneem is in fishing country (trout and salmon abound in the river and nearby mountain lakes), the church's weathervane sports a salmon. Stop after the bridge to look at the river tumbling over the rocks below, quite gently usually, but spectacular after a heavy rain. Just beyond is the very attractive Italianate, 19th-century Catholic church on the right. You'll also want to stop at the *Blue Bull* — a pleasant country pub and restaurant — if only for a quick drink.

EATING OUT: *Blue Bull* – This charming pub has three different rooms. The walls are decorated with fascinating old prints of County Kerry scenes, and, appropriately, a straw blue bull's head also commands attention. In the summer, a back room becomes a seafood restaurant, and there's music on most weekends throughout the year. Sneem (phone: 064-45231). Moderate in the restaurant; inexpensive in the pub.

En Route from Sneem – The Ring of Kerry route turns southeast toward the shore of the Kenmare River. A mile down the road a detour signposted "Oyster Bed" (so called because oysters grow here) leads down to a pier where you can savor the calm of the approaching garden spot before returning to the main road and driving the remaining mile to Parknasilla. Known for its lush trees, shrubs, and beautiful seascape, Parknasilla owes its subtropical vegetation to its position in a sheltered curve of coastline backed by the 895-foot Knockanamadane Hill. The *Great Southern* hotel, on the grounds of the onetime summer home of Charles Graves, Protestant bishop of Limerick and grandfather of the poet Robert Graves, was a favorite holiday place of George Bernard Shaw. From Parknasilla, the Ring of Kerry road runs east toward the upper end of the Kenmare River. Beyond Blackwater Bridge, in a forest on the right, is Dromore Castle, the seat of an old Gaelic family, the O'Mahonys, and the subject of a haunting lullaby. Also on the right, on a rock 2 miles out of Kenmare, are the ruins of Dunkerron Castle, a stronghold of the O'Sullivan family, branches of which occupied both sides of the Kenmare River from the early 13th century until they were driven out by the Cromwellians in the 17th century.

 CHECKING IN: *Great Southern* – George Bernard Shaw stayed here at least twice annually for a period of almost 15 years; more recently, Queen Juliana of the Netherlands has been a guest. This luxury hotel (not to be confused with Killarney's *Great Southern*), built on the verdant grounds of a former private estate in 1896, is carefully and splendidly done in Victorian style, while amenities are up to the minute. There are 60 rooms with private bath, a private (9-hole) golf course for guests, a heated indoor swimming pool, and fishing or boating on the bay. The cuisine is very good. Closed November through March. Parknasilla (phone: 064-45122). Expensive.

KENMARE: This attractive town sits in a limestone niche surrounded by old red sandstone at the point where the River Roughty runs into the head of the sea inlet known as the Kenmare River. The location makes it an ideal base for touring either the Iveragh Peninsula to the north or the Beara Peninsula to the south. Kenmare is a planned, landlord's town, laid out according to the instructions of the first marquess of Lansdowne in 1775. A number of houses are built of the local limestone and there is a fine Roman Catholic church with striking roof timbers. Next to it is the Convent of the Poor Clares, founded in 1861 and well known because of its lacemaking school; the famous point lace and other types produced here are on display daily. The town's oldest monument, the Druid's Circle, is beautifully placed on the banks of the River Finnihy on Kenmare's outskirts and dates back to the Beaker folk, copper miners who arrived from Spain 4,000 years ago. This is a circle of 15 stones with a large boulder in the center, an example of a form frequent in and mainly confined to this peninsula. Such circles were places of worship, but may also have had secular, ceremonial use as well as astronomical significance — and there is some evidence that human sacrifice was practiced in them.

Kenmare shares the mild climate common to the south coast and the subtropical foliage evident at Parknasilla is to be seen here, too. There is bathing in the sheltered coves west of the town, extensive salmon and trout fishing, and opportunity for deep-sea fishing. The annual Fruits de Mer Festival, usually held in September, underscores all this aquatic abundance with lots of deep-sea fishing, seafood exhibitions and banquets, and a wide range of entertainment.

CHECKING IN: *Park* – Widely recognized as one of the country's finest hotels, the *Park* is on its own palm tree–lined grounds on Kenmare Bay, just at the edge of the village. Guests are greeted like royalty as they sit down to register at an early Georgian partners desk in the lobby. There are 50 rooms, all with bath, including 6 master suites with four-posters, hand-carved armoires, etc. The restaurant, with romantic bay views on long summer days and candlelight in winter, specializes in seafood, especially salmon and shellfish. Kenmare (phone: 064-41200). Expensive.

Kenmare Bay – This hotel has 68 airy and modern rooms, a pleasant bar, and a good restaurant. During the Fruits de Mer Festival, it can be very crowded. Closed November through March. Sneem Rd., Kenmare (phone: 064-41300). Moderate.

EATING OUT: *Remy's House* – A renovated 19th-century bank is the setting for this French restaurant, beautifully decorated in shades of blue. Especially worth trying is the *mille-feuille d'épinards aux moules* (creamed mussels and spinach in pastry); the seafood, pork rib, and rack of lamb are also good. Dinner only. Open mid-March through mid-October. Top of Main St., Kenmare (phone: 064-41589). Expensive.

Lime Tree – An old stone schoolhouse (1821) is the setting for Kenmare's newest restaurant rendezvous, right next to the grounds of the *Park* hotel. There's a choice of dining in the cozy downstairs area, with its warming fireplace, or in the skylit gallery overhead. On both levels, paintings by modern Irish artists line the walls. The menu ranges from poached monkfish, trout almondine, or fish mousse to rack of lamb with spicy plum sauce. Open April through October. Shelbourne St. (phone: 064-41225). Expensive to moderate.

Jugs – A modern and airy place, it serves steaks and seafood as well as the "Gourmet Dinner," in which customers cook slices of beef, pork, turkey, and lamb at a grill wheeled to the table; various sauces are provided for dipping. Lunch and dinner daily, mid-March through October. Sneem Rd., Kenmare (phone: 064-41099). Moderate.

Purple Heather Bistro – Seafood is the specialty of the house, with meals served in the comfortable bar. Closed from the end of October to March. Henry St., Kenmare (phone: 064-41016). Moderate.

En Route from Kenmare – By the time you reach Kenmare, you will have covered 90 miles of the Ring of Kerry route, excluding detours. From here, the most direct road back to Killarney is N71 north, a distance of 21 miles. This will take you over the mountains through Moll's Gap and via Ladies View, a lookout point with a panorama of the wonderful lakes of Killarney that is supposed to have gotten its name because it particularly pleased Queen Victoria's ladies-in-waiting.

Route N71 south leads across the Beara Peninsula to Glengariff (17 miles) and Bantry (29 miles from Kenmare). If pressed for time, it is possible to head directly to Bantry and pick up the West Cork route there (or at Ballylickey, 3 miles north of Bantry). Otherwise, extend your tour to take in the Beara Peninsula, a thinly populated, very underdeveloped region that is also very beautiful and the least frequented of the three great southwestern peninsulas. The full circuit can fill at least a day, but it can be shortened by cutting across the center of the peninsula on the spectacular Healy Pass Road. Leaving Kenmare on Route N71, you'll have fine views of the Kenmare River, adrift with swans, and of the surrounding mountains. The road follows the valley of the River Sheen for several miles, then crosses the River Baurearagh and begins to climb through a series of tunnels, the longest one passing under the border between County Cork and County Kerry. Beyond the main tunnel, far to the right, is Barley

Lake, a striking glacial corrie filled with water, with an improbable road snaking up to it. The tortured Caha Mountains are on the right and the great stretch of Bantry Bay is visible below, with the tip of Whiddy Island barely discernible. The road then descends through a valley into Glengarriff.

GLENGARRIFF: Its name means "rough glen," a description that is only partially true of this lovely village snuggled into a deeply wooded glen at the southeastern corner of the Beara Peninsula. There is nothing rough about it, and sheltered as it is from any harsh winds by mountains on three sides, the village has a justly famous reputation for mild weather and luxuriant vegetation. Arbutus, eucalyptus, fuchsia, rhododendron, and blue-eyed grass are among the plants and trees that flourish in the glen, and on Garinish Island in Glengarriff Harbour, the growth is subtropical. Until the early part of this century, the island was bare, but its owners then began to transform it with an extraordinary richness of flowers and foliage laid out in beautiful, Italian-style formal gardens. At the highest point of the island is a martello tower, the first of many to be built around Britain and Ireland against the expected Napoleonic invasion of 1804–5. The island, which was given as a gift to the nation, is now open to the public (admission charge for the gardens). Boats leave Glengarriff daily from 9:30 AM to 6 PM (Sundays from 1 to 6 PM) from March through October. There is excellent sea and river fishing in and around the village and bathing is good along the nearby coves, one of which, Poulgorm ("blue pool") is an extremely picturesque spot just a 2-minute walk from the post office. Glengarriff also has tennis courts, a golf course, and unlimited terrain for riding and walking.

CHECKING IN: *Eccles* – Overlooking Glengariff Harbor, this traditional but updated hotel offers 35 rooms, all with bath; also self-catering apartments. Open early April through September. Glangariff (phone: 027-63003). Moderate.

Casey's – This small and pleasant family-owned and -run place has 20 rooms (only 4 with bath) and a dining room serving fine food. Open late May through September. Glengariff (phone: 027-6310). Moderate to inexpensive.

En Route from Glengarriff – Route R572 twists west into poor and rocky country along the south coast of the Beara Peninsula. When you reach Adrigole village, 12 miles from Glengarriff, take the signposted road (R574) to the right for the Healy Pass.

HEALY PASS: Work on this road began as a relief project during the famine years of the mid-19th century but stopped shortly thereafter. It was resumed in 1928 at the direction of Tim Healy, the first governor-general of the Irish Free State (a native of Bantry), and finished 3 years later. The road climbs to a height of 1,084 feet as it crosses the Caha Mountains (and, again, the border between County Cork and County Kerry) to provide rewarding views over Mizen Head and Sheep's Head to the south, and Derreen, Kilmakilloge Harbour, the Kenmare River, and the mountains of the Iveragh Peninsula to the north. In early summer the soft ground beside the pass will be spattered with the blooms of the pinguicula grandiflora, the large-flowered butterwort. The road descends to Lauragh on the northern coast of the peninsula but if you wish to extend your exploration to the isolated region farther west, turn back, admiring the splendid sight of Bantry Bay as you drop down to Adrigole.

En Route from Adrigole – Proceed west on R572. The route to Castletownbere is dominated by the lean, well-named Hungry Hill (a reminder of the famine of 1845 and, at 2,251 feet, the highest point on the peninsula), while Bere Island, with its two martello towers, emerges to the left in Bantry Bay. The island was named for Beara, a Spanish princess married to Eogan, a partly legendary and partly historical figure who landed here during the course of an invasion of Ireland. Eventually, the whole peninsula was named for the princess. Despite the spare countryside, note that holly and sally trees flourish and fuchsia is rampant; in early summer, great drifts of white lilies make a stunning show.

CASTLETOWNBERE: This village — no more than a string of houses along both sides of the street — grew up at the beginning of the 19th century when the copper mines at Allihies, west of town, were opened. Its sheltered natural harbor continued to earn it a living as the site of a British naval base until 1938, and it is now becoming one of Ireland's main fishing centers, with tourism increasing. Look at the seven dormer windows, like elegant ships' portholes, over the three houses facing the pier — they are a feature of the area. The ruins of the 15th-century Dunboy Castle, the stronghold of the branch of the O'Sullivans who were lords of this peninsula (the main branch occupied most of the Iveragh Peninsula) are about 2 miles west of town.

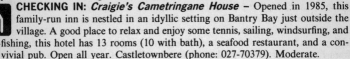

CHECKING IN: *Craigie's Cametringane House* – Opened in 1985, this family-run inn is nestled in an idyllic setting on Bantry Bay just outside the village. A good place to relax and enjoy some tennis, sailing, windsurfing, and fishing, this hotel has 13 rooms (10 with bath), a seafood restaurant, and a convivial pub. Open all year. Castletownbere (phone: 027-70379). Moderate.

En Route from Castletownbere – Continue on Route R572 west for about 6 miles. When the road divides, with a sign pointing each way to Allihies, take the road to the right, R575. There are good views of the two Skellig Rocks and of Scariff and Deenish islands at the end of the Kenmare River. The road passes the abandoned Allihies copper mines, first worked by Iberian miners some 4,000 years ago and reopened during the Napoleonic wars by the Puxley family, who made a great fortune. The Puxleys employed no fewer than 1,200 people at a time before the operation succumbed to competition in 1886, and when Daphne du Maurier wrote her book about the mines, *Hungry Hill,* she used Puxley family papers to research it, though naming it for a mountain some miles away. After skirting the little village of Allihies, now a shadow of its former self, follow the signs to Eyeries, then on to Ardgroom and to Lauragh, at the head of Kilmakillage Harbour and the border of County Kerry. On a good day this stretch of the route will provide some of the most striking scenery in all of West Cork and Kerry. It is, however, narrow and twisting most of the way.

LAURAGH: The Healy Pass road across the peninsula joins the scenic sea road, L62, at Lauragh. Close to the village is the estate of Derreen House, whose beautiful subtropical gardens are open to visitors three afternoons a week (Sundays, Tuesdays, and Thursdays, 2 to 6 PM) from early April through September. The gardens — much less formal than those of Garinish Island or Muckross House — are remarkable for rhododendrons, camellias, tree ferns, bamboos, and eucalyptus.

En Route from Lauragh – Route L62 passes the Cloonie lakes and Lough Inchiquin — well stocked with salmon and sea and brown trout — as it continues east along the coast to Kenmare.

The Dingle Peninsula

The Dingle Peninsula is the northernmost of the mountainous promontories that stick out into the Atlantic from Ireland's southwest coast like toes extended to test the water. It is a jumble of old and varied peaks and cliffs, glacial valleys and lakes, headlands and bays, islands, strands, and great sand dunes stretching 30 miles west from the lowlying country around Tralee through mountains that turn to wild hills and meet the sea in splendid coastlines. The peninsula is blessed with a remoteness that has been an inspiration to poets and religious ascetics alike. It was on Dingle that John Millington Synge wondered why anyone was left in Dublin or London or Paris, and whether it wouldn't be better to live "with this magnificent sea and sky, and to breathe this wonderful air, which is like wine in one's teeth."

Dingle's dramatic rendering of nature's bare essentials never ceases to delight visitors. On a clear day there are stunning views: great panoramic expanses of green stopped by shimmering ribbons of water in the distance, then the farther gray-blue outline of the next peninsula, island, or rocky point, itself backlit by the phosphorescence of fine, silver-edged cloudings. On a less clear day when the depth of the scene diminishes, the eye is drawn to the hedgerows by the roadside, made up in spring of white hawthorn or yellow-flowering furze bushes, of languorous drapings of honeysuckle or purplish fuchsia just burst into bloom. Where they part, they reveal the patchwork of fields beyond, and an ample sampling of Ireland's green.

Dingle's topography is mountainous, but not in the alpine way. It rises — from the eastern Slieve Mish Mountains to the western Brandon Mountains — to rounded and treeless peaks, the effect the same as if some primordial giant had thrown down a heavy carpet to soften the contours and soothe his aching feet. This possibility is not entirely implausible because Dingle is alive with legend and folklore, its remote fastnesses the stamping ground of mythological heroes such as Cu Chulainn, its ports guarded by the larger-than-life Finn MacCool and his warrior army, the Fianna. Visitors may see only innumerable sheep ranging down valleys and over the distant hills, but to locals with longer memories, the land is the home of giants as tall as the tales.

The peninsula is also particularly rich in antiquities, especially prehistoric and early Christian remains, among them *galláns,* or standing stones; *ogham* stones, or pillars inscribed with the earliest form of Irish writing; and *clocháns,* or circular beehive huts. The latter may be the most suggestive. Grouped in fraternal clusters or alone as solitary cells, monks isolated themselves in these stone huts on Ireland's lonely western fringes in the early days of Irish Christianity. The eremitical offshoot of Irish monasticism was nowhere stronger than it was in Kerry, and it's not hard for visitors to see why. Perched on the ledge of a wave-pounded rock or on the quieter summit of a deserted hill, the hermit monks could ponder at length both the awesome and the gentle face of God and perhaps, in a radiant flash of sun on sea, witness their own immortality.

Not all beehive huts are ancient, however. Farmers continue to copy the technique for modern animal shelters and sheds, one of many ways Dingle's timeless appearance endures to confound seekers of authenticity. Almost two decades ago, when scouts were searching for a location to film *Ryan's Daughter,* a story that was supposed to have taken place in 1916, the peninsula was chosen because it looked as though it hadn't progressed much beyond that date, though none of its tiny villages had quite the look of abject poverty required (a model village was built).

Time has also stood still on Dingle in the matter of language. Its western reaches are part of the Gaeltacht, the collective name for the few surviving Irish-speaking areas of Ireland where geography protected what was lost elsewhere under British rule. The native Irish tongue can be heard in villages such as Dunquin and Ballyferriter, whose people use it daily, though they also speak English. During the summer, students come from all over the country to attend the Irish language schools here.

The scenic route around the peninsula is roughly in the shape of a figure eight, with the town of Dingle at the crossing. Roads are narrow and twisting but they're easy to negotiate just the same, and you'll have no trouble with traffic — though you may round a bend and come upon a traveling bank truck or a collie herding the cattle home. The drive is best on a very bright (not necessarily dry) day and to be avoided, if possible, in mist or continuous rain. You can see it all in a long day trip of approximately 100 miles from Tralee and back, including time for lunch in Dingle Town, through which the route passes twice. Though Tralee, where our route begins, is the usual gateway to Dingle, you could stay out on the peninsula itself — there are plenty of bed-and-breakfast houses and farms, plus small hotels and guesthouses, and, in Dingle town, a modern A-category hotel.

As elsewhere in our Irish listings, a double room in an expensive hotel will cost $80 and up; in a moderate one, from $50 to $75; and in an inexpensive one, $40 or less. A meal for two in an expensive restaurant will cost $50 and up; in a moderate one, from $30 to $45; and in an inexpensive one, $30 or less.

TRALEE: This friendly, busy trading center of 18,000 people is the chief town of County Kerry and one of the most active in southern Ireland. It grew up around the 13th-century Desmond Castle, but because the town was destroyed at the end of the 17th century, its remains — such as the Georgian terraces on Denny Street and in Day Place and St. John's Cathedral Church — are mainly from the 18th and 19th centuries. Its major antiquity is the ruined Rathass Church, about a mile east, dating from the 9th and 10th centuries. Inside there is a stone commemorating an 8th-century notable in ogham, the earliest form of Irish writing. Ogham consists of groups of strokes and dots related to a spinal line and it arose, probably in this peninsula, about the beginning of the Christian era.

Tralee has a racecourse and a new 18-hole golf course designed by Arnold Palmer, plus salmon and trout fishing in its rivers, excellent deep-sea fishing, a choice of beaches, sailing, skin diving, and riding. Tralee is also the home of Siamsa tíre (pronounced Shee-am-sah teer), the National Folk Theatre of Ireland (phone: 23055), which brings to life the customs of the Irish countryside through a program of music, singing, dancing, and mime several nights weekly from June through September. Its greatest attraction, however, is the Rose of Tralee International Festival, otherwise known as the Festival of Kerry, a week of carnivallike pageantry at the end of August or the beginning of September. This is Ireland's biggest bash and its highlight is the crowning of the Rose, the loveliest young woman of Irish descent in the world and the one who best exemplifies the qualities of the original Rose of Tralee from the song by William Mulchinock, who was born and died here.

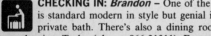 **CHECKING IN:** *Brandon* – One of the largest hotels in County Kerry, this is standard modern in style but genial in its operation. All 162 rooms have private bath. There's also a dining room, coffee shop, and nightclub with dancing. Tralee (phone: 066-21311). Expensive to moderate.

Ballygarry House – This recently refurbished country inn with private garden has an old world look, complete with open fireplaces. All 16 of the individually decorated bedrooms have private bath. The restaurant serves mostly Continental cuisine. 1½ miles from town on the Tralee-Killarney road. Leebrook, Tralee (phone: 066-21233). Moderate.

EATING OUT: *Barrett's Cordon Bleu* – The menu at this casual and unhurried eatery offers a surprising range of well-prepared dishes, from (of course) veal Cordon Bleu to seafood vol-au-vent (in pastry). The Square, Tralee (phone: 066-21596). Moderate.

Ocean Billow – Shades of ocean blue dominate the decor at this upstairs seafood restaurant. Candlelight dinners include pineapple seafood curry, seafood soufflé, and a velvety cream of salmon soup. Lunches, too. 29 Lower Castle St., Tralee (phone: 066-21377). Moderate.

Oyster Tavern – Visit this pub for seafood cooked in a straightforward manner. Favorites include cockle and mussel soup and grilled crab claws. About 3 miles west of Tralee at Spa, where there was a famous watering place in the 18th century. Spa (phone: 066-36102). Moderate.

Slatts – For lunch or dinner, try this comfortable lounge and bar with an open-hearth fire and delightful staff. Background piano music in the evenings is a pleasant accompaniment. Boherbee, Tralee (phone: 066-22126). Moderate.

Tankard – This restaurant with sweeping seascape views offers shellfish from Tralee Bay, as well as steak, duck, chicken, and quail. Open for lunch and dinner all year. 6 miles west of Tralee. Fenit (phone: 066-36164). Moderate.

Brogue Inn – This big barn of a pub — strewn with agricultural instruments — is a good place for a light lunch. Rock St., Tralee (phone: 066-22126). Inexpensive.

En Route from Tralee – The road to Dingle (T68) runs along the 19th-century ship canal to Blennerville, which is unusual for its ruined windmill and famous among bird-watchers for its mudflats in Tralee Bay. Less than a mile farther on where a roadway comes from the left, the 12th- to 13th-century Annagh church is hidden on the right on a site claimed to be the birthplace of the 6th-century St. Brendan the Navigator, reputed to have discovered America even before the Vikings. (Fenit, across Tralee Bay, is the more likely birthplace.) Continuing out onto the peninsula, along its northern edge, there are wonderfully scenic views. The Slieve Mish Mountains are inland to the left and to the right a sweep of green tilts gently down to magnificent beaches on the bay, the green scattered with grazing cattle and sheep to the very edge of the pale gold sand.

The remains of the old Tralee and Dingle railway are along the route, now on one side, now on the other. Where the road divides just before Camp, going right for Castlegregory and left for Dingle, take the left fork and then turn left again under the broken arch of the old railway line and head straight across the peninsula toward Aughils. The mountain to the left of this road is Caherconree and, near its summit, the curious rock formation with cliffs on three sides and a narrow approach cut off by a substantial wall is a promontory fort dating from the Iron Age (which began in Ireland about 500 BC and lasted till the arrival of St. Patrick in the 5th century AD). It is notable not only because it is inland, while the many other promontory forts on the peninsula are on the coast, but also because it was the home of Cu Roi Mac Daire, a figure from a cycle of legends dealing with Iron Age heroes. Cu Roi was killed by Cu Chulainn, a small, fierce, brave man and a womanizer, after the former had stolen the beautiful Blathnaid, a woman for whom Cu Chulainn had set his cap. There are breathtaking views from the fort, reached via a marked trail that begins some distance farther along the road, and there are equally memorable views — of Dingle Bay and the Iveragh Peninsula — as the road descends to Aughils and Inch. When you reach the sea road at Aughils, turn right and Inch is only another 4 miles away.

INCH: This sheltered seaside resort is at the base of the Inch Peninsula. Its name to the contrary, the peninsula provides a 4-mile strip of firm, golden sand that is excellent for bathing and was the setting for some of the beach scenes in the film *Ryan's Daughter*. The beach is backed by high dunes that have yielded evidence of mysterious sandhill dwellers who lived here in Iron Age times and perhaps earlier. In the 18th century, this same sandy spit stretching out into Dingle Bay was used to wreck ships from the West Indies. A lantern on the head of a moving horse would fool captains into thinking there was another ship ahead, not a sand bar.

ANASCAUL: Four miles west of Inch, the inland village of Anascaul is known as the location of the *South Pole Inn*. Now a pub where you can stop for a drink (no food served), this was once the home of Thomas Crean, who was a member of Robert Falcon Scott's last and fatal expedition to Antarctica (1910-12). A signposted detour north from the town leads, in about 2 miles, to the beautiful Anascaul Lake in a boulder-scattered valley about which there is another Cu Chulainn story. A giant was carrying off a girl, Scál, but Cu Chulainn came to her rescue. From the mountains on either side of the lake each threw great stones at the other. Cu Chulainn was wounded and Scál, thinking him dead, drowned herself in the water.

En Route from Anascaul – Here you can rejoin the main Tralee-Dingle road (T68). Continuing west, it next passes through Lispole. Less than a mile farther, look left for the standing stone, or gallán, of Ballineetig, about 100 yards from the road. This Bronze Age gravestone is the largest in the peninsula. The roughly pointed tip shows that it was a monument for a man — for women the tips were scooped out.

Still farther, where there is a good view of Dingle Harbour, turn left after a sign for an accident blackspot (a place with a bad record for auto accidents), then again sharp left at a house. A third of a mile beyond this in a field on the left is the little burial place of Ballintaggart, an important site for the study of ogham stones. Inside the circular wall are nine of them, rounded, with the base, or spinal, line unusually omitted. The inscription of one stone commemorates the "three sons of Mailagnos," the next has a long Latin cross, and two others have short Greek ones, possibly added later as Christianity began to take over from paganism. Before leaving Ballintaggart, take a moment to enjoy the splendid sight of the Skellig Rocks off the coast of the Iveragh Peninsula in the distance. Then return to the main road and drive the remaining 1½ miles into Dingle.

DINGLE: The peninsula's chief town lies at the foot of a steep slope on the north side of the harbor and is bounded on three sides by hills. It was the main port of Kerry in the old Spanish trading days, and in the reign of Queen Elizabeth I it was important enough as an outpost to merit a protective wall. In the 18th century, Dingle became a smuggling center, and during the French Revolution, a local man, Colonel James Rice, was the linchpin of a plot to rescue Marie Antoinette and spirit her to "the highest house on the hill," on Main Street. She refused when she learned her family would not come with her and the house has since been replaced by the Catholic presbytery. Today Dingle's population of 1,400 is dependent on fishing and tourism. Deep-sea fishing facilities are excellent, there is good bathing at various beaches in the vicinity, and there is pony trekking into the surrounding hills. You may be able to catch traditional Irish music sessions at the rough-hewn and barnlike *O'Flaherty's Pub* on Bridge Street; order a Guinness, pull up an orange crate, and sit down and listen. Also worth a visit is *Richard MacDonnell's* on Church St. Known locally as "Dick Mack's," this has to be the only place in Ireland where you can buy shoes, boots, and leather belts (hand-fashioned by octogenarian Dick) on one side of the room and enjoy a freshly drawn pint of Guinness on the other. The pub side has two old-fashioned snugs that alone are worth a look. Dingle is also the gateway to the West Kerry Gaeltacht, the Irish-speaking district, as well as a good base for extended exploration of the archaeological antiquities of this rich area. Begin with the enormous rock called a *bullaun* on Main Street. It has holes in it and was probably used for grinding hard wheat in early Christian times.

 CHECKING IN: *Alpine House* – A modern, centrally heated guesthouse with 15 rooms, about half with private bath/shower. At the entrance to Dingle town, with pleasant views, a lounge, and a dining room. Open March through October. Dingle (phone: 066-51250). Inexpensive.

EATING OUT: *Doyle's Seafood Bar* – In a small town known for its fine restaurants, this is the leader; its award-winning specialties include crab bisque, éclairs of smoked mackerel pâté, local lobster, and a popular seafood mornay. If you want to picnic, you can buy homemade brown bread and smoked salmon to go. The addition of 8 guestrooms in the adjoining house is planned for the spring of 1988. Open for lunch and dinner; closed Sundays and November through February. John St., Dingle (phone: 066-51174). Moderate.

***Greets* –** Just west of town, perched on a hill overlooking Dingle Bay, this new addition to the Dingle dining scene is operated by the same couple who own *Gaby's* in Killarney. A modern wide-windowed bistro, they feature sole on the bone, lobster, trout, and haddock, as well as creative meat dishes. On warm days al fresco dining on the patio is a pleasant alternative. Lunch and dinner daily, May through September. The Wood, Dingle (phone: 51214). Moderate.

***Half-Door* –** Right next to *Doyle's*, it's not as renowned as its neighbor but is a good alternative. The menu features the best of the local catch, imaginatively prepared in such combinations as sole with banana and chutney, trout in blackberry and vermouth sauce, and salmon in ginger butter. Lobster is featured here, too, as is at least one meat selection. Closed Tuesdays and later November to early March. John St., Dingle (phone: 066-51600). Moderate.

***An Cafe Liteartha* –** Serving simple fare such as salads and sandwiches, this place is best known for its bookshop, with an excellent section on Ireland and the Irish. An Daingean (phone: 066-51380). Inexpensive.

En Route from Dingle – Head west out of town, and when you come to a junction, take the road in the direction of Slea Head. Just beyond a modern cemetery at Milltown there is an interesting set of antiquities inside a gate on the right. The site, an ancient burial ground referred to as the "gates of glory," consists of a great gallán, along with two others that have fallen and broken pieces of more stones. The mysterious scribings on top of one of the fallen galláns were made by early metal workers who came to Ireland from Spain some 4,000 years ago. The scooped-out hollows are called cup marks. Many such stones can be found in Kerry, but no one has yet given an adequate interpretation of them.

VENTRY: About 4 miles from Dingle, this little village has a delightful beach. In Irish legend, Ventry Harbour was the scene of a great battle won by the hero Finn MacCool and his warriors, the Fianna, against the forces of the "king of the world," Daire Donn, who crammed the harbor with his ships and was held off for a year and a day before being wiped out to the last man. Keep an eye open for *Quinn's Ventry Inn,* a modern pub with panoramic views, for a congenial place to have a drink or a cup of coffee. Beyond the harbor, the road continues to Slea Head on the lower slopes of Mt. Eagle, providing lovely coastal views of Dingle Bay. This cliff-hugging part of the route is particularly scenic and will, again, be familiar to filmgoers who have seen *Ryan's Daughter.* The village of Kirrary, which appeared in the film, was along the coast west of Ventry, but don't look for it, because it was built from scratch for the filming and destroyed afterward to preserve the landscape. The area from Ventry to Slea Head is also rich in archaeological remains.

DUNBEG AND FAHAN: Just under 4 miles from Ventry, an Iron Age promontory fort, Dunbeg, can be seen below the road to the left. In addition to the wall that cuts off the triangular promontory, there are four earthen defensive rings, an underground escape passage (or souterrain) at the entrance, and remains of an inner house. Dunbeg may have been the first bridgehead established by the people who built the ancient town of Fahan, the greatest collection of antiquities in all Ireland. Fahan consists of over 400 *clocháns* (circular beehive huts constructed without mortar of overlapped or corbeled stones), cave dwellings, standing and inscribed stones and crosses, souterrains, forts, and a church — more than 500 remains in all — strewn along an old road above the main road for a distance of about 3 miles. To best see this settlement, which was possibly a full-fledged community between the 6th and 10th century, as large then as Dingle is now, keep to the main road until you've passed the small ford at Glenfahan, after which there is a sign indicating beehive huts. These are among the most interesting and convenient, but the owners of the property expect a small payment from visitors.

SLEA HEAD: The road from Dingle continues to Slea Head at the tip of the peninsula, where the view of the Blasket Islands, the westernmost point in Europe (except for Iceland), is spectacular. In September 1588, four ships of the Spanish Armada were driven by storms through Blasket Sound. Two reached shelter, but a third, the *Santa Maria de la Rosa,* came flying through the sound with its sails in tatters, crashed onto a rock, and sank, as did the fourth, the *San Juan de Ragusa.* (The remains of the *Santa Maria de la Rosa* were found at the bottom of Blasket Sound in the late 1960s.) The beach between Slea Head and the next promontory, Dunmore Head, is Coumeenole strand, attractive but dangerous.

BLASKET ISLANDS: This is a group of seven islands, inhabited by an Irish-speaking community from prehistoric times but now deserted. The largest, Great Blasket (4 miles long and ¾ mile wide), was "the next parish to America" until 1953 when the remaining population of barely 100 could no longer support itself after several disastrous fishing seasons and was resettled on the mainland. Blasket islanders were adept at the art of storytelling and produced a number of books. The best-selling *Twenty Years A-growing* by Maurice O'Sullivan, *The Islander,* a masterpiece by Thomas O'Crohan, and *Peig* by Peig Sayers were all written by island natives. Boats to the Blaskets can be hired in Dunquin, north of Slea Head.

En Route from Slea Head – The road leaves the seacoast to cut across Dunmore Head, then continues north to Dunquin along a coast where many forms of fossils can be found. At Dunquin Harbour, the colored silurian rocks in the cliffs date from 400 million years ago. From Dunquin there are fairly regular sailings in summer to the Blaskets. Typically, the boat is a *curragh,* a light, canvas-covered canoe painted with tar which, if properly handled, is an extraordinarily seaworthy revival of the ancient boat originally made of skins. After Dunquin, the route passes Clogher Head and turns inland toward the village of Ballyferriter. Watch for the pottery workshop at Clogher (*Potadóireacht na Caolóige*). You can stop and see the potters at work here, as well as buy some of the simple, colorful pieces they produce.

BALLYFERRITER: This is a small, mostly Irish-speaking village whose population is increased in summer by students taking part in Irish language schools. The ruined Castle Sybil, the home of the Anglo-Norman Ferriter family, is about 2 miles northwest of the village just above Ferriter's Cove. The castle was the birthplace of Kerry poet and patriot Piaras Ferriter, an insurgent leader who was hanged by the Cromwellians in 1653. Castle Sybil is said to be named after Sybil Lynch of Galway who eloped with a Ferriter. When her father sought her out she was hidden in the cave beneath the castle and was drowned by the rising tide.

Smerwick Harbour is about a mile north of Ballyferriter. The *Dún An Óir* — a pleasant hotel popular with families — is named for the small, long-gone fort of Dún An Óir, the "golden" fort that once stood on a promontory in the harbor. In 1580, an expedition of some 600 men financed by the pope — mainly Italians, but also Spanish, Irish, and English — entrenched at the fort to support the cause of the Catholic Irish against the Protestant English in what was the first significant invasion of the British Isles for many centuries. The English (led by Lord Grey and including Edmund Spenser and, possibly, Sir Walter Raleigh) bombarded the fort from land and sea and soon its defenders capitulated. Once disarmed, they were slaughtered and the massacre of Smerwick rang throughout Europe, a warning to anyone who might again attempt to invade the queen's territory.

En Route from Ballyferriter – Follow the main road east, keeping to the left (avoid the narrow road that bears right up a hill). Turn right over the bridge at a gasoline pump, and, almost immediately, right again. The recently excavated eremitical and monastic site of Reask is a short distance farther along (about ¾ mile east of Ballyferriter). This gives a good idea of the layout of an early, perhaps 7th- or 8th-century, monastery — the beehive huts, the oblong foundation of a boat-shaped oratory (a small church), the cross-pillars (upright stones incised with crosses), and the wall separating the upper, or consecrated, part of the monastery from the rest. Then go back down the road, turn right, and follow the signposts for the Gallarus Oratory, about 4 miles northwest of Dingle.

GALLARUS ORATORY: This small, rectangular church in the shape of an upturned boat is the best example of dry-rubble masonry in Ireland and probably the most perfect piece of early Irish architecture extant. Oratories are standard in monastic sites, but everywhere except here and on the remote Skellig Rocks, the unmortared roofs have fallen in from the great weight of their stones. Gallarus is still completely watertight and may date from as early as the 8th century, though the mastery of the corbel technique used in its building suggests a later date to some of the experts — perhaps as late as the 11th or 12th century. Besides a cross-pillar, signs of an early monastic settlement around it have yet to be found.

KILMALKEDAR: At the crossroads above Gallarus, turn sharp left for the remains of Kilmalkedar Church, a fine example of Irish Romanesque. The nave was built in the mid-12th century, the chancel a little later, and it once had a corbeled stone roof, a development of the Gallarus style. Even before the church was built, there was a Christian settlement here, dating from the late 6th and early 7th centuries. Look inside the church for the "alphabet" stone, crudely carved with a Latin cross and the Latin alphabet, used for instruction in an early-7th-century school. There must have been an even earlier, pagan, settlement on the site, too. A holed stone inside and another with ogham outside recall Indian yoni stones through which worshipers would have to pass to achieve regeneration. Reminiscent of these practices, the east window of the medieval church is known as the "eye of the needle," through which the faithful must pass to be saved. A well-carved pre-Christian sundial, and a large, crudely cut cross, one of the few in Kerry, are also outside.

Just north of the church is a roadway and, where it forks, the 15th-century St. Brendan's house is on the left. This was probably a presbytery for the church and had nothing to do with St. Brendan. The old Saints' Road, which ran through this area bisecting the fork, however, did. It led to the top of Mt. Brandon, named after St. Brendan, who is said to have had his retreat there. After his death, it was used for pilgrimages to his shrine, a practice which has since died out except for occasional revivals.

En Route from Kilmalkedar – Continue on the road beyond town and, at the T-junction, turn right and follow the signposts for Brandon Creek. It was from this spot that St. Brendan is reputed to have set out on his 6th-century voyages searching for the Land of Promise and, it seems, discovering America. Two 9th-century manuscripts, one recounting the story of his life and the other the story of his travels, were immensely popular in early medieval Europe and an inspiration for many voyagers, including Columbus, though at least as far as his travels are concerned, there may have been some confusion between the name of St. Brendan and that of the hero of an Irish pagan story, *The Voyage of Bran.* Bran and his Kerrymen companions traveled to magical western islands and, returning from one voyage, put ashore at Brandon Point, northeast of here. By this account, it was Bran, and not St. Brendan, who gave his name to the great Mt. Brandon.

From Brandon Creek, turn back toward Dingle. Just 2 miles along you'll cross the Saints' Road again. If you turn left and drive up as far as you can, you will reach the spot from which the 3,127-foot summit of Mt. Brandon, Ireland's second highest peak, is most easily accessible. It's about a 3½-mile walk to the top and on a clear day, the views are magnificent. If you're not up to this strenuous trek — which thousands of pilgrims before you have made — return to Dingle and take the Connor Pass road out of town.

CONNOR PASS: Driving this road demands great care and it should be avoided in bad weather. Leave Dingle by the unclassified road marked Connor (or Conair) Pass, climbing northeasterly between the Brandon and the central Dingle groups of mountains. At the summit (1,500 feet), there are magnificent views in both directions, south over Dingle town and Dingle Bay, north to the bays of Brandon and Tralee, the great beaches of north Kerry, and on to the mouth of the Shannon. The road descends between cliffs and valleys and then, below the pass, continues east running parallel to beautiful beaches on Brandon Bay. At Stradbally, take the left fork for Castlegregory.

CASTLEGREGORY: The castle from which this tiny village got its name is now gone. It was built in the 16th century by a local chief, Gregory Hoare, whose daughter-in-law came to grief in 1580 when she poured out all the castle's wine rather than offer it to her country's enemies in the person of Lord Grey and a party of English troops lodging at the castle on their way to attack the fort at Smerwick Harbour. Her husband killed her in a fit of rage and the next day he, himself, died suddenly. The village is at the neck of a sandy spit of land that separates the Tralee and Brandon bays. Beyond the limestone tip of the spit are the Maharee Islands, also known as the Seven Hogs. On one of these, Illauntannig, as on nearly every remote outcropping of rock in western Kerry, remains of an early Christian monastic settlement have been found. It is possible only with difficulty to arrange a boat to the island (and the ruins are in poor condition), so content yourself with a drive out along the spit from Castlegregory or a visit to Lough Gill, west of the village, an attractive lake noted for its waterfowl including a species of swan that comes all the way from Siberia to winter here.

En Route from Castlegregory – Continue east, and at the town of Camp, take T68 back to Tralee, from where you are only 20 miles north of Killarney, the gateway to the *Ring of Kerry and the Beara Peninsula* route.

Clare

Clare, in the middle of the west coast of Ireland, is an "island" county; the Atlantic washes its north and west shores, the encircling River Shannon guards it on the east and south. What is left unwashed in the northeastern quadrant is guarded by a chain of hills. In its isolation Clare has retained much of the past — a sturdy political and economic independence, a music livelier and more varied than that of other parts of Ireland, a tenacious grasp of folk traditions, a speech dotted with the remnants of Irish language forms.

Clare landscape is varied, a microcosm of the Irish west coast generally, but with features that give it an original twist. Heading inward from the coast, Clare terrain changes strikingly, from the wild rocky seacliffs to the marshy uplands behind them, to the central limestone plain dotted with lakes, to the great brown hills of the east. In the very north is the Burren country, a stony moonscape plateau.

History has left many interesting remains in Clare. Scattered over the northern hills are more than 150 dolmens, or Stone Age tombs, of the farmers who migrated here from France 5,000 years ago. There are nearly 3,000 circular forts in earth and stone, the fortified settlements of their Celtic successors. And over 200 castles are still extant, the earliest ones built by the Normans, the later by the Irish. Traces of the early Catholic church are found in Clare. Most "churches" are of the eremitical type; a collection of them is on St. Senan's monastic island in the mouth of the Shannon, and they dot the islets and the hillsides up the coast. Such ruins are particularly plentiful in the Burren where the early hermits found the isolation they desired; here the stony desert is dotted with oratories, "saints' beds" or shrines, wells, and stone crosses.

Claremen are mature and practiced politicians who sum up a situation and pragmatically choose a leader. In the tenth century they picked Brian Ború, head of an obscure clan called the Dal gCais. They fought for him until he became first king of Munster and then High King of Ireland; they died with him as he defeated the Vikings on the coast of Dublin Bay. At the great upsurge of Irish democracy in the nineteenth century they voted in Daniel O'Connell as Member of Parliament for Clare, and they supported Charles Stewart Parnell in the Land League Movement. In this century they elected Eamon de Valera, who was prime minister and president of an independent Ireland.

Although most Clare folk still pursue a rural lifestyle on small dairy farms, they are gradually adapting to a new world. Many country market towns are beginning to expand with factories, and more people are working in the transport, tourism, and service industries. The international airport at Shannon has not only established a duty-free zone and nurtured an industrial park with many welcome new jobs, but has also made County Clare the major western gateway to Ireland.

The route suggested below begins in Limerick City, which is where most people spend their first night after landing at Shannon. From here, you'll travel to Ennis, capital of Clare, then along the Shannon River through numerous little towns out to the lonely peninsula of Loop Head. From this wild Atlantic seascape, the road turns north to the resort towns of Kilkee and Lahinch, and on to the great Cliffs of Moher. An eastern leg explores the wonderland of the Burren with its unusual rock formations, caves, flora, and ruins.

Although the Limerick City area has many new large hotels, accommodations in Clare tend to be small hotels or B&Bs. You can expect to pay $80 and up for a double in those places listed as expensive; from $50 to $75 in moderate; and under $40 in inexpensive. A meal for two, excluding wine, tips, or drinks, will cost about $50 and up in places listed as expensive; $30 to $45 in moderate; and under $30 in inexpensive.

LIMERICK CITY: For a detailed report on the city, its hotels and restaurants, see *Limerick,* THE CITIES.

En Route from Limerick – About 12 miles down the main Limerick-Ennis road is the tiny village of Newmarket-on-Fergus, which owes its name to a track-crazy 18th-century landlord who renamed it after the great center of English horse racing. The long demesne wall beyond the town encloses Dromoland Castle and is well worth a look. It was once the home of the O'Briens, earls of Inchiquin, descendants of the high king, Brian Ború, and is now the deluxe *Dromoland Castle* hotel.

ENNIS: This county seat of Clare (pop. 8,000), with its narrow winding main street intersected by even narrower lanes, has a lively medieval charm. Off Francis St. are the ruins of a Franciscan Friary founded about 1240 by Donough Mor O'Brien. A monument to Liberator Daniel O'Connell, who secured Catholic emancipation and sat in parliament for Clare, is in O'Connell Sq. The modern De Valera Library and Museum, which was ingeniously adapted from a disused church, is on Harmony Row. Outside town on the Limerick road, you'll see signposts to Clare Abbey, the now undistinguished and abandoned ruins of an Augustinian monastery established in 1189 by Donal Mor O'Brien, King of Munster.

CHECKING IN: *Old Ground* – An ivy-clad, centrally located hotel dating from the 17th century. One of its rooms used to be Town Hall and another was once the town jail. Recently upgraded, it now has 61 rooms with bath, some with antiques and other more modern in decor. There is a warming fireplace in the lobby and the *Poet's Corner* bar is a great spot to meet the locals. O'Connell St., Ennis (phone: 28127). Expensive.

West County Inn – This large, modern hotel has 120 rooms with private bath, a coffee shop, a restaurant, a nightclub, and a sauna. Dinner dances are held every Saturday evening and Irish cabaret shows are staged on summer evenings. Clare Rd., Ennis (phone: 065-28421). Moderate.

EATING OUT: *Brogan's* – This atmospheric old pub serves steaks, smoked salmon, soup and sandwiches. 24 O'Connell St., Ennis (phone: 29859). Moderate.

Lenthall's Inn – Soups, salads, sandwiches, and Irish stew or shepherd's pie are served in the pub lounge during the day. Dinner is served in the upstairs restaurant, and the house specialty is steak Considine (named after the proprietor, who created it) — beef cooked with cream and brandy and served aflame. Abbey St., Ennis (phone: 22933). Moderate.

Cloister – Next to Ennis Abbey, this landmark building houses both a homey pub and an adjoining fine dining room. The pub is noted for its all-day lunch menu including fisherman's pie and hot crab claws; the restaurant is quite another matter, with specialties like salmon in champagne sauce, spiced braised duckling, filet of lamb en croûte, and Gaelic steak. Save room for chocolate rum mousse, creme de menthe cheesecake, or a melon frappé. A pianist or harpist entertains nightly. Abbey St., Ennis (phone: 29521). Restaurant: expensive; pub: inexpensive.

En Route from Ennis – The L51 travels along the bank of the Shannon estuary all the way to Kilrush. The landscape is gentle and pastoral and there are fine views across "the Shannon spreading like a sea" of the little wooded harbor town of Foynes, of Glin with its Regency castle, and of Tarbert with its lighthouse and electric power station. At Killimer a car ferry crosses every hour on the hour to Tarbert on the Kerry shore.

KILRUSH: The chief market town of southwest Clare, it has a number of small industries, including a factory for processing seaweed. Just outside Kilrush is Cappagh Pier, formerly the terminus for the river steamers that plied the Shannon from Limerick. From here you can take a boat to Scattery Island, the monastic retreat founded in the 6th century by St. Senan. On the island are five early churches dating from the 9th to 11th century and a 120-foot round tower, the tallest in Ireland.

EATING OUT: ***Orchard*** – A pleasant hotel lounge at the southern edge of Kilrush that serves homemade soups and sandwiches as well as hot dishes. Watercolors of the area adorn the walls; sing-alongs are usually on tap Saturday nights. Killimer Rd., Kilrush (phone: Kilrush 401). Moderate to inexpensive.

Crotty's – A favorite with traditional musicians. At the corner of the square, Kilrush. Inexpensive.

En Route from Kilrush – Taking T41 toward Kilkee, you pass through the rushy, windswept landscape typical of south Clare. About 6 miles out there's a sign for a holy well; turn left and in 2½ miles you'll see a tidily kept holy well dedicated to St. Martin. Turning back from the well, go straight east parallel to the estuary.

The first hamlet you pass through, Doonaha, was the birthplace of Eugene O'Curry, a pioneer 19th-century Irish scholar and topographer. When the road hits the estuary again, you'll come to Carrigaholt, a picturesque village wrapped around a crescent of beach with a tall O'Brien castle guarding the little harbor. Another 8 miles farther down the spine of the peninsula is the last village, Kilbaha, and 4½ miles beyond that is the lonely lighthouse of Loop Head. From the headland there are superb views to the south of the mountains of Kerry — the Macgillycuddy Reeks crowned by Carrantuohill, the highest point in Ireland, and Mt. Brandon at the west end of the Dingle Peninsula. To the north you can see the whale-backed Aran Islands in Galway Bay and the saw-toothed peaks of Connemara. Below the lighthouse are some rocks separated from the shore by a deep chasm. Across this, legend has it, the Irish hero Cu Chulainn made a bold leap when pursued by a persistent female.

On the return journey from the head, branch left at the village of Killbaha for a mile to Moneen church. In a baptistery chapel on the left of the altar is a fascinating relic of the period of anti-Catholic discrimination in Ireland. What looks like an old-fashioned bathing machine, a little wooden hut with a canvas roof and windows, is in fact the only church allowed in this area in the first half of the 19th century. A bigoted landlord refused to allow a church to be built, so the parish priest — lifting the idea from a horse-drawn carriage in which he had traveled from Kilrush to Ennis —

had this structure built. Each Sunday it was drawn onto the beach, where he said Mass and his congregation knelt in the open. Known as "the Little Ark," the wooden chapel is still an object of veneration and the incident is illustrated in stained glass over the church door.

Just beyond the church there is a storm beach of huge rounded boulders; a half-mile farther on, a signpost directs you to the parking lot for the Bridges of Ross. These are curious rock formations carved out by the sea.

Another half-mile beyond the village of Cross, take a right turn on a narrow road, which after 2 miles reaches the coast and the top of Oldtown hill and gives you a view of miles of rugged cliffs ahead. The road soon begins to hug the cliff tops and the next 5 miles into Kilkee are a dramatic unfolding panorama of rock stacks and precipices. Occasionally you'll see remains of castle towers and stone forts in inaccessible places in the rock. The most striking phenomenon of all is Bishop's Island, a sheer stack of rock that's been cut off from the mainland but retains a beehive oratory and house associated with St. Senan.

KILKEE: This little resort town, with its charming rows of Regency-Gothic houses, has been a popular vacation spot for well-to-do people from Limerick since they came by Shannon steamer in the early 19th century. Its powdery, horseshoe-shaped strand is protected from the full force of the Atlantic by two bold headlands and offers safe bathing and boating. Because most of Kilkee's visitors rent houses, there are very few hotels. It's best to stop here for a dip and a drink at *Scott's, Marrinan's,* the *Greyhound,* or *Fitzgerald's,* some pubs with good conversation.

En Route from Kilkee – The road to Lahinch runs inland for the next 20 miles, but if you have time, detour to see the high cliffs of Ballard Bay guarded by an O'Brien tower or the White Strand beyond the village of Doonbeg. In the small fishing village of Quilty, one of the pubs, the *Leon,* is named after the Spanish Armada ship that was wrecked off nearby Mutton Island. The distinctive stone walls you will see on the beach here are for drying seaweed — a valued crop.

MILTOWN MALBAY: This village is a strong traditional music center that hosts each July the Willie Clancy School of Piping (named after a beloved local piper). Featured here are the *uilleann* pipes — the Irish type played with a bellows under the elbow. They have a wide melodic variation and none of the shrieking shrillness of their cousins, the Scottish warpipes. On a Sunday or a holiday, and particularly during the school term, almost any of the bars in Miltown Malbay will have traditional music, as will those in nearby villages such as Mullagh, the Crosses of Annagh, or Quilty. Be warned, however: Traditional music happens rather than is planned, and you have to stalk it.

The nearby resort of Spanish Point commemorates sailors of the Spanish Armada who drowned here in September 1588. Those whom the sea did not claim were butchered by the followers of Loyalist Sir Turlough O'Brien of Liscannor.

LAHINCH: Prettily set on the shores of Liscannor Bay, Lahinch is a cubistic composition of pastel houses perched on a cliff; it has a somewhat exotic Mediterranean look. There's plenty to do: surfboards can be rented at the beach; bicycles can be hired at *Tomo's Laundromat,* on Station Rd., (phone: 81022); boats are available, both for deep-sea and freshwater fishing; and a celebrated 18-hole championship golf course, open to guests (phone: 81003).

CHECKING IN: *Vaughan's Aberdeen Arms –* An oasis of comfort, this hostelry has 48 rooms with bath; the bar serves periwinkles, not peanuts; and the restaurant offers some very fine seafood — try the Clahane lobster broth or the poached Inagh salmon. Open April to October (phone: 81100). Moderate.

En Route from Lahinch – Take the coast road past the ruined tower house of Dough set among the golf greens on the left; on the right in the sandhills are the "tiger" holes of the golf course. Legend has it that fairy king Donn of the Sandhills rides his horse here on moonlit nights.

The ruined medieval church of Kilmacrehy is about a mile on, to your left. Its founder, St. Mac Creiche, fought dragons, cured plagues, and was buried between high and low tide at a spot called "Mac Creiche's bed."

LISCANNOR: An ancient O'Brien tower guards this fishing village and birthplace of John P. Holland, inventor of the submarine and founder of the Electric Boat Company (which became General Dynamics). There is a small museum and library of memorabilia. The road climbs steadily out of Liscannor and at one point you come abreast of a tall urn-crowned column on the left. This is a good stopping point. Below you is Liscannor Bay, and all the billowy coast toward Miltown Malbay. The column was built to honor local hero Cornelius O'Brien. Beside it is *Dabhac Bhrighde*, St. Bridget's Well, a vernacular folk shrine still much visited by pilgrims. Its rushing waters, its quaint whitewashed courtyard surrounded by scarlet fuchsia, even the ex-voto offerings of pictures, rosary beads, and a pair of crutches attest to an abiding religious feeling that dates to pre-Christian times when this was a spring sacred to an ancient Celtic goddess.

EATING OUT: *Captain's Deck* – On the upper level of an antiques shop overlooking Liscannor Bay, this rustic restaurant is earning a far-reaching reputation for its fresh seafood — from "stowaway's delight" (cod in the rough) to local lobster, salmon steaks, crab claws, and surf and turf. Open every night for dinner and weekends for lunch. Liscannor (phone: 81385). Moderate.

CLIFFS OF MOHER: Two miles from the well, you turn right into the parking lot for the Cliffs of Moher. You'll see a visitors center with restaurant and craft shop. Follow the path up the hillside to the little tower, built by Cornelius O'Brien, a Clare landlord and patron, who intended it as a teahouse "for the entertainment and refreshment of lady visitors." Now it's just a lookout, but the view from the top is spectacular: You look north to the Aran Islands and the Connemara mountains and south toward the Cliffs of Moher, a great curtain of sheer cliff face, rippling 5 miles along the coast and hanging over 600 feet above the sea.

En Route from Liscannor – Back on the road and past the Cliffs of Moher, you'll again catch some marvelous vistas out toward the Aran Islands. On Inisheer, the nearest, you'll see an O'Brien Castle and a lighthouse to the left, and a village to the right. The inhabitants of Inisheer speak Irish, farm and fish for a living, and retain many of the customs described in the plays and essays of John M. Synge and in the novels of Liam O'Flaherty.

The hills on the right of the road produce a slate flag — called Liscannor or Moher flag — which is used for roofing stables and outhouses and for decorative work in architecture. About 5 miles from the Cliffs of Moher is a detour 2 miles to the left to the village and harbor of Doolin. The village is a single row of thatched fisherman's houses. Beside them is a pub, *Gus O'Connor's*, which is famous for traditional music. From Doolin Harbor you can cross by motor launch (or in a curragh, if you want to go hazardously native) to Inisheer.

EATING OUT: *Ivy Cottage* – Also known as "Ilsa's Kitchen," this splendid little ivy-covered stone house is just a few doors down the road from Gus O'Connor's music pub. Specializing in wholefood dishes and locally caught seafood, this health food oasis also doubles as an art gallery. Open for dinner,

Wednesdays through Sundays, May to September. Doolin (phone: 74244). Moderate.

Killilagh House – A country house restaurant-cum-crafts gallery serving delicious meals. Open April through September for lunch and dinner. Roadford, Doolin (phone: 74183). Moderate.

Bruach na hAille – Here you'll fine simple but satisfying meals — fresh mackerel, scallops, crab, and other seafood. Doolin (phone: 74120). Inexpensive.

LISDOONVARNA: Beach hotels and boarding houses have been part of this spa resort since the 18th century due to its curative sulfur and iron springs. Lisdoonvarna is patronized by area residents in autumn, when, in addition to taking the waters, they play music, dance, and generally enjoy themselves. The *Spa Wells Health Centre* (phone: 74062) is open from June to October; a sulfur bath is £5. Lisdoonvarna also plays host to a folk festival during the second weekend in July, a nonstop music event — folk, rock, traditional, and country. In September, the *Matchmaking Festival of Ireland* is held here. (For festival information, contact the local tourist office during summer or the Limerick City tourist office year-round.)

CHECKING IN: Lisdoonvarna hotels are simple to the point of primitive, but guesthouses are uniformly good. The best of the lot is *Keane's,* which has 12 rooms, most of which have a bath. The owner is a botanist and Burren enthusiast and usually caters to a distinguished clientele (phone: 74011). Inexpensive.

En Route from Lisdoonvarna – You may take either of two routes to Ballyvaughan, either the scenic coast road to Black Head or the Corkscrew Road through the Burren country.

About a mile out on the former, you'll see the 15th-century O'Brien castle, Ballynalacken, a roofless but walled ruin. From the castle's parapets you have a great view west across the bay to the Aran Islands and east over the gray hills of the Burren. Continuing north from Ballynalacken, the road runs along a shelf between the sea and overhanging limestone terraces. It's about 10 miles to the lighthouse at Black Head, from which you have fine views across Galway Bay to the mountains of Mayo and Connemara. Another 5 miles takes you into Ballyvaughan.

The aptly named Corkscrew Road is a narrow, tortuous lane clinging to the Burren hillsides. The vistas are nothing short of breathtaking, with soft mists rising prismlike from the neighboring valleys. The Burren takes its name from the Irish word *boireann,* meaning "rocky." It is literally a rocky desert of silvery gray limestone. General Ludlow, a commander of Cromwell's, returned after a reconnaissance to report that it had "not enough wood to hang a man, earth to bury a man, or water to drown a man!"

The Burren arrived at its present denuded state through the actions of ice, water, air, and frost over scores of centuries. The final effect is unique, and not by any means depressing. The color of the rock ranges from a somber pewter to a light silver and it has been rubbed and carved into marvelous shapes. Long fingers of green reach between the crags to provide relief for the eye and summer grazing for cattle.

Because of the absence of trees or of heavy vegetation the Burren is open to broad untrammeled light, the combination of which with all the other weather factors produces the Burren's final glory — its wildflowers. In late spring, at the end of May, this desert blooms. The sparse patches of earth and grass on the bare rock face suddenly become bejeweled with as exotic a collection of flora as can be seen anywhere in the world. Clumps of creamy gold mountain avens from the Arctic grow side by side with tall red and white orchids or the scarlet splash of bloody cranesbill from the Mediterranean. Beside these are the intense blue stars of the spring flowering gentian, which also grow in the alps. Small wonder that the monks of nearby Corcomroe named their abbey St. Mary's of the Fertile Rock.

BALLYVAUGHAN: A little coastal village that is nestled in one of the green valleys that slope down from the Burren hills. Two miles southeast of town is Aillwee Cave, the only one in the burren you can visit. Its remarkable stalagmites and stalactites and mysterious bear pits draw over 100,000 visitors a year. Open daily year-round; for information, call 77036. A tea shop, restaurant, craft shop, and the Burren Gold Cheesemaking center are all at the entrance to the caves.

CHECKING IN: *Gregan's Castle* – There's a charming homey feeling about this antique-filled castle at the foot of Corkscrew Hill, overlooking the Burren country and Galway Bay. It has 16 cozy rooms, 12 with bath. Open March through October (phone: 77005). Moderate.

Hyland's – A clean, cheerful, and small (12 rooms, most with bath) inn, run by the seventh and eighth generation of Hyland's, with a dining room that features seafood. Open April to October (phone: 77037). Moderate.

EATING OUT: *Manus Walsh's Gallery and Restaurant* – At this jewel of a restaurant, Manus sells paintings and crafts and his wife, Claire, serves up scrumptious lobster, crab, mackerel, and homemade breads and cakes. Open for dinner only, April through September (phone: 77029). Moderate.

Some atmospheric pubs in town include: the *Ballyvaughan Inn,* which offers folk music and talk; *MacNeill O'LocLainn's,* another tiny and traditional pub; and the *Monk's Harbour Bar,* a place at the pier with seafood and music.

En Route from Ballyvaughan – About 3 miles on is a spectacular tomb, the Poulnabrone Portal dolmen, well worth stopping your car and walking across the field to view. A few miles farther are signposts to the right for Caherconnell, a well-preserved *caher,* or stone ring fort, which protected four Iron Age and early Christian settlements. At the next crossroad stands Leamaneh Castle, a tower house built by the O'Briens in the 15th century, enlarged and fortified in the 17th century, and abandoned in the 18th century in favor of Dromoland Castle. Features of Leamaneh — a fireplace and gateway — were subsequently moved to Dromoland.

A 4-mile digression into the village of Kilfenora is recommended for a look at the remains of its 12th-century cathedral whose chancel has some very good stone carving. In the cemetery are the three Irish high crosses carved with Bible scenes and Celtic and Scandinavian interlace ornamentation. The crosses are very typical of Irish art. The Kilfenora Burren Display Centre is a very worthwhile stop. Here, the unusual and fascinating flora of the Burren is reproduced in wax and silk, with special lighting and models to help explain what is special about the area and how it came to be. It's open daily from mid-March through October (phone: 88030).

Return to the crossroads and turn south on the main road toward Corofin, where you can visit the Clare Heritage Centre, housed in St. Catherine's Church. This museum portrays the history of western Ireland from 1800–60, a significant period of famine and mass emigration to the US. The collection includes genealogical tracts, local sculptural exhibits, archaeological artifacts, and photographs (open daily mid-March to late October; admission charge; phone: 27955 and 27632). From Corofin, it's 13 miles back to Ennis.

EATING OUT: *Maryse and Gilbert's* – A half-mile north of Corofin on its own grounds, this farmhouse restaurant specializes in French and Italian dishes, with garden-fresh Irish ingredients. Menu items include chicken cacciatore, lamb primavera, filet of beef *en moutarde,* pork steak *au citron,* pasta carbonara, and tagliatelle with smoked salmon. Dinner only; closed Mondays. Corofin (phone: 27660). Moderate.

An alternative to returning to Ennis would be to continue southeast from Ballyvaughan toward Gort and Thoor Ballylee, after which you could connect with the *Connemara* tour route.

Continue along the coast road from Ballyvaughan for 9 miles and turn right at

Bell Harbour, where there is a green monument signpost for Corcomroe Abbey. The abbey is reached by a narrow lane (signposted) just beyond the post office. Corcomroe, or St. Mary of the Fertile Rock, was founded in 1196 for the Cistercians by Donal Mor O'Brien, king of Munster. The church is distinguished by some vigorous Irish Romanesque carving on its columns, and there is an important tomb of Conor O'Brien, grandson of the founder.

Some 15 miles farther is Kinvara, home of the 15th-century Dun Gaire Castle, which overlooks Galway Bay and offers delightful medieval banquets on summer evenings. (For information or reservations, call 61788).

Take a sharp right turn along the road signposted for Gort, which is about 11 miles distant. Then, about a mile outside Gort, on the Galway road, turn left following signposts into Coole Park, the estate of Lady Augusta Gregory, the playwright and founder of the Abbey Theatre, and hostess to such literary lights as W. B. Yeats, George Bernard Shaw, John M. Synge, and Sean O'Casey. The house has been demolished, but the garden, with its autograph tree, survives. Walk by the lake and through the woods so often described by Yeats in his verse.

After Coole Park, continue along the Galway road for another mile and turn right at the signpost for Thoor Ballylee; follow the narrow road for a mile or so.

Thoor Ballylee, a 16th-century tower house built by the De Burgo family, was Yeats's home from 1917 to 1929 and a frequent symbol in his poetry. It's open daily during the summer; for information, call 091-31436. Stop in the bookshop for a look and in the tea shop for a cup and a slice of "barm brack" — raisin cake.

From here, it's just 21 miles on the main road to Galway City.

Connemara

There's scarcely any other part of Ireland where you come so intimately in touch with the past as in Connemara. That ancient Gaelic kingdom of bogland and mountain stretches across west Galway to the rocky rim of the wild Atlantic. It lies many removes from the modern world, a haunted mystical land where some kind of time warp seems to have made the centuries come to a halt.

Most Connemara people still speak the ancient Erse language. Now called Irish, it is the mother tongue that has been nearly stilled throughout other parts of Ireland. In Connemara, you will find the biggest Gaeltacht — a region where Irish is the everyday language — in Ireland. But the reality nowadays is that most of the population, particularly the young, is bilingual, fluent in both Irish and English. And, with English emerging as the international medium of communication, Irish is increasingly threatened by extinction. However, the mother tongue *does* live and any visitor going into Connemara who has taken the trouble to learn a few Irish phrases will win an appreciative and warm welcome and won't go short of a drink.

It isn't merely the language that causes the echoes of other days to ring plangently through the glens and mountains of Connemara. This rugged and tempestuous land is a rich repository of many facets of the Celtic past. Everywhere there is a brooding sense of Ireland's ancient culture and tradition. And also to be found are vestiges of a way of life that was common to all European peasant societies many centuries ago.

Since those great mountains were sculpted against the western Irish sky and those glens were chiseled deep into the earth, the Connemara landscape has hardly changed and man has barely fixed his stamp on it. It is a stark and unyielding place that has shaped its people into strong and independent individuals with a stoic and earthy eye to the rest of the world.

The land was always begrudging to yield its beggarly substance, but the Connemara peasants farmed every crevice of its flinty earth. In the old days they lived off potatoes, and when the horrendous potato blight fell upon Ireland in the 1840s, they suffered more than most others from the famine that followed. Thousands died in their thatched hovels or out in the stony fields and wild bogs, and thousands more fled westward to the shores of "Amerikay." Since then the region has been sparsely populated, the drain on its people continuing through emigration until today, when industrialization has slowed the flight from the land.

The sea is the other mighty element Connemara people have to wrestle with, and their battles have inspired such writers as John Millington Synge and Liam O'Flaherty to powerful prose and poetry. Until recent times, Connemara fisherfolk rode the Atlantic breakers in fragile curraghs to farm the sea. (The *curragh* is a boat of immemorial vintage, which originally was made from hides but now is sheathed in tarred canvas.) You can still see curraghs, powered by sinew and oar, off the Connemara coast today. They look like black scimitar blades knifing through the waves, seemingly frail and vulnerable but, in fact, ingeniously crafted to ride out the angriest of storms. They are widely used yet by the Aran Islanders.

Nobody should ever go to Connemara without also visiting the Aran Islands. They lie west of the mainland, facing the open mouth of Galway Bay, three rocky islands stripped bare of all trees by the Atlantic winds. Their isolation helps to preserve ancient traditions even more perfectly than in Connemara. Much of the primeval peasant lifestyle remains intact on the islands — even down to the dress worn by the old people. The biggest island, Inishmore, which attracts the preponderance of outside visitors, is developing beady-eyed commercial instincts, but the other two, Inishmaan and Inisheer, still almost totally maintain the ambience of another age.

The rapidly developing technologies of the twentieth century are only now beginning to come into Connemara. There are at last factories for the young people to work in instead of being forced onto the emigrant ship. The fishing industry is gradually being taken out of the curragh age. A measure of affluence has come upon the land. The old thatch cottages with their lime-washed stonewalls are coming down to be replaced by rather alien-looking "mod-con" (that is, modern convenience) bungalows.

But in Connemara the elemental link between man, the earth, and the sea is still a force. The old ways still survive and man faces nature with tools that are not much more advanced than those used at the dawn of civilization. And man somehow seems inconsequential out there on the Connemara landscape with its great gnarled mountains rearing into the sky, lone and level bogs spreading out toward desolate horizons, rivers racing toward the freedom of the sea, and valleys that have been lost to the outside world.

Our route starts in Galway City and heads northwest from there into

Connemara territory. The road coils in a serpentine circle through valleys and mountains, at times verging the Atlantic and going through most of the untamed and rugged areas of unsurpassed beauty that have made Connemara famous. We travel along the edge of Galway Bay to get back into Galway City and then we take off for the Aran Islands.

An opening word of utmost caution: The roads you will be traveling over are for the most part narrow, winding, and poorly surfaced, in addition to which Irish drivers display an unnervingly cavalier attitude at the wheel. So, drive slowly, keep very much to the *left,* and at all times be prepared to encounter flocks of sheep or herds of cattle around that next bend.

A double room in a hotel listed as expensive will cost $40 to $55 or more a night; moderate means $30 to $40. Dinner for two (with wine) in the moderate category will run $30 to $40; expensive, more.

GALWAY CITY: For a complete report on the city, its sights, restaurants, and hotels, see *Galway,* THE CITIES.

En Route from Galway City – Take N59 to the village of Oughterard, 17 miles away. This road runs almost parallel with Lough Corrib, a marvelous fishing lake that is on your right all the way to Oughterard (pronounced ookther-ard). Most of the side roads to the right will take you to the shores of the lake, and it is easy enough to hire rowing or powered boats for pleasure trips on the lough or for fishing. (See *Sources and Resources,* GALWAY.)

OUGHTERARD: When you get to Oughterard it is worth visiting the 16th-century Aughnanure Castle, which is signposted and 2 miles southeast of the town. It was the redoubt of the ferocious O'Flaherty tribe who exhibited sanguinary instincts similar to the Borgias, once dispatching a dinner guest through a flagstone trap door into the river beneath the banquet hall. The castle has been restored.

But angling is the life and soul of Oughterard. Wander into any of the pubs or hotels and you will quickly find yourself immersed in the great terminological inexactitudes of fishing lore. Angling tourists from all over Europe come here to pursue the trout and salmon of Lough Corrib and the fish landed sometimes have been known to be even more immense than the ones that got away. Wander into *Keogh's* emporium on the main street (phone: 091-82212) and arm yourself with a rod bought or rented and get onto the lake for great thrills.

One period of the year, around about mid-May, is known as the time of the "carnival of the trout." That is when great clouds of newly hatched mayflies hover over the lake, and the trout go mad for them. Anglers capture masses of the mayfly, impale them on hooks, and "dap" them on the surface of the water with the aid of a special fishing line; the trout come out with their hands up.

CHECKING IN: *Sweeney's Oughterard House* – A delightful ivy-smothered Georgian house with a deserved international reputation, this family-run hotel offers superb cuisine. Its sumptuous dinners are for hotel guests only, but casual visitors can feast on a rich range of unusual fare in the lounge-bar. Through the town, turn right over the bridge beside the church, left again, and you're there (phone: 091-82207). Expensive.

Connemara Gateway – A classy, modern motel that has recently been refurbished, with 48 comfortable rooms, an outdoor swimming pool, pretty gardens, and a fairly good restaurant featuring some homemade specialties. The staff is extremely friendly. On the main road from Galway City, just before entering Oughterard (phone: 091-82328). Moderate.

Currarevagh House – An aristocratic home on Lough Corrib, now a peaceful and relaxing guesthouse. Open only from April to October. Reservations necessary. Second right turn on entering Oughterard, signposted for the 4 miles to the lakeside (phone: 091-82313). Moderate.

 EATING OUT: *Silver Teal* – Seafood is the specialty here; try the fresh salmon. Moycullen village, 7 miles north on the road to Oughterard (phone: 85274). Expensive.

Drimcong House – A lovely old country house now serves as the backdrop for one of Ireland's best restaurants. Like the decor, the cuisine is elegant yet unpretentious, and the service super-efficient yet unobstrusive. Specialties include excellent wild game, spiced beef, salmon, and oysters. It is a dining experience not to be missed. One mile north of Moycullen village on N59 (phone: 85115). Expensive.

En Route from Oughterard – Still traveling northwest on N59, you are beginning to move into Connemara, but in this particular area the Irish language is rarely heard and you must travel much farther to reach the Gaeltacht areas. The land beyond Oughterard is desolate and bare, though in a valley to the left there are a number of small lakes. Ten miles out, you reach Maam Cross, an intersection where you turn right onto L100, a very precarious road where you carefully — *very* carefully — make your way into the lonely valley of Maam.

When Orson Welles passed this way at the age of 17 — long before becoming the *enfant terrible* of American radio, stage, and screen — he came riding on a donkey, probably the very best way to travel here. Motorists should stop often and get out and sit on a rock or a stone bridge, just to immerse themselves in the atmosphere or maybe to talk to a passing farmer. There is also much to see *above* the land itself. Look upward because artists have come from many lands to do just that in Connemara. Unless there is heavy sea mist or fog or impenetrable overcast, the sky above Connemara is a living mural of constantly changing cloud patterns with an astonishing interplay of light, color, and shadow, never for a moment the same and always a source of impassioned inspiration and agonizing frustration for painters.

Five miles farther on, you reach Maam Bridge and turn left to head toward the village of Leenane, 9 miles away. You are now deep in the Maam Valley, with the craggy Maamturk Mountains that dominate the Joyce Country on your left and the hills of south Mayo to your right. Two diversions might be worth venturing on here. From Maam Bridge you can take a road south into the Joyce Country until you come to the hill of Maumeen where legend says St. Patrick slept and where a sacred well named after him is still a place of pilgrimage. It is just 10 miles away amid magnificent mountain country. Or, 5 miles along the road to Leenane, you can turn right at the signpost for Lake Nafooey, which lies 5 miles away in a sequestered valley of bogland grandeur. You won't find anything closer to Shangri-La than Nafooey, outside the pages of a book.

CHECKING IN/EATING OUT: *Peacocks* – A sort of Celtic bazaar at Maam Cross, but offering a valuable service to tourists. There's a big bar for booze and fast grub; a more sedate sit-down restaurant with good fare; a shop with the whole bag of stereotypical Emerald Isle souvenirs — tweeds, wools, pottery; a small supermarket; a car accessories shop; and a filling station. You can even stay overnight. Maam Cross (phone: 091-82306). Moderate.

LEENANE: This lovely village is lost at the bottom of a bowl of mountains, one of whose peaks is called "the Devil's Mother." Leenane also lies close to Killary Harbour, the only true Scandinavian-style fjord to be found in Ireland. The long arm of water reaches deeply in between giant mountains for 10 miles, and roads lining each side of the inlet provide dramatic panoramas of land and sea. The road north from Leenane goes into Mayo; walk 3 miles up this road for a view of the Aasleagh Falls on the Erriff River, and maybe to fish for salmon there, too.

En Route from Leenane – Head west on the road to Clifden, which runs along the shore of the Killary fjord. But there is much to view in between and a few byways to explore. Ten miles down the road you pass by Kylemore Abbey, a modern gothic building across a lake on your right. This was built by a doctor in the 19th century as an adoring and lasting monument to his wife, and is now a high-toned school for girls run by Benedictine nuns. They'll show you around the castle library, church, and pottery. They also serve the daintiest of teas.

CHECKING IN: *Kylemore House* – Not to be confused with the *Kylemore Pass* hotel, this is a truly superior place to stay, one of a number in this area. It's worth a visit if only to see the precious antique furniture and paintings that adorn it. Absolute luxury, 7 acres of woods, 3 private fishing lakes with salmon and trout, and a table par excellence. A real find. Reservations essential. 3 miles east of Kylemore Abbey on N59, the main Leenane-Clifden road (phone: 095-41143). Moderate.

RENVYLE: About 1 mile west of Kylemore, you'll see a signpost on the right for Renvyle, 6 miles away. This will take you north of the main route to the precarious verge of the Atlantic Ocean, where the rocky headland juts defiantly out into the water. Locals say that if while standing there you look directly west and squint hard, you'll see the next parish — Brooklyn! Out on the promontory is yet another ruined castle of those terrible O'Flahertys. All round this area are some very lovely and safe beaches. On the way into Renvyle you will have passed through another village called Tullycross and here you can see modern versions of the traditional thatched Irish cottages that have been fitted with comforts and conveniences unknown to the peasantry of yore. These cottages can be rented at moderate rates though reservations far in advance are essential. (For information, call Áras Fáilte at 091-63081.)

CHECKING IN: *Renvyle House* – At this elegant hotel perched above the sea, the decor is of another age and an air of graciousness prevails. It once was the country residence of the great Irish wit, Oliver St. John Gogarty, the prototype of the character Buck Mulligan in Joyce's *Ulysses.* Closed January, February, and most of March. Signposted on the right, 1½ miles past Tully Cross (phone: 095-43434 or 43444). Moderate.

LETTERFRACK: It's about 8 miles from Renvyle back through Tullycross into Letterfrack village, back to the main road from Leenane to Clifden. Letterfrack is a crossroads village of great charm. Visit most any of the pubs in the evening and you'll hear some of the best genuine Irish music played on fiddle and tin whistle. The village also lies in the shadow of the towering range of mountains called "the Twelve Bens." Just recently, the Irish government has taken over 3,800 acres of this wild mountainous terrain and turned it into a national park. It shouldn't be missed. The entrance is only about 100 yards south of the main street of Letterfrack. There are wide-open spaces in which to pitch camp, and Diamond Mountain — reaching heavenward in the middle of the park — just begs to be climbed. While at the national park, you can also get a close look at the famous Connemara ponies. Indeed, these sturdy and tough little horses, renowned for their endurance, jumping powers, and amiability, can be found roaming all over Connemara. Some people believe that they are descended from Spanish horses that swam to the safety of the Connemara coast from ships wrecked in the Spanish Armada and interbred with local strains. Others say they have Egyptian bloodlines. Whatever the true story, the Connemara pony is now a breed of international celebrity, and there are Connemara pony societies all over the world, including the US.

 CHECKING IN: *Rosleague Manor* – Run by two more of the famous Foyle family, this gracious Georgian manor overlooks a quiet bay. Unusually good food. Open Easter through October. 2 miles west of Letterfrack on N59, the main road to Clifden (phone: 095-41101). Moderate.

 EATING OUT: *Doon* – Hidden behind hedges so you can easily miss it, *Doon* is a great find: fresh orange juice, lobster salads, chocolate cream slices, fresh fish, and more served from 12:30 to 3 PM only. 4 miles west of Letterfrack, watch carefully for a tiny notice that says "Doon" stuck in the hedge, and turn right (phone: 095-41139). Moderate.

CLIFDEN: This town, on the main road 9 miles from Letterfrack, is cradled in a glen at the head of an Atlantic inlet into which a river rushes. Though it has a population of little more than 1,000, Clifden is called the capital of Connemara, a label that might be challenged by people in southern Connemara where scarcely anything but Irish is spoken. Clifden is an English-speaking town, a legacy of the days when it was a favorite seaside summer resort of the British gentry. Many army officers from Dublin Castle (the former seat of British rule in Ireland) built or bought landed manors in and around Clifden, and some of those splendid residences are among the better hotels we have cited in this chapter.

Almost forgotten now is the fact that the first wireless messages from Europe to America were sent from Clifden. The inventor of radio, Marconi, set up a station in Derrygimlagh Bog, 4 miles south of the town. Marconi himself spent much time in Clifden. The buildings that housed the transatlantic wireless station were destroyed during the Irish civil war of the early 1920s, but some of the transmitting masts are still standing. The same bog has claim to another historic distinction. It was on its peaty surface in 1919 that the aviators John William Alcock and Arthur Whitten Brown landed their biplane, after having flown from Newfoundland to complete the first nonstop transatlantic flight. A pile of stones marks the spot today, and nearby there's a more imposing limestone monument of a tailplane commemorating the event. These sites are well marked; travel about 4 miles out of the Ballyconneely road to get to them.

Anyone visiting Clifden must ascend the dizzying heights of the Sky Road, well named because when you're toiling up its steep slope you feel you may well reach the sky. The road is signposted from the town's central square; it's narrow and heart-stoppingly sheer and requires skilled gear-shifting if you're in a car. As you ascend, a fabulous view of Clifden Bay and the savage rocky west coast spreads out beneath you; farther out, you can see the small islands nestled like humpbacked whales in the Atlantic. At the highest point there's a walled-in car park where you can rest to take in the view at leisure and maybe have a picnic.

The fishing village of Cleggan, 7 miles to the northwest, should also be visited when you're in Clifden. Double back on the main road to Leenane and at Streamstown turn left. Cleggan is the embarkation point for Inishbofin Island, which in recent times has become a haunt of poets, philosophers, and artists from many lands. The mail boat that leaves Cleggan every noon — the temperamental Atlantic permitting — will carry you to the island. If a really bad storm brews up, though, you may be marooned on the island for days or even weeks, but in view of the hospitality and friendliness of the islanders, you could meet worse fates. The ruins of a monastery founded by St. Colman in the 7th century are still there, and the island also was once in the possession of those terrible O'Flahertys. The daring sea queen of the western waters, Grainne Ui Mhaille (pronounced *grawn*-ya ee *whal*-ya and translated as "Grace O'Malley"), also found shelter for her warships here in the days when she rebelled against the sovereignty of

Queen Elizabeth. The iron gauntlet of Cromwell fell on the island in 1652 and the barracks where his Roundheads were billeted stands at the harbor entrance.

CHECKING IN: *Abbeyglen Castle* – This place was dignified with the name of a castle after architectural tinkering added castellated turrets to what was a charming old mansion needing no such cosmetics, but it's still a great place to stay. It is tucked away in a beautiful setting of gardens, waterfalls, and streams, with the monumental Twelve Bens forming a breathtaking backdrop. Sumptuous suites overlook the Atlantic, and the dining room cuisine, with a decidedly French accent, has won several prestigious awards. Sky Road, Clifden (phone: 095-21070). Expensive.

Rock Glen Manor House – A converted 19th-century shooting lodge set amid sylvan glades and stony mountains on the edge of the Atlantic, this is a beautiful and restful retreat where guests are given warm personal attention. There's a spacious drawing room stuffed with antiques, an old-fashioned billiards and snooker room, a small intimate bar, and a marvelous restaurant. The owner, John Roche, does all the cooking, specializing in shellfish, salmon, trout, and mountain lamb. One mile south of Clifden on L102, the Ballyconneely Rd. (phone: 095-21035 or -21393). Expensive.

Alcock and Brown – Named after the two flyers who made the first nonstop transatlantic flight from Newfoundland to Clifden, this is a very good modern hotel set right in the center of Clifden town. All the creature comforts are provided, including a commendable table graced mostly by fresh fish and mountain lamb. Market Square, Clifden (phone: 095-21086). Moderate.

Celtic – Exceptionally friendly house where management and staff go out of their way to ensure your comfort. Pleasant rooms and a good restaurant. Main St., Clifden (phone: Clifden 115). Moderate.

Clifden Bay – The original hostelry founded by the Foyle family already mentioned, and a place of warm informality, with music sessions on many evenings, lovely rooms, and fine food. Main St., Clifden (phone: Clifden 128). Moderate.

EATING OUT: *D'Arcy Inn* – Charming pub and eating place. Downstairs for the drink and the singing; upstairs for the toothsome delicacies, many of Continental inspiration. Main St., Clifden (phone: Clifden 202). Moderate.

High Moors – Exceptionally fine dinners — with local lamb, fish, and homegrown vegetables — are served in this quaint old house with magnificent views across Clifden Bay. Dooneen, Clifden, ¾ mile outside town on L102, the Ballyconneely Rd., signposted (phone: 095-21342). Moderate.

O'Grady's Seafood – All creatures great and small, shelled and unshelled, from the surrounding Atlantic, find their way onto the tables of this quintessential fish specialty house, among the very best in Ireland. Market St., Clifden (phone: 095-21450). Moderate.

En Route from Clifden – Head roughly southeast toward Galway City on the "low road," L102, which hugs the jagged northern coast of the bay almost the whole way. It takes you quickly into the Gaeltacht area where most of the signposts are in Irish, but you're not likely to get lost for any great length of time and most people can speak English anyway to get you back on the track. Besides, it's a nice place to get lost in.

ROUNDSTONE: This is one of the loveliest sea villages in Connemara and in summertime it is crowded with tourists from across the globe. Its Irish name is *Cloch nah Ron,* which means "Rock of the Seals," and in the evening you can indeed see the whiskered heads of seals bobbing in the bay. Two granite piers built in the 19th century jut into the bay to protect the fishing boats. Rising almost directly behind the main street is Errisbeg Mountain, which is easy to ascend and from its summit you can see just about all of the west coast. The two finest beaches in Connemara are off the main road, less than 2 miles west of the village.

BALLYNAHINCH: Continue on the coast road from Roundstone for 10 miles to Ballynahinch, which is signposted and where you'll find the splendid Castle of Ballynahinch amid woodlands behind turreted gates. In a way, this is the true capital of ancient Connemara, because here resided the powerful albeit eccentric Martin family who were simply granted just about all of Connemara by an English king in the 18th century. (One of the Martins had a very nimble intuition: He pledged the right allegiance to the right royal house at the right time.) The dispossessed O'Flahertys (yes, those wild ones again) hated the Martins and put to the sword any that crossed their path, though the Martins themselves were no mean swordsmen. One of them, Dick Martin, won notoriety as a duelist, but redeemed his reputation by founding the Society for the Prevention of Cruelty to Animals, thus earning the name "Humanity Dick." The castle, now a hotel, has a magnificent setting among mountains, lakes, and woods. The Ballynahinch Fishery is world famous for salmon angling.

Leaving Ballynahinch Castle, double back on the road until you reach the signpost for Cashel and continue southeast along the coast once more. Cashel is lush with vegetation and shrubbery and provides a warm contrast with the stonier and starker face of the Connemara landscape. The view seaward is breathtaking.

CHECKING IN: *Ballynahinch Castle* – Ancestral home of the Martin dynasty and now a hotel that echoes with history. Truly striking scenery and some of the best salmon fishing anywhere. Much frequented by American visitors. Open June 1 to October 12. 10 miles from Roundstone as you head for Galway City (phone: Clifden 135). Expensive.

Cashel House – Often cited as one of Ireland's best hotels. Charles de Gaulle stayed here. Sheltered gardens, monastic quiet, and delicious food. Book well in advance. On the coast road from Roundstone to Galway City, 14 miles from Roundstone (phone: Cashel, Co. Galway 9). Expensive.

Zetland – The feeling is warm and hospitable at this hotel set in a lushly wooded ground. It has its own fishing facilities (for salmon and sea trout) and a fine dining room. 14 miles from Roundstone on the coast road to Galway City (phone: Cashel, Co. Galway 8 or 34). Expensive. *N.B.: Make sure you specify Co. Galway because there's another Cashel in Co. Tipperary.*

CARNA: About 10 miles south of Cashel, this sea village is in the heart of the Irish-speaking district. July, when there are a number of festivals of a maritime flavor, is a good time to be in Carna. The old sailing boats called "hookers" and "pucauns," along with the curraghs already mentioned, gather off Carna for regattas and races. Carna is also a marvelous place for traditional Irish music. You'll be welcome to join the informal sessions in the pubs or to go to an Irish dance which is known as a *ceili* (pronounced *kay*-lee). It's also worth taking a trip out to MacDara's Island, the resting place of St. MacDara, protector of fishermen who still dip their oars in salute as they sail past the island. From Carna continue along the meandering coast road through Kilkieran to Gortmore and turn right here at the signpost to Rosmuc.

ROSMUC: This isolated area is a venerated place in modern Irish history. It was in a cottage here that the mystic poet and philosopher Padraig Pearse, who led the 1916 Rising against the British in Dublin, sought seclusion to contemplate Ireland's Celtic past and to dream of revolution and a free nation. Many leading political figures of those times joined him in the cottage to ponder Ireland's destiny. After the rising, Pearse and the other leaders were shot, but their action led to independence for the southern part of Ireland within 5 years. The cottage is a national monument open to the public.

Returning to Gortmore and the L102, turn right and travel as far as Screeb, 3 miles away, then right again until you come to Costelloe. Detour northwest here following the signpost to Carraroe.

CARRAROE: This village set amid furze-clad hills and stony fields is a place where the lingering charm of the past is at its strongest. Irish is the lingua franca and in the small farms, the old traditional ways of cultivating the land are still used. Children from all over Ireland come here in summer to gain fluency in speaking Irish. There are a number of pristine beaches tucked away in niches along the rugged shoreline, including a small coral strand less than 2 miles from the village. Return now to Costelloe and head southeast on L100. Just before the village of Inverin, the road straightens out and runs directly east to Galway City, 16 miles away, and for the entire run you have Galway Bay on your right.

 CHECKING IN: *Ostan Cheathru Rua* – Pronounced *oh*-shtawn kah-roo roo-ah, which means "Hotel Carraroe," this is the only hostelry that can, with an easy conscience, be recommended in this locality. It is up-to-date and most comfortable and the cuisine is good. Very often there are enjoyable sessions of Irish music. Open May 29 to October 2. A highly visible signpost on the village's main street points the way. Carraroe (phone: 091-95116). Expensive.

Ostan Charna – Comfortable, pleasant, and quite affordable; the food is nothing fancy, but it's fresh and wholesome, with particularly good lamb and fish. In Carna village (phone: Carna 21 or 22). Inexpensive.

 EATING OUT: *Boluisce* – Lobster and prawn are the shellfish of choice at this restaurant specializing in seafood. In the village of Spiddal, on the coast road, 100, from Carraroe to Galway City (phone: 091-83286). Moderate.

ARAN ISLANDS: Galway City is the best jumping-off spot for the Aran Islands and you can travel either by sea or plane. In summertime when the weather is good, the sea voyage in the motor vessels that sail from Galway harbor is the most enjoyable way to go as you get a chance to mingle and maybe share a pint with some of the islanders.

All three of the Aran Islands seem like geographical relics of the stone age abandoned in the Atlantic. They are hewn out of solid rock with a penurious layer of soil in some places, while in others there is no grass, only great slabs of stone. When the celebrated American film maker Robert Flaherty made a documentary of life on Aran in the thirties, one sequence showed a farmer grinding rock to dust and sprinkling it over his fields as topsoil. That was Flaherty indulging in undue artistic license to highlight the hardship of island life; such things never happened, but, still, the rigors of wresting a subsistence from the land and the sea around were heartbreaking.

The islands are named Inishmore or the big island; Inishmaan, the middle island; and Inisheer, the eastern island, which is the smallest. All three have their own charms and their barren isolation has impregnably immured them in the past. They keep extant a way of life that has long since passed away in almost every other part of Europe. The big island, Inishmore, which has more constant and active contact with the mainland and attracts most of the tourists, is slipping more rapidly into the modern age than its two sister isles. The influx of free-spending tourists on Inishmore has uncovered a mercenary streak there. But the two smaller islands, Inishmaan and Inisheer, are the more fascinating ones for any visitor. On both of those many of the older inhabitants still dress in the colorful garb worn by their forefathers centuries ago.

The islands were inhabited in prehistoric times, possibly by the race known as the Fir Bolg, and on Inishmore is the spectacular remains of an ancient civilization — the great fort called Dun Aengus. It is a savage symphony in stone spread over 12 acres on a cliff high above the Atlantic. There is another massive fort called Dun Chonchuir (pronounced Doon Krah-hoor) on Inishmaan and exploration of both those fortresses is quite rewarding.

On Inishmaan and Inisheer it would be almost sacrilegious to move around other than on foot — not that there's much choice as the automobile is still alien to these places. You can ride around on a horse-drawn jaunting car or on bicycles. Inishmore has a few taxis and one or two minibuses. But walking also allows you to get closer to the pre-Christian and early Christian ruins that are everywhere to be found. The islands were a stronghold of the very special Irish monasticism of the 6th and 7th centuries.

Apart from safaris back into the Celtic past, there are many other intriguing things to see and do on the island. The tiny little pubs, some of them roofed in thatch, are scenes of boisterous merriment and song. You can fish off the coastal rocks or get a fisherman to take you out for a ride in a curragh, which can be quite a thrill. Some propitious fate has decreed that the waters washing the beaches of Inishmore be a little warmer than off the mainland, so the swimming can be good on hot summer days. The sheer cliffs rising from the ocean will test the nerve of anyone with a mountaineering spirit.

To get to Aran by plane, call Aer Arann at Áras Fáilte (the tourism office) off Eyre Square in Galway City; phone: 091-65119. There are several flights each day from Carnmore Airport, 5 miles north of the city off the Monivea Road.

The sea trips to the island are run by Córas Iompair Éireann (CIE), the national transport agency. During summer they sail daily with the tide to Inishmore, with stopoffs at the other two islands. At other times of the year, there are sailings only twice a week. For details contact CIE at the Railway Station, Eyre Sq., Galway City; phone: 091-62141.

There is an alternative daily sea route from Rossaveal Harbour in Connemara, serving the three islands. Arrangements for these trips can be made by contacting the Áras Fáilte office, off Eyre Sq., Galway City; phone: 091-63081.

CHECKING IN: Most accommodation on the islands is provided in private homes and is of a generally high standard. Arrangements can be made for bed-and-breakfast or for partial board (includes dinner in the evening) or full board (includes both lunch and dinner). The map *Oileain Arann,* mentioned above, has an almost complete list of all the homes offering accommodation. Bed-and-breakfast for two averages $25 to $30 a day, partial board $40 to $45, and full board about $55 to $60. A list of homes approved by Board Failte, the Irish Tourist Board, is available at the Galway City office, Aras Failte, off Eyre Square (phone: 091-63081 or -65201 or -65202).

Johnston Hernon's Kilmurvey House – A comfortable 8-bedroom guesthouse, close to Dun Aengus. Nothing pretentious in the cuisine, but the food is wholesome and usually there's excellent fresh fish. Kilmurvey village, abut 6 miles west of Kilronan, Inishmore (phone: 099-61218). Inexpensive.

Inisheer – Newly built, this is the only true hotel in Aran and quite a good one, although it has only 10 rooms. The food is commendable if very traditional with no frills. A few hundred yards south of the landing pier, Inisheer (phone: 091-65226 or -65227). Inexpensive.

EATING OUT: *An tSean Cheibh (pronounced "Un Chan Kayve" and meaning The Old Pier)* – As might be expected, fish, in endless varieties, is the strong point of the house, although native lamb and beef dishes, conjured up with French flair or in traditional home-cooked style, are top rate. The restaurant is in the style of an Aran cottage, with lime-painted stone walls and an outdoor terrace overlooking the sea for al fresco dining. By far the best restaurant on the islands, it is open from morning until late at night from May to September. A 3-minute walk from the landing pier, Kilronan, Inishmore (phone: 099-61228). Moderate.

Dun Aonghusa – Very good food, with fish predominant, in pleasant old-fashioned surroundings, with timbered stone walls and an enormous open fireplace. Beside the landing pier, overlooking Galway Bay, Kilronan, Inishmore (phone: 099-61104). Moderate.

Southern Mayo

 Above brooding Connemara, the Mweelrea and Partry Mountains and the Sheeffrey Hills of southern County Mayo give way to a gentler landscape that wraps its way around the beautiful, island-studded Clew Bay. Croagh Patrick, the stately mountain where St. Patrick is said to have prayed and fasted for forty days for the salvation of the Irish people, is the dominant feature of the bay's southern shore, while Achill Island, Ireland's largest offshore island, guards the northwestern reaches of the bay. Inland, a series of lakes, most notably Lough Mask, which feeds into Lough Corrib near Mayo's border with County Galway, offer anglers excellent trout fishing. Southern Mayo's natural amenities and leisure facilities present traditional Ireland at its best, and many names associated with its heritage are famed in song and story.

The coastline, which presents a succession of sandy beaches, rugged headlands, and dramatic cliffs, is steeped in the legends of Grace O'Malley (Grainne Ui Mhaille), the 16th-century warrior sea queen who made herself ruler of the district that surrounds Clew Bay and its islands after the death of her father. While some doubt the veracity of her legendary exploits, they have been handed down in the spoken tradition of the islanders and in the historical novel *Queen of Men* by William O'Brien. One of the most interesting tales concerns a marriage contract she made with her second husband, MacWilliam Oughter. They agreed that either party could dissolve the union after one year merely by saying, "I dismiss you!" Grace O'Malley took advantage of the escape clause at the end of the year, but not before she had garrisoned all of Oughter's coastal castles with her own followers to make her position as ruler of the area even stronger.

And while the authenticity of Irish history reaches back no farther than the 7th century, the plain of Southern Moytura near Cong is said to have been the scene of the first battle between two mythical tribes that ruled this area 3,000 years ago, the Fir Bolg, a race of small dark men, and the fair Tuatha De Denaan, said to be a race of magicians. Though the Denaan were victorious here they were later overcome in the Celtic conquest. Legend says the defeated Denaan changed themselves into fairies and ever since have inhabited the hills, forts, and caves of Ireland. Beneath the rocks of Cong, there are more than forty dark, unearthly looking caves, and not a few locals will tell you that it is likely that many of the "little people" went to live there.

There is more historical certainty about the role that Mayo men played in the agitations of the Land League, formed to help tenant farmers resist tyrannical and rent-racking landlords. Michael Davit, one of the founders of the league, was born at Straid, near Castlebar, and Captain Charles Boycott, one of the league's targets, lived at Lough Mask House on the shores of the southern Mayo lake.

This route begins at Cong, just over the border from County Galway and a pleasant 20-mile drive from Galway City, and skirts the western edges of Lough Mask beneath the Partry Mountains, heading north to Castlebar. From this busy town in the heart of the limestone plain country, the route goes west to take in Achill Island and south again around Clew Bay to the lovely planned town of Westport and along the curving bay to Louisburgh. From here the road leads south to Killary Harbour and dips into Joyce Country before following the northern shore of Lough Corrib back to Cong.

Expect to pay $40 to $90 for a double room at an expensive hotel, and from $30 to $40 at a moderate one. Dinner for two at *Ashford Castle* will cost a minimum of $50; at moderately priced restaurants, two can dine well for from $25 to $40.

CONG: This tiny village on an isthmus between Lough Mask and Lough Corrib is best known for the ruins of the 12th-century Cong Abbey and the luxury hotel, *Ashford Castle.* It may also be familiar to Americans as the setting for that quintessential Irish-American movie *The Quiet Man,* which was filmed in these precincts.

Cong Abbey, founded for Irish Augustinians by Turlough O'Connor, king of Ireland, is considered one of the finest examples of early architecture in Ireland. The ruins preserve several doorways and windows of a type transitional between Romanesque and Gothic and are best seen from the cloisters garth. Behind the west end of the abbey garth is a small stone house constructed so that the Cong River flows through a gully beneath the floor. The structure is known as the Monks' Fishing House because monks from the abbey supposedly fished through a trap door in its floor.

The ruins of the abbey are beside one of the entrance gates to the lovely grounds of Ashford Castle, which commands some of the finest acreage along Lough Corrib. The oldest part of the castle was built in the 18th century, but the castellated towers and a bridge on the river's edge were added later by Sir Benjamin Guinness. There are some 25 miles of landscaped walks through the demesne of the castle, which was converted into a hotel in 1939. Parts of the grounds are open to the public.

Besides the abbey there are several interesting historic artifacts and monuments connected with Cong and its environs. The celebrated Cross of Cong (now in the National Museum in Dublin) was discovered in a chest in the village early in the last century. Made of oak plated with copper and decorated with beautiful gold filigree work of Celtic pattern, it is a masterpiece of religious art. The little ruined church and the ancient Stone of Lunga on the low wooded island of Inchagoill in Lough Corrib belong to the age of St. Patrick. The stone is a 2.5-foot-high obelisk that bears ancient Roman characters thought to be the oldest Christian inscription in Europe outside the Catacombs.

The stream connecting Lough Mask and Lough Corrib has three parts of its short course underground at Cong and the subterranean channel is accessible from a number of caves that honeycomb the plateau of cavernous limestone between the lakes. The Pigeon Hole is the most accessible of the caves of Cong. It is reached by turning right onto New Saw Mill, a mile west of the village. At the first cottage on the right there is an iron gate that opens to a field and a short way from the gate, 61 stone steps lead down to the underground chamber.

Another underground curiosity is the Dry Canal, which was built as a relief scheme during the Great Famine of 1846 with the idea of connecting Lough Corrib and Lough Mask to extend navigation. When it was completed, however, it was discovered that despite the cut-stone banks and locks, the canal was incapable of holding water because of the porous limestone bed.

About a half mile from the village on all three approach roads to Cong, the visitor may notice small mounds of wooden crosses, called *crusheens*. For centuries it has been the practice of funeral corteges to stop at these spots to say a prayer and add another cross to the pile.

About 4 miles north of Cong, the ruins of a castle that belonged to Captain Charles Boycott can be seen on a minor road along the shores of Lough Mask. The name of Boycott, a retired British army officer who was unpopular with his tenants, came to stand for ostracism and isolation because workers refused to help him during the harvest season during the Land League agitation in the 1880s.

Cong is a center for hunting and fishing. Lough Mask is noted for large trout and pike; Lough Corrib — Ireland's second largest lake — is renowned for brown trout, pike, and salmon. The season for salmon and trout fishing in the lakes runs from February 15 to September 30 and on the rivers from March 1 to September 30. Fishing is free on both lakes with the exception of part of the Cong River within Ashford Castle grounds. Horses can be hired for riding in the area from the Cong Riding Centre (phone: Cong 29), and there is a secluded sandy cove for bathers that can be reached from an approach road off the Cong-Clonbur Road, 1 mile west of the village.

CHECKING IN: *Ashford Castle* – One of the finest castle hotels in Europe, its public rooms have paneled ceilings and impressive woodcarvings and stonework, set off by period furniture, Waterford chandeliers, and military memorabilia. Each of the 77 rooms has a view of the lake or the hotel's formal gardens and wide lawns, and there is a 9-hole golf course on the grounds. The dining room, which is walled in mirrors and looks out over the lake, serves elaborate French cuisine. Although it is possible to dine at the castle even if you aren't staying there, reservations must be made well in advance. On Highway 98A just east of Cong (phone: 094-22644). Expensive.

En Route from Cong – The route north to Castlebar follows a minor road along the western bank of Lough Mask beside the Partry Mountains, passing through Tourmakeady, a small Irish-speaking village. At the village of Partry, take the N84 about 3½ miles north, where a road on the right leads to the largely restored Ballintubber Abbey, which has been in almost uninterrupted use as a place of worship since it was founded for members of the order of St. Augustine in 1216. The abbey consists of a cruciform church with nave transepts and choir. Three blocked windows of Norman design with double dog-tooth moulding are over the altar. The monastic buildings are at the end of the south transept, and in a chapel to the south of the choir there is an elaborate altar tomb with a row of figures on the pediment Return to N84 and continue north to Castlebar.

CASTLEBAR: The administrative capital of County Mayo, Castlebar is a thriving commercial center that began as a settlement where a castle was built by the de Barra family. It became famous during the 1798 Rebellion because a joint Irish-French force defeated the British army here in a battle known as the Races of Castlebar. The remains of John Moore, president of the Republic of Connaught that was proclaimed after the battle, are buried in the town's pleasant tree-lined Mall. The Castlebar Tourist Information Office (phone: 094-21207) is open only during the summer season.

In the pretty village of Turlough, 3 miles northeast of Castlebar on the N5, there is a well-preserved round tower beside the ruins of a 17th-century church.

CHECKING IN: *Breaffy House* – An elegant Georgian mansion with modern additions, it's set in 60 acres of wooded parkland. There are 43 pleasantly appointed rooms and a schedule of evening entertainment during the summer months. 2 miles from Castlebar on the Castlebar-Claremorris road, N60 (phone: 094-22033). Expensive.

EATING OUT: *Davitt* – Excellent steaks and other regular fare in a well-run open-kitchen eatery. Rush St., Castlebar (phone: 094-22233). Moderate.
Castle Bistro – Seafood is one of the specialties at this attractive restaurant and bar reminiscent of a French bistro. Food is also served in the bar area all day long. Castle St., Castlebar (phone: 094-22809). Moderate.

En Route from Castlebar – Newport, an angling center on the northeast corner of Clew Bay beneath the Nephin and Nephin Beg Mountains, is 12 miles northwest on the L138. Two miles farther, a road to the left leads to the well-preserved Burrishole church of the Burrishole Friary, built in 1450 by Richard Burke. The central tower of the cruciform church remains and there are some good examples of pointed arches. About 2 miles farther west on the highway, an unpaved road on the left leads to the square tower of Grace O'Malley's castle of Rockfleet, where the warrior queen dismissed her husband after a year of marriage. Mulrany, a picturesque resort with a good bathing beach on the margin of Clew Bay, lies on the narrow isthmus that joins the mountainous Curraun Peninsula to the mainland. The main route to Achill Island follows the north shore of the peninsula, but the road along the southern rim of the peninsula is recommended for its fine seascapes.

 CHECKING IN: *Newport House* – A 21-room, white Georgian house with Regency decor, situated bayside. The French chef prepares superb food, serving fresh produce from the hotel's own gardens, farms, and fishery. Newport (phone: 098-41222). Moderate.

ACHILL ISLAND: The largest of Ireland's offshore islands, Achill is a popular holiday center, though little known to foreign visitors. It is dominated by three mountains, and its coast is marked by dramatic cliffs, as well as several charming resort villages with long, broad sandy beaches. The town of Achill Sound, just across the bridge from the mainland, is the island's principal shopping center and has facilities for bathing, boating, and fishing. Beyond Achill Sound, the Atlantic Highway bears right off L148, the island's main road, and passes a keep of the O'Malleys. This road traverses the windswept tracts of peat bog that cover much of the island and supply fuel to the islanders. Black-faced sheep dot the rolling bogs and occasionally block the winding road. Dooega, a small village at the mouth of a valley on the west side of the Minaun Mountain, is a convenient place from which to climb the mountain or the Minaun Cliffs, rising to 800 feet.

Just before reaching Keel, the island's main resort town, you pass the spectacular Cathedral Rocks, water-carved cliffs that resemble a Gothic cathedral jutting up from the ocean. Keel, on a curving bay sheltered by Slievemore Mountain on the north and Croghun Mountain on the west, is a center for surfing and underwater sports. In addition to its 3-mile-long sandy beach, it has a 9-hole golf course and tennis courts.

Two miles farther on are the whitewashed cottages of Dooagh, on a bay famous for salmon netting. Keem Bay, which has a wide beach of fine sand, sheltered by the steeply rising Moyteoge Head, is 3 miles farther west. Basking sharks frequent Achill waters in spring and are trapped in nets at Keem Bay and then killed with lances by island crews working from small canvas-covered curraghs. A steep road leads from Keem Bay to the summit of Croghun Mountain, with its 4-mile line of superb cliffs reaching as high as 2,000 feet above the ocean.

Heading back through Keem Bay, a road to the left leads north across the island to Dugort, a north shore village from which boatmen take visitors to the Seal Caves that extend far into the cliffs under Slievemore Mountain, a mass of quartzite rock and mica that rises to 2,204 feet.

In addition to sea angling, there is fishing for trout in Achill's lakes and the Dooega River, and in recent years the island has become a popular hang-gliding center. There are numerous small hotels and guesthouses on the island open to visitors in summer. May and June are the best months to visit Achill, but Tourist Information Offices are open at Achill Sound (phone: Achill Sound 51) and Keel (phone: Keel 27) throughout the summer.

En Route from Achill Island – The N59 follows the curve of Clew Bay south from Mulrany to Westport, 8 miles below Newport.

WESTPORT: This charming seigneurial town in a hollow on the arm of Clew Bay was planned for the marquess of Sligo by James Wyatt, a famous British architect of the Georgian period. Its main street, known as The Mall, runs along both sides of the gentle Carrowbeg River, which is crossed by several picturesque stone bridges and sheltered by a colonnade of lime trees. Westport is an important center for sea angling and was the scene of a meeting at which the Irish Land League was formed in 1879. The town also provided the setting for a number of novels by George A. Birmingham, the pen name of James Owen Hannay who was rector of the Church of Ireland here from 1893 to 1913. A mile and a half west of the town center in a lovely demesne overlooking Clew Bay and the Atlantic Ocean is Westport House, a fine Georgian mansion that was the home of the marquess of Sligo. The house is open to the public April 1 through October 5 (phone: 098-25141 or 098-25430). Designed by the German architect Richard Cassels in 1730 and altered 50 years later by Wyatt, it houses fine collections of old English and Irish silver; paintings by Sir Joshua Reynolds and James O'Connor (perhaps the best of Irish landscape painters); Waterford crystal; and fine old furniture. The attractive marble staircase was built by Italian artisans brought here specifically for that purpose. In a basement area, there is a warren of shops, an amusement arcade, and a tea shop. Ireland's first zoo park is on the grounds, and Westport House Country Estates has holiday homes, horse caravans, and campers for hire.

Just outside the gates to the grounds of Westport House is Westport Quay, where boats may be rented for boating and fishing on Clew Bay. On Collanmore Island in the bay, there is a sail-training center for beginners and intermediates. (For information, contact Glenans Irish Sailing Centres, 1 Kildare St., Dublin 2; phone: 76775, 760938, or Carrowholly 728). The Westport Golf Club (phone: 098-25113), 3 miles from town, has an 18-hole, par-73 championship course that winds around the precipitous slopes of Croagh Patrick. One of its most interesting holes is the par-5, 15th hole with a carry from the tee across Clew Bay.

Each June, a 4-day international sea angling festival and the 3-day Westport Horse Show, one of Ireland's most important, are held here. In August, the Cailin Deas Festival includes sporting events, art displays, and a variety of musical entertainment and dancing. Westport has three dance halls, and ballad sessions are held in some hotels and pubs during the summer. The Westport Tourist Information Office is on The Mall (phone: 098-25711).

CHECKING IN: *Westport* – The best standards in town are maintained at this modern, 49-room hotel. The staff is exceedingly friendly, and the cuisine is of estimable quality. Westport, across the bridge at the bottom of James St., entering Newport Rd.; take the first left turn (phone: 098-25122). Moderate.

Westport Ryan's – The largest (56 rooms) of the 6 hotels in town, it offers modern accommodations. Westport, on the road from town to the quay (phone: 098-25811). Moderate.

EATING OUT: *Ardmore House* – Specializing in fresh seafood, this small, intimate, candlelit restaurant overlooks Clew Bay. Owner-chef Pat Hoban prepares excellent Continental and Irish dishes, and his wife, Noreen, gives her personal attention to the dining room. Reservations recommended in summer months. Rosbeg, Westport, 1 mile from the town center (phone: 098-25994). Moderate.

Chalet Swiss – Very fine European cooking blended with traditional Irish dishes in a cozy, friendly atmosphere. Excellent value. The Quay, Westport (phone: 098-25874). Moderate.

En Route from Westport – The graceful Croagh Patrick, Ireland's holy mountain 5 miles west of town off R335, is one of the most impressive landmarks in the west of Ireland. From its 2,510-foot summit, there is an inspiring view of the island-dotted bay, making the 2-hour climb worth the effort. St. Patrick is said to have spent 40 days and 40 nights in prayer and fasting atop the mountain in 441, and each year Catholics make national pilgrimages to the mountain on the last Sunday in July. The route up the mountain begins near the Murrisk Abbey, which was built in the 14th century for the Augustinians and has a notable east window.

Eight miles farther west is Louisburgh, a pleasant fishing village at the mouth of the Bunowen River. There are several good sandy beaches nearby at Old Head, Carramore, Berta, Carrowniskey, and Thallabawn. In addition to several small hotels and guesthouses, there are ten self-catering cottages available through Rent an Irish Cottage Ltd.; for details, write to Shannon Airport House, Shannon International Airport, Co. Clare, Irish Republic; phone: 61580/61588. The local Tourist Information Office (phone: Louisburgh 50) is only open during summer months.

A minor road west from Louisburgh leads to Roonah Quay where boats are available for trips to Clare Island.

CLARE ISLAND: Steeped in the legends of the 16th-century sea queen Grace O'Malley, Clare Island guards the entrance to Clew Bay and offers the visitor a sense of peace and remoteness. Grace O'Malley's massive square castle on the east coast of the island above the harbor was converted into a coast guard station over 150 years ago and is not particularly interesting. Tradition says that the ferocious Grace was interred in Clare Abbey, a small 15th-century church about a mile and a half southwest of the harbor, but even if this is untrue it is worth seeing for its frescoes. There is only one small hotel on the island, but day-trippers can take advantage of several good beaches for bathing or picnics. There is a colorful regatta held at Clare Island every year in July.

En Route from Clare Island – Back on the mainland, the route south from Louisburgh crosses a desolate moor and climbs past Cregganbaum before descending to the Delphi Valley, which has a series of lakes and is flanked by the Sheeffrey Hills (2,504 feet) on the left. A sharp turn south brings you to the northern shore of Killary Harbour (see the *Connemara* route) and to the handsome waterfall where the Erriff River comes down from the mountain. At Leenane, a sparse fishing village at a bend in the Killary, the road to the right (L101) leads back to Cong through Joyce Country and along the northern banks of Lough Corrib and back to Cong. Alternatively, follow R336 to Maam, then pick up N59 south to Galway City.

Donegal

Donegal seems forever haunted by its history — harking back to the days when it was a proud and independent enclave ruled by its own kings and chieftains. Spiritually remote from the rest of Ireland, the area retains a strong individuality and an awareness of its former glory.

The sense of isolation is emphasized by the towering mountains that hem in the county. They are part of the same earth folds that make up the Scottish Highlands, a fact that may help explain the close affinity that exists between

Donegal people and the Scots. All this is not to suggest that the Donegal people are not Irish; they are, but they are Irish in their own way.

Donegal people even look different from everybody else in Ireland, and they are very easy to spot. Remarkable hair color — sandy to flaming red — cleanly chiseled features, penetrating blue eyes, and lips curled on the brink of whimsicality are some of the giveaway characteristics. Their speech has been set to music in the Ulster mode, more easily understood in the northern capital of Belfast than in the southern one of Dublin. The skirling lilt of the Scots brogue sometimes creeps in, too, because so many Donegal people have spent time in Scotland, forced there not only by hard times but by a kinship that goes back centuries.

The word *Dún na nGall* (Donegal) means "the fort of the foreigners," and is believed to refer to the Vikings who constantly raided Irish coastal areas during the 9th and 10th centuries. They may have established the fort that existed where Donegal Town now stands on the River Eske. There's also convincing evidence that this northwestern region of Ireland was settled long before the Norsemen came. The migrant races of the ancient world made successive incursions into Ireland, and traces of some of them have been found in Donegal including crude Stone Age weapons and tools.

Originally, Donegal was known as *Tirconnaill* (pronounced Cheer-*kuhn*-il) or the "Land of Conall." The name comes from Conall Gulban, son of an Irish king known as Niall (Neil) of the Nine Hostages because he always took prisoners when he raided foreign lands. This piratical king endowed his favorite son, Conall, with the wild territory of Donegal, and it was Conall who founded the Kingdom of Tir Connaill in the 5th century. A line of kings reigned until 1071.

The most glorious era in Donegal's history began with the emergence of the O'Donnell dynasty around 1200. The mighty O'Donnells held sway over Tirconnaill for four centuries, wielding powerful influence not only in Donegal but throughout Ireland. At a time when the old Gaelic chiefs were feuding among themselves, the O'Donnells maintained their independence in Tirconnaill by virtue of their superior war skills and with no little help from the "gallowglasses" — mercenary soldiers from the Scottish Isles.

In 1587, one of the clan, young Red Hugh O'Donnell (the second), was kidnapped by an agent of Queen Elizabeth and held hostage in Dublin Castle in an attempt to extort loyalty to the Queen from his father. When Red Hugh escaped after 5 years, he became the hero of Gaelic Ireland. He and another great chieftain, Hugh O'Neill of Tyrone, combined with a Spanish invading force in a final effort to defeat the armies of Elizabeth. Instead, they were themselves crushed at the disastrous Battle of Kinsale on Christmas Day 1601. This was the final death rattle of the old Irish chiefs. O'Donnell fled to Spain where he died, apparently by poisoning. His brother and successor, Rory O'Donnell, along with O'Neill, sailed in exile from the Donegal port of Rathmullan in 1607, an event known as "the Flight of the Earls." With their departure, all hopes of a revival of Gaelic dominance were quenched forever.

These stirring events of a past age are a vital part of the folk memory of Donegal and have helped shape the character and personality of its people.

The O'Donnells may be gone but their splendid empire of mountain and glen and wild coast is in the good keeping of their descendents. Most of these people live off the land or the sea, and some still make a living weaving the Donegal tweeds that find their way to the fashion salons of the world. There are parts of the county where Irish is spoken as it was in the time of the first Red Hugh.

Our tour, which starts at the most natural departure point, Donegal Town, covers about 200 miles and could be driven comfortably in 4 days. We'll head northeast from here to make a huge straggling circle, girdling the entire county and returning at the end to Donegal Town. The greater part of the tour is along the seacoast that has some of the most dramatic scenery in Ireland, but it also takes in Donegal's magnificent mountains and valleys and lonesome bogs. The roads are not great at any time and in some stretches would unnerve a stunt driver, so ease off the gas pedal.

The price categories for the hotels listed in this route are expensive, $40 to $55 or more a night for a double room; moderate, $30 to $40; and inexpensive, $20 to $30. Dinner for two with wine in an expensive restaurant will run $45 and up; in moderate, $30 to $40; and in inexpensive, under $30.

DONEGAL TOWN: This is the town from which the entire county got its name. It is thought that the Vikings built a fort here and on that site the O'Donnell chieftains erected their own stronghold toward the end of the 15th century. That castle still stands though not in its original state; it was greatly added to in the 17th century by the Brookes, the English ruling family who supplanted the O'Donnells. The castle is now a national monument and open to the public daily. Bridge St. beside the stone bridge that spans the River Eske.

Donegal is a small town with a population of only 1,500 so it is easy to see all in a day. The obvious starting point is the Tourist Information Office on Quay St. (phone: 073-21148), which is open from May to September and where you can get all the advice and literature you need about the entire northwestern area of Ireland.

On the quay beside the tourist office you'll see mounted on a block a huge anchor from a French ship that was part of an expedition sent by Napoleon in 1798 in an abortive bid to help the Irish in a rising against the British. Local legend says the anchor was cut from the frigate *Romaine* as she fled from Donegal Bay back to France.

Farther along the quay toward the sea are the ruins of a Franciscan friary built by one of the O'Donnells in the 15th century and repeatedly plundered after the fall of the clan so that little remains today. Some of the monks of this friary, led by lay brother Michael O'Cleary, compiled the great historical work on Celtic Ireland called *The Annals of the Four Masters*.

A few steps north of the tourist office is the Diamond, the central point of the town. (Diamonds, rather than the commonplace town squares, are distinctive architectural features of many towns in the northern part of Ireland.) The Donegal Diamond was laid out by British colonist Sir Basil Brooke when he took over the town in 1603. There is a red granite obelisk in the Diamond that commemorates the friars who compiled the *Annals*. Here also is one of the most notable stores in Ireland, *Magees,* the home of the handwoven Donegal tweed, which carries the work of weavers from all over the county. A demonstration of hand-weaving is usually in progress at the *Magee* store, and there are morning and afternoon tours of the factory every weekday (phone: 073-21100).

From Donegal Town take the road northeast toward Letterkenny. Just 7 miles out you'll enter the Barnesmore Gap, which is a passageway through the Blue Stack

Mountains and joins the southern and northern parts of the county. In olden days the gap was a lucrative hunting ground for highwaymen and other assorted brigands who preyed on travelers making their way through the mountains. The road also passes through the twin towns of Ballybofey and Stranorlar through which runs the Finn River, excellent for salmon and trout. Just before Letterkenny turn right at the signpost for Ramelton and from that village go on to Rathmullan.

CHECKING IN: *Hyland Central* – The best hotel in Donegal Town, its staff is friendly, courteous, and efficient. On top of that, it has good food and comfortable rooms. The Diamond, Donegal Town (phone: 073-21027). Moderate.

Gallagher's – A small, old-fashioned, and very comfortable place to stay that is right in the center of town; meals include extra large helpings of fresh foodstuffs. Main St., Letterkenny (phone: 074-22570). Moderate.

Kee's – A fine, homey hostelry where the cuisine is simple but of a high order. Main St., Stranorlar, 18 miles north of Donegal Town on the N15 (phone: 074-31018). Moderate.

EATING OUT: *Biddy's O' Barnes* – Unusual and quaint pub at the entrance to the Barnesmore Gap. A refurbishment has sadly stripped away much of its original charm, but it's still a pleasant place to relax with good food and drink. Home-baked brown bread is still the specialty of the house and hearty fresh soups from the kitchen tureen are a joy. Barnesmore Gap, 7 miles north of Donegal Town on the N15 (phone: 073-21402). Moderate.

RATHMULLAN: There is scarcely a lovelier seaside village than Rathmullan in all of Ireland — certainly, there's no other tiny spot so richly awash in history. It was here in 1587 that the young Red Hugh O'Donnell (the second) was kidnapped at the behest of Queen Elizabeth; the youngster was lured aboard a British ship anchored off Rathmullan, chained in the hold, and taken to Dublin where he was held for 5 years before he escaped and made his way back to Tirconnaill to rally his warriors against Elizabeth.

This was also the scene of one of the most tragic events in Irish history: the Flight of the Earls, when the great chieftains O'Donnell and O'Neill, attended by a retinue of followers, boarded a ship to sail in exile to Europe in 1607. They were the last of the Gaelic chiefs and their departure cleared the way for the final phase of the English conquest of Ireland.

History swept up on Rathmullan's shores again in 1798, when the French fleet planning to invade Ireland and aid a native rebellion against the British came to grief in Lough Swilly. Aboard one of the captured French ships was the leading insurrectionist, Wolfe Tone, a revered Irish patriot. Tone died, possibly by his own hand, while in prison awaiting execution.

The bay of Lough Swilly on which Rathmullan is located is one of the deepest sea anchorages in Europe. Although men o' war no longer sail into the long, deep harbor, in summertime hundreds of yachts, speed boats, and motor launches knife through the sheltered waters. There's great fishing offshore and every June fishermen from many lands gather in Rathmullan for the sea-angling festival.

CHECKING IN: *Fort Royal* – A delightful country house with its own beach on Lough Swilly, riding stables, tennis courts, and fine food. About ½ mile from Rathmullan on the Portsalon road, immediately beyond the gates of Rathmullan House, with a sign indicating the narrow road that leads to it (phone: 074-58100). Expensive.

Rathmullan House – This magnificent, rambling old mansion hidden away amid trees and close to the shores of Lough Swilly is one of the loveliest hotels in Ireland; very good food. About ½ mile from Rathmullan on the road to Portsalon, watch for sign on gates at right (phone: 074-58117). Expensive.

EATING OUT: *Mirabeau Steak House* – Gracious candlelit dinners are served in this Georgian period house looking out on an inlet of Lough Swilly. As the name suggests, steak is the strong point but there's also a toothsome line in fresh fish. Open only for dinners 6 to 10 PM. The Mall, Ramelton (phone: 074-51138). Moderate.

Water's Edge – Perched on the brink of the ocean, this superb dining place makes the most of the fish that's readily available. Not without reason it has won the top award of Ireland's fish promotion agency. Boned duckling in an exotic sauce is another specialty. Ballyboe, on the L77 as you approach Rathmullan (phone: 074-58182). Moderate.

En Route from Rathmullan – You can walk for miles unhindered along the sandy shore of Lough Swilly, or you can get into your car and go north toward Fanad Head, taking the Knockalla Coast Road. Follow the signposts (the road is unnumbered) to Portsalon, 8 miles away. It's a precipitous and thrilling drive, for the road first climbs a coastal cliff towering above the Atlantic and then suddenly dips and sweeps downward to Ballymastocker Bay, a crescent of golden sands. As a spectacle, it's something of a heart stopper. North of Portsalon, the road turns really mean, but it's worth chancing the final 3 miles to Fanad Head just to take in the view from the top of the cliffs there. Then turn south and drive to the village of Tamney, continue down along the eastern fringe of beautiful Mulroy Bay to Kerrykeel, and from there to the town of Milford.

 SHARING A PINT: *Moore's Inn* – Flavorsome 19th-century pub where the welcome is warm. Good drink and snacks. Main St., Milford (phone: 074-53123). Inexpensive.

En Route from Milford – Go north along the western edge of Mulroy Bay on R245 toward Carrigart, 10 miles away. The bay is a narrow, elongated inlet like a Scandinavian fjord and, with trees edging its shore, is a lovely sight. Three miles from town, the road winds by Cratlagh Wood, where in 1878 one of the most hated landlords in Ireland, the third earl of Leitrim, was murdered along with two of his servants. Follow the road up into the Rosguill Peninsula, one of the many Gaeltacht pockets of Donegal where Irish is still a living language, spoken mostly by the old people. When you get to Carrigart, turn left, and then just on the edge of town, turn right (north) at the signpost for Rosapenna. This takes you onto the headland of Rosguill, where another spectacular seascape unfolds along the circular Atlantic Drive. The drive goes through an ecologically devastated "desert" where not a blade of grass grows and around lovely Dooagh Bay. As you leave the Rosguill headland and return to Carrigart, turn right (southwest) onto the road to Creeslough.

CHECKING IN: *Rosapenna Golf* – Its 18-hole golf course is a great attraction; a splendid table. Signposted right turn on the edge of Carrigart, 1 mile in on the Rosguill headland (phone: Downings 4). Expensive.

Carrigart – Noted for its conviviality and warm informality, this hotel also serves good food. Top of the Main St. in Carrigart (phone: Carrigart 6). Moderate.

DOE CASTLE/CREESLOUGH: About 6 miles southwest of Carrigart, at the village of Cashel, turn right (north) at the signpost to Doe Castle; it's 1 mile down the side road. Perched on the edge of the sea, Doe Castle is one of the finest fortresses left in Ireland; to explore it, ask for the key in the second house up from the entrance. In the early 16th century, Doe Castle was the stronghold of the MacSweeneys, a clan of "gallowglasses" from Scotland who came to Donegal to fight for the O'Donnell chieftains and gained a foothold in the county themselves. Before he was kidnapped, Red Hugh O'Donnell lived here briefly under the fosterage of the MacSweeneys. Survivors of the Spanish Armada who swam from their wrecked ships to the Donegal coast found a haven in this castle. The road from Doe Castle runs into Creeslough, a pretty town overlooking the coast. Creeslough is a convenient base for Muckish Mountain expeditions. Muckish must be climbed because it's there, and from its peak 2,000 feet up, you can look down on all of the north of Ireland — a magnificent sight.

 EATING OUT: *Corncutters' Rest* – One of the few pub-cum-fast-food eateries in Donegal that can be relied on for cleanliness and efficiency. Snacks downstairs during the day and an à la carte menu upstairs in the evening. Main St., Creeslough (phone: Creeslough 67). Moderate to inexpensive.

En Route from Creeslough – Some 3 miles north, on the road to Port-na-Blagh and Dunfanaghy, the texture of the landscape changes suddenly and dramatically, the stark, rugged barrenness giving way to a soft, green-wooded peninsula that juts into Sheep Haven Bay. This is the Ards Forest Park, which is open year-round to everybody. It is a relaxing shaded idyll where you can cut yourself off from the outside world amid ancient trees that stand sentinel above the bay. There are walks that wander through the woods and clearings that make perfect picnic places. At the edge of the forest there are white strands running down to the sea, where you can swim on those rare days when the sun brings the water up to a bearable temperature.

Port-na-Blagh and Dunfanaghy are delightfully unspoiled seaside resorts surrounded by beaches. Again, sadly it must be noted that while the whole jagged coast of Donegal is a treasure trove of beaches, they are hardly ever used because the rainy and windy weather discourages all but the most valiant of spirit. Just beyond Dunfanaghy, swing right to take the signposted road to Horn Head for another of those drives around the cliffs above the Atlantic. For Horn Head, you need a strong heart and a steady hand on the steering wheel, because up at the very top, at the brink of the ocean, you can look down those cliffs and get a glimpse of eternity. The massive cathedral cliffs also provide a nesting haven for thousands of seabirds in midsummer; this event attracts bird-watchers from many countries.

Back on N56 again, head southwest to Falcarragh, which is 7 miles away and part of the Gortahork Gaeltacht. Falcarragh has much of a Gaelic flavor because Irish is still widely used and many students come here every summer to study the native tongue. It is also another point from which to climb Muckish Mountain (see entry for Creeslough above). Turn left (south) at the village crossroads and travel the side road 6 miles to the mountain.

 CHECKING IN: *Port-na-Blagh* – The dining room at this large, modern hotel perched on a cliff looking out over Sheep Haven Bay is particularly good on fish. On the left as you drive in to Port-na-Blagh from Creeslough (phone: 074-36129). Moderate.

TORY ISLAND: Just 9 miles off the coast in the Falcarragh area lies Tory Island about which there are many legends. One dating back to antiquity tells of an ancient race of giants known as the Formorians inhabiting the island. Their chief was the feared "Balor of the Evil Eye," who was said to have supernatural powers and the remains of whose castle still stand on the cliffs at the eastern side of the island. More civilized influences prevailed after the arrival of Christianity, and there are some ruins where Donegal's most famous saint, Columcille, once presided over a settlement of monks.

Today there are only about 250 Tory islanders left and their life-style is much the same as that of their ancestors. They speak an Irish that has undertones of Scots Gaelic because of the age-old connection between Tory and Scotland. The islanders live in small, thatched cottages and cultivate the meager soil on their tiny holdings, raising oats and potatoes in those parts of the island protected from the fierce Atlantic storms.

No trees grow on the island at all, but some wild flowers manage to bloom in the stony soil. The menfolk still go to sea on fishing expeditions in frail curraghs — the tarred-canvas-covered boats used for centuries in Ireland.

To relieve this hard and bitter life, there are some rather fascinating compensations. For instance, you'll find no rats whatever on Tory Island. The reason for this — according to the islanders — is that St. Columcille banished rats from Tory and blessed the soil so they daren't return. Even better — and perhaps more pertinent today — the islanders don't have to pay any taxes.

While on the island, try to scale the two *tors* (steep hills) from which it gets its name; the view is splendid. On top of one there's a holy stone upon which, it is said, if you stand and turn around to the right three times you'll be granted any wish that you make.

There are a number of ports from which you can sail to Tory, and Falcarragh is as convenient a one as any. Contact James Ferry, phone: 074-35177. If you don't want to get marooned on the island, make sure that no bad weather is in the offing on the day you make your trip. Wild Atlantic storms are frequent, and Tory is often cut off from the mainland for 2 or 3 weeks at a time. But the people are extraordinarily kind and hospitable, so that an enforced stay can be a happy experience.

En Route from Tory Island – Returning to the mainland, we get back on the N56 in Falcarragh and head southwest to Gortahork. At this point take the signposted road to Meenaclady that runs along the northern coast toward the promontory known as Bloody Foreland. Again, there are magnificent seascapes all along this stretch. Bloody Foreland is at the extreme northwestern tip of the Gaeltacht region known as Gweedore and got its name from the blood-red color of the rocks as they are struck by the setting sun. Painters and photographers come to Bloody Foreland in summer hoping to catch one of these remarkable sunsets. The road swings around the headland and then turns south through the seaside resorts of Derrybeg and Bunbeg. The latter is a particularly attractive village, tucked away beneath tall cliffs and has one outstanding curiosity: the smallest harbor in the world. There is also a beautiful and very safe sandy beach here surrounded by sand dunes and crags that invite exploration.

Turn left (west) in Bunbeg and follow the signpost to Gweedore village; that brings you back to N56, the main route. From Gweedore, it's 2 miles east to Dunlewy. Errigal Mountain is immediately north of the village.

CHECKING IN: *Gweedore* – Perched dizzyingly on the brink of a cliff way above a golden beach, this is a smart, ultramodern hostelry with all the creature comforts. Good food. A signpost on Bunbeg's main street points the way to the hotel (phone: Bunbeg 85). Moderate.

McFadden's – A venerable and classy family-run hotel where friendliness and personal attention are the winning points. The food can be recommended too. Main St., Gortahork (phone: 35267). Moderate.

MT. ERRIGAL/DUNLEWY: People unskilled in mountain-climbing should not attempt Errigal unless they are accompanied by a local guide. From the summit of this 2,466-foot mountain you can see as far away as the Scottish highlands. While in Dunlewy, you should also take the opportunity to walk south of the village into a strange exotic valley called the "Poisoned Glen." Poisonous weeds known as spurge grow prolifically in the glen and they have contaminated a lake making it unsafe to drink the water. Another peculiarity is that there are no birds in the valley, so that when the weather turns hot in summer all sorts of creeping and flying insects infest the place, making it feel uncomfortably like a rainforest, only without the trees!

Return to the main road, N56, and continue southwest to the Rosses.

THE ROSSES: This area, called "the Rosses," meaning the promontories or head-lands of which there are countless numbers hereabouts, has large and lonely stretches of uninhabited bogland. Its very bleakness has an appeal of its own and it draws many tourists every summer.

About 3 miles south of Gweedore is the village of Crolly, which is famous for doll-making and exports Crolly Dolls all over the world. You can visit the doll factory and buy a doll at cut rates. If you walk south of Crolly on the Dungloe road, be prepared for a deafening crash as you pass by a giant glacial boulder. This is the "Big Stone of the Leaping Fox" and legend says it will come tumbling down when an honest person passes it — so you've been warned. Instead of taking this road from Crolly to Dungloe, however, turn right at the signposted road to Annagary, which will lead you in a circle around the coast through Kincasslagh, Burtonport, and Dungloe, the real heart of the Rosses.

Turn right at the signpost for Burtonport, one of the busiest fishing ports in Ireland, landing more salmon and lobster than anywhere else. At the height of the fishing season, it is fun to watch the activity on the pier as the trawlers come in from the Atlantic to unload their catches. Also from Burtonport, you can take a boat out to the island of Arranmore, 3 miles offshore. Boats depart frequently from 10:30 AM; for information, call Arranmore 5. If you want to relax and do a bit of fishing you can catch rainbow trout in Lough Shure; contact Philip Boyle, phone: Arranmore 8. If you're fit you can try the 4-mile walk to Rinrawros Point, crossing a small mountain as you go. The point is a lovely spot dominated by a lighthouse.

Although it's considered the capital of the Rosses, Dungloe is an unremarkable town of 900 people. There's some very good trout fishing in the lakes and rivers around the town.

 CHECKING IN: _Ostan Na Rosann_ – It's a good, modern hotel with an indoor pool; the dining room serves wholesome food in enormous portions. Just outside Dungloe on the road to Burtonport (phone: 075-21088). Moderate.

 EATING OUT: _Viking House_ – The accent here is on seafood fresh from the Atlantic outside the door. Very popular in summertime so you need to book in advance, preferably the day before. 7 miles from Crolly on the coast road, watch for prominent sign on left-hand side of road once you've passed village of Kincasslagh (phone: Kincasslagh 3). Moderate. _Note:_ This is also an inexpensive guesthouse with 8 rooms, a fine place to stay — if you can get a reservation.

En Route from Dungloe – Take N56 south to Maas, 13 miles away, and turn right (west) to travel into the pretty villages of Narin and Portnoo, both high above Gwee-barra Bay. You can find real solitude in this area because it has not yet been overrun by tourists, and there are a number of secluded beaches and coves along the coast. When the tide is out, you can walk across the sands from Narin to the island of Iniskeel on which there are the ruins of a 6th-century church.

Travel around the circular road from Portnoo through Rosbeg until you come to a junction and turn right (south) for Ardara, a village that just might well be the loveliest in all of Donegal. Ardara is tucked away in a deep valley where the Owentocker River races over rocks and boulders into Loughros More Bay. It is an area renowned for the weaving of Donegal tweed and there are many shops in the village where real bargains are to be had in tweed goods. For the more adventurous, signposts point the way to the Maghera sea caves where moonshiners used to ply their illicit art in olden days. Exploring these caves is an exciting experience, but first check the tidal schedules or you could be in great danger. Make sure to visit the Church of the Holy Family, which contains a very fine work in stained glass by the artist Evie Hone.

Two miles south of Ardara on the main road, turn right at the signpost for Glen-columbkille and when you reach Crobane 3 miles farther on, take the right fork of the road. This runs through the Glengesh Pass, a thrilling drive as the road climbs 900 feet into the clouds and then plunges dizzily down to the valley below. When the landscape flattens out, you're in Glencolumbkille.

 EATING OUT: *Portnoo* – This fine hotel commanding a majestic view of the sea has a gracious, Old World air about it. The cuisine is admirable, particularly the fish. On the seafront in Portnoo (phone: Clooney 10). Moderate.

Nesbitt Arms – A traditional inn where the comfort of the guests is always in mind. Great food and a good buy. Main St., Ardara (phone: Ardara 51). Inexpensive.

GLENCOLUMBKILLE: This is the lost valley where the patron saint of Donegal, Columcille, came in retreat from the world. He built a monastic prayer house here in the 6th century and even today there are relics and reminders of his presence scattered around the glen. The whole place has a timelessness about it, as well as a slower tempo. The outside world scarcely intrudes.

On St. Columcille's feast day, June 9, hundreds of people make a 3-mile pilgrims' tour of the glen, stopping to pray at ancient stone crosses along the way. At one of those crosses, beside the Protestant Church, the pilgrims kiss the stone and then peer through an opening in the top in pursuit of a belief that if they are without sin they may be given a glimpse of the next world.

But it isn't only Christian memorabilia and artifacts that are to be found in Glencolumbkille. There's also much evidence of an earlier presence. Something close to 50 monuments traceable to pre-Christian times are scattered throughout the glen, including underground passages and burial places.

Some years back, in order to provide employment and halt emigration from the glen, the local people formed a cooperative to develop home crafts and industries and to attract more tourists. The results have been one of the more encouraging success stories of rural Ireland. One such enterprise was the building of a village of traditional thatched cottages. Visitors can rent these for any length of time at costs that run from inexpensive in off season to moderate during high season. Information about this community, which is not related to the Rent-An-Irish-Cottage scheme, can be obtained from the Glencolumbkille Cooperative Society, Glencolumbkille, Co. Donegal (phone: 5 or 24). If you want to see what life was really like beneath the thatched roofs of Irish cottages in other eras, there's a folk village close by where the past has been reconstructed in fine detail, well worth a visit.

 CHECKING IN: *Glencolumbkille* – The only hotel in the valley offers a reasonable degree of comfort and has an exceptionally friendly staff and good food (phone: Glencolumbkille 3). Moderate.

En Route from Glencolumbkille – To complete the tour circuit back to Donegal Town, take the road from Glencolumbkille to Carrick, Kilcar, and Killybegs. Killybegs is of interest because it's Ireland's most important fishing port, and one of the great spectacles is to see the fishing fleet coming home in the evening with thousands of seagulls shrieking above it. Just north of Killybegs, rejoin N56. From here it's a 17-mile run into Donegal Town.

INDEX

Index

Abbey Theatre (Dublin, Irish Republic), 522–23

Abbotsbury, England, 648

Abergavenny, Wales, 725–26

Aberystwyth, Wales, 729

Accommodations and reservations, 86–93

Achill Island, Irish Republic, 815–16

Adamton Courte (Monkton, near Prestwick, Scotland), 601

Aherne's Pub & Seafood Bar (Youghal, Irish Republic), 572–73

Airplane travel, 18–28
  on arrival, 27–28
  bucket shops, 28–29
  charter flight(s), 24–26
    bookings, 25–26
  consumer protection, 27
  discount travel sources, 26
    trip cancellation and interruption insurance, 65–66
  flight insurance, 66–67
  handicapped travelers, 68–69
  intra-European fares, 28
  net fare sources, 26–27
  scheduled flights, 18–21
    baggage, 24
    fares, 19–22
    flying with children, 23
    gateways, 18–19
    getting bumped, 23–24
    meals, 23
    reservations, 22
    seating, 22–23
    smoking, 23

Aldeburgh Festival (Aldeburgh, England), 529

Alderney, Channel Islands, 640

Althorp (near Northampton, England), 592

Alveston Manor Hotel (Stratford-upon-Avon, England), 580

Ambleside, England, 675

American Museum in Britain (Bath, England), 505

Anascaul, Irish Republic, 790

Angel Hotel (Lavenham, England), 566

Angler's Rest (Drewsteignton, Devon, England), 598

Anglesey, Isle of, 736

Annual Bottle Kicking and Hare Pie Scramble (Hallaton, England), 531–32

Antelope (London, England), 566

Antiques and auctions, 538–50
  fairs, 540–41
  flea markets, 541–44
  shops and antiques, 539

Antrim Coast, Northern Ireland, tour, 739–49

Aran Islands, Irish Republic, 810–11

Arbutus Lodge (Cork, Irish Republic), 582–83

Architecture
  Britain, 144–48
  Ireland, 176–78

Arklow, Irish Republic, 756–57

Arran Island, Scotland, 708–10

Art Gallery and Museum (Glasgow, Scotland), 511–12

Arts, performing, 516–25
  England, 516–21
  Irish Republic, 522–25
  Northern Ireland, 525
  Scotland, 521–22
  traditional Irish music, 178–81, 522–25

Arundel, England, 632

Arundel Festival (Arundel, England), 529–30

Arundell Arms Hotel (Lifton, England), 474, 476, 577–78

Ashford Castle Hotel (Cong, Irish Republic), 582

Ashmolean Museum (Oxford, England), 511

Assembly House (Norwich, England), 599

Auctions, *see* Antiques and auctions

Audley, The (London, England), 566–67

Automobile insurance, 67

Avebury Stone Circle (Avebury, England), 551

Avoca, Irish Republic, 756

Avondale, Irish Republic, 755–56

Avon River (England), 191, 449, 465–66

Ayr, Scotland, 693–94

Badminton Horse Trials (Badminton, England), 452–53

Bailey of Duke Street, (Dublin, Irish Republic), 570–71

Ballingeary, Irish Republic, 769

Ballinskelligs, Irish Republic, 780

Ballintubber Abbey (Ballintubber, Irish Republic), 557–58

Ballybunion Golf Club (Ballybunion, Irish Republic), 446

Ballycastle, Northern Ireland, 743

Ballyferriter, Irish Republic, 792–93

Ballylickey House (Ballylickey, Irish Republic), 586–87

Ballymaloe House (Midleton, Irish Republic), 584

Ballynahinch, Irish Republic, 809

Ballyvaughan, Irish Republic, 801–2

Banquets, historical, 599–602
  England, 600–601
  Irish Republic, 602
  Scotland, 601
  Wales, 601–2

Bantam Tea Rooms (Chipping Campden, England), 598

Bantry, Irish Republic, 770–71

Barbican Centre (London, England), 517

Barmouth, Wales, 732

Barn (Sidmouth, England), 597

Barringtons, *see* Great Barrington; Little Barrington

Bath, England, 187–98, 670
  antiques and auctions, 544–45
  essay, 187–88
  hotels, 195–96, 585
  local transportation, 191

  museums, 189, 190, 191–92
  music, 194
  nightclubs and nightlife, 194
  pubs, 198
  restaurants, 196–98
  shopping, 192–93
  sights and activities, 188–91
  sins, 194
  special events, 193
  sports, 193–94
  theater, 194
  tourist information, 191

Bath International Festival of Music (Bath, England), 530

Battle, England, 629–30

Bayham Abbey, England, 631

Bay Tree (Stamford, England), 599

Beara Peninsula, Ring of Kerry and, Irish Republic, tour, 773–86

Beaulieu Abbey and Palace House (near Lyndhurst, England), 591

Beaumaris, Wales, 736–37

Bed-and-breakfast inns (B&Bs), 87–88

Beefeater by the Tower of London (London, England), 600–601

Belfast, Northern Ireland, 199–206
  antiques and auctions, 549
  essay, 199–200
  hotels, 205
  local transportation, 202–3
  museums, 201, 202, 204
  music, 204
  nightclubs and nightlife, 204
  pubs, 206
  restaurants, 205
  shopping, 203
  sights and activities, 201–4
    city center, 201
    environs, 201–2
  special events, 203
  sports, 203–4
  theater, 204
  tourist information, 202

Belfast Festival at Queen's (Belfast, Northern Ireland), 537

Bell Inn (Aston, Clinton, England), 575

Betws-y-Coed, Wales, 734–35

Bibury, England, 661–62

Biking, 52–54, 481–87
    best areas for, 482–86
    holidays, 487–88
    tour, planning, 487
Birmingham Museum and Art Gallery
    (Birmingham, England), 505–6
Birmingham Repertory Theatre (Bir-
    mingham, England), 516–17
Black Swan (Stratford-upon-Avon, Eng-
    land), 568
Blake's of the Hollow (Enniskillen,
    Northern Ireland), 573
Blasket Islands, Irish Republic, 792
Blenheim Palace (near Woodstock, Eng-
    land), 593
Bodmin Moor, England, 656
Books and magazines, recommended,
    114–15
Boughton House (near Kettering, Eng-
    land), 590–91
Bourton-on-the-Water, England, 663–64
Bowness, England, 672–73
Box Tree, The (Ilkley, England), 577
Brazen Head, The (Dublin, Irish Repub-
    lic), 571
Brecon, Wales, 726–27
Brighton, England, 207–18, 632
    essay, 207–9
    hotels, 215–16
    local transportation, 212–13
    museums, 210, 211, 212, 213
    music, 214
    nightclubs and nightlife, 214–15
    pubs, 217–18
    restaurants, 216–17
    shopping, 213
    sights and activities, 209–12
        central city, 209–11
        environs, 211–12
    sins, 215
    special events, 213
    sports, 214
    theater, 214
    tourist information, 212, 632
Brighton Festival (Brighton, England),
    530
Brighton Museum and Art Gallery
    (Brighton, England), 506

Bristol, England, 219–30
    antiques and auctions, 545
    essay, 219–20
    hotels, 227–28
    local transportation, 224
    museums, 221–22, 222–23, 224–25
    music, 227
    nightclubs and nightlife, 227
    pubs, 229–30
    restaurants, 228–29
    shopping, 225–26
    sights and activities, 221–24
        central city, 221–22
        Clifton, 223
        environs, 223–24
        harbor, 222–23
    special events, 226
    sports, 226
    theater, 226–27
    tourist information, 224
Britain, 119–59, 621–738
    architecture, 144–48
    banquets, 600–601
    festivals, 523–33, 537
    food and drink, 153–59
    genealogy hunts, 110–12
    history, 119–35
    literature, 135–48
    museums, 505–11
    music and dance, traditional, 148–53
    performing arts, 516–21
    See also England; Northern Ireland;
        Scotland; Wales
British Museum, (London, England),
    506–7
Broadway, England, 666–67
Budweiser Irish Derby (Kildare, County
    Kildare, Irish Republic), 454
Bunratty Castle (Bunratty, Irish Repub-
    lic), 602
Burford, England, 662
Burghley House (near Stamford, Eng-
    land), 592–93
Burrell Collection (Glasgow, Scotland),
    512
Bus, touring by, 41–44
    handicapped travelers, 69–70
    passes, 42–44

Business hours, 99
Buxton Festival (Buxton, England), 530

Cadbury Castle (South Cadbury, England), 554
Caernarfon (castle) (Gwynedd, Wales), 556–57
Caernarvon, Wales, 735–36
Cahernane Hotel (Killarney, Irish Republic), 587
Cahirciveen, Irish Republic, 779–80
Callander, Scotland, 699–700
Cambridge, England, 231–44
   essay, 231–32
   hotels, 241–42
   local transportation, 238
   museums, 233–34, 236, 238–39
   music, 241
   nightclubs and nightlife, 241
   pubs, 243–44
   restaurants, 242–43
   shopping, 239
   sights and activities, 233–37
      colleges, 233–36
      other sights, 236–37
   sins, 241
   special events, 239–40
   sports, 240
   theater, 240
   tourist information, 237–38
Camden Festival (London, England), 537
Camera and equipment, 107–9
Camping, 50–52
Canals, Britain's, 466
Canterbury, England, 245–53, 625
   antiques and auctions, 545
   essay, 245–46
   hotels, 251–52, 625
   local transportation, 250
   museums, 248, 250
   nightclubs and nightlife, 251
   pubs, 253
   restaurants, 252–53
   shopping, 250
   sights and activities, 246–49
      Canterbury Cathedral, 247–48
      environs, 249
      within old city walls, 248
      outside perimeter, 248–49

sins, 251
sports, 251
theater, 251
tourist information, 249–50
Caravans, 50–52
   horse-drawn, 52
Cardiff, Wales, 254–63
   essay, 254–56
   hotels, 261–62
   local transportation, 259
   museums, 256–57, 258, 259
   music, 261
   nightclubs and nightlife, 261
   pubs, 263
   restaurants, 262–63
   shopping, 259–60
   sights and activities, 256–58
      city center, 256–57
      environs, 257–58
   sins, 261
   special events, 260
   sports, 260
   theater, 260–61
   tourist information, 258–59
Carmarthen, Wales, 727–28
Carna, Irish Republic, 809
Carnoustie Golf Club (Carnoustie, Scotland), 445
Carraroe, Irish Republic, 810
Car rentals, 33–36
   fly/drive, 35
   handicapped travelers, 67–70
   local, 35
   from U.S., 33–34
Carrickfergus, Northern Ireland, 740–41
Carrickfergus Castle (County Antrim, Northern Ireland), 561–62
Car travel, 33–36
   gasoline, 36
   handicapped travelers, 69–70
   insurance, 67
   touring by, 33–36
Cashel, Irish Republic, 558, 767–68
   See also Rock of Cashel
Cashel House Hotel (Cashel, County Galway, Irish Republic), 587
Castlebar, Irish Republic, 814–15
Castlegregory, Irish Republic, 794

Castle Hotel, The (Taunton, England), 586

Castle hotels, *see under* Hotel(s)

Castle Howard (near Malton, England), 591–92

Castletownbere, Irish Republic, 786

Cavendish Hotel (Baslow, England), 475, 585

Cecil Higgins Art Gallery (Bedford, England), 505

Chain stores, 603

Channel Islands, England, tour, 635–41
  Alderney, 640
  Guernsey, 638–40
  Herm, 641
  Jersey, 636–38
  Jethou, 641
  Sark, 640–41
  tourist information, 105, 635–36

Charles Bingham Fishing, Ltd. (Coryton, near Okehampton, England), 474

Chatsworth (near Bakewell, England), 589–90

Cheddar Caves, England, 659–60

Chedworth, England, 661

Cheltenham, England, 667–68

Cheltenham International Festival of Music (Cheltenham, England), 530

Chester, England, 264–73
  antiques and auctions, 544
  essay, 264–65
  hotels, 271
  local transportation, 268
  museums, 268–69
  music, 270
  nightclubs and nightlife, 270
  pubs, 273
  restaurants, 271–73
  shopping, 269
  sights and activities, 265–68
  sins, 270–71
  special events, 269–70
  sports, 270
  theater, 270
  tourist information, 268

Chester Beatty Library (Dublin, Irish Republic), 512–13

Cheviot Hills and Scottish Border Country, England, 458

Chewton Glen Hotel (New Milton, England), 578–79

Chichester, England, 633

Chichester Festival Theatre (Chichester, England), 530–31

Children, hints for traveling with, 70–72
  accommodations, 72
  on airplanes, 23
  getting there and getting around, 71–72
  packing, 71
  planning, 71
  what to see and do, 72

Chilham, England, 625

Chipping Campden, England, 665–66

Cirencester, England, 668–69

Citizens' Theatre (Glasgow, Scotland), 521–22

City of London Festival (London, England), 532

Clare, Irish Republic, tour, 795–802

Clare Island, Irish Republic, 795–802, 817

Cleveland Way (from Helmsley to Filey, England), 497

Clifden, Irish Republic, 807–8

Climate, 12–13
  and clothes, 62

Clivedon (Taplow, Buckinghamshire, England), 585

Clonmel, Irish Republic, 765–67

Close, (Tetbury, England), 586

Clovelly, England, 657

Cobh, Irish Republic, 761–63

Cockermouth, England, 679–80

Cockney Club, The (London, England), 601

Coffee Shop (Yarm, England), 599

Coldstream, Scotland, 685

Coleraine, Northern Ireland, 745

Coliseum (London, England), 517

Combe House (Gittisham, England), 576–78

Cong, Irish Republic, 813–14

Coniston, England, 674

Connemara, Irish Republic, tour, 496, 802–11

Connemara Pony Show (Clifden, Irish Republic), 454
Connemara Trail, Irish Republic, 458
Connor Pass, Irish Republic, 794
Consular services, 81
Conwy Castle (Conwy, Wales), 557
Coombe Abbey (near Coventry, West Midlands, England), 600
Cork, West, Irish Republic, tour, 495, 768–73
Cork (city), Irish Republic, 274–84, 768–73
  essay, 274–75
  hotels, 281–82
  local transportation, 279
  museums, 276, 277–78, 279
  music, 281
  nightclubs and nightlife, 281
  pubs, 283–84
  restaurants, 282–83
  shopping, 279–80
  sights and activities, 275–78
    flat of the city, 276–77
    north bank, 277
    south bank, 277–78
  sins, 281
  special events, 280
  sports, 280–81
  theater, 281
  tourist information, 278
Cork International Choral and Folk Dance Festival (Cork, Irish Republic), 538
Cornwall coast, North, England, 656–57
Costs, calculating, 56–59
  accommodations, 57–58
  food, 58
  local taxes, 58
  service charges, 58–59
  transportation, 57
Cotswolds, England, 660–70
  antiques, 545–46
  biking, 483
  essay, 660–61
  tour, 660–70
Cotswold Way (from Chipping Campden to Bath, England), 497–98
Cottage in the Wood (Malvern Wells, Malvern, England), 578

Cottage Teashop (Tintagel, England), 599
County Sligo Golf Club (Rosses Point, Irish Republic), 447
Courtauld Institute Galleries (London, England), 507
Crathes Castle (Banchory, Scotland), 593–94
Credit and currency, 82–85
Credit cards, 83–85
Creeslough, Irish Republic, 821–22
Crocnaraw Country House (Moyard, Irish Republic), 587
Crown Saloon (Belfast, Northern Ireland), 573
Cruises, waterways and coastal, 461–67
Culloden Hotel (Craigavad, Holywood, Northern Ireland), 588
Culloden House (Inverness, Scotland), 586
Culzean Castle, Scotland, 693
Currency and credit, 82–85
Cushendall, Northern Ireland, 742–43
Cushendun, Northern Ireland, 742–43
Customs and returning to U.S., 102–3
Cycling, see Biking

Dales Way (from Ilkley to Bowness-on-Windermere, England), 498
Dance, see Music and dance, traditional
Dartmoor, England, 649–50
Dartmouth, England, 651
Davy Byrne's of Duke Street (Dublin, Irish Republic), 571
Deal, England, 626
Denbigh, Wales, 737–38
Department stores, 604
Derby Stakes (Epsom, England), 453
Derry, Northern Ireland, 747–49
Devil's Bridge, Wales, 729–30
Devon coast, North, England, 657–58
Dinas Mawddwy, Wales, 731
Dingle Peninsula, Irish Republic, tour, 786–94
Dingle Peninsula Trail, Irish Republic, 458, 790–91
Dirleton, Scotland, 683
Dirty Dicks (London, England), 567

Documents, entry requirements and, 59–60

Doe Castle (Creeslough, Irish Republic), 821–22

Doheny & Nesbitt's (Dublin, Irish Republic), 571

Dolgellau, Wales, 731–33

Donegal, Irish Republic, tour, 817–25

Donegal Town, Irish Republic, 819–20

Dorchester, England, 647–48

Doune, Scotland, 699

Dover, England, 626–27

Downhill, Northern Ireland, 745–46

Doyle's Seafood Bar (Dingle, Irish Republic), 583

Drinking, 100–101

Dromoland Castle (Newmarket-on-Fergus, Irish Republic), 479, 584–85

Drugs, 101–2

Druid Lane Theatre (Galway, Irish Republic), 524

Drumnadrochit, Scotland, 703

Dublin (city), Irish Republic, 285–301, 751
  antiques and auctions, 549
  biking, 485–86
  essay, 285–87
  hotels, 297–98
  local transportation, 293
  museums, 288, 290–91, 293–94
  music, 296
  nightclubs and nightlife, 296–97
  pubs, 300–301
  restaurants, 299–300
  shopping, 294–95
  sights and activities, 287–92
    north downtown, 290–91
    south downtown, 288–90
    suburbs, 291–92
  sins, 297
  special events, 295
  sports, 295–96
  theater, 296
  tourist information, 293
  wine bars, 301

Dublin Horse Show (Dublin, Irish Republic), 454

Dublin Theatre Festival (Dublin, Irish Republic), 534

Dublin to New Ross, Southeast Ireland, tour, 750–58

Duck Inn (Pett Bottom, England), 579

Dulwich College Picture Gallery (Dulwich, London, England), 507–8

Dumfries, Scotland, 690–91

Dunbar, Scotland, 684–85

Dunbeg, Irish Republic, 792

Dundrum House Hotel (Dundrum, County Tipperary, Irish Republic), 587

Dun Laoghaire, Irish Republic, 751–54

Dun Laoghaire Summer Festival (Dun Laoghaire, Irish Republic), 534–35

Dunlewy, Irish Republic, 823

Dunluce Castle, (Antrim Coast, Northern Ireland), 745

Dunnose Cottage (Luccombe, Isle of Wight, England), 598

Dunster, England, 658–59

Durty Nelly's (Bunratty, Irish Republic), 570

Eagle (Cambridge, England), 566

East Anglia, England, 482, 546

Eastwell Manor (Ashford, England), 574

Edinburgh, Scotland, 302–14, 682–83
  antiques and auctions, 548–49
  essay, 302–4
  hotels, 311–12
  local transportation, 308–9
  museums, 305–6, 307, 309
  music, 310
  nightclubs and nightlife, 311
  pubs, 313–14
  restaurants, 312–13
  shopping, 309–10
  sights and activities, 304–8
    beyond Royal Mile, 306–8
    Royal Mile, 305
  sins, 311
  special events, 310
  sports, 310
  theater, 310
  tourist information, 308

Edinburgh Festival (Edinburgh, Scotland), 533

Edinburgh International Folk Festival (Edinburgh, Scotland), 537
Edith's Café (Marlborough, England), 598
Electricity, 100
Elms Hotel (Abberley, England), 574
El Vino (London, England), 567
England, 9–10, 621–738
  antiques, 544–48
  banquets, 600–601
  biking, 482–85
  canals, 466
  festivals, 523–33, 537
  fishing, 465, 469, 471, 472, 474
  hunting, 452–53, 458, 459–60
  monuments and ruins, 551–55
  museums, 505–11
  pub crawling, 565–69
  rivers, 465–66
  rural retreats, 574–81, 585–86
  theater, 517–21
  tourist information, 104–6
  See also Britain
England, Lake District, tour, 483–84, 670–80
England, Northeast, 484
England, Southeast, tour, 483, 621–35
England, Southwest, tour, 484, 641–60
Ennis, Irish Republic, 796–97
Enniskerry, Irish Republic, 754
Entry requirements and documents, 59–60
Erddig House (near Wrexham, Wales), 594
Erne Waterway, Northern Ireland, 467
Ever Ready Derby Stakes (Epson, Surrey, England), 453
Exeter, England, 649
Exmoor Forest, England, 658–59

Fahan, Irish Republic, 792
Fairford, England, 662
Fair Head, Northern Ireland, 743
Fairs, 528–38
Farmhouses, 88
Faversham, England, 624
Festivals, 528–38
  England, 523–33, 537
  Irish Republic, 534–37, 538

  Northern Ireland, 537
  Scotland, 533–34, 537–38
  Wales, 534, 538
Fishguard Music Festival (Fishguard, Wales), 534
Fishing, 467–81
  coarse, 471–72
  game, 468–71
    hotels, 474–81
  schools, 474
  sea angling, 472–73
Fitzwilliam Museum (Cambridge, England), 506
Flea markets, 541–44
Flight insurance, 66–67
Focus Theatre (Dublin, Irish Republic), 523
Food and drink
  Britain, 153–59
  Ireland, 181–82
Foreign exchange, 85
Fort Augustus, Scotland, 702–3
Fort William, Scotland, 701–2

Gaiety Theatre (Dublin, Irish Republic), 523
Gallarus Oratory, Irish Republic, 793
Galloway Forest Park, Scotland, 692–93
Galway (city), Irish Republic, 315–23, 804
  essay, 315–16
  hotels, 320–21
  local transportation, 319
  museums, 316, 319
  music, 320
  nightclubs and nightlife, 320
  pubs, 323
  restaurants, 321–22
  shopping, 319
  sights and activities, 316–18
  sins, 320
  special events, 319
  sports, 319–20
  theater, 320
  tourist information, 318–19
Galway International Oyster Festival (Galway, Irish Republic), 535
Ganton Golf Club (Ganton, England), 444

Garden House Hotel (Cambridge, England), 585–86
Gardens, 588–99
  great, 588–94
  tea, 594–99
Gate Theatre (Dublin, Irish Republic), 523
Gateway Cakeshop (Evesham, England), 596
Genealogy hunts, 110–14
  England and Wales, 110–12
  Republic and Northern Ireland, 112–13
  Scotland, 112
  special problems, 113–14
George of Stamford (Stamford, England), 580
Giant's Causeway, Northern Ireland, 744–45
Glasgow, Scotland, 324–36
  essay, 324–26
  hotels, 334–35
  local transportation, 330
  museums, 327, 328, 329, 331
  music, 333
  nightclubs and nightlife, 334
  pubs, 336
  restaurants, 335–36
  shopping, 331–32
  sights and activities, 326–29
    by Clydeside, 329
    Medieval Glasgow, 327–28
    Modern Glasgow, 328
    Old Merchants' City, 328
    Victorian Glasgow, 327
  sins, 334
  special events, 332
  sports, 332–33
  theater, 333
  tourist information, 330
Glastonbury, England, 659
  hotels, 659
Glastonbury Abbey (Glastonbury, England), 551–52
Glenbeigh, Irish Republic, 778–79
Glencoe, Scotland, 700–701
  hotels, 701
Glencolumbkille, Irish Republic, 825
Glendalough, Irish Republic, 754–56

Gleneagles Hotel (Auchterarder, Scotland), 581
Gleneagles Hotel Golf Course (Auchterarder, Scotland), 445
Glenelg Brochs (Glenelg, Scotland), 555
Glengarriff, Irish Republic, 785
Globe Inn (Dumfries, Scotland), 569
Glyndebourne Festival Opera (Glyndebourne, England), 531
Golf courses, 443–48
Gorey Arts Festival (Gorey, Irish Republic), 535
Gougane Barra, Irish Republic, 770
Granary Tavern (Limerick City, Irish Republic), 602
Grand National (Aintree, near Liverpool, England), 452
Grand Opera House (Belfast, Northern Ireland), 525
Grasmere, England, 675–77
  hotels, 676–77
Gravetye Manor (near East Grinstead, England), 576
Great Barrington, England, 663
Great Southern Hotel (Parknasilla, Irish Republic), 583
Greenwich Festival (London, England), 531
Grenadier, The (London, England), 567
Grianán of Aileach (Burt, Irish Republic), 559–60
Groes Hotel (Ty'n-y-Groes, near Conwy, Wales), 570
Guernsey, Channel Islands, England, 638–40
  hotels, 640
Guesthouses, see under Hotel(s)
Gullane, Scotland, 683

Hadrian's Wall (near Newcastle-upon-Tyne, England), 553–54
Hambleton Hall (Hambleton, England), 579
Handicapped travelers, hints for, 67–70
  on airplanes, 68–69
  by car, bus, or train, 67–70
  planning, 67–68
  by ship, 69
  tours, 69–70

Harewood House (near Leeds, England), 591

Harlech, Wales, 733

Harris Island, Scotland, 712–14
hotels, 713–14

Harrogate International Festival (Harrogate, England), 532

Hasting, England, 629–30

Hawick, Scotland, 687–88

Hawkshead, England, 674

Haxey Hood Game (Haxey, England), 531

Healy Pass, Irish Republic, 785–86

Henchy's (Cork, Irish Republic), 570

Herm Channel Islands, England, 641

Herne Bay, England, 624–25

Highlands, Scotland, 485, 694–706

Hiking, 54–55, 491–503
group trips, 501–3
locations, 493–96
long-distance footpaths, 496–500
maps and more information, 500–501

History
Britain, 119–35
Ireland, 160–68

Hobby Horse Celebrations (Padstow, England), 533

Hole in the Wall (Tunbridge Wells, England), 569

Homes, stately, and great gardens, 588–94

Honourable Company of Edinburgh Golfers (Gullane, Scotland), 445

Horse(s), 450–61
drawn caravans, 52, 459
and hunting, 459–61
meets, shows, and races, 451–55
post trekking, 457–59
riding holidays and pony trekking, 455–57

Horse with the Red Unbrella (Dorchester, England), 598

Horse of the Year Show (Wembley, near London, England, 454

Horsted Place (Uckfield, East Sussex, England), 580

Hotel(s), 86–93
bed-and-breakfast inns (B&Bs), 87–88
castle, 87
costs, 57–58
farmhouses, 88
flats, homes, and cottages, 88–89
game fishing, 475–81
guesthouses and inns, 86–87
home stays, 89–90
hunting, 490–91
reservations, 90–92
rural retreats, 573–88
England, 574–81, 585–86
Irish Republic, 582–85, 586–88
Northern Ireland, 588
Scotland, 581, 586
Wales, 581–82
See also hotels *entry under names of individual cities*

Hunting, 488–91, 551–55
booking agencies, 489–90
England, 452–53, 458, 459–60, 551–55
Irish Republic, 454, 458, 460
Northern Ireland, 461
Scotland, 458–59

Hwyrnos (Swansea, Wales), 601

Hythe, England, 627–28
hotels, 628

Inch, Irish Republic, 790

Inns, 86–87

Insurance, 64–67
automobile, 67
baggage and personal effects, 65
combination policies, 67
default and/or bankruptcy, 66
flight, 66–67
personal accident and sickness, 65
trip cancellation and interruption, 65–66

International Musical Eisteddfod (Llangollen, Wales), 534

Inverlochy Castle (near Fort William, Scotland), 581

Inverness, Scotland, 703–6
hotels, 704–5

Ireland, 11, 160–82, 750–825
architecture, 176–78
banquets, 602
biking, 485–86

festivals, 534–37, 538
fishing, 470, 471, 472–73
food and drink, 181–82
history, 160–68
hunting, 454, 458, 460
literature, 168–76
monuments and ruins, 557–61
museums, 512–15
music and dance, traditional, 178–81, 525–28
performing arts, 522–25
pub crawling, 570–73
rivers, 466–67
rural retreats, 582–85, 586–88
tourist information, 106
Ireland, Southcentral, tour, 758–68
Ireland, Southeast (Dublin to New Ross), tour, 750–58
Irish Agricultural Museum (Wexford, Irish Republic), 514–15
Irish National Ballet (Cork, Irish Republic), 522
Irish Sweeps Derby (Kildare, Irish Republic), 454
Island Hotel (Tresco, Isles of Scilly, England), 586
Isle of Anglesey, Wales, 736
Isle of Man, 105
Isle of Wight, England, 105, 633–34
hotels, 634
Isles of Scilly, England, 654–55
hotels, 655
Iveagh Bequest (London, England), 508

Jedburgh, Scotland, 686–87
Jersey, Channel Islands, England, 636–38
Jethou, Channel Islands, England, 641
Johnstown Castle (near Wexford, Irish Republic), 757

Keepers Restaurant (Haworth, England), 597
Kelso, Scotland, 685–86
Kendal, England, 672
Kenmare, Irish Republic, 783–85
Kennet and Avon Canal, England, 191
Kerry (County), Irish Republic, 495

Kerry, Ring of, and Beara Peninsula, Irish Republic, tour, 773–86
Keswick, England, 677–79
hotels, 678
Kilkee, Irish Republic, 798
Kilkenny Arts Week (Kilkenny, Irish Republic), 535–36
Kilkenny (city), Irish Republic, 337–45
essay, 337–38
hotels, 343–44
local transportation, 341
museums, 340, 341, 342
music, 343
nightclubs and nightlife, 343
pubs, 345
restaurants, 344–45
shopping, 342
sights and activities, 339–41
sins, 343
special events, 342
sports, 342–43
theater, 343
tourist information, 341
Killarney, Irish Republic, 774–78
Killarney Golf and Fishing Club (Killarney, Irish Republic), 447
Killorglin, Irish Republic, 778
Kilmalkedar, Irish Republic, 793–94
Kilrush, Irish Republic, 797–98
King's Head Hotel (Richmond, England), 579–80
King's Lynn Festival (King's Lynn, England), 532
Kinsale, Irish Republic, 772–73
Kirkcudbright, Scotland, 691–92
hotels, 692
Knappogue Castle (Quin, Irish Republic), 602

Lahinch, Irish Republic, 798–99
Lahinch Golf Club (Lahinch, Irish Republic), 447
Lake District, England, tour, 483–84, 670–80
Lake District National Park (Cumbria, England), 493–94
Lampeter, Wales, 728–29
Language hints, 115–16

Larne, Northern Ireland, 741–42
Lauragh, Irish Republic, 786
Leenane, Irish Republic, 805–6
Legal aid, 80–81
Le Manor Aux Quat' Saisons (Great Milton, Oxfordshire, England), 577
Letterfrack, Irish Republic, 806–7
Lewis Island, Scotland, 714–15
  hotels, 715
Limavady, Northern Ireland, 746–47
Limerick City, Irish Republic, 346–53, 796
  essay, 346–47
  hotels, 351–52
  local transportation, 349–50
  museums, 347, 348, 349, 350
  nightclubs and nightlife, 351
  pubs, 353
  restaurants, 352–53
  shopping, 350
  sights and activities, 347–49
    city center, 347–48
    environs, 348–49
  sins, 351
  special events, 350
  sports, 350–51
  tourist information, 349
Liscannor, Irish Republic, 799
Lisdoonvarna, Irish Republic, 800
Liss Ard House (Skibbereen, Irish Republic), 587–88
Listowel Writers' Week (Listowel, Irish Republic), 536
Literature
  Britain, 135–48
  Ireland, 168–76
Little Barrington, England, 663
Lizard, England, 653–54
Llandeilo, Wales, 727
Llanidloes, Wales, 730–31
Llanwrtyd Wells, Wales, 728–29
Lochearnhead, Scotland, 700
London, England, 354–84
  antiques and auctions, 546–48
  biking, 482
  essay, 354–57
  hotels, 375–79
  local transportation, 366–67
  museums, 358, 359, 360, 361, 362, 363, 364, 365, 368
  music, 373–74
  nightclubs and nightlife, 374
  pubs, 384–85
  restaurants, 379–84
  shopping, 368–71
  sights and activities, 357–65
    city, 362–63
    other attractions, 363–65
    Westminster, 358–62
  sins, 374–75
  special events, 367
  sports, 371–72
  theater, 372–73
  tourist information, 365–66
  wine bars, 385
Londonderry (city, also called Derry), Northern Ireland, 747–49
  hotels and restaurants, 749
Londonderry Arms (Carnlough, Northern Ireland), 588
London-to-Brighton Veteran Car Run (London, England), 532
Longueville House and President's Restaurant (Mallow, Irish Republic), 583–84
Lord Mayor's Procession (London, England), 532
Lough Derg Trail (Cos. Clare, Tipperary, and Galway, Ireland), 458
Lowlands, Scotland, 680–94
Lygon Arms (Broadway, England), 575–76
Lyme Regis, England, 648–49
  hotels, 649

Macroom, Irish Republic, 769
Maes Howe (Mainland, Scotland), 556
Magazines and books, recommended, 114–15
Maidstone, England, 623
Mail, 99
Malahide Castle (Malahide, Irish Republic), 594
Malmesbury, England, 669
Malvern Festival (Malvern, England), 532

Man, Isle of, 105

Manchester, England,

Marlfield House Hotel (Gorey, County Wexford, Irish Republic), 587

Mayo, Southern, Irish Republic, tour, 812–17

Medical aid, 78–80

Melrose Abbey (Melrose, Scotland), 555–56

Miller Howe (Windermere, England), 580–81

Miltown Malbay, Irish Republic, 798

Miner's Inn (Acomb, England), 565–66

Mitchelstown, Irish Republic, 760–61

Moffat, Scotland, 689–90

Moher, Cliffs of, Irish Republic, 799–800

Monaghan County Museum (Monaghan, Irish Republic), 514

Monasterboice, Irish Republic, 292

Money, 82–85

Monmouth, Wales, 724–25

Monuments and ruins, ancient, 550–62
    England, 551–55
    Irish Republic, 557–61
    Northern Ireland, 561–62
    Scotland, 555–56
    Wales, 556–57

Moran's Oyster Cottage (The Weir, Kilcolgan, Irish Republic), 572

Moreton-in-Marsh, England, 665

Mt. Errigal, Irish Republic, 823

Mourne Mountains (County Down, Northern Ireland), 496

Muckross House Folk Museum (Muckross, Irish Republic), 514

Mulligan's of Poolbeg Street (Dublin, Irish Republic), 571

Museum of Mankind (London, England), 508

Museums, 504–15
    England, 505–11
    Irish Republic, 512–15
    Northern Ireland, 515
    Scotland, 511–12
    Wales, 512
    See also museums entry under names of individual cities

Music and dance, traditional

Britain, 148–53

Irish Republic, 178–81, 522–25

See also music entry under names of individual cities

National Folk Theatre of Ireland, Siamsa Tíre (Tralee, Irish Republic), 524–25

National Gallery (London, England), 508

National Gallery of Scotland (Edinburgh, Scotland), 511

National Maritime Museum (Greenwich, London, England), 508–9

National Museum (Dublin, Irish Republic), 513

National Museum of Wales (Cardiff, Wales), 512

National parks, 493–96

National Pilgrimage to Croagh Patrick (Westport, Irish Republic), 536

National Portrait Gallery (London, England), 509

National Theatre (London, England), 517–18

Natural History Museum (Dublin, Irish Republic), 513

Near Sawrey, England, 673–74

Neary's of Chatham Street (Dublin, Irish Republic), 571–72

Newgrange (Newgrange, Irish Republic), 560–61

Newmarket-on-Fergus, Irish Republic, 796

New Ross, Dublin to, Southeast Ireland, tour, 750–58

Nightclubs and nightlife, see nightclubs and nightlife entry under names of individual cities

Norfolk Broads, England, 465

North Berwick, Scotland, 683–84

North Downs Way (from Farnham to Dover, England), 498

Northern Ireland, 11, 739–49
    antiques, 549
    biking, 486
    essay, 739–40
    festivals, 537
    fishing, 470–71, 473–74

Northern Ireland (*cont.*)
hunting, 461
monuments and ruins, 561–62
museums, 515
performing arts, 525
pub crawling, 573
rivers, 467
rural retreats, 588
tourist information, 106
See also Antrim Coast, Northern Ireland, tour
Northleach, England, 661
Northumberland National Park (Northumberland, England), 494–95
North Wales Music Festival (St. Asaph, Wales), 538
North York Moors, England, 483
North York Moors National Park (Yorkshire, England), 494

Offa's Dyke Path (from near Chepstow to Prestatyn, Wales), 499–500
Old Bakery (Woolpit, England), 599
Old Course, The (St. Andrews, Scotland), 444–45
Olde Cheshire Cheese (London, England), 567–68
Older travelers, hints for, 76–78
discounts, 78
packing, 76
planning, 76–78
Old Fire Engine House (Ely, England), 596
Old Lace Shop (Beer, England), 598
Old Original Bakewell Pudding Shop (Bakewell, England), 597–98
Old Vic, The (London, England), 518
Olympia Theatre (Dublin, Irish Republic), 523–24
Open Air Theatre (Regent's Park, London, England), 518
Open markets, 603–4
Opera houses, 519
Original Maids of Honour Shop (Kew Gardens, England), 597
Orkney Island, Scotland, 715–18
Osprey Fishing School (Aviemore, Scotland), 474

Oughterard, Irish Republic, 480, 804–5
Owain Glyndwr Hotel (Corwen, Wales), 569–70
Oxford, England, 386–98, 661
antiques, 548
essay, 386–88
hotels, 395–96
local transportation, 392
museums, 388–89, 391, 392–93
music, 394
nightclubs and nightlife, 394
pubs, 398
restaurants, 396–98
shopping, 393
sights and activities, 388–91
heart of Oxford, 388–91
offbeat Oxford, 391
sins, 394
special events, 393
sports, 393–94
theater, 394
tourist information, 392
Oyster Tavern (Cork, Irish Republic), 570

Package tours, 44–50
European, booked in Britain, 48–50
for handicapped travelers, 69–70
sample, to Great Britain and Ireland, 46–48
Packing hints, 61–63, 71, 76
Paddy Burke's (Clarenbridge, Irish Republic), 582
Padstow, England, 655
Parks, national, 493–96
Passports, 59–60
lost abroad, 60
Peak District, England, 483
Peebles Angling School (Peebles, Scotland), 474
Pembrokeshire Coast Path (from St. Dogmaels to Amroth, Wales), 500
Pennine Way (from Edale, England, to Kirk, Yetholm, Scotland), 498
Penrith, England, 680
Penzance, England, 654
Pike and Eel (Needingworth, England), 568

Pitlochry Festival (Pitlochry, Scotland), 537–38

Planning a trip, 60–61
  biking, 487–88
  handicapped travelers, 67–68
  older travelers, 76–78

Plough and Sail (Paglesham, England), 568

Plymouth, England, 651–52

Portmarnock Golf Club (Portmarnock, Irish Republic), 447

Portmeirion, Wales, 733–34

Portmeirion Hotel (Portmeirion, Wales), 581–82

Portrush, Northern Ireland, 745

Post-Christmas and July sales, 603

Prestwick Golf Club (Prestwick, Scotland), 446

Priory Hotel (Bath, England), 585

Pub crawling, 563–73
  England, 565–69
  Irish Republic, 570–73
  Northern Ireland, 573
  Scotland, 569
  Wales, 569–70
  See also pubs *entry under names of individual cities*

Queen's Gallery (London, England), 509

Rathlin Island, Northern Ireland, 743–44

Rathmullan, Irish Republic, 820–21

Rathmullan House (Rathmullan, Irish Republic), 587

Renvyle, Irish Republic, 806

Reservations and accommodations, 86–93

Restaurant costs, 58
  See also restaurants *entry under names of individual cities*

Retreats, rural, 573–88
  England, 574–81, 585–86
  Irish Republic, 582–85, 586–88
  Northern Ireland, 588
  Scotland, 581, 586
  Wales, 581–82

Ridgeway (from Overton Hill, near Avebury, to Ivinghoe Beacon, England), 498–99

Rivers
  England, 465–66
  Irish Republic, 466–67
  Northern Ireland, 467
  Scotland, 466

Rob Roy Country, Scotland, 458–59

Rochester, England, 622–24

Rock of Cashel (Cashel, Irish Republic), 558

Romney Marsh, England, 628

Rose and Crown (Tewin, England), 568–69

Rose of Torridge Café (Bideford, England), 598

Rose of Tralee International Festival (Tralee, Irish Republic), 536

Rosmuc, Irish Republic, 809–10

Rosses, Irish Republic, 824–25

Rottingdean, England, 212

Roundstone, Irish Republic, 808–9

Royal Albert Hall (London, England), 518

Royal Albert Hotel (London, England), 518

Royal Ascot (Ascot, England), 452

Royal Birkdale Golf Club (Southport, England), 444

Royal County Down Golf Club (Newcastle, Northern Ireland), 448

Royal Court Theatre (London, England), 519

Royal Crescent (Bath, England), 585

Royal Dornoch (Dornoch, Scotland), 445

Royal Dublin Golf Club (Dollymount, Irish Republic), 447

Royal Dublin Society Concert Hall (Dublin, Irish Republic), 524

Royal Exchange Theatre (Manchester, England), 520–21

Royal Festival Hall (London, England), 519

Royal International Horse Show (Birmingham, England), 453

Royal Liverpool Golf Club (Hoylake, England), 444

Royal Lytham & St. Annes Golf Club (Lytham St. Annes, England), 444

Royal Oak (King's Bromley, England), 566

Royal Oak (Winsford, England), 569

Royal Opera House (Covent Garden, London, England), 519

Royal Porthcawl Golf Club (Porthcawl, Wales), 446

Royal Portrush Golf Club (Portrush, Northern Ireland), 447–48

Royal St. George's Golf Club (Sandwich, England), 444

Royal Shakespeare Theatre (Stratford-upon-Avon, England), 521

Royal Troon Golf Club (Troon, Scotland), 446

Royal Tunbridge Wells, England, 631

Royal Windsor Safari Park (near London, England), 365

Ruins, see Monuments and ruins, ancient

Rural retreats, see under Hotel(s)

Ruthin Castle (Ruthin, Wales), 586, 601–2

Rydal, England, 675

Rye, England, 628–29
 hotels, 629

Sadler's Wells Theatre (London, England), 519

Sailing, 461–63
 charters, 462
 events, 464
 schools, 462–63

St. Andrews, Scotland, 444–45

St. David's Cathedral Bach Festival (St. David's, Wales), 538

St. Leonards, England, 629–30

St. Mawes, England, 652–53

St. Patrick's Week (country-wide, Irish Republic), 534

Salisbury, England, 644–45

Salisbury Festival (Salisbury, England), 533

Saltee Islands, Irish Republic, 423

Sandwich, England, 625–26

Sandycove, Irish Republic, 753

Sark, Channel Islands, England, 640–41

Savill Garden (near Windsor, England), 365

Scilly, Isles of, England, 654–55

Scotland, 10, 680–721
 antiques, 548–49
 banquets, 601
 biking, 485
 festivals, 533–34, 537–38
 fishing, 469–70, 472, 474
 genealogy hunts, 112
 golf, 444–46
 monuments and ruins, 555–56
 museums, 511–12
 performing arts, 521–22
 pub crawling, 569
 rural retreats, 581, 586
 tourist information, 105–6

Scottish Highlands, tour, 485, 694–706

Scottish Islands, tour, 707–21

Scottish Lowlands, tour, 680–94

Seagan ua Neachtáin, Tabharneoir (Galway, Irish Republic), 572

Selkirk, Scotland, 688–89

Settle (Frome, England), 597

Severn River (England), 449

Shakespeare's Tavern and Playhouse (London, England), 601

Shannon Ceili (Bunratty Folk Park, County Clare, Irish Republic), 602

Shannon River (Irish Republic), 466–67

Sharrow Bay Hotel (Pooley Bridge, England), 579

Sherborne, England, 646

Sherlock Holmes (London, England), 568

Shetland Isles, Scotland, 718–21

Ship, traveling by, 29–33
 ferries, 32–33
 freighters, 30–31
 handicapped travelers, 69
 inland waterways, 31–32

Ship's Lights Tearoom (near Bridport, England), 596

Shooting and stalking, 488–91
 booking agencies for, 489–90
 hotels for, 490–91

Shopping, 93–94, 538–50, 602–18
 antiques and auctions, 538–50

best buys, 606–17
  bagpipes, 606
  baskets, 606
  books, 606–7
  china, 607–8
  chocolate, 608
  crystal and glass, 608–9
  curiosity shops, 609
  designer clothing, 609–10
  fabrics, 610
  food and liquor, 610–11
  guns, 611
  handicrafts, 611–12
  hats, 613
  jewelry, 613
  maps and prints, 613–14
  menswear, 614
  music, 614
  paper goods, 614
  perfumes, 614
  rainwear, 615
  riding equipment, 615
  sheepskins, 618
  shoes, 617
  sporting goods, 618
  tobacoo, 618
  toys, 618
  woolens, 615–17
chain stores, 603
department stores, 604
duty-free shops, 95
how to shop abroad, 94–95
open markets, 603–4
post-Christmas and July sales, 603
special streets and districts, 604–5
value added tax (VAT), 95–96
what to buy, 93–94
where to shop, 603–6
See also shopping *entry under names of
  individual cities*
Siamsa Tíre, The National Folk Theatre
  of Ireland (Tralee, Irish Republic), 524–25
Silk Cut Derby (Hickstead, West Sussex,
  England), 453–54
Single travelers, hints for, 73–76
Sir John Soane's Museum (London, England), 509–10

Skara Brae and Maes Howe (Mainland,
  Scotland), 556
Skeabost House Hotel (Skeabost Bridge,
  Isle of Skye, Scotland), 581
Skellig Rocks, Irish Republic, 780
Skibbereen, Irish Republic, 771–72
Skye, Isle of, Scotland, 710–12
Slane, Irish Republic, 292
Slea Head, Irish Republic, 792
Sneem, Irish Republic, 782–83
Snowdonia National Park (Gwynedd,
  Wales), 495
South Downs Way (from Eastbourne to
  Harting, near Petersfield, Eng-
  land), 499
Southwest Way (from Studland to Mine-
  head, England), 499
Special events, 13–18
  Great Britain, 14–16
  Irish Republic and Northern Ireland,
    16–18
  tickets for, 107
  See also special events *entry under
    names of individual cities*
Sports, 96–98
  biking, 52–54, 481–86
    best areas for, 482–86
    holidays, 487–88
    tour, planning, 487
  cricket, 97
  curling, 97–98
  fishing, 467–81
    coarse, 471–72
    game, 468–71
    schools, 474
    sea angling, 472–73
  Gaelic football, 98
  golf, 443–48
  Highland games, 98
  hiking, 54–55, 491–503
    group trips, 501–3
    locations, 493–96
    long-distance footpaths, 496–500
    maps and more information, 500–
      501
  horses, 450–61
    drawn caravans, 459
    and hunting, 459–61

Sports (*cont.*)
    meets, shows, and races, 451–55
    post trekking, 457–59
    riding holidays and pony trekking,
       455–57
  hunting, 488–91
  hurling, 98
  polo, 97
  rugby, 96–97
  sailing, 461–63
    charters, 462
    events, 464
    schools, 462–63
  soccer, 96
  tennis, 448–50
  See also sports *entry under names of
    individual cities*
Stable Door (Middleham, England), 598
Stag's Head (Dublin, Irish Republic), 572
Staigue Fort, Irish Republic, 782
Stalking and shooting, *see* Hunting
Stirling, Scotland, 697–99
Stone Cross Cottage (Godshill, Isle of
    Wight, England), 598
Stonehenge (Wiltshire, England), 554–55
Stow-on-the-Wold, England, 664–65
Stratford-upon-Avon, England, 399–409
  essay, 399–401
  hotels, 406–8
  local transportation, 404–5
  museums, 402, 403
  music, 406
  nightclubs and nightlife, 406
  pubs, 409–10
  restaurants, 408–9
  shopping, 405
  sights and activities, 401–4
    other attractions, 402–4
    Shakespeare Birthplace Trust, 401–2
  sins, 406
  special events, 405
  sports, 405–6
  theater, 403–4, 406
  tourist information, 404
Sunningdale Golf Club (Sunningdale,
    England), 443
Sutherland House (Southwold, England),
    599
Swansea Festival (Swansea, Wales), 538

Tara, Hill of (near Navan, Irish Repub-
    lic), 560
Tate Gallery (London, England), 510
Tea shops/tea gardens, 594–99
Telephone, 100
Tennis, 448–50
Terms, British and Irish, and American
    translations, 115–16
Thames River (England), 465–66
Theater(s), 515–25
  tickets, 107
  See also theater *entry under names of
    individual cities*
Theatre Royal (Bristol, England), 517
Theatre Royal (Glasgow, Scotland), 522
Theatre Royal (London, England),
    519–20
  Drury Lane, 519–20
  Haymarket, 520
Theatre Royal (Norfolk, England), 521
Three Choirs Festival (Gloucester, Here-
    ford, and Worcestershire, Eng-
    land), 531
Tilted Wig (Edinburgh, Scotland), 569
Time zones, 98–99
Tip packs, 83
Tipperary, Irish Republic, 454–55,
    759–60
Tipperary Racecourse (Tipperary Town,
    County Tipperary, Irish Repub-
    lic), 454–55
Tipping, 92–93
Tory Island, Irish Republic, 822–23
Totnes, England, 650–51
Tourist information offices, 104–6
  Channel Islands, 105
  England, 104–5
  Irish Republic, 106
  Isle of Man, 105
  Isle of Wight, 105
  Northern Ireland, 106
  Scotland, 105–6
  U.S., 104
  Wales, 106
  See also tourist information *entry
    under names of individual cities*
Tours, *see* Package tours
Tower of London (London, England),
    552–53

Towers Hotel (Glenbeigh, Irish Republic), 572
Train, touring by, 36–41
  further information, 41
  Great Britain, 37–39
  handicapped travelers, 69–70
  Ireland, 39–40
  passes, 40–41
Tralee, Irish Republic, 788–89
Transportation, local, *see* local transportation *entry under names of individual cities*
Transportation costs, 57
  See also Airplane travel; Bus, touring by; Car, driving own; Car rentals; Ship, traveling by; Train, touring by
Travel agents, how to use, 63–64
Traveler's checks, 82–83
Tregaron, Wales, 728
Turnberry Hotel Golf Course (Turnberry, Scotland), 446

Ulster Folk and Transport Museum (Holywood, Northern Ireland), 201, 515
Ulster Museum (Belfast, Northern Ireland), 515
Ulster Way, The (around Northern Ireland), 500
Up-Helly-Aa (Lerwick, Shetland Isles, Scotland), 533–34
Upper Slaughter, England, 663

Valentia Island, Irish Republic, 780
Value added tax (VAT), 95–96
Ventry, Irish Republic, 791–92
Victoria and Albert Museum (London, England), 510–11
Vintage (Kinsale, Irish Republic), 583

Wales, 10–11, 721–38
  banquets, 601–2
  biking, 485
  essay, 721–24
  festivals, 534, 538
  fishing, 469, 472
  monuments and ruins, 556–57
  museums, 512

pub crawling, 569–70
  rural retreats, 581–82
  tour, 721–38
  tourist information, 106
Walks, *see* Hiking
Wallace Collection (London, England), 511
Waterford (city), Irish Republic, 411–19
  essay, 411–12
  hotels, 417–18
  local transportation, 414–15
  museums, 412–13, 415
  music, 417
  nightclubs and nightlife, 417
  pubs, 419
  restaurants, 418
  shopping, 415–16
  sights and activities, 412–14
  sins, 417
  special events, 416
  sports, 416
  theater, 416
  tourist information, 414
Waterford (County), Irish Republic, 765
Waterford International Festival of Light Opera (Waterford, Irish Republic), 414
Waterside Inn (Bray-on-Thames, England), 575
Waterville, Irish Republic, 781–82
Waterville Golf Club (Waterville, Irish Republic), 447
Waterways and coastal cruises, 461–67
Weald, The, England, 630–32
Wells, England, 659
Welsh Folk Museum (St. Fagan's, Wales), 258
Welsh Marches, England, 484–85
Wensleydale Heifer, The (West Witton, England), 586
Wentworth Golf Club (Virginia Water, England), 443–44
Westbere, England, 625
West Penwith, England, 653–54
Westport, Irish Republic, 816–17
Wexford, Irish Republic, 420–28, 757–58
  essay, 420–21
  hotels, 426–27
  local transportation, 423–24

Wexford (*cont.*)
  museums, 422, 423
  music and nightlife, 425
  pubs, 428
  restaurants, 427–28
  shopping, 424
  sights and activities, 421–23
  sins, 426
  special events, 424–25
  sports, 425
  theater, 425
  tourist information, 423, 757–58
Wexford County Museum (Enniscorthy, Irish Republic), 514
Wexford Festival Opera (Wexford, Irish Republic), 536–37
Wheatsheaf Coffee Shop (Morpeth, England), 598–99
Whitstable, England, 624–25
Wicklow Mountains (Counties Wicklow and Dublin, Irish Republic), 495
Wicklow Way (from Marlay Park, near Sandyford, to Luggala, near Sally Gap, Irish Republic), 500
Wight, Isle of, England, 105, 633–34
Wigmore Hall (London, England), 520
Wimbledon Lawn Tennis Championships (Wimbledon, England), 450
Winchcombe, England, 667
Winchester, England, 643–44
Windermere, England, 672–73
Windrush, England, 663
Windsor Castle (Windsor, England), 365, 537

Windsor Festival (Windsor Castle, England), 537
Wine bars
  Dublin, 301
  London, 385
Wolds Way (from Filey to North Ferriby, England), 499
Woodenbridge, Irish Republic, 755

York, England, 429–40
  antiques and auctions, 548
  essay, 429–30
  hotels, 437–39
  local transportation, 434–35
  museums, 431–32, 433, 435
  music, 437
  nightclubs and nightlife, 437
  pubs, 440
  restaurants, 439–40
  shopping, 435–36
  sights and activities, 431–33
  sins, 437
  special events, 436
  sports, 436
  theater, 437
  tourist information, 434
York Early Music Festival (York, England), 533
York Festival and Mystery Plays (York, England), 533
Yorkshire Dales, England, 484
Youghal, Irish Republic, 763–65
Young Vic Theatre (London, England), 520